P9-ELF-840

DATE DUE

MY 17 '85	MY 17 '96		
JA 2 '90	MY 30 '96		
MY 29	DC 29 '96		
MY 27 '90	DE 20 '96		
NO 16 '94			
MR 15 '96			
	NO 27 '96		

ML
1711
B67
c. 2

Bordman, Gerald
Martin.

American musical
theatre

RIVERSIDE CITY COLLEGE

LIBRARY

Riverside, California

OCT 84

DEMCO

AMERICAN MUSICAL THEATRE

AMERICAN MUSICAL THEATRE

A Chronicle

GERALD BORDMAN

Riverside Community College
Library
4800 Magnolia Avenue
Riverside, CA 92506

NEW YORK • OXFORD UNIVERSITY PRESS • 1978

Copyright © 1978 by Oxford University Press, Inc.

Library of Congress Cataloging in Publication Data

Bordman, Gerald Martin.
    American musical theatre.

        Includes index.
        1.   Musical revue, comedy, etc.—United States.
I.   Title.
ML1711.B67   782.8′1′0973   77-18748
ISBN 0-19-502356-0

Second printing, 1979

Riverside Community College
Library

Printed in the United States of America

PREFACE

I had long been aware of the need for a thorough, accurate history of the American Musical Theatre. Fine students of the field, notably Stanley Green, have published excellent works covering selected areas, but there has been no truly comprehensive work. I also became aware that young people in particular seemed unaware of the great songwriters who made those old musicals so memorable, not only someone like Vincent Youmans but even, I found to my horror, Jerome Kern!

Since there is no sense in doing things by halves, I decided to start with the first musical done in America and cover everything up to the moment the printer required the last page of typescript. So many early texts are lost, and the coverage of plays in those early years often so scant, that the seasons before 1866 are best covered in a summary—a summary that nevertheless offers a number of extended discussions and extracts from the more important or interesting musicals of the epoch.

In considering the whole range of the American Musical Theatre, these early years can be viewed as a prologue to the five great acts, four intermissions, and an epilogue that follow. Accordingly, this book has been divided into eleven chapters. The second chapter—or Act I—begins with *The Black Crook*. From there on, the book moves season by season, show by show, to cover every musical done on Broadway. Because Boston, Philadelphia, Chicago, and other cities were active in producing their own shows before World War I, the spotlight occasionally swings to light up their efforts. This is particularly true of the lively, under-rated Chicago musical theatre that flourished from the turn of the century until 1914. Because three of the five acts are so long, these three have been divided into two "scenes." The division point in Act I is obvious and natural, but in Acts IV and V the choice was admittedly arbitrary. Where an opening date and theatre are not mentioned in the text they appear in parentheses directly after the show's title. When a show is mentioned later, in passing, its original opening date is provided. Similarly, in the case of revivals when the revival date is mentioned in the text, the original opening date but not the theatre will be found immediately after the title. With a few exceptions, original opening dates are omitted from all but the first mention of importations. Speaking of importations, Continental readers may be taken aback on reading some of the plot synopses. The story outlines given in this book are those employed for the American production and in a few instances bear only the most remote resemblance to the originals. I have excluded shows that opened out of town and then closed before their anticipated Broadway openings, as there was no way to obtain accurate information on many of these shows.

Just as opening dates and theatres are given after titles, in plot synopses performers' names appear in parentheses after characters they portrayed. A number of performers changed the spelling of their names at some time during their careers, and as a rule I have employed only the best-known spelling. Thus Miss Brice will always be Fanny, and Miss Miller, Marilyn. Programs and reviews are maddeningly inconsistent in the case of a few minor names. Just how did Henry Leone, or Henri Leone, or Henry Leoni, or Henri Leoni spell his name?

Although I have recorded as many dates and names as possible, a complete listing of all statistics for every show would have doubled or tripled the length of this book. As a result, a companion volume, listing every vital fact and figure, is projected under different authorship some years from now. Readers anxious to know the names of authors not mentioned here, or who designed the shoes or served as stage manager for any show will find the answers in that volume.

A few minor points:

Rather than burden this book with the scholarly *sic,* typographical errors have been corrected. Similarly, to avoid a plethora of quotation marks, critical comments culled from reviews have been incorporated into the text. For example, if a score is labeled mediocre or a production called lively the adjective was almost always picked from a notice to represent a consensus of the major critics.

Since few readers will want to read this book from beginning to end, but will rather "dip into" it, we have, in a handful of instances, repeated some important or interesting points.

We apologize for a few omissions. Nowhere could we find satisfactory biographical material for two major figures, William Gill and Richard Barker. In Barker's case even his alma mater, D'Oyly Carte, was unable to unearth suitable dates and background for us. And somehow, despite inquiries to all major theatre collections, not a note of music from *Adonis,* the first musical to run over 500 performances in New York, has surfaced. Nor has a copy of the libretto. But the saddest omissions of all were some 500 examples of music and lyrics we had hoped to include. Most of these were under copyright, and the cost of permissions would have inflated the price of the book beyond reason.

Among the twenty-two libraries and theatre collections consulted, special thanks must go to three. Hobart Berolzheimer, head of the Literature Department at the Free Library of Philadelphia; Mrs. Geri Duclow, librarian of its theatre collection, and her assistant, Mrs. Elaine Ebo, offered invaluable help. Manny Kean of the Kean Archives in Philadelphia provided constant and much needed advice and sheet music. Last, but certainly not least, was the professional aid provided by Paul Myers and his large, knowledgeable staff at the Theatre Collection, Library and Museum of the Performing Arts at Lincoln Center, a division of the New York Public Library. Among my many friends and associates who offered their personal assistance, particular thanks must go to Dr. Kenneth Goldstein and Stuart Tipton Cooke. To the many names unmentioned, please know you are neither unremembered nor unappreciated.

Yellow Wood Farm
Kirk's Mills, Pa.
June 1978

Gerald Bordman

CONTENTS

Contents

AMERICAN MUSICAL THEATRE

PROLOGUE
Origins to 1866

Music and drama have gone hand in hand from the beginning. Ancient Greeks and Romans sang or, at least, intoned much of their theatre. The medieval mystery plays' doggerel was often recited to an accompaniment of fife and tambour. By Elizabethan times songs in comedy, if not in tragedy, were commonplace. Shakespeare's lyrics remain familiar even if the poet might not recognize any melodies that now accompany his words. In the late 1600s Italy heard the first serious attempts to set an entire theatrical tale to music. With time these operas became the supreme achievement of the lyric stage. As the 17th century gave way to the 18th a rage for ballad operas struck England. These were dramas and comedies in which the plot was developed in dialogue rather than in recitative and in which songs were interspersed to underline the play's sentiments. In many instances melodies for these songs were not created for the entertainment but borrowed from popular airs by the librettist-lyricist, a borrowing openly acknowledged. There were, however, some original composers such as Charles Dibdin (who wrote his own librettos), Michael Arne, and William Shields who earned contemporary acclaim for their melodic efforts.

Since the rise of ballad opera coincided with the primitive beginnings of theatre in America, the first bit of musical theatre performed in the colonies was, not surprisingly, one of that genre. O. G. Sonneck, compiler of several scholarly catalogs of early American stage musicals, believed an English performer named Tony Ashton may have imported the first London ballad opera to Charleston as early as 1703. But Sonneck readily admitted to the absence of proof. Nonetheless the first recorded performance of such a musical was in Charleston—thirty-two years later. On February 8, 1735, an advertisement in the *South Carolina Gazette* read, "On Tuesday the 18th inst. will be presented at the Courtroom the opera 'Flora, or Hob in the Well' with the Dance of the two Pierrots, and a new Pantomime entertainment, called the adventures of Harlequin Scaramouch. . . ."

By 1753, when Mr. and Mrs. Lewis Hallam established New York's first permanent playhouse—the New Theatre in Nassau Street—their troupe was prepared to offer not only *Flora* and the most enduring of ballad operas, John Gay's *The Beggar's Opera*, but such full-length or shorter works as *Devil to Pay, Damon and Phillida,* and *Virginia Unmasked,* as well as a number of harlequinades. The shorter musicals generally served as afterpieces for major mountings of now forgotten or neglected works on the order of Baker's *Tunbridge Walks,* Otway's *Venice Preserved,* and Farquhar's *The Constant Couple.* Of course they also followed performances of evergreens such as *The Beaux Stratagem* and *Romeo and Juliet* (the latter performed in David Garrick's revised version).

What was apparently our first native musical work—it advertised itself as "a new Comic Opera" —was entitled, with bittersweet appropriateness, **The Disappointment.** Announcements of its imminent premiere began to appear in Philadelphia newspapers on April 6, 1767. These notices promised local theatregoers that on April 20 the American Company—a band of traveling players who also entertained in New York and as far south as Charleston—would present the novelty at the New Theatre in Southwark (generally called simply the Southwark Theatre). But something went wrong. On April 16 a curt statement informed Philadelphians that *The Disappointment* "as it contains personal reflections, is unfit for the stage" and was being withdrawn from rehearsal. Sonneck surmises, "Evidently the parties reflected had brought pressure to bear on Mr. Douglass [head of the American Company] who could not afford to lose the good will of influential people in a city where the opposition against the theatre just then was very strong." Who the injured parties were will probably never be known. Certainly the text gives no obvious clues. Nor does it really matter, for the work, with all its faults, is adequate enough on its own. In the common practice of the time the offering had a subtitle, *The Force of Credulity*. Either name gave a reasonable hint of the plot. The curious were able to learn details of the story quickly, for in the same week that the piece was originally scheduled for production in Philadelphia the text was published in New York.

As readers discovered, *The Disappointment* had a simple plot and an even more elementary subplot. Three practical jokers—Hum, Parchment, and Quadrant—decide to gull Raccoon, "an old Debauchee" whose cowardice is exceeded only by his greed. Their plan is to allow a fraudulent letter (purporting to reveal the location of a hidden treasure chest) to fall into the hands of Raccoon and his friends, Washball, Trushoop, and M'Snip. To make their efforts more credible the conspirators enlist the aid of Rattletrap, whom they set to "poring over the canto of Hudibras and Sydrophel in order to furnish himself with a set of hard words, which added to his knowledge in the mathematics, will sufficiently gratify him for a modern conjurer." Raccoon falls for the ruse, although in his joy he proves not as totally selfish as his teasers imagined. "Dis will make me cut de figure in life," he remarks, "and appear in de worl de proper importance; and den I'll do something for my poor ting." His "poor ting" is Moll Placket. He reiterates his promise directly to her, taking his oath to the tune of "Yankee Doodle":

O! how joyful shall I be
　When I get de money
I will bring it all to dee;
　O! my diddling honey!

With the "help" of Rattletrap the dupes retrieve the chest. Their joy is short-lived. Carrying it home and opening it, they find it filled with stones and recognize the trick that has been played on them. The subplot has Washball's niece, Lucy, reject her uncle's offer of a substantial dowry to marry the man of his choice. She elopes with her true love, Meanwell. To express their feelings the lovers also put new lyrics to old airs. The text suggests an obviously familiar tune, which it lists solely as "My fond Shepherds etc," to furnish the melody as the young couple plight their troth:

My dear Lucy, you ravish my heart,
I am blest with such language as this
To my arms then, oh, come, we'll ne'er part
And let's mutually seal with a kiss.

The play ends not with the humiliation of Raccoon and his friends but with Washball's acceptance of his niece's husband and with the wedding feast he provides.

Throughout the piece there are elementary but valid attempts to give characters some individuality. For example, Trushoop speaks with an Irish accent unique to him, "before" becoming "bafare"; "leave" becoming "laave"; and the "s" sound in "place" and "bliss" becoming "plashe" and "blish." Raccoon, despite his name and what a 20th-century reader would take for a Negro accent, was seen by contemporaries as speaking English as a Frenchman might. (Shakespeare employed a similar speech for his French ladies in *Henry V*—"Oui, dat de tongues of de mans is be full of deceits.") Musically, the piece was perhaps less sophisticated. As Sonneck notes, "attempts at ensembles and choruses are exceedingly few and feeble. To improvise or to write 'accompaniments' for the 'Disappointment' cannot have been a very interesting task and we hardly regret not to know the name of the musician whose duty it was to do so." Sonneck adds there are "only eighteen" ballads used in the work, but "the introduction of Yankee Doodle is especially noteworthy, being probably the earliest reference to the tune in American literature." If the composer—or, more likely, the conductor—who was to tie together the music remains unknown, the author of the libretto and lyrics can be identified. Both the first and second editions of the musical listed his name as Andrew Barton. Scholars have questioned that attribution, crediting the work instead either to one Colonel Thomas Forrest of Germantown (an area now part of Philadelphia but then a separate village) or to John Leacock, a Philadelphia coroner. Since none of these names reappear in the history of the American Musical Theatre the matter can be dismissed as academic.

By way of a footnote, four nights after *The Disappointment* was scheduled for production, the American Company did raise the curtain on an event of historical importance. Perhaps as compensation for the earlier cancellation, the troupe mounted Thomas Godfrey's *The Prince of Parthia,* the first play written by an American to be performed professionally.

If *The Disappointment* clearly represents an American endeavor at native ballad opera, its calling itself a comic opera initiates a confusion of nomenclature that will plague our musical stage throughout its history. Only in retrospect can some of the "name-calling" be rectified, and only in retrospect could it be seen that this vernacular ballad opera deserves to be considered one of the precursors of musical comedy.

The next native work did not appear until fourteen years and one revolution later. It too served as a forerunner, but of a different genre—the spectacle or extravaganza. Francis Hopkinson called his work **The Temple of Minerva** and described it as an "oratorical entertainment." It was not a full-blown work, being given merely as part of a concert offered in Philadelphia on December 11, 1781, by the French minister in honor of George Washington. In two scenes it told how the Goddess Minerva and her High Priest unite the Genius of France and the Genius of America. Promising perpetual alliance they end by singing a paean to General Washington. Patently descended from the masques of a century before, the form evolved in the century ahead into the set pieces and transformations for the lavish mountings of *The Black Crook* (9-12-66) era, and in the first quarter or so of the 20th century became the tableaux of Ziegfeldian revues. Hopkinson's music—which can be considered the first original material composed for our musical stage—has, unfortunately, been lost.

There was an inkling of another great tradition of our lyric stage when **The Blockheads; or, The Fortunate Contractor,** was published the next year, 1782. Its publisher called it "An opera in two acts" and claimed it was printed "As it was performed at New York." No record of any performance survives. But the text is a travesty of *The Blockade of Boston* which General Burgoyne wrote and had performed while he occupied that city. Burlesque had come early to American boards, even though its heyday was a hundred years or more away.

On April 16, 1787, Royall Tyler became the first American to have a comedy of his own produced for American audiences. **The Contrast** was first unveiled at the John Street Theatre in New York and soon performed in Baltimore, Philadelphia, and Boston. While indisputably a straight play, it bowed to conventions of the day by including at least two songs. Early in the first act the heroine, Maria, is discovered singing a plaintive tune whose lyrics have nothing to do with the story:

The sun sets in night, and the stars shun the day;
But glory remains when their lights fade away!
Begin, ye tormentors! your threats are in vain,
For the son of Alknomook shall never complain.

In the third act, the principal comic figure, the bumptious Jonathan, following in Raccoon's footsteps, offers new lyrics to "Yankee Doodle."

The success of *The Contrast* undoubtedly led to the mounting a month later of a second Tyler work, **May Day in Town; or, New York in an Uproar.** Advertisements in New York papers announced a "comic opera in 2 acts. . . . The Music compiled from the most eminent Masters. With an Overture and Accompanyments." The play was a one-performance failure. Never published, the text is lost. Nor do we know who the eminent masters might be. George O. Seilhamer, a 19th-century student of our stage, suggests it was "a skit on . . . the much dreaded May-movings."

Three years elapsed before another domestic musical work was announced. Like *The Disappointment,* Peter Markoe's "comic opera" in two acts, **The Reconciliation; or, The Triumph of Nature,** was slated to be produced in Philadelphia by the peripatetic American Company and abruptly discarded. The reasons for the change of heart were never made known, although a reading of the work and a published critique of the period suggest the piece may have proved too stilted for even so formal an age as the 18th century. But the musical is interesting on several counts. First, it pioneered, at least in domestic creations, the practice of making a lyrical evening from a straight play. In this instance, Markoe chose a translation of a short German play, *Erastus.* He turned it into a full evening's entertainment by increasing the dialogue and interspersing a fair number of songs. The story, like the story of *The Disappointment,* was simple, and this time devoid of any subplot. When young Wilson makes a marriage displeasing to his father, the older man disinherits his son. For twelve years Wilson and his wife live in poverty, although somehow retaining

3

the wherewithal to keep two servants. The elder Wilson becomes ill, and seeing death approaching, realizes how unjustly he behaved. He sets out to find his son but while seeking him is robbed of half his money. The thief turns out to be the son's servant, Simon, desperately attempting to keep his master from starving. A reconciliation follows. Perhaps more interesting is the untitled song which has survived and which offers both some idea of popular stage music of the time and an even better idea of why the text was considered "less fit for the stage than for the closet."

1793 witnessed the production of two works by **Raynor Taylor.** Taylor was an Englishman who emigrated to America and had become an important figure on the musical scene by the turn of the century. He was instrumental in founding the Musical Fund Society in Philadelphia. His biographer notes, "As a speciality he cultivated burlesque olios or 'extravaganzas' which came dangerously near being music hall skits. He strikingly illustrates the fact that the American public of the 18th century was not horrified by secular tendencies in an organist, outside of the church walls." His 1793 efforts included the "Mock Italian Opera, called **Capocchio and Dorinna** . . . Dressed in Character . . . Consisting of Recitative Airs and Duets . . . the whole of the music original and composed by Mr. Taylor," which was announced for presentation in Annapolis on January 20, and his "comic burletta" **Old Woman of Eighty Three** which was performed at the same city on February 28. Regrettably, like much of this early music, none of Taylor's secular theatre pieces seems to have survived.

Needs Must; or, The Ballad Singers raised its curtain at the end of the same year, on December 23. The celebrated actress Mrs. Pownall wrote the "trifle" as a vehicle for herself while she was bedridden with a broken leg. She turned to Anne Julia Hatton, a sister of Mrs. Siddons, for lyrics and some of the music.

Just over two months later Mrs. Hatton served as the librettist and lyricist for a more ambitious enterprise when the John Street Theatre offered its public the first performance of **Tammany; or, The Indian Chief** on March 3, 1794. Mrs. Hatton's motives were not entirely artistic. By glorifying Tammany she helped promote the Tammany Society and the Antifederalist cause. Mrs. Hatton's collaborator was James Hewitt, a violinist, composer, and ultimately a highly successful music publisher. Again the plot was simple. Tammany (John Hodgkinson) loves Manana (Mrs. Hodgkinson). But the villainous Ferdinand (John Martin) abducts her.

When Tammany rescues the girl, the Spaniards return and burn the two of them to death in their cabin. Some comic relief was provided by another Indian, Wegaw (W. H. Prigmore). The fundamentally tragic nature of the work places it on the fringe of popular musical theatre. But it must be remembered that tragic opera had a much more general vogue in the 18th and 19th centuries than in recent years. If a few of Mrs. Hatton's lyrics had a familiar ring, there is no reason to condemn the lady. The premium the romantic era set on originality had yet to become pervasive:

> The sun sets in night and the stars shun the day
> But glory unfading can never decay,
> You white men deceivers your smiles are in vain;
> The son of Alkmoonac shall ne'er wear your chain.

With something approaching scholastic integrity, Mrs. Hatton noted this duet between Tammany and Manana was "Altered from the old Indian Song," a point Royall Tyler apparently assumed his readers took for granted when he published *The Contrast*. On her own, Mrs. Hatton was not a bad lyricist, given the traditions of the epoch. For example, Ferdinand sings;

> Fury swells my aching soul,
> Boils and maddens in my veins;
> Fierce contending passions roll
> Where Manana's image reigns.

The lines throb with life if not with poetry. How well Hewitt's music coupled with the words can only be guessed. Although many of his compositions survive, nothing from *Tammany* has surfaced. But if the sounds of *Tammany* are silenced forever, the mind's eye can still form a tentative picture of how the production looked to 1794 audiences, for William Dunlap left a sketchy description of the mounting in his *History of the American Theatre*. His point was that *Tammany*'s scenery marked a small breakthrough in set design. Until its opening New York sets had been culled from tired "old stock [that] were originally of the lowest grade, and had become black with age." (Dunlap records that Philadelphia scenery of the period was far superior.) Charles Ciceri, a young man who in time became New York's best scene painter and machinist, apparently made his debut with his designs for *Tammany*. Dunlap noted, "They were gaudy and unnatural, but had a brilliancy of colouring, reds and yellows being abundant." Even at this early date musicals were a feast for the eye.

The Sicilian Romance, which was offered to Philadelphians in 1795 and to New Yorkers a year later, exemplifies still another practice which would become distressingly common with time. A London success, its William Reeves score was largely jettisoned and more "American" music by its coproducer Alexander Reinagle interpolated. Reinagle's score, like Hewitt's, is apparently lost.

No work of the American Musical Theatre before *The Black Crook* (9-12-66) has received more attention than **The Archers.** Numerous scholars have devoted extensive space to it, and Julian Mates has made it the center of his full-length study of the lyric stage of the time. Neither its quality nor its success justifies the disproportionate attention it has received. In fact, its quality is minimal. *The Archers* is competent hack work; little more. Nor was its success exceptional. Only five performances —three in New York and two in Boston—are definitely known to have taken place, although students surmise from various hints that another half-dozen or so representations were given in various cities.

The attention *The Archers* has won can be attributed largely to William Dunlap, who supplied both dialogue and lyrics.

. . .

William Dunlap has long been known as "The Father of the American Stage." Born at Perth Amboy, New Jersey, on February 19, 1766, he abandoned his New York City china shop at the age of thirty and purchased a substantial interest in the old American Company. He held the position of manager until bankruptcy forced him to resign in 1805. He retired to indulge his second love, painting. Dunlap had been a pupil of Benjamin West and become a founder and vice-president of the National Academy of Design. He returned to the theatre briefly in 1827. During his two theatrical stints he wrote or translated more than fifty plays. A dozen of his translations helped make August von Kotzebue almost as well known in America as he was in Germany. His other talents notwithstanding, Dunlap's major achievement may well have been his *History of the American Theatre,* published in 1832, seven years before his death.

. . .

The Archers was one of Dunlap's earliest efforts. It betrays not only something of his inexperience but also the general level of uninspired professionalism which he was never to rise above. Dunlap chose the William Tell legend as the basis for his plot. The story of Tell's struggle for Swiss freedom had great appeal for playgoers in a newly liberated land. Two years earlier, in 1794, Hewitt had composed an overture and song for another version, now lost, called *The Patriot; or, Liberty Asserted.* Dunlap's prologue proclaimed "We tell a tale of Liberty tonight." The tale is set in Altdorf. Cecily (Mrs. Hodgkinson), a basket seller, enters, singing of her wares. She is followed by her sweetheart, Conrad (Lewis Hallam), who appears leading his jackass. Conrad is also a street vendor, and he, too, sings of his trade:

> Here are bowls by the dozen, and spoons by the
> gross,
> And a ladle or two in the bargain I'll toss.

But the Austrians are impressing young Swiss men into service and a lieutenant (Joseph Jefferson, grandfather of his more famous namesake) arrives and orders Conrad seized. After a trio in which Conrad and Cecily bemoan their lot while the lieutenant sings a cynical rationale, the scene changes to Tell's home. Tell (John Hodgkinson), too, is unhappy. But his sorrow is for his whole nation. Unlike the comic pair Tell is prompted to action. He tells his wife (Mrs. Melmoth) and his young son (played as a trouser role by an ingenue, Miss Harding):

> How glorious 'tis in spite of time
> In spite of death, to live sublime.

By the Lake of Uri leaders of various groups of Swiss Archers meet and exhort their men. These leaders include Werner Staffach (Hallam, Jr.), Walter Furst (John Johnson), and Arnold Melchthal (Joseph Tyler). Furst's daughter, Rhodolpha (Miss Broadhurst), enters. She is dressed as a huntress and surrounded by young ladies. (Did her huntresses parade in a manner later generations called an "Amazon march"?) She begs to be allowed to fight alongside the men and her request is granted. Her motive is not entirely patriotic, for she is in love with Melchthal. The second act begins in front of the castle at Altdorf. The tyrannical Gesler (Mr. Cleveland) has ordered all the townspeople to kneel before his hat, which he has raised to the top of a pole. When Rhodolpha catches a pusillanimous burgher bowing to Gesler's orders she makes the embarrassed villager kneel to her and to liberty instead. At a town meeting Tell exhorts the citizenry much as he had earlier incited his wife and son to action. Gesler orders Tell's execution and is deaf to the pleas of Tell's wife. Only news of the emperor's death and the uncertainty of what will follow induce the tyrant to alter his edict. Tell will be spared if he can shoot an apple off his son's head. Tell succeeds, but the treacherous Gesler fails to keep his word. Tell and his guards embark in a boat with Gesler to cross the lake. A storm churns the waters and only Tell is able to bring the boat to safety. Jumping ashore he grabs his bow, shoots and kills Gesler, and escapes into the woods. Returned to his men, he leads the Swiss forces against Austria. In their joy, the lovers, Rhodolpha and Melchthal, sing not of their own passions but of their admiration for their leader:

> Where none are lords, and none are slaves,
> There look to find a Tell.

The Swiss triumph. The principals join in a concerted finale extolling the virtues and rewards of bravery and liberty. Only Cecily, given practically the last word, thinks in more immediate terms:

> Now war is o'er, and Conrad mine
> I'll make baskets neat and fine.

The chorus ends the work by repeating the sentiments Tell had expressed moments before:

> When heaven pours blessings all around
> O! May mankind be grateful found.

Although publication has permitted Dunlap's text to survive, Benjamin Carr's score for the piece, like so much of this earlier music, is largely lost. Of the little that remains the best is the song Melchthal sings to Rhodolpha on learning of her determination to join the soldiers, "Why Huntress Why."

. . .

Benjamin Carr was an Englishman who followed in the footsteps of Hewitt, Taylor, and Reinagle, emigrating to America in 1793. Moving to Philadelphia he became an organist, a composer, concert manager, and publisher. He joined Taylor in helping to found the Musical Fund Society, which long remained the prime lyric organization in Philadelphia.

. . .

In *The American Musical Stage Before 1800* Mates suggests Charles Ciceri may have designed the sets for the mounting. If, as seems likely, his surmise is correct, it would be worth noting how Ciceri's art had matured since his work on *Tammany*. Edwin Duerr, in an article on Ciceri in *Theatre Arts Monthly* (December 1932) records, "Ciceri, and his aides, often made use of the new transparent scenery, perfected in England by de Loutherbourg in 1780. From him, also, they had learned to build up their stages with scaffolding or carpentry for such elaborate spectacles that required practicable stairways, doors, windows, mountain passes, bridges, Gothic halls, and moun-

tain torrents. The New Yorkers probably experimented with dioramic, or moving scenery; and perhaps Dunlap and Ciceri knew side walls on their stage." Mates adds, "Ciceri also utilized artificial figures and was facile in the use of stage transformations." How many of his new skills Ciceri applied to *The Archers* is not known. But if tables and chairs were no longer painted on flats, for the most part scenery was still rarely architecturally conceived; flats, wings, flies, and drop curtains predominated. *The Archers* was first performed at the John Street Theatre on April 18, 1796, when it was advertised as "a new Dramatic Piece," but in his own history and in the published text Dunlap called the work "an opera." This was another early instance of the looseness with which musical works would be stamped throughout the history of the American Musical Theatre.

A one-performance failure of the same year was **Edwin and Angelina,** a musical version of the ballad found in Goldsmith's *The Vicar of Wakefield.* The libretto was by Elihu Hubbard Smith, a young doctor who died some months later of yellow fever at the age of twenty-seven. The music was by Victor Pelissier, who, with Hewitt, was long a composer and arranger for the old American Company. Slightly simplified, the plot details how the wicked Earl Ethelbert (John Martin) drives his erstwhile friend Sifrid (John Hodgkinson) into outlawry and causes Edwin (Joseph Tyler) to become a hermit. In the end both men are reunited with their loved ones: Sifrid with Emma (who never appears in the work), and Edwin with Angelina (Mrs. Hodgkinson). Ethelbert reforms. And so, grudgingly, does Sifrid's band.

Sonneck writes, "In 1797 a form of operatic entertainment was introduced in New York for which I believe the Americans to be peculiarly gifted: the melodrama." These were exaggerated and overwrought stories played out to a musical accompaniment. For the most part they were no more lyric theatre than the films and television programs of our own era that employ musical backgrounds, although a few slowly evolved into the spectacles so popular in the late 19th century. Surely the example Sonneck proffers as initiating the reign of melodrama does not fall legitimately into our field. The advertisement for *Ariadne Abandoned by Theseus, in the Isle of Naxos* called the work "a piece, in one act," adding, "Between the different passages spoken by the actors, will be Full Orchestra Music, expressive of each situation and passion. The music composed and managed by Pelissier." Although some of the music may have been in the form of songs it seems unmistakable that the advertisement was calling the public's attention to what today we would label background music.

If the rise of the melodrama began at the end of the 18th century, the demise of the ballad opera occurred simultaneously. Left for the public's pleasure were several forms of musical entertainment. Spectacles with "incidental Song" such as John Hodgkinson's **The Launch; or, Huzza for the Constitution** ("The Musick selected from the best Composers") and **Americania and Elutheria; or, A New Tale of the Genii** continued to hold sway. The latter, first done in Charleston in February 1798, was typical of the allegorical bent of so many of these works. In the piece a wood nymph demands to meet a mortal and when a satyr brings the nymph an ignorant old hermit, the Genius of America appears and commands her domestics teach the recluse how Elutheria, Goddess of Liberty, flew to the arms of Americania. Into these patriotic and allegorical representations a new twist was introduced at the turn of the century. As Sonneck records, "just then began the era of the American circus; and the novelty of equestrian and acrobatic feats combined with pantomimes sumptuously gotten up, like 'Bucephalus' and 'Don Juan' presented year after year."

Straight plays, too, might have a song or two for seasoning or variety. And about the same time French and Italian operas began to find their way into the playhouses. There were no auditoriums devoted solely to opera as there are today, nor was there sufficient demand or theatregoers to justify establishing such separate houses. As a result playgoers took in these early operas as part of a theatrical repertory. However alien the operas might have been, they were often the most artful, cohesive musical works available, and would remain so for nearly a century.

The early years of the 19th century were barren indeed for the American Musical Theatre. The paling forms of 18th-century lyric stage art—their lifeblood fast draining away—were virtually all the musical theatre audiences had to enjoy. To some extent this dearth persisted throughout the first two-thirds of the new century, although here and there sparks of life, small promises of a renascence to come, momentarily brightened the era's candle- and gas-lit stages. In a way, this lack of creativity and productivity is puzzling, for music and musical performers were near at hand in almost every 19th-century playhouse. Major theatres, even those with no intention of mounting musical offerings, kept full orchestras in their pits at all times, to entertain patrons before the first curtain and between acts. Many houses kept singers and dancers on their payrolls specifically to provide audiences with entr'acte diversion. In resident companies a particularly talented member of the acting ensemble often would double in brass to perform the chore, but if such a member were not already on the payroll, one would be hired. For example, for 1853 theatre historian Odell lists Adelaide Price as "the stock *entr'acte* dancer of the [Broadway] theatre." The Broadway was then a leading home of serious drama.

For all its atrophy or apathy the musical theatre was not totally moribund. In retrospect, the first gleamings of the future become evident. The prototypes of late 19th-century comic opera, farce-comedy, and extravaganza, and of 20th-century operetta, musical play, musical comedy, and revue are all to be seen. Four types stand out.

On March 3, 1823, the Park Theatre, then the finest of New York's two playhouses, was host to a hit from England, Pierce Egan's **Tom and Jerry; or, Life in London.** Jerry is Jerry Hawthorn (Mr. Cowell), a lad from the country come to London to visit his cousin, Corinthian Tom (Mr. Simpson). With Tom's friend, Bob Logic (Mr. Watkinson), the boys embark on a whirl around town. After visiting the high spots (the Burlington Arcade, Tattersal's) they become embroiled in a street melee and are hauled into court. But their adventures are not over. At a gambling house they lose their money. Fortunately, Jerry's country sweetheart, Sue (Miss Johnson), comes to take him home while Kate (Mrs. Bancker) helps restore Tom's fortune and leads him to the altar. As George Odell noted in his *Annals of the New York Stage,* "The gist of the matter is found in rapidly shifting scenes, great diversity of city types of character, and a large amount of consequent spectacle, song and dance. The dances included waltzes and quadrilles." The plot's somewhat slapdash nature allowed musical numbers and spectacular stage effects to be inserted or dropped at will. Although the era of "runs" was still several decades in the future, *Tom and Jerry* was repeated frequently for the remainder of the season. (Plays were still offered in repertory. The show's success was attested to by the haste with which a band of Negro players produced a version, and by the compliment of a burlesque, *The Death of Life in London; or, Tom and Jerry's Funeral,* brought out in the summer of 1824.

Eleven years later Charles Matthews arrived at the same Park Theatre with a show he called his

Comic Annual. Little more than a series of sketches in which Matthews introduced his audiences to a parade of city and country characters, the entertainment suggests how the loose structure of Tom and Jerry shows could be loosened further still into an incipient revue. Matthews, in what was almost a one-man show, gave patrons his version of celebrated critics discussing the poetry of Burns, Byron, Scott, and Shakespeare, told "The Old Scotch Lady's Leetle Anecdote," and portrayed Josephus Jollyfat, a Gastronomer Astronomer. Besides recounting in song the "Humors Of A Country Fair" and "A Police Report," Matthews filled the evening "with Welsh, French, Scotch, Irish, Indian, Swiss, and English airs."

In the spring of 1848 three shows opened in quick succession to take New York by storm. All three centered on a young Bowery fireman called Mose ("a true specimen of one of the B'hoys"), all three bustled with characters from the high and low life of the day, and all three used Tom and Jerry frames. All three also featured the tall, well-built, ruggedly handsome Frank Chanfrau as Mose, "with his red shirt, his soap-locks [hair plastered down with soap], his 'plug' hat [a top hat], and his boots, into which the trousers were tucked at will." The first to arrive was **A Glance at New York in 1848,** to a text by B. A. Baker. In Baker's tale George Parsells (G. Clark), a "Green-horn" from the country, comes to visit his city cousin, Harry Gordon (G. J. Arnold), and is quickly subjected to the wiles of every conceivable New York sharper. The principal sharper was Jake (W. Conover), proprietor of Loafer's Paradise. Other figures included Major Gates, a literary loafer; Mrs. Morton, president of the "Ladies' Bowling Saloon"; and six lovely members of the "saloon," who constituted a sort of primitive chorus line. Cabmen, Applewomen, and Newsboys provided local color. The show opened at the Olympic on February 15 and ran for 24 performances until a revised version, **A New Glance at New York,** was ready on March 15. Additions included "luscious-voiced" Mary Taylor as Eliza Stebbens, "one of the Gals." Her inclusion allowed the development of a love interest in this primitive *Guys and Dolls,* a love interest told in the slang of the time. Liza refuses Mose's invitation to see "de wawdeville plays," but she offers him an alternative:

Liza: . . . I'd rather go to Christy's. Did you ever see George Christy play the bones? Ain't he one of 'em?
Mose: Yes, he's some.

This prompts Liza to sing one of Christy's minstrel songs. *A New Glance* was even more successful than its parent, running 50 nights at the Olympic. Chanfrau had a third Mose saga ready at the Chatham on April 17 (it is unclear who replaced him as Mose at the Olympic). By this date excitement was such that the *Spirit of the Times* reported the police had to be called in on opening night to quell the boisterousness of the real "B'hoys" (members of rowdy gangs, composed largely of Irish immigrants) who packed the pit. Once more a country yokel, William Twill (Mr. Herbert), arrives from the country to spend a week with his city cousin, Charles Meadows (Mr. Stafford), and encounters a variety of unpleasant city types. The evening ended with Mose rescuing a child from a burning building. Sets took audiences to Chatham Square, the Chatham Theatre, the Old Dutch Church, a Soup House, City Hall, and the Catharine Fish Market. Songs included Meadows' singing of "Come Miss, Stir Your Stumps," while dances—besides jigs and a quadrille—included a "Nigger dance for eels." The show ran until mid-June. In September, Chanfrau played Mose in H. P. Grattan's *The Mysteries and Miseries of New York,* but this piece, at the National, failed.

Three years later, the celebrated W. E. Burton, whose troupe was briefly the finest in New York, offered his loyal patrons a similar piece, **The World's Fair; or, London in 1851.** Beginning February 15, 1851, at his own theatre, Burton as William Waggles spent several weeks showing audiences the sights of the metropolis and introducing them to We-Peek, Lo-Po-Te, Pete Gotobed, Mrs. and Miss Smudge, Fatima, the Greek Slave, and Light of the Morning. Three more years passed before Burton ventured another such vehicle, on December 11, 1854. For **Apollo in New York** Burton mixed burlesque elements with his Tom and Jerry tour. The gods visit New York in disguise (a similar plot would be used in 1910 for *Up and Down Broadway*). Apollo (Miss McCarthy) becomes Apollini, an Italian tenor, and courts a young society belle. New Yorkers of the day recognized the courtship as a thinly veiled parody of a real romance between the singer Signor Mario and one Miss Coutt. Burton played Jupiter, come to earth as Sandy Hook, but afterwards disguised as Mrs. Partington at a Women's Rights Convention. According to the *Evening Post,* Miss McCarthy's Apollo "inclines strongly to the Know-Nothing principle in politics, and opposes foreign intervention with a good deal of force." The action moved from Sandy Hook (with Lighthouse), where the gods land and

8

where Jupiter decides on a name, to the Staten Island ferry, to a Tavern, and finally to the women's convention. The *Evening Post* concluded the work owed its success "to localization rather than brilliancy." In fact, its success was negligible, so Burton withdrew it after 11 nights.

On August 18, 1856, a fascinating figure entered the Tom and Jerry lists, John Brougham.

. . .

John Brougham was born in Dublin, Ireland, on May 9, 1810. Financial problems forced him to abandon medical studies, and he made his theatrical debut at London's Tottenham Street Theatre in July 1830 in a production of *Tom and Jerry*. After acting for several seasons at Covent Garden he became manager of the Lyceum and began writing plays as well as performing. In 1843 he arrived in America, hoping to fill the place left vacant by the retirement of another great Irish star, Tyrone Power. But Power had been a brilliant, penetrating actor, while Brougham was essentially a showman. Brougham's American managerial efforts all ended in failure, but as an actor and a writer whose work ranged from farce to serious drama he was to play a major role in the American theatre for the next thirty-five years. Short, round-faced, with a high forehead and a conspicuous moustache, he soon became a beloved figure.

. . .

The entertainment Brougham offered at the Bowery transposed Egan's play to America, rechristened **Life in New York; or, Tom and Jerry on a Visit.** Assigning the parts of Tom and Jerry to lesser performers (Messrs. Fisher and Dunn), Brougham appeared in a number of guises, notably Fitzgammon Bowlingreen. His redaction took audiences from Collins Wharf, to Canal Street, the Astor House, and Mrs. Codfishe's ballroom (with dances and ballets choreographed by B. Yates and danced by the Henrarde Sisters). A finale at City Hall featured a fireworks display.

These vernacular Tom and Jerry romps led in time not only to the great Harrigan and Hart shows, but provided much of the impetus for both modern musical comedy and revue.

Another form that contributed significantly to both revues and musical comedies was burlesque, a more patently outlandish art that had, as we have seen, flourished sporadically even in the 18th century. Two figures dominated the art in the first half of the 19th century: James Robinson Planché and William Mitchell. Planché began earlier and outlasted Mitchell. His work seems more "classic," less wildly impudent than Mitchell's. Because both were

so prolific (Mitchell offered as many as 86 works in a single season!), we will offer only a sample of their art.

Planché's pieces were rarely full length. They were offered as merely one part of the elaborate bills our forefathers demanded, or at least sat through. In company with a drama called *The Hunchback,* Planché's "burletta" **The Deep, Deep Sea** was offered to patrons of the Park on November 15, 1834. The plot centered on Triton (Thomas Placide), who comes ashore in New England and announces himself to the strains of "Yankee Doodle." The entertainment presented parodies of opera arias such as "Non Piu Mesta" and "Di Tanti Palpiti," "mingled with Ride a Cock-Horse to Banbury Cross, or Oh, What a Row, What a Rumpus and a Rioting, as musical setting for the absurd quarrels of Neptune [W. H. Latham], Amphitrite [Mrs. Vernon] and Cassiope [Mrs. Archer], and the rescue of Andromeda [Mrs. Gurner] by Perseus [Mrs. S. Chapman] from the dread sea serpent." If Planché's music is forgotten, it must have enjoyed some contemporary vogue, for advertisements in the *Evening Post* informed readers, "Books containing songs of the Burletta, for sale at Box Office. Price 6 cents."

William Mitchell took over the Olympic on December 9, 1839, and for the next eleven seasons tremendously enlivened New York's theatre scene. Typical of his first season's offerings were **The Roof Scrambler,** a parody of Bellini's *La Sonnambula,* and **The Musquitoe,** a take-off of the ballerina Fanny Elssler's triumphs. The *Spirit of the Times* reported, "MITCHELL plays *Amina,* under the English, if not the more euphonious, name of *Molly Brown.* And how irresistible is the lovely *Molly,* whether in simpering gladness she engages in soft dalliance with her swain, *Swelvino* . . . whether scrambling over house-tops, or descending by pump-handles and water casks—or, more than all, sinking with decorous and innocent grace upon the couch of *Rodolpho.*" The paper continued, "And then the musical charms of the 'Roof Scrambler'— the glad voices which mingle in the swelling chorus to hail *Swelvino's* marriage; and the *silent* one which so eloquently describes to *Rodolpho* the mysteries of the enchanted chamber! And the grand *finale,* how mellifluously does *Molly Brown* glide from the exulting and rapturous burst of 'Ah! do not mingle' into a fitting, a joyous double shuffle!" Mitchell's own advertisements detailed scenes from *The Musquitoe,* warning, "This ballet is founded upon the well-known properties of the Musquitoe, whose bite renders the patient exceedingly impatient, and throws him into a fit of scratching, slapping and swearing delirium." The notice further advertised, "The MUSIC had been begged, borrowed, and stolen from all sorts of Opera and Ballets, in the most impudent and free and easy style—by the Musical Director, Mr. *George Loder*."

Mitchell's second season successes included **1940!; or, Crumbles in Search of Novelty** (which displayed Niblo's "a hundred years hence" and men flying routinely in balloons), and a spoof of the successful ballet, *La Bayadère; or, The Maid of Cashmere*, retitled *Buy-It-Dear, 'Tis Made of Cashmere*. Dances for the latter included the entrance of Buy-A-Brooms, Grand Broom Dance, Procession of the Palanquin, and the Grand Trial Dance. Rarely were these pieces full length. For example, Mitchell's bills generally coupled *1940!* with *Buy-It-Dear*. As the excerpt from his advertisement to *The Musquitoe* suggests, Mitchell's fun began long before his audiences entered his house. Notices for *Billy Taylor* announced "Produced without an Immense Expense, the entire cost being considerably under TEN THOUSAND DOLLARS!!! The new Scenery is painted on less than 50,000 SQUARE FEET OF CANVAS, and it has not been MANY MONTHS IN PREPARATION!!!" Clearly, the hasty reader, glancing solely at the capitalized words, would be misinformed. But Mitchell's private ledgers are still extant and they reveal another side of the theatre of the day. The Olympic's top price was for its dress circle—50¢, the going top price for all the years before the Civil War. Balcony seats cost 25¢, while a place in the pit went for 12½¢. To allow for such prices no one but Mitchell was paid more than $25 a week.

When Planché's **King Charming** opened at the Broadway on December 24, 1855, it was extended the courtesy of relatively long notices by both the New York *Times* and the *Spirit of the Times* (for the most part reviews at this time were maddeningly uninformative about details of production, and these were no exception). Both papers relished Planché's story of the king (H. C. Watson), blessed with eternal youth, who grows bored after three or four centuries, so decides to take a wife. He heads for King Henpeckt's court, where the princesses quickly battle each other for his hand. A good fairy (Mme. Elizabeth Ponisi) sees to it he wins the best of the girls. The *Times* quoted one couplet as typical of Planché's wit:

A wife like this I could not live a day with
She's one to run away from, not away with.

The paper also suggested what the era looked for in the genre, noting, "Mr. Planché may be con-

sidered the father of the modern school of Burlesque. In his hands a fairy tale preserves all its delicate outline of imagination. It is, for a child, the same wonderful creation it ever was. But his labors do not end there. He has to add something for the carping appetite of mature age. Pointed jokes, smart scraps of sarcasm, quick telling local allusions; all these have to be interwoven with the original texture without impairing its delicacy." (Years later, reviewing a burlesque of *Cinderella* which opened at the Winter Garden on September 9, 1861, the *Times* by indirection implied how far the insertion of sarcasm and local allusions had been carried when it praised the work for not containing a single reference to New Jersey or to "lager-bier.")

Curiously, the *Times* gave shorter shrift to, and the *Spirit of the Times* virtually ignored, an opening at Wallack's the same evening *King Charming* premiered, an opening many scholars have come to view as far more significant in the development of the American Musical Theatre. That show was Brougham's **Pocahontas; or, The Gentle Savage.** The evening featured Charles M. Walcot as Captain John Smith, Georgina Hodson as Po-Ca-Hon-Tas, and Brougham as Pow-Ha-Tan I. Other characters, whose names give something of the flavor of the work, were Cod-Livr-Oyl, Ip-Pah-Kak, Kal-O-Mel, Kross-As-Kan-Bee, Lump-A-Sugah, and Poo-Ti-Pet. Musical numbers were largely parodies of popular songs—only Smith's comic version of a song called "Widow Machree" was singled out by critics—while dances were apparently confined to brief jigs and a clog number. The musical ran as part of ever-changing, longer bills until February 23; it was replaced, two nights later, by a new Planché work, *Knights of the Round Table*.

Happily, the success of *Pocahontas* prompted reviewers to devote more attention to its successor a year later, this one written not by Brougham but by Walcot. Indeed, Brougham seems to have played no part in **Hiawatha; or, Ardent Spirits and Laughing Water,** either on stage or behind the scenes. Walcot naturally assumed the title role, playing, as the program noted, "a character strikingly more in the style of a School-boy than of a Long-fellow." The *Times* advised its readers, "He has interpolated jokes and puns of the most agonizing kind, and utterly regardless of historical truth makes 'Hiawatha' a critic, a censor, a satirist, a singer of comic songs, and a dancer of absurd jigs." The *Spirit of the Times* added that there was an excellent hornpipe as well as jigs. It noted the evening was laced with "songs, choruses and concerted" passages, praising especially an "opening glee and chorus, a parody on the

'Chough and Crow' from 'Guy Mannering.' " But Walcot turned out to be far from the star of his own effort. Encomiums were lavished on a slender, sloe-eyed young lady making her New York debut, Mrs. John Wood. Her excellent singing and adroit clowning as Minnehaha soon made her a star in her own right. Kind words were also awarded to a second young woman who would become famous, although not in musicals, Mary Gannon. She portrayed Pooh-Pooh-Mammi, "an indescribably self-willed young lady." Burlesque tradition loved to dress men in women's clothes, so *Hiawatha* enlisted Mr. G. Holland to play the hero's "grandmamma," No-Go-Miss. When *Hiawatha* closed after a month's run, Mrs. Wood went into another burlesque, *Shylock; or, The Merchant of Venice Preserved*, with herself as Portia and her husband as the Jew.

The list of burlesques presented in the period just covered would fill several pages. Most likely these works, if they are extant, deserve a serious scholarly examination. But as these examples suggest, the art of burlesque was vitally alive. In time, along with the competing minstrel burlesque tradition, it led to Weber and Fields, and, even in a constricted form, to the hilarities of later revue skits.

The Negro theatre mentioned earlier and the minstrels alluded to also influenced the American musical. A playhouse catering to blacks existed in the early 19th century in New York, led by the first major black actor in America, James Hewlett. The level of its artistry can be garnered from descriptions of its performances of *Richard the Third* and *Othello*. In *Richard*, King Henry and the Duchess were played by the same actor, one speech began "Gib me noder Horse," and "Several fashionable songs" were added. In *Othello*, Desdemona danced a hornpipe, while Othello and Iago put aside their enmity long enough to raise their voices together in "The Rival Beauties." Odell, suggesting "the verses . . . look like the beginnings of negro minstrelsy," quoted one couplet: At dancing school I next was sent, all muffled up with care,/Where I larnt to dance a minuet as graceful as a Bear!

Few, if any, white men attended these entertainments. But interest in the Negro as a stage character was growing. This interest was heightened appreciably in 1832 when T. D. Rice "jumped" his "Jim Crow" between the acts of whatever shows were on the bills of houses at which he was appearing. Indicative of the mélange of entertainment and moods early 19th-century theatregoers were prepared to face in a single evening, Rice made his New York debut on November 12 between performances of

two serious dramas, *The Hunchback* and *Catherine of Cleves*. Regardless of the expressive verb "jump" that immediately became associated with "Jim Crow," the dance seems to have been a shuffle, with the feet generally on the ground and upper-body movements contorted. Rice is said to have developed the routine after watching a crippled black stablehand in Louisville entertain himself. Some scholars dispute this story, especially since Rice is said to have also appropriated the Negro's tune. These scholars argue that tune is too similar to an Irish folk tune and an English stage song. They apparently assume that because Rice is said to have derived the tune from the Negro, the melody by implication must be black in origin. In any case Rice added his own words.

Wheel about, turn about
  Do jes so,
An' ebery time I wheel about
  I jump Jim Crow.

The dance along with its music and lyrics became what Robert Toll, in his history of the minstrel show, *Blacking Up*, labeled "the first of many Afro-American dances to become a worldwide success." For years afterwards Rice appeared in shows such as *Jim Crow in London* and *The Virginia Mummy*, their advertisements often promising "he will sing his celebrated song of Jim Crow."

Although blackface artists such as Rice were precursors of minstrelsy, the minstrel show, as an entire evening's entertainment, did not take to the stage until February 1843, when Billy Whitlock, Frank Pelham, Frank Bower, and Dan Emmett, billing themselves as the Virginia Minstrels, offered an extended exhibition of the "oddities, peculiarities, eccentricities, and comicalities of that Sable Genus of Humanity." Curiously, the term "minstrels," which has ever since been linked with burnt cork amusement, was given its vogue by this group. Until its arrival most blackface performers were known as "delineators," often, more specifically, "Ethiopian delineators." The new band borrowed the last half of its name from the Tyrolese Minstrel Family, which had just toured the land to great acclaim. Although the Virginia Minstrels disbanded within a year, its success was so great that imitators sprang up everywhere. For the most part these early minstrel groups stayed close to their home auditoriums. However, only a year after the debut of the Virginia Minstrels, a troupe known as the Ethiopian Serenaders trucked its luggage to the White House for a command performance.

While blackface seems to have originally been

used in theatricals in the South and Midwest, the evening-long minstrel show that first saw the footlights in New York also saw its principal development there. Toll believes this was "because the intense competition eliminated poor performers and forced innovations." What did evolve was the first genuinely American Musical Theatre, the first great indigenous entertainment. But only in the most liberal sense of the term could a minstrel show be a work of art. As Toll noted, "It had no characterization to develop, no plot to evolve, no musical score, no set speeches, no subsidiary dialogue—indeed no fixed script at all. Each set—song, dance, joke, or skit—was a self-contained performance that strived to be the highlight of the show." The show was held together by an external framework—what today's jargon would call a format—rather than by any internal cohesion or organically dictated form. Its devil-may-care indifference to even the vaguest dramatic unities helped establish a not altogether healthy slapdash tradition in the American Musical Theatre.

The pattern that did quickly settle into place was simple. The show was divided into three parts. The first part, with its semicircle of performers flanked by comic end men Tambo and Bones and presided over by a centrally seated interlocutor, was the section that came to typify minstrelsy. Tambo and Bones received their names from the tambourine and clackers they held and which they rattled to express their approval of a song or a joke. Their comedy routines and songs were interspersed with the more serious romantic melodies rendered by the fourth principal, the balladeer. The second part of the performances was an olio. Like the opening section, it was essentially a variety bill, made less formal by the absence of the interlocutor and end men. The difference between the two parts was more of degree than of kind. Its most noteworthy feature was a "stump speech," a comic monologue. Toll quotes one that began, "Feller-fellers and oder fellers, when Joan of Ark and his broder Noah's Ark crossed de Rubicund. . . ." The final portion of the show was an extended skit. At first these skits were simple scenes of plantation life laced with songs and dances, little more than a third type of vaudeville. Within a decade, however, George Christy of the Christy Minstrels and his copiers supplanted scenes of life in the South with lampoons of current events or, with increasing frequency, of current plays. The sensational vogue of *Uncle Tom's Cabin* inevitably demanded spoofing, and afforded an excellent and easy transition from plantation scenes to travesties of stage plays. Under such titles as "Uncle Dad's Cabin's," "Aunt Dinah's Cabin," "Life Among the Happy" (Mrs. Stowe's subtitle had been *Life Among the Lowly*), or "Happy Uncle Tom," minstrels presented a cheerily deranged version in which Uncle Tom was usually not sold down the river, in which Simon Legree often failed to appear, and in which Topsy, Eva, and all the other famous figures found ample opportunity for songs and jigs. As one lyric announced:

Oh, white folks, we'll have you to know
Dis am not de version of Mrs. Stowe;
Wid her de Darks am all unlucky
But we am de boys from Old Kentucky.

No small part of these curious inversions reflected an underlying and persistent sentiment of minstrelsy: its fundamentally anti-Negro attitude. However good-natured the kidding might be, by and large minstrel shows had little truck with abolitionist sentiment. The Civil War forced a certain change of attitude, but not a change of heart. With Reconstruction many a minstrel company briefly dropped their satirizing of stage successes to mock carpetbaggers and over-ambitious Negroes.

Within the pattern there was ample scope for a variety of songs, humor, and dance. Some of the most long-lived jokes in the American repertory seem to have first been tried on minstrel audiences. While no conclusive records exist it is probable that a minstrel first asked why a chicken crossed the road and told his amazed foil the answer, "To get to the other side"; and that a fellow blackface performer first asked why a fireman wears red suspenders and informed his straightman it was "To hold up his pants." Toll points to some humor which was double-barreled, evidently to reassure patrons that it was all a masquerade as well as to provide a joke. " 'Why am I like a young widow?' a comedian asked. After the line was slowly repeated, he fired back: 'Because I do not stay long in black.' " Later, when the popularity of minstrelsy began to wane, immigrants' dialects and traits were also parodied.

Minstrel songs ranged from racial lampoons to political satire to treacly 19th-century sentimentality. Obviously the coon songs came first. Many of these, especially in the beginning, appropriated standard melodies. "Jim Crow" was not unique. A number of successful minstrels claim to have carefully studied native Negro song patterns, and to have sometimes borrowed Negro melodies and verses. But how much genuine black material audiences heard remains moot. Although political satire employed darky speech it was clearly the product of professionals.

Of songs of a more sentimental nature, those that bear the signature of Stephen Foster are sung and loved to this day. Foster had played in minstrel shows as a young man and took readily to minstrel styles. All his songs were popular on the minstrel stage, although some, such as "Oh, Susanna!," "Old Black Joe," or "Camptown Races," were not necessarily composed with the stage in mind. But "Massa's In De Cold Cold Ground" and his masterpiece, "Old Folks At Home" ("Way Down Upon The Swanee River"), seem to have been composed at the behest of the Christy Minstrels, and the latter was first issued with E. P. Christy listed as composer. But Foster's material was the cream of the crop. More typical of the everyday melodies with which theatregoers of the era were regaled were the works of William Shakespeare Hays. While he is now all but forgotten, the remarkably prolific Hays was esteemed in his own day. "Early In De Morn'" exemplifies his work.

A few other songs from the minstrel stage have retained their popularity. For some, such as "Polly Wolly Doodle," their hold on public affection grows shakier with time. But "Dixie," which was written by Dan Emmett and introduced by him with Bryant's Minstrels on April 4, 1859, and soon employed to rally the Confederacy, has become a classic.

Most of the dancing—such as that employed with "Jim Crow" or "Essence Of Old Virginia"—derived from the same Negro shuffle that eventually led to the "buck and wing" and the "soft shoe." For the most part they were a white man's attempt to theatricalize a black man's art. But significantly the most highly praised of early minstrel dancers reversed the procedure. William Henry Lane, who performed as "Master Juba," was a Negro who based his routines on an Irish jig. From their inception, minstrel troupes composed of Negroes were generally most admired for their high stepping. Here was another pattern established early on! Apart from the clowning of a great comedian on the order of Bert Williams, it would be years before anything from a Negro musical but its dances would be taken seriously.

Although the minstrel show remained popular until the turn of the century, its heyday ended with the Civil War. The new musical entertainments that erupted just after the war offered novelty, more spectacle, and ultimately, the comfort of something that passed for a story. Leading minstrel impresarios were quick to appreciate the change of tastes. They attempted to compete by adding parades, more spectacular mountings of their own, more

non-Negro materials, and, in cases such as Francis Leon of Kelly and Leon's Minstrels, by offering female impersonations in their burlesques. But in 1883–84, when J. H. Haverly, the last of the great minstrel impresarios, bought out New York's final surviving resident troupe, the oddly named San Francisco Minstrels, the great era of blackface came to a close. Haverly increased the size of his companies, advertising 40 Mastodon Minstrels, and he unveiled a scene of a "Turkish Barbaric Palace in Silver and Gold" transformed before audiences' eyes into a King's Palace. He claimed to have spent as much as $1500 on a single costume when the whole shows cost no more to produce. But his efforts were to little avail. Those who followed him—Dumont, Dockstader, and their associates—generally contented themselves with playing to elderly audiences in houses that were not always the most desirable.

While Tom and Jerry shows, burlesques, and minstrels occasionally touched on less pleasant sides of life, their approach was essentially sunny, if tongue-in-cheek. Two other forms took themselves more seriously: spectacle and opera. Ultimately spectacle joined with burlesque to evolve into the revue-extravaganzas of the early 20th century. Technological advances and economics eventually drove it from the stage. Opera took two roads. One, uncompromising and lofty, led it away from popular stages to the confines of a few great auditoriums such as the Metropolitan Opera. The other, flexible and seeking a broader audience, abandoned recitative for dialogue, subdued its arioso flights, minimized the tragedy, and emphasized the romance of its stories. This road led straight to comic opera and operetta.

In the days before cinematographic realism and electronic trickery, scene painters and machinists vied with each other to see who could create the most startlingly life-like effects or the most magical flights of fancy. Audiences generally accepted the results with delight and enthusiasm. Even the most serious drama (although we might scoff at it today as absurd melodrama) featured these spectacular moments. And since most theatres maintained orchestras and a small troupe of dancers, these efforts could be embellished readily with music and ballet to make them even more thrilling. One example of this sort of serious drama-cum-spectacle must suffice. On January 11, 1836, the Bowery offered Louisa Medina's **Norman Leslie,** the saga of a man falsely accused of murder and his long struggle to vindicate himself. The story took its characters and its audience to, among other places, the American Hotel on Broadway, a magnificent Ball Room, Mr. Temple's house [on fire], an Italian Palazzo and Gardens by sunset, St. Peter's, a Carnival in Rome, the Coliseum in Ruins, and a Grand Denouement. The ballroom was the scene of quadrilles, waltzes, and gallopades; the Palazzo, of a peasant dance. At St. Peter's the hymn "Ave Maria" was sung by a large chorus. At the Carnival—where masqueraders romped as Alexander the Great, Shylock, Richard III, Hamlet, Julius Caesar, Achilles, Mahomet, and others—"sixteen ladies and gentlemen" performed a Russian dance, one Madame Trust did a Spanish dance with castanets, and a group performed a comic "Morice" Dance.

On July 4, 1828, William Niblo, who had successfully operated a popular coffee house and an entertainment park, purchased a large plot of land on the northeast corner of Broadway and Prince Street. He converted one building on the property into a theatre, naming it the Sans Souci. A year later he turned the playhouse into a concert hall and erected a large, new theatre next door. He rechristened his complex Niblo's Garden and Theatre, which his public promptly shortened to Niblo's Garden. His audiences for the most part lived so far away that the entrepreneur was forced to provide stage coach service between his far uptown establishment and the Battery. When the theatre was destroyed by fire in 1846 Niblo determined to retire, but he was persuaded instead to remain in business and erect a new house. With the city moving steadily north the adjacent ground was soon occupied by the Metropolitan Hotel and the theatre was entered through the hotel's lobby.

Almost from its inception Niblo's Garden regularly awed its patrons with lavish mountings of less seriously dramatic entertainments. For example, on April 21, 1841, no less an artist than Charlotte Cushman assumed the title role in Burton's **The Naiad Queen.** Neither the *Evening Post* nor the *Spirit of the Times* gave away the plot, but the latter hailed the scenery as "gorgeous in the extreme." Unfortunately, neither paper, nor the *Herald,* quoted by Odell, described the sets. Nor were the papers any more informative nearly a decade later when the house mounted Brougham's "spectacular new and original operatic drama," **Home,** in May of 1850 or the more light-hearted, fantastic **Island of Jewels** in the following month. That the latter was more comic can be judged from its cast of characters which included such names as King Giltginger-bread the Great, Prince Prettiphello (a trouser role), and Fairy Benevolenta.

But three other spectacles have left some glimpses behind, and they are worth noting. **Faustus; or, The Demon of the Dragonfels,** which opened at the Broadway on January 13, 1851, and ran six weeks, told of the downfall of the King of Naples. Early in the story a ship is wrecked and, as the audience watches, the wreckage is transformed into Venice at Carnival, "with Gondolas passing and repassing" and with "150 persons in Grotesque and Sumptuous Costumes." The evening ended with "the intrusion of Venetians seeking redress against the base Seducer! Wizard!! Murderer!!! The Steps are Red with Blood!! Repentance comes too late. The Demon claims his own. The Palace disappears, disclosing Pandemonium! Terrific Denouement!" All this was interspersed with ballets by Mons. Schmidt that featured Adeline as principal *danseuse,* Checkini as chief grotesque dancer, and La Petite Carman.

Faustus was followed at the same house on April 7 by **The Vision of the Sun,** an Inca legend in which a maiden is sacrificially drowned in a lake. Odell found a yellowing program for the work which noted, "The waters become agitated and rise, and in their progress to the whole height of the Stage, they assume various tints, till a most Brilliant Palace rises out of the Water!"

Even the renowned actress Laura Keene was not above turning her house over to such spectacles. She had the longest run of her career when **The Seven Sisters** (based on an older German work translated as *The Seven Daughters of Satan*) began a stay of 253 performances on November 26, 1860. Promising the best of all worlds, she billed her attraction as a "Grand Operatic, Spectacular, Musical, Terpsichorean, Diabolical, Farcical Burletta." She herself portrayed Diavoline, one of the seven sisters who come from hell to see the sights of New York. Her "terpsichorean" offerings included a ballet, a Zouave drill, and a shadow dance by Polly Marshall (who played another sister, Plutella). The evening ended with a lavish transformation scene— "The Birth of the Butterfly in the Bower of the Ferns." Odell found a description of it in the New York *Express*: "Emerald light, water as clear as crystal (it was represented by looking glass), water lilies, fern leaves, revolving pillars . . . welded together by the genius of the scene painter [James Roberts, from the Theatre Royal, Covent Garden] in one brief and delicate vision of fairyland." Clearly, all that was lacking to turn *The Seven Sisters* into the runaway success of *The Black Crook* (9-12-66) was the lush prosperity the oncoming Civil War would bring, and a bevy of girls in pink tights.

Opera remained a popular entertainment, not, as in later years, confined to a single house that served as museum as much as theatre. It was, as everyone agreed, by far the most artful form in the lyric theatre. While Rossini might switch overtures and arias from opera to opera with an abandon that shocks purists today, opera remained the most conscientiously coherent lyric art form, attempting generally to integrate words and music into a meaningful whole. Of course, America, far removed from the sources, sometimes took a more freewheeling attitude, as it would in future decades with lighter importations. Both this freewheeling approach and signs of change were evident in the 1833–34 season. The season was interesting musically in two particulars. Mrs. Joseph Wood, the celebrated English singer, made her American debut, and New York's first auditorium designed exclusively for the presentation of opera raised its curtain. Mrs. Wood arrived first. In 48 performances scattered from early September to the end of May, the lady offered such varied fare as *The Barber of Seville, Cinderella,* and *Robert the Devil* as well as English pieces on the order of *Love in a Village.* What artistic integrity her mountings displayed is questionable. *Robert the Devil,* for example, was not sung as Meyerbeer wrote it, but in an adaptation by Rophino Lacy. An idea of theatrical economics of the day is afforded by the grosses Mrs. Wood attained. Though her opening pulled a strong $1,679, and her eight benefits averaged $1,167, her 39 regular performances achieved receipts of only about $500 apiece. Some blame for the poor showing undoubtedly belonged to the competition provided by the new Italian Opera House, at Leonard and Church streets. Although its career was brief—to a large extent because it was erected in an out-of-the-way and unfashionable area—for much of its initial season it was society's new pet. From its opening on November 18 until it closed in financial trouble at the beginning of summer, it offered interpretations of seven operas—all, naturally, Italian. They inclued such now obscure works as Pacini's *Gli Arabi nelle Gallie* and Rossini's *Matilde di Shabran e Coradino.*

Within a few years English operas had a brief, pyrotechnic renaissance. Although their stories were hardly different from those of contemporary Italian and French works, something indefinably native in them allowed American audiences to feel an affinity for the works. William Michael Rooke's **Amilie,** first sung here at the Park on October 15, 1838, told a story much like that of Bellini's *La Sonnambula* and concluded with a voguish mad

scene for the soprano. An especially fine singer, Jane Shirreff, was America's first Amilie. Her "I'm Over Young To Marry Yet" and another aria, "John Anderson, My Jo," were whistled much as show tunes of a later era were.

The greatest of the English composers in this new school was unquestionably Michael William Balfe. His masterpiece, **The Bohemian Girl,** was given its first American performance at the Park on November 25, 1844, and was so warmly received it held the boards until mid-December. In its libretto a Polish exile, Thaddeus, rescues a young girl, Arline, from an attacking stag. When Thaddeus and his gypsy friends are abused by Arline's noble father they kidnap the girl and raise her as one of their own. Years later, when she is returned to her father, she refuses to marry anyone but Thaddeus. Edward Seguin and his wife sang the gypsy leader and the heroine, while one Mr. Frazer was Thaddeus. Out of this opera came one of the most popular songs of the day, long a standard in concerts, Arline's "I Dreamt That I Dwelt In Marble Halls." Balfe's **The Enchantress,** which premiered at the Chatham on May 25, 1846, was almost as popular, while other of his works were brought forth with varying success.

A third major English composer was Vincent Wallace. His greatest work, **Maritana,** was first performed in America in Philadelphia in 1846, then two years later brought to the Bowery on May 4, 1848. Gypsies and nobles mingled in its plot much as they had in *The Bohemian Girl.* In this case the gypsy girl, Maritana, and a young noble, Don Caesar, go off to consummate their marriage despite the intrigues of Don Jose on behalf of the lascivious King of Spain. Since the Seguins didn't offer the work until the last three nights of their repertory season, *Maritana*'s first run was brief. But once again the man in the street was soon whistling new operatic arias—the soprano's "Scenes That Are Brightest" and the tenor's "Yes, Let Me Like A Soldier Fall." Their popularity assured frequent revivals.

Inevitably, American composers tried their own hand at similar offerings. On September 27, 1855, Niblo's Garden played host to the world premiere of **Rip Van Winkle,** an opera with a libretto by J. H. Wainright and music by George Bristow. The *Times* could only recommend it to its readers on the grounds that native opera needed support even when it was indifferently executed. The paper damned the score with faint praise, dismissing it as "pretty." Adding that it was "pervaded with a martial manner," the paper rued its lack of period flavor. Amusingly, the reviewer seemed confounded by a second act which had no basis in Irving's story, but showed instead the fantasies dreamt by the sleeping Rip. A Mr. Stretton sang the role of Rip. The opera was sung nightly until October 6, when it entered a repertory that included *The Bohemian Girl, Maritana,* and—something of a surprise—*The Beggar's Opera.*

Since early works such as *The Archers* are probably closer in form to later comic operas and operettas than these English and American operas, the influence of these lyric pieces can be easily overrated or overlooked. Doubtless they were neither the sole nor the direct progenitors of the lighter lyric works of the late 19th century. But in softening the bravura, florid lines of Italian and French opera, in emphasizing and sentimentalizing romance, they helped ease theatregoers into a ready acceptance of a new form.

Although the Civil War was probably the most cataclysmic upheaval in our history, its effect on the American Musical Theatre was slight and indirect. The last wartime season, and the last season, but one, before the first great era of native musicals, 1864–65, witnessed no major changes in the musical scene. The news of the day—the surrender at Appomattox and Lincoln's assassination—was far more dramatic than any fiction occupying the boards. The most significant theatrical events of the year were not the premieres of any new masterpieces but the long runs recorded. These runs were occasioned by New York's exploding population and, more urgently, the tremendous war-born prosperity of the Union. The noted comedian John Sleeper Clarke had a record run of 101 performances in a repertory of his best loved pieces; this was bettered by John E. Owens, who compiled a stay of thirty-three consecutive weeks with his own repertory, but notably with his playing of the old Yankee farmer, Solon Shingle, in *The People's Lawyer.* Neither of these extended visits meant as much to theatregoers of the time as Edwin Booth's 100-performance run in a single play, *Hamlet.* Together the three men monopolized two of New York's seven principal houses for the bulk of the season. Booth was Clarke's brother-in-law. Tragically, he was also John Wilkes Booth's brother. Edwin, John, and Junius Brutus played in *Julius Caesar* on November 25, 1864. This was the night before Edwin began his run in *Hamlet.* It was the last time John appeared on the New York stage.

Musically, the theatre offered "more of more of the same." The Academy of Music at 14th Street and Union Square had long since replaced the virtually forgotten Italian Opera House. From September through May it offered New Yorkers the finest —and sometimes the latest—in German, Italian, and French operas.

Spectacle and pantomime were available to entertain younger playgoers and those seeking less high-minded diversions. Among the amazing hodge-podge of pleasantries P. T. Barnum offered at his Museum was a "musical fairy romance," **The Ring of Fate; or, Fire, Air, Earth and Water.** Beginning on December 26, 1864, Princess Eveline and Arnulph braved the elements and the supernatural on their way to the altar. It remained as the main feature on Barnum's extensive bill for a month and reappeared intermittently thereafter. At the Bowery, home of slapstick farce and roaring melodrama, a "new and gorgeous pantomime" entitled **Old Dame Trot and Her Comical Cat** headed the bill for eight weeks beginning January 30, 1865. G. L. Fox, soon to be famous as Humpty Dumpty, portrayed Sappy Saponaceous and Clown; his brother, C. K. Fox, played Antiquated Solderwell and Pantaloon; one Mons. Baptistine appeared as John Stout and Harlequin, while Mlle. Martinetti frolicked as Little Bo-Peep and Columbine. A female impersonator played Old Dame Trot to young Master Timothy's cat.

The two most prestigious minstrel houses were Bryant's and Wood's. Both opened the 1864–65 season on September 12. Throughout the year their bills changed to constantly spoof the rage of the moment. Bryant, for example, acknowledged Booth's triumph with a skit called "Evenings with Shakespoke," thereby competing with Wood's burlesque "Booth's Dane." The flood of actresses playing Mazeppa was mocked when Bryant appeared as Ada Leo Kate Fisher Hudson Menken Mazeppa. Bryant also doffed his hat to Owen by enacting Sole-Owen Shingle. Wood had notable success with a take-off on *The Streets of New York* and with an elaborate skit, "Petroliamania, or Oil on the Brain." Among the lesser troupes Campbell's Minstrels became Hooley and Campbell's and finally merely Hooley's. Sam Sharpley's Minstrels, advertised as "the famous Ironclads" and "the Monitors of Minstrelsy," made a brief appearance at the end of the season. But history would show the most significant event in minstrelsy was the opening of the San Francisco Minstrels on May 8, 1865, at 585 Broadway. The troupe—led by Charley Backus, "Billy" Bernard, "Billy" Birch, and "Dave" Wambold— came on the scene too late to be truly innovative, but in the waning years of minstrelsy it retained the highest standards of performance and production, and it went down in history, as we have mentioned, as the last great resident company in New York.

Hardly noticed at the time but of vital importance in the ensuing years was the transfer of another minstrel hall in which Sharpley's entourage had so briefly entertained to the aegis of Tony Pastor. Variety had just begun to supplant minstrels as the popular mass diversion. But it still had a low reputation. Much of the entertainment was suggestive if not lewd, and auditoriums in which it was offered saw a substantial part of their profits derive from liquor service. Pastor threw out the bars, cleaned up the entertainment, and made a point of inviting ladies to the shows. His success was too obvious to be ignored. Variety, or vaudeville as it was later called, served as training ground and sometimes as pasturage for the great names in the American Musical Theatre.

Of course a large number of the era's "straight" plays continued to have songs. Dan Bryant aban-

doned his blackface troupe for a time in July and August of 1865 to play a season in plays catering to an Irish-American audience, plays such as *The Irish Immigrant, The Colleen Bawn,* and *Born to Good Luck.* All the plays found places for Bryant to sing Irish or Irish-sounding ballads. Maggie Mitchell appeared in the title role with which she was identified all through her career. *Fanchon the Cricket* told of a waif—condemned because her mother is the village pariah—who wins everyone's love and respect by her goodness, and by her occasional singing and dancing. But all of these shows were primarily dramas and comedies, their songs attesting to the less strictured theatrical rules of the time.

Nowhere in the theatrical writings or dramatic reviews of this day does there seem to have been a cry for a new form of native stage musical. But in just over a season the postwar boom and a curious accident would combine to excite managers to its possibilities and to initiate, historically if not aesthetically, the American Musical Theatre.

2

ACT ONE
Early Successes

Scene One
OPÉRA BOUFFE AND NATIVE ELEMENTS
1866-1878

By the beginning of the 1866–67 season the Civil War had been over and Reconstruction under way for almost a year and a half. Prosperity prevailed, but harmony and integrity were in short supply. This war-engendered prosperity buoyed the American theatre to no small extent and helped produce what George Odell in his *Annals of the New York Stage* labeled "A Season of Sensations." Given conditions in our native theatre at the time, no one complained if most of the sensations had something of a foreign flavor. A few—such as the American debut of the celebrated Italian actress Ristori—attested simply to the dollar's growing power to import leading talents. Other events betrayed their foreign influences less blatantly. The season's dramatic success was Joseph Jefferson in *Rip Van Winkle*, Washington Irving's tale which had been dramatized many times before. Jefferson, then still a rising figure on the comic stage, had himself

played in several versions. This latest one—one that gave him a vehicle for the remainder of his life and became one of the best-loved stage pieces in American history—was prepared for the actor by Dion Boucicault. Although Boucicault had just spent several profitable years in the United States and with time would return to end his days here, the author was Irish born and London trained. He and Jefferson presented their new version in London for a season before bringing it to New York.

The few sensations that seemed to have no foreign connection were disasters—namely, the fiery destruction of the Winter Garden and of the New Bowery theatres. These were the fourth and fifth auditoriums to burn in Manhattan since the end of the war. It was the holocaust at the Academy of Music the previous spring that gave rise to the greatest sensation of all and to what is generally looked on as the birth of the American Musical Theatre: **The Black Crook** (9-12-66, Niblo's). In a way, this sensation, like Jefferson's *Rip Van Winkle* and Ristori's debut, had a foreign tinge about it. Two impresarios, Henry C. Jarrett and Harry Palmer, had imported a French ballet troupe to perform *La Biche au Bois* and had booked the Academy to display its art. Suddenly without a stage, in desperation they approached William Wheatley, the manager of Niblo's Garden, hoping to obtain his house. They discovered Wheatley had committed himself to a second-rate melodramatist, Charles M. Barras, and was preparing to mount the author's piece of ersatz German romanticism. Luckily for the annals of our stage, Jarrett and Palmer's frantic cajolery induced Wheatley to merge the two offerings. The result was a five-and-a-half-hour spectacle (in many ways similar to earlier Niblo spectacles we have mentioned) which made all three men, as well as the initially reluctant Barras, comfortable for life.

Barras' story was a rather wooden variation of Carl Maria von Weber's romantic opera *Der Freischütz*. The "Arch Fiend" Zamiel (E. B. Holmes) induces Hertzog (C. H. Morton), the Black Crook, to deliver a human soul into his power each twelfth month just before midnight on New Year's Eve. Count Wolfenstein (J. W. Blaisdell) has imprisoned the painter, Rudolf (spelled in many programs Rodolphe, and played originally by G. C. Boniface). Hertzog arranges for Rudolf's escape and promises to lead Rudolf to a cache of gold. The grateful Rudolf accepts, not understanding the nature of the bargain. On his way to the gold Rudolf saves the life of a dove. The dove proves to be Stalacta (Annie Kemp Bowler), the Queen of the Golden Realm. She alerts him to his dangers, takes him to fairyland, and ultimately sees to it he wins the hand of his beloved Amina (Rose Morton).

Barras probably never understood how lucky the unwanted additions were for him. His very plot was modeled on a type even then going out of vogue. His gift for characterization was minimal and his way with dialogue heavy-handed, although not exceptionally so in an age of stilted stage speech:

Rudolf: If this indeed be not a dream, tell me, bright being, you whose simple motion seems to sway the moves and passions of this Elfin Band, who art thou, and where am I.

Stalacta: I am called Stalacta, Queen of this dazzling realm, the glittering wonders that assail thine eyes are not creations of phantastic dreams, but nature's handiwork, wrought with the cunning fingers in a bounteous mood.

Not all the dialogue was so wordy. But even in fairly short speeches tricks of Victorian rhetoric prevailed. When Hertzog discovers his efforts are to prove fruitless he rails, "Foiled, tricked, crossed in the hour of my victory." The nature of the story and the demands of the large-scale spectacle allowed little play for comedy. The chief comic figure was Von Puffengruntz (J. G. Burnett), Wolfenstein's valet. Most of his laughs were gotten visually. He faints into his wife's arms, has his wig unexpectedly lifted, and receives a drubbing from his wife. What little dialogue he had ran to the order

of "You snore, Madame Von Puffengruntz, you snore loud enough to split the drums of my ear and rip out the seams of my night-cap." Musically the show was a hodgepodge. Extant librettos record only two lyrics, a villagers' chorus in the first act and Stalacta's spell in the second. The villagers sang:

> Hark, hark, hark
> Hark, the birds with tuneful voices
> Vocal for our lady fair
> And the lips of op'ning flowers
> Breathe their incense in the air.

There are, however, a number of musical cues. They indicate ballet music or melodramatic backgrounds. While much of the music, as it had been in the old ballad opera tradition, was derived from the better-known and well-loved compositions of the day, several composers contributed new melodies, notably one Giuseppe Operti. For the most part, the songs failed to catch the public's fancy. They were replaced at intervals all through the long run and the subsequent revivals. The only tune singled out for praise by the New York *Times* reviewer was a number he called "The Naughty Men," which was published as "You Naughty, Naughty Men" (G. Bicknell/T. Kennick). It was a simplistic ditty drifting along on an elementary ABC or A^1 A^2 A^3 pattern. The sheet music announces it was "composed for and sung by" Millie Cavendish, a young English entertainer who played Carlina, Amina's maid.

The *Times* critic noted the song was encored. But he also noted the principal ballet was "encored twice." Indeed, the ballets with girls in pink tights proved the sensation of the evening. David Costa devised the choreography, patterned in the romantic style of the day, assigning his choicest conceptions to four principal ballerinas: Marie Bonfanti, Rita Sangalli, Betty Rigl, and Rose Delval. Odell exclaimed, "the ballet, the wonderful ballet . . . was the thing." The critics and the public agreed. Costa also presented a line of tall girls in carefully staged drills, proffering in these "Amazon marches" the "dance" form that most seriously rivaled classic ballet on our musical stage for forty years, until the waltzes of *The Merry Widow* (10-21-07) swept it away.

The *Tribune* dismissed the book as "rubbish," the *Times* damned it as "trashy." But the *Times* hastily added, "No similar exhibition had been made in an American stage that we remember, certainly none where such a combination of youth, grace, beauty and *elan* was found . . . decidedly the event of this spectacular age." The *Tribune,* equally impressed, went into more detail: "Some of the most perfect and admirable pieces of scenery that have ever been exhibited upon the stage are employed in this piece." After extolling a storm scene painted by R. Smith, the paper turned its attention to the second-act finale: "A vast grotto . . . extending into an almost measureless perspective. Stalactites depend from the arched roof. A tranquil and lovely lake reflects the golden glories that span it like a vast sky. In every direction one sees the bright sheen or the dull richness of massy gold. Beautiful fairies, too, are herein assembled—the sprites of the Ballet, who make the scene luxuriant with their beauty." *The Black Crook* made transformation scenes (major scene changes executed while audiences watch) de rigueur for spectacle mounting. Once again the *Tribune* attempted to convey its grandeur to the paper's readers, noting the effects were devised by the Drew Brothers of London. "One by one curtains of mist ascend and drift away. Silver couches, on which the fairies loll in negligent grace, ascend and descend amid a silver rain. Columns of living splendor whirl, and dazzle as they whirl. From the clouds droop gilded chariots and the white forms of angels." Almost as an afterthought the paper noted "two bits of painting are especially remarkable," listing these as D. A. Strong's "A Wild Pass in the Hartz Mountains" and James E. Hayes' "Valley at the Foot of the Hartz Mountains."

The word "painting" is significant. Years were to pass before sets were architecturally conceived. The great scenery of this era was, with few exceptions, simply flats with perspective painted on. Unless absolutely essential to the play's action—as, say, the balcony in *Romeo and Juliet*—balconies, stairs, columns, trees, even animals and, sometimes, people, were merely oil on flat canvas. For the most part, in these decades of cheap labor, performers, not scenery, filled the stage. Moreover, as credits for *The Black Crook* demonstrate, no one man was responsible for the total integrity of the sets. Artists specialized in one type of scene and usually were allowed to design only that set which depicted their specialty. For its day, these practices worked superbly.

Odell is undoubtedly correct in stating, "the show revolutionized ballet spectacle in America." But it can seriously be questioned whether *The Black Crook* was the beginning of musical comedy in America. Textually, the early American ballad operas have as much claim. They, too, combined song, drama, and, to a lesser extent, dance into a total evening's entertainment. Nor did the more successful musicals that followed in the dozen or so years after *The Black Crook* opened seem significantly influenced by its style and tone. Rather, it was the profit the producers made on their at that time enormous investment of $50,000 and the phenomenal run of 475 performances that alerted other producers to the money to be made from such lavish productions. Another practice initiated by *The Black Crook* was the periodic revision of the production, freshening sets and costumes and introducing new material and performers. These "improvements" became known as reconstructions. The first occurred on May 25 when two new ballets "The Bouquet" and "The Water Lily" were incorporated to display the artistry of new dancers supposedly imported from La Scala, San Carlo, and Covent Garden.

Of course there were other musical entertainments to divert theatregoers in 1866–67. The San Francisco Minstrels opened their season on September 3, the night of Joseph Jefferson's premiere. Three weeks later the troupe interpolated a burlesque of *The Black Crook.* The travesty so delighted audiences it was retained on the bill for most of the remaining season. While the San Francisco Minstrels had quickly established a reputation as "the most dignified, the most settled" of blackface bands, demands for their sort of entertainment held steady enough to allow a number of other organizations to flourish. In New York, Kelly and Leon's Minstrels and George Christy's company provided season-long competition. On March 2 a new playhouse, known in its first year both as Lingard's and as Wood's Theatre Comique, opened with an attempt to have the best of both worlds. It presented for its patrons' amusement "minstrels, pantomimists and ballets." Both managements failed, although in a few years the house was to know a brief period of glory.

Apart from *The Black Crook* the most enduring musical of the season was **The Doctor of Alcantara.** This so-called "opéra bouffe" had its premiere four years earlier on April 7, 1862, at the Museum in Boston, Massachusetts. Its score was the work of Julius Eichberg; its libretto by Benjamin Woolf. Eichberg figured insignificantly in the history of our musical stage, but Woolf played a more prominent role, although most of his activity was confined to Boston.

. . .

The obituaries that appeared the day after **Benjamin Edward Woolf**'s death in Boston on February 7, 1901, give no clue as to the date of his birth, offering only the information that he was born in England and emigrated to America at a very early age. Here he apprenticed as an engraver, but left that calling to become a violinist in the orchestra his father conducted at Burton's Theatre in New York. He soon moved to Boston to himself conduct a pit band, at that city's Museum. As the Boston *Herald* noted, "He early developed the brilliant and versatile talent found so often in the race to which he belonged." His poetry was published in book form, his art presented at leading galleries and, between about the time of the onset of the Civil War and the mid 1890s, he wrote over thirty shows for production in Boston. Curiously, for all his musical skill and knowledge, he seems to have confined himself largely to contriving librettos. At one time or another he served as drama critic, art critic, or music critic to a succession of Boston papers, for a brief period covering drama and music for both the *Saturday Evening Gazette* and the Boston *Globe* simultaneously.

. . .

Woolf and Eichberg's piece suggests that perhaps a distinct musical genre was slowly evolving from European ballad opera, sing-spiel, or opera buffa and that with time the form would have become both sufficiently artful and native to enjoy a success equal to the vogue of a mindless spectacle such as *The Black Crook.* Just such a development did occur thirteen years later in England, when *H.M.S. Pinafore* became the rage.

For the moment, Woolf employed stale Continental motifs to assemble his story. Basically the plot revolved about two young lovers, Isabella and Carlos, who are ordered by their respective fathers, Doctor Paracelsus and Senor Balthazar, to marry mates they have never seen. None realize that the lovers and the selected mates are one and the same. Woolf resorted to several common—and Shakespearean—ploys for comic relief and dramatic tension. At one point Carlos gains entrance to Isabella's house concealed in a basket. When the basket is thrown out a window into the river Carlos is presumed drowned. Later Carlos is again mistaken for dead when he drinks one of the doctor's sleeping potions. Woolf's dialogue was, no doubt, spunky for its day. In one scene Isabella's mother, Lucrezia, attempts to persuade her to accept her father's selection:

Isa: A pretty sort of gentleman he must be to have his wife selected for him.

Luc: That is an especial proof of his trust in you.

Isa: Nonsense! It is an especial proof that he is a fool. Obedience in such a case is no merit.

Eichberg's music is typified by "I Love, I Love," which Carlos sings to a baffled Lucrezia on popping out of the basket.

Three companies mounted the work successfully in New York at one time or another during the season. The American Opera offered it as part of its repertory on September 25, at the French Theatre. Eichberg himself conducted the ensemble at the New York Theatre for two weeks beginning October 3, while Caroline Richings included it among her bills at the French Theatre in the spring. At the New York it was followed by a week's run of the same composer's *A Night in Rome* and then by a two-week stay of an English rendering of Donizetti's opera *The Daughter of the Regiment.* In keeping with the practice of the time, the musicals were merely the main course in a theatrical feast that also included a short farce such as *Wanted, 1000 Milliners* or *Rum-ti-Foo-zle* as well as diversions between the acts and sometimes between scene changes. With time the Donizetti work gravitated to the confines of opera houses, but *The Doctor of Alcantara* held its audiences' affections and was revived with some frequency in ensuing years at regular legitimate theatres.

On November 2 the Brothers Brough took over the New York Theatre with their London burlesque *Perdita.* The next musical offering was also from their shop. Irene, Jennie, and Sophie Worrell began the first of two visits on January 14 with *Camaralazman and Bedoura.* These ladies, whom Odell says were "the first to give here *opéra-bouffe* in English," clearly possessed the diverse skills necessary to keep a mid-19th-century entertainer employed. Their act included banjo solos and a cobbler's hornpipe. When their rather unattractively titled vehicle showed itself to have limited appeal, the sisters hastily converted to pantomime. Their double bill of *Cinderella* and *Aladdin* premiered on January 14 and ran a month at the Broadway. Demand was such that, after honoring commitments on the road, the sisters returned on May 6, this time to the New York Theatre, and embarked on a two-month stay during which *Cinderella* was coupled with any one of three works: *Aladdin, The Elves,* or *The Invisible Prince.*

Caroline Richings also began the first of her two visits on January 14. Miss Richings' art was on a higher plane than that of the Worrells. The bills of her initial stay at the Olympic included *Maritana, The Bohemian Girl, Rose of Castile,* and the "beautiful musical drama" *The Blind Man's Daughter.* Except for *The Bohemian Girl* the works are forgotten today, although their own age viewed them with respect as exemplars of popular lyric art. When Miss Richings returned the first night in April she added *Crown Diamonds* and the ubiquitous *Doctor of Alcantara* to her repertory.

German operas such as *Zar und Zimmermann* and *Stradella* also made the Olympic's rafters ring during a short season that began on February 4.

The last musical offerings of the season were presented by P. T. Barnum at the Old Bowery—not to be confused with the New Bowery, which had burned. The pantomime *Jack and Gill* had a brief vogue while *Little Boy Blue* began a successful stay on April 1.

1867-1868

Perhaps the most surprising feature of this season was the dearth of pieces imitating *The Black Crook*. The lone work following in its path, *The White Fawn*, was mounted by *The Black Crook*'s producers and was disappointing. Its relative failure suggested the success of the first work was a little freakish. Although coming seasons did bring spectacles mounted in the *Black Crook* tradition, especially at Niblo's, only *The Black Crook* itself and *Around the World* (8-28-75) engendered sufficient loyalties to allow for a long history of successful revivals. Another genre burst on the musical scene in September 1867 to claim theatregoers' attention. More cohesive and artistically thoughtful than the haphazard opulence of *The Black Crook*, this new genre—opéra bouffe—deserved its popularity. Despite the evident artistic integrity of the new form, American writers, for the most part, continued to produce contrived claptrap pieces that nevertheless retained the allegiance of New York theatregoers.

The musical that started the rage was Jacques Offenbach's **La Grande Duchesse de Gérolstein,** a tongue-in-cheek history of a great lady's love for a common soldier. She promotes him all the way to general before she realizes she can never win his affections away from his simple sweetheart. Paris had first heard the work only five months earlier on April 12, 1867, at the Théâtre des Variétés, with the celebrated Hortense Schneider in the lead. Its American premiere came about in a curious fashion. Ristori had returned early in September for another season at the French Theatre. But like many of the reigning stars of the time, she refused to perform every night. On one of the nights when the theatre would have been dark, September 24, the impre-

sario H. L. Bateman mounted *La Grande Duchesse* for Lucille Tostée. Tostée and the show "took the town by storm. 'Voici le sabre de mon père' and other airs of La Grande Duchesse were hummed, whistled, played until the ear was worn to shreds." Since New York's few theatres were generally booked ahead for most of the season, Batemen was forced to fit in performances wherever and whenever a house became available for a night or two. As a result, although the mounting achieved a "run" of 156 performances before it was withdrawn on March 25, it did so in a happenstance repertory with Ristori and other productions. The record was impressive for the time—all the more impressive since the work was sung in French. (Hereafter, with some exceptions that should be obvious, opéra bouffe titles will be given in the language used to sing the mounting. General discussions will use the English title.)

Niblo's sequel to *The Black Crook,* **The White Fawn,** premiered on January 17. Its fate augured ill for the future of sequels in the American Musical Theatre. James Mortimer provided the libretto, while the music was again the work of a number of hands. The story retreated from the adult, metaphysical romanticism of Barras' plot to a lighter, fairy-tale-like world. In a sense, the story hinted at the long reign to come of librettos for adults that employed stories and motifs from childhood. The basic plot was simple. For her disobedience, Princess Graceful (Jennie De Lacey) is sealed in a dark tower by her father, King Dingdong (Mark Smith). Otherworld creatures aid her to flee into the arms of Prince Leander (Lucy Egerton). *The Black Crook*'s Germanic names gave way to comic contrivances such as King Salmon and Lord Twaddledum. At times this otherworldliness was brushed aside in the interests of topicality. The *Times* noted of the audience, "Light words inflamed them and the faintest political hint fired them. Quite a small conflict of cheering and hissing occurred during the third act over an allusion to Gen. Grant and the dialogue was not permitted to be proceeded until the General and the President received the conventional number of hurrahs." But spectacle and ballet remained the dominant attractions: "Gold, silver, silk and electricity—all the effulgence and gradation of light and color mix one with the other in the midst of an admirably arranged confusion, where probably has nowhere else been seen . . . fairy creatures caper about with torches on their heads which they agitate in such a manner as, notwithstanding the gracefulness of the action, makes one tremble lest they should set themselves on fire." Circus elements were fast invading Niblo's thinking. A first-act finale had children and midgets, as carpenters, masons, and other laborers, erecting the tower. Like *The Black Crook* the show was inordinately long. On opening night the fourth act did not begin until 12:05. First-nighters never saw the final grand transformation; it was discovered all too late that "eighty carpenters and twenty gasmen could not work it perfectly." *The White Fawn* was not a failure, but its run of 150 performances, coming after the year-long stay of *The Black Crook,* marked it as a major disappointment.

The minstrels who had been entertaining New Yorkers all season long brought out their biggest guns in February. The scandal-ridden Kelly and Leon's Minstrels (Kelly had shot a rival performer at the Fifth Avenue Theatre) came to life when Leon returned to the stage in "The Grand Dutch 'S'." "Mounted with a lavishness hitherto unknown in such things," the skit enjoyed the longest consecutive run in minstrelsy, February 3 to June 6. In the cast was George Christy, now without his own troupe and making what proved to be his final Manhattan appearance. A week later the San Francisco Minstrels unveiled their most popular skit of the season "Under the Kerosene Lamp," a takeoff on Augustin Daly's popular *Under the Gaslight.* Earlier in the year they had also enjoyed some success with a travesty of Robertson's *Caste* rechristened "Caste from Memory."

Although *The Grand Duchess* inaugurated a decade-long rage for opéra bouffe, some of which are performed to this day, the season's runaway success was a native effort derived from an older British tradition. With G. L. Fox as star and librettist of **Humpty Dumpty** (3-10-68, Olympic), American pantomime reached its peak.

· · ·

George Lafayette Fox was probably the first real "star" of the American Musical Theatre. He was born in Boston, most likely on July 3, 1825, although his obituary lists his birth year as 1823. Since he was "52 years, 3 months and 21 days" old when he died on October 24, 1877, the later date seems more accurate. He came from a family of "actors of a mediocre kind such as used to delight rural New England audiences but rarely appeared before city theatre-goers." After his Boston debut at the age of seven in *The Hunter of the Alps,* he roamed with his family troupe until shortly before making his New York debut in 1850 in *The Demon of the Desert.* A long stint playing Gumption Cute and Deacon Perry in *Uncle Tom's Cabin* was ended so that he could try his hand at pantomime. He scored successes in *Magic Pills* and *The Devil's Doctor,* left to serve briefly in the early years of the Civil War and returned to attract attention to himself in repertories of *Jack and the Beanstalk* and other such pantomimes. He had increasingly lengthy stands, culminating in a season-long stay at the Old Bowery beginning in September of 1865. Lean, with pointed features that reflected his name, he eschewed brash comedy. Instead he drew both sympathy and laughs with performances that contained as much pathos as humor. His popularity was such that when *Humpty Dumpty* was at its height he was the highest paid actor in America. His yearly income exceeded a then remarkable $20,000.

· · ·

For Americans who have forgotten the pantomime tradition, it is important to point out how far it strayed from Mother Goose. The action of *Humpty Dumpty* begins in the "Abode of Romance" where Romance (Mrs. C. Edmonds) and Burlesque (Alice Harrison) decide to follow the antics of a group of children. The children are Humpty Dumpty (Fox), Goody Two Shoes (Emily Rigl), Goody's beau, Dan Tucker (C. K. Fox), and One Two Button My Shoe (F. Lacy). The course of the puppy-love affair between Goody and Dan does not run smoothly, complicated as it is by the suit of the Honorable Grandeur Dignity. Goody rejects him violently, toppling him backwards. When Goody and Dan are finally allowed to come together, Burlesque, in accepted pantomime fashion, turns the children into Clown, Columbine (with a twelve-inch skirt and silk tights), Pantaloon, and Harlequin (in spangled trunks and patchwork fleshings). Also, in accepted pantomime fashion— especially in its American reincarnation—topical references abounded. In an allusion to the growing political graft and to the postwar inflation, the children pay a call on New York's new $100,000,000 City Hall. At one point our "manifest destiny" was acknowledged when nurses carried two babies on stage. The babies were called Alaska and St. Thomas. In others of the sixteen scenes the cast skated and demonstrated its finesse at billiards. Sets conveyed audiences from Romance's abode (by moonlight) to the Farm of Plenty, an Enchanted Garden, New York sights such as the Olympic Theatre by Night, a Candy Store, City Hall, and, just before the Grand Transformation, to the Retreat of the Silver Sprites. As he had for both *The Black Crook* and *The White Fawn,* David Costa devised the choreography, which ranged from elaborate ballets to a simple contredanse, a country style dance with participants ranged facing each other. As the months of the run went by, *Humpty Dumpty,* like *The Black Crook,* incorporated anything that its producers felt would appeal to playgoers. In April a champion skater, E. T. Goodrich, joined the cast, along with La Petite Ravel. By June a major "reconstruction" added a Zouave drill and bayonet combat. One new scene had three dozen people in formal dress, each carrying a shield with the name of one of the states, invite a lady named "Cuba" to join them. In the next season, the producers felt they had made enough revisions to advertise the presentation as the "second volume." These changes included ballet girls making music with wooden and straw sticks and the same young ladies dressed as men. Musically, the evening was probably even more vapid. The score, advertised as "all new," was attributed to A. Reiff, Jr., although much of his task admittedly consisted of selecting suitable airs from the standard repertory. His original material was banal and ignored in most reviews. Virtually nothing was published. It was primarily on account of the magic of Fox's cavortings that *Humpty Dumpty* recorded a first run of 483 performances and grossed $1,406,000 in New York and on its initial tour. Because Fox understood the show's appeal to children he inaugurated a series of Wednesday matinees. These proved so successful that within a few years even plays catering solely to adults began midweek afternoon performances (only *Uncle Tom's Cabin* during its 1853 run at the National had employed midweek matinees successfully before). The show was to have frequent remountings over the next two decades, and Fox himself played the lead 1,128 times, until his insanity caused him to be forcibly removed from the stage. Whatever its failings as a piece of artful writing, *Humpty Dumpty*'s success underscored the lesson of *The Black Crook:* a vast audience awaited native lyric works tailored to the taste of the American public.

The night after H. L. Bateman withdrew *La Grande Duchesse,* he offered Tostée in a second Offenbach work, **La Belle Hélène** (3-26-68, Français). In France this retelling of the Trojan War legend disguised political barbs that were lost on American audiences. Neither critics nor theatregoers were taken with it as much as they had been with the earlier opéra bouffe. But the musical was by no means a failure, running from March 26 until May 2. A month after it closed Kelly and Leon's Minstrels honored it with a spoof, "La Belle L.N." Kelly, released from jail, played Paris while Leon assumed his customary drag to portray Helen. The skit was successful, but just as *La Belle Hélène*

failed to equal the vogue of *La Grande Duchesse,* "La Belle L.N." fell short of the appeal of "The Grand Dutch 'S'."

An opéra bouffe company was hurriedly rushed in from New Orleans, but its productions of Offenbach's *Orphée* (*Orphée aux Enfers*) and *La Grande Duchesse* seemed provincial to New Yorkers, and the company left almost as abruptly as it appeared.

May brought Caroline Richings back to sing much of the same repertory she had offered the preceding year.

Undaunted by the disappointing showing of *La Belle Hélène* and the fiasco of the New Orleans troupe, Bateman organized the H. L. Bateman's Opéra Bouffe Company and, with the folding of *The White Fawn,* presented the American premiere of Offenbach's **Barbe Bleue** (7-13-68, Niblo's). In this Gallic version Bluebeard is tamed by his sixth wife, the country wench Boulotte. M. Aujac and Mlle. Irma starred. Bateman's faith and determination were justified. The work was a resounding hit, running twelve weeks. *Barbe Bleue*'s popularity assured the reign of opéra bouffe over the musical stage for the next several seasons. But its success did something else. The people flocking to Niblo's box office convinced many a manager that audiences would buy musical entertainments even during hot weather when they would not attend "legitimate" attractions. Within a year even Wallack's, the most august of the "legitimate" houses, offered its summer-darkened auditorium to producers of lyric pieces. The notion of the frivolous, space-filling "summer musical" was born.

1868-1869

There were changes aplenty in the new season, but none that obviously signaled major advances. The heart of the theatrical district was moving to the area between Union Square and Madison Square (14th to 23rd Streets), a stretch soon to be known affectionately as "The Rialto." When the old Broadway Theatre was demolished in April of 1869, only Niblo's and the Olympic, the sites of the first two long runs in the American Musical Theatre, were left below 13th Street. Two fine, important new playhouses opened—Booth's Theatre and Pike's Opera House. Both were to have star-crossed existences, although the gutted Booth stood late into the next century as a housing for stores and lofts, while

Pike's, under a series of names, became a "combination" house and a grind movie palace. Wood's Museum also opened its doors for the first time. Patterned after Barnum's, it opened every morning at 11 o'clock to exhibit its collection of oddities, a bonus of sorts for theatregoers coming to see the attractions in its auditorium at regular hours. The rapidly growing audience, with its ever-increasing purchasing power, demanded not only more auditoriums for its entertainment but more performances. Wallack's, the last holdout, capitulated and initiated Saturday matinees in line with its competitors. Meanwhile competition raced a step ahead by offering midweek matinees that had proved so successful for *Humpty Dumpty* and would help fill the coffers of Lydia Thompson.

Musically, the French and the English dominated the season. H. L. Bateman's mounting of Offenbach's *La Grande Duchesse* with Tostée was honored with the opening night at Pike's. Before the season was finished Bateman had two companies presenting opéra bouffe on whatever stage became available. Other producers quickly followed suit. Maurice Grau struck gold at the Théâtre Français with an eleven-week run of Offenbach's melodic version of the legend of a falsely accused wife, *Geneviève de Brabant,* beginning on October 22. He followed with almost as successful stagings of Herve's *L'Oeil Crevé* on January 11 and Offenbach's glittering grand tour of the City of Light, *La Vie Parisienne,* on March 29, the latter at the then astounding top of $3.00, double the customary price. New Yorkers, it seemed, could not get enough of Offenbach. His charming tale of a Peruvian street-singer, *La Périchole,* had its American premiere on January 4. At least a dozen other examples of opéra bouffe found a place in the season's repertory. They ranged from Offenbach's still popular *La Belle Hélène* to such now forgotten works as *Monsieur Landry, La Chanson de Fortunio,* and *Le Maître de Chapelle.* Their vogue was not lessened by the fact that they were all still being done in French.

But their vogue was challenged by something theatregoers could more readily understand, a troupe of beautiful blonde girls, often dressed seductively in tights, who clowned and crooned in English. "Small, brisk and clever" Lydia Thompson, aided by several other attractive young ladies from the British Isles, inaugurated the last of the three great musical fads of the decade: the "blonde burlesques." Their vehicle was **Ixion, or, The Man at the Wheel** (9-28-68, Wood's Museum), an English extravaganza by F. C. Burnand. The piece had been first performed in America two years earlier in Brooklyn, but in a more straight-faced production. The new producer, Samuel Colville, retained the basic tale of a mortal man's pursuit of a goddess and of his punishment tied to a perpetually revolving wheel, but filled the production with references to contemporary and local happenings, added popular American airs and dances, and staged the whole work tongue-in-cheek. The British blondes quickly replaced the coryphées of *The Black Crook* in the hearts of Broadway's gay blades. In *Ixion* and other musical burlesques such as *The Forty Thieves* or *Sinbad,* the girls happily assumed the trouser roles that exploited their shapely limbs. When the engagement at Wood's concluded, they opened an equally profitable one at Niblo's. The two stands carried them through the season.

Neither opéra bouffe nor blonde burlesques went unnoticed by the minstrels. Earlier spoofs such as "The Grand Dutch 'S' " had proved so rewarding that the troupes were devoting an increasing amount of time to their burlesques and less and less space to olios. Bryant's Minstrels, the San Francisco Minstrels, and Kelly and Leon all promptly inserted travesties of the latest hits in their evenings. Kelly and Leon had the biggest success with "Barber Blue," which allowed Leon, the best-known female impersonator of the time, to don a blonde wig and to kid Miss Thompson and Offenbach at the same time.

Apart from the minstrels, native talents for the most part ignored the musical stage. When W. H. Lingard reopened his renovated Theatre Comique on February 1, the bill included an extended skit, *Pluto.* This burlesque extravaganza was derived from Byron's *Orpheus* by Henry B. Farnie. Its songs were by Dave Braham, whose career at the Comique would be long and glorious. The spoof allowed Alice Dunning to lighten her hair and put on tights to play Orpheus, while Lingard cavorted as Pluto.

Earlier, John Brougham had offered a burlesque called *Much Ado about the Merchant of Venice* (10-14-68, Pike's) as an afterpiece. This bit of musical fluff was received unkindly and, while revived briefly at the Fifth Avenue, was soon forgotten. But later in the season Brougham had mounted another afterpiece that bears some scrutiny. Following the premiere of his new comedy, *Better Late Than Never,* he appended a performance of a curious piece with a curious title, **The Dramatic Review for 1868** (1-25-69, Fifth Ave.). Of course, Brougham could have no inkling of the dated annuals called revues that would flood Broadway half a century later. Nonetheless in a small way this short collection of skits had something of the feel of the later spectacles. It opened with an allegory whose principal figures were Manhatta and Brooklyna, "the oldest of Manhatta's family, and a remarkably forward young lady . . . holding but ferry little intercourse with her Ma, and that she means to abridge." Other characters included New Jersia, North Rivero (a fluent individual), East Rivero, Public Opinion, and Captain Jinks. Succeeding skits twitted various opéra bouffe ("Bouffe à la Mode"), *Humpty Dumpty* (as "The Fox's Nest"), new theatres, and new straight plays. Effie Germon sang a song teasing the velocipede craze.

To be right too soon is to be wrong. Some years later, when the first *Passing Show* (5-12-94) established the revue tradition in America, hardly anyone remembered Brougham's little mélange of skits and songs. Brougham himself wrote a number of longer plays interlarded at times with melody in the Tom and Jerry tour-of-a-city tradition. These plays undoubtedly helped smooth the way for Harrigan and Hart and other early vernacular musicals. But Brougham most certainly never thought of himself as a writer of musicals.

On May 10, 1869, thousands of miles west of New York, in Ogden, Utah, a golden spike driven into a rail signaled the completion of America's first transcontinental railroad connection. Although many years passed before touring companies routinely played the West Coast, long-range effects of the event—demographic changes, the opening up of California to a young movie industry—were to bear significantly on our lyric stage.

Just before the hot weather arrived, *Humpty Dumpty* took its final fall on May 15. Three nights later, however, G. L. Fox was back with many of the same players, in a sequel called **Hiccory Diccory Dock** (5-18-69, Olympic). Like its predecessor it reveled in the pantomime tradition. Fox once again assumed the title role and as Hiccory visited with Mrs. Jack Spratt (C. K. Fox), climbed the beanstalk with another Jack (F. Lacy), and romped with Little Red Riding Hood (Mlle. A. Laurent). In the second half a transformation scene allowed Hiccory to become Clown and his cohorts to change into Pantaloon, Harlequin, Columbine, and—a rare addition—Sprite. Spectacular sets depicted a Palace of Dazzling Light, the Haunt of Fancy, and, as a finale, Hiccory's Aerial Voyage by the First Flying Velocipede. Lavish ballets, devised by David Costa, were led by Mlle. Sangalli. She offered her Dance of the Lily in the Grand Ballet of Coral Nymphs. Haniola, Imre, and Bolossy Kiralfy whirled through a Magyar Czardas in the Palace scene. But the spectacle and high jinks suffered the fate of so many sequels—not unlike *The White Fawn* that had followed *The Black Crook*—*Hiccory Diccory Dock* was a disappointment. Fox's popularity saw to it that the evening was not a total loss. His followers came in sufficient numbers to allow the musical to run into the first week of September. In the long haul, the evening's most important contribution was the debut of the Kiralfy brothers. Hungarian immigrants, they arrived in this country as dancers. Within a short term they became the principal producers of spectacle in New York.

The coming of summer allowed the Lauri family to mount some musical pantomimes at Wallack's. The Lauris wisely invited several of the British blondes to join them. The month-long festival included *Little Boy Blue, Mother Hubbard or Harlequin Little Bo-Peep*, and *Coralline, or, Sir Rupert, the Reckless.*

1869-1870

Writing in 1936, theatre historian George Odell proclaimed, "A new era in New York theatricals begins in the year 1869." He concluded his introduction to the decade of the seventies with a statement that would startle modern scholars, "Those years . . . seem to me almost the very palmiest days of the drama in New York." Throughout his career Odell had little time for the lyric stage. But even if he had been more favorably inclined toward musicals, the ten seasons beginning with 1869–70 would have afforded him small pleasure. They were years of uncertain groping for formulas, meager in their lyric offerings, stingy with their triumphs. And 1869–70 itself was no exception. Only a fluke in the theatrical calendar allowed it to claim one of the most popular of the 19th-century's proto-musicals.

Certainly the most obvious and baffling circumstance of the season was the abrupt and all but total disappearance of opéra bouffe from the Broadway stage—almost as if the surfeit of the preceding session precluded so much as a four-bar phrase in the new year. The Théâtre Français housed the few exceptions, mounting *La Grande Duchesse* briefly in January, *Geneviève de Brabant* for a week in February, and one performance of a double bill of *Barbe Bleue* and *Le Sourd*. However, the disappearance was momentary. By 1870–71 opéra bouffe renewed its lease on theatregoers' affections.

On the other hand serious opera fared well on commercial stages all year long. The very first musical event of importance was the opening of the Carl Rosa–C. D. Hess Company on September 11 at the Théâtre Français. The company's curtain raiser was the American premiere of Balfe's *The Puritan's Daughter*. Some may have considered it only just that opera in English was being presented at the Théâtre Français after so much opéra bouffe had been sung in French at more traditionally named playhouses. The Rosa-Hess repertory also included *The Bohemian Girl, La Sonnambula,* and *Martha*. In late October a troupe of Germans spent a week at the same house singing *Faust, Martha, The Magic Flute,* and *Robert the Devil*. Caroline Richings returned as Caroline Richings-Bernard on November 15 to offer her own season at the Grand Opera House. Her programs included many of the same works the Germans and the Rosa-Hess organization had offered, as well as *Fra Diavolo, Il Trovatore,* and *The Huguenots*. The restored Academy of Music also provided opera lovers with a season.

Virtually all the other musical offerings served up at the commercial houses were burlesques. Wood's Museum began the parade of travesties at the beginning of September. Its most notable and successful offerings were *Wip Wan Winkle,* twitting Joseph Jefferson's version then finishing its run at Booth's and a "second company" of British blondes in *Ixion* and newer material. Since the blondes were being spoofed by minstrels and other burlesquers they decided the height of fun might be to spoof themselves. They did so in their own version of an old hit *The Fair One with the Golden Locks,* which they reworked as *Dora Bella, the Mill, the Mystery, the Mission, the Miss, the Minstrel and the Dyed Hair*. Alice Oates employed the same old play when she appeared for a summer season at the Olympic. Her version was called *The Fair One and the Blonde Wig*. Lydia Thompson herself returned from a tour of major American cities to begin a two-month stay at Niblo's Garden on April 4. Her opening bill was *Pippin, or King of the Gold Mines,* one of her London successes, adapted for American tastes. After a brief fling at serious melodrama, Miss Thompson and her band reverted to burlesque with revivals of *Ixion* and *The Forty Thieves*.

But the year's most successful burlesque was G. L. Fox's **Hamlet.** Fox worked together with T. C. De Leon, his collaborator on *Humpty Dumpty* and *Hiccory Diccory Dock,* to contrive what the *Times* hailed as an evening of "uproarious laughter." Edwin Booth had opened in his great *Hamlet* on January 5 and was still playing to packed houses when Fox romped onto the stage of the Olympic on February 14. Inevitably, Fox dressed as much like Booth as possible. But not for long. Reacting to Francisco's complaint " 'Tis bitter cold," Fox stopped the proceedings to don a gigantic fur hat, brightly colored woolen socks, and oversized mittens. Those intervals when Fox could not be on stage were filled with music, everything from sentimental ballads to a wild Danish cancan. The piece ran two months. But when Fox tried to follow on April 18 with a mock mounting of Booth's version of *Macbeth* he met with a poor reception. The failure of a sequel was nothing new to Fox, but this time he had the small consolation of knowing Booth's *Macbeth* also fell far short of the success of the actor's *Hamlet*.

Apart from Fox's *Hamlet,* the major hits of the year were outside the burlesque world. Both appeared rather late in the season. The financier, "Big Jim" Fisk, had taken over the Grand Opera House (formerly Pike's) on West 23rd Street. Slightly off the beaten path, the theatre's location made its success precarious. Fisk was determined to give its uncertain fortunes a boost. On February 7 he helped unveil the most expensive production to that date in America, a $75,000 mounting of **The Twelve Temptations.** The piece was unmistakably meant to be in the tradition of *The Black Crook*. Its story was based on the Walpurgis Night legend and adapted for the stage by Joseph C. Foster. Once again a tempter claims a lost soul, and once again the soul is rescued at the last moment. Intentionally or not a principal figure was named Rudolph. Of course, the Rudolf of *The Black Crook* had been the hero, the Rudolph (E. L. Tilton) of *The Twelve Temptations* was the villainous tempter. In the end the hero, Ulric (G. C. Boniface), is rescued not by a fairy queen but by Justice (Fanny Lovelace), Faith (Nannie Egbert), Hope (Flora Leland), Charity (Nelly Jarman), and Purity (Marion Herbert). David Costa, the era's leading choreographer, staged the dances amid revolving temples, a fiery underworld, and the final glorious transformation. In keeping with contemporary practice, new spectacular scenes, new dances, and new artists were inserted at various times during the run. At one point a troupe of Spanish dancers was hired. All the lavishness was rewarded, and *The Twelve Temptations* ran profitably until July 9, achieving just over 150 showings. Unfortunately Fisk's assassination less than two years later put an end to his plans for the house and helped undermine its already shaky reputation.

But the most enduring work of the season did

not appear until by normal reckoning the season was long finished, when Joseph K. Emmet opened in **Fritz, Our Cousin German** (7-11-70, Wallack's).

· · ·

Joseph K. Emmet was born in St. Louis on March 13, 1841. His father died when the boy was ten, and young Joseph was apprenticed to a sign painter. Joseph soon found himself making frequent visits to neighborhood theatres, since his employer also painted sets for provincial playhouses. This taste of the other side of the footlights led Emmet to create a variety act as "a song and dance artist." After a brief stint on the minstrel stage Emmet returned to variety in a "Dutch" (German) act, wearing a green blouse and cap and wooden shoes, and singing in broken English.

· · ·

Charles Gayler, the play's author, assuredly conceived of the work as a sentimental melodramatic comedy. There was no music, nor were there lyrics in his original manuscript, although places were designated for the singing of "Home, Sweet Home" and a "Guitar Song" that soon evolved into the famous "Lullaby." But Emmet was known for his fine singing voice and playing ability. A note at the beginning of the manuscript reads, "Curtain when music played once through." This suggests an overture. However, it must be remembered that in a time of cheap labor all major houses—even those devoted exclusively to straight plays—had orchestras in their pits to entertain before the show and at intermissions.

Gayler's plot is complicated and covers a substantial stretch of time. Fritz (Emmet) arrives in America to seek his long-lost sister and to locate the money their father left with the girl. During the crossing he falls in love with another immigrant, Katarina (Georgia Langley). But Katarina is also sought by Colonel Crafton (Charles Fisher), whom the manuscript lists as the "leading heavy." Some years earlier Crafton had adopted an immigrant girl. Of course, the girl is Fritz' sister. Elias Grim (C. H. Rockwell), Crafton's attorney, discovers the relationship and understands that Crafton hopes to have all his adopted daughter's money. Grim demands the hand of Crafton's real daughter in return for his silence. Crafton lures Katarina away from Fritz and locks her in a house he owns, but Fritz, disguised as a washerwoman, comes to see Katarina. He alerts the girl to Crafton's plan to drug her. Katarina switches drinks on Crafton and when he is unconscious she and Fritz flee. Grim, furious at Crafton for his refusal to give his consent, sneaks Fritz into Crafton's house to see if Crafton's

adopted daughter is the woman Fritz claims she is. Fritz sings a lullaby he and his sister loved as children, and her recognition of the old song seals the identification. Later Fritz and Katarina wed. They have a child. Crafton, impoverished, attempts to kidnap the infant but Fritz kills Crafton. The killing occurs at a mill, where Fritz springs a trapdoor. The villain falls through, and moments later his lifeless body is seen caught in the mill wheel. Gayler's dialogue employed all the rhetoric of melodrama:

Katarina: Oh in Heaven's name forbear—take all we have—strip us of everything—but do not injure one hair of that loved darling's head.
Crafton: You plead in vain—now I will be avenged for all.

Gayler's humor was equally of his time. Fritz wins the audience's affection with his "Dutchisms." He says "foolosipher" for "philosopher" and refers to English as the "United States Language." But the bulk of the evening's comedy went to an unimportant character called Julius Snow (Mr. Kyle), listed in the manuscript as "negro—first comedian." The part was played in blackface, and a typical speech ran:

Evening parties when giben regardless of expense is a great engine of cibilization—dey open de hearts of mankind—and make dem gib de footman a dollar—when he hands de hats and de coats at de door—by de way—I must not forgit to mix up dem hats and de coats in de hall— dere are shabby persons who if dey can find dere own hats and coats for demselves—will sneak wid out gibben de footman a red cent.

While the story clearly appealed to Victorian tastes, it was Emmet's singing, playing, and acting that remained the evening's prime attraction. Songs listed in the program, and credited to Thomas Baker, included "Valking Dat Broadway Down" and "Oh, Schneider, How You Vas?" There is no reason to be certain that the half-dozen songs named were all that were offered although they may well have been. Because playbills of the era often failed to list musical numbers, it cannot be determined exactly when Emmet's "Lullaby" became a part of the show. Although a place for it was clearly there from the start, the song was not copyrighted until 1878. Whenever it was introduced it quickly became popular and has remained one of the longest-lived melodies to emanate from our musical stage. This original production ran until September 10. But for more than a decade Emmet kept busy in revivals and revisions of the work and in a series of similar pieces.

1870-1871

Perhaps the four years that elapsed between the July 1870 debut of *Fritz, Our Cousin German* and the July 1874 premiere of *Evangeline* (7-27-74) illustrate most cogently that *The Black Crook* (9-12-66) did not initiate a spate of creativity in the American Musical Theatre. The four years seemed desultory and aimless on the lyric stage. At best it was a time of small consolidations. In this period all three of the immediate postwar hits—*The Black Crook, Humpty Dumpty* (3-10-68), and *Fritz*—had their first major revivals. The success of the three revivals showed that the popularity of the originals was not a season's quirk. But the revivals also illustrated how different each work was, how essentially unrelated and unconnected their styles were. *The Black Crook* was romantic, melodramatic spectacle, with its prime musical emphasis on ballet; *Humpty Dumpty* was transposed English pantomime with an element of *The Black Crook*'s spectacle appended; *Fritz* was sentimental, melodramatic comedy with light songs interspersed. All three plays found imitators, the latter two were most successfully reworked by their original stars and authors.

The season of 1870–71 offered distressingly slim pickings for lovers of the lyric stage. The schedule of opera at the Academy of Music was "the leanest in its history." Miss Richings offered three weeks of opera at Niblo's Garden, beginning October 24. The San Francisco Minstrels got off to an early start on August 29 but their audience petered out and their year ended on April 1. Their competition, both occupied with opening new auditoriums, started later. Kelly and Leon's raised its curtain on September 12, but financial problems forced the troupe to move to Brooklyn in December. Bryant's new house nearby Booth's was not ready until November 23. Once opened, Bryant outlasted his principal competitors, running happily until June 7. Indicatively, far longer seasons were chalked up by the new variety houses, with Tony Pastor's in the lead and the Theatre Comique not far behind.

That beloved curiosity, the diminutive Lotta (Lotta Crabtree), arrived in *Heart's Ease* (9-12-70, Niblo's). In this and the other plays in her repertory Miss Crabtree strummed her banjo, sang her simple ditties, and danced a bit. It can be argued whether or not her vehicles were in fact musicals. The fairest answer seems to be they were essentially straight plays tailored to include outlets for Lotta's abundant store of specialties. They differ from, say, Emmet's *Fritz* plays in that a man such as Emmet was primarily a singer and the songs in his vehicles were worked in with more care. Although there were exceptions, other artists rarely sang or danced in these stars' pieces, and choruses or concerted passages were unknown.

Of more conventional lyric theatre there was precious little. Most were mounted at the Grand Opera House, where a seven-and-a-half-month season of opéra bouffe ran from September 26 to May 20. Although Tostée reappeared and the session saw the New York premieres of two more Offenbach works, *Les Brigands* and *Les Géorgiennes,* it was the debut on December 21 of Tostée's great rival and successor, Marie Aimée, that was the highlight of the stand.

G. L. Fox had a new pantomime ready for his followers. A happy-go-lucky mélange of Mother Goose, classical legend, and wild imagination, **Wee Willie Winkie** (10-5-70, Olympic), let its hero meet Old Grain (George A. Beane), "The Jolly Miller on the River Dee"; Leander (R. Honeywood), "a youth of Hellespont in love with Blondette"; and Blondette (Fannie Beane), who was the miller's daughter and "not a blonde." In twenty-two scenes Wee Willie's travels took him from a Fairy Dell to as far as China, and he participated in two elaborate transformations. The first was "The Glory of Florisette," the second—the grand finale—whisked the cast to the "Realms of Light and Beauty." The antics found Clown and Harlequin battling their own shadows, and in a minor comic "transformation" Harlequin metamorphosed into a sandwich. With music "composed and selected by Mon. F. Strebinger," the piece sang, danced, and mimed its merry way until February 4. One interesting sidelight was the lack of apparent changes during the run. Neither programs nor newspaper announcements suggested the deletions and additions so common in the musical theatre of the time. Apparently audiences at the last performance saw much the same entertainment first-nighters had applauded. A certain sense of artistic integrity may have been creeping into the American Musical Theatre.

On October 12 the self-advertised "prince of comedy and song," M. W. Fiske, opened at the Bowery in *Little Dick, the New York Bootblack,* a vehicle not unlike Lotta's or Emmet's in conception. It was withdrawn after four nights and a burlesque of *The Grand Duchess* substituted.

Jarrett and Palmer gave *The Black Crook* (9-12-66) its first major revival on December 12, just in time to capture the holiday trade. They captured far more, and theatregoers again flocked to Niblo's in sufficient numbers to keep the show running until April 8 (122 performances). Advertised as costing $45,000 ($15,000 for scenery alone), it featured the acrobatic Majiltons and a team of skaters, Moe and Goodrich—another early sign of how quickly circus elements were coming to dominate these extravagant mountings. Marie Bonfanti was back as prima ballerina, while one of Lydia Thompson's most beautiful girls, Pauline Markham, played Stalacta. W. T. Voegtlin, for the next decade or so one of New York's most sought-after scene painters, led the list of designers. The eye-filling depictions of "The Ravine of Zamiel" and "The Palace of Dew Drops" (this latter painted by the Drew Brothers of London) amazed audiences with "Dutch metal [imitation gold leaf], red fire, thunder and lightning, gongs, atabals and other instruments of optical and auric delectation." Unlike Fox at the Olympic, Jarrett and Palmer followed contemporary fashion by announcing frequent changes in cast and spectacle.

G. L. Fox himself attempted another burlesque on the order of his *Hamlet* travesty when he replaced *Wee Winnie Winkie* with his spoof of Booth's *Richelieu*. Called **Richelieu of the Period,** its hero appropriated its star's initials, appearing as Cardinal G. L. Richelieu, a man of "obvious Cardinal Virtues." But, *Hamlet* excepted, Fox never appealed to the public at large except in more traditional pantomime. The work disappeared on March 18.

Only one other American lyric work appeared during the entire season. After opéra bouffe left the Grand, the house attempted on May 22 to offer a successor of sorts to its popular *The Twelve Temptations* (2-7-70), another romantic spectacle, **The Three Hunchbacks.** Its producers succeeded in luring many performers from the recently closed revival of *The Black Crook,* including prima ballerina Marie Bonfanti and the skaters Moe and Goodrich. Despite its florid Arabian Nights setting and the injection of pantomime features, the work failed to win public affection. Critics complained of the lack of integration between the main story and the pranks of Clown, Harlequin, and their crew. Changes were made, but they were unavailing. The show left after one month.

The season closed as it had opened, with opéra bouffe. But there were two important differences. The operas were housed at the renowned Wallack's and were done in English with the principal performer being, to the surprise of many, Lydia Thompson. Her repertory included the premiere of another Offenbach opera, **The Princess of Trébizonde,** on September 11. Its plot centered on a prince caught up in a whirl of circus people. Hearing opéra bouffe in English stunned the reviewer for the *Herald.* Prudish and shortsighted he cried:

> *Opéra bouffe* may well be said to have seen its palmiest days. The lower school of music, which it made the rage of the European capitals for the past few years, has proved, like the intoxication of French champagne, to be only a passing exhilaration. Like champagne, too, in large doses, it has proved nauseating. Manifestly the product of the lower empire and its loose ways, this deification of the *demi-monde* has almost passed away. . . . It is safe to say that had a knowledge of the French language been more widespread the grossness and *equivoque* of its *dialogue* would have sooner earned for it a public condemnation.

Miss Thompson's engagement, which by today's calendar would belong to the following season, ran, with disappointing returns, from August 16 to September 23.

1871-1872

The new season was even more lackluster than its predecessor. The New York stage's circus aspect, whose intrusion the theatre historian O. G. Sonneck had noted began three-quarters of a century before, seemed especially marked, perhaps because there were no new pieces of merit. With Kelly and Leon's gone, only Bryant and the San Francisco troupe remained as blackface regulars. They were augmented on and off throughout the theatrical year by the brief appearance of other bands. These included one black troupe, the Georgia Minstrels, who began a month's stay at Lina Edwin's Theatre at the end of the season.

Variety fared a little better. In retrospect its bills contain tantalizing previews of the future. The program of the Globe Theatre for the week of October 16 found Edward "Ned" Harrigan and Tony Hart on the bill. In the future much of their material would be unveiled at this very house. Six months later, on April 15, the Vokes Family arrived from England with their comedy of high life below stairs, *The Belles of the Kitchen.* Interlarded with the troupe's songs and specialties, the evening was one of the biggest successes of the season. Its popularity played no small part in initiating the vogue for farce-comedy, the somewhat deceptive name for a collection of songs, dances, and other acts tied together with a loose plot. All variety houses at this time offered musical playlets, little more than skits, which nonetheless hinted at more fully fleshed vehicles to come. Unfortunately, most of these shorter offerings are lost. If enough could be found, a careful study might furnish some interesting sidelights on the development of vernacular musical comedy.

The regular playhouses reopened in August, with Joseph K. Emmet starring in a month-long run of *Fritz, Our Cousin German* (7-11-70). He raised his curtain at Niblo's Garden on August 21.

One week later an ex-minstrel, G. Swayne Buckley, relit the Bowery with *On the Track.* Although Buckley played "ten instruments, sang twelve songs, and executed six dances," critics reviewed the piece as straight melodrama. Buckley, like Lotta and Emmet, employed vehicles that defied easy classification.

Three nights later, August 31, when the Olympic began its season, G. L. Fox was once again playing it safe with *Humpty Dumpty* (3-10-68). His caution was rewarded. *Humpty Dumpty* added another 300 performances to its record before it closed on June 11. During the eight-plus months that the musical remained on the boards it was twice advertised as "remodeled." First-nighters on August 31 saw the evening begin with a burlesque prologue in which the personification of Burlesque (Lulu Prior) confronted the personification of Tragedy (Annie Yeamans). These two ladies argued for supremacy before a court that included America (Flora Lee), Europe (Miss R. Melnotte), and Asia (Miss H. Naylor). The main part of the show offered a cornucopia of performers. The Kiralfys were back with lavish ballets. The Marten family performed "Tyrolean eccentricities, including a cat duo." Another band of performers was known as the Zig-Zags. A four-year-old with the stage name of Young Adonis performed a pas de deux with a two-year-old named Little Venus. On January 8 the first of the wholesale revisions took place. The burlesque prologue was changed to a two-character piece in which the Sun Spirit (played by the same lady who had impersonated Burlesque) vied with the Ice King (George Beane) to see who could conjure up the most spectacular effects. Specialties

included a couple "who walk on a ceiling head downwards." The Kiralfys introduced a colorful "Warriors' Dance" in which the women, dressed as Amazons, climbed a staircase made by the men holding their shields above their heads. Similar changes occurred April 1.

On September 18 Emmet replaced *Fritz* with **Carl, the Fiddler.** The play, like *Fritz,* was by Charles Gayler and centered on an immigrant's attempt to find a long-lost sister. The recognition scene once again came to pass when the hero sang what was in this version called "The Brother's Lullaby." Gayler was credited with writing the songs as well as the libretto. For Emmet this play initiated a series of successors to *Fritz* that were little more than minor variations on the same theme. Generally, the public proved indifferent to the changes, content with familiar figures and Emmet's fine singing. But neither the critics nor the public were especially kind to *Carl.* The *Times* was annoyed by a "dialect drama" in which the hero "wandered about the stage for three hours with a guitar strung across his back." Reviews of this nature kept theatregoers away. *Fritz* was hastily revived to alternate with *Carl* until Emmet's engagement ran its course on September 30.

Opéra bouffe held sway at Lina Edwin's Theatre from October 9 through February 3. With Aimée as the principal attraction, a number of works fast becoming old favorites were revived: *La Grande Duchesse, Barbe Bleue, La Périchole.* Two new offerings were added to the repertory as well, although neither gained lasting affection: Charles Lecocq's *Fleur de Thé* and Offenbach's *Le Pont de Soupirs.*

Jarrett and Palmer again revived *The Black Crook* (9-12-66) on December 18 at Niblo's Garden, advertising with relish increasingly Barnumesque interpolations. These included a trio of Egyptian Jugglers, the St. Felix Parisienne Infant Ballet ("Children from 5 to 10 years of age dancing with the proficiency of adults"), and Professor Samwell's trained animals. The revival ran until February 24. This was the last time the musical played on the stage where it had originally opened. On May 6 a fire left only the rear of Niblo's standing, Manhattan's ninth major theatre fire in seven years. The Niblo's Garden that rose from the ashes was a grander auditorium, despite the growing distance the years were putting between it and the main theatre area.

The season closed with the return of Lydia Thompson and her repertory of burlesque. The opening attraction at Wallack's on July 15 was

Robin Hood, followed in August by *Blue Beard* and in September by a revival of *Ixion* coupled with *A Happy Pair.* On September 21, the last week of her stay, Miss Thompson brought out a spoof of Sir Walter Scott's *Kenilworth.*

One extra-theatrical event of interest to theatregoers also occurred in July. A figure Broadway would soon admire for his legitimate offerings appeared briefly as a conductor of three special concerts of his orchestral pieces at the Academy of Music. He was Johann Strauss.

1872-1873

There are few seasons as intriguing as the theatrical year of 1872–73; intriguing in its manifestations of lost possibilities for the American Musical Theatre. For in this season one of the towering figures of the 19th-century American stage— Augustin Daly—took a sudden interest in musicals. Daly was not only the manager of one of New York's most prestigious playhouses, but an indefatigable translator and adapter of plays, plays that were considered the last word in dramaturgy for their time. In this season, besides keeping occupied with his Fifth Avenue Theatre and his adaptations, Daly assumed temporary control of the Grand Opera House. On August 26 he inaugurated the year with a lavish mounting of Offenbach's **Le Roi Carotte.** His star in the work was John Brougham, whose Tom-and-Jerry-style slices of New York life, prototypical revues, and *Pocahontas* (12-24-55) had taken their places as precursors of modern musicals. Despite Daly's retention of the French title, the work was offered in translation and "Brougham played, with his Irish brogue, King Carrot, the vegetable monarch who rose out of a garden bed in a single night" to save a prince from revolution. The original was larded with political innuendo; the American interpretation presented the story more at face value. The show ran until the end of November, after which Daly had even more interesting offerings in store.

Wood's Museum attempted to present Daly with serious competition when it raised its curtain on September 9 with **Chow Chow, or A Tale of Pekin.** The extravaganza was written by the theatre's stage-manager, James Barnes, and had music "arranged by W. H. Brinkworth." Based loosely and irreverently on the adventures of Byron's pirate chief in a

harem, it featured Lisa Weber as Conrad and Pauline Markham as Maimounie. Characters not found in Byron included Prince Pretty Bill, Cupid, and Glowworm (Alice Atherton). Only the briefest bow was made to the subtitle when late in the last act Conrad and his friends arrived in Pekin to meet Chow Chow (a comparatively minor role played by G. C. Charles), Pig-Taili, and Sing Sing. Although the cast included several of Lydia Thompson's most popular blondes (who had made their memorable debut at this very house) and a future star such as Miss Atherton, its disappointing run lasted less than a month. Aimée opened the season at the fading Olympic on October 14 with a four-week repertory of opéra bouffe that introduced no new works. She was followed by Lydia Thompson and her blondes in their own four-week stay that gave New Yorkers a chance to see *Aladdin II* and a revival of *Kenilworth.* By December 9 Aimée was back. This time she did mount a novelty, Lecocq's tale of demi-mondaines who answer their government's call for virgins to settle an island, *Les Cents Vierges* (on December 23). Aimée and her company remained until January 11.

Meanwhile, at the Grand Opera House, Daly had one of his own adaptations ready on November 25. Based loosely on *La Tour du Cadran,* a French vaudeville by H. Cremieux and H. Bocage, which sent its hero on a tour of Paris, **Round The Clock, or New York by Dark,** took its own protagonist, Roderick Killgobbin (John Brougham), on a whirl around Manhattan. Transferring the action of his adaptations to America was a common practice of Daly's. In his pursuit of Ernesta Hardacre (Emma Howson), Roderick visited a number of boutiques, the Grand Union Depot, a Liederkranz Society Ball, and Niblo's Garden during a performance of *The Black Crook* (during which Mrs. John Wood imitated the Majiltons). At one point the action was stopped for a sumptuous tableau entitled "The Daughters of Eve" depicting five thousand years of fashions in dress. The evening ended with a joyous cancan "taken from the French." The show kept the box office busy for two months. One interesting sidelight was the ruckus raised by patrons offended by an action-packed prizefight. The *Times* rushed to Daly's defense, assailing the "fastidious" who objected to some manly boxing but remained silent about the increasing violence in other shows. No one, the paper pointed out, was shot in the back, as was the case in several other plays then or recently on the stage. Collectors of theatrical trivia might note that the law firm of Ketchum and Cheatum was making what was probably its first of many appearances in the American Musical Theatre.

While *Round the Clock* took its audience to the old Niblo's, the new Niblo's Garden threw open its doors on November 30 with a ballet extravaganza in the dependable tradition of *The Black Crook*— **Leo and Lotos.** The story told how a wicked seneschal fails to keep the lovers apart. But the plot was so thin the *Times* warned audiences it must be prepared to "derive pleasure from music, sets, and costumes" alone. Prince Leo was sung by Mlle. Diani "from the Paris Opera." Her fellow artists included Henry Collard, a dwarf famous for his imitations of great tenors, E. D. Davies, a ventriloquist, and the inevitable acrobats. The evening was "rich in marches, counter-marches and groupings of lovely Amazons." It also featured one particularly sumptuous stage picture, "The Palace of Jewels." The still popular style of mounting, and excitement over the new auditorium, helped the entertainment run until the end of March.

The irrepressible *Humpty Dumpty* (3-10-68) returned to the Olympic for another run on February 17. Assisting G. L. Fox with their specialties were a harpist and violinist, a wirewalker, a pair of skaters, and ten "Bedouin Arabs." Young Adonis and Little Venus were back, a year older. With inevitable cast changes and new stage business, Fox and his company cavorted until June 7.

The night after *Humpty Dumpty* returned, Daly presented his last production of the season with substantial singing and dancing. Like *Round the Clock*, **Roughing It** was said to be based on a Parisian show, one Daly failed to identify. Although the source was Parisian, Daly again followed his customary practice of transferring the action to America. But in this instance his canvas was considerably larger than the limited tour of New York he had offered earlier. Antoinette (Mrs. John Wood), the daughter of Denis MacDuffie (Brougham), elopes with poor but social Aubrey Van Dollas (J. C. Peakes). They lead her father on a chase that takes them from Manhattan to the Rockies and then, just before the almost requisite final transformation scene, to a Chinese opium den. There Mrs. Wood had a splendid comic "death scene," recovering miraculously the moment her father consents to her marrying Denis. At one point Mrs. Wood was honored with the flattery of impersonation, when Annie Deland portrayed her as "the queen of comedy and song." Annie Yeamans, in a few years to be Harrigan and Hart's leading lady, won applause in the cameo role of Mother Terror, an "opium crone." Sets included

"a very animated view of the Grand Central Depot," a transformation scene depicting the four seasons, and, most highly praised of all, Wild West stage pictures of a barroom on the plains and an Indian encampment. Western settings allowed Daly to incorporate scenes from Mark Twain and to appropriate Twain's title.

The New York *Times* informed its readers "[the evening] resembles more closely the order of plays known in Paris as revues. . . . In a revue a story as slender as that of a fairy-tale, but having for personages mortals only, binds together a number of varied situations." Although the composer was listed in the program as A. Predigam, critics ignored his contribution. Clearly neither Daly nor the critics could foresee the vogue for revues that would begin with *The Passing Show* (5-12-94) twenty years later. But Daly's productions used the same formula these early revues employed, tying together specialties with a slim plot. Only the emphasis was different, and, perhaps, the fundamental approach that considered the later mountings as primarily musicals. Nor was the public quite ready. *Roughing It* was withdrawn after four weeks. Daly was to have precious little luck with his musicals until late in his career. Did he understand that he had touched the future only to step away? James T. Powers, the turn-of-the-century comedian, recorded Daly's feelings about this time: "Mr. Daly told me he was beginning to like musical comedies, as he realized that they require more talent than legitimate plays—especially the comic portion; 'for,' he said, 'in the straight plays the fun comes mostly from the pen of the author, while in musical comedies, it generally originates in the brain of the comedian.' " No doubt Powers was moved by the flattery implicit in the remark, but Daly's view held true as long as great clowns flourished.

A spectacular pantomime, **Azreal, or The Magic Charm** (4-28-73, Niblo's), featured James S. Maffitt as Clown, the same Maffitt who soon endeared himself to a generation of theatregoers as The Lone Fisherman in *Evangeline* (7-27-74). A major feature of the production was the child gymnast, Lulu, advertised as "the eighth wonder of the world in 'The Wonderous Flight Through Space.' " Lulu's most sensational moment took the gymnast from an apparent standing position in one sudden bounce to a high platform, then in a triple somersault from a bar into a net. But Lulu soon embroiled the show in a minor scandal when the athlete was unmasked as a boy. *Azreal*'s magic charms worked on Niblo's faithful audiences until June 9, when the cast dropped the plot and stayed on to offer a simple variety show.

Of course, for pleasure seekers preferring minstrelsy both the San Francisco Minstrels and Bryant's Minstrels provided the expected entertainment. Bryant's troupe was augmented by Kelly and Leon. They played from August 26 to June 25. The San Francisco Minstrels opened their season on the same night as Bryant's. But their season ended March 1. Lack of business was not the reason. They had sold their house to make way for the new Fifth Avenue Theatre; their new home was not yet ready to receive them. Although minstrelsy was slowly being strangled by variety, it was still profitable enough to think in terms of new houses. Variety also continued to expand. Tony Pastor's opened September 16, with Harrigan and Hart on the bill, but the team soon switched to the Theatre Comique, where they would soon take over and rise to glory.

1873-1874

The new season was an unhappy one. The Panic of 1873 spread hard times across the land. Only the best playhouses enjoyed prosperous returns, largely because those people who still had money and work sought to forget the problems around them. During the season every major theatre gave benefits for its less fortunate neighbors.

Artistically the American Musical Theatre languished, as unproductive as the economy. Only at the very end of the year did a lone work appear to revitalize the lagging creative forces of the lyric stage. As with *Fritz, Our Cousin German* in 1869–70, it arrived so late that by modern calculations it belonged in the next season.

Niblo's began the year with a revival of *The Black Crook* (9-12-66). Specialty acts, increasingly important to any mounting of the piece, included the "great French caricaturist," M. Régamey; the ventriloquist, E. D. Davies; the Girards in "Leg-Mania"; the Female Swabian Nightingale Quartette; and the infant Vedeys (gymnast sisters) in "mid-air exploits." Undergoing the expected "reconstruction" in mid-run, it tallied over 100 additional showings before it closed on December 8.

A nonmusical footnote enlivened the early season. On August 19 a production of **A Midsummer Night's Dream** was unveiled at the Grand Opera House. The sumptuous Victorian-style mounting included several ballets. More to our point the evening featured G. L. Fox as Bottom and, in her New York debut, Fay Templeton, still a tot, as Puck.

Two importations got the musical season into full gear six nights later. In one, Daly presented theatregoers with Aimée in the American premiere of Lecocq's **La Fille de Madame Angot** (8-25-73, Broadway). Its simple plot had a rather refreshing ending, when the daughter of a fishmonger realizes the man she loves is perfidious and accepts her mother's choice of a mate for her. Sung in French, it ran for three weeks to excellent business and then went into repertory with *La Grande Duchess* and *La Périchole*.

Downtown the Olympic raised its curtain the same night on Lydia Thompson in a burlesque extravaganza ridiculing just such opéra bouffe as Aimée was singing, **Mephisto and the Four Sensations** (using much of Lecocq's score to *La Fille de Madame Angot*). In George Fawcett Rowe's text, Miss Thompson as Pluto prepared to lure Frou-Frou, Camille, Belle Hélène, and Geneviève de Brabant to the netherworld. Theatre historian Odell undoubtedly expressed the sentiments of many "highminded" playgoers of the day when he lamented, "One might think the world would have been utterly weary of such concoctions until one remembers the persistence, in later years, of such epidemics as London Gaiety musical farces, comic opera, musical revues, etc." Miss Thompson held the stage for a month in a repertory of her new piece and her older favorites. She was succeeded on September 29 by a company offering opéra bouffe in English. Its repertory included *The Grand Duchess,* and the first translation of *Mme. Angot's Child.*

Joseph K. Emmet returned in another variation of his Fritz theme. This time his singing of a childhood lullaby helps him find not a long-lost sister, but a long-lost father. The public accepted **Max, the Merry Swiss Boy** (10-6-73, Broadway) no more than it had accepted *Carl* (9-18-71). The work, by Henry J. Bryan, was hastily withdrawn. Emmet, guitar, dialect and all, rushed back to the safety of *Fritz.*

Three weeks later Daly gave *Round the Clock* (11-25-72) a brief revival.

A spate of *Humpty Dumpty* (3-10-68) spin-offs marked the season. The first was mounted on November 25 by Daly at the Grand Opera House. G. L. Fox and many of his loyal associates were back. But the nature of the evening was changed. It was not quite the old familiar pantomime. De-emphasis of the story created an impression of vaudeville. Daly also added an important amount of spectacle. This allowed **Humpty Dumpty Abroad** to fall more in the category of burlesque-extravaganza or even to be considered a light-hearted version of the *Black Crook* school. The evening included much-applauded panoramas in which the children of the tale were carried from China to the North Pole to Italy. A Chinese lantern festival was hailed as "decidedly the most effective piece of stage-grouping ever seen in this city." In the "Palace of Instruments on the Isle of Harmony" the cast paraded dressed as brasses, wood winds, cellos, and drums. Betty and Emily Rigl led the ballets, but the Martens family's Tyroliennes, "encored four times," almost stole the show.

When the musical closed at the beginning of February, it was replaced on the 9th by a double bill, **Jack Haraway at Sea** and **Humpty Dumpty at School,** with many of the same principals and a new batch of specialty acts. There was virtually no story in either piece. In *Jack* a tobacconist named Tobias Shortcut (Fox) has to impersonate a sea captain during a naval engagement; in the second part Humpty Dumpty leads his fellow pupils into mischievous stunts. The *Times* viewed the bill as a succession of "athletic performances, a *ballet d'action,* Tyrolean ballads, Ethiopian minstrelsy, remarkable tight-rope exercises." Odell branded the pair "a highly sublimated 'Variety' bill—it was nothing else." The producers apparently drew the same conclusion. Before long the main title for the whole evening was changed to *A Round of Pleasure,* its original subtitle. After a two-month run, during which constant revisions of the program took place, Daly and Fox separated. Fox took over management of the Broadway from Daly and moved Humpty and his friends to the house. In the last Humpty Dumpty of the season, **Humpty Dumpty at Home,** Goody Two Shoes and Tommy Tucker pursued their on-again, off-again romance with the connivance of Humpty all during the first act. The critics agreed the story was completely forgotten in the second act, which was merely a succession of specialty acts. These included bell ringers and Reardon's Tumblericon (musical glasses). Audiences were not too pleased. The run, which began on April 6, terminated abruptly at the beginning of May when Fox's backer withdrew his support.

While Humpty was changing costumes and vehicles a number of importations came in to offer competition. The Vokes offered their popular English extravaganza, *The Children in the Wood* (12-8-74, Niblo's). At the Olympic the English Opéra Bouffe Troupe entertained patrons with *The Grand Duchess, The Bohemian Girl,* and *La Sonnambula.* The definition of opéra bouffe was obviously elastic. But purists could rest content when Aimée returned on March 9 for a month's engagement, singing seven of her most dependable roles.

A ballet-rich version of *The Lady of the Lake* debuted at Niblo's on May 25. But a careful reading of reviews suggests it was primarily a straight play, making an expensive bow to Niblo's tradition of musical spectacle.

Nothing more of musical interest appeared until July 27. And even then the musical that opened at Niblo's received discouraging notices and ran a mere two weeks. But that musical was **Evangeline.** A Boston creation, it slowly found an adoring public and became one of the most frequently played, best-loved musicals of the last quarter of the 19th century. Billed as an extravaganza, listed on its sheet music as an opéra bouffe, it was treated by the critics as a burlesque—which it was. The New York *Times* reviewer took the occasion to damn the entire genre. Evaluating *Evangeline* as "tolerably fair," he went on to suggest the work represented the sort of theatre that required "unquestioning good-nature to take kindly to." It was a sort, he lamented, filled with "atrocious puns . . . indifferent music," concluding, "Even Terpsichore is but a halt jade." However, the day before the work opened, this same *Times* advised its readers that *Evangeline* promised to be a considerable departure from customary burlesque: "The music is original throughout, and the fun is brisk and piquant." In a way, both journalists were correct.

Suggested by Longfellow's poem, the libretto had the heroine (Ione Burke) and her lover Gabriel (Connie Thompson) seek each other not just in the locales of the original but in the Wild West and a wilder Africa as well. Before the lovers clasp hands in a happy ending that has no basis in Longfellow, Evangeline is also pursued by an amorous whale and cavorts with a dancing heifer. This heifer dance became one of the most popular scenes in the work, and at least one major comedian of the American Musical Theatre, Francis Wilson, spent a season of apprenticeship as half of the cow. Equally cherished by audiences was another figure not found in Longfellow, The Lone Fisherman. Taciturn to the point of not speaking a word all evening, he nonetheless intruded everywhere in the action, often straining to view through his oversized telescope a sea thousands of miles away. Although J. W. Thompson (or Thoman) originally played the role, James Maffitt soon became so identified with it that he played little else for the remainder of his career. In keeping with the burlesque tradition, Gabriel was a trouser role for a woman, and the part of the obese, clownish Catherine was given to a man (Louis Mestayer). In the latter instance another famous performer of the time, George K. Fortesque, became identified with the role, although he, like Maffitt, was not the original. The author of these shenanigans was J. Cheever Goodwin. With Goodwin we come to the first professional librettist to leave his mark on the American Musical Theatre. Unfortunately, as is the case for several early figures, precise biographical information is hard to come by.

. . .

J. Cheever Goodwin was born into comfortable middle-class surroundings in Boston about 1852. Educated at Harvard, he took employment with the Boston *Traveler* shortly after graduation. At the same time he began tinkering with an idea for a light-hearted musicalization of Longfellow. Through circumstances now unknown he met E. E. Rice, a onetime actor then a printer of advertisements. Rice was so delighted with Goodwin's plans, he abandoned printing and collaborated with Goodwin in bringing *Evangeline* onto the stage of Boston's Globe Theatre.

. . .

Musically the show was equally interesting. Advertisements promised "songs, duets, trios, full chorus, etc."—in short, a complete musical scoring. But more important, all the songs were original and by one composer-lyricist, Rice.

. . .

Edward E. Rice was born in Brighton, Massachusetts, in 1849. Forced by poverty to find work while still a minor, he joined a troupe of itinerant actors. He apparently performed all sorts of odd jobs and soon came to know well every facet of theatre. But for some reason he elected to make a career elsewhere, moving from one profession to another until just before he met Goodwin.

. . .

If Rice's songs were not so memorable as to be whistled years later, they were still more than merely "indifferent." Relatively simple, sweetly melodic, appropriately theatrical, they helped impart a sense of cohesion and knowing stage craftsmanship to the evening. The heifer's dance, with its triplets and elementary syncopations, foreshadowed the style of musical composition that would in later years become associated with animated cartoon music.

All season long, variety flourished. At the Theatre Comique, Harrigan and Hart presented their skit "The Mulligan Guard," initially little more than a clownish drill routine. Out of this playlet grew the Harrigan–Braham works of coming years. It was brought back off and on all season as part of a number of variety bills at the house. Pastor's flourished as well, with Harrigan and Hart even bringing "The Mulligan Guard" there for a benefit performance. Minstrels fared less happily than vaudeville. The San Francisco Minstrels, learning their new house would not be ready for the season, spent the year on the road. Bryant had the field virtually to himself. His skits included one called "Mme. Angot's Kids."

1874-1875

Once again the American Musical Theatre mirrored the national scene in general. Both remained sluggish. Revivals and importations comprised the majority of the sparse lyric offerings. In this respect the musical theatre ran counter to the quality and success of other stage offerings. The theatrical year was filled with notable performances (including Charlotte Cushman's farewell and John Drew's debut) and premieres of some of the epoch's most important plays—*The Shaughraun, The Big Bonanza, The Two Orphans,* and *Colonel Sellers.*

Maurice Grau, who later figured importantly at the Metropolitan Opera, opened the season on August 24 at the Lyceum when, in partnership with C. A. Chizzola, he starred Aimée in a repertory of opéra bouffe. The program included the American premiere of Leon Vasseur's **La Timbale d'Argent** (in which rivals for a silver bowl in a singing contest fall in love despite vows to the contrary) as well as performances of *La Princesse de Trébizonde, La Fille de Madame Angot,* and *La Périchole.* The company remained until October 17. Many of the same opéra bouffe offerings were heard on the very same stage two weeks later. However, on this occasion they were sung in English by a troupe starring the English soprano Emily Soldene. Her program included one novelty, the American premiere of Hervé's tale of Merovingian intrigue and romance, *Chilpéric.* Miss Soldene and her fellow artists kept the Lyceum lit until January 2. Nine nights later at the Park, Chizzola and Grau brought their own troupe back, minus Aimée. Her roles were taken principally by another young French singer, Coralie Geoffroy. This return engagement was significant primarily for the New

York premiere of Lecocq's **Giroflé-Girofla,** which had premiered in Paris only the past November and which in New York held the stage alone from February 4 to March 20. Its story recounted the kidnaping of one of two lovely twins on the morning both girls were to be married.

The Kiralfy brothers, who till now had been prominent dancers in the spectacles at Niblo's and elsewhere, turned producers to relight the same Niblo's with **The Deluge** on September 7. Advertised as a "grand spectacular drama" but with "500 ballet and auxiliaries on stage," it was actually a musical pageant. Its source was a French drama performed in Paris some ten years earlier that related stories from the Old Testament: Adam and Eve, Cain and Abel, and the great flood.

By the time the Kiralfys had raised the curtain on their American version, the piece ran five hours, starred a "large, imposing" English lady, Julia Seaman, as Satan, and was marked by a "prodigious quantity of action . . . in Pandemonium and on earth, by much dialogue, and by dances, marches and tableaux." It was also marked, at least on opening night, by mechanical problems. One reviewer chortled at "stage carpenters wrestling with . . . unruly scenery and [after a mishap in the final Deluge] wading into the wings in full sight of the spectators." Despite these first-night problems, the work caught the public's fancy and ran over two months. It was no sooner taken off the boards than the Kiralfys had a second production ready. The ambitious brothers took over management of the Grand Opera House and on November 23 mounted a revival of *The Black Crook* (9-12-66). Once again Marie Bonfanti was on hand to lead the dancers, while the growing horde of specialists included the Benton Family (acrobats), the London Madrigal Boys, the Persian Twin Sisters, and the Vaidis children (probably the same troupe listed in the 1873 revival as the Vedeys). Significantly neither advertisements nor pre-opening announcements listed the actors who portrayed the principal figures in the story. Although this was the third revival in four seasons it demonstrated the continuing attraction of the work. The spectacle played from November 23 to January 2.

Another spectacle in the same tradition was **Ahmed** (3-30-75, Grand Opera), written by Mrs. Julia E. Dunn and based loosely on Washington Irving's *The Pilgrim of Love.* It was dismissed by the *Times* as "simply a vehicle for exhibiting a long series of tableaux and for introducing a number of dances." The tableaux included an elaborate grotto setting that undoubtedly recalled *The Black Crook*

to many in the house, while the dancing offered "a *pas de quatre* by four tiny *ballerine*" that catered to the circuslike tone demanded by so many ticket-buyers. For all its pandering to popular taste *Ahmed* found only modest public support. It closed on April 28. Two weeks later a revival of *The Twelve Temptations* (2-7-70) was rushed in to keep the house open. It ran for ten nights, and with its close the Grand Opera House's season ended.

In a few short seasons the presence of Harrigan and Hart on its bills had made the Theatre Comique "the most popular 'Variety' hall in the city," temporarily eclipsing Tony Pastor's. Much of Harrigan and Hart's success stemmed from playlets Harrigan contrived, usually with a song or two by David Braham. On May 31 Harrigan and Hart abandoned the Comique for the moment to mount a longer—although not quite full length—play at Wallack's. Probably to satisfy their less adventuresome followers, as well as to fill out the entire evening, they offered a small variety bill with the play. But this play, **The Donovans,** was the first stop on the team's rise to fame and fortune. Its story was suggested by one of the most sensational events of the day, the kidnaping of young Charlie Ross. In Harrigan's work Michael and Norah Donovan (played by Harrigan and Hart, respectively) find the search for their missing child takes them not only around New York City but to a Kentucky plantation as well. The play ended with the rescue of the child at a railroad viaduct moments before an oncoming train might have spelled tragedy. The various locations of the tale, clearly in the school of Tom and Jerry playwriting, took its principals on a whirlwind tour. For Harrigan they had the advantage of opening up the story sufficiently to allow for the reasonable insertion of a number of additional variety acts such as the Peak Bell Ringers and Baby Bindley. If these specialties hampered any serious consideration of the adventure no one probably cared. After all, the sight of the bereaved mother played by a man in drag hardly sets a high tone.

Minstrelsy had its ups and downs during the season. The gaiety was occasioned by the return of the San Francisco Minstrels, displaying their art in what they joyously advertised the "Most Beautiful Theatre in the World." They ran out the year. But Bryant's troupe and theatre passed on with the death of Bryant himself in April. For the rest of its history in these waning years of minstrelsy the San Francisco entourage would have the field virtually to itself.

Little footnotes enlivened the season. On December 14 the police raided the variety show at the Metropolitan Theatre to stop the cancan there. But the cancan continued. And on November 20, Mrs. Leonowens, "late governess of the royal family of Siam," lectured at Steinway Hall, never dreaming she would eventually become the heroine of one of Broadway's most sucessful musicals, *The King and I* (3-29-51).

1875-1876

As America prepared to celebrate its centennial, the American Musical Theatre languished. And the lyric stage was not alone in its woes. Theatre historian George Odell noted that these were "Hard Times for the Theatres" in general. Niblo's, increasingly out-of-the-way, remained dark all season. And while Americans across the land heard more than their normal quota of facilely optimistic speeches in the course of the season, they also witnessed the horrors of the Molly Maguires and the ignominy of Custer's Last Stand.

The theatrical year season was framed by opéra bouffe. The Henderson and Colville company opened the season on August 19 with a reworking of *Barbe Bleue* called *Boulette*. The piece ran until the beginning of September when it was replaced first by *The Grand Duchess* and later by *Giroflé-Girofla*. At the same time Daly's boards played host to the Mexican Juvenile Opera Company, headed by an eight-year-old prima donna, Moron Carmen. The youngsters sang their interpretation of *The Grand Duchess* as well as Offenbach's *Robinson Crusoe*. More traditional performances began at the Lyceum (once the Théâtre Français) on September 6 when the Grau and Chizzola troupe, again starring Coralie Geoffroy, presented *Madame l'Archiduc*, *La Fille de Mme. Angot*, *Giroflé-Girofla*, *Le Canard à Trois Becs*, and *Le Petit Faust*. The season's close found the doomed Booth's housing a revival of *La Vie Parisienne* for the week of June 12. Offenbach himself conducted the opening night, with Aimée across the footlights singing the principal role.

August also saw competing versions of **Around the World in Eighty Days,** one at the Grand Opera House (a failure, running only September 16 to September 28) and one at the Academy of Music. Both laced their adaptations of Jules Verne with ballets, songs, and specialty acts. The mounting at the Academy on the 28th was by the Kiralfys and

was the more successful of the two. In eighteen spectacular scenes it took Phileas Fogg (Owen Marlowe) from his London club room through the Suez into the interior of a "Hindoo" bungalow and to an elegant Calcutta hotel. Thereafter a "procession of Brahmins and worshippers" at "The Great Religious Festival of the Suttee" led up to a "startling" pyre and a "Grand Funeral Pageant." As if this were not enough, the "Wreck of the Henrietta" depicted "the total disappearance of the steamer under the waves." While scenes were being changed a novel curtain—of the sort we would call a show curtain today—formed an immense fan and concealed the movement behind it. Scene-painter Matt Morgan was praised both for his inventiveness and his taste. The ballets were lauded, but so were performers in the story, notably Marlowe for his dignity and *sang-froid*. When, along with *The Black Crook* (9-12-66), this extravaganza would prove sufficiently popular to merit regular revivals, critics would hereafter ignore actors in the tale, and devote their notices to the increasingly elaborate dances and circuslike specialties that soon came to dominate productions of *Around the World*.

One of the season's few "original" native musicals, **Humpty Dumpty in Every Clime** (10-25-75, Booth's), gave audiences another chance to see G. L. Fox in his most beloved part. Most theatregoers could not know this was to be their last, brief chance to do so. There was virtually no plot, and the second act, in which the audience was transported around the world in eighty minutes, was branded as little more than an olio. However, the *Times* review affords an interesting picture of Fox's technique and the style of his final offering:

> [Humpty Dumpty] is sent by *Old One Two* with a letter to the nearest post office, *Clown* faces in the right direction, and then boldly marks time as though he were walking for a wager. Meanwhile the scenery moves, houses disappear, fields and a long lane are passed, and by and by the actor who has apparently travelled over a long road, reaches his goal. But just as he is depositing the letter the ever attendant *Harlequin* taps on the floor with his magic blade and, presto, the post office disappears, and where it was there stands the same house whence *Clown* set out minutes before.

This business was gone through three times. But Fox was becoming more erratic than the clown he played, in one instance attacking members of the audience for no obvious reason. On November 15 his insanity became so apparent that James Maffitt was called in to finish the performance. Fox returned and continued to act until November 27. Committed then to an institution, he never appeared before the public again and died shortly thereafter. With him died the chief impetus for traditional pantomime in America.

At the new Eagle Theatre at Sixth Avenue between 32nd and 33rd streets, some distance above the regular theatre district, the bill for the week of November 15 included an "original and dramatic cantata." The "cantata" had music by an Englishman, Arthur Sullivan, and words by another Englishman, W. S. Gilbert. What scant attention it received was not especially favorable, and it quickly left the scene. Time forced a reconsideration of this saga of a faithless lover judged by a faithless magistrate, for the "cantata" was **Trial by Jury.**

A "Grand Christmas Pantomime" called **Nimble Nip** came in for the holiday trade. The evening featured the Worells. Sophie Worell played Prince Sweet-as-Sugar to her sister's Princess Ever-So-Fair. Neither the villainies of Blunderbore nor the temper tantrums of King Grumble-Grone stand in the way of their finding romance. Advertised attractions included "one hundred charming children" and a "fairy fountain of real water." Offering "a tolerable medley of songs and dances" and a "grand transformation scene" the show ran three weeks. It departed from the general practice of pantomime by not having the principals turn into Clown and his friends. These roles were played by minor performers.

As Odell notes: "Negro minstrelsy, once all raging, was reduced in New York, in 1875–1876, by that new 'rage'—'Variety'—to only one permanent company. . . ." Five important houses offered "that new rage" to New Yorkers. Their programs included burlesques and musical comediettas by promising young writers such as Sydney Rosenfeld.

1876-1877

There was little to distinguish this season from the preceding one—or from the one to follow. The lyric stage remained in the doldrums. The creative spurt that began almost accidentally with *The Black Crook* (9-12-66) seemed to have exhausted itself. To aggravate matters, the horrendous Brooklyn Theatre fire on December 5 seriously affected theatre attendance for the remainder of the season,

thereby coupling the artistic vacuity with economic hardship.

In the long run the most significant event of the season came at the very start, the assumption by Harrigan and Hart of management of the Theatre Comique. Their original intention seems to have been to retain it as a vaudeville house, but the popularity of sketches Harrigan inserted in the bills soon irrevocably altered their plans. Most of these skits, with names such as "Down in Dixie," "Walking for Dat Cake," "The Blue and the Grey," or "An Editor's Troubles," were hastily, if professionally, composed and just as hastily discarded. But a few contained the nucleus for later, more extended, efforts. Out of "Old Lavender Water" came the character who was to be Harrigan's personal favorite. More importantly, a skit called "Centennial Marksmen, or, the International Rifle Match by the Four Picked Teams"—celebrating the multinational shooting matches then in progress—pitted the Queen's Invincibles and the Ginger Blues against two of the most beloved creations of Harrigan's fertile imagination, The Skidmores and The Mulligan Guards. At one point Harrigan gave yet another hint of things to come when he offered a full-length play on the bill of November 20. The play was a "romantic drama" entitled *Lascaire*, different in style from Harrigan's later works but alike in ambition.

The years of Harrigan and Hart's triumphs were just ahead. The season at hand got under way with more old-fashioned efforts, spectacles squarely in the *Black Crook* tradition. **Baba** (9-18-76, Niblo's) had a libretto by "Arnold and Sherwood," names now lost in the ancient pages of theatrical history, and music by Max Maretzek, still remembered as an important figure of the late 19th-century musical scene. A number of critics singled out the marches he wrote for this piece, the *Times* insisting they were "far superior to that of most spectacles." The same reviewer bewailed that in the ten years since the premiere of *The Black Crook* an unfortunate pattern had developed emphasizing spectacle over plot. He could, with equal accuracy, have suggested spectacle had come to dominate over everything else as well, including the music. The story he felt was relegated to a secondary place told how Baba (W. H. Crane), the adopted son of the Vizier, and his young friend fall in love with two princesses. Their pursuit of the young ladies takes them to "The Grotto of the Emeralds," "The Crumbling Palace," "A Field of Mushrooms," and onto a "Magic Ship." The piece played to diminishing returns until December 11, when the effect of the Brooklyn fire proved fatal and an audience of a mere thirty patrons had its money refunded.

The Kiralfys took over the house and mounted another spectacle, **Azurine,** on Christmas night. The story recounted the plight of "the daughter of the king of a realm in the sky ordered to spend a year on earth." But the story was plainly not the thing. The Kiralfys boasted of a cast that included "300 young ladies" and a spectacular moving panorama of the city in the sky. Only a handful of ballerinas were deemed worthy of being listed by name, an honor, as usual, not even accorded the authors of the piece. It was a two-week failure. The brothers rushed in a revival of *Around the World in Eighty Days* (8-28-75) on January 22, but this, too, met with little interest. Booth's relit on August 14 with an adaptation of Byron's **Sardanapalus,** replete with ballets, songs, twenty-four Negro boys, and forty-eight "extra" ladies.

For playgoers seeking more artful lyric theatre opéra bouffe troupes came and went throughout the season. The Alice Oates Opera Company inaugurated the parade on September 18 at the Grand Opera House, singing in English their repertory of standards. A week later Aimée returned after a brief vacation. In three visits at three different houses she repeated many of her old favorites and offered New Yorkers their first opportunity to hear Lecocq's *La Petite Mariée* and Offenbach's *La Boulangère a des Écus.* Mid-season, on March 14, the Kiralfys wed opéra bouffe and extravaganza with their elaborate mounting at Booth's of Offenbach's **A Trip to the Moon,** in which King Pin and his son, Prince Caprice, take the journey to break their mundane monotony. Although it boasted of "a chorus of one hundred," tepid notices and the effects of the Brooklyn holocaust told quickly. The show closed after ten nights.

Two plays in the Tom and Jerry tradition also scored successes during the season, *Fifth Avenue* and *Life.* **Life** was Augustin Daly's adaptation and combination of two French plays, *Le Procès Veauradieux* and *Loulou.* A mélange of farce, spectacle, specialty acts, and ballet, it displeased many of Daly's more traditional customers, but nevertheless found enough of an audience to run from September 27 to November 18. Daly's great farceur, the carrot-topped James Lewis, played a sport, Pony Mutual, and found an excuse to imitate Marie Bonfanti. His final leap was so magnificent he disappeared into the flies. This Tom and Jerry tour ended at a theatre with a set depicting fairyland on its stage. This allowed no other than Miss Bonfanti herself, as the Spirit of the Sun, and Augusta

Sohlke, as the Spirit of the Snow, to dance together in an elaborate "Snow Ballet" (using music from a work New York had yet to see, Offenbach's *A Trip to the Moon*). Daly regulars in the cast included Maurice Barrymore, Georgiana Drew (Barrymore's wife, and the mother of Lionel, Ethel, and John), Charles F. Coghlan, Emily Rigl, John Brougham, and the beloved old trouper, Mrs. Gilbert. **Fifth Avenue** (2-5-77, Booth's), which had a five-week run, was more arguably a straight play, with a melodramatic plot. Richard Blake (George Rignold) wins the hand of Olive Schuyler (Maud Granger) after proving his worth by rescuing her from a shipwreck, saving her father from bankruptcy, and clearing himself of a false accusation. The shipwreck provided a challenge to the set painters; reviewers felt they met it handsomely. For all that it was a straight play, the show was larded with turns by performers from the up-and-coming vaudeville world. As "boss of all the bill-posters," Charles T. Parsloe, Jr., led a comic song and clog dance. John Wild in blackface is reported to have stopped the show, although unfortunately no critic detailed his act. Wild would go on to become one of Harrigan and Hart's favorite regulars. In his autobiography, the distinguished British actor, Frederick Warde, then a member of Daly's company, recalled the equally show-stopping antics of George S. Knight. His description of Knight's turn suggests how ideas of humor change, for he applauded Knight's "wonderful acrobatic imitation of a German immigrant seized with an epileptic fit." As Odell noted in his theatre history of the time, "the songs and specialties of these clever people were encored until the perpetrators were breathless, while the principals waited in the wings for the tumult to die."

With G. L. Fox gone, a performer named Grimaldi briefly assumed the crown of pantomime. On the very stage where Fox once reigned—at the Olympic—from March 12 he and his troupe offered a month of repertory alternating between *Jack and Jill* and their version of *Humpty Dumpty.* Their mountings were coupled with olios, and when their run ended they moved over to Tony Pastor's.

Indeed, all season long variety was the most flourishing form of entertainment. Minstrelsy had dwindled to a lone stronghold, the San Francisco Minstrels, although Kelly and Leon did attempt a brief comeback late in the season at Darling's Opera House. Ironically, Darling's had long been Dan Bryant's theatre. Both variety and minstrelsy continued to spoof the hits of the season and in these skits continued to tinker with the forms of future revues and musical comedies. Odell also takes notice of some of the entertainers mentioned earlier who enlivened their more or less straight vehicles with song and dance. He remarks that Lotta's revival of **Little Nell and the Marchioness** offered "real negro serenaders" and her "unrivalled clog dance." He concludes: "Had she belonged to the 1920s, Lotta might have been drafted into the Ziegfeld Follies, the Scandals or some such froth."

The year ended when *Evangeline* (7-27-74) returned on June 4 to begin a two-month run at Daly's. This run marks the real beginning of New York's affection for the piece. Eliza Weathersby sang Gabriel, while Lizzie Harold was Evangeline. As Capt. Dietrich, George S. Knight was made up to resemble the celebrated Civil War soldier, General Benjamin F. Butler. Two future stars, N. C. Goodwin and Henry E. Dixey, appeared in minor roles, and during the second month of the stay George K. Fortesque donned Catherine's garments again. Looking back years later on the cast, Odell concluded that "a baker's dozen names about to be listed in the near future as the most potent to draw lovers of burlesque" graced the bill.

1877-1878

The new season resembled the calm before the storm. Musically, it was the least active season in more than half a dozen years. Lydia Thompson returned after a marked absence to open the year with a repertory of burlesques at Wallack's on August 18. Old favorites such as *Blue Beard* appeared first. But they were soon replaced by newer works, **Oxygen, or Prince Fritz of Virgamen** (8-27-77) and **Robinson Crusoe** (9-12-77). Both librettos were by H. B. Farnie, the earlier in collaboration with R. Reece. *Prince Fritz* made only passing reference to J. K. Emmet's Fritz, following instead the adventures of a student prince (Miss Thompson) and his friends. They encounter mad Dr. Ox (Horatio Saker), who has found a way to use oxygen to conquer the world. Of course, Fritz and his most important friends were trouser roles. The cast, which included Willie Edouin, Alice Atherton, and Kate Everleigh, later prompted Odell to look on it much as he had the preceding *Evangeline*'s and remark, "Almost every woman in that cast won a high place in our theatre, either in burlesque or musical comedy, or both."

Defoe would have scarcely recognized his Crusoe story. In this 1877 version the hero and Jim Cox are jilted by their sweethearts and run away to sea. A shipwreck and their sweethearts follow, as does a reconciliation, but not before a number of musical adventures overtake the principals. These include meetings with lady pirates such as Tarr, Pitch, and Rosin. For many the clowning of Willie Edouin as Friday was the evening's most memorable feature. But Friday was only one of a number of strange inhabitants of the isle on Wallack's stage. Characters such as Queen Ylang-Ylang, Jes-so, Wai-ho, O-wy-o-wy, and O-pop-i-nax also cavorted throughout the piece.

The year's most important work, Ned Harrigan's **Old Lavender,** premiered on September 3. At this point it was not quite a full-length play but rather an extended sketch based on a shorter piece he had used earlier. Harrigan dickered with these medium-long efforts all season, bringing forth *The Rising Star, Sullivan's Christmas*, and the burlesque *A Celebrated Hard Case*, among others. All contained songs by David Braham. It was only during the week of April 22—the last week of Harrigan and Hart's season at the Theatre Comique—that Harrigan offered a more fully fleshed version of *Old Lavender,* beginning the career of the play and the character that ever after remained his personal favorite. Harrigan's story was condemned by the *Herald* and others as old hat, but the public couldn't care less. Paul Cassin (F. A. Blackburn) and John Filbert (T. E. Egbert) attempt to swindle Phillip Coggswell (F. Chippendale), a banker, out of a large sum by use of fraudulent checks. To abet his machinations Cassin pretends to court Coggswell's wife, Laura (Annie Mack). When Coggswell discovers the deception he concludes his brother George, who introduced Filbert at the bank, is party to the scheme. George is a middle-aged bachelor affectionately known to his friends as Old Lavender (Harrigan). Laura and George are reduced to poverty. Phillip, too, falls on hard times. But Lavender's old mining stock proves to be valuable and when, through a warning given him by the Negro bootblack, Dick the Rat (Tony Hart), Old Lavender is able to prevent a robbery, matters end happily. Some critics also complained about florid dialogue. Lavender, for example, describing a hangover, asserts, "The density of the atmosphere, weighing upon an individual after a night of recreation, is quite sufficient to flush a goddess." None of Braham's songs from *Old Lavender* earned a high place in his canon, nor were they as urgent to the story as in later works. Hart, who generally played the principal comic role, either in blackface or in drag, here took the relatively minor role of Dick.

Indeed a few performers who were soon to be pillars of the company—notably Annie Yeamans—were seen in this production in only minor parts.

Two competing companies arrived in October to offer New York a choice of opéra bouffe. Aimée came in on the 1st, singing her repertory in French. For novelty she offered the American premiere of Lecocq's **Marjolaine,** its tale of an erstwhile rake who boasts of his new bride's fidelity, based loosely on Shakespeare's *Cymbeline,* and Johann Strauss' first operetta, **La Reine Indigo,** recounting the love of the Queen's slave girl for the Queen's jester. Two weeks later the Hess Opera Company, with Emilie Melville as star, presented opera and opéra bouffe in English at the Fifth Avenue Theatre. The company returned for a second engagement, this time at the Union Square Theatre, from May 21 to June 8.

Lydia Thompson also played a return engagement, although not at so desirable a house. Her stay at the Eagle began on November 12 with *Robinson Crusoe.* On the 21st she introduced **Piff-Paff,** playing Prince Glamour in the court of King XXXVI of Gramercie. Alice Atherton (Mrs. Edouin) as Queen Folichonne had the hit of the evening, singing "Oh, Naughty, Naughty." When the run closed on December 15, the Edouins left the company and mounted **Babes in the Wood, or Who Killed Cock Robin?** on December 24. The parting clearly had been amicable, for Miss Thompson was credited with designing the costumes. More significantly, William Gill, who played comic villain, was credited with collaborating in the adaptation of this Drury Lane piece with Edouin. Gill's reworking was so slapdash that the *Times* suggested he could have just as easily called the affair "Fifth Avenue, or the Cataract of the Ganges." Edouin won a solid round of applause as a female circus rider, performing on a wooden horse and unerringly caricaturing the mannerisms of circus prima donnas. One critic was prompted to compare him with G. L. Fox, noting that Edouin's style was far brasher, lacking Fox's pathos and naiveté. Before the principals were turned into Clown, Pantaloon, and their friends, doors changed places, carpet-bags sprouted legs, and a transformation scene transported the cast from the arctic to the tropics. However slipshod Gill's writing was at the moment, he soon became an important librettist in the early American Musical Theatre.

Just over a week before the Edouins unveiled *Babes in the Wood,* Thomas Edison's tinkerings had reached the point where on December 6 he spoke into his primitive recording device and minutes later heard his own voice reciting "Mary Had a Little Lamb." In time, records not only helped popularize songs from the American Musical Theatre but perpetuated the very sounds of our lyric stage and its artists. Unfortunately this was a quarter of a century away, and it was the English who first recognized the value of original cast recordings.

April 22, the night that saw Harrigan's expanded *Old Lavender,* witnessed the return of J. K. Emmet in **The New Fritz, Our Cousin German** at the Standard. The "new" injected into the title announced the addition of several scenes and a full complement of songs. The added scenes included a prologue showing the stealing of Fritz's sister. Among the songs offered were "Oh, He Hit Me In De Nose," "Meet Me At The Garden Gate," "Sauerkraut Receipt," "She Fainted Away In My Arms," and "Oh, Don't Tickle Me." Of course none of these tunes achieved the popularity of Emmet's "Lullaby." But whether or not the "Brother's Lullaby" listed for this version was the beloved melody copyrighted in the following year or the song used years before in *Carl, the Fiddler* (9-18-71) remains moot. As if the "new" Fritz was not enough, Emmet announced an "amended" version on May 25, with new songs; and then on June 20, just before ending his stay, the star advertised he was performing the "London" version.

Like Grimaldi in the preceding season, Robert Frazer attempted to claim the Fox inheritance with his production of **Humpty Dumpty's Dream** (5-21-78, Fifth Ave.). Fraser had played Humpty in backwaters for some years and even appeared for a week in 1875–76 at the Olympic pantomime. His new vehicle was on a double bill with a version of Dickens' *Christmas Carol* called *The Miser.* It recorded Humpty's (and Clown's) adventures in a dream world of animals and sprites. Apparently audiences were not too disturbed by the telling of a Christmas tale in spring. The pair ran until June 5.

Minstrel shows continued to be represented by the San Francisco Minstrels, while variety theatres emerged in all parts of the city. The Olympic, converted to variety, helped give a new word for the form currency when, on November 19, it began advertising "Genuine Vaudeville." But more importantly, variety or vaudeville was obviously becoming a spawning ground not merely for future stars of the musical theatre but for plotted musical theatre comedy itself. Nowhere was it more obvious than at Harrigan and Hart's. But even Tony Pastor's hinted at the coming deluge. On April 8 his bills boasted an "original operetta," *May Moving Time* (shades of Royall Tyler's *May-Day in Town* ninety years before). "Operetta," like "vaudeville," was a word just coming into playgoers' vocabularies.

Scene Two
H.M.S. PINAFORE AND THE GREAT TRANSFORMATION 1878-1892

1878-1879

In the theatrical terms of the day, the 1878–79 season represented a "Grand Transformation," a spectacular scene change effected before the eyes of awed spectators. The uncertain, almost fortuitous triumphs of the late sixties and early seventies gave place that year to an outpouring of lyric offerings until then inconceivable in the American Musical Theatre. Almost imperceptibly at first, the popularity of old, favored types began to decline. Pantomime found no advocate as skillful or well liked as G. L. Fox. Overly elaborate spectacle came to seem cumbersome and vulgar. Most imitators of J. K. Emmet generally offered fewer musical numbers in their evenings—straight plays with at best a song or two interpolated. Perhaps the least affected genre was burlesque. Yet even its evolution was slow. As seasons passed, it blended with vaudeville skits, Harrigan and Braham's musicals, and the freewheeling, song-studded "farce comedies" to help create a native musical comedy.

Initially, few of the new musicals were any more artful or cohesive than musicals of the old school had been. And, given the increasing amount of competition, few enjoyed the runaway successes of *The Black Crook* (9-12-66) or *Humpty Dumpty* (3-10-68). But if many of the better new works failed to run as long as these old warhorses had, they nonetheless were usually highly profitable.

Moreover, they gave their creators not only fortune, but fame. Composers and librettists before them had rarely become famous in their own right. Probably not one theatregoer in ten could say who was responsible for *The Black Crook*'s music, while Barras became a name more familiar to theatrical historians than to his own contemporaries. Fox and Emmet were remembered as performers rather than collaborators, and their partners were largely ignored. Both J. Cheever Goodwin and E. E. Rice did enjoy a certain recognition, but it came with time and with an accumulation of successes. Soon, new writers coming on the scene received more instant renown. And this burgeoning fame brought with it a sense of responsibility. When failure diminished a man's reputation as readily as it hurt his pocketbook, he became doubly careful. But the principal impetus for all the new creative change and activity, the spark for the real beginning of the American Musical Theatre, was a foreign work. The unprecedented popularity of Gilbert and Sullivan's *H.M.S. Pinafore* remains the pivotal landmark in the story of our lyric theatre. However, the English comic opera did not arrive until midseason. A few interesting pieces preceded it.

Harrigan and Hart relit the Theatre Comique on August 19, each bill offering a Harrigan playlet as a major attraction. Most of these extended sketches came and went after a week, sometimes returning a month or a season later. But on September 23 **The Mulligan Guards' Picnic** began a month's run. (There was some spelling inconsistency about some early Harrigan titles. For example, on sheet music one play was called "The Mulligan Guard Ball." On the program, the same play was listed as "The Mulligan Guards' Ball." For purposes of consistency in this book the latter form will be used wherever a confusion exists.) Harrigan depicted a bad day in Dan Mulligan's life. Not only does the tailor shorten Dan's trousers to the point of absurdity, but the picnic he had planned is disrupted by the claims of a Negro society to the picnic grounds and by a wild fight between Gustavus Lochmuller (Harry Fisher) and Tommy Fagan (William Gray). The Full Moon Union has planned a balloon ascent, singing, in "Second Degree, Full Moon Union":

Sail way up in a balloon
It's dar you hear dem colored people
Shoutin' glory in dat fiery moon.

The fight develops because Lochmuller has mysteriously disappeared and, assuming him dead, Tommy has announced he will court his "widow."

A hasty trial is held at Squire Cohog's Grocery and Court, where sassy, black Rebecca Allup (Hart) proves a hilariously hostile witness. As he would so often in ensuing years, Harrigan not only wrote the play but also acted the part of Mulligan.

. . .

Edward Green Harrigan was born on October 26, 1844, in the then predominantly Irish Lower East Side of Manhattan. His father was the son of Irish immigrants who settled in Labrador as fishermen. The elder Harrigan ran away to sea, renouncing his parents' Catholic faith and becoming a determined Mason. He married the daughter of a seaman, and they settled in New York at 31 Scammel Street. Apart from a brief period in the 1850s when his father tried farming in New Jersey, young Ned was reared in the city. Ned's mother encouraged his early fascination with the theatre, but when his parents were divorced and his father married a stern Methodist, the atmosphere at home changed. At eighteen Ned left New York, winding up several years later in San Francisco. He made his first song and dance appearance there at an amateur night at Dashaway Hall, but within a short span he was well known on the bills at the city's regular variety houses. After a time, Harrigan teamed with Alex O'Brien, until the latter's heavy drinking broke up their act. Ned then joined with Sam Rickey to form a duo billed as "Noted Californian Comedians." They offered a sketch, "The Little Frauds," about a baker and a coquettish fräulein. When Rickey proved as undependable as O'Brien, Harrigan was forced to look for a new partner. He found one quickly.

. . .

Tony Hart was born Anthony J. Cannon to a poor Irish family in Worcester, Massachusetts, on July 25, 1855. The shortest member in a large clan, he became the butt of jokes and slights. His retaliations grew so out of hand he was sent to reform school. He soon ran away, coming to New York and accepting singing and dancing jobs in saloons. A brief stint with a traveling circus was followed by spells with several minstrel companies. Sometime during this period he adopted his stage name. He was only sixteen years old when he met Harrigan and persuaded him that he would be an excellent replacement for Rickey. His shortness and almost femininely beautiful face made him a natural for drag roles, while his masculine approach meant his "women" tended to be raucous and combative.

. . .

October 14 at the Standard saw the return of J. K. Emmet and his "new" *Fritz.* He, too, enjoyed a month's run. By some curious coincidence at several turning points in the history of the American Musical Theatre, producers, however unintentionally, offered something approaching a recapitulation of the past. By the year's end, three of the four major hits of the post-Civil War period were presented to playgoers for their reconsideration. Only *Humpty Dumpty* would be missing.

Harrigan had another success and another month's run beginning November 25, at the Comique with a full-length play, **The Lorgaire.** It told a story not unlike *Fritz.* The manuscript explains that "lorgaire" is Irish for detective. The sleuth in this case is Cornelius Dempsey (Harrigan) of Scotland Yard. Dempsey ascertains that Squire Ryan (Welsh Edwards) bribed a young girl to switch his child with his lord's child so that his own youngster might have a better upbringing. In the course of his work Dempsey falls in love with Norah Mullahey (Lizzie Rich) and wins her hand by the final curtain. Hart played Norah's brother, Terry. Musically the show was the richest to date at the Theatre Comique. David Braham wrote seven original songs and adapted three old Irish airs. The musical numbers included something rare in these Harrigan and Braham compositions, an opening chorus ("Listen To The Anvil"). More importantly they included one of Braham's most popular melodies, one which years later he told an interviewer had always remained his personal favorite, "Dolly, My Crumpled Horn Cow."

. . .

David Braham was born in London in 1838, scion of a musical family. He migrated to America when he was sixteen. Intending to become a harpist, he is said to have switched to the violin when a stagecoach operator refused to transport a bulky harp. The young musician obtained a position as violinist with Pony Moore's Minstrels, then became conductor of Robinson's Military Band and for several theatres, finally settling at the Comique while it was still known as Wood's. Braham composed all his songs on the violin. (In time his daughter married Harrigan. One nephew, John, conducted the first American performance of *H.M.S. Pinafore,* while another, Harry, married Lillian Russell.)

. . .

A holiday revival of *Evangeline* (7-27-74) came into Booth's from December 16 to early January. Clara Fisher was Evangeline and Nellie Larkelle was Gabriel, but more importantly, the production gave New Yorkers their first chance to see James S.

Maffitt in the role he would always be identified with, The Lone Fisherman.

On December 23, Minnie Cummings' Drawing-Room Theatre was opened to the public. If the theatre was short-lived, its initial attraction had an even shorter life. **Manhattan Beach; or, Down Among the Breakers**—an operetta, opera, or operatic lark, depending on which advertisement one read—had music by Edward Mollenhauer and book and lyrics by Charles Barnard. Barnard based his story on a popular French work, *Niniche,* which recounted how a wily wife wins back a roving husband. The text may well have been more a translation than an adaptation for at least one critic insisted the only thing American about the piece was a passing reference to clams at Coney Island.

Two companies brought in revivals of the preceding year's *Babes in the Wood.* The Colville Burlesque troupe opened on December 23, like *Evangeline* in time for the holiday trade. It also revived *Robinson Crusoe* on January 9. Rice's Surprise Party—its entourage including the Edouins, W. A. Mestayer, Louis Harrison, and Henry Dixey—played three slightly separate engagements in the spring. The fluidity of pieces such as *Babes in the Wood* can be gauged by comparing the casts of characters in the various playbills. About half the figures in the story change from production to production. The Queens of Songbirds and Tragedy disappeared after the 1877 mounting, while Dr. Bigfee, Dr. Littlepill, Dr. Callagain, and Dr. Overpaid pranced through the latest edition. Had musical numbers been listed, a similar revision would probably have been evident.

January 6 presented New Yorkers with a choice of opening nights, both revivals. The Lyceum offered playgoers a second *Evangeline.* This version offered Venie Clancy and Lizzie Webster as the maid and her lover, Harry Hunter as The Lone Fisherman, and George K. Fortesque as Catherine. It ran until *H.M.S. Pinafore* pre-empted it in the middle of its third week. At the same time, down at the Bowery, a revival of *Baba* (9-18-76) was mounted at an advertised cost of $50,000. It survived only a half week longer than the Lyceum's *Evangeline.* Shortly after *Baba* closed, the Bowery —an important playhouse for fifty-three years— left the English-speaking fold and began offering foreign-language mountings for the immigrants who had clustered nearby.

The week starting Monday, January 13 marked a major turning point in the American Musical Theatre. Even if *H.M.S. Pinafore* had not had its tumultuous American premiere on Wednesday, given time, the success of **The Mulligan Guards' Ball,** which occupied the Comique from January 13 to May 24, might well have hastened the evolution of the lyric stage. In any case it consolidated the fame of Harrigan, Hart, and Braham. Their company's halcyon days began with this production. The play was still not full length and was presented each week with a different vaudeville bill. One of these bills included George M. Cohan's father, Jerry. And like most musical works of the time the piece remained fluid, with Harrigan adding and subtracting scenes during the run. Basically it dealt with two problems confronting Dan Mulligan (Harrigan). The first of these stems from the arrangements for the Mulligan Guards' Ball. Dan is especially proud of the group, which he boasts was "christened after me." But a younger element is trying to take over. Compounding matters, the hall Dan's brigade has booked for its annual ball has been booked for the identical night by a black group, the Skidmore Guards. (This was the same device Harrigan had employed in the *Mulligan Guards' Picnic.)* The blacks finally consent to use the upstairs room, while the whites remain below. In one of the most famous of all Harrigan scenes, the black revelries become so wild the floor gives way and the Skidmore comes toppling down into the Mulligan party. Dan's second problem is the romance of the Mulligans' son, Tommy (Hart), and the Lochmullers' daughter, Katy (Nellie Jones). The mothers, Cordelia Mulligan (Annie Yeamans) and Bridget Lochmuller (Annie Mack), detest each other, and Dan's hackles are raised by the prospect of mixing Irish and German blood. Dan's prejudices are not completely justified since Bridget is Irish. The children decide to elope. The elopement brings the battle between Dan and Gustave Lochmuller (H. A. Fisher) to a head. Like Fritz, Lochmuller was an early comic "Dutchman." At one point he warns Cordelia, "Mrs. Mulligan, don't add reputation to insult." But once the newlyweds return, their *fait accompli* helps reconcile family differences.

Harrigan was excellent at characterization. The older Mulligan, like many figures Harrigan created for himself, was inclined to be garrulous, but warm and sensible. Dan's speech to Tommy asking the youngster not to forget his father's old cronies is typical:

They wanted me to tell ye that they were pioneers in the old guard before the war and they've saved the battle axes and russian hats and they want to march to the ball ahead of the Young Mulligans. Lave them. I owe McSweeney five and Gilmartin ten. 'Twill aise them up.

The children are more impetuous; their talk more colloquial:

Tommy: I'll tell you now how we'll fix the snap. We'll go down to Maggie's now and we'll talk it over with her about standing up with you tomorrow night.

Kitty: We can't get married at the ball.

Tommy: Hold on, let me get to the end of the story. We go to the ball together, don't we?

Kitty: Yes.

Tommy: And during intermission we'll go to Judge Walsh's home.

Harrigan's Negroes spoke a stage dialect that was probably not too far from black speech of the day, for while he employed stereotypes Harrigan always injected sympathetic notes. His Negroes may have been exaggerations but they were not minstrel grotesqueries. The dialogue between Simpson Primrose (John Wild) and Palestine Puter (Billy Gray) as they plan the Skidmore decoration is believable:

Simpson: I spect we'll have it decorated wid nice ingredients.

Puter: Oh, yes. Dar's a large chromo of Abraham Lincoln to go over de door and de floral tributes are something gorgeous.

Simpson: I understand leftenant Newlumber's Sister Ruth is gwine to stand for de Goddess of Liberty when de Skidmores march in de hall.

Puter: She'll have to stand on a flour barrel.

All these characters appeared again and again in later Mulligan episodes. Harrigan generally remembered their histories and kept his delineations consistent from play to play. Sometimes a line from one play gave a hint of a future story. For example, in *The Mulligan Guards' Ball* Cordelia notes, "I have a Silver Wedding the night after the ball," and before long *The Mulligans' Silver Wedding* entered the repertory. Theatregoers with an attentive ear and a good memory would also come to realize that Harrigan had favorite lines which he repeated, wittingly or not, from one show to another. One of the minor characters in the play complains the corned beef was so bad, "I've corns on me teeth from ateing it." Later figures made identical complaints. With time, Harrigan fleshed out all his better efforts, but their multi-scened construction, their debt to Tom and Jerry shows, allowed a certain looseness that left little sacred. One thing that never changed

once established was Braham's hit songs. Although "The Mulligan Guard" was written in 1873 for a short vaudeville skit, it was forever after incorporated into this play and often used in other Mulligan plays. It was unquestionably the most popular and enduring number to come from the Harrigan and Braham partnership. But a second favorite was written specifically for this production, a melody typical of the sentimental tunes found in all the Harrigan and Hart shows, "The Babies On Our Block."

Unlike *The Lorgaire*, *The Mulligan Guards' Ball* had no opening number. The first song did not come until the end of the first scene when Dan offers Cordelia's lady friends refreshment from "The Pitcher Of Beer." Obviously standard formulas had yet to be arrived at. But the evening was clearly a musical entertainment well on its way to becoming a full-fledged musical comedy.

Two nights later **H.M.S. Pinafore** burst upon New York. But New York was not the first American city to embrace the work. The active Boston theatre had grabbed that honor with its version on November 25, 1878. San Francisco was applauding it by December 23 and Philadelphia by the first week of 1879. The first New York performance took place at the Standard Theatre on January 15, and just over a week later the Lyceum offered a competing production. Since it takes more than a week to assemble and rehearse a cast, managers clearly expected the show to be a hit. Because of the period's loose copyright laws competing companies were not unheard of. What was unheard of was the sweep that Gilbert and Sullivan's comic opera made of the New York theatre scene. By February 8, less than four weeks after the premiere, the *Dramatic Mirror* could remark, "The constant spread of 'H.M.S. Pinafore' has led to the report that every house in New York is to do the opera within two weeks." No such monopolization came to pass. Nevertheless, on May 3 this same theatrical sheet did look back and note that at one time or another eleven major houses—Wallack's, the Fifth Avenue, the Standard, the Globe, the Olympic, Niblo's, the Lyceum, the Academy of Music, Tony Pastor's, the Germania, and the Windsor—all had played host to the piece. In its excitement, the paper overlooked a twelfth theatre, the Broadway. Some weeks as many as three companies were running simultaneously—this at a time when there were rarely more than a dozen principal houses lit in any one week. There was even an all-black troupe and a company composed solely of children. The young man who played Sir Joseph Porter in the latter was the son of a famous trouper, E. L. Davenport, and himself became a musical comedy favorite, Harry Davenport.

In W. S. Gilbert's deliciously preposterous yarn, subtitled *The Lass That Loved a Sailor,* the lass is Josephine, daughter of the *Pinafore*'s captain. She is sought in marriage by none other than "the ruler of the Queen's navee," Sir Joseph Porter, K.C.B. His account of his rise from office boy, carefully polishing the handle of the big front door, to his current exalted position fails to move the young lady. Nor do his assurances that "love can level ranks" have any effect. Josephine remains loyal to her real love, the common sailor, Ralph Rackstraw. Josephine's plight is resolved only by Buttercup, a fat, homely, jovial old woman, reduced to selling sailors "snuff and tobaccy, and excellent jacky." She confesses that many years ago she had practiced baby-farming. To her dismay she "mixed up" two children—one patrician and one of low birth. The high-born babe was actually Ralph, the captain was the other! Ralph is hastily made the *Pinafore*'s new commander, and, allowing love to level ranks, marries Josephine. Her father, now a mere sailor, weds Buttercup, while Sir Joseph settles for a lady named Hebe.

American theatregoers were exposed to a rare, but not new, kind of musical theatre in which book, lyrics, and music combined to form an integral whole. What made the show distinctive was the literacy and wit of its words, and the artistry and almost unprecedented melodic invention of its music. W. S. Gilbert carried the absurdities of his story to the brink of acceptable extremity, while Arthur Sullivan infused old forms such as ballades, sea chanties, jigs, and octettes with such irresistibly catchy melodies that most people sang them readily and happily, unaware of the artistry behind them. Together they devised the finest patter songs (in this case Sir Joseph's history, "When I Was A Lad") the popular musical stage has ever known. Not everyone knew how to take such drollery at first hearing. The *Times* recorded: "During the first act everyone seemed more or less at sea—chorus, orchestra and soloists. The audience scarcely knew whether to accept the love-making as serious or humorous, and in consequence some very pretty passages excited general hilarity." The original American cast—which chalked up 175 performances—had Thomas Whiffen as Sir Joseph Porter, Eugene Clark as Captain Corcoran, Henri Laurent as Ralph Rackstraw, W. Davidge as Dick Deadeye, Eva Mills as Jose-

phine, and Blanche Galton as Buttercup. Given the era's freewheeling ways, not all productions were faithful to the original. The Lyceum company, under E. E. Rice's management, gave the work a tongue-in-cheek mounting. Although lovely Lizzie Webster sang Josephine, Buttercup was George K. Fortesque. Reviews mention frequent interpolations of popular American songs. And, of course, minstrels and variety houses had a field day with satirical pieces. For example, Tony Pastor, besides offering the English work, produced a burlesque called *T.P.S. Canal Boat Pinafore,* which included characters such as Sir Joseph Lager and Dick Deadbeat. New York, by the way, was not alone in burlesquing the *Pinafore* rage. Typically, while *H.M.S. Pinafore* was delighting patrons at Philadelphia's Broad Street Theatre, that city's 11th Street Opera House, a short walk away, was regaling its customers with *Shadboat Pinafore.*

For all the infidelities and burlesques, the extraordinary success of *H.M.S. Pinafore* alerted producers and writers to the possibilities of musicals with more coherence and artistic sensibility than heretofore. Although the days of musicals contrived almost haphazardly as stage pieces and conceived in terms of immediate theatrical values were far from over, a new approach to the American musical stage became unavoidable. Perhaps nothing ever written for our native stage surpassed the intelligence and brilliance of Gilbert and Sullivan's masterpieces, but from 1879 on Americans would at least try. Two problems presented themselves at once. As the theatre chronicler George Odell noted, "the mad rush for *Pinafore* caught all unprepared; a race of singing actors needed to be developed." More importantly, composers and writers with both talent and integrity had to appear. Happily, with time these creators and interpreters made themselves known.

One immediate result of *Pinafore*'s popularity was a rush to stage other Gilbert and Sullivan works. On February 21 the Broadway raised its curtain on an earlier comic opera previously shunted aside, *The Sorcerer.* When the work failed to provide a second *Pinafore,* the house withdrew it on March 8 and hastily brought up a company of *Pinafore* from Philadelphia. But the failure hardly tarnished Gilbert and Sullivan's bright star. As one commentator suggested, even *Trial by Jury,* "which was rated rather dull when produced here three years ago, has in the light of recent events become a great work."

March 5 witnessed a revival of *The Black Crook*

(9-12-66) at Niblo's. Marie Bonfanti was once again prima ballerina. By now—thirteen years after she danced at its premiere—she must have come to look upon the work as her private annuity. One of the specialty acts assisting her was Professor Swan, billed as a "man alligator." The spectacle's return caused the *Dramatic Mirror* to suggest, "The era of the spectacle, which seemed a logical outcome of the ways, wealth and prodigality which succeeded the late war, ended aruptly with the financial crash of 1873." The statement was only partly true. Few new spectacles on the order of *The Black Crook* followed, but *The Black Crook* itself held the boards and the hearts of theatregoers for the rest of the century. This particular revival ran until May, with a "Grand Reconstruction" announced for the final week. It closed suddenly when the manager absconded with the payroll.

For all its success, *Pinafore* could not eject opéra bouffe from the stages. All through the spring companies performing in English or French found harbor in one house or another. Besides the old standbys, they added Lecocq's **Le Petit Duc** and von Suppé's **Fatinitza** to their lists. Lecocq's piece enjoyed a vernacular production at Booth's on March 17, and, when it left, Aimée came into the house to sing it in the original. She sang the part of a young nobleman whose plans to rescue his sweetheart from her seminary are thwarted when he is called to arms. *Fatinitza*'s American premiere took place on April 14 at the Germania, a house devoted appropriately to productions in German; its debut in English occurred eight nights later at the Fifth Avenue. The displacement of French opéra bouffe by German operetta began with this piece. Now long forgotten, it remained a favorite for over a decade. Franz von Suppé has been called the German Offenbach, although his works were generally more sentimental, less laden with burlesque and political satire. But the vogue for trouser roles required *Fatinitza*, first sung in Vienna on January 5, 1876, to resort to at least one feature of burlesque—dressing a woman as a man. Cleverly, it introduced an element of triple tension by allowing its leading lady in the role of a man to have to pose as a woman. Its story told of a Russian general who falls in love with a beautiful girl, never suspecting the lady is actually one of his lieutenants, heading for a masquerade. By comic opera coincidence the lieutenant and the general's niece are sweethearts. Jeannie Winston sang the title role.

Minstrelsy remained primarily in the hands of the competent San Francisco Minstrels. They, too, joined in the fun at the expense of Gilbert and Sulli-van. Their spoof was entitled "His Mud Scow Pinafore." The ranks of vaudeville houses continued to swell, introducing one major new emporium, Koster and Bial's at 23rd Street and Sixth Avenue.

The season ended in May with the return of Rice's Surprise Party and the arrival of the Salsbury Troubadors. In **The Brook** (5-12-79, San Francisco Minstrels' Hall), the work the Salsbury troupe presented, many scholars have detected one of the origins of modern musical comedy. The piece and the company initiated a vogue for what were soon called "farce-comedies." These were plays with the merest trifle of a plot, just enough frame to provide an excuse for songs, dances, and specialties by the small band that comprised the company. In essence they were loosely justified vaudeville, differing from variety in that a performer did not merely do his act and disappear for the evening but rather assumed a number of guises and presented parts of his or her repertory at intervals during the show. And, of course, vaudeville rarely pretended to have a story to tell. Scholars who see in the Troubadors the seeds of later musical comedy are correct, but seeds for the 20th-century revues were there as well. *The Brook* was subtitled *A Jolly Day at the Picnic*, a subtitle which gave away the whole plot. Three men and two women arrive at the "I-Flow-on-for-ever" brook with their picnic baskets. The picnickers bore names such as Festus Heavysides, Percy Montrose, and Blanche Sylvester. Out of their baskets came not only their meal but costumes, juggling balls, and all the other paraphernalia for their acts. For many the darling of the evening was Nellie McHenry, whose "laugh was a long ripple of merriment," cavorting as Rose Dimplecheek. Both the public and the critics agreed with the *Dramatic Mirror*, which found the evening "without plot, character, motif, or, we might almost add, incident, but all the same, very funny." Soon Rice's Surprise Party, Colville's Folly, The Tourists, and a host of other bands were offering similar pieces. While Rice's troupe, which arrived a week after the Salsbury entourage, opened at the Union Square with *Babes in the Wood,* they changed to William Gill's "burlesque extravaganza," **Horrors, or The Marajah of Zogobad** on May 28. Its paper-thin plot booked a young man, mistaken in the belief he has inherited a harem, on an eastbound liner. The passengers he meets provided the specialties. Willie Edouin shone as a "premiere danseuse" trying to perform on a ship pitching and rolling at sea. A season or two passed before the troupe officially switched to farce-comedies, although many would justifiably tag *Horrors* as a farce-comedy.

1879-1880

For George Odell, in his history of the New York stage, the 1879–80 season marked the beginnings of "A Changing Theatre." Nowhere was that change more evident than on the lyric stage. If opéra bouffe repertory companies each count as a single entry, the seasons between *The Black Crook* (9-12-66) and *H.M.S. Pinafore* (1-15-79) averaged about eight musical mountings. Not until the 1950s was such a low figure again recorded. From the dozen or so offerings in 1878–79 of the American Musical Theatre, the number jumped to over thirty in 1879–80. Of course many were importations, revivals, or return engagements. Further, many American works took pride in advertising that their directors, their designers, and even their sets were from abroad. Nor was so dramatic an increase in activity matched by any similar rise in quality. It took a while before American authors and composers assimilated the aesthetic lessons Gilbert and Sullivan had offered them.

That the Mulligan plays had become a successful series was demonstrated by advertisements which called **The Mulligan Guards' Chowder** (8-11-79, Comique) "Volume the Third." Ned Harrigan once again was Dan and Annie Yeamans, Cordelia; while Tony Hart not only played their son Tommy, but Mrs. Welcome (Rebecca) Allup as well. However, the principal plot of the evening pivoted on the behavior of two other characters, for when Walsingham McSweeny (M. Bradley) is selected as head cook of the chowder over Snuff McIntosh (Edward Burt), the explosive Snuff vows to wreck the event. His intentions are unwittingly abetted by the black Skidmores, whose Decoration Day plans call for them to celebrate on the same small piece of turf the Guards have chosen. This was the third time Harrigan had employed the device of conflicting arrangements. The blacks' march, "The Skids Are Out Tonight," was the hit of the show. Other songs included "Oh, Girly, Girly," "Never Take The Horseshoe From The Door," and "The Little Widow Dunn." None of Braham's songs for this piece ranked among his best. Nonetheless on November 2 the *Times* noted, "The melodies which form such an attractive part of 'The Mulligan Guard Chowder' . . . are played on every side. If popularity is a species of present immortality, then the composer, Mr. David Braham, should be a happy man." How curious that Harrigan and Hart were never known as Harrigan, Hart, and Braham! The actors' visibility worked to their fame. The *Chowder* was served up for the 100th time on November 5 and closed ten nights later.

Colville's organization—called for the moment the Opera Burlesque Company—brought in **The Magic Slipper** (8-25-79, Haverly's Lyceum). The story recounted how the Baron de Boulevard's (Ed Chapman) stepdaughters—especially the wicked Clorinda (R. E. Graham—an actor!)—humiliate his own daughter, Cinderella de Boulevard (Eme Roseau). Naturally Cinderella triumphs, abetted or hindered in her triumph by Prince Popette (a trouser role played by Alice Hastings), Daffydownilla, Sweetcornia, and Wheatina. The dialogue ran to such lines as "men who play polo never get married" to snatches from *Pinafore,* while the score was a similar hodgepodge. The troupe remained in town for three weeks. After a long road tour it returned with the same offering in May.

Maurice Grau's band of opéra bouffe interpreters began the first of three separate engagements on September 1st. Together the three stays (at the Fifth Avenue, Booth's, and the Academy of Music) added up to over four months. At first Aimée was the star, but she was soon replaced by Paola Marie, sister of an earlier opéra bouffe favorite, Irma, and sister, as well, of Bizet's original Carmen, Galli-Marie. The repertory offered nothing new. Its works were the opéra bouffe standards of the day, from *La Grande Duchesse* on.

When the Kiralfys mounted **Enchantment** (9-4-79, Niblo's), a "grand operatic spectacle" in the *Black Crook* tradition, their advertisements promised "celebrated English singers, renowned Italian ballet premieres and extraordinary specialty features." They also offered their customarily elaborate stage effects. In this instance the effects were so complicated they caused several delays in the opening date. A number of critics questioned whether it was worth the wait. The *Times* lamented that the "silly" evening "abounds in side shows." To tie the spectacle and specialties together the work told a tale of troubled love. Andre (C. J. Campbell), a young fisherman, loves the governor's daughter, Angeline (Jessie Greville). The governor opposes the match. The enchantress, Rayense (Mlle. Cassati), leads the lovers to the Land of the Ephemerals, the Isle of Mystery, and other unearthly places before she prevails on the girl's father to give his consent. A large segment of the public ignored the *Dramatic Mirror*'s pronouncement of the preceding year and the critic's reservations. Their way to Niblo's made easier by the new elevated railway, they flocked in sufficient number to allow *Enchantment* to offer its 100th performance on November 25 and continue until the middle of December.

Augustin Daly remained hopeful that part of his season could be devoted to a musical presentation. His hopes suffered a setback when he mounted **Newport, or The Swimmer, the Singer and the Cypher,** as part of a double bill on September 17. The *Times* knowingly informed its readers "a musical comedy it is called" and added, somewhat mysteriously, that it was the work of "an American writer living abroad." The writer remained unidentified even in the program, but was later discovered to be Olive Logan Sykes. She based her play on *Niniche,* the same source used the year before by Edward Mollenhauer in *Manhattan Beach* (12-23-78), and used again years later by Harry B. Smith for *The Little Duchess* (10-14-01). The woman who has to go about winning back her straying husband (Charles Leclercq) was called Mrs. Porter (Catherine Lewis). Music was by a number of composers, but one new song, sung by the wife, caught the critics' and public's fancy, surviving the show's two-week run. The song had the odd title of "Crutch And Toothpick," and twitted the dandified "dudes" of the time. Even at this early date Daly was thoughtful enough to fill his stage not just with attractive scenery, but with "a host of pretty girls."

The season's first farce-comedy troupe raised its curtain on September 29 at a theatre known briefly as Wood's Broadway—but soon to be the Bijou. Padgett and Bassett's **Bric-A-Brac** used a reception as an excuse for its jokes, specialties, and music. In keeping with general practice the songs came from everywhere, "music from 'Fatinitza,' ballads more or less familiar, some original songs." Also in keeping with the practice of these pieces the cast was small. Padgett and Bassett needed only two other performers to help them play all the parts.

A similar, but slightly more elaborate, mounting followed. **Hobbies** (10-6-79, Lyceum), a farce-comedy, was commissioned by Nat Goodwin and written by Ben Woolf, the same Woolf who had provided the libretto for *The Doctor of Alcantara* (9-25-66). Woolf was also the author of the successful play *The Mighty Dollar.* Goodwin had just organized his own farce-comedy band, Goodwin's Froliques. According to Goodwin, Woolf threw off the piece in five days but gave Goodwin and his five fellow players four years' work. Goodwin's imitations of other actors were generally the most praised specialty in the evening, although Jennie

Weatherby was lauded for her bit as an old lady unwilling to accept the fact that she is no longer a languid beauty. The show represented the first peak in Goodwin's erratic, scandal-plagued career.

The initial revival of *H.M.S. Pinafore,* by the Juvenile Opera Co., at Wood's Broadway, occurred on October 20, though a better *Pinafore* was not far off.

J. K. Emmet returned with a new Fritz play, **Fritz in Ireland** (11-3-79, Park). William Carleton's story was complicated and preposterous, leading up to the inevitable recognition scene. Baroness Hertford, feeling her husband (J. H. Rennie) has never loved her, leaves her estate to her sister, Lady Amelia (Lenore Bigelow), in case she dies before her child reaches maturity. Both she and the child do die, but the conniving Lawyer Priggins (John Mackay) persuades the baron to kidnap and substitute another child, since the baroness' sister has never seen her niece. The blackmailing Priggins attempts to force the baron to assign his wealth to him. But the baron reminds Priggins of his suspicious actions when he was sent to seek Lord Seaton's lost son in Germany. The real son was to marry Lady Amelia. Of course, Priggins wanted to prevent the wedding. He was determined to marry Amelia himself, if the inheritance did finally fall into her hands. Years pass. Fritz arrives, seeking his kidnaped sister. In dialogue almost word for word from *Fritz, Our Cousin German* (7-11-70), the baron's "daughter" (Emily Baker) responds to Fritz's singing an old lullaby:

Louisa: Oh, how beautiful!
Fritz: Dot song make you cry.
Louisa: The melody is so soft and sad.

Reunion follows. How much melodrama and spectacle was included in these pieces can be gauged from the following note in the prologue of the manuscript:

> After Priggins steals the child, Fritz discovers the theft, Priggins can make his escape on horseback pursued by Fritz, he overtakes Priggins on a dock at the waters edge, big fight Fritz knocked off dock into water, Priggins escapes in row-boat to 55 foot Yawl yacht in waiting, Fritz swims to a launch climbs in, starts engine, and races after Yawl, over-hauls it, another fight, is thrown over board, Yawl makes its escape, and Fritz is rescued by fisherman.

The action is cinematographic rather than theatrical, but prefilm audiences accepted as realistic effects that today would be risible. Musically the show marked no advance over the earlier Fritz efforts, and Emmet usually incorporated his by then famous "Lullaby" in the recognition scene. New songs included "The Bells Are Ringing," "The Cuckoo Song," and "The Love Of The Shamrock." This edition ran eight weeks and returned in May for an additional run. By this time, the shape of Emmet's future career seemed clear to him, and he was eager to convey his intentions to his audience. In the program for the Park Theatre for the week of November 14 he inserted a "Notice To Public." The notice ran, "It is Mr. EMMET'S intention to make an alteration yearly in his character of 'FRITZ,' by giving him sketches and incidents of his experience during his travels around the world, and introduce new scenes and music, making, if not an entire new drama, an entertainment not to be excelled." Possibly excluding the last value judgment, Emmet was true to his word. Emmet was plainly astute enough to gauge accurately his audiences' tastes, and he was determined enough never to veer from his stated plans. Even after his death, his son and others would be able to thrive for a number of years by rigidly following this 1879 dictum.

The same night *Fritz in Ireland* premiered, a third farce-comedy troupe, The Tourists, settled in for a two-week visit at Haverly's Lyceum with their most successful piece, **A Pullman Palace Car.** After a first act in which a collection of socialites plan a trip west, the second and third acts take place on the train, where the travelers and assorted passersby perform their turns. Typical of how these small bands made a cast seem larger was W. A. Mestayer's switching from the role of T. Henry Slum in the first act to impersonate Richard Morgye, Faro Jack, and the Western Guerilla in the last two acts. Delightful vignettes included M. H. Watson's drunken butler, Jennie Reifferth's maiden aunt, and J. N. Long's "red-striped-shirt polo player with bogus English accent, elbows and hips thrown backward to the point of breaking." Songs included a scene from *Pinafore*, "The Old Kentucky Home," a chorus from *The Chimes of Normandy,* a serenade from *Cox and Box,* "The Skids Are Out To-day" (from Harrigan and Hart), and "original with the Tourists," "Poor Cock Robin." Later programs show a markedly different collection of musical numbers, including the addition of a title song. The Tourists returned to Haverly's in their *Pullman Palace Car* on January 5 for a six-week sojourn.

A month-long revival of *Fatinitza* (4-14-79) opened at the Standard on November 17, competing with **The Mulligan Guards' Christmas** for first-nighters' attention. Undoubtedly the more sedate opéra bouffe drew a more stately crowd. The new work dealt with the arrival in America of Bridget Lochmuller's brother, Planxty McFudd (Welsh Edwards). To the resigned dismay of the Mulligans (Harrigan and Annie Yeamans), he courts and wins Dan's sister, Diana (Marie Gorenflo). Among the new characters Harrigan created for this play was Macaulay Jangles (Edward Burt), a slightly demented figure given to grand malapropisms. As usual Annie Mack played Bridget; Hart, Rebecca Allup; John Wild, Simpson Primrose; and Billy Gray, Palestine Puter. David Braham's songs included "The Sweet Kentucky Rose" (Hart's major song), "The Skids Are On Review," "The Mulligan Braves," "Tu-ri-ad-i-lum, Or Santa Claus Has Come" (sung by Harrigan). If Odell is correct, Harrigan again sang "The Pitcher Of Beer" in this work. Not quite full-length, *The Mulligan Guards' Christmas* was accompanied by an olio as it ran until February 14.

On December 1 at the Fifth Avenue Gilbert, Sullivan, and D'Oyly Carte showed Americans how they meant *H.M.S. Pinafore* to be done. They brought with them J. H. Ryley to sing Sir Joseph Porter, Hugh Talbot for Ralph, Furneaux Cook to be Dick Deadeye, and Alice Barnett as Buttercup. In a gesture of transatlantic courtesy they hired two Americans: John Cook, who performed under the name Signor Brocolini, for Captain Corcoran, and Blanche Roosevelt as Josephine. The Englishmen's crossing was not, however, purely in the name of aesthetics or altruism. Their principal reason for making the still hazardous journey was to stop the rampant pirating of their works. To this end they were determined to secure the copyright to their latest work, **The Pirates of Penzance,** by mounting it here first. They did so on New Year's Eve, December 31, 1879, again at the Fifth Avenue.

Gilbert's young hero was Frederick, whose wet-nurse, Ruth, somewhat hard of hearing, misunderstood his father's request to apprentice the boy to pilots, and apprenticed him instead to pirates. Though by his own reckoning Frederick has reached his twenty-first birthday and therefore is a free man, his mentors insist that since he was born on February 29, his birthday comes once every four years and he is merely a five-year-old. The beautiful Mabel falls in love at first sight with Frederick, whom she labels a "Poor Wandering One." Mabel's guardian is Major-General Stanley, "the very model of a modern Major-General," who, while up on "information vegetable, animal, and mineral," knows no more of things military "than a novice in a nunnery." A happy ending is arranged when the docile pirates yield to a band of timid police in "Queen Victoria's name." The song of the pirates, "With Cat-like Tread," soon swept the nation (with new lyrics) as "Hail, Hail, The Gang's All Here."

The cast was led by Talbot as Frederick, Ryley as Major-General Stanley, Cook as Samuel, Brocolini as Richard, and Miss Roosevelt as Mabel. If the reception of the new work by the public was disappointing—it ran only until March 6—the Englishmen could at least leave knowing they would no longer be so easily cheated of their royalties. Doubtless despite its relatively short run, the new comic opera had some further positive influence on American writers. In construction, wit, and melody it remained far above anything the native talent was offering. Critics, if not theatregoers, were sensible of its superiority. The *Herald* hailed it "a great improvement of 'Pinafore' . . . it is brighter, prettier and more artistic." The *World,* the *Sun,* and others echoed the *Herald* almost word for word.

The very next musical to open suggested American authors had the will if not the creative means to follow in Gilbert and Sullivan's paths. This "comic military opera" was New York's initial exposure to what it soon came to term derisively "the Philadelphia school"—a school Broadway saw as given to inane dialogue and banally simple music. **The First Life Guards at Brighton** had premiered on November 3, 1879, at Philadelphia's North Broad Street Theatre, and after winning generally enthusiastic notices, chalked up a two-month run before beginning its East Coast tour on January 5, 1880, at Wood's Broadway. The musical was written by J. S. Crossy and presented by his own ambitious J. S. Crossy American Comic Opera Company. In Crossy's tale Sir Charles Courtland loves a young lady who refuses to marry him because she is uncertain of her own history. Her mother had been killed in India, and she had then been separated from her father. Two down-at-the-heel rogues appear—a major (with a red nose) and a newspaperman. The reporter writes an article for Colonel Preston's local paper. This article, assailing Sir Charles' First Life Guards, leads to a duel between the colonel and Charles, and the duel in turn leads to the discovery that the colonel is the long-lost father of Charles' fiancée. Florence Ellis was the leading lady, with Eugene Clarke, Edward Connell, Charles F. Lang, and Charles Foster in principal male roles. The *Times* treated it as a "trifle," a word it often used to describe the farce-comedies, and dismissed it in a one-paragraph review as a "fiasco."

Crossy kept the work on the boards for two weeks and then turned his Americans over to a presentation of *Madame Angot's Daughter.*

Evangeline (7-27-74) returned for a brief stay at the Standard the same night as the Crossy work opened. The day before its revival, the *Times* predicted hard going for it, suggesting, "in these days of 'Pinafore,' burlesque will hardly kick its heels and grind out its old tunes to advantage." But *Evangeline* had developed a faithful following. It did satisfactory business during its two-week stay and came back again in May for another fortnight.

The font that *Fatinitza* had opened received replenishment on January 28 when New Yorkers were given their first opportunity to hear **The Royal Middy,** an English version of Zell and Genée's *Der Seekadet* (also spelled *Seecadet*), a tale of a gypsy girl who becomes a sailor to find her lover. Its producer was Augustin Daly, and his success with the work allowed him to gratify at one and the same time his urge to mount musicals and his penchant for German theatre. Daly awarded Catherine Lewis the title role and even utilized his rising star Ada Rehan in an ancillary role. Daly's orchestra leader, Mollenhauer, adapted the piece, retrieving in its acclaim much of the esteem he had lost the preceding year with *Manhattan Beach.* Another orchestra leader was less fortunate. Operti was ejected from Daly's, allegedly for taking notes for a rival production. Daly might have spared himself the lawsuit that followed had he known how his rivals were to fare. Daly's *Royal Middy* ran two months to excellent business; Sidney Rosenfeld's version, **The Sea Cadet,** opened June 7 at the Fifth Avenue and closed June 12.

February 2 afforded playgoers a choice of musical openings. Rice's Surprise Party brought back *Horrors* (5-28-79) for a three-week run at the Standard, while the Broadway watched Caverly's English Folly Company begin a month-long run with the burlesque, *Princess Carpillona.*

A new version of *Humpty Dumpty* (3-10-68) arrived the following night. It acknowledged the passing of time, even in the world of Mother Goose, when it pitted Humpty Dumpty Sr. against Humpty Dumpty Jr. Of course, the old favorites were present—Goody Twoshoes (Pauline Barretta), Tommy Tucker (J. F. Raymond), Old One-Two (W. H. Bartholomew), as well as Old Three-Four (N. D. Jones). A stray from *The Black Crook* (9-12-66), Stalacta, also had her moment. Humpty Senior was played by James Maffitt, who once had been called in to replace the incapacitated G. L. Fox as Humpty, on one of his vacations from the role of

The Lone Fisherman. Junior was clowned by another old hand at Humpty, Robert Fraser. But the hit of the evening was a specialty act, a troupe of Spanish youngsters singing as they accompanied themselves on guitars and mandolins. The happy hodgepodge delighted New York theatregoers for eight weeks. *The Black Crook* itself was revived briefly, as a stop-gap booking on the 16th at Niblo's, with one of the Kiralfys dancing Dragonfil.

The Theatre Comique's final offering of the season also bowed on February 16. **The Mulligan Guards' Surprise** dealt with Dan's unhappiness after Cordelia (Annie Yeamans) persuades him to leave his beloved neighborhood and move to more pretentious quarters. Dan (Harrigan) embarrasses Cordelia and her family by getting roaring drunk. But Rebecca Allup (Hart) helps extricate him from his agony. The basic situation was the same Harrigan would reuse a few seasons later in what is generally conceded his best work, *Cordelia's Aspirations* (11-5-83). That Harrigan, Hart, and Braham were establishing the first ongoing traditions in the American Musical Theatre can be seen from the reviews. Years later, discussing *McAllister's Legacy,* the *Times* vividly depicted a typical Harrigan and Hart audience: "The enthusiasm began to display itself at an early stage in the proceedings. No sooner was Mr. Braham seen than he was greeted with applause and cheers. To this followed a concerted shout of 'How are you, David Braham?' When Mr. Harrigan came on the stage, which was early in the first act, he met with such a continuous round of cheers and applause that the acting had to be suspended. After the audience or a large portion had finished their shout of 'How are you, Mr. Harrigan?' he was forced to respond to the good natured greeting before the play could proceed. He said he hardly knew what to say. He had been very busy during the week and was fortunate in having a new play for them. Whether the manuscript of it should have perished in the flames which destroyed the Theatre Comique or should be handed down to future generations was for them to say. He, having said so much, could do no more than return thanks and 'curl up into Dr. McAllister'—which he did at once, amid loud applause. Mr. Hart's greeting was no less warm. He was met with 'One! two! three! How do you do, Mr. Hart?' To which he responded by placing his right hand over his heart and observing that there was too much effervescence there to express his feelings, and that he was glad they were not compelled to leave New York for some time to come at least. Mrs. Annie Yeamans and John Wild also came in for their share of applause on appear-

ing. . . . At the close of the first act Mr. Braham was presented with a valuable violin in the place of the one lost by him at the Comique fire. A lawyer of this city made the presentation speech, but although Braham was urged to reply, he wisely forbore, and let his orchestra speak for him. At this point a large number queried, in chorus, 'When was David Braham?' and responded with 'First in war, first in peace, and first in the hearts of his countrymen.' Similar remarks were also made concerning one George Washington."

In offering *The Mulligan Guards' Surprise* the first extended notice it ever gave to the Comique, the *Times* remarked that while the house's balconies were still filled with raucous fans who often interrupted the action with prolonged cheers, applause, and even comments (to which the players not infrequently responded), the ground floor was attracting an increasingly cultivated crowd. The *Times* was willing to accept partial credit for this improvement, suggesting its brief Sunday notices had helped call attention to the freshness and integrity of Harrigan and Braham's material. The paper, praising and listing Braham's songs, concluded that they "will take their places with 'Sallie Waters' and 'The Little Widow Dunn.' " The paper was a little less happy with Harrigan's writing. It saw the evening as "a superfluity of coarse fun and cheap wit, and a tiresome diffuseness of dialogue." But its criticism did not prevent it from enjoying the entertainment or allowing that the public would enjoy it even more. The public, in fact, enjoyed it for just over 100 performances, until it closed on May 15.

Another totally native work, **Hiawatha** (2-21-80, Standard), advertised itself as an "entirely original American operatic extravaganza." Actually it was another burlesque in the *Evangeline* tradition. Longfellow would no more have recognized this adaptation of his poem than he would have the earlier one. As before the entertainment was largely the work of the busy E. E. Rice, this time in collaboration with Nathaniel Childs. Their story told how Romulus Smith (Henry E. Dixey) and Remus Brown (Louis Harrison) conspire with William Penn Brown (Willie Edouin) to gull Hiawatha (Alice Atherton) and Minnehaha (Marion Singer). An audience must have had to be especially alert for the librettists' puns, which probably were not as obvious to the ear as they were to the eye. At one point Penn is said to have "penn-etrated the forest, not for-rest but for plunder." The songs of *Hiawatha* were a far cry from *The Song of Hiawatha,* including as they did "Bubble, Bubble," "Indians Never Lie," and "Tea, Toast, And Kisses." Whatever flaws the writing possessed, the performance was lively. One critic grudgingly conceded the audience didn't share in his chagrin at the "brazen" foolery of Miss Atherton, and he acknowledged the growing attraction of comely chorus lines, admitting how enthusiastic theatregoers could become when "short skirts, well-displayed limbs, and not over-modest young women mingle under the searching glare of the limelight." Picturesque sets by W. T. Voegtlin, the era's leading scene painter, depicted a wigwam with a waterfall behind it, and a snow storm. (Unlike the Kiralfys' very wet cascades, Voegtlin's falls seems to have been entirely oil on canvas.) But weaknesses of conception told. The show failed, even though the cast was studded with some of the brightest talent of the 1880s.

A revival of *The Brook* (5-12-79) was booked into Haverly's Lyceum on February 23 for three weeks. On March 8 *Robinson Crusoe* was hurriedly restaged by Rice to supplant the failed *Hiawatha*. March and early April also saw visits by performers in plays that straddled the line between musical and straight drama. Lotta came in with her repertory, and Maggie Mitchell reappeared in her perennial *Fanchon*.

On March 1 a troupe known as the Boston Ideal Opera Company made its first New York appearance. Probably few in Niblo's that night dreamt of how successful and influential this ensemble would grow. The organization first confronted Boston with its version of *H.M.S. Pinafore* on April 14, 1879. So skillful was the production, it ran a then-unheard-of nine weeks. A second operetta, *Fatinitza*, followed with equal success. This second triumph convinced the band's founder, Miss Ober, to set up a permanent troupe. Some inkling of the company's artistry can be gathered from the *Times* pronouncement that its sole offering on this visit, *Pinafore*, was "the most perfect, musically at least, that has yet been given in the City." Captain Corcoran was sung by the "celebrated oratorio singer," Myron Whitney, Adelaide Phillips was Josephine, and Mary Beebe played Buttercup. But even at this early date, the troupe included the great comic baritone who would be the company's real bulwark virtually until its dissolution, its Sir Joseph, Henry Clay Barnabee.

. . .

Henry Clay Barnabee was born in Portsmouth, New Hampshire, on November 4, 1833. He quit school to accept work as a dry-goods clerk, but occasional appearances in amateur theatricals, concerts, and lyceums convinced him his future lay behind the footlights. His enchanting autobiography, *My Wanderings,* describes one of the primitive mu-

sicals in which he barnstormed New England for many years. This one was first peformed in his hometown on May 24 and 25 of 1868: "An 'operatic cantata' had its inception at this period. It was a mongrel, nondescript affair, compounded of gush, nonsense, and impossible scenery, and entitled 'The Haymakers.' . . . The work of a farmer, both in music and in scenario. The 'action' consisted of a number of chorus men, supposed to be mowing in a hay-field. . . . The book called for two farmer's daughters, soprano and contralto, and two hired men, tenor and bass, to fall in love with them, and incidentally to engage in a series of musical mix-ups, such as duos, trios and quartettes. . . . Snipkins, a city boy gapes at the countryside and a farmer responds, 'Say, I s'pose if I should go daown to Boston, I'd gawp araound same as yew do up here?' " Other early musicals Barnabee toured in included Julius Eichberg's *The Two Cadis,* a tale of two rogues determined to outwit each other, and *Marmaduke Mouser,* a romp of high life below stairs that Barnabee himself adapted from a play called *Betsy Baker.* The slightly horse-faced comedian claimed to his dying day he could not read a note of music, but his lovable villains and his sense of artistic integrity won him the respect and affection of his generation.

. . .

The last day of March saw a British double bill at the Bijou. The Bijou was the old Broadway, refurbished and renamed by John A. McCaull, a former Confederate officer and Baltimore lawyer. Under his aegis the house was soon to be a major stage for musicals and McCaull himself termed "the father of comic opera in America." A group called the Opera di Camera presented two English works: *Ages Ago* by W. S. Gilbert and Frederick Clay and *Charity Begins at Home* by Bolton Rowe and Alfred Cellier. Cellier had conducted the D'Oyly Carte's New York production of *H.M.S. Pinafore* and was embarking on his own career as a comic opera composer. The double bill provided a delightful surprise, and thus started McCaull's new house off happily, running until May 15.

The Colville Opera Burlesque returned on May 3, offering first *The Magic Slipper* it had presented at the start of the season, then switching on May 10 to a burlesque of Verdi, *Ill Treated Il Trovatore* which had Manrico as a trouser role (played by Eme Roseau) and threw in everything else laughable. Verdi's music was presented along with material from *Pinafore, Der Seekadet,* and the minstrel stages. The show ran a week before the troupe moved on.

The season's final hit was Franz von Suppé's **Boccaccio,** in which the poet's actual romance with the so-called Fiametta, really the Princess Maria of Naples, was given a fictitious happy ending. Jeannie Winston and Alice Hosmer sang the hero and heroine. Opening on May 15, it consolidated the season-old vogue for middle-European operettas. *Boccaccio* ran four weeks, until hot weather withered trade.

William C. Mitchell's Pleasure Party bucked the same heat to end the theatrical year with their farce-comedy, **Our Goblins.** Its author, William Gill, and a future star, Francis Wilson, were two of the five members of the troupe. In Gill's story Benjamin Franklin Cobb and four friends go picnicking near an old, deserted castle on the Rhine. Gill as Cobb falls asleep and dreams of the ancient revels held in the castle. Obviously, the story was only a variation of that used in the first of the farce-comedy successes, *The Brook.* As usual in these works, disparate sources were culled for the songs.

On other musical stages, the San Francisco Minstrels kept the torch of blackface entertainment aflame. Some indication that even this torch sputtered now and then can be gleaned from a notice in the *Times* on January 4 advising playgoers to attend a performance, since "the patient gentlemen of the San Francisco Minstrels have discovered two new jokes, which will be utilized until further notice." Their efforts for the season included a spoof entitled "The Pirates of Sandy Hook." In the increasingly large and competitive vaudeville field, Tony Pastor, noting the success with which Harrigan and Hart were moving away, attempted to imitate the masters with playlets such as *Murphy's Wedding* and *The Parade of the Rafferty Blues.* When these failed, Pastor turned to farce-comedy. On his bill for January 19 he included *The Emigrant Train, or Go West!* by the author of *Fritz in Ireland,* William Carleton. In the end Pastor came to the sensible realization that he was the master showman of variety. Although he later attempted innovations, he was careful never to drift too far from his basic vaudeville format.

1880–1881

The new season was much like the old. The lyric stage bustled with activity, but offered little in the way of creative novelty. Ned Harrigan and David Braham continued their Mulligan series, farce-comedies abounded, a procession of importations

from France, Germany, and England graced the boards. Odell lamented, "Tourists and Troubadours and Surprise Parties, with their trifling wares, and comic opera generally were killing the taste for serious plays."

An indication of the musical theatre's new life was its busy August schedule. Seven musicals raised their curtains, while an eighth work, *Edgewood Folks,* a straight play, stopped its action at a number of points to allow its star, Sol Smith Russell, to sing his songs. One might complain that three of the shows were revivals and a fourth an enlargement of an earlier piece. None of this obviates the fact that in one month as many lyric entertainments were mounted as had been the case in entire seasons before the arrival of *H.M.S. Pinafore* (1-15-79).

The season began with an importation. Wallack's prestigious house, nearing the end of its great career, relit on August 5 with a "Grand Pantomimic Burlesque Extravaganza" from London, **Grim Goblin.** In H. Spry and George Conquest, Sr.'s plot a princess loses a cherished keepsake and promises to wed the man who retrieves it. Conquest and his son, George Jr., were acrobats who filled the evening with their feats. One breath-taking bit was the "Wonderful Phantom Flight" which "consisted of the performer flying from floor to ceiling, where he grasped a swinging trapeze, to which a rope was thrown, and which he descended to the stage as quickly as possible." The elder Conquest was to assume a number of roles: Grim Goblin, Hick-Hac-Hoc, Prince Pigmy, and Nix, the Demon Head. Unfortunately on the very first night he broke his leg in a fall. His son, too, was injured several times. George Sr. was unable to return to the Cobweb Cave of the Grim Goblin, but his son performed, at times conspicuously bandaged. One way or another, this English mélange of childlike nonsense and spectacle held the stage until September 11, when Wallack's company was ready to resume.

Farce-comedy made its initial appearance of the year four nights after *Grim Goblin,* when **Fun on the Bristol** (8-9-80, 14th St.) began a two-week stand. The *Times* reviewer recorded that music for this version "ranges from selections from Verdi's, Donizetti's, and Bizet's operas, through Offenbach and Lecocq to popular ballads and negro minstrel jigs."

Harrigan and Hart reopened their Theatre Comique on August 9 with an enlarged but not quite full evening's version of their early success, *The Mulligan Guards' Picnic* (9-23-78). Braham's contributions included "Sandy-Haired Mary In Our

Area," "Mary Kelly's Beau," "Locked Out After Nine," "All Aboard For The M.G.P.," and "The Second Degree Full Moon Union." Accompanied by ever-changing curtain-raisers, the work ran well over 100 showings, closing November 20.

Monday, August 23, saw the premiere of *Edgewood Folks* as well as the return of *Fritz in Ireland* (11-3-79), the latter at the Grand. The very next Monday witnessed three musical first nights. The peripatetic *Evangeline* (7-27-74) replaced *Fun on the Bristol* at the 14th Street, the Kiralfys revived *Around the World* (8-28-75) for five weeks at Niblo's, and *Dreams* made its first New York appearance at the Bijou. The *Evangeline* 1880 playgoers enjoyed was not quite the same earlier patrons had seen. A revised libretto introduced several new characters such as Peter Papyrus (Charles Groves). E. E. Rice announced he had written ten new songs for the revision. More importantly, the updated dialogue was by a new librettist, J. J. McNally.

. . .

John J. McNally was born in Charlestown, Massachusetts, in either 1854 or 1853 (his age was given as seventy-seven when he died in March, 1931). Although he earned a law degree at Harvard, he soon abandoned his practice to enter journalism, accepting a post as drama critic for the Boston *Herald*. His very first attempt at playwriting, the farce-comedy *Revels,* was an immediate success, although it reached Broadway after his reworking of *Evangeline*.

. . .

Around the World unveiled a succession of spectacular sets, beginning with the arrival of a steamer —complete with whistles and steam—and culminating in a jewel-studded Oriental necropolis. One absurdity was a "teutonic Borneo brass band."

Having long worked for others, Willie Edouin broke away to form his own company of farce-comedy players. He and his wife, Alice Atherton, led the company. With Rice's recent collaborator, Nathaniel Childs, Edouin concocted a piece called **Dreams, or Fun in a Photographic Gallery.** An old farmer and his wife are about to celebrate their sixtieth wedding anniversary. They begin to reminisce about their courting days. The aged husband soon grows tired, falls asleep and dreams of taking his bride-to-be to a photographer's studio. (No one seemed to be bothered by the anachronism of an 1820 photograph.) A group of other customers come and go. Eventually the groom suspects the photographer of flirting with his bride and a fight ensues. The photographer calls the police, but just as they appear the farmer awakes from his dream.

Friends arrive to help celebrate the anniversary. The second act, set in the photographer's shop, contained the main business of the evening. As each customer entered to have his picture taken he would first perform his specialty. Even the husband and wife got into the spirit of things. Edouin did a turn showing all the ways to tip a hat to a lady, while Miss Atherton impersonated Buffalo Bill, George and Martha Washington, and Rip Van Winkle. Edouin and his wife each played several other characters as well as the farmer and his wife, while lanky Jacques Kruger cavorted as the photographer, Pickleback Grabiball. The costume changing must have been just short of frantic. Looking back years later, James T. Powers, a turn-of-the-century favorite who first came to New Yorkers' attention in this piece, confirms the impression. In his autobiography he wrote, "In one scene the entire company did a specialty, making quick changes of costume for each song; the last number was patriotic, and Lotta Belton, who had an extraordinary baritone voice, sang the song; the company marked time as they stood behind her. . . ." If in retrospect farce-comedies seem all of a piece, critics and playgoers of the 1880s discerned distinctions. For example the *Dramatic Mirror* compared Edouin's Sparks to Salsbury's Troubadours and found the earlier entourage closer to variety, Edouin's troupe more given to coherent burlesque. Like all farce-comedy troupes, the Sparks drew their songs from diverse sources. One, "Lardy Dah," seems to have been new and heavily applauded. Like "Crutch And Toothpick" from the preceding year, it twitted the pretensions of some dandified men-about-town:

> He wears a penny flower in his coat, Lardy dah!
>> And a penny paper collar round his throat, Lardy dah!
> In his hand a penny stick, In his mouth a quill toothpick
>> Not a penny in his pocket, Lardy dah! Lardy dah!
> Not a penny in his pocket, Lardy dah!

In its initial Broadway stay, *Dreams* ran six weeks. New Yorkers would see it again.

The evening of Monday, September 13, like that of August 30, saw three musical offerings make their bow. The 14th Street Theatre had already housed two musicals in the still young season. With the main theatre area moving steadily north it found itself increasingly out of the way and having to be content with a rapid turnover of bookings. From September 13 to October 2 it offered M. B. Leavitt's Grand English Operatic Burlesque Company in

Carmen, or Soldiers and Seville-ians, a London piece adapted for American tastes. New Yorkers had seen their first mounting of Bizet's five-year-old opera only the preceding season.

The other two offerings the same night had more dignity and significance. Maurice Grau's French Opera Company inaugurated its season of opéra bouffe by unveiling the first New York showing of Offenbach's nine-month-old **La Fille du Tambour-Major** at the Standard. In the opéra bouffe's story a duchess, who had once been a laundress and had been married to a painter, wants her daughter by that marriage to wed a marquis. But the daughter loves a common soldier, and, with the help of her father—now a drum major in the army—marries her own choice. Paola Marie starred. She also starred in the company's other premiere, Laurent de Rillé's tale of rural love, **Babiole,** on October 21. In the five intervening weeks several old standards were revived. A competitive version of *La Fille du Tambour-Major* played the 14th Street the week of October 4.

Even more important was the New York visit of the Boston Ideal Opera Company at Booth's. Of course, *Pinafore* and *Fatinitza* were part of the program. However, a third offering, *The Pirates of Penzance*, served as the opening night bill. Myron Whitney was back, this time to sing the Pirate King, and Henry Clay Barnabee portrayed Major-General Stanley. Samuel was sung by another artist who would remain loyal to the group until the end, W. H. MacDonald. Two fine performers who proved almost as steadfast were George Frothingham (as the Sergeant of Police) and Tom Karl (as Frederick). Mary Beebe was Mabel; Adelaide Phillips, Ruth. Quibblers complained that Whitney's "oratorio style" was unsuited to such comic material and that Barnabee's "little voice" probably couldn't be heard in the far reaches of the house, but few theatregoers shared their opinions. The company was respectfully received by most critics and played nearly a month.

To avoid conflicting with three other musical openings, the premiere of Alfred Cellier's London success **The Sultan of Mocha** changed its opening at the Union Square to the next night, September 14. Considering its fate it might have been better off losing itself in the crowd. The show was withdrawn after its second week, but while it probably had no influence (unless it suggested an exotic setting for *The Mikado* to Gilbert), it was a harbinger of a fashionable new locale for later comic operas and musical comedies. Its story told how Dolly (Leonora Braham) is sold by her greedy guardian, Cap-

tain Flint (Harry Allen), to the sultan (William Hamilton). Her dashing sailor sweetheart (Eugene Clarke) rushes in with his buddies to rescue her, and when she is kidnapped and returned to the sultan, the sailor, disguised as a pilgrim, rescues her again.

September closed with the arrival from Boston of another farce-comedy, Ben Woolf's "peculiarity," **Lawn-Tennis** (9-20-80, Abbey's Park). Its construction was peculiar indeed, for its second act was a playlet within a play. Alfred Puddifoot (Digby Bell), a dramatist, and his hosts, the Cornwallis Algernon Prouts (John Howson and Hetty Tracy), go to the all-female Man-Tamers' Club in search of material for a play. By coincidence costumes for a comic opera have been delivered to the club, so Puddifoot and the Prouts watch as the group's members perform the "operettina," Djack and Djill. The playlet spoofed the lyric stage of the day. King Stupidenko XIV's daughter, Djill, loves Djack despite her father's objections. The king refuses to believe his wicked seneschal when the old man reports the youngsters have been silly enough to go *up* a hill to fetch a pail of water. But the king's heart melts on learning Djill purposely tumbled down the hill so that Djack's misstep would not embarrass the young man. Neither the published text, the advertisements, nor the reviews indicate who wrote the music for the evening, but given Woolf's musical background it remains conceivable that he was at least partly to credit. The piece enjoyed a number of engagements of varying length at different houses all through the season.

The celebrated Brooklyn organist, Dudley Buck, attempted his hand at a native comic opera when he wrote a score to W. A. Croffut's libretto for **Deseret, or The Saint's Difficulties** (10-11-80, 14th St.). Its story treated a Mormon and his wives as if they were a Sultan and his harem. Such levity disgusted the *Times,* which insisted Mormon polygamy deserved scorn not comic sanction. Other papers concentrated on the piece's artistic merits. Although the *Tribune* saw it as "the first really successful American opera" and the *World* hailed it as "a veritable American Pinafore," most critics and the public at large disagreed. The work was hustled over to Brooklyn on the 25th and disappeared from theatrical history after a week's run there. *Deseret* was probably no more influential than *The Sultan of Mocha,* but like the English work it foreshadowed a theatrical fad. For the next thirty or forty years Mormons would appear on the American lyric stage solely as figures of ridicule.

The night after *Deseret* opened, Booth's housed

a popularized version of Rossini's *Cinderella,* replete with specialty acts and interpolations of contemporary songs. However more highminded critics might react, the public attended in sufficient numbers to let the piece survive until November 6.

A revival of *Boccaccio* with Jeannie Winston at the Grand showed Americans how they might better write or treat a comic opera. But Americans went blithely on their way with farce-comedies, spectacles, and vernacular musicals. The farce-comedies came the week after the von Suppé revival when Rice's Surprise Party began a stay in a whole repertory of its pieces. The first was new. It found Edouin and his wife again working under E. E. Rice's aegis. In J. J. McNally's **Revels** (10-25-80, 14th St.) Bon Ton George loves Maryanthus, ward of Sir Ramesgate Bramblewig. Sir Ramesgate was a pork butcher whom circumstance had made majordomo to the king of Egypt. George's brother Rufus also loves Maryanthus. Rufus makes waves, but George ultimately wins his beloved. A subplot described the argumentative romance between the Bramblewigs' maid, Isis, and Calapat. Isis wants him though she admits he is "such a dorg," always chasing skirts. The work suggests how farce-comedy was borrowing from burlesque to develop more intricate stories. Its debt to burlesque was also evidenced by the fact that both George and Rufus were trouser roles. Another sign of development was that most performers played only one part in the course of the evening. Edouin was Calapat, Miss Atherton was George. But they were not the only fine performers. Rice provided them with such associates as the English star Topsy Venn, and Henry E. Dixey. *Revels* further indicates the growing vogue for "Oriental" settings. The Surprise Party's repertory included a revised version of *Horrors* (5-28-79) called *Prince Achmet,* a redoing of the failed *Hiawatha* (2-21-80), and *Babes in the Wood.*

On November 15 the Kiralfys replaced their revival of *Around the World* with a remounting of *Enchantment* (9-4-79), using many of the same artists they had used the previous year. The spectacle played three weeks.

Harrigan, Hart, and Braham had another hit with **The Mulligan Guards' Nominee** (11-22-80, Comique). The title is odd since it makes no reference to the principal plot or the subplot. In the main story, Bridget Lochmuller (Annie Mack) returns from a vacation in Ireland, trailed by an officer of the law who believes she is a revolutionary. The confusion arises from the initials of her benevolent group, the Florence Nightingale Association. These initials match letter for letter those of the Fernia National Army. As a result Bridget, Cordelia (Annie Yeamans), and their friends are arrested on the Albany nightboat for "belonging to a secret order designing the capture of Canada." The subplot details Rebecca's stratagems for winning Palestine Puter (William Gray) away from the voluptuous Caroline. Like Rebecca (Hart), Caroline was played by a man (James Tierney, in both blackface and drag). The political contest between Lochmuller (Harry Fischer) and Dan (Harrigan) for Alderman-at-large took a back seat. But it did provide the most quoted line from the show. When Dan's friend McSweeny is arrested in an election brawl, Dan shouts at the policeman, "Raylease him. I'm 200 votes ahead of Lochmuller and I'll say no more." McSweeny is released. The show ran until February 21, bolstered by such Braham numbers as "Down In Gossip Row," "Hang The Mulligan Banner Up," "A Nightcap," "Mulligan's Promises," "The Skidmore Masquerade," and the most popular of all, a song introduced during the run of *The Mulligan Guards' Chowder,* "The Skids Are Out Tonight." (For their march the "blacks" were dressed in spanking new cream-colored uniforms.)

Although minstrelsy was past its heyday, a number of bands still flourished. Several of these had come under the banner of J. H. Haverly, who also ran Niblo's and the 14th Street Theatre. As a result two minstrel troupes made rare appearances at houses normally given over to more standard fare when Haverly's Genuine Colored Minstrels played Niblo's from December 6 to December 18 and Haverly's Mastodon Minstrels returned from Europe in March to further applause at the 14th Street. Since minstrel burlesque followed closely on recent successes the same play or opera often found itself travestied a number of times in short order. The Mastodon Minstrels joined the field in spoofing *Il Trovatore.* With the well-liked Billy Emerson leading the funmakers, they called their version "Ill-True-Bad-Doer," with Emerson as Man-Wreck-Oh. The villain was Count Di-Loony (E. M. Rayne) and the heroine, played by a man, Lean-O'er-Her (Paul Vernon).

The Negro minstrels at Niblo's made way for the next-to-last musical of 1880, a revival of the preceding year's *Humpty Dumpty* (2-3-80), with Maffitt and Fraser once again father and son. Some of their thunder was almost literally stolen from them by one of the specialty acts, a young lady named

Zazel who was shot from a cannon at each performance. The show came in on December 20, just in time for the holiday trade, and stayed until January 8.

An importation from France closed out the year. This show was Audran's **Olivette** (correctly, *Les Noces d'Olivette*) which had its premiere at a matinee performance on December 25. In its two and a half hours it recorded how Olivette wins her soldier-lover despite disguises, mistaken identities, kidnappings, and parental objections. An instant success, it ran five weeks at the Bijou and moved to the Fifth Avenue to continue its run. A rival troupe mounted the work at the Park on January 17 but ran only three weeks. A third company, led by Selina Dolaro and W. T. Carleton, played briefly at the Bijou beginning March 19. The Bijou's first production affords a good example of the versatility of the period's players, for it was staged by the Comley-Barton Company, a troupe that switched with apparent ease from their farce-comedy, *Lawn-Tennis,* to this opéra bouffe. Catherine Lewis sang the title role, supported by J. C. Armand, Digby Bell, and John Howson. J. C. Duff's production at the Park offered a less attractive cast.

The Salsbury Troubadours ushered in the new year with a return engagement of *The Brook* (5-12-79). They played the piece for two weeks beginning January 3 and then showed that they, too, were versatile by staging their version of *Widow Bedott*. This was a popular comedy of the day. The Troubadours performed it essentially as a straight play, although they could not resist interpolating a few songs.

Another straight play, partially musicalized, raised its curtain at Niblo's on January 12. **Black Venus,** based on a piece by Adolphe Belot, and advertising a collection of wild animals and three ballets (with "250 young ladies") kept the house lit for a month. Set in Africa, the evening recounted how a slave girl wins the hand of King Morenza. Although one paper, looking at the size of the cast listed in the show's advertisements, warned readers "managerial announcements are not always to be believed," most likely the production's most bally-hooed scene did indeed have forty lady riders in a "Battle of the Amazons"—a refreshing change from the traditional march of the tall chorus girls. One intriguing question remains unanswered. Given the setting and the plot, did the performers appear in blackface?

Emma Abbott brought her opera company to the Fifth Avenue on January 17 in a repertory that ranged from *Lucia di Lammermoor* and *Faust* to *The Bohemian Girl* and *The Chimes of Normandy*. Miss Abbott sang for a fortnight and went her way. But much of her repertory was heard again at the same house from February 28 to March 12, this time interpreted by the Max Strakosch–A. D. Hess English Opera Company. Meanwhile, on January 17, Tony Pastor began to include a series of extended burlesques on his variety bills. The first was a take-off of Robertson's play, *School,* done as "Our School Girls." It was followed in due course by "The Pie-rats of Penn Yann" and "All of It." Two young ladies called themselves to audiences' attention in these burlesques. Both soon became stars in the musical stage: May Irwin and Lillian Russell. The nature of the parts they played can be gleaned from Miss Irwin's role in the Gilbert and Sullivan travesty. Her Freddy was set down as an "indentured prowler."

Since the 19th-century policy of opening whenever possible on Monday led to another cluster of first nights on January 17, the American premiere of Genée's *Nisida*, called in this country, **Zanina, or The Rover of Cambaye,** was abruptly put back to the next night. Why its producer and adapter, Augustin Daly, also changed its name is lost in history. If it stemmed from some fear the name was not attractive enough, this fear may well have spilled over onto the text itself. Daly, again for reasons now lost, threw out much of Genée's music and helped give currency to a dubious practice by interpolating numerous new songs his orchestra leader, Edward Mollenhauer, composed. One song, "In The North Sea Lived A Whale (The Torpedo And The Whale)," became the rage. At best the libretto still clung to the story of a fickle officer torn between an opera singer and an Indian princess. Laura Joyce sang the title role. Her husband-to-be, Digby Bell, lead the comedians. Daly regulars included the beloved red-headed farceur, James Lewis, and the radiant Ada Rehan. Daly filled the stage with real Indian Nautch dancers, magicians, and snake-charmers. Still the work proved a disappointment and a quick failure.

On February 19, New Yorkers heard for the first time the popular English work, **Billie Taylor.** It won American hearts and remained before the footlights on and off for several decades. When Billie is shanghaied in the middle of his wedding, his bride disguises herself as a sailor in order to look for him. Surprisingly the faithless Billie ends by marrying another girl, while his sweetheart marries his kidnapper. Presented by D'Oyly Carte in conjunction with E. E. Rice, the cast included J. H. Ryley (by this time a permanent American resident) as the kidnapper, Arnold Breedon as Billie, and Carrie Burton as his sweetheart. *Billie Taylor* introduced America to Edward Solomon, an English composer who became Lillian Russell's husband and wrote several of her musicals, the successes of which were usually attributable to Miss Russell. In America at least, Solomon never repeated the small triumph his *Billie Taylor* afforded him.

Three wholly native offerings competed for attention on February 21. Two were making return stands: Goodwin in *Hobbies* (10-6-79) and The Tourists in *A Pullman Palace Car* (11-3-79). The third was the latest "volume" in the Mulligan series, **The Mulligans' Silver Wedding.** Harrigan's newest effort showed how careful and thoughtful he was in developing his history. Cordelia Mulligan had alluded to her impending anniversary as far back as *The Mulligan Guards' Ball* (1-13-79), while Dan's recent victory at the polls was acknowledged by listing him as Alderman Mulligan. Unfortunately, Harrigan's growing sense of playcraft deserted him momentarily. *The Mulligans' Silver Wedding* had less plot and more vaudeville than most of its predecessors. One might almost detect the loosening influence of farce-comedy on its construction. The play centered on the Mulligans' plans for their forthcoming celebration. When a peeping Tom seems to be hovering about, a keyhole is blackened. Not one, but three black eyes are soon evident. The show's most famous scene had Cordelia attempt to kill herself by swallowing some "rat poison." The "poison" is merely whiskey Dan had falsely marked to keep it out of Rebecca's hands. When Dan is unmoved by her "death scene" Cordelia becomes doubly agonized. This very scene was later resurrected by Harrigan in *Cordelia's Aspirations* (11-5-83), where it played to stronger effect because it fit so well into the plot. As a lyricist, however, Ned Harrigan remained observant and affectionate. His "South Fifth Avenue," sung by Tony Hart, observed the changing scene and certain New Yorkers' reactions to it:

Oh, Dear me, Mister Puter,
　Just loan me your cologne,
I wish to scent my handkerchief,
　Passing dis saloon.
De vapor's quite distressing,
　From dat Italian crew,
Dis padrone emigration,
　To South Fifth Avenue.

"Wheel The Baby Out," which Harrigan sang, had

a grown man unselfconsciously singing nursery rhymes in his joy at fatherhood:

High diddle, diddle,
　The cat's in the fiddle,
How are you Mister Mulligan
　You'd hear the neighbors shout,
The little doggy laughed
　For to see such funny sport,
I was always singing
　When I'd wheel the baby out.

The 3rd, 4th, 7th, and 8th lines remained the same while the nursery jingles were altered in each of the five choruses. Once again the *Times* noted the high-class patrons Harrigan had begun to draw downstairs, although cheaper seats still lured vocal, unruly elements. Staid or raucous, the Comique's loyal followers overlooked flaws in the play and packed the house from February 21 until the end of April. Their enthusiasm was no doubt whetted by the fact that, at a top of seventy-five cents, Harrigan and Hart offered the cheapest top ticket in town.

Daly, who earlier had lost quite a large sum on *Zanina,* recouped some of his losses when he mounted a second musical at his house on March 5. **Cinderella at School** was a full-length lyric version of the same Robertson play Pastor had spoofed two months before. The music and, apparently, the book and lyrics were by Woolson Morse.

· · ·

Henry Woolson Morse was born in Charlestown, Massachusetts, on February 24, 1858. Of old New England stock, he was distantly related to Samuel F. B. Morse, the inventor of the telegraph. He was educated at Noble's, an elite private school, then studied music at the Boston Conservatory. He furthered his training abroad, working under Gerome and Henner. Returning home he wrote *Cinderella at School,* but found no producer willing to risk a mounting. As a result, Morse himself paid for an amateur production at Springfield, Massachusetts. Word of its success somehow reached Daly.

· · ·

The action begins with the young ladies attending Papyrus Seminary listening to Niobe (May Fielding), a charity pupil, tell them the tale of Cinderella. An English peer, Lord Lawntennis (Charles Leclercq), arrives with his nephew, Arthur Bicycle (Harry Lacy), and Arthur's friend, Jack Polo (John Brand). The lord has come seeking a long-lost granddaughter. Suddenly a bull chases Niobe past where the men are standing, and Niobe loses her shoe in the rush. As everyone could guess from thereon, despite the machinations of the comic "head usher and chief husher," Syntax (James Lewis), charming Arthur weds Niobe. Consanguinity was blithely ignored. The chorus concludes:

Oh, isn't it delightful
Her cup of joy is quite full.
Love's magic power
Is greater far
Than that of Fairy grandmamma.
Now in silks and satins
She'll attend the matins!

With Laura Joyce, Ada Rehan, and Mrs. Gilbert assisting, the musical ran out the season.

While new forms were ineluctably taking over the musical stage, old favorites retained much of their appeal. *The Black Crook* (9-12-66), so rusty and bedraggled in the eyes of critics, still found a ready public. The evening's Stalacta was Pauline Markham, who had come to America with Lydia Thompson and who had assumed the role of the fairy queen in the first major revival. Ballets were lead by Mlles. de Rosa and Cappalini, and by Arnold Kirafly. One interesting addition was Prince Awata Katsnoshin, a magician. From March 7 to April 9 the production at Niblo's brought back happy memories for many in the house.

Jules Verne's *The Children of Captain Grant* was dramatized and set to music as **Voyagers in Southern Seas** (3-21-81, Booth's). The production had originally been staged in its home town by the Boston Theatre Company. But this troupe, despite the presence of Marie Bonfanti and "the Flying wonder" Ariel heading the ballets, was a far cry from the Boston Ideal entourage. Rejected as shabby and amateurish, it quickly returned home and in a short while disappeared from the theatrical picture.

March closed to the capers of W. C. Mitchell's Pleasure Party, once more calling to life *Our Goblins* (6-14-80). The irrepressible Lotta went through much of her repertory in April, while the Vokes, whom many scholars believe gave Salsbury the idea for farce-comedy, played a stand with their own old favorites, beginning with *The Belles of the Kitchen*.

In midseason the Bijou had won the race with its mounting of Audran's *Olivette,* beating the Park by three weeks. It reasserted its primacy on May 5 with its staging of a second Audran work, **La Mascotte.** Its margin of victory was less ample this time. The Park had its mounting of *The Mascot* ready four nights later. The public found that first was best. The Park Theatre's production ran only a month, while *La Mascotte* kept the Bijou lit well into August. In any case, Audran was indisputably the season's darling. Despite the Bijou's retention of the French spelling, both campanies translated this tale of a country girl faithful to the shepherd she loves in the face of abductions and promises of high honors. No major names graced either cast.

The theatrical year ended with the New York premiere of von Suppé's **Donna Juanita** (5-16-81, Fifth Ave.), whose heroine (first played in America by Jeannie Winston) must dress as a French cadet to win her lover. It ran three weeks.

1881-1882

By the end of this new season it became clear a pattern was emerging. The lyric theatre was busy. But the business was deceptive. The bustle was created by a constant parade of revivals and importations. There were not even half a dozen original, substantial native musical works. Had Harrigan and Braham not been so productive, the record would have been sorry indeed. But the activity—foreign or rehashed—did accustom the public to a regular flow of musical theatre and did suggest how many stages could be kept lit, how many performers kept occupied, and how many cash registers kept ringing.

Harrigan and Hart opened the season on August 29 with a double novelty. One was a new play; the other was a new theatre. This "new" Theatre Comique at 728–730 Broadway had been a theatre under various names for some years. Its career had been ill-starred. Harrigan and Hart gutted the premises and installed a completely rebuilt auditorium. Not everyone was pleased by the results. One critic ruefully described the décor as "extravagant bronze and bric-a-brac style . . . much too gaudy." For a while at least the new house did seem to chase the jinx. To inaugurate his latest playhouse Harrigan made a sharp, surprising departure. He dropped the Mulligans and their neighbors and wrote a noticeably original part for himself, **The Major.** Roguish and flamboyant, Major Gilfeather was a far cry from steady, dependable Dan. He lived by his wits, hoodwinking even his friends when necessary. Thus, though Mrs. Pinch (Annie Mack) has given him a retainer to locate Enry Iggins (Tony Hart), the man who had eloped with her daughter, the Major has no compunctions about accepting a sum from Iggins to keep his whereabouts secret. David Braham's tunes included "The Veteran Guards' Cadets," "Clara Jenkins' Tea," and a title song. Increasing costs forced the team to raise their top price to $1.00 a seat. The higher prices were readily accepted by Harrigan and Hart's loyal followers. Indeed, "Nothing could exceed in heartiness and friendliness the fashion in which Mr. Harrigan and other favorites of the familiar company were received, and several of the noisily hailed comedians were forced to acknowledge the public welcome in a few informal words." The piece had the longest run of any Harrigan and Hart work to date, over 150 showings.

The era's loose copyright laws and intense competition often resulted in several theatres offering their respective versions of a single piece at the same time. The first instance of this in the 1881–82 season occurred right at the start. The Jules Verne–Adolph d'Ennery melodrama of a patriot's suffering on the retreat from Moscow, **Michael Strogoff,** was presented at three houses in very close succession: the Tivoli's production premiered on August 29, the Booth's staging on August 31, and the Academy of Music's interpretation on September 3. None was especially successful. But the spectacle at the Academy of Music was in the hands of the Kiralfys. As was their wont, they filled their evening with ballets, occasional songs, and elaborate sets. However, a reaction was clearly developing against the overwhelming stage pictures. The *Times* complained that mechanical snowfalls and waterfalls "as a competition with nature, are somewhat ridiculous."

The popularity of Audran's *The Mascot* continued high all during the season. Its first revival appeared on September 5. This mounting at the Bijou advertised that the work was being played "with for the first time here the composer's original orchestrations." *The Mascot* sang on happily for two months and returned, in the hands of one company or another, three more times during the season.

Le Voyage en Suisse (9-12-81, Park) was a French musical extravaganza adapted for the London stage and produced here largely as a vehicle for a family of five acrobats, the Hanlon-Lees. One member of the family lit a cigarette as he somersaulted from the top of a stagecoach; another fell through the floor of a railway car traveling at regulation speed and slid along its bottom among the wheels, while the whole family turned an elegant hotel dining room into a storm of spinning plates, tureens, and food. The affair was an immediate hit. Although it moved to three different theatres it played continuously from its opening night until the end of 1881.

Monday, September 19 found another French work competing for attention. Lecocq's **Mme. Favart,** recounting an imaginary romance of a real

18th-century prima donna, debuted at the Fifth Avenue. Its star, Catherine Lewis, had played the leading roles in *The Royal Middy* and *Olivette.* But good things did not come in threes. *Mme. Favart* was a two-week failure. When it closed, Catherine Lewis' star fell with it.

But **Patience** (9-22-81, Standard) was a different story. For a while it seemed as if the wild triumph of *H.M.S. Pinafore* stood to be repeated. A visit by Oscar Wilde to America fanned interest in this lark about a dairymaid who must choose between a Wilde-like poet and an idyllic poet. D'Oyly Carte's largely American cast included J. H. Ryley as Bunthorne, James Barton as Grosvenor, A. Wilkinson as Murgatroyd, W. T. Carelton as Calverly, Carrie Burton as Patience, Alice Burville as Angela, and Augusta Rooke as Jane. This "definitive" version ran uninterruptedly until March 4 and then for a month more continued as part of a Gilbert and Sullivan repertory. By the time it closed it had made a $100,000 profit for the Englishmen, $40,000 more than *H.M.S. Pinafore* had earned on its initial voyage. Additional sums filled the British coffers when the rights were magnanimously awarded to several other producers. While the original *Patience* was still running, E. E. Rice's Comic Opera Company brought its touring troupe into Booth's for two weeks starting November 14, while Haverly brought his road company into his 14th Street Theatre for a fortnight commencing February 6. After the Englishmen had sailed home, the Bijou put on the boards its own interpretation on June 5. Although it was judged inferior as ensemble to D'Oyly Carte's, it confirmed the claim to stardom of its own Patience, Lillian Russell. Miss Russell had gotten her start at Tony Pastor's and only recently had portrayed the milkmaid in Pastor's spoof. She had been given her first principal Broadway assignment earlier in the season. With her appearance in this Gilbert and Sullivan work she began her two-decade reign as the first queen of Broadway musicals.

. . .

Lillian Russell was born in Clinton, Iowa, on December 4, 1861, the daughter of a prominent printer. Her real name was Helen (Nellie) Louise Leonard. When she was three her family moved to Chicago, where her mother soon became active in the growing women's rights movement. At sixteen Helen left her convent school to make her stage debut in Chicago in *Time Tries All.* Shortly thereafter her parents separated, and Lillian moved to New York with her mother. While studying music with Leopold Damrosch she obtained a small role in *Evangeline,* where she caught Pastor's eye. More than the leading comic opera artist of her era, she was also one of its chief ornaments—a glittering beauty with the classic, if slightly buxom, lines admired by Victorians.

. . .

The death of President Garfield cast a momentary pall over the Rialto. (The President had been shot in July, but survived until September 19.) All Broadway shows shut the evening of his death and again the evening of his funeral. Emma Abbott and her opera company resumed the parade of lyric works on October 3. Her bill ran from old operas such as *Lucia di Lammermoor* to new opéras bouffes such as *Olivette*. She remained at the Grand for two weeks.

The next Monday welcomed the first *Humpty Dumpty* of the season. Curiously it was the opening attraction at Tony Pastor's new theatre on 14th Street, near Irving Place. Pastor did not begin his first season at the new house until October 24. Why he chose not to open his own house himself and why he permitted a minor touring company of the pantomime to have the honor are puzzling. A second touring company, headed by Tony Denier, played a week at the Windsor in January. *Humpty Dumpty* (3-10-68) was having a great fall, indeed.

The work in which Lillian Russell initially assumed a major part was Audran's **The Grand Mogul,** (10-29-81, Bijou), also known as *The Snake Charmer*. Audran's first success—mounted in Marseille in 1877—New York saw this tale of a ruler's love for the snake-charmer, Irma, before Paris. Selina Dolaro starred as Prince Mignapour—a part originally conceived for a tenor, while Miss Russell sang the puzzling American transcription of Irma, D'Jemma. Although Miss Russell suffered from noticeable opening-night jitters, she called attention to herself, her voice and, most of all, her beauty, and helped the opéra bouffe run until New Year's Eve.

Haverly's touring troupe, the Mastodon Minstrels, made the first of two brief appearances during the theatrical year at the 14th Street Theatre on October 31. (They returned to the house in March.) Waning interest in minstrelsy had, as has been noted, forced Haverly to offer increasingly elaborate productions with larger and larger companies. His current band boasted over 100 performers. Among them were men like Lew Dockstader who would attempt to keep blackface alive to the very end. Inevitably the troupe acknowledged the raging success of *Patience* with its burlesques, "Thompson Street Aesthetics" and "Patient Wilde." In the latter, Leon, once of Kelly and Leon's, donned his customary drag to play Miss Patient Wilde, a young lady partial to sunflowers.

Two opéra bouffe companies were the sole lyric entries in November. H. B. Mahn's Comic Opera Company performed in English at Niblo's, while Maurice Grau's French Opera Company sang in the original language at Abbey's Park. The Mahn group's two-week stand offered *Donna Juanita, Boccaccio,* and *The Mascot*. Grau's organization also played a two-week stand, returning in April for three additional weeks at the Fifth Avenue. In those brief visits the repertory changed almost nightly, with nearly a dozen works offered. These included *La Mascotte, Les Mousquetaires au Convent, Mignon, La Fille du Tambour-Major,* and *Si J'etais Roi.*

December brought no novelties whatsoever. On the 5th, *Fritz in Ireland* (11-3-79), with J. K. Emmet of course as the principal attraction, made the first of three seasonal visits to New York. The others came in January and April. The December visit was at the 14th Street Theatre, the others at Niblo's. Advertisements carried the seemingly inevitable announcement of Emmet's plays—"entirely rewritten." Whether Emmet or his claims of novelty were the real attraction, the show's initial three-week stay grossed $30,000, "the largest amount of money ever played to by any dramatic star in the same length of time at the prices prevailing." *Olivette* was revived in mid-month. And the day after Christmas the Vokes family brought their song-filled playlets back.

Just as Harrigan, Hart, and Braham got the season off to an excellent start, they began the new year on the right foot as well. **Squatter Sovereignty** (1-9-82, Comique), like its predecessor, broke away from the Mulligan series. In the background of the story was the conflict between the owners of the land close to the East River and the squatters who had made their homes there. One is the Widow Nolan (Hart). She would have her daughter, Nellie (Gertie Granville), marry Terrence (M. Bradley), the son of the "astronomer" Felix McIntyre (Harrigan). But Nellie and Terrence have plans of their own. Nellie is fond of Fred Kline (James Tierney). Unfortunately, Fred's father (Harry Fisher) is one of the landowners determined to evict the squatters. When the Widow's goat gets loose, wanders over to the elder Kline's mansion, and eats his basement curtains, Kline has the goat seized. McIntyre arranges an entertainment at Kline's dinner party with his telescope, planning to break away while the guests are star-gazing and to release the Widow's animal. The matter is complicated when young Fred escorts Nellie to the dinner. He presents her under an assumed name. The older Kline, who has advertised for a bride, believes she is answering his advertisement. Matters are cleared up in time for Fred and Nellie, and Felix and the widow, to wed. The dialogue was brisk. Its humor still leaned heavily on wordplay:

Felix: Wid the aid of that wonderful instrument, I could show you Uranus, Venus, Mars and Jew-Peter.
Widow: Has he come down?
Felix: Who?
Widow: Jew-Peter
Felix: He never wint up.
Widow: But he did
Felix: When?
Widow: Six months ago, for stealing an overcoat.

In small ways Harrigan's feeling for ethnic characters eluded him. For example, he called an Italian "Pedro." Musically there were fewer songs than usual, and they were not as well integrated. One of the best-loved numbers from the show, "Paddy Duffy's Cart," was used as the opening to the third act, where it announced Duffy's arrival. But Duffy was a very unimportant figure in the play. His arrival seemed to have been necessitated by the song rather than the other way round. Still the number and "Widow Nolan's Goat" remained popular as long as the generation that first heard them survived.

The songs helped *Squatter Sovereignty* surpass the run of *The Major*. It celebrated its 150th performance on May 17 and continued until the beginning of June. Its success meant that Harrigan and Hart had needed only two shows to keep their house lit for the entire season.

While the Theatre Comique grabbed the lion's share of attention on January 9, at the Fifth Avenue the Comley and Barton Opera Company initiated the first of two visits during the theatrical year. With Alfred Cellier conducting, the players offered *Olivette, Mme. Favart,* and, for their final week, the first New York production of Lecocq's *Le Jour et la Nuit,* retitled **Manola,** on February 6. The French title gave away more of the plot, which centered on a man who has one wife by day and another by night. The company played five weeks and returned for two more in March.

A week later, on January 16, Willie Edouin's Sparks offered *Dreams* (8-30-80). Its two-week stand at the Bijou in January was followed by a week's engagement at the Grand in May. Edouin, his wife, and James T. Power were all back to re-create their original roles.

Dreams' first visit ended on January 28. Two nights later the Bijou offered a new American comic opera. **L'Afrique** was by Wayman C. McCreery and W. Schuyler, both newcomers. It was an amateurish botch of an evening. The *Times* referred to it as a "comic (?) opera," complaining, the "singing is simply torture," and exclaiming, "who ever saw coconut palms at the Cape of Good Hope!" The story related Mynheer Arent Van Zwickenboot's determined efforts to win the hand of Georgina (Marie Glover), daughter of the English Capt. Montague-Jones (Fred W. Lennox). Georgina prefers Lieut. Geoffry Plantagenet Hamilton de Bracy (Philip Branson). Van Zwickenboot (Harry Standish) kidnaps the Captain and leads Zulus against the British. Defeated, he claims he was temporarily insane. He offers half his fortune by way of apparent contrition. His apology and money are accepted:

Capt.: . . . since you are now perfectly sane—as your last action has proved—why, go in peace. There will always be a seat at our mess table for you.
Mynh: A thousand thanks. [aside] That was a pretty expensive little affair. Curse them!

FINALE

Lieut.: All our dangers now are over,
  All our troubles they are past:
Capt.: [joining the hands of Lieut. and Geo.]
  Now then, take her, you deserve her,
  And may your happiness last
Geo.: Now in peaceful pleasure living,
  May our loving never end.
Mynh.: While I know that any woman
  Shall never my heart strings rend.
Cho.: Yes, he'd better leave women alone.
Alice: [to Tops] Now my Tops, we too shall marry.
Tops: Yes, no longer must we tarry.
Cho.: Yes, we all shall now be married,
  And we'll live so happy together;
  By no storms our lives be harried,
  But all be summer weather.

Curtain.

Despite an almost universal drubbing, the musical managed a three-week run before collapsing.

The Boston Ideal Opera, its fame and its repertory growing, paid New York another call starting on February 6 at Booth's. Not yet embarked on its attempt to promote native works, the company presented *Fatinitza, The Chimes of Normandy, The Mascot, Czar and Carpenter, Olivette, The Pirates of Penzance, H.M.S. Pinafore,* and *The Bohemian Girl.* All in a two-week visit! When the New Englanders left, Max Strakosch's Grand Italian Opera took over.

Yet another repertory company emerged a fortnight later when the Emilie Melville Opera Company settled into the Bijou for a five-week stand. Not as prodigal as some other touring troupes, it opened with a revival of *The Royal Middy,* switched on the 25th to the Manhattan premiere of Millöcker's **Apajune, or The Water Sprite** (in which mistaken identities muddle the lives of a soldier, a rustic maid, a comic nobleman, and the boarding-house keeper who wants to marry him), and then contented itself with singing its rendering of *The Pirates of Penzance* from March 13 to April 1.

Because the Standard Theatre was under contract to mount Edward Solomon's **Claude Duval,** the house faced the prospect of having to cut short *Patience*'s successful engagement. A compromise was reached. On Monday, March 6, Solomon's work had its premiere. From that time until *Patience* was withdrawn at the end of the month, *Claude Duval* was sung on Monday, Tuesday, and Wednesday nights, and Wednesday matinees; Gilbert and Sullivan were left with the choice late-week evenings and Saturday matinee. When *Patience* left, *Claude Duval* continued on its own for five weeks. This tale of a romantic highwayman who saves the life of his pursuer, Charles Lorrimore, and even helps him win his lady, was beautifully mounted by W. T. Voegtlin with scenes that ended in tableaux designed after famous paintings. One had Duval and the lady, Constance, dancing a minuet alone in a field. W. T. Carleton sang Duval to L. Cadwallader's Lorrimore and Carrie Burton's Constance. J. H. Ryley and A. Wilkinson played leading comic roles. The encore mania had long been established and on opening night at least one song, "William's Sure To Be Right," had to be sung six times.

Away from the main stem, the Windsor, a "combination" house—that is, a house booking touring attractions—offered an original comic opera on March 13. **The Jolly Bachelors** (also called *Twelve Jolly Bachelors*) had a book by John A. Stevens and music by Edward A. Darling. It starred "pretty and vivacious" Jeannie Winston as Prince Cosmos in quest of "plump and pleasing" Amy Gordon as Princess Florida. A first-act drinking chorus gave delight "with the peculiar effect produced by the clinking of the metalic drinking cups." One week and the show was gone.

Not every fledgling native effort tried its wings on the Rialto. For the next thirty years a number of other American theatrical centers would regularly mount home-grown presentations. Boston, Philadelphia, and especially Chicago would contribute significantly to the American Musical Theatre. On March 25, 1882, a minor premiere but important debut occurred in Washington, D.C. **The Smugglers** had a libretto by Wilson J. Vance and songs by John Philip Sousa.

. . .

John Philip Sousa was born in Washington, D.C., on November 6, 1854, son of a Portuguese father and Bavarian mother. While at grammar school, he was enrolled at a private music conservatory run by John Esputa, Jr. At the age of thirteen he ran away to join a circus band. Returned to his parents, his father enlisted him as an apprentice musician in the U.S. Marine Band. He remained with the band for nearly seven years, all the while furthering his studies with George Felix Benkert. He then accepted work in various theatre orchestras, mostly in Philadelphia. On October 1, 1880, he was called back to become the Marine Band's fourteenth leader, a post he held until 1892.

. . .

Vance and Sousa had worked together in 1878 and 1879 on a comic opera that was never produced, *Katherine.* The early dates are a trifle startling, suggesting as they do that an independent tradition of comic opera might have developed even without the coming of *H.M.S. Pinafore* (1-15-79). Yet it was *H.M.S. Pinafore* that precipitated the creation of *The Smugglers.* In 1879 Sousa had been hired to lead the orchestra for a New England tour of the Philadelphia Church Choir Company's staging of the Gilbert and Sullivan work. After a time the group added Sullivan and Burnand's *The Contrabandista* to their program, supplementing the English score with original Sousa melodies. On leaving the Philadelphia players, Sousa decided to use Burnand's story as the basis for an otherwise entirely new operetta.

In Vance's libretto a photographer named Stubbs loses his way in the Spanish mountains. He is seized by a band of smugglers and forced to marry their queen. The queen believes that her husband has died and that Stubbs fulfills a prophecy that the next king of the smugglers will be a stranger. Stubbs' protestations that he is a married man go unheeded. Love interest is provided by Violante, a kidnapped heiress held for ransom, and Enrique, her sweetheart, who has joined the band to protect her and help her escape. A happy ending for everyone comes with the arrival of the Spanish army, led by the queen's supposedly dead husband and bearing pardons for all.

The show, performed largely by amateurs, gave only a single performance in Washington. It moved to Philadelphia, where it was given five times, and then to Lancaster, Pennsylvania, for one final playing. Sousa felt his score deserved a more widespread hearing. Throughout his career he reused melodies from this show. A song called "Sighing, Ah Sighing" was heard as "Sweetheart, I'm Waiting" in *El Capitan* (4-30-96), while "Let Us March Along" became the source of "The Lambs' March."

Another revival of *The Black Crook* (9-12-66), advertised as the "best of the 2,387 productions of this great spectacle," appeared briefly at Niblo's starting April 3. Dismissed as "hardly more than a variety show," the *Times* could nonetheless see it as "a last, lingering spasm of the fine old days of leg-drama, when a woman's talents lay chiefly in her heels."

On April 13 Augustin Daly sent his resident company out on tour. To keep his home box office busy he mounted a new opéra bouffe, Auguste Coedès' *Girouette,* in which King Pepin helps two pairs of lovers to the altar. Both the men and women who took the final vows were sung by young ladies. Renamed **The Weathercock,** it proved diverting enough to allow the theatre to remain open until the end of May.

The season's last touring repertory band, the C.D. Hess Acme Opera Company, closed the year at the Standard with a month's stand that began May 1. The schedule included *The Mascot, H.M.S. Pinafore, The Chimes of Normandy,* and the premiere on May 8 of Calixa Levellee's **The Widow.** A duke who would prevent his niece's marriage finally not only allows it but marries the widow who helped bring it about. The new work was a quick failure, withdrawn after four nights. (On May 8 J. W. Norcross' competing troupe offered its version of *The Mascot* with W. T. Carleton, J. H. Riley, Pauline Hall, and Fay Templeton.)

Revivals and importations brought the season to an end. Rice's Surprise Party switched to something a bit more substantial than the farce-comedies and burlesques it had hitherto specialized in. Its ranks momentarily swelled, the group mounted a revival of *Cinderella at School* (3-5-81) for two weeks at Booth's from May 8 to May 20.

Although Johann Strauss was a world-celebrated figure, his operettas remained virtually unknown to the American public. Some theatres catering to German audiences had staged a few of his pieces. *Die Fledermaus,* for example, was first sung in New York in 1879. But these operettas had not made their way into the major houses as had French opéra bouffe, either in English or in the original. On June 29 the Germania, a house that had once been Wallack's and was now given over to German-language productions, offered, as part of the J. W. Norcross Opera Company's program, an English translation of *Der lustige Krieg.* As **The Merry War** the work delighted playgoers willing to travel to a slightly out-of-the-way and unfashionable house. The fracas erupts after two cities both announce a famous dancer will appear at their respective opera houses on the same night. The dancer solves everything by appearing at neither. Word of mouth proved surprisingly effective and when the mounting exhausted its booking it was immediately transferred to the Metropolitan Concert Hall for an additional run. W. T. Carleton, Dora Wiley, Richard Golden, and a German comic, Gustav Adolfe, led the cast. All told, *The Merry War* ran seven weeks. Without fanfare the world of Strauss operetta had begun its hold on the American stage. Curiously, Strauss' masterpiece, *Die Fledermaus,* encountered little success or acclaim here until after the composer's death when the vogue for his lesser works had subsided.

The year's last offering suggested that the American Musical Theatre had a way to go before it lost completely its circus tinge. On July 31 the New Miniature Opera Company, a Boston troupe composed solely of child performers, presented New Yorkers with its version of *Patience.* Enough New Yorkers found the version sufficiently droll to brave the heat and keep the show on the boards for five weeks.

Just off center-stage, minstrelsy continued to wane and vaudeville to flourish. According to Odell, "minstrelsy had become a fountain of burlesque." The San Francisco Minstrels' programs included "Hamlet, Prince of Dunkirk" and "Patients, or Bunion-Valve's Bride." Pastor, always an innovator, attempted plotted vaudeville, again bringing his house closer to the legitimate fold. But the experiment was no more successful than his earlier tries and was soon abandoned.

1882-1883

All signs pointed to the continuing growth and health of the American Musical Theatre, even if a native element was not yet solidly evident. The lyric stage remained busy. In fact the 1882–83 theatrical year was by far the busiest to date. Counting repertory companies as single offerings, Broadway playgoers could chose from over forty musical first nights. Admittedly, almost all were still either importations or revivals. But soon this dependence would prove to be a passing phenomenon. The onrush of lyric pieces resulted in three of New York's playhouses devoting virtually the entire season to musical offerings. More significantly, for the first time a legitimate theatre was constructed as a showcase for popular musical entertainments. In its early seasons the Casino housed only importations, but its stage stood ready to receive American works. At the same time, one by one, the first great, enduring names of the American Musical Theatre came into the spotlight. If, sadly, E. E. Rice, Harrigan, Hart, and Braham mean little to anyone but scholars, the names of Lillian Russell, Fay Templeton, John Philip Sousa, and Reginald De Koven still carry some of their first magic.

The Theatre Comique led off the season on August 26 with a type of offering new to the house. **The Blackbird** was a melodrama set in Ireland. It was closer in style to the plays performed by J. K. Emmet and later W. J. Scanlan, Chauncey Olcott, and their ilk, than to the vernacular roughhouses Harrigan and Braham normally provided. In fact, Harrigan was not even author of the piece. A sometime member of the company, George L. Stout, received credit. And Braham's contribution was minor. Even Harrigan's fine scene painter, Charles Whitham, abandoned his customary cityscapes for cascades and whirlpools in moonlight. Stout's tale followed Colonel Raymond Darcy (De Wolf Hopper) in his attempt to escape pursuers after the battle of Culloden. Displeased, the Comique's regulars withheld their patronage. *The Blackbird* was withdrawn when Harrigan and Braham had a new work ready at the end of October.

Two nights after *The Blackbird* premiered, *Billie Taylor* began the long procession of the season's revivals at the Bijou. Its stay was short. Two weeks later Lillian Russell was again singing *Patience* at the house.

The Salsbury Troubadours, led by Nate Salsbury and Nellie McHenry, brought farce-comedy back to Broadway for a week at the Windsor on September 4 and for a month's fun beginning April 9. Their piece was called **Greenroom Fun,** a title that reveals the entire plot. One character was Booth McForrest, a tribute to three tragedians—Edwin Booth, Edwin Forrest, and the now forgotten John McCullough. The first generation of farce-comedies was nearing the end of its vogue. But it was by no means exhausted, and a more mature second generation was soon to follow.

Opéra bouffe made its first appearance of the year on September 11. Maurice Grau had organized a new company around the talents of his latest protégé, Madam Theo. His plan had been to give her the honor of opening the new Casino, but construction delays forced him to present his new star at the Fifth Avenue instead. The hasty booking revisions this change necessitated meant that for the rest of the season Madam Theo and her entourage were shunted from theatre to theatre. By the summer Grau's troupe had played five separate engagements in one New York house or another.

On September 14, before his regular season started, Tony Pastor booked a double bill of *The Beautiful Galatea* and *Trial by Jury* for his 14th Street house. Indifferently received and apparently ill-financed, the bill shuttered without finishing out the week. Four nights later, down the block at Haverly's 14th Street Theatre, **My Sweetheart** opened as a vehicle for Minnie Palmer and R. E. Graham. Miss Palmer, "talking" her songs, was looked upon as something of a "second Lotta," while Graham playing a German dialect, was viewed as another Emmet. *My Sweetheart*—advertised as "the difference between the love of a good, pure girl and the designs of a woman of the world"—was a straight play, adapted to the stars' requirements by William Gill. These requirements included spots for their specialties. But in the end *My Sweetheart* was no more a musical than Lotta's pieces and considerably less so than Emmet's mountings. More music was added to the work when Miss Palmer took the show to London. Cordially received there, it far surpassed its American run. After a week in New York the show was replaced by Hague's Great British Operatic Minstrels, who themselves moved on with equal speed. At the same time Tony Pastor rushed in a replacement for his disastrous opening. The Boston English Opera Company sang its version of von Suppé's *Donna Juanita* until Pastor was ready with his vaudeville bills two weeks later.

The "English" in the Boston troupe's name referred to the fact that the works they sang were translated into English. Something more exotically English followed the New Englanders two nights later at the Standard. Thanks largely to Gilbert and Sullivan, the D'Oyly Carte was London's stellar lyric troupe. But because Gilbert and Sullivan loomed so grandly in its success, the extent of

Rupert D'Oyly Carte's enterprise and the diversity of his presentations are often forgotten. When the company arrived for an 1882–83 visit, its trunks and cases included costumes and sets for three works, only one of which was by its premiere creators. Somewhat bravely it opened with Bucalossi's *Les Manteaux Noirs*. The reception was disappointing and a month later the company raised the curtain on Robert Planquette's *Rip Van Winkle*. This, too, had only a modest success—perhaps the result of a $2.00 top. By the time it offered the first American performance of Gilbert and Sullivan's **Iolanthe** on November 25, D'Oyly Carte's once glittering reputation appeared a bit tarnished. Masterpiece though it was, *Iolanthe* failed to arouse the enthusiasm *H.M.S. Pinafore* and *Patience* had engendered. Still, enough appreciative theatregoers responded to permit the comic opera to hold the boards through the end of February. Gilbert and Sullivan's account of a fairy's tinkering with English romance and politics was superbly cast. W. T. Carleton sang Strephon; J. H. Ryley, Lord Chancellor, and Marie Jansen, Iolanthe. Curiously, if accounts in E. E. Rice's obituaries are correct, his mounting of this same work for Boston was far more successful, establishing what was then a record of nineteen weeks there. A warning to scholars about trusting critics' accuracy can be learned from reading the *Times* review, where the unidentified critic assured his readers that the show had "no plot."

October 2, the Monday after the D'Oyly Carte's arrival, four musical offerings bowed. When one recalls that New York at this time had only thirteen principal theatres, plus a few combination houses, the figure is even more impressive. The Kiralfys resurrected *Around the World in Eighty Days* (8-28-75), playing Niblo's for three weeks, and returning to a second house in April for an additional fortnight. Solomon's **The Vicar of Bray,** in which a vicar is comically blackmailed into allowing his daughter to marry the man of her choice, was a one-week flop at the Fifth Avenue, while the Norcross Opera Company presented two weeks of *The Merry War* at Haverly's 14th Street Theatre. The final entry among the foursome was Max Strakosch's English Opera Company, "English" again signifying works sung in translation. Its repertory at the Grand consisted of *The Bohemian Girl, Fatinitza,* and *Carmen*.

To replace the failed Solomon work, a more beloved piece of his was hurried back. The peripatetic *Billie Taylor* came to life again for a week until Madam Theo's troupe could be moved to the house.

Friend or Foe (10-16-82, Windsor) helped make a star of a new figure, W. J. Scanlan. Scanlan, like J. K. Emmet, was known for his fine singing and he appeared primarily in straight plays, such as this Bartley Campbell effort, generously supplied with melodies to display his talent. Scanlan's career was brief. His departure from the stage and his death resulted from paresis and its consequent insanity. In this respect his end was like so many of the early stars of the lyric stage—G. L. Fox, Emmet, and Tony Hart, for example. The story of *Friend or Foe* centered on Carrol Moore, an Irishman living in France. He falls in love with the daughter of the family with whom he boards. Carrol's rival for her hand is the owner of the house, who threatens to turn the family out if his suit is denied. Carrol accepts $15,000 to fight as a substitute for his rival in the Franco-Prussian War. He is caught in this subterfuge and sentenced to be shot. But his sweetheart prevails on the commanding officer and he is saved. This sort of romantic play—merely a variation of the type Emmet offered—long retained a large following. When Emmet and Scanlan were no longer available to play them, Chauncey Olcott provided similar entertainment for another generation.

Once passed over, *The Sorcerer* was revived on October 17 to capitalize on Gilbert and Sullivan's vogue and the excitement generated by the impending premiere of *Iolanthe*. Happily, it was no ordinary revival. Produced by John McCaull at his own Bijou Theatre, it was sumptuously mounted and featured Lillian Russell as Aline, John Howson as Wells, Laura Joyce as Lady Sangazure, George Olmi as Marmaduke, Digby Bell as Dr. Daly, and Charles J. Campbell as Alexis. The response kept the work before the footlights until January 9, a run of 92 performances. After a four-month tour it returned for a brief run at the Casino in April.

The Casino itself, after long, costly, and heartbreaking delays, announced it was finally ready to open its doors on October 21, 1882. The house that McCaull and his partner, Rudolph Aronson, erected at 39th Street and Broadway, diagonally across from where the Metropolitan Opera House would rise one year later, was something of an oddity. It capitulated to the momentary fad for Moorish design, a surrender that quickly dated the building architecturally. Even odder was its placing its auditorium on the second floor, forcing patrons to climb at least one flight of stairs. Later the inside of the building was gutted and the orchestra brought down to street level. But McCaull and Aronson were too anxious to give Broadway its first theatre built especially for musicals. Their anxiety led to immediate, serious embarrassment—beyond, of course, the opening delays. The critics who reviewed the first attraction, Johann Strauss' **The Queen's Lace Handkerchief,** remarked disparagingly how unready the house was for patrons. A number of ticketholders conveyed their displeasure in turn. Heating didn't work, carpets were missing, myriad little malfunctions beset the house. Fearing to lose all they had set out to achieve, McCaull and Aronson closed the theatre after one week's operation and put their production in storage. When "America's Handsomest Place of Amusement" advertised it would reopen on December 30, its owners knew that everything was in working order. One important change of cast had taken place in the interim. Young Francis Wilson left off playing farce-comedies to assume the comic lead and begin his rise as one of America's better musical comedy clowns. In his autobiography Wilson gave a fascinating glimpse of the movements and pacing in the staging of the times. The passage incidently shows that even Strauss was not safe from having other men's songs inserted into his score:

. . . the baritone William T. Carleton sang an interpolated song entitled "Woman, Fair Woman," the cue to which was, "Oh, Woman, lovely Woman, what would we not do for thy sweet sake!" Having delivered himself of which he would make the conventional up-stage tour gazing most unnaturally at the muslin clouds and sky, returning to the front at the exact moment for the first note of the ballad.

The plot of the show gave the real Cervantes an imaginary romance that ended happily when he aids his imprisoned queen to escape. Strauss later used themes from this show for his "Roses from the South." Signor Perugini was the first Cervantes, replaced on the reopening by Carleton. Lilly Post was the Queen, and Mathilde Cottrelly, Cervantes' fiancée.

Theatregoers, especially devotees of the Theatre Comique, had a second shock in store for them five nights after the Casino opened. On October 26 Harrigan, Hart, and Braham had their latest effort ready. Unlike *The Blackbird,* this play had a libretto and lyrics by Harrigan himself and a fair complement of Braham tunes. But its story revolved around an ethnic group that Harrigan had previously paid scant attention to—the Jews. Harrigan assumed the title role of **Mordecai Lyons,** a Jewish pawnbroker. Lyon's daughter (Annie Mack), much against his will, has left home to become an

actress. When she is "ruined" and deserted by her lover, she receives only curses from her father. But the lover discovers he has deserted Esther to court a girl who turns out to be his own daughter. Contrived reconciliations follow. By and large the critics were no happier with the new play than was the public. The *Herald* branded it unequivocally as the team's "first distinct failure." Curiosity, loyalty, and the need to prepare a replacement kept *Mordecai Lyons* going for a month.

Neither Harrigan, Hart, and Braham, opéra bouffe nor farce-comedies could destroy the appeal of *The Black Crook* (9-12-66) for some audiences. A touring version came in to the 14th Street Theatre on November 13 to cater to their pleasure. But the circus element that increasingly overwhelmed the spectacle seemed particularly strong in this version. The mounting featured "Tyrolean warblers," a ventriloquist, and a trio that specialized in "grotesque eccentricities." The side shows coupled with the spectacle, ballet, and melodrama found welcome for three weeks and then continued traipsing around the country.

Seemingly just as indestructible, the Vokes family returned with *Belles of the Kitchen* and the rest of their proto-farce-comedy repertory to delight the audiences at Niblo's from November 20 to December 2.

Gilbert and Sullivan's *Iolanthe* premiered on November 25; Harrigan and Braham's **McSorley's Inflation** on November 27. Like *Iolanthe, McSorley's Inflation* was at once a success and a disappointment. It gave Ned Harrigan and Tony Hart their most profitable run of the season, but it was a run that fell short of the best the Comique had known or was to know. The play closed on March 31, having celebrated its 100th performance on February 19. Although the Mulligan gang was missing, the story of the play was more in line with the Mulligan tradition than any of the other works the Comique mounted during the year. Harrigan seems to have used "inflation" in the sense of swelling pride. Peter McSorley (Harrigan), a candidate for coroner, wants his wife Bridget (Hart) to give up her stall at the Washington Market. He deems it unbecoming a candidate's wife. Bridget's brawny exuberance wins the day. A subsidiary plot recounted the turmoil at a black political convention, while other scenes raised mayhem in Chinatown (with one Chinese flying through a second-story window) and a Salvation Army office. Braham's "I Never Drink Behind The Bar," "McNally's Row Of Flats," and "The Old Feather Bed" won instant popularity. The title of another song seems forty years ahead of the times. But "The Charleston Blues" referred to a black para-military band like the Skidmores of the Mulligan Guards shows.

December brought little for lovers of the musical stage, offering only the indefatigable, aging Lotta in her standard repertory. Nor did 1883 get off to an exciting start. On New Year's night Tony Denier romped into the Windsor with a *Humpty Dumpty* (3-10-68) that predated Lotta, while J. K. Emmet arrived at the 14th Street Theatre in something of a novelty, **Fritz among the Gypsies.** The evening might have seemed more novel had not the plot, like virtually every one Emmet used, revolved around a recognition scene. The principal novelties and attractions of the evening turned out to be the cavortings of a "$2,500 sagacious giant dog" and a new tune which became one of Emmet's best loved, "Sweet Violets."

The play ran six weeks. Emmet, keeping the promise made years before in his programs, returned off and on during the season in various versions of his Fritz plays. For example, he performed *Fritz in England and Ireland* briefly at Niblo's and appeared in *Fritz in Ireland* later at the Cosmopolitan. Both plays were probably largely the same. Emmet rarely trod the boards of major houses anymore. Haverly's 14th Street Theatre may be viewed as a borderline house, but Niblo's was past its heyday, and the Cosmopolitan at 41st Street and Broadway was then considered far uptown. Emmet's place in the theatre of his day was clearly one shared by a number of his fellow players. Disdained by most "sophisticates," he nonetheless had such a loyal following that he could have all the bookings he chose in any but the gilt-edged houses. His type of show continued popular until the first motion pictures drew away its faithful attendants.

Solomon's second new work of the year, **Virginia or Ringing the Changes** (1-8-83, Bijou), told a tale of switched babies and Mephistophelian machinations. American critics rejected it as watered-down Gilbert and Sullivan. Apart from *Billie Taylor,* Solomon was never to enjoy the same acclaim here as in London. But despite tepid notices *Virginia* played five weeks to decent business and then toured.

A revival of *The Black Venus* (1-12-81) at Niblo's inaugurated a busy February on the 5th. "Forty secundas and coryphées, a caravan of lions, tigers, camels, zebras, horses, goats, and Nubian slaves made the actors seem very unimportant." The same night that saw the opening of *The Black Venus* offered one of the many borderline plays that filled the stages of the time. *Zara* was a romantic melodrama written by Fred Marsden for Annie Pixley. Later in the season Marsden performed a similar service for Lotta when she returned to town in *Bob. Zara*'s story described the unsuccessful attempt to deprive the heroine of her inheritance. Seven or eight songs were included. None was written for the show, one critic shrugging them off as "time honored chestnuts." But they suggest how musical a "straight" play of the era could seem, especially when one remembers that most legitimate theatres still maintained orchestras to play overtures and frequent background material.

One week later, February 12, a German language production of Millöcker's **Countess Du Barry**—depicting the rise of a callous milliner's assistant to the king's favorite—was brought to the Fifth Avenue for a week. The show had originally been produced at the Thalia in the Bowery, a house catering to the large German population of New York, who still preferred to take their entertainment in their native tongue. Competing versions of Lecocq's *La Coeur et la Main* bowed eleven nights apart. They opened in a hail of charges, countercharges, and lawsuits. McCaull got his version to the public first, opening it at his Bijou on February 15 as **Heart and Hand.** James Duff, owner of the Standard, used his mounting to replace the faltering *Iolanthe.* Duff presented his mounting as **Micaela** on February 26. Neither production caught theatregoers' fancies and both ran less than a month, leaving each manager to blame the other for the lack of success. In both versions a duke is reluctant to marry a princess, perferring a servant girl he has met. Of course, the girl turns out to be the princess in disguise.

Between the controversial openings, the Boston Ideal Opera Company slipped into town on what was becoming an annual visit. For the 1882–83 season it brought with it *Fatinitza, The Musketeers, The Mascot, The Pirates of Penzance, Patience,* and *The Marriage of Figaro.*

On the 29th, the evening of *Micaela*'s premiere, Thatcher, Primrose, and West's Minstrels climbed onto Niblo's stage for a week of good, old-fashioned blackface.

March opened with one of the most interesting native efforts of the year, **The Dime Novel** (3-5-83, Bijou). Called a "musical comedy," it had a book by A. C. Gunter and songs by Jesse Williams. The libretto, insisting "bad books make bad boys," spoofed the effects of reading cheap fiction. When a well-intentioned young man behaves like the heroes of pulp novels he reads, he finds himself in difficulty. Although it was well received, the public refused to respond. The show folded at the end of a single week, leaving the Bijou unexpectedly dark for some time.

Vying for attention on March 5 was a pasted together opera company that included Henry E. Dixey and Marie Jansen. It kept the Fifth Avenue lit for nearly a month with its renditions of *Iolanthe* and *The Mascot*. After a week's respite, during which Catherine Lewis came in to sing *Olivette* and Lecocq's *Prince Conti,* it staged a week-long revival of *Cinderella at School* (3-5-81), and then disappeared from the musical scene.

The failure of *Micaela* prompted a hasty revival of *H.M.S. Pinafore* at the Standard on March 17, succeeded on the 26th by *Patience*.

Harrigan, Hart, and Braham had a new work ready, **The Muddy Day** (4-2-83, Comique). Mary Ann O'Leary (Hart) is a widow, courted by two mud-scow captains, Roger McNab (Harrigan) and Herman Schoonover (Harry Fisher). She decides to marry the wealthier. Her search to find out the financial status of her suitors takes her to a party on a barge, and the barge promptly sinks. At another point she even resorts to dressing as a man to learn the facts. In the end, she chooses Roger. Some of the more skittish critics were shocked by Mrs. O'Leary's entrance in only a barrel and some underwear. But most of the audience undoubtedly relished the absurdity as well as the almost Shakespearean triple-tension of a man disguised as a woman disguised as a man. Braham's tunes were not top-drawer, but they were "sung heartily" and danced "forcibly." Harrigan and Hart's large, sustained company scuffled through the proceedings until May 19. Like so many shows during the season, *The Muddy Day,* while not a failure, disappointed by not achieving unmitigated success.

French opéra bouffe was also nearing the end of its brightest era. Even with Lillian Russell in the principal, if not the title, role, Offenbach's *The Princess of Trébizonde*—"the romance of a prince caught among a swirl of circus performers"—could not accrue more than a month's stand at the Casino. However, the impetuous Miss Russell's abrupt departure may have shortened its run more than any other thing, even though an able supporting cast included Digby Bell, John Howson, Laura Joyce, and Madeline Lucette. *The Queen's Lace Handkerchief* was brought in from the road to keep the Casino lit.

Boston was not alone in providing New York with occasional entertainment. On May 9 the Barton English Opera Company came from San Francisco with Balfe's twenty-five-year-old *Satanella*. The troupe suffered another of the disappointments so pervasive this season, departing the Standard on May 19.

A week later Haverly brought his Mastodon Minstrels into his 14th Street Theatre for a two-week stand. The following Monday, May 21, Rice's Surprise Party introduced one of the most popular of farce-comedies, **Pop.** Originally produced in San Francisco, it may well have attracted Californians partly by the glamor of its second-act setting, the salon of a great Cunard ocean liner. But its infectious fun and generally excellent songs soon found a universal welcome. Again the story line was simple. Adolphus Pop (John A. Mackay), a playwright, decides to make an ocean crossing. The people he meets provide little in the way of complications but much in the way of specialties. As his audiences expected, Mackay himself presented imitations of the best-known actors of the day, offering "encores until he was obliged to decline from sheer exhaustion." George K. Fortesque danced in his elephantine fashion, while "The Dudes And The Dude Prince" presented "a number of girls marching as 'dudes'—that latest development of male fashion or folly." For a finale the cast gathered to sing a medley of songs from current comic operas.

A new name first came to Broadway's attention on June 4, Ludwig Englander.

• • •

Ludwig Englander was born in Vienna in 1859 and received his first musical training there. He later moved briefly to Paris, where he worked under Offenbach. Coming to America in 1882, he obtained the position of conductor at the Thalia, one of several New York auditoriums catering to German-speaking audiences.

• • •

It was at the Thalia that his first work, **Der Prinz Gemahl,** was produced on April 11. His librettist was Julius Hopp. Its reception was encouraging enough to prompt the company to move it to Wallack's Theatre. For the benefit of non-German-speaking patrons the program translated the title as *The Prince Consort,* although the work was still sung in German. When Broadway was not interested, the piece closed after two weeks. The failure nevertheless quickly provided Englander with a springboard to commercial success on the English-speaking stage.

Englander's countryman, Johann Strauss, fared more happily when the Casino brought forth its final offering of the season, **Prince Methusalem,** on July 9. The prince of the title must win back his principality from revolutionaries before he can conclude the wedding the revolution interrupted. Her quarrel with John McCaull and Rudolph Aronson settled, Lillian Russell returned to star in the title part. The role was her second trouser role in succession, the only way a lady had at this juncture to show her shapely legs. More than any other management the Casino was able to appreciate the possibilities of summer runs for musicals. This very first attempt of the house in its maiden season to span the summer more than paid off. *Prince Methusalem* ran into October, surviving yet another tempestuous Russell departure in September.

The Casino's first season coincided with the last full season of minstrelsy in New York. Minstrels now seemed too far removed from contemporary rhythms and complexities to remain viable. As they had in recent years, the San Francisco Minstrels relied heavily on burlesquing popular plays. *Iolanthe,* for example, reappeared as "High and Lengthy." The play on words seems not especially funny. But comedy is one thing to one generation, another to a second. Still, there was evidence even to contemporaries that exhaustion had set in. The season ended on March 24, significantly earlier than customary. In June, Charlie Backus, a surviving founder, died. There were rumors on the Rialto that Billy Birch, the last original member, was eager to sell the troupe and its building. Of course, the theatre was changing in less musical spheres. The theatrical center continued to move uptown. Booth's, opened seventeen years before with glimmering hope, was converted into a dry-goods store. Niblo's, now distant from the main stem, could have advertised "last years."

1883-1884

After four consecutive seasons of unprecedented activity the lyric stage slackened its pace a bit, but only a bit. Depending on how one considers certain borderline cases, approximately thirty musical mountings vied for attention, more than triple the average count before *H.M.S. Pinafore* (1-15-79). As usual, importations and revivals constituted the bulk of the fare.

Harrigan and Hart inaugurated the season with a full-length revision of Harrigan and Braham's earlier success, *The Mulligan Guards' Ball* (1-13-79), using old material from *The Mulligan Guards' Nominee* (11-22-80) and new Braham melodies to stretch the evening. The lessons of the preceding year had been well learned. The entire schedule of the Theatre Comique for 1883–84 was devoted to the Mulligans. By now Harrigan and Hart's troupe was filled with beloved performers identified with specific roles. Besides the stars, favorites included Annie Yeamans, who usually played Cordelia, and John Wild, most often cast as Simpson Primrose. No company, not even Wallack's or Daly's respected organizations, seemed to stay together so loyally nor enjoy a more devoted following. The revival of *The Mulligan Guards' Ball* held the stage from August 6 to September 22.

The Devil's Auction, a Philadelphia production in the *Black Crook* tradition, came into the 14th Street Theatre for a two-week visit on August 18. The show was based on a melodrama that had played the nation's theatres just after the Civil War, at the very moment *The Black Crook* (9-12-66) became the rage. Its story recounted how Carlos (Dore Davidson), a poor shepherd, loves Madeline (Kate Girard), a farmer's daughter. Mephisto (James S. Maffitt) would help Count Fortune (W. H. Bartholomew) win Madeline, but Crystaline, a good fairy, prevails. In the course of the evening spectators were transported to the Volcano of Hades and to the Golden Palace of the Pasha. Adele Cornalba led the ballets. At one point this exotic tour came to a momentary halt while the cast regaled playgoers with "The new American Singing and Dancing number, entitled 'The Wild And Wooly West.' " If the producers had hopes that popular acclaim might extend their stay, their hopes were disappointed.

Three nights after the premiere of *The Devil's Auction,* the Kiralfys relit Niblo's Garden with a Parisian importation, **Excelsior.** It, too, was of the *Black Crook* school, melodrama heavy with spectacle and ballet. Not a word was spoken in this depiction of Darkness (Ettore Coppini) defeated by Light (Mlle. Nani). The Kiralfys and Niblo's were far more alluring than their neighbors. *Excelsior* ran until December 15.

Chicago, a great city once again after its fire, was rapidly becoming an important producing center. On August 21, the same night *The Devil's Auction* opened, Chicago sent one of its earliest efforts for New York's inspection. S. G. Pratt's **Zenobia,** first done the preceding season in its hometown, was termed a "lyric drama" in its advertisements and "grand opera" in pre-opening synopses. Reviews suggest the latter description may have been the more accurate. Pratt's tale recounted how the proud rebel, Zenobia (Dora Hennings), is spared death when the king (E. Connell) falls in love with her daughter (Helen Wallace). Housed at the minor, out-of-the-way 23rd Street Theatre, it was condescendingly received and hastily withdrawn after its first four performances grossed a mere $129, $60, $55, and $33 respectively. Its reception, moreover, hinted at the indifference with which New York would almost always greet an arrival from the Middle West. Perhaps in this case the coldness was justified. Not a trace of the text seems to remain.

A revival of *Heart and Hand* closed August, while September was ushered in by an importation, G. R. Sims and Frederick Clay's **The Merry Duchess.** Telling of a jockey who wins the hand of the Duchess of Epsom Downs, the evening featured John Nash, Selina Dolaro, and Henry E. Dixey. Dixey portrayed a comic villain, Brabazon Sykes, who connives unsuccessfully to poison the duchess' mount. This English foolery pleased audiences at the Standard until mid-October.

On September 10 Maurice Grau, with Aimée once again his star, brought in the first of the season's numerous opéra bouffe troupes. Lecocq's **La Princesse des Canaries** was the curtain raiser. Its saga of a general who ousts a usurper so a princess may regain her rightful throne allowed Aimée to display "her winks and kicks and nods and smiles, and her abundance of quiet suggestiveness." By summertime, lovers of the genre had been given one or more opportunities to hear such works as *La Mascotte, Les Cloches de Corneville, Boccaccio,* and *The Bohemian Girl.*

September's final offering was a second Theatre Comique revival, *The Mulligan Guards' Picnic* (9-23-78). Again the original piece had been reworked into a full evening's entertainment, by utilizing scenes from earlier Harrigan plays and by new Braham tunes, in this case "Hurry, Little Children, Sunday Morning" and "Going Home With Nellie After Five." The play ran just over a month.

Revivals and minstrels accounted for all of October's openings except its last. *Fritz in Ireland* (11-3-79) played a week at a combination house beginning October 1, to be followed seven nights later at the same auditorium by a week's return of Rice's Surprise Party doing *Pop* (5-21-83). The Thatcher, Primrose, and West Minstrels arrived on the 15th for the first of three brief stands. Their later runs came in late January and late February. On October 22 competing opéra bouffe entourages raised their curtains. Grau's troupe at the Standard sang in French; the Wilbur Opera Company at the People's sang in English. Only October's closing entry was a novelty. With *Prince Methusalem* fi-

nally departed, the McCaull Opera Company at the Casino offered the New York premiere in English of Millöcker's **The Beggar Student.** The show was an instant hit, achieving a profitable run of 107 performances. In Europe it remains a repertory standard to this day. A general, rejected in his suit of a countess' daughter, dresses a poor soldier as a prince and sends him to court the girl. W.T. Carleton and Bertha Ricci sang the lovers.

When compared with busy October, November was quiet indeed. But its first offering was the high point of the season so far as native lyric pieces were concerned. On November 5 the Theatre Comique presented its first new work of the season, the work generally judged Harrigan's best, **Cordelia's Aspiration.** In a sense even this play was not new. Harrigan had employed the same basic story earlier in *The Mulligan Guards' Surprise* (2-16-80), while he had tried out the evening's most celebrated scene in *The Mulligans' Silver Wedding* (2-21-81). Cordelia's brother Planxty (H. A. Fisher) and her sisters come to America. They are determined to share in Cordelia's good fortune. As Planxty proclaims, "Cordelia's living in clover—we must be in the field when it's ripe." Although Cordelia (Annie Yeamans) has sailed first class on the same ship that brought her family across and although she had sent them all sorts of comforts to cushion their second-class passage, she feels impelled to live up to their exaggerated ideas of her wealth. She prods Dan (Harrigan) to move to more elegant quarters and travel in more elevated society. Planxty attempts to get Cordelia to sign all her property over to him. To this end he forges a woman's love letter to Dan and arranges for Cordelia to find the letter. Driven to distraction by Planxty's machinations and by Dan's social gaffes, Cordelia gulps down a bottle of "Roach Poison." Of course, the poison is merely Rebecca Allup's cache of booze. Cordelia's death scene comes to naught when Rebecca (Hart) confides in Dan the real contents of the bottle. Planxty is sent packing, and Cordelia realizes she is happier with her old friends in her old home. Harrigan's comedy was typical of its period, full of puns and racial caricatures:

Cordelia: Many's the little luxury I sent them on the ship—incognito.
Rebecca: No, you didn't send it dat way. You sent me wid it.
Cordelia: I paid the steward well, but Rebecca—not a word to my brother and sisters, they mortify.

Rebecca: The mortar would have to be pooty hot to fry dat big Planxty.

Some humor was merely vaudeville jokes, hardly pertinent to the story. One player remarks, "That barkeeper—he's not fit for the counter. He's a counterfit." Strange as some of the humor may now seem, some of the pacing may well seem even stranger. The end of Cordelia's famous drunk scene would undoubtedly have been more abrupt had the scene been written a generation later:

Dan: Cordelia's dying. She drank the roach poison from the bottle.
Rebecca: She drank out of dis bottle?
Dan: Cordelia's dead.
Rebecca: Drunk.

At this point, instead of a blackout, Rebecca and Simpson Primrose (John Wild) take the bottle, drink from it, and launch into "Whiskey, You're The Devil." The song finished, the curtain rose and fell on two stage pictures—each accompanied by a reprise of the song's chorus. None of Braham's melodies for the evening was among his best. However, they were serviceable. *Cordelia's Aspirations* recorded 176 showings before it closed on April 5.

November's last musical was the preceding season's *Friend or Foe* (10-16-82), making the first of two brief return visits. The second visit came merely a month later. The first was at the Windsor, the second at the Grand.

Over the summer the old Bijou had been demolished and a new house had been constructed on its site. The new Bijou was ready to receive its first patrons on December 1. Again, an importation was given the honor of opening a theatre built for musicals. Offenbach's *Orpheus and Eurydice* (now generally called *Orpheus in the Underworld*) was the premiere attraction. Filled with names, such as Amelia Summerville and Digby Bell, that became household words to theatregoers of the age, it ran just over 100 performances.

Thirteen nights after the new Bijou opened the old Standard burned to the ground. The third major theatre fire in a little over a year, it frightened away a sufficient number of potential ticket buyers to dampen business on Broadway for the rest of the year. To some extent the fire and the resultant scare may account for the drop in the number of musicals during 1883–84. At the time of its destruction the Standard had only begun to play host to a new comic opera from England, **Estrella.** With music by Luscombe Searelle and a libretto by Walter Parke, the piece had raised its curtain three nights earlier, December 11. To watch how his bride will react, a suspicious count disappears shortly after their wedding. When his bride, believing him dead, marries the young man she had wanted in the first place, the count finds to his chagrin he cannot reclaim her. Hubert Wilke, W. S. Rising, and Amy Gordon sang the principal roles. The work's reception was at best lukewarm, and when its costumes and sets were consumed in the fire no attempt was made to re-create them. However, *Estrella* did not completely disappear. The traveling Wilbur Opera Company added it to its repertory. On and off for the next several years it appeared on the company's programs at various combination houses in the city.

On Thursday, November 29, the *Herald* sadly acknowledged, "This is the last week of the Old San Francisco Minstrels." Two nights later, December 1, 1883, minstrelsy disappeared forever as a permanent part of the New York theatre scene. But permanent companies remained elsewhere, in Philadelphia, for example. And New York would still have seasonal visits from a number of traveling companies. In fact some of the defunct troupe's performers could be seen at the People's, a combination house, on December 17, when Haverly's American-European Consolidated Spectacular Mastodon Minstrels arrived for a week's stand.

At other combination houses, including Haverly's own in Brooklyn, J. K. Emmet could be heard in January and February of 1884 offering still another variation of his beloved Fritz stories, **Fritz, the Bohemian.** This new edition was written for Emmet by the drama critic of the Buffalo *Courier,* Thomas Kean. Kean borrowed a bit from Rip Van Winkle by having his Fritz fall into a long, deep sleep. However, this new Fritz awakens from his sleep to learn he is a prince. Emmet once more featured his dog, Rector, although Rector's value had become suddenly inflated to $4,000 and he was billed as "the largest in the world."

At more central, important houses there was little new activity until February 4, when the Casino revived Strauss' *The Merry War* for a two-month run and the Fifth Avenue presented the American premiere of **Princess Ida** a week later on February 11. The only Gilbert and Sullivan work in three acts rather than two and the only one with a libretto entirely in blank verse, this tale of a women's seminary bent on forever keeping its doors closed to men was performed by some of the era's most skillful players. J. H. Ryley was King Gama; Cora S. Tanner, Ida; Wallace Macreery, Hilarion; W. S. Rising, Cyril; Charles F. Lang, Florian; Signor Brocolini, King Hildebrand; and Genevieve Reynolds, Lady Blanche. In keeping with the common, fashionable practice of the day, an Englishman—in this instance Frank Thornton—was brought over from London's West End to stage the production. The new effort failed to recapture the appeal of some of its predecessors, achieving a modest six-week run.

Occasionally a combination house would find time to book one of the odd-ball enterprises that touring impresarios threw together for the less demanding hinterlands. On February 13 the Cosmopolitan announced **On the Yellowstone,** a musical concoction with the rather uninviting subtitle, *Realistic Scenes of the President's Trip to the National Park.* This vaudeville-cum-travelogue promised music by Operti and featured the once glamorous Pauline Markham, at this point near the end of her career. It ran a week and a half and then, apparently, toured.

March brought in a lone musical entry, a revival of Offenbach's *La Vie Parisienne* which lasted 50 performances. In its cast was Richard Mansfield, soon to be a giant of serious dramatic acting, but then still a minor singer. In the pit conducting was Gustave Kerker, also soon to have a prominent career.

Ned Harrigan had a new story ready on April 7, one he wryly called **Dan's Tribulations.** Did he mean to imply Dan's tribulations emanated from Cordelia's aspirations? Certainly it is Cordelia who is responsible for Dan's problems in both plays. The Mulligans have moved back downtown. Dan (Harrigan) has a grocery store, and Cordelia (Annie Yeamans), ever determined to be the lady, runs a "Frinch" academy. To avoid a foreclosure Cordelia sells the Mulligans' property to Mrs. Lochmuller (Jennie Christie) for one dollar. Almost at once Cordelia and her sometime friend have a falling out, and for a time it seems the Mulligans will be evicted anyway. With help from their son, Tommy (Hart), matters are righted by the final curtain. In a subplot, Rebecca's husband dies, and Rebecca (also played by Hart) sells his corpse to a medical school. She decides to have the funeral at night because it is cheaper and because her cronies may not notice the absence of the corpse. However, she concludes that a corpse is necessary, so she persuades Simpson Primrose (John Wild) to act the part of the body. Since he is hiding from the police he grabs the opportunity. In the show's most hilarious scene, he also grabs the wallets of the mourners as they pass the bier. Although Hart played two wildly different roles, Harrigan spared him frantic costume changes. Rebecca appeared

only in the first two acts; Tommy (weighted down with gold on his return from the West) only in the third. Another pleasing David Braham score, with songs such as "My Little Side Door," "Coming Home From Meeting," and "Cobwebs On The Wall," helped *Dan's Tribulations* run to the season's end.

H. B. Farnie, whose adaptation of *La Vie Parisienne* was still running at the Bijou, had a second translation unveiled on April 4 at the Casino. His version of Francis Chassaigne's **Falka** proved an even greater delight. It ran well into the summer, recording over 100 showings. The musical's complicated plot basically told how a girl disguises herself as her brother so that she can be abducted in his stead. Bertha Ricci, Mathilde Cottrelly, and Frank Tannehill, Jr., headed the cast.

Although Johann Strauss' **A Night in Venice** had been a fiasco at its Berlin premiere the preceding fall, this did not hinder its American chances. That it failed in New York, too, when it opened at Daly's on April 19 was the result of a mediocre production more so than of any overriding weakness in its libretto or score. What its producer, James C. Duff, hoped would be a summer-long run terminated instead on May 24.

The busy Farnie had a third adaptation ready on May 6 when his version of Offenbach's *Blue Beard* came before the footlights at the Bijou. With Jacques Kruger in the title role, it ran six weeks.

Some understanding of how sound the theatrical economics of the period were can be gathered from Broadway's willingness to mount a musical that had been a disastrous failure at its first showing. Another suggestion of this same fiscal security was offered by **Madam Piper** (5-12-84, Wallack's). Madam Piper (Elma Delaro) is the old woman who lived in a shoe. Her husband turns out to be King Cole (John Howson). In his visits to her he discreetly disguises himself as a miller. The king finally acknowledges his paternity and moves his family to the palace. But neither he nor Madam Piper will permit their children to marry mates of their own choice. The youngsters take up arms to win their way. Two better-known figures of the lyric stage of the day created the work—librettist J. Cheever Goodwin and composer Woolson Morse. Their names on the playbill failed to prevent a cool reception. Shortly after the opening the *Dramatic Mirror* reported, "The Management are forcing a run for the purpose of securing prestige for the road." In his autobiography De Wolf Hopper reflected that this was a common practice of the period, "The Broadway engagement frequently was played at a loss, but what of it? Six months' losses in New York could be retrieved usually in three months on the road." *Madam Piper* ran no six months but merely five weeks; nor is there a record of how profitable its subsequent road tour was. Still, losses were the exception rather than the norm in those halycon days.

On May 19 hefty George K. Fortesque bounced into the Fifth Avenue with a burlesque of Sardou's *Fedora,* appropriately rechristened **Well-Fed Dora.** Of course, Fortesque waddled about as Dora Roamin' Off while Hetty Tracy donned trousers to play the hero. A grab bag of songs gave the piece the texture of a farce-comedy.

The season's final novelty was a more extended burlesque that winked at the Tom and Jerry (tour of the city) tradition and the *Black Crook's* tradition of spectacle as well. **Penny Ante, or The Last of the Fairies** (6-9-84, 14th St.) had book and lyrics by Jeff S. Leerburger and music by Fred J. Eustis. In Leerburger's tale a group of New Yorkers are arrested in a melee over prices at a dry-goods store. They are taken to the Tombs and from there to a fairy grotto. The title role of Penny Ante was played in expected burlesque tradition by Charles H. Drew in drag. *Penny Ante* folded unexpectedly after two weeks and disappeared from history.

Gustave Kerker, the Bijou's conductor, in conjunction with John Donnelly, offered a repertory of opéra bouffe and light opera at the house for a month beginning July 21. Their program included *The Chimes of Normandy, The Bohemian Girl, Fra Diavolo,* and *Maritana.* Kerker was quickly expanding his horizons and making a name for himself.

Variety continued on its prosperous path all season long, but the ever-restless Tony Pastor insisted on experimenting. Often during the year his variety bills played second fiddle momentarily to extended playlets with music: for example, *The Dude* for two weeks commencing November 5; *Two Gay Benedicts,* which succeeded on November 19; *Have You Seen Lilly?* on November 29; and *The Mother Goose Party,* in time for the Christmas trade on December 24. But most important of all, from April 14 to May 3, Pastor's boards held a new play, *A Rag Baby,* by Charles H. Hoyt. Hoyt's first successful work, *A Bunch of Keys,* had burst on New York the preceding year, with Willie Edouin, Alice Atherton, James T. Powers, and Julian Mitchell in the cast. *A Rag Baby* featured another future star of the musical stage, Frank Daniels. Both works were straight plays, and their surviving texts give no indication of any singing. But Hoyt had apprenticed with Edouin in his first farce-comedy

days, and reviews suggest that songs were indeed interpolated into both plays at the whim of the producers or the stars.

One interesting sidelight of the season was the visit of the great English favorites Henry Irving and Ellen Terry. Though their repertory was comprised wholly of straight plays, they packed houses while asking a $3.00 top. Thirty years had to pass before any Broadway musical dared charge so much.

1884-1885

Once again the season witnessed a slight slackening of musical activity. It also watched in horror as another of the epoch's endemic theatre fires destroyed the Comique. As there had been with earlier holocausts, there may have been a connection between a general drop in attendance after the fire and a falling off of production. And once more three-quarters of the entries must be classified as importations or revivals—or both. But a bright side was evident, too. In *Adonis* the season boasted one of the runaway successes of the American Musical Theatre. Moreover, historians reviewing the year may come away with a feeling that there was less slapdash in the original offerings. Americans were increasingly able to offer their countrymen evening-long musicals with plots sufficiently developed to maintain interest, and scores written with the story or, at least, the performers in mind.

Determined to keep its stage occupied for as full a year as possible, the Casino began the season with a midsummer revival of *The Little Duke* on August 4. Its hopes were realized, and *The Little Duke* played merrily on until the beginning of October. The musical's military milieu allowed the producers to insert an Amazon march. Oddly, in this French piece sung in English, they awarded the title role to one Fraulein Januschowsky, who had been a favorite at New York's German-language theatres and who sang with a thick German accent.

August 18 found competing versions of **Sieba and the Seven Ravens** vying for first-nighters' attention. Loose copyright laws allowed the Kiralfys to mount their version at the Star, while the Kiralfys' former home, Niblo's, brought forth its own. Based on a Hans Christian Andersen tale, both versions were translations of a dramatization popular all over Europe. Somehow the Kiralfys permitted Niblo's to outshine them. Niblo's troupe and scenery were purported to be from Vienna. (More German accents!) The house claimed to fill its stage with a chorus of 600 and a field of 110,000 perfumed roses! Perhaps theatregoers' eagerness to see how close the theatre could come to its patent exaggerations gained Niblo's a three-month run compared with the Kiralfys' two-month stay at the Star. But the Kiralfy version was published, and two quotations from the text forcefully bring to life the textures of both the work and its genre. The first reveals the basic plot, the second illustrates something of the period's staging:

Her name was Sieba. Her mother, in a rage,
Had cursed her seven young and gentle brothers.
This curse gave me full power over them—
And I transformed the seven pretty lads
Into as many black and croaking ravens.
The mother died of dire remorse and horror,
While little Sieba ran after the poor birds,
Wringing her hands in piteous lamentation,
When night closed in, she dropped from sheer
    exhaustion,
And in a lonely forest 'twas I found her.
I gave her back her strength, and then she told me
In trembling accents all about her woes.
I bid her hope and pointed out a way
To break the charm and to set free her brothers.
I made her promise that for seven years
She should not utter word of mouth or speech,
And, furthermore, that she, within that time,
Should spin and weave, in silence, seven gar-
    ments,
All in the seven colors of the rainbows,
And of a size to clothe her seven brothers.
If this task she accomplished, I agreed
That she and all her brothers should be happy.

FINALE

Ruperta: Put torches to the pyre.
    (*Harold sinks down in his chains.*)
The faggots are lighted. It has grown dark. The torches shed an uncertain light upon the scene.
Then are heard eight successive and very distinct strokes of a bell, accompanied by orchestra.
Sieba: (*listens intently to the strokes, then gives a shout of joy with the last stroke.*) Harold, husband! Save me!
Flourish: Loud thunder.
Music full and forte.
The walls sink.
    At back is seen a beautiful wood (after Schwind.)
    The fetters fall from Harold. His stake sinks out of sight.

He rushes to Sieba and embraces her feet. The flames go out by themselves.
Around the pyre, on ascending ground, are grouped Sieba's seven brothers in garments of the seven colors of the rainbow, mounted on splendid chargers, their swords raised as if to protect Sieba.
L. of Sieba Puck appears in splendid fairy costume with Rosalind's children in her arms.
Above this, Savanta floats as if in a cloud. In front, all kneel.
The torches are extinguished, giving place to the red light of the setting sun.
Note.—As a matter of course, the main effect depends upon quickness in producing the above.
Ruperta kneels and takes her coronet from her head, as if offering it to Savanta.
    (*Music pianissimo.*)
Rosalind (*to soft music.*) My own beloved Arthur, come to me that I may weep with joy upon your bust.
(*Arthur mounts the pyre, kneels and encircles her waist.*) You, and my children, and my brothers all! To perfect joy has turned our distress, And nothing e'er shall cloud our happiness.)
    (*Music forte.*)

TRANSFORMATION

The scene changes to a fairy paradise of gorgeous beauty and splendor.
The pyre changes to a throne, on which Ros. and Arthur stand in ecstatic embrace.
Rosalind's dress transforms into a white robe, adorned with jewels and flowers. A coronet sinks down upon her head.
The back scene rises.
The Fairy queen is seen in the far perspective, enthroned and surrounded by her court. At L. of her is Savanta, at whose feet, Rough crouches in submission. At R. Pigwidgeon with the children.
Magic light on all.
The persons in front have remained kneeling. During this:

CHORUS

Hail to the faithful
Who, for her brother
Lovingly suffered!
Sing her all hail!

Harrigan, Hart, and Braham had a new work ready on September 1. The Mulligans were given a rest, but the characters that filled **Investigation** were virtually next of kin. Bernard McKenna (Hart), a glue manufacturer with a penchant for politics, and

D'Arcy Flynn (Harrigan) seek the hand of a rich widow, Mrs. Belinda Tuggs (Annie Yeamans). D'Arcy wins. The broad panorama that almost any Harrigan story covered permitted the insertion of seemingly outlandish scenes. The most famous bit in the show came when D'Arcy and Belinda found themselves having to portray Romeo and Juliet. The vain Belinda, recalling the English triumph of the preceding season, thinks nothing of interrupting Shakespeare's verse to ask, "Do I look like Miss Terry?" But neither Terry nor Irving ever suffered with a recalcitrant spotlight that refused to do proper honor to either Flynn or Tuggs. There is, by the way, an Elizabethan richness to the names of many characters that fill the invariably lengthy personae of a Harrigan play. *Investigation* included Orion Overhoe, Oscar Onderdonk, Rev. Jonah Woolgather, Adelaide Foglip, Alexis Canfruit, and Gaspard Pitkins. Some critics discerned a lessening of melodic invention in David Braham's songs. None entered Braham's canon, although on opening night "every piece of music had to be played three or four times." What critics could not see was that *Investigation* marked the beginning of the end for Harrigan, Hart, and Braham. The play closed when its sets and costumes were destroyed along with the Theatre Comique two nights before Christmas. Hart's syphilis-spawned problems were coming to the fore. This, coupled with apparent recriminations over the origin of the fire, led to a coolness between Broadway's most celebrated pair and by the end of the season led to a permanent split. Harrigan-Hart's opening coincided with Jacques Kruger's return in a revival of *Dreams* (8-30-80) at Tony Pastor's.

Adonis opened at the Bijou on September 4, 1884. Slated by the theatre's management for a three-month run it succeeded beyond everyone's expectations. When it closed on April 17, 1886, it had compiled a record of 603 showings, far and away the longest run in Broadway history up to that time. The show was the work of some of the most renowned names of the time. Written and produced by E. E. Rice and William Gill, it catapulted Henry E. Dixey to fame and fortune.

. . .

Henry E. Dixey was born in Boston on January 6, 1859. He made his stage debut at the age of nine in 1868 in Daly's *Under the Gaslight* at the Howard Athenaeum. He played mostly comedy and drama in the Boston area until E. E. Rice spotted him and gave him a small part in *Evangeline*. Several years under Rice's tutelage followed. The boyishly handsome, gracefully built young Dixey first opened in *Adonis* on July 6, 1884, at Hooley's Theatre in Chicago.

. . .

Dixey also accepted credit for collaboration on the book, although most of his contribution seems to have come from his expanding his own part. The play's action starts when the sculptress Talmea (Lillie Grubb) persuades the goddess Artea (Louise V. Essing) to bring to life the statue of Adonis (Dixey). (He comes to life first with merely a sly wink, then with a dance on his pedestal.) Both Talmea and her patroness, the Duchess (Jennie Reiffarth), fall in love with the young man. So does every girl who sees him. (Ladies in the audience also succumbed, especially when Dixey pranced about fetchingly in tights—a turnabout on the coryphées and prima donnas of the day.) But he has eyes only for a simple, if extravagantly buxom, country girl, Rosetta (Amelia Summerville). Rosetta passes her time "eating huckleberries all day long, and learning how to love." For all her learning she is a little overwhelmed by Adonis' overtures, although she is by no means at a loss for words. She replies to his fluent advances, "I see that you can be as elegantly phraseological as you are physically majestic, and we rustics are unused to such bewildering conjunctions!" Unfortunately, Adonis cannot escape from his horde of pursuers, even though he resorts to one clever disguise after another. When he realizes the hopelessness of living the life of his choice, he returns to stone.

The disguises that Adonis assumed let him roam broadly in the burlesque tradition. Most famous of all was Dixey's spoof of Henry Irving. This bit of foolery was not confined to one brief moment, but employed at length. For example, at one point, still dressed like Irving's Hamlet, Dixey played the part of an unscrupulous milkman, pumping water into his milk cans, and "in Irving's manner" informing audiences, "They tell me in the village that I sell bad milk! It may be bad water, but it can't be bad milk." Some of the burlesque may have been less broad, suggesting how close knit was the community of theatre folk and theatregoers in the eighties. For example, at one point chorus girls entered four at a time, each foursome dressed in apparently familiar costumes used by chorus girls of other musicals. One reviewer was able to recognize dresses that had adorned girls in *The Merry War, Orpheus and Eurydice, The Queen's Lace Handkerchief,* and *Olivette*. Of the songs, two now forgotten numbers enjoyed wide and instant appeal, "The Susceptible

Statue" and "It's English, You Know." The latter, added after the show opened and sung by Dixey while still in his Irving make-up, noted

> O the queer things we say, and the queer things we do, / Are English, you know, quite English, you know.

Following the practically inevitable custom of the time, periodic changes were made in the show during its run. But Dixey remained a stalwart feature for the length of the run as well as in subsequent revivals. Her playing of Rosetta consolidated Amelia Summerville's fortunes.

Wallack's Theatre inaugurated its season with a five-week visit by Maurice Grau's opéra bouffe ensemble, this time starring Mme. Theo. When its stay was terminated, it moved for an additional week to the Bijou. Later in the season Gustave Kerker also offered a brief repertory of opéra bouffe. However, as Odell observed, in his theatre history, "This form of entertainment, so popular for nearly twenty years in New York, was entering on its last stages here; Gilbert and Sullivan and Strauss and Millöcker sang the temporary eclipse of Offenbach and Lecocq and Audran." Excepting that Audran and Lecocq seem to have been permanently eclipsed in this country, the statement is just.

Revivals of both schools followed in quick order. Millöcker's *The Beggar Student* commenced a month's run at the Casino on October 6, while Offenbach's *Orpheus and Eurydice* played a one-week fill-in at the Fifth Avenue.

Just before *The Beggar Student* settled in, **A Parlor Match** opened a two-week visit at Tony Pastor's. With it the short reign of the second generation farce-comedies can be said to begin. The difference, as so often happens, was one of degree not kind. This second generation was largely the work of Charles H. Hoyt, who was far and away the best writer of claptrap farces at the end of the century. Until *A Trip to Chinatown* (11-9-91), songs in his plays were taken from any available source, much as the early farce-comedies had done. But Hoyt was a sturdier playwright than his predecessors. His plays, like Harrigan's later writings, were conceived as full-length works. However, Hoyt was more careful and compact, usually requiring only one set per act instead of the kaleidoscope of scenes Harrigan employed. (Of course, this may have been an inheritance from the simple settings of earlier farce-comedy.) Moreover Hoyt eschewed ethnic material, preferring to write about native Americans familiar to most theatregoers around the country.

In his latest play Hoyt dealt with a tramp who blithely walks in and out of a house stealing merchandise, with the busy family oblivious to his presence. When he fears detection he hides in a drawer. A somewhat inebriated member of the household discovers him there. But the tramp escapes because the drunk hysterically concludes he is having delirium tremens. In the last act a spiritualist is called in to set things right. The show, featuring the team of Charles Evans and William Hoey, played a one-week return stand in April.

Early in November the Casino replaced *The Beggar Student* with a new work, Planquette's **Nell Gwynn** offering Mathilde Cottrelly in the title role. But Americans did not take to this Frenchman's interpretation of an English figure. The show was a quick failure. On the other hand a bevy of tangible English beauties, supplemented by some American ones, closed out November at the Comedy Theatre with **An Adamless Eden.** Even the orchestra players were women. Music ran from Arditi's "L'Estasi" to songs from *The Beggar Student*. If Lilly Clay and her troupe (including Pauline Hall and Topsy Venn) hoped to repeat the stir Lydia Thompson had created in the sixties they were disappointed. After a month's run and a modest tour they returned to England.

December proved happier. A revival of *Prince Methusalem* bowed at the Casino on the 15th, while eight nights afterwards the rebuilt Standard opened its doors with von Suppé's **A Trip to Africa.** In a complicated plot Titania finds love with Antaxid while on a Nile journey. Another indication of how small and familiar the theatre was is evident from the fact that the producer of the piece, James C. Duff, was Augustin Daly's father-in-law. Despite a lack of "names" in the cast, Duff's production enjoyed moderate business; it closed February 21.

The old school of farce-comedy was represented by **We, Us and Co. at Mud Springs** (12-23-84, Star). Just hours after the smoking ruins of the Comique signaled a turn in Harrigan and Hart's fortunes, William A. Mestayer and Charles Bernard presented their example of another vanishing form. They also demonstrated how complex the staging if not the plotting had grown. A party of hypochondriacs comes to Mud Spring under the care of a quack physician. Their hotel is unusual to say the least. It is constructed atop a railroad turntable to allow all rooms some exposure to the sun. Its revolutions lead to a series of confused guests, who seem invariably to enter the wrong room at the wrong time. Much of these comings and goings are prompted by all the men patients' infatuation with the same young lady. Although Mestayer's initial visit was brief, lasting less than a month, the piece provided him and his entourage with employment for several years.

The new year was ushered in by the latest Harrigan and Braham work, **McAllister's Legacy.** By a stroke of luck, sets and costumes for the play, which was being rehearsed at the Comique when the house burned, had not yet been delivered to the theatre. Harrigan and Hart hastily booked a seeming white elephant, the Park Theatre, and opened there on January 5, 1885. Critical reception was restrained. It was as if the private tensions developing between Harrigan and Hart were evidenced in the quality of their material. But if professional aisle-sitters were reserved, Harrigan and Hart's loyal public was not. In an almost column-long notice, quoted earlier in discussing *The Mulligan Guards' Surprise* (2-16-80), the *Times* devoted extensive space to describing the give and take between the performers and their steadfast patrons. *McAllister's Legacy* told a simple tale, although it was filled with the multiple scenes and song-inducing complications dear to all Harrigan creations. An old man dies and leaves some tenement property to two relatives. One is a veterinary surgeon, Dr. McAllister (Ned Harrigan). The other is rambunctious Mollie McGouldrich (Tony Hart). Mollie feels she has been given the lesser share and sets about unleashing complications. McGouldrich undoubtedly was a slight slap at the financier Jay Gould, although some programs spelled it McGoldrick. As Eddie Foy wrote in his autobiography, many Irish of the time felt Fisk was their friend and harbored grave suspicions about Gould. The name Mollie allowed Harrigan and Braham to write one of the innumerable songs of the day celebrating the name. But neither the play nor its songs caught on. Harrigan and Hart moved the work to what they hoped would be a more desirable house, the old 14th Street Theatre. The transfer failed to help business, and the show was withdrawn on March 14.

In order not to compete with a Harrigan and Hart opening, E. E. Rice delayed the first night of **A Bottle of Ink** at the Comedy until the following evening, January 6. Written by George H. Jessop and William Gill, the play was one of the last of the old style farce-comedies to brave New York. Their day was over, and *A Bottle of Ink* suffered as well from being an inferior example of the genre. Jefferson Jingo (John A. Mackay) is a Wild West newspaper man, as wild as the West he covers. A number of irate figures confront him, and each confrontation invariably leads to a specialty number. One angry young man who confronts Jingo is Hermann Zwugg—played by an actor listed on the program as Jeff De Angelis. Tiny Ida Mulle sang songs from *Princess Ida,* and Maud Beverly belted out a medley of cockney music-hall ditties. Dismissed by the *Times* as a rehash of *Pop* (5-21-83), it lingered less than a month. Despite the tremendous success of *Adonis,* Rice, like Harrigan and Hart, was approaching the end of his heyday.

January's third and final musical was an importation. A revival of Millöcker's *Apajune* (1-16-85, Casino), produced by John McCaull, entertained the Casino's growing band of loyalists for two months. W. S. Rising, Mathilde Cottrelly, Francis Wilson, and Belle Archer headed the cast.

A revival of *Gasparone* at the Standard was February's sole entry. The next lyrical first night occurred on March 9 when the Boston Ideal Opera Company returned after a season's absence. Included in their repertory were *Fatinitza, H.M.S. Pinafore, The Bohemian Girl, The Musketeers, Fra Diavolo,* and *Giroflé-Girofla*—all in a brief two-week visit at the Fifth Avenue.

Monday, March 16, presented competing first nights. Both were revivals; both had short runs. The Casino put on *Die Fledermaus,* with the rising De Wolf Hopper cast as Franke. Mark Smith played Eisenstein; Irene Perry, Prince Orlofsky; Rosalba Beecher, Rosalind; and Mathilde Cottrelly, Adele. Fine as this cast was, it could not make *Die Fledermaus* a rousing hit. Until after the turn of the century, this greatest of all Strauss operettas inexplicably failed to dazzle audiences in the same way now forgotten Strauss works did. To make employment for their company after the disappointment of *McAllister's Legacy,* Harrigan and Hart returned *The Major* (8-28-81) to the boards.

Another revival of *H.M.S. Pinafore* docked at the Standard on April 4. Sung by the same troupe that had presented *Gasparone,* it played merrily for two weeks. Two nights after the Standard opening the Thatcher, Primrose, and West Minstrels came in for a brief stay at the Fifth Avenue.

A domestically made "comic opera," **Twins,** replaced Gilbert and Sullivan at the Standard on April 20. It starred John A. Mackay, long the leading comedian in Rice's farce-comedies. Mackay played both the pious churchman, Dr. Titus Spinach, and his impious brother, Timothy, whose misbehavior constantly embarrasses the clergyman. Filled with tunes gathered from diverse sources, it was more a farce-comedy of the sort Mackay was known for than the "comic opera" it claimed to be.

On its opening night it competed with the second Harrigan, Hart, and Braham revival of the year, *Cordelia's Aspirations* (11-5-83). The three-week run marked the last time Harrigan and Hart ever performed together on Broadway. They played out a short commitment in Brooklyn in June, then went their separate ways.

A happier opening took place on the next Monday, April 27. At the Casino E. E. Rice brought in his Gaiety Opera Company with Lillian Russell as star and J. H. Ryley as its droll patter-song comedian. The vehicle was a new comic opera by Miss Russell's English husband, Edward Solomon, **Polly, or The Pet of the Regiment.** Taking hints from both Gilbert and Sullivan and from Donizetti, its plot told how a buffoonish major general makes Polly his regiment's mascot. The show ran until June 18. Then the same troupe closed its engagement by reviving Solomon's *Billie Taylor* for a week beginning June 20. Miss Russell again starred.

May's first lyric offering was the month's only hit. John McCaull had split with Rudolf Aronson at the Casino. On May 4 he moved his company of players—mostly recruited from the Casino—to Wallack's, where he presented Sydney Rosenfeld's adaptation of yet another Millöcker work, *Der Feldprediger*. Retitled **The Black Hussar** for American audiences, it ran over 100 performances with Mark Smith, De Wolf Hopper, and Digby Bell as the principal comedians. The story told how a Hussar, fomenting insurrection, diverts suspicion onto a pestiferous magistrate.

Ned Harrigan, now going it alone, suffered one of the worst humiliations of his career when his **Are You Insured?** opened on May 11 at the 14th Street Theatre and folded five nights later. Actually, the play lacked not only Hart, but Harrigan himself. Had he acted in his own work, the *Herald* might not have written that the evening "gives one a higher opinion of the abilities of Hart." Harrigan's story related the problems two hustling life insurance agents, Philander Dividend (Charles Stanley) and Sarsfield Per Annum (W. H. Fitzgerald), encounter when they marry Sheriff Bouncer's roaring daughters. The critics did no more than mention David Braham's songs in passing.

Apart from Gustave Kerker's opéra bouffe troupe, the only other May arrival was J. K. Emmet, once more playing *Fritz in Ireland* (11-3-79). The show played three weeks at an out-of-the-way house generally given over to German entertainment.

Three shows came in during June. The first two were revivals. At Niblo's the Kiralfys once more remounted *Around the World in Eighty Days* on the 1st, while *Billie Taylor* returned, as mentioned earlier, for a week. By this date revivals of *Around the World* (8-28-75) were customarily passed over with the briefest reviews. In a one-paragraph assessment, the *Times* assured the faithful they would still find the evening replete with "bright scenery, glittering costumes, and whirling phalanxes of more or less shapely coryphees." The month's lone novelty, however, proved a resounding hit. The Zell-Genée operetta **Nanon** was produced at the Casino with Sadie Martinot, Pauline Hall, and W. T. Carleton in the leading roles in a tale of two ladies, Nanon and Ninon, in love with the same marquis. It ran from June 29 to November 14, suggesting that the Casino had more than won the battle to keep its stage lit throughout the year.

The season ended in a curious mixture of triumph and ignominy. Hoping to be the first with the best, Sydney Rosenfeld rushed in a presentation of Gilbert and Sullivan's **The Mikado** on July 20, 1885. His glee at beating out his rivals was short lived, however. An injunction was obtained, Rosenfeld was jailed for unauthorized production, and his production disappeared after its initial showing at the Union Square.

. . .

Sydney Rosenfeld was long a colorful, controversial figure on the American theatrical scene. Born in Richmond, Virginia, on October 26, 1855 (or 1856), son of a prosperous merchant, he claimed to have run a Civil War blockade so that he could attend private school in New York. At fifteen he began supplying short stories to boys' magazines, and by 1874 his first play, a burlesque of *Rose Michel*, saw the footlights. Thereafter he kept busy as author, translator, producer, or director. While pursuing his various theatrical activities he still found time to write for the *Sun*, the *World*, and, eventually, to become the first editor of *Puck*.

. . .

All through the season variety continued to flourish, even though many houses followed Tony Pastor in occasionally breaking their parade of vaudeville bills by introducing longer pieces. For example, on its August 16 program Koster and Bial's offered a short operetta, *Love in ye Days of Charles ye Second.* Meanwhile Hyde and Behman's became a refuge for many old minstrels, although its confused bills were anything but pure minstrelsy.

1885-1886

Moving season by season one can almost feel how long-lived were the growing pains of the American Musical Theatre. Apart from the deluge of productions that followed in the wake of *H.M.S. Pinafore* (1-15-79), even landmark musicals left little but the record of their own success behind. Not one of the great hits of this early period established a reigning style as did, say, *The Merry Widow* (10-21-07) or *Oklahoma!* (3-31-43) in later years. True, *The Black Crook* (9-12-66), *Humpty Dumpty* (3-10-68), and the Fritz plays offered their own sequels and encouraged a number of imitations. But neither the sequels nor the imitations approached the originals in popularity. The season of 1885–86 continued the pattern of the preceding years—a musical roster top-heavy with revivals and importations. Two English creations, *The Mikado* and *Erminie,* dominated the season. But rumblings of nascent domestic creativity were evident, even if the rumblings were first heard miles from Broadway.

The season began in earnest with the simultaneous entry of several musicals on August 17. Millöcker's *Die Naherin,* done as **Chatter,** opened at Wallack's. This tale of a loquacious seamstress whose gabbing throws an estate into turmoil featured a droll comic performance by De Wolf Hopper as an "elderly gentleman of gallant proclivities." Mathilde Cottrelly was praised for her superb, understated clowning in the principal role. At Niblo's, Bartley Campbell's old warhorse, *Clio,* detailing the love of a duke's daughter and an artist, appeared bedecked with lavish ballets led by Adele Cornalba and tinseled with light songs. Among its spectacular effects was a palace destroyed by an earthquake. Both shows were quick, costly failures.

Actually one show came in a week before, on Monday, August 10. This was a mounting of *The Mikado* at the People's Theatre. It ran just a week. Curiously the house was owned by Henry Miner, and one week later Miner somehow managed to reassemble the production Rosenfeld had brought in a month before, presenting it again at the Union Square. Why Miner used two different casts and, possibly, two collections of sets and costumes remains obscure. In any case, this *Mikado,* which opened concurrently with *Chatter* and *Clio,* survived a mere fortnight. Legal threats precipitated its shuttering, but the arrival at the Fifth Avenue of

D'Oyly Carte's own mounting of the Gilbert and Sullivan masterpiece two nights later on August 19 undoubtedly confronted Miner with insuperable competition. The production was an immediate triumph, and compiled 250 performances before it closed on April 17. Under Richard Barker's excellent direction, this story of a Mikado's disguised son who agrees to be beheaded if he can spend a month married to the girl he loves was capitally performed by F. Federici as the Mikado, the "vest-pocket tenor" and matinee idol, Courtice Pounds, as Nanki-Poo, F. Billington as Pooh-Bah, George Thorne as Ko-Ko, Geraldine Ulmar as Yum-Yum, and Elsie Cameron as Katisha. Sullivan's timeless melodies were heard in his original orchestrations, not in the "alternately thin and brassy" treatment the pirated versions had offered. Songs included Nanki-Poo's showpiece, "A Wandering Minstrel," Nanki-Poo and Ko-Ko's "The Flowers That Bloom In The Spring," and Ko-Ko's "Willow, Tit-willow." Sullivan came to the country and conducted some performances in September. But the success of the work was assured without his presence.

Although short of the records accrued by a few phenomenal successes, the run was one of the longest in the New York annals up to its time. Yet it fell far short of the more than 600 performances *The Mikado* achieved in London. Oddly, Alfred Cellier's *Dorothy,* produced almost at the same time in London, markedly exceeded even that record. Down through the decades London seems to have regularly given its greatest hits far longer support than New York gave its hits. Just how much these longer runs influenced the early flowering of the English musical and how much the shorter runs on this side of the Atlantic retarded American development will probably never be known. The American "road," while highly profitable, was far more constricted than in its heyday. (The number of touring performers and companies peaked immediately after the turn of the century, just before films first lured away significant patronage.) At this time, the road could not always fully compensate for the relatively brief New York runs, despite the De Wolf Hopper comment cited earlier. Moreover England had the "provinces" to offer against our "road."

In one respect *The Mikado* had over 250 showings. D'Oyly Carte was not monopolistic. Although he fought unauthorized productions, he allowed competition to flourish—possibly in the knowledge that no one could really compete with his own style and know-how. Five nights after his own mounting premiered, D'Oyly Carte permitted James

Duff to unveil his version at the Standard. Adequate but inferior, it ran three months, after which Duff moved it to Chicago, whence Rosenfeld's illicit production had come. D'Oyly Carte even permitted a touring company to visit Niblo's in March for a month, ignoring complaints that its version was filled "with local gags and very little Gilbert." A German-language version gave forth at the Thalia. While the superior wit, melody, and coherence of *The Mikado* undoubtedly acted as a goad to challenge aspiring young American authors, the show's most immediate and most enduring influence was probably to consolidate the vogue for musical librettos with exotic, usually pseudo-Oriental, settings. Earlier *The Sultan of Mocha* (9-14-80) and *Revels* (10-25-80) had hinted at possibilities of just such a fashion. Things Oriental had become so modish in Victorian circles that in London Gilbert could have Bunthorne proclaim in that same spring of 1881, "I do not long for all one sees / That's Japanese."

The following Monday, August 31—almost all openings continued to be on Monday nights—Harrigan began his solo career with a revival of *Old Lavender* (9-3-77), his own personal favorite among his plays. Harrigan again leased the old Park, refurbishing it slightly and renaming it Harrigan's Park Theatre. The play also underwent revisions while Harrigan's father-in-law, Braham, composed a number of new songs. One of these, "Ebb And Flow," was an instant best seller. With its improvements, *Old Lavender* ran on sturdily until the end of November.

The failure of *Chatter* prompted John McCaull to bring back *Die Fledermaus* (9-14-85, Wallack's), using many of the principals the Casino had employed the season before. The revival lasted only two weeks. When it closed Maurice Grau brought in a season of opéra bouffe beginning Oct. 1. His star was Mme. Anna Judic, whom Odell in his theatre history judged "perhaps the most artistic representative of the species ever seen in this country." She, alone of the French singers who graced our boards during opéra bouffe's ascendancy, was a major star in Paris, singing the premieres of numerous original productions there. The repertory included *Mlle. Nitouche, Lili, La Femme à Papa, Niniche, Le Grand Casimir,* and *La Mascotte.* The vogue for opéra bouffe may have been waning, but in three separate engagements scattered throughout the season the company played a total of six weeks.

The Thatcher, Primrose, and West Minstrels romped into Niblo's on October 5. It was the first of several visits this troupe and other touring minstrels would make to Manhattan during the year. These led Odell to see "the revival, in 1885–86, of the black-face art." True, there was an unusual bustle of activity. Thatcher, Primrose, and West's ensemble alone spent a total of two months in five separate stays. But their evening consisted largely of a burlesque of *Adonis* (9-4-84), called simply *Black Adonis.* They and the troupes that played lesser, more out-of-the-way houses all deviated noticeably from the old, traditional formula, which most audiences had tired of. If the minstrels were busy they were occupied not with preserving classic forms but with establishing acceptable new entertainments. Extended burlesques and vaudeville seemed the answer.

Evangeline (7-27-74) returned for a stay at the 14th Street Theatre beginning October 7. In keeping with the creative fluidity of the era, the work happily announced substantial revisions. As best as can be determined these were largely cosmetic: a few new melodies, minor new scenes and dialogue and, of course, new sets and costumes. The slim Fay Templeton was Gabriel and the hefty Amelia Summerville, temporarily departed from *Adonis,* played Hubert. (Interestingly, her role in *Adonis* had been assumed by George K. Fortesque, playing in drag.) James Maffitt was at his post as The Lone Fisherman. Although *Evangeline* was indisputably one of the most successful and beloved works of the era, it oddly enough never had a really long run in New York. In this respect it was much like the Fritz plays and, in a few years, *Robin Hood* (9-28-91). Its 1885–86 run of 201 performances marked its lengthiest stay in New York.

On November 2 the Thatcher, Primrose, and West Minstrels briefly dropped their twitting of *Adonis* to poke fun at *The Mikado* instead. In their retelling it came out *The Mick-ah-do.* Later in the year they returned to perform *The Black Mikado,* which may have been the same spoof with another name. On this January visit they also reached far back to kid *Humpty Dumpty* as *Hughey Dougherty.* The burlesque reflects the continuing popularity on the road of the old pantomime, even if New York had seen the last of it. However, a careful look at minstrel programs shows the form had degenerated into little more than variety. The bill that included *The Mick-ah-do* also regaled its patrons with the boy soprano Master Witmark (later a famous music publisher) singing "Baby's Lullaby," with trained dogs, drum majors' parades, and acrobats. Variety, too, was offering spoofs of *The Mikado* on the very night the minstrels presented theirs. At Koster and Bial's the travesty listed such

83

characters as Pity Sing Sing, Yum Yum First Ward, and High Kockey (made up to resemble General Ben Butler).

Amorita followed (11-16-85, Casino). Its heroine would have been forced to marry the wicked usurper in Florence had not his overthrow occurred moments before the finale curtain. A sense of time and place was a matter of indifference to clowns of the era, so Francis Wilson won his biggest laughs nightly with a comic game of stud poker. Madeline Lucette (in the title role), Pauline Hall, and Rose Beaudet assisted. Now utterly forgotten, the operetta enjoyed a moderate three-month run.

A week later Nat Goodwin offered New Yorkers another farce-comedy, **The Skating Rink** (11-23-85, Standard). Perhaps nothing so well reveals the attitudes and methods of farce-comedy producers as Goodwin's memoirs:

> My idea was to ascertain if any of the company had a specialty that could be injected into this porous play. It permitted all sorts of pioneering. The plot stopped at eighty thirty! . . . Two or three of the young ladies interpolated some of the latest New York ditties, Fanny Rice and I cribbing the See-Saw duet. I also introduced the entire act of a play called "The Marionettes," assisted by one of the [trick] skating trio, an Irish song written by a Jew, "Since Maggie Learned To Skate," and a burlesque of "Camille." I appeared as the coughing heroine! [Then] disappearing as the dying lady on one side of the stage to return from the opposite as the Irishman in search of his daughter, Maggie.

As if all this were not enough, Goodwin adds that he inserted a number of his famous imitations and hired a man who first swallowed and then disgorged lit cigars. Obviously Goodwin knew his audiences. The piece gave him employment on and off for several years.

Both the Kiralfys and Harrigan had new works ready on November 30. The Kiralfys fell back on the Pied Piper story for **The Ratcatcher,** filling it as was their wont with an amalgam of spectacle, ballet, and vaudeville specialties. Starring the baritone Hubert Wilke as Singold the Piper, it kept Niblo's lit for two months. Harrigan's **The Grip** ran only slightly longer. In Harrigan's tale two Civil War comrades, Col. Patrick Reilly (Harrigan) and Capt. Phil Clancy (Harry Fisher), promise each other that their children will wed each other and seal the promise with a grip. Years pass. Clancy announces he and his son John (H. A. Weaver, Jr.) are coming East to allow John to wed Reilly's daughter,

Rosalind (Stella Boniface). But Reilly had heard the Clancys are now in bad odor. He persuades his family to behave with outlandish vulgarity. Nonetheless, John and Rosalind fall in love. By curtain time the Clancy name is cleared and everyone is happy. No outstanding Braham songs helped the evening. Nonetheless, Harrigan regulars on both sides of the footlights kept *The Grip* firmly at the Park until mid-February.

December offered only two revivals: *The Black Hussar* (12-9-85, Star) and *Mlle. Nitouche* (12-14-85, Standard), the latter sung in English by, surprisingly, Lotta. Lotta's visit also proffered revivals of her expected repertory. The first month of the new year brought nothing at all. Not until February 15, 1886, did another lyric first night occur. And then a trio of shows opened at once.

One was Ned Harrigan's final effort for the season at the Park, **The Leather Patch.** To be rid of a shrewish wife (Annie Yeamans), McCarthy (Harrigan) decides to play dead. Before his "burial" he writes a codicil to his will, leaving everything to his son, then he places the will in a leather patch on a pair of trousers. After McCarthy's "death" Roderick McQuade (John Sparks), an undertaker, courts the Widow McCarthy. When Roderick needs a pair of trousers to bury an Indian, the widow gives him the pair with the patch. Jefferson Putnam (John Wild), a Negro graverobber, steals them. McCarthy's "ghost" eventually returns to right matters and reform his wife. The free-flowing give and take offered opportunities for slices of contemporary life such as a jubilant black wake and "a lively illustration of the methods of Baker-Street clothing dealers." Characters allowed their brief moment on the stage included, to name only a few, "the seedy shyster, the convivial Police Justice, the negro vagabond, the Sixth Ward gin seller." The *Times'* critic rued the conspicuous advertising of a particular brand of whiskey, a commercial intrusion for which Harrigan was probably compensated, but which could be defended as another bit of realism. In its afterthoughts, several weeks later, the *Times* praised the work for presenting "as much broad humor and local color as 'The Beggar's Opera,' without a touch of the immorality of the amusing work that set London in a furor in 1725. Harrigan has found a new field as surely as John Gay did." No doubt heartfelt and well-meant, the praise was a little late in the day. Again Braham produced no hits. But *The Leather Patch* was sufficiently diverting to run until May.

At the Casino first-nighters heard a more enduring work, Johann Strauss' **The Gypsy Baron.** The

Casino brought over William Castle from grand opera to sing Sandor and awarded the role of Zsupan to the up-and-coming Francis Wilson. Wilson clowned in a German accent and introduced "a topical song" written by the operetta's translator, Sydney Rosenfeld. Rosenfeld at least remained faithful to the original story of a nobleman who returns from exile and falls in love with a gypsy, a young lady unaware she, too, is of noble birth. But the work enjoyed only a modest success, running until May 10. Its three-month stay was about average for the Casino. Hindsight makes it difficult to understand how Strauss' best works—operettas like *The Gypsy Baron* and *Die Fledermaus*—achieved merely middling receptions, while lesser, virtually forgotten Strauss pieces such as *Prince Methusalem* were greater hits.

The last and certainly least of the openings was **Three of a Kind.** The three are dry-goods clerks on a spree at a country boarding house. One finds romance. Nellie McHenry and Nate Salsbury led the antics. It was offered for a week by the recently voguish Salsbury's Troubadours at the Grand Opera House, by this time also past its heyday. With so much better to choose from, New Yorkers had discarded as old hat these strolling players and their contrivances.

The newer, more acceptable generation of farce-comedies was represented when William Gill's **A Toy Pistol** bowed (2-20-86, Comedy). Gill's story was a variation and elaboration on the one he had used the previous year in *A Bottle of Ink* (1-6-85). To save his failing paper, the *Toy Pistol,* editor Isaac Roost sends himself fraudulent telegrams and disguises himself as an Italian musician, a clerk, a washerwoman, and a "Milesian Mikado." In keeping with the old practice of doubling in roles so dear to farce-comedy, one actor (D. G. Longworth) portrayed three characters with typical musical stage names of the period: Ernest Seeker, J. Lancelot Hustler, and Primrose Path. A few critics singled out such songs as "Collar Cuffs" and "I Give It Up" as praiseworthy, although everything from the show—culled, again in farce-comedy fashion, from myriad sources—has been forgotten. The reason for Gill's revisions was to create a vehicle for Tony Hart, and for most 1886 theatregoers it was Hart's name that loomed as the principal attraction. He was welcomed as effusively as he always had been when he played with Harrigan. One critic noted, "A large majority of spectators yelled with delight, others stamped their feet, hammered their canes, and clapped their hands. Floral tributes in profusion were handed to Mr. Hart." His best mo-

ment came when, as the Irish washerwoman buying a bit of tea, he subjected the defenseless sales clerk to a long, rambling history of trials and tribulations. Unfortunately Gill's work, lacking Harrigan's verisimilitude and artistry, was patently theatrical. Hart played Broadway for five weeks and then went on tour.

We, Us and Co. (12-29-84) returned on March 8 for a week's visit to the Standard.

Another popular artist arrived in a starring vehicle one month after Hart. Lillian Russell played the title role in **Pepita, or The Girl with the Glass Eyes** (3-16-86, Union Square). Pepita was the daughter of the eccentric Professor Pongo, fabricator of performing automata. When his robot prima donna breaks down just before the performance of an opera, Pepita takes its place. The leading male automaton soon malfunctions, and Pepita is happy to substitute her real lover in the part. Unlike many other musical queens, Russell was always careful to surround herself with the best available talent. Professor Pongo was played by Jacques Kruger (who had written the spoof of *Patience* that made Miss Russell famous), while the young hero was played by a youthful minstrel performing for the first time on the legitimate stage, Chauncey Olcott. To Kruger fell the newly voguish "topical song," twitting the day's national and local foibles, even when they bore no relation to the plot. At least one critic recorded that Olcott's "nasal tones were inopportunely mirth provoking," although everyone was surprised when Miss Russell suddenly disclosed a violin and accompanied herself in one number. The material was by Alfred Thompson and Miss Russell's husband, Edward Solomon. Solomon was no doubt delighted when "almost all the numbers of the score were encored." *Pepita* held the stage until May 22 and enjoyed a profitable tour.

A more interesting and more successful work followed Miss Russell by two weeks. When **The Little Tycoon** opened at the Standard on March 29, it had already been running three months in Philadelphia. The original cast was transferred to New York, while a new contingent continued the Philadelphia stand, playing there until early June and returning the next season for several shorter engagements. *The Little Tycoon* was the work of a Philadelphia socialite, Willard Spenser.

. . .

Willard Spenser was born in Cooperstown, New York, apparently in 1852. Scion of a wealthy family, he attended the best private schools. After his marriage he settled in St. Davids, then an elite suburb of Philadelphia. His obituaries mention no occupation, but state that he had had select schooling by the best available teachers of music he could find. Spenser came to represent to New York the figurehead of the "Philadelphia school" of musical theatre. Savagely criticized, he allowed only his first two musicals a New York hearing. On the other hand both Philadelphia and the road gave all his musicals warm receptions as late as 1912.

. . .

Spenser's simple plot assuredly recalled *The Bourgeois Gentleman*. General Knickerbocker (R. E. Graham) and his daughter, Violet (Carrie M. Dietrich), are returning from Europe accompanied by the flatulent nobleman whom Knickerbocker has selected to be his daughter's husband, Lord Dolphin (E. H. Van Veghten). But Violet's heart is given to Alvin (W. S. Rising). By no coincidence Alvin is on the same crossing. Lest Alvin and Violet meet, the General has his daughter locked in her cabin. Violet's lady friends obtain a passkey to free her. Furious, the General announces his daughter will wed the lord immediately upon their return to Newport. However, once home, the General receives a letter from "His Royal Highness Sham, The Great Tycoon of Japan," announcing his imminent appearance at the Knickerbocker mansion. Overwhelmed by the potentate and the "craze for everything that's Japanase" (it was, after all, the year of *The Mikado*), the General forgets his English favorite and presents his daughter to the monarch. Of course, the Tycoon is merely Alvin in disguise. Lord Dolphin's domineering mama, the Marchioness of Pullhimback, angrily hurries off with her milk-toast son. The music, lyrics, and dialogue were simple almost to the point of being puerile. Much of the humor came from outrageous puns. The General entertains the Tycoon by singing "The Cats On Our Back Fence":

> Oh! the cats on our back fence!
> Politicians they of sense.
> Win they with cooperation,
> With con-catty, ratty-oscination.

The Tycoon requests the General sing some more. Flattered, the General is soon at the monarch's beck and call:

Gen. Knickerbocker: Any other request the Great Tycoon can make I pledge myself to grant.
Lord Dolphin: Oh, Ah!
Alvin: Show-im-up, tight squeak, Ki-yi; Choke-im-oph Tycoon yah-yah, ki-yi! Chum-yah, boojum-snark hop-scotch Tycoonee,—yum yum.

Gen. Knickerbocker: Yes, I understand. You have my unqualified consent, your majesty.
 (*To Rufus*) But what does he say?
Rufus: Great Tycoon ask for hand of General Knickerbocker's beautiful daughter.
Lord Dolphin: (*In consternation*) Oh, ah!
Gen. Knickerbocker: I swoon! How very unfortunate! My daughter's hand is promised to Lord Dolphin.
Lord Dolphin: (*Despairingly*) Oh, ah!
Gen. Knickerbocker: But hold. Never was there such a craze for everything that's Japanase. She's yours.
Lord Dolphin: (*Despairingly*) Oh, ah!

Dolphin's two monosyllables were his only sounds throughout the work. With Alvin and Violet hand in hand the company reprised the little waltz that was the most popular melody in the show, "Love Comes Like A Summer Sigh."

Originally slated for a five-week stay, *The Little Tycoon* ran until June. Although a success, it was by no means the phenomenon it had been in Philadelphia. To New York it stood as a distressing example of "the Philadelphia school," with its inane librettos, driveling dialogue, and elementary music. Critics even assailed Philadelphia for capitulating more readily to audience demands for encores. Most galling to Spenser was the charge he had borrowed the setting and many of his ideas from *The Mikado*. Spenser replied by showing he had copyrighted the musical on October 24, 1882—three years before *The Mikado*'s premiere. He contended he had offered the work to a Colonel Morse, D'Oyly Carte's agent, and that Morse had retained the manuscript for several years before returning it. The best part of the production was the colorful Japanese costumes, judged equal to the handiwork of New York's costumers.

March's only other entry was yet another revival at Niblo's of *The Black Crook* (9-12-66), adding another month's run to its history. Its additions for this revival included the Mignani family, performing the March from *Aida* on sweepers' brooms, and a "Mikado Ballet"—these in a work set in Germany.

Washington, like Philadelphia and Boston, was mounting its own productions. On April 12 a short new John Philip Sousa work, **The Queen of Hearts, or Royalty and Roguery,** opened on a double bill with *Trial by Jury*. Sousa conducted. Edward M. Taber's libretto took as its source the Mother Goose rhyme in which the Knave of Hearts steals the Queen's tarts. All the characters were cards in the deck. The piece was not a success and was never revived after its brief three-performance run.

W. J. Scanlan came into Niblo's on April 26 in **Shane-na-Lawn,** another of those Irish romantic dramas laced with song out of which he made a career. Shane was a clever Irish lad who clears a girl of false charges of murder and wins himself a bride. Scanlan's offering competed for attention with a new William Gill effort, **Arcadia** (4-26-86, Bijou). Like several other librettists during the year, Gill had recourse to childhood favorites for his tale. Tom, Tom, the Piper's Son (George Richards) runs away from home, visiting the Garden of Trumpetta's Palace and Mephistopheles' Country Seat before trudging back to his own hearth. Gill wrote himself a part that allowed him to traipse in and out playing bagpipes. The show lacked a centralizing figure such as Adonis and suffered as well from a bad score. David Braham's brother John "selected and arranged" the music. The most notable number was "Hic-hiccough Hic-hiccough," its new words attached to Sullivan's "Willow Tit-willow" from *The Mikado.* The show was a flop, closing after a three-week stand.

Four shows with varying degrees of musical seriousness opened May 3. At Wallack's John McCaull offered the most musically cohesive of the arrivals, Rudolph Dellinger's reworking of *Maritana,* **Don Caesar.** Bertha Ricci and Mathilde Cottrelly were featured. But critics and audiences did not take to the importation and it was soon withdrawn. The Vokes returned in a repertory of their song-studded farce-comedies: *In Honor Bound, My Milliner's Bill,* and *A Christmas Pantomime Rehearsal.* But the most successful "musical" was something of a curiosity. Richard Mansfield, heretofore a figure in the middle ranks of musical performers, began his career as a dramatic star with **Prince Karl.** To smooth the transition from the lyric to the dramatic stage, he inserted several tunes. The compromise pleased playgoers, and the show ran through the summer at the Madison Square.

May 3 also welcomed a new Charles Hoyt contrivance at the Standard, **A Tin Soldier.** It was typical of the works he was writing and producing at the time. A young couple attend a masked ball. The husband (George Boniface, Jr.) has got himself up in an array of kitchen utensils to look like a mock knight. He returns home early, and his servant, Rats, dons his master's costume. Rats runs off to the ball, where the obvious complications and confusions ensue. The ball setting allowed for the free and easy introduction of a number of vaudeville turns. As the *Dramatic Mirror* noted, the evening

metamorphosed into "a sugar coated variety olio punctuating the act with charming inconsistency." One character was named after the spanking new masterpiece that was the talk of New York. To this figure, Brooklyn Bridge (Paul Arthur), fell the "inevitable topical song with verses ad libitum." Led by young James T. Powers as Rats, the performers played for two months, after which the road extended a vigorous welcome.

The following Monday, May 10, brought in the biggest hit of the year, a show that remained popular for close to half a century. The Casino's mounting of an English work, **Erminie** (Harry Paulton/Edward Jakobowski), that had premiered only the preceding November 9 at London's Comedy Theatre gave it its longest run—571 performances—and secured the stardom of its principal comic, Francis Wilson.

. . .

Francis Wilson was born in Philadelphia on February 7, 1854, and made his debut at that city's historic Chestnut Street Opera House in 1878. At first he played mostly in dramas and comedies, but a prolonged stint with *Our Goblins* convinced him his future lay with musicals. His performances in early Casino shows such as *The Queen's Lace Handkerchief* and, especially, *Erminie,* gave him a firm leg up in the field. He sang the role of Cadeaux from *Erminie* nearly 1300 times. Unlike rubber-faced clowns of James T. Powers' ilk or an overwhelming hulk of a man such as De Wolf Hopper, the well-proportioned, finely featured Wilson, while as acrobatic as clowns of the day had to be, relied on an exceptional grace of movement and on a more intellectual approach than his great associates. In later years, when he felt he was too old for energetic antics, he became a successful lecturer and scholarly author. He also served Actors' Equity as founder and its first president.

. . .

Erminie was based on a long-popular play, *Robert Macaire.* Macaire and his cohort, Jacques Strop, were a pair of murderers who tie up a groom and steal his bride. For the heroine, her kidnapping is a blessing in disguise, freeing her from a marriage she hadn't wanted. In Paulton's retelling the menacing murderers became two harmless vagabonds, Ravennes (W. S. Daboll) and Cadeaux (Wilson). Pauline Hall played the heroine, Erminie. Daboll portrayed Ravennes as a dashing, plausible rascal, while Wilson emphasized Cadeaux's sympathetic, wistful side. Together the men won encores with

"We're A Philanthropic Couple." Erminie's delicate balance of the romantic and the picaresque established a model for a generation of comic operas. The show made comic rogues light-opera stereotypes, its pink ballroom set made pink as popular for rooms as *The Black Crook* (9-12-66) had made it for tights, and its "Lullaby" (Dear Mother, In Dreams I See Her") became one of the best-loved songs of the generation.

Lydia Thompson attempted to capitalize on the perennial appeal of nostalgia with a revival on May 17 of *Oxygen* (8-27-77). Judging by the reception, she would have been best advised to let aging playgoers survive with their memories intact. Two weeks at the 14th Street Theatre and she was gone.

McNish, Johnson, and Slavin's Minstrels followed the successful practice of troupes such as the Thatcher, Primrose, and West entourage by concentration on burlesque. They chose the still-running *The Little Tycoon,* distorting it under the name *Little Fly Coon.* The company was rewarded with two weeks of good business.

A pair of rival translations of Audran's *Le Serment d'Amour* opened two nights apart: **The Crowing Hen** at Wallack's on May 29 and **The Bridal Trap** at the Bijou on May 31. The latter was by the rambunctious, trouble-prone Sydney Rosenfeld. Broadway was more amused by the battle outside the houses than by the opéra bouffe itself. The Bijou and Wallack's faced each other across Broadway. Rosenfeld and his producers, Miles and Barton, put a stereopticon on the roof of the Bijou and projected insulting comments about *The Crowing Hen* on Wallack's facade. McCaull, the producer of *The Crowing Hen,* hired calcium lights to blot out the insults and then procured his own stereopticon to throw insults at the Bijou. The antics did little for the shows. *The Bridal Trap* closed on June 26, *The Crowing Hen* two weeks later. During their short stays both told how a peasant girl wins a count despite his aunt's stratagems. McCaull's cast, featuring Bertha Ricci, Mathilde Cottrelly, Signor Perugini, and De Wolf Hopper, was by far the better of the two.

An even worse flop was Millöcker's **The Maid of Belleville,** which opened at the Star on June 24 and closed July 7. Its love story was played out on a lower social level than was Audran's, for here a coy village lass settles for the sergeant of her dreams. June ended with another of the era's many comedies that sneaked a song or two into their action, *Humbug.* Then the season came to quiet finish in July with a revival of *Falka* at Wallack's.

1886-1887

There was little reason to cheer during this season. Wallack's great company, for example, was in its last year. When it disbanded, an institution and an era passed. Musically, the year again offered little but importations and revivals. New domestic contributions were few and far between. Neither they nor the imported novelties were particularly exciting.

August was busy, despite hot weather. Minstrelsy headed the parade when Lester and Allen's troupe arrived August 9 for a fortnight. The Bijou, like the Casino, eagerly eyed the possibility of keeping open all year long. When *Humbug* closed, the theatre, on August 16, offered its patrons a bit of summer fluff billed as a "musical comedy," **Soldiers and Sweethearts.** George Schleiffarth wrote music to Owen Westford and Susie Russell's scissors-and-paste book. Major Ashley (Westford) is worried about the irresponsible behavior of his son, Lt. Ashley (Frederick Darell). The young soldier's lady friends stage an amateur performance of *Satanella* (it occupied the whole second act) and then disguise themselves as soldiers to enter the barracks. The settings afforded an excuse for the standard Amazon march, while the newly de rigueur "topical song" was awarded to Henry V. Donnelly, who sang it with a conspicuously "Yankee twang." The show lasted three weeks, just long enough to keep the Bijou occupied until the next booking was available.

A more promising work failed even more miserably when it opened at the Standard the same night, August 16. **The Maid and the Moonshiner** had a libretto by Charles Hoyt and music by Edward Solomon. It starred two reigning favorites of the day, Lillian Russell and Tony Hart. Few new American musicals at the time offered a more encouraging lineup. Yet everything seemed to go wrong. Atrocious notices, heat, and backstage bickering toppled the piece after a dismal two-week run. For that short time, Upton O. Dodge (Hart), a bungling assistant moonshiner, helps his boss, Bourbon Miller (John E. Brand), win the hand of Virginia (Miss Russell) from a rich plantation owner (James Radcliffe). The action moved from a steamboat landing (showing the boat arrive), to a plantation, to a still in the Blue Ridge Mountains. Hart stopped the show with a comic number, "Flag

Of Truce," while Miss Russell won critical kudos for her "easy-going style." No one mentioned the name of the young man who assisted Hoyt in staging the work, Julian Mitchell. His efforts marked the beginning of a forty-year career that would make him the most prolific director in the history of The American Musical Theatre, although his value would not be appreciated until he flourished under the aegis of Weber and Fields. There is one amusing footnote to the fiasco. All Hoyt's early successes had titles beginning with the indefinite article "A." The failure of *The Maid and the Moonshiner* convinced him the indefinite article was his lucky talisman, and for the rest of his career all his shows had titles starting with "A."

Two revivals followed. The Kiralfys threw open the doors at Niblo's on August 21 with a remounting of *Around the World in Eighty Days* (8-28-75), while on the 31st Ned Harrigan began his season with a brief return of *Investigation* (9-1-84). The Kiralfys inserted the same "Mikado Ballet" they had used the preceding season in *The Black Crook*. Clearly it belonged here more naturally than in an international tour.

August's final entry was an importation. John McCaull brought over Victor Roger's **Josephine Sold by Her Sisters** (8-30-86, Wallack's) and enjoyed the profits from the French piece to mid-October. A janitress' daughter becomes an opera singer, but her jealous sisters arrange for an Egyptian pasha to kidnap her under the pretense of offering her a place at the Cairo opera. Louise Parker sang Josephine, Mathilde Cottrelly was the ringleader of the sisters, and De Wolf Hopper was the pasha.

The Bijou began its new season on September 13. From then until the end of April one man dominated its stage, Nat Goodwin. By and large his vehicles were much like *The Skating Rink* (11-23-85) he had offered the preceding year. In fact, *The Skating Rink* held the boards for a month beginning February 26. But for his opener Goodwin selected a new English work, **Little Jack Sheppard.** Loie Fuller assumed the title role, finding an appropriate moment to include her flowing-skirt dance. Yet Goodwin saw to it his part of Jonathan Wild remained pivotal. He stopped the show with an interpolated "topical song," sang a spoof of sentimental ballads and imitated the more celebrated performers then on Broadway. Critics accepted the work for the light frippery it was, although the *Times* did feel obligated to call attention to the increasing "display" of "limbs" by the chorus girls.

The not quite full-length musical was played until December with one or another additional short pieces.

With the Bijou booked, *Adonis* (9-4-84) played its first return engagement at the Fifth Avenue. Opening September 20, it arrived before many loyalists expected it. Great hopes had been held that *Adonis* would repeat its American success in London, but the London reception was cool, the run brief—150 performances. Dixey and his statue lingered in New York for two weeks before embarking on a national tour. The production returned again in May, recording an additional two months at the Bijou.

The run of *Erminie* was forced to suspend for the month of October when a previous commitment required the Casino to house **The Commodore,** an adaptation of Offenbach's *La Creole*. This story of an old seaman who would force his daughter to marry a man she doesn't like was brought over from England by the Earl of Lonsdale with an entirely English cast led by a young lady with an apparently notorious reputation, Violet Cameron. "One of the worst failures in the history of the Casino," there was no outcry to extend its planned stay. The commitment honored, Offenbach's work disappeared from Broadway annals, and *Erminie* resumed its run.

The following Monday, October 11, Ned Harrigan had his first new work of the year ready for inspection. Bernard O'Reagan, a saloon-keeper (Harrigan), receives a surprise visit from his English cousin and namesake (Joseph Sparks), who has come to America to collect for the Parnell fund. The American gives the Englishman a thousand dollars. The saloon-keeper is engaged to Bedalia McNeirney (Annie Yeamans), but in a change of heart has secretly married Bedalia's daughter, Kate (Amy Lee). Suspecting as much, Bedalia "borrows" the Parnell fund money to bribe the truth from Bernard's cronies. The money gets lost—stuck to some plaster—and the efforts to recover it lead to a series of brouhahas. These take the cast to Chinatown and the Salvation Army Headquarters and cause the black leader, Silas (John Wild), to fall through a skylight and into a fire. His wife, Lulu (Dan Collyer), protests she doesn't like "roasted coon." David Braham's best efforts are "The U.S. Black Marines" and "The Trumpet In The Cornfield Blows." Although **The O'Reagans** was not one of Harrigan and Braham's better efforts, it enjoyed a satisfactory run of sixteen weeks.

October also played host to a return visit of the

Thatcher, Primrose, and West Minstrels. The group returned in February for a second short stay. But lovers of minstrelsy could take heart when what promised to be a new permanent blackface band settled in as Dockstader's Minstrels. Both groups continued to give increasing emphasis to the burlesque portion of the bill. For instance, Dockstader rushed in his spoof, *Little Black Shepherd,* just two weeks after Goodwin's opening.

November's only entries were both revivals and both by Gilbert and Sullivan. *The Mikado* bowed on November 1, giving way three weeks later to *Princess Ida. Ida,* too, stayed for three weeks. Courtice Pounds, Geraldine Ulmar, and Signor Brocolini led both casts at the Fifth Avenue.

Goodwin had a new bit of foolery ready at the Bijou on December 11. In **Turned Up** Caraway Jones, a bibulous undertaker, with "carroty locks and goatee and a crimson nose," marries Sabina Medway (Jennie Weatherby), whom he believes to be the widow of a sea captain. But the knot is no sooner tied than Sabina's "dead" husband (C. B. Bishop) returns. The captain's chagrin is increased when an African queen appears who contends she is his wife. Jones brings about a happy ending by leaving with the Negress to run a plantation. Typical of Goodwin's business was his appearance as "a bridegroom in all his splendor." Moments later he is dunked in a river, and on emerging he fishes a cigar stub from his pocket and attempts to relight it with his waterlogged matches. The piece was by Mark Medway, with its songs borrowed from the usual variety of sources. Coupled with *Turned Up* was Goodwin's travesty of Henry Irving, *Those Bells.*

1887 began in a buzz of activity. Five musicals appeared in January led on the 3rd by yet another visit of *Evangeline* (7-27-74). It played a single week at Niblo's, departing to make room on the 17th for an even older favorite, *The Black Crook* (9-12-66). Featured were D'Alvini, a juggler, and an "Operetta Ballet," to music from then current or recent comic opera hits. Stalacta wove her magic for three weeks.

Most critics ignored the revival, preferring to give their attention to **Indiana** at the Star. Its name notwithstanding, *Indiana* was basically a French work with music by Audran. Its story centered on a heroine who complicates her life by resorting to disguises in order to spy on a fiancé she has never seen. Lilly Post assumed the title role, while Digby Bell was in charge of the comedy. H. B. Farnie's adaptation was not to New York's taste. Its producer, the busy John McCaull, did not accept the

judgment. Although he removed it after three weeks, he sent it touring, then brought it back for reconsideration in July. New York refused to reconsider.

For a change of pace, Goodwin dropped his brand of farce-comedies and mounted a production of *The Mascot* on January 24. Of course, given Goodwin's school of theatre, the presentation was far less faithful to the original than other mountings of the work New York had seen. While the insertion of specialties and interpolations had become commonplace in all but the most conscientiously staged importations, Goodwin carried domestication further than most performers. He showered patrons with imitations of celebrities, topical songs, and local allusions. But his audiences loved it. *The Mascot* ran a month and had a return engagement in late March.

January closed with Harrigan's second and last new work of the season, **McNooney's Visit.** In going to pay a call on Widow Gilmartin (Annie Yeamans), McNooney (Harrigan) inadvertently exchanges carpetbags with the man seated next to him on the train. The bag contains burglar's tools. McNooney is arrested, jailed, escapes, gets into a brawl, and is arrested and jailed again. Besides bringing in another widow, Harrigan resorted to one more old favorite device, a goat. Braham, too, was content to rest on his laurels, writing only three new songs. Not even as good as *The O'Reagans,* the play was nevertheless able to sustain itself on Harrigan's loyal following for ten weeks at the Park.

At the beginning of February John McCaull granted an interview to the *Times.* His pessimistic assessment of the lyric scene embraced both sides of the footlights. He knew of no Americans who could write good music, and insisted "we haven't even an American librettist as yet." His "as yet" was mildly hopeful, but he felt no urgent need for a fine native wordsmith: "My audiences will stand any amount of gags, and topical songs. It doesn't matter in the least how bad they are. Sometimes I think the worse they are the better they are appreciated." But McCaull did feel that "the music they require, however, must be good." If nothing else, the producer saw some didactic value in the lyric stage, concluding, "comic opera at the present time is far ahead of anything as a musical educator."

The irrepressible Nate Salsbury and his Troubadours practiced their fading art in a new piece, **The Humming Bird.** The *Times* insisted it could have been called "The Mongoose" or "The Ibis" with equal pertinence. Its specialties took place when some New Yorkers meet by chance at Shakespeare's statue in Central Park. Three weeks, and they were gone.

The season's most durable lyric work raised its curtain at the Fifth Avenue on February 21. As might be expected it was an importation. And as might also be guessed, it was another in Gilbert and Sullivan's great series. **Ruddigore** (spelled *Ruddygore* in contemporary programs and advertisements) has never ranked high in the Savoyard canon. In this, history has reflected the 1887 evaluation. But even second-best Gilbert and Sullivan was notably superior in wit, melody, style, and coherence to anything else then gracing the stage. D'Oyly Carte's ensemble played this story of a young man's over-coming a fatal, familial curse until only April 9. Principals included Courtice Pounds, George Thorne, Geraldine Ulmar, Kate Foster, and Fred Billington.

J. K. Emmet also opened on February 21 at the Standard, and surprisingly ran just one week less than *Ruddigore*. His vehicle was his old standby, *Fritz, Our Cousin German* (7-11-70), advertised with the seemingly inevitable "new songs" and "new scenes." The nuances of Emmet's career are probably lost forever. Still, it is curious to see him, after so many years of playing short engagements at backwater houses, once again enjoying a reason-ably extended stay at a major theatre. Was there a sudden wave of nostalgia or perhaps some premoni-tion that Emmet's days were numbered?

The next Monday, February 28, also welcomed a pair of musicals. McCaull supplanted *Indiana* at the Star with yet another importation, Rudolph Dellinger's **Lorraine,** adapted by W. J. Henderson. Perhaps rashly, McCaull had contracted for this story of Louis XIII's natural son finding romance at Louis XIV's court before its German premiere. Signor Perugini, De Wolf Hopper, Mathilde Cot-trelly, and Gertrude Griswold sparked the proceed-ings. But their antics were not enough. The musi-cal fared even less well than its predecessor, fad-ing away after two weeks. Competing with it for first-nighters was the return of *The Skating Rink* mentioned earlier.

The season's last original work arrived on March 31. It was the closing salvo in Nat Goodwin's series of farce-comedy plays. **Big Pony, or The Gentle-manly Savage** had a book by A. C. Wheeler and music by Edward Darling. Goodwin played an In-dian—in dress suit and soft hat—whose attempts to settle some family quarrels take him not just to the Wild West but to Mexico and Spain as well. He was assisted again by Loie Fuller in her nimble skirt dances. The piece played three weeks until

Goodwin decided to bring back *Little Jack Shep-pard* for a week to close his stay.

By April the season was effectively finished. Eight more musicals followed. All were revivals. In order of their appearance they were *A Trip to Africa* on April 11; *Cordelia's Aspirations* (11-5-83) (the only native work) on April 18; *The Gypsy Baron* on May 2; *The Black Hussar,* May 7; *Gasparone,* May 16; *Iolanthe,* May 30; *Falka,* May 31; and *The Beggar Student,* July 25.

Away from the heart of Broadway the season saw constant activity. None of it was really impor-tant, most of the plays seem hopelessly lost; yet it should be given a moment's notice. For example, in his history of the New York stage, Odell re-cords the two-week engagement at a minor combi-nation house of *The Red Fox,* "another of those frequent Irish plays of political and sentimental in-terest, interspersed with an occasional song." At the Oriental Theatre, once the Bowery Gardens, musicals catering to the area's Jewish audiences were beginning to be mounted. The leading com-poser appears to have been Joseph Lateiner, and the year's programs included his "musical drama" *Emigration to America* and his "historical oper-etta" *Joseph and His Brothers.* The former began with a pogrom in Balta and took those who escaped to Ellis Island, to an East Side ghetto, and to a triumphal wedding. Clearly, both the Irish and, more slowly, the Jews—two definitive influences on the American Musical Theatre—were preparing the way for the future.

1887-1888

In retrospect the 1887–88 season seems distress-ingly lackluster. Yet in its own day it clearly marked an improvement over the preceding year. If no novelty as enduring as *Ruddigore* appeared, it must be remembered that *Ruddigore*'s premiere was a disappointment. The event of the year was un-theatrical: the great blizzard of March 12. It pro-vided New Yorkers with lifelong memories far more vivid than those afforded by any musical of the day. In the theatre itself the most newsworthy oc-currences were the burning of the Union Square Theatre in February and two benefits. The first of these benefits was held for Tony Hart at the Acad-emy of Music. Originally scheduled for March 15, it was postponed a week by the blizzard's after-effects. On May 21 the Metropolitan Opera House was the scene of a similar gala for the great actor and impresario Lester Wallack. Both men were seriously ill and Hart by this time hopelessly insane. Neither ever again played for their public.

August gave the season a sluggish opening. The Kiralfys relit Niblo's on the 17th with their version of John Brougham's old melodrama, *The Duke's Motto.* They rechristened the work **Lagardère,** filled it with ballet and spectacle, and gave the popular Maurice Barrymore the title role of a duke who disguises himself as a hunchback to achieve his ends. A gypsy ballet and a ballet based on Shakespeare's seven ages of man offered diversions from the plot. The Kiralfys were rewarded with a two-month run.

John McCaull and his comic opera company had almost as long a stay with their importation of a minor German operetta, Ralba's **Bellman.** The fine singer-actor Hubert Wilke, Marion Manola, and two rising young comedians, De Wolf Hopper and Jefferson De Angelis, headed the cast. Wilke played the title role, a poet who loves and wins a countess. De Angelis and Harry MacDonough played two Jewish powder-makers. Jews as comic figures—often passed off as Dutchmen—would soon become stock-in-trade of musicals. But these were among the first, and the *Times* was at once appalled and amused at how much time they were allotted. Hopper cavorted as an upstart, pompous millionaire. The work ran at Wallack's from August 22 to October 8. Its first night coincided with the return at the Star of McNish, Johnson, and Slavin's Refined Minstrels.

A trio of musicals appeared on September 12. The least musical, if not the least substantial, was a burlesque, **The Wily West,** in which John T. Kelly amused patrons at Harrigan's Park Theatre. Its hero, inspired by tales of Buffalo Bill, gives up a position as a dry-goods clerk and goes west. On the same night, one of the final offerings of Rice's Surprise Party, **A Circus in Town,** romped into the Bijou. The faithful John A. Mackay was in the lead. Edward Holst and Woolson Morse concocted the piece, but the work was too much of a fading school to win acceptance. Oddly enough, though, the story touched gingerly on a new, ominous, social problem—labor unrest. Circus performers call a strike. One performer writes a love note to the circus owner's wife and spends the rest of the evening contriving its return after he learns his boss is insanely jealous. Nonetheless, several reviewers insisted the piece had no sustained plot. The *Times* recorded, "The music included a drinking chorus,

a rather effective 'dude quartet' and a sentimental solo." The show was abruptly withdrawn in a rare mid-week closing on September 22, and a similar troupe with a similar piece, Salsbury's Troubadours in *The Humming Bird,* dutifully filled the remaining three weeks of the stand. This time around it offered Nellie McHenry's take-off of Ophelia.

The third opening was important, although the play itself was minor and not especially successful. The show was a Chicago mounting, **The Arabian Nights, or, Aladdin's Wonderful Lamp.** It was a traditional burlesque-pantomime in which the hero was played as a trouser role. In this instance Loie Fuller portrayed Aladdin. The show's importance lay in its Chicago origins. The city was rapidly becoming a major production center. Under the aegis of David Henderson, the producer of the work, an era was beginning there. Henderson was determined to present musicals of the highest quality at the newly built Chicago Opera House and decided on elaborate spectacles in the English tradition as the best way to impress Chicagoans. And impressed they were! When the Imperial Burlesque Company (as Henderson initially called his troupe) opened there on June 4, 1877, lavish effects such as a widow's shanty transformed into a glittering boudoir elicited such applause that the play was forced to halt while the scene painter was called on stage for a bow. Henderson's career was to be brief, but more than any other man he probably pioneered the now virtually forgotten and dismayingly underrated school of Chicago musicals. *The Arabian Nights* ran until the end of October. Its failure to repeat its Chicago success in New York continued a sad and only occasionally broken precedent.

The Casino's season got under way with another of the house's importations, **The Marquis.** For this American version of Paul Lacombe's *Jeanne, Jeanette et Jeanneton,* the heroines' names were changed to Mae, Marie, and Marion. The French title more accurately reflected the plot which centered on three country girls who arrive together in Paris. One sets up a cabaret, one becomes a dancer, while the third marries into the nobility. Bertha Ricci, Isabelle Urquhart, and Sylvia Gerrish were aided in unfolding the story by Mark Smith, Courtice Pounds, Max Freeman, Henri Leoni, and James T. Powers. Despite so fine a cast of Casino favorites, the show failed to repeat the runaway success of its precedessor, *Erminie* (5-10-86). Even so, it ran profitably from September 19 to December 3.

September closed with the season's lone visit of an opéra bouffe company to the city. Although

Maurice Grau was the producer, he no longer had a glittering star to lead his entourage. He was, moreover, presenting an art form fast losing vogue. Grau seems to have acknowledged opéra bouffe's waning popularity by including in his repertory one German operetta, *Fatinitza*. The French works included *Le Grand Mogul, Serment d'Amour, La Fille de Mme. Angot,* and *La Mascotte.* The troupe departed Wallack's after three weeks of disappointing business.

With Hart gone, Ned Harrigan's creative abilities inexplicably continued to wane. He came to rely increasingly on revivals of his old favorites. To open his 1887–88 season he brought back *The Leather Patch* (2-15-86) for a month's run beginning October 10.

A far more successful and an original work by E. E. Rice and John Braham opened at the Bijou on the 18th. At least, **The Corsair** was original in that it was new. A travesty of Byron's poem, it featured Amelia Summerville as Conrad. Frank David as a sub-Corsair was given the requisite topical song. Equally requisite was an Amazon march. A trick dancing mule and a telephone that summoned with a cowbell added humorous touches. As a result, the production by Henry E. Dixey, in association with Miles and Barton, was so sumptuous and the evening so lively that patrons ignored its general critical rejection and flocked to the show for 180 performances. Dockstader's Minstrels spoofed the work as *The Coarse Hair.*

November 5 witnessed the American premiere of **Dorothy** at the Standard. This comic opera by Gilbert and Sullivan's erstwhile conductor, Alfred Cellier, had outrun *The Mikado* in London. Two young English ladies condescend to act as barmaids during a harvest festival. They fall in love with two customers. One of the men, Geoffrey, prefers his newfound country wench to the girl his rich uncle demands he marry, someone named Dorothy. Circumstances lead the girls to disguise themselves as men and challenge their new beaux to duels. Of course, in the end Dorothy and one of the serving girls prove to be one and the same. The two pairs of lovers wed. Lillian Russell sang Dorothy; Marie Halton was her conspirator-cousin. Harry Paulton, Eugene Oudin, John E. Brand, and William Hamilton were the principal males. New York foretold *Dorothy*'s future reckoning by judging it pleasant, but inferior. It enjoyed only modest returns, playing until December 17.

Two nights after *Dorothy*'s arrival, Harrigan brought in his second offering of the year and his second revival, *Cordelia's Aspirations* (11-5-83). Apparently a stopgap booking, it stayed for just two weeks until Harrigan had his lone new work ready to present.

For the second time in the season a minor work of great significance raised its curtain in New York. John McCaull's company gave New Yorkers their first view of **The Begum** (11-21-87, Fifth Ave.), thereby introducing theatregoers to two new names that would loom large in the future—Reginald De Koven and Harry B. Smith.

* * *

Reginald De Koven was born in Middletown, Connecticut, on April 3, 1859. When he was thirteen his clergyman father moved his family to England. The young man was educated at Oxford and then went to Germany and France to pursue his musical studies. In Paris he worked under the tutelage of Leo Delibes. He returned to America, settling in Chicago. After a brief stint in business, a marriage to a wealthy girl allowed him to abandon day-to-day drudgery and concentrate on composing.

* * *

Harry B. Smith was born in Buffalo, New York, on December 28, 1860. His family moved to Chicago, where he began earning a living as a newspaper man. Stints as a music critic and then as a drama critic whetted his appetite for the stage. In time he became the most prolific librettist and lyricist in history. By his own estimate he wrote (alone or with collaborators) books for over 300 shows and lyrics for some 6000 songs. He was the first American lyricist honored by the publication of an anthology of his lyrics.

* * *

Smith's first libretto set the style that he would follow for the rest of his long career. The Begum of Oude has a simple way of disposing of a husband who has come to bore her. She merely makes him her General-in-Chief, declares war, and sends him off to die in battle. But when her latest spouse, Howja-Dhu, engages the enemy, he returns unobligingly victorious. She has no choice but to accept the results. Mathilde Cottrelly portrayed the Begum and De Wolf Hopper played Howja-Dhu. Besides Howja-Dhu, the cast of characters was filled with absurd names so beloved by writers of the day. Hubert Wilke enacted Klahm-Chowdee; Digby Bell, Myhnt-Jhuleep; and Jefferson De Angelis, Jhustt-Naut. This journeyman effort failed to please New Yorkers (although the *Times* praised both the show and McCaull's courage in mounting an American work), but the sensible economics of the time allowed McCaull to pack the show on to Chicago, where De Koven's social standing enabled the producer to have a profitable run and recoup his costs.

Harrigan's only new work of the season, **Pete,** bowed on November 22. When he was in partnership with Hart, he often wrote blackface roles for his associates, notably Rebecca Allup for Hart. But he rarely assumed black roles himself. Now he created and played the principal role of a faithful Negro servant. Pete is an ex-slave and the guardian of a supposedly illegitimate girl (Dan Collyer). He proves her legitimacy to enable her to receive an inheritance. In one great scene Harrigan won vociferous approval telling in pantomime how the girl's father had died in battle. David Braham's best numbers were "The Old Black Crow" and "The Old Barn Floor." Although closer than most Harrigan works to serious Victorian melodrama, the show was an immediate hit, running 170 performances before it closed on April 21. Harrigan's still loyal following was not upset by his opening night apology for not completely forgetting some of his Irish mannerisms.

December's solitary entry, on the 5th, was still another in the Casino's continuing parade of importations, Lecocq's **Madelon.** Lillian Grubb, Bertha Ricci, Isabelle Urquhart, Mark Smith, James T. Powers, and Courtice Pounds (condemned by the *Herald* for his "high collar" voice) acted out this interweaving of romantic and comic liaisons, in which, for example, an innkeeper's wife plans to elope with a sausage maker. It opened on December 5 and played for just over a month.

If the Casino remained steadfast in its dependence on importations, the Kiralfys stuck with equal tenacity to their peculiar brand of musical spectacle. They ushered in 1888 with one more of the type, **Mazulm, the Night Owl.** Adapted from an old pantomime, its cast of 300 traveled to "The Palace of Jewels" and watched a "Japanese Ballet." The mounting occupied the spacious Academy of Music from January 9 through March 10.

The Boston Ideal Opera Company returned for one of their periodic visits on January 16. The program consisted largely of works that today would be confined to grand opera houses—*The Elixir of Love, The Daughter of the Regiment, Martha, Carmen,* and *Fra Diavolo.* In a slightly lighter vein they also offered Firmin Bernicat's *François la Basbleu* as *Victor, the Bluestocking.* After a month at the Fifth Avenue they moved to Niblo's for a final week and then set off again for the hinterlands. Their opening night coincided with the return of

Erminie to the Casino, where the work chalked up an additional 136 performances. Pauline Hall, Francis Wilson, and W. S. Daboll were back to recreate their original roles.

Just before the Boston company spent its week at Niblo's, the Thatcher, Primrose, and West Minstrels played a week at the house. They were the second blackface entourage to entertain there, the Progressive Minstrels, a lesser touring band, having played the house for a week in November. But minstrelsy was undeniably dying. Dockstader's Minstrels, who had attempted to follow in the path of the San Francisco Minstrels by offering New York a permanent company, threw in the towel in February and took to the road.

February's only other musicals were brief returns by the Salsbury Troubadours in *Three of a Kind* (2-15-86) and Nat Goodwin in *Turned Up* (12-11-86). Goodwin continued to turn up in this and his other pieces at combination houses—theatres devoted to touring plays—for the next several seasons, but Nate Salsbury was preparing to leave the theatre to run Buffalo Bill's traveling Wild West show.

March, like December, had only one musical arrival. And as in December, the piece was a work by Lecocq. A revival of *The Pearl of Pekin (La Fleur de Thé),* laced with interpolations by Gustave Kerker, was made moderately welcome, keeping the Bijou lit until the end of May.

The Kiralfys had yet one more of their unique mountings at Niblo's ready on April 2 when they unveiled their version of Sardou's *La Patrie* as **Dolores.** Incongruous ballets, such as a gypsy number with the principals all in black, and "Dresdenia" with the ensemble made to resemble Dresden china, bore little or no relation to a tale of a Flemish count who is forced to take no action on his wife's infidelity lest he reveal he is a revolutionary. The mounting lasted two weeks.

Rosina Vokes also made an appearance in April. She offered the same fare her family had been regaling playgoers with for nearly two decades. April's last entry was another revival, Harrigan's *Old Lavender* (9-3-78). The public refused it the affection Harrigan bestowed on it, and Harrigan closed the play in two weeks' time, closing his season as well.

The first musical to play the new Broadway Theatre at 41st Street arrived on May 2. Although the theatre for years was to be one of New York's principal homes of musicals, its opening had been awarded to Fanny Davenport in *La Tosca,* Sardou's play. But the initial lyric attraction had luminaries enough, with Camille D'Arville and Lillian Russell sharing starring honors. Like *La Tosca,* **The Queen's Mate** had started its career as a Parisian hit, Lecocq's *La Princesse de Canaries.* This retitled revival was presented in an adaptation by Harry Paulton, who had collaborated on *Erminie.* Paulton also played a major role in the company. The show was a resounding hit. Except for a brief summer vacation it ran on steadily into the fall.

McCaull and his company were soon ready with another new American work. **The Lady or the Tiger?** (5-7-88, Bijou) was based on Frank R. Stockton's short story of the same name. The new work had a book by Sydney Rosenfeld and music by Julius J. Lyons and McCaull's conductor, Adolph Nowack. In the original tale the hero and emperor's daughter are in love, but the hero is to be fed to the lions. There are two doors in the arena. One opens to unleash the hungry lion and bring the hero instant death. The other opens to bring forth a beautiful maiden and instant marriage. In either case, the emperor's daughter will lose her beloved. She indicates which door to choose and the hero opens it. The story ended there, leaving the reader to guess what was in the princess' mind. The most celebrated change made by Rosenfeld was to let the audience see the princess' selection. It turns out to be an old hag. Although the show was coolly received by the critics, it played comfortably until the end of June. No doubt the presence in the cast of De Wolf Hopper, Jefferson De Angelis, and Mathilde Cottrelly (this time as the old crone) induced playgoers to ignore the critical verdict.

A week later the Casino displayed its summer attraction—Francis Chassaigne's **Nadjy.** The love of a margrave's nephew for his Nadjy triumphs over his emperor's command to marry a girl the monarch has kidnaped for him. Richard Barker, D'Oyly Carte's assistant, who became the era's leading transatlantic director of musicals, staged the work, with Marie Jansen in the title part and Isabelle Urquhart, Mark Smith, and James T. Powers in support. The Casino's faith in the work was justified and the piece played merrily on until mid-October.

John McCaull's band closed the season with a revival of Johann Strauss' *Prince Methusalem.* It ran for a month, and but for one instance should be no more than a passing footnote in the history of the American Musical Theatre. Sometime during the run and somewhere in the second act, De Wolf Hopper departed from the text and inserted a poem, "Casey at the Bat," by Ernest Lawrence Thayer. Just how Hopper justified the insertion of this bit of baseball lore into an operetta will prob-

ably never be known. But his reading drew insistent encores, and for the rest of his career there was hardly a performance in which Hopper was not called on to recite the piece. The interpolation vividly illustrates the freewheeling attitudes of late 19th-century authors and performers, and the easygoing acceptance of their audiences. In later years, when consistent stylistic tone and creative integrity came to matter more, Hopper often found the poem had to be recited at intermission or during curtain calls instead of in mid-performance. Hopper, for the record, recalled the date of his first recitation as May 13, 1888—a Sunday when there was no regular performance. Even so, this would make his first reading of the piece take place during the run of *The Lady or the Tiger?* But Hopper insisted *Prince Methusalem* was the show.

All through the season combination houses offered works with musical interludes. For example, W. J. Scanlan, his career almost at its end, appeared in *The Irish Minstrel* by Fred Marsden. Scanlan, like J. K. Emmet, generally took credit for the songs in his pieces. But so responsible and good-natured a scholar as Odell alluded to persistent accusations when he wrote of them, "each purveyor was declared to have composed his most popular melody." Odell unwittingly recorded the uncertain vagaries of fame when, writing in his history of the New York theatre in 1941, he added that both Emmet's "Lullaby" and Scanlan's "Peek-A-Boo" were still sung. He could not have reiterated the statement thirty-five years later.

1888-1889

In number and in quality the preceding season had marked the lowest ebb since the onrush that followed *H.M.S. Pinafore* (1-15-79). There was a slight upturn in the new season, but it was deceptive. There were simply more revivals or return engagements. And a small rise in quality was largely attributable to a single importation: *The Yeomen of the Guard.*

The season got off to a slow start. Only two musical offerings bowed in August; only two in September. Each month disclosed one novelty and one revival. The first new musical of the year was a Kiralfy production. But in this instance it was produced by just one of the brothers, Bolossy. His private family bickerings scarcely affected the mounting the public saw. **Mathias Sandorf** was a typical period melodrama bedecked with typical Kiralfy splendour (there was real water in the waterfall) and studded with typical Kiralfy specialty acts and ballets. In true Kiralfy fashion "the ballet took precedence of dramatic values." The story followed the perilous career of a Hungarian patriot. Condemned to death, he escapes, makes a fortune overseas, and uses his wealth to take revenge on his betrayers. Of course, as with most of the family's productions, *Mathias Sandorf* was housed at Niblo's, enjoying the theatre's shelter from August 18 through October 13.

The two revivals followed in short order. Dellinger's *Lorraine* arrived two nights after *Mathias Sandorf*. It played for just a fortnight and was replaced at the same house, Wallack's, by a month-long run of von Suppé's *Boccaccio*. Marion Manola, De Wolf Hopper, Jefferson De Angelis, and Annie Myers figured prominently in both, with Digby Bell joining them in the second.

Waddy Googan, Harrigan and Braham's only original effort for the season, opened on September 3, the same night *Boccaccio* returned. Ned Harrigan's compassion for the underdogs of any racial or religious group was again asserted in his simple story. Waddy Googan (Harrigan) is a hack driver. His wife Mary (Annie Yeamans) keeps a small restaurant. Together they see that justice is done to Bianca (Annie O'Neill), an Italian waif they have adopted, and that punishment is meted out to her harasser, Shang Wilkins (Charles Sturges). But Harrigan could put his personally generous feelings aside to record accurately the prejudices of his characters. One figure remarks, "De Irish is de wise man, de German is de fool," while another comments, "the Irish can crowd the Dutch out dead or alive." Unwittingly Harrigan also demonstrated how one century's complaints and problems are repeated in the next. At one point this bit of dialogue occurs:

Mary: ... that's the garbage fleet
Waddy: Yes and when they dump the garbage they choke the channels of our harbor.
Mary: Yes and kill all the fish.

Later Mary explodes, "Bad luck to the street gangs I say. They're like two armies fighting, when school is out." Harrigan's exceedingly large cast of characters often surpassed the resources of his good-sized company. This, plus probably the desire for a small *tour de force*, prompted Harrigan to play not only the title role but the minor part of Joe Cornello as well. Reviews of the era rarely mentioned the dancing in Harrigan and Hart musicals,

but the *Times* noted that a tarantella stopped the show and that a march by the midnight police squad at the second precinct also won applause. Abetted by David Braham's pleasant melodies, *Waddy Googan* survived until December 3.

The Star Theatre played host to a new farce-comedy, **Zig-Zag,** for two weeks beginning October 1. The slightest of plots took patrons of a Turkish bath for a spree on Mount Olympus. Its reception was more enthusiastic than either its producers or the theatre had expected. Although the *Herald* sneered, "unutterable trash," the public disagreed. Previous commitments forced it to be pulled when its initial booking ended, but word-of-mouth enthusiasm brought it back for two more engagements later in the season: one at Niblo's and one at the Bijou.

October's next entry was a second farce-comedy. Charles Hoyt's **A Brass Monkey** bowed at the Bijou on October 15 and compiled a run of 104 showings before it closed on January 4. An old auctioneer named Doolittle Work (Alf M. Hampton) has always ridiculed his superstitious friends who have insisted the brass monkey he forever carries has caused the breakup of his four marriages. He dies, bequeathing his estate to his nephew, Dodge Work (Tim Murphy), on the condition the young man retain the brass monkey. When the nephew's own marriage starts to come apart he puts the monkey up for auction. The show was the first of three Hoyt works to be staged during the year. *A Tin Soldier* (5-3-85) was revived at the 14th Street Theatre on December 24 with a cast that included the young Marie Cahill, while *A Midnight Bell* premiered at the Bijou on March 5, offering in its cast Thomas Q. Seabrooke, who later starred in a number of musical comedies, and introducing a sixteen-year-old Maude Adams, who went on to fame in less lyric enterprises. Although a comedy, *A Midnight Bell* was a more serious attempt by Hoyt at playwriting. The specialties that Hoyt contrived to inject in his other pieces were omitted.

October 15 also witnessed Lydia Thompson's second attempt at a comeback. Like *Ixion* (9-28-68) just twenty years before, **Penelope** resorted to classic legend for its plot. Miss Thompson was garbed as Ulysses to show her still attractive features to best advantage. But librettist H. P. Stevens and composer Edward Solomon concocted a weak vehicle that only emphasized the passing of a once fresh art. *Penelope* folded forlornly after a single week at the Star.

The first of two happy gifts from England arrived at the Casino on the 17th. Gilbert and Sullivan's **The Yeomen of the Guard** demonstrated the continuing vitality of the English musical stage. Richard Barker directed this tale of a jester's unrequited love, with J. H. Ryley as Jack Point, George Broderick as Sir Richard, Henry Hallam as Colonel Fairfax, George Olmi as Sgt. Meryll, Charles Renwick as Leonard Meryll, Fred Solomon as Wilfred Shadbolt, Bertha Ricci as Elsie Maynard, Sylvia Gerrish as Phoebe, Isabelle Urquhart as Dame Carruthers, and Kate Uart as Kate. Perhaps because the musical touched on tragedy its reception was somewhat restrained. But it ran into January, inscribing 100 performances in the record book and winding up on the happy side of the ledger.

An older English masterpiece, *A Midsummer Night's Dream,* closed out the month at the Star. Of course it was not really a musical, but in keeping with a common practice of the day this production was prodigal in its presentation of ballet and occasional songs.

While Lew Dockstader made another effort to establish a permanent company at the auditorium that once housed the San Francisco Minstrels, he had to tinker desperately with traditional formulas to keep his box office humming. The whole month of January was devoted to a farce-comedy, *Kitty,* and when it closed the bills that followed looked very much like standard variety. The lone visit by a minstrel troupe presenting anything that resembled the old format occurred when Thatcher, Primrose, and West began a brief stay on November 5.

Starting November 12, Henry E. Dixey and *Adonis* (9-4-84) paid a two-week visit to the Star just below the heart of the theatrical district that then ran from Union Square to slightly above Herald Square. The show and its star were also available to theatregoers unwilling to stray far from their home neighborhoods. For example, in May the production visited the Grand Opera House, now given over almost wholly to touring attractions. During the season this same house played most to the preceding season's hits—*The Irish Minstrel* (4-9-88), *The Corsair* (10-18-87), and an opéra bouffe troupe.

Just a month after Lydia Thompson's failure and the Savoyard success, England offered America a new delight. The fame of George Edwardes' London Gaiety Burlesque Theatre, of its cheery musicals and, most of all, of its lovely dancing girls, whetted appetites and stimulated advance sales at the Standard. When **Monte Cristo, Jr.** opened on November 15 the great expectations proved a

stumbling block. An uneasy sense of disappointment set in. Most of the regrets were directed toward the quality of the work itself, a travesty in doggerel verse of Dumas' tale. But the English girls, led by small, slender, husky-voiced Nellie Farren and augmented by a number of American beauties, elicited the happiest applause and began a new rage on the lyric stage. As Odell records, "a bevy of young and beautiful English girls introduced us to a new style of dancing in long, swishy skirts that immediately caught our fancy and started a fashion, a craze, that lasted here several years. Tights went out and the lovely skirt dancing came in." Actually, the flowing grace of this style of choreography already had been seen by Americans in the dancing of Loie Fuller. But she was a solo performer. It was the cumulative effect of an entire line of lovely young ladies in movement that so strongly impressed itself on susceptible theatregoers. The impression was reinforced when the English company replaced *Monte Cristo, Jr.* with a more acceptable piece, **Miss Esmeralda,** on December 17. This burlesque of the Esmeralda-Captain Phoebus romance from *The Hunchback of Notre Dame* ran until January 5 when contracts took the company on tour. It returned with both shows in two other engagements during the winter and spring.

Chicago, too, was prepared to offer New York its wares. On November 26, that city's version of the Cinderella tale traveled east after a six-month run at home. Alfred Thompson and Harry B. Smith made the adaptation and David Henderson mounted it. In **The Crystal Slipper** Cinderella (Marguerite Fish) is a "slavey" in the castle of Baron von Anthracite (R. E. Graham). Her only friends are the Baron's valet, Yosemite, and the Baron's mouser, Thomas Cat. Of course, the good Prince Polydore von Prettiwitz (Mamie Cerbi) comes to her rescue. Although the New York run of four weeks fell far short of its home stand, the visit did call New Yorkers' attention to two rising stage clowns. Yosemite was played by Eddie Foy and the cat by George Ali. Ali, as Foy recalled in his autobiography, "spent almost his entire career inside a caricatured imitation of some animal's skin." Miss Fish added an exotic touch to the evening. Only recently arrived from Vienna, she played Cinderella with a German accent.

Apart from *A Tin Soldier* and *Miss Esmeralda,* the only December offering to be classed as a musical was the revival of *The Lorgaire* (11-25-78). Harrigan and Braham apparently no longer had the creative drive to produce a string of new plays each season. But it remains to Harrigan's credit as a producer that he did not attempt to fall back comfortably on one or two of his biggest hits to complete his season. Harrigan drew from the whole range of his canon. But Harrigan's audiences were not as brave nor were they as willing to rehear anything but the best. As a result Harrigan had to make frequent changes on his posters throughout the season. His 1878 work gave way to his year-old *Pete* (11-22-87) on January 31 and this in turn to a work from a year earlier, *The O'Reagans* (10-11-86), on March 4. When this failed, Harrigan endeavored to present an old acquaintance under a new name. *4-11-44,* which opened on March 21, was merely a minor rewriting of *McNooney's Visit* (1-31-87). Three weeks later he rushed in *The Grip* (11-30-85). This lasted only a week when a discouraged Harrigan abruptly terminated the season and announced he was leaving the Park.

January 1889 was almost entirely given over to revivals and return engagements. Both *The Queen's Mate* and *The Pearl of Pekin* paid return calls on the 7th. On the 21st the Casino brought back its production of *Nadjy* for an additional three months. And *Pete* closed out the month at the Park. The sole new "musical" was **Myles Aroon** by George Jessop and Horace Townsend. It was a vehicle for Scanlan in which he introduced a handful of songs into the romantic piece as was his wont. The work remained for just two weeks at the 14th Street, since Scanlan's most loyal followers took their patronage to more outlying houses.

In contrast to January, February had a number of novelties and no revivals. Two openings occurred on the 11th. Bolossy Kiralfy mounted still another spectacle at Niblo's, **The Water Queen.** This saga of the Queen of the Rhine's love for a mortal lasted only three weeks. **Later On,** which debuted at the Star, fared even more unhappily, surviving a single week. On February 25 the same house brought in **Said Pasha.** Although the show had apparently been mounted independently in San Francisco, this production had originated in Philadelphia, and New York chose to view it as another horrible example of the "Philadelphia school." Sung to Richard Stahl's music, Scott Marble's story told how the Pasha (Francis Gaillard) attempts to circumnavigate the globe in record time. His daughter Serena (Helen Dingeon) accompanies him to be with her lover, Hassen Bey (R. N. Dunbar). A Mexican (Hubert Wilke) in search of a perfect woman almost persuades Serena to change her affections. The music was undistinguished, although far more sophisticated than Spenser's. But some of Marble's dialogue could have justified New York-

ers' seeing a Philadelphia influence in the work. For example, just as one character in *The Little Tycoon* (3-24-86) grunted his way through the story, a comic figure named Nockey (Stanley Felch) spent the evening giving every possible inflection to a single word, "why." To drive the knife home, critics found the harem of chorus girls especially unattractive. Although the production played only a fortnight, it returned after a road tour for a second Rialto engagement in April.

March reverted to the safety or necessity of revivals. All stays were brief. Harrigan's presentations aside, the month welcomed a touring company of *Evangeline* at the Star and John McCaull's production of von Suppé's *Boccaccio* at Palmer's. This latter house had been Wallack's, but with Broadway's lack of respect for the past and pandering to raging egos it had been renamed the moment Wallack died.

April was surprisingly busy. In a way it was also varied, even if much of the variety stemmed from works written years before. The openings of the 1st were illustrative. McCaull replaced *Boccaccio* at Palmer's with another importation, Czibulka's *The May Queen.* At the same time, the sturdy *Erminie* came in to Niblo's for a week. Seven nights later Harrigan's *The Grip* also began a week's stand.

Two novelties vied for attention on April 22. One was an American operetta, **Dovetta.** Its authors were Betsy Banker and Charles Raynaud; its composer, Mrs. E. Marcy Raymond. In their story Dovetta (Fatmah Diard) was an American Indian, torn between her love for the Indian brave, Rainbow (Joseph Lynde), and Lt. Robert Brambleton (W. S. Rising) of the U.S. Army. When she learns she is actually white, adopted by the chief after a raid on a settlement, she selects Robert. Some of Robert's fellow officers were Clubby and Broomy, played by Hattie Delaro and Ruby Stuart as trouser roles. Together the girls led the expected Amazon march. The work barely managed to stay alive beyond its first week at the Standard, lingering only for a few matinees. The *Times'* treatment of the work indicates the fundamental disbelief then held in many quarters in our native ability to match England's musicals. On the front page of its Sunday edition for May 21, the paper devoted a long article —with review—to the London opening of Alfred Cellier's *Doris.* In the theatre news on page 5 the paper noted tersely, almost incredulously, that *Dovetta* would open the following night and that "there is opportunity for the success of an American work and it is to be sincerely hoped that new production will be found excellent." Two days later a one-paragraph review dismissed the piece without any kind words, suggesting as a parting shot that New York could create musicals every bit as bad as Philadelphia's.

The other newcomer was an immediate hit. **Fritz in a Madhouse** gave J. K. Emmet his first new vehicle in several years. The plot was preposterously involved. Fritz is the son of the Baron von Wolfenstein (Harold Hartsell). The baron disowns the boy after he is jailed. What the baron does not know is that his son was jailed fighting in defense of a lady. Fritz loves Collie (Louise Balfe), a daughter of rich, uncouth Joe Parker (Edmund D. Lyons). Mrs. Parker (Ethel Greybrooke), a social climber, disdains her husband and his affectionate daughter. She has sent her son (C. D. Bennett) away to be educated out of reach of his father and sister's compromising influences. A letter leads Mrs. Parker to think her husband is having an affair. Fritz eventually must show her that it was her son, not her husband, who was the subject of the letter and that it was her son's attempt to abuse a lady that landed Fritz in a fight and in jail. Although the last act was set in a madhouse the setting was only an incidental accommodation to the title. The real source of the title was a line of Fritz's in the play, ". . . dis world is one great madhouse—and love is de only disease worth catching." Actually the original title had been *Uncle Joe*. The emphasis and the title were changed when Emmet saw possibilities in the story. Devotees flocked to the 14th Street Theatre for seven weeks before Emmet adjourned for vacation and a planned road tour.

The two novelties were followed on April 29 at the Standard by Imre Kiralfy's revival of *The Black Crook* (9-12-66), still a dependable, albeit fading, standby. It was good for a two-week stand. Kiralfy's staging ignored a growing reaction against the old piece. The *Times* exemplified this new feeling when, in its review of *The Water Queen*, it gratuitously branded *The Black Crook* "probably the stupidest stage play ever invented."

By May producers and theatre owners began to be concerned about keeping their houses lit throughout the summer. For the most part the better managers and theatres were lucky in the summer of 1888, although none of their successful offerings are especially remembered a hundred years later. John McCaull hit the jackpot first on May 8 with his production at Palmer's of von Suppé's **Clover,** in which a reckless noble and his faithful servant rebound from bankruptcy. Von Suppé's vivacious score kept the box office busy until early October, particularly as enlivened by Miss Cottrelly, Oudin, De Angelis, and Hopper.

One night later the Casino raised its curtain on a lavish revival of Offenbach's *The Brigands,* using W. S. Gilbert's translation. Lillian Russell and statuesque Isabelle Urquhart were its principal beauties and singers. Until mid-September they helped the Casino's patrons forget the heat.

The third summer-spanning success arrived four nights later. Sydney Rosenfeld's adaptation of Lecocq's *La Jolie Persane* was rechristened **The Oolah** to cast attention on the role portrayed by its star, Francis Wilson. Marie Jansen was the pretty Persian and Hubert Wilke her lover. The show had the "Oriental" setting so prevalent in musical librettos of the era and a plot about comic divorces not unlike *The Begum* (11-21-87). When divorces for women become too easy and too frequent in old Persia the ruler decrees that before a divorced woman could remarry a man of her choice, she must marry a public servant called an oolah. Royal ladies were assigned a special oolah, Hoolagoolah. Wilson not only secured his hold on stardom with the show but introduced several lines that quickly obtained common currency. As Hoolagoolah he demanded women "think twice about divorcing once." He proudly admitted, "I have been married a hundred and fifteen times and not once deceived. I have known men who have been married but once, but who were deceived a hundred and fifteen times."

A revival of *Mazulm* (1-9-88) appeared on the same night *The Oolah* opened. The Kiralfy mounting lasted a mere week.

A comic-opera fiasco ended the year. A week's run beginning June 3 was all that **Ardriell** could muster at the Union Square. The show was based on *La Poupée de Nuremberg* and so told the same tale as *Pepita*. Odell says the music was by J. A. Norris, writing under the penname J. Adahm, but newspapers of the day insist Adahm was German.

1889-1890

In his theatre history, Odell judged the new theatrical year "A Very Brilliant Season." As usual, his evaluation did not take into account lyric enterprises. By and large it was another distressing season for musicals. Yet in retrospect historians can catch faint glimmers, hear tentative stirrings of better things to come.

Niblo's inaugurated the season on August 17 with one more of its gargantuan mountings, **Antiope.** Bolossy Kiralfy adapted and expanded the work from a shorter piece that had been done at London's Alhambra. He retained the story of an Amazonian queen's unrequited love for a neighboring prince. The youth prefers the queen's demure young sister, Antiope. When the queen would wrathfully destroy the lovers, a *deus ex machina* (in pink tights) sets things right. The extravaganza's main claim to fame is that it served to introduce Carmencita to New York audiences. Although the *Times* singled her out as "an agile, graceful, mercurial woman, with flashing eyes and mobile features," the dancer was apparently lost amid Niblo's swollen casts and overwhelming scenery. Not until she joined Koster and Bial's variety bill later in the year did she embark on her meteoric rise. The rest of the cast was panned, especially for its "coarse, unpleasant" singing. Spectacle included Niblo's umpteenth Amazon march and a luxurious barge that "moved forward and backward with equal facility." For all its unevenness, *Antiope* was something of a hit, running until the end of September.

Frank Tannehill, Jr.'s farce-comedy, **Bric-A-Brac,** held Tony Pastor's stage briefly from August 25 before Pastor's regular variety season opened. Its songs and dances were attached to the story of a millionaire who invites a group of "geniuses" to a ball. The most flamboyant genius is a writer of comic operas. A runaway balloon carries the party to Africa where circus people, seeking animals, rescue them. Specialties included Alf Hampton's imitations, Maude Giroux's love ballads, and an unidentified "darky" whistler.

August's only other musical entry was an importation by the authors of *Erminie*, Harry Paulton and Edward Jakobowski. Called **Paola** (8-26-89, Fifth Avenue), it totally failed to win the affection that had been showered on its predecessor. Paulton, Louise Beaudet, and Chauncey Olcott (praised for his "light, sweet tenor") romped through the adventures of a comic coward assigned to execute a Corsican vendetta. It ran until October 5 before its producer, the J. C. Duff Opera Company, withdrew it.

McKenna's Flirtation opened at the Park on September 2. The title and the house suggest it was a new Harrigan and Braham work, but in fact Harrigan had temporarily retired from the theatrical scene. Its plot was fairly simple, recording complications that follow fast when McKenna, a Harlem contractor, is mistakenly delivered a love note Mrs. Ryan (Marie Cahill) has meant for another man. Dramatic representations of an elevated train and of ships sailing into port embellished the story. The producers and the author, Edgar Selden, employed

the practice of farce-comedies and some other, older shows by borrowing music from a number of sources, most often the variety stages. With a cast also recruited largely from vaudeville favorites of the time, notably short, stout, and red-haired William Barry (as McKenna) and tall, thin Hugh Fay (as Mr. Ryan), 104 performances were chalked up before it closed on November 30. For Miss Cahill, her excellent notices marked the beginning of a career that would keep her a star for nearly a generation.

If *McKenna's Flirtation* depicted the more riotous side of Irish life, **The Fairy's Well** (also advertised as *The Fairies' Well*) recounted its more romantic side. The work was of that type so popular with Irish audiences of the time. Essentially a straight play, it punctuated its most dramatic moments with song. The show had been on tour for over a year. In 1888–90 it had made several stops in Brooklyn. It arrived at the 14th Street Theatre, a house that often played host to Irish plays, on September 9 and lingered for two weeks before resuming its peregrinations. Its appearance so close to the main stem prompted the *Times* to attack the genre as a whole:

> There is not an original idea in the play, and the auditor is confronted at every turn with familiar scenes, incidents, characters and dialogue. The hero is the traditional servant in corduroy, who makes pert answers to his social superiors and sings and dances without excuse or apology in the most inappropriate places. The heroine is a peculiar young woman who is beset on the one hand by a hard-hearted mortgage holder and on the other by a villain with papers that reflect the character of her departed mother.

Carroll Johnson, long a minstrel, led the undistinguished cast. An "Irish jaunting car" was featured on stage.

More solid lyric material was heard the following Monday night when the Casino represented its first offering of the season, a revival of Offenbach's *La Fille de Tambour-Major,* translated as **The Drum Major.** The adaptation was by Max Freeman and Edgar Smith. Freeman doubled as director and Smith as a performer. Pauline Hall and James T. Powers were prominent in the cast, but even their talents could not overcome a mediocre, humorless translation and an indifferent reception that made it known pretty stage pictures were not enough. The piece had a slightly forced run of eight weeks.

Two return engagements brought September to a

close, *Zig-Zag* (10-1-88) and *The Pearl of Pekin.* Both stayed only a week.

The Seven Ages (10-7-89, Standard) was conceived in the hope of providing Henry E. Dixey with a vehicle that might approach the success of *Adonis* (9-4-84). Unfortunately, *The Seven Ages* suffered the fate of most sequels, falling far short of its predecessor's triumph. In fact, so many mishaps—lines muffed, long scene changes, a scene halted while a costume was changed—occurred opening night that few would have been surprised had the show been an immediate failure. But Dixey was too stalwart a professional to surrender to such happenstance misfortunes. Rehearsals and revisions quickly knocked the show into shape, and, while *The Seven Ages* never turned into a runaway hit, it nonetheless enjoyed a highly satisfactory run of 152 performances and a profitable road tour. As in *Adonis,* the curtain rose to reveal a living statue. However, instead of Dixey as a white marble Greek, playgoers beheld a supporting actor, George Howard, as a bronze Shakespeare. The statue comes to life to begin Bertie Van Loo on a journey covering his entire history, taking Bertie not only back to his infant days in a baby carriage but into the future to see himself as an old man of ninety. In between Bertie cavorts as a lover, a soldier, and a justice of the peace.

The Seven Ages was October's only musical. November was scarcely more generous, bringing in only two lyric works, both revivals. On the 11th W. J. Scanlan began a four-week visit in *Myles Aroon* at the Star, while on the 20th the Casino quickly remounted *Erminie* to replace the faltering *Drum Major.* With Francis Wilson occupied elsewhere, the part of Cadeaux so identified with him went to James T. Powers.

Kajanka premiered at Niblo's on December 2. "Another attempt to recapture some of the fine careless raptures of *The Black Crook* and its Niblo successors," the piece had an initial run of five weeks. But unlike some of its ilk which enjoyed longer first runs, *Kajanka* caught the fancy of a number of cities on the road and held up so well on its tour that it came back a year later for a second stay. The libretto, by a famous clown of the period, George D. Melville, told a straightforward tale with pantomime trappings. The wicked son of a bad fairy attempts to kidnap Kajanka (Edith Craske). Good fairies, assisted by Clown and Pantaloon, save the girl. As always, Niblo's filled the show with specialty numbers. Four young ladies in long, flying skirts performed a butterfly dance and the Donazettis were hailed as "the best tumbling

act ever seen here." Even principals doubled in brass. William Ruge, who played the wicked son, "give a remarkable exhibition as acrobat and contortionist."

For a second season in a row performers from London's Gaiety Theatre crossed the Atlantic to display their act. Their vehicle for this occasion was **Faust up to Date.** Some important cast members (notably Florence St. John, slated to play Marguerite) were too ill to perform at the opening, and their absence dampened the work's reception. But the beguiling line of Gaiety girls ("a frank display of the lower limbs") went a long way to compensate for the missing principals. The show held the stage at the Broadway for a month, beginning December 10, toured major cities, and returned in April for a short farewell stay.

A revival of *The Brigands* (12-26-70) ushered in the new year and the new decade on January 6, 1890. Its presence on the Casino stage was interesting for two reasons. For one, it was the second of a string of revivals the house found it necessary to resort to during the season. The year was probably the most difficult the house had endured since its opening. Few novelties of merit seemed to be available to it; indeed, few novelties of merit seemed to be available at all. Secondly, it was an opéra bouffe. Although newspapers of the time and scholars of a later day both had long considered the opéra bouffe a waning vogue, many of the best examples of the genre still found a large audience. What had largely disappeared was the opéra bouffe repertory company, playing different pieces each night—playing them rather faithfully and often singing them in French. These new opéra bouffe mountings reflected both management's and performers' contentments with the larger profits and comforts of long runs. They were generally staged with a freedom that disconcerted purists, adding alien interpolations and business on a scale that jolted those who knew and loved the originals.

Another jolt was in store for devotees of a kindred art form the night after *The Brigands'* return. The long-awaited American premiere of Gilbert and Sullivan's **The Gondoliers** took place at the Park on January 7. This last of their masterpieces told a lighthearted yarn of two gondoliers whose romances are interrupted when a misunderstanding makes them kings for a day. Although it was an "authorized" production, it was so badly bungled critics shook their heads in dismay. Advance sales and some forcing allowed the mounting to run until February 13. Then D'Oyly Carte, who had hurried over, recast and restaged the work, and reopened it at Palmer's, where it ran for an additional two months. Principals in this "definitive" version included Fred Billington, Richard Temple, Richard Clarke, Kate Talby, Norah Phyllis, and Esther Palliser.

Eddie Foy, fast rising to prominence, was the source of much of the mirth at Niblo's in **Blue-beard, Jr.,** the third of David Henderson's elaborate Chicago extravaganzas to visit New York in as many years. The libretto by Clay M. Greene (to music by Fred Eustis and Richard Maddern) played loose with the famous pirate's story, centering mainly upon his marriage to Fatima. Bluebeard, or Ben Ali Barbazuli (Frank Blair), purchases Fatima (Alice Johnston) from her cynical father, O'Mahdi Benzini (Foy). Before the marriage can be consummated, the bride is rescued by her lover. Bluebeard is not put to death for the murder of his other wives. A more diabolical punishment awaits him. His slain wives are resurrected and return to the harem to torment him. The production catered to the insistent demand for spectacle with a grand ballet, "The Light of Asia," and "The Ballet of the Birds and Insects." Seventy Amazons marched "in armor that really clanked." Over 200 performers filled the stage. On its Chicago opening the preceding June 11, the *Tribune* happily reported "the art of using electric lights to advantage was never better illustrated . . . the pictures by this means were toned and varied." New York critics apparently took such wonders for granted, ignoring both the lighting and Richard Barker's lively staging. The producer and authors also kept a careful eye on the large children's audience, introducing in the "Glittering Grotto of Fantastic Fancy" Jack, the Giant Killer, Puss in Boots, the Babes in the Wood, and the Old Woman Who Lived in a Shoe. Most New Yorkers welcomed the piece, for a month starting January 13, but meddling do-gooders from the Gerry Society prevented the children of the old lady in the shoe from performing.

On January 25 the Casino brought forth a particularly elaborate revival of *The Grand Duchess* with Lillian Russell as star. Gustave Kerker conducted. For want of better novelties to compete with, the work ran up 100 showings.

One of the biggest hits of the season, **The City Directory** (2-10-90, Bijou), had a libretto by Paul M. Potter and music by "the old minstrel man," W. S. Mullaly. Potter's libretto was a cross between the old Tom and Jerry theme and the farce-comedies of Hoyt, with perhaps a touch of Harrigan's slices of New York life thrown in. It dealt with the confusions that ensue when a Chicago detective, John Smith (Charlie Reed), comes to New York to arrest a local crook, John Smith. Before the evening is over, nearly a dozen John Smiths are caught up in the muddle, and a tour of Manhattan has been made. The other John Smiths in the play include a businessman (John W. Jennings), an athlete (Alf Hampton), a ballet-master (Ignacio Martinetti), an actor (William Collier), a messenger boy (Joseph Jackson), an elevator operator (a new calling) (Josie Sadler), and a "bunco-steerer" (a confidence man) (William F. Mack). As the ballet-master, Martinetti was able to prance about like "a veritable jumping jack," in contrast to the more graceful dancing of Amelia Glover, then at the beginning of a brief period of celebrity. *The City Directory* compiled 152 performances, marking its 100th showing by announcing that it had been "rejuvenated" with new sets, new bits, and new songs.

Adolph Muller's imported operetta **King's Fool** (10-17-90, Niblo's) was a typical work of the time, with the heroine in a trouser role of a princess everyone determines to pass off as a boy until a court jester comes to her aid. It was also a two-week failure. Its small place in the history of the American Musical Theatre has been secured solely because it marked the debut of Della Fox, who would briefly rival Lillian Russell as a prima donna.

While *The Gondoliers* slowly won a loyal following, Savoyards could see two older favorites when *The Mikado* and *The Pirates of Penzance* each played a week at the Broadway in the spring. *The Mikado* opened on March 31, *The Pirates* two weeks later. Both were touring companies making New York just another stop on their journeys.

De Wolf Hopper saw his name above the title when **Castles in the Air** premiered at the Broadway on May 5. He was not only the star but was at least the nominal head of the De Wolf Hopper Comic Opera Company which produced the work.

. . .

William De Wolf Hopper was born in New York City on March 30, 1858. Never getting beyond the equivalent of high school he took turns trying various trades before he made his debut as an actor in 1879 in *Our Daughters*. A small legacy enabled him to turn actor-manager, but his tour failed and he soon exhausted his funds. Although he hoped to become a serious dramatic actor, he was so toweringly tall other performers were reluctant to have him in their company, where he would only dwarf them. By 1884, when he accepted a role in Sousa's *Desiree,* he was resigned to confining his booming basso voice to the musical stage. Increasingly adroit performances in shows such as *The Begum* and *The Lady or the Tiger?* speedily consolidated his reputation.

. . .

Castles in the Air had a libretto by C. A. Byrne. His story reminded the *Dramatic Mirror* of the plot for Offenbach's *Les Bavards,* although the trade paper dutifully, if unbelievingly, reported that the show's program insisted Byrne drew his idea from Cervantes' one-act intermezzo, *Los Dos Habladores.* Cabolastro (Thomas Q. Seabrooke) offers the debt-ridden Bul-Bul (Marion Manola) a disguise to help him elude his creditors on the condition that Bul-Bul outtalk Cabolastro's garrulous wife (Rose Leighton). Bul-Bul consents, since he loves Cabolastro's daughter, Blanche (Della Fox). Interestingly, Hopper played none of the pivotal roles, appearing instead off and on throughout the evening as a freethinking judge, Filacoudre. Most of his laughs came from his broad clowning in scenes that had little to do with the tale. One was a hilarious pantomime billiard match played—sans table, cues, or balls—with Miss Fox. Given Byrne's dialogue, Hopper's comic skills were sorely needed. Byrne's idea of humor ran to lines such as, "All old men die at an advanced age; it is only the young who have a chance to die early." The score was by one of the most prominent figures of the turn-of-the-century American Musical Theatre, Gustave Kerker.

. . .

Gustave Kerker was born in Hereford, Germany, on February 28, 1857. He began his studies as a cellist at the age of seven and continued his musical education when his family moved to Louisville, Kentucky, three years later. As a young man he played in the city's theatre orchestras, rising soon to be a conductor. In 1879 he composed his first operetta, *Cadets,* which played briefly in the South. E. E. Rice caught a performance and offered the composer-conductor a chance to work with him. Moving to New York he soon became the principal conductor at the Casino. On occasion he interpolated his own numbers in importations of the period both at the Casino and elsewhere, most notably, in Lecocq's *The Pearl of Pekin.*

. . .

Della Fox's performance in the role of Blanche skyrocketed her to fame. The swiftness of the rise, coming so soon after her debut, suggests how intimate the confines of Broadway remained. *Castles in the Air* played to satisfied audiences until August 16, recording 105 performances.

The same evening as Byrne and Kerker's piece opened, the reunited Kiralfys restored to Niblo's stage their ever ready *Around the World in Eighty Days* (8-28-75), still featuring the Mikado Ballet. It lasted a month.

A rousing revival of *H.M.S. Pinafore* completed May's musical entries. Featuring Digby Bell, Chauncey Olcott, and a cast of 200, it filled the large Academy of Music from May 12 to May 30. On June 2 the same company gave the New York season its second interpretation of *The Mikado.*

Uptown at the Casino, Chassaigne's **The Brazilian** arrived the same evening as *The Mikado.* Marie Halton, Edith Ainsworth, Grace Golden, George Olmi, and Richard F. Carroll were featured in this saga of a wily lady's maid who lands spouses for herself and her mistress after they are captured by Brazilian bandits. If the management had hoped to span the summer with the work they were disappointed. The work received only a moderate run, closing in mid-August.

Palmer's, too, brought in a musical that seemed to have been slated for a summer run and failed. Richard Stahl's operetta, **The Sea King,** was even less well attended than *The Brazilian.* Hubert Wilke, Edwin Stevens, Esther Palliser, Lena Merville, Annie Myers, and J. C. Miron could do little to save this tale of a wandering Dutch seaman who lands in Spain, finds a lady who had been waiting all her life for him and wins her over her uncle's objections. It opened on June 23 and folded August 3.

No better indication of the fading of minstrelsy and the telling influences of the new English shows could be offered than the fate of the old San Francisco Minstrels' Theatre. Rechristened Dockstader's in recent years, Lew Dockstader himself appeared there only from October to December. The house closed at the end of 1889 only to reopen in February of 1890 as the Gaiety!

Away from the mainstream a number of prototypical musicals played at other houses. For example, on October 14 Tony Pastor's sheltered the Burton Stanley Opera Company's *Mrs. Partington,* the text of which is apparently lost, while Wild and Collier's Comedy Theatre presented a number of song-larded farces such as *Running Wild, The Mashers,* and *A Legal Holiday.* These works, too, seemingly left no trace.

1890-1891

The number of new musicals dropped noticeably as the new decade began. But, as frequently happened, a drop in numbers was coupled with a rise in quality. The new season and the following one brought the first great act of the American Musical Theatre to a close with several native creations which gave assurances that, even if the domestic lyric stage had not totally found itself, it was confidently on the right track.

Before New York's season got under way, Chicago played host to an elaborate new musical on July 23. Henry E. Dixey, looking for another *Adonis* (9-4-84), turned his attention to Washington Irving's evergreen, *Rip Van Winkle,* which had been serving Joseph Jefferson as a drama vehicle for so many years. But Dixey's *Rip* retained little of the original story except the name of the central figure, the long nap, and a few quaint spellings. A real estate broker unable to sell his Kaatskill Mountains for one cent an acre persuades a happy old man to promote it by a marathon snooze. Rip falls asleep, wakes up to find himself young, and sells the property for a large sum. One interesting feature of the show was its architecturally conceived sets. Old-fashioned drops were minimized. The mountain started at the footlights and climbed as it moved backstage. But the sets were more interesting than the rest of the evening. Dixey was never able to whip the show into suitable shape for a New York visit.

August's activity was testimony to the failure of the late spring musicals to survive the summer. Palmer's, the Broadway, and the Casino all needed new mid-summer attractions. Palmer's brought its offering in first, presenting **The Red Hussar** on August 5. Its book by H. P. Stevens and score by Edward Solomon were not particularly noteworthy. But the part of Kitty Carroll, a young lady who disguises herself as a Red Hussar in order to follow her sweetheart to France, was played by Marie Tempest, making her American debut. She created what the papers love to call a "sensation" and almost singlehandedly kept the box office humming until she had to return to England in mid-October.

On the 14th the Casino revived one of the earliest opéra bouffe favorites, shortening its title a bit to *Mme. Angot.* It ran concurrently with *The Red Hussar,* even closing on the same night, October 11.

Francis Wilson completed the trio of August

openings with his second starring vehicle, **The Merry Monarch** (8-18-90, Broadway). J. Cheever Goodwin based his libretto on *L'Etoile* (*The Star of Fate*). Its plot dealt with the curious fate that binds King Anso IV (Wilson) to one of his subjects. The king selects the saucy street vendor, Lazuli (a trouser role played by Marie Jansen), to be the annual human sacrifice. His astrologer, Sirocco (Charles Plunkett), discovers Lazuli's horoscope is so tied to Anso's that if one dies the other will die. The rest of the evening is spent frantically trying to keep the reckless boy alive. Wilson, like Beatrice Lillie years later, was a master at puncturing spurious claims to dignity. His first entrance was one of the highlights of the show. Brought in on a majestic palanquin, he promptly tumbled down the steps in descending. His constant refusal to finish a thought, but rather to leave it hanging with an "and so forth and so on" not only justified the king's name but predated the same peculiarity in a later stage ruler—the king of *The King and I* (3-29-51). A number of the songs by Emile Chabrier and Woolson Morse became the delights of the day, notably, "When I Was A Child Of Three," "The Ostrich Song," and "Love Will Find A Way."

In his autobiography Wilson casts a further sidelight on what a grab bag of talents and materials these old shows often developed into. While in Washington Wilson spotted two young Negro boys dancing in the street for pennies. He was so taken with their improvisations that he took them with him to New York and incorporated their routine in the show—until some killjoys of the anti-child-labor movement who had troubled *Bluebeard* a year before deprived theatregoers of a novel specialty act and the two youngsters of a legitimate income. With or without the boys *The Merry Monarch* held court until October 4. The show was one of the many of the era directed by Richard Barker, an Englishman whose reputation for staging musicals earned him frequent transatlantic crossings.

Two nights before *The Merry Monarch* premiered, *Kajanka* (12-2-89) returned to Niblo's. It added an additional two weeks to its record. Vying for attention with Wilson's vehicle was an extravaganza by William Gill and Robert Frazer, **Hendrik Hudson** (8-18-90, 14th St.). With trouser roles all the rage, the title part was given to Fay Templeton.

. . .

Fay Templeton was born into a theatrical family on Christmas Day 1865, in Little Rock, Arkansas. She made her first stage appearance less than four years later on August 16, 1869, as Cupid. New

York first saw her in 1873 as Puck in *A Midsummer Night's Dream*. In 1880 she joined a juvenile company of *H.M.S. Pinafore,* and within a year graduated to romantic leads in musicals such as *Evangeline, The Mascot,* and *Billie Taylor.* For the most part she served her apprenticeship on the road. In 1886 she was featured prominently in the original London mounting of *Monte Cristo, Jr.* Her vivacity and her fetchingly throaty delivery so endeared her to her generation that not even a persistent weight problem, making her notably buxom in an era of buxom beauties, could alienate its allegiance.

. . .

In *Hendrik Hudson* Miss Templeton made her entrance in much talked-about bottom kid leggings, "the newest and most artistic amplification of the Sarah Bernhardt kid gloves." Her Hendrik was a faithless husband who goes to Florida with his bevy of chorus girls. When he finds Columbus (Eva Randolph) living in retirement there, he signs the old man for appearances at the forthcoming World's Fair. Other characters were Miss Manhattan (Toma Hanlon), the Marquis Perfecto de Cubanas (Edw. G. Whalen), and Kill von Kull, editor of the *New Amsterdam Kicker* (Edwin Stevens). Miss Templeton won encores singing a topical song, "The Same Old Thing," but at least one critic felt most of her performance was "merely twaddle and tights." Miss Templeton was not yet star enough to save a generally disdained show. The producers withdrew the piece after just sixteen performances. The withdrawal did not, however, mark the end for the musical. The era's healthy theatrical economics allowed the show to be taken on the road for repairs and to be brought back for a reconsideration on October 27 at the Park. The consensus found the repairs inadequate, and *Hendrik Hudson* had its final curtain after a second fortnight.

The first of minstrel bands to play New York followed *Hendrik Hudson*'s initial visit at the 14th Street Theatre. The Cleveland Minstrels featured Billy Emerson and Barney Fagan. Their format was a reversion to more traditional blackface bills, minimizing the recently expanded burlesque portion and concentrating on old, beloved songs. Their two-week stand was part of a national junket. George Thatcher had broken away from Primrose and West during the preceding year. Both in 1889–90 and in 1890–91 Primrose and West made several appearances in outlying combination houses, but Thatcher's troupe succeeded in getting a week's booking at the Bijou beginning November 3. John Wild, so long the leading player of blackface roles in the Harrigan and Braham shows, costarred with Thatcher.

On the same night the Cleveland Minstrels bowed, September 1, an importation called **The Seven Swabians** raised its curtain. But the curtain that rose was far uptown at the Harlem Opera House. This theatre was essentially a combination house, offering its stage to touring attractions and post-Broadway runs. Yet, situated as it was in an area of elegant, upper middle-class brown-stones, it was judged ideal for the sort of tryouts later reserved for Philadelphia or Boston or New Haven. *The Seven Swabians* was just this sort of tryout. Mounted with panache by the McCaull Opera Company and featuring many of the company's leading players such as Mathilde Cottrelly and Chauncey Olcott, it quickly proved to be one of those errors in judgment even the best of managements makes. It never reached the heart of the Rialto. But the Harlem Opera House would soon witness a far more important and successful tryout.

September's only other entry was a curiosity, suggesting that Broadway had not yet completely shed its circus aspect. The cast of **The Pupil in Magic** consisted of a band of troupers known as The Liliputians. As the name suggests, the appealing performers were midgets, who had been playing as an ensemble for several seasons in Berlin. They ranged in age from eighteen to forty-three years, in height from twenty-eight to thirty-eight inches. The principal members were Selma Gomer, Adolf Zink, and Franz Ebert. Ebert, "a droll little fellow with a face that is comedy in itself," quickly became the darling of both critics and public. The play was by Robert Breitenbach with music "selected and arranged" by Carl Joseph. In Breitenbach's story, Fritz (Miss Gomer), on a visit to his toymaker uncle, falls asleep and dreams he signs a bargain with Puck (Ebert) that wins him the love of every woman he encounters. Near the end, a vision of his mother searching for him fills Fritz with remorse. A transformation scene carries him back to the toymaker's shop. Spectacular dream sequences included a grand ballet depicting the wedding of Princess Lydia (Minchen Becker) to Fritz, a trip to the North Pole, and a tour of Paris. The company regaled audiences for five weeks at Niblo's, returning in December for another month at the Bijou. In between these engagements and afterwards, *The Pupil in Magic* played several of the city's combination houses and toured around the country. The Liliputians were no ninety-day wonder. Their appeal proved surprisingly long-lived. When they and their audiences tired of one vehicle they had another play ready to offer.

The only full-fledged musicals to arrive in October were a revival of *The Chimes of Normandy,* retitled *Paul Jones,* and **Poor Jonathan.** Both opened on the 6th. *Paul Jones* starred Agnes Huntington in another of the era's many trouser roles. The piece played a month, attesting again, as did *Mme. Angot,* to the market that remained for selected opéra bouffe.

The arrival of Millöcker's *Poor Jonathan* at the Casino ended that house's string of bad luck for the time being. Lillian Russell and Jefferson De Angelis headed the cast, while Harry Macdonough and Fanny Rice helped De Angelis spark the comedy. The plot, which told how an American millionaire, deserted by his protégé, is tricked out of committing suicide by his loyal cook, was typical turn-of-the-century frippery. Yet the show was unusual in one way. It was a German operetta with an American setting. But the adapters were aghast at some scenes of the original, such as Negroes picking cotton in New York City. They quietly moved the first act setting from Manhattan to West Point, substituting lively cadets for the cavorting blacks. Obviously there were limits to the absurdities even comic opera could tolerate. Or perhaps it was simply that absurdities were acceptable only in alien settings. In any case, *Poor Jonathan* was the biggest hit at the Casino since *Erminie,* compiling 202 performances before it was recast for a tour at the beginning of May.

The busy night of October 6 brought in another interesting work, but one that was not really a musical. *Blue Jeans* was one of the great thrillers of the age, most famous for a scene in which its hero is strapped to a treadmill moving ever closer to a menacing saw while the villain demands the heroine's attentions. But *Blue Jeans* included in its cast a number of veterans of farce-comedies and other light musical efforts, such as Jacques Kruger and Jennie Yeamans. Further, it had a number of mood-setting tunes, old and new, "composed and arranged" by the same old minstrel who had provided melodies for *The City Directory* (2-10-90), W. S. Mullaly. The piece vividly illustrates the difficulty of drawing a clear-cut line between musicals and straight plays of the time.

At Niblo's the Casino's erstwhile performer, director, and adapter, Max Freeman, mounted **Claudius Nero** on October 22. Based on Ernest Eckstein's romance, *Nero,* it was another of Niblo's ballet and song embellished spectacles (with real lions on stage). It closed unexpectedly in mid-December when its leading dancer walked out, claiming substantial unpaid back salary. After some refinancing and recasting the show moved on to the Broadway for three additional weeks.

The musical which *Claudius Nero* supplanted when it moved uptown was J. Cheever Goodwin's second creation to appear during the season. **Pippins** (11-26-90, Broadway) featured the mammoth Amelia Summerville as the lithe Atalanta. Of course the title came from the apples dropped to distract Atalanta during her race. The show, badly hurt by unfavorable notices, was crippled hopelessly when Miss Summerville was injured in an accident. As a result the record shows the piece ran only to December 6 before fading into oblivion.

A more successful novelty ushered in December. **Ship Ahoy** (12-8-90, Standard) was billed as an "operatic extravaganza" with a libretto by H. Grattan Donnelly and a score by Fred Miller. A comic-opera troupe is shipwrecked on an island. The men would set up a kingdom with themselves in charge, but the ladies of the ballet, led by Mlle Auburni Ernani (Bertha Ricci), revolt and establish their own republic. In an ending that ten years later would become a cliché, the troupe is rescued by the U.S. Navy. Because the show was a Philadelphia mounting, New York critics came down hard on it. The *Times* insisted the dialogue was traditional Philadelphia drivel, while the *Dramatic Mirror* heard Gilbert and Sullivan in every song. The trade paper cited the tune sung by Commodore Columbus Cook (Edward M. Favor) of the *U.S.S. Cuckoo* as a direct steal from a song it called "The Ruler Of The Queen's Navee" ("When I Was A Lad"). The loose plot allowed a flood of vaudeville turns to be inserted, and several critics insisted these were the mainstay of the evening.

New York usually did applaud Philadelphia productions for the excellence of their sets and costumes. *Ship Ahoy* was no exception. A stage picture of the white squadron sailing out of Chesapeake Bay won general approbation. Willard Spenser and other Philadelphians had long since learned that New York's rejection was rarely repeated on the road. After five weeks the company embarked on a tour that brought it back to several other New York theatres during the season. On its return it sought to assure patrons its songs were not cacophonously modern, but were "music with melody."

While *Ship Ahoy* was being unveiled at the Standard, the Harlem Opera House far uptown was hosting another tryout. But this show was soon to make history: Charles Hoyt's **A Trip to Chinatown.** Hoyt was a conscientious craftsman by the standards of the time. With his straight play, *A Texas Steer,* one of the joyous hits of the 1890–91 season, he saw no reason to rush his new work downtown. Instead, he took it on the road for nearly a year. Its phenomenal run was part of the next season's record.

The J. C. Duff Opera Company arrived at the Broadway on December 22 to entertain holiday crowds with a repertory of Gilbert and Sullivan works: *The Pirates of Penzance, Patience,* and *Iolanthe.*

On December 29 a rejuvenated Edward Harrigan returned to the New York scene with two new attractions. The first was his new theatre, called simply Harrigan's, at 35th Street and Broadway. The second was his (and Braham's) new work, **Reilly and the Four Hundred.** "The Four Hundred" was the phrase coined by social arbiter Ward McAllister to define the limits of high society. Wiley Riley (Harrigan), a pawnbroker, sets up his son, Ned (Harry Davenport), as a lawyer so that the young man may have entrée into this high echelon. Reilly hopes Ned will marry Emeline (Isabelle Archer), the niece of his rich fellow Irishman, Commodore Toby Tow (James Radcliffe). Ned does, and Reilly marries the commodore's sister, Lavina (Hattie Moore). But before the weddings can take place Reilly must expose Herman Smeltz (Harry Fisher), a sausage tycoon and one of the four hundred, as an ex-ship's butcher who had been dismissed for stealing. The plot was obviously the next step after the Mulligans' own efforts to enter society. It reflected the view of high society that, while upstart parents might not enter the charmed circle, their children could be considered. Harrigan's dialogue and characterization were as fine as ever, though occasionally Harrigan did stretch theatrical coincidence in the name of theatrical brevity. For example, the commodore's servant pawns an old ship's log that belonged to his master. It reveals Smeltz' crimes to Reilly. Reilly no sooner reads the incriminating passage than Smeltz himself walks in. Nor were the songs always well motivated. The hit of the evening was one of Braham's classics, "Maggie Murphy's Home." But Maggie was a very minor figure in the play. Referred to as a "chippie," her brief scene consisted merely of her announcement that she will indulge in a "challenge jig" at a benefit ball. The song is sung at the opening of the next scene, Foley's benefit at Casey's Hall. Some indication of the

staging of the time can be garnered from a note in the typescript at the end of the song. It reads "after each chorus, waltz. Bus[iness] of perspiration etc., after the song." An indication of how long audiences of the time could be expected to sit quietly in their seats is given at the beginning of the same typescript where the "time of acting" is listed as "three hours." Harrigan was able to reassemble most of his old associates such as Annie Yeamans (as an Irish housekeeper) and John Wild (as an argumentative black). Newcomers included two future stars, Ada Lewis, who quickly became a favorite in "tough girl" parts, and Harry Davenport. *Reilly and the Four Hundred* gave Harrigan and Braham one of their greatest triumphs, running 202 performances.

The final musical of 1890 arrived the night after the Harrigan premiere. **The Babes in the Wood** (12-30-90, Niblo's) was a resuscitation of the old pantomime with William A. Mestayer and George K. Fortesque as the Babes. One ludicrous moment found Fortesque, a behemoth of a man, abducted by a two-and-a-half-foot dwarf. Spectacle included a Shakespearean tableau. Despite the evening's better moments, the musical failed miserably (its scenery seized for nonpayment), ending the year on a downbeat note.

The game, aging Lydia Thompson (the *Times* ungallantly announced that she was fifty-five) tried again with a vehicle called **The Dazzler.** Other papers attempted to be kinder, although Miss Thompson clearly had seen her best days. The *Dramatic Mirror* noted, "Her voice is a thing of the past . . . but she can dance with all, or nearly all of her pristine nimbleness." When, late in the first act, she donned her old Robinson Crusoe costume, "the bald-headed contingent smiled with reminiscent satisfaction, and went out between the acts to talk over the halcyon days of their vanished youth." In the show's simple plot a wild, uncouth Irishman named Mulligan (Thomas J. Grady) somehow manages to woo and win the actress Kitty Starlight (Miss Thompson). Miss Thompson's persistence was rewarded with a modicum of success. She occupied the Park for a week beginning January 12, and the Standard for most of February, and then she came back for brief stays at other houses.

The closest thing to a musical to appear in January was J. J. McNally's farce, **A Straight Tip** (1-26-91, Bijou). It dealt with the inheriting of a hotel; the inheritance only settled when Dick Dasher bets on the right horse following a tip. James T. Powers was the show's star, inserting a number of songs, dances, and an imitation of Carmencita into Mc-Nally's material. One or two other specialties were also interpolated. The show also served to call attention to Peter F. Dailey in the supporting role of Jack Postsand Poole.

March brought in little more than January or February, being noteworthy only for the return of W. J. Scanlan presenting a week each of *Myles Aroon* (1-21-89) and *The Irish Minstrel* (4-9-88) at the 14th Street Theatre, and for another of the many song-studded farce-comedies, **U and I** (3-23-91, Standard). Its excuse for its specialties was to have John Ungerblotz (Gus Williams) and O'Donovan Innes (John T. Kelly), back from a toot, fall asleep in the apartment of a voice coach, Mlle Vermicelli (Gertrude Zella). Miss Zella was "rapturously encored" for her kissing song, while Kelly won applause for dancing a jig and for singing (in a thick brogue). Typical of how other specialties were introduced was the appearance of the janitor to check on the apartment. He turned out to be an acrobat. At one point a group of girls entered dressed as rosebuds. *U and I* was presented by George Lederer, who would shortly make his mark as a producer of more genuinely musical enterprises.

By April, managers were clearly biding their time, awaiting the propitious moment to bring in those spring offerings they hoped would turn into "summer musicals." The lone voice raised in song belonged to Joseph Murphy, a minor player in the tradition of Emmet and Scanlan, who offered a month-long repertory at the 14th Street Theatre that included *The Kerry Gow, Shaun Rue,* and *The Donagh.*

The most successful summer entertainment not only spanned the summer, but enjoyed later revivals and long held the affection of those who saw it. **Wang** (5-4-91, Broadway) had J. Cheever Goodwin's third libretto for the season and his second in less than a year done in collaboration with composer Woolson Morse. Its principal characters were stock favorites of the era's musicals: the grotesquely made-up clown and the hero played as a trouser role. It was set in the Orient, which had become almost the *sine qua non* of comic opera. All that Goodwin overlooked were the outrageously punning names so often given characters of the time. Wang (De Wolf Hopper) is the comic, conniving regent of Siam. While the young prince, Mataya (Della Fox), bridles at his elder's machinations, he is more preoccupied by his romance with Gillette (Anna O'Keefe). Gillette is the eldest daughter of La Veuve Frimousse (Marion Singer), the widow of a former French consul, who has managed to secure in her custody the entire treasury of Siam. Although her daughters are so numerous they compose an entire chorus line and although she is anxious to marry them all off, she suspects that Mataya courts Gillette only in the hope of retrieving his country's money. But Mataya convinces her and her daughter of his sincerity by renouncing the throne. At this point Wang grabs the throne and the hand of the susceptible widow, taking from her hand at the same moment the precious royal coffer. Goodwin's lyrics and Morse's melodies are exemplified by two songs. "A Pretty Girl" (sung by Mataya early in the first act) juxtaposes a simple, charming tune with an equally simple lyric that turns unexpectedly cynical.

The work's principal comic number (sung near the end of the evening by Wang, Mataya, and a French Colonel) was "Ask The Man In The Moon," a song that in keeping with common practice of the time was most meaty in its verse, with only a rudimentary chorus. Also in keeping with then common practice, the song satirized contemporary affairs in New York, ignoring entirely the problems of the plot. One verse ran:

> New York is a city of wealth,
> Millionaires we can count by the score;
> And can boast of a host
> Who have hundreds of thousands or more.
> But Grant's monument tho' isn't built—
> If you'd ask a subscription they'd swoon;
> Will the Washington Arch, be completed
> next March,
> You must ask of the man in the moon.

When a real Siamese king visited America in the 1930s, he is said to have requested to hear songs from the show. As Wang, Hopper reached what is generally acknowledged as the pinnacle of his career. His entrance—not unlike Francis Wilson's in *The Merry Monarch* (8-18-90)—and his extended opening monologue, even on paper, capture some flavor of the great clowning of the period. Wang first appears on an elephant "over whom a gorgeous canopy is held by six slaves."

CHORUS OF WELCOME.

(At end of Chorus, Pepat [played by "tiny Alfred Klein"] endeavors to have the elephant kneel).

Pepat: Hurri gurry baloo masam!
    (*Elephant declines to kneel; Pepat jabs him*

with pike; elephant raises trunk and trumpets. Pepat continued jabbing and elephant shows annoyance)

Wang: Say! What are you trying to do with this elephant anyway? Make him do a song-and-dance! Are you aware that your monarch is patiently awaiting to descend?

Pepat: But he won't kneel, sire!

Wang: Won't kneel—scoundrel! In the bright lexicon of middle age there is no such word as Won't! What are you on the salary list for, anyway? Make him kneel!

(Pepat jabs elephant again, who, with a flourish of his trunk, knocks Pepat over. Crowd manifest alarm)

Serves you right! I wish he had broken every one of the two hundred and forty eight bones in your wretched carcass. You know as much about elephants as a black cat does of dummy whist! Hand me that fish spear up here!

(Pepat, picking himself up, hands pike, with fear and trembling to Wang, who shouts to elephant)

Enteuthen exelaunei parassangas dekas!

(As he jabs elephant, the latter again trumpets and stampedes about stage, crowd dodging him with screams, in great confusion; finally, with a last blast of rage, he rushes off R. 4. E., leaving Wang, who has stood up to prod him, clinging to branch of tree L. I. E., facing audience)

(Clinging to branch, to Pepat) Come here! come here! you moon faced concentration of imbecility! and let your monarch fall on you! Do you want me to break the royal neck?

(Pepat dodging Wang's legs, gets under him so the latter can rest his foot on the former's shoulders; when Wang lets go of branch, Pepat collapses with him; Fracasse hastens to assist Wang to arise. Pepat is cowering with fear, on his hands and knees)

[Wang launches into a song "The Regent Wang," and when it is finished he chases away the crowd and dismisses his retainers.]

(Addressing audience) Between ourselves, what I want to be alone for, is to think; I never can think in a crowd, and I have got enough to think about to kill a cat. When my brother, the late king, died six years ago, he left the royal coffer a howling vacuum. What in the name of Daniel Dancer he did with all the shekels he raked in during his reign, staggered me. He didn't take them with him, I'll swear, for I had a post mortem made that developed nothing except a quarrel among the surgeons. For six years I have hunted high low Jack and the game and not found a sign of them. The result has been, I have lived the life of a royal pauper. I have not been able to reign, I have only sprinkled. I have borrowed right and left; I have plastered the palace with mortages, and worst of all in a moment of reckless extravagance, I purchased a sacred elephant from the king of Cambodia, and confound his colossal impudence, he absolutely wants to be paid for it. An embassy from that besotted monarch dunning me for the price, has stuck to me closer than a porous plaster for the last one hundred and eighty four days. I don't dare behead them for he would go to war and lick me out of my royal boots. The result is, I'm obliged to do the sneak act and play hide and seek with them all over my kingdom. Dodging them is one of the things that brings me here today. The other and far more important one, is this letter addressed to Mataya—*(taking letter from pocket)*—which is the first ray of hope which has trickled into my atmosphere of chronic, cold, black gloom. *(Reads letter)* Paris, November 17th. My dear Prince: Shortly before your royal father's death, distrusting as he did, your uncle's honesty—*(spoken)*—I would not have had my brother's suspicious nature for $17.50!—*(reads)*—He confided to me a chest, with instructions to deliver it to you upon your coronation. My hours are numbered and I shall never see Siam again; but I send you the enclosed key, and have charged Madame Frimousse with the sacred duty of seeing that the chest it unlocks reaches you on the day named. Its contents are unknown to her, as they are to me—*(speaking)* well, you can wager your saccharine existence that they won't be unknown to me long, once I interview Madame Frimousse! *(Read)* My sight fails—farewell; follow in your father's footsteps and emulate his example. *(signed)* Frimousse. *(Restoring letter to pocket. Rising)* There can't be any doubt about it, that chest contains the treasure I have hunted for six long weary years! and as Mataya hasn't got any idea of its existence, he won't lose anything by not getting it. What does he know about the value of money, anyway? He's got enough to occupy his mind, smoking cigarettes and raising a moustache; whereas let yours truly once get his fingers on it and I'll make things hump! Let's see! I've got the key, I hope! *(Produces key and returns it to*

pocket) That's all right! and now to tackle the widow Frimousse and secure the chest. (*Goes to house L. H. and raps. Widow appears at door*) I beg your pardon—

Widow: If you want anything to eat, you'll have to go round to the back door! (*Slams door in his face*)

Wang: First blood for the widow! But at the call of time, the Siamese Chicken came up smiling! (*Raps again at door of house, L. H.*)

Widow: (*Again appearing at door L. H.*) If you don't go away, I'll set the dog on you! (*As she goes to again slam door, Wang puts his foot in it and prevents her*)

Wang: No, you don't! What do you take me for, anyway, a book peddler or a junkman? Don't you know a real live Regent when you see him?

Widow: Mon Dieu! Mon Dieu! Can I ever forgive myself? (*Curtseys*)

Della Fox as Mataya, like Hopper, confirmed her claim to stardom. Of course the show easily lasted through the summer and then left for an extended tour.

The Casino hoped to repeat the welcome success of *Poor Jonathan* with its mounting on May 7 of another German work, Joseph Hellmesberger's **Apollo.** Divine law states that if the lady elected to serve as Apollo's oracle during a festival is kissed, disaster will follow. The evening was spent keeping the lady and her lover apart until the festival finished. Although the cast included the principals who had shone so brilliantly in the earlier production, especially Lillian Russell and Jefferson De Angelis, it failed fully to please either critics or playgoers. The piece, called a "burlesque operetta," survived only until July 11. One telling footnote was the presence of Gustave Kerker on the conductor's podium. Composing American comic operas was still an uncertain livelihood.

But Harry B. Smith was slowly and surely making the composition of librettos pay. For Digby Bell and the McCaull Opera Company he wrote **The Tar and the Tartar** (5-11-91, Palmer's) in collaboration with a young Baltimore conductor-composer, Adam Itzel, Jr. Smith resorted to an age-old motif, the disappearance of a ruler and the substitution of a commoner who resembles him. Smith acknowledged the antiquity of his basic plot, but later proudly pointed out that his version appeared three years before *The Prisoner of Zenda*. Once again McCaull and Palmer's knew the pleasure of watching a production run comfortably through the hot weather.

May's last offering was another free and easy farce-comedy larded with songs and specialty acts, **A Knotty Affair** (5-18-91, Park) by Herbert Hall Winslow. A newspaper's search for the source of an anonymous tip led the cast from an editorial office, to a swank apartment, to a "Kirmess" hall. The search continued nightly for just two weeks.

The season ended on July 11 with the arrival of *The Grand Duchess,* revived by the distressed Casino to fill the void left in the aftermath of *Apollo*'s failure. Lillian Russell and Jefferson De Angelis were again the principals. But even this Offenbach revival fell short of expectations, running just until August 22.

1891-1892

The preceding season's revival of *The Grand Duchess* in July was the only break in an unusually long hiatus that lasted from mid-May until August. Critics rued that what little plot a farce-comedy called **A High Roller** (8-3-91, Bijou) contained collapsed by the end of the first act, leaving the last act an "ordinary variety show." The *Times* itemized some of the musical numbers: "It contains a decidedly revelatory dance to set things going. . . . Four queer young men sing amusingly, and another dance, introducing the inevitable Amazon March, leads up to a 'Tar and Tartar' chorus and the curtain."

Two traditional musicals and one traditional spectacle in the Niblo style arrived during the week of August 24. All three were disappointments; the first and the last to arrive, outright failures. The first was a work written by Americans but with its heart and inspiration patently in the Old World, where a handsome young noble, Marcel (Edward Webb), falls in love with a flower-girl (Mamie Smith). He courts and wins her at a Students' Ball where everyone waltzed bedecked in colorful masks and dominoes. *Fleurette*'s libretto was by one Mrs. C. Doremus and Edgar Smith; its music was by Emma R. Steiner. Miss Steiner was apparently something of a musician, for besides composing the score she conducted the orchestra. However, her labors were to little avail. **Fleurette** (8-24-91, Standard) lacked the requisite wit, melody, and flair for success. It closed after a single week.

The night after *Fleurette*'s premiere, the Casino

mounted a production of Johann Strauss' *Indigo,* an operetta with a trouble-plagued history of failures and rewritings. Troubles of a sort plagued it at the Casino, too. Most of the house's stars, performers such as Francis Wilson and Lillian Russell, had moved elsewhere. Only Jefferson De Angelis remained of its stellar roster. As a result, critics and public generally viewed the new presentation as a lackluster effort. It ran just over a month, closing on October 3.

Niblo's spectacle, opening on the 27th, was advertised as an operetta and was called **The Khedive.** It proved another in the string of "Oriental" subjects so popular in the musicals and straight plays of the time. The son (Wallace McCrery) of an American-born Khedive of Turkey (Ferris Hartman) revolts when he cannot marry the girl (Lotta Gilman) of his choice. Both Niblo's and its distinctive mountings were nearing the end of their days; neither would linger into the new century. *The Khedive*'s fate reflected the waning power of both the theatre and the genre to attract patrons. It ran a mere week and a half.

When *Reilly and the Four Hundred* closed just before the height of summer, Ned Harrigan concluded its appeal had hardly diminished. As a result he soon announced the show was "on vacation," not permanently shuttered. His judgment was vindicated when the work relit Harrigan's Theatre on September 14 and played an additional 100 performances before giving way to *The Last of the Hogans* in December. In the spring, shortly before Harrigan ended his 1891–92 season, Reilly and his friends came back for still another visit, albeit a brief one of three weeks.

The night of Reilly's return in September also marked the return of W. S. Cleveland's Minstrels. Theirs was an art falling as rapidly out of vogue as Niblo's spectacles. The Minstrels' single week at the Park was all the blackface entertainment the Rialto was offered during the season, at least in any semblance of the old minstrel show.

J. J. McNally's farce-comedy **Boys and Girls** (9-21-91, Park) replaced Cleveland's troupe the following Monday. The plot revolved around a hero (James A. Sturgis) left $50,000 on the condition he spend it all. If he fails the money goes to his friends and relatives. Naturally they throw obstacles in his way. Its cast included a number of names soon to move to the top in musical comedy circles, although not always as performers, notably May Irwin (as a tough girl) and Julian Mitchell (as director). The dancer Ignacio Martinetti delighted with his graceful leaps and the Leopolds won applause

for more purely acrobatic turns. But the show was not accepted, and disappeared after a single week.

Competing with *Boys and Girls* for first-nighters was a second bit of contemporary pseudo-Orientalia, Bill Nye's **The Cadi** (9-21-91, Union Square). Nye at least attempted something different in "Orientalia," allowing his exotica to take place in New York. A mischievous boy (Minnie Dupree) leads a Wyoming postmaster to believe he has been made Turkish consul in Manhattan. Enlivened by the cavortings of Thomas Q. Seabrooke as the postmaster and Charles Parsloe as a pig-tailed, pigeon-English-speaking Chinese, the piece played until December 19.

September 28, 1891, brought two musical openings. Both were hits and one a landmark in the history of the American Musical Theatre. The lesser of the two was **Mavourneen,** a vehicle written for W. J. Scanlan by George H. Jessop and Horace Townsend. Scanlan played Terence Dwyer, a young Irishman whose betrothed is abducted. Dwyer goes to America, becomes rich, and returns home to use his money to retrieve his girl. The show introduced the song which next to "Peek-a-Boo" is most associated with Scanlan, "Molly O!" As was his custom, Scanlan took credit for both the words and music. The show gave every indication of being a smash hit and lifting Scanlan to new heights. But his behavior during the run grew increasingly odd, and forced him to close the show on Christmas night. The following week he was committed to an insane asylum, dying of paresis (syphilis-induced insanity) seven years later. Only a month before his removal from the stage Tony Hart had died from the same cause.

Robin Hood (9-28-91, Standard) was the first successful American comic opera or operetta cast in a mold that could be recognized as contemporary, or, at least, could have been so recognized while operetta held a place on the musical stage. Curiously, like several mid-19th-century hits such as *Evangeline* (7-27-74) and *Fritz, Our German Cousin* (7-11-70), its New York stays were brief. In *Robin Hood*'s case there were two reasons for its relatively short runs. First of all, the work was produced by the Boston Ideal Opera Company, a troupe, as we have seen, based in Boston and devoted to touring the nation with its repertory. New York was simply another stop in the itinerary. Second, the company (increasingly referred to just as The Bostonians) had reservations about the piece. The troupe had long wanted to stage an American work. The preceding season it had mounted *Don Quixote* with a libretto and lyrics by

Harry B. Smith and music by Reginald De Koven. The work had enjoyed only a small success but seems to have been removed from the schedule more because of backstage politics than any true failure. Nonetheless when De Koven and Smith presented the company with a second work, the Bostonians were so unsure of its feasibility that they used costumes and settings from other productions. If Smith's memory served him well, the total expenditure for the original production was $109.50. Its enthusiastic reception prompted the management to buy new sets and costumes to the tune of $5,000. This redecked mounting was what New Yorkers saw. Since the show grossed $12,000 a week at the Standard, the investment was quickly repaid. While critics, as was then their wont, failed to describe the physical production, they were unstinting with their praise of the performance—praise often begrudged groups based outside New York. The *Times* hailed the troupe as "a genuine operetta company, equipped with voices and method." Nor was this praise meant solely for the principals, for the paper continued, "There is probably not another operetta chorus, which, after three or four minutes of dialogue, could pick up the refrain of the song, and without orchestral support, sing it in tune and in the original key."

Smith's story was reasonably faithful to the old legend. The Sheriff of Nottingham (Henry Clay Barnabee) wrongfully deprives Robert, Earl of Huntington (Tom Karl), of his lands, conferring them upon his protégé, Guy of Gisborne (Peter Lang). Guy is also awarded the hand of Maid Marian (Caroline Hamilton), the sheriff's ward. In despair, Robert takes to outlawry. Under the name of Robin Hood he assumes leadership of a band of rather mild brigands. The treachery of one of the band leads to Robin Hood's capture, and he is condemned to die, but only after he witnesses the marriage of Marian to Guy. At the same wedding the sheriff plans to forcibly wed Annabel (Lea Van Dyke), the sweetheart of another of Robin Hood's band, Alan-a-Dale (Jessie Bartlett Davis). As the wedding is about to take place, Alan-a-Dale reminds his betrothed of their vows by singing "Oh, Promise Me" from his hiding place. Before the ceremony is finished Robin Hood's band—including Friar Tuck (George B. Frothingham), Little John (W. H. MacDonald), and Will Scarlet (Eugene Cowles, in his debut)—comes to the rescue. They have with them a pardon from Richard the Lion-Heart, who has newly returned from the wars. Something of the tenor of Smith's piece can be gauged by the fact that he wrote the part of the

Sheriff for the most beloved of the Bostonians, Barnabee, making the Sheriff into a comic, and not unlikable, villain:

(*The Sheriff enters with Guy and six journeymen tinkers.*)

Sheriff: Ah, here we are on the borders of Sherwood Forest, where the outlaw Robin Hood commits his fearful crimes. What is the matter with the Earl of Huntington? If you tremble like that you will shake down some of these trees. You seem to think you have got to be shaken before Robin is taken.

Guy: But I'm thinking of the desperado, Robin Hood Br-r-r (*trembles*).

Sheriff (*imitating him*): Br-r-r. What are you doing?

Guy (*trembling*): I am quaking at the dreaded name of Robin Hood. They say he sticks at nothing.

Sheriff: I don't care if he sticks at everything. Robin Hood never robs from the poor—sensible man; they have nothing worth taking. As journeymen tinkers we are too poor to attract his attention. Perhaps we will get a chance to capture this Robin, whoever he may be. You seem to forget that I have my eagle eye with me.

Guy: Which is your eagle eye?

Sheriff: The left—and it's a wonder. Trust to my colossal intellect, friend Guy, and we will not only bring Marian back so you can marry her, but we will hang Robin on a highly ornate and commodious gallows.

Much of the success of *Robin Hood* and possibly the main reason it held the stage for so long over the years was the popularity of "Oh, Promise Me." The song was not written for *Robin Hood* and was added only when it was felt another song was needed for Alan-a-Dale. In his memoirs Barnabee wrote, "It was taken from an old Italian melody, known and sung by every peasant in that lovely land of music. It is said it was unconsciously plagiarized by Reginald De Koven." Since De Koven remarked, in an interview, several years after *Robin Hood* opened, that much of his music was imitative, there may be a certain truth in Barnabee's story. Strangely, the pervasive lack of confidence in the work and its authors almost kept the song out of the show. Jessie Bartlett Davis, who had been assigned the trouser role, at first refused to sing it. Only when De Koven transposed the key and made some minor revisions did she acquiesce.

The other great hit of the show was a convivial drinking song, "Brown October Ale," in which Little John led a stirring male chorus. Its vogue led to similar numbers in later operettas. The songs of the day's better comic operas were not looked on merely as catchy melodies tailored to be easily sung by the man-in-the-street. Both composers and students of the time took a more artful, considered approach. They understood the classic forms around which they wrote their melodies and sought an interesting and pertinent variety of these classic forms to fill out their musical selections. In his *Standard Light Operas,* George P. Upton listed a duet, a quartet, a quintet, a tantara, a waltz, and a romance among *Robin Hood*'s numbers. *Robin Hood* did superb business during its strictly limited one-month run. This brisk trade encouraged the Bostonians to pay a second call later in the season for an additional five weeks. Whenever they returned thereafter, *Robin Hood* was almost certain to be in their repertory.

At a matinee on October 1 Rudolph Aronson offered his patrons a type of work fast fading from regular Broadway stages—grand opera. Beating out the impresario Oscar Hammerstein by a matter of hours, he gave New Yorkers their first exposure to Mascagni's *Cavalleria Rusticana.* The opera had had its world premiere in May of 1890 and its American premiere in Philadelphia on September 9, 1891. Hammerstein, who believed he had sole New York rights, hauled Aronson into court, but he lost on a technicality. Legal problems out of the way, Aronson put it on a regular bill, coupled with a translation of Carl Zeller's *Der Vogelhändler.* Misunderstandings and petty jealousies keep a bird handler and his sweetheart apart and flirting with royalty until just before the final curtain. The operetta was renamed **The Tyrolean** and starred Marie Tempest. The double bill began a run at the Casino on October 5. Mascagni's opera was dropped on December 5 but *The Tyrolean* ran until January 11, chalking up 100 performances.

October 5 brought in two other musicals. One was a three-month return of Francis Wilson in *The Merry Monarch* (8-18-90). The other was a curious pastiche that combined Thatcher's Minstrels with Rich and Harris' Comedy Company in a spoof of high society called **Tuxedo.** It was essentially a vaudeville that resulted from assorted characters, including a tough, Irish upstart (Hugh Dougherty), being thrown together on the porch of a grand hotel. At one point two principals spoofed President Benjamin Harrison and ex-President Grover Cleveland—in blackface. Its opening number had been extracted from *A High Roller* (8-3-91). The wild mélange played only a month in its original stay, but its popularity brought it back to several other houses over the season and in later years.

The quick closing of *The Khedive* had left Niblo's dark at one of the best moments of the theatrical year. Not until October 12 did the house reopen its doors. And then it played host to "one of the most dismal failures ever seen in New York." The show was **Beautiful Star,** with a libretto by William H. Day (a successful scene designer) and a score by Charles Puerner. Brutally panned, this tale from the Arabian Nights lasted a mere four nights.

Lillian Russell, until recently a glittering fixture at the Casino, returned to New York on October 26 at the head of her own company in Audran's **La Cigale.** The grasshopper of the title is a simple maiden who wins a chevalier away from a scheming duchess. For 112 performances Miss Russell delighted her admirers at the Garden Theatre, singing not only Audran's music but a number of interpolations by young Ivan Caryll, a Belgian who would soon take his place in the world of operetta.

November 2 saw the premiere of a straight play destined for years of popularity, **Hoss and Hoss.** But the amount of music in many straight plays of the period can be perceived by the songs thrown into the piece. On opening night they included, "Annie Laurie," the quartet from *Rigoletto,* a "kangaroo dance," and a take-off on Carmencita.

More Audran music was heard when David Belasco and Charles Frohman joined forces with Mrs. Leslie Carter to present **Miss Helyett** (11-3-91, Star). In this American version Mrs. Carter, an "oriflamme of red hair in an incredible braid far down her back," played (and sang, although not well) a simple American girl from Verity Village, Pennsylvania, who goes on a spree in Paris. Since Belasco, Mrs. Carter, and, at this early date, Frohman, were known entirely for their straight mountings, no one need have been surprised when pre-opening announcements insisted the piece was "not a comic opera, but a quaint and amusing comedy with 'musical attachments.' " But these same announcements noted, "The orchestra has been enlarged to thirty musicians and is under the direction of William Furst. There are twenty musical numbers."

A Trip to Chinatown (11-9-91, Madison Square) reached the heart of the New York theatre district after nearly a year on the road and became the biggest hit of the season. Nearly a quarter of a century elapsed before a straight play broke its record of 657 performances, and nearly thirty years went by before *Irene* (11-18-19), the first musical to surpass its stay. As originally conceived, the show had a libretto and lyrics by Charles Hoyt and music by Percy Gaunt. Its plot was simple. Rashleigh Gay (Lloyd Wilson), Wilder Daly, and their lady friends plan to spend an evening at a masquerade ball. Daly's young lady is Rashleigh's sister, Tony (Lillian Barr). But Rashleigh and Tony fear their Uncle Ben (George A. Beane) will not let them out for so riotous a night on the town. So they tell him they are going on a tour of Chinatown. They have dutifully invited a widow, Mrs. Guyer (Anna Boyd), to act as chaperone. But her letter of acceptance inadvertently gets delivered to Uncle Ben. Thinking he has made a conquest of the vivacious widow, Ben allows the youngsters to go on their tour, and he goes out to meet Mrs. Guyer at the restaurant she has mentioned in her letter. Of course, the restaurant is the very one Rashleigh and Wilder have booked for their own pre-ball dinner. At the restaurant Ben becomes increasingly intoxicated while waiting for his lady to appear. Only when Mrs. Guyer and the youngsters have gone off to the ball does he learn the widow had been there all the while. His embarrassment increases when he realizes that in his rush to the tryst he had forgotten his wallet. All the principals meet at the end of the evening. Uncle Ben would chastise his wards for their deception, but they have learned of his escapade, so there is mutual forgiving. To string out the thin story Hoyt used his arsenal of farce-comedy and vaudeville tricks. For example, he employed a series of running jokes. The servant Slavin Payne (Harry Gilfoil) is forever put down when he attempts to be helpful:

Slavin: Is anything required of me?
Rashleigh: Yes, Get out!
Slavin: Anything else I can do?
Ben: Yes. Keep out!
Slavin: Any service I can perform, sir?
Ben: Yes. Leave the room!

A number of characters are almost vaudeville vignettes. The most important figure apart from the youngsters, Ben, and the widow was a hypochondriac named Welland Strong (Harry Conor). He knows that everything he loves is killing him, so he keeps a notebook to record how each rich meal or each cigar lessens his life expectancy. But Hoyt does manage to impart a certain extra dimension while maintaining his running gags and stock humor. Here is how he takes what is really a vaudeville monologue and turns it into part of the play's regular dialogue:

Ben: Have a glass of wine?
Strong: I will! Wine is harmful to me. It shortens my life. But I'll take it! (*drinks*)
Ben: You don't look badly, old man!
Strong: No! That's the exasperating thing about it!
Wilder: Which lung is affected, sir?
Strong: Neither as yet. But the left one probably will be by Saturday night.
Rashleigh: Do you cough much?
Strong: Not at all! That's a very serious feature. My malady is so deepseated that I can't bring the cough to the surface. But instead I feel a sensation which, in a well man would be called a thirst for liquor.
Tony: And what do the doctors say?
Strong: No two agree.
Ben: And who shall decide when doctors disagree?
Strong: Usually the coroner. Why, I had seven of them. One fool said that nothing ailed me. Do you know, the only man who really understood my case was a horse doctor! He said if I stayed in Boston I'd die in sixty days. Out here I'd live two years if I obeyed certain rules. Here's the book of rules and it tells how much I shorten my life each time I break one. That glass of wine shortened it nineteen hours.

The persistently freewheeling ways of the era's musical theatre are interestingly illustrated by surviving texts of Hoyt's libretto. In them the setting for the third act differs and the relationships among the characters vary slightly. Significantly, while Wilder Daly plays a major, balancing role in all extant texts, he appears in no programs! Musically the freewheeling is also evident. One of the show's most popular numbers was Gaunt's adaptation of an old sixteen bar melody to new words by Hoyt, "Reuben And Cynthia." Typical of its many choruses was:

Reuben, Reuben, I've been thinking,
What a strange thing that would be,
If the streams of drinking water,
All turned salty as the sea.
Cynthia, Cynthia, I've been thinking,
You can safely take my word,
More than half the population,
Wouldn't know it had occurred.

Many of the lyrics were remarkably fresh and natural. The opening verse to "The Widow" runs:

Do you know her? Have you met her?
If so, you'll ne'er forget her—
The pretty little widow with the laughing eyes of brown.

Demure in her sobriety,
Severe in her propriety,
But the life of all society,
The jolliest thing in town.

If some of the words are no longer current usage, they were more commonplace at the turn of the century. But the best remembered of the Hoyt-Gaunt songs is assuredly "The Bowery," sung as a reminiscence by Strong to the partying couples.

Another illustration of the era's freewheeling practices occurred when road companies were sent out. While the first of the touring companies was in Milwaukee, Charles K. Harris' "After The Ball" was added and soon became one of the show's musical numbers wherever the show was performed. (See the discussion when *A Trip to Chinatown* returns in February 1894.) It was easy to insert and remove songs. For the most part the lead-ins were so generalized that with few exceptions, such as possibly "The Widow" or "The Chaperone," almost any song might have followed. "Reuben And Cynthia" is treated almost as a drinking song, led into simply by a universal "Drink hearty!" A simulated "coon" song, "Push Dem Clouds Away," is sung after Uncle Ben says, "I want you four young people to get 'round the piano and sing me my favorite quartette." And even though "The Widow" fits logically into the plot, the song is actually brought up by Wilder's comment, "That's a great song Billy Parker wrote and dedicated to her." In short, there was still some instinct prompting librettists to look at songs as extraneous, something to be kept formally apart. This attitude was underscored in the directions and staging. After "The Bowery" Hoyt's directions read, "exit à la militaire," while one unidentified song comes with the following directions: "Musical introduction. Tony and Flirt down C. and sing. Then the two boys join them. Then as they go up R. and L., Widow enters R.U.E. in white Chinese dress and does Chinese specialty. Then Strong, who is getting pretty drunk, down C. and sings with widow, all joining in chorus and dance at finish." However loosely incorporated, Hoyt saw to it the musical numbers were well done. Tiny, young Ollie Archmere won especially large applause for her pert dances. (In February 1892 Loie Fuller joined the cast to swirl her skirts more widely than she had before, in an elaborate imitation of butterfly wings. She was replaced the following October by Bessie Clayton, a young lady whose winning manner and stunning legs soon made her a favorite at Weber and Fields.) But whatever sort of dancing momentarily halted the plot, Hoyt saw

to it the evening as a whole was tautly staged. The *Times* reported the "piece gallops from start to finish."

An elaborate pantomime of **Cinderella** filled the Academy of Music from just before Thanksgiving until the day after Christmas. Romping with Cinderella (Fanny Ward) and her young-lady-in-trousers prince (Bertha Ricci) were such unusual characters as The Insect Queen and Baron Stone Broke. Naturally, since this was pantomime, Clown, Pantaloon, Harlequin, and Columbine were also present.

The Last of the Hogans, Harrigan and Braham's only new work of the season, bowed on December 21. The title throws the evening slightly out of perspective, since there were two stories running concurrently and that dealing with the Hogans was neither as important nor as entertaining as the other. Judge Dominick Murray, a "sporting" Irishman (Harrigan), is handling two cases. One concerns a will leaving a substantial fortune to "the last of the Hogans." He proves to be a bricklayer. The judge's other case concerns a group of Negroes attempting to sell their church. One of the church members, Esaw Coldstream (John Wild), runs an illegal society—The Mystic Star—dedicated to exterminating Italians who charge less for shoeshines than Negroes do. During a meeting on a barge, their scow is cut loose and collides with a tug on which the judge is holding an illegal prizefight. After the yacht's bowsprit crashed through the barge's rotten timbers the curtain fell on a "capitally devised scene of comic consternation." Ada Lewis assumed several roles, appearing first as a "froway" servant and later as a hard-boiled music hall artist, while Annie Yeamans, in a noteworthy change of pace for her, portrayed a warmly sentimental spinster. The *Times,* which not long before had compared Harrigan to Gay, now compared him to Hogarth and Dickens. As theatre historian George Odell noted, audiences must have loved "a stage full of sidewalks of New York" for the show enjoyed four profitable months at the box office.

An even more successful musical followed in just over a week. In **The Lion Tamer** (12-30-91, Broadway)—an American version of Lecocq's *Le Grand Casimir*—Francis Wilson found another vehicle to delight his loyal admirers. Wilson played Casimir a timid lion tamer who also owns a failing circus When he feigns suicide to leave his wife debt-free, complications ensue. With most of Lecocq's music discarded, the *Times* lamented that Richard Stahl's score was "commonplace" but resignedly accepted that "no one expected him to suddenly develop the faculty for melodic inventiveness." What luster the music displayed came from John Philip Sousa's orchestrations. During the run, Marie Jansen, Wilson's leading lady, became ill and a chorus girl who was her understudy had to go on. Truth is often as amazing as fiction. This popular motif of 1920 Broadway musicals and 1930 Hollywood musicals unfolded on the very real Rialto of 1892. The chorus girl who called attention to herself in such storybook fashion was Lulu Glaser.

. . .

Lulu Glaser was born in Allegheny City, Pennsylvania, on June 2, 1874. The buoyancy with which she threw about her long hair and displayed her attractive legs so delighted Wilson that he agreed to hire her for his chorus, even though she confessed she had had no previous professional experience. It was this same buoyancy and these same legs (which for years she displayed in light brown tights) that kept her a star for a quarter of a century.

. . .

Odell records another interesting footnote, one that demonstrates the danger of trusting to autobiographical memories. Wilson remembered the incident of the two young Negro entertainers in connection with *The Merry Monarch* (8-18-90), but Odell lists their names and the roles they played in *The Lion Tamer* as well as details of the Gerry Society's action against them after they opened the show. Other cast changes notwithstanding, Wilson was *The Lion Tamer* for Broadway's audiences until early May.

The first three months of 1892 were occupied with either revivals or importations. The Casino revived *Nanon* for Marie Tempest on January 12 and then tried a French novelty, Audran's **Uncle Celestin,** on February 15. Its story centered on an effete young man who hopes to marry the daughter of a snobbish baron but who learns he will lose the inheritance left him by his uncle unless he agrees to run a common tavern. Even Jefferson De Angelis' genial clowning could not infuse enough life into the piece to please New Yorkers. It had a slightly forced run of two months. On that same February 15 Agnes Huntington appeared in Planquette's **Captain Therese** at the Union Square. She played a lady who must dress as a man in order to rescue her falsely imprisoned lover. A poor reception necessitated her switching to *Paul Jones* on February 29. She played this revival for a week and then returned to the road.

Robin Hood's story claimed the stage again, but this time it was the legendary hero's fellow Englishmen who created the work. **The Foresters** (3-17-92, Daly's) was a play by Alfred Tennyson, embellished with songs and background music by Arthur Sullivan. It ran from mid-March until late April.

Three musicals opened on April 18. Millöcker's **The Child of Fortune,** with a libretto about the love life of a bohemian photographer, began an unrewarding run at the Casino. A. C. Gunter provided the libretto for a "fantastic operetta," **Polly Middles,** for which W. W. Lowitz composed the score. Polly (Annie Pixley), a "Drury Lane soubrette," and a group of fellow tourists in 1877 Pompeii drink a potion offered them by a German scientist. Suddenly they are transported back in time to Pompeii in its gaudy heyday. The shock of Vesuvius' great eruption sends them back to 1877. Richard Barker directed. The third opening was a farce-comedy, **A Jolly Surprise,** which played briefly at the Bijou.

The increasingly busy Harry B. Smith was librettist and lyricist for **Jupiter** (5-2-92, Palmer's), in which Digby Bell starred. Its score raised Julian Edwards from the ranks of conductors into the more select circle of composers.

. . .

Julian Edwards was born in Manchester, England, on December 11, 1855. After studying music in Edinburgh and London he accepted a post as conductor with the Carl Rosa Opera Company. J. C. Duff invited him to America to be his musical director.

. . .

Smith's tale for *Jupiter* was much like the one used decades later in *Amphitryon 38* and its musicalization, *Out of This World* (12-21-50). Jupiter assumes the guise of a hard-drinking shoemaker in order to seduce the shoemaker's wife (Laura Joyce Bell). The proprieties of the day led at least one critic to damn the show as sacrilege. Other critics had a more legitimate complaint: the show did not represent a noteworthy achievement on the part of either Smith or Edwards. However, at least one critic was so pleased with the scenery he devoted a few words to describing it—a rare practice at this time. The first act, done primarily in buff and blue, was set in a Roman square, with a triumphal arch at center stage. (On opening night Bell accidently knocked over the arch on his first entrance.) The second act was set on "Mount Olympus among silver-lined clouds and an eccentric moon." This setting provided a background for E. Forrest Jones as Marcus Coonius to sing a medley of minstrel songs. The cast included a still relatively unknown young lady, Trixie Friganza. But it was largely Bell's antics that kept the work on the boards for two months. Ignoring his ancient Roman toga, Bell joked about poker and baseball, and sang "Annie Rooney."

The next Monday, May 7, saw another great clown, De Wolf Hopper, return for an additional four weeks of *Wang* (5-4-91).

A "lyric-comedy" called **Elysium** (5-16-92, Herrmann's), based on Marie Uchard's *My Uncle Barbassou,* recorded the consternation of a young man (Clement Bainbridge) on learning he is heir to his uncle's estate—a harem. A eunuch (Max Figman) provided the comedy. The hero's consternation was small compared with that of some of the critics. "Positively indecent," the *Times* wailed. The public seemed to agree and the piece left hastily.

The abysmal failure of *Beautiful Star* left its composer, Charles Puerner, undiscouraged. He tried again on May 28 with a comic opera, **The Robber of the Rhine.** His librettist was a figure more often thought of as an actor in straight plays, Maurice Barrymore. This variation of the Robin Hood legend, peopled with gypsies and German brigands, was selected to open the new Fifth Avenue Theatre. Although it was staged by the capable Richard Barker and gave New Yorkers their first major glimpse of Hayden Coffin and Marie Dressler, the work met with a cool welcome. It ran only until the beginning of July.

June was ushered in on an unhappy note. The Broadway Theatre had hoped **King Kalico,** a comic opera with a book by Frank Dupree, and a score by Fred Solomon and R. L. Scott, would keep it lit through the summer. Edwin Stevens and Eva Davenport played the leads. Instead, the musical, which opened on the 7th, was a two-week flop. Its chief novelty was its setting, the Sandwich Islands (Hawaii)—a locale its librettist called home.

The Casino had better luck with another in its procession of importations, **The Vice Admiral.** The titular hero is a young man willed a fortune provided he marry before his twentieth birthday. The success of Millöcker's operetta made amends for the disappointment of his *The Child of Fortune.* Again, Jefferson De Angelis' clowning sparked the evening. *The Vice Admiral* sang his way into New Yorkers' hearts from June 18 until September 10.

The Garden Theatre also found itself a summer-long attraction in its mounting on June 27 of a lavish spectacle, **Sinbad.** The "$10,000 beauty,"

Louise Montague, played the title role. Spectacular sets took playgoers beneath the ocean and to the Valley of Diamonds. The construction of the piece was not as careful as the construction of its sets. The dialogue was filled with puns that were considered old hat and outrageous even in an era that was tolerant of old and strained puns. Its songs were culled from numerous sources and changed at intervals during the run. But the management could only remind the musical's critics that the audiences who flocked to the house until October 8 obviously didn't share the detractors' concern.

Henry E. Dixey brought the season to a close with a series of revivals. Opening on July 18 with *The Mascot* he later switched to *Patience, Iolanthe,* and a double bill of *Trial by Jury* and *The Sorcerer.* Dixey's company included Trixie Friganza. In the pit Julian Edwards conducted. Like Gustave Kerker before him, Edwards clearly was determined to play it safe until he was sure composing alone could bring him a dependable income. The troupe played until October 1.

Away from the mainstream, theatregoers could attend a number of minor efforts. For example, at the Thalia the Liliputians tried out a piece called *The Dwarfs' Wedding.* Deemed unworthy of better houses, the play was soon withdrawn and a new Robert Breitenbach work substituted. At Koster and Bial's the bill for October 19 included *Carmen up to Date,* a spoof not completely in the Gaiety tradition. At the London, another vaudeville house, McIntyre and Heath offered *Way Down South.* McIntyre and Heath were the earliest blackface act to make a mark in the legitimate theatre, although most of their career was spent in vaudeville. They were almost certainly the most enduring of blackface pairs. One of the great stories of the backstage world was their famous feud. While they acted and starred together for decades, an early disagreement led to their never speaking to each other off stage for most of their careers. Another future vaudeville great, Willy West, was a principal in their troupe. In their extended skit, McIntyre played an old colored woman named Hannah, Heath played a "fly coon" and a poacher, and West portrayed a porter.

One sad note was the appearance of *Fritz in Ireland* (11-3-79) at the Grand Opera House. The title role was played by J. K. Emmet, Jr., son of its originator. The young Emmet spent a number of years touring in his father's old vehicles and in some new ones, such as Sydney Rosenfeld's *Fritz in Prosperity.* He never won the love or fortune bestowed on his father, but for a while made a respectable living from the pieces.

3

INTERMISSION
Further British Influences
and New Stirrings

1892-1902

By the early nineties the great musical circus began to lose its appeal. Audiences had become jaded with more color than content. Freaks seemed less curious, clowns all of the same ilk, and spectacles appeared much like preceding spectacles. Another generation had to pass before audiences and economic conditions chased vestiges of carnival glitter and tricks from the musical stages. These vestiges survived as long as they did because a new group of brasher clowns came to tickle changing fancies, while spectacle found an outlet in a form that made its first tentative appearance at the beginning of this intermission, the revue. To a small extent vestiges still survive, attesting to the undying appeal of some theatrical extravagance and outlandishness.

All through this period future patterns quietly continued to take shape. For the first time a separation of lyric works into operetta, musical comedy, and revue could be discerned, although the pattern is clearer in retrospect than it was to critics and playgoers of the time. Musically, the stage remained under the influence of London. Two great hits, *A Gaiety Girl* and *Florodora*, flanked the period, reasserting the hegemony won for the English musical stage by Gilbert and Sullivan. The influence of the Gaiety musicals, coupled with the vogue of American farce-comedy, led directly to modern musical comedy. Both the American and English pieces reveled in the vernacular. They dealt not with royalty or unworldly figures but with more or less everyday men and women in more or less everyday difficulties. The English pieces had style

and a certain cohesion; the American works offered zest and more pertinent domestic material.

Theatrical royalty and its friends found refuge in comic opera, clothed in that genre's universally higher musical pretensions. The higher social order of its characters and its loftier musical aims were the genre's unifying traits. As often as not the form was not even accorded the courtesy of a generally accepted name. One playgoer's comic opera was another's opéra bouffe and a third's operetta. To some extent this confusion of nomenclature stemmed from the multiple sources of the American works, or, perhaps more accurately, from the blending and refashioning of these sources by American writers. The earliest Offenbachian opéra bouffe used mythological and other outlandish settings to mask sharp political commentary. Offenbach's successors brought their settings closer to contemporary France and substituted sentiment for satire. English comic opera, its standards set by Gilbert and Sullivan, generally kept its brilliantly witty and literate satire—satire more often social than specifically political—in the forefront. Its music, however artful, tended to be less arioso than either French or Viennese scores. Viennese operetta was the most carefree and playful. Its gay plots were more frivolous than preposterous. And far more so than either the French or English school, the Viennese works were determinedly contemporary. Almost every major Viennese operetta purported to take place in the very world its audience inhabited. American comic opera at this time clearly owed its main debt to Gilbert and Sullivan. But American writers, lacking Gilbert and Sullivan's genius, reduced Gilbert's great satire to buffoonery and Sullivan's magnificent melodies to tinkly pleasantries.

Acrobatic clowns and prima donnas dominated the musical stage of the period. The clowns were almost always in grotesque make-up and the prima donnas as often as not in tights, both thereby underscoring the traditions out of which they came. For most of the period their supremacy was acknowledged by having whole show companies named for them. The Francis Wilson Comic Opera Company or the De Wolf Hopper Comic Opera Company or the Alice Nielsen Comic Opera Company visited a town, as much as *Half a King* or *El Capitan* or *The Fortune Teller*. But hard times, brought on by the Panic of 1893, combined with an all too loose system of theatrical bookings, prompted a number of theatre magnates to merge their offices, forming what soon became known as "The Trust" or "The Syndicate." For better or worse this group completely changed producing and booking practices in the decade that followed. One of its initial coups was to end effectively the reign of the actor-manager, although, in fairness to the Trust, many a performer was undoubtedly thankful to be relieved of responsibility for his own ledgers.

Neither the Trust nor the stars could create the geniuses to write their material. It became evident during this intermission that Reginald De Koven was never to write a second *Robin Hood*. John Philip Sousa, in many ways a better and more theatrical melodist, had only modest luck with his stage pieces and soon tired of them. Theatre orchestra conductors who hastily donned composers' mantles—Ludwig Englander, William Furst, Gustave Kerker, as well as one man who was not a conductor, A. Baldwin Sloane—were musicianly, competent enough to orchestrate their own works, but basically they were hacks. When Victor Herbert appeared, the public and press alike were quick to appreciate his melodic gifts, and he would set the standards for American operetta composition for nearly a quarter of a century. No librettists or lyricists of similar magnitude emerged during this era.

Mounting changed little. Most musicals still relied on flats with perspective painted on. "Well-painted" remained a conventional expression of critical praise. Architecturally conceived sets were few and far between. Nor was one man customarily responsible for all the sets of a single evening. Specialists evolved, one painting little but garden scenes, a second called in for interiors, a third

known for his street scenes. Even the Casino, generally credited with the best producing staff, filled its stage with people rather than scenery. (In an age of low-paid performers, casts ranged from 60 to 200.) The first use of motion pictures to advance the action appeared. But film was offered more for its novelty than for its functional advantages. Its potentials and its implications largely passed unrealized.

Outside the theatrical mainstream a phenomenon occurred that would have more significance in the long run than anything else in the period. Afro-American music became popular. Ragtime's origins were untheatrical. Ben Harney first brought the infectious rhythm to New York in 1896. His success, while not as dramatic as sometimes thought, was immediate. Ragtime spread with remarkable speed in the burgeoning vaudeville circuits, and before long singers were interpolating so-called ragtime into loosely structured farce-comedies and the new revue form. The popularity of ragtime helped briefly to revive old songs from the waning minstrel tradition. Together they were responsible for the "coon" song rage of the turn of the century.

1892-1893

Appropriately, if unwittingly, the season was one of reminiscence and recapitulation. Over half the lyric pieces presented in 1892–93 were revivals. Off and on throughout the theatrical year the best-loved offerings from the first harvest of American musicals graced Broadway's stages. By summer New York had been given the opportunity to enjoy once more all the major native successes except *Evangeline* and *Humpty Dumpty*. New Yorkers who chanced to visit other cities at the right time could have caught these two favorites playing before packed houses across the country. They also could have caught a road company of *A Trip to Chinatown*, which began its tour on August 29 at the Harlem Opera House. The original cast, of course, continued at the Madison Square until April.

The first three musicals to arrive were past favorites. One of the most recent hits, *Wang*, with De Wolf Hopper still heading the cast, returned for a month's engagement at the Broadway on August 15 (and later for a week at the same house beginning November 14). A touring company of *Around the World in 80 Days* performed for a week starting August 27 at the fading Niblo's. But the biggest and perhaps the most surprising success among the older works was the remounting of *The Black Crook* (9-12-66) on September 1. Its original performers and scenery had long since disappeared, and since neither programs nor reviews detail the musical numbers, probably many of the 1866 songs had been replaced. Nonetheless the new production remained faithful in spirit to the sensation of a quarter of a century earlier. The settings were lavish and, besides the actors cast for the dramatic roles, the company included a host of ballet artists, acrobats (tightrope walkers, head balancers, etc.), and a contingent of French quadrille dancers. New songs included "Ta-Ra-Ra-Boom-Dee-Ay" (Henry J. Sayers). With an oddly fitting irony the show opened at the Academy of Music, whose burning in 1866 had led to the creation of the musical. Curiosity and nostalgia helped pack the auditorium for the whole season. When *The Black Crook* closed on May 20, it had added another 306 performances to its record and had grossed an additional $375,000.

The skimpy parade of new American musicals began on September 19 with the arrival of *Puritania* and *Candy*. **Puritania** was written by C.M.S. McLellan and Edgar Stillman Kelly for the prima donna of *Evangeline*, Pauline Hall. McLellan's book described how in 1640 Elizabeth (Louise Beaudet), a Salem maiden, is condemned as a witch. She is saved by a young English earl, Vivian George Trevelyan (Miss Hall), who carries her off to England. But she goes mad from her experience and in front of King Charles (John Brand) recites a mock incantation. At that very moment an anti-Royalist conspirator, Killsen Burgess (Harry Macdonough), sets off a bomb. To the king this validates the judgment against Elizabeth. In the end Burgess turns out to be Elizabeth's father. He is pardoned; she is cleared. She and the earl wed. It was a satisfactory vehicle for Miss Hall, and it remained at the Fifth Avenue Theatre until November 5 when it headed out into the hinterlands.

Candy, at the Union Square, was the latest in the series concocted by Robert Breitenbach for the Liliputians. It told how Sam Nollendorf (Mr. Durand) offers the hand of his daughter, Kitty (Minchen Becker), to anyone who can cure her addiction to candy. Tom Klapps (Franz Ebert), a bootblack, disguises himself as Prince Ole Hugh Ham and rids the young girl of her habit. Everyone then sails for Africa with the real prince (Mr. Kahn) to quell a revolution. They take a band of Amazons with them. Having restored the prince to his throne, they prepare to sail home on their steamer, S. S. *Microscope*. A storm shipwrecks them on a cannibal shore, but the grateful prince comes to their rescue. The first and last of the four acts ended with transformation scenes. At the Nollendorf home the guests were whisked off to "a candy palace" for a ballet; at the end the cast became part of an elaborate "Rose Festival." The musical stage could still support these theatrical freak shows, so when it became obvious that the show was settling down for a small run, one of the most popular midgets, Adolf Zink, was given "Ta-Ra-Ra-Boom-Dee-Ay" to interpolate as well as a prizefight with his fellow Liliputian, baby-faced, "tottly" legged Ebert. The German origins of most of the people associated with the show—as well, probably, as a good share of the audience—were acknowledged when the piece was published with English and German texts side by side.

One old standby, *Squatter Sovereignty*, opened the same night as *Candy* and *Puritania*. It signaled an entire season of revivals at Harrigan's, a tacit admission that the great showman had passed his most fruitful years. Hart was dead. Dave Braham's newer songs never enjoyed the general vogue of his former melodies, and, while Ned Harrigan continued to write effective material, he was never again able to assemble it with the compelling theatricality his better offerings displayed. His later works were all to be "comparative failures."

Rudolph Aronson suggested just how pervasive the feeling of creative exhaustion was when he removed the Casino from the legitimate fold and reopened it on September 26 as a vaudeville house. Since the theatre had been given over from its inception to importations, his action hinted that the font of foreign inspiration had run as dry as the native one. Vaudeville proved unpopular at the theatre. By November comic opera once more held its stage.

On September 24, the *Dramatic Mirror* announced that William Hoey was now singing a new song in the touring company of *A Parlor Match*. The song was "The Man Who Broke The Bank At Monte Carlo" (Fred Gilbert). The trade paper noted happily that the song "proved very funny, and aided by capital make-up, it received several encores." The song was ever after identified both with Hoey and the show. In later years, even when he was appearing in straight plays such as *The Globe Trotter,* Hoey found a way of inserting the song into his material.

A return of *The Lady or the Tiger?* was October's sole musical entry, filling the bill at the Broadway between *Wang*'s two engagements.

November opened with a visit to the Garden Theatre by the Bostonians, singing their greatest hit, *Robin Hood* (9-28-91). It cheered New York in this sluggish season from November 7 until Christmas Eve and then again from May 22 until the first of July, with a one-week break. For seekers of novelty, Smith and De Koven, the authors of *Robin Hood,* had a new work ready one week after the revival of their masterpiece. **The Fencing Master** (11-14-92, Casino) gave Broadway several causes for small celebration. The show marked the return of the Casino to the legitimate realm and also marked the first American musical ever to play the theatre. It was as well the first new lyric piece of the season to enjoy an unqualified success. But though it was American in origin it was set in the lavish palaces of 15th-century Milan and Venice, its scene and mood even more alien to our shores than Sherwood Forest. The play's principal figure was not its fencing master, Torquato (William Broderick), but his daughter Francesca. She is in love with Fortunio (Hubert Wilke), who would be Duke of Milan had not the spendthrift Galeazzo Visconti (Charles Hopper) usurped the throne. Unfortunately, since Francesca has been raised as a boy, Fortunio has no idea of her true sex and has found romance elsewhere. His heart is given to the Countess Filippa (Grace Golden). When the bankrupt duke sells Filippa's hand in marriage to a Venetian and orders Fortunio to escort the countess to her wedding, Fortunio plans an elopement. He reveals his plan to Francesca and she, in desperation, betrays him. Fortunio challenges her to a duel and only when she is injured is her real nature ascertained. She takes the blame for the duel and is imprisoned. A marchesa who loves the supposed boy and is unaware of the truth helps Francesca escape. At a masked ball Fortunio realizes he loves Francesca. The duke and his astrologer (Jerome Sykes)—two more of Smith's comic villains—are overthrown and Fortunio's rights restored. De Koven carefully filled his score with appropriate Mediterranean styles—tarantellas, barcaroles, habaneras, and maranescas—and while many of the melodies were attractive, none proved lastingly popular. Probably the best were "Ah Yes, I Love Thee" and "A Wild Bird That Singeth." With Marie Tempest starred in yet another trouser role, *The Fencing Master* delighted New York until the end of February.

November's third and final lyric piece was Harrigan's *The Mulligan Guards' Ball* (1-13-79). It proved far and away the most popular of his four revivals, running from November 30 to March 18.

Another of the season's new successes, **The Isle of Champagne,** followed on December 5, although its relatively short run belies its popularity around the turn of the century. With a text by Charles Alfred Byrne and Louis Harrison and with music by W. W. Furst (long the pit leader at San Francisco's Tivoli), the musical recounted how King Pommery Sec makes his fortune when a ship is wrecked off his island. The king's domain flows with champagne but water is unknown. The wrecked vessel has a large supply of water on board which Pommery Sec promptly commandeers. Other characters had such likely names as the Baron Heidsic and the Marquis Mumm. As an added attraction the mounting offered "stage pictures prolific in gold, silver, and silk tights." Starring Thomas Q. Seabrooke, the show played until January 21 at Hammerstein's 2600-seat Manhattan Opera House and, after touring Harlem, Brooklyn, and points farther afield, returned on May 29 for a summer run at the elegant Fifth Avenue. With or without its original star *The Isle of Champagne* played constantly for over a decade.

Audran's *La Cigale* was revived the night after Christmas at the Garden for two weeks, but the booking was clearly a stop gap until **The Mountebanks** was ready to raise its curtain on January 11. This joining of W. S. Gilbert with Alfred Cellier, who years before had conducted some of Sullivan's scores in New York, piqued Broadway's curiosity. At least it did before the curtain went up. Even with Lillian Russell and the American-born English favorite, Hayden Coffin, singing the leads, the show, which detailed the complications produced by a magic philter that makes "everyone who drinks it exactly what he pretends to be," proved mildly disappointing. Nonetheless, the musical ran a month and a half, then toured. If London and New York tastes were not always the same, there were cases where, for better or worse, they did coincide. Gilbert's complaint in *The Mountebanks* that many a song has "twenty verses and each verse has a chorus" suggests that pandering to the demand for excessive encores was as prevalent in England as it was in America.

A more important event for the New York stage, if not for the American Musical Theatre, occurred two weeks later when the Empire Theatre first opened its doors at 39th Street and Broadway on January 25, 1893. With time this house became one of the most venerated in theatrical annals, occupying a niche alongside Wallack's and Daly's, and enduring far longer. Its grandeur may have given its proprietor, Charles Frohman, even more grandiose ambitions, for no sooner had the theatre opened than he was in secret consultation with a number of other theatre owners. To the extent that Frohman hoped to end the chaos in national bookings his plans were admirable. Most theatres were independently owned. A few more aggressive entrepreneurs owned a handful of houses. But anything like the transcontinental chains of later years was unknown. As a result to book a national tour required long, elaborate correspondence with a large number of house managers. If bookings were made late or had to be changed suddenly a company often found itself skipping its way back and forth across the country. By grouping together important theatres across the land and handling all their bookings from one office, troupes could move from city to city with some geographic logic. Moreover, given a long view of a season, dark weeks could be minimized. Unfortunately, the men with whom Frohman conferred—notably Abe Erlanger—were not highly ethical. Out of these talks came the infamous "Trust" or "Syndicate," a booking monopoly that shortly had marked effects on theatrical practices, including those of the American musical. Anyone refusing to bow to the dictates of the monopoly found whole cities with no available theatres.

No more musicals bowed until February 27, when André Messager's **The Basoche** replaced *The Fencing Master* at the Casino. Its plot recounted the rocky road a marriage takes after a husband and wife each suspect the other of being unfaithful. The *Basoche* of the title was a French legal fraternity. The evening proved a harsher disappointment than *The Mountebanks* and was withdrawn after two weeks. The same night saw the opening of **A Mad Bargain,** a farce comedy filled with names working their way to the top of the lyric stage: J. J. McNally and Julian Mitchell (its authors), James T. Powers, Peter F. Dailey, and Richard Carle. McNally's plot recounted the plight of a would-be suicide. Lacking the courage to take his own life he persuades his cousin to arrange an "accident." When he has a change of heart, he cannot locate his cousin to stop the arrangement. His contrivances to keep out of death's way comprised much of the fun. In keeping with the farce-comedy tradition extraneous songs were interpolated.

March saw nothing but revivals. Lillian Russell began a month's run on the third in *Giroflé-Girofla;* *The Gondoliers* was rushed in on the 16th at the Casino to fill the vacancy created by the failure of *The Basoche;* and on the 20th Harrigan returned

Cordelia's Aspirations (11-5-83) to the footlights.

The burlesque traditions of the seventies and early eighties had become passé, especially those based on classical models. But minstrels and variety performers, as we have seen, kept the art alive, if truncated. A harbinger of its revival appeared on April 3 when Charles Brookfield's full-length parody of **Lady Windemere's Fan** was unveiled at the Garden. In that it occupied the whole evening it was an even more ambitious undertaking than later Weber and Fields spoofs. It advertised itself simply as a burlesque of Oscar Wilde's play, eschewing the delicious possibilities of twitting the title as well as the story. Typical of its changes, Lady Agatha was rechristened in honor of her most indicative line. She became Lady Yesmama, and May Robson, who played the role, had little else to do except walk across the stage uttering the phrase. The "little else," however, included a takeoff on Loie Fuller's skirt dance, employing a third leg. Besides characters based on Wilde's figures, audiences beheld a bard (Harry Mills), Hamlet (Max Figman), Ophelia (May Irwin), a fairy (again Miss Irwin), and an actor impersonating Wilde himself (Henry Miller as Oscar O'Flaherty Wilde). The famous men's scene was filled with minstrel jokes. The evening amused knowledgeable playgoers for nearly two months.

At the Casino, Rudolph Aronson's worst fears were being realized. His attempt at vaudeville was a failure, and now he was "having trouble finding musicals." When the revival of *The Gondoliers* drew only middling attendance, he hurried in a revival of *Adonis* on April 18, frantically adding the strongman Sandow as an added attraction on June 12 in a final attempt to save the house. But his maneuvers went for nought, and after he put the theatre into receivership his stockholders successfully petitioned to have him removed. More than any other incident, this vividly illustrates the plight of the musical theatre at the time and its lack of resourceful talent. Thomas Canary and George Lederer took over the management.

. . .

George Lederer was quickly to outshine his associate. He was born in Wilkes-Barre, Pennsylvania, in 1861. Although he began his career as an actor, he soon tried his hand at producing, sending a play called *Florimel* on national tour. His partner in this fledgling effort was Sydney Rosenfeld, with whom he would work at the Casino.

. . .

The last of Harrigan's revivals, *Reilly and the 400* (12-29-90), competed on May 1 for the attention of first nighters with De Wolf Hopper's newest vehicle, **Panjandrum** (5-1-93, Broadway). Written for him by the same team that had provided him with *Wang,* J. Cheever Goodwin and Woolson Morse, it fell short of its predecessor's raging popularity but even so kept the Broadway lit through the summer until September 30. The plot was preposterous. On an island in the Philippines, Pedro (Hopper) fails as a bullfighter and thus forfeits the affection of Paquita (Della Fox). To win the girl back he agrees to help in an elopement Paquita has planned for the ward of a Spanish grandee and a coach driver. The party is captured by a savage tribe. Their king is Panjandrum. Unbeknownst to all but a few in the tribe, the king has been dead for six years. Pedro looks remarkably like him and is persuaded to take his place. He does so admirably. The *Times* rather cruelly condemned Miss Fox, "who can neither act nor sing and who is not pretty," but nevertheless felt the show would be successful, and "Every one in town will go to see De Wolf Hopper imprison a tiger in a hogshead by tying a knot in his tail." The show followed the then still fashionable practice of making constant revisions in an effort to lure satisfied patrons back more than once, announcing a "second edition" on June 28 just before the worst summer heat was expected. In his memoirs Hopper stated the title was cynically arrived at in a determined effort to publicize his name. As he remembered, "We purposely called the play by the meaningless syllables, 'Panjandrum.' Rather than stumble over 'Panjandrum,' the public asked for seats for Hopper, as we intended they should." Although Hopper may have been unaware the syllables had taken on a meaning since Samuel Foote first employed them, this statement's real significance is to demonstrate that the play was patently not the thing; it was merely a vehicle for a star's special talents. On the very day *Panjandrum* premiered, President Cleveland pressed a button to open Chicago's year-late Columbian Exposition. But the celebration was short-lived. On May 6 National Cordage, a speculative stock which had hit 147, collapsed, and the Panic of 1893 began.

As so often happened a half-century or so later, the season's biggest hit came virtually last. Called **1492** (5-15-93, Palmer's), it was, like the Chicago Fair, a year late with its honors, but few cared. The work originated in Boston where its creators, E. E. Rice and R. A. Barnet, scoured the upper echelons of vaudeville for performers. They were not so careful in seeking out a composer, settling all too easily on Carl Plueger. Walter Jones essayed

the dual roles of King Ferdinand and the tramp Charlie Tatters. Richard Harlow, popular as a female impersonator, played Queen Isabella. "Specialists" included Theresa Vaughn, cast vaguely as "Fraulein," bringing over from her variety turn her singing of English and American songs (such as "Annie Rooney") in an arch German. Like *Panjandrum, 1492* underwent frequent alterations. Two weeks after the opening, for example, a fashion show-cum-ballet called "Six Daily Hints from Paris" was inserted. It was so well received that on November 13 of the next season "Six More Daily Hints from Paris" was added along with a dance of store window mannequins. New York audiences applauded the show in one form or another for 354 performances.

During their late season return the Bostonians offered the newest De Koven–Smith effort, **The Knickerbockers** (5-29-93, Garden). Miles Bradford (W. H. MacDonald) comes to New Amsterdam to court the governor's daughter, Katrina (Camille D'Arville). But because he helps a fellow Puritan escape from jail he is accused of being a spy. His friend, Hendrick (Edwin W. Hoff), persuades Miles to disguise himself as Hendrick's fiancée, Priscilla (Jessie Bartlett Davis), and to flee. The governor (Henry Clay Barnabee) gets wind of the plan and sends soldiers to arrest Miles. Instead, they arrest the protesting Priscilla. She escapes, disguising herself as a British soldier. Miles, in yet another disguise, takes service as the governor's bodyguard. But he becomes jealous of a British soldier he believes is receiving too much of Katrina's attention. Of course, the "soldier" is Priscilla. A happy ending follows. Although the *Times* hailed the work in its review headlines as "A REAL NEW YORK OPERETTA," "A Genuine American Work," and "an Event," the text of its notice was more reserved, rating the music as "cold and uninspired" and complaining that Smith ignored the possibilities of local color. The public agreed with the reservations, and after a single week the Bostonians were again singing *Robin Hood.* Interestingly, the critics, while praising old favorites such as Barnabee and Miss Davis, were most lavish in their praise of a recent addition to the troupe's roster, Miss D'Arville. The reasons why Miss D'Arville, who had shared starring honors with Lillian Russell, was content to lose herself in the relative anonymity of a traveling repertory company are lost. One answer may lie in the dearth of stellar roles available to her. But her reputation suffered not at all. Within a year her name was again above a title.

The season's final lyric offering was Robert Planquette's **The Talisman** (6-21-93, Manhattan Opera House), which had premiered only six months before in Paris. Most critics and advance notices overlooked the plot—as did Florian Bruyas in his history of French musicals—all suggesting the feeble story line was merely an excuse for sumptuous Louis XV sets and costumes. In New York it proved an insufficient excuse. The piece folded two weeks later, and Hammerstein sold his auditorium to Koster and Bial, who moved their vaudeville up from 23rd Street.

1893-1894

While the number of musical works reaching New York in this season jumped by more than half over the figure of the preceding year—from two dozen to better than three dozen—the increase did not mean higher standards. Rather it attested to the turnover prompted by both the generally mediocre quality of the new works and the effects of the Panic of 1893. Well above a third of the productions were revivals. A lone, small note of encouragement came from the drop in the percentage of importations. Americans were not writing very good musicals, but they were writing more of them.

All of August's entries were old favorites. *The Black Crook* (9-12-66) returned to the scene of its 1892–93 triumph where its cast cavorted on the stage of the Academy of Music from August 14 to September 23. Twelve nights later *1492* relit Palmer's after a summer vacation, while a touring company of *A Night at the Circus* (12-21-91) began a two-week stay at the Park. On the 28th, Harrigan reopened his house with a revival of *Dan's Tribulations* (4-7-84), the first rehearing the play had received in seven years. It was greeted politely, but without real enthusiasm, by both critics and the public, inaugurating a sadly unsatisfying year for Harrigan. He kept it on the boards only until October 7, when his sole original offering of the season was ready.

September's four lyric works were all new, or tried to be. The ambivalent arrival was **The Brand New City Directory** (9-5-93, Bijou), a fresh mounting of the recent hit (2-10-90) that kept the show's original frame but filled it with new specialties and dialogue. The original's three acts were compressed into two, with much of the second half devoted to a burlesque of a Faust rehearsal in which Willis

Sweatnam, long of the minstrel stages, portrayed a stage manager and half-sang, half-talked a song. Rubber-faced William B. Wood brought over from variety his monologue justifying his nailing his suspenders to his shirt. Nellie Parker introduced the "latest" London successes, while Amelia Glover performed her lively dances.

"A spectacular play," **A Trip to Mars** (9-8-93, Niblo's), opened three nights later. The mounting was a vehicle for the Liliputians, written for them, as always, by Robert Breitenbach. Its music was by Fritz Krause. The plot reveled in the preposterous science fiction of the time. Professor Heddison devises a pill that "miniaturizes" people. By way of a secret cabinet he sends his small folk to Mars. On the way back they visit the clouds and a marvelous grotto reminiscent of *The Black Crook* (9-12-66). They return to earth, landing on the dome of the World Building. The trip to the clouds offered a much publicized effect, advertised as "The Flying Heads," in which only the midgets' heads, with wings attached, were seen flying across on the stage. Other noteworthy moments devised by Carl Rosenberg included "The blinding glories of an electrical apotheosis, the novel beauties of a snow-bird dance," and a chariot drawn by the "smallest ponies in the world." The electrical apotheosis occurred on both sides of the footlights, for Niblo's proudly announced that the auditorium was lit by electricity.

William Gill's **The Rising Generation** (9-11-93, Park) was a farce-comedy that tipped its hat both to the growing social standing of the Irish and to the burgeoning musical comedy. In a story larded with "rollicking music" and specialties it traced the rise of Martin McShayne from a lowly bricklayer to a successful contractor. After three weeks it headed for the road.

The month's most eagerly awaited musical raised its curtain at the Casino on September 25. But **The Rainmaker of Syria,** besides being an artistic disappointment, soon became embroiled in the legal battles raging around the house. Its book and lyrics were by Sydney Rosenfeld and its music, somewhat surprisingly, by Rudolph Aronson, who had been temporarily restored to his old hegemony at the theatre by court order. Rosenfeld's libretto was period exotica. The Egyptian Amosis (Mark Smith) pretends to be a rainmaker. Studying past droughts he discerns a pattern and correctly predicts when the next rain will arrive. King Thesaurus (Harry Davenport) would award him the hand of an ugly princess, but Amosis demurs. He prefers "King" Hatchupoo (also spelt Hatshepu) (Bertha Ricci) whom he knows to be an attractive woman in disguise. The show closed on October 12 when Rosenfeld broke his own connections with the Casino and refused to pay the cast. The incident also left Aronson once again out of office.

October was the season's busiest month, but it was not especially fruitful. A revival of *Erminie* (5-10-86) with Francis Wilson, Lulu Glaser, and Christie MacDonald ushered in the month and kept audiences at the Broadway delighted into December.

Harrigan's only novelty of the year was **The Woolen Stocking** (10-9-93, Harrigan's). In his customary blend of comedy, melodrama, and sentimentality, Harrigan retailed the plight of Paddy Dempsey (Edward Mack), who saves a mine owner, is made his heir, loses the deed to the mine, and goes blind. Larry McLarney (Harrigan), a stevedore boss, retrieves the deed for Dempsey. Larry also woos and wins Widow Hickey (Annie Yeamans), a hotel-keeper. Besides Harrigan and Miss Yeamans, other regulars, such as John Wild, Joseph Sparks, and Paula Edwards, assumed roles of various importance. If the substance of Harrigan's story and the drift of Braham's songs were the same as they long had been, the added spark that had once spelled success was wanting, and the very sameness now told against the work. "Little Daughter Nell" and "The Sunny Side Of Thompson Street" enjoyed small, brief vogues, but neither entered the canon of Braham favorites. Harrigan kept the piece going until he could prepare a revival of his own best-loved work, *Old Lavender*. After *The Woolen Stocking* was withdrawn on December 16, Harrigan promptly settled down to revise it. He brought it back on February 19. Unfortunately the revisions changed its reception not a jot. Harrigan closed it after one week and abruptly ended his season. The early closing was another sad indication of his falling star.

A new Fritz play, **Fritz in Prosperity** (10-23-93, Grand Opera House), like so many offerings of the period, revealed changes in the wind. Critics complained about the "Americanization" of Fritz in this latest opus of the busy Rosenfeld and also noted the virtual absence of song. *Fritz in Prosperity* was as close as any of the series came to being a pure straight play.

On October 25 Lillian Russell returned to the Casino in a musical written for her by the same team that had provided Thomas Q. Seabrooke with *The Isle of Champagne* (12-5-92) the preceding season. Set to William Furst's music, Charles Alfred Byrne and Louis Harrison's book for **Princess Nicotine** told of the marriage of a pretty cigarette

maker, Rosa (Miss Russell), to a rich tobacco planter, Chicos (Perry Averill). The local governor, Don Pedro (Digby Bell), had wanted Rosa for himself. He arranges for Chicos' arrest and goes to woo Rosa. But just in front of the honeymoon cottage he falls into a stream. Rosa rescues him. In her innocence she sets his clothes out to dry and invites him into her house. Chicos escapes, returns, and seeing the governor's clothing outside, misconstrues the situation. Explanations follow in time for a happy ending. For her endeavors Miss Russell received a salary of $700 a week, plus half the profits. But she undoubtedly earned every penny of it, for she kept this musical of such modest achievement before the footlights for three full months. Assisting her, at considerably less pay, besides Bell, were Dan Collyer and Marie Dressler.

Another reigning musical queen brightened the Rialto the next night, when Marie Tempest arrived as star of **The Algerian** (10-26-93, Garden). If her star twinkled a little less brightly than did Miss Russell's, her luck in having a Reginald De Koven score to sing was a hoped-for compensation. Once again in this glum season hopes were dashed. Although for many years afterwards De Koven insisted this was his favorite score, his public did not agree. Moreover, instead of assigning the book to Harry B. Smith, who had served him honorably for so long, he entrusted it to a newcomer, Glen MacDonough. MacDonough later went on to write a number of remunerative librettos, but his work for *The Algerian* betrayed his lack of experience. Not that his basic plot line was much different from the run-of-the-mill comic opera tale. He chose the safe setting of the mysterious "Orient," supposedly basing his tale on an unnamed Alphonse Daudet novel. In Algiers the impecunious Prince of Montenegro (Joseph Herbert) establishes a fake harem to lure tourists. He hires his "wives" from the chorus of a stranded opera company. One visitor, Col. La Grange (Julius Steger), falls in love with a supposed concubine, but Celeste, the Countess of Monvel (Miss Tempest), who loves La Grange and who was once a member of the opera company, exposes the hoax. Miss Tempest and De Koven still drew well enough at the box office to keep the show in New York until mid-December.

Julian Edwards' continuing seriousness of purpose was manifest on November 22 when his **King Rene's Daughter** joined Gounod's *Philemon and Baucis* on a double bill at Herrmann's Theatre. The two works were to have opened together a week earlier, but the illness of Eleanor Mayo, who was to sing the title role in Edwards' work, forced a week's separation in the premieres. Count Tristan (Charles Bassett) comes to King Rene's court to marry the king's daughter, Iolanthe. At the court he falls in love with a winsome blind girl who has never been told other people are not blind. Tristan demands King Rene (William Pruette) cancel the wedding so that he can marry the young lady, only to discover she is Iolanthe. The libretto was derived from Henrik Hertz' drama, which was also the source of Tchaikovsky's opera *Iolantha*. If the story was not much different from many on the boards at the same moment, the music attempted to be. It elicited a not unexpected outcry from some of the critics, the *Herald* bewailing it "wallows in Wagner." But the *Dramatic Mirror* hailed it as "musicianly and musical." The public seemed to side with the *Herald,* for the double bill was withdrawn after two weeks.

December played it safe with three revivals for the holiday crowds. The preceding season's success, *The Fencing Master* (11-14-92), returned briefly on the 11th, without, of course, Miss Tempest, who had taken *The Algerian* on the road. A week later Harrigan revived his personal favorite, *Old Lavender* (9-3-77), for a month's run at his house.

December 23 witnessed the start of a month-long engagement of a French work, **The Voyage of Susette,** mounted as a spectacle at the American.

The popular Bostonians came to town on Christmas night, opening with their most popular piece, *Robin Hood* (9-28-91). They offered the work until January 15, celebrating their 1200th representation of it on January 8. Two less important, but new pieces also opened on Christmas night. One was the premiere at the Bijou of a farce-comedy with musical interpolations, **A Country Sport.** With Peter F. Dailey, May Irwin, Ada Lewis, and Richard Carle among the pranksters, the show became one of the biggest hits of the season, running until the spring. Dailey played Harry Hardy, of Jokersville-on-the-Hudson, who is left his uncle's considerable fortune on the condition he prove himself "a thoroughbred sport." With a phony preacher, Con Connelly (Carle), he heads for the Bowery's fun spots. He resists efforts to convert him to the cloth and manfully shows he is entitled to the inheritance. Dailey's high jinks included inviting the wax figure of a policeman at a dime museum to dinner (and having him accept!) and, in company with Miss Irwin, waltzing with wire dummies at a cheap clothing store.

The same night saw George Thatcher's troupe present something between a farce-comedy and a minstrel show, **Africa.** In an age of musicals filled with gimmicks, *Africa* was no exception. All the characters in the show had names beginning with "M"—Mr. Medikus, Mark Mansfield, Moses Merrill, Miggs, Maggs, Muggs, and so on. No author came forward to take credit for the nonsense. What little plot the musical had seems to have allowed Thatcher, as a quack doctor, Medikus, to take his patients for a cure to an island he tells them is off the coast of Africa but is actually a stage set he has built on an island off the American shore. A touring production, it lingered briefly, returned in January for two weeks at the Park, then went its way.

New Year's night, 1894, brought back the Liliputians in a revival of *The Pupil in Magic* (9-15-90). The show was the last that could be called a musical ever to play Niblo's. At the end of the next season, the old house that once sheltered *The Black Crook* (9-12-66) and *Evangeline* (5-10-86) was demolished. Bad times coupled with the theatrical center's move northward had sealed its doom.

The Bostonians, too, were soon to pass from the scene, and no small part of their demise was their inability to find a number of strong follow-ups to *Robin Hood.* Henry Clay Barnabee and his associates were aware of their difficulty and attempted to counter it by commissioning three works that "waved the starspangled banner of native art." One of these, *The Knickerbockers* (5-29-93), had reached New York the preceding season. The other two were included as part of their 1893–94 visit. **The Maid of Plymouth** (1-15-94, Broadway) was offered first. Clay M. Greene's version of the Priscilla Alden and Miles Standish legend was set to music by Thomas P. Thorne. Their romantic adaptation was a far cry from the arch burlesque treatment Rice had given *Evangeline.* The text was competent by the standards of the time and the lyric rose to a popular poetry:

> Amid the storm they sang,
>   And the stars heard, and the sea
> And the sounding aisles of the dim woods rang
>   With the anthem of the free.

On the other hand, Greene's Indians often spoke (and sang) in the "metre and style of 'Hiawatha.' " This led the *Times* to view both the work and the production as a travesty and to condemn its "shopworn patter." Most other papers took the work more seriously, even if they could not wax enthusiastic over it. Almost without exception, they viewed Thorne's music as serviceable, but not memorable. Eugene Cowles sang Miles; Margaret Reid, Priscilla; Edwin W. Hoff, John Alden. Barnabee played an Elder, while Jessie Bartlett Davis portrayed an Indian.

One week later—on January 22—Harrigan replaced *Old Lavender* with a revival of *The Leather Patch* (2-11-86), and still another week later **Prince Kam, or A Trip to Venus** (1-29-94, Casino) premiered. Originally mounted in Boston in September and unfavorably received, it spent the intervening months on the road attempting to whip itself into shape. Its librettists were those of *Princess Nicotine*, Byrne and Harrison, and its composer, Gustave Kerker. The title role was a trouser part for Camille D'Arville. As Prince Kam of Thibet she takes a flying machine to Mars (William Pruette), where the prince falls in love with Venus (Fannie Johnson). Venus follows Kam back to earth. Pruette and Miss Johnson, a vivacious blonde, stopped the show singing a song that took a jaundiced view of love, while Miss D'Arville won applause for her pyrotechnical rendition of "A Leap From The Earth To The Sky." E. E. Rice produced the evening with an éclat typical of both him and the Casino. As one satisfied critic noted, "the young ladies of the chorus were innumerable, the costumes rainbows and jewels." A month's run was followed by a tour.

February opened with one of the season's many revivals, *A Trip to Chinatown* (11-9-91), which began a seven-week stay at the Madison Square Theatre on February 12. In the course of its travels it had picked up one major interpolation, "After The Ball" (Charles Harris). The song was spectacularly successful. It reputedly sold five million copies. Isadore Witmark attributed to the money Harris made as his own publisher "the establishment of mushroom publishing houses financed on a shoestring." With "Reuben And Cynthia" and "The Bowery" still on the program, no American show up to this date could boast so many songs that have remained part of our active musical heritage.

The second of the Bostonians' new American works, **The Ogallallas** (2-19-94, Broadway), claimed to be the first major musical to center on the American Indian. *Pocahontas* (12-24-55), *Hiawatha* (12-25-56), *Dovetta* (4-22-89), and other works were apparently forgotten. The new piece offered a tale that must have reminded many of a section from *The Last of the Mohicans*. General Andover (Henry Clay Barnabee) is escorting a group of ladies across the prairie when they are captured by Indians. Captain Deadshot (Edgar Temple) is also captured when he attempts to rescue them. Deadshot, an Indian known as War Cloud (W. H. MacDonald), and a Mexican bandit,

Cardenas (Eugene Cowles), all court one of the young ladies, Edith (Bertha Waltzinger). Edith decides on Deadshot just as the army arrives to free the prisoners. As she had in *The Maid of Plymouth*, Jessie Bartlett Davis found herself cast as an Indian. The novelty of Young E. Allison's subject was the principal attraction along, perhaps, with the fame and quality of the troupe. Waller's music was nondescript. Barnabee was forced to admit, "American art languished on its native hearth." The Bostonians were able to revert to *Robin Hood* before heading out once more to the hinterlands.

On February 19 Harrigan brought back *The Woolen Stocking*. Confessing he was in trouble, Harrigan had already leased his stage to an outside attraction, so the revival was a one-week stopgap.

About Town (2-26-94, Casino) had a somewhat unusual history. As *Der Corner Grocer aus Avenue A* it had been running as a straight play down at the Germania Theatre on 8th Street since the middle of October. Its author, Adolph Philipp, played the title role in this slice of German and Yiddish life. The evening recounted the rise of a barber (Jacques Kruger) and his move uptown to Fifth Avenue. He and his newly rich friends have more money than *savoir-faire*. The cast of characters was filled with names such as Waldorf Metropole (played with "open-mouthed imbecility" by David Warfield) and Houston Streets (W. F. Mack). Willis P. Sweatnam inserted a minstrel monologue, Amelia Glover "danced her prettiest," while sad-miened Dan Daly injected his special brand of lugubrious humor. Harriet Sterling paraded about in a "gleaming golden satin gown eliciting gasps from the audience." Although in outline *About Town* appears to be a variation of a popular Harrigan theme, it was, essentially, another farce-comedy, "an offshoot, in form and substance, from *The City Directory* and other haphazard melees of riotous fun, song, and dance." But the looseness of its construction was markedly more noticeable than in most farce-comedies and at least one critic considered it "a new kind of entertainment . . . a hodgepodge of music, vaudeville, and fun." In short, *About Town* was another unwitting precursor of the revue, the form the same Casino would introduce to New Yorkers later in the season. But this first dip in new waters failed to please uptown theatregoers and the show closed after three weeks.

The evening *About Town* opened, an old part of the Fritz series, *Fritz in a Madhouse* (4-22-89), appeared at the American. *Au courant* theatregoers had long since lost interest in the series, but J. K. Emmet, Jr., continued to trek profitably across the country and in and out of Manhattan's combination houses with one or another of his father's plays. With the arrival of *Fritz in a Madhouse,* the American entered the ranks of combination houses.

The early closing of Harrigan's season made his theatre available unexpectedly. On March 5 Pauline Hall starred in a revival of *The Princess of Trébizonde,* "modernized almost beyond recognition." The *Times* bewailed that what was "once an opéra bouffe with music by Jacques Offenbach [and a libretto filled with] Gallic wit had degenerated into an evening of cheap horse play!" leaning heavily on snide contemporary references. It added that Miss Hall was past her prime and had no business appearing in "a garment of black gauze of astonishing transparency." Better or worse, the old opéra bouffe ran out the month.

Three weeks later Lillian Russell also returned in an old French work, *Girofté-Girofla,* filling the void left by the failure of *About Town* at the Casino. She, too, lasted a month. Miss Russell had to compete for attention on opening night with the latest Gilbert and Sullivan premiere, **Utopia, Ltd.** (3-26-94, Broadway). Although the work has been relegated to a low place in the Savoyard hierarchy, this early example of the havoc Western culture wreaks on an idyllic South Sea world was patently superior to most of the drivel forthcoming at the time. Audiences appreciated its superiority and the D'Oyly Carte production ran until mid-May. A cast of performers who never really made it to the top included a Mr. Peterkin as Captain Corcoran, J. J. Dallas, Kate Talby, and Clinton Elder.

1492 had moved from Palmer's to the Garden Theatre on February 5, adding new songs to celebrate the change of house. In late March it introduced another novelty, "living pictures" or tableaux. The earliest mountings re-created such then popular works of art as Bouguereau's "Cupid and Psyche," Canova's "Diana," and Cott's "Springtime." These posed moments caught on and before long musical after musical felt it necessary to have at least one such set piece in the show.

The Idea, an extravaganza with Fred Hallen and Joe Hart, began a three-week engagement at the Park on April 9. Many of the characters were named after New York hotels—Hoffman Howes (Hallen), Gilsey Howes (Donald Harold); another was named Peach Blow (Fanny Bloodgood) after the much publicized Chinese vase of the time. Still other figures had stage names typical for the era. One young lady was called May B. Quiet. The evening was a sort of primitive *Guys and Dolls* (11-

24-50). In a Tom and Jerry frame it told how a young man was saved from a life of dissipation. A transformation scene moved from a gambling house to a Salvation Army meeting.

April's only other lyric offering was an English burlesque extravaganza, *Cinderella.* It opened at the Abbey on April 23 and delighted audiences until June 16.

May's first two musicals swelled the total of revivals. On the 7th, Henry E. Dixey romped into Palmer's for a two-week visit with *Adonis* (9-4-84) and Chauncey Olcott began a week's run with *Mavourneen* (9-28-91) at the 14th Street Theatre.

At the end of the same week, on Saturday, May 12, 1894, the most significant show of the season premiered at the Casino. **The Passing Show** was, in fact, a milestone, a breakaway, for it was the first American revue. When it referred to itself as such —and it didn't bandy the new term about—it spelled it "review." The *Times,* discussing the work the Sunday before it opened, put the evening in an interesting perspective—reminding theatregoers of some stage history which they might have forgotten. The paper described the show as "a kind of entertainment little known in this country, and not attempted since John Brougham's time. It is a review, in dramatic form, of the chief events of the past year—political, historical and theatrical." Of course, the *Times* could have no way of foreseeing that *The Passing Show,* unlike Brougham's efforts, which failed to produce successors, would be the real progenitor of a half-century of revues. Indeed most critics judged the work as just another entertainment, not as an essentially new theatrical form. But then the producers themselves branded the evening "a topical extravaganza" more urgently than they advertised it as a revue. One exception, the *World,* recording the evening's French antecedents and spelling "revue" accordingly, granted that "the scheme had merit" but found the execution dull. The chic French spelling had to wait for more than a decade for general acceptance. But the French spelling would have been appropriate, since George Lederer and Sydney Rosenfeld did, as the *World* reported, derive much of their inspiration for the evening from the raging Parisian vogue, and not from Brougham.

The Gallic revue, like its American cousin, was only a few steps removed from another French theatrical child, vaudeville. It had become the popular Paris theatre attraction when something was needed to replace the waning demand for opéra bouffe. Unlike vaudeville each entertainer did not make a single appearance offering material he (or she) had often written himself or had commissioned especially for his act. Instead each performer appeared off and on throughout the evening performing dialogue and songs written by librettists and composers responsible for the entire work. Of course, specialties found their way into the show, particularly in the early years. To dress up the affair and make it more "legitimate," the shows were elaborately mounted. Moreover, with virtually no exceptions, early revues were tied together with plots, however gossamer, to further a sense of legitimization. These early revues also evidenced their debt to the burlesque tradition by leaning heavily on take-offs of current stage hits.

The Passing Show was responsible for shaping the first generation of revues. Two shows Rosenfeld selected for twitting were Pinero's *The Amazons* and *Sowing the Wind*. In the Pinero piece a mother raises her daughters as boys, giving them such names as Thomasin and Noeline. Rosenfeld changed their names to Lady Tom-A-Line (Madge Lessing), Lady Dick-A-Line (Lillian Thurgate), and Harry Line (no "Lady" or "A") (Belle Stewart). In *Sowing the Wind* Lord Brabson (Paul Arthur) attempts to wreck the reputation of his ward, Rosamond (played for the first two weeks by Adele Ritchie, thereafter by Jessie Carlisle), to prevent her marrying. Rosenfeld retained the names of the principals but changed a minor character such as Watkin to Weebit (Lucy Daly). In fact, Rosenfeld used the characters from *Sowing the Wind* to provide the slim plot for the evening. Rosamond's father (Jefferson De Angelis) and a detective (J. E. Henshaw) he hires, search the town for the girl. The performers stayed in character all evening long interweaving the songs and dances and extraneous material with the satire. This extra material included "living pictures," allusions to the headlines of the day in a song on the order of "Coxey's Army," the comedy of the Tamale Brothers (they had a song, "Hot Tamales"), and the acrobatics of the Amazons. "L'Enfant Prodigue" was recast as a ballet with four Pierrots and four temptresses. In a lighter vein, "Round the Opera in Twenty Minutes" embroiled Tannhäuser, Escamillo, Pagliacci, and other notable operatic characters in a comic melee. A hit of the evening was "Old Before His Time." The construction of the song marked no advance. Its chorus was a simplistic Ludwig Englander melody that covered a single sentence, repeated once, "Yes, that is one thing, yes, that is one thing makes a man old before his time." The meat of the song remained in its verse. Although it blamed premature aging on such things as "that everlasting tariff, out of reason out of rhyme," it saved its sharpest barbs for a whole verse assailing the new school of writing and acting:

The modern school of acting's
    such a thing of pure delight [is],
The heroine has consumption,
    the hero meningitis.
The villain, yellow jaundice;
    oh, his sufferings are fearful.
The scene's laid in a hospital,
    to make it nice and cheerful;
And the happ'nings, tho' abnormal,
    are supported by statistics.
It's a school of realism,
    and endorsed by realistics;
And the audiences are wading
    thro' the mire and the slime,
As they feel themselves grow old
    before their time.

With a cast of 100, the show ran into August and then embarked on an extended tour.

The season ended the week after *The Passing Show* arrived when a revival of *The Mikado* began a run at the Fifth Avenue that kept the house lit the entire summer, and Thomas Q. Seabrooke opened in **Tabasco** (5-14-94, Broadway). Originally mounted for Boston, with a book by R. A. Barnet and music by George W. Chadwick, it was another of the era's virtually countless bits of pseudo-Orientalia. Hot-Ham-Head-Pasha, the Bey of Tangiers (Walter Allen), beheads any chef who fails to put enough tabasco in his food. Dennis O'Grady assumes the post of chef. His problem is made difficult by a scarcity of the seasoning, until he discovers two tramps (Robert E. Bell and Edward Smith) with a case salvaged from a shipwreck which they are peddling as hair tonic. He tries to keep the bey's palate satisfied and to woo a native girl, Lola (Elvia Cox), at one and the same time. By a series of comical contrivances, he succeeds.

The move northward that doomed Niblo's removed the Union Square as well from the legitimate fold. But the theatre was not demolished. Instead it became one of B. F. Keith's major vaudeville houses. Interestingly, when Keith reopened it he included shortened versions of Broadway musical successes as part of the bill. *Said Pasha, The Mascot, The Princess of Trébizonde,* and *The Mikado* were all offered at one time or another. But the experiment proved a disappointment, and by the middle of the season it was dropped.

1894-1895

Artistically and financially the doldrums persisted throughout the new season. The nation could not shake off the effects of the 1893 panic nor could the American Musical Theatre rouse itself from its lethargy. New lyric pieces fell slightly in number, but a precise figure is difficult to agree on with so many offerings still falling into borderline categories. Still, there were hints of happier seasons ahead, for those perspicacious enough to see them. *A Gaiety Girl* sailed in from London to infuse musicals with a new sense of style and tone, and to start a decade-long vogue for English musical comedy. Even more significantly, Victor Herbert, the first truly enduring name in the history of our musical stage, made his initial appearance as a comic-opera composer. For those not gifted with foresight the season nevertheless offered its share of ephemeral delights. Several shows, now all but forgotten, were applauded, and awarded long and profitable runs.

The season (now following the divisions in Burns Mantle's *Best Plays* series at mid-June each year) began with the arrival of **Dr. Syntax** (6-23-94, Broadway), a rewriting of the 1881–82 success *Cinderella at School*. Once again a waif at a boarding school lands a wealthy young man despite the machinations of the titular comic villain. A vehicle for De Wolf Hopper, it had been announced as being in the works the preceding September when disappointing grosses on the road for *Panjandrum* warned that show would not prove as long-lasting as *Wang*. Since Woolson Morse had done the original score for *Cinderella at School* as well as for *Wang* and *Panjandrum,* he was naturally called upon to make the musical revisions, while J. Cheever Goodwin, Morse and Hopper's associate in their last two outings, brought the book "up to date." Hopper's happy relationship with his writers stemmed not only from his theatrical success but from his fidelity to the material they proffered him. He was not given to originating too much business of his own. In an 1894 interview Hopper noted, "as a general thing I am simply interpreting the libretto of Cheever Goodwin." But he could not resist confessing that he did add a line to a young lady having difficulty on a ladder, admonishing her, "Don't stutter with your feet." Text and ad-libs combined to satisfy New York audiences for 169 showings.

No further musicals premiered until **Miss Innocence Abroad** (8-25-94, Bijou) arrived by way of Paris and London. Miss Innocence was so naïve she was unaware of her noble birth and humbly accepted a position as a milliner. (Sweet young milliners soon became stock heroines of the musical stage.) Rose Beaudet, Melville Stewart, and Fanny Rice led the cast. New Yorkers found the evening less entertaining than the Parisian play or the London musical on which it was based, and it disappeared after 33 showings.

Two nights later a revised edition of *1492* (5-15-93) opened for a brief stay prior to an extended road tour. With a roster continually in flux, this time around it offered, among other changes, an interpolation of a Strauss waltz, "Ich Liebe Dich." For the road, the show changed its title slightly and voguishly to *1492 up to Date*. Down at the 14th Street Theatre other first-nighters sat through a comedy-drama called *Coon Hollow,* a straight play nonetheless replete with songs and specialties.

The Casino began its season on August 30 with **The Little Trooper** (also called *Little Miss Trooper*). Originally a French musical with text by Raymond and Mars and music by Victor Roger, it was heavily revised by Clay Greene and William Furst to serve as Della Fox's first solo starring vehicle. Jefferson De Angelis was featured, and Richard Barker staged the evening. Barker and his principals were responsible for whatever success the show enjoyed in its 68-performance stay.

Broadway's mite of cheer increased a bit when Francis Wilson unveiled **The Devil's Deputy** (9-10-94, Abbey's). Richard Barker was again the director. Like Hopper, Wilson cavorted to a Goodwin libretto. In this instance Goodwin based his tale on the old German belief in good devils as well as bad ones. An actor named Lorenzo (Rhys Thomas) is caught in a backstage embrace with the wife of General Karamatoff (J. C. Miron) and forced to flee, still wearing a devil's costume. He comes to a provincial inn, where he tells a band of wedding guests he is a good devil. Seeing Karamatoff approach he convinces the groom, Melissen (Wilson), to change places with him. But Karamatoff has come merely to bring him before a princess (Adele Ritchie) for a command performance. The princess falls in love with the actor, not realizing he is someone other than the man she has sent for. Luckily, Lorenzo is able to engineer one more exchange of place with Melissen. The groom returns to his bride (Lulu Glaser), and the actor wins the princess. Although Wilson spread his jollity for 72 performances—still a healthy run for the time

—the joy might have been greater had Wilson's original plans for the work been fulfilled. The Syndicate would soon largely destroy the importance of the actor-manager, but Wilson at this day called his own shots. The evening was his conception and his production. Wilson had first approached John Philip Sousa with Goodwin's partially finished text, hoping the march king would create the show's score. But Wilson, in his own way, was as tough in financial transactions as the Trust he so despised. He refused to allow Sousa to share in the royalties, and when Sousa then offered to compromise for a flat fee of $1500—the equivalent of about 15 percent of just one week's gross—Wilson adamantly refused to go above $1000. Since by his own admissions it cost no more than $25,000 to mount a comic opera, the additional cost was not excessively burdensome. Wilson turned to *Erminie*'s Edward Jakobowski, who gave him adequate if lackluster songs. No one can say how much that $500 cost the comedian. But for some reason the affair must have rankled. Wilson, intentionally or otherwise, ignored the show in his autobiography.

The theatrical economy, unhealthy by the standards of the day, was enviably sound by the criteria of another century. As a result the American Musical Theatre time and again in this period saw cities all around the nation mount their own offerings. On the same night New Yorkers first applauded *The Devil's Deputy*, Clevelanders witnessed the premiere of **By King's Command,** a comic opera by a local journalist, W. S. Rose, with a score by Edward Beach. If the production was not up to the best of the time—the reviews said the mounting needed no apology—the plot was quite typical of the nonsense so beloved by the era. Two principalities, Pam and Mirande, prepare to go to war over a land dispute. The King of France orders the argument settled by mating the respective prince and princess—who had loved each other all along but were kept apart by their feuding houses.

Humpty Dumpty still retained his theatrical allure. The night after *The Devil's Deputy* opened, Robert Breitenbach reincarnated him and his world as a playground for his Liliputians. In **Humpty Dumpty up to Date** (9-11-94, Fifth Ave.), a wealthy wine dealer and his servant whip a fairy who has helped the merchant's daughter elope. As punishment they are turned into Humpty Dumpty and Pantaloon. "That ripened and cynical baby," Franz Ebert, played Humpty—played it, if the *Times* is correct, mostly in German. He and his fellow midgets romped with giant pigs and living tulips. Young and old were entertained for eight weeks.

One of the most important musicals in the history of the American Musical Theatre opened the following week—September 18, 1894, at Daly's. Like so many early milestones in our theatrical history it was imported as well as important. **A Gaiety Girl** had a libretto by Owen Hall, lyrics by Harry Greenbank, and music by Sydney Jones. The show was not the first of the so-called Gaiety musicals, originated in the West End by the great English producer, George Edwardes. In fact, *A Gaiety Girl* did not even play his Gaiety Theatre. It had been preceded by *In Town* and was followed by *The Shop Girl* (both of which were housed for at least part of their runs at the Gaiety). *In Town* was a loosely structured affair. The looseness of its story allowed for interpolations and occasional program changes. But the success of its contemporary story and setting pointed the way. The story of *A Gaiety Girl* was tauter and more complex, yet still broad enough to allow for specialties, additions not by the authors, and alterations. It told how a group of chorus girls from the Gaiety are shunned at an elegant party until they consent to perform. A young officer falls in love with one of the girls, but a rival for his affections plants a diamond comb in the actress' pocket and accuses her of theft. The officer helps clear her.

Curiously, most English scholars (who consider Edwardes the originator of English musical comedy or even of musical comedy as an international theatrical genre) select either *In Town* or *The Shop Girl* as the landmark work. But it was undoubtedly the year-long London run of *A Gaiety Girl* that assured the continuation and legendary status of the series. *A Gaiety Girl* combined the vernacular appeal of farce-comedy with the integrity of comic opera. Interpolated specialties were limited, songs bore a more discernible relationship to the story, and the audience could identify more easily with the characters and the situations than with the royalty and absurdities of the comic opera. Puns were minimized. The chorus line was young, svelte (by standards of the day), and moved with grace. All the cast dressed stylishly in the latest fashions. Both in England and America, Gaiety shows quickly set standards for clothes-conscious playgoers.

For the next ten years or so good English musicals were always given the heartiest welcome and, far more so than the otherwise influential *H.M.S. Pinafore* (1-15-79), the flattery of constant imitation. Not all critics were impressed. The *Times* called *A Gaiety Girl* "nondescript" and at best ranked it with the old Hoyt pieces. In America the show, with Blanche Massey and W. Louis Bradfield in the principal roles, was produced by Augustin Daly, who not many years before had pioneered in modern musical mountings.

But the latest vogue could not stifle the appeal of older traditions, and *The Black Crook* (9-12-66) played to two weeks of good business when it came into the Grand Opera House on September 24 as part of its annual road tour. Some of the additions to this version are startling. Despite its Continental setting one production number was "The American Roll Call of Honor." "Want And Abundance" introduced social commentary in "twenty-two distinct pictures" featuring eighty performers.

October 1 brought in two entertainments that by modern lights would not fall into the musical mainstream. Comstock's Minstrels began a week's run at St. James Hall. More importantly, Chauncey Olcott appeared at his customary berth in the 14th Street Theatre with **The Irish Artist,** another of the sentimental melodramas that allowed him to please his followers with half a dozen songs. Scholars generally feel it was this show that firmly established Olcott as "successor to Emmet and Scanlan" in romantic Irish melodramas and determined the style of production he would be most often associated with thereafter. Olcott portrayed Maurice Cronin, who returns to his home in Wexford after a successful career in London. He finds an old buddy has turned against him and would jealously shame Cronin and his family. Critics noted Olcott was "cheered with vehemence" and "admired vociferously." Nineteenth-century audiences were apparently far less restrained than contemporary ones, and audiences for Irish plays least restrained of all.

· · ·

Although he usually played a staunchly Catholic native of Ireland, **Chauncey Olcott** was born in Buffalo, N.Y., on July 21, 1860, and educated in the city's public schools. He made his debut at the Buffalo Academy of Music, listed on the program as a "ballad singer." His Broadway debut was opposite Lillian Russell in *Pepita*.

· · ·

The text of Charles Hoyt's farce-comedy, **A Milk White Flag** (10-8-94, Hoyt's), included only four songs plus spottings for several musical drills. But Hoyt advertised it as a musical comedy, and its audiences undoubtedly looked on it as such. The story detailed the rivalry between two social clubs with fashionable military bents, a story not unlike the early Harrigan and Hart, acted out on a higher

social plane. The Daly Blues have constantly outshone the Ransome Guards, and the Guards are out for vengeance. They decide to hold the biggest, gaudiest funeral the town has ever seen. All they lack is a corpse. Their problem is solved when Piggott Luce (R. A. Roberts), a shady contractor, agrees to go through with a fake burial and flee town. In fleeing town he will also escape the law and a wife who is suing him for divorce and alimony. His "death" of course upsets his widow (Isabelle Coe). If her divorce has been granted, she cannot be his heir; if it has not been granted, she must publicly and hypocritically grieve. Hypocrisy is a small price to pay for the inheritance, but it would also interfere with her courtship by the club's "colonel" (Charles Stanley). All ends happily. The hoax is exposed and the divorce granted. The "widow" and her "colonel" agree to wed, while Piggott claims the hand of his ex-wife's best friend (Lillie Deaves). Unlike *A Trip to Chinatown*, no songs from *A Milk White Flag* set the country humming. Except for "Love's Serenade" they were either humorous or martial, or both. The verse of "Wouldn't You Like To Fondle Little Baby?" ran:

My Uncle Freddie bought a box of roses
To send his sweetheart, a pretty Kitty Lee.
In the box he put a note,
And this is what he wrote:
"My dearest when you wear them think of me."
He left the box alone for half a minute;
The roses I was mean enough to sneak,
And a pair of papa's trousers I put in it.
Now Uncle Fred and Kitty never speak.

The wit in "Warriors Bold" was more succinct, vaguely Gilbertian:

Our thirst for blood
And our love for mud
Cannot be called extensive;
And we don't like storms
For our uniforms
Are horribly expensive.

Staged by Julian Mitchell, *A Milk White Flag* entertained New York for six months.

The English musical stage celebrated the 400th anniversary of Columbus even more roundaboutly than did the American. Its **Little Christopher Columbus** (10-15-94, Garden), for which Ivan Caryll did the London score, actually dealt with a cabin boy who turned out to be Columbus' descendant. The book was modified slightly for New York taste, with Gustave Kerker called in to supplement the original music. Shortly after the show opened its title was contracted to *Little Christopher*. A large cast included Charles Bigelow, Harry Macdonough, Helen Bertram, Henri Leoni, and Alexander Clark. However little real homage it paid to Columbus, like *1492* it caught the public's fancy, running almost the rest of the season, then touring successfully.

More minstrelsy enlivened New York when Primrose and West, combined for the moment with Dockstader's organization, raised the curtain at the Grand Opera House on October 27. But the merger of the two groups betrayed the fact that the heyday of the minstrels had ended.

The season's biggest hit, **Rob Roy** (10-29-94, Herald Square), was to prove Reginald De Koven's longest New York run. Although at its debut it evoked a storm of argument over whether or not it was superior to *Robin Hood,* posterity, if it has chosen at all, has relegated it to second place. Harry B. Smith's book was confused and drifting. While Rob Roy (William Pruette) is the titular figure, the comic mayor of Perth (Richard F. Carroll) holds the piece together as much as anyone. He is another in Smith's long line of comic villains. He changes sides and costumes with every change of fortune in the Scottish and English war. He marries his daughter Janet (Juliette Cordon) first to a Scotsman and then to an Englishman, blissfully unaware that all the while she is married to Rob Roy. Concurrently Flora MacDonald (Lizzie MacNichol) and the besieged Prince Charles (Baron Berthald) pursue their own romance. When the prince is in danger of capture Flora dons his clothes and is jailed in his stead. Rob Roy, Lochiel (W. H. McLaughlin), and their Highlanders eventually see that both Charles and Flora escape to France. Once more, none of De Koven's songs appealed to the public for long, although one of Janet's songs—probably "The Merry Miller"—was "three times encored" on opening night. But the professionalism of the piece was valued highly enough to give it a run of 253 performances in two briefly separated stays.

November's first offering was an importation, **The Queen of Brilliants** (11-7-94, Abbey's), for which Edward Jakobowski composed the music. Lillian Russell, Hubert Wilke, and Digby Bell enacted a tale of a countess who runs away from home to join a variety troupe. Even Miss Russell's potent allure could not overcome its languors, and it left after 29 showings. When it closed Miss Russell rushed into a revival of *The Grand Duchess* to fill her contracted engagement.

Less promising but far more successful, **The Brownies** tapped the children's market and ran for 96 performances at the out-of-the-way 14th Street Theatre beginning November 12. In its calcium-lit never-never-land the villain, Dragonfels (G. L. Broderick), attempts to thwart the marriage of Prince Florimel (Alice Johnson), an adopted Brownie, to Princess (or Queen) Titania (Marie Louise Day). When the Brownies attempt to aid Florimel, a demon ensnares them. But they escape and set all wrongs right. The critics of the day were especially impressed by the "dazzling" spectacle the house was able to mount, notably a first-act deluge and a second-act earthquake. Specialties included five men imitating a German band.

Genius of a far more dazzling sort was partially responsible for the next offering to appear, although none could see it at the time. Victor Herbert's name first graced a New York program when **Prince Ananias** bowed on November 20, 1894, at the Broadway Theatre.

. . .

Victor Herbert was born in Dublin on February 1, 1859. After his father died, when Victor was three, his mother moved to England to live with her father, Samuel Lover, a novelist of some repute. She began Herbert's musical training early, and when she remarried and moved with her new husband to Stuttgart, her son was enrolled at the local conservatory to study cello, his principal instrument for the rest of his life. While working as a cellist with the Stuttgart Opera, he fell in love with the leading soprano of the company, Theresa Förster. She accepted a contract with the Metropolitan on the stipulation that Herbert be engaged there as a cellist. She and Herbert were married shortly before they sailed. Herbert soon supplemented their income by composition and conducting, rising to the post of bandmaster with the 22nd Regiment Band. How he came to the attention of the Bostonians is uncertain, but in the summer of 1894 he and a librettist, Francis Neilson, signed a contract to provide the famed organization with a new comic opera, receiving a $500 advance and royalties of no less than 5 percent. Herbert imposed an unusual condition for an unknown, demanding that "no changes shall be made in the libretto or music" without his consent. Here was a theatrical figure with integrity! Herbert always was to insist on this clause, and the one time it was accidently omitted an absurd contretemps ensued.

. . .

Neilson's story was set in 16th-century France, where a band of strolling players headed by one La Fontaine (Henry Clay Barnabee) are ordered to appear before the king and amuse him or suffer the consequences. They fail, but a poet traveling with them dispels the king's depression, and they are forgiven. The poet is named Louis (W. H. Mac-Donald), though he is affectionately called Prince Ananias by the players. The vagabond prince's reward is the hand of the leading lady of the strollers, Idalia (Jessie Bartlett Davis). Almost to a man New York critics damned the libretto as too long and trite, but praised the music as above average. Herbert's best number was Idalia's wistfully melancholy "Amaryllis" early in Act II. The Bostonians were never to duplicate the success of *Robin Hood,* but *Prince Ananias* remained in their repertory for two years, including this New York run of 55 showings.

In **The Flams** (11-26-94, Bijou) the popular comic William F. Hoey cavorted as Marmaduke Flam, a good-hearted impostor. The play was studded with interpolated songs and living pictures.

The same night *The Flams* arrived, the name of another composer made its first Broadway appearance. But Alfred G. Robyn's light was to shine more dimly and briefly than Herbert's, although he was only a year younger and survived Herbert by more than a decade. In **Jacinta** (11-26-94, Fifth Ave.), the St. Louis-born organist and his librettist, William Lapere, told a singularly undemocratic story, perhaps revealing the imperialist sentiments growing in an era of revived manifest destiny. Two naval officers, Miguel (Stuart Harold) and Morrelos (Signor Perugini), are condemned to die for their efforts to overthrow the Mexican republic and are spared only when the emperor's son restores the monarchy. As a reward Miguel wins Blanca (Cecile Essing) and Morrelos weds Jacinta (Louise Beaudet). Jacinta and the marching chorus won encores nightly with "A Soldier Need Not Fear." Signor Don Giovanni Perugini, who, one paper observed, "shone in . . . three satin and lace suits," was not an Italian. He was an American named Jack Chatterton. For a brief time he was also Lillian Russell's husband until in a scandalous, acrimonious divorce he accused her of using his make-up and monopolizing his mirror. Miss Russell not only won the case, she won general sympathy at a time when divorce was still customarily frowned upon. Chatteron's career was shattered.

Ned Harrigan and David Braham came a cropper with **Notoriety** (12-10-94, Harrigan's), December's only new lyric piece, even though more than one critic felt Harrigan remained "still unrivaled in his peculiar line." The conflict between whites and blacks which Harrigan had handled so good-naturedly before again provided the basis for his plot. A black "Accident Society" sends Fred Hoffman a letter threatening to blow off his head unless he pays them $100. Because the signature reads merely "A.S." Hoffman suspects the "A" stands for anarchist. Harrigan as Barry Nolan, a retired policeman and now a barkeeper, solves the problem. Annie Yeamans was on hand to impersonate a rich New York Irish junk dealer, while Joseph Sparks gained applause as a forlorn, but aggressive "female darky trance medium." Braham's songs used the stylish expressions of the day in numbers such as "The Girl That's Up To Date" and "Out On A College Rah Rah," while still finding a place for the requisite sentimentality in "The Old Neighborhood." Excellent scenery effectively evoked night in the seething Tenderloin district and the lawn of a Hudson River villa—where a comic rendering of "As You Like It" ended the evening. But the efforts were to no avail. By February, Harrigan had replaced *Notoriety* with a revival of *The Major.*

Not every new show in Boston was mounted by the Bostonians. **Westward Ho,** with a libretto by a Boston attorney, Richard Ware, and music by Benjamin Woolf, bowed at the Boston Museum on New Year's Eve. Their story recounted the adventures of Hair Trigger Hal—actually the Earl of Ravenswood in disguise—when he visits Maverick, Wyoming, a town run by women. The Earl wins the mayor-elect for a bride, and the Earl's brother, Sir Lionel, who follows him, wins the hand of the district attorney. The show, well-received at home, never reached New York. Another show that never reached the main stem was **Off the Earth,** a musical that got only as close as Harlem and Brooklyn. A slapdash affair, it was praised largely for the clowning of Eddie Foy.

New York, like Boston, would not neglect the modern woman. On January 25, Sydney Rosenfeld and Ludwig Englander brought their newest creation into the Bijou. This first musical of 1895 was entitled, a little prematurely, **The 20th Century Girl.** But its more than "up to date" title couldn't save it from a critical drubbing. It quickly closed. The brash Rosenfeld was not easily daunted. He rewrote his story of Percy Verance (Helen Dauvray), who sets herself up as a "girl bachelor," dresses like a man (prompting her infuriated guardian—Edwin Stevens—to dress like a woman), runs for Congress, and leads a carefree life, and reopened it with only slightly more success in May. During both runs the press singled out A. H. Wilson for his comic yodeling in the dialect role of Professor Blinderbogen. Critics also praised the songs which the multi-talented Rosenfeld was said to have composed, calling special attention to "The Play's The Thing," "The Ambitious Magpie," and "The Antidote."

Stanislaus Stange and Julian Edwards had better luck with **Madelaine, or The Magic Kiss,** which followed *The 20th Century Girl* into the Bijou, beginning a ten-week run on February 25. Stange's story was another of the epoch's preposterous concoctions. On his 100th birthday the Baron de Grimm (Aubrey Boucicault) discovers that each kiss he receives from a virgin will take 25 years off his life. Three kisses reduced him to 75, 50, and 25. But when Madelaine (Camille D'Arville), his young bride, kisses him he fears he will be reduced to a baby. Happily hers is "The Kiss of Love" and all ends well. On this simple plot Edwards, as conscientious if not as talented a composer as Herbert, hung a number of pleasant tunes such as "Heart, Foolish Heart" and "I Would Have Told Thee Long Ago." In singing the title role, Miss D'Arville once again saw her name above the title. Indeed, the lobby of the Bijou was ringed with flowers in honor of the occasion.

No major houses offered new musicals in March. But uptown at the Harlem Opera House, Thomas Q. Seabrooke appeared briefly beginning March 4 in a sequel to *Tabasco* called **The Grand Vizier.** Seabrooke once again played Dennis O'Grady, this time using whiskey instead of hot sauce to win love and position.

David Henderson, who made a name for himself in Chicago with his elaborate spectacles, brought in one of his biggest hits, **Aladdin, Jr.** (4-8-95, Broadway). Not all the people on the program were strangers to New York. The libretto, for example, was by J. Cheever Goodwin. In spite of the "Jr." in the title, the plot was the one that had served pantomime so well with the usual setting in Peking, the expected villain, Abanazar (Henry Norman), and Widow Twankey (rechristened Widow Bohea) (Ada Deaves). Another character was the delicious Tu Tee Fru Tee (L. Easton). Anna Boyd played Aladdin. "An immense amount of well-painted scenery" took audiences from Peking to a magic cave, to a "gilt and amber" glen as well as a laundry, gardens, and an Egyptian palace. A jumble of song writers added their melodies, and the show delighted youngsters of all ages for six weeks.

April's only other musical was a revival at Abbey's of Offenbach's opéra bouffe *La Périchole*

with Lillian Russell as star. The engagement was a holding action while Miss Russell and Abbey's management prepared a new musical they hoped would erase the stain of their November failure.

Less delightful, apparently, was the revival of *The Bohemian Girl,* which came into the Star as part of a light opera repertory and folded after a single performance.

A "Spectacular Comic Opera," **The Viking** (5-9-95, Palmer's), retold the adventures of Eric the Red and Leif Ericson. Its librettists admitted their plot was "largely drawn from the rosehued chambers of fancy." Eric (Bernard Dyllyn) is slated to marry Princess Njarda (Beatrice Goldie), but he prefers Thora (Grace Reals) and Njarda loves Bjohnson Bjones (Harry Dietz). The lovers get their way. The show had two strikes against it from the start. Instead of opening in the evening and charging standard prices ($1.50 top), the producers elected to have an afternoon opening at $5.00 top for charity. As a result, the premiere was poorly attended, the balconies virtually empty.

Lillian Russell's new vehicle was ready on May 16 at Abbey's. In this instance, "ready" might not have been the happiest term, for the press bewailed a patent lack of rehearsals, noting the fact that even Miss Russell at times had to be audibly prompted. **The Tzigane** had a book by Harry B. Smith and a score by Reginald De Koven. Miss Russell played a Russian gypsy, Vera. She loves a young officer, Kazimir (Hubert Wilke). But Kazimir's uncle commands Vera to marry Vasili (Jefferson De Angelis), a serf. Vera suspects Kazimir is behind the order. She runs away. Years later, after Napoleon's retreat from Moscow, Vera returns. She is now a lady of some wealth and position. She discovers Kazimir has remained faithful and marries him. Critics complained that the book was static and that Smith ignored the colorful possibilities of the 1812 setting much as he had the opportunities of 17th-century New Amsterdam in *The Knickerbockers* (5-29-93). If Smith ignored possibilities, Henry E. Hoyt, a distinguished scene painter of the day, did not. His work, especially an encampment scene for which he drew startlingly lifelike horses, was showered with praise. Smith himself blamed the show's failure on the fact that ticket buyers could not remember its name. But this was undoubtedly rationalization. They could as easily have called it the Russell show as they had *Panjandrum* (5-1-93) the Hopper show. Curiously, Miss Russell's leading comedian, De Angelis, insisted in his autobiography that it became the chic thing to pronounce the title correctly. Unfortunately, it never became chic enough to help *The Tzigane* last out the month of June.

A touring revival of *The Lily of Killarney* stopped for a week at the Grand.

Three of the four closing offerings leaned to burlesque. Two in fact were extended full-length burlesques of single shows, suggesting the popularity of the 1892–93 travesty of *Lady Windermere's Fan* had prompted composers and authors into some new naughtiness. **Hamlet II** (5-27-95, Herald Square) rejected one cliché of the older burlesque formula by allowing a man to play the hero. Mixing Shakespeare with contemporary slang, it offered its patrons a "Trilbyesque" Ophelia and song such as "What's The Matter With Ham?" In the scene with the players the strolling actors twitted nontheatrical celebrities whose notoriety had earned them places on variety bills of the day. One player confessed he was hired after he tried to jump off a bridge (Steve Brodie had appeared in variety after his escapade on the Brooklyn Bridge), another was a former prizefighter (Bob Fitzsimmons led a parade of fighters before the footlights), while the soubrette announced she had been divorced eleven times in ten years.

The busy J. Cheever Goodwin and Englander combined their talents to interrupt the chain of burlesques with the season's last traditional comic opera, **A Daughter of the Revolution** (5-27-95, Broadway). Starring Camille D'Arville, and set in 1776, it followed Marion Dunbar as she pretends to be a renegade in order to pass through enemy lines. She wins the affection of the British General Grumm (Hallen Mostyn) and his wife (Miss Sidney Worth), and then frees her lover, Captain Arthur Lee (Clinton Elder), who has been arrested as a spy. Even though Miss D'Arville was one of the leading prima donnas of her day, neither she nor the authors received the lion's share of attention. In a day when there were no films or television to provide spectacular scenes, all aspects of the theatre were called upon to satisfy the demand. Comic opera was often no exception. The first scene of the third act depicted Washington crossing the Delaware. Only loosely connected with the plot, the scene nonetheless won what little attention *A Daughter of the Revolution* earned. But it was not enough to tide the show over the hot weather. Curiously, like *The Tzigane* before it, the show was assailed as ill-rehearsed.

George du Maurier's best-selling novel *Trilby* (1894) inevitably found itself the subject of an extended burlesque as **Thrilby** (6-3-95, Garrick).

Joseph Herbert, who wrote the libretto to Charles Puerner's music, assumed the title role. Set in the studio of three privateers and then at a theatre, it turned Svengali into Spaghetti (Alexander Clark); and the rest of the characters had such names as Butter-Scotch and Madame Sans Ragene, allowing Sardou as well as du Maurier to be ribbed between songs and specialties. At one point du Maurier (A. G. Andrews) determines to eliminate Spaghetti. He succeeds in forcing the villain to climb one side of the proscenium. From an upper box Spaghetti sings a sardonic farewell. Noisy scene changes, so common in the era, prompted a gag that provoked some of the evening's biggest laughs. At the end of a scene in a laundry the lights were blacked out and the inevitable clatter ensued. But when the lights went on again, audiences saw the identical set with the identical players in their identical spots.

Both *Madame Sans Gene* and *Trilby* were also twitted on June 8 in **The Merry World,** the Casino's sequel to its well-thought-of *Passing Show*. Hoping to profit from the best of both merry worlds, the house called its offering both a burlesque and, using the spelling of the day, a review. The fledgling form still used skits much longer than would eventually be the norm and utilized a theatrical tour as a slim plot. Besides spoofing straight plays of the day, the show parodied the season's musicals. In one skit Dr. Syntax's daughter Madelaine is engaged to Rob Roy. A superb cast included Dan Daly, Amelia Summerville, Virginia Earle, David Warfield, Louis Harrison, and Louis Mann. Since so many shows still opened "cold" in New York during this period, no one quibbled at *The Merry World*'s premiere if "at midnight a third of the show had not been given." (Shades of *The Black Crook!*) Edgar Smith and Nicolas Biddle wrote the dialogue, while William Furst contributed most of the songs the specialists didn't contribute themselves.

1895-1896

Little changed for the American economy or the American Musical Theatre in the new season. At least little change was apparent. But subtle, not immediately obvious, transitions were in the wind. With time what became known as Gaiety Theatre musicals—although not all were actually mounted at London's Gaiety—shamed American writers and managers into devising more thoughtful, more tasteful lyric offerings of their own. But unlike many turning points in our later musical history, no hue and cry accompanied the improvements. Reading interviews with writers and performers of this period, and following criticism of the time, one is left with an impression that by and large America was satisfied with the entertainment it created for itself. It was especially appreciative and happy when a superior piece such as *El Capitan* premiered late in the season, but it was not about to complain of the string of mediocrities that preceded or trailed this success.

The ever-active Boston stage provided New York with its only musical novelty in July when **The Sphinx** began what it hoped would be a summer run at the Casino on the 8th. The Near East was to *fin-de-siècle* American musicals what Italy was to Elizabethan drama, a setting at once exotic and commonplace. Into this world the authors injected a bit of local pride when Harvard's Professor Papyrus (Edwin Stevens) discovers a woman's seminary whose pupils are preparing to elope with a band of Bedouins. They will visit the Sphinx, where each couple will be presented with a riddle. Papyrus' request to join them is disdained until his valet, Ptimmins (Tallmadge Baldwin), reveals that the professor has a book filled with answers to the puzzles. The riddler is a woman, Hathor (Marie Millard), who falls in love with Papyrus and is condemned to ask him a riddle not answered in the book. Papyrus inadvertently gives the correct reply. He and Hathor wed. The evening was sumptuously and ingeniously mounted, with Hathor's first entrance, seeming to float out of the Sphinx, particularly impressive. But the writing was not as fetching as the story, and, while the show ran four weeks in the summer heat, it was at best a modest success.

St. Louis was far from the cultural hubbub of Boston or New York but it, too, could mount its own lyric works. On July 15 its Uhrig's Garden presented a new comic opera called **Ollamus,** whose story coupled the popular theme of feminist agitation with the popular setting of never-never-land. Miss Jones, an unsuccessful candidate for the U.S. presidency, lands in Utopiana and attempts to overthrow the king, Ollamus. She uses a trick phonograph to let people believe they are eavesdropping on private conversation. Her plan is foiled, but Ollamus is forgiving.

Back in New York the new season began in earnest with the arrival of a second Boston success, **Kismet** (8-12-95, Herald Square). Unrelated to the famous Otis Skinner vehicle, it did, however, play out its story in the same "Oriental" splendor. A Sultan decrees that the first boy born to any of his wives shall be chief of state but that all boys born thereafter must be put to death. The Princess Ramadamus (Rose Leighton) gives birth to a girl. Determined to be a power behind the throne, she announces the child is a boy and names it Kismet (Lizzie MacNichol). When her second child is in fact a male, she is forced to name it Haidee and raise it as a girl. Both children are kept in ignorance of their true sex. Kismet becomes sultan and sends for suitors to woo Haidee (Richard F. Carroll). In the end Kismet marries one of Haidee's suitors and Haidee assumes the throne. There was little comment about Gustave Kerker's undistinguished score, but several other matters disturbed the critics. The *Times* complained that Carroll, who was also the librettist, cheapened the evening by playing to the gallery. A number of critics decried what they considered unnecessarily suggestive innuendoes in the dialogue. The *Dramatic Mirror* rushed to the show's defense, arguing it was less suggestive than many. When the debate had no effect on ticket sales, the show folded after three weeks.

Three nights after the opening of *Kismet,* Alfred Cellier's London favorite, *Dorothy,* began a delayed, trouble-plagued (last-minute cast changes, costumes unready) revival at the Standard. The next night *The Merry World* was rushed back to the Casino after a disappointing Chicago stand and proved even more in demand as a cool-weather ticket than it had originally. It compiled an additional 148 performances.

Fleur-De-Lis (8-29-95, Palmer's), a comic opera by J. Cheever Goodwin and William Furst, starred Della Fox in the title role and Jefferson De Angelis. Barker was the director. The Count Des Escarbilles (De Angelis) and the Marquis De Rosolio (Arthur Wheelan) go to war over their claims to a duchy. One of the noblemen has a daughter (Miss Fox), the other a son (Melville Stewart). The lovers manage to wangle a peace agreement despite the frequent interference of the count's uncooperative foot, which develops a nervous kick whenever he and the marquis are on the verge of reconciliation. The plot was a spoof of the dying tradition of melodrama that filled the evening with besieged castles (the hero made a thrilling 40-foot jump in the course of the evening), lost wills, and ghosts. For De Angelis his billing finally moved him from years as a featured player to stardom.

· · ·

Jefferson De Angelis was born in San Francisco on November 30, 1859. He made his first stage appearance at the age of twelve in early vaudeville at Baltimore's Odeon Theatre. In the early eighties he toured the world with his own dramatic company. But his ambition to be a serious actor, like De Wolf Hopper's, gave way to the realization that his métier lay elsewhere. New York first applauded him in *A Bottle of Ink* (1-6-85). Increasingly important roles followed in musicals such as *The Begum, The Lady or the Tiger?, Poor Jonathan,* and *Apollo.*

. . .

The *Times,* which had recently been attacking Miss Fox in her appearances, continued its apparent hate affair when it snidely noted no improvement in her "babyish face and plump figure." But the paper, as it had in its previous criticism, leaned backward to confess it was clearly in the minority in its dislike of the star. Indeed, it was. This time, most critical complaints were leveled at Furst's latest colorless score. The same *Dramatic Mirror* that defended the librettist of *Kismet* now bewailed: "It is time that orchestral leaders of the Kerker and Furst order should cease to figure as operatic composers." Once again the public and the *Dramatic Mirror* went their separate ways. *Fleur-De-Lis* had a satisfactory run of 65 performances and a season-long tour.

Four musicals of one sort or another competed for attention on September 2. A return engagement of *Rob Roy* (10-29-94) relit the Herald Square, recently vacated by *Kismet.* The Fifth Avenue offered a one-performance fiasco called **The Bathing Girl**. It told of Miss Terriberry (Grace Golden), a bathing girl, who arrives at a resort hotel where country bumpkins try to pass themselves off as potentates. She finally finds romance with J. Klingsbury Boats (William Stevens). The humor heard on that single presentation ran to the order of:

—Where is your yacht?
—Why, she's in the water, where she yacht to be!

A moonlit beach provided a suitable background for romantic scenes, while on a brighter stage "a bevy of girls in bathing costumes, costumes known only to the comic artists, twirl about."

Only slightly more successful was *The White Crook,* billed as "A Grand Spectacular Extravaganza," although it was as much commonplace vaudeville as anything. Affection remained for *The Black Crook* (9-12-66), but the day when it could be imitated with some promise of a ready audience was long gone. The press awarded the evening at the Gaiety mere passing notice.

Among the offerings, only **Princess Bonnie** enjoyed a moderate success. Written by the same Willard Spenser who had achieved fame with *The Little Tycoon* (3-24-86), the show had been a Philadelphia hit, running at the Chestnut Street Theatre in Spenser's home town from March 26 to July 7, 1894. A subsequent road tour—of which the New York stay was a brief part—chalked up nearly 1000 additional performances. *Princess Bonnie* recounted the heart-warming history of an infant rescued from a shipwreck by a Maine lighthouse keeper (F. Lennox, Jr.). Named Bonnie (Hilda Clark), she grows up and falls in love with a rich summer resident, Roy Stirling (W. M. Armstrong). But the Spanish Admiral Pomposo (J. S. Greensfelder) comes to claim her as a princess and take her to Spain. She is saved from an undesirable marriage when Shrimps (the lighthouse man) and Roy follow her to Spain and again rescue her. Philadelphia continued to mount occasional musicals of its own, even though few ever reached New York. Their reception there was generally so cool that Philadelphia, like Boston and Chicago, came to feel a musical's provenance, not its quality, determined New York's judgment. Spenser apparently had been vocal in his conclusions, prompting the *Times* to scoff at any suggestion "some of the New York papers formed a cabal against his work because it came from Philadelphia." The *Times* insisted Spenser himself was at fault. It wrote of his music, "simplicity is its chief characteristic. A child might have written it, provided the child were not Mozart." By no means a failure—it ran 40 performances at the Broadway—*Princess Bonnie* fell far short of the popularity of *The Little Tycoon.* With it, Spenser quietly retired from the New York musical stage, although he continued to write for Philadelphia productions.

A week after the rash of openings **The Chieftain** (9-9-95, Abbey's) raised its curtain. The importation narrated the comic plight of a tourist taken prisoner by bandits whose "chieftainess" falls in love with him. In good comic-opera fashion the man's wife appears. Audiences of the time were attracted by its star, Francis Wilson, its director, Richard Barker, and by its composer, Arthur Sullivan. But Sullivan was no longer in top form and his librettist, F. C. Burnand, no match for Gilbert. Still, the show was pleasing enough to run until early November.

May Irwin, the great "coon-shouter," interpolated a number of "coon" songs into the "farcical conceit" J. J. McNally created for her, **The Widow Jones** (9-16-95, Bijou). The show was the first to honor her with stardom. The press was happy to note "elevation to stardom has not changed her in any respect. She is as round, as blond, as innocent looking . . . and as blue-eyed as ever." To underscore the event, Miss Irwin introduced what is often considered her best number, Charles E. Trevathan's "The Bully Song." Its lyrics recited in Negro dialect the singer's determined search for "dat nigger dat treated folks so free." Miss Irwin played Beatrice Byke, who escapes her fortune hunting suitors by running off to Maine and pretending to be the widow of a man drowned the year before. She soon finds herself saddled with the man's debts, his daughter, and, eventually, the "drowned" man himself.

Early in October combination houses such as the Grand and the 14th Street began advertising returns of the preceding seasons' musicals. *The Irish Artist* (10-1-94), *Mavourneen* (9-28-91), and the inevitable *Black Crook* (9-12-66) all made one or more appearances. The enviable resiliency the healthy theatrical economics of the time allowed is shown by the appearance at intervals of the panned and troubled *20th Century Girl* (1-25-95). One curiosity of the month was the American premiere of Humperdinck's opera *Hansel and Gretel* at Daly's. Anton Seidl conducted.

Gilbert, with a new partner, Osmond Carr, fared less happily than Sullivan had with Burnand. Gilbert's plot centered on a governor given to practical joking. He makes a commoner the butt of his humor, unaware the commoner is his king in disguise. **His Excellency** (10-14-95, Broadway) was a quick failure; its rapid closing hastened by public resentment at its producers' attempt to charge $2.00 top instead of the customary $1.50.

Leonardo (10-21-95, Garrick) also flopped in short order. Richard Mansfield, the distinguished actor and manager, produced the work, attesting once again to the fascination the early musical stage held for serious artists. A "romantic comic opera" with music by the composer of *The Maid of Plymouth* (1-15-94), Thomas P. Thorne, it presented the historical da Vinci in an imaginary love affair. The Duke of Milan (Hobart Smock) travels to Florence to commission a statue of himself from Leonardo (George Devoll). But when the duke discovers his daughter, Beatrice (Marguerite Lemon), has become enamored of the artist, he banishes the young man. The duke encounters hard times as Leonardo's star rises. Leonardo helps restore the duke to power, and by curtain time he is granted Beatrice's hand.

One week later, Ivan Caryll's London success

The Shop Girl (10-28-95, Palmer's) premiered. Those English scholars who look on *The Shop Girl* as the first real musical comedy cite its relatively tight book as a principal argument. The story was simple enough, recounting the search for Bessie Brent by her late father's friend. Bessie, unaware of the wealth now hers, works happily as the shop girl of the title. Bessie's fiancé loves her as much when he learns she is an heiress as when he thought she was poor. In London, George Edwardes' production at the Gaiety broke the house record with a run of 546 performances. In New York the stay was far shorter. Another $2.00 top may have hurt business, but one English history student has suggested Britain's territorial dispute with Venezuela, deemed a violation of the Monroe Doctrine, disturbed a sufficient number of American playgoers to cut down attendance. Although new songs were advertised in celebration of the 50th performance, the run was terminated two weeks later. Two London originals repeated their roles for Broadway. Seymour Hicks re-created his role as Bessie's suitor, Charles. George Grossmith, Jr. (the son of the great Gilbert and Sullivan favorite), made both his West End and Rialto debuts as a man-about-town, Bertie Boyd.

The Wizard of the Nile (11-4-95, Casino), Victor Herbert's second comic opera, established him as a name to be reckoned with. At the same instance it secured fame and fortune for its star, Frank Daniels, long a popular figure in farce-comedy. And it also introduced Herbert to Harry B. Smith, a librettist with whom he would work so often in the future. For the second time in the season Egypt provided the setting. Moreover, Smith's plot was a variation of the story Rosenfeld had used two years before in *The Rainmaker of Syria*. Drought plagues the land. But a cheeky traveling magician, Kibosh, offers to bring rain. He does. Unfortunately the rain will not stop and disastrous floods ensue. The king (Walter Allen) orders Kibosh sealed in a tomb, only to discover his zealous courtiers have sealed him in as well. He is so grateful to escape alive that in his enthusiasm he pardons Kibosh. A romantic subplot depicts the fond feelings shared by Cleopatra (Dorothy Morton) and a musician, Ptarmigan (Edwin Isham). But defying comic opera tradition the lovers do not wed in the end. Instead, Cleopatra settles down to await the arrival of Mark Antony. Daniels had to look to his laurels, for many a critic was captivated by "childish faced, innocent" Miss Morton, playing Cleopatra in a blond wig.

Herbert's score was less operatic than his music

for *Prince Ananias,* but that was only in keeping with the lighter nature of the piece. All through his career Herbert endeavored to adopt his style to the nature of his libretto. There were few of the waltzes Herbert was later associated with, but much martial music—a reflection of his experience as a band leader as well as of the story. Nonetheless, one waltz, "Star Light, Star Bright," was the hit of the show. The pleasant, simplistic melody is forgotten today because so much finer material poured from Herbert's pen in later years.

Also forgotten, sadly, is Herbert's skill as an orchestrator. Like all the more musicianly composers of his time Herbert orchestrated his own works. Although he sought primarily rich, well-balanced sound, Herbert always pursued novel instrumental effects. He hit on one of his happiest for a minor number from this piece. The accompaniment to the "Stonecutters' Song" was composed for piano and xylophone—"a glittering, chipping combination." Unlike Kerker in *Kismet,* Herbert contrived enough passages of psuedo-Oriental colorings to draw delighted comments from reviewers. The show ran 105 performances in New York, changing some of its initial post-Broadway bookings in order to satisfy the demand for seats. Daniels retained the role of Kibosh for two years, and when he left other lesser comedians kept the road pleased for a decade.

The Merry Countess (11-2-95, Garrick), an importation based on a French hit, *Niniche,* which had served as the source for *Newport* (9-15-79) and would serve again for other shows later, closed abruptly in the middle of its second week. In its short stay it allowed sad-faced Dan Daly, fleeing a jealous husband, to knock over furniture, take refuge in a bathhouse whose floor promptly collapses, and then desperately try to wheel the contraption into the safety of the audience.

Fast upon the heels of *A Gaiety Girl* (9-18-94), *The 20th Century Girl* (1-25-95), *The Bathing Girl* (9-2-95), and *The Shop Girl* (10-28-95), **The Bicycle Girl** wheeled into New York on November 18. This "musical farce-comedy" was designed primarily as a touring attraction, and its brief New York stay was at the Grand, a combination house. The musical's title reflected the bicycle craze that was sweeping the nation. The story was commonplace. Grace Fordyce (Nellie McHenry) inherits the Briarwood Bicycle Company from her late father. She is courted by the so-called Baron Byke, who is actually the disguised son of the president of Briarwood's arch rival. Stephen Forster, a modest young student, also seeks her hand. A bike race

determines which man she shall wed, and, of course, Stephen wins. At best the evening had some fun with feminist agitation. A "new" girl sang "See The Conquering Shero," while a "new" man wore bloomers and a bonnet, and carried a baby. The show treated its songs in the same commonplace fashion it handled most of its libretto. As the *Dramatic Mirror* noted, "The incidental music comprised a topical song called 'Long Ago,' with a talking chorus, a clambake song, medleys and parodies on popular songs, and many other melodious selections." But in one respect the mounting was not commonplace. The bike race was depicted by means of "Kinetoscope," an innocent glimpse of a not so innocent future. Edison's "Vitascope" would not be unveiled at Koster and Bial's until five months later, April 20, 1896.

A week after *The Bicycle Girl* bowed, another traveling farce-comedy came in from the hinterlands. In **A Happy Little Home** (11-25-95, 14th St.), Owen Moore (plump George W. Monroe) dresses up as a girl and takes a job as an Irish housekeeper so that he may be near his sweetheart, Miss Gayfeather. He soon learns he must ward off the advances of his girl's father. The slapdash nature of farce-comedy construction was illustrated by the fact that most of the songs were in the third act. As usual they were essentially vaudeville specialties, with performers arriving at the Gayfeather house in the guise of visitors. Indeed the affair was so slapdash that the author refused to allow his name on the program. He was Charles Klein, whose greatest success was just a few months away.

Excelsior, Jr., the season's biggest success, opened on November 29. It was a double-barreled opening, for it also allowed New Yorkers to gape for the first time at the attractions of Oscar Hammerstein's new Olympia Theatre, a house the financially reckless impresario was soon to lose. Originally conceived in Boston, *Excelsior, Jr.*'s libretto was by R. A. Barnet. Its music was largely by E. E. Rice—the last show he helped write, although his career as producer and director had another decade to run. Additional new tunes were by several hands, including A. Baldwin Sloane. Old tunes—"of which there were many"—were also offered. Neither the program nor the press identified them. The titular hero is left a large fortune with the stipulation he must first scale a mountain as his father had done before him. He goes to Switzerland, where he meets the operator of a shooting gallery, William Tell ("whose overture is much admired"). The young man is courted by Bertha, the innkeeper, and by an elderly Venetian lady who hears him sing and believes he is serenading her. But Excelsior has eyes only for Mary Vanderbuilt Lamb, an American heiress. He climbs the mountain and wins Mary. Bertha settles for Tell, and the Venetian lady is left sadder but wiser. The title part was played as a trouser role by Fay Templeton. One critic rued Miss Templeton had "grown formidably corpulent," undoubtedly unaware the performer's contract stipulated she must remain under 150 pounds. Marie Cahill and Richard Carle used smaller parts to move toward stardom. In keeping with the fashion of the day, new songs were added at intervals. A spring announcement advised that the role of the St. Bernard had been expanded by popular request.

In an era when successful shows recouped their investments quickly and even short-lived productions often turned a small profit, the creative fever could hit small towns. On December 16, for example, Baldwinsville, N.Y., mounted its own comic opera. **Next Year** took place at a college reunion. One of the grads has invented a flying machine and with three of his old buddies flies to another planet. Written by Harry P. Bigelow, who never made it to Broadway, it was a local hit. The correspondent for the village reported in the *Dramatic Mirror* that "a foot-ball chorus and a polar bear dance" were the most applauded numbers.

A musical travesty called **A Stag Party, or A Hero in Spite of Himself** (12-17-95, Garden) enjoyed a fortnight's run. Bill Nye and Paul Potter wrote the book; Herman Perlet, the music. Members of a gun club prepare to hunt a stag, but a neighboring landowner seizes the animal. The club decides to retrieve it and complications ensue. The large cast included a number of up-and-coming talents: Marie Dressler, Louis Harrison, Leo Ditrichstein, and John Slavin. Richard Barker staged the work.

Two more London successes arrived at the end of 1895. **An Artist's Model** (12-23-95, Broadway), with music by Sidney Jones, won favor; **The School Girl** (12-30-95, Bijou) did not. The artist's model jilted her poor painter to marry a rich suitor. Widowed, she is rebuffed by the artist, but eventually wins a reconciliation. The school girl wins a man her mother hoped to grab for herself. Minnie Palmer was the lucky pupil.

January 6, 1896, witnessed a pair of musical openings. Another English hit, **Gentlemen Joe**, seemed about to be a quick failure at the Fifth Avenue. With the law harassing its star, M. B. Curtis, a substitute had to go on opening night. The show was shuttered after 10 performances. Revised,

and with James T. Powers in the lead, it reopened at the end of the month and enjoyed a limited vogue. Powers, a man of many comic faces, portrayed a hack driver in league with servants cavorting while their masters are away.

But Charles Hoyt's **A Black Sheep** was a hit at Hoyt's from the start. The story line was thin. Goodrich Mudd, alias Hot Stuff (Otis Harlan), a Wild West lush, is bequeathed a fortune provided he returns to the East and marries his cousin. He is satisfied to remain where he is, so a local paper arranges a mock lynching to scare him out of town. Bessie Clayton's attractive legs and lively dances were "much admired," while Harlan won encores with "Some Things Are Better Left Unsaid." The *Times* rejoiced that songs such as Harlan's were not incorporated in the all-too-common "I'll sing you a song that will tell you all about it style." On the other hand, the *Dramatic Mirror* insisted the show's musical numbers were hardly related to the plot, sung, as they were, by members of a burlesque troupe stranded in Hot Stuff's village. But Hoyt persisted in advertising his show as "a musical comedy," and the public flocked to it for the rest of the season.

A touring show that had originated at Detroit's Whitney Opera House stopped briefly at the People's Theatre on January 27. **Down on the Suwanee River** was a musical spectacle by R. H. Stephens. Forty of the forty-two performers in its cast were black. Essentially a pageant of black history it moved its players from Africa to a Southern plantation to Rafferty's Hall in New York, where the evening ended with a giant cakewalk. Although *Down on the Suwanee River* played an out-of-the-way house, interest in black music seems to have exploded all over New York's theatrical heartland in the following month. Several times during February, 1896 the *Times* carried notices such as this:

New Negro Melodies. Flora Irwin will sing in the second act of "Gentleman Joe" at the Bijou Theatre to-night two new and original darky songs, which have been composed and written for her. They are called "Honey Does Yer Love Yer Man" and "Nigger with a White Spot on His Face."

On February 16 newspaper advertisements for Keith's Union Square Theatre announced that the next day would mark the "Debut on the High Class Vaudeville Boards of the noted Western Entertainer," Ben Harney. Harney, a white man, accompanied by his black stooge, Strap Hill, first regaled Broadway audiences with a new form of black musical composition, ragtime. Listed eleventh on a bill of fifteen acts, Harney failed to elicit so much as a simple notice from reviewers of the *Times,* the *World,* or the *Herald.* But the public was taken with the new style. Ragtime, more than any other black musical form of the era, fueled the coon song rage and permanently established Afro-American modes as the main influence on American popular song. By the end of the month Primrose and West revealed they had hired Madison Square Garden for an evening of cakewalking, with 200 dancers.

Another importation, **The Lady Slavey** (2-3-96, Casino), was the eighth English musical of the season. Dan Daly starred. Daly played a lackadaisical sheriff ordered to seize the estate of a bankrupt Englishman. The Englishman (Henry Norman) desperately tries to marry one of his four eldest daughters (Virginia Earle), who, with the help of a flighty music hall singer (Marie Dressler), bags a wealthy young heir (Charles Dickson). The show's producer, George Lederer, followed the pattern of the day by allowing American textual revisions and musical interpolations. But Lederer went to extremes. His "Americanized" book was "practically new" and his entire score was by Gustave Kerker. Apparently, not a note of John Crook's original score was heard. The plump bulldog-miened Miss Dressler and the tall, thin, lugubrious Daly combined their abundant talents to stop the show nightly with an acrobatic waltz, "The Human Fly."

With *Excelsior, Jr.,* moved to another house, Oscar Hammerstein was able to present his own creation, **Marguerite,** at the Olympia on February 10. Hammerstein's libretto played havoc with the Faust legend. Faust (Thomas Evans Green) becomes a painter and Marguerite (Alice Rose) his wife. Mephisto (Adolph Dahm-Peterson) appears and, with his magical dragon-headed staff, brings Faust's paintings to life. Later Faust and his wife are transported to Mephisto's summer home, "The Palace of the Flowers." If a number of the critics had unkind things to say about the book, most of the reviewers treated Hammerstein's gifts as a composer with surprising respect. Hammerstein filled the evening with appealing stage pictures. He introduced each major dance number with a voguish "living picture." These tableaux (apparently Faust's paintings) came to life to allow pretty girls to dance at the court of Louis XV, to display a Hussar march and drill as well as to permit a cancan, a peasant dance, and an Oriental dance. One special effect illuminated 1,700 electric bulbs hanging from the ceiling and from strips dangling down to the floor. But Hammerstein had been unwise to let the profitable *Excelsior, Jr.* leave his new house. The comparative failure of *Marguerite* contributed to the flamboyant Hammerstein's bankruptcy.

Robin Hood (9-28-91) returned the same evening as *Marguerite* premiered to initiate a rash of late winter revivals. As might be expected, the production was the Bostonians' venerated interpretation, with Henry Clay Barnabee, W. H. MacDonald, Eugene Cowles, and Jessie Bartlett Davis repeating their great roles. But another name had been added to the troupe's roster, "a young Californian, to whom is entrusted the minor soprano role [of Annabel]." There was no foreseeing the damage Alice Nielsen would inflict on the company that brought her to public attention.

Only one fresh piece broke the chain of revivals. Lillian Russell suffered her third failure in two seasons when she and her handpicked company offered **The Goddess of Truth** (2-26-96, Abbey's). The critics complained that Stanislaus Stange's retelling of the Pygmalion legend lacked wit and that Julian Edwards' score lacked memorable melodies. Indeed, the *Times* took the opportunity to comment on the generally "barren days" for the musical theatre and even to assail Miss Russell, especially the "narrow range of her abilities as an actress." The paper professed the star was at her best only "when she poses in her ornate draperies in the revealing glare of the calcium light." The show left after a somewhat forced run of 45 showings.

On March 2 Chauncey Olcott returned to the 14th Street Theatre in a revival of *The Irish Minstrel,* inexplicably rechristened *The Minstrel of Clare.* (Did Olcott fear audiences might confuse *The Irish Minstrel* with *The Irish Artist?*) *1492* (5-15-93) visited the Grand during the same week. To fill out her scheduled stay at Abbey's Miss Russell hastily mounted *The Little Duke* for a fortnight beginning April 6. Another Fritz play, *Fritz in Love,* appeared on the combination circuit in April.

The year's most enduring work, **El Capitan** (4-20-96, Broadway), had a book by Charles Klein (who in November had provided the American text for *The Merry Countess* and later in the month had disclaimed credit for *A Happy Little Home*). More importantly it had a score by John Philip Sousa. Sousa and Tom Frost collaborated on the lyrics. Although in later years Sousa insisted on calling Klein's book the finest libretto America had ever produced, it was, at best, little better than average.

Certainly in outline it seems barely distinguishable from myriad other contrivances of the time. A rebel band led by El Capitan is determined to overthrow Don Medigua, viceroy of Peru. But Medigua (De Wolf Hopper) captures El Capitan, secretly executes him, and assumes his place in disguise. When the rebels capture Pozzo (Charles Klein), his chamberlain, and mistake the servant for the viceroy, Medigua is at no pains to enlighten them. But Medigua's wife (Alice Hosmer) and daughter (Bertha Waltzinger), hearing of his apparent capture, set out to rescue him, assisted by the daughter's suitor, Count Hernando Verrada (Edmund Stanley). Meanwhile Estrelda (Edna Wallace Hopper), daughter of a former viceroy, falls in love with the supposed El Capitan. To further complicate Medigua's life the Spanish army arrives to help him against the rebels. As El Capitan he leads the rebels in circles until they are too tired to fight. His family arrives in time to explain his and Pozzo's true identities to the Spanish commander. Medigua himself has a little explaining to do to his wife regarding Estrelda. But everything ends happily. Estrelda is given to the man who loves her, Scaramba; the count wins the daughter; and Medigua and his wife once again reign over Peru. Much of Sousa's lovely score was culled by him from earlier works. "The Legend Of The Frogs" (cut before the show opened) had been "The Fable Of The Frogs" in *The Queen of Hearts,* and the lovers' beautiful "Sweetheart, I'm Waiting" was a revision of "Sighing, Ah Sighing" from *The Smugglers.* But the enduring masterpiece of the evening was El Capitan's own march, derived from "El Capitan's Song," sung by Medigua and the chorus.

The show gave its star and producer, De Wolf Hopper, "in wondrous garb and 'make-up'" as a bearded, plumed conquistador, the greatest success of his career. Its first New York run tallied 112 performances. With or without him as star it played virtually without interruption throughout the country for four years. It ran six months in London, and over the years has enjoyed several notable revivals.

The year's last original work was the Casino's third annual summer "review," **In Gay New York,** which arrived on May 25. Since revues still had to have plots, *In Gay New York* described a visit by newlyweds from Maine (how librettists loved to bring in Maine!) to New York. They visit Grand Central, the Waldorf, Coney Island, and the Casino—where they see bits from the season's most popular plays satirized. The plays twitted included *The Heart of Maryland* (in the revue's version David Warfield became entangled in the bell ropes)

and Henry Irving's *Macbeth.* Besides the numerous vaudeville specialties, the evening included a "Newspaper Ballet" and an "Icicle Ballet." Virginia Earle, Madge Lessing, Julius Steger, Walter Jones, Lee Harrison, Warfield, Richard Carle, and John Slavin were part of the large cast. With dialogue by Hugh Morton and music by Gustave Kerker, the evening lasted till midnight.

Two opera companies also appeared at the end of May with traditional repertories that ranged from operetta to grand opera. But the financial climate told and by mid-August, when *In Gay New York* shut down for vacation, not a single musical was playing on Broadway. Lovers of lyric theatre or nostalgia in the New York area could, however, have taken themselves to Manhattan Beach, where a well-attended revival of *Evangeline* (7-27-74) was advertised as "just pure and simple—NOT up to date."

1896-1897

Economically and creatively, the theatre continued to tread water. The new season brought nothing to compare in merit and durability with the preceding April's *El Capitan.* However, with the opening of Weber and Fields' Music Hall it did witness one last extended flourish of a more or less classic burlesque tradition.

The only summer entries were all-star revivals of Gilbert and Sullivan's *H.M.S. Pinafore* and *Patience* at the Herald Square. Lillian Russell, Henry E. Dixey, and W. T. Carleton headed the roster. But Miss Russell, accustomed to being the center of attention, received a rude shock, probably made doubly painful by her recent failures. Sadie Martinot caused an outpouring of gasps and comments when she appeared as Lady Angela, wearing what is reputed to have been the first strapless gown seen on the New York stage.

The main season began poignantly with a Ned Harrigan and David Braham offering. Harrigan's day had passed, and he had fallen on hard times. His theatre had been taken over by Richard Mansfield, who had rechristened it the Garrick. No Harrigan play had reached Broadway in 1895–96. One work, *My Son Dan,* had been tried out, only to fold on the road. The mere fact that Harrigan felt the need to take a new show on the road suggested his own awareness of his faltering flair. Harrigan had always opened his new pieces confidently in New

York. Coincident with the closing of *My Son Dan*, Harrigan had announced a "temporary retirement." But by August 31 Harrigan had a fresh opus ready to inaugurate the season at the Bijou. **Marty Malone** (Harrigan) is an Irish sailor who has renounced a chance to be Prince consort of Ghoola-Ghoola and who befriends a street waif, Pauline Jordan (Pauline Train). Pauline becomes a music hall singer, then proves to be an heiress and leaves Marty to marry rich and handsome Lord John Foxwood (John Hollis). Marty finds solace with a girl attached to some Cuban revolutionaries. Harrigan's tale began in a dilapidated sailor's home in the harbor slums and ended, much as *Notoriety* had, on the lawn of a great estate, with painted yachts "sailing" in the distance. The cliché-filled tale, with perhaps a hint of Chaplin's film *City Lights*, disappointed Harrigan's faithful, even though they greeted the piece with "noisy acclaim." Nor was Braham able to come up with a truly popular song, although "Savannah Sue"—"neatly executed" by Dan Collyer, Dave Braham, Jr., and Gussie Hart (as a "darky damsel")—was much applauded, like the show itself, at the premiere. When *Marty Malone* closed, Harrigan drifted into a less publicly proclaimed retirement, returning only intermittently to the stage.

September was an unusually busy month. Ten musicals bowed. The month began inauspiciously with Ludwig Englander and Harry B. Smith's **The Caliph** (9-3-96, Broadway). Smith professed to have based his libretto on the legend of Haroun Al Raschid, but in fact it was merely another of the comic contrivances set in pseudo-Oriental splendor so dear to the time. With crime rampant in Baghdad, the caliph, Hardluck XIII (Jefferson De Angelis), is persuaded by his cynical vizier to spend some time in disguise among criminal elements so that by better understanding their methods he may more readily eradicate them. Before long the caliph himself has committed every crime in the book. His plans for reform are thwarted, however, when he is abducted by his younger brother, Brikbrak (Alfred C. Whelan). The young man will release the caliph only if he is allowed to marry Djemma (Minnie Landers)—the very girl the caliph had hoped to wed. The caliph agrees and officiates not only over the marriage of Brikbrak and Djemma but of his own daughter and her fiancé as well. For De Angelis the show was his first solo starring part. In a day of broad physical comedy, the press was happy to note that "as an acrobat he can hold his own with any star comedian on our stage." His

funniest moment found him hopelessly entangled in a hammock. Richard Barker directed. *The Caliph* had been scheduled to run until October 26. Poor notices and poorer attendance closed the show ahead of time, with a loss of most of its $16,000 investment.

On September 5, 1896, the three-year-old Imperial Music Hall on Broadway at 29th Street was reopened as Weber and Fields' Musical Hall. Both the stage and the auditorium were small. The house held only 665 seats, and audiences watched performers do their bit on a stage a mere sixteen feet deep. At $1.50 top a sold-out performance could realize no more than $700. But backstage costs, with one exception, were low. At first costumes and sets were rented, and a stage crew of nine drew a total of $132 a week in salaries. But principals asked as much as $200 a week. Thus with actors' fees included, it cost almost $700 a performance to keep the house open. The new music hall was never to be the moneymaker standard-size musical houses were. But at the moment Weber and Fields were not eyeing long-term riches. Their experiences in variety had been artistically enriching and on occasion financially rewarding, but more often uncertain. The young clowns were looking for steady employment.

. . .

Lew Fields (Lewis Schanfield) was born in New York City's Bowery on January 1, 1867, to immigrant parents of modest means. **Joe Weber** (his first name was actually Morris) was born a few blocks away from the Fields' home just over seven months later, August 11, 1867. His parents, too, were immigrants. The boys were childhood friends. They first performed together at the age of ten, doing a "Dutch" act not very different at heart from the dialect clowning they would use the rest of their lives. They moved from amateur to professional variety, rising almost to the top before they decided to borrow money and try their hand as legitimate performers and impresarios. In their act the tall, thin Fields and the shorter, stockier Weber customarily made up with chin whiskers, dressed in gaudily checkered suits (Weber's heavily padded) and sported derbies.

. . .

The renaissance of the burlesque tradition had begun a few seasons earlier with Charles Brookfield's parody of *Lady Windemere's Fan* (4-3-93), its rebirth coming at virtually the same moment as the birth of the revue. Both dealt in travesty, but burlesque aimed its mockery at a single principal target while the revue shot its barbs all over the map. The limitations of the burlesque tradition constrained and eventually killed it, while the revue's open flexibility allowed it to evolve and flourish for half a century. Curiously, when Weber and Fields eventually abandoned burlesque they turned to book shows, almost never to revues. The relative cohesion and discipline of their tradition dictated their futures. But the opening attraction at their new house suggested they were willing to compromise. The first part of their evening was a pure, unalloyed olio; only the second part was a sustained burlesque. This practice of opening night obtained as long as the music hall flourished. For their first burlesque the team chose the same show so well spoofed in *In Gay New York—The Heart of Maryland.* They called their version **The Art of Maryland.** Mary Land became a cook, the creator of chicken à la Maryland. But the material was weak, missing even the obvious opportunity to have fun with Mrs. Carter's swinging on the clapper of the church bell to ensure "The bell shall not ring!" When the London hit, *The Geisha,* opened in September and immediately became one of the outstanding successes of the new season, Weber and Fields hastily dropped *The Art of Maryland* and substituted their first major triumph, **The Geezer.** In the burlesque, Li Hung Chang (a Chinese official with that name had visited America earlier in the year) comes seeking an American heiress as bride for his emperor. The heiress' dowry must be sufficient to pay off the indemnity demanded by Japan after the 1894–95 war. Other characters included a teahouse keeper, Two-Hi (played by Sam Bernard), who offers all comers "one pie-cee beer mit pretzels." Occidentals were kidded as well. The famous reporter Nellie Bly became Nellie Fly; the actress May Yoke, whose marriage had made her Lady Francis Pelham Clinton Hope, found herself kidded as Ladies Faith, Hope, and Charity; the ubiquitous police commissioner, Teddy Roosevelt, gave his name to all the policemen in the cast—A. Roosevelt, B. Roosevelt, etc. The tradition of comic opera out of which *The Geisha* came was made fair game in the opening chorus, a spoof of opening choruses:

Hurrah! Hurrah! We laugh and sing,
So loudly let the welkin ring.
We must admit, though far from slow,
What welkin is, we do not know.

But musical traditions alien to comic opera and *The Geisha* also found a place. "Miss Lucy" honored the raging coon song vogue with lyrics Wordsworth might not have disdained for his Lucy:

The bees hum in the blossom vine,
The birds break out in song.
The sun, he say, "Ise obleeged to shine,"
When Miss Lucy pass along.

The text was by Joseph Herbert, who left Weber and Fields at the end of the season, but the music was by the composer who remained loyal to the house until his death, John Stromberg. One other change Weber and Fields introduced in their second week was an "animatograph," an early, primitive form of motion pictures. In doing so they were catering to that new fad that had begun the preceding season. Days earlier, Tony Pastor had offered his patrons a "kineopticon" and the Union Square a "cinematograph." Weber and Fields discarded their film show after a short time, preferring to satirize its flickering, jerky movements by rapidly changing the screens in front of their calcium spots. It was the first use of a device that would soon become a commonplace.

Sidney Jones' London hit **The Geisha** opened on September 9 at Daly's. Owen Hall wrote the book; Harry Greenbank, the lyrics; and Lionel Monckton supplied additional melodies. The story told of the love of a naval officer—whose uniform would be appropriated by a decade or more of musical heroes—and a geisha at a tea house. The lovers are parted at the end, but not tragically. The Englishman weds a comely English girl, and O Mimosa San marries an Oriental. Dorothy Morton and Van Rensselaer Wheeler were featured, while one of the evening's dancers was Isadora Duncan. Because of various commitments, Daly was not able to allow *The Geisha* to run uninterruptedly. However, in a series of engagements during this season and the next it compiled over 200 performances. For reasons no longer clear it also underwent constant cast changes.

If burlesque was renascent, minstrelsy continued to wane. When the Cleveland Haverly Minstrels came to town the same night as *The Geisha,* they were relegated to the Star Theatre, once a major house but by this date a less important auditorium.

Englander and Smith had a second comic opera, **Half a King** (9-14-96, Knickerbocker), ready a week after the *Caliph* premiere. By the lights of the time they served Francis Wilson and Lulu Glaser better than they had Jefferson De Angelis, although nothing from *Half a King* has remained popular. In this musical version of Chivot and Duru's *Le Roi* *de Pique,* two mountebanks, Tireschappe (Wilson) and Mistris (Peter Lang), attempt to foist the waif Pierrette (Miss Glaser) on the Duke de Chateau Marguax (J. C. Miron). They kidnap the duke's intended bride and send Pierrette in her place. But Pierrette bungles her chance and returns to her mountebanks. Wilson, like De Angelis, was praised for his "acrobatic humor," although it was generally conceded that Wilson's style was the least broad and most cerebral of the major clowns of his day. Wilson had fun with a trick donkey and delighted audiences with a topical song in which he instructed real kings of the day how to run their realms. Henry E. Hoyt painted a beautiful outdoor view of Paris, while Richard Marston contributed his painterly skills to a palace interior. Richard Barker again directed. Whatever posterity has thought of the piece, Wilson's commission kept him profitably occupied for two months in New York and the rest of the season on tour. The show was the first to play Abbey's under its new and more enduring name of the Knickerbocker.

On September 21 Victor Herbert suffered one of the worst failures of his career when **The Gold Bug** opened at the Casino on Monday and closed the next Saturday. Although only three musical numbers were published, Herbert was not to blame for the show's failure. In fact, one number, "The Gold Bug March," is still heard occasionally. Much of the show's troubles stemmed from delaying the opening night several times. Even on that first night many costumes were not ready. A shaky performance accentuated the libretto's flatness. This book by Glen MacDonough, with whom Herbert collaborated more happily in later years, revolved around Willet Float (Max Figman), the Secretary of the Navy, and "a man with a past." The skeleton in his closet is the Indian wife he deserted. His daughter by her, Wawayanda (Molly Fuller), appears and blackmails him into abetting her romance. Characters included Lady Patty Larceny (played by young Marie Cahill), Doolittle Work (Henry Norman), and a politician called Constant Steele (Robert Fisher). For many, Miss Cahill was the delight of the evening. She assumed the part of a young woman who still pursues the perfect mate, even if she has been divorced fifteen times. Her song, "When I First Began To Marry, Years Ago," her cancan and her cachuca with her ex-mates were all show-stoppers. Two performers not given characters to play and not even listed by name on the program were nonetheless shortly to make an indelible mark on the history of the American Musical Theatre: Bert Williams and George Walker.

J. Cheever Goodwin and Woolson Morse, deprived of De Wolf Hopper's talents, nevertheless managed to delight Broadway with **Lost, Strayed or Stolen** (9-21-96, Fifth Ave.). The show was a musical version of Grange and Bernard's *Le Baptême du Petit Oscar.* A nurse gives a child about to be baptized to a soldier, and the soldier disappears. The baby's father and three godfathers go in search of the child, encountering special complications (as well as specialties) when they arrive at the apartment of Rose D'Ete (Georgia Caine), an actress who is also the soldier's mistress. The comic highlight of the evening was a scene in which Rose, as each new caller arrives, shoves his predecessor into a single, minuscule closet. One popular song, "Ootchy Kootchy," was not sung to the baby. With so many soldiers among the principals, the producers could not resist the inevitable marches and drills, but their excess elicited cries for moderation.

Two other important debuts occurred when Anna Held made her first American appearance in a revival of Charles Hoyt's *A Parlor Match* (9-21-96, Herald Square). The show's young producer, Florenz Ziegfeld, Jr., had only recently called attention to himself in Chicago.

· · ·

Florenz Ziegfeld was born on March 21, 1869. His father, an austere martinet, headed the Chicago Musical College, one of the city's many music schools. Ziegfeld's reaction to a heavy dose of classical music was a lifelong aversion to great musical masterpieces and an indifference to music in general. Although in later years Ziegfeld always sought out the best composers for his shows as a matter of sound business practice, his attitude toward them and their music was often infuriating and alienating. Ziegfeld fell in love with show business when Buffalo Bill and Annie Oakley came to Chicago in 1883. Ziegfeld later claimed he played hookey from school several days running to see the troupe. At twenty-two he staged a show called *The Dancing Ducks of Denmark* until the SPCA forced a closing of the attraction. (He had induced the ducks to dance by heating the bottoms of their feet.) He became secretary-treasurer of his father's school, but his spendthrift recklessness caused him to be removed quickly. When his father was made musical director for the 1893 Columbian Exposition in Chicago, young Ziegfeld was sent to secure performers. The elder Ziegfeld was appalled at the collection of jugglers, acrobats, and circus bands his son signed. On his return Ziegfeld also signed the strong-man Sandow. It was as Sandow's promoter at the fair and on the tour that followed that Ziegfeld first came to the public eye. For his first Broadway venture Ziegfeld decided to reunite the once famous comedy team of Charles Evans and William Hoey in a revival of their old favorite, the Hoyt play. Ziegfeld and Evans went to Europe seeking new faces. In London they saw Anna Held at the Palace.

. . .

Anna Held professed to be a native of Paris, but records suggest she was actually born in Warsaw in 1873. Her father was a French-Jewish glove maker; her mother was Polish. Her father died when she was still a child, and she and her mother moved to London, where they found employment in the garment industry. A young admirer wangled her a job as a chorus girl. She soon moved over to the more serious Yiddish theatre, then to Dutch and Parisian music halls. When Ziegfeld and Evans saw her, Miss Held had just returned to the stage after an unhappy marriage that produced one child. Miss Held and Ziegfeld hoped to marry after the opening of *A Parlor Match,* but Anna's first husband, a Catholic, refused her a divorce. Ziegfeld and Miss Held lived together as husband and wife until their union was recognized in common law in 1904. Acknowledging that her first entrance evoked "a prolonged and sincere 'Oh!' " from her audience, one critic proceeded to describe her: "Mlle. Held is not very tall; she has lots of hair, not quite black, and combed back loosely from a smooth low brow; her costume was a radiant combination of pale blue and pale salmon, heavily embroidered . . . . Her eyes are long, narrow, and heavily circled; her nose is straight; her mouth perfect . . . . Her voice is not as charming as she is, but it will do." The diminutive coquette skyrocketed to the same glittering stardom as Weber and Fields, and Bert Williams.

. . .

In his fiscal high-flying Oscar Hammerstein foreshadowed Ziegfeld. Deep in financial difficulties, Hammerstein still found time to write both libretto and music for another comic opera, **Santa Maria** (9-24-96, Olympia), and to unveil it at the house he was about to lose. Camille D'Arville was the star. The title had nothing to do with saints or Columbus; it was, for no special reason, the heroine's name. A gypsy informs the king of Holland that years before, while the king was away at war, his wife bore him a child, but gave it away. The king sends a trusted lieutenant in search of the child, hoping to identify it by an unusual birthmark. The lieutenant returns with a beautiful girl, who falls in love with him. The grateful king makes the two his

heirs. James T. Powers provided much of the comedy as a judge in a land where offences against women are tried by all-female juries. The judge sees to it his jurors are especially comely, and keeps them in hand by squirting seltzer from a soda fountain built into his bench at girls who misbehave. Critics complained that the songs had as little to do with the story as did the title. But the public ignored the carping. They flocked to the theatre long enough to let the show run 100 performances and salve some of Hammerstein's wounds.

Robert Breitenbach and his composer, Carl Pleininger, closed out the month with **The Merry Tramps** (9-28-96, Star). It was one more vehicle for the Liliputians, with the midgets performing in "colloquial German and American English" and with the program boasting the scenery was painted in Germany. In another of the period's fantastic science-fiction plots, Professor Willard (A. Durand) invents a magic machine that tells him who in all the earth is best qualified to marry his daughter, Mary (Bertha Jaeger). Willard, Mary, and a man-ape set out on a magic train and airship to test three leading prospects. Each is given a sum of money, and the one that does best with it will win. Two squander their capital. The third man, Jim (Adolf Zink), increases it. Franz Ebert, generally conceded the most beloved of the little people, assumed a number of roles, appearing "as a drunk, a lady-killer in pink coat and knee smalls, an old Jew, a frivolous woman, and Adonis taking a shower." The show played five weeks at the house and then embarked on a tour.

October's first entry was a revival of *Evangeline* (7-27-74), with Henry E. Dixey as the Lone Fisherman and George K. Fortesque once again playing Catherine. The show featured a dozen pretty chorus girls and a grand "Amazon March." Eleven nights later, October 12, the Casino acknowledged that farce-comedy was unmistakably evolving into musical comedy when it presented its patrons J. J. McNally's latest effort, **A Good Thing.** McNally's tale described Billy Biddall's embarrassment when his love letters to Minnie Millett (Agnes Milton) fall into her mother's hands and the old lady presumes they are meant for her. Peter F. Dailey, soon to be a pillar of strength at Weber and Field starred as Billy. The songs were all interpolations and the specialties included five girls in a bicycle dance. The principals took time off from the plot to burlesque grand opera, while Flora Irwin stepped front and center to introduce the latest coon songs. But Casino patrons wanted more cohesive material. *A Good Thing* survived a mere three weeks.

Yet, in spite of failures and of the slapdash nature of some of the hits, musicals were voguish and profitable. When a revival of *A Night at the Circus, Brian Boru,* and *In Mexico* all raised their curtains on October 19, half of the sixteen shows playing the main stem were musicals by standards of the time.

The extent to which shows were conceived for special audiences can be gauged when it was noted that **Brian Boru** was the first show since the days of Dion Boucicault with a totally Irish story aimed at more than the local Irish trade. And the story was indeed Irish. In glens filled with fairies and banshees, Brian Boru (Max Eugene), the Irish king, is tempted by the British princess, Elfrida (Amanda Fabris), to betray his own people. She fails, and Brian leads his forces to victory. But if Stanislaus Stange's story was Celtic, Julian Edwards' music was not. Still theatregoers of all backgrounds made the show a modest hit at the Broadway, relishing in particular the scene in which the thwarted Elfrida turns on the king:

Rude barbarian, wild uncouth!
Elfrida now to thee speaks truth—
I never loved thee—thou wert my tool;
I hate and scorn thee, poor weak fool!

Indeed, Miss Fabris "trilled with a vigor that moved the audience to wild applause." Older theatregoers could take special delight in the presence of Amelia Summerville as an "elderly baby." The once mammoth comedienne had become probably the first major celebrity to undertake a publicized, rigid diet. At least one amused critic compared the relatively slim Miss Summerville with the unromantically burly hero.

In Mexico was part of the Bostonians' repertory. The group's fortunes had begun to fail, and they were shunted off to a new, but somewhat out-of-the-way house, the Murray Hill. The story was set in the Mexican War. When the wounded Captain Selden (William E. Phillip) falls in love with his nurse, Marquita Mason (Hilda Mason), Ramon Falcon (W. H. MacDonald) would force the girl to marry him by threatening to make public compromising letters her guardian had written. She is spared when a peasant named Theresa (Jessie Bartlett Davis), a girl Falcon has wronged, stabs him to death. Other Bostonian stalwarts took lesser roles, Eugene Cowles appearing as a faithful half-breed and Henry Clay Barnabee as a "Varmount sutler" (Vermont settler). With a book by C. T. Dazey and music by Oscar Weil—who had earlier composed *Suzette* for the Bostonians—it was originally produced as *A Wartime Wedding.* The *Times,* in an interesting observation, suggested the Mexican War was a poor setting for a tale, noting that since the war had never been "cherished" by Americans it would elicit no patriotic fervor. Its repertory nature allowed the company to keep weak works on its program, often with the hope of slowly improving them. In his autobiography, Barnabee recalled that the musical "seemed to fit our organization like a glove, and yet proved an incorrigible misfit with regard to the patronizing public." The Bostonians immediately replaced the work with *The Bohemian Girl* on October 26 and finished their engagement.

On November 2 the Casino replaced its own failure, *A Good Thing,* with **Jack and the Beanstalk,** a children's extravaganza—another genre new to the house—and was awarded with two months of good holiday business. R. A. Barnet's fable found Jack, Old Mother Hubbard's (Madge Lessing) son, selling his cow with the crumpled horn to buy a beanstalk. He climbs it with Sinbad the Sailor (E. Gerard) and together they visit Cloudland, where King Cole (H. V. Donnelly), Miss Moffett (Merri Osborne), and Puss 'n Boots (Marie Godoy) live. Miss Osborne won encores with two coon songs, one sung straight and the other rendered as an English coster might do it. The show was the first with a complete score by A. Baldwin Sloane, although a number of his songs had been heard the preceding year in *Excelsior, Jr* (11-29-95).

. . .

A. Baldwin Sloane was born in Baltimore on August 28, 1872, receiving his musical training there from various professors. An early fondness for the lyric stage made him one of the founders of Baltimore's Paint and Powder Club, a semiprofessional theatrical group, which mounted some of his fledgling efforts. Moving to New York, he began composing in accepted Tin Pan Alley style, and soon found his songs being interpolated into musicals and employed by vaudevillians. Sloane's melodies were devoid of distinction, but he was genial and prolific, and quickly found increasing call for his services.

. . .

Harry B. Smith had yet another libretto ready—with another Oriental setting—for **The Mandarin** (11-2-96, Herald Square). His mandarin (George Honey) disguises himself as Fan-Tan (G. C. Boniface, Jr.), a carpenter, in order to woo Fan-Tan's beautiful wife (Bertha Waltzinger). But the police come to arrest Fan-Tan, who has been out on a spree. Naturally they haul in the disguised mandarin despite his protests. The mandarin's cohorts then mistakenly hustle Fan-Tan to the safety of the mandarin's home and twelve wives. But when the real Fan-Tan has his saviors bring him his own wife, he falls afoul of a law permitting a man no more than a dozen mates. Only the mandarin's confession saves Fan-Tan from the block. The score was another disappointment by Reginald De Koven, who was beginning to be assailed as a once-lucky hack. De Koven, in an interview, defended himself as best he could from critical complaints that his music was increasingly derivative. He insisted all composers are "imitative" and that it was too soon to expect our still young nation to develop a fresh style of its own. Either ignorant of or ignoring the Negro influence beginning to be felt all about him, he pontificated, "what we need is music in America, not American music." *The Mandarin* departed after five weeks.

The season's runaway hit was E. E. Rice's mounting of Ivan Caryll's London success *The Gay Parisienne,* retitled **The Girl from Paris** (12-8-96, Herald Square). The libretto concerned the troubles of an austere old Englishman (Charles A. Bigelow) who returns from a Continental tour to find himself sued for breach of promise by a young French lady (Clara Lipman). The musical ran into the summer.

No further musicals appeared until December 28, when another London favorite, **Dorcas** (for which *Erminie's* Harry Paulton collaborated with Edward Paulton on the book, while Watty Hydes and Clement Lockname did the score), opened at the Lyric the same evening Gustave Kerker and Hugh Morton's **An American Beauty** arrived at the Casino. The London musical described how an Englishman, engaged to a girl he has never met, determines to evaluate her by visiting her in disguise. She gets wind of the ploy and pulls one of her own. The Casino's show was plainly tacked together as a vehicle for Lillian Russell and had the virtue of not trying to call itself a comic opera or anything else on its program. Miss Russell played Gabrielle Dalmont, a young lady who goes riding, forgetting it is her wedding day. Circus proprietors Bangle, Budd, and Bingle spot her and offer her employment as the circus queen. She politely rejects the offer. But she conceives the idea of giving a circus ball. The Earl of Beverly (Harold Blake) falls in love with her and disguises himself as a gardener, hoping to woo and win her without the glamor of his station. When she declines his hand, he obtains a magic flower which causes anyone inhaling its fragrance to sleep and to fall in love with the first person she sees on waking. Of course the Earl arranges that it is he Gabrielle sees. But the groom Gabrielle has forgot-

ten, Prince Schwepps (Owen Westford), convinces the Earl that Gabrielle has learned his identity and is bluffing. The Earl leaves, only to return and win Gabrielle again. Miss Russell made her entrance at the ball on a stage elephant and lingered to watch a line-up of specialties that filled out the ballroom scene. Her followers kept ticket sales brisk until the end of February, when she took the show on the road.

A completely different sort of lady arrived at the Bijou December 29, the night after Miss Russell's opening. May Irwin, the leading singer of coon songs, stalked on stage in John J. McNally's newest farce-comedy, **Courted into Court.** Dottie Dimple (Miss Irwin), an actress, decides to divorce her husband, Worthington Best, Jr. (John C. Rice), when he becomes jealous of the attention his own father (Raymond Hitchcock) pays to Dottie. The Judge (Joseph M. Sparks), hoping to marry Dottie himself, insists on granting the divorce even after Dottie reconsiders and wants the case dropped. Clara Palmer, Ada Lewis, and Jacques Kruger virtually completed the cast—an all-star line-up. Although on opening night Miss Lewis as a German dancer won the loudest applause for "The Oompah," two of Miss Irwin's biggest hits came from songs added to the play: "Mister Johnson Turn Me Loose" (by the same Ben Harney who had brought ragtime to New York) and "All Coons Look Alike To Me" (Ernest Hogan).

The first new show to appear in 1897 was also a farce-comedy, Charles Hoyt's **A Contented Woman** (1-4-97, Hoyt's). But it was unusual in that instead of culling its songs willynilly as was farce-comedy's wont, it seems to have had a score by a single composer, Richard Stahl. Of course Hoyt had earlier used Percy Gaunt to write whole scores for his farce-comedies, but few of his fellow farceurs copied him. Hoyt resorted to the popular motif of a woman's rebellion for his story. When Benton Holme (William H. Currie), a mayoral candidate, rudely tears off a button his wife (Caroline Miskel-Hoyt) has sewn on incorrectly, she decides to run against him on a reform ticket. With women's suffrage in the air Hoyt found a receptive audience, although the success of *A Contented Woman* fell short of some of his earlier hits.

The preceding season's flop, *Kismet* (8-12-95), was revived the same night *A Contented Woman* premiered. It failed once again, but the mere fact it was revived further illustrates the relative freedom from critical and financial burdens this epoch's musical theatre enjoyed.

The next night, January 5, an importation,

Shamus O'Brien, began a two-month run at the Broadway.

Charles E. Blaney's **A Boy Wanted** (1-18-97, Star) became the second farce-comedy in a row to have songs by a single composer. In this case the music was by Harry James. Blaney's story unfolded the escapades of Phoney Dice in his efforts to find a soft berth and an easy buck. But neither the music nor the play was up to Broadway standards, and the show, after a week at the Star, returned to the hinterlands for which it had been conceived.

The 14th Street Theatre, like the Star, was generally looked on as a combination house. Every now and then, however, it played host to an attraction not quite right for Broadway. More often than not these were plays designed for specific ethnic groups, usually the Irish. Just such a play opened on January 25 when Chauncey Olcott appeared in Augustus Pitou's **Sweet Inniscarra.** It called itself a romantic drama, but in keeping with Olcott's practice half a dozen songs were written for the piece. Olcott portrayed Gerald O'Carroll, who returns to Ireland from London high life to woo Kate O'Donoghue (Georgia Busby). Although Kate's father has other plans for her, love triumphs. If this, like most Olcott vehicles, was more straight play than musical, with "Sweet Inniscarra," "Kate O'Donoghue," and "The Old Fashioned Mother" it showed greater concern with the pertinence of its songs than most farce-comedies or some more pretentious efforts demonstrated. The 14th Street Theatre was often content with bookings of one week or a fortnight. *Sweet Inniscarra* remained there the rest of the season.

At Gay Coney Island, one more farce-comedy, appeared for a week beginning February 1 at a combination house, the Columbus. Mistaken identities lead its stars, the team of J. Sherrie Matthews and Harry Bulger, a merry chase around the resort. Matthews and Bulger, along with Maurice Levi, composed most of the songs.

All through this period Boston continued actively mounting local productions. The success of the Bostonians had prompted a number of groups to form there in hopes of emulating their early prosperity. One was the Boston Cadets, and for this ensemble R. A. Barnet created a variation of *Jack and the Beanstalk,* calling it **Simple Simon.** In Boston the good Fairy Queen helps Simple Simon in his courtship of Curly Locks, whose heart has been turned to stone by a witch.

By 1897, English musicals had supplanted French opéra bouffe as the reigning musical mode. While French plays frequently served as the in-

spiration for American librettos, few new French lyric works found their way across the Atlantic. Although sung in German *Ta Ta-To To,* opening at the Irving Place on February 11, was an exception. The piece departed quickly. A second French importation, **La Falote** (3-1-97, Casino) confirmed the disfavor the Gallic pieces had fallen into when it struggled through a two-week run. Its silly plot was no help. A flirtatious baroness disguises herself as a "castle-haunting spook." Even J. Cheever Goodwin's adaptation was to no avail.

Between the two debacles, Weber and Fields changed bills at their music hall. One of the current theatrical hits was Stanley Weyman's *Under the Red Robe,* a play about Richelieu. At the music hall it became **Under the Red Globe,** and its hero was Fishglue. The action now took place in Gaily's Gambling House, which audiences of the day understood as Daly's next door. Audiences themselves were changing at Weber and Fields. "Music Hall" had long connoted food, and, more especially, drink service, during the performance. To attract a better element the team announced service would be suspended while the play was on, and shortly thereafter service was discontinued altogether. While some patrons undoubtedly rued the loss of such amenities, Weber and Fields did succeed in attracting more couples, more women, and a generally higher social stratum than customarily attended music halls. Just how successful they were and how rapid their success was suggested when one reviewer noted the theatre was "packed to suffocation, every seat and every inch of standing room being occupied."

The extent to which the word "musical" in the title added box office appeal was shown when one of the most popular of all American actresses, Ada Rehan, revived Charlotte Cushman's once popular vehicle, *Meg Merrilies,* calling it not a "romantic melodrama" but rather a "romantic musical play."

The last outstanding success the Bostonians were to enjoy was Victor Herbert's **The Serenade** (3-16-97, Knickerbocker). It had been given its world premiere in Cleveland a month earlier and then had been taken to Chicago with the rest of the Bostonians' repertory while it was polished. Looking back over the musical stage years later, the greatest of the Bostonians, Henry Clay Barnabee, concluded the work was "the best American contribution to genuine comic opera—as distinguished from musical comedy, which I consider 'Robin Hood' to be—up to now revealed." Barnabee's strange classification of *Robin Hood* (9-28-91) probably stemmed from his belief that the comic part of the villainous sheriff was the pivotal role, whereas comic elements were secondary in *The Serenade*. Herbert's scholarly and thoughtful biographer, Edward N. Waters, shares some of Barnabee's sentiments, "The score was one of the best Herbert ever did, and he never surpassed some of its concerted and dramatic numbers." The public of 1897 most certainly fell in love with Herbert's melodious songs, especially the famous serenade itself, "I Love Thee, I Adore Thee." Harry B. Smith's libretto, while not on a par with Herbert's music, sufficed. Unfortunately, Herbert was never to collaborate with a first-rate librettist.

In *The Serenade* everyone loves the ravishing Dolores (Jessie Bartlett Davis). Her guardian, the Duke of Santa Cruz (Barnabee), would keep her for himself; Alvarado (W. H. MacDonald), the dashing baritone of the Madrid Opera, courts her; and Romero (Eugene Cowles), president of the Royal Madrid Brigandage Association (he is a brigand on alternate days, a monk the rest of the time), also pines for her. Alvarado's life is complicated by Yvonne (Alice Nielsen), whom he jilted but who still loves him. The Duke hides Dolores in a convent. With the strains of the Serenade to guide them, Alvarado and Dolores eventually are able to rush into each other's arms. Yvonne must be content with Lopez (William E. Philip), secretary to the brigands. The show played to packed houses until May 22 when previous commitments forced the Bostonians to move on. The success of Nielsen as Yvonne encouraged her to leave the Bostonians and form her own company. Taking Cowles with her, she inflicted a wound on the Bostonians that hastened their demise. But the ambitious Miss Nielsen was to prove no more loyal to the comic opera stage than she had been to the group that nurtured her.

Vaudeville still eyed legitimate musicals with uncertainty. Farce-comedies in particular were draining away some of the best talents from the variety stage. So it is not too surprising that vaudeville houses continued to seek ways of identifying themselves with the legitimate arena. Koster and Bial's, instead of performing miniature comic opera, tried approaching the revue format by giving a bill a title and by having a librettist and composer tie the specialties together. On March 22 they called the bill **In Gayest Manhattan or Around New York in Ninety Minutes.** The indefatigable Harry B. Smith wrote some lyrics and dialogue and Ludwig Englander wrote some songs. Smith's slim plot had a retired tragedian, Delsarte Flam—played by Henry E. Dixey—audition potential pupils. Somehow an excuse was discovered to allow a grand march by chorus girls dressed to represent firefighters and also to permit a glimpse of the sort of spectacle early 20th-century extravaganzas would offer when the girls posed to form a gigantic "floral fountain." But the novelty had no noticeable appeal; no one was deceived or no one cared. In a few weeks the house quietly dropped the title.

Miss Manhattan (3-23-97, Wallack's) was an extravaganza with a plot suspiciously like the one *Miss Philadelphia* had used in the City of Brotherly Love the year before and which Broadway would see in the following season. Of course, William Penn gave place to Father Knickerbocker, who visits Chollie Knickerbocker in a dream to admonish the young man's spendthrift ways and who finds himself taken on a tour of the town. He is beset by bicycles, flying motor-carriages, and a cable car ("realistically depicted rounding Dead Man Curve"). At one point an up-to-date Miss Manhattan kicks off his hat. (Kicking off hats seems to have been modish in this theatrical year. Earlier, in *An American Beauty*, Lillian Russell had sung of a saucy French demimondaine who teased erring husbands by promising them "I keek off ze 'igh chapeau/Wiz ze wee little point of my toe, Papa!") Knickerbocker's progress was further halted as a women's brass band provided accompaniment for yet another Amazon drill. The cast was filled with minor names destined to remain unimportant. The score was by various hands, but the librettist was a writer new to the musical theatre—one who would remain around some while —George V. Hobart.

Two weeks later Stanislaus Stange and Julian Edwards brought in their second offering of the season, **The Wedding Day** (4-8-97, Casino). Actually it was an adaptation of Audran's *La Petite Fronde,* and in this instance Edwards merely supplemented the score. In its story a French peasant girl, a lady, and a baker combined their efforts to secure a Franco-Spanish treaty. Although it offered three top stars in the same show—a rarity at the time—it was something of a disappointment. Jefferson De Angelis, Della Fox, and Lillian Russell combined could not earn it more than 72 performances, in two separate engagements.

For a few weeks Herbert had two works running simultaneously when *The Wizard of the Nile* (11-4-95) played a popular return engagement beginning April 19.

Miss Manhattan was in her last days when Weber and Fields offered her a mate, **Mister New York, Esquire.** The new bill, their last for the season, marked a departure from the burlesques they had rapidly made famous. They called it a "travesty" to suggest that it mocked things in general and was not built around a specific play. Audiences were not appreciative. Good businessmen that they were, Weber and Fields withdrew it and never used the term "travesty" again.

Ivan Caryll and Lionel Monckton's London hit, **The Circus Girl** (4-23-97, Daly's), arrived as April's last offering, delighting Anglophile New York at its producer's own theatre almost as much as it had charmed the West End at Edwardes' Gaiety. James T. Powers led the fun-making, in a tale of a schoolgirl in love with a circus performer who turns out to be an heir. But a German musical, **At the French Ball** (5-3-97, Bijou), met with a cooler reception. The production was "a traveling show," stopping only briefly in New York, which featured Fanny Rice ("moderation is scarcely her watchword") as a shoemaker's wife who dreams of owning a silk gown. It lingered only a month. The vogue for almost anything English was acknowledged in the columns of "The Matinee Girl," a weekly feature in the *Dramatic Mirror*. Its anonymous authoress asked, "Why is it that the English composers send us over such dainty verses and tripping airs in comparison to some of the domestic stuff we get?" The lady concluded, "I am getting to be a bit of an Anglomaniac so far as musical comedies are concerned." History has not shared her judgments. Like her male contemporaries she mistook the high style and cohesion of English offerings for genuine, overriding quality.

Having catered since late January to its Irish audience, the 14th Street Theatre apparently aimed at a different crowd when it presented **The Widow Goldstein** on May 17. Another farce-comedy with songs from various sources it recounted how Hettie Goldstein (Jennie Reiffarth) outtricks the sly, greedy Cyrus Russell (R. F. Cotton), thereby allowing a number of young lovers to wed. It also included, as did so many of its type, jugglers, a waiter turned magician, a "collegate" band, and other variety acts.

The Bijou replaced *At the French Ball* on May 24 with a repertory company to play old favorites such as *Erminie* and *The Chimes of Normandy* for "a summer season." A further sign hot weather was at hand was the back to back (and side by side) arrival of two revues. **A Round of Pleasure** raised its curtain at the Knickerbocker on May 24, while **The Whirl of the Town** romped into the Casino the next night. Both, of course, had plots. Sydney Rosenfeld's, for the former, was the simpler of the

two. The Duke of Marlinspike (Richard Carle) is shown around America by Welkin Ring (Jerome Sykes) and his daughters, Aurora (Marguerite Sylva) and Niobe (Marie Celeste). What the Duke saw was "over 100" performers (and 200 mechanical horses in a miniature Madison Square Garden Horse Show). He witnessed a dagger dance, and "Dutch" clowning by Gus and Max Rogers. The Duke reciprocated by parodying Hamlet. Ludwig Englander provided everyone with music. The show received a divided press—although its advertisements were quick to acknowledge the *Herald*'s praise of "one real round of Pleasure" in an early use of excerpts from notices in daily ads. But the criticisms apparently told. By June 19 substantial revisions had been announced, and soon ads advised "Something New Every Night." The show lasted six weeks, closed for vacation, then reopened as *One Round of Pleasure* for a fortnight prior to touring.

Hugh Morton and Gustave Kerker's *The Whirl of the Town* at the Casino met with a happier response. Audiences were coming to look forward to the house's annual summer revue, and the house was perfecting its presentations. Morton's plot was not much different from Rosenfeld's. Bibulous, kleptomaniacal Willie Badboy (Dan Daly) steals Dimples (Madge Lessing), a mermaid, from the aquarium and takes her on a trip around New York. Pursued by her keeper (Louis Harrison), as well as by a detective (David Warfield) and the multi-disguised proprietors (John Slavin and Harry MacDonough) of a freak museum, they visit a cable car, the Rialto, the Met (where they watch a "vaudeville"), and the Cave of Jewels off Coney Island. Typical of Morton's dialogue was the half-high Willie's response to the mermaid's urgent need for a tank. He assures her he's quite a tank himself. Mimics, jugglers, and other specialities filled the scenes. *The Whirl of the Town* far outstripped its next-door neighbor, compiling 127 showings.

While *A Round of Pleasure* was soliciting first-nighter's approval in New York, the Bostonians, out on the road, offered their faithful followers a new American comic opera. But their musical adaptation of *Rip Van Winkle* suffered the same unkind reception most of their native material was accorded. The troupe quickly dropped the piece.

The economy and generally lax quality of the year's shows were not the only things adversely affecting attendance. As early as March 27 trade journals were lamenting that "bicycle fever" was hurting theatres, and on May 29 the *Dramatic Mirror*'s Chicago correspondent bewailed "Those bicycle legs are beginning to knock the everlasting spots out of the big downtown playhouses." By July the number of active roof gardens had dwindled by half compared with the preceding season, and few regular theatres were open.

1897-1898

The number of new musical shows dropped noticeably during the new season. The lessening vogue for farce-comedy was partly responsible. To the extent that the decline in numbers reflected the passing of these relatively haphazard concoctions it meant a step forward for coherent musical comedy writing. Unfortunately, the decline resulted more from the continued creative exhaustion of the lyric stage as a whole. Economic doldrums, the third cause of the falling off of production, ended abruptly in March when the *Maine* was blown up in Havana harbor. Bicycle fever speedily succumbed to war fever. A month later we were officially at war, and the economy began to hum again.

A freakish affair was the first entry of the new season. Although **Captain Cook** was billed as a "comic opera"—and did indeed have a comic opera plot and score—it was primarily a gigantic spectacle. It was mounted not at one of the standard legitimate houses but in the huge arena of Madison Square Garden on July 12. The premiere was attended by Queen Liliuokalani of Hawaii. The story, if it could be heard in the unmicrophoned vastness of the building, depicted Captain Cook's reception as a god when he arrived in Hawaii. The captain is awarded Princess Ia Ia. But Oponuii, who loves the princess, leads a rebellion to discredit and expel Cook. His rebellion coincides with an eruption of Mauna Loa, convincing superstitious islanders that Oponuii is opposed by the gods. But the kindly Cook assures the natives that Oponuii is a good man. He gives the princess in marriage to the youthful rebel and sails away. Written by inexperienced hands, the show was a quick failure.

No other musicals made an effort to buck the long summer, so it was not until August 30 that two more musicals appeared. **Very Little Faust and More Marguerite** raised its curtain at the same Olympia Theatre in which Hammerstein had offered his own *Marguerite* two seasons before. The new work was a French burlesque adopted for the American stage and originally presented at Man-

hattan Beach for a summer run prior to its Broadway sally. Broadway felt something was lost in the sea crossing, and the show survived just 24 showings.

But J. J. McNally's latest farce-comedy, **The Good Mr. Best** (8-30-97, Garrick), had an even shorter stay, just two weeks. Between the various incidental songs and specialties McNally unfolded the confusion created when an uncle gives twins large allowances on the condition they never marry. Tom does marry—his uncle's ex-wife, in fact. But he hides both his marriage and his twin brother's death from his generous relative. When the uncle shows up Tom is forced to impersonate his late brother, Tim. He discovers his brother was even naughtier than he.

Weber and Fields' Music Hall relit on September 2. The principal attraction was **The Glad Hand, or Secret Servants,** which managed to twit both the Yukon Gold Rush, then at its height, and William Gillette's popular *Secret Service*. While Weber and Fields' spy waited for his all-important dispatch a little gambling seemed in order. Only the gamblers—Sam Bernard, Peter F. Dailey, Charles J. Ross, and John Kelly—apparently flustered by the tension of the wait, got their games confused. A brouhaha ensued when one of the players threw his dice and insisted he rolled a flush. Mabel Fenton arrived on the scene to insert a spoof of the famous demimondaine, Cleo de Merode. Oddly, the material was by an Englishman, Kenneth Lee. It was his first and only effort for the house. But a far more important figure also made his debut at the theatre with the same production. Julian Mitchell took over as stager. Under his reign the productions, despite the minuscule stage, achieved an opulence and style that made them the talk of the town. His chorus line rapidly established a reputation as more eye-filling than even the Casino's. In their day his girls basked in much the renown that Ziegfeld's were to have a generation later, and it was not accidental that Ziegfeld hired Mitchell to stage his early *Follies*.

• • •

Julian Mitchell, the most prolific of all musical stagers, was born in 1854 and while still a youngster began his theatrical career as a call boy at Niblo's. He soon found himself on the other side of the footlights, dancing in an early revival of *The Black Crook*. By the time he was twenty he was producing and dancing in his own touring productions. But a growing deafness—which became almost total with time—forced him to abandon performing. Charles Hoyt hired him to direct

The Maid and the Moonshiner and *A Trip to Chinatown.*

. . .

The London hit, **In Town** (9-6-97, Knickerbocker), had a libretto by Adrian Ross and James T. Tanner, and melodies by Osmond Carr. The evening proved a disappointment to New Yorkers. *In Town* is generally acknowledged as the first of George Edwardes' new style of Gaiety shows and as such is often considered the first English musical comedy. It premiered in London October 15, 1892, one day short of a year before *A Gaiety Girl*'s premiere. Like its successor it opened at the Prince of Wales Theatre, but unlike *A Gaiety Girl* (which opened in New York 9-17-94) it did eventually move to the Gaiety. Its libretto told how the out-of-pocket Captain Coddington invited all the ladies of the Ambiguity Theatre to lunch. The captain's friend, Lord Clanside, agrees to foot the bill on the condition he can join the party. A group of uninvited guests appears and everyone moves to the Ambiguity to watch a rehearsal. Coddington woos and wins the prima donna. The looseness of the story allowed for numerous interpolations and changes. W. Louis Bradfield, who had played the lead in *A Gaiety Girl,* was Coddington.

Francis Wilson brought *Half a King* (9-14-96) back for a brief engagement at the Broadway on the 20th. Another importation from London, **The French Maid** (9-27-97, Herald Square) had the longest run of any of the season's musicals—160 performances. E. E. Rice produced and staged the work for which Walter Slaughter wrote the music and Basil Hood the libretto whose exasperatingly complicated plot (the *Times* devoted half a column attempting to dissect it) begins when the British send a freeloading Indian prince to a French spa. Marguerite Sylva headed a cast that included Anna Robinson and Eva Davenport.

The same night as *The French Maid* premiered, **McFadden's Row of Flats** began a one-week stay at the People's, a combination house normally outside the range of this history. All summer long its producers had taken large, illustrated ads in trade journals urging theatre bookers around the country to schedule it into their houses. Typically, it differed from shows designed to play the great Manhattan houses more in degree than in kind. The story, by E. W. Townsend, found Tim McFadden and Jacob Baumgartner rivals for alderman. A tie vote can be broken only by the flats' poet, Terrence McSwatt. McFadden gets Mrs. Murphy to consent to her daughter Mary Ellen's marrying McSwatt,

thus winning the election. The music was largely by one Ivan L. Davis. In extending the show the courtesy of a review, the *Dramatic Mirror* singled out the songs as "pretty." *McFadden's Row of Flats* was not the only 1897–98 creation intended primarily or wholly for the hinterlands. The list of touring musicals setting out in September included *Bimbo of Bombay, In Old Madrid, Bo-Peep,* and *Darkest Africa.* None, except a heavily revised *Bo-Peep,* ever approached the Rialto, and most, apparently, left no record at all behind. A number of trade journal listings were artists' companies rather than individual shows. The De Wolf Hopper Opera Company or the Francis Wilson Opera Company played the big time. But a dozen or so lesser names, long forgotten, took smaller, generally seedier, contingents around giving one- and two-night stands.

September's last offering, **The Belle of New York** (9-28-97, Casino), is a curious, fascinating anomaly. Another Hugh Morton and Gustave Kerker contrivance (which George Lederer not only produced, but also staged), it was greeted with middling enthusiasm and racked up a New York run of only 56 showings. But after its American tour it traveled to London, where Englishmen were as taken with it as Americans had been for the past several seasons with West End musicals. It played there for 674 performances, the first American musical to ever run a year or more in the West End. Long runs in Paris and Berlin followed. Both Paris and London have entertained periodic revivals. Morton's story had Violet Gray (Edna May), a fashion-conscious Salvation Army belle, mend the spendthrift ways of Harry Brown (Harry Davenport), who has been cast out by his hypocritical, "reformist" father, Ichabod (Dan Daly). The elder Brown is the president of an organization known as (depending on which text one reads) either the "Young Men's Rescue League and Anti-Cigarette Society of Cohoes" or the "Anti-Cigarette and Enjoyment League Against All Amusements." So grateful is the elder Brown that he is prepared to annul Harry's marriage to Cora Angelique (Ada Dare) and force his son to wed Violet. The Salvation Army belle realizes that Harry and Cora are genuinely in love, and that she could not earn Harry's affection, so she purposely alienates Ichabod with a risqué French ditty, "At Ze Naughty Folies Bergère (My feet zey fly up in ze air)." Before he meets his salvation, by honest labor as a soda jerk, Harry encounters a variety of clowns, including an infuriatingly polite lunatic (David Warfield). The first-act finale was set in Chinatown and began with a "showy, bizarre ballet." Kerker's music, as undistinguished as always, was nevertheless as good as he wrote and exemplified by the title number. The song was introduced by "a mixed-ale pugilist," Blinky Bill (William Cameron), to announce Violet's initial appearance—in the Chinatown scene just before the first-act curtain!

The attitudes and styles of Morton's guys and dolls in "The Anti-Cigarette League" (sung by Ichabod) or "The Purity Brigade" (Violet's principal number) contrasted strikingly with those of Frank Loesser's a half-century later:

I hope I do not shock
My late converted flock
By changing to a costume that could be described
    as snappy,
I would not have you think
That I would ever sink
From my high state of piety, to anything clap
    trappy.

In both New York and London young Miss May rocketed to stardom in the title role.

Having tired of playing Kibosh in Victor Herbert's *The Wizard of the Nile* (11-4-95), Frank Daniels handed his role over to a replacement and commissioned Herbert and Harry B. Smith to write a new operetta for him. Although the first announcements insisted the show would be a sequel to the earlier show and that Daniels would again impersonate the magician, it arrived with a different tale. In **The Idol's Eye** (10-25-97, Broadway), Daniels played Abel Conn, "an aeronaut who seeks and finds adventure." He finds it in India after Jamie McSnuffy (Alf C. Whelan), "the last of the McSnuffys of Castle McSnuffy," a kleptomaniac, drummed out of a Highlands regiment, steals a sacred £100,000 ruby from the eye of an idol. The ruby magically makes everyone love the possessor. The ruby's mate, a stone that makes its owner hated, lies not far away in the jungle. Ned Winner (Maurice Darcy), an American novelist, is in India to court a Cuban beauty, Maraquita Tabasco (Helen Redmond). Her father (Will Danforth) insists Ned must earn £100,000 before he will consent to her marrying Ned. At this juncture Conn appears on the scene. He picks up the wrong ruby, causing the lovers to have a falling-out. The two gems change hands from moment to moment, realigning emotions faster than Abel can handle them. The show succeeded largely on the strength of the genial Daniels' clowning, including a first appearance dropping from the flies in a balloon and landing on an idol. He stopped the show—and ulti-mately provided the basis for a future vehicle—singing of "The Tattooed Man":

He had designs upon himself,
    She had designs on him;
And she loved to look at the picture book
    Which he had on ev'ry limb.

The song recounted the resourcefulness of the unfaithful "human picture gallery," concluding with one of the word-plays so beloved of the era, "You can beat a tattoo,/But you can't beat a tattooed man!" Herbert's unpretentious score marked a falling off from the richness and fine melodies of *The Serenade* (3-16-97). But the critic of the *Evening Post*, waxing unduly ecstatic, nevertheless glimpsed the immediate future when he wrote of Herbert, "Indeed, now that Suppé is dead, Sullivan written out, and Strauss practically quiescent, he has no superior in Europe." After two months in New York the show headed out for another of Daniels' extended road tours.

Two productions of Audran's **La Poupée** came to town during the season. In both instances the story told of a monk in an impoverished monastery who learns his uncle will make the monastery rich if the monk will leave it and marry. The monk attempts to honor both his vows and his uncle by marrying a doll, but the uncle, learning of the plan, slyly substitutes a real girl. The first, and more successful, version opened October 21 with Anna Held at what until a few weeks before had been the Olympia and now, under new management, was called the Lyric. The second appeared briefly at Daly's in mid-April.

By November of 1897 the Trust or Syndicate had become so visible and so obnoxious in its methods that the *Dramatic Mirror* began a series of weekly supplements recounting its brutalities and adding horrified and saddened commentaries by those theatrical figures affected. It seemed at the time the new monopoly would drive its enemies from the boards and kill any show not bringing a handsome return. History recorded otherwise, but the shock of the Syndicate's initial actions still threw much of Broadway into a panic. Henry Clay Barnabee, Francis Wilson, and a number of other artists claimed the Trust brought an end to the era of the performer-manager. And it is true that within a few years musical stars no longer produced their own shows. But the healthy salaries stars were beginning to draw, coupled with their willingness to let others take the financial risks and managerial bothers, probably had more to do with the decline of the actor-manager than did any machination of Klaw, Erlanger, Frohman, and their cohorts.

May Irwin arrived with another of the song-filled comedies she was known for. Its story was reminiscent of an earlier Irwin vehicle, *Courted into Court* (12-26-96). In **The Swell Miss Fitzwell** (11-15-97, Bijou) she played a poor American girl who marries a French count. The count's father disinherits him. Miss Fitzwell sets up a shop, but a misunderstanding there with her spouse leads to a divorce suit. When the misunderstanding is resolved the divorce action proves infuriatingly difficult to withdraw.

November's only other musical was the first of two Philadelphia hits to reach Manhattan during the season. **1999** (11-15-97, Casino) had been mounted at the Chestnut Street Theatre the previous April, ran out the season, and returned after a summer hiatus for a fall engagement. Called the "most complete, costly and up-to-date musical" the city had ever seen, it had book and lyrics by Herman Lee Ensign and music by Edward Holst, two names otherwise unknown to Broadway. Set at a coeducational institution in a world dominated by women, it recounted the complications that ensue when the school's lady astronomer, Professor Brent (Clara Alene Jewell), invites a group of Martians to visit the earth. Professor Brent hopes to make marriages for her daughters Electra (Claresse Agnew) and Corona (Bertha Waltzinger). She succeeds, but she herself also wins the hand of the king of Mars. A subplot depicted the arrival by a flying machine of a Spanish Countess (Mathilde Cottrelly) to woo a bogus millionaire. The subplot nearly wrecked the show at its New York opening when the flying machine became stuck in its tracks and could not be made to operate. *1999* had been rushed in to fill the vacancy left by *The Belle of New York* and remained at the Casino for five weeks.

December's first offering (on the 2nd) was **Pousse Café,** Weber and Fields' replacement for *The Glad Hand*. Its subtitle, *The Worst Born*, poked fun at one of the season's great straight play hits, David Belasco's *The First Born*, although the musical had fun at the expense of *La Poupée* and J. M. Barrie's *The Little Minister* as well. Even its scenery was contrived to resemble sets from shows that were travestied. The evening tied its burlesques together with a plot which bravely aimed its barbs at the Trust. Bierheister (Fields) and Weishaben (Sam Bernard) form a "skindecat" to cheat Weinshoppen (Weber) out of royalties from a mechanical doll he has invented. Bierheister invites Weinshoppen to sign a contract sight unseen:

Bierheister: Here is der disagreement papers . . . Now I von't read der commencing of der contract to you because dere are a few tings I vish to write in after you sign your name to it.

So successful had the team become in less than two seasons that they were able to raise the price of seats for the first ten rows to $2.00 without serious complaint.

Another in the decreasingly fashionable farce-comedies began a brief stay when William Gill's **My Boys** (12-6-97, Manhattan) opened. Using music by assorted, uncredited composers, it told of Silas Plummer's plans to marry off his five sons when unbeknown to him the five boys are married. Silas (George Richards) spent much of the evening in a running gag tripping over any steps that crossed his path. Gill's dialogue ran to such repartee as,

Son: Well?
Silas: You don't look it.

Another December 6 arrival, at the American, was one of the three companies of the Castle Square Opera Players, another group whose repertory ranged from comic to grand opera. They, too, played out the season. (A second contingent of the Castle Square Players was in the midst of a two-year stay in Philadelphia.)

The most successful American musical of the season bowed next. At the time, the popularity of **The Highwayman** (12-13-97, Broadway) bolstered greatly Reginald De Koven's sagging reputation, even though it has since joined all of De Koven's scores except *Robin Hood* in obscurity. Its Harry B. Smith libretto told a tale not unlike that earlier hit. When Sir John Hawkhurst (Edwin White) ruins Dick Fitzgerald (Joseph O'Hara) at the gaming tables, Fitzgerald becomes a highwayman under the name of Captain Scarlet. He and Lady Constance (Hilda Clark) fall in love. Hawkhurst seizes a pardon meant for Fitzgerald, but Constance retrieves it from him at gunpoint. If the comic villain, the Sheriff of Nottingham, was for many the principal delight of *Robin Hood*, the equally comic, conceited constable, Foxy Quiller, stole the new comic opera. In hefty Jerome Sykes' hands he became such a popular figure that Smith and De Koven later were prompted to write a second work about him. Smith's autobiography reveals something of the caliber of the period's bit players as well as of the era's idea of humor. According to the librettist an actor was chagrined when a line of his received one of the biggest laughs of the evening each night. The line, delivered by a young sailor, read, "I would rather be Lord High Admiral of England's navy with *you* for a wife than a common sailor without you." The actor, chagrined or no, at least had steady employment, for *The Highwayman* ran out the season.

New Yorkers failed to greet E. E. Rice's production of **The Ballet Girl** (12-21-97, Manhattan) as enthusiastically as had Londoners. The musical's plot described the rivalry between a fortune-hunting father and his carefree son for the affections of a ballet dancer. David Lythgoe, Louise Willis-Hepner, Allene Crater, and Thomas Ricketts helped enliven J. T. Tanner's book, Adrian Ross' lyrics and Carl Kiefert's music.

Two more young ladies bounced in six nights later. **The Telephone Girl** (12-27-97, Casino) was another Gustave Kerker and Hugh Morton collaboration, one New Yorkers took to more eagerly than they had the team's *Belle of New York* (9-28-97). The show's initial run of 104 performances almost doubled the stay of the other show, and in June it returned for an additional three weeks. Estelle Coocoo (Clara Lipman), a telephone operator, is furious at the attention Beauty Fairfax (Eleanor Elton) pays to Estelle's young man. Estelle eavesdrops on phone calls between Beauty and the man who is keeping her, Colonel Goldtop (Charles Dickson). She disguises herself as Beauty's maid, gets incriminating evidence, and persuades Beauty to give up chasing her beau. Clara Lipman's husband, Louis Mann, another of the many German-dialect comedians taking over as Broadway's principal funnymen, played a telephone repairman, Hans Nix. Nix thinks nothing of making a phone call to the warden of Sing Sing to accuse him of harboring thieves. He also flustered the other principals by hiding behind a screen and squirting seltzer at them.

Miss Philadelphia premiered the same night. The musical had been done originally two seasons before at Philadelphia's Chestnut Street Opera House. It was such a success it went through two "editions" and then spent most of the 1896–97 season on the road. It had featured one rising young comedian, William Collier, for most of its early run, but by the time it reached New York another rising young star, Joseph Cawthorn, had replaced Collier. As has been mentioned, the story was similar to the one used later by *Miss Manhattan*. William Penn returns to visit a young man called William Penn, Jr., and together with Ruth Springarden (Springarden was then a fashionable street in Philadelphia) they embark on a tour of the city. They call at the Union League, the Mint, Wanamaker's De-

partment Store, and an inn on the Wissahicken (all actual places). Among characters they meet are Dodge Trolleys, "a rapid young man about town"; Prestissimo, an Italian street singer; and Etta Candie, "a real sweet thing." The show played briefly at one of New York's combination houses, the Star, and continued on its tour.

Apart from some German operetta sung in German at the Irving Place Theatre, the only musical of sorts to arrive in New York in January 1898 was another farce-comedy. **A Hired Girl** (1-10-98, Star) by Charles E. Blaney slanted toward burlesque; its title role was played by James T. Kelly in drag. The role had little to do with the main story line in which Lord Green Goods is pursued by a female detective, U. Bet Gilbert. When she realizes he is innocent of the crime he has supposedly committed, she marries him. The musical side of the evening featured an old minstrel, Willis J. Sweatnam, who, in the role of Link Missing, sang many of his old minstrel favorites.

R. A. Barnet continued to work with the Cadets in Boston. On February 7 they presented his latest work (with music by E. W. Corliss) at the Tremont there. **Queen of the Ballet** marked a departure from the children's extravaganza he had done the preceding year. The story was right out of the English and burgeoning American musical comedy tradition. Conspirators deprive Jack Hardwicke (Walter S. Hawkins) of his fortune. When he retrieves it he also wins Beatrice Jerome (Sheafe C. Rose), Queen of the Jollity Ballet.

Both new musicals arriving in Manhattan in February were failures. A German operetta, **Lilli Tsi** (2-17-98, Daly's), survived 35 performances as curtain raiser to a straight play, while **A Normandy Wedding** (2-21-98, Herald Square) fell three performances short of that dismal figure. The show had initially opened in the Midwest in September as *Papa Gou Gou*. Its librettists, J. Cheever Goodwin and Charles Alfred Byrne, and its composer, William Furst, spent the next five and a half months trying to whip it into shape. Thomas Q. Seabrooke had originally starred, but by the time Broadway saw the musical Richard F. Carroll had replaced him as an unprincipled old cider-maker determined to get rich and find a wealthy husband for his daughter. Based on a French play, translated as *The Goose Girl*, and filled with American slang that made no effort to retain any Gallic flavor, the musical abandoned its travels after New York rejected it.

Weber and Fields introduced their final change of bill on St. Patrick's Day. One of the hits of the year was Paul M. Potter's *The Conquerors,* the story of a cynical Prussian officer's attack on a French maiden. She defends her virtue in Gallic style, throwing the wine she had been ordered to drink in the officer's face. In the new version, **The Con-Curers,** the girl is ordered to eat a pie. According to Weber and Fields' biographer, this is the earliest recorded instance of a man getting a pie in his face. One more favorite Weber and Fields trick also made its first appearance here—a statue smoking a cigar.

Another London offering, Talbot's **Monte Carlo** (3-21-98, Herald Square), began a disappointing run on the same evening that the English hit, *The Geisha,* opened a return engagement at Daly's. *Monte Carlo*'s producer and director, E. E. Rice, added a number of his own songs and gave Marie Cahill some new comic material in a vain effort to enliven Sidney Carlton's original tale of gaming and romance.

One week later, on March 28, *In Gay New York* (5-28-96) returned to the Casino, while down at the 14th Street Theatre **Fun on the Pacific Mail,** a farce-comedy based on *The Overland Route,* came in briefly from the hinterlands. The passengers on the transpacific steamship were largely vaudevillians displaying their specialties. They included the popular singer, Maggie Cline, and a more pretentious artist, Madame Alexa.

A lone new offering appeared in April. It appeared at an otherwise obscure, out-of-the-way theatre; and it appeared only briefly. But **A Trip to Coontown,** which opened at the Third Avenue Theatre on April 4, was a landmark in that it was entirely written, performed, and produced by blacks. It was the creation of two particularly talented Negroes, Bob Cole and Billy Johnson. Johnson played Jim Flimflammer, a "bunco steerer" (what today we would call a "con man") who tries to fleece old Silas Green out of a $5,000 pension, but is outsmarted by the old man. Cole played a tramp called Wayside Willie. The show created no stir on Broadway, but New Yorkers would shortly pay more respectful attention to Cole and the two Johnson brothers (Rosamond and J. W.) with whom he worked.

For the moment it gave more respectful attention to a musical that opened one week later, John Philip Sousa's **The Bride Elect** (4-11-98, Knickerbocker). Because Charles Klein was ill, Sousa decided to write the book himself. That proved a mistake. His inferior libretto was inordinately complicated. In as simple terms as possible, the death of a pet goat leads to war between two kingdoms. King

Papagallo XIII (Albert Hart) of Tiberio wins, and demands the hand of Princess Minutezza (Christie MacDonald) of Capri. But Minutezza loves Papagallo's nephew, Guido (Frank Pollock), Duke of Ventroso. Minutezza arranges for a female brigand, La Pastorella (Nella Bergen), to abduct the king. Minutezza's mother, Queen Bianca (Mabella Baker), thinking Papagallo has kidnapped Minutezza, marches on La Pastorella's camp and releases the prisoners. Minutezza is allowed to marry Guido, while Papagallo settles for the widowed Bianca. The show, which had been touring profitably since December, played 64 performances to generally good business, until hot weather closed it. It toured again the next year.

Sousa disdained a small fortune by refusing an offer of $100,000 made by the managers of the New Haven Theatre in which it gave its world premiere for exclusive rights to the show. He also rejected an offer of $10,000 from the New York *Journal* for permission to publish "The Bride Elect March," a song based on the show's second-act finale, "Unchain The Dogs Of War." In later years Sousa is said to have considered this the best march he had ever written. First-night audiences also awarded encores to Minutezza's lullaby, "The Snow Baby."

The remainder of April was filled with revivals. Led by James T. Powers and Virginia Earle, the second company of *La Poupée* bowed at Daly's on the 15th, the same evening *The Wedding Day* began a return stay. On April 25 *The Lady Slavey* reappeared.

A "Chinese-Japanese opera," **The Koreans** (5-3-98, Herald Square), was May's only original full-scale musical. It opened and closed in the same week. The plot revolved around the contrast of Oriental and Occidental cultures, a theme that was to become increasingly popular. But *The Koreans* played no part in making the motif so popular. In its tale, George Washington Tree (Richard F. Carroll) writes his proposal of marriage to Fidelia (Alice Holbrook) on his cuff, but inadvertently sends the shirt to a Chinese laundry. The laundry's owner absconds, taking all the clothing in the shop with him. George and Fidelia follow him to Korea. There George, a union organizer, organizes an ancestor worshippers' union. The show had first been mounted the previous spring in Boston, where it had been known as *The Walking Delegate.* A year's overhauling proved futile.

A more popular piece with an Oriental setting, *The Mikado,* returned the same night as the opening attraction of the American Opera Company's "summer season" at the Star. The troupe later performed *The Bohemian Girl, Olivette,* and *Pinafore,* among others. Taking no chances on its audiences not receiving value for money, it offered a vaudeville bill before each main presentation. On May 16, the Royal Italian Opera came into Wallack's bringing with it two Puccini operas, the two-year-old *La Bohème* and the first New York performance of *Manon Lescaut.*

Thomas Q. Seabrooke returned on the 18th with his dependable *The Isle of Champagne* (12-5-92) at the Broadway, and five nights later Francis Wilson, Henry Dixey, and Lulu Glaser revived *Erminie* (5-10-86) at the Casino.

By rights, **A Cook's Tour at Koster and Bial's** should be dismissed as a vaudeville. But since the management again decided to give the evening a title and a "plot" some passing notice is justified. The plot had a theatrical producer, Mr. Klawlanger, take his company on a world tour. A few current plays were spoofed in between specialties. Earlier in the season the house had gone one step further, offering **Au Bain,** its own translation of a supposed French musical. (Bruyas lists no such show in his detailed history of the French musical theatre.) Adele Ritchie played a young lady who hides in the water rather than wed her cousin. In what was apparently a shocking scene for its time the calcium sputtered as the triumphant miss emerged from the water in her bathing suit at the end of the evening. The *Times'* priggish critic could only lament archly that the parents of playgoers who enjoyed the moment "used to go to church and pray." Oscar Hammerstein also embellished his Olympia vaudeville with airs of legitimacy. On May 16 he offered **War Bubbles,** a "patriotic extravaganza," as an afterpiece. This virtually plotless hodgepodge included trained Boston terriers playing football, a comic Yiddish military drill, and a "Spirit of '76" finale concluding with "The Star Spangled Banner." When the piece promptly folded, Hammerstein's losses caused him to lose the Olympia.

1898-1899

The Spanish-American War revitalized the national economy and gave the theatre a necessary stimulus in the process. By April the theatrical year was being hailed as "the most successful season the American theatre has ever known." If musicals shared in the general prosperity they did so somewhat indiscriminately. There was no noticeable change in the number of new lyric pieces, nor was there an appreciable difference in quality over preceding years. But two shows—*The Fortune Teller* and *The Romance of Athlone*—contained songs that remained popular long after.

The Casino monopolized the beginning of the season. Its roof opened for the summer on June 18 with a entertainment staged by E. E. Rice and titled simply **Rice's Summer Nights.** These nights were essentially vaudeville but part of one of the bills made it a theatrical landmark. On July 5, 1898, the evening ended with an extended afterpiece called **The Origin of the Cake Walk or, Clorindy.** The playlet had a libretto and lyrics by Paul Laurence Dunbar and music by Will Marion Cook. Its cast of forty (later reduced to thirty) was led by Ernest Hogan. All were blacks. The premiere marked the first time an all-black effort played at a major house —albeit a roof garden—patronized exclusively by whites. The piece itself was so wildly successful it remained on the bill most of the summer. Relatively short though it was, it followed the practice of longer shows by making revisions intermittently from July 25 on. Its popularity—which the *Times* called "sensational"—prompted imitations. Rice himself quickly had black material performed by others on his changing bills. In August the main attraction at Koster and Bial's was Cole and Johnson's **Kings of Koon-dom,** with "over twenty of the Darktown contingent." At least one long popular, if now forgotten, song, "Darktown Is Out Tonight," came from *Clorindy*'s score. But while the show represented a successful breakthrough, its artistic importance is sometimes overstated. The cakewalk and ragtime had both been working their way into the theatrical mainstream. And, as *A Trip to Coontown* demonstrated, black artists were already venturing into full-fledged musical works. Although prejudice kept them out of the better houses, these longer shows were the real precursors of later black musicals.

When hitches developed in preparations for the Casino's annual revue, *The Telephone Girl* (12-27-97) was called in off the road and made comfortable for a brief return stay. By July 25 the new revue was ready. **Yankee Doodle Dandy** was another Hugh Morton and Gustave Kerker collaboration. Morton modishly incorporated the anti-Spanish sentiments of the hour into his plot. Teddy Two-shoes (Edna Wallace Hopper in a trouser role) falls in love with a girl depicted in the stucco ceiling of the New York Academy of Design. The molding comes to life. She announces her name as

Honoria (Madge Lessing) and declares that she was once a young Roman matron. Teddy, Honoria, and an inventor, Gideon Terwilliger (Thomas Q. Seabrooke), scour the town seeking two Spanish spies, Don Alfonso de Alcantara (J. C. Miron) and Don Pascuale de Mackerel (Richard Carle). A $10,000 reward has been offered for their capture. Honoria disguises herself as a Spanish girl to trap the villains. The case takes everyone to a platform of the El and to Printing House Square at night (with offices lit and war bulletins being issued). A visit to the Battery prompted a "Yankee Doodle Ballet," with figures from colonial times up to the moment prancing across the scene. A collegiate ballet, and a ballet in which dancers broke out of eggs in an incubator were also offered. In a salute to Teddy Roosevelt chorus girls marched as "Tough Riders." The finale took everyone to Washington, where, at the White House, they participated in the booming new rage for ragtime. A cakewalk to "Coon Chowder Party" brought down the curtain. The show was looked upon as something of a disappointment. In keeping with the practice of the day, changes were made regularly and, given the lukewarm press, perhaps more frequently than would otherwise have been the case. Titillating hints of prurience became evident when the *Dramatic Mirror* noted a month after the opening, "Clara Betz, an artist's model, was introduced last week in *Yankee Doodle Dandy* at the Casino, posing to considerable applause."

A name out of a fast receding past, Imre Kiralfy, appeared for a few nights on the program of the Madison Square Garden when he mounted a two-a-day spectacle, *Our Naval Victories*. But the event could in no way be considered a musical, and the Kiralfy name makes its last appearance in this history.

Also fading rapidly and soon to seem as distant as the old extravaganzas were the decade's farce-comedies. They were increasingly relegated to combination houses and the road. In 1898–99 only two would play a prime house. The first farce-comedy, **In Atlantic City** (8-13-98, Star), told for all eight performances how a prospective father-in-law goes about winning the affection of his son's bride-to-be.

The season had its first smash hit when James T. Powers clowned his way through Ivan Caryll and Lionel Monckton's London success, **A Runaway Girl** (8-25-98, Daly's). Powers, continuing to rely heavily on importations, played a jockey smuggler who helps the romance of a convent girl passing for a street singer.

Five evenings later **A Day and a Night in New York** (8-30-98, Garrick) began a 63-performance run. The story was simple. Marble Hart (Otis Harlan), a young prig, is brought to his senses when a trip to New York reveals that his rich, snobbish fiancée was once a show girl. As always the scenes were larded with interpolated songs. This was one of the two farce-comedies to play a major house and also the last new Charles Hoyt work New York was ever to see. Like so many important theatrical figures of the 19th century (Fox, Hart, Scanlan), Hoyt became insane. He died at the age of forty-one in November 1900.

The season's first full-fledged American hit was **The Charlatan** (9-5-98, Knickerbocker), although its run of only 40 performances may seem to belie its success. John Philip Sousa wrote the songs while recuperating from a nervous breakdown brought on by his hectic activities during the war. To ease his load, he also utilized songs from his earlier shows. Luckily, Charles Klein had recovered from the illness that kept him from helping with *The Bride Elect* and provided a better libretto than Sousa might have created on his own. From its inception the work was designed for De Wolf Hopper and his opera company. In Klein's story Prince Boris (Edmund Stanley) must marry someone of his own station or forfeit his estate. His treacherous uncle, Gogol (Mark Price), tricks him into marrying the daughter of a traveling charlatan, Demidoff (Hopper), by passing off Demidoff's daughter (Nella Bergen) as Princess Ruchkowski. Gogol assumes that the name is fictitious. But a real Princess Ruchkowski (Adine Bouvier) appears with the Grand Duke (Arthur Cunningham). Demidoff exposes Gogol's machinations, and the Grand Duke assures everyone he will persuade the czar to allow a happy ending. In the custom of the time the show was completely booked for its road tour long before its New York premiere. Its post-Broadway journey broke record after record, grossing more than $10,000 a week in Baltimore, Washington, and Boston. It returned for an additional New York run in May.

Another hit opened three nights later, September 8, when Weber and Fields began their third season. The opening attraction was **Hurly-Burly.** Harry B. Smith joined Edgar Smith in providing dialogue and lyrics to accompany John Stromberg's songs. Two of Stromberg's successes emerged from the score, "Emmaline" and "Dinah," the latter introduced by one of the house's great comedians, Peter F. Dailey. A pair of newcomers added their talents and glamor to the roster: Fay Templeton and David

Warfield. Given his later fame as a serious actor in Belasco's plays, it is easy to forget Warfield began as a "Dutch" comedian. The main plot of the evening featured Dailey as an American theatrical agent about to take over all the regular London music halls. But his rival in love puts on free vaudeville at lesser theatres and hurts Dailey's trade. Into this Weber and Fields bring a mummy of Cleopatra they own. Warfield resuscitates the dead queen (played by Miss Templeton), and she takes them all back to ancient Egypt, where they meet such figures as Octopus Sneezer (John T. Kelly). The evening began with the customary, although somewhat shortened, olio and did not end until midnight.

The Castle Square Players inaugurated their second season of light and grand opera at the American the same night the music hall was relit, while up at the Herald Square the return of *The French Maid* offered first-nighters a third musical.

When Klein and Sousa were creating a new vehicle for Hopper and his company, Harry B. Smith and Ludwig Englander were writing one for Francis Wilson and his group. Their effort, **The Little Corporal** (9-19-98, Broadway), ran a month longer than *The Charlatan* in New York but shattered no records on the road. Smith's story managed to combine quaint European characters with another Egyptian setting. Honoré St. André (Denis O'Sullivan) and his valet, Petipas (Wilson), while ardent royalists, are forced to join Napoleon's Egyptian expedition as professors of science. St. André writes a lampoon on Bonaparte and is arrested. To save his master, Petipas disguises himself as Napoleon, intending "personally" to free the prisoner. While he is in the disguise, the Arabs attack and are convinced they have caught the commander. The valet and his master are sentenced to death, and the real Napoleon scornfully rejects pleas for help. Petipas effects their escape. St. André marries his loyal sweetheart, Adele (Maud Lillian Berri), and Petipas wins Adele's foster-sister, Jacqueline (Lulu Glaser). Although Americans wrote and performed the show, the pervasive English hold on our musical stage was evidenced by Wilson's proud announcements that Percy Anderson, an English water colorist, did the sets and that the English director, Richard Barker, staged the work, "as usual."

A touring extravaganza called **Wine, Women, and Song** (9-19-98, Grand Opera House) visited New York for a week. Its story followed Rip Van Winkle's two brothers in their search for him, and its musical numbers were "composed chiefly of a series of ballets by young women in decidedly abbreviated costumes." Rip was also the subject of a burlesque mounted the same night at Koster and Bial's as part of a double bill. Preceded by an olio, **In Gotham** featured Rip (Dick Bernard) traveling through the city trying to find proof of his identity. A young lady in the cast named Eva Tanguay attracted considerable attention, as did a song by Alfred E. Aarons, "Rag Time Liz." Ragtime was sweeping the musical stage. Every loosely structured musical that could incorporate a ragtime tune did so. Even sedate comic operas were soon to capitulate.

At the end of the preceding season Sam Bernard had left Weber and Fields to try his luck as a solo star in a new musical.

. . .

Sam Bernard was born in Birmingham, England, on June 3, 1863. His real name was Samuel Barnett. Brought to America as a child, he started a children's playhouse in an old barn behind his home at 72 Bayard Street in New York. His first professional appearance was at the Grand Duke's Theatre in the rough and tumble Five Points section. He moved swiftly up the professional ladder, playing the New York Museum and other more important variety stages before joining Weber and Fields.

. . .

Bernard's new vehicle turned out to be **The Marquis of Michigan** (9-21-98, Bijou), for which Glen MacDonough contrived the book and Edward W. Townsend composed most of the score. It had a month-long shakedown on the road that began in Poughkeepsie (it is easy to forget that every modest size American town had its legitimate theatre in this era). The story was the sort Bernard would spend the rest of his life making funnier than it truly was. Hermann Engel, an artist, is captured by brigands. His life is spared when he tells the outlaws he is the Marquis of Michigan. He makes a marriage of convenience with Etna Vesuvius (whose temper, naturally, is always erupting). Later, believing Etna (Alice Atherton) has died, Hermann takes a second wife. A fuming Etna appears. Fortunately the Chevalier Maginnice (William Burress) discovers through hypnosis that Etna is his own long-lost wife. In a subplot Dan Collyer played a man accused of stealing a bracelet. He is acquitted thanks to a brilliant defense by an all-admiring, all-believing, female lawyer (Harriet Sterling). She is brought down to earth when the only payment he can offer is the bracelet he had denied stealing. Most critics had very kind words for Bernard, if not for the show. But some singled out A. B. Sloane's interpolations, often in mock ragtime, as above average. Audiences enjoyed the evening, for all its faults, and it stayed for six weeks before moving on.

The operetta that next raised its curtain displayed none of the lapses of taste so common to the time. Its great songs have survived although the inferior ragtimes inserted into most Broadway musicals of the season have passed into oblivion. The work was Victor Herbert's **The Fortune Teller** (9-26-98, Wallack's). Out of it came "the most famous gypsy music in American operetta literature": "Romany Life" and "Gypsy Love Song."

The score "fitted the dramatic action well, and there was scarcely a number that failed to propel the play along." If there was anything to carp about it was that Harry B. Smith's latest book needed all the propeling it could get. Written for Alice Nielsen and her new opera company, it allowed the star to play the roles of two look-alikes: Musette, a gypsy fortune-teller, and Irma, an heiress studying ballet in Budapest. Musette is loved by a gypsy musician, Sandor (Eugene Cowles). Irma and a handsome Hungarian hussar, Ladislas (Frank Rushworth), are in love, but Irma is being pressed to marry the Count Berezowski (Joseph Herbert). Their similarity in looks gets both girls in trouble with their sweethearts, but in the end helps extricate Irma from the Count's clutches and provide a happy ending. An up-and-coming comedian, Joseph Cawthorn, cavorted as Musette's father, while an equally fast-rising figure, Julian Mitchell, staged the work. The great songs were carefully distributed. Ladislas and an actress friend of his (Marguerite Sylva) were given the lovely waltz, "Only In The Play." As Irma, Miss Nielsen sang a coy profession of injured innocence, "Always Do As People Say You Should," then as Musette she led the chorus in the fiery "Romany Life." The comic opera's great hit, "Gypsy Love Song," fell to Sandor. Like many shows of the time, its New York engagement was looked upon merely as part of its national tour. It remained in Manhattan only five weeks before moving on its appointed rounds.

A forgotten farce-comedy, *A Sure Cure*, premiered the same night as *The Fortune Teller*, staying only a week before it, too, went to its next booking.

October's first offering was the American version of *L'Auberge Tohu Bohu*, a London and Paris hit, known here as **Hotel Topsy Turvy** (10-3-98, Herald Square). Eddie Foy, Marie Dressler, and Aubrey Boucicault presided over a tale of rival woolendrapers whose children fall in love and, with the help of a comic count, reconcile the families. Billed

as a "vaudeville operetta," it appealed to New York as well as Europe, playing twelve weeks to good houses. Its opening coincided with the arrival of yet another specialty-filled farce-comedy, John F. Byrne's **Going to the Races,** at the Grand Opera House and Haverly's Minstrels at the 14th Street Theatre. Byrne was a member of an acrobatic family and wrote the piece as a vehicle for them. He contrived a spectacular fire scene that allowed performers to leap from high windows and to form a human ladder. Haverly's contingent offered imitations by the Nichols Sisters, Buck Shaffer, and Nellie O'Brien in "Cotton Field Frolics," and a mini-operetta, "The Princess of Madagascar."

A fourth musical opening the same night was the Castle Square Players production of *Patience*. In a way the Gilbert and Sullivan work was just another of the many operas and comic operas this troupe presented week after week during the several years they remained at the American. But the cast of this mounting may give some hint of the organization's probable excellence and certainly attests to its astuteness in spotting potential talent. Murgatroyd was played by Frank Moulan, Bunthorne by Raymond Hitchcock, and Angela by Lizzie Macnichol. Both men were to become stars in their own right.

The next Monday—October 10—provided three openings. Yet another farce-comedy, Herbert Hall Winslow's **A High Born Lady,** came in for a week at the Star. The play told how Willie Du-Much is sent to Europe by his uncle to prevent his marrying Flossie O'Shaughnessy. Flossie marries a millionaire, and when he dies she and Willie marry. The tune critics singled out for praise was one more coon song, "The Doodle Doodle Wagon's Done Got You At Last." West's Minstrels replaced *Going to the Races* at the Grand, and the Royal Italian Opera began a brief season at the Casino, offering such works as *La Bohème* directly across the street from the Metropolitan. West's troupe advertised that it was offering "up-to-date" ballads and "witticism mostly of contemporary interest."

On November 3 Weber and Fields rushed in their parody of Broadway's newest hit, *Cyrano de Bergerac*, calling it **Cyranose de Bric-a-Brac.** The *Times* praised "a troop of Gascons and gentlemen of France who for beauty and amiability have never been surpassed." Weber and Fields' chorus line was quickly gaining the reputation that it retained as long as the Music Hall thrived, and the *Times* quotation almost assuredly refers to girls dressed as men rather than to any male members of the company. Fields may have been amiable, but he was anything but attractive in his Cyranose makeup. He gave audiences a chance to see it close up by making his entrance from the rear of the house, running down the aisle to the stage. For good measure he and Weber added a lampoon of Hall Caine's *The Christian, The Heathen.* An actor impersonating Caine protested volubly from the balcony.

The Star offered another farce-comedy on November 7. **The Finish of Mr. Fresh** dealt with a comic divorce case presided over by Judge E. Z. Mark. So little was thought of it by its producers and author that no writer was given credit for the text in the program. But the piece is not without passing historical interest, for its score was by one composer, David Braham. Undoubtedly it marked a sad decline in his once solid reputation. Braham was more at sea without his son-in-law Harrigan than Harrigan was ever at a loss without Hart. In an interview shortly after the play opened, Braham never referred to the new piece, talking only about his halcyon days at the Comique. He mentioned that all his songs were written for specific performers, not necessarily for specific dramatic situations. In a sense that should have enabled him to write well for the loosely plotted musicals still rampant. But in his years with Harrigan, years in which the same performers came back to play in show after show, he developed a familiarity with his artists that was impossible in the newer casting system.

When the Italians left the Casino, a Viennese work, known in Sydney Rosenfeld's translation as **A Dangerous Maid,** settled in for a two-month run starting November 12. The story told of a poor girl who dreams she has a rich lover. More interesting than the plot was a comment in the *Times* on the performance, "The managers of the Casino have a rule against the abominable encore nuisance, and last night it was bravely inforced, in spite of considerable opposition in the audience." It would be years before the nuisance would be eradicated, and even the Casino would have to make strategic retreats from time to time.

Two evenings afterwards the team of Stanislaus Stange and Julian Edwards had another comic opera ready for Jefferson De Angelis and his troupe, **The Jolly Musketeer.** Richard Barker was the director. The plot revolved around the complicated marital arrangements necessary in the class-conscious world of operetta librettos. Henri, the musketeer Count of Beaupret (De Angelis), loves a commoner, Yvette (Maud Hollins). The count's father will not allow him to marry a low-born girl, so the Marquis de Chantilly (Van Rensselaer Wheeler),

who has been condemned to die for his part in a duel, agrees to marry the girl and leave her a widowed marquise. But after the wedding the marquis is pardoned. He and Yvette realize they are in love. Henri obligingly accepts Yvette's cousin instead. The *Times,* apparently deeming comic opera more high-minded and cohesive, lamented, "how fast this species of entertainment is going down hill toward operetta." The critic's major complaint was that the roughhouse clowning of Harry MacDonough and De Angelis had no pertinence to the plot. De Angelis was almost as great an attraction as De Wolf Hopper or Francis Wilson was, and his new show was good, if unexceptional, in its comedy, music, and staging. He kept it in New York at the Broadway for a month then braved the hinterlands, returning for a brief stay in June.

Another father's objections to his son's marriage plans provided the springboard for the action in **The Little Host** (12-26-98, Herald Square). Edgar Smith and Louis De Lange, who had worked together at Weber and Fields', created the book, while W. T. Francis and Thomas Chilvers composed the music. In the story Jack Dashington's stuffy father (R. E. Graham) wants him to marry Susie Jones (Mabel Bouton). Jack (Hugh Chilvers) prefers Margery Dazzle, an actress. Margery, dressed as a man, throws a party, inviting both Susie and the elder Dashington. Their unseemly behavior forces the father to consent to Jack and Margery's marriage. Comic bits included "a waltz song by Alice Johnson, with a noiseless but violently acrobatic piano accompaniment by John Slavin," as well as a drunk who, told to take a cab home, walks into a refrigerator. Della Fox again donned trousers to assume the title role. Keeping in mind the *Times'* comment in its review of *The Jolly Musketeer* one suspects the term "operetta" may have fallen into disrepute for some reason during the season. In its preopening publicity *The Little Host* went out of its way to assure potential patrons it was a musical comedy and not an operetta. Its very plot would mark it as musical comedy, though, of course, heretofore Miss Fox had only been identified with more arioso forms. Whatever the reasons, the show, announced from the start as playing a limited run, met with only a modest reception and was soon gone.

The Star kept turning over farce-comedies like pancakes. Charles E. Blaney's **A Female Drummer** was its Christmas week attraction. Johnstone Bennett, a female impersonator, embraced the old burlesque tradition as he played Haza Bargain, a female corset-drummer who takes her male customers out for a night on the town, then blackmails them into ordering her complete line. The former minstrel, Willis P. Sweatnam, again found employment in the genre, this time singing his old songs in the character of Super Stitious.

Chauncey Olcott brought his latest piece of fustian claptrap into the 14th Street Theatre on January 9. In **A Romance of Athlone** Augustus Pitou told a more than ordinarily complicated story. Amid gypsy bands, abductions, and duels, Dick Ronyane rescues his older half-brother Francis (Dustin Farnum) from the machinations of Standish Fitzsimmons and wins the hand of Rose Manning (Olive White). Complaining about the story, the *Dramatic Mirror* added, "what the audiences wanted was not a good play, but an opportunity to hear Mr. Olcott sing." Why Olcott limited the number of songs in his plays remains puzzling. But in this instance he gave his loyal public one of his most endearing melodies—one he wrote himself—"My Wild Irish Rose." The quick turnover of shows at the 14th Street Theatre generally came to a halt whenever an Olcott vehicle arrived. *A Romance of Athlone* was no exception. The play stayed on the boards at the old house for eleven weeks.

A revival of Offenbach's *La Belle Hélène*, starring Lillian Russell and Thomas Q. Seabrooke, began a 52-performance stand at the Casino on January 12. The mounting emphasized music and spectacle, relegating the work's veiled political references and humor to secondary roles. Both the *Times* and the *Dramatic Mirror* noted with chagrin that nobody dared stop Miss Russell from breaking the Casino's no-encores rule.

A "spectacular extravaganza" with a plot as fustian as Olcott's came into the Grand on January 16, but lasted only one week. **The Evil Eye** belonged to Evil Eye Warburg who kidnaps Gerta after slaying her father and who is hounded to death by her acrobatic brothers, Nid and Nod. Most of its songs were adopted from music long known to its audiences.

Unable to think of a properly funny distortion, Weber and Fields offered their latest burlesque on January 19 with the same title as the show it lampooned, **Catherine.** The original play was something like Cinderella, played on a more starkly realistic level and with an unhappy ending. In the travesty Fay Templeton was the poor working girl. Rose Beaumont was her wicked sister, "trying to make herself sick by smoking cigarettes in order that Catherine may have more work to do." David Warfield was their lazy father, "sent out for a walk in the vain hope that a cable car may run over him."

Peter F. Dailey impersonated a duchess, while Weber and Fields appeared as kids in "trousers-nightgowns."

January's last new entry provided another Harry B. Smith libretto. **The Three Dragoons** (1-30-99, Broadway) had a score by Reginald De Koven. While De Koven was by no means as prolific as Smith, both were beginning to be attacked for the dreary mechanical nature of their productions. Julian Mitchell's staging helped gloss over the general mediocrity, and rotund Jerome Sykes, who had come to the public's attention as Foxy Quiller in *The Highwayman*, put a further comic sheen on the evening as Don Bambola Bambolio, king of Portugal—whose presence in the story is never really explained. The show was not a failure, but public and critics alike had now been given a new standard of musical composition by Victor Herbert, even if no really striking, original librettist had appeared to better Smith's obviously uninspired material. In his latest story, three British dragoons who save the life of an old Frenchman are left his fortune with the stipulation that his niece may pick one as a husband. Since all three have fiancées this would seem to present a problem. But one of the men, Jack (Joseph O'Mara), has loved the very girl who turns out to be the man's niece, Inez (Marguerite Lemon).

Two more farce-comedies played briefly in February. **Brown's in Town,** dotted with the voguish coon songs, which told of a mismanaged elopement, and with no character named Brown, stayed two weeks at the Bijou, while **Johnny on the Spot** lasted a week at the out-of-the-way Columbus.

J. Sherrie Matthews and Harry Bulger, in their first starring roles, pleased Broadway with **By the Sad Sea Waves** (2-28-99, Herald Square), a musical for which they wrote much of the dialogue. In their plot Palmer Coin and Boston Budge, desperate for work, present themselves as an athletic instructor and a music professor in what they believe to be a school. It is, in fact, a lunatic asylum. The staff and patients provided vaudeville turns that filled out the evening, and, along with the stars, sang "a mixture of airs from 'The Mikado' and popular 'coon' songs." Turns included "the violin playing of Josie De Witt with the soft violet calciums illuminating her shapely arms" and the ragtime piano of Edward Wayburn (later Ned Wayburn, the famous director and choreographer). Anna Held joined the cast shortly before the show closed. Bulger and Matthews—"music hall performers of the kind known technically as 'sidewalk conversationalists'"—were not destined to survive long as a team. Matthews took ill, retired, and died young, leaving Bulger to fend for himself as best he could.

Gus and Max Rogers were another comic pair whose stardom was to have a relatively short span. Just as Matthews' illness broke up his act, Gus' sudden death put an end to the brothers' partnership. But their act survived long enough to be a thorn in the side of Weber and Fields, although some critics felt it served merely as a foil to demonstrate Weber and Fields' excellence. The pair was backed by the Syndicate, apparently nettled at being parodied in *Pousse Café* (12-2-97). Of course, the Trust was also aware of how successful Weber and Fields were, and undoubtedly hoped for a share of their ticket sales. As a result, on March 2, 1899, **A Reign of Error** was given the honor of opening the group's new Victoria Theatre—the first major theatre built on 42nd Street. How closely the Rogers Brothers' act was patterned on Weber and Fields was hinted at in the persistent legend that Tony Pastor's demented manager, Harry Kernell, had given the Rogers Brothers their start by standing at the back of the house while Weber and Fields performed, writing down every bit of business the comedians used and teaching it to the young brothers. Like the older team they always appeared as "Dutch" comedians. To their credit the Rogers Brothers never slavishly imitated the successful burlesque formula Weber and Fields had devised for their music hall. Instead they used a wispy plot, which often changed course between acts, to tie together the evening. Their earliest librettos were the work of the successful farce-comedy writer, J. J. McNally. In *A Reign of Error* Gus played Hans Wurst and Max was Carl Leetlewurzer. They were pursued by Dr. Dago Daggeri—described in the program as "a consistent stage villain if specialties permitted." The specialties included La Petite Adelaide's Rag-Time Toe Dancers. One comic bit offered Ada Lewis as a seasick clairvoyant, while Georgia Caine, "with her languid way of frisking," sang several songs. Maurice Levi, the show's conductor, wrote the songs, among them "I Am A Dago," "Bonnie Little Johnnie," and what had almost overnight become a requisite, the fresh Negro rhythms, "The Origin Of The Coon Song" and "I Wonder What's That Coon's Game."

Joseph M. Gaites, who, like McNally, turned eventually to musical comedy librettos, saw one of his farce-comedies, **The Air Ship,** fly briefly across the scene at a combination house in mid-March.

Parental interference reared its head once more during the season with **In Gay Paree** (3-20-99, Casino). Adapted by Clay M. Greene from a French farce, its audiences watched Emelie Bartavel (Margaret Warren) and the boulevardier, Henri Distrait (Harry Davenport), attempt a trial honeymoon to please Papa Bartavel (George Beane). During the test Henri runs off with an old flame, Louisette (Mabel Gilman), leaving Emelie free to marry the man she wanted in the first place, Theodore Lacour (Edward B. Tyler). Since the setting was Paris, the first act offered a lively cancan, but also found time for Miss Gilman to win encores with a song about letters from her "Tootsie Wootsie Woo" and for Charles Dickson as a flirtatious German, Hector Von Donnerblitz, to sing a kissing duet with Marie George. In the second act "The English dancer, Violet Holmes . . . turned cartwheels and did high kicking in a costume of lemon and salmon and black, and kept herself in a perpetual halo of lingerie while she was in view." Ludwig Englander provided music to Grant Stewart's lyrics. The last regular new book show of the season, the evening achieved a satisfactory run of six weeks.

Helter Skelter arrived April 6 to bring Weber and Fields' season to a close. It combined spoofs of several of the town's straight play hits: *Lord and Lady Algy, Zaza, The Great Ruby,* and *The King's Musketeers.* Fay Templeton played a sleepwalker who mistakes David Warfield (as Detective Nosenstein) for Apollo. The mistake convinces Fields, a jewel thief, that Miss Templeton is in fact asleep. Mabel Fenton employed Mrs. Carter's mannerisms and costumes in playing Zaza. Odd-ball performers included a pantomimist named Gernella as a poodle. In this curious mélange space was found for Miss Templeton and Peter F. Dailey to sing John Stromberg's latest coon songs such as "What? Marry Dat Gal?" Thrilling was the word one critic used to describe "the Oriental and saltatorial finale, with nimble Bessie Clayton."

Three extravaganzas and three revivals wrote an end to the 1898–99 season. The most successful of the spectacles was the first to arrive, **The Man in the Moon.** It opened on April 24 at the New York Theatre (until then the Olympia Music Hall, next door to the former Olympia Theatre). Its array of then glamorous names should have assured success. Louis Harrison and Stanislaus Stange collaborated on the book, while Englander, Kerker, and De Koven were listed as composers. George Lederer, besides producing the work, followed his occasional practice of staging it. The cast included such rising young talents as Marie Dressler, Christie MacDonald, and Sam Bernard. The story was not much different from the frames used for summer revues. Willie Billion (John E. Henshaw) loves the statue of Diana atop Madison Square Garden. She (Miss MacDonald) comes to life, and joins Willie on a tour of New York ending at the "Temple of Freedom" and "The Golden Halls of Columbia." They are followed everywhere they visit by an infuriated Viola Alum (Miss Dressler), attended by a violinist who expresses all her emotions for her on his violin. The evening was a veritable three-ring circus, offering, as it did, an Orchid Ballet and a Pony Ballet as well as introducing a wild assortment of characters ranging from Sherlock Holmes (Ferris Hartman), Conan Doyle (Bernard), Continuous Porter (Walter Jones), Psyche, and Dewdimple. The hodge-podge delighted young and old for 192 showings.

An Arabian Girl and Forty Thieves (4-29-99, Herald Square) was a reworking for New York of David Henderson's long-popular Chicago mounting of *Ali Baba.* Julian Mitchell staged the spectacle. In one scene real water cascaded down into a moonlit glen. The forty thieves drilled in unison, the *corps de ballet* formed a gigantic dragon, and both the chorus and ballet dancers combined for some showy calisthenics in Baghdad's public square. J. Cheever Goodwin's libretto narrated how Ali Baba defeats the forty thieves, who are in league with the corrupt police chief, Arraby Gorrah. As a reward Ali is made Caliph of Baghdad and wins the hand of Morgiana, a slave girl. Ali Baba was a trouser role in the pantomime tradition. If the young lady who played it (Dorothy Morton) caused no stir, a rising comedian did. Several reviewers singled out the clowning of Edwin Foy as Cassin D'Artagnan. Foy sat in a collapsing chair, tripped down slippery stairs, and did a comic turn with a donkey.

. . .

Eddie Foy was born in Greenwich Village on March 9, 1856. His real family name was Fitzgerald. When he was a youngster his family decided to move to Chicago. Jim Fisk had promised them all free passage and had told them to pick up their passes on a Saturday. On the preceding Friday Edward Stokes killed Fisk. Foy's mother nonetheless sent young Edwin to see what could be done. Foy discovered that Fisk had made out the passes moments before he was shot. (Foy's determined mother later served as Mary Todd Lincoln's nurse during Mrs. Lincoln's last years.) Young Foy started his career in newsboy theatricals. He adopted his stage name when he and Jack Flanegan became a pair of acrobatic clowns. They toured western mining towns, breaking up the act when

Foy determined to return to Chicago to try the big time there. He quickly secured comic roles in Henderson's productions.

. . .

Less successful than *An Arabian Girl* was **Mother Goose** (5-1-99, 14th St.), which folded after 10 performances when its actors refused to work without pay. The show had been ill-starred from its inception. Originally mounted as *Bo-Peep,* it had failed on the road during the preceding season. Edgar Smith and Louis de Lange attempted to salvage it. Both Bo-Peep and Mother Goose figure prominently in the plot. Mother Goose (Frank Blair) escapes from her book and flees to Banbury Cross in time for Banbury Fair. There Jack Horner (Olive Redpath) and Bo-Peep (Marie Celeste) fall in love and wed.

Henry E. Dixey returned with *Adonis* (9-4-84) on May 9, but its day was over and Dixey could only keep it on the boards for two weeks. The same night saw *Erminie* (5-10-86) back at the Casino. This was the third summer in a row a revival of the old musical had come to New York. Francis Wilson re-created his original role, assisted by Lillian Russell and Thomas Q. Seabrooke. There were complaints about the raggedness of the scenery, and howls that the pink ballroom was no longer pink. But fans of the old piece were happy to have it back, so well cast. It stayed a month, giving place to the season's final entry, a return on June 5 of *The Jolly Musketeer* (11-14-98).

1899-1900

An even twenty musicals arrived on the Rialto for this end-of-the-century season: three revivals, two importations, and fifteen American originals. It would be the lowest figure for several decades. The number represented less than a fourth of the total legitimate offerings. Sadly, there was no remarkable quality to compensate for the comparatively low quantity, although by and large the productions offered the lighthearted diversion theatregoers sought.

Only one "summer" musical was introduced. **The Rounders** was unveiled July 12 as the Casino's annual hot weather offering and proved attractive enough to linger into the fall. With Charles McLellan away in London for the English edition of *The Belle of New York,* Harry B. Smith was asked to write the book, which he adapted from the

French comedy *Les Fêtards*. The philandering Marquis de Baccarat (Harry Davenport) is married to an American Quaker, Priscilla (Mabel Gilman). When she discovers the dancer Thea (Phyllis Rankin) is her husband's mistress, Priscilla swallows her pride and her modesty, dons one of Thea's scanty costumes, and makes the Marquis sit up and take notice. Other characters included a Duke du Pay de Clam (Dan Daly), Siegfried Gotterdammerung (Joseph Cawthorn), and Maginnis Pasha (Thomas Q. Seabrooke). Besides his dialect comedy Cawthorn made an appearance playing the concertina. The sad-faced Daly won applause for his comically agile dances, while Seabrooke emphasized his Irish brogue in his search for laughs. But not all was perfect in these premicrophone days. While most critics praised Miss Gilman's fine singing voice, several complained about her diction. Englander, who was becoming a sort of composer-in-residence, replaced Roger's French score with one supposedly more in the American idiom.

No other regular musical opened until mid-September, but **The Last of the Rohans** (8-31-99, Academy of Music), in keeping with the practice of so many Irish pieces of the time, had a number of songs for its star, Andrew Mack.

The summer doldrums ended when two shows opened simultaneously on September 18: **Cyrano de Bergerac** and **The Rogers Brothers in Wall Street.** The musical version of *Cyrano* was the first of four new Victor Herbert scores heard in this single season. It opened at the Knickerbocker less than a year after the American premiere of Rostand's play and less than two years after its world premiere in Paris. It also followed by less than a season Weber and Fields' hilarious burlesque (11-3-98). As a result it found itself in immediate difficulties. Because the comic opera's stars were two outstanding comedians (Francis Wilson as Cyrano, Lulu Glaser as Roxane), the singing of Herbert's music suffered. On the other hand Herbert's lovely, romantic songs were often inimical to the piece's comedy. Herbert's biographer noted audiences "never made up their minds as to whether they had seen a great play travestied or a mediocre burlesque almost ennobled." Removed after 28 performances, an extended road tour had to be curtailed when the provinces also rejected it.

The Syndicate, still anxious to cut into the popularity of the independent Weber and Fields, brought **The Rogers Brothers in Wall Street** to the Victoria. The boys played the proprietors of a couple of warships in a fireworks display who ultimately peddle shares in a donkey to a promoter who is convinced he is purchasing a stake in the fabulous "Little Don Key" mine. Ada Lewis was featured in another tough-girl role, although this time her Bowery toughie was a yellow journalist. J. J. McNally's book had so little to do with Wall Street, the *Times* argued, the evening "might have been called most anything with equal propriety." The immediacy of some of McNally's lines must have delighted first-nighters and startled at least one of them. The Tammany leader, Richard Crocker, attended the opening, possibly to get his mind off charges of corruption being flung at him from all sides. If so, he was thwarted, for one character remarked, "It's a dull day in the city. Richard Crocker hasn't been accused of anything." One short-lived hit, "The Belle Of Murray Hill," emerged from Maurice Levi's lackluster score. Not all the music was new. Louise Gunning "warbled old Scotch songs daintily," Sousa marches and Stephen Foster songs were heard, and there was even a medley of tunes from *A Runaway Girl.* (Sousa's marches served as background for the showy drills that were de rigueur in the era's musicals.) Levi, like Stromberg at the Music Hall, doubled as conductor. *The Rogers Brothers in Wall Street* ran three months before embarking on a tour of the Syndicate's houses.

Weber and Fields did not take the new competition sitting down, and when they relit their music hall on September 21 with **Whirl-i-gig** they added a stellar attraction to the roster—Lillian Russell, the leading singing beauty of the Gilded Age. As a result seats for opening nights were in such demand that the management finally determined to put them up for auction. Jesse Lewisohn paid $1000 for two boxes, while Stanford White, William Randolph Hearst, and the scandal-ridden Mr. Crocker bid as high as $750 for top locations. Ordinary orchestra seats brought $100. The comedian-entrepreneurs were not above active participation in the wild speculation that ensued, for they had just given their tiny house a costly renovation, and, even more pressing, Miss Russell's contract called for the staggering sum of $1,250 a week. The first part of the evening was the customary vaudeville, with Miss Russell attempting her first coon number, "When Chloe Sings Her Song." The second half was a burlesque of the French farce *The Girl from Maxim's,* which Charles Frohman had brought into the Criterion three weeks before. In the original an amoral grisette upsets a sternly conventional society. Weber and Fields, as was their wont, reversed the situation, placing a prim, innocent young lady in the midst of a gay

Newport set. When objections were raised to Miss Russell appearing in bed in a low-cut gown at the opening of this burlesque, the scene was hastily restaged. But no one complained of the comedy:

Uneeda: The captain is my ideal of a hero.
Sigmund Cohenski [Warfield]:—A hero! Is dot a business? A tailor is a business, a shoemaker is a business, but a hero? Better you should marry a bookkeeper.
Uneeda: A bookkeeper? I suppose you think the pen is mightier than the sword.
Cohenski: You bet your life! Could you sign checks with a sword?
Fifi [Russell]:—You might bring me a demi-tasse.
Cohenski: Bring me the same, and a cup of coffee.

In December the burlesque was changed to spoof Clyde Fitch's *Barbara Frietchie* as *Barbara Fidgety.* The candidate for mayor of Frederick runs on the platform "To the victims belongs what is spoiled." He promises Weber a job as tax collector, and, as Weber described the position, "I have to go along the street and whenever I see a tack, I should collect it so the bicycles wouldn't get punctured." Still later, *Sapho* was burlesqued as *Sapolio,* but Weber and Fields had concluded Miss Russell was not a strong comedienne and confined her appearances to the opening act. *Whirl-i-gig's* 264 performances far outstripped the Rogers Brothers' run, even with allowances for the larger house they played in. When the show went on the road Weber and Fields made such large profits that from then on they limited their Broadway stays. Although they proved just as riotous and just as popular in the big road theatres, they could never bring themselves to move to a more spacious house in New York.

October's sole musical was Victor Herbert's **The Singing Girl** (10-23-99, Casino), his second vehicle for "the piquant little star" Alice Nielsen. Stanislaus Stange's book was the sort of driveling nonsense that perpetually beset Herbert. When the Duke of Linz (Eugene Cowles) is jilted he decrees all would-be lovers must first obtain a license to woo. Youngsters caught kissing must promptly marry or be imprisoned for life. But Greta, the Singing Girl, and her Count Otto (Richie Ling) prevail on the Duke to live and let live. Herbert was not able to rise above this dross, although his score was superior to anything else being played on Broadway. With Nielsen's help it sounded pleasing enough to keep the show in New York eleven weeks (with only one matinee a week) and then, coupled with a revival of *The Fortune Teller,* to tour successfully.

Three musicals raised their curtains in November. The first was a revival of the preceding season's *In Gay Paree* (3-20-99), chalking up an additional 48 performances at the New York.

At Florenz Ziegfeld's urging, busy Harry B. Smith, who had done the book and lyrics for *The Rounders* and the lyrics for *Cyrano, Whirl-i-gig,* and *The Singing Girl,* did both the lyrics and the book for **Papa's Wife** (11-13-99, Manhattan), combining plot elements from two Hervé works, *La Femme a Papa* and *Mam'zelle Nitouche.* Smith told how an innocent bride learns her husband cannot be faithful even on his honeymoon and how she sets about curing him. Reginald De Koven supplemented the original score. Ziegfeld produced the piece as a vehicle for his wife. The flamboyant Miss Held stopped the show with "I Wish I Really Weren't, But I Am" and made a sensational exit in an 1899 automobile. Most historians agree with Smith, "It was with this play that Mr. Ziegfeld first revealed himself as a connoisseur of pulchritude. There were only sixteen girls in *Papa's Wife,* but they were all highly decorative and in their costuming economy was not considered." The show ran 147 performances, a figure surpassed only by *Whirl-i-gig.*

The London success, **A Greek Slave** (11-28-99, Herald Square), with music by Lionel Monckton and Sidney Jones, closed out November. Its tale of a statue come to life undoubtedly brought back memories of *Adonis* (9-4-84) to many playgoers. Kate Michelena, Hugh Chilvers, Minnie Ashley, and Albert Parr figured prominently in the cast.

A third Victor Herbert piece, **The Ameer** (12-4-99, Wallack's), united Herbert with an old associate, the happy, clownish Frank Daniels. Although critical consensus branded the new work inferior to *The Wizard of the Nile* (11-4-95) or *The Idol's Eye* (10-25-97), the public responded avidly. For 51 performances in New York and a year and a half on the road, Daniels portrayed Iffe Khan, the Ameer of Afghanistan who is compelled to marry a rich woman in order to pay his annual tribute to the English. His courtship of a young American is frustrated when she marries the British commanding officer, but Iffe flushes out a wealthy native woman in time for a proper curtain.

Three Little Lambs was a Christmas present from the Boston Cadets at the Fifth Avenue Theatre. Three crooks—David Tooke, Hungry Jim, and Phyllis Argyle—try to con Jack Hardwicke and Beatrice Jerome out of their inheritances. They get Jack drunk, forcing him to forfeit his rights to an unknown lady. Furious and ashamed, Jack joins the navy and sails for Puerto Rico. There he woos and wins Beatrice, discovering at the same time she is the unknown girl to whom he has lost his fortune. If the names of the principal characters sound familiar, theatregoers had already been introduced to them in 1898. The show was a rewriting of *The Queen of the Ballet* (2-5-98), some of the details and settings changed to acknowledge America's pride in its newly acquired territory. With a book by R. A. Barnet, music by E. W. Corliss, and a cast of attractive, youthful performers including Marie Cahill, Adele Ritchie, and Raymond Hitchcock, it played 49 performances. The success of the Boston Cadets was little short of phenomenal, even if it sadly suggested that the company's tinselly theatrical artifice was more rewarding than the Bostonians' soul-searching artiness. In February the *Dramatic Mirror* noted, "Since 1892 Mr. Barnet's extravaganzas have netted $168,000 for the Cadets."

Another holiday present was offered New Year's Day, 1900, when the extravaganza **Chris and the Wonderful Lamp** opened at the Victoria. It was the only score that the march king, John Philip Sousa, ever composed for children. Its book was by Glen MacDonough, who would later collaborate with Victor Herbert on youngsters' shows. Chris Wagstaff (Edna Wallace Hopper) buys Aladdin's lamp. He removes his sweetheart Fanny (Ethel Irene Stewart) from school and in the company of the genie (Jerome Sykes) they visit Aladdin's home, Etheria. Aladdin (Emile Beaupre) falls in love with Fanny and steals the lamp in order to keep the girl with him. But she rubs the lamp, sending herself and Chris back to Earth. Children and adults applauded the show for 58 performances.

A second children's extravaganza, **Little Red Riding Hood** (1-8-00, Casino), was imported from London. It lacked the appeal of *Chris and the Wonderful Lamp* and was withdrawn after 24 showings.

Fay Templeton had been conspicuously missing from the season's Weber and Fields' high jinks. But when she appeared in **Broadway to Tokio** (1-23-00, New York), she recalled her earlier appearance in *Hurly Burly* (9-8-98) playing Cleopatra's mummy. For that show provided the germ of the new musical's plot, in which the mummy travels from New York to San Francisco and back again, and then to Japan, to search for the heart that has been removed from its wrappings. Reginald De Koven wrote some of the songs, but most of the score was A. Baldwin Sloane. Miss Templeton's mummy cakewalked with Otis Harlan and imitated

a French singer shouting a coon song. Stage-encompassing dance numbers included a "Golden Gate Ballet" (with changing light effects) and a "Cherry Blossom Ballet." Somehow a place was found to burlesque Eleanora Duse's *Camille*. For all her imperfections the mummy had enough life left to continent-hop for 88 performances. The era's changing theatrical vocabulary was made evident by a comment in the *Times* that "Max Freeman, in the technical slang of the hour, staged the piece." The newsman might also have noted that the term "manager" was giving way to "producer."

Kirk La Shelle, who had collaborated with Frederick Ranken on the book of *The Ameer* (12-4-99), alone supplied the libretto for Julian Edwards' score for **Princess Chic** (2-12-00, Casino). La Shelle's tale told how Princess Chic of Normandy (Christie MacDonald), disguised as a peasant, warns Charles the Bold (Winfield Blake) of King Louis' plans to make trouble. Charles falls in love with the maid and learns her true station in time for a happy ending. The show survived only 22 performances.

One day short of a month after his music was heard in *Broadway to Tokio*, a "full" if "commonplace" Sloane score was heard in **Aunt Hannah** (2-22-00, Bijou), and he enjoyed a quick if fleeting success with the requisite coon song, "My Tiger Lily." During the dance for this song "the calcium, shining through a painted medium, threw the shadow of a big tiger lily on stage." An unbilled soloist stopped the show with "When The Cat's Away The Mice Will Play." The plot of the "musical farce" recorded how sedate, religious Aunt Hannah (Agnes Findlay) goes on a trip, leaving her mansion in the keeping of her nephew, Jack (Frederick Hallen). Over the servants' protests, Jack decides to throw a grand party. Aunt Hannah returns unexpectedly, and Jack must desperately try to make things look like what they are not. An old flame of Hannah's is at the party and sets everything right. The show ran 21 performances.

Even though there were many who objected to the "questionable character" of young Richard Carle's brand of comedy, he had a large following on the road both as a performer and writer. It was solely as a writer that he was represented by the musical comedy **Mam'selle Awkins** (2-26-00, Victoria). Carle described the plight of an impoverished noble (Will Armstrong). Secretly married, he must fend off the demands of his prime creditor to marry the daughter (Mamie Gilroy) of a rich, cockney soap-manufacturer. The lord hires a number of friends and acquaintances to impersonate him in such a fashion as to drive away the girl. The score was by producer Alfred E. Aarons, with additional melodies by Herman Perlet. The mam'selle could muster only 35 representations.

Long before Florenz Ziegfeld began glorifying the American girl, the Casino Theatre was as famous for its line of beauties as was the Gaiety in London. When a new attraction was needed for the Casino, George Lederer once more called on Harry B. Smith to provide a libretto, this time suggesting it center on one of the theatre's famous beauties. What Smith concocted and called **The Casino Girl** was not a backstage tale, but a formula book of an American in an exotic setting. Laura Lee (Mabel Gilman, now spelling her name Mabelle), a former Casino chorus girl, flees to Cairo to escape a pestering English earl (Virginia Earle). She opens a millinery store and prepares to settle down, when her pursuing earl reappears. After complications brought on by a comic Khedive (Sam Bernard) and some clownish thieves, she realizes she does indeed love the Englishman. The already time-worn plot bothered no one, nor did the hodgepodge score by a number of hands. One number, "How Actresses Are Made," won encores nightly. Knowing audiences recognized in the duet by Miss Gilman and Miss Earle veiled references to the methods Lederer employed to make Edna May a star. Although the show, which opened March 19, was revised several times during its run, with one very substantial revision by Harry's brother Robert, audiences loved it in every form and it ran 131 performances, toured, and even crossed the Atlantic to the West End.

The Viceroy (4-30-00, Knickerbocker), the season's last musical, almost sneaked in, arriving as part of the Bostonians' repertory, which included *Robin Hood* and *The Serenade*. The story recounted how the pirate Tivolini (Helen Bertram), in reality the rightful viceroy, regains his patrimony from his treacherous cousin (Henry Clay Barnabee), wins the hand of Beatrice (Grace Cameron), and magnanimously offers his villainous cousin a share of the government. Harry B. Smith's dreary book was coupled with a less than sterling Victor Herbert score, although some scholars have admired Tivolini's serenade, "Hear Me."

1900-1901

The new century was being looked forward to and the nation was preparing for another presidential election. All of William Jennings Bryan's silver-tongued oratory would not win him the White House while his countrymen felt safe and sound with William McKinley. Twenty-eight new musicals vied for Broadway's favor—nearly a third of all the plays mounted during the season. While two chalked up far and away the longest runs of the year, theatregoers were by and large not uncritically receptive. Although a dozen straight plays tallied 100 or more performances, apart from the two musical smashes, only two other lyric pieces achieved long runs. In retrospect some regular comedies and dramas that caught New Yorkers' fancies appear worthless, but the public taste that rejected most of the season's musicals seems unquestionable. It was a dismal season.

Two importations opened the season. **The Cadet Girl** (7-25-00, Herald Square), a Parisian hit adapted by Harry B. Smith, enjoyed a 48-performance run. Dan Daly, Christie MacDonald, and Adele Ritchie enlivened a complicated rigmarole about a will and a medallion. Arthur Sullivan's **The Rose of Persia,** with its tale of a sultan's wife who goes on the town disguised as a dancer and with most of its original London cast, opened at Daly's September 6, but failed to find an audience.

Sullivan's comic opera made the mistake of competing with the most popular first-night in town, the fall reopening of Weber and Fields. They called their 1900's nonsense **Fiddle-dee-dee,** and filled it with a topflight cast including both Lillian Russell and Fay Templeton, as well as De Wolf Hopper, David Warfield, John T. Kelly, and Bessie Clayton. Backing the principals was another dramatically beautiful chorus line. The year's burlesque was a takeoff on the preceding session's dramatization of *Quo Vadis,* called in comic Dutch *Quo Vas Iss?* In it the Emperor Zero, alarmed that the W.C.T.U. has succeeded in closing all the bars in Antium and is threatening to burn Rum, has the beautiful Lythia of the local W.C.T.U. chapter tossed to the wild borax. Her would-be rescuer, Fursus, is so weak he cannot break loose from his chain of pretzels and sausages. Several of the stars shone in small roles. Hopper appeared "as the suave and formidable, Petrolius, who finds opening his veins cheaper than opening a jackpot . . . Warfield as an impressive and astonishingly soiled Greek philosopher; and Fields an obstreperously Roman bad boy." In mid-October a spoof of the new season's *Arizona* was inserted. It caused something of a furor because the chorus girls entered dressed shabbily as travel-worn soldiers. It is often forgotten that along with the Casino the music hall had the reputation of displaying the most beautiful line in New York. In December the Arizona travesty was removed and a new second act burlesqued not one, but several of the town's latest hits, including the runaway smash, *Florodora*. Out of *Fiddle-dee-dee* came the two most popular songs to emerge from John Stromberg and the music hall series, "I'm A Respectable Working Girl" and "Ma Blushin' Rosie." Fay Templeton introduced both. Social reforms have blunted the urgency of the working girl's plight and relegated the former to a period piece. But a succession of great minstrels and songsters from Al Jolson to Judy Garland have kept "Ma Blushin' Rosie" something of a standard. The show ran 262 times, outdistanced only by the *Florodora* phenomenon.

The Monks of Malabar (9-14-00, Knickerbocker), a comic opera with music by Ludwig Englander, ran 39 performances. It was the only musical to open between Weber and Fields and their new rivals, the Rogers Brothers. The staid title belied the show's farcical carryings-on. In the book J. Cheever Goodwin created for Francis Wilson the central figure is Boolboom, a French merchant living in India. To rid himself of his shrewish wife, he goes into hiding and has broadcast the news that he has been eaten by a lion. Only too late does he discover that by Indian law his own death ordains his wife's cremation. He cannot come forth and reveal the truth, or he will be put to death for lying. In a series of disguises he manages to delay his wife's execution until they are both rescued by the French army.

Unlike the music hall show, **The Rogers Brothers in Central Park** (9-17-00, Victoria) did not open cold but tried out in the hinterlands. It arrived as a tightly knit entertainment held together by J. J. McNally's thin story of "two innocent Germans having been bunkoed into buying Central Park, Missouri, thinking it was Central Park, New York." As usual much of the humor was topical:

(*1st man*): This town seems to be for McKinley and Roosevelt.
(*2nd man*): How's that?
(*1st man*): There's only McKinley and Roosevelt banners on Broadway.
(*2nd man*): Well, what of it? Banners can't vote.
(*1st man*): No, but they show which way the wind blows.

Maurice Levi's music was equally simple and direct. In this edition he began a series of "Reuben" songs depicting the plight of the hapless yokel in the big city, a series apparently prompted by the continuing success of "Reuben And Cynthia" from *A Trip to Chinatown* (11-9-91). Cole and J. W. Johnson interpolated "Run Brudder Possum Run." Young Richard Carle helped with both lyrics and music. But the boys on 42nd Street were no real match for Weber and Fields. They took their show back on the road after 72 performances at the Victoria.

The talents who had combined to make a success of *The Casino Girl* (3-19-00) brought **The Belle of Bohemia** into the 39th Street house on September 24. George Lederer was again the producer. The book and lyrics were by Harry B. Smith and the music by Ludwig Englander, with another assist from Harry T. MacConnell. Sam Bernard, who had scored so effectively as the Khedive, was given the pivotal, if not the title role. His brother, Dick, supported him. Smith's story smacked of Plautus and Shakespeare. A prosperous brewer (Sam) and a humble tintype photographer (Dick) look so alike that when the brewer is jailed for the photographer's misdeeds, the bohemian must take the entrepreneur's place at an important society function. The score included the inevitable coon songs, love songs, topical tunes, waltzes, and a lullaby, but nothing of consequence. Ballets were eschewed, allowing lively clogs and waltzes to propel the entertainment. The show's 55-performance run fell far short of *The Casino Girl*'s stay.

A Million Dollars (9-27-00, New York) employed a slim plot that harked back to one used by *About Town* (2-26-94). Once again a barber (Ignacio Martinetti) comes into sudden wealth and goes on a spending spree. Produced and written by the same team responsible for *Broadway to Tokio* (1-23-00), it was a distinct failure. Dancing highlighted the evening. The first act featured an Amazon march known as "The Allies"; the second a "Coney Island Ballet"; while almost the whole of the third act was given over to a ballet called "The Roses" and mounted in gold, silver, and, appropriately, rose. The musical had the first of four A. Baldwin Sloane scores to be heard during the season. So rapidly was Sloane earning an unenviable reputation, that the *Times* could already knowingly complain that his latest score "was not equal to his modest best." Critics would soon look back longingly to Victor Herbert's four inferior efforts of the preceding year. One reason the American lyric season was so dismal was that Herbert was preoccupied as conductor of the Pittsburgh Symphony, and it would be several years before he could be persuaded to return to the musical stage.

Five musicals premiered in October. The first

was Sidney Jones' London hit **San Toy** (10-1-00, New York), still trafficking in the fading Oriental vogue *The Mikado* had sparked a generation before and which Jones himself had most profitably pursued in *The Geisha*. Marie Celeste sang the title role while James T. Powers served as principal comedian. In runs interrupted by booking difficulties *San Toy* totaled 168 performances.

Alfred E. Aarons wrote the score for **The Military Maid** (10-8-00, Savoy), which George V. Hobart adapted from the French. Josephine Hall was the star, playing Fleurette D'Norville, an attractive, sought after young lady who invites her pesky suitors—and their wives—to a dinner party. Besides the inevitable drills the title promised, the evening offered a show stopper for Miss Hall in a song entitled "Sister Mary Has The Measles." But the drills and the song were not enough, and the show was an eight-performance fiasco.

Hobart was also responsible for the book of **Hodge, Podge, & Co.** (10-23-00, Madison Square), this time adapting it from a German play *Im Himmelshof*. Hodge, Podge, & Co. receive a cryptic letter advising that one of their employees has deserted his wife and children. The writer announces she will send her son Rudolf with further details. When one Rudolf Roastemsum appears, he is taken for the man mentioned in the letter. A series of confused identities follows. Since one act took place in the "model room" of a poster studio, a parade of "comely young woman in varied and sometimes startling attire" was offered. Weber and Fields' favorite, Peter F. Dailey, was costarred with Christie MacDonald. The "plump and impertinent" Dailey appeared in a "spring suit," in a kilt, and as a toreador. He bantered with chorus girls as he danced and talked confidentially to the gallery. Miss MacDonald displayed her "pert vivacity with a mere hint of fervor" as she sang and performed. A number of composers contributed a share of the music, with John W. Bratton writing most of the score. Although it was all undistinguished, the show sang and kicked its heels gaily enough to keep audiences happy for over two months.

Another "Belle" show, **The Belle of Bridgeport** (10-29-00, Bijou), had a cast that included the hefty "blond personification of good humor," May Irwin, still a leading "coon" singer, and Raymond Hitchcock. In Glen MacDonough's book Ariel Smith saves her father's secretary, Malcolm Crane (Bert Thayer), from a false charge of theft. With Miss Irwin to belt out the black-derived material in her "customary 'semi-mezzo' voice," some of the finest young black talent (Bob Cole, J. W. Johnson,

and J. Rosamond Johnson) combined to help with the score. When she wasn't singing or propelling the plot Miss Irwin talked with audiences about trout-fishing and department-store methods. Reviewers failed to note whether she approved of the way great retail outlets functioned, but the press did disapprove of a certain commercialism evident in *The Belle of Bridgeport* and "more and more common" in other shows. This was the brazen advertising of special products. In Miss Irwin's vehicle a brand of whiskey and a make of typewriter were ballyhooed.

Two nights later a burlesque of *Nell Gwynn*, called **Nell Go In** (10-31-00, New York), was part of a triple bill (the other two acts were ballets) that began a brief stay. Even the burlesque itself ran heavily to dance, including a "skipping-rope" dance, "coon" steps by Pat Rooney and Mayme Gehrue, and a showy, lively "Bal Champêtre." A Shadow pantomime was also featured. Music included opera arias ("Di quella pira," "The Jewel Song" from *Faust*). A. Baldwin Sloane composed what new tunes were required.

Jerome Sykes had scored so memorable a success as Foxy Quiller in Reginald De Koven's comic opera *The Highwayman* (12-13-97) that Klaw and Erlanger commissioned De Koven and Harry B. Smith to write a new musical around the character. **Foxy Quiller** (11-5-00, Broadway), with the rotund Sykes as star, suffered the fate of most written-to-order sequels. It was a 50-performance disappointment. A young sailor, Ned Royster (W. G. Stewart), has his money stolen by a dwarf (Adolph Zink). Abel Gudgeon (Louis Cassavant), the father of Ned's fiancée Daphne (Grace Cameron), refuses to allow the pair to wed until the money is recovered. Foxy Quiller is called in and, always talking of himself in the third person, promises to solve the crime by "deductive, inductive, and seductive" reasoning. When he finds the money in his own valise he arrests himself and sentences himself to be shot. Luckily, the real thief confesses. For many, the thief, played with such engaging mischief by the erstwhile Liliputian, Zink, almost stole the show from Sykes.

Florodora opened one week later, November 12, at the Casino. Although it soon became a legend, it was not an immediate success. Its critical reception was mixed, seemingly justifying the fears of all the leading managers who had rejected the show despite its London success. It was left to a new managerial team, Dunne, Ryley, and Fisher, to gamble with it on the Rialto. For the first two or three weeks, it was better than even money that they had lost their entire investment. But the sextette, "Tell Me, Pretty Maiden," became wildly popular. (Technically, a double sextette for six men and six women, it was the first major hit tune from a Broadway show not sung by any of the principals.) With the *Sun* plugging the show daily, *Florodora* eventually found an audience. Before long it was playing to absolute capacity ($10,000 a week) and turning prospective ticket buyers away. When it closed after 505 performances, it was the second musical in New York history to exceed the 500 mark. By running longer in New York than in London it had strikingly reversed the pattern of the day. The show's popularity undoubtedly launched the vogue for South Sea settings that soon replaced the Orient as a favorite of librettists. Florodora was an island in the Philippines, famous for its perfume. The island and the rights to the perfume belong to the heroine, Dolores (Fannie Johnston), but the villainous magnate, Gilfain, attempts to cheat her out of her property. Dolores and her fiancé, Frank Albercoed (Bertram Godfrey), abetted by the clownish Tweedlepunch, thwart Gilfain's plans. The part of Gilfain was first played in New York by R. E. Graham, who had created the part of General Knickerbocker in *The Little Tycoon* (3-24-86). Tweedlepunch was played by the actor who originated the role in London. He was an old American favorite long absent from New York, Willie Edouin.

A vaudeville, **Star and Garter** (11-26-00, Victoria), was compiled primarily as a showcase for "The Marvelous Agoust Family" of jugglers. The Agousts did not make their first appearance until the beginning of the second act, in a restaurant scene which found one of the family as the maître d'hôtel, a second as a waiter, and two others as diners. While the scene at first was deceptively serene, before long, cutlery, dishes, and food were flying across the stage. The first act featured travesties of *David Harum, The Gay Lord Quex,* and *Richard Carvel* with the mocking led by Marie Cahill, Otis Harlan, and a young American who would become the toast of London as Danilo in *The Merry Widow,* Joseph Coyne.

Boisterous Lulu Glaser starred in **Sweet Anne Page** (12-3-00, Manhattan), a colorless piece set in the reign of James II of England. Anne Page runs away from a miserly uncle (Fred Frear) and the prospect of an unhappy marriage. She joins a troupe of strolling players. Anne's real love is Tom (Arthur Donaldson), a yeoman supporting William of Orange. When William succeeds to the throne, Tom is knighted and Anne learns she is a noble-

man's daughter. The musical failed to run out the month.

May Irwin returned in a farce with music, **Madge Smith, Attorney** (12-10-00, Bijou). Among the composers credited with the songs was the increasingly ubiquitous A. Baldwin Sloane. But in a unique departure from common practice, the songs were not scattered throughout the plot. Instead they were all offered in a single extended medley.

Sloane also write the score for **The Giddy Throng** (12-24-00, New York), a burlesque revue with dialogue by Sydney Rosenfeld, which opened as the principal attraction on a four-part bill. The rest of the bill included a comedy act, a ballet, and a "musical sketch" by George V. Hobart and Sloane called "After Office Hours." Revues of the day still had plots to tie their numbers together. *The Giddy Throng* was no exception. Producer Noble Rhoman (Joseph Harrington) goes looking for a hit show, but the characters from current Broadway successes get in his way. For example, David Harum (William Gould) stops the action attempting to sell Gay Lord Quex (Louis Harrison) a real horse. The cast was led by May Yohe and Harrison, a jack-of-all-trades who had supplied the books for earlier Sloane shows and for the recently staged *Madge Smith, Attorney.* Many in the audience came merely to gape at Miss Yohe, whose recent marriage had made her Lady Francis Hope. She made only two brief appearances, first wearing a yellow and white dress and laden down with what she professed to be the Hope family jewels; then in a pink gown. She sang just two songs, "Kiss Me To Sleep" and "Down By The River," in a voice which the *Times* snidely rued had once possessed three notes, but had, since her marriage, lost two of them. Up-and-coming youngsters in the cast included Emma Carus and Pat Rooney. Oldtimers such as Amelia Summerville brought their years of experience. This bright array of talent helped make the show a smash hit. Its 164 performances were the fourth longest run among the season's musicals.

A Royal Rogue (12-24-00, Broadway) had a book by Charles Klein, who had not been active as a librettist for some time, and a score by W. T. Francis. Klein's story centered on Baptiste Ballou, who in 1792 ran a Paris restaurant and ran it into debt. Ballou is an antiroyalist cutthroat, while his daughter is a social-climbing snob who pretends her father is the Duc de Chartres. She hopes her pretense will help her win the hand of George Girodet (F. Newton Lind). Complications arise when the revolutionary band to which Baptiste belongs selects him to assassinate the Duc de Chartres. Jefferson De Angelis and Josephine Hall starred, and while De Angelis had an explosive first entrance—blown through a kitchen door—neither the stars nor a chorus "liberal in its display of hosiery" could breathe sufficient life into the piece. It languished for a month, then disappeared.

Nor could Marie Dressler, Jobyna Howland, or Bessie Clayton inject the needed gaiety into **Miss Prinnt** (12-25-00, Victoria), a musical comedy with the refreshing tale of Helen Prinnt, a woman editor who determines to stir up the sleepyheads at her newspaper. She eventually marries Richmond Blackstone (Theodore Babcock), a lawyer who had fought her tactics. But George V. Hobart's development was not as fresh as his basic idea, and John Golden's music and lyrics were trite. At best an irrelevant "coon" song by Miss Dressler and the chorus at the end of the first act won four encores. The show closed at the same time as *A Royal Rogue*.

The Burgomaster arrived from Chicago on New Year's Eve, bringing with it two names new to New York: librettist-lyricist Frank Pixley and composer Gustav Luders.

· · ·

Gustav Luders was born in Bremen, Germany, on December 13, 1865. A thoroughly trained musician, he emigrated to America in 1888, settling first in Milwaukee and then in Chicago, in time to play an active role in the musical events at the 1893 World's Fair. When a season of opera he conducted failed at the Schiller he agreed to keep the house open by writing a musical in conjunction with Harry B. Smith. Unfortunately, *Little Robinson Crusoe,* with Eddie Foy as star, didn't keep the box office humming either. Luders teamed up with Pixley, a local newspaperman. Together they wrote *King Dodo,* but could find no one to produce it.

· · ·

Their second effort, **The Burgomaster** (12-31-00, Manhattan), however, was readily accepted and proved an immediate hit. Pixley's libretto had Peter Stuyvesant (Henry E. Dixey) and his secretary, Doodle Van Kull (Knox Wilson), fall into a drunken sleep. They are awakened in 1900 when workmen come across them while digging in City Hall Park. The pair are taken on a tour of the town. Luders' score provided a gay, endearing accompaniment to the story. Its outstanding melody, "The Tale Of The Nangaroo," began a parade of Pixley-Luders "Tale" and "Message" songs and helped spread the vogue for anthropomorphic animal tunes.

New Yorkers had developed a conditioned disdain for Chicago offerings, and *The Burgomaster* was unable to override the prejudice. This aversion is surprising in this instance, given the show's New York setting. But the producers compounded their difficulties by offering a tacky mounting. The same backdrop, depicting old Dutch ships in the harbor, was used for both the 1660 and 1900 scenes. At least the press was able to find kind words for the performers, not merely for Dixey's nimble clowning but for such stellarly played bit parts as Raymond Hitchcock's vain, loquacious actor, E. Booth Talkington. *The Burgomaster*'s stay at the Manhattan was a disheartening 33 performances.

The 20th-century's initial musical did not arrive at the Herald Square until January 7. **The Girl from Up There** starred Edna May as a young lady who has lain frozen in a cloth-of-gold gown at the North Pole for 500 years and is released by a bolt of lightning to face the modern world. She must find the "Gold Cup of Olaf" within ninety days or she will die. Learning that pirates have stolen the cup, she dons tights and masquerades as a buccaneer. Hugh Morton's book was serviceable, filled with theatrically meaty roles. Harry Conor wandered in and out of the story as a disagreeable man who carries a pepper shaker in a town that forbids sneezing, while Harry Davenport staggered around as a tipsy officer. Edna Aug won applause for her "rainbow dance" as she sang "Seraphina And Her Concertina." But most significantly, Morton's story allowed two young young comedians, Dave Montgomery and Fred Stone, playing "a brace of pirates," to catch the public's eye and embark on one of Broadway's happiest careers. But the book was not sacrosanct. When Otis Harlan and Harry Kelly left the cast, their roles (King Flash and King Flush) were conveniently combined into one for Dan Daly. And serviceable may well be the kindest word for Gustave Kerker's score. The *Times* reflected the prevailing dissatisfaction with the run of Broadway composers (as it had earlier in its comments about Sloane) when its critic lamented, "Mr. Kerker's music is obviously and persistently Mr. Kerker's. It is the same old music." Once more a fine cast of solid professionals figured importantly in lengthening the run of a show. *The Girl from Up There* missed entering the charmed circle of 100 performances by a mere four showings.

On the same night—January 7—**Garrett O'Magh** raised its curtain downtown at the 14th Street Theatre. Garrett (Chauncey Olcott) attempts to mollify an importuning young lady (Edith Barker) by eloping with her and behaving disgracefully so she will call off the marriage. But Garrett winds up falling in love. Essentially a straight play, it contained just enough songs to please Olcott's large Irish following.

A hastily thrown-together "musical comedy," **The Night of the Fourth,** was rushed into the Victoria on January 21 to fill a two-week gap in its bookings. The show had originally been done the previous summer in San Francisco and most of its plot seemed to have been left there. New York was offered little more than a vaudeville in which Maud Courtney sang Stephen Foster melodies, Walter Jones pranced through a comic fandango, and Harry Bulger, deprived of his former partner Sherrie Matthews, now held "sidewalk conversations with Joe Coyne." Acrobats, jugglers, and a magician filled in the gaps. No cry to extend the engagement beyond its announced limits was heard, so the show quickly disappeared.

Two nights later a rarity for the day, a Viennese operetta, was unveiled. Despite some lovely Johann Strauss music, the public was not receptive to **Vienna Life** (*Wiener Blut*) (1-23-01, Broadway). Its story detailed how a countess is ready to end her marriage when she believes the count has taken up with a dancer. Six years would pass by before another show revived interest in the Viennese school. At that time Ethel Jackson, who played the forlorn countess, would appear more happily as a merry widow.

Another lively cast that included Clifton Crawford, Lotta Faust, Charles J. Ross, and Eva Tanguay propelled **My Lady** (2-11-01, Victoria), an extravaganza by R. A. Barnet, with music by assorted writers, to a 93-performance run. A Boston show, originally done there as *Miladi and the Three Musketeers,* it was, as its earlier title suggests, a burlesque of Dumas' tale. The show's idea of humor was to change Porthos' name to Pork House. Showstoppers included a song sung in a moving automobile and a dance by the queen's scrubwomen.

The season's most important musical opened at the Savoy on February 25. Although the Savoy was "uptown" at 34th and Broadway, it was not considered a major house. At the time no one was aware of the show's importance: neither the critics, who were not overwhelmed, nor the public, who bought only enough seats to keep the show going 32 performances. If one person alone appreciated the occasion's significance he was undoubtedly the author of the "musical farce," twenty-two-year-old George M. Cohan. Cohan had fashioned his new

musical from a vaudeville sketch he had written for his family act, "The Four Cohans." Vaudeville and the theatre were in Cohan's blood.

. . .

George M. Cohan was born in the proverbial trunk in Providence, Rhode Island, on either July 3 or July 4 (depending on whose story you accept) in 1878, the son of two vaudeville troupers, Jerry and Nellie Cohan. Carried on stage as part of their act, he soon branched out as "Master Georgie" in an enlarged act. The act was further enlarged when his sister, Josephine, was included, and with time a fifth Cohan, George's wife, Ethel Levey, was added. George had no formal musical training. But his invaluable experience and native intelligence combined early on to produce a unique talent.

. . .

Cohan's fleshing out of the act into **The Governor's Son** revealed both his remarkable theatrical know-how and his as yet incomplete artistic maturity. The faults, to do the critics and public justice, were most obvious. The book was a confusing narrative labyrinth. The principal plot does not involve the governor's son. Instead it relates the efforts of Bill Swift (N.J. Sullivan) to locate his runaway brother-in-law, Dicky Dickson (Will H. Sloan). He hires a detective, Martin McGovern (James H. Manning), unaware that McGovern is all the while helping Dicky to hide. Dicky mischievously disguises himself as a detective and hires himself out to Swift under the alias Rudolf Schlitz. A second unhappy couple are the Curtises (Jerry and Nellie Cohan). When Mrs. Curtis becomes jealous of her husband's flirting with other ladies, Mr. Curtis hires the governor's son, Algy Wheelock (George M.), to flirt with his wife and to let him catch the pair at it. But Algy confuses Mrs. Curtis with Mrs. Dickson (Josie Cohan). Everything ends satisfactorily. The couples are reunited, and Algy wins the hand of Emerald Green (Ethel Levey). The dialogue was often singularly colloquial and snappy:

Swift: What'll I do if I catch him?
Dickson: Kick him in the shins.
Swift: All right, kiddo, I'm for you. You lead the league with me.

Too often, however, Cohan fell back on two-a-day clichés. "Oh, Mr. Brown. Come over here, dear, under the AnheuserBusch." It was, of course, his songs that gave Cohan his enduring fame. In

The Governor's Son his flowing, vernacular lyrics were already evident:

> Push me along in my pushcart
> Push me along with the crowd
> What a sensational feeling one feels
> It beats all the airships and automobiles.
> Oh, what a chance with your sweetheart
> Closer and closer you shove.
> If you got the "cush" get in the push
> With the girl you love.

But his music, while jaunty and singable, still lacked Cohan's unique stamp. In one respect, Cohan did give audiences a glimpse of his future flag-waving when he sang "Yankee Doodle Doings." The five Cohans toured with the show for two years, while George improved his material and mulled over his second Broadway offering.

If Willard Spenser had despaired of achieving recognition or real acclaim in New York, he nonetheless remained steadfastly welcome in his home town of Philadelphia. On April 15 **Miss Bob White** premiered at the Chestnut Street Theatre there. Spenser's earlier works had told tales comfortably in the comic opera tradition. Moving with the times, his latest libretto smacked clearly of then contemporary musical comedy. After losing a bet, two millionaires, Billy Van Million (John Slavin) and Artie Tre Billion (Raymond Hitchcock), must live as tramps for two months. They head for a farm, followed by Clare Livingston (Ethel Jackson), an heiress. She disguises herself as a milkman, Bob White, and by the final curtain she has won Artie. Not even the onset of hot weather wilted Philadelphia's delight in the show, although, before its 136-performance run was over, outside romantic interests had forced Miss Jackson to withdraw. Her replacement was Marguerite Sylva.

Two musicals, one in April and one in May, closed out the season in New York. Lulu Glaser returned in **The Prima Donna** (4-17-01, Herald Square), a musical farce Harry B. Smith and Aimee Lachaume designed for her, but it proved no more satisfactory than her *Sweet Anne Page* and quickly folded. Miss Glaser portrayed Angela Chumpley, the star of the Frivolity Theatre. When she marries Meyerbeer Supnoodle, her father disinherits her. She is not in the least disconcerted. An Egyptian pasha falls in love with her and invites her to Cairo. A series of the mistaken identities so rampant in the librettos of the age filled out the evening. The *Times*, noting that "the silly season" of summer musicals was at hand, could find little to praise and suggested

the show was attempting to get by with only "high kicking and low dressing."

Sydney Rosenfeld and A. Baldwin Sloane had only slightly better luck with another burlesque revue, **The King's Carnival** (5-13-01, New York), which recessed for the hot weather and resumed briefly in the fall. Some semblance of a story revolved about the mix-up of a royal baby and a commoner. The story soon disappeared, prompting Louis Harrison, as King Philip of Spain, to remark, "The plot grows thinner." With its disappearance the evening was given over to spoofs of such popular plays as *In the Palace of the King, When Knighthood Was in Flower, The Climbers,* and *Under Two Flags.* Besides Harrison the excellent assemblage of comics included Emma Carus, Harry Bulger, Marie Dressler, Amelia Summerville, and Adele Ritchie.

1901-1902

From Broadway's point of view there remained much to cheer about. Of twenty-three musicals offered only five were importations. Almost half the new lyric pieces ran over 100 performances. If, as happened in about every season of this period, the longest run by far was racked up by an English musical, that in no way gainsaid the stirrings of a native art. A number of domestic works were greeted with perhaps unjustified enthusiasm, but this very enthusiasm could not help encourage American composers and librettists on to better efforts. One further indication of the American Musical Theatre's growing success and confidence was the absence of any revivals, so often a sign of contemporary creative exhaustion.

The Strollers (6-24-01, Knickerbocker), another Harry B. Smith—Ludwig Englander concoction, opened the season. Smith's libretto followed closely the story of an 1899 Viennese hit *Die Landstreicher,* although it was deemed prudent to discard the score. The story followed a pair of vagabonds, husband and wife, in their social elevation after they assist in recovering a valuable necklace a prince has thoughtlessly bestowed on a dancer. The piece was tailored to the needs of Francis Wilson, who had reluctantly come to terms with the Syndicate. Wilson's wife in the production was "graceful and piquant" Irene Bentley, who shortly afterward married Smith. Eddie Foy had an important role as a comic jailer, Kamfer. Englander's new music was no better than the rejected Ziehrer material, although "A Lesson In Flirtation" and the evening's theme, "The Song Of The Strollers," enjoyed a passing popularity. With virtually no competition, the show ran through the summer.

It was September 2 before another musical offering appeared, and it was the by now annual Rogers Brothers carnival that came into the Knickerbocker to get the season really under way. The plot of **The Rogers Brothers in Washington** told how a present meant for one lady is mistakenly given to a second young woman who keeps turning up with it at awkward times. The story line was so tenuous McNally called the evening a "vaudeville farce." Composer-conductor Maurice Levi continued the "Reuben" series with "The Wedding Of Reuben And The Maid" (lyrics by Harry B. Smith), but produced nothing outstanding. The principal attraction remained the "Dutch" clowning of Gus and Max Rogers, although a number of reviewers singled out young Nora Bayes for special praise. She and a chorus dressed as watermelons sang and danced "Watermelon Party." Pat Rooney's "grotesque dances" also came in for some notice, as did Gus A. Weinberg's imitation of De Wolf Hopper. This edition was certainly not all the brothers hoped it would be. They played a relatively short 49-performance stand before taking to the road, from where they could watch Weber and Fields, who followed into New York hot on their heels, chalk up a rousing 225 performances.

Hoity-Toity, which opened September 5, had a plot to tie together its olio portion. De Wolf Hopper arrives in Monte Carlo with six marriageable daughters, while Weber, Fields, and Sam Bernard (replacing David Warfield) played three East Side delicatessen owners who had cornered the sauerkraut market and come to the Riviera to gamble their winnings. Their encounters with the Hopper clan provided the continuity. Out of this vaudeville came one of Weber and Fields' most famous sketches, their routine on how to start a bank. As Herman Kaffekuchen and Frederich Schnitzel respectively, Fields and Bernard get Weber, in the role of Philip Sauerbraten, to put up money to open the bank. They assure him there will be no difficulties. At worst a bank inspector "comes around occasionally and overlooks the books." The jargon of high finance is explained. For example, "A joint note is a note signed by three or more people who all become unreliable for the full amount." When Sauerbraten sets himself up behind a teller's barred window, Kaffekuchen warns him if he is not careful

he might spend a good many years behind bars. Kaffekuchen and Schnitzel each make a "posit" of five dollars, then each writes a check for $200. Sauerbraten pays out but then complains they are overdrawn. Each writes a second for far more, demanding the difference in cash. Before long the bank's reserves are exhausted and a run ensues. But Kaffekuchen and Schnitzel run even faster. On opening night the skit ran five minutes. By the end of the season, the boys were milking it for nearly half an hour. "The Pullman Porter's Ball" was also heard in the first act. Once again Lillian Russell, Fay Templeton, and Bessie Clayton headed the bevy of beauties. The eagerly awaited second-act burlesques this season turned inside out *The Man from Mars, The Girl and the Judge* (as *The Curl and the Judge*), and *Madame Du Barry* (as *Madame Du Hurry*). What virtually no one knew was that Weber's displeasure with his part in *The Man from Mars* travesty prompted him to stop speaking to Fields. While for over a year the team carefully concealed the fact, the rupture proved irreparable.

The day the reviews for *Hoity-Toity* appeared, the national telegraphs clicked away with more pressing, shocking news. President William McKinley had been shot by an anarchist at the Pan-American Exposition in Buffalo, New York. The President hovered between life and death for a week, but he succumbed on the 14th, and Theodore Roosevelt succeeded to the presidency. Two importations raised their curtains on the 16th. In fact, one set of curtains was the fabled golden drapery at the Metropolitan Opera House, where Alfred E. Aarons presented Ivan Caryll's **The Ladies Paradise** for 24 performances. The plot led a young lord and an opera singer to the altar despite objections from the groom's parents. Queenie Vassar and Templar Saxe were supported by an stellar cast that included John Hyams, Josephine Hall, Richard Carle, and Dave Lewis. Aarons apparently exhausted his limited funds in hiring his cast, for several critics professed to recognize the scenery as bought or borrowed from older shows. More Caryll music, written in conjunction with Lionel Monckton, graced **The Messenger Boy,** which began a 128-performance stay the same evening at Daly's. James T. Powers starred as a courier assigned to deliver a message from London to Cairo. Fearing interference, he adopts a number of comic disguises which prevent the senders from finding him when they have to stop delivery.

Harry B. Smith approached Klaw and Erlanger, asking to be a coproducer of the next show he did for them. When they accepted, he set to work on

The Liberty Belles (9-30-01, Madison Square). In his autobiography he tells what followed:

> With a crafty economy which I had never considered before I evolved a piece for which the costumes in the first act should cost nothing and those in the second very little. The scene of the first act was to be the dormitory of a girls' school, the pupils getting together for a supper party after the authorities had retired for the night. The girls were to wear nightgowns, pajamas and negligees, and the economical theory was that each would prefer to buy her own in order to look as pretty as nature would allow. The scene of the second act was to be a cooking school and the girls were to wear dainty but inexpensive frocks. The only outlay for costuming was to be for summer gowns in the last act.
>
> I wrote the piece, lyrics and all, in three weeks. This important fact was afterward paragraphed and one friendly reviewer in Chicago said that he thought it quite remarkable till he saw the play and then he wondered what I had been doing all that time.

The cast included Lotta Faust, Harry Davenport, John Slavin, Harry Gilfoil, and twenty-one ladies —"as pretty girls as can be found on the stage"— called in the program "Klaw and Erlanger's Troubadours." A number of composers contributed music —John Bratton, Clifton Crawford, Aimee Lachaume, Harry Von Tilzer, and A. Baldwin Sloane. But the slapdash piece pleased enough tired businessmen and their wives to run three months.

Another Ludwig Englander score was heard when **The New Yorkers** (10-7-01, Herald Square) bowed, but this time his collaborators were Glen MacDonough on the book and George V. Hobart for the lyrics. In MacDonough's adventure Upson Downes (Dan Daly) is an out-of-work New Yorker scrounging his way around Paris. When Downes hears rich De Long Green (George A. Schiller) announce plans to marry his daughter Olive Green (Virginia Earle) to a baron, Downes puts on an appropriate disguise and courts the girl. In the end a real baron appears to win Olive. Will Marion Cook contributed the expected coon song.

An inanity called **Sweet Marie** (10-10-01, Victoria) came and left quickly. The story centered on Marie and Adele Malonie (James and John Russell), sisters who run a bird store in France. They are engaged to two ne'er-do-wells, the meek Edward Gumpshion (Louis Montgomery) and the tricky François Sceemere (Albert La Mar). When the boys learn the girls are to receive fortunes they rush

the weddings. In the middle of the dual ceremony a man comes and reads their uncle's will. The document states that only the second sister to marry will be heir to his fortune. The first to marry will receive nothing. The contretemps that follows lets the girls see their suitors for the money-grabbers they really are. The *Times* felt the Russell Brothers, celebrated as female impersonators on the less critical two-a-day circuits, "were conspicuous by the rudeness of their methods and their cheerful innocence of the meaning of humor." Although one "W. Brown" was credited with the book and a certain "R. Jackson" with the music, the *Dramatic Mirror* reported the actual author was probably the show's producer, Oscar Hammerstein.

October's final premiere was **The Little Duchess** (10-14-01, Casino), which Florenz Ziegfeld mounted for his wife, Anna Held. The apparently tireless Harry B. Smith took his book from the vaudeville-operetta *Niniche*. When the work was first performed in Paris nearly a quarter of a century earlier, the great French star Anna Judic created a sensation by appearing in a bathing suit. Miss Held also wore a bathing suit, but created no stir with it. She also "rolled her eyes and posed . . . in front of a divan for minutes at a time while the limelight man threw his brightest rays on her scintillating jewels." Girls in rosebud dresses adorned a pink boudoir and, in a double sextette that may have approached Judic's bit for titillation, removed their stockings. The story told how an actress masquerades as a duchess to avoid creditors. So slim a story seems unlikely to hamper an evening's fun, but when the show played a return engagement at the Grand Opera House a year later, the program included the astounding statement, "Owing to the length of the performance the plot has been eliminated." In a day when musicals often meandered their leisurely way until 11:30 or midnight, such drastic pruning would seem an irresponsible slap at the piece's integrity. But indifference to a story line was commonplace even when most shows went into rehearsal with a clear tale to tell. All through the season the *Times* had reflected on the hapless plight of the libretto:

> There is a dark and mysterious plot in the play, so dark and mysterious that no one discovers it, and no one tries. (*Hoity-Toity*)
>
> Its plot is woefully thin. (*The Liberty Belles*)
>
> . . . the three detectives who wandered aimlessly through the two acts could not have located that little bit of plot. (*The New Yorkers*)

There was not much to cheer in Reginald De

Koven's score, so Ziegfeld rushed in a number of interpolations which were only better by degree. Ziegfeld gave special care to every aspect of his mounting. When one scene called for his chorus girls to do a bit of fencing, he gave them all fencing lessons to assure a supple grace in their movements. Miss Held's allure and Ziegfeld's fine production kept the show going for over four months, breaking Lillian Russell's old house records in the process. It then embarked on an extended tour.

November's sole arrival was the London pantomime, **The Sleeping Beauty and the Beast** (11-4-01, Broadway), which John J. McNally and J. Cheever Goodwin refitted for American tastes. It tapped the huge children's market so successfully it ran out the season.

On December 23 **The Supper Club** began a 40-performance stay at the Winter Garden on the roof of the New York Theatre. Another of Sydney Rosenfeld's slapped-together confections, it offered the slim plot of an upstart millionaire taking his friends on a tour of New York. Few patrons remained for the whole tour. The roof supposedly seated 2,000 customers, yet only two small elevators were available to move playgoers up and down. As a result there was constant traffic during the performance, while those willing to wait out the finale found they had to linger as long as an hour before they could get down to the street.

Ivan Caryll and Lionel Monckton found themselves with another hit when 1902's first show, **The Toreador** (1-6-02, Knickerbocker), began a five-month run. Francis Wilson starred in a cast that featured Christie MacDonald, Adele Ritchie, Queenie Vassar, Maud Lambert, Melville Ellis, and Joseph Coyne. The story told how a discharged servant is driven by circumstances to challenge the bulls. He also finds himself embroiled in a mad anarchist's bomb schemes. In London the show was the last to play the beloved, original Gaiety. Broadway was no respecter of even established London hits, and an American coon song was worked into this English piece set in Spain.

But Broadway did respect Julian Edwards and warmly welcomed his musicalized version of the Dolly Varden story from Dicken's *Barnaby Rudge* —a musicalized version that also incorporated motifs and and names from *The Country Girl*, Garrick's rewriting of Wycherley's *The Country Wife*. When her guardian, John Fairfax (Albert Parr), would prevent Dolly (Lulu Glaser) from marrying Capt. Belleville (Van Rensselaer Wheeler) and keep her for himself, Dolly furtively alters a letter of renunciation Fairfax has made her write and

contrives to have Fairfax himself deliver the letter. There was praise all around—for Stanislaus Stange's handling of the libretto and Miss Glaser's "buoyant" characterization and "rippling laughter" in the title role. One lone sour note was the "execrable taste" displayed by the scene painter who colored a ballroom with garish purple columns and "very ugly" blue walls. But the public was happy to overlook such minor lapses for **Dolly Varden** (1-27-02, Herald Square) had a satisfactory run of 154 performances.

There was less satisfaction when Harry B. Smith and Reginald De Koven, undeterred by the failure of earlier sequels, revisited the forest of Arden, hoping **Maid Marian** (1-27-02, Garden) would prove as rewarding as *Robin Hood* (9-22-91). The piece had been commissioned, not without a certain desperation, by the Bostonians, whose best days had clearly passed and who soon would disappear forever from the American stage. Old ties and the presence of old favorites such as Henry Clay Barnabee and W. M. MacDonald were sufficient drawing cards to allow a 64-performance run. Smith's plot recounted the troubles that develop after Richard the Lion-Hearted sends Robin Hood (Frank Rushworth) to the Crusades. Left alone, Marion (Grace Van Studdiford) is again assailed by the Sheriff of Nottingham (Barnabee) in the interests of Guy of Gisbourne (Will Fitzgerald). Robin Hood's friends led by Little John (MacDonald) take Marion to join her lover. She is captured by Saracens. When Robin Hood comes to her rescue he and his band are betrayed into the Saracens' hands by the Sheriff, who has continued to pursue her. Marion and Robin Hood escape, return to England, and mete out justice to the Sheriff and his cohorts. Writing in 1902 in his *Standard Light Operas*, George P. Upton suggested the music for *Maid Marian* was of a higher order than that for *Robin Hood*, concluding it "occasionally approaches grand opera in its breadth and earnestness." Upton especially praises two second-act numbers: Alan-a-Dale's graceful "Tell Me Again, Sweetheart" and Marian and Robin's waltz, "True Love Is Not For A Day." Although none of De Koven's melodies have remained in the public's ken, the press noted that on opening night "ever solo [was] encored." The reviewer for the *Dramatic Mirror* called the piece "the best work turned out by the librettist and composer since *Robin Hood*" and then turned his attention to a summary of the season to date. He hailed *Dolly Varden* as "the truest comic opera we have had the honor to see in many years" and called Weber and Fields' entertainments "the best burlesques that the world have ever seen." The public does not seem to have shared the critic's sentiments. It took a middle ground, rejecting such extravagant praise on the one hand while on the other hand passing over other papers' reservations.

The night *Maid Marian* opened, an old-fashioned farce-comedy **The Head Waiters** flitted briefly across the stage of the Grand.

Sydney Rosenfeld, George V. Hobart, and A. Baldwin Sloane hit a small jackpot with **The Hall of Fame** (2-3-02, New York). When the Goddess Fame (Amelia Summerville) informs a fame-starved actor (Louis Harrison) there is no real glory until after death, the furious performer decides to play a trick. He announces he will go over Niagara Falls in a barrel. The barrel is found empty, and he is taken for dead. He immediately gains the fame that had eluded him, but when he reappears to have the last laugh he is grabbed and hauled away by Lady Oblivion (Marie Dressler). The musical's theatrical milieu prompted a rash of imitations. Dan McAvoy mimicked Dave Warfield, Frank Doane aped John Drew, and Annie Lewis gave her impression of Mrs. Fiske. Lady Oblivion sang of one man's moment of glory, describing what happens "When Charlie Plays The Slide Trombone." The show's hit tune, "My Pajama Beauty," suggests there was some sort of vogue for pajama-clad girls on the season's stages.

R. A. Barnet and H. L. Heartz had only moderate luck this time around with **Miss Simplicity** (2-10-02, Casino), a vehicle for a happy-go-lucky clown, Frank Daniels. Daniels cavorted as a trolley car conductor, My Man Blossoms, abruptly elevated to a king's valet, and then made king for a day. Daniels raced about in a "gas-buggy" which finally exploded noisily, and he earned his encores singing "The Chesnutty Language Of Lovers." But despite the roughhouse comedy on the brightly lit, gaudily colored stage, the supporting material was not up to snuff, forcing Daniels and his company to hit the road after 56 showings. Interestingly, when Barnet and Heartz first mounted *Miss Simplicity* in Boston a year before no character called Blossoms was in the cast, and the story centered on a royal romance.

Primrose and Dockstader's Minstrels competed for first-nighters with *Miss Simplicity*. Obviously aware of how provincial they had become, the entertainers let it be known that there would be no semicircle, no bones or tambourine, and no plantation set. Instead, these modern minstrels used a Mediterranean setting as background! Critics suggested the odd scenery only underscored how American the material was. This material included Dockstader monologues; twin midgets, Johnny and Willy Foley, in an old-fashioned double clog; and the Jackson Family, a troupe of dancing women.

Foxy Grandpa (2-17-02, 14th St.) fared better. R. Melville Baker dramatized stories from the *Herald*, and Joseph Hart set the book to music. Hart also starred. The book was cracker-barrel hokum in which a Signor Bolero (Eugene Redding), "a facial artist who makes a living by looking like other people," is persuaded to substitute for Grandpa after the old man has fallen for the snares of the blackmailing Signorina Colonna (Beatrice Lieb). Grandpa outfoxed everyone for four months. For example when some mischievous boys fill his hat with water they discover Grandpa has built a flap into the top of the hat, so the water drains out before he puts it on. Asked to test a trick "lung-testing machine," he first inhales air from a bicycle pump, then blows it into the machine with such force the contraption explodes. But perhaps the foxiest person was Hart. Reaction to his composing was so cool he never again wrote for Broadway.

A. Baldwin Sloane composed at least some of the music for a short "musical comedietta," **The Belle of Broadway** (3-17-02, Winter Garden). Thomas Q. Seabrooke played Hannibal Jerome, a quack inventor who persuades Mrs. George Washington Honeywell and her guests at Manhattan Beach to buy stock in his company.

Another disappointment was the second Barnet-Heartz offering of the season, **The Show Girl** (5-5-02, Wallack's). The show was beset with problems from the beginning. E. W. Corliss was called in to write additional tunes and did produce the evening's most popular piece, "Psyche." D. K. Stevens provided more lyrics. Even after the opening, there were more than the usual cast changes, and everyone associated with the show was undoubtedly relieved when it closed early in July. The show had originally been produced as *The Cap of Fortune* in Boston by the Cadets, apparently without difficulties. Ironically, it told of a troubled theatrical troupe. Stranded in Greece, the company's manager, Dionysius Lye (Frank Lalor), finds a magic cap and brings Psyche (Paula Edwards) back to earth. She helps the troupe out of its troubles. She also aids Cecilia Gay (Marion Parker), the Show Girl, in her rocky romance. Yet for all its faults, critics found things to like in this E. E. Rice production. Many agreed with Rice that his new discovery, Lalor, was "a natural-born comedian." They also praised Miss Edwards' "wax-doll beauty" and Amorita's toe dancing. Even a military band on stage to accompany the expected drills elicited approval.

Trouble of another sort blossomed when **The Wild Rose** opened at the Knickerbocker, the same night as *The Show Girl*. The musical was by some of the same tightly knit coterie of hacks who dominated the lyric stage of the day. Harry B. Smith did the book and many of the lyrics, with George V. Hobart assisting on the rhymes. Smith's wife, Irene Bentley, appeared as the belle of a gypsy camp, rescued from an unwanted marriage by a comic hypnotist, Paracelsus Noodles (Eddie Foy). They flee to a rathskeller where German and French troops hang out together. Ludwig Englander tossed off his third score of the season, a score filled with " 'coon' rhythms [interpolations] alternating with the lilt of the Viennese waltz." Over the authors' objections and their threats of a suit, George Lederer allowed Marie Cahill, as an "aeronaut's lady friend," to interpolate "Nancy Brown," a song by the young actor-writer Clifton Crawford, who was then appearing in *Foxy Grandpa*. The *Evening Telegram* recorded, "Miss Cahill made the hit of the evening with her 'Nancy Brown' song," and the *Herald* counted six encores. Since so many other outside tunes were incorporated into the show, it is hard to determine why there was so much fuss over this one song in particular. If the whole thing was not a publicity stunt, then Smith and Englander were among the very first artists to tackle the problem head on. Until this time only Victor Herbert, Julian Edwards, Reginald De Koven, and, apparently, John Philip Sousa had been forceful or prestigious enough to demand contracts that barred other men's songs from being inserted into their shows. But this vanguard of artistic and stylistic integrity had a long up-hill fight ahead. Miss Cahill won this battle hands down, and for the rest of her career she insisted on interpolating at will. But her later foes proved more determined and she retreated from some of her battles badly scarred. No fuss was made about the show's other hit, "The Little Gypsy Maid," an interpolation which Smith's wife sang. The song had music by Will Marion Cook and lyrics by Smith and Cecil Mack—not, as is often believed, by Paul Laurence Dunbar. For all the controversy and all its faults, the show proved entertaining enough to span the summer.

The success of *The Burgomaster* had sent managers fighting for the rights to do **King Dodo** (5-12-02, Daly's), the Frank Pixley-Gustav Luders work they all had rejected earlier. By the time it reached New York, it had been delighting audiences in Chicago and parts west for a year. The story was just the captivating nonsense the rather appropriately named Pixley excelled at. King Dodo of Spoojuland discovers an elixir which allows him to turn the clock back thirty years. But he is forced to revert to his real age when his queen insists that she prefers him as he was. Even makeup which made the older Dodo resemble a duck would not discourage her. The king's ward and a soldier supply the love interest. Luders furnished another sweet, simple score, although an ominous warning of repetitions to come could be seen in the "Tale Of The Bumble Bee," a close parallel to the preceding year's "Tale Of The Kangaroo." New Yorkers could still not find it in their hearts to give a wholehearted welcome to a midwestern creation, but the 64-performance run was not bad in light of the hot weather. With his performance as Dodo, the genial Raymond Hitchcock secured his position as a leading musical comedy man.

. . .

Raymond Hitchcock was born in Auburn, N. Y., on October 22, 1865. He came to the theatre at the comparatively late age of twenty-five, having tried his hand unhappily at a number of other trades, spending several years as a shoe clerk. The sharp-featured, lanky, raspy-voiced comedian quickly called attention to himself in *The Brigands* and *The Golden Wedding*. These appearances landed him a juicy role in the original American production of *Charley's Aunt*. Larger roles in New York and Philadelphia musicals followed.

. . .

However never-never-landish were the plots of so many of the era's musicals, they often inserted much topical material. Hitchcock was badly beaten up in Providence, supposedly by hirelings of the meat trust, for injecting the following lyrics:

Another King has risen up
  To contest the rights of Dodo.
The Beef Trust's now to the front, you'll note,
  Much scornful of King Dodo.
But its life will be a brief one,
Our King's not to be by beef done;
The finish will be Swift,
Unless Dodo's lost the gift
Of breaking through such Armour as the beef one.

Pixley-Luder shows, like earlier David Henderson extravaganzas, were conceived and mounted for Chicago. In the following season New York would applaud a show that had been entertaining Chicagoans at the Studebaker Theatre since March 11, *The Sultan of Sulu.* These New York runs were essentially happy afterthoughts, an extra reward for special merit. They were not the only musicals produced for Chicago, but the less successful had never ventured far from the Midwest. Probably the first really successful Chicago musical not to brave the Rialto was **The Storks,** which opened at the Dearborn Theatre on May 18. Like most Chicago musicals up to its time it was brought in as a summer attraction to keep an otherwise dark house both lit and profitable. It more than achieved its purpose, running handsomely for seventeen weeks—a substantial run in 1902 even in New York. The piece had a score by Frederick Chapin and a book by Guy F. Steely and Richard Carle. Carle was also the star.

. . .

Richard Carle, born Charles Nicholas Carleton in Somerville, Massachusetts, on July 7, 1871, spent his early years in local amateur theatricals. His New York debut was at the Bijou on September 20, 1891, in *Niobe.* He rose quickly, playing important roles in *A Round of Pleasure* and *A Greek Slave.* At the same time his name began appearing in author credits on shows such as *Mam'selle Awkins.* Shortly before *The Storks* premiered he had delighted Chicago audiences in a less successful musical, *The Explorers,* impersonating Bonaparte Hunter in his encounters with a lady lion-tamer.

. . .

Carle's story for *The Storks* recounted how the magician Malzadoc turns King Bungloo into a stork to avenge an unjust imprisonment. Bungloo cannot remember the magic word necessary to turn him back into human form. Lady Violet is transformed into an owl when she attempts to tell Bungloo the word. The word (Mutabor) is accidentally dropped in time for a happy ending in which everyone is properly mated and Malzadoc renounces sorcery. Carle's reception in *The Storks* prompted him to make Chicago his base of operations as long as a separate Chicago musical theatre flourished. Indeed, the success of *The Storks* may have played a small part in inaugurating the great era of Chicago musicals, an era that coincided with a renaissance of the American Musical Theatre in New York and that for a brief moment gave promise of outlasting it.

While the season was fast drawing to a close, its biggest musical hit had yet to open. It arrived by boat from London (where it had become the first show to surpass 1000 performances) and settled into a full year's run. George Dance's story fol-

lowed Simon Pineapple and his bride on their unorthodox wedding trip in **A Chinese Honeymoon** (6-2-02, Casino). When Simon gives a kiss to a young lady in China, he learns he must marry her, too. Since American producers who could leave well enough alone were nonexistent, several interpolations by William Jerome and Jean Schwartz were inserted. One of these, "Mr. Dooley," became as well liked as anything from the original Howard Talbot score. A superb cast included Thomas Q. Seabrooke, Amelia Stone, Edwin Stevens, Adele Ritchie, William Pruette, and Van Rensselaer Wheeler. Perhaps the most important feature about this production was the legend carried over its title in the playbills, for the show was the first musical presented by a name just being heard on Broadway, Sam S. Shubert.

The score for the season's final lyric piece, **The Chaperons** (6-5-02, New York), was by the music publisher, Isidore Witmark. The plot Witmark set his music to was typical turn-of-the-century fluff, perhaps recalling a bit *The Prima Donna* (4-17-01) from the preceding year, or an even earlier effort, *The Casino Girl* (3-9-00). Adam Hogg (Harry Conor) is a Cincinnati pork curer. He is also the head of the society to suppress vice. Hearing horrible tales of decadence in Paris, he hurries there to see for himself. He falls in with an opera troupe, a sultan, and a rich American contractor. They all head to Cairo for further explorations. Witmark's tribulations, poignantly recorded in his autobiography, *From Ragtime to Swing,* discouraged him from ever trying his hand on Broadway again. His reluctance is surprising since his score was well received and the show's hit, "My Sambo," made a star of Eva Tanguay. Moreover, if his memory is correct, at least one company of the show remained on the road for five seasons, even though the New York run was a meager 49 performances. But Klaw and Erlanger's grip on the best houses was such they not only could demand revisions, but, before they would book a piece, also demand a royalty for suggesting the revisions. Witmark complied, stopping short only when they attempted to add songs by other composers. When George Lederer, who had been brought in at the Syndicate's instance, added a tune while Witmark was on business elsewhere, Witmark took them to court, even though his legal expenses set him $3,000 out of pocket. Witmark was famous for harboring grievances. He never again spoke to Lederer, and writing of the incident at nearly forty years' remove still branded the pioneer producer "a henchman of the magnates."

4

ACT TWO
The Emergence
of American Talent
1902-1907

The enthusiastic reactions of the *Dramatic Mirror* to the lyric stage during the preceding season were by no means universally shared. If anything they were a minority viewpoint. The *Times* was, perhaps, more representative of the prevailing consensus. But by September 7, 1902, the paper's reserve had itself slid into an extreme pessimism. An article headed "Musical Comedies' Vogue Said To Be on the Wane" recorded "the general opinion was that in the not far distant future the musical comedy and its kin will be found among the 'have beens' so far as concerns New York. Nearly all agree that the cycle is dead." As if to challenge so dire a judgment the American Musical Theatre in 1902–03 burst brightly into a brief, tentative era of hope and achievement. The reasons for this happy, if short-lived, renaissance are not thoroughly apparent, even in retrospect. Undoubtedly President Theodore Roosevelt's forceful optimism provided some sort of indirect stimulus. America's economic picture was rosy—deceptively so, as the summer of 1903 would prove. And the simple coincidence of several brilliant young talents reaching maturity simultaneously played no small part.

Actually the changes wrought were not revolutionary. The improvements manifest were more of degree than of kind, often more hope than achievement. Here would be a small attempt at greater integrity; there a more daring breakthrough—blacks in a black-created show at a principal white house. At least two composers—George M. Cohan and Victor Herbert—showered Broadway with magnificent melodies and in so doing gave Irish writers their last glorious reign in the musical theatre. Comic opera remained arioso, sentimental, and, thanks usually to a dialect comedian, comic. Musical comedy remained boisterous, loose-jointed, and filled with specialties that generally had little or nothing to do with the matter at hand. Scenery was rarely, albeit increasingly, conceived architecturally. Painted flats predominated, and "well painted" was frequently the highest encomium awarded set designers' work. The painting was often garish and just as often clashed with equally gaudy costumes. Not scenery but casts of 60 to 100 or more filled musical stages. Marches and clogs dominated the "choreography." But here one major change did occur. If the *Enciclopedia dello Spettacolo* is correct, sometime in 1903 Ned Wayburn, tiring of heavy-footed clog dances, put small metal plates on the bottom of dancers' shoes for a lighter, steelier sound accomplished with slighter, more graceful movement. Tap-dancing was born.

1902-1903

The season opened with **The Defender** (7-3-02, Herald Square), a musical comedy detailing the machinations of a British betting syndicate, headed by the villainous soap magnate, Ivory D. Queers (Alexander Clark), to influence the outcome of the race between Sir Thomas Ceylon Teaton's yacht, *Hibernia,* and the American yacht, *Constitution.* But Jellie Canvas (Paula Edwards) and the detective Pinky Winkerton (Charles Wayne) foil the scheme. At one point the villain captures Jellie and ties her to railroad tracks, knowing an express train is on the way. The approach of the train and Jellie's rescue were depicted in a Biograph film interlude. The dialogue was turgid, even for the time ("Don't attempt to bribe me with your filthy lucre"), the jokes were labored ("Have you ever used Queers' soap?"), and the regular score insipid. Harry Davenport was Teaton, and Emma Carus also had an important role. What success the show enjoyed was due largely to one interpolation, "In The Good Old Summer Time" (Ren Shields/George Evans). The song, which had already been heard on a few vaudeville stages, was introduced in the show by Blanche Ring. It catapulted her to fame. She was heard from again—and again, and again—during the season. In years to come, when she was not busy on the two-a-day circuits, she propped up many a faltering vehicle by reinterpolating this and other numbers she soon made her own. "Mister Dooley," used successfully in *A Chinese Honeymoon,* was also interpolated in *The Defender.*

July's only other entry was a revival of *The Mikado* (7-14-02, Madison Square Roof Garden), noteworthy because its producers felt compelled to add a plotless spectacle, *Japan at Night,* to the bill. Together the two pieces rolled up 70 performances.

Marie Cahill, who arrived in **Sally in Our Alley** (8-29-02, Broadway), was very much like Blanche Ring, although she devoted far more time than Miss Ring to the legitimate stage.

. . .

Marie Cahill was born in Brooklyn, but the exact date of her birth has apparently been lost. She was fifty-nine when she died in late 1933, so it seems safe to assume she was born in 1874 (although Stanley Green, a trustworthy scholar, gives the date as February 7, 1870). Brought up in a strict, religious home, she was nevertheless a sufficiently iron-willed youngster to prevail on her parents to let her study voice and ballet. Later she studied acting under Frederick Ward. She made her debut in Hoyt's *A Tin Soldier.* Her strong personality rarely bent to the role assigned; instead the character she was supposed to play assumed her attributes. This same forcefulness, coupled with firm moral convictions that she retained from her girlhood, caused her, while playing rambunctious young ladies, to reject the leering humor and suggestiveness so common to such roles. Her shows were generally praised as clean. If her personality caused any problems, it was in her constant battle with composers for outstanding tunes.

. . .

The ruckus over the interpolation of "Nancy Brown" in *The Wild Rose* (5-5-02) had convinced her of the usefulness of carefully selected interpolations and, as if to confirm the point, she scored the hit of the evening with "Under The Bamboo Tree" (Bob Cole). For the second time in four months she helped relegate an Englander score to a back seat. George V. Hobart's complex story reminded the *Times* of old Harrigan and Hart days with one significant modification, "the typical Bowery boy has become a yid of the Dave Warfield type, and the Bowery girl his daughter." In this case the Jew is Izzy (Dan McAvoy), proprietor of the Heterogeneous Emporium. Although Izzy called his daughter Sarah, her friends felt "Sally" was more modish. So good a girl is Sally that she pretends her neighbor's baby is her own when the neighbor seems to be in trouble; she even steals some papers to help acquit a man of forgery. McAvoy gave the lively Miss Cahill able assistance, not only with his dialect clowning, but with some grotesque dancing in which he burlesqued a flamboyant conductor of the day ("If Creatori and his sort delight us/what a leader would have been St. Vitus."). It took four hours on opening night to tell the story and sing the songs, although by the end of the two-month run a reasonable amount of excess had been pruned.

The Rogers Brothers at Harvard (9-1-02, Knickerbocker) offered another of this series' thin plotlines designed to hold together songs and vaudeville specialties. The plot had two old rakes as guardians for two young blades. With two French milliners and "two young women to whom virtue is too easy," they become "entangled in a double quadrille, in which the cry is always 'Change partners.'" Scenery, which followed the customary practice of one set for each act, portrayed upper New York City with a view of Grant's Tomb, the Eden Musée's entertainment hall and, finally bowing to the title, Harvard Yard. Maurice Levi's score included the latest in the Reuben series, "The Troubles Of The Reuben And The Maid"—with lyrics for this installment by the venerable J. Cheever Goodwin. But the music was flat and the jokes none too fresh. More than one critic suggested the Rogers Brothers proved how excellent Weber and Fields were.

Some of Sir Arthur Sullivan's last compositions were also heard September 1, when **The Emerald**

Isle was brought into the Herald Square by Sam S. Shubert. It was his second musical mounting. Although the story centered on the successful courtship by an Irish rebel of the daughter of Ireland's Lord Lieutenant, the star of the evening was Jefferson De Angelis in the role of a buffoonish professor. Neither the comedian nor the comic opera elicited much interest, and they quickly departed.

King Highball (9-6-02, New York) also had only a brief stay. Based on Rupert Hughes' *The Understudy*, it told another of the preposterous, never-never-land tales so beloved by the era. An astronomer who has been seeking to communicate with Mars finally attracts the attention of a young Martian lady. She succeeds in bringing him and his assistant to the planet, where they learn the law states if ever an Earthling arrives he shall be made king. Complications ensue when the assistant, who is an older man, claims he should become the ruler. They are both expelled and return to Earth. Frederick Bowers' score was as undistinguished as Charles Horwitz' dialogue. To impart a suitably unearthly aura chorus girls danced on a darkened stage lit only by tiny light bulbs twinkling on the girls' dresses. The most rewarding moments of the evening probably came when its star, Marie Dressler, displayed her rambunctious brand of clowning. She played none of the figures mentioned in the summary of the plot (which, incidently, required more than a full page of the program to outline its convoluted details); instead she walked off with comic honors as the king's "46th wife."

A revival of *Robin Hood* (9-28-91), with several of the original players (notably Henry Clay Barnabee, W. H. MacDonald) still singing their roles, came in on September 8 to begin a four-week stand at the Academy of Music.

Weber and Fields gave Broadway its first major hit of the season when they relit their Music Hall on September 11 with **Twirly-Whirly**. For the first time they called their evening a "musical comedy," thereby aligning themselves squarely with the forces of the future. A pall was cast over the opening by the realization that this was the last Stromberg score, for John Stromberg had committed suicide in July. But he had succeeded in composing an outstanding number for Lillian Russell—"Come Down, Ma Evenin' Star"—and, although she was too overcome by emotion on opening night to finish the song, it afterward remained identified with her. Other problems beset this star-crossed production. De Wolf Hopper and Sam Bernard had left for bigger salaries elsewhere and, most ominous of all, rumors were beginning to spread about the personal coolness between the stars, despite their efforts to keep it quiet. But on the brightly colored stage the treasured absurdities seemed as hilarious as ever. Tourists and natives in Seville can only talk about Mrs. Stockson Bond's purchase of the big, local castle, until Hanki Panki Poo (Will Archer), a monkey, distracts them with a seltzer siphon. (One successful interpolation in *The Defender* had been "Pinky Panky Poo.") The monkey's owner, McCracken, rues his lot in a number which in keeping with the Weber and Fields pattern was rather well integrated into the story, "Strike Out, McCracken." After a series of vaudeville repartees between McCracken and Winger, a vaudeville impresario, Mrs. Bond (Lillian Russell) arrives, announcing she is "The Leader Of Vanity Fair":

You must take up the fad I start
Whether it be racing or Delsarte
Though it seems hollow, still you must follow
The leader of the set called "smart."

Before she exits she advises her friends she will hold a gala that evening. She has asked all the resident nobility. Michael Schlaatz (Weber) and Meyer Ausgaaben (Fields) arrive in an airship. They are quickly invited to the party to replace some nobles who have determined to cut the American upstart. Meyer appears for the soiree pulling Mike in an automobile. Mrs. Bond is informed Hanki Panki Poo is drunk. She laments, "the life of a society star is not a path of roses. I envy the little stars up there. They can stay out every night and not lose their sparkle." And she beckons, "Come Down, Ma Evenin' Star." But Schlaatz and Ausgaaben are bored. To escape from the party and to have a little excitement at the same time they decide to to set off a bomb. Meyer prepares the explosive and gives it to Mike to detonate: "I tell you it is easy. Go right up and kick it and as soon as you hear the explosion, step to one side and let it go past." The blast sends the monkey and the furniture flying. A tattered pair of comedians run across the stage as the curtain falls. Typical of the outrageous stage business Weber and Fields employed so skillfully was the trick sailor suit worn by one of the performers while talking to the pair. When he faced Weber, the side of the suit was black, as were his wig and moustache, and he spoke in a gruff, deep voice. When he turned to face Fields, he had a white suit, blond hair and a high-pitched voice. Antics of this sort regaled audiences for 244 performances.

September's final offering was another of the numerous importations from London, Lionel

Monckton's **A Country Girl** (9-22-02, Daly's). It played four months and then toured. The respect American critics held for these English pieces can be seen by the amount of space the *Times'* reviewer gave to it, especially his detailed discussion of the plot. Plots in American shows were given short shrift at best. Perhaps in the case of *A Country Girl* the attention was merited, not so much for the quality of the work as for the way some of its characters hinted at the future. Its hero, a handsome young man called Geoffrey Challoner, was a naval officer. The leading comedian appeared in the guise of the Rajah of Bhong. Come December, New York would rejoice in some homemade nonsense from Chicago featuring an American naval officer and a Sultan.

On October 4 Chicago welcomed a new show and a new theatre. The show, *Chow Chow*, would come to New York at the end of the season with a change of title; the theatre, the New Orpheon, would, of course, remain in Chicago. But it, too, would undergo a change of name and become the most important lyric house in the heyday of the Chicago musical.

A less successful new musical and a less successful new theatre were unveiled in New York two weeks later when **Tommy Rot** opened the short-lived auditorium known as Mrs. Osborn's Playhouse on October 21. The musical was paired with a Joseph Herbert parody of *Iris* called *Cryris*. *Tommy Rot* had an all-too-simple plot. Eric Leicester loves Phoebe Dare, but a will keeps them apart until the curtain falls. With so little story to dwell on, those critics who did not rail at what they considered an unseemly title found plenty to complain about in the weak score and crude jokes that ran to the order of, "The boys at the club call one of the twins Inanimate and the other In-a-minute." Only Blanche Ring, playing a young lady with the inappropriate name of Innocence Demure, received general praise and with "The Belle Of Avenue A" added another song to her lifelong repertory. The show closed quickly, was revised and reopened on November 27 as *Fad and Folly*. But the reworking was insufficient, and the show soon folded for good.

Another English importation, Leslie Stuart's **The Silver Slipper** (10-27-02, Broadway), enjoyed a five-month run. A saucy young lady of Venus kicks her slipper out of Venus' orbit, so is banished to Earth. Intercourse between Venus and Earth apparently was more stageworthy than between Earth and Mars. Stuart's score was somewhat hand-me-down, clearly hoping to capitalize on his *Florodora* vogue with numbers like "Come Little Girl And Tell Me Truly." The gowns for this sextette were said to cost $3,000. Still, the biggest success of the evening was an American interpolation, "Tessie, You're The Only, Only, Only" (Will R. Anderson) —a song inexplicably adopted by the Boston National baseball team as its theme, although it had nothing to do with baseball or Boston.

The same October 27 saw Chauncey Olcott arrive at his customary harbor, the 14th Street Theatre, with still one more of his sentimental Irish melodramas, **Old Limerick Town.** Neil O'Brien loses his wealth, retrieves it, and finds love with a comely Irish lass. As usual, Olcott sang a handful of Irish-American melodies to please his roisterous and loyal brigades.

Apart from *Fad and Folly,* only a single musical appeared in November, **The Mocking Bird** (11-10-02, Bijou), with book and lyrics by Sydney Rosenfeld and music by A. Baldwin Sloane. When the king of France fails to advise the governor of his Louisiana Territory that the land has been ceded to Spain, the local citizenry rebel, led by the "gentlemanly" pirate, Jean La Farge (Frank Doane). To signal one another the rebels whistle "Listen To The Mocking Bird." In the end they make the king sit up and take notice, and Jean wins the hand of Yvette Millet (Mabelle Gilman), the French ward of a wealthy New Orleans man whose advances she has spurned. The critics were more taken with the evening than the public was. The dialogue was certainly adequate and Rosenfeld's lyrics were as good as were then being written—possibly a mite better. He could not always escape the inversions, imageries, and fustian rhetoric of the time, and he did produce phrases such as, "When gentle night in sable mantle dressed." But he could also draw some fetching, natural pictures:

> The bullfrogs huddle near the old bayou
> And they croak as in a dream;
> And the owls hoot grimly "To whit, to whoo!"
> In the fireflies' fitful gleam.
> And the frogs and the owls and the flies on wing
> Seem possess'd of a solemn fright;
> They are all of 'em asking the self-same thing—
> "What's the matter with the moon to-night?"

Sloane's score was as good as any he ever did. Restricted, almost pinched, in range and persistently uninspired, it was nonetheless not unpleasant. On the opening night the finale for the first act, "Glorious France," stirringly sung and marched to, won the most encores. There was much public to-do over Rosenfeld's supposed rediscovering the "long lost"

"Listen To The Mocking Bird." Whether the old minstrel tune had indeed been as completely forgotten as some of the advance notices suggested or whether it was simply the sort of clever publicity Rosenfeld was noted for is moot.

Three musicals arrived in New York in December. The first was a fascinating work, at once artistically important and artistically disappointing. **When Johnny Comes Marching Home** (12-16-02, New York) told a straightforward, if melodramatic, tale of the War between the States. It told it with a surprising compassion for both sides and with a minimum of the buffoonery so commonplace in the period's lyric efforts. Indeed, some critics complained of a lack of humor in the piece. Kate Pemberton (Zetti Kennedy), a southern belle, falls in love with a Union colonel, John Graham (William G. Stewart). But Kate's ardor for the Confederate cause is such that her young brother (a trouser role played by Julia Gifford) has little difficulty in persuading her to pilfer important papers from the pocket of General Allen, even though Allen's daughter (Maude Lambert) has been Kate's friend. Though Graham steps in and takes the papers, he is understanding. And in the end, when it is discovered that John is the long-lost son of Felix Graham (Albert McGuckin), on whose plantation much of the action unfolds, the youngsters are united. The excessive melodrama and far-fetched turns of Stanislaus Stange's plot vitiated some of the artistic pretensions of the work. Similarly, Julian Edwards' score was the best of his not overly distinguished career, containing some above average work. "My Own United States" was sung nightly by John to fervent applause.

Equally fervent applause greeted the stirring, military first-act finale—this one set at a Confederate Ball. Both Edwards and Stange were too much of their own time to rise above the conventions of the day. "My Honeysuckle Girl," "Sir Frog And Mistress Toad" and "Fairyland" were all bows to the era's theatrical conventions. And while no interpolations were permitted to spoil what integrity the musical possessed, the show's producer nonetheless felt compelled to advertise it as "a spectacular military opera" and an "American spectacular comic opera." Although it ran only 71 performances, *When Johnny Comes Marching Home* enjoyed revivals in later years.

Chicago's New Orpheon Theatre retained its original name for only a matter of weeks. Shortly after *Chow Chow* closed, the playhouse was rechristened the La Salle and under this name served as the flagship for the Chicago musical theatre. The renaming coincided with the opening of a new musical on December 21. **The Paraders** had book and lyrics by Raymond Peck and music by Joe Howard. Peck shortly disappeared from the lyric scene, but Howard stayed on to become the most prolific and best of the Chicago-based composers.

. . .

Joe Howard was born in 1867, the son of an Irish saloon keeper on New York's Lower East Side. Placed in an orphanage after his parents' death, he ran away to St. Louis. After a stint as a newsboy, he joined McNish, Johnson, and Slavin's Refined Minstrels, leaving this group to launch a vaudeville act in which he boxed with former heavyweight champion, Bob Fitzsimmons. Settling in Chicago, Howard embarked on a career as a songwriter to supplement his income as a performer. He quickly scored one big hit, "Hello, Ma Baby." Two of his songs, "The Queen Of The Track" and "Coffee," had been inserted into *Chow Chow*.

. . .

The Paraders recounted how an old cowboy, Major Ben Bluster, has a run-in with the spendthrift, foppish Baron von Blitzen. Wiener Schnitzel, a Buffalo lawyer, arrives to complicate matters, but a pretty American heiress, Melba Million, sets everything right. The Chicago *Tribune* dismissed the work as "an extended sketch," and *The Paraders* was withdrawn after a run of just over a month. But in one respect the *Tribune* admired the work and correctly predicted a future for similar musicals, if they were better written. The paper's critic suggested, "there is a place in Chicago for the more modest musical production provided it is thoroughly wholesome."

A conventional show, **The Billionaire** (12-29-02, Daly's), met with immediate success in New York, although it was quickly forgotten after its final curtain. The run-of-the-mill songs Gustave Kerker and Harry B. Smith ground out covered the requisite range—"pretty songs, coon songs, semi-classical, sentimental, and topical . . . ." Smith's plot focused on John Doe (Jerome Sykes), the richest man in the world. In Nice he meets a young American, Pansy Good (Nellie Follis), who is studying for the stage. He becomes so fond of her he builds her a theatre in New York. Later, back in France, Doe attempts to ride his own horse in a race. Since he is too fat, Pansy takes his place and wins. Smith's idea of humor, despite his years of professional success, was often no better than the amateurish material of, say, *Tommy Rot*. One character announced, "I will now sing a song written expressly for me, by an expressman," while a later bit of dialogue ran:

—You're so refined.
—I ought to be; my father used to own a refinery.

An even more successful musical opened at Wallack's on December 29, the same night as *The Billionaire*. A Chicago musical which began a long run there at the Studebaker on March 11, 1902, it was one of the rare Chicago triumphs that New Yorkers openly embraced, and for many it has remained the exemplar of its type—the interaction of American mores, generally represented by the American navy, and the strangely utopian ways of a far-off tropical isle. More often than not the isle was ruled over by an outlandish clown of a king, either a befuddled foreigner accidently placed there or a curiously freethinking native. Ki-Ram (Frank Moulan) fills the bill to a tee. He is **The Sultan of Sulu,** a dot of land somewhere in the Philippines. As the curtain and the sun rise his reluctant wives gather before his hut to sing an exotic reveille. Ki-Ram's major-domo, Hadji (Fred Frear), sees to it the wives, willing or not, behave correctly before their master:

Hadji: Daily catechism. Do you love your husband?
Selina [a wife]: What is the answer?
Hadji: The answer is "I adore him."

But for all Hadji's careful preparation, Ki-Ram's day will not be just another round of insouciant bliss. Lt. William Hardy (Templar Saxe) of the U.S. Navy appears to announce his country has bought the island and a navy contingent led by Colonel Budd (William C. Mandeville) will arrive momentarily to take over. Budd, admonishing his men, conveys the ambivalence of Yankee attitudes, "For the first time you are about to stand in the presence of royalty. Stiffen yourselves for the ordeal, and remember, no deference, for each of you is a sovereign in his own right." Ki-Ram is advised that changes will have to be made, for "the constitution follows the flag." But the Sultan sees no need for the slightest alteration. He enumerates the virtues of "The Smiling Isle" to the puzzled sailors:

We've not a single college
Where youth may get a knowledge
  Of chorus girls and cigarettes, of poker and
  the like;
No janitors to sass us

No bell-boys to harass us
  And we've never known the pleasure of a
  labor-union strike.

But the Americans are not impressed, especially their new judge advocate, Pamela Francis Jackson (Blanche Chapman). She is determined to put an end to the Sultan's bigamy. Ki-Ram, hoping to have things his way, woos her, insisting the world has become full of color and sweet fragrance "Since I First Met You." The stern Miss Jackson has all but melted and acquiesced when she realizes Ki-Ram simply means to add her to his harem. Her vengeance is as awful as it is swift. She decrees he must pay alimony to his wives: half his total income to each—or, as he quickly calculates, three times his total revenues. Ki-Ram begs for mercy, pleading his difficulties stem from the fact that more than the constitution follows the flag:

Ki-Ram: When the Colonel took me aside in there he said he was going to make me acquainted with one of the first blessings of civilization. He told me that the constitution and the cocktail follow the flag. Then he gave me an amber-colored beverage with a roguish little cherry nestling at the bottom. And, oh, little friend, when I felt that delicious liquid trickle down the corridors of my inmost being, all incandescent lights were turned on and all the birds began to sing.

But Miss Jackson's heart has hardened. Fortunately, word from Washington informs Colonel Budd that the Supreme Court has declared "the constitution follows the flag on Mondays, Wednesdays and Fridays only" and since the navy has imposed itself on an off day Ki-Ram is free to govern as he wishes. The New York *Times,* summarizing the plot, suggests Sulu and American values will prevail on alternate days. If the critic's summary is accurate, then deviation from the printed text had taken place. The show confirmed Frank Moulan as a star and enhanced the popularity of its librettist-lyricist, George Ade. But though Alfred G. Wathall's music was as good as anything on Broadway at that moment, Wathall never provided another score for the New York theatre.

1903's first musical did not arrive until January 19 when a melodized Dickens, **Mr. Pickwick,** with book by Charles Klein and music by his brother, Manuel, had a 32-performance stay at the Herald Square. Even the commanding presence of De Wolf Hopper, for whom Klein had written the book of *El Capitan,* could not save the day. Nor could a host of excellent supporting performances

—Digby Bell (Weller), Louise Gunning (Arabella), and Marguerite Clark (Polly).

While *Mr. Pickwick*'s opening was attracting attention on the main stem, the once important Star Theatre offered a week's run of **Zig-Zag Alley**, virtually the last of the once important farce-comedy genre. The piece dealt with the problems of mistaken identities that plague four eloping couples in Atlantic City. Its best number was "Under The Bamboo Tree," which New Yorkers had heard earlier in *Sally in Our Alley*.

The season's biggest hit, **The Wizard of Oz** (1-20-03, Majestic), was adapted for the stage by its creator, L. Frank Baum, with music by Paul Tietjens and A. Baldwin Sloane. Julian Mitchell staged the entertainment. Its story was not quite that of the original nor that made famous by the movie version thirty-odd years later. Long ago an Earthling arrived in Oz by balloon. He deposed King Pastoria (Gilbert Clayton) and sent him into exile back on Earth. A gigantic cyclone, which opens the show, whisks the old King back to his homeland. Caught up in the same storm are little Dorothy Gale (Anna Laughlin) of Kansas and her cow, Imogene (Edwin J. Stone). The King's girl friend, Trixie (Paula Edwards), has also been transported by the winds to Oz. With the help of his old ally, General Riskitt (Harold Morey), the King sets about reclaiming his throne. Meanwhile Dorothy, aided by a Witch and the former court poet, Dashemoff Dailey (Bessie Wynn), heads for a meeting with the Wizard, who alone can send her back to her Kansas farm. On the road they encounter a Scarecrow, looking for a brain, and a Tin Man, looking for a heart. (They also encounter a lion. But in this version his part is minuscule.) Together they continue on to the Wizard. Their path is not an easy one. At one point enchanted plants ensnare them, and only the Witch's magic breaks the spell. In the end Pastoria captures the Wizard (Bobby Gaylor). But the King, too, is reluctant to let any Earthling return, even Dorothy. Once again the Witch comes to her aid, threatening to brew a worse storm than before if the King prevents the little girl's leaving.

The dialogue and the music were banal. The most popular songs were two interpolations: "Sammy" (James O'Dea/Edw. Hutchinson) and "Hurrah For Baffins Bay" (Vincent Bryan/Theodore Morse). However, the spectacle and the story intrigued not just regular playgoers, but the children's market as well. Mitchell's opening cyclone rivaled David Belasco in its realism and beauty, exposing "twenty-seven heavens and nine hells of

scenery" by allowing one rapidly opening curtain after another to display the progress of the storm and the uprooting of Dorothy's house. Although advertisements for the show warned playgoers that if they were late and missed the opening cyclone they missed the most spectacular part of the evening, for many who saw the original production the most memorable moments of the evening were the carryings-on of Fred Stone and Dave Montgomery as the Scarecrow and the Tin Man. Coming after their initial success in *The Girl from up There*, it established them as stars. For the rest of their career they played similar roles in similar shows, taking what bygone times would have turned into pantomime and making it into a unique musical comedy genre. Time and again their offerings were to prove the major success of the season; and while they had a few imitators they had no rivals.

. . .

Dave Montgomery was born in St. Joseph, Missouri, on April 21, 1870. His early professional experience was in dramatic stock. Playing in Galveston in 1894 when Haverly's Minstrels came to town, he left his stock troupe to join the entourage, finding Stone in its company.

. . .

Fred Stone had been born in Denver, Colorado, on August 19, 1873, but spent most of his childhood in Topeka, Kansas. He and his brother joined a circus in 1886. During their stint they served as roustabouts, acrobats, and clowns. Fred left to enter the legitimate theatre, where his first role proved to be Topsy in *Uncle Tom's Cabin*. He soon transferred his allegiance to the minstrel stage. Shortly after Montgomery and Stone met, Haverly disbanded his company. The two young men tried out a new act at a New Orleans saloon and quickly moved up to Chicago vaudeville. From there their progress took them to New York and London before they attempted their first legitimate musical.

. . .

In his autobiography Stone devoted much space to describing the acrobatics he used in later shows. However, much of his discussion of *The Wizard of Oz* centered on his makeup, vividly recording the grotesqueries so typical of clowns of the day. "We had worked out a makeup which in every particular resembled the illustrations of the fairy tale. I used a thick flesh grease paint which obliterated all the lines of my face, eyebrows, eyelashes, and features, and applied heavy streaks of black to accentuate the straight mouth and nose. One eyebrow was drawn low and the other high, with black circles around the eyes, one large and one small."

A great solo clown, Eddie Foy, had almost as big a success the next night with a revision of David Henderson's old Chicago hit, *Mr. Bluebeard* (1-21-03, Knickerbocker). The revision went back to its English source to restore the part of Sister Anne for Foy. Foy had a field day with a recalcitrant bustle that seemed to have a mind of its own. The bustle persisted in wagging at embarrassing moments and often in directions exactly opposite from the way in which the rest of Foy was moving. The show's "pony" Ballet with music by Jean Schwartz heightened the vogue for the diminutive chorines. But Foy's luck ran out when the show moved to Chicago. For it was during a performance of *Mr. Bluebeard* on December 30, 1903, that the disastrous Iroquois Theatre fire took place.

Raymond Peck and Joe Howard had a musical ready on February 1 to replace *The Paraders* at Chicago's La Salle Theatre. In spite of a title suggesting an American Indian setting, **Tom-Tom** followed a group of Americans to Japan as they search for a legendary jewel. Curiously, the hit song was "Ragtime Chinaman." Howard himself and Al Shean were featured prominently. But the show was no more successful than its predecessor.

Blanche Ring returned to New York as **The Jewel of Asia** (2-16-03, Criterion). While hers was the title role, she was not yet listed above the show's name. The official star of the evening was James T. Powers as Pierre Lerouge, an artist who is forced to become a waiter and ultimately finds himself with a harem all his own. But Zaidee, the Jewel of Asia and the wife of the minister of police, Simon Pasha (George O'Donnell), straightens everything out. There was no real show-stopper for Miss Ring in the evening as there had been in her two earlier productions. The book and lyrics (by Frederic Ranken and Harry B. Smith) and the music (by Englander) were lackluster. What shine the evening had came from its performers, who kept it on the boards until another musical was ready for Miss Ring.

Marie Cahill, for the second time in the season, followed hard on Miss Ring's heels. Cashing in on her controversial interpolation in *The Wild Rose* (5-5-02), Miss Cahill reentered the arena as **Nancy Brown** (2-16-03, Bijou), a marriage broker who arrives in the financially distressed land of Bally Hoo in time to furnish needed rich heiresses. The libretto was tailored to Miss Cahill's measurements by Frederic Ranken, in collaboration this time with George Broadhurst, and the otherwise unknown

Henry Hadley provided a score. Since Miss Cahill was calling the shots, there were no difficulties about interpolations. She brought back "Under The Bamboo Tree" and had the dependable Cole and Johnson supply another number to add to her permanent repertory, "Congo Love Song." She kept encoring it for 104 performances.

On February 18, 1903, the New York Theatre was the scene of one of the most important events in American Musical Theatre history. **In Dahomey** opened. This was the first full-length musical written and played by blacks to be performed at a major Broadway house. There had been some misgivings in theatrical circles. The New York *Times* opened its review with the startling report, "A thundercloud has been gathering of late in the faces of the established Broadway managers. Since it was announced that Williams and Walker, with their all-negro musical comedy, 'In Dahomey,' were booked to appear at the New York Theatre, there have been times when trouble breeders foreboded a race war. But," the paper concluded with relief, "all went merrily last night." It was impossible for most reviewers to separate the show and its artists. However, when they did, by and large they reached the conclusion that the material was ordinary, even though the lyrics were by the distinguished black poet Paul Laurence Dunbar and the music by Will Marion Cook. Cook's numbers included a cakewalk in which the audience by its applause determined the winning pair of dancers. The *Times'* man felt "the whole was well up to the not very exalted average of this kind of show," while *Theatre Arts'* reviewer, who had a few more days to make an evaluation, employed almost identical words, "It is about on the same level with the average Broadway show." J. A. Shipp's libretto told how a group of unscrupulous Boston blacks form the Get-the-Coin Syndicate and broadcast their ambitions to colonize Africa with down-and-out American blacks. They send the hustling Rareback Pinkerton (George Walker) to Florida to bamboozle a senile old man out of his fortune. A good-natured simpleton, Shylock Homestead (Bert Williams), accompanies Rareback. But Rareback makes the amazing discovery that Shylock is worth far more money than the doting old fool he has been assigned to cheat. Rareback fast-talks the slow-witted Shylock into making him his trustee, and before long Rareback is strutting his way in the latest peacock clothes in the cream of Florida and Dahomey society. When the boys are made governors the natives break out in an orgy of wild African dancing. Inevitably, Rareback loses all sense of proportion and restraint, till even the tolerant Shylock rebels:

Rareback: Shylock, I really must have the ten thousand dollars.

Shylock: And I say "No."

Rareback: Do you mean to say that you refuse?

Shylock: No, I don't refuse. "No" and "refuse" is two diffunt words. They don't sound alike. You don't even spell 'em alike. I say "No." N-O-E. No!!

Critics agreed "the headliners were the whole show, Williams in particular . . . ." In fact *Theatre Arts* went so far as to pronounce Williams "a vastly funnier man than any white comedian now on the American stage."

. . .

Egbert Williams was born in Nassau, in the British West Indies, sometime between 1873 and 1876, but most likely on November 12, 1874. Coming to America as a young man, he soon found work as a banjo player in minstrel shows. Light-skinned, educated, and well spoken, Williams hoped to carve a niche for himself in the legitimate theatre. But the prejudices of the times precluded any such career for a black man. Williams was forced to darken his face with burnt cork and to assume the mannerisms and speech of the accepted stage "coon." While working on the West Coast he met George Walker, and the two created a vaudeville act that became popular on western circuits. With time the team moved east and began to appear in musical comedies written for the handful of theatres catering to blacks. *In Dahomey* had been created originally for these same houses.

. . .

Although Williams and Walker remained a popular and successful team, disparities bred of discrimination prevented their ever achieving the sustained runs that Montgomery and Stone enjoyed. The 53-performance run of *In Dahomey* can nonetheless be regarded as a triumphant breakthrough. A year later, when the show went to London, it was received with open arms and ran seven months.

Raymond Peck had a third musical ready for Chicago's La Salle Theatre on March 16, but this time he collaborated with a new composer, Robert Hood Bowers. Their **Rubes and Roses** related the complications that ensue when two "Dutch" comedians are sold a plot of land which straddles the Illinois-Indiana border. Al Shean and Dave Lewis were the principals. The show was soundly thrashed and closed quickly. *The Paraders* was rushed back in until another work could be readied.

One of the best loved turn-of-the-century musicals, **The Prince of Pilsen,** bowed a month later, on March 17 at the Broadway. In a sense there are three princes of Pilsen in the story. The first is Hans Wagner (John W. Ransome), a major Cincinnati brewer and alderman of the city's tenth ward. He goes to Nice with his daughter, Nellie (Lillian Coleman), to visit his son, Tom (Albert Parr), who is serving in the American navy—suddenly a necessary affiliation for many musical comedy leading men. For different reasons both Hans and Tom are mistaken for Prince Carl Otto, who has coincidently booked into the same hotel. The real Carl Otto (Arthur Donaldson) arrives and, quickly sizing up the situation, decides he can have more fun if no one recognizes him. Hans finds time to court a rich American widow, Mrs. Madison Crockers (Helen Bertram), and Tom falls in love with a college girl, Edith (Anna Lichter). Everything is pleasant until a secret map falls into the elder Wagner's hands, and he is accused of being a spy. At this point Carl Otto is forced to identify himself. But he also reveals he will marry Nellie, whom he has been courting in his disguise as a commoner. The show gave Frank Pixley and Gustav Luders their biggest hit. Two of Luders' top numbers, "The Heidelberg Stein Song" and "The Message Of The Violet," came from his fine score. Interestingly, the latter, the hit love tune, was sung not by the principal lovers but by the secondary leads, Tom and Edith. Luders supplied some novel orchestrations. Several of the choral numbers, notably the stein song, were sung without instrumental accompaniment, while, when the full orchestra was playing, the percussions ("kettle drums, bass drum, snare drum, and cymbals") were given "a full evening's work" to emphasize the melodies' rhythms. One or more companies remained on the road for five consecutive seasons, and several revivals followed. It was only when later, lustier operettas offered *The Prince of Pilsen* strong competition that its popularity faded.

Still another important piece opened down at the 14th Street on April 27, the month's lone musical. While George M. Cohan's first musical show had not been much of a success, the popular Four Cohans had been able to keep *The Governor's Son* alive and well for over two years. Now young George took a second of his vaudeville sketches and expanded it into a full evening's entertainment, **Running for Office.** The story was simple and, as a Cohan biographer has said, "perfectly symmetrical." John Tiger (Jerry Cohan) decides to marry, even though he is in the middle of a campaign for mayor of Tigerville. He has been a widower for fifteen years, and the new Mrs. Tiger (Nellie Cohan) is a widow of an appropriate age. John has a grown, single daughter, Madeline (Josie Cohan), and his wife an eligible bachelor son, Augustus (George M. Cohan). Unfortunately the newlyweds forget to tell their children of their plans. While Madeline and Gussie are attracted to each other, they are kept apart by their innocent misconstructions of their parents' actions. Everything is explained, and both pairs are united in time to celebrate John's victory at the polls.

Cohan filled the show with neat touches. Tiger's opponent wants desperately to lose since he has bet $1000 on John. Cohan's dialogue was racy and slangy—and this raised the hackles of a number of critics. It, too, bore some nicely humorous twists, as when John, who has run on a "Dry" ticket, says to a friend after the votes are in, "I've made a temperance town out of Tigerville. Let's go and get a drink." Cohan had not quite found himself musically, but the easy cadence of his best lyrics and the toe-tapping lilt of his better tunes were foretold in songs such as "If I Were Only Mister Morgan."

Curiously, even though Cohan's unique stylized dances became one of his trademarks, in *Running for Office* the airy dancing of Ethel Levey and the lively stepping of a chorus of "unusual sprightliness and good looks" were singled out for most praise.

The *Times* critic hinted at the excitement conveyed by the speed and brashness of Cohan's production ("Who are the four Cohans; where have they come from, why has it taken them so long to arrive?"), but Broadway was not bowled over. The show's 48 performances at the 14th Street Theatre were only 16 more than *The Governor's Son* had attained.

On the other hand, a claptrap affair called **The Runaways** came in from Chicago, with much fanfare and at a well-advertised cost of $75,000, to pique Broadway's fancy and chalk up 167 performances. According to the *World*, it was "a production that out Anna Helds David Belasco." (In time Chicago critics came to insist some local productions were better mounted than the best New York shows.) The *Times*, on the other hand, thought little of the physical production, allowing that the costumes were elaborate, but damning the scenery as "crude." *The Runaways'* story was a variant on *The Sultan of Sulu* theme. The dyspeptic General Hardtack (Alexander Clark) wins big by betting on a horse called The Runaway. With his winnings he transports the entire cast of 160 to the Island of Table d'hote, "that much overrun fictitious island of the South Pacific where musical comedy authors always rush pellmell for scenic effect." There he is promptly made king, only to discover that he must marry his predecessor's widow or die. The American navy, which seems to have spent much of its time behind the footlights, comes to the rescue. The cast contained a large array of specialists. For example, Walter Stanton, Jr., entertained dressed as a rooster. His clog dance caused his feathers and tail to bob animatedly. Arthur Dunn, a midget, brought a comic pickpocket act over from vaudeville. The score marked the inauspicious debut of Raymond Hubbell, a composer Broadway would hear much from and remember little of.

. . .

Raymond Hubbell was born June 1, 1897, in Urbana, Ohio, and moved as a young man to Chicago, first to study music and then to lead a dance orchestra. He took a job as staff composer with Charles K. Harris' organization. This show, which was known in the Windy City as *Chow Chow*, had opened the playhouse that soon became the La Salle Theatre.

. . .

That same La Salle Theatre played host to a new show the very night *The Runaways* opened in New York. **The Voyagers** may have consciously been chosen as a title that suggested *The Paraders*, but it represented the efforts of a single author who had not been connected with that earlier show. Frieda Pauline Cohen's story described the lengths to which a father would go to prevent what he deems an undesirable marriage for his daughter. He hires a ship for a world cruise. But his daughter's fiancé will go to equal lengths. He comes aboard in disguise. Love wins. The show had little appeal, and by late June a new show had replaced it.

On June 1 Oscar Hammerstein opened his Paradise Roof Garden for the hot weather crowds with an extravaganza for which he claimed authorship, **Punch, Judy, and Co.** Critics insisted there was no plot to speak of and no music to praise. An all-female cast employed no dialogue; everything was sung or danced. Some suggested Hammerstein would be best advised to remain an impresario. The *Herald* described the "Stork Ballet," which it considered the hit of the evening, as follows: "Four nursemaids wheel in empty baby carriages, and after doing some high kicks fall asleep. Miss Elsa Hartung in a really frightful costume (that she must have been paid a large salary for wearing) dances in on her toes driving four storks and places a baby in each carriage." Few musicals of the era could escape march numbers, so a pretty chorus of soldiers paraded and Hoosier Zouaves staged an army drill. Trained donkeys and a trick horse assisted. Even so, the show ran out the summer.

In New York, the season ended on June 8 as it began—with Blanche Ring (her fourth show of the year). This time she was assisted by Harry Conor of *A Trip to Chinatown* fame. The piece was called **The Blonde in Black** (6-8-03, Knickerbocker), although it was originally to have been known as *The Gibson Girl*. The title was changed after Charles Dana Gibson and *Life Magazine* threatened court action. The title really didn't matter. Gaston Roulette (Conor) uses his wife's Parisian dressmaking shop as home office for his matrimonial agency, the Domestic Fidelity Trust Co. He promises to forfeit his fee to any husband whose wife flirts within six months of marriage. Into the shop walks Flossie Featherly (Miss Ring), a vaudeville performer who has come to Paris in a black wig ostensibly to promote the cakewalk, but really to become a great actress and play Camille. Before she is aware of what has happened, Gaston has paired her with an artist named Van Dyck Beard (Charles H. Bowers). A number of Gaston's couples meet at Van Dyck's atelier, and it takes Flossie a whole act to unravel the misunderstandings. Unfortunately, there was nothing Flossie or Miss Ring could do about Gustave Kerker's third-rate music and for some reason no workable interpolation was found. Miss Ring did find a way to work in a spoof of *Camille,* and the chorus delighted audiences with a mock banjo serenade. No instruments were used. The boys and girls simply made sounds that mimicked strumming. The two sets allowed George Lederer to parade thirty show girls, first as dressmakers' models, then as artists' models. But these happier moments were not sufficient to save *The Blonde in Black*. Miss Ring doffed her wig for good after 30 performances. In the following season Eva Tanguay toured with the piece, under the title *The Sambo Girl*. Harry B. Smith and Gustave Kerker, who wrote the work in the first place, came up with a number of new songs for their new star.

In Chicago one more La Salle production closed the season. **Lunatics and Lovers** was so little thought of by its authors that they neglected to put their names on the credits. The story these anonymous scribes told portrayed the confusions that arise when three women, all named Nell, come to visit at a house situated next door to an insane asylum. It closed quickly, ending an undistinguished initial season for the small house.

1903-1904

The success and excitement of the preceding season prodded New York managers. As a result, the 1903–04 season saw a substantial jump in the number of musicals: thirty-two lyric attractions appeared. But critics and public alike detected a decline in quality, and only eight new pieces ran over 100 performances. Two events outside the Broadway arena contributed to the shorter runs. The panic of 1903, coming so soon after the nation had recovered from the 1893 crisis, deprived many theatregoers of dollars they might have passed across box office counters. The panic hit in the summer, and by August even President Roosevelt admitted it was particularly "ugly." Then in December the holocaust at Chicago's Iroquois Theatre, claiming hundreds of lives, frightened many still affluent playgoers into staying away from patently unsafe and overcrowded auditoriums. The crackdown on fire code violations that came in its wake closed a number of theatres. New York's most notable casualty was the cramped music hall in which Weber and Fields had so long regaled customers.

Because Abbey's Theatre recently had been renamed the Knickerbocker, some playgoers were quick to assume that the musical opening at the Herald Square on June 15 would be in the tradition of *A Gaiety Girl* and *The Casino Girl*. It was not. **The Knickerbocker Girl** used "Knickerbocker" in its older meaning—a resident of Manhattan. The show's libretto aspired to some novelty by taking its heroine, Mahitable Merton (Josephine Hall), to the as yet theatrically unexplored world of South America. There Mahitable helps catch the man who absconded with money from a mineral water company owned by her family. She also finds romance. The musical, with a book by George Totten Smith and music by Alfred E. Aarons, had been touring for some months. But Broadway's Brahmins felt even the weeks out of town had not whipped it into shape. *The Knickerbocker Girl* picked up her skirts and left after a mere two weeks.

A double bill of burlesques, **The Darling of the Gallery Gods** and **The Dress Parade** (6-22-03, Crystal Gardens), was the sole attraction to brave the height of the summer heat. A bit of everything was thrown in to make audiences forget the weather. Vaudeville turns included Pat Rooney's soft shoe dances, Da Kolta's magic act, and music by the Hebrew Orphans' Band. Ned Wayburn devised a miniature minstrel show for seventeen girls. Dialogue in "The Minstrel Misses" ran:

Miss Bones: Do you know how Anna Held feels?
Interlocutor: No. Tell us how she is feeling.
Miss Bones: Well, better than Zieg-felt.

The bill managed a mere 30 showings. A farce about a show girl, *Vivian's Papas*, offered a number of songs and specialties, but was, essentially, a straight play.

The season began in earnest when two English importations premiered. Edward German's **A Princess of Kensington** (8-31-03, Broadway) failed to win a large audience, although it boasted James T. Powers as the star of a tale that begins when a fairy steals a banker's clothes and embarks on a masquerade. Paul Rubens' **Three Little Maids** (9-1-03, Daly's), which followed, quickly found favor and profited from the first long run of the year— 130 performances. Broadway relished the adventures of three daughters of a curate as they take on London sophisticates.

The Rogers Brothers in London (9-7-03, Knickerbocker) arrived for an eight-week stay. Its plot revolved about a magic diamond which rewarded any owner with good luck but cast a curse on anyone holding it unlawfully. Their pursuit of the jewel took Gus and Max aboard an ocean liner (Act I), to Trafalgar Square (Act II), and finally to a Trenton, New Jersey, department store (Act III). The brothers resourcefully found excuses not merely for their "Dutch" routines, but for Negro and cockney bits as well. In most respects the production displayed the standard accouterments of the day, including dancing that was the "acme of gymnastics, but not of grace" and costumes "strikingly brilliant and variegated, but in no wise beautiful." A major change was the replacement of Maurice Levi by Max Hoffmann (this year assisted by M. Melville Ellis). Hoffmann's bloodless music was hardly distinguishable from Levi's, but like his predecessor he produced one or two moderately popular tunes for each edition. "By The Sycamore Tree" received as much play as any of his melodies for *The Rogers Brothers in London* and exemplifies his output.

A number of critics found kind things to say about George Ade's book for **Peggy from Paris** (9-10-03, Wallack's). The *Times* called it "fruitful in social satire," suggesting "the secret of its charm is the racy and unmistakably vernacular quality of the whole plot." But the reviewer regretted it was not "worked out with mature and intelligent craftsmanship." Ade's Peggy (Georgia Caine) was a young lady from Illinois (this was another Chicago show) who goes to Paris to train for a career in singing. After six years she returns as Fleureth Caramelle. She is exposed by her hayseed father (George Richards) at her Chicago debut. Flustered, she insists that her German maid (Josie Sadler) is Peggy. In the end, of course, she acknowledges her identity. Sadly, Ade once again collaborated with an inferior composer. In this case it was William Lorraine, who offered nothing better than "I Like You, Lil, For Fair." Critics praised Richards' "sincere and whimsical" interpretation of the father, adding it gave the whole evening a "grateful touch of human comedy." More typically, they also enjoyed Arthur Deagon (as a bouncer) who employed "grotesque mugging and contorted dancing." Perhaps even more typically, reviewers rued "garish and crude" sets and costumes. The show's run fell far short of *The Sultan of Sulu*'s (12-29-02).

Two nights after Peggy arrived in New York, her hometown welcomed a new musical at the La Salle. **The Isle of Spice** was the latest work in *The Sultan of Sulu* tradition. More importantly it was the first smash hit the still young house enjoyed. In fact, *The Isle of Spice* was so successful it did something many New York shows had done before it, but no Chicago production had dared. It sent out a second company! It was this contingent, supplemented by some of the original Chicago players, that reached Broadway in the 1904–05 season.

Blanche Ring threatened to repeat her persistence of the preceding season when she arrived in **The Jersey Lily** (9-14-03, Victoria). For the first time her name was above the title. George V. Hobart's book cast her as an actress from Trouville who returns to her Jersey home to rearrange some other people's matrimonial plans to her own liking. It wasn't much of a story, and the dialogue was rarely more than competent. The *Times'* man insisted the most enjoyable moments of the evening came whenever George Ali, playing the part of Miss Ring's parrot, was on stage. Miss Ring dutifully sang the drab songs Reginald De Koven provided for her and then quickly fell back on the repertory of personal favorites she was building, and on new interpolations, of which "Bedelia" (William Jerome/Jean Schwartz) was the best, achieving a sale of 3 million copies. But her strong vocal chords were not enough to carry so weak a show. Three weeks, and it was gone.

While most aisle-sitters saw no weakness in the annual Weber and Fields' insanity for 1903–04 labeled **Whoop-Dee-Doo**, first-nighters on September 24 apparently spread their lack of enthusiasm. *Whoop-Dee-Doo*'s 151 performances fell far short of the best runs the boys had compiled. Weber and Fields classified the evening as a "Musical Extravaganza" instead of a burlesque or a musical comedy. In another change, W. T. Francis was enlisted to replace the much mourned John Stromberg. He provided nothing of worth. Edgar Smith's plot unfolds at the Kaiser Wilhelm Bier Haus—on the Seine, in Paris. The opening chorus immediately establishes the situation:

> Hoch! Hoch! Hoch!
> It would seem at a casual glance
> That Hoch! Hoch! Hoch!
> Is an odd salutation for France.
> A beer garden perched on the banks of the Seine
> Gives consistency quite a hard poke
> While adjacent Paree scarcely seems to agree
> With Hoch! Hoch! Hoch!

The owner of this bedraggled stube, Pilsener Hofbrau (Louis Mann), does his best to unload the establishment on Michael Suppegreetz (Weber), a retired grocer, and Michael's friend, Meyer Schwartzgeezer (Fields). The complicated maneuvers that ensue require Mike and Meyer to pose as statues, one of their most famous routines. Trying to get a bite to eat during this imposture they are forced to suspend their movements while one has a mouthful of bread and the other a chicken pierced on his sword.

Harry Von Tilzer, one of the legendary Tin Pan Alley greats, rarely bothered with Broadway. He was already an established name (with songs such as "A Bird In A Gilded Cage"). In 1902, he had opened his own music publishing house. On October 5 at the Victoria he presented his first full score in **The Fisher Maiden.** Although Tin Pan Alley had close ties with the burgeoning musical comedy form, the new show was, as its title hints, a comic opera of the old school. That Von Tilzer should associate himself with comic opera instead of musical comedy may seem surprising at first sight. But his allegiance falls into place when one realizes how quickly and totally Von Tilzer disappeared from the musical scene a few years later when newer, jazzier forms claimed musical comedy for their own. The piece had a standard comic opera plot. Marjory Sax (Edna Bronson), the daughter of a New England innkeeper (Al H. Weston), loves Bob Bobstay, although he is almost old enough to be her father. When Sir George Gidding (Robert Lett) is advised by his doctor to witness a wedding in order to restore his health, he has someone impersonate Bobstay, while Bobstay himself is kept

away by members of a secret society. Of course in the end love triumphs, when Marjory falls in love with the young impersonator. The book was as dreary and dumb as the plot outline suggests, and, though Von Tilzer's music was praised in many quarters, nothing caught the public's fancy. The show lingered on for a month, and Von Tilzer never again wrote a complete score for the New York stage.

Just over a week later New York celebrated Victor Herbert's return to the musical theatre. Herbert had been missing from the Broadway scene for nearly three years while he served a not always serene term as conductor of the Pittsburgh Symphony. His tenure at an end, he returned with two scores in hand. The first was for **Babes in Toyland** (10-13-03, Majestic). The show had been commissioned by Fred R. Hamlin and Julian Mitchell as a successor to their production of *The Wizard of Oz* (1-20-03). Curiously *Babes in Toyland* was only the second show by Herbert written with a New York presentation primarily in mind. Except for his quick failure, *The Gold Bug* (9-21-96), his pieces had been created for essentially itinerant companies—although none of these troupes begrudged an extended stay in New York. But times were changing, and New York was surely if imperceptibly asserting its ultimate dominance. Yet times had not changed enough to ignore Chicago, so the show opened there at the Grand Opera House on June 17, 1903, playing through the summer and up to its premiere at the Majestic. The "Babes" were Jane (Mabel Barrison) and Alan (William Norris), who find themselves shipwrecked through the machinations of their wicked Uncle Barnaby (George W. Denham). Luckily, they are stranded in Toyland, where they meet Contrary Mary, the Widow Piper and her eldest son, Tom Tom, Jill, Bo Peep, Miss Muffett, Boy Blue, Simple Simon, and a host of other Mother Goose figures as well as tree spirits, fairies, life-sized dolls, and talking flowers. Uncle Barnaby appears to court Contrary Mary (Amy Ricard) and to further his wicked schemes with the help of the nefarious Toymaker (Dore Davidson). But Jane and Alan are aided by all their Mother Goose friends, and one by one Barnaby's tricks are foiled. Justice is finally meted out at a Toyland court.

The plot was not particularly original, and Glen MacDonough's dialogue was arch when it was not leaden. Still, the mediocrity of the libretto in no way hindered the success of the evening. The spectacle was magnificent—among the best Chicago and New York had ever seen—Barnaby's farm followed by the shipwreck and proceeding through Mary's garden, the Spider's forest, the floral palace of the Moth Queen, the Christmas Tree Grove, a street in Toyland, the Toymaker's workshop, his castle, and the Toyland Palace of Justice. In variety and opulence the mounting harked back to *The Black Crook* (9-12-66) and *Humpty Dumpty* (3-10-68)—a far cry from the one-set-per-act musicals increasingly common at the time. Best of all, *Babes in Toyland* had a perfect Herbert score. His biographer, Edward Waters, calls the music that underscored the shipwreck "equivalent to a symphonic poem." To excerpt all the tunes that are still cherished would be to quote from most of the score. The songs ranged from the stirring "March Of The Toys" to the patently cute "I Can't Do That Sum" (with Miss Barrison and the chorus tapping away on slates) to the sentimental "Toyland" (sung in the original by Bessie Wynn as Tom Tom). The show ran out the season, and several companies, of varying opulence, toured the country for years. The work marked the beginning of Herbert's great period as one of the masters of the American Musical Theatre.

October's last offering was a revival of *Erminie* (5-10-86) on October 19 at the Casino. Francis Wilson was once again Cadeaux, while Marguerite Sylva sang the title role. Jessie Bartlett Davis, once a pillar of the now defunct Bostonians, was featured. The musical was well received, attesting to its enduring appeal.

Two shows debuted simultaneously at the beginning of November. **The Girl from Kay's** (11-2-03, Herald Square) was an importation from London and a smash hit. It had a score by Ivan Caryll and a book by Owen Hall. The action took place in a millinery shop where all the customers conveniently added their own vaudeville specialties to the entertainment. A misconstrued kiss created the complications, but a Mr. Hoggenheimer elicited most of the laughs. Sam Bernard and his fans found the Hoggenheimer role so congenial that it wasn't long before American authors sat down to write a further evening of his adventures.

A second well-liked comic, Frank Daniels, was the star of the competing premiere. It was designed around his talents by Harry B. Smith and Ludwig Englander. Smith "Americanized" a French farce, calling it **The Office Boy** (11-2-03, Victoria). In his version Daniels played Noah Little, an office menial in the firm of Ketchum and Cheatum. When Noah falls in love with an office girl, he lies to her father that he is a member of the firm. Later he is confused with a famous jockey and forced to ride

in a race. Daniels had a droll first entrance. Just before closing time, the offices of Ketchum and Cheatum are humming with activity—girls typing and boys busily running errands. A bell sounds and the staff leaves, wondering where Noah has disappeared to. The office manager turns out the lights and the office is dark and still. Burglars enter through a window. They head directly for a large safe. Failing to jimmy it, they blow it open. Out rolls a sleeping Noah. But Daniels was not the sole attraction. Louise Gunning's lovely voice and Eva Tanguay's abandoned dancing also earned encores. However bright and tuneful Englander's music was, it contained nothing that flourished outside the house. The hit of the evening was an interpolation—a fate Englander was long accustomed to. Daniels stopped the show nightly with "I'm On The Water Wagon Now" (Paul West/J. W. Bratton). But even this piece languished without Daniels' personable projection. Still, Daniels was funny enough to give the show a two-month run and a decent tour. Though theatregoers could not foresee it, *The Office Boy* was the first in a long line of musicals produced by Charles Dillingham.

• • •

Charles Dillingham was born in Hartford, Connecticut, on May 30, 1868, the son of an Episcopalian clergyman. Dillingham rejected college, preferring early employment in the field in which he hoped to make a career, journalism. A stint with a local paper was followed by positions in Washington and Chicago, and, finally, with the New York *Evening Sun*. Soon after his arrival there he was made the paper's drama critic, his first real exposure to the stage. In 1896 he wrote and produced a play called *Ten P.M.* The show was a failure, but it caught the attention of Charles Frohman, who offered Dillingham a position in his organization. Dillingham accepted. For the next several years he served Frohman as a press agent and production assistant.

• • •

The Red Feather (11-9-03, Lyric) suffered a perplexing failure. Two of the most venerated old hands in the musical field collaborated on it: Charles Klein wrote the book and Reginald De Koven wrote the music. And that relative newcomer, Florenz Ziegfeld, mounted it with stunning panache, filling it, as one newspaper noted, with "the resonance of a chorus singing at the top of its voice, a dazzling splendor of superb costumes, and an abundance of handsome, young women." Most of its reviews would today be considered raves. But it lasted only 60 performances in New York, and while on tour, where it fetched more ecstatic notices, business was erratic but generally disappointing. Its story was elementary. The dashing Capt. Trevor (George L. Tallman) of the Romancian army doesn't realize his sweetheart, Countess Hilda Von Draga (Grace Van Studdiford), is also the bandit known as "The Red Feather," whom he has been ordered to pursue. When the truth comes out it is accompanied by an acceptable explanation, and the lovers are free to unite. Thomas Q. Seabrooke handled the comic role of Baron Bulverstrauss. Perhaps significantly, Seabrooke's name was no longer above the title. Miss Van Studdiford, a Bostonian alumna, alone was starred. The *Times,* less enthusiastic than most papers, may have touched on the reason for its poor showing when it generalized, "the name of comic opera, as well as the thing itself, has fallen into disfavor." If the reviewer was correct he was an astute and sensitive observer, for a number of shows that announced themselves as, and indeed were, comic operas had long, profitable runs in the next several years. But this does not gainsay that the term if not the genre was obsolescent. Within five years fewer and fewer pieces would assume the name, and after World War I the term was relegated to theatrical history.

In an interesting sidelight, *The Red Feather* was the first musical to play the lovely new Lyric on 42nd Street. The Shuberts built the house to alternate as home for both Richard Mansfield's dramatic company and the American School of Opera, which none other than De Koven had recently founded. Given De Koven's conservative bent, the school was obviously superannuated from the start. Neither Mansfield nor De Koven occupied the house for long, although De Koven did have one of his last hits there. Mansfield had been given the honor of opening the house the previous month. He selected *Old Heidelberg* as the initial attraction. Of course *Old Heidelberg* will return to this history in musical form as *The Student Prince* (12-2-24).

A second disappointment followed in short order: in this instance for Harry B. Smith, Victor Herbert, and their new star, Fritzi Scheff.

. . .

Fritzi Scheff was born on August 30, 1880, in Vienna, where her mother, Anna Jaeger, was a prima donna at the Imperial Opera House. The youngster was educated at Hoch's Conservatory in Frankfort and then made her debut in Munich in 1898, singing the title role in Flotow's *Martha*. Her success was immediate and shortly she was invited to sing at the Metropolitan Opera in New York. She made her first appearance there on January 11, 1901.

Miss Scheff had been lured from the Metropolitan Opera by the show's fledgling producer, Charles Dillingham. In fact he stole her not just from the Met but from Ziegfeld, who had sought her for *The Red Feather*.

. . .

Babette (11-16-03, Broadway) is a village letter writer in Antwerp during the days of Spanish domination. With the help of a soldier of fortune, Mondragon (Eugene Cowles), she enlists the aid of the king of France (Errol Dunbar) to overthrow the despotic rule. The critics were enraptured with the petite, volatile Miss Scheff. She was at once a fine actress and superb singer. As the *Times* recorded, "her archness and coquetry and flow of animal spirits exercise their full potency." Accolades for Herbert's music were equally warm. The *Evening Post* began by comparing Herbert favorably with Johann Strauss, concluding, "The Broadway Theatre is only a block from the Metropolitan Opera House, and lovers of good music and singing will find them not too far apart musically either." The praise was not far-fetched. Herbert was always careful to tailor his scores to the artists who were to perform them. Miss Scheff's range and skill allowed Herbert a breadth of composition often denied him. He took intelligent advantage of it. In all the shows he wrote for Miss Scheff he included at least one extended showpiece designed to display his star's talents. For *Babette* Herbert gave his heroine "Letters I Write All Day," in which she describes various letters she is called on to set down. Herbert gave each letter a melody appropriate to its content. For example, the music for the greedy landlord's correspondence was "crabbed, monotonous, harsh." Later this sort of number in *Mlle. Modiste* (12-25-05) was to provide Miss Scheff with the greatest hit of her career. Lamentably, the book was bad. Harry B. Smith was getting an undesirable reputation, even in this era of hack librettists and tolerant critics. The *Times* was biting: "Mr. Smith is known as one of the largest manufacturers in this country of comic opera librettos, which of late years have been remarkably free from comic spirit in their conception and of wit in their dialogue, and the book of *Babette* has little that will tend to injure the reputation." The show ran only 59 performances. The claim that it was meant to be a limited engagement cannot hold, for even if Miss Scheff had other commitments someone would have been found to continue and then tour in the piece had the box office warranted.

Frederic Ranken and Gustave Kerker, utilizing an importation by the authors of *Erminie*, put together a bit of fluff entitled **Winsome Winnie** (12-1-03, Casino). An American actress, Winnie Walker (Paula Edwards), is stranded in Montenegro. To earn return fare she agrees to pose as Marjorie Bell, Lord Poverish's ward. She is abducted by comic bandits but talks her way out of their den. With the show's labored humor ("This is a viper from the bottom of a pen. A regular pen viper in fact") and mediocre songs poor Winnie could neither talk nor sing her way into a run. She left after 56 representations.

On December 2, just in time for the holiday trade, **Mother Goose** alighted at the New Amsterdam. The magnificent New Amsterdam, for over two decades the supreme musical house in New York, had opened a month earlier with a prestige production of *A Midsummer Night's Dream*. Musicals were still considered backwater affairs and straight play openings were preferred. The house was the fourth to rise on 42nd Street and the first on the south side of the street. The Lyric had opened a few weeks before, the older, pioneering Victoria in 1899, and the Republic in 1900. But it was this great pseudo-baroque masterpiece that signaled the inevitable primacy of the block. On its mahogany-paneled walls and splendid green onyx staircase were allegorical figures and ancient gods and a lush abundance of tropical plants and animals. On the vaulted ceilings Homeric heroes mingled with the tragic kings and queens of Shakespeare. *Mother Goose* boasted a smart array of young and old talent: Harry Bulger, Joseph Cawthorn (in the title role!), Clifton Crawford, Leila McIntyre, and Pat Rooney. Although it was an importation from London's Drury Lane, it was drastically revised for this side of the Atlantic, primarily by J. J. McNally. At one time or another in its 105-performance run nearly two dozen songs by native writers were interpolated. George M. Cohan provided "Always Leave 'Em Laughin' When You Say Goodbye" and "I Want To Hear A Yankee Doodle Tune," while Cole and Johnson contributed an "Evolution Of Ragtime" number.

Just one day short of a month after he offered *The Red Feather*, Ziegfeld presented **Mam'selle Napoleon** (12-8-03, Knickerbocker) as a vehicle for his wife. Anna Held portrayed Mlle. Mars of the Comédie Française. Her affair with Napoleon (Arthur Lawrence) takes a dangerous turn when the Emperor learns she has another lover, a common soldier (Frank Rushworth). But his fury relents after she is abducted and the young soldier disgraced. He allows them to go off together. By way of novelty Miss Held recited La Fontaine's fable of the lion and the mouse as a second-act curtain. She recited it in French! Ziegfeld surrounded his wife with a lavish production that included a set of an island with shimmering water in the distance, a sumptuous Opera Ball, and, at the very end, a tableau depicting Napoleon's return from Elba. The show had pleasant, if minor, music by Gustav Luders. But all its attractions could not lure enough patrons to keep it on the boards beyond 43 performances.

Taking in stride all the criticism he was receiving for the librettos he was grinding out, Harry B. Smith once again assumed the burdens of producer when he brought in **The Girl from Dixie** (12-14-03, Madison Square), a collection of clichés he threw together for Irene Bentley (Mrs. Smith). The story, which he claimed came to mind when he heard a restaurant orchestra applauded for playing "Dixie," was just enough to see the show through the last curtain. Kitty Calvert comes from an old, but impoverished, Maryland family. She is the apple of Lord Dunsmore's eye, but she politely rejects him. Her own choice is a young man who believes she is an heiress. When he realizes no money will be forthcoming he makes his excuses and retreats, leaving Kitty to reconsider Dunsmore's overtures. Dunsmore was played by Frederick Gottschalk. The musical featured a beautiful chorus line, although the producers, concluding the term "show girl" had been overused, referred to them as "young women of haughty mien and proud carriage." The music, as one Chicago paper noted, was by "nearly all of the living American composers . . . and several dead ones." Cole and Johnson led the credits with six contributions. Opening on December 16, it was 1903's last New York show. It barely made it to the new year.

Just before Christmas two musicals opened an evening apart in Chicago. The first appeared on December 20 at the Great Northern Theatre, a Chicago combination house. **A Son of Rest** was advertised as a "smart operatic storyette." Written by George Weston and Max Witt as a vehicle for Nat Wills, it recounted the adventures of a tramp and his cat. **The Belle of Newport,** which replaced *The Isle of Spice* at the La Salle, was a curious piece in that it was basically a rewriting of *The Defender,* with more emphasis on Sir Thomas Teaton's courtship of Mrs. Jack Orchard (for which audiences of the time could probably read Mrs. Jack Gardner, Boston's famous art patron). It also offered several Ben Jerome songs not sung in New York. The production was staged by Gus Sohlke, son of the popular 19th-century ballerina, Augusta Sohlke.

For the next several years Sohlke's chorus lines were to enjoy the same reputation in Chicago that the Casino and Weber and Fields' lines enjoyed in New York. But few Chicagoans were to be entertained by *The Belle of Newport*. The Iroquois Theatre fire struck just over a week after the new musical opened. All Chicago theatres were immediately closed, and when, after rigorous inspection and reconstruction, they began to reopen in late winter poor attendance threatened to close them once more. *The Belle of Newport* was one of the casualties of these hard times.

If the old year in New York had ended with a musical set in the postbellum South, 1904's first song-and-dance entertainment was a visit to the Victoria on January 4 by Lew Dockstader's Minstrels. But the day was long gone when Bryant, Kelly and Leon, and the San Francisco Minstrels all could play full seasons in competition with the regular theatrical attractions. Dockstader paused briefly to spoof everything from Mayor McLellan to the gossip at Sherry's (by means of "magic wireless") and then returned to the road.

Three English musical comedies followed in rapid succession. Two Sidney Jones' works, **My Lady Molly** and **The Medal and the Maid**, premiered on the 5th and the 11th respectively, while **An English Daisy** opened on January 18. *My Lady Molly,* which featured the London favorite Vesta Tilley, had its heroine disguise herself as a man to be near her beau. Although James T. Powers was starred in *The Maid and the Medal,* its principal plot revolved about complications created when an heiress and a flower girl exchange places, using a medallion as a recognition token. *An English Daisy* offered a first-rate cast, including Charles A. Bigelow, Templar Saxe, Frank Lalor, Henri Leoni, Christie MacDonald, and Truly Shattuck. They sang and danced a tale of two lodgers about to be evicted for nonpayment who are allowed to remain provided one marries the landlord's homely niece. Not one of the three shows was a rousing hit, although the last two tried to ingratiate themselves by interpolating "coon" songs. *The Medal and the Maid* inserted "In Zanzibar" (Will Cobb/Gus Edwards), while *An English Daisy* used the busy Cole and Johnson's "Big Indian Chief."

The 18th also witnessed the opening of **Sergeant Kitty** at Daly's, with book and lyrics by R. H. Burnside and music by A. Baldwin Sloane. Kitty La Tour (Virginia Earle) loves Lucien Vallière (Albert Parr), and he loves her. But their lives become complicated in true musical comedy fashion when Henri de Morrilac (Harry Stone), who will be dis-

inherited by his rich uncle if he marries before he is twenty-five but who is already secretly wed, passes off his own bride (Estelle Wentworth) as Lucien's. Furthermore, Kitty has a difficult aunt (Carrie E. Perkins) who insists that her niece marry. Kitty marries Lucien by proxy so her aunt can see a marriage certificate. The book was generally branded as dull, while Sloane was fast acquiring the same dubious reputation as a composer that Smith had long since won for himself as a librettist. Kitty and chorus girls paraded around for seven weeks and then marched away.

Another London hit, **Glittering Gloria,** unpacked its bags on February 15 at Daly's. Local allusions, American slang, and interpolations were added. Adele Ritchie was starred as an actress who finds herself in hot water after she asks a married man to price a jewel necklace for her. In spite of all the rewriting done to make it acceptable to Broadway, its stay was brief.

One week later, on the 22nd, two new musicals came in for inspection. **The Tenderfoot** was a Chicago musical which furthered the national celebrity of the versatile Richard Carle. Carle wrote both the book and lyrics besides starring as Professor Pettibone, who leaves the effete East to experience the more virile pleasures of the Wild West. But he experiences more than he bargained for when he is captured by Indians and almost burned at the stake. H. L. Heartz' music was pallid stuff. Still, Carle made a show-stopper out of "My Alamo Love." The *Times* reported the song had received "seven or eight encores" every night during its Chicago stay and sold 30,000 copies in its first ten weeks. Some of Carle's lyrics were praised. Yet for all his popularity in Chicago and on the road Carle was looked on as an easy mark by the New York critics, who found his humor too obvious and too often dependent on off-color *double-entendres*. For those who found Carle not to their taste, Helena Frederick offered a diversion with her hilarious impersonation of an heiress so exasperated by her husband that she dresses as a man and challenges him to a duel. "Yelling cowboys, swaggering Texans, and taciturn Indians" filled the stage. Although *The Tenderfoot* had run twenty weeks in Chicago, its 81-performance run at the New York Theatre was as long an unbroken Broadway visit as Carle ever enjoyed during his heyday.

Another fine young comic, Raymond Hitchcock, reconfirmed his right to stardom the same night in the title role of **The Yankee Consul** (2-22-04, Broadway). Hitchcock impersonated Adijah Booze, the lazy, bibulous American representative at Puerta Plata. In courting Donna Teresa (Eva Davenport) he gets himself mixed up in a marriage-for-revenge agency and a brewing Latin revolution. The revolution is stymied by Donna Teresa's daughter, who fears its outbreak will coincide with the governor's ball. The arrival of the U.S. Navy, led by handsome Jack Morrell (Harry Fairleigh), squelches the incipient rebellion. Booze wins the Donna's hand, and Morell wins her daughter (Flora Zabelle). Although it called itself a "comic opera," *The Yankee Consul* was, like *The Sultan of Sulu* (12-29-02), a choice example of early musical comedy. (Indeed, with its chorus girls dancing in pink tights it reminded more than one critic of still a third genre, *The Black Crook* (9-12-66) and its successors.) The book was by Henry Blossom, who quickly became, as John Golden wrote, "one of the best musical-book writers that America ever developed."

. . .

Henry Blossom was born in St. Louis, Missouri, on May 6, 1866. He attended private schools, but spurned college to enter his father's insurance company. He soon turned to writing novels, left the insurance business, and entered the theatre with a dramatization of his own novel, *Checkers*. Most of Blossom's best work was to be with operetta, but he had little trouble making the easy transition to the lighter, brasher musical comedies.

. . .

Alfred Robyn's music was light and often brassy, if not brash. The *Times* dismissed it as "bimmity-bang." "My San Domingo Maid" was the hit of the show. Robyn's was a minor light that flickered only a short while on Broadway. His last years were spent as an organist in the great motion picture palaces. *The Yankee Consul* ran 115 performances, the first long run for an American creation since *Babes in Toyland* opened in October.

There were no March musicals. A third great comic, Eddie Foy, opened at the Casino on April 2 with the season's biggest hit, **Piff! Paff!! Pouf!!!** The plot revolved around another musical comedy will. This one prevents Augustus Melon (Joseph Miron) from inheriting his late wife's fortune until their four daughters marry—in order of age. The daughters are Nova (Mabel Hollins), Cora (Grace Cameron), Encora (Hilda Hollins), and Rose (Amelia Stone). The three oldest girls are the problems, for each attaches a condition to her falling in love. One will have only a man who's never been kissed, the second wants a man who has achieved some sort of greatness, while the third wants a man of almost impossible virtue. Luckily three men

named Piffle (Templar Saxe), Paffle (John Hyams), and Poufle (Foy) meet the bill. The fourth daughter is more than content with a pleasantly everyday newsman. Alice Fischer and R. E. Graham were prominent in Foy's large supporting cast. But Foy dominated the evening, most notably in a scene in which he was supposedly buried in the sand and then paraded around as a sand castle. The music was the first full score Jean Schwartz composed for Broadway.

. . .

Jean Schwartz was born in Budapest on November 4, 1878. His sister, a pupil of Liszt, cultivated his love of music and gave him his first lessons. The family moved to New York while Jean was still in his teens, and he was quickly put to work to earn his share of their support. Odd jobs in a cigar factory and a Turkish bath soon gave way to more congenial employment as a pianist with an orchestra at Coney Island, as a song-plugger at the Siegal-Cooper department store on Sixth Avenue, and for the music publishing house of Shapiro-Bernstein. He formed a partnership with the young lyricist, William Jerome, and before much time passed their tunes were being interpolated into Broadway shows. "When Mr. Shakespeare Comes To Town" was used in *Hoity-Toity* (for which Schwartz was accompanist), "Rip Van Winkle Was A Lucky Man" in *The Sleeping Beauty and the Beast*, "Mister Dooley" in *A Chinese Honeymoon*, "Hamlet Was A Melancholy Dane" in *Mr. Bluebeard*, and "Bedelia" in *The Jersey Lily*.

. . .

Their biggest hits in the new show were Foy's comic number "The Ghost That Never Walked" (a theatrical term for being stranded in the sticks) and a production number, "Radium Dance", with chorus girls in luminescent costumes jumping luminescent ropes. The piece ran well into the next season.

De Wolf Hopper, the fourth great comedian to head a musical cast in less than two months, returned in a revival of *Wang* (5-4-91) to close out April.

May brought three musicals; all flops. **The Man from China** (5-2-04, Majestic) told of a family of Florida fruit-growers who hope an eccentric Chinese they have invited to be their guest will bail them out of their financial woes. They mistake an itinerant one-man band (Charles A. Bigelow) for their expected Oriental and welcome him in style. The bewildered wanderer readily agrees to lend them millions he does not have in return for their luxurious yacht. By the time he is exposed, his hosts' daughter (Vera Michelena) has fallen in love with him. "Fifty-seven Ways To Catch A Man" was the hit of the evening, sung by the show's principal comedienne, Stella Mayhew, in her role of Anastasia Giltedge. Although librettist-lyricist Paul West and composer John W. Bratton were both experienced, their drollery lacked the necessary flair to capture the warm weather audience.

An incredibly old-fashioned, fustian piece, **A Venetian Romance** (5-2-04, Knickerbocker), had even less allure. A renaissance Venetian girl is forced to masquerade as a boy to win the attentions of the young nobleman she loves. Even brigands cannot stand in her way. Not only was the show badly written, it displayed a disheartening lack of style and tone, filled as it was with mediocre vaudeville turns.

The Southerners (5-23-04, New York) called itself "A Musical Study in Black and White." General Preston's old slave, Uncle Daniel—played in blackface by Eddie Leonard—falls asleep to dream of thrilling events at the plantation fifty years before, in 1830. Young Leroy Preston (William Gould), after a tiff with his sweetheart, Polly Drayton (Elfie Fay), leaves the homestead to join the navy. He gives instructions that the slaves are not to be sold to strangers—especially to the boorish Irish Turk, Brannigan Bey (Junie McCree), who lusts after the light-skinned black, Parthenia (Vinie Daly). Preston would prefer to set his slaves free, but he knows society will not allow that. A repentant Polly disguises herself as a naval officer to follow Leroy. Preston returns to the plantation in time to foil Bey's maneuvers and to reconcile his differences with his sweetheart. The preceding season a cast had balked at including a black in their show, (even though Negroes had acted in white variety bills and musical shows), but *The Southerners* bravely employed a whole black chorus for one scene. The awesome tension of their first appearance was caught by the *Times* critic, who reported, "When the chorus of real live coons walked in for the cake last night at the New York Theatre, mingling with the white members of the cast, there were those in the audience who trembled in their seats." The *Times'* man seemed almost relieved to add "the negro composer of the score, Mr. Will Marion Cook . . . succeeded in harmonizing the racial broth as skillfully as he had harmonized the score." But Cook's music was not enough to overcome an otherwise claptrap show.

The season ended June 6 when an excellent vaudeville, entitled candidly, **A Little Bit of Everything,** opened on the New Amsterdam Roof.

"Everything" ranged from Offenbach to a second chance to hear Cole and Johnson's "Evolution Of Ragtime." With a stellar cast headed by Fay Templeton and Peter F. Dailey it played merrily through the summer.

1904–1905

Three musicals opened in New York during the hot months, two in July and one near the end of August. Chicago also welcomed a new piece. **Paris by Night** premiered under the stars at the Madison Square Garden Roof on July 2. It was a lively vaudeville with a thin tour-of-the-city story line to hold the turns together. The principal tourist was Isaac Goldstein (Ben Welsh). Something of a pennypincher, he complains that three months in Paris have cost him $30. His sightseeing allows him to meet a Russian detective (Henry Vogel), who is looking for Japanese spies, and Steve Hickey (Hugh Cameron), a Bowery tough posing as a South African millionaire. Steve prefaces a courtship by informing his girl, "I've a bunch of talk to hand out to you, Mamey." There were enough pleasant evenings and interest at the box office to keep the roof lit for 50 nights.

Guy Steely and Frederick Chapin, who, along with Richard Carle, had given Chicago *The Storks* in 1902, had another musical ready there on July 4 at the Dearborn Theatre. Benjamin Barclay, the breakfast-cereal tycoon from Battle Ax, Michigan (the great Kellogg interests were centered in Battle Creek), takes his niece, Dorothy Fairfax, on a voyage to **The Forbidden Land** of Tibet. A handsome young Englishman, Tom Wilkinson, accompanies them. Their party is taken prisoner and told it will be released only if Wilkinson consents to marry Mina Doma, daughter of the Tibetan potentate. Kinkaboo, executive head of the Amalgamated Association of Asiatic Robbers, smuggles a machine into prison. The contraption allows the group to escape. Shortly after the musical opened, the lead article in the theatre section of the Chicago *Tribune* noted a marked decline in the quality of "light opera," blaming this decline on the rise of the comedian and the scarcity of good singers. The article failed to notice the local tradition of musical comedy that was evolving to replace the waning comic opera.

Meanwhile, Carle himself had found a new collaborator. The irrepressible comedian stopped briefly in New York to entertain his followers with **The Maid and the Mummy** (7-25-04, New York). Its story centered on Washington Stubbs, a failed actor, and now a failing curio dealer. Given to manufacturing whatever "antique" his customer is seeking, Stubbs forces his man-of-all-work, Bolivar (Edward Garvie), to pretend he is a mummy so that Doctor Dubbins (George A. Beane), the wealthy inventor, can test an elixir on him, and bring him back to life. For many, an old favorite and a new favorite stole the show. The veteran was Annie Yeamans of Harrigan and Hart fame. Her first entrance as Dubbins' flirtatious spinster sister was greeted with a "storm of applause." The newcomer was Janet Priest. She portrayed a street urchin, Mugsy, trying to be profane, but succeeding only in creating comic malapropisms. As became his custom, Carle provided the book and lyrics as well as playing the lead. R. H. Bowers wrote the humdrum music. As usual, New York was not as receptive as Chicago or the road. *The Maid and the Mummy* headed off to greener pastures after 42 showings.

A second piece from Chicago followed, this time by way of an extended stay in Boston. On **The Isle of Spice** (8-23-04, Majestic) Bompopka (Alexander Clark), king of Nicobar, "retires" his wives to a "Tomb of Silence" when they reach thirty-five. He is about to put away Kamorta (Mattie Martz) and marry Teresa (Blanche Buckner), a young American who has come to the island, when the U.S. Navy arrives. The sailors are greeted as sun gods, but Bompopka's awe vanishes quickly after he realizes their arrival will scuttle his marriage plans. Teresa is happy to change allegiances and marry Lt. Harold Katchall (George Fiske). The show attempted some unusual choreography. In a "limelight dance" a chorus of "the prettiest and most graceful girls that ever came eastward on the pike" dressed as witches in pantalettes and danced with brooms. Even the inevitable military drill offered some novelty—at least on opening night. Seventeen marines from the Brooklyn navy yard performed "hay-foot-straw-foot," earning themselves several encores. Although the book and Ben Jerome's music were condemned as "a rehash of all the nothings known to the musical stage" the show managed a ten-week stay.

English pride in its navy had long made naval officers heroes in its plays, and lately in its musicals. Now the impressive might of America's growing naval arm was to be manifest increasingly in the American Musical Theatre. It took the Great White Fleet a week and a day to sail from the Majestic at Columbus Circle, where *The Isle of Spice* basked in a calcium sun, to 42nd Street. Its presence was required there after the Rajah of Oolong (Henri Leoni), over an imagined slight, summarily beheads **The Royal Chef** (9-1-04, Lyric). Heinrich Lempauser (Sam Collins), a Chicago alderman on a Cook's tour, is not quite voluntarily enlisted as the dead chef's replacement by the obstinate Rajah, who refuses to accept that a Cook's tour is not a chef's tour. The navy lands to effect a rescue, and Lt. Harry Parker (John Park) falls in love with the rajah's daughter (Amelia Stone). They override a revolution, and a happy ending ensues. The criticisms leveled at *The Isle of Spice* could have been equally well brought against *The Royal Chef*. And indeed they were—with a vengeance. For this was another Chicago offering (with another Jerome score) and a genuinely bad one all around. While Chicago and Boston had embraced the musical (giving it twenty-three- and sixteen-week runs respectively), it disappeared from New York after just 17 performances.

At the same time the navy was securing the Lyric, the English sailed in with the season's first real hit, **The School Girl** (9-1-04, Daly's). Leslie Stuart's score was heavily laced with domestic interpolations by at least a half a dozen different songsmiths. American Edna May and English George Grossmith, Jr., enlivened this tale of a convent-trained girl's adventures in Paris for 120 showings.

Two musicals elbowed each other for attention the next Monday. Lulu Glaser arrived in a Harry B. Smith–Ludwig Englander musicalization of Charles Major's novel *When Knighthood Was in Flower*, retitled **A Madcap Princess** (9-5-04, Knickerbocker). When King Henry (William Pruette) decrees Mary Tudor, who loves Charles Brandon (Bertram Wallis), must instead marry the king of France, Mary suspects that King Henry is bluffing. She calls his bluff and wins. The comic opera's 48-performance run was not bad considering how strained the comedy was:

King Henry [*angry*]: I lack words.
Mary: You lack breath. You ought to try breathing exercises. My, aren't kings wearing high collars today . . . That collar is an awful thing to get hot under.

Nor was the music of a higher order, but Miss Glaser, dressed as a page to effect an elopement, brought down the house with her blustering rendition of "A Typical Cavalier."

The princess' rivals were **The Rogers Brothers in Paris** (9-5-04, New Amsterdam). It was a typical McNally-Hobart-Hoffman "Vaudeville Farce." The practically nonexistent story had Rudolph Kahn (Gus) and Adolph Finkeleiner (Max) go not only to Paris, but to the St. Louis World's Fair. En route they help Marjorie Keller (Josephine Cohan) win Walter Leonard (Fred Niblo) over Papa Keller's (John Conroy) objections. A high spot of the evening was an automobile race, with two real cars spinning wildly around an imaginary Place de la Concorde. As usual nothing distinguished came from the score, even though, as sung by Dorothy Hunting and George Austin Moore, "Under The Old Oak Tree" had to be "encored time after time." The boys clowned for nine weeks before embarking on a cross-country tour.

By rights **Mr. Wix of Wickham** (9-19-04, Bijou) —a saga of an Australian heir and a Parisian modiste—should be given the shortest shrift. It was an importation and a flop. But one thing gives it an undying importance. Five songs were added to the original English material. They gave Broadway its first chance to hear melodies by the man who became the finest, most significant composer in the American Musical Theatre—Jerome Kern. These songs, however, gave little clue to his future greatness. Kern was only nineteen at the time.

. . .

Jerome Kern was born in New York City on January 27, 1885, into prosperous middle-class surroundings. His father had major water-sprinkling concessions in Manhattan and some outlying areas. It was his mother, herself a pianist, who began Kern's musical training. When the Kerns moved to Newark, New Jersey, ten years later, so his father could run a merchandising house, Kern continued his studies under private music teachers until his graduation from high school. His mother and his teachers prevailed on his reluctant father to let him attend the New York College of Music. There he was so eager a pupil he also took extracurricular lessons in theory and harmony from Austin Pierce. However, at his father's insistence he finally entered the family business. Legend has it that his father sent him to the Bronx to buy two pianos, only to have young Jerry return later in the day to announce he had purchased two hundred. As a result the young musician was left to continue his musical studies, this time in Germany. He soon gravitated to England, gave up plans to compose serious music, and prevailed on Charles Frohman to interpolate some of his melodies in shows the trans-

atlantic impresario was presenting in London. "Susan" was typical of Kern songs 1904 first-nighters heard.

. . .

One other important figure debuted in *Mr. Wix of Wickham* when Julian Eltinge made his first appearance in a legitimate work as a female impersonator. If Kern and Eltinge were making inauspicious debuts, one major figure was making an equally sad farewell. *Mr. Wix of Wickham* marked the final mounting of E. E. Rice, virtually the first great producer and director (and, to a lesser extent, author) of the American Musical Theatre. Not only had he been part-author of two milestone shows, *Evangeline* (7-27-74) and *Adonis* (9-4-84), but he had been the first to offer audiences such future great stars as Henry E. Dixey, Lillian Russell, and Fay Templeton. Since he lived another twenty years, he at least had the satisfaction of knowing that both Kern and Eltinge would be added to his list of credits.

Della Fox had the briefest run of her career in **The West Point Cadet** (9-30-04, Princess), four performances. She played the roles of a brother and sister. Their resemblance is so close she wears his uniform to elope. Miss Fox's penchant for trouser roles, the era's love of military drills, and a West Point setting all conspired to fill the stage with more march routines.

Even if theatre owners with new houses slated to host mostly musicals felt it more honorable to open their auditoriums with straight plays, the lyric stage had become prestigious enough and certainly profitable enough to begin to lure the great names from the top ranks of the musical world. October's first entry, **Love's Lottery** (10-3-04, Broadway), was written by Stanislaus Stange and Julian Edwards as a vehicle for the distinguished Mme. Ernestine Schumann-Heink. She stepped down from the world of Wagnerian opera to portray Lina, a German laundress in 1818 England, who wins a lottery and the heart of Sergeant Bob Trivet (Wallace Brownlow) as well. Turgid pieces such as "My First True Love" were the best the serious but poorly endowed Edwards could provide for her. The prima donna was anything but austere. Several times on opening night she stopped to ask the audience, "Is my English goot?" Apparently it was adequate, even if her vehicle wasn't. After 50 performances she returned to Schubert and Schumann and Brahms.

The same night as Mme. Schumann-Heink premiered, Lew Dockstader returned to Broadway. Only the first half of his entertainment was pure, old-fashioned minstrelsy. In the second half Dockstader parachuted down from the flies and launched into a series of skits and songs on New York Life. The skits twitted the slowness of Manhattan's rapid transit; the songs sang of "Seeing New York On A Rubberneck Hack."

The first American hit followed a week later with **The Sho-Gun** (10-10-04, Wallack's). It marked the fourth Chicago production to debut in the still-young season. Like *The Isle of Spice* and *The Royal Chef* before it, it placed an American in an exotic society on the other side of the globe—in this instance, Korea. Both the setting and the story prompted the *Times* to compare it to what the reviewer referred to curiously as that "forgotten classic," *The Mikado*. Apparently the *Times'* man had himself forgotten its successful revival just two seasons earlier. George Ade provided the delicious book, as well as the lyrics. Ade's American is William Henry Spangle (Charles E. Evans), the "Goo-Goo" Chewing Gum King and "the man who put Ioway on the map." By his own description he was "born in Chicago and bred at the Waldorf-Astoria." He travels to Ka-Choo, Korea's imaginary capital, to persuade the Sho-Gun (Edward Martindell) to chew "Goo-Goo." But the Sho-Gun, Flai-Hai, is away on a pilgrimage, and an incipient revolution threatens to elevate Spangle into the royal seat or onto the chopping block. The difficulties in which Hanki-Panki (Thomas C. Leary), the royal astrologer; Omee-Omi (Georgia Caine), an amorous widow; and Hunni-Bun (Christie MacDonald), a princess, entangle the foreigner seem almost insurmountable until the U.S. Navy arrives to restore order and let Spangle sail away.

In an interview with the Milwaukee *Sentinel* during the show's tryout, Gustav Luders professed to rate this as the best of his scores. But this was undoubtedly press-agentry. He also insisted the music was thoroughly American, since he had "never heard of a Corean school of music." Moreover the *Times* felt throughout the evening "a little local color [was] gained by sparing use of the five-note scale." And Luders clearly did attempt something of what he knew his audience would accept as an Oriental flavor in production numbers such as "Hi-Ko, Hi-Ko" as much by choppy rhythm as by tonal color. Most of the regular songs were what his admirers had come to expect, and if Luders deceived himself into thinking they were all 100 percent Yankee no harm was done. But much of the score indeed echoed the pleasant Americana of the day. For example, Spangle courts Omee-Omi with "She's Just A Little Different From The Others That I Know."

Higgledy-Piggledy (10-20-04, Weber Music Hall), another hit, presented Weber without Fields, for their split had come into the open, and the great clowns had gone their separate ways. Initially, Ziegfeld collaborated with Weber on the production, bringing to it his ever-increasing flair and his wife, Anna Held. Weber was probably astute in joining with Ziegfeld, for Weber was generally considered to have had less production acumen than Fields— a reputation that time did nothing to disprove. But the Ziegfelds and Weber could not get along, and when the show went on tour Weber was the sole producer and Trixie Friganza replaced Miss Held. Most of the old Weber and Fields regulars were absent, but Marie Dressler was added to the roster. The story, which was pretty much what the old team had always employed, had two rich Americans traveling in Europe with two young ladies. Adolf Schnitz (Weber), the mustard merchant, has brought along his daughter, Philopena (Miss Dressler), while Gottlieb Gesler (Harry Morris), "President of the American Swiss-Cheese Sandwich Trust," escorts a new-found friend, Mimi de Chartreuse (Miss Held). The boys are unhappy with the "Bedecker" they have purchased. Schnitz deplores the "closefisted printing," while Gesler admits, "I read a little but its a rotten story." Nevertheless Philopena assures them without it they would know nothing of "Versales and the Plats de Can Can, where Mary Ann Tonette was beheaded." Gesler is impressed:

Gesler: My! but ain't your daughter stuffed with education?
Schnitz: She ought to be. She served two years and six months in a very fine ladies' cemetery.

Gesler's name gets them involved in an insane William Tell dialogue, and the evening ends in the customary brawl. Neither the Ziegfelds nor Weber walked off with the most critical cheers. They were saved for Miss Dressler, notably in a song "A Great Big Girl Like Me," "an operatic chant varied by elephantine gambols." Maurice Levi, who had served the rival Rogers Brothers, did the score. It was pleasant enough for the evening but without anything memorable.

A London importation, Monckton's **The Cingalee** (10-24-04, Daly's), offered one more story set in an exotic land, this time revealing the bittersweet romance between an Englishman and a native girl. It failed to find favor.

But an all-American George M. Cohan returned to give the American Musical Theatre one of its unforgettable evenings. **Little Johnny Jones** (11-

7-04, Liberty) was responsible for a number of firsts for the brash young musical comedy man. It was his first show with Sam Harris, who was to be his longtime partner; his first show to play a major uptown house; his first solid hit; his first book with the flag-waving chauvinism he used so uniquely time and again thereafter; his first score to include some of his undying favorites. His father and mother were again given important parts, as was his wife, Ethel Levey. But Josephine Cohan and her husband had left to join the Rogers Brothers. A new name was on the roster, Donald Brian—a rising young singer and dancer who by some luck or other was on stage whenever important musical theatre history was made during the next decade. A few critics complained that *Little Johnny Jones* was more "musical melodrama" than "musical comedy." They were right, but they had no cause to berate Cohan, who had correctly advertised the work as a "musical play" or simply as a "play with music." The idea for the plot came to Cohan when he read of the exploits of Tod Sloan, an American jockey who rode a royal mount in the 1903 English Derby. In Cohan's theatricalization Sloan became Johnny Jones, the cocky, slangy, identical twin of his creator. Johnny comes to London to ride in the Derby. He is pursued by a whole chorus of attractive girls unconcerned by the knowledge that Johnny is engaged. He has no time to play around with them, but he is thoughtful enough to offer them a helpful hint. When they go to the races, he advises them "Pawn your jewelry, go in hock, and play Yankee Doodle to win," adding, confidently, that he is "The Yankee Doodle Boy." But Johnny's ingratiating smiles belie troubles behind the scenes. Anthony Anstey (Jerry Cohan) is prepared to bribe Johnny to throw the race. Johnny indignantly refuses. When Johnny loses the race after all, the vindictive Anstey nonetheless spreads the word that Jones lost on purpose. When he shows up at the Southampton docks to sail away, Johnny is met by an angry crowd. His patriotic hackles up, he orders his luggage removed from the ship and prepares to remain in England to clear his good name and his country. A detective friend remains on the ship to search for evidence of the frame-up. If he finds any he will signal Johnny with a rocket from the ship. As the vessel disappears Johnny bids all his friends on board, "Give My Regards To Broadway." In a "transformation" scene that became so famous Cohan had a mural depict it in the lobby of the theatre he later built, the stage darkened to indicate the passing of time. When the lights went up, Johnny was alone on the pier, lean-

ing against a piling. Before long the ship appears out at sea, slowly making its way across the horizon. Just as Johnny is beginning to despair, the rocket is fired. The jubilant Johnny does a high-kicking reprise of "Give My Regards To Broadway" as the curtain falls. But Anstey's villainy is not ended. He kidnaps Johnny's girl, Goldie Gates (Miss Levey), and Johnny must trail them both to, appropriately, San Francisco, where Anstey runs a gambling house. At first he can find no trace of them in the hustle and bustle of Chinatown, and in a moment of temporary tranquillity he pauses to soliloquize "Life's A Funny Proposition After All":

> Did you ever sit and ponder, sit and wonder, sit and think,
> Why we're here and what this life is all about?
> It's a problem that has driven many brainy men to drink,
> It's the weirdest thing they've tried to figure out;
> About a thousand different theories, all the scientists can show,
> But never yet have proved a reason why.
> With all we've thought, and all we're taught,
> Why all we seem to know is we're born and live a while and then we die.
>
> Life's a very funny proposition after all,
> Imagination, jealousy, hyprocrisy and all;
> Three meals a day, a whole lot to say;
> When you haven't got the coin you're always in the way.
> Ev'rybody's fighting as we wend our way along,
> Ev'ry fellow claims the other fellow's in the wrong;
> Hurried and worried until we're buried and there's no curtain call,
> Life's a very funny proposition after all.

But Johnny is not one to philosophize all night. He is quickly back on the trail and soon succeeds in freeing Goldie and giving Anstey a well-earned comeuppance.

Little Johnny Jones was as fine and progressive a musical as 1904 New York had ever seen. At times, such as the "transformation" at the close of Act II, it harked back to *The Black Crook* (9-12-66). But in most older pieces the transformation was pure spectacle. Cohan used it for a stunning dramatic climax. In giving his heroine the name Goldie Gates, Cohan was capitulating to the theatrical clichés of the time. And much of the humor, largely in the hands of the detective (played by burly Tom Lewis as if he were on a perpetual jag), was a series of vaudeville routines. But Cohan's melodramatic yarn was carefully wrought and never lost sight of.

Act Two: The Emergence of American Talent, 1902–1907

Its dimensions were human: the characters had blood that rushed to their cheeks and their dialogue was vibrant. And all the excellent Cohan songs—not just the classics—were a telling adjunct to the story line. Most critics were unkind. They condemned Cohan for using genuinely contemporary dialogue, though they often complained the talk in most musicals was absurdly stilted. They belittled his attempts at seriousness, while elsewhere they bewailed the frivolousness of the musical stage. Some even assailed his flag-waving as a poor substitute for the sugary confections of the English importations. The show's initial run was only 52 performances, but Cohan brought the work back in May for four more months, and again in November of 1905 for an additional month, giving the piece over 200 performances, or more than all but two other of the season's lyric efforts.

The same night Cohan opened in *Little Johnny Jones,* May Irwin premiered in George V. Hobart's comedy, **Mrs. Black Is Back** (11-7-04, Bijou). The show resembled Pinero's *The Magistrate,* in which a widow lies about her age, forcing her to pretend her grown son is a toddler. Like all Miss Irwin's vehicles the piece was really a straight play. But as was her wont, Miss Irwin found room for several songs.

With a title that must have recalled happy memories for a generation of old playgoers, **Humpty Dumpty** frolicked into the New Amsterdam on November 14. The show was not the old 1868 G. L. Fox extravaganza, but a Drury Lane pantomime adapted for domestic consumption by J. J. McNally and with a number of American songs interpolated. The most popular were by Cole and Johnson. Their "Sambo And Dinah" told of how, "Without respect to grammar . . . dusky lovers bill and coo." With Frank Moulan as the star the show ran through the holidays and almost up to spring.

Harry B. Smith, his brother Robert, and composer Alfred E. Aarons had an embarrassingly quick flop with **A China Doll** (11-19-04, Majestic). The doll was an automaton loved and lost by Pee Chee San (Helen Royston), who refuses to marry an "Americanized 'Chink,'" until it is found. The production was beautifully mounted, especially a second act set of a Chinese palace overlooking a lake and hills beyond. The palace itself was painted to resemble porcelain. Yet stage design technique was still relatively primitive, so at least one critic felt the illusion was hampered somewhat by "the glare of white lights."

Another quick flop was **The Baroness Fiddlesticks** (11-21-04, Casino), a dreary affair in which a parvenu's chances for acceptance are jeopardized if it becomes known the baroness he is entertaining is an impostor. The score was by Emil Brugière, his only one to get a Broadway hearing. It was one of three musicals to open on November 21.

Some of the top professionals of the day also had bad luck with their adaptation of Oliver Goldsmith's *She Stoops To Conquer,* the second of the evening's openings. Stanislaus Stange moved the setting to the Continent and changed the heroine's name to Rose Decourelles. The affair was also given a new title, **The Two Roses** (11-21-04, Broadway). But Stange was as heavy-handed a librettist as Smith. His dialogue included jokes on the order of, "Too many crooks spoil a policeman," and, "Getting married is like going to a fire. They run there and walk back." Neither Ludwig Englander nor Gustave Kerker, who collaborated on the score, was capable of rising above such mediocrity. Englander, who did the bulk of the music, could do no better than saccharine dainties such as "What's A Kiss?" Significantly, Fritzi Scheff as Rose drew the loudest applause of the evening when she interpolated two arias from her operatic repertory at the end of the evening. Yet even the enchanting Miss Scheff could not save the show.

The happiest of the three November 21 premieres was Frank Pixley and Gustav Luders' **Woodland** at the New York. Though it was a Chicago show, it eschewed the Oriental settings that were beginning to appear a Chicago trademark. Instead it chose a field farther removed from Western civilization, the woodland domain of the birds. All the characters were feathered creatures, though their behavior was singularly manlike. Prince Eagle loves Miss Nightingale, but the King of the Birds disapproves of the match. The Blue Jay, disgruntled for other reasons, attempts to lead a revolution. But the Prince helps his father quell the uprising, so the grateful King allows his son to marry the Nightingale. There were complaints about Pixley's earthbound dialogue and the team's persistence with "Message" and "Tale" songs—in this case "The Message Of Spring" and "The Tale Of The Turtle Dove." But the story was charming and refreshing, and Luders' lightweight grace engaging. The piece ran nearly three months.

One Chicago musical that never made it to New York was **His Highness the Bey.** Its failure to reach Broadway belies its importance, for it was the first musical written by the trio that created most of the great Chicago musicals: Will M. Hough, Frank R. Adams, and Joe Howard. Of course, Howard had already made a small name for himself, nationally as well as locally. Hough and Adams were still students at the University of Chicago. On November 21 their classmates packed a La Salle Theatre that had been drastically rebuilt on orders of the Chicago fire department. The story the collegians told began with the announcement that the Bey has fled his country in fear of an enemy attack. A new leader must be found. Who should wander innocently into the crisis but a bandmaster from Kankakee, Louie Wurtzelheimer (Al Shean). The world tour he is making with his wife comes to an abrupt halt when he is drafted into the job of Bey. The complications that follow find Louie prepared to arrest his spouse as an enemy spy. Luckily, the war stops because the papers find they haven't any more room for war news. The real Bey returns and the reconciled Wurtzelheimers are permitted to go on their way. *His Highness the Bey* settled in to begin a three-month run, while Hough-Adams-Howard started work on its successor.

When Lew Fields broke with Weber, he promptly formed a new association with Fred Hamlin and Julian Mitchell. Together they established the Lew Fields Stock Company and began construction of a Lew Fields Theatre on 42nd Street. Victor Herbert was commissioned to write the scores for their mountings. Their first effort, **It Happened in Nordland,** inaugurated the new house on December 5. It was an instant success, but it was soon to cause Herbert and the company public anguish and become a landmark case. The story was simple enough, its opening not unlike *His Highness the Bey*. The Queen of Nordland disappears rather than accept an unwelcome marriage. When the new American ambassadress, Katherine Peepfogle, turns out to be the Queen's double, she is pressed into impersonating her so that Nordland will not be embarrassed. Katherine discovers her long-lost brother Hubert (Fields) and extricates him from all sorts of problems before the Queen returns and Katherine can resume her correct role. Mitchell and Fields had long since gained a reputation for lavish, tasteful productions. *It Happened in Nordland* was no exception. In an era when choruses of thirty, forty, or fifty girls were common, the men saw to it every girl was a beauty—"even in the last row." Lovely stage pictures were capped by a brilliant second-act carnival scene. Herbert's score was a charmer. Fittingly, it was less operatic than most of those he had done before, closer in style to his material for Frank Daniels' vehicles. The numbers were shorter and less arioso. There were fewer concerted pieces. The hit of the evening was "Absinthe Frappé." In the carnival scene Herbert inserted a fully orchestrated version of his earlier piano work, "Al Fresco."

In writing his contract for the show Herbert made a ghastly mistake. He neglected to include his customary clause prohibiting interpolations—a particularly dangerous omission when he knew Marie Cahill was to play Katherine. As early as the first night of the Harrisburg tryout, Miss Cahill added extraneous songs. Herbert fumed, but he was helpless. The animosities grew. At the very end of the New York run Herbert came for several nights to conduct in place of the ailing Max Hirschfeld. But he would only conduct his own music. Before Miss Cahill began each interpolation Herbert ostentatiously handed his baton to the concertmaster. This so unnerved Miss Cahill that during the final New York performance on Saturday, April 26, she broke down in the middle of something called "Any 1905 Old Tree." She left the stage to regain her composure, and, while she did finish the performance, she demanded a showdown. To her dismay Fields took Herbert's side. She withdrew from the show, and the following Monday in Boston her understudy went on. Blanche Ring was eventually brought in to play Katherine. Amazingly, she ignored the implications of the earlier contretemps and insisted on adding her own interpolations. When Fields in turn fired her, the fiery Miss Ring stalked out—taking all Katherine's costumes with her. Both incidents received wide publicity. They failed to bring an end to the haphazard desecration created by willful performers. But they did announce the battle had been joined. The more conscientious of the established composers became increasingly careful to insert clauses prohibiting interpolations.

A second 18th-century English classic, *The School for Scandal*, was set to music by A. Baldwin Sloane as **Lady Teazle** (12-24-04, Casino). But neither Sloane nor his librettist and lyricist could approach Sheridan's brilliance. In their version Joseph Surface's profligacy was demonstrated by his cavorting with a bevy of girls in short pink and white skirts, the sale of the family portraits was conducted in song and rhyme, and when Lillian Russell—their more than ample Lady Teazle—was discovered behind a screen she sought refuge in a French accent and a song that began, "I am ze dainty milliner." W. T. Carleton played Sir Peter Teazle; Clarence Handyside, Sir Oliver; and Van Rensselaer Wheeler, Charles. Yet neither Miss Russell, her fine supporting players, nor eighty-six beautiful chorus girls could help. The piece lasted only 57 performances.

The musical was the first to carry above its title the announcement "The Messrs. Shubert present." The "Messrs." were Sam, Lee (for Levi), and J. (for Jacob) J. Shubert. As was the case with so many immigrants the dates and places of their birth are in question.

. . .

Sam Shubert was generally conceded to be the oldest, but the year of his birth is given as 1876, a year after Lee's official birth date of March 15, 1875. **Lee Shubert** is known to have admitted privately that he was born several years earlier, possibly 1873. **J. J. Shubert's** official birth date is given as August 15, 1880. The dates were apparently altered so that all three brothers could claim American birth. Most likely, they were all born in Lithuania. Their father, David Szemanski, a ne'er-do-well, alcoholic pack-peddlar, fled Czarist pogroms, taking his family as far as England and then, coming alone to America, settling in Syracuse. He brought his family over a year later. Sam and Lee began peddling papers in front of one of Syracuse's theatres. Before long Sam was inside the house, selling programs and souvenirs. Ambitious, bright, and energetic, the five-foot-tall Sam soon became assistant treasurer at a more important house and within months treasurer at a still better one. A meeting with Charles Hoyt prompted him to visit New York to purchase road rights to Hoyt's *A Stranger in New York* and *A Texas Steer*. The success of the first brought Lee into the picture and Jake followed shortly thereafter. With profits from the plays the boys were able to take over houses in Syracuse. Rochester and Utica soon had Shubert-run theatres. At this point Sam tried to establish a mutually satisfactory arrangement with the Syndicate by sitting down with Abe Erlanger. What seemed to be an excellent deal was quickly worked out. But Erlanger reneged, a treachery the Shuberts never forgot or forgave. Inevitably, the boys set their sights on New York. In 1900 they leased the Herald Square Theatre. Soon the Casino was under their management. Their great building spree began when they erected the Lyric Theatre. When Sam was killed in a 1905 train accident, Lee took over the running of the organization the brothers had created. J. J. would remain the lesser of the survivors in the company, but it would be his love for operetta that gave the Shuberts some of their greatest hits.

. . .

However startling the number of chorus girls in *Lady Teazle* may seem to theatregoers in our less generous era, the figure was not much above the norm for musical extravaganzas at the turn of the century. The New York *World* ran an article on a survey it had conducted of the girls in *Lady Teazle's* line. It affords insights into why even the usually niggardly Shuberts could be so prodigal. The ages of the young ladies ranged from sixteen to a discreetly omitted top. Most important, though the girls claimed they averaged only twenty-weeks-a-year employment, they were content to receive only $18 for each of the weeks they did grace the boards. The girls and the *World's* article made it clear that a prominent place in an attractive chorus line was merely a means to an end. Forty-eight of the ladies acknowledged "independent means," seventy-eight boasted of their jewelry and furs, while seven even owned newfangled, expensive automobiles, and another seven were driven to the show each night in private carriages. In short, many chorus girls didn't need large salaries. They were "kept women." Of course, many young ladies (and young men) of the chorus were not kept. They were willing to survive on a relative pittance in hope of future glory and wealth. But well-provided-for chorus girls were not unique to this era or even to New York. Years earlier "Practical John" Hollingshead, the original proprietor of London's Gaiety, had posted what became a famous notice on his bulletin board—"Ladies drawing less than 25 shillings a week are politely requested not to arrive at the theatre in broughams." The notice was posted in the 1860s!

Two more former Weber and Fields' names—Fay Templeton and Peter F. Dailey—invited their fans to visit them **In Newport** (12-26-04, Liberty). Their musical told how old henpecked Bankwell (Lee Harrison) hires detective Alert Pincherton (Dailey) to retrieve a letter he has written to a French girl (Miss Templeton) and thwart a blackmail scheme. Pincherton disguises himself as an ordinary policeman and winds up watching a rehearsal of a play filled with vaudeville acts before he can earn his pay. Joseph Coyne was featured as a "traditional English nincompoop." One well-received number employed a large segment of the chorus in a mock football game. J. J. McNally wrote the book, while Bob Cole, with both J. W. and J. Rosamond Johnson, did the songs. But for all the excellent talent something went wrong. They all packed their bags and left after just three weeks.

The same night *In Newport* opened, Fritzi Scheff reappeared. Rather than risk another failure in an untried piece, she sang a repertory of opéra bouffe,

Fatinitza, Giroflé-Girofla, and *Boccaccio.* The old favorites retained sufficient appeal to give Miss Scheff a three-month run.

Chicago welcomed the first musical hit of the year on January 9. And a curious one it was! **The Girl and the Bandit** was a rewritten, recast, and re-titled version of a musical New York had already rejected, *A Venetian Romance.* Even Chicago the-atre managers were not prepared for its reception. Forced out of one theatre by a previous booking, it moved to another house only to find it must va-cate that one because of a previous booking there. In three separate runs the musical chalked up fif-teen weeks. It toured the Midwest for two seasons.

Fantana (1-14-05, Lyric), a musical with Chi-cago connections, quickly became the season's smash hit. Sam S. Shubert was not only its pro-ducer but its co-librettist, sharing credits with Rob-ert B. Smith. Smith felt he had done all the work, though he admitted Shubert had given him the original story line. He finally prevailed on Shubert to acknowledge how small his contribution was. But Shubert never changed the published credits. Shubert's story related the adventures of Commo-dore Everett (Hubert Wilke), a retired naval offi-cer and now successful owner of the "Fantana" vineyard. He proposes to take his daughter and the Japanese Ambassador to Japan to teach viniculture. But the trip seems abortive when the Ambassador learns he will be beheaded if he returns. What the Commodore fails to reckon with is the determina-tion of his daughter, Fanny (Adele Ritchie), who is set on seeing her fiancé (Frank Rushworth), a lieu-tenant serving with the U.S. Navy in Japan. She persuades Hawkins (Jefferson De Angelis), her father's valet, to pose as the Ambassador, and they all sail away. It takes the navy to save Hawkins from losing his head. Since the show's plot was the sort Chicago had been so receptive to, and since both Smith and the composer, Raymond Hubbell, had close ties to the city, Shubert wisely opened the tryout there. By the time the show reached the Lyric it was in tip-top shape, with Jefferson De Angelis' broad clowning winning the loudest ap-plause. His disguise as the Japanese ambassador af-forded De Angelis a chance to chase a tassel on his hat about the stage. The tassel was quicker than the comedian, often swinging around from behind to slap him in the face. Two youngsters also called attention to themselves: Julia Sanderson and Doug-las Fairbanks. Hubbell's tunes were trite, but agree-able. The show's biggest hit, added for the New York run, was the already popular "Tammany"

(Vincent Bryan/Gus Edwards). The show ran into the next season.

Two nights later Ivan Caryll's London hit **The Duchess of Dantzic** (1-14-05, Daly's), a musical version of Sardou's *Madame Sans Gene,* began a profitable stay.

George Lederer closed out January in Chicago with **Smiling Island** (a title which just may have been taken from the song in *The Sultan of Sulu*). The show opened at Hyde and Behman's on the 30th. Unfortunately, the critics could find no plot nor anything to like in the work. Its main attraction seemed to be the lavishness of the production with, as the advertisements proclaimed, "100 in cast MOSTLY GIRLS." The girls were not enough to save the show; it closed quickly.

On February 12 Chicago's leading combination house, the Great Northern, played host to Florence Bindley in **The Street Singer.** By today's standards the show would be a melodrama with musical in-terpolations. But in its day it was looked on as an addition to the roster of the lyric theatre. In fact, it was looked on with a certain pride. The Sunday before the show opened, the Chicago *Tribune* noted, "The play is said to contain a coherent plot of more than average effectiveness and musical numbers are introduced without serious jog to the dramatic proprieties." Even in 1905 the integra-tion of book and music was a serious considera-tion, although perhaps more of a hope than of an achievement. The plot into which the songs were added told of Violet, a young street-singer whose father works for a rich man. The rich man has two sons, one good and one bad. Both eye Violet, but by the end of the evening the good young man has won her hand.

Two shows opened in Chicago in mid-March one night apart. On March 13, **Me, Him and I** came in for a brief stay at the Great Northern. Its plot followed three stranded comedians on their adven-tures in the Yukon Gold Rush. The following night witnessed a much more important premiere when Hough-Adams-Howard's second show bowed. **The Isle of Bong Bong** was set on Lord Percy's hunting estate in the theatrically voguish Philippines. In order to court Marjory Gray, the young American secretary of his uncle, Lord Percy changes places with his valet. At the same time the Sultan of the floating island of Bong Bong comes ashore to court the thrice-widowed Mrs. Renssalaer-Rennsalaer. A wizard, a bandit, pirates and a hungry off-stage lion place obstacles in the lovers' way. Everything ends happily, with the Sultan consenting to anchor his island near civilization. The show had fun with other musicals of the era and with local figures. At one point Bong Bong's ruler speaks kindly of his "sometime neighbor," the Sultan of Sulu. In the first act Marjory sings lovingly of "My Illinois," mentioning in passing "Clark Street ticket scalpers" and the White Sox. Joe Howard took a role in the cast, but more importantly the show called the attention of Chicago theatregoers to two artists who became Chicago favorites, Cecil Lean and Florence Holbrook. The musical settled into the La Salle for a comfortable run.

While these shows had been opening in Chicago, New York's musical scene had been quiet. A new musical finally arrived on April 12, 1905, but its arrival was overshadowed by the new theatre that housed it. The show was **A Yankee Circus on Mars.** The theatre was the Hippodrome. Built on Sixth Aveune between 43rd and 44th Streets, it accelerated the northward movement of the theatrical district. But its site on the east side of the avenue established an eastern boundary beyond which no other playhouse was ever raised. The Hippodrome was the largest legitimate theatre in the world. The statistics it claimed for itself were staggering. It accommodated over 5,000 customers at one time. The depth of its stage from foot-lights to back wall was 110 feet, while in length the stage exceeded 200 feet, nearly equal to a whole city block. The stage was lit by 5,000 incandescent lights and 53 calcium lights. The staff of over 1,000 required to run the house included 78 electricians and 22 engineers. It employed a permanent ballet of 200 as well as 400 chorus girls and 100 chorus boys. The vastness of the house precluded ordinary entertainments. John Golden, who wrote words for some of the songs presented there, despaired, "the Hippodrome was so big that audiences could never hear the lyrics." Nor could they hear most of the dialogue. Spectacle was all the house could properly offer and, in its heyday, all it presented. George V. Hobart wrote the "libretto" for the opening. But there was no real story line. The evening was essentially a series of circus acts and ballets that must have recalled *The Black Crook* (9-12-66) to the oldsters in the auditorium. But it was far grander than anything Niblo's Garden or the Kiralfys could set before playgoers. Horses plunged into the theatre's giant tank; elephants pulled outsized automobiles. The piece was coupled with a "tableauxdrama" originally called *Andersonville: A Story of Wilson's Raiders,* but soon shortened merely to *The Raiders.* The horrors of the prison camp were depicted, followed by a Northerner's escape, a secret visit to the plantation

of his southern sweetheart, and a Civil War battle scene. From the beginning the Hippodrome offered spectacular scenes of carnage in which spectacle effectively served to water down blood and gore. Manuel Klein and Jean Schwartz composed the music. It took a season or two before the Hippodrome shows developed a pattern and found a niche for themselves. By that time Frederic W. Thompson and Elmer S. Dundy, who conceived the whole affair (and who also had created Luna Park in Coney Island), were bankrupt. Part of the problem was the lateness of the opening. Hot weather was just around the corner. Hippodrome shows did not hit their full stride until later producers offered them early in the fall.

The English hit, **Sergeant Brue** (4-24-05, Knickerbocker), with Frank Daniels capering about in the title role, repeated its London popularity. Daniels played a London bobby who will come into a large inheritance if he can earn the rank of sergeant. Blanche Ring stopped the show nightly with an interpolation, "My Irish Molly O" (Jerome/Schwartz).

Sam Bernard and Hattie Williams also produced enough laughter to keep **The Rollicking Girl** (5-1-05, Herald Square) titillating New Yorkers until autumn. Miss Williams was Iona, who runs away on the eve of her wedding and takes refuge in the house of the wigmaker, Schmaltz. She and Schmaltz have theatrical ambitions; together they go to the Royal Theatre. In the end, however, she realizes she loves her groom-in-waiting, and Schmaltz returns to his wigs. Much of the humor was the "Dutch" variety Bernard had mastered during his stay with Weber and Fields:

Schmaltz: Valk on this way and say, "My Lady, the letter has came."
Iona: I shall say come, not came.
Schmaltz: Not at all. You already want to teach the author his bizness. Now, ven the author says "came" he just wants to show that the maid don't know how it is to speak the words gramatic.

Joe Coyne, falling into a pattern that only *The Merry Widow* would rescue him from, donned a shiny baldpate wig to impersonate another English buffoon. The critics praised both Sydney Rosenfeld's book, which he adapted from *A Dangerous Maid* (11-12-98), and W. T. Francis' score.

Two musicals came in to entertain Chicago in May. Both failed. William A. Brady presented "a topsy turvy in two acts" called **All around Chicago** on May 1 at the McVickers. In a slim Tom and Jerry frame the piece offered everything from a

Sherlock Holmes travesty to a Moulin Rouge can-can. On May 21 **Kafoozelum** opened at Hyde and Behman's. Set in Turviana, a land inside the earth, it recounted problems that develop when Earthlings arrive.

Two roof garden attractions opened in New York in June. **Lifting the Lid** (6-5-05, New Amsterdam Roof) was little more than a vaudeville, with its entire second act devoted to scenes and songs from Gilbert and Sullivan. Still, it was pleasing enough to run until fall. **When We Were Forty-one** (6-12-05, New York Roof) was Robert B. Smith's burlesque of Henry V. Esmond's popular *When We Were Twenty-One,* which Nat C. Goodwin had been touring around the country since 1900. It told how mad Dr. Hasler (Harry Bulger) attempts to put everyone over forty to sleep. Gus Edwards composed the necessary tunes. The piece was part of a longer bill presented for 66 performances.

Chicago had the last word of the season when **The Woggle Bug** appeared at the Garrick on June 18. The work had a score by Frederick Chapin and a book by the creator of *The Wizard of Oz* (1-20-03), L. Frank Baum. In another of his never-never-lands, the Princess Ozma is transformed into a boy named Tip. Jack Pumpkinhead, a seahorse, and the Woggle Bug himself help her to resume her rightful state. The critics praised the show, the man from the *Tribune* suggesting Chapin's score was so fine Victor Herbert had better look to his laurels. But attendance was disappointing. Too many parents remembered the holocaust at the Iroquois Theatre.

1905-1906

If Chicago had had the last word in 1904–05, it also got the new season well under way before New York came to life. The first musical to arrive raised the curtain of the La Salle on August 12. Like the two shows that followed, it told of an American who is reluctantly elevated to the leadership of a foreign country. Cecil Lean was made **The Yankee Regent** of Wiener because he is the "32nd cousin —twice removed" of Princess Olive. Olive must choose between a prince and the regent, or abdicate. Naturally she chooses the handsome American. The show was not by Hough-Adams-Howard. Instead the libretto was by Charles Adelman and I. L. Blumstock; the score by Ben M. Jerome. The musical was a modest success, helping to keep the

La Salle lit until Hough-Adams-Howard had a new show ready.

The Rajah of Bhong came into the Great Northern on August 20. There had been a Rajah of Bhong in *A Country Girl,* but apart from the curious coincidence of the names there appears to have been no connection between the two shows. This American piece had a libretto by William Roberts and music by Hal L. Campbell. Its story told of a New Yorker who escapes an unhappy love affair by taking a cruise. He is shipwrecked and made rajah by the natives of the island on which he is cast ashore. The next evening **The Geezer of Geck** opened at the Garrick. The show, for which Robert Adam wrote the book and Paul Schindler composed the music, echoed the plot of *His Highness the Bey.* A reluctant Julius Schmidt is made Geezer and finds he must buy his wife back at an auction. But he spends so much money purchasing his harem that he has no cash left when his wife comes on the block.

The New York season opened with **The Pearl and the Pumpkin** (8-21-05, Broadway). There is a pumpkin famine, even in Davy Jones' locker, where Bluebeard's stomach aches from a lack of pumpkin pie. A lad who knows how to grow them is turned into a pumpkin when he refuses to reveal the technique. A wild chase to a newly discovered pumpkin patch finds the Flying Dutchman, Captain Kidd, and a group of Vermont farmers among the racers. John Bratton's tunes and Paul West's lyrics were of an appropriate order. All in all, a pleasant children's show—except that it wasn't! The moralizing *Times* reflected: "The tendency of the nowadays musical comedy producers to utilize little-boy-and-girl lore is a more or less delightful departure from the Gallic flavor of the comic opera of the past." The paper saluted the change as "more wholesome." Apparently the *Times'* man did not recall the day when the original *Humpty Dumpty* (3-10-68) outran the most successful new opéra bouffe. The run of *The Pearl and the Pumpkin* matched neither, a modest 72 performances.

Easy Dawson, which opened the next night, was looked upon by most critics as an attempt by Raymond Hitchcock to build a bridge for himself from musical comedy to straight play. There were four or five songs in the piece, by various composers, none particularly germane to the action on stage.

Two lyric pieces bowed the next Monday. Edna May was **The Catch of the Season** (8-28-05, Daly's). This retelling of the Cinderella tale in contemporary dress had been a London hit and now became a transatlantic success, helped not only by

Miss May but by three attractive Jerome Kern interpolations, "Raining," "Won't You Kiss Me Once Before I Go?" and "Edna May's Irish Song."

The popular blackface duo, McIntyre and Heath, sparked a musical vaudeville called **The Ham Tree** (8-28-05, New York), which recounted the misadventures of two picaresque Negroes, Henry Jones (Heath) and his not very bright friend Alexander Hambletonian (McIntyre), after they are stranded in a small town and present themselves as a rajah and his minister in order to get free room and board. The *Times* noted the evening contained all the requisite blackface bits—the principals sitting on a trunk by a railroad track, searching for food in a spooky, dark woods. William Jerome and Jean Schwartz' songs did little to suggest the minstrel antecedents of the piece, and the hit of the evening, "Good-bye Sweet Old Manhattan Isle," could have come from almost any show. But audiences loved *The Ham Tree,* and McIntyre and Heath were able to revive it profitably whenever another vehicle failed them or vaudeville routings were not to their liking. In this original production, a young comic juggler, W. C. Fields, won applause and good notices as Sherlock Baffles.

Miss Dolly Dollars (9-4-05, Knickerbocker) was the first of the season's three Victor Herbert shows. It was written for Lulu Glaser. She portrayed Dorothy Gay, who is familiarly known as "Dolly Dollars," since her father is the condensed-soup tycoon, Sam Gay (Charles Bradshaw). Sam takes Dolly to the Henley regatta and to Paris, where she falls in love with the seemingly penniless Lord Burlingham (Melville Stewart). But Burlingham turns out to have enough money to save Sam when his business fortunes take an unexpectedly bad turn. If this Harry B. Smith story "offered many an opportunity for social satire of a delicious sort," Smith disappointed none of his detractors when he "ignored every possibility." Nor was Herbert's score top drawer. Even a real automobile chasing real people, dogs, and chickens about the stage was looked on as a device long since "worn threadbare." The musical stayed in Gotham less than two months and then took to the road for the rest of the theatrical year.

Gus and Max Rogers had better luck when they brought **The Rogers Brothers in Ireland** (9-4-05, Liberty) to 42nd Street. This edition had Heinrich Punk (Gus) and Nicholas Knox (Max) go to Ireland to fetch the Blarney Stone for exhibition in America. They will use the money they make to help free Ireland. John J. McNally's plot suggested that heavy Irish theatrical patronage extended even

to these "Dutch" comedians, but none of the numerous Anglophiles who served as daily reviewers at the time complained of the story line, although a number deplored the persistently inferior quality of the Rogers material. Actually, the reception accorded the latest edition was relatively kind, suggesting either the brothers were improving or the critics were growing indifferent. The sets were especially praised, particularly a well-painted view of the Lakes of Killarney. Gus and Max made one entrance in a pony cart and sang Irish folk songs in their German dialect. They also participated in a travesty of the reigning hit song of the moment, "In The Shade Of The Old Apple Tree." Gus and Max made New Yorkers happy for 106 performances before they too embarked on a long tour.

The Duke of Duluth (9-11-05, Majestic) was a three-week flop. The latest in *The Sultan of Sulu* (12-29-02) school of musical comedy transported a tramp named Darling Doolittle by submarine to the Island of Wot, where a prophet has predicted his arrival and where safety compels him to assume a number of disguises until the navy can effect a rescue. Popular Nat M. Wills played Doolittle. Wills' costumes garnered as many hefty laughs as any of his stage business. His first appearance was in an outlandish sailor's suit. Later he paraded pompously around the stage dressed as an English gentleman—in a bright green cutaway and with his face made up to resemble Mr. Hyde. At one point Wills, wearing thick glasses, rode in on horseback and saluted Teddy Roosevelt in "Strenuous" ("Let our Teddy bite the Isthmus; He can cut through it by Christmas"). His star's popularity was great enough to convince producer-librettist George Broadhurst that the vehicle could be saved. A tour followed, but when the show returned the week of December 4 it survived only one week.

Reginald De Koven was still listed on the program as proprietor of the Lyric when his **Happyland** raised the house's curtain on October 2. The librettist was Frederic Ranken, working alone. The star was De Wolf Hopper. Hopper cavorted as King Ecstaticus of Elysia, a land where, according to the typescript, everything is in the style of Alma-Tadema. The monarch is bored to distraction by the happiness overflowing his kingdom:

No little scandal e'er comes in
  To cheer and comfort me.
They hand me love in wholesale lots
  And tons of ecstasy.

To make matters bad he orders everyone to marry. He also promises to marry his son to a neighboring potentate's daughter. But since he has no son, Ecstaticus commands his own daughter, Sylvia (Marguerite Clark), to masquerade as one. She flees. The king realizes that unhappiness can exist in Elysia and decides to let well enough alone. Once again the De Koven score was pleasant, but as juiceless as most of the theatrically accepted music of the day. Still, with little better around and with Hopper to put his delightful personal stamp on the proceedings, *Happyland* gave De Koven one of his longest New York stays—136 performances in two slightly separated runs.

Although the elder Emmet was long gone, the fame of Fritz endured, prodding J. J. McNally, William Jerome, and Jean Schwartz to reincarnate him for Joseph Cawthorn. Together they landed **Fritz in Tammany Hall** (10-16-05, Herald Square). In order to split the district vote, Pat McCann, the district leader, has Fritz nominated for alderman. To everyone's surprise Fritz wins. Nothing memorable came out of the Tin-Pan-Alley-like score, although Ada Lewis, in another of her tough-girl roles, won encores with "East Side Lil." Still, for six weeks the show pleased old timers as well as playgoers too young to remember the original series.

Victor Herbert, Glen MacDonough, and Julian Mitchell, who had been responsible for the music, lyrics, and libretto, and the staging of *Babes in Toyland* (10-13-03), had for some time planned a sequel. MacDonough agreed to write a story combining *Alice in Wonderland, Through the Looking Glass,* and Grimms' "The Twelve Dancing Princesses." Initially it was called *Alice and the Eight Princesses.* The story had Alice, a street urchin who sells matches, dream she is in **Wonderland** (10-24-05, Majestic). The princesses are mysteriously disappearing, and Alice solves the mystery. Out-of-town reviewers were scathing. The book was hastily, drastically, and ineptly revised. By the time it reached New York, Alice and all the Carroll figures had been dropped, and so had any attempt at a consistent story line. The *Times* saw it simply as "a very elaborate sort of vaudeville entertainment," while the reviewer for the *Evening Post,* praising, as did all his fellow critics, the performance of the trick horse operated by two men within the costume, suggested the horse could have written a better libretto. Nor was Herbert's score of much assistance. Some songs, such as "Jografree," were too reminiscent of his *Toyland* compositions, while other pleasantries remained incontestably second-string. However, audiences again proved more tolerant than the critics, and after a 73-performance stay, *Wonderland* began a cross-country tour that

kept box-offices busy for not one, but two full seasons.

One of the many musicals to spend a week at Chicago's principal combination house, the Great Northern, and then quickly move on was **The Belle of the West.** Unlike many touring shows that played the house this musical was probably meant to reach New York eventually. Harry B. Smith was the librettist and lyricist. Florence Bindley was its star. Had the show succeeded it would have introduced a new name to Broadway, Karl Hoschna. But the drubbing the musical took from the Chicago critics after its October 29 opening was such that the show was quickly withdrawn. No critic mentioned the plot, and Harry B. Smith ignored the work in his autobiography. Possibly the runaway success of Belasco's *The Girl of the Golden West* at the same time put the final nail in the musical's coffin.

In New York two musicals closed out October on the 30th. Marie Cahill and her interpolations romped into the Liberty with **Moonshine** while Messager's **Veronique** graced the Broadway's stage. The latter story recounted the adventures of two noble youngsters who run away from home rather than accept arranged marriages. Naturally they fall in love not knowing they were the very mates their parents had selected.

The first act of *Moonshine* was set at the Henley Regatta—a popular locale in the 1905–06 season—where Miss Cahill portrayed another popular stage figure, the detective, or, specifically in this case, the ex-Secret Service agent who utilizes her police knowledge to save the reputation of the man she loves. In what seemed to be developing into a pattern, Cole and Johnson provided her with a hit in "The Conjure Man." Benjamin Hapgood Burt also struck paydirt for Miss Cahill with "Robinson Crusoe's Isle." The best the composer of the main score, Silvio Hein, could come up with was a pseudo-coon song, suspiciously like a watered down version of Miss Cahill's 1902 "Under The Bamboo Tree."

. . .

Silvio Hein was a curious, somewhat pathetic figure on the musical scene. Hein was born in New York City on March 15, 1879. Although he came from a musical family he had no formal musical training. Entirely self-taught, he confined his writing to the simplest tried-and-true lyric forms.

. . .

Klaw and Erlanger continued their policy of importing Drury Lane's pantomime-spectacles when they ushered in **The White Cat** (11-2-05, New Amsterdam). Harry B. Smith adapted the book, while William Jerome and Jean Schwartz added seven songs. The waning vogue for the genre and the inferior quality of the new mounting in particular gave the piece an extremely short run. Klaw and Erlanger were to heed the warning.

Another English importation fared far more happily. Ivan Caryll's **The Earl and the Girl** (11-4-05, Casino), with genial Eddie Foy in charge, came into the Casino two nights later to begin a 148-performance run. Foy portrayed a traveling salesman (always toting two puppies he described as bloodhounds) who changes places with an earl so the earl can court a commoner. The suave Caryll's score was charming, but it never produced anything as popular as one of the many interpolations, "How'd You Like To Spoon With Me?" The song marked the first real commercial success for young Jerome Kern. It is almost forgotten today because it was simply a better-than-average period tune, with none of the beguiling lyricism that was soon to set Kern's music apart. In the show it was sung by chorus girls on flower-strewn swings, led by Georgia Caine.

Benton Scoops is **The Press Agent** (11-29-05, Field's) who takes a party of chorus girls on an excursion boat with the idea of throwing a girl overboard as a stunt. But the ship is hijacked by a band of South American revolutionaries, who force the vessel and the girls to sail to Concarne. The American navy has to rescue them. The story was a refreshing, if preposterous, variation on one of the period's most acceptable musical comedy plots. But even its star, Peter F. Dailey, couldn't surmount the tired jokes and equally fatigued William Lorraine score. Just as damaging, the *Times* noted, "The women in the cast cannot sing and the men cannot act . . . and the costuming is garish." The show, done originally with a different cast in Chicago as *The Filibuster,* came in at Thanksgiving time and was gone by the New Year.

On December 2 Chicago's La Salle Theatre offered its patrons what proved to be far and away the biggest musical hit the city had ever seen. **The Umpire** was the latest Hough-Adams-Howard collaboration. Cecil Lean and Florence Holbrook were again the featured performers. Lean portrayed Johnny Nolan, an umpire who makes such an outrageous call he is forced to flee to Morocco. There, at a football game, he redeems himself. He also wins the hand of the center, when it turns out this star player is a lovely young lady named Maribel Lewton. The show established Lean as the leading musical comedy actor in Chicago and confirmed beyond

any doubt the supremacy of Hough-Adams-Howard in the pecking order of Chicago's lyric stage. But the show also brought a new name to the city. On October 31 the *Tribune* noted that the La Salle had been sold to the Singer Brothers, young men who had risen prominently in the Milwaukee and Minneapolis theatre worlds. It fell to one of these brothers, Mort Singer, to run the La Salle. Under his aegis the musicals at the La Salle came to enjoy a reputation for quality and success virtually unmatched in the city's annals. *The Umpire* began these triumphs by tallying more than 300 performances—a run half again as long as that earned by any 1905–06 New York musical with the exception of the Hippodrome spectacle.

In New York, December's first musical was another Richard Carle vehicle, **The Mayor of Tokio** (12-4-05, New York). As was his wont, Carle wrote the book and lyrics. He called on W. F. Peters for the music. Carle's fable found a comic-opera troupe, Kipper's Konsolidated Komiques, stranded in Tokio. They are mistaken for royalty, and the mayor's daughter falls in love with their leading man. The leading man's wealthy father appears on his yacht to rescue them. It was a typical Carle affair, with typically minor Peters music. Once more New Yorkers were not as enthusiastic as Chicago or the road, although one critic reported the audience "piled up encores three and four deep." The show stayed only 50 performances.

The Hippodrome began to find itself when the Shuberts were called in to take over the house. **A Society Circus**—which depicted what happens when Lady Volumnia (Rose La Harte) decides to stage an elaborate party—opened on December 13, at the height of the season instead of toward its end. Twice-a-day performances became the rule. And the spectacle was changed at intervals during the run, much in line with the "reconstructions" of the 19th-century extravaganzas. Speciality acts came and went. At one time or another audiences could watch fountains of "dancing waters," the Hippodrome chorus transform itself into a huge floral bouquet, and an elaborate tribute to the newfangled flying machines (called "Motoring in Mid-Air"). Perfume was sprayed over the auditorium during the flower number. Gustav Luders joined Manuel Klein to compose the score, and Klein came up with the first of the modest hits he produced in his decade at the house, "Moon Dear." It could almost pass for a spoof of the songs of the time, though it was presented as a serious ballad. The show compiled 596 performances, far and away the longest run of the season. During their heyday Hippodrome spectacles almost invariably walked off with each year's long-run honors.

Another jumble of fairy tales, **The Babes and the Baron** (12-25-05, Lyric), was one of three Christmas night offerings. An English show, it was laced with interpolations by Aarons, Burt, Goetz, Hubbell, and Kern, among others. It survived 45 performances.

A similar American piece, termed a "Fairyesque" by its creators, Frederic Ranken and A. Baldwin Sloane, bowed the same night. **The Gingerbread Man** (12-25-05, Liberty) described how the flavorful King (Eddie Redway) of BonBonLand lives in fear of being eaten. He was once human, but was turned into gingerbread by the evil Machevavelius. Santa Claus arrives (on a sled pulled by eight chorus girls dressed as reindeer), and Mrs. Santa Claus turns up to set everything straight. The hit of the evening fell to the Gingerbread Man himself. His song, in which he longs to be a typical "John Dough," was encored half a dozen times on opening night. The musical stayed only long enough to profit from the holiday trade and went on the road. It returned later in the season for a second two-week stay.

The third Christmas night offering was its best. It was also the biggest musical hit of the season, excepting the unique Hippodrome mounting. **Mlle. Modiste** (12-25-05, Knickerbocker) is best remembered for its lovely Victor Herbert score and its radiant star, petite Fritzi Scheff. But no small part of its initial success must be credited to its book by Henry Blossom, generally conceded the best librettist Herbert ever worked with. Blossom's story was simple. The romance of Fifi, the charming little salesgirl at Mme. Cecile's hat shop on the Rue de la Paix, and of Capt. Etienne de Bouvray (Walter Percival) faces two obstacles. Mme. Cecile (Josephine Bartlett) expects her employee to marry her son (Leo Mars), while the Compte de St. Mar (William Pruette), Etienne's uncle, forbids his nephew to wed beneath his station. But one day a free-spirited American millionaire, Hiram Bent (Claude Gillingwater), bursts into the hat shop. At first Fifi suspects another masher:

Hiram: I'm sorry to frighten you, Mlle. Modiste. I merely wanted to ask you a question.
Fifi: "No" is the answer.
Hiram: Then you can't tell me?
Fifi: Tell you what?
Hiram: The quickest way to the Louvre.

Fifi: The quickest way is to run.
Hiram: Now just for that I'll stay.
Fifi: Monsieur, I don't have the pleasure of your acquaintance.
Hiram: And you don't want to have, I guess.
Fifi: Monsieur, I am too polite to disagree with you.
Hiram: See here. There's a sign in your window "One Speaks English Here." I guess I'm the one.
Fifi: I "guess" you're not. You don't speak English. You speak American. Englishmen don't guess, they know.

Hiram is taken by Fifi's pert replies, and Fifi realizes Hiram's inquiries are unfeigned. Before long they have told each other their respective backgrounds. Fifi describes at length how she would perform, "If I Were On The Stage." The delighted, open-handed Hiram offers to underwrite Fifi's musical studies. A year later a charity bazaar is held at the count's estate. The count is a gruff, purposeful fellow, avowing to all who will listen, "I Want What I Want When I Want It." He is overwhelmed by the singing of Mme. Bellini, and when he discovers she is none other than Fifi, the modiste, he gracefully withdraws his objections to a marriage. Etienne rushes over and kisses Fifi on the forehead. Fifi steps back:

Etienne: Oh, Fifi, have I offended you? Twas only on the forehead!
Fifi: Well, I'll have to call you down a little!

When Etienne grasps Fifi's meaning, he gives her a proper kiss.

Herbert's great number from the operetta was "Kiss Me Again." Herbert had written the waltz several years earlier and put it away until he could find a desirable spot for it. Over the complaints of Miss Scheff, Blossom, and producer Dillingham, he insisted it be retained as part of Fifi's first-act tour de force, "If I Were On The Stage," in which she sings in various styles to suggest the range of her dramatic characterizations. Miss Scheff remained identified with the song for the rest of her life. The count's song, "I Want What I Want When I Want It," became a bass-baritone standard for years. The rest of the score was almost as good, including as it did Etienne's "The Time And The Place And The Girl" and Fifi's "The Mascot Of The Troop," with its quotation from "La Marseillaise." *Mlle. Modiste* ran until vacation time and then resumed in September until a previous booking for another Herbert show forced it on to the road. It toured for three full seasons.

The first show of 1906 was equally important and equally good, although not nearly as successful. By the time **Forty-five Minutes from Broadway** opened at the New Amsterdam on January 1, the nation was already singing its three great hits—"So Long Mary," "Mary's A Grand Old Name," and its title song. The "Gentlemen Of The Press" are gathered at the Castleton home in New Rochelle to interview Tom Bennett (Donald Brian), Castleton's nephew, who stands to inherit a vast fortune if his uncle died, as he apparently did, intestate. Bennett announces he will be married to his actress-sweetheart, Flora Dora Dean (Lois Ewell), as soon as she arrives. The interview disappoints the townspeople who have also gathered at the house, for they had expected Castleton to leave his wealth to his long faithful servant, Mary (Fay Templeton). Matters are made unhappier for Mary by Dan Cronin (James H. Manning), who courted her when he expected her to inherit the Castleton wealth and now makes no bones about his loss of interest in her. Bennett assures everyone, "I Want To Be A Popular Millionaire." No one is brazen enough to tell Tom that one quick jump toward popularity would be to rid himself of his wise-guy secretary, Kid Burns (Victor Moore). Kid has no false modesty, even on his first entrance:

Kid: I'm the real noise around this man's residence, understand? I'm the real noise. I'll make these rubes around here pay a little attention to me yet. Forty-five minutes from Broadway, Gee, its got some of them towns in Texas tied to a post.

Mary arrives, depressed. Andy (Louis R. Grisel), the butler, tries to console her. Their dialogue is pure vaudeville, including a favorite of Cohan's, playing with nouns in apposition. But Cohan has learned how to make it all apply to the plot:

Andy: You know I knew your father, Mary.
Mary: You mean my mother, Mary. My father's name was Oscar.

. . .

Andy: How long have you been fond of Cronin, Mary?
Mary: It's three years now since he first told me that I loved him.
Andy: And nobody knew that you were engaged?
Mary: No, I didn't know it myself until he called it off.

Mary and Kid meet and discover that Kid's mother was also named Mary. The maid assures the secretary, "Mary's A Grand Old Name." Burns agrees. He suggests they might go out together for a night on the town. Ruefully, he suspects an evening of such fun is impossible "Forty-five Minutes From Broadway." Bennett reappears with Miss Dean and her snobbish mother (Julia Ralph). But it seems the snobbery is meant to camouflage her past, and part of that past was crooked Dan Cronin, who threatens to reveal her history. Burns witnesses this conversation but hasn't much time to think about it for he has stumbled on Castleton's will. Reading it he confirms that the heir is—as the orchestra, not Burns, announces—Mary. Mary enters with her luggage, but Burns, who is falling in love with her, persuades her to stay, although he doesn't mention the will. At a dinner party Bennett and Mrs. Dean fight over Mrs. Dean's dislike of Kid Burns. Bennett remains loyal, while growing angrier:

Bennett: And if you don't like it, you can go right straight to—
Flora: Tom!
Mrs. Dean: Let him say it! Let him say it!
Bennett: Oh, Hell.

Bennett finally agrees to keep Burns out of sight, only to have the bitchy Mrs. Dean start in on Mary. Cronin demands Mrs. Dean get him the combination of the Castleton safe. Cronin then phones Bennett, pretending to be his lawyer's secretary and insisting he return immediately to New York. Burns warns Bennett that Mrs. Dean and her daughter are up to no good, but Bennett refuses to listen and breaks with the Kid. Mary and Burns agree to take a train together in the morning. In a dumb show Cronin attempts to rob the house but is foiled by Mary. At the railroad station the crowds wait to see Cronin taken to jail. While they wait they gossip that Mrs. Dean and Flora Dora have packed their bags and vanished. Mary arrives with her friends, who bid her, "So Long Mary." Burns arrives and shows Mary the will. She concludes that Kid, like Cronin, really only wanted her inheritance. But Kid assures her he would marry her despite it. She rips up the will.

Here was Cohan at his peak. His story was good and not unbelievable; his earthy dialogue, albeit a little coy or a little vaudevillian at times, a far cry from even the better-than-average material Blossom had provided the week before in *Mlle. Modiste*. Cohan, moreover, was brazen enough to put all his songs in the first and third acts, leaving the second act for pure melodrama. In a sense this was as retrogressive as it was daring, suggesting the piece, like so many mountings of the preceding generation, was primarily a play, with songs tacked on.

Even though Cohan worked the story and music together far more skillfully than most of his more slapdash predecessors, his efforts were not universally applauded. Some papers objected to a comedienne making an audience cry or to mixing melodrama and musical comedy. The *Times* saw it as "a case of oil and water." But even the *Times* grudgingly conceded there were "four or five capital songs." The initial New York run of 90 performances fell short of the Chicago tryout. It was not just Chicago-made shows New Yorkers disdained, but New York material in the homespun, forthright Chicago style. For all the exciting innovations in some domestic musicals, English and French shows, and American creations conceived in their unmistakably Continental mold, continued to receive the most serious attention and favor. It was a curious blind spot for Broadway, and would continue to be so for another decade. This xenophilia failed to hurt Cohan financially. *Forty-five Minutes from Broadway* cost a mere $10,000 to produce and was in the black a few days after its New York opening.

One more or less American musical form, the rowdy "Dutch" comedian burlesque, was still well received in Manhattan. Perhaps the clowns' dialects, even in mockery, gave the requisite Continental tinge to the evening. In any case, **Twiddle-Twaddle** (1-1-06, Weber's Music Hall), which opened the same night as *Forty-Five Minutes from Broadway,* chalked up 169 performances in two separate runs. Knowledgeable theatre-buffs would immediately and correctly spot the title as more Weber and Fields' nonsense, although of course Fields had gone his own way. The main plot was also typical. A multimillionaire sausage-maker takes his daughter to Europe to find her a titled husband. Edgar Smith's libretto was not without its Cohanesque chauvinisms: "We changed the words to that ["God Save The King"] and came pretty near making you British change your tune . . . Hurray, I'm a Yankee." Broadway clearly had strong but ambivalent feelings. A highlight of the evening was Marie Dressler's travesty of a Spanish dance. She danced close to the footlights, but she stomped so hard a trick chair collapsed at the rear of the stage. The principal burlesque offered a double spoof, "The Squawman's Girl of the Golden West." Maurice Levi's score was serviceable at best.

Broadway gave scant attention to **Comin' Thro' the Rye** (1-9-06, Herald Square) on which George V. Hobart and A. Baldwin Sloane did the lion's share of the work. Hobart's plot had a Newport society queen (Alice Fisher) entertaining penniless artists in hopes of stumbling onto a genius. One of the artists (John Park) has painted a picture, "Comin' Thro' the Rye," using as a model a young girl (Georgie Kelly) whose irate father (Dan McAvoy) suddenly appears. The expected misunderstandings and a number of specialty acts rounded out the evening. To allow Dan McAvoy another "Dutch" role, the father was called Ippy Ipstein and the girl was his "long-lost" offspring. McAvoy fans no doubt recalled he had portrayed Izzy, the father of Sally of our Alley three seasons back. The looseness of the plot allowed for some absurd theatrical *non sequiturs*. Although the first half was set in an artist's loft and the second at the Newport Casino, Nena Blake, dressed in a white cowgirl outfit, galloped on stage on a white pony to sing "My Broncho Boy." As usual Sloane's score was never more than adequate. The show moved out after 35 performances.

Lew Dockstader and his minstrels returned on January 15. Once again only about half his program was traditional blackface material—this time including Dockstader's own rendition of Bert Williams' "Nobody." The rest of the entertainment was more up-to-date material, hinging largely on satires of the New York political scene.

Racing the still newfangled automobiles had become so popular that a Vanderbilt offered a cup to the winner of one of the more important meets. The musical stage was quick to use it for plot material. A country girl, Dorothy Willetts (Dorothy would be a popular name for musical comedy racers), is sent for by her brother (Henry V. Donnelly), who has made a fortune in New York. She upsets the intrigues of Clarinda Larkspur (Edith Decker) who, in revenge, bribes the Willetts' chauffeur (Henry Bergman) to lose the race for **The Vanderbilt Cup** (1-16-06, Broadway). But Willetts' car wins with Dorothy and her lover (Aubrey Boucicault) behind the wheel. The show not only utilized the latest sports headlines for its story, it employed the newest theatrical gimmicks in the story's unfolding. Dorothy's trip east was shown to the audience by means of another newfangled device—moving pictures. For the race itself, two real cars were brought on stage, apparently on a treadmill, and drop after drop was raised to suggest the passage of scenery. The last drop, at the finish line, portrayed a group of shouting spectators—an addition to the large chorus that several papers felt was artificial and redundant. At the end of the race Barney Oldfield, the famous auto-racer, doffed his goggles to reveal he was one of the contestants. Since Oldfield was not listed in any of the programs, this was probably simply an opening-night stunt. Elsie Janis, a former child star, just coming into maturity, played Dorothy. She brought over from her vaudeville act a series of imitations, including Maude Adams as Peter Pan. Otis Harlan also won applause, in his case for an eccentric dance in which he accompanied himself with a "whistling obbligato." Unfortunately it fell to Miss Janis' lot to have to put over a weak score. However, her theatrical élan, Sydney Rosenfeld's book, and the superb, inventive staging made a hit of the evening.

If the Shuberts and their writers for *Fantana* (1-14-05) hoped to repeat their success with **Mexicana** (1-29-06, Lyric), they were badly disappointed. They disappointed theatregoers as well. "Book Stupid; Music Dull," read the *Times*' headline. The book followed a New Yorker to Mexico, where he discovers he is the victim of a Porfirio Diaz swindle with a bogus mine called "Mexicana." He engineers a revolution. Raymond Hubbell's music had no more of a Mexican flavor than his songs for *Fantana* savored of Japan. *Mexicana*'s leading players, Thomas Q. Seabrooke and Christie MacDonald, were unable to improve matters.

George Washington, Jr. (2-12-06, Herald Square) was the first of two February musicals. When he unveiled his latest work, Cohan attacked the twisted, pervasive belittling of American virtues so evident in criticism of his plays. This was the flag-waving Cohan of *Little Johnny Jones* (11-7-04) back in full stride. Senator Belgrave (Jerry Cohan), an Anglophile boastfully contemptuous of the country he serves, is determined that his son George (George M.) will marry Lord Rothburt's languid, arrogant daughter, Evelyn. But George loves Dolly Johnson (Ethel Levey), the niece of the straightforward Senator Hopkins (Eugene O'Rourke). They have all come to Mount Vernon to show the Rothburts some Americana. If Dolly is a bit naive about Washington's mores, George couldn't care less. He will be happy to educate her:

Dolly: Do the Senators get a big salary?
George: That's all according to what corporation they represent.
Dolly: There are no female politicians, are there?
George: There are lots of old ladies in the Senate.

Hopkins hears George is to marry Evelyn and warns Dolly. Dolly's coolness upsets George and he finally breaks with his father:

George: I disown you as a father. Now what do you think of that!

Belgrave: You're a disgrace to the name of Belgrave.
George: Then take your name! I don't want your name! To hell with it! I'll take my own name!

And, taking heed of the estate on which they are standing, he then and there calls himself George Washington, Jr., Hopkins enters and Belgrave snarls at him, "You did this." To which Hopkins replies, for a first-act curtain, "No, you're wrong, Belgrave. The man who used to live there [pointing to Mount Vernon] did this." Hopkins is still not completely satisfied that George is the right boy for Dolly. He informs George he will not give his consent until there's a monument to George Washington, Jr. But Hopkins himself is not beyond reproach. Lord Rothburt and Evelyn are frauds hired by him to embarrass Belgrave. George gets wind of the machinations in the nick of time, and despite their quarrel, warns his father. Belgrave sees the error of his ways, and when in gratitude he offers to erect a monument to his son, Hopkins consents to the marriage. The hit of the show was "You're A Grand Old Flag"—called "You're A Grand Old Rag" until the sort of patriots Cohan hated objected and he was forced to change the lyrics. The song was the first one written with a specific musical in mind to sell over a million copies of its sheet music. Dolly was also given a show-stopper, "I Was Born In Virginia." Although it was almost as good as *Forty-five Minutes from Broadway* and with its full complement of songs closer to accepted musical comedy, *George Washington, Jr.* didn't even attain the former's 90 performances. Once again the road was more welcoming to Cohan than his own beloved Broadway. Both musicals played return Broadway engagements, but neither added appreciably to the number of New York showings.

The second February musical was **Abyssinia** (2-20-06, Majestic). It was as important as the Cohan piece, almost as well realized, yet far less popular. Assembled by the team that created *In Dahomey* (2-18-03) for many of the same players, including the stars, Williams and Walker, it marked an obvious advance in writing and staging techniques for the group. After Rastus Johnson (Bert Williams) wins $15,000 in a lottery, Rastus and Jasmine Jenkins (George Walker) decide to visit the land of their ancestors, which they have determined was Abyssinia. (The stage Abyssinia displayed real water pouring down a waterfall in a mountain pass, and a colorful bazaar with a "property lion and camel and real asses.") Their ignorance of foreign ways leads Rastus and Jasmine into several misadventures culminating before the throne of Abyssinia's iron-fisted monarch, Menelik. They are brought there as a court of last appeal after they have "borrowed" a priceless vase. If Menelik sounds a gong three times, the "borrowers" must die, if he sounds it four times, they are pardoned. The long wait between the third and fourth gong provided a memorable scene, at once comic and terrifying. One interesting feature of J. A. Shipp and Alex Rogers' libretto and lyrics was the way African blacks and American blacks were contrasted. Apparently Shipp and Rogers wanted to suggest that coming to America marked a falling away from grace, if not from perfection. The Africans speak the King's English. Indeed some of their dialogue and lyrics are so stilted they smack of parody:

Soldiers of the King are we,
   We bow to his supremacy,
We know naught of disloyalty,
   Hence can not spare an enemy.

On the other hand the Americans speak lines straight out of minstrelsy:

Jasmine: And you's a philosophy?
Rastus: Philospher
Jasmine: What's the duty of a philoso- philoso- (*finally add pede*)
Rastus: To look on the bright side of other people's troubles when you haven't any of your own.

Will Marion Cook and Williams supplied the score. No long-lived favorites emerged from it, but it represented the best black popular musical writing of the period, with native and international styles in reciprocal influences. Negro shows had to be particularly careful. No serious love interest could be included. No "suggestion" was allowed. Even Cohan's coy profanity was taboo. Notwithstanding their concern at offending a white audience's sensibilities, these fine black talents could win over only a handful of ticket buyers. Thirty-one performances was all *Abyssinia* could attain.

Although **His Majesty** (3-19-06, Majestic) professed to be a musicalization of *Man and Superman,* it most certainly was not. Bernard Shaw was not about to give his consent to an adaptation. And a show written around Blanche Ring's gaudy talents stood small chance of reflecting the balanced debates that comprised Shaw's scenes. What was presented on the stage of the Majestic on March 19 was a most un-Shavian concoction about an opera company killed in a railroad wreck. In Hell, its prima donna, Mrs. Brown of Chicago, finds all six of her ex-husbands. She gets her revenge on one who reneged on his alimony payments. The score, by the otherwise unheard-from Shafter Howard, offered nothing of merit, nor could Miss Ring find a first-rate interpolation to add during the brief three-week run.

Harry B. Smith, collaborating with composer Stafford Waters, had a new musical, **The Three Graces,** ready for inspection at the Chicago Opera House on April 2. Smith's story told of three thieves' stealing clothes so they can pose as gentlemen at a Catskill hotel. The clothes contain papers that help them discover a missing heiress. Though several critics compared the plot—and the show—unfavorably to *Erminie,* it proved acceptable to many Chicagoans. The show ran into the hot weather.

The front page of **The Social Whirl** (4-7-06, Casino), a notorious scandal sheet, discloses that "J. E." was seen wining and dining the Broadway star Viola Dare (Adele Ritchie) at a discreet country inn. At least four men in her circle have those initials, and three of them are married. Each tries to throw suspicion on the others. All that really took place was that Viola took both James Ellingham (Frederic Bond) and his son Jack (Willard Curtis) in her car so that she could persuade the elder Ellingham she was a fit match for his boy. Small parts were excellently cast. Ada Lewis played yet another toughie. Charles J. Ross and Joe Coyne portrayed a father and son, with Coyne singing about a girl who plays love songs on a calliope; while Maud Raymond earned several encores with a song describing a black who has to dance whenever he hears a band play. Blanche Deyo and Mabel Fenton offered "crowd-pleasing" dances. The chorus whirled through a ballet done all in crimson, a hunting dance, and a routine in which the smaller girls impersonated bootblacks shining the taller girls' shoes. There was another Gustave Kerker score relegated to the sidelines by interpolations. The most popular were "You're Just The Girl I'm Looking For" (E. Ray Goetz) and "Old Man Manhattan" by the husband-and-wife team of James O'Dea and Anne Caldwell. They were typical vaudeville melodies, stronger fibered than the watery Kerker stuff. With so solid a cast of favorites the show ran from early April into the fall.

John Philip Sousa returned to the theatre after a six-year absence to write the score to Harry B. Smith's tale of **The Freelance** (4-16-06, New Amsterdam). In Smith's story the Duke of Graftiana (Albert Hart) arranges for his son Florian (George Tallman) to wed Yolanda (Nella Bergen), daughter of the Emperor of Bragadocia (Felix Haney). The children balk. Yolande flees, changing places with Griselda (Jeanette Lowrie), a goose girl, while Florian, not knowing of Yolanda's actions, switches stations with Griselda's husband, the goatherd, Sigmund Lump (Joseph Cawthorn). When Sigmund discovers he is not to wed a real princess, he sighs, "Everytime I'm invited out to dinner, I always get just what I have at home." Smith's tale left Sousa uninspired. As the librettist noted, the best number in the show, the closing march "Drums Are Beating," never stirred a soul except on opening night, when Sousa himself conducted and was hailed back for six curtain calls. While the show helped secure Cawthorn stardom, even his clowning could not push it beyond 35 performances.

. . .

Joseph Cawthorn was born in New York on March 29, 1867. He made his debut in variety at the age of four and appeared one year later with Haverly's Minstrels. Taken to England when he was nine, he spent the next four years performing a child act in British music halls. His first appearances on his return to America were also in vaudeville, but he soon moved over to legitimate musicals, appearing in *Excelsior, Jr.* (11-29-95), *Miss Philadelphia* (12-27-97), and *The Fortune Teller* (9-26-98) among others.

. . .

Philadelphians still enjoyed patronizing local productions, especially Willard Spenser's sporadic musicals. Spenser unveiled a new one—with an unusual setting—on April 23 at the Chestnut Street Theatre. **Rosalie** planted its principals in the midst of the Russo-Japanese War in Manchuria. Rosalie (Clara Maentz) finds time from nursing the wounded to win the hand of an American reporter (Albert Parr). The musical ran into June.

Joe Howard, the Chicago favorite, braved New York with **The District Leader** (4-30-06, Wallack's). His story was a down-to-earth, if melodramatic, slice of American politics. Tim Halloran, a candidate for the state senate, loves Grace Lowton, daughter of the Republican candidate for the same post. Halloran's manager, Sam Grady, betrays Tim and drugs his twin brother, Jim, in a Chinatown opium den. But Tom Cole, a newspaperman and Grace's brother, exposes Grady's scheme. Howard took credit for the book and lyrics as well as the music. The critics were impressed with none of it. But songs such as "Won't You Be My Girlie?"

carry the melodic stamp and lyric directness that endeared Howard to his Chicago fans. Howard also appeared in the show, but he took none of the major roles, contenting himself instead with singing a single song while sitting placidly on a park bench. He didn't have to sit for long. He could hurry back to Chicago after an ignominious one-week run.

Politics were also the order of the day in **His Honor the Mayor** (5-28-06, New York), the only musical to bow in May. His Honor (Clarence Harvey), it develops, is not very honorable. When it comes out that the mayor of Kankakee bought the election, he is forced to leave town. Amazingly, all the action takes place in Paris and at a Hungarian spa. Spearheading the reform and the evening was the indefatigable Blanche Ring. Nothing from Julian Edwards' score really stopped the show, but Gus Edwards gave Miss Ring a fairly good tune in "Come Take A Skate With Me," and Will Cobb and Ren Shields offered an even better number in "Waltz Me Around Again Willie." To play safe she also revived "My Irish Molly O!" During several encores for this song she was abetted by the grotesque dancing of Harry Kelly and the unicycling of Henri French. Together they cavorted through the hot weather.

The season's final production was a loosely-strung-together vaudeville called **Seeing New York** (6-5-06, New York Roof). Cool rooftop breezes must have been as much of an attraction as the show itself. A hackneyed Sloane score and the thinnest of story lines by Joseph Hart and Clifton Crawford about another yokel on tour needed all the help they could get from the performers (including Mr. Crawford) and the weather. The other performers included the Six Proveanies in their bicycle act and Salerno, the juggler. A "policeman" chorus sang while a burglary progressed (the burglar ran off taking one policeman's shield with him), while a chorus of red-gowned young women, supposedly standing in the wind at 23rd Street and Broadway, had their skirts ballooned by air blown from beneath the stage. As it turned out the evening had little other serious roof garden competition and made it through the summer.

1906-1907

The season got off to a lurid start. **Mamzelle Champagne** (6-25-06, Madison Square Garden Roof) was never able to complete its first performance.

During the second act Harry Thaw shot and killed the Garden's architect, Stanford White, in a dispute over Thaw's wife, the musical comedy starlet, Evelyn Nesbit. The scene and some of its background was described in a letter by the librettist, Edgar Allan Woolf, to Burns Mantle:

"Mamzelle Champagne" was my Columbia varsity show, and was transported by a manager, Henry Pincus, to the open Madison Square Roof with a professional cast. Of course, when the college boys played it, with such lines as "I'm a good girl—you can't insult me," every line was a howl, but spoken by actresses the howls were missing. In addition to this calamity, the wind was blowing down Madison Ave. on the night of the opening—blowing all the dialogue with it. My mother and father were sitting in the front row, and through the remarks of the people behind them, they knew the show was dying, and that the author was in ill repute. When the three shots fired by Harry Thaw rang through the air, my mother jumped up in her chair and screamed, "My God, they've shot my son!"
Although poor Pincus thought his show was ruined by the murder, the next night you couldn't get near the Garden, and the seats at the table where Stanford White sat, sold at a premium.

Curiosity seekers continued to keep the otherwise vapid evening alive for 60 showings.

There were no new shows in July. But five musicals arrived in August, and three of them were rewarded with long runs. First to arrive was the London hit **The Little Cherub** (8-6-06, Criterion). That show's star, Hattie Williams, played a young lady who must first charm a snobbish earl before she can marry his son. Besides the regular Ivan Caryll score, Miss Williams sang songs by Marie Doro, Jerome Kern, and Jean Schwartz. She sang them 155 times in New York before repeating them in other cities.

The first solid American-made hit, **The Tourists** (8-25-06, Daly's), had book and lyrics by R. H. Burnside and music by Gustave Kerker. Burnside's fable, a variation of the popular American-in-exotic-parts plot, was inordinately complicated. John Duke (Alfred Hickman) of Plymouth, Massachusetts, is registered as the Duke of Plymouth at the Oriental Hotel in Rangapang. He is evading his tutor, Mr. Todd (Richard Golden), and courting Dora Blossom (Julia Sanderson), whose American father (Phil H. Ryley) is seeking a titled marriage for her. Todd somehow discovers John's whereabouts and telegraphs that he is on his way. Jambo-

Ree (also called Ram-Dow, and played by Alfred Cahill) arrives. His master, Boojam, was to have married the Rajah's daughter (Vera Michelena) but, according to Jambo-Ree, Boojam has been eaten by a tiger and Jambo-Ree has decided to impersonate him. The hotel manager, recognizing Jambo-Ree as a rebel with a price on his head, drugs him and prepares to claim the reward. This suggests an escape to John. He writes Todd, claiming he has been kidnapped by Jambo-Ree and must be ransomed. A battered, road-weary Todd soon appears:

We traveled thru France
　But I hadn't a chance
to see it—for I had malaria.
　And while we were in Spain
I was nearly insane
　with the grip, which I caught in Bulgaria.

Mr. Blossom offers Todd some reassurance, "You can sue the Government for keeping the roads in such bad condition and get damages." But Todd isn't interested, "I've got all the damages I want—what I need is repairs." Todd is blindfolded and led around the hotel courtyard, which he is told is the rebel's cave. After his negotiations with Jambo-Ree (actually John faking an Oriental accent), he is "returned" to the hotel. The Rajah (William Pruette) enters and falls in love with Dora, insisting he will abduct her if she will not marry him willingly. He accuses Todd, who has been gotten up in native dress, of being another rebel. Todd claims he is Boojam, only to have Boojam turn up hale and hearty. Everything is finally explained, and the lovers are allowed to go their own way:

Todd: Jack, I want to congratulate you—this is the happiest day of your life!
Jack [John]:—You are too previous, old man, I am not to be married until tomorrow!
Todd: That's what I say—This is the happiest day of your life.

Kerker's music was his usual run-of-the-mill melodies with the expected love ditties, such as "It's Nice To Have A Sweetheart" and the apparently requisite paean to the Rialto, "Dear Old Broadway."

The authors also demonstrated the persistent influence of *Florodora*, when they gave "Which One Shall I Marry?" to a "double quartet." The *Times* ruefully concluded "that Gustave Kerker long ago gave up any idea of going down to fame by reason of anything he might write." But the paper, which four years before had predicted the demise of musical comedy, still found little attractive in the whole school. "A mystic maze of brilliant color, popular melody, obvious comicality, with the inevitable girls, girls, girls, . . . when one has said that what more is there to tell about any of the so-called musical comedies?" "Nothing," contented theatregoers seemed to respond, as they stood in line for seats during the show's four-month run.

Marie Cahill came in two nights later as **Marrying Mary** (8-27-06, Daly's). Although Mary Montgomery is a much-married young lady, her marriages never last more than an hour or two, when she runs away in fright. She has already married a Senator, a Mormon, and a lush. At a vacation retreat she meets Ormsby Kulpepper (William Courtleigh) and his father, Henry Clay Kulpepper (Eugene Cowles), both of whom would marry her, though the elder Kulpepper heads the Anti-Divorce League. Just as she is trying to decide between the two, all her past mates appear. She finally realizes which one she really loves and promises this time to stay around for at least a week or so. On paper *Marrying Mary* would seem like the usual Cahill vehicle. Instead of a "Congo Love Song" or an "Arab Love Song" Benjamin Hapgood Burt and Silvio Hein presented her with "The Hottentot Love Song." And once again an interpolation, "He's A Cousin Of Mine" (Cecil Mack/Chris Smith and Silvio Hein), often got the biggest applause. Mary reprised the chorus whenever she was caught with the wrong man. But most of the critics, even the ones who customarily had reservations about Miss Cahill, were free with their praise. They lauded the show for its sense of tone and scale (there wasn't a big chorus line or any large, stagy numbers), and they praised Miss Cahill for playing a part instead of herself. Nonetheless the show stayed only six weeks before it headed to the profitable hinterlands. There is a tantalizing footnote to the show. One of the songs was "Is There Any One Here By The Name Of Smith?" Years later, Fritzi Scheff starred in *Pretty Mrs. Smith* (9-21-14), using an almost identical plot, except that all her former husbands had been named Smith. Was there any connection?

Lew Fields struck gold with an elaborate vaudeville, **About Town** (8-30-06, Herald Square), held together by the required gossamer story line. The Duke of Slushington (Lawrence Grossmith) must choose between the saucy adventuress Fancy Frivol (Edna Wallace Hopper) and pert Gertie Gibson (Louise Dresser), who is, appropriately, a Gibson girl. He is aided by a brash cab driver (Fields), who suddenly finds himself elevated to the presidency of the All-Night Bank. Fields gave his eye-filling chorus a variety of routines. They marched as soldiers in red and then again as cadets in gray. They sang and danced as Dutchmen, Gibson girls (in white and blue), and nursemaids (in polka dots). At one point Fields divided the ladies of the ensemble into two groups: the first in red frocks and black stockings, the second all in blue. He then made the chorus boys choose a group. Whichever group was chosen, the other crossed the stage and began to rip off their clothes in a jealous pique. For the times, it was very naughty and revealing. Sketches, songs, and even the performers came and went during the 138-performance run. Besides Fields, entertainers included Jack Norworth, Vernon Castle, Miss Hopper, Miss Dresser, and, later, Peter F. Dailey and Blanche Ring. Though no hit song developed, the roster of credits included, at one time or another, Victor Herbert, Gus Edwards, Albert Von Tilzer, Raymond Hubbell, Gustave Kerker, and A. Baldwin Sloane. When business started to fall off, Fields harked back to his music hall days and inserted a burlesque of *The Great Divide,* which he rechristened "The Great Decide."

The Man from Now (9-3-06, New Amsterdam) offered one of the primitive science-fiction plots the age so relished. Professor Forecasta (Edward B. Martindell) invents a machine to let people see 1000 years ahead and then concocts a potion that allows the drinker to visit the future he has seen. A visit to Gassar, a 30th-century women's college, discloses that women dominate the world. The men quickly return to the comfortably male-dominated 1906. This summary gives no hint that the star of the show was Harry Bulger, who ambled in and out of the action as a tramp called "Waffles." But the plot, as was so often the case, served only as an insubstantial frame on which to hang tours de force, specialties, and anything else that came to mind. For example, Helen Hale was brought on to sing "My Gasoline Maid" dressed as a motorcar. Chorus girls, as college girls, played a choreographed football game, exercised with dumbbells, and marched and countermarched "statuesquely." The show arrived in New York only after an extended road tour, during which it was known as *2905 or To-morrow Land*. But its Broadway run was brief and the show was gone long before 1907 arrived.

The plot of Paul Rubens' London hit, *Lady Madcap,* retitled **My Lady's Maid** (9-20-06, Casino), was something of a novelty, though at best it was merely a British variation of the sort of tale told in *His Highness the Bey* (11-21-04) or *It Happened* *in Nordland* (12-5-04). In this instance a maid is forced to impersonate her mistress when the madcap lady disappears.

The Red Mill (9-24-06, Knickerbocker) was the smash hit of the season and remains one of the joys of the American Musical Theatre. If it was different, it was a difference of degree, not kind. Stripped to essentials, it was merely another of the many musical comedies that had fun with Americans in a foreign setting. But for 1906 audiences it also had the brilliant clowning of David Montgomery and Fred Stone, while for posterity it had a superior Henry Blossom book and an unforgettable Victor Herbert score. Con Kidder (Stone) and Kid Conner (Montgomery) are two aggressive young Americans. They've come to "do" Europe, but find the Continent has undone them. They are broke. Arriving at a little Dutch port of Katwyk-ann-Zee, they nonetheless take lodgings at the inn on the square, within sight of an old, legendary red mill. The town is lorded over by a stern burgomaster, Jan Van Borkem (Edward Begley). He has promised his daughter Gretchen (Augusta Greenleaf) to the handsome governor of Zeeland, though both men know her heart belongs to the equally handsome sea captain, Doris Van Damn (Joseph M. Ratliff). Con flirts with the innkeeper's daughter, Tina (Ethel Johnson), hoping she will help soften the blow when he and Kid are revealed as penniless. Tina is as spunky as Con and Kid, but the three agree there is a double standard and the only way a woman can publicly vent her anger is to "Whistle It." Gretchen and Doris meet and talk together longingly of "The Isle Of Our Dreams." But the burgomaster's sister Bertha (Allene Crater), while she sympathizes with the lovers, warns Doris that Van Borkem will lock Gretchen in the mill and its terrifying history will repeat itself:

Doris: I don't believe that foolish story.
Bertha: It's true. It happened hundreds of years ago. King Johann locked the Princess Wilhelmina in this mill over night to keep her from the man she loved and she disappeared and no trace did they ever find of her.

Con and Kid dream of another island, and they recapitulate the pleasures to be found on "The Streets Of New York." Van Borkem discovers Gretchen and Doris have seen each other and fulfills Bertha's warning by locking Gretchen in the mill. Alone at night on the deck of the mill she prays "Moonbeams" will send her message of love to Doris. But Con manages to enter the mill and lowers Gretchen to freedom on a mill sail. The gover-

nor (Neal McCay) arrives at the burgomaster's house, with a bevy of beautiful admirers. Though he is engaged, he happily proclaims, "Everyday Is Ladies' Day To Me." Nor is he above fancying another young lady in private, merely, as he tells her, "Because You're You." But Gretchen's escape forces both the burgomaster and the governor to face reality. The burgomaster gives Doris and Gretchen his reluctant consent, and the governor goes looking for more willing girls. Van Borkem's reluctance further melts when he learns Van Damn will inherit a large fortune. Con and Kid are hauled in for attempting to leave without paying, but Tina helps to get them a pardon.

The summary overlooks a number of Con and Kid's actions. The acrobatic Stone made a much-applauded first entrance seeming to fall down a two-story-high ladder. In the course of the evening Con and Kid disguise themselves as Italian musicians and as Sherlock Holmes and Watson. Herbert's music was of the lighter sort he created for pieces he considered musical comedy, rather than comic opera. As a comparison of "Dear Old Broadway" or "Good-bye Sweet Old Manhattan Isle" with "The Streets Of New York" demonstrates, Herbert could compose in a more Tin Pan Alley style and beat the Tin Pan Alley boys on their own grounds. Some mystery has surrounded a minor number that Montgomery and Stone sang as the Italian musicians, "Good-a-bye, John." It was printed with Blossom and Herbert's names but it bears an uncanny resemblance to "Good-a-bye, John" sung earlier in *The Belle Of Avenue A* and credited to Harry Williams and Egbert Van Alstyne. Waters' thesis that Stone or Montgomery slyly hummed the tune while suggesting a type of song needed for the scene cannot hold water for it fails to account for the identical lyrics. The mystery remains. Outside the theatre *The Red Mill* can stake its claim to a famous first. With the show a success, Charles Dillingham constructed a large mill in front of the Knickerbocker, with electrically moved arms. He hung lights on the revolving parts, giving Broadway its first moving illuminated sign.

Two more Herbert scores followed. On Christmas night Weber presented himself at his own house in a double bill **Dream City** and **The Magic Knight.** Herbert had several times spurned offers to write for the old Weber and Fields' Music Hall. Some quirky personal pigeonholing led him to consider music halls beneath his dignity. But now that the partners, in going their separate ways, were producing more traditional fare in regular theatres, the composer was delighted to accommodate both of them. *Dream City* was flippantly listed in the programs as "a dramatic 'pipe' in two puffs." It was set in "the immediate future according to current real estate advertisements." J. Billington Holmes (Otis Harlan), a fast-talking promoter, convinces Wilhelm Dinglebender (Weber) that his farm at Malaria Center, Long Island, will make the perfect site for an elaborate housing development. In a dream Dinglebender visualizes the fabulous new town and attends a performance at its new opera house. He is so disillusioned by the opera and the people he meets there that he refuses to sign the property transfer. Weber filled the evening with delightful bits of his Dutch clowning. In one scene he went fishing, casting into a tiny bucket. Told he can't possibly catch fish that way, he replied, "I know dots. I vass shust teaching der vorm to swim." *The Magic Knight,* a brilliant spoof on *Lohengrin,* was originally intended to have been part of the second act, the opera Dinglebender witnesses. But Weber, fearing many of his regulars had never seen an opera and would miss the satire, insisted it be given as an afterpiece. As Herbert's biographer notes, the evening "received as much critical acclaim and enthusiasm as any work Herbert ever wrote; yet none of his scores is now more forgotten and ignored." The *World* hailed the bill as "high art" and the *Tribune* blessed it as "a triumph of musical fooling." With the passing of time the *Dream City* seems less awesome, however pretty. But the Lohengrin burlesque, in capable hands, could be hilarious. Lohengrin ("a professional rescuer of distressed maidens") arrives in a cab drawn by a swan. To his "Mein Lieber Schwan" Frederick (Ortrud's "hen-pecked uncle") can only respond "Quack, Quack." Maurice Farkoa sang Lohengrin; Otis Harlan, Frederick; Cora Tracy, Ortrud; and Lillian Blauvelt, Elsa. Time and again Herbert took Wagnerian airs and subtly twisted them into hints of popular tunes. For all the kudos in the press, the show could only manage 102 performances, and when it took to the road Weber's fears proved well founded. Small city audiences were baffled by *The Magic Knight* and began walking out in distressing numbers. Weber quickly dropped it. When, after the first season's tour, another producing unit bought the rights for the one-night stands, Herbert was horrified to learn that the producers intended to drop all his music as too advanced for the backwaters and had commissioned Maurice Levi to create a more transparently tinkly score. Herbert sued and ultimately got the new material removed. But the show held no charms for small-town crowds and shortly folded.

Herbert's third score was composed for Frank Daniels, with whom he had worked so often in the past. In **The Tattooed Man** (2-18-07, Criterion) Daniels portrayed Omar Khayam, Jr. Omar rules Persia during the Shah's frequent absences. But he has a peculiar birthmark and it has been decreed that if ever another man appears with the same mark both men must die together. Fatima (May Vokes), rebuffed by Omar, tattoos the mark on not one, but two other men, and Omar must spend the rest of the evening designing ways to avoid the inevitable. Though he does avoid losing his head, he meets a fate worse than death when the returning Shah (Herbert Waterous) orders him to marry Fatima. Daniels' broad, low comedy delighted his followers, and he could make a line such as "Early to bed and early to rise—and you never meet any prominent people" seem hilariously observant. But Daniels was not the whole show. Miss Vokes won applause for her comic wallflower, while Sallie Fisher, who had attracted attention with her dancing and singing some weeks before in *The Man from Now,* again won praise as Leila "beloved of Omar, but nothing doing." When the principals were offstage, there was still "much of song and dance, grouping and marching, by girls in glittering golden gowns, delicate shell pink, yellow and brown, and rich combined tints of green and red." The score was not one of Herbert's best. Still, he was always looking for new ideas and, somewhat bravely for the era, eschewed an overture, opening instead with forty bars to set the mood for the opening in which a muezzin calls the faithful to prayers. The run was cut short when a fire at the neighboring New York Theatre resulted in water damage to the Criterion. It was taken on the road and toured for a year and a half.

Both October regular musical entries were also hits. Richard Carle put in his annual appearance, this time as star of **The Spring Chicken** (10-8-06, Daly's). Appearances might be a more accurate word, since his 115 New York performances were divided among three separate engagements. Bessie McCoy, Blanche Deyo ("both fine dancers"), and Adele Rowland were prominently featured. In one respect *The Spring Chicken* marked a notable departure for Carle. Although he was credited with "Americanizing" the material, the show was originally a London hit with a book by George Grossmith, Jr., and music by Ivan Caryll and Lionel Monckton. The Englishmen in turn borrowed their story from a French farce, *Coquin de Printemps.* Given Carle's penchant for suggestive material, the story of a young lawyer so flirtatious that he jeopardizes his own marriage was obviously appealing to him. Inevitably Carle added his own songs, and in another change wrote some of the tunes as well as some of the lyrics. His biggest hit, to words by M. E. Rourke, was "A Lemon In The Garden Of Love."

Although he was American by birth, there was also English blood in **The Rich Mr. Hoggenheimer** (10-22-06, Wallack's), which Harry B. Smith and Ludwig Englander wrote at the request of Charles Frohman. Sam Bernard had made a success of the Hoggenheimer character in Frohman's 1903 importation, *The Girl from Kay's*. Now a whole vehicle was created around the part. "Piggy" Hoggenheimer's plans for his son Guy's marriage to Lady Mildred are spoiled when the boy (Edwin Nicander) goes to America to study modern business methods and falls in love with a poor girl, Amy Leigh (Marion Garson). Pretending to be on assignment from the War Office, Hoggenheimer rushes to the States. Because her husband's actress friend, Flora Fair (Georgia Caine), is on the same ship, Mrs. Hoggenheimer books passage as well. In various disguises Hoggenheimer tracks down and spies on his son's fiancée and in the end approves of the marriage. He also helps Flora win the man she has her eye on, Percy Vere (Percy Ames). Bernard's best scenes came when disguised as a cabbie he finds he has picked up his own wife as a fare and when he revises the wording on a telegram to give it precisely the opposite meaning. Next to the Hippodrome spectacle and *The Red Mill, The Rich Mr. Hoggenheimer* was the biggest hit of the season. Three things accounted for the smashing success. Most of all there was Bernard's performance—considered by many the high point of his career. Secondly there was the fetching Georgia Caine as Flora. And lastly, there were several popular and universally praised songs—none by Englander. One was "Any Old Time At All" (Jerome/Schwartz), sung by Guy and Flora. Equally well-liked were Jerome Kern's insertions. Kern had rapidly established a practice of interpolating in Frohman importations, tunes that were as bright and fresh as anything being offered by all but the very best. Songs like Flora's "Don't You Want A Paper, Dearie?" and "Poker Love" (sung by two minor players, one, Flossie Hope, dressed as a man), so applauded and hummed when new, are forgotten today, largely because Kern himself later turned out superior material.

The same night *The Rich Mr. Hoggenheimer* opened, Chauncey Olcott debuted in **Eileen Asthore** (10-22-06, New York). In this instance Olcott played a young man who squanders his patrimony, outwits a villain who would thwart his attempts to earn a second fortune, and ultimately wins the hand of Eileen O'Donnell. To many the story seemed merely a rehash of *Old Limerick Town* (10-27-02). It was typical of the romantic pieces with which he enthralled his followers for many years. They were not really full-blown musicals, usually containing only four or five songs. But some of these songs became standards. None from *Eileen Asthore*.

Another London hit was Talbot and Rubens' **The Blue Moon** (11-3-06, Casino). Its story told of a prince who loves a girl who loves another man. The great rubber-faced clown, James T. Powers, continuing to throw his lot with imported London works, was starred, assisted by a fine cast that included Clara Palmer, Ethel Jackson, Grace La Rue, Templar Saxe, and Phil Ryley. With the expected American additions, the musical repeated, albeit on a smaller scale, its West End success.

Still further English influences were seen in Robert B. Smith's and Raymond Hubbell's **Mamselle Sallie**, which John C. Fisher produced on November 26 at the slightly out-of-the-way Grand Opera House down on 23rd Street. Several critics felt the plot was a rehash of *The Medal and the Maid* (1-11-04), which Fisher had coproduced. In Smith's retelling, Muriel Oliver, a young student at Mme. Woodbury's seminary, and Emile Martell, a French military cadet, have both been bequeathed large fortunes in Thessaly and have been given identical lockets as recognition tokens. The lockets are lost and stolen. But Mamselle Sallie, a laundress, disguises herself as a brigand to retrieve them and to tie the marriage knot for the young heir and heiress. Robert was no better a librettist than his brother, Harry. He was capable of passing off as a joke lines such as, "I can't eat peas, they roll off my knife." As was so often the case with musical comedies of this era, the lovers were not the stars. Top billing in *Mamselle Sallie* went to little John Slavin as a waiter impersonating a lawyer and brash Katie Barry as a comic hairdresser. Chorus girls, whirling across the stage in orange and black gowns, were supplemented at one point by "English Butterfly Dancers." Even a move to the more centrally located New York Theatre could not gain the show more than a three-week run. But Smith and Hubbell were strong-willed hacks, and *Mamselle Sallie* would be heard from again.

In **A Parisian Model** (11-27-06, Broadway), which left first-nighters gaping, Florenz Ziegfeld surrounded Anna Held with a large chorus of breathtakingly beautiful girls, bedecked in gorgeous costumes and set in sumptuous mountings. He reserved for Anna some of the most elaborate gowns yet seen on the stage. The effects he and Julian Mitchell contrived were the talk of the town. In a scene set in an artist's studio the chorus girls entered in long, elegant cloaks. Stepping behind easels they dropped their cloaks, revealing their bare shoulders and legs. Sixteen of the chorus girls, led by the flamboyant Gertrude Hoffman, lay on a revolving stage, kicking their legs and ringing bells tied to their ankles. Later Miss Hoffman, dressed as a boy, danced with Miss Held. But the *pièce de résistance* was naturally given to Anna, who in one number wore a different gown for each chorus of the song she was singing—and she sang six choruses. Anna played a painter's model who comes into a fortune through an old lady's will. But her artist lover, Julien (Henri Leoni), suspects her newfound wealth has other origins. Furiously jealous, he publicly courts another young lady, Violette (Truly Shattuck). But Anna wins him back by shocking him into the realization that he loves her best of all. A comic character named Silas Goldfinch (Charles A. Bigelow) appeared throughout the evening in various disguises—Paderewski, a Mexican, an old woman—trying to give money away. Although Max Hoffman wrote the score, it was her two interpolations that Miss Held would use for the rest of her short, tragic life. "It's Delightful To Be Married," for which she is reputed to have written the lyrics to V. Scotto's music, and "I Just Can't Make My Eyes Behave" (Cobb/Edwards).

A triple bill opened at the Hippodrome November 28. It consisted of a one-act circus, a three-scene melodrama called **Pioneer Days,** and a three-scene "Operatic extravanganza," **Neptune's Daughter.** The melodrama, "Belasco's Golden West, four times magnified," filled the stage with cowboys, lawmen, Indians, and, when an alarm was raised, a troop of cavalry charging on their horses. The "Operatic extravaganza" was set in a Breton coastal village where a one-legged man hobbles on and sees in a red sky the portent of a storm. The storm follows quickly, creating a shipwreck from which a child is dramatically rescued. Mermaids and Neptune arise from a golden barge to still the waters. In *Neptune's Daughter* the famous Hippodrome water tank (situated between the main stage and the orchestra pit) was employed for the first time to receive a flock of bathing beauties instead of men and horses. Trick mechanical devices allowed chorus girls to dive into the tank and disappear. Manuel Klein wrote the songs for both the

melodrama and *Neptune's Daughter*, producing for the latter one of the hits of the day, "Red Sky." The bill, with changes, ran 288 performances.

The procession of London hits resumed with Leslie Stuart's **The Belle of Mayfair** (12-3-06, Daly's). Produced with a fine American cast led by Irene Bentley, Christie MacDonald, Bessie Clayton, and Valeska Suratt and with an unaccustomed faithfulness to the original story of a Romeo and Juliet romance that ends happily, it ran into spring.

Lew Dockstader's Minstrels displayed their wares beginning December 17. The interlocutors and end men and all the old standbys lingered a paltry 26 performances, then headed back to the road.

Herbert's *Dream City* came in a week later.

The next night Frederic Ranken, Stanislaus Stange and Reginald De Koven offered Broadway **The Student King** (12-25-06, Garden). Its far-fetched romantic story had Francis (Henry Coote), a Prague University student, elected "king for a day." Princess Ilsa (Lina Abarbanell) falls in love with him, although she is already betrothed. Happily, Francis turns out to be the king's long-lost son. The king (Alexander Clark) abdicates in his favor, and Francis makes Ilsa his queen. De Koven provided a wearisome score that more than one critic branded "reminiscent." In just over a month it was gone. But in that short time it gave theatregoers an opportunity to watch Miss Abarbanell, a young lady they would see much of, as well as two fine comedians, Clark and Detmar Poppen. Miss Abarbanell had called attention to herself first in German-language productions of operettas at the Irving Place Theatre, then as Hansel at the Metropolitan Opera.

The Princess Beggar (1-7-07, Casino) followed hard on *The Student King*'s heels, arriving as 1907's first musical show. It had a similarly absurd plot, with the sexes reversed. Prince Karl (Bertram Wallis) would marry Elaine (Paula Edwards), a girl of the woods who saved his life. Empty royal coffers argue against this love match. Furthermore, the villainous Baron Lombardo (Stanley L. Forde) is conniving to put another family on the throne. But Elaine is discovered to be a real and rich princess, permitting a very happy ending. Paulton and Robyn had even less finesse and panache than the authors of *The Student King*. Yet *The Princess Beggar* ran exactly as long—40 performances.

Things got worse. In fact the *Times* headlined its review for **The Mimic and the Maid** (1-11-07, Bijou), "Rock Bottom Reached." Its story of a courtship during the rehearsal of a play in a small town was simply another excuse for a number of specialty acts. In *A Parisian Model* Anna Held had sung a tune to two man-sized Teddy bears. *The Mimic and the Maid* filled the stage with small, mechanized ones. But nothing helped. Two performances, and the show was withdrawn. Even A. Baldwin Sloane, who composed whatever numbers the specialty acts did not bring with them, must have been especially embarrassed by debacle. Prolific till now, he was not heard from again for three years.

The Belle of London Town (1-28-07, Lincoln Square) was also a quick flop—16 performances. But it received some good notices. The plot, praised as "able to stand alone," was a little different. Sir John Manners marries Belinda for her beauty and she marries him for his money. But he loses his money at the same time Belinda comes into a large inheritance. She leaves him and becomes the belle of the town. But after a misunderstanding about some unsigned love letters actually meant for Belinda's cousin, they are reconciled. Like *Marrying Mary* at the beginning of the season, the show had no chorus. But the well-thought-out story and the novel intimacy proved no incentive to ticket buyers. The weaknesses of Julian Edwards' score were only underlined by Stanislaus Stange's awkward titles and lyrics such as "Drink With Me The Night Away" and "I Should Have Been Offended If My Waist You Hadn't Squeezed." If the show was one of the last for the fading Camille D'Arville, it marked a step up the ladder for Orville Harrold.

Messager's *The Little Michus* (1-31-07, Garden) failed to find favor and ran only 29 performances.

A second Julian Edwards' score was heard a week after his music for *The Belle of London Town,* when **The Girl and the Governor** opened February 4 at the Manhattan. It, too, received some good notices, though on this occasion the praise was for Edwards' songs and for the star, Jefferson De Angelis. The plot was simple. A foppish 16th-century Spanish governor in South America captures an English girl (Estelle Wentworth) and decides to marry her. She seems to acquiesce, asking only that the governor hire an English sailor to help with her chores. Of course, the sailor is her lover, and they elope. The evening failed to catch the public's fancy, and it stayed for only 26 performances.

Twenty-six performances were also all **The Rose of Alhambra** (2-4-07, Majestic), which opened the same night, could muster. Based on a Washington Irving story of a girl (Agnes Caine Brown) who dwells in a town with an old aunt, it started life in Chicago, where it was not too cordially greeted. The critic for the Chicago *Record* left the theatre at 11:00 P.M., noting that a whole act remained to be played. The *Chronicle's* man also had his watch out, recording "only two hearty laughs between 8:15 and 9:30." One of these would seem to have been a monk's reply to the accusation he was "seeking young maids to roast them alive." In reply he insisted, "No. I'm not a roaster. I'm a friar." Things had not improved much by the time the show reached New York. The music comprised the only score by Lucius Hosmer ever to be sung on Broadway.

Gustave Kerker had a second score ready for Broadway when **The White Hen** (also known as *The Girl from Vienna*) was unveiled at the Casino on February 16. The plot recounted Hensee Blinker's difficulties after his lawyer (Ralph Herz) persuades Hensee (Louis Mann) to visit a marriage broker (Carrie E. Perkins). The lawyer's secretary (Lotta Faust) and the contracted wife (Louise Gunning) change places without Hensee's knowing it. Before long Blinker has two wives. The show delighted audiences for three months largely because of the droll clowning of Mann, Herz, and Miss Faust, as well as the lovely singing of Miss Gunning.

The Tattooed Man displayed his attractions beginning February 18.

Over a month passed before another musical appeared, and then from Chicago came one more American-in-foreign-parts story. George Washington Barker, a circus fakir stranded in Honolulu, makes a balloon ascent and lands on the Island of Inde. A Buddist ceremony is in progress, and Barker is mistaken for **The Grand Mogul** (3-25-07). The real Grand Mogul arrives, but Barker is rescued by a Yankee gunboat. More than the story was familiar. Frank Pixley's book and lyrics, and Gustav Luders' tunes were pleasant, but derivative. Furthermore, Baker was played by an old hand at this sort of thing, Frank Moulan. Moulan's balloon entrance had him crashing through a temple roof. He was forever pushing "Mrs. Mogul" out of his way in order to mingle with a chorus of beautiful girls. He and Maud Lillian Berri "encored many times" their "Nestle By My Side." After a five-week stay the show resumed its national trek.

Eleven months after the fiasco of his *District Leader* Joe Howard returned to New York with a show in which he and his wife, Mabel Barrison, starred. But **The Land of Nod** (4-1-07, New York) was not a solo effort. It was a children's extravaganza written with the two men with whom he created most of his major lyric pieces, Frank R. Adams and Will M. Hough. It had been a Chicago success. Taking no chances, the producer had

George V. Hobart "rearrange" the work for New York audiences, and for good measure, he added an operatic skit Hobart and Victor Herbert had written for a Lambs Club Gambol, "The Song Birds." But New York wasn't interested in Bonnie's visit to dreamland and her infatuation for the Jack of Hearts (a trouser role by Helen Bertram). Bonnie (Miss Barrison) is caught up in the wicked Sandman's scheme to steal everyone's heart and destroy the card castle. But Jack vanquishes the Sandman (William Burress), turning him into a bundle of rags. The humor was of the arch variety so beloved by writers of children's pieces. When a star falls at the Moon's feet, he (Howard) advises Bonnie, "Don't be frightened. That's only a little message from my wife, Rory Bory Alice. Alice is always throwing things." He opens the star and reads the message inside. "If you are not back before morning I will go home to Mars! What do you think of a lady who uses that kind of grammar. No wonder I left." For the "swingers" of the era there was a wisecracking chorus girl (Carrie De Mar), whose offhand name-dropping must have been lost on tots in the audience. A similar girl had been used as a foil in *The Wizard of Oz*. Even with Hobart's and Herbert's names on the credits, *The Land of Nod* had little appeal.

The following Monday ushered in the London hit, **The Orchid** (4-8-07, Herald Square). In London this Ivan Caryll and Lionel Monckton musical had been awarded the honor of opening the new Gaiety Theatre. (The old Gaiety had been condemned to make way for urban redevelopment.) The story told of an explorer who stumbles on a seemingly priceless rare orchid, loses it, and finds another in a London florist shop. Eddie Foy starred in the New York version, and his supporting cast included such popular vaudevillians as Trixie Friganza and Irene Franklin. In a day of high public piety and propriety Foy nonetheless made a showstopper of one interpolation, "He Goes To Church On Sunday" (Vincent Bryan/E. Ray Goetz):

He goes to church on Sunday,
  He passes round the contribution box;
But meet him in the office on a Monday,
  He's as crooked and as cunning as a fox,
On Tuesday, Wednesday, Thursday, Friday,
    Saturday
  He's robbing everybody that he can;
But he goes to church on Sunday,
  So they say that he's an honest man.

Although many of the day's musicals were written in incredible haste—often thrown off in a week

or two—some of the most frivolous-seeming actually were the result of prolonged and intensive reworkings. **Fascinating Flora** (5-20-07, Casino), which ran through the summer, fills four volumes of typescript versions. The cast of characters in this R. H. Burnside and Joseph Herbert libretto lists everyone's love interest. Gulliver Gayboy (Fred Bond)—"In love with his money"—bankrolls Flora Duval (Adele Ritchie)—"In love with America"— after she has left her husband because he is too much of a homebody. "You were the light of my life," she tells him, "but you never went out." Flora has no false modesty:

I really think it must be fate
  That I was born to fascinate
And so they call me Fascinating Flora.

She would become an opera star under Gayboy's aegis, but she admits she finds most operas boring and has no qualms about enlivening them by adding "anything with dash and go." Gayboy is also planning to marry his daughter to Jack Graham (Arthur Stanford)—"In love with Dolly"—unaware his child has secretly made a happy marriage of her own. Unluckily, Gayboy is flimflammed, and the shares with which he hoped to support his opera company turn out to be mere railroad timetables. Flora returns to her home-loving spouse. And Jack does marry Dolly (Ella Snyder). The score was Gustave Kerker's third of the season, a figure matched only by Ivan Caryll and Victor Herbert. But neither Kerker's music nor Hapgood Burt and Jerome Kern's interpolations were more than serviceable.

At the very start of the season the *Times* discreetly acknowledged Cohan's incontestable vogue on September 2, 1906, when it described the returning *Little Johnny Jones* as "ever popular." To end the season Cohan brought back another of his pieces, *Running for Office*, on June 3, revising it to suit the requirements of the New Amsterdam Roof and retitling it *The Honeymooners*. His fast pacing had often ruffled his critics, and when he made little allowance for the summer heat the *Morning Telegraph* commented snidely, "If Cohan would play fair and give his audience a chance to catch its breath it might make a few unkind remarks." But most unkind words came from the aisle-sitters. Appreciative audiences packed the house all summer.

If Chicago theatres have been missing from this account of the 1906–07 season, that is not to be construed as any indication of the lack of activity. The truth is quite the opposite. The city's leading combination house, the Great Northern, was frequently lit for a week or two with traveling musicals New York never saw. Far more important were the two musicals Hough-Adams-Howard wrote for Mort Singer at the La Salle. *The Girl Question* ran longer than had *The Umpire,* while *The Time, the Place and the Girl,* by chalking up a run of over 400 performances, established a record in Chicago that went unbroken for many years. Both of these musicals braved New York in forthcoming seasons.

5

INTERMISSION
Viennese Operetta
and the American Retreat
1907-1914

The seven-season period that began with the 1907–08 theatrical year was at once rich and distressing. It would be absurd to write off an era that witnessed the creation of *Naughty Marietta, Sweethearts, The Firefly, Madame Sherry,* or *The Pink Lady* (to name five of the "domestic" masterpieces of the day), or that brought from overseas treasures such as *The Chocolate Soldier, Sari,* and, most of all, *The Merry Widow.* But the rage for these Viennese confections so overwhelmed the stages of the Western world that even the best local creations swiftly became imitative. For seven years all the best works offered by American composers were in this unmistakably arioso style that we would now brand "operetta." Those writers who could not or would not write in this gay, sweeping Central European idiom met with increasing disappointments. Native musical material was still presented regularly, but it often seemed intimidated by the cavalier elegance of the Viennese school.

Still, in a way, America was lucky. This seven-year retreat gave our young native talent time to regroup, rethink, and develop. When World War I broke out in Europe at the end of this period, our young composers and librettists were alive with fresh, original ideas. Every now and then during this intermission hints of things to come were heard and seen. And one new form—the revue—advanced to just short of maturity.

Europe was not so fortunate. The war that gave American musical comedy writers their chance stifled the French and English musical stages, and inflicted a lingering, ultimately fatal wound on Viennese operetta.

There was a certain symmetry to this seven-year period. Its three most intriguing seasons were its first, its last, and the one that fell right in the middle, 1910–11. Although *The Merry Widow* overwhelmed the opening session, a number of other productions bore importantly on the future of the American Musical Theatre. The last theatrical year would produce little of interest aside from three exceptional works. 1910–11 also offered three magnificently achieved works, but time and again its minor hits and failures contained fascinating hints of better things to come.

1907-1908

On June 22, almost a year to the day after the lurid opening of *Mamzelle Champagne,* the Madison Square Garden Roof presented another summer musical, **The Maid and the Millionaire.** Its plot was a rehash of *The Billionaire* (12-29-02). The setting was changed to a new outpost of the expanding American empire, Guam, but the story still recounted how a stage-struck tycoon helped a young actress on her way. Both the show and its first night were uneventful. The piece distracted its patrons from the summer heat and doldrums for 72 performances.

July 8 brought in the **Follies of 1907.** The *Follies* would soon include the name of their creator, Florenz Ziegfeld, in the title, and for a quarter of a century be a resplendent jewel of the musical theatre scene. But this first edition was relatively modest. Bankrolled by Klaw and Erlanger, Ziegfeld mounted the evening for $13,000—an unexceptional figure for its day. Although it became a national institution "glorifying the American girl," the *Follies* professed to be Continental in its tone and style. Its very title called to mind the Parisian *Folies Bergère,* and for playgoers who failed to make the connection the New York Theatre Roof was rechristened the Jardin de Paris. Ziegfeld's European wife, Anna Held, originally convinced him that something like the voguish Parisian revue might appeal to New Yorkers, although, curiously, the title may not have been derived from the French *Folies* but from a column written by the show's first librettist, Harry B. Smith. Smith's column had been called "Follies of the Day," and Smith suggested using a similar title for the show, "Follies of the Year." Since Ziegfeld had previously found good luck in titles of thirteen letters (excluding the article), he compromised with the thirteen characters of *Follies of 1907.* In his early programs, Ziegfeld acknowledged his superstition by numbering each letter and digit in the title, starting with a "1" under the "F" and climbing to a "13" under the "7". Smith, in honor of the Jamestown Exposition, named his compère and commère, John Smith and Pocahontas. He described the highlights of the "libretto" in his autobiography: "Theodore Roosevelt, then at the height of his popularity, was prominent among the characters, wearing his Rough Rider uniform and displaying a spectacular array of teeth. Mr. Roosevelt was in the audience one evening and laughed louder than anyone. In a scene at Grand Central Station, Chauncey Depew was in charge of the 'Misinformation Department.' The rival impresarios, Oscar Hammerstein and Heinrich Conried, fought an operatic duel supported by their respective companies; and in a court scene Caruso was found guilty of misdemeanor on account of his much-advertised adventure at the Central Park monkey house. Anthony Comstock, Commodore Perry, Andrew Carnegie, John D. Rockefeller, Edna May, and other celebrities were among the dramatis personae. There was just enough story to hold the scenes together, the theme being the introduction of Pocahontas and Captain John Smith to . . . modern life."

Fifty lovely chorines, the first in the long parade of breathtaking beauties made even more dazzling by their association with Ziegfeld, were billed as "Anna Held Girls" in an effort to convey to them some of the exotic, mischievous glamor of Ziegfeld's wife. The most famous name in the cast was Nora Bayes. Nothing of any lasting value emerged from the evening. "Budweiser's A Friend Of Mine" (Vincent Bryan/Seymour Furth) and "Handle Me With Care" (William Jerome/Jean Schwartz) were probably the most popular numbers in the show. Even more quickly forgotten were "I Think I Oughtn't Auto Anymore" (Bryan/E. Ray Goetz), "The Gibson Bathing Girls" (Paul West/Alfred Solomon), and "Bye Bye Dear Old Broadway" (Will Cobb/Gus Edwards). During the run of this first edition, performers and numbers were added or dropped in a way inconceivable today. Miss Bayes, for example, stayed with the show for only about half its run. In fact, Ziegfeld boasted in his advertisements of weekly changes. His feature for the week of August 11 was typical, offering Annabelle Whitford and her "Gibson Bathing Girls." The show was hardly better than many of the other producer-assemblages Broadway regularly accepted, especially in the hotter months. Trade papers reviewed it under "Vaudeville Acts." Ziegfeld's taste, imagination, lavish hand, and persistence would eventually turn the *Follies* into a legend. It played through the summer and toured briefly. Its profits were so large Ziegfeld determined to offer an even better edition the next year.

The first of August's six musicals came from Chicago. It was one of the best of the Will M. Hough, Frank R. Adams, and Joe Howard series— and one of the few to travel as far east as New York. It was no reflection on their quality that these musicals were never as enthusiastically welcomed on the Rialto as they were back home. They were solidly crafted. Their librettos generally put reasonably real people in conceivable difficulties and let them talk their way out of their problems with dialogue that was easy on the ear. If some of the early, expository speeches were long and even naïve by later standards, they were so racily colloquial that the drawback was overlooked. The lyrics, too, were far superior to the run-of-the-mill of the day. Within limitations imposed by matter and rhyme, they were refreshingly natural, managing to avoid involutions, obsolescent imageries, and other contrivances of the period's hacks. Howard's music was totally American, and in its field the best being written. **The Time, the Place and the Girl** (8-5-07, Wallack's) recounted how Tom Cunningham (George Anderson), a rich young man-about-town, and his gambling buddy, Happy Johnny

Hicks (Arthur Deagon), take refuge in a sanatorium after fleeing from a nasty drunken brawl:

Johnny: You were bound to go into Glad Hand Murphy's gambling joint and mix in on a poker game. The ante was two-bits and the roof was the limit. I came in. They cleaned me in about forty-five minutes, but I wasn't exactly dirty when I blew in. Thursday always was my Jonah Day. By this time you was buyin' nothin' but grape and you was keepin' one eye shut so's not to count your money double. There was cheatin' goin' on in the game and when I gets wise and tips you off, you reaches over and pinches all the coin in sight, not knowin' just what you was doin'. The young guy opposite gets riled and says you're a shine sport, and sayin' he can lick you or any other man in Boston, he wades in to do it. Just as somebody douses the light I see you hit him over the head with a bottle and he drops like a shot. Then an awful bag of cats is stirred up and we mixes it up general all over the place, everybody taking a hand. You can guess the answer. Us sittin' in the middle of the street listenin' to an owl car comin' up the pike about half a mile away. I dunno how we got there but maybe we fell out of a window. I didn't know how bad that guy was hurt that you dropped with the bottle, but I thought we'd better leave Boston for a while, and as you said you wanted to come here, it was us on the caboose for Virginia. The mountains can't come too high for me.

Tom: You're a brick, Johnny,—for seeing me through this scrape.

Johnny: Take that noise away.

At the same sanatorium Tom discovers his childhood sweetheart, Margaret Simpson (Violet McMillan), and John whiles away the hours with the head nurse, Molly Kelly (Elene Foster). The budding romances suffer an unpleasant setback when Johnny and Tom learn the man they fought was Molly's brother. What saves the day for John and Molly, and also gives Tom the chance he needs to court Margaret, is a police-imposed quarantine, when an infectious outbreak is suspected. By the time the quarantine is lifted, the lovers are set to be wed. "Thursday Is My Jonah Day" typified the colloquial flow and native humor of the Hough and Adams lyrics:

Thursday always was my Jonah day;
   Never struck any luck, any time,

If it's Thursday when I pass away,
   Then I know they'll "hand me mine."

The lines to Howard's excellent melody for "Blow The Smoke Away" are equally natural and expressive. They demonstrate the abrupt endings Hough and Adams often employed to good effect —a somewhat less difficult trick in the days before the AABA form overwhelmed popular song:

Of course you're only dreaming,
   Blow the smoke away,
You know you can't win her,
   Things don't ever go that way.
Still you keep on dreaming,
   Might as well, no doubt—
Then your pipe goes out.

The best song, a melody still occasionally heard, was Howard's wistful "Waning Honeymoon."

Both "Blow The Smoke Away" and "Waning Honeymoon" were sung by minor characters and the chorus. The first was performed by Laurie Farnham (James Norval); the second by Mrs. Talbot (Harriet Burt). Even if New York's critics condemned the evening's "heavy-handed" sentimentality, they found kind things to say about various aspects of the production. Miss Burt won praise for her German-style dances, danced in a dress of bright "Spanish" red to the strains of "Dixie." The chorus imitated the sounds of horse races, wind in the trees, a motor car, and even imitated an audience applauding (without the chorus boys and girls actually clapping their own hands). To the *Times'* critic, the hotel setting seemed contrived to resemble the Orangerie at the Hotel Astor, "with a sort of miniature natural bridge of rocks, where the musicians' balcony should be." *The Time, the Place and the Girl* stayed a month at Wallack's, a far cry from its record-breaking 400-performance run in Chicago.

The Shoo Fly Regiment (8-6-07, Bijou) was an all-black show by Cole and Johnson, designed to entertain "an audience composed mostly of whites." It found many critics willing to praise its music, but few who could say anything good about its book. The story followed a regiment recruited from the Lincolnville Institute into the Spanish-American War. The boys' lady friends ("vermilion-cheeked colored girls in scarlet gowns") accompany them. Much to their own surprise, the young soldiers win a battle and return as heroes. One outstanding number was "Lit'l Gal," a song written for *The Cannibal King,* an earlier Cole and Johnson effort that never reached the big time. Oddly, the published lyrics are credited to Paul Laurence Dunbar, although he is not given credit elsewhere. The song, written in a relatively free-flowing AA B pattern, makes remarkable use of alternating major and minor chords. The regiment marched off after two weeks.

Two shows opened on August 12. **The Alaskan,** at the Knickerbocker, was a 29-performance failure in New York; **The Yankee Tourist,** at the Astor, was the season's first long-run hit. Yet in history's so commonly perverse way, the flop was the more interesting of the two. The *Dramatic Mirror* rejoiced, "There is more originality, freshness and downright charm in 'The Alaskan' than in ten ordinary musicals put together. At last a new locale has been found [and] best of all the new field is our own—Alaska." Up in the Yukon, Richard Atwater has been staked in his mining operations by a New Yorker, Mr. Eaton. A letter from Eaton's daughter, Arlee (Agnes Cain Brown), announces her father's death and her intention to become Atwater's partner. She arrives, but mistakes Atwater for the mine foreman. When the mine fails she leaves, without learning who the foreman really is. But Atwater has fallen in love, and when another mine of his is successful he reveals his identity and wins Arlee for his wife. The "new locale" did indeed allow for some novel bits. The show opened with a sled pulled by twelve real huskies crossing the snow and starting a climb up a mountain. At one point the "pony" chorus appeared dressed as Eskimos. But the moment that "roused even the wilting Summer night crowd to enthusiasm" found the entire chorus dressed as totem poles while Totem Pole Pete (Edward Martindell) led them in, appropriately, "The Totem Pole" ("My father's father was an eagle"). When, seventeen years later, critic after critic raved about a similar production number in *Rose-Marie* (9-2-24), none of the reviewers apparently retained any recollection of *The Alaskan*'s version. Atwater was played by the show's composer, Harry Giraud. Although he and his librettists, Max Figman and Joseph Blethen (Blethen was also the lyricist), displayed a certain precocious integrity in handling their story and in refusing to allow interpolated material, their inexperience and lack of inspiration told against them. Not too many others agreed with the *Dramatic Mirror*'s man, and the authors never again tried their hand at Broadway musicals. However, like so many New York failures of the day, *The Alaskan* moved on to a successful road tour.

The *Dramatic Mirror* critic was far less taken with *The Yankee Tourist,* a piece which exposed all the weaknesses of typical turn-of-the-century musical comedy. "It is rather a shock," he observed, "to have the action of the play suddenly halted for the insertion of a more or less relevant song . . . but since the action does not depend on probabilities, the shock is not lasting." Nor did the reviewer think much of the music (mostly by Alfred G. Robyn) which interrupted the action. His kindest words were for the lyrics and the star, Raymond Hitchcock. Hitchcock played Copeland Schuyler, who assumes the name and role of Kirke Warren, a famous correspondent in the Greco-Turkish War of 1897. Schuyler feels the imposture is his best way to keep near his fiancée Grace Whitney (Flora Zabelle), a nurse. Warren's pursuers—creditors, admirers—now pursue Schuyler, and Schuyler's troubles are compounded when he is captured by the Turks. The play was based on a hit of the preceding season, *The Galloper,* by a real and famous war correspondent, Richard Harding Davis. Again, the trade paper was in the minority. Still, for those who might share the paper's reservations about the integrity of the book and the quality of the music, the production offered compensations. Almost at the beginning came a spectacular effect, with a "realistic" ship sailing away from a "realistic" dock. An attractive chorus line, called "Teddy Girls" in the program, danced as ship stewardesses, Turks in baggy trousers and tasseled fezes, and as soldiers in a snappy gun drill. The limelights changed colors as Miss Zabelle (she was also Mrs. Hitchcock) and the chorus girls fluttered scarves and danced while singing "Rainbow." The public flocked to the Astor for 103 performances; then the show went on a long tour. Just before the cross-country trek began, Wallace Beery replaced Hitchcock.

One week after the double opening, **The Lady from Lane's** (8-19-07, Lyric) arrived. The *Dramatic Mirror*, once again at odds with the public response, saw it as "the fourth attempt already this season to put musical plays on a more rational basis, where consistency of plot is made, relatively, of as much importance as songs and chorus girls." The other attempts were listed as *The Alaskan, The Time, the Place and the Girl*, and, with a curious inconsistency, the show the paper had panned a week earlier, *The Yankee Tourist.* The book the *Dramatic Mirror* admired watched millionaire Singleton Seabrook (Thomas Wise) pursue a forger. A woman detective, Adelaide Forster (Truly Shattuck), is also stalking the criminal. She believes Singleton to be the forger. She woos him, hoping he will drop his guard and make a slip. Then she arrests him. He clears himself and the two realize they are in love. George Broadhurst's dialogue and Gustave Kerker's music were second rate. *The Lady from Lane's* left after six weeks.

Charles Frohman advertised **The Dairymaids** (8-26-07, Criterion) as his "annual musical production," implying that musicals were uniquely festive events outside the on-going theatrical mainstream. He might just as easily have considered the show his annual musical importation, for despite the native talent emerging around him, Frohman, with his impressive connections on both sides of the ocean, played it safe by bringing New York major London musical entertainments. More often than not he came to depend on one young American, Jerome Kern, for additional numbers to give his importations an added fillip and something of a domestic flavor. *The Dairymaids* was no exception. Kern added six songs. All were better than anything in the original, but none was outstandingly melodic. The best, "I'd Like To Meet Your Father," enjoyed a brief vogue. The story was reasonably simple. When two girls decide to pass some time at their rich aunt's model dairy farm, two young English lords disguise themselves as young ladies so they may be close to the girls. The show featured Julia Sanderson and marked the American debut of the nimble English patter artist, Huntley Wright.

The Rogers Brothers in Panama (9-2-07, Broadway), more so than any of the earlier Rogers Brothers' affairs, approached what the age understood as musical comedy. In their 1907 escapade the U.S. Canal Commissioners are captured by revolutionaries. Two young men take their place and make admirals of their valets (Gus and Max). The fraudulent sailors and servants are exposed and jailed, but they drug the villainous jailor and escape to an island. The erstwhile valets ultimately return to mainland Panama and stage a bullfight. Humor remained as broad as always—and often had little to do with the story. Since Max played a character called Hugo Kisser, while Gus was known as A. Gustave Windt, several routines tinkered with puns on their names. Nor did Max Hoffman's music, despite titles such as "In Panama," "Under The Jungle Moon" and "Way Down In Colon Town," offer any local color. Although electric lights had been used on Broadway for some time, the *Times* could still note with a certain fresh joy that "in a painted bay there are painted ships . . . and they have real lights on them at night." Like

so many other musicals of the year, the show offered Spanish dances by ladies in bright red dresses. *The Rogers Brothers in Panama* ran 71 performances and embarked on a national tour. The happiness of many theatregoers at the return of the brothers was shattered when Gus died suddenly. Astute showpeople had always considered Gus the lesser of the pair and assumed Max would succeed on his own, but he seemed colorless without his brother. Max did not retire immediately, but the Rogers Brothers soon passed into theatrical history.

Unfortunately for comedienne Lulu Glaser, **Lola from Berlin** (9-16-07, Liberty) was not a particularly good vehicle. J. J. McNally, who for years had contrived the Rogers Brothers' books, slapped together a stock of clichés and passed it off as a libretto. Lola, an immigrant and an heiress, is mistaken for an applicant for a maid's job. She is finally recognized and accepted into the home of John Westervelt (Dodson Mitchell), her late uncle's lawyer. When a note of Mrs. Westervelt (Florence Lester) to her lover is intercepted, Lola gamely claims she wrote the letter. This alienates her admirer, Arthur Paget (Jack Standing), but in the end everything is resolved. Jean Schwartz' wooden score was no better than McNally's book. Miss Glaser played her role in dialect, as did eight flaxen-haired chorus girls, dressed in "Gretchen" costumes. (The eight chorus boys were American college students.) Ralph Herz won some of the best laughs and applause for his delineation of a comic blackmailer. But the evening's virtues were few and far between. Thirty-five performances and Lola left town.

Another collection of clichés comprised the story of **The Hurdy Gurdy Girl** (9-23-07, Wallack's). The daughter of a rich sausage-maker is stolen by an Italian organ grinder. But the Italian's drunken wife takes the child to a foundling home and brings back another child. The sausage-maker is about to claim his second tot when the truth comes out. A small scar identifies the real girl. By coincidence, the girl's name was Lola (Bertha Mills). But more than one critic felt the most noteworthy playing of the evening came from another young lady, Adele Rowland, who, the *Times* announced, smiles, sings, dances, and talks "engagingly." In a cameo appearance, a much older lady, Annie Yeamans, the beloved Cordelia of the Harrigan and Hart shows, brought down the house in a role not much different from that of the sharp-tongued wife that had made her famous. Once again the music was as dreary as the book. One "realistic" setting, depicting dawn in Times Square, attracted some favorable comment, even if milkmen crossing the square in Buster Brown costumes elicited titters. The show's three-week run was even shorter than *Lola from Berlin*'s.

The Girl behind the Counter (10-1-07, Herald Square) was a smash hit. The work was an importation thoroughly revamped by Edgar Smith for Lew Fields. Fields played Henry Schniff, who dons a series of disguises to help his stepdaughter, Winnie (May Naudain), marry American Charley Chetwyn (Joseph Ratliff) rather than her mother's choice, a titled Englishman. The basic show was solid, if unoriginal. Each night Fields garnered the biggest applause of the evening with a much-talked-about soda fountain scene in which he matched the color of his customers' sodas to the dress or tie the patron was wearing. When a difficult young man insisted his striped tie be duplicated, it was. But most likely, one song could also claim some credit for the show's eight-month run and profitable tour. The song was Paul Lincke's "The Glow-Worm," inserted into the show after its opening. The song had already become popular, and Fields, pleading an old superstition against disturbing success, refused to insert the song—unless publisher Edward Marks paid him a thousand dollars to include it. Marks refused, but he offered to pay Fields if the song failed to stop the show and stimulate ticket sales. Fields agreed. As Marks wrote, " 'Glow Worm' went in; Miss Naudain sang dozens of encores every evening; and I didn't have to pay."

Since revues were still not plotless at this early stage in their history, **The Gay White Way** (10-7-07, Casino) sent an amateur detective (Jefferson De Angelis) to the Hotel Rooseveltia (Act I), an Actors' Fund Fair at the Metropolitan Opera House (Act II), and a 42nd Street restaurant (Act III) in search of the identity of a headless photograph. Before he ascertains its identity he views a collection of loosely introduced vaudeville turns. Blanche Ring had many of the evening's best moments. In a turnabout from her usual brassy delivery, she softly sang a Negro lullaby while dressed as a gamin and seated down by the footlights. She also portrayed the heroine in a travesty of *The Great Divide*. She and De Angelis combined for a hilarious spoof of the great sawmill scene from *Blue Jeans*. While the tethered De Angelis was dragged ever closer to a spinning papier-mâché saw, Miss Ring babbled incessantly to the audience about her concern for his whereabouts. For those artists who didn't bring their own songs, Ludwig Englander provided some mediocre new tunes. Faulty as it may have been as a good revue, the good vaudeville in *The Gay White Way* was enough of a draw to keep the Casino lit for 105 performances.

With Fields performing at the Herald Square, Weber reopened the old Music Hall on October 10 without his oldtime partner. The house had been substantially rebuilt as a result of the new fire laws that followed the Iroquois Theatre disaster. **Hip! Hip! Hooray!** attempted to revive Weber and Fields' old formula after a year's absence, even though, like the recent Rogers Brothers' offering, it employed a bit more plot than formerly. Two German professors (Weber and Dick Bernard) attempt to introduce a new breakfast cereal, "Excited Oats," at Doolittle College and become involved in love affairs with a widow (Valeska Suratt) and a village belle (Bessie Clayton). Miss Clayton's sprightly, high-kicking dancing allowed her to display her still famous, still beautiful legs, while the stylish Miss Suratt paraded about modeling exceptionally large hats dwarfed only by her elaborate larger coiffures. (The size of her hats suggests that "Merry Widow Hats" were coming into fashion even before *The Merry Widow* opened.) The lone Weber was by no means the failure that Max Rogers had been, but without Fields an electric give-and-take was missing. The production had a forlornly short run of 64 performances.

Two shows came in on October 19. **The Hoyden,** at the Knickerbocker, was an English importation, starring Elsie Janis. To suit Miss Janis and her American audiences, the show was altered until, as John Golden (one of its American lyricists) noted, "There was nothing left of the English composers' music or lyrics, and very little of the original book." That book described how the heroine falls in love with a man she believes has jilted her sister and whom she sets about humiliating. How unimpressed the rewriting left the public was evidenced by *The Hoyden*'s modest seven-week run.

The Top of the World, at the Majestic, was a musical extravaganza, written with an eye on the younger audience. The music was by Manuel Klein (of the Hippodrome) and by Anne Caldwell, who married the show's lyricist, James O'Dea, and who, about this time, gave up composing to write lyrics and librettos. In Mark E. Swon's book, Jack Frost (George Majeroni) is a policeman attached to Aurora Borealis (George W. Monroe), Queen of the North. Jack objects to people in the land of Illusia and turns them to ice. But Westinghouse Morse (John McVey) follows Jack around with a can of tropical atmosphere and thaws out Jack's victims. Two love stories were interwoven into the plot. In one a fairy prince loves Maida (Kathleen

Clifford), a girl who must find a wishing pole; in the other Stalacta (Blanche Wayne) loves the explorer Shellman (Harry Farleigh). Typical of the show's knowing touches was a number in which five young ladies asked five real collies, "How'd You Like To Be My Bow-wow-wow?" The collies gave their answer by dancing with the girls. The show delighted young and old for twenty weeks.

So far it had been an interesting season—long on promise, short on distinction. But the promises, implicit in shows such as *The Alaskan; The Time, the Place, and the Girl;* possibly even in the *Follies of 1907,* were intriguing enough to excuse the momentary absence of real merit. However, two nights after *The Top of the World* opened, another show arrived and radically changed the whole direction of the musical theatre—not just for the season, but for years to come. The show that opened at the New Amsterdam on October 21, 1907, was **The Merry Widow.**

Since its Viennese premiere on December 30, 1905, *Die lustige Witwe* had swept the Western world, becoming a legend in its own time. Curiously, like *H.M.S. Pinafore* in London and *Florodora* (11-20-00) in New York, the work was not an immediate hit in Vienna. Some of its original notices were very unkind. But just as Sullivan had popularized his show's tunes at concerts, Franz Lehar saw to it his lovely melodies received constant playing. In a short time the theatre was selling out nightly, and *The Merry Widow* was on its way. Singlehandedly, it revived the moribund Viennese operetta. The show triumphed in Berlin. London welcomed it on June 17, 1907. Sensing its importance and its reception, the New York *Times* gave the production a full-page spread on the Sunday prior to its premiere. Indeed, in America its success was phenomenal. Trade sheets of the period were not as informative as they have since become, and the records are confused and scattered. Yet within months after its premiere at the New Amsterdam, no less than three, and possibly as many as six, road companies were carrying its gorgeous strains across the land. Only one Viennese work had premiered in the preceding seven years. *The Merry Widow* made operetta the rage of the musical theatre. America's fondness for English musical comedies cooled appreciably. The older, more stolid, comic opera and the new, struggling native musical comedy were stifled. Comic opera never recovered. The American musical had to bide its time for seven years. *The Merry Widow*'s relatively cohesive book, its pervasive sense of style and tone, and, best of all, its magnificent Franz

Lehar score set new standards. "The Merry Widow Waltz" ("I Love You So"), "Maxim's" and "Vilja" quickly became classics. In its excitement the *Dramatic Mirror* forgot its earlier, hopeful assessment of the lyric theatre, damning what weeks before it had praised. But this time it accurately evaluated the influence the new show would have:

> Coming at the end of an epoch of inane musical comedy—grant that it is at an end!—the operetta is twice welcome, on account of its own excellence and because it may start a new era in musical entertainment. The music is tuneful, bright and original, the humor fresh and genuine; the story clear and vigorous, and the characters exaggerated only a trifle beyond probabilities.

The "clear and vigorous" story told how Prince Danilo is ordered to court a rich widow, Sonya, lest her millions be lost to his country's treasury. Reluctant at first, he soon finds he is wooing the widow for herself and not for her money. The show made overnight stars of its two principals, Ethel Jackson and Donald Brian. Miss Jackson's star soon flickered, but Brian's remained bright for many years.

• • •

Donald Brian was born in Saint John's, Newfoundland, on February 17, 1877. Handsome, with a dimpled round face and wavy hair, he made his stage debut in Lawrence, Massachusetts, in 1896. Thereafter he played in stock and toured in straight plays until he landed a small role in a touring company of *The Chaperones.* Appearances followed in *The Supper Club, The Belle of Broadway, Florodora, The Silver Slipper,* and *Myles Aroon.* George M. Cohan spotted the actor, who had become an excellent dancer and an adequate singer, and gave him important parts in *Forty-five Minutes from Broadway* and *Little Johnny Jones.* Brian's association with *The Merry Widow* has caused many writers to look on him as primarily a singer, although in fact his singing was secondary to his acting and dancing. Coincidently, London's original Danilo was Joseph Coyne, another American known more for his general stageworthiness than for any special vocal talents.

• • •

Even outside the theatrical world the musical's influence was enormous. In fashion, feathery, oversized "Merry Widow Hats" became de rigueur. Its irrepressible waltz had no small part in initiating what was quickly tagged "the dancing craze."

If Harry B. Smith's recollections are correct, there was a startling irony to its commanding vogue, for Smith contended that *The Merry Widow* was rushed into its original Viennese production when a principal's illness delayed what was to have been the first Austrian mounting of a major American work, *Robin Hood* (9-28-91). The truth of Smith's closing comment on the story was soon made clear. "Lehar's opera made a fortune for Colonel Savage, its producer. Eventually it cost American managers a number of fortunes, because, for several years afterward, they produced every German and Austrian operetta they could get, in the vain hope of finding another 'Merry Widow.' "

The third financial panic in fourteen years struck home forcefully two days after *The Merry Widow* opened when the Knickerbocker Trust Company closed its doors on October 23. The glittering success of Lehar's piece both in New York and in its many road companies contrasted noticeably with the fiscal gloom. This contrast undoubtedly hastened the rash of importations from Vienna and the American imitations that followed.

Boston still remained a production center, and one week after *The Merry Widow* arrived, the Boston Cadet Corps brought its latest effort down to New York. **Miss Pocahontas** (10-28-07, Lyric) played havoc with a favorite bit of American folklore, turning Captain John Smith (Walter Jones) into a braggart, condemned to die or marry a withered old Indian crone. He chooses death. Pocahontas (Marie Dupuis) rescues him, though she really loves John Rolfe (George Fox). Pow-Ha-Tan (George Le Soir) was given an Irish father to fill the need for a traditional musical clown. New Yorkers didn't take to the show and it was withdrawn after two weeks.

Edward German's **Tom Jones** (11-11-07, Astor), the popular English comic opera, was November's first musical. It was followed a week later by a new American comic opera, Reginald De Koven's **The Girls of Holland** (11-18-07, Lyric). Each new De Koven piece made it embarrassingly evident that De Koven was written out. His best new melodies were still pretty enough, but they did not survive constant repetition. The weakness of the music was emphasized by Stanislaus Stange's stodgy, silly book and lyrics. To prove the worth of his elixir and to win the love of the niece of Frau Van Biere (a brewer's widow!), Dr. Franz (Harry Fairleigh), with the help of Mephisto's female cousin, Ariella (Vera Michelena), brings to life the statue of Snowdrop (Edward M. Tavor). Snowdrop proves a nasty surprise, demanding the niece for himself. He is summarily returned to stone.

Another week later, on November 25, the third annual Hippodrome production appeared. Like the preceding season's Casino hit, *The Vanderbilt Cup*, **The Auto Race** cashed in on the fast-growing vogue for sporting cars. The vastness of the Hippodrome stage and its unsurpassed technical facilities allowed it to mount an even more spectacular chase than *The Vanderbilt Cup* could. For good measure, a naval battle, a ballet called "The Four Seasons," a gigantic garden party, and another Hippodrome circus were also staged. Of course, for that very reason, Hippodrome shows could never tour in anything approaching their original form. Their audiences had to come to them. Theatregoers came in droves—enough to keep the 5000-seat house showing a profit twice a day for 312 performances.

Chicago remained active all season. But many of its productions are recorded as they arrived in New York. Meanwhile, the city's primary combination house, the Great Northern, continued to offer local traveling shows that never reached Broadway. For example, the week beginning December 1, 1907, the house offered its patrons **Busy Izzy, the Mazuma Man** with George Sidney as star. Izzy Mark doesn't care about money. Nonetheless, Izzy manages to save a bank from failure, only to squander his reward.

The first of the season's three George M. Cohan musicals, **The Talk of New York** (12-3-07, Knickerbocker), continued the adventures of Kid Burns, with Victor Moore once again playing the Kid.

· · ·

Victor Moore was born in Hammonton, New Jersey, on February 24, 1876. His first "theatrical" experience seems to have been at the age of ten, when he carried a banner in a local minstrel parade. Shortly thereafter his parents moved to Boston. There he obtained employment as a super in *Babes in the Woods* for $3.50 a week. A few years in stock followed. In 1902 he purchased the rights to a vaudeville skit entitled "Change Your Act, or Back to the Woods," paying $125 for it. The skit chronicled the end of a seedy, hard-luck vaudeville team, just handed their notice and heckled as they attempt to make their way through their final performance. Ignoring the injunction of the title, Moore used the skit off and on for the next twenty-five years, whenever no suitable legitimate vehicle offered itself. His partner was usually his wife, Emma Littlefield. Cohan signed Moore for *Forty-five Minutes from Broadway* after watching the young comedian in this act.

· · ·

Kid Burns, rich from his racetrack winnings and his investments, falls in love with Geraldine Wilcox

(Miss Littlefield). (Mary, his love in *Forty-Five Minutes from Broadway* (1-1-06), has, for theatrically imperative reasons, been forgotten.) Any talk of marriage is opposed by her brother, Joe (Jack Gardner). Joe loves Grace Palmer (Gertrude Vanderbilt), whom Kid exposes as a blackmailer. When Joe hears Grace accepting his father's money to leave him, Joe shoots her. Kid takes the weapon and the blame. On his release from jail he finds a repentant Grace and a Joe who approves of his marrying Geraldine. The book was well written, with Cohan's sharp, idiomatic dialogue. But Cohan's score was the weakest he had done in some while. Not one standout emerged, though "When A Fellow's On The Level With A Girl That's On The Square" had some vogue. Nonetheless, *The Talk of New York* gave Cohan his first experience with a long New York run, just under twenty weeks.

Cohan brought in his second show two months to the day after *The Talk of New York*. It was a more than usually emotional opening. Cohan had long idolized Ned Harrigan of the old Harrigan and Hart shows. Harrigan had retired from the stage, and Broadway had more or less forgotten him. But Cohan had remembered and invited him to the first night. There Harrigan discovered that one of the principals of **Fifty Miles from Boston** (2-3-08, Garrick—originally Harrigan's!) was named in his honor. Cohan's Harrigan (George Parson) loves Sadie Woodis (Edna Wallace Hopper), but she prefers Joe Westcott (Laurence Wheat), the baseball hero of Brookfield, Massachusetts. Sadie's brother, Jed (John Westley), has stolen $400 from the post office and lost it in a bet. Harrigan offers to supply Jed the money if he will persuade Joe to give up Sadie. But Sadie remains true to Joe. Just as Jed thinks he will go to jail, the post office burns down. Harrigan, realizing how ignoble his position is, gives Jed the money anyway. *Fifty Miles from Boston* was a peculiar show. Cohan himself called it a "play with music," as he had some of his earlier works, and as he had in *Forty-Five Minutes from Broadway,* he distributed its songs unevenly. Its first two acts were largely songless melodrama. Most of the tunes were saved for Act III. The songs were better than those Cohan had written for *The Talk of New York*. One stopped the show—especially the first night with the old trouper in the house. "H-A-Double R-I-G-A-N" (published simply as "Harrigan") was the last song Cohan wrote for Broadway that entered into his classic canon. It was sung by James C. Marlowe. The song is rarely sung as written. Cohan's triplet over the word "double," per-

haps under the influence of the very word, has long since been reduced to two notes. Despite the hit tune, the show ran only four weeks.

Cohan's third show, **The Yankee Prince** (4-20-08, Knickerbocker), was even less successful. The title suggested the Yankee Doodle boy was succumbing to the glamor of Europe. But the story was vintage Cohan, with the Cohans themselves starred. Franklyn Fielding (Jerry), a rich Chicagoan, takes his daughter Evelyn (Josephine) to Europe in search of a titled husband. She meets and falls in love with Percy Springer (George), an American. Even though her father finds a willing earl, Evelyn marries Percy. With another hand-me-down Cohan score, the show ran only 28 performances.

Raymond Hubbell and Robert B. Smith had a resounding hit with **A Knight for a Day** (12-16-07, Wallack's). The evening was a rewrite of their 24-performance flop of the preceding year, *Mamselle Sallie* (11-26-06). The plot of *A Knight for a Day* was trite enough, again making a whole evening out of an attempt to mate matching lockets and thereby inherit a fortune. The lockets fall into the wrong hands—the antagonists' and the comics'—before the finale resolves everything. John Slavin and May Vokes led the clowning, while Sallie Fisher and Percy Bronson played the romantic leads. Hubbell's score was a proper match for the libretto, pleasurable and forgettable. Its mating made a fortune for all involved, for this time the show chalked up 176 performances. Its success was a commentary on the healthy theatrical economy of the era. Chicago remained an independently rewarding production center as did some other cities. As Cohan and others showed time and again, if Broadway failed to embrace material meant for it, there was often a highly lucrative welcome waiting on the road. But even Broadway was customarily easy-going enough to reconsider efforts it had only recently rejected. Although the ten or fifteen thousand dollars it cost to raise the curtain on a well-produced musical was not an inconsiderable sum when bread cost a nickel for a one pound loaf, a good pair of shoes was $3.75, and a popular novel sold for $1.50, the few forms of competition and pre-union wage scales kept weekly expenses so low that some extra effort could be repaid many times over.

Paul Rubens' **Miss Hook of Holland** (12-31-07, Criterion) arrived from London to become an immediate hit, helped by Christie MacDonald in the leading role of a brewer's daughter loved by a bandmaster.

A fifth consecutive hit followed two nights later

on January 2 when Weber brought **The Merry Widow Burlesque** into his theatre, getting 1908 off to a happy start. Weber used Lehar's music—with the composer's permission—and had George V. Hobart "retranslate" the original. In the new version Prince Danilo became Dandilo, while Margot, Clo-Clo, and Frou-Frou were joined by cuddly Goo-Goo. While Charles J. Ross was Dandilo and Lulu Glaser the first widow, most of the cast was recruited from old Weber and Fields stalwarts: Peter F. Dailey, Bessie Clayton, and Mabel Fenton. When Miss Glaser left the cast during the run, Blanche Ring was called in to replace her. The new widow brought with her the one song from the show to become a hit, "Yip-I-Addy-I-Ay" (Will Cobb/ John H. Flynn). The burlesque ran out the season.

Funabashi (1-6-08, Casino) told one of the era's most popular stories—the romance of an American naval officer serving in the Orient. In this instance the officer was Jack Carter (Walter Percival), and he falls in love with a fellow American, Dolly Rivers (Vera Michelena). But Jack's father, the Secretary of War, orders him to marry Gwyndolin Hillary-Hoops (Margaret Rutledge). A family friend, Nan Livingston (Alice Fischer), persuades the Secretary to marry Gwyndolin himself, freeing Jack to marry Dolly. Unlike many earlier musical comedies of its sort, *Funabashi* neglected to utilize fully its setting. Japan figured only slightly in the story and was used primarily for background color. References to it were typically half-respectful, half-condescending. And in this era of a revived "manifest destiny" and "the big stick" it was not surprising to find one stirring martial air saluting "The Girl Behind The Man Behind The Gun." A refreshing change, noted by several of the critics was the absence of a grotesque comedian. Whatever the show's virtues, Broadway had become too crowded with hits, so *Funabashi* moved on after a brief stay.

January's next musical came in two weeks later. **Lonesome Town** (1-20-08, New Circle) was a brave title in an era when musical titles were gay, or, at best, noncommittal. Its book was in the picaresque American minstrel tradition. Chico Brown (C. William Kolb) and Bakersfield Bill (Max M. Dill), two tramps, are chased into Watts by a wild bull. They encounter an old friend, Fresno Phil (Ben T. Dillon), who reports that Mr. Watts, the town's absentee landowner, is dead and has left no known will. Fresno poses as a lawyer, while Chico and Bill pretend to be Watts and his son. They are ultimately exposed and go on their way. Although there was no particularly good music to assist in

putting over the material, *Lonesome Town* recorded a satisfactory run of eleven weeks.

Oscar Straus' **A Waltz Dream** (1-27-08, Broadway) was well received and quickly caught up in the new rage for Viennese operetta, running until the warm weather. The story told of a young man's unhappy marriage to a foreign princess and of his sneaking off to listen to the music of his homeland, played by an all-girl orchestra in a park. The original leads were Magda Dahl and Edward Johnson, but they were soon replaced by Vera Michelena and Frank Rushworth. Several newspapers made much of Johnson's departure, announcing he was leaving to further his voice studies in Italy so that he might try his luck at opera. Of course, none of these papers could foresee that his luck would one day make him general manager of the Metropolitan Opera.

The Soul Kiss (1-28-08, New York) was a vehicle for Adelaide Genee, whom Ziegfeld, the show's producer, advertised as "the world's greatest dancer." While she may not have been at the very top of her profession, she was a highly regarded, serious artist, and more than one reviewer was distressed to find her in such a commercial assemblage. The book was by Harry B. Smith, who at the time was writing the scripts for the new *Follies*. Suzette, a model, will not kiss the sculptor, Maurice (Cecil Lean). J. Lucifer Mephisto (Ralph Herz) wagers a million dollars that Suzette (Florence Holbrook) cannot keep Maurice faithful for one year. He tempts Maurice with historical and fictitious beauties—Carmen, Marguerite, and Cleopatra. Maurice falls in love with "The Dancer" (Genee), and they decide to marry. Suzette marries an American millionaire, and Mephisto goes off to the Bal Tabarin with a chorus girl. The music, culled from various composers, but mainly by Maurice Levi, was of the same mediocre order as the book. One of the songs gave a generous plug to the reigning hit of the season, happily at another syndicate house, "Since My Mariutch Learned The Merry Widow Waltz." Ziegfeld was already making a name for himself with his lavish touch. The brilliant Bal Tabarin set won approval as did an autumn hunting scene with real hounds and with girls in white hunting frocks. (Not even stiff hunting boots prevented Genee from dancing gracefully in the hunting ballet.) The star, glorified by Ziegfeld's production and promotion, proved a potent draw; the show ran sixteen weeks.

February 3 brought two solidly American shows: *Fifty Miles from Boston* and **Bandana Land**. For the latter, Ray Comstock, one of the most enlightened producers in Broadway history, brought together much of the leading Negro talent of the day. Williams and Walker were the stars. Most of the music was by Will Marion Cook, with supplemental numbers by Williams and by Chris Smith. Alex Rogers, who did most of the lyrics, combined with J. A. Shipp to write a libretto that told a typical Williams and Walker tale. Mose Blackstone (Alex Rogers) organizes a syndicate to buy Amos Simmons' farm and sell it to the street railway company, but he cannot raise all the needed cash. He learns rich Skunkton Bowser (Williams) is stranded with a small minstrel company and gets him to contribute the rest. Blackstone sells half the farm to the railway. The rest he turns into a black man's park and advises the railway the Negroes will make all sorts of noises and trouble unless the railway pays an exorbitant price for the remaining half. At the last minute Skunkton and his "guardian" Bud Jenkins (Walker) withdraw from the deal and handle the whole arrangement themselves. The play was good, clean fun. Williams and Walker lead a show-stopping cakewalk at the end of Act I. The lyrics, in frequently resorting to Negro dialect, were more patently racial than the music. Although one pedant was offended by black actors wearing straight-haired wigs, insisting their performances would have been "just as vigorous with kinks," the show was well received and played eleven weeks at the Majestic.

Nearly a Hero (2-24-08, Casino) was another producer-assemblage with a number of composers providing the tunes for another inane Harry B. Smith libretto. Jabez Doolittle (Sam Edwards), in order to explain an absence from home, claims to be the unknown hero who rescued Harold Montague (Edgar Norton) from drowning. But Harold is not thankful, claiming his rescuer robbed him. He demands Doolittle's arrest. Ludwig Knoedler (Sam Bernard), who boards with the Doolittles, is jailed by mistake. By Act III everything is explained. Enlivened by a superb cast that also included Ethel Levey, Ada Lewis, Zelda Sears, and Elizabeth Brice, *Nearly a Hero* pleased sufficient crowds to run 116 performances.

On March 23 Mort Singer gave Chicagoans still another Hough–Adams–Howard hit at the La Salle, **Honeymoon Trail.** Cecil Lean and Florence Holbrook again were starred, while a figure new to the series, Ned Wayburn, directed. The action was set at a hotel in California, which had recently passed a law granting divorce after six months' residence. Yet love and marriage were at the forefront of the plot. Tightfisted, much-divorced George Mason,

the canned-bean tycoon, won't hear of his daughter, Edna, marrying Perkins, the head of advertising at a rival cannery. To mollify her father Edna feigns interest in Bill Dudley, her stepmother's former husband. Dudley tricks Mason out of $50,000. Perkins gets Mason, who is usually averse to gambling, to bet him a similar sum. Perkins knows he will lose his own bet. Then Perkins arranges for the hotel manager, who is also a justice of the peace, to marry him and Edna while they pretend to say goodbye. Although some of Hough and Adams' lyrics were untypically stilted ('Tis here that hearts long since grown weary/of wife dearie, gain their liberty), their dialogue was as crisp and witty as ever:

Edna: You had no business kissing me.
Perkins: It wasn't business—it was pleasure.

On April 20 New York was offered **The Flower of the Ranch,** a Chicago hit that Joe Howard wrote without his usual collaborators, Hough and Adams. It told the melodramatic tale of "Little Flower" (Mabel Barrison), whose father was killed by Toni Miguel (Ike Oliver) when she was still a baby and whose property was seized by Bob Branden (Frederick Knight). When she is grown, she is given papers for safekeeping by Jack Farnum (Howard). Branden gets Miguel to steal the papers. But when he learns of the reward offered for them, Miguel attempts to return them. Branden shoots him to thwart the return. However, Branden has an "awakening of conscience" and confesses all. Once again New Yorkers would not buy the Chicago school of musicals. *The Flower of the Ranch* lasted only two weeks at the Majestic.

Cohan's *The Yankee Prince* also opened April 20. Five nights later, **The Merry-Go-Round,** a revue with enough of a plot to allow the evening to be called a musical comedy, came into the Circle Theatre. The plot followed another tour, this time of the sights of a country fair. Chicago favorite, brash Mabel Hite (described as a female George M. Cohan), sang and danced a comic song describing her efforts to be a lady in Weehawken. Ignacio Martinetti earned several encores for his energetic dances. The Circle Theatre was temporarily rechristened Gus Edwards' Music Hall in honor of the show's composer. But none of Edwards' songs lasted much beyond the show's run.

The Gay Musician (5-18-08, Wallack's) was anything but gay. He was an unknown comic opera composer, Eugene Dubois (Walter Percival), who invites a prima donna, Maude Granville (Amelia Stone), to hear his latest work, at the same time forcing his wife, Marie (Sophie Brandt), to play the part of his maid and slapping her when she makes a gaffe. She leaves him. In the second act Eugene and Maude are to be married, as are Maude's father and Marie. But Maude and Eugene quarrel, and he goes away with Marie. Although the book and the Julian Edwards score were praised, the public withheld its support. The show folded after just two and a half weeks.

The season's last musical in New York, **Mary's Lamb** (5-25-08, New York), was based on the French farce *Mme. Mongodin*. It was a vehicle for Richard Carle, with book, lyrics, and music by Carle himself. Carle played "Leander Lamb, a martyr." Lamb is henpecked by a wife (Elita Proctor Otis) who displays a large framed knife she calls "The Shrine of Virtue." She boasts she once used it to discourage a too ardent lover. Leander accepts his wife's opinion of herself, referring to her as "My better two-thirds." The first time Mr. Lamb is caught with Sylvia Montrose (Henrietta Lee), Mrs. Lamb accepts his excuse of sleepwalking. But the second time she goes for the knife. At that moment an old schoolmate of Lamb's arrives. He turns out to be the old "ardent lover" and tells the true story of the knife. After that Mr. Lamb has the upper hand. *Mary's Lamb* was another of the many musicals adored on the road and rejected on Broadway. Carle, in shows of his own writing or by others, toured the country ceaselessly, as one of the most popular entertainers of the day. New York critics generally found his material "raw," and a torrid, if comic, dance he did in *Mary's Lamb* with a burlesque queen did nothing to let them change their minds. As a result, his Broadway runs were almost always short—although rarely as short as the two-week stand of *Mary's Lamb*.

The continuing success of the Hough–Adams–Howard musicals prompted the Singer brothers to erect a second Chicago theatre to house the shows. They opened the Princess Theatre on June 1 with the latest work of the trio, **A Stubborn Cinderella.** Its popularity meant that Hough–Adams–Howard had two hits running in Chicago at once. Although *Honeymoon Trail* never reached New York, *A Stubborn Cinderella* did. But its run there in no way matched its stay of over 300 performances in Chicago.

Not all of the commercial activity was confined to the principal houses in Chicago and New York. In New York itself, away from Broadway, there were numerous theatres promoting homegrown musicals that provided pleasure to their neighborhoods and experience to their artists. Up at the

Yorkville, opening-nighters on October 28, 1907, applauded L. B. Parker's musical melodrama **The Candy Kid,** in which "Yalie" Eddy Edson saves Bonnie Bosworth and her brother from the machinations of Emanuel Lopez. Lopez tries to have the brother seduced and murdered, and attempts to kidnap Bonnie. Neither Parker nor his musical made it downtown. But Flournoy Miller and Aubrey Lyles, who wrote the libretto for the all-black musical, **The Oyster Man,** which played Negro neighborhoods in November, did eventually receive their share of Broadway acclaim. In December, the New Circle Theatre, a house that served Broadway and its hinterlands, brought in **Playing the Ponies.** Its plot suggests the show was aimed at an ethnically mixed audience. Pincus and Plonsky each think McGuiness is his long-lost child. They explore his background at Act I's race track and Act II's Luna Park. It turns out McGuiness' father was Mr. McGuiness. **The Bad Boy and His Teddy Bear** ("Teddy" was still in office) described how a "prankish lad" befriends a family of bears. The action takes place at a hotel operated by Badly Cook, who has a rain-making invention which he wants to sell to Harrington, the railroad magnate. A love affair between Harrington's son and Cook's daughter helps the transaction. Brooklyn also produced its own musicals. **The Girl from Williamsburg** met with an enthusiastic reception when it opened at Payton's in May. But the day of the neighborhood musical was virtually over. By March 1908 there were 400 movie houses in New York City alone, and a good number of them had very recently been marginal legitimate theatres. The trend was national. In the May 30 issue of *The Dramatic Mirror* a large ad appeared, headlined, "Turn Your Opera House Into A Moving Picture Nickelodeon This Summer." Many "summer" nickelodeons never returned to the legitimate fold.

1908-1909

1908–09 got off to a promising start, and then collapsed, at least artistically. Commercially, there could be little complaint, for a third of the season's musicals ran over 100 performances. But this success reflected simply the musical theatre's skill in brightening the lives of the tired businessman and his wife. Aesthetic considerations were few and far between at this time in Broadway's history.

Two musicals appeared on June 15, the traditional date for separating the seasons. One was a revue; the other was a book show. Both were smash hits. Indeed, **Three Twins,** at the Herald Square, was the season's biggest hit (excepting as usual the *sui generis* Hippodrome spectacle). The musical was adapted by Charles Dickson from Mrs. R. Pacheco's *Incog.* Tom Stanhope (Clifton Crawford), disinherited by his father because of his love of Kate Armitage (Alice Yorke), disguises himself to resemble a photograph he has found. The photo is of Molly Sommers' sweetheart, Harry Winter (Willard Curtiss). Harry has a slightly demented twin brother. And so Molly (Bessie McCoy) is never sure which of the three twins she is dealing with. The complications are ironed out in time for Molly and Harry, and Tom and Kate to wed. The libretto was clean and cheerful, but what really made the show was Bessie McCoy and two outstanding songs. The show, in turn, made Miss McCoy a star, and made the lyricist, Otto Hauerbach, and the composer, Karl Hoschna, names to be reckoned with.

. . .

Otto Hauerbach (later **Harbach**) was born to Danish immigrant parents in Salt Lake City, Utah, on August 1, 1873. After graduation from Knox College he taught English and public speaking at Whitman College in Walla Walla, Washington. He arrived in New York in 1901 to work toward a doctorate at Columbia. Failing eyesight forced him to abandon his plans and take odd jobs, mostly in the newspaper field. He met Hoschna in 1902 and together they wrote an operetta, *The Daughter of the Desert,* that was never produced.

. . .

Karl Hoschna was born in Kuschwarda in Bohemia on August 16, 1877. Leaving the Vienna Conservatory with honors, he accepted a post as an oboist in the Austrian army band. In 1896 he emigrated to America and soon found work under Victor Herbert. An uncontrollable fear that oboe playing would affect his mind led him to accept work as a copyist with Witmark. In this job he began composing popular songs. Three operettas followed, all folding before they reached New York.

. . .

One of Hoschna's song hits in *Three Twins,* "The Yama Yama Man" (lyrics by Collin Davis), is now nearly forgotten. It is a choice example of the benign infantilism that remained voguish all through this period. Miss McCoy introduced it in a satin clown outfit topped by a cone-shaped hat. A second hit from the show still enjoys periodic revivals—"Cuddle Up A Little Closer, Lovie Mine." Although the song is endearingly intimate, it was given an elaborate, formal staging with "A unique chorus setting representing the seven ages of lovers from infancy to old age." Theatrical effect rather than consistent tone governed musical mountings. The rest of the score was trippingly melodic. The show scored 288 performances.

Another standard came out of Ziegfeld's **Follies of 1908,** June 15's other premiere. Nora Bayes introduced "Shine On Harvest Moon," which she and her husband, Jack Norworth, wrote. A second of their numbers, "Over On The Jersey Side," teasingly condescending, suggested the show still expected to cater to a largely local audience who would understand the lyric's parochial sentiments and allusions. Both songs were interpolations. The official score was by Maurice Levi, who had written for the defunct Rogers Brothers' burlesques. The most played of his numbers was the martial "Song Of The Navy," its Harry B. Smith lyrics boasting, "Red, White, and Blue is ready for peace or war," a feeling close to the heart of a nation and its "big stick" President. How new and tentative the form was could be seen in several ways. For example, its sheet music clung to the older spelling, "review." Several years still had to pass before the French spelling was universally accepted. And the revue had a book—by Smith. This year's compère and commère were Adam and Eve. Their experiences viewing their progeny's accomplishments provided the thread that tied together the selections and production numbers. These numbers included a view of a tunnel being dug between Manhattan and New Jersey, followed by a view of the Jersey marshes, with Ziegfeld's beauties as giant mosquitoes. The girls later appeared as taxicabs whose lights glared out into the auditorium. Important political figures of the day were impersonated in a scene that re-created the Chicago convention. The show's success assured its continuance. It ran 120 performances at the Jardin de Paris, almost twice as long as the first edition. With this second mounting, the *Follies* started on the way to becoming both an institution and a legend.

On the Madison Square Garden Roof, a weak musical entitled **Ski-Hi** had a brief 25-performance run beginning June 20. Little more than another revue with the slimmest of plotlines, it took its titular hero (William Conley) to the Orient and then to Jupiter. It was the last of the summer musicals to play the roof. The house had never had particularly good luck with its selections, and the shooting of Stanford White on opening night two summers before had added notoriety to its ill fortune. Moreover, the theatre district was ineluctably moving away from Madison Square, dooming even more fortunate theatres.

If the critics were not speaking loosely when they said **The Mimic World** (7-9-08, Casino) hadn't "even the semblance of a plot and makes no pretense of any," then the revue would have been years ahead of its time. Some thin thread to tie together the songs and sketches, however fragile, was still in order. The sketches were basically old-fashioned burlesques on the plays and players of the day (George M. Cohan, Kid Burns, Prince Danilo) interspersed with vaudeville turns. It satisfied a public seeking light, summer entertainment.

Two shows opened August 3. One was the **Cohan and Harris Minstrels,** at the New York. Cohan, the great musical comedy innovator, was also Cohan, the knowledgeable traditionalist. His love and respect of Harrigan had already been made evident, and in a few years his feeling about Weber and Fields, and their burlesque tradition, would have important effects on the American revue. Now Cohan and his partner, Sam Harris, boldly attempted to resuscitate a dying tradition. Their minstrels included George Evans, Eddie Leonard, and the great female impersonator, Julian Eltinge. Because political conventions were then in the news, Evans acknowledged the applause greeting his first entrance by shouting, "I accept your nomination." Eltinge performed a Salome dance. Much of the second act was occupied by Cohan's one-act musical comedy, "The Belle of the Barbers' Ball." Although the 24-performance run was a limited booking from the start, grosses were disappointing. Cohan and Harris were not discouraged. They promised to bring the troupe back again the next year.

The second August 3 opening was **The Girl Question** at Wallack's. As they had the previous August, Hough, Adams, and Howard brought in another of their Chicago hits for New York's inspection. Once again their welcome was lukewarm, with critics again suggesting Chicago was too partial to melodrama and sentimentality. Con Ryan (Junie McCree), headwaiter at the restaurant where all the action takes place, loves Elsie Davis (Isabel D'Armond), the cashier, and is loved by Jo Forster (Georgie Drew Mendum), a waitress. Elsie marries Harold Sears (Jack Henderson), son of a railroad magnate. Sears senior forecloses the mortgage on the restaurant to turn it into a broker-age office. But Jo comes into an inheritance and sells her railroad stock to Sears in return for the restaurant. Con and Jo marry. *The Girl Question* had all the virtues of Hough-Adams-Howard shows: slangy dialogue; simple, natural lyrics; and good homespun melody. Still, the show stayed only a month before moving on.

In January the trio tried again with **A Stubborn Cinderella** (1-25-09, Broadway). It was to be the closest they would come to repeating their Chicago popularity in the big town. Lady Leslie (Sallie Fisher), an amazingly unworldly young Scot, is traveling with a bodyguard through America on her way to a marriage with a Russian Grand Duke. She stops at Columbus College, where she agrees to unveil a statue. At the ceremony she meets Mac and, assuming he is the sculptor, asks him to make a statue of her. They head for California after being delayed by a landslide in Colorado. To while away the time, Mac tells her the story of Cinderella, and she decides he can be her Prince Charming, even though he has botched the statue. If the book was a bit less cohesive than their earlier efforts, Howard's songs were as good or better. The best was a melodic waltz, "When You First Kiss The Last Girl You Love." *A Stubborn Cinderella*'s run of 88 performances was the longest the team ever enjoyed in New York. One reason may have been the actor who played Mac. Several critics singled him out, predicting a bright future for him in musical comedy. He was John Barrymore.

August's final musical, **Algeria** (8-31-08, Broadway), had a gorgeous, romantic Victor Herbert score and a dreadful Glen MacDonough book. The story told how the Sultana Zoradie (Ida Brooks Hunt) falls in love, sight unseen, with the poet of "Rose of the World." Three Foreign Legion deserters each claim to be the author, but each in turn is proven false. The poet is found to be a French captain, De Lome (George Leon Moore). Zoradie and De Lome wed. The libretto flipped back and forth between arch romance and slapstick. The deserters had names used over and over again for comic characters—Carrol Sweet, De Long Greene, and Van Cortlandt Park. A pair of comedians were presented as Mr. and Mrs. Billings F. Cooings. Outstanding among Herbert's melodies were two numbers that remain part of his classic canon, "Rose Of The World" and "Twilight In Barakeesh." In fact, Herbert's score was so fine more than one critic pleaded for a rewriting of the show. Frank McKee, the producer, closed the show after six weeks and sold the rights to Lew Fields, who promptly set about making revisions.

Ivan Caryll and Lionel Monckton's **The Girls of Gottenburg** (9-2-08, Knickerbocker), a London hit, began a 14-week run. The production featured the winsome London favorite, Gertie Millar, as a girl whose disguise as an inn-keeper's daughter forces almost everyone else into some disguise or other. Will R. Anderson, Harry Von Tilzer, and Jerome Kern all contributed interpolations.

Sporting Days, the annual Hippodrome spectacular, arrived September 5. Under the Shuberts the series had quickly settled into a pattern. Each year the mindless extravaganza had a theme, which could easily be stretched if a good song or an unrelated production number was judged worthy of inclusion. There were appropriate tunes: "Rowing," "Racing Game," and others that could fit in anywhere: "I'm Looking For A Sweetheart And I Think You'll Do." Two highly praised set pieces were a ballet, "The Land of the Birds," and a disingenuous but cruelly prophetic depiction of a 1950 air war, "The Battle in the Skies." As it would do on several occasions the Hippodrome mounted displays of carnage with such beguiling spectacle audiences were entranced rather than shocked. Enough New Yorkers and tourists stood in line for the twice-daily performances to give the house its longest run since *A Society Circus*—448 performances.

Just as Hough, Adams, and Howard seemed to have consolidated their hold on Chicago, their efforts began to flag. When **The Girl at the Helm** opened at the La Salle on September 5, their names were missing from the credits. The new musical had a book and lyrics by Robert B. Smith and music by Raymond Hubbell. The plot recounted another racing saga. Colonel Higginson challenges Countess Von Hertz to a motor boat race. The colonel would also have his daughter Dorothy marry the young German he was hired to run his boat. (Here was another Dorothy as heroine of a racing plot!) But the Countess lures the young man away. Dorothy's real flame, Fred Stanhope, wins both the race and Dorothy. With Cecil Lean starred, *The Girl at the Helm* settled in for a five-month run.

New Kern songs were heard when **Fluffy Ruffles** (9-7-08, Criterion) opened. J. J. McNally, at liberty with the closing of the Rogers Brothers' series, based his funny, impudent book on cartoons from the *Herald.* Uncle Dave Dill (John Bunny) believes, "If a woman can do a man's work let her do it. And if she can do it as well, let her receive the same pay." He offers his nieces an even better deal

—$500,000 apiece if they can learn a trade and stick to it for six weeks. His beautiful but difficult niece, Fluffy (Hattie Williams), is offered $1,000,000. Fluffy alone fails, claiming her bosses fired her because the men at work paid more attention to her than they did to their jobs. When all but Fluffy are taken to Europe as a bonus, Fluffy sneaks aboard ship as a maid. Uncle Dave would marry Mme. Shonts (Lida McMillan), but she was once married to a man named Franconi (Edward Durand), who disappeared after the wedding, and Dave himself was married to one of the Maloni twins (Mattie O'Brien). He has never been sure which, since both also ran away after the nuptuals. While Dave and Mme. Shonts are chaperoning the nieces, their old spouses reappear. But Dave believes he has the situation well in hand:

Noggy [one of Fluffy's suitors]: What's the word?
Uncle: Do you want to do something useful?
Noggy: I don't want to, but I will.
Uncle: Well, look through the grounds and if you find a man named Franconi—
Noggy: Franconi, yes—
Uncle: Kill him. And if he has a woman with him named Maloni—
Noggy: Kill her too?
Uncle: Kill her twice, she's twins.

Maloni and Franconi go off together, allowing Uncle Dave and Mme. Shonts to wed. Fluffy reveals she has been a newspaper reporter for the *Herald* all along. She wins the hand of Augustus Traddles (George Grossmith, Jr). For all its snappy dialogue the book betrayed the haphazard construction peculiar to the time. "Willy's Got A New Girl Now" was introduced with a one-line lead, "I am having more trouble with my situation than Willy had with his girls," though Willy has not been mentioned before and is forgotten with the last bar of the song. The typescript included an "Eating Act" for the performer who played Noggy (spelled Noggie in the program and performed by Bert Leslie), commenting, "The act is very funny." And a team of specialty dancers, the Swizzle Sisters, wandered aimlessly in and out of the plot to do their bits. Much top Broadway talent was associated with the show. Charles Frohman produced it, a noteworthy change from his hitherto invariable importation. *Fluffy Ruffles* lingered six weeks, then toured.

Gus Edwards, flushed with the success of *The Merry-Go-Round,* hoped to make his renaming of the Circle Theatre after himself a permanent change. But the name didn't stick, nor did his follow-up show. **School Days** (9-14-08, Circle), capitalizing on the title of his 1907 hit tune, described how Izzy Levy (Herman Timberg) comes to an East Side school and falls in love with a seeming waif, Nonnie (Janet Priest). When he breaks a window and is about to be arrested, she pays for the window with a half-dollar. Nonni, it develops, is an heiress. The plot left room for a cast of almost forty young, aspiring stars to show their stuff. Their stuff ranged from Gregory Kelly's imitations of Back Bay Brahmins to Joe Keno and Agnes Lynn's acrobatics. It was at heart a glorified amateur vaudeville show. Old and new songs by Edwards were not enough to help the evening beyond a four-week run, so it was hastily abbreviated into a suitable piece for the vaudeville circuit.

Mlle. Mischief (9-28-08, Lyric), a Viennese importation, was rewritten around Lulu Glaser's talents. Miss Glaser played a brazen young girl who bets she can masquerade for twenty-four hours as a soldier at the local barracks. Her smart performance kept the show on the boards for 96 performances.

Frank Pixley and Gustav Luders had less success with **Marcelle** (10-1-08, Casino), which ran eight and a half weeks. Although they called it a musical comedy, it was a comfortably traditional operetta. Indeed, one of its major failings was the apparent replaying of Pixley and Luders' earlier material. The plot was old hat even at this early date. Baron von Berghof (Jess Dandy) must produce a son or lose his estate to his nephew (Frank Rushworth). The baron claims he has a son in Paris and sends Dumm (Henry Norman), his cellar master, there to abduct someone, neglecting to mention the victim must be a young man. Dumm brings back Marcelle (Louise Gunning), an actress, who agrees to change her dress and impersonate the fictitious son. When Marcelle and the nephew fall in love, a happy ending follows. Dialect comedians provided the evening's happiest moments. *Marcelle*'s most memorable scene occurred when the Baron and his nephew's lawyer Herr Schwindle (Joseph Cawthorn) try to get each other drunk by spiking a punch bowl. Of course, each only pretends to drink from his own glass, taking every opportunity to empty the contents in a potted palm. Their increasingly frantic spikings and their growing amazement at the other's drinking prowess provided a crescendo of laughs, culminating as the two watch in dumb bafflement while the palm withers and dies. Luders' music, however light and lovely, seemed even more derivative than the book. Pixley didn't help matters with his lyrics—especially when the show's best number, "The Message Of The Red, Red Rose" so flagrantly echoed *The Prince of Pilsen*'s "The Message Of The Violet." Both Pixley and Luders seemed to be running dry.

Four nights later, the premiere of **The American Idea** (10-5-08, New York) suggested that George M. Cohan, too, had taken to repeating himself. The plot, another of his chauvinistic parables, did little more than change names and settings. This time Dan Sullivan (Walter Le Roy) and Herman Budmeyer (Gilbert Gregory), rival millionaires from Brooklyn, arrive in Paris and are persuaded to find French counts for their daughters. But two Brooklyn boys, disguised as nobles, win the girls. Cohan filled the evening with snappy dances and marches, and gave Trixie Friganza as Mrs. Waxtapper a show-stopper, singing and prancing to "Cohan's Pet Names." Both the words and music of Cohan's songs underlined the show's hand-me-down feeling. There was a spelling song, "F-A-M-E," not unlike *The Yankee Prince*'s "M-O-N-E-Y," *The Talk of New York*'s "M-A-Double R-I-E-D" and, of course, "H-A-Double R-I-G-A-N." Again after "Harrigan," *The American Idea* sang of "Sullivan," while the show's slated hit, "Too Long From Long Acre Square," recalled "Forty-five Minutes From Broadway" and "Fifty Miles From Boston." "Just like all the other Cohan pieces," one critic complained, but he added carefully that there was "no mistaking Mr. Cohan's knowledge of what will appeal to popular taste." Popular taste kept the show in New York for eight weeks, after which it went on a cross-country trek.

When **The Golden Butterfly** (10-12-08, Broadway) came into the Broadway one week after *The American Idea,* it further underscored the sad state of domestic creativity. Harry B. Smith's book was as cumbersome as it was complicated. Ilma Walden's lover, Franz (Walter Percival), goes to Paris to make his fortune as a composer. Baron von Affenkoff (Louis Harrison) tells Ilma (Grace Van Studdiford) Franz has met with instant success and has forgotten her. The baron invites her to sing the lead in his new opera, "The Golden Butterfly," if she will marry him. Franz returns and, not wanting to hinder Ilma's career, masquerades as a Russian prince. The real prince (Louis Cassavant) appears. He demands Franz be arrested as an impostor. Franz discloses why he has disguised himself, so the prince relents. The baron's opera is discovered to be a work the baron had stolen from Franz shortly after Franz had completed it. Ilma and Franz are reunited. More dismaying than Smith's dreary libretto was Reginald De Koven's colorless score. The composer, who orchestrated his own work and conducted on opening night, used Wagnerian-like brassy orchestrations that seemed designed to cover up the lack of fine melodies. There was no escaping De Koven was written out, and it was increasingly obvious by this time that, for all his popularity, he would go down as the creator of only a single masterpiece, *Robin Hood* (9-28-91).

De Koven's popularity could take credit for one last hit he did participate in later in the season. **The Beauty Spot** (4-10-09, Herald Square) had a libretto every bit as complicated as *The Golden Butterfly*, but less heavy-handed. It also had the well-liked Jefferson De Angelis and his company to perform. Joseph Herbert's story found General Samovar's daughter, Nadine (Marguerite Clark), engaged to Nikolas Kromeski (Frank Doane) but in love with Jacques Baccarel (George MacFarlane), an artist the general hates because of Jacques' *avant-garde* notions of painting. The general (De Angelis) is unaware that Baccarel had once painted his wife and called the picture "The Beauty Spot." Samovar is also unaware that Nikolas has returned from overseas, bringing a bride with him. Jacques and Nikolas exchange disguises, and the new Nikolas convinces the general to buy "The Beauty Spot" after some more clothing has been painted on the model. In the end Samovar is reconciled to Jacques' and Nadine's marrying. Only the least bit superior to *The Golden Butterfly*, *The Beauty Spot* nonetheless gave De Koven his last run of any length—137 performances.

Smith was the librettist and lyricist for October's final entry. Neither his material nor Victor Herbert's score for **Little Nemo** (10-20-08, New Amsterdam) was distinguished. But there remained a place for a pleasant children's entertainment, and this musical adaptation of Winsor McKay's cartoons filled the bill. Alone of the month's lyric pieces, it enjoyed a passing success, running 111 performances. Little Nemo (Master Gabriel—reputedly a thirty-one-year-old midget with the stature and voice of a ten-year-old boy) goes to Slumberland to recover the elixir of youth stolen by Dr. Pill's dancing missionary (Harry Kelly). A storm carries Nemo to a cannibal isle, where his tin soldiers fend off the hungry natives. He awakes and is told he must stay in his room because he has been naughty, but King Morpheus (W. W. Black) of Slumberland appears to conduct him on more adventures. The show was opulently mounted. A red and pink "Land of Valentine" was presided over by a bevy of lovely ladies.

Snow fell and wind blew through a "weather factory," where human raindrops splashed in a merry ballet. "A Boy's Dream of the Fourth of July" offered "flowery bouquets of rockets and roman candles and brilliant fire." Chorus girls in brightly colored army uniforms marched in precision. On a lighter side, Collins and Hart displayed their comic acrobatics. Joseph Cawthorn (Dr. Pill), Billy B. Van, and Harry Kelly joined forces for a comic boasting session in which each proclaimed his success as a hunter. The animals they claimed they bagged had never been seen before, or since. One described a "Peninsula," the only bird to lay square eggs, while another spoke of a creature who lives on canned meat and thereby develops such Armour and becomes so Swift that he can only be laughed to death. One night when backstage problems forced Cawthorn to stall for time he hastily invented a water-dwelling creature and described its habits of gobbling food. Cawthorn named the animal a "Whiffenpoof." Some Yale students were captivated by the name and when they founded a singing society in the following year they called it after Cawthorn's creature.

The Boys and Betty (11-2-08, Wallack's) was a vehicle for the exuberant Marie Cahill. She played Betty Barbeau, who runs away to Paris to escape her selfish husband. Betty sets up shop and soon is wealthy. Her husband arrives, insisting he is entitled to half her fortune. Luckily, Betty learns he has remarried. She obtains a divorce and marries the best of the boys, Paul Gerard (Edgar Atchison-Ely). George V. Hobart's book was workmanlike, as was Silvio Hein's score. But in "Marie Cahill's Arab Love Song" Hobart and Hein succeeded in giving their star a bigger applause-getter than any of the interpolations she added as a matter of course. Miss Cahill didn't monopolize the applause. Clara Palmer was called back for bows after her bizarre Oriental dance. The scenery, too, won kudos. The bright colors of a Parisian flower shop were contrasted effectively with a snow storm outside, while the last act opened "with a realistic picture of a sudden Summer shower . . . [and] the breaking out of a rainbow." *The Boys and Betty* stayed seventeen weeks before it embarked on a long tour.

On November 21 Chicago hailed the opening of a new theatre, the Garden. The owners of the house promised it would offer pieces to compete with the La Salle and the Princess. A new musical, **A Winning Miss,** was awarded the honor of being the house's first attraction and was advertised proudly as "Made in Chicago." Harold Atteridge created the book and lyrics, while W. F. Peters composed the score. Atteridge's yarn centered upon another yacht race. But the author took a novel approach, making all his characters caricatures of figures from popular plays of the day. Thus the heroine, Mary Willington, a sometime kleptomaniac, was drawn from the heroine of *The Thief.* The novelty of Atteridge's approach failed to entertain Chicagoans. The show was a quick flop, and the owners of the theatre, going back on their word, converted the Garden into a vaudeville house.

Miss Innocence (11-30-08, New York) was a vehicle for Ziegfeld's wife Anna Held. Her vehicles had quickly established a mystique and pattern of their own, so that audiences buying seats for "an Anna Held Show" knew they would watch a titillatingly risqué story unfold in beautiful and elaborate mountings. (While critics praised the show's beautiful costumes and scenery, none, alas, apparently described them.) The plot was trivial. Anna has been kept in a girls' school of remarkable innocence since she was three years old. She runs away to Paris with Captain Montjoy (Lawrence d'Orsay), who promises to find her parents and does, after two acts complicated by the machinations of a bogus detective (Charles A. Bigelow). Though Ludwig Englander wrote the official score, the hit of the evening was an interpolation with a typical Held title, "I Wonder What's The Matter With My Eyes" (Harry Williams/Egbert Van Alstyne). Another long-lived tune was in the show for a while. On February 20, 1909, long after the second edition of the *Follies* had left New York, the *Dramatic Mirror* reported: "Nora Bayes and Jack Norworth of F. Ziegfeld, Jr's. Follies of 1908 company have written another new song which was introduced in *Miss Innocence* yesterday. It bears the name 'Shine On, Harvest Moon,' and was sung by Lillian Lorraine early in the first act." A Jerome Remick advertisement in the same edition of the trade paper for music from *Miss Innocence* included the song in its list. The ad makes no mention of the *Follies.* Either memories were short (the song had first been sung in the *Follies of 1908*), or more likely, *Miss Innocence* was looked on as a more important show. But the song played no part in the evening's success. Together Miss Held and Ziegfeld delighted audiences for 176 performances.

Victor Herbert's second operetta of the season opened on the same night as *Miss Innocence.* **The Prima Donna** (11-30-08, Knickerbocker) starred Fritzi Scheff. But if Henry Blossom (its author),

Herbert, and Miss Scheff hoped for another *Mlle. Modiste* (12-25-05), they were rudely disappointed. Blossom's libretto was straightforward enough, without vaudeville turns or horseplay, but also without any overriding merit. An auto accident strands Mlle. Athenée (Miss Scheff), prima donna of the Paris Opera, in front of a night club. While waiting for repairs, she consents to sing a song written by Lt. Armand, Count de Fontenne (William Raymond). He falls in love with her and, when she repulses the advances of Captain Bordenave (William K. Harcourt), agrees to renounce his fiancée and marry Athenée.

The mediocre Herbert score was even more of a letdown than the unimaginative libretto. The evening was beautifully designed, from the vitality of soldiers and grisettes at play in Montmartre to the staid elegance of a clubhouse and lawn fete. But the principal attraction remained "Fritzi Scheff stamping her little feet and showing the real Fritzi Scheff temper (stage temper, of course); Fritzi Scheff beating a long roll on a tenor drum; Fritzi Scheff in short skirts and long." But Fritzi Scheff was not enough. The piece could muster only 72 performances.

R. H. Burnside and Manuel Klein, of the Hippodrome, brought in the season's second entertainment designed for children on December 3. They brought it into the Majestic, the house that had so often in the past delighted children with trips to Oz and Toyland. Now the youngsters in the audience could join the children of Hamelin and **The Pied Piper** (De Wolf Hopper) in the Piper's City of Innocence. Here, with Father Time (Warren Fabian) benignly overseeing matters, everything is idyllic until the chauffeur and cook of an airship (Edward Heron and Grace Cameron) steal the pipes. Of course the pipes are found by curtain time and tranquillity restored. Some of Klein's music was the same being sung nightly at the Hippodrome's *Sporting Days.* But in the easy give-and-take of the day's theatrical practices no one cared. Unfortunately not enough people cared for *The Pied Piper,* either. Its 52 performances fell far short of the record *Sporting Days* was compiling.

An inane work called **The Queen of the Moulin Rouge** (12-7-08, Circle) completed a twenty-week run despite some devastating notices. Its book detailed how the Princess Marotz (Flora Parker), smarting from the indifference of her betrothed, King Sacha of Orcania (Carter De Haven), goes to Paris and wins the King's affections disguised as Queen of the Moulin Rouge. Its music was no better than its book. However, the staging was zesty and sometimes pleasantly risqué. Cancans and lively "student" dances helped impel the story, while one set allowed half a dozen chorus girls to disrobe behind a gauze curtain.

Peggy Machree (12-21-08, Broadway) called itself a "comedy with music," although its sheet music listed sixteen songs from the score. Peggy was an alias used by Lady Margaret (Adrienne Augarde) in her love affair with young Barry Trevor (Joseph O'Mara). Years pass, and Barry, now rich and renowned, falls in love with Lady Margaret, seemingly forgetting his old flame, Peggy.

Still another musical conceived as a vehicle for its star's talents arrived as 1908's last offering. **Mr. Hamlet of Broadway** (12-23-08, Casino) found Eddie Foy portraying Joey Wheeze, a circus performer stranded with his sassy, trained bear (James F. Cook) at an Adirondacks hotel. Joey is drafted into playing the melancholy Dane when the actor who was to take the lead telegraphs the hotel that he is ill. Joey's frightened prince soliloquizes, "To flee or not to flee." It wasn't much of a plot, even by 1908 standards, but as long as Foy was on stage his followers were happy. Some of his followers may have remembered that Foy had touched on Hamlet before, singing "Hamlet Was A Melancholy Dane" in the star-crossed *Mr. Bluebeard* (1-21-03).

Only two musicals opened in January, both on the 25th. One was *A Stubborn Cinderella*. The second was the London hit **Kitty Grey,** at the New Amsterdam, graced by some minor Jerome Kern interpolations. *Kitty Grey* used as its source *Les Fêtards,* the same play Smith had used years before to fashion *The Rounders* (7-12-99). In the new version Kitty Grey (Julia Sanderson) is an actress who teaches a troubled wife how to keep a husband.

February also brought in two musicals. Again one was American and one English. Both were hits, although the British piece's run of 272 performances (exactly twice as many as the American piece attained) made it the second biggest hit among the regular entries. Only *Three Twins* ran longer.

The American piece, **The Fair Co-ed** (2-1-09, Knickerbocker), had the second Gustav Luders score to be sung in New York during the season, but it was Luders without his customary collaborator, Frank Pixley. Instead the popular humorist George Ade provided the book and lyrics. Ade set his plot in his beloved Bingham College (the locale of his play *The College Widow*). His heroine, Cyn-

thia Bright (Elsie Janis), could have been first cousin to the earlier work's Jane. Cynthia is Bingham's only co-ed, a concession to her father's importance to the school. When her father dies suddenly, it is discovered his will stipulates Cynthia must marry a Bingham graduate. It's a worrisome clause since her fiancé, Davy Dickerson (Arthur Stanford), seems certain to flunk out. But learning of the requirement he makes a determined effort to succeed. Ade's humor more than Luders' songs gave the show its vogue. But time plays havoc on humor as much as anything else, and much of the fun seems hopelessly of the period:

Old Grad: Why do you fellows make such a noise?
Boys: So people can see we're college boys.
Old Grad: They could tell that by your passionate socks.

One big production number found Cynthia and the chorus girls attending a military ball dressed in naval uniforms—a foretaste of the army clothes Miss Janis would one day sport as the "Sweetheart Of The A.E.F."

Havana (2-11-09, Casino), the London Gaiety Theatre hit, with music by Leslie Stuart, offered James T. Powers, who had spent the last several years clowning in English importations, as an Englishman embroiled in a Cuban revolution.

Two Hough–Adams–Howard shows opened a week apart in Chicago. **The Prince of Tonight** premiered on March 9, **The Golden Girl** on March 16. *The Prince of Tonight* was greeted with disappointing notices, the first such Hough, Adams, and Howard received. The notices were probably accepted grudgingly. But Howard was to receive a further blow to his ego. His song, "Her Eyes Are Blue For Yale," was reprised several times each evening, in the expectation that it would be the show's hit. It wasn't. Instead audiences encored the biggest success ever to come out of a Hough–Adams–Howard show, the titular hero's "I Wonder Who's Kissing Her Now." Only a handful of insiders knew that Howard had not written the song. He had purchased the rights to the melody from its composer, Harold Orlob. Although Howard for years took both credit and royalties from the song, Orlob eventually brought him to court and won belated recognition. In Hough and Adams' story an impecunious college student, Jim Southerland (Henry Woodruff), comes to Palm Beach as a lifeguard. He falls in love with Virginia Stuart (Georgia Caine), but the young heiress spurns him. Jim learns that the nectar from a blooming century plant can turn him into a prince for a night. He courts and wins Virginia in this guise, and manages to retain her love in the morning. The production had been announced as the "second of the Princess Theatre musical comedies," clearly indicating its producers and authors had every hope of many more shows to come. It was not a failure, but its four-month run was the shortest a Hough–Adams–Howard show had received. Apart from *The Golden Girl,* it was the last the trio would ever take credit for without others being involved.

Even *The Golden Girl,* although it was generally praised, elicited critical comments that suggested Chicagoans were beginning to tire of the shows. In his review for the Chicago *Tribune* Burns Mantle saluted the La Salle as "first of the small musical comedy playhouses in Chicago," but, he continued, "these playhouses are directed by one management, furnished with entertainment by one firm of amusement purveyors, and patronized practically by one public." The musical itself, he concluded, was "as good as anything Hough and Adams have done, which is saying much or little, depending upon your admiration of these young men—or lack of it." Hough and Adams' story for *The Golden Girl* forced Dorothy Hale to choose between two West Point cadets—a boy who had been her childhood sweetheart and slim, suave John Fiske. A golden girl appears in a vision and persuades Dorothy to select John. The musical ran six months; its run, too, was shorter than those awarded Hough, Adams, and Howard's biggest hits. Undoubtedly a certain sameness was telling. But the growing number of vaudeville houses and, more urgently, motion picture theatres were just as assuredly exerting an unfortunate influence. Yet the malaise was balanced by a certain pride Chicago could still take in its active theatre. On March 7, the *Tribune* ran as article headed "Chicago Best Source For Musical Comedy." The article claimed that of 100 successful touring companies crossing America 20 were presenting Chicago musicals. The article added, "Chicago's musical comedy output has been the most successful that had gone over the circuits this year." Even if the well-rounded figures are suspiciously vague, there can be no gainsaying that the Chicago musical theatre in the last years of its heyday was still noticeably vigorous.

For the second time in the season a comic strip provided the impetus for a new musical when **The Newlyweds and Their Baby** opened at the Majestic on March 22. It was really a vaudeville. The substituting of a dwarf named Major Knott Much for the newlyweds' baby, Napoleon, and their subsequent search to reclaim their infant was sufficient plot on which to hang a grab bag of songs, dances, and specialty acts. Aimed at a more adult audience than *Little Nemo,* it managed a five-week stay.

April's first two offerings were *The Beauty Spot* and a well-received revival of the 1881 success, *The Mascot,* starring Raymond Hitchcock and Flora Zabelle. The month closed with the arrival of **The Candy Shop** (4-27-09, Knickerbocker). George V. Hobart's book recorded the adventures of Jack Sweet (Leslie Gaze) after his own father accuses him of theft. Jack and his friends go to Coney Island, where Jack obtains a job as a waiter, falls in love with Hilda Noble (Maud Fulton), who turns out to be an heiress, and clears his good name in time for a happy ending. John Golden, not yet aware his real future lay in producing, wrote the words and music (assisted quietly by Henry Blossom). One novel set depicted Coney Island "with carousels, the chutes and miniature taxicabs and motors spinning across the stage." Apart from that, nothing about the evening was out of the ordinary. It played seven weeks.

May's initial musical was a failure, although many observers thought it, or at least its score, deserved a lengthier hearing. A black show, written by Bob Cole and J. Rosamond Johnson as a showcase for their own talent and those of their friends, **The Red Moon** (5-3-09, Majestic) told how Minnehaha (Abbie Mitchell), daughter of an Indian chief and a black woman, is taken back to the reservation by her father and then returned to her mother through the contriving of Slim Brown, a bogus lawyer, and Plunk Green, a quack doctor. Cole and Johnson played Brown and Green. Whatever the faults of the claptrap book, the songs were excellent. The *Dramatic Mirror,* often especially hard on Negro shows, admitted, "the score is often quite ambitious and always pleasing to hear." The music publisher Edward B. Marks was even more enthusiastic, insisting in his autobiography, published in 1934 after many more all-black shows had been produced, that *The Red Moon* remained "the most tuneful colored show of the century."

The Midnight Sons (5-22-09, Broadway), a musical by Glen MacDonough and Raymond Hubbell, was brought in by Lew Fields as a summer attraction. It proved so popular it ran into 1910. Its success had little to do with its plot. Senator Constant Noyes (George A. Schiller), as he is about to leave on an African junket, informs his four playboy sons—Tom (Harry Fisher), Dick (Fritz Williams), Harry (Denman Maley), and Jack (Joseph Ratliff)—they must find steady jobs or he will disinherit them. One becomes the proprietor of a hotel, the second manages a theatre, the third launches a shoe business with the fourth as a shoe salesman. Hubbell contributed a "whistleable" score. But what made the show was Fields' elaborate production and a fine cast, recruited in a large part from vaudeville and headed by Blanche Ring. One of her interpolations, "I've Got Rings On My Fingers (And Bells On My Toes)" (Weston and Barnes/Maurice Scott), became the outstanding hit. Miss Ring used it as long as she performed. Vernon Castle attracted attention with his "amusing disjointed dances." Fields' imaginative staging started the moment the curtain rose. The audience in the theatre found that it was staring at another audience in another theatre, "with orchestra, balcony, gallery, and boxes filled." In fact the real audience could imagine it was sitting on a stage, for a row of footlights glared at the real patrons, while performers playing to the other audience kept their backs to the paying playgoers.

Richard Carle, with some assistance from M. E. Rourke and H. L. Heartz, brought in **The Boy and the Girl** (5-31-09, New Amsterdam). The show was a rarity in that it was one of the few Carle shows Chicago disdained. In New York, it was a 24-performance flop. In neither Chicago nor New York did the major critics give a hint of the plot. What little space they expended on the entertainment was devoted to praising Marie Dressler's roughhouse antics—again, sadly, without specifics.

The season's final musical was the 1909 edition of the **Follies** (6-14-09, Jardin de Paris). Although Florenz Ziegfeld and Harry B. Smith had traveled to Europe looking for fresh ideas for the revue, they confessed they returned empty-handed. The most important addition to the series was Lillian Lorraine, whom Ziegfeld had used in *Miss Innocence* (11-30-08) and who now became the *Follies*' first incontestable dazzler. Nora Bayes returned, and Eva Tanguay appeared briefly. No major song hits came out of this edition, even though Ziegfeld interpolated "By The Light Of The Silvery Moon" for a while. "Moving Day In Jungle Town" allowed Ziegfeld to offer the first of the many jungle spectaculars the series would offer. In the second act an airship, with Lillian Lorraine at the controls, circled over the audience. The show's most memorable production number suggested each state should present the nation with a battleship (all battleships at the time were named for states), and each chorus girl was dressed to represent a state, her hat modeled after the dreadnoughts of the day. One Philadelphia paper was so thrilled it seriously suggested the nation accept Ziegfeld's scheme as a quick and easy way to enlarge the fleet.

1909-1910

The new season confirmed the triumph of Viennese operetta and the frustration of the American Musical Theatre. Julian Edwards exemplified this frustration. He offered three scores, including the music for the season's opener, *The Motor Girl*. Nothing he contributed to the shows was especially original or distinguished, and none of the shows was an outstanding success. Edwards, like Reginald De Koven and so many other American composers of the period, was fast falling into the ranks of writers who would be remembered for one superior show —or perhaps only one song. Oddly, the songs Edwards composed this season were far less in a comic opera vein than most of his earlier ones. As the arioso operetta took over, Edwards turned unexpectedly to lighter forms.

The Motor Girl (6-15-09, Lyric) hoped to find success in the same world of rich men's sporting cars that served *The Vanderbilt Cup* (1-16-06) and *The Auto Race* (11-25-07) so well. The show almost made it. It told how Dorothy Dare (Georgia Caine) dons her brother Arthur's clothes and wins the Paris auto race after she ascertains Arthur has been villainously detained. (Note how often racing musicals had heroines named Dorothy!) Much of the action was set in Holland, allowing Adelaide Sharp to dress as a "Deutscher maid" and lead a "German" chorus not unlike several the preceding season. Elizabeth Brice had fun as a countess whose action required her to appear in various disguises. The show's 12-week run matched that of **The Girl and the Wizard** (9-27-09, Casino), more a "comedy with music" than a musical comedy. Besides Edwards' tunes, audiences heard interpolations by Jerome Kern and Louis Hirsch. But what the audiences had really come to hear and see were J. Hartley Manners' story and Sam Bernard. Sam Bernard didn't disappoint his followers. Manners did. His story centered on Herman Scholz, a dealer in old gems and a confirmed bachelor, who lives only for his nephew Paul (William Roselle). When Paul announces his determination to marry, Scholz sends him away. A man who is in debt to Scholz offers the dealer his daughter, Murietta (Kitty Gordon), as a wife in the hope of erasing the debt. To his surprise, Scholz accepts. But Paul returns, rich on the royalties of a gun he has invented, and claims Murietta (Flora Parker), the girl he wanted in the first place. Scholz gives in, and all ends happily. In this day of loosely constructed plots no one seriously objected when the gem dealer's funniest scene had him portraying a screaming stage manager endeavoring to instruct some thick-headed actors, or if there was little excuse for Kitty Gordon's parading in beautiful gowns that exposed her famous back. Edwards' third score was for **Molly May** (4-8-10, Hackett). The show had the thinnest of story lines. Molly May (Grace LaRue) is queen of the artists' models. A letter of hers meant for old Senator Sparks (James E. Sullivan) is mistakenly thought to be for Sparks' son-in-law, Jack Willoughby (Sydney Grant). The complications that ensue are resolved by curtain time. The *Dramatic Mirror* predicted, "The book, lyric and music will add fame to no one." It made no one rich, either, running only 27 times.

On the other hand, not all Viennese pieces made the grade. **The Gay Hussars** (7-29-09, Knickerbocker) introduced Broadway to Emmerich Kalman, a name it later embraced. The operetta's plot recounted the determination of a Hussar to win back a girl who jilted him for a wealthier older man. Although the show was produced by Henry W. Savage, who had done so well by *The Merry Widow* (10-21-07), critics complained the work was tackily mounted and that poor voices failed to do justice to the generally appreciated score. Qualified notices and hot weather hurt. The show barely made it through five and a half weeks.

Egbert Van Alstyne and his lyricist, Harry Williams, provided the songs for two musicals, one at either end of the season. **A Broken Idol** (8-16-09, Herald Square), with an abysmal book by the inexperienced Hal Stephens, managed 40 performances. The show had originally been mounted for Chicago. A noble Englishman hires an American to teach him American ways so he can court a Yankee. But when the peer learns the young lady has lost her money he jilts her. She marries the newsman she has wanted all along. In June, **Girlies** (6-13-10, New Amsterdam), with a better book by the more knowing George V. Hobart, offered satisfying summer entertainment and ran 11 weeks at the New Amsterdam. Summer plots tended to be more frivolous than the plots of shows meant to run through the fall, winter, and spring seasons. But in a day when frivolity didn't condemn a show the difference between the plots of summer and

winter offerings was often a matter of imperceptible degree. The degree of difference was a bit more perceptible in *Girlies*. Dr. Speil (Joseph Cawthorn) teaches botany at Hightonia Co-ed College. He courts the directress, who insists she will marry only a hero. Speil decides he can be that hero if he can live for a time in a suit made entirely of newspapers. With his dog Blitzen (David Abraham), he gets himself into complications that parodied then current Broadway shows. These plays included *Madame X, The Witching Hour,* and *The Spendthrift.* "Swift and lively" dances embellished the attraction. Besides his fine dialect clowning, Cawthorn won applause for his concertina playing. The evening was helped greatly by the attractive performances of Jed Prouty, Ernest Truex, and Maude Raymond.

The same night as *A Broken Idol* opened, **The Cohan and Harris Minstrels** made their promised return. The entertainment included beloved old songs of the minstrel era such as "Down Where The Watermelons Grow" and "The Rose Of Killarney." Clog dances and "an old-fashioned breakdown" were offered as part of "Scenes from Blackville." A contingent of blackfaced soldiers marched in front of a drop depicting lighted battleships at sea. For two weeks tambourines jingled and end men joked at the New York, but this was the last time a more or less traditional minstrel show played the heartland of Broadway. The minstrel show era was over.

But blackface acts were far from finished. Two weeks later McIntyre and Heath, probably the most popular blackface duo of the day, presented their new vehicle **In Hayti** (8-30-09, Circle). Both J. J. McNally's book and William Jerome and Jean Schwartz' songs were conventional. Heath portrayed Jasper Johnson, an ambitious wheeler-dealer, determined to make his pliable buddy Geronimo Jobbs (McIntyre) president of the island republic. The production displayed the homey, down-on-the farm ambience blackface shows customarily affected. Chorus girls dressed as roosters sang about "Chicken," while McIntyre and Heath carried two chickens on and off throughout the evening as pets. The show played seven weeks and toured.

Savage failed again with his second Viennese offering of the season, Edmund Eysler's **The Love Cure** (9-1-09, New Amsterdam), the first of September's six musicals. Opera lovers knew a similar plot had been used in *La Traviata.* However, in the operetta the heroine is an actress not a courtesan.

Still, she disillusions her lover at his father's moving request. Eysler was no Verdi; *The Love Cure* ran less than five weeks.

The annual Hippodrome offering arrived September 4, and, as was so often the case with the great house's simple-minded spectacles, it tallied far more performances than any other musical during the season. Although part of the evening was devoted to a voyage *Inside the Earth* and to a *Ballet of the Jewels,* the principal portion was **A Trip to Japan.** R. H. Burnside called his extravaganza a "melodrama with music," but what little drama there was served solely as a frame for the stunning effects. These effects included a large steamship sailing out of port, a "Feast of [Japanese] Lanterns," and two waterfalls, one on each side of the stage, cascading down bathed in "prismatic lights." The story reflected the thinking of a world that viewed war as more glorious and romantic than ominous. It recounted how the Japanese hire a circus to disguise their shipments of submarines back to their homeland.

The next two Monday evenings witnessed the openings of the two Viennese operettas that, following on the phenomenal success of *The Merry Widow* (10-21-07), established the hegemony of this mode through the next several seasons. The first of the pair was Leo Fall's **The Dollar Princess** (9-6-09, Knickerbocker). Operettas are so much of their period they are frequently thought of as having been born old-fashioned. In their time the best were in every way the last word. *The Dollar Princess* was set in the business world of its day—the opening number saluting the modern "type-writer girls." So determined were its authors to suggest the story was as new as the century they eschewed a Graustarkian setting, placing their taming-of-the-shrew tale in the United States. Valli Valli sang the title role, but Donald Brian garnered the best notices on the strength of his charm and his light footwork. Leo Fall's score was lovely, but it has not retained the affection of Americans in the way the second offering's songs have. That next entry was **The Chocolate Soldier** (9-13-09, Lyric). It softened the antiwar satire of its source, Shaw's *Arms and the Man,* but its story of a warrior who prefers eating chocolates to fighting was still a refreshing change from the rampant militarism of the day. Ida Brooks Hunt and J. E. Gardner sang the romantic leads, while William Pruette supplied the comedy in his role as Popoff. Oscar Straus' marvelous songs, notably "My Hero," remain standards. Excepting the Hippodrome spectacle, the two shows were the runaway hits of the season,

The Dollar Princess compiling 288 performances; *The Chocolate Soldier,* 296.

The next Monday ushered in the promised revision of the preceding year's *Algeria* (8-31-08), rechristened **The Rose of Algeria** (9-20-09, Herald Square). Frank Pollock replaced George Leon Moore as De Lome, and since the original Zoradie, Ida Brooks Hunt, and the original first comedian, William Pruette, were busy with *The Chocolate Soldier,* Lillian Herlein and Eugene Cowles assumed their roles. Youthful Anna Wheaton drew attention to herself as Mrs. Cooings. The revisions were not as drastic as many critics felt necessary. Disappointment in the absence of significant changes cut sharply into its ticket sales, as did the striking success of the other new arrivals. The work added just 40 performances to its record.

The last Monday in September saw the premiere of Edwards' *The Girl and the Wizard.*

October's only musical was **The Man Who Owns Broadway** (10-11-09, New York), George M. Cohan's lyrical version of his own straight play failure, *Popularity.* Although he changed the names of its main characters, Cohan retained the original story line of a brash but well-liked young actor (in this musical version, a musical comedy star) who overrides intrigue and backbiting to win a rich man's daughter. (More than one critic saw something autobiographical in the hero, Sydney Lyons.) Cohan also retained two stunning effects he had used in his original. Cohan exposed the actual brick wall at the rear of the stage to give the audience an authentic backstage feeling. Furthermore he goaded his audience into playing the make-believe audience that applauds so insistently Lyons is induced to make a curtain speech. It was a well-written, jargony book, in which Cohan was not above spoofing theatrical conventions ("My boy, the villains are never handcuffed until 11:00.") and boosting his favorite song-and-dance man ("I'll stick to musical comedy as long as George Cohan will write them for me."). Cohan's lyrics were as natural and idiomatic as his dialogue, now and then disclosing the sort of impudent rhyming wit Broadway rarely heard before Ira Gershwin, Cole Porter, or Lorenz Hart. In "I'm All O.K. With K. And E." Lyons bets "two bits" that he'll "paralyze the Shuberts." Cohan's music was filled with pleasantries, lacking only that something extra that pulsated through his earlier hits. The personable Raymond Hitchcock portrayed Lyons. Hitchcock could not approach Cohan in dancing agility, but he did successfully execute a soft shoe. Cohan saw to it the chorus compensated for his absence with its lively stepping. *The Man*

Who Owns Broadway, for which Cohan retained a warm spot the rest of his life, ran 128 performances and enjoyed a long tour.

Two musicals opened in Chicago in October. One, **The Kissing Girl,** was an immediate failure even though it had a book by Stanislaus Stange, lyrics by Vincent Bryan, and music by Harry Von Tilzer. A misconstrued kiss was the source of the evening's complications. The show opened on October 25 and left two weeks later. **They Loved a Lassie** opened on the 31st and fared better. The work had music by Benjamin Hapgood Burt and a book by George Arliss. In Arliss' tale two married men on a business trip find their footsteps dogged by an old flame both had once loved. Troubles arise when the men's wives appear on the scene. At the end of its run at the Whitney Opera House, the show listed its post-Chicago itinerary in its advertisements. The ads revealed the tour would take it to towns such as Burlington and Muscatine, Iowa.

The Flirting Princess premiered at Chicago's Princess Theatre on November 1. Although the show was billed as an "Adams–Hough–Howard Musical," Harold Orlob was publicly acknowledged to have written nearly half the score. The intrusion of a fourth figure into the established trio was a major change, but it was not the only one. The *Tribune*'s new drama critic, Percy Hammond, noted that the librettists had "departed from their usual formula." There was no "hefty romance . . . no dreams, little slang." Hammond concluded the musical was "a sort of review, but a blunt review." If the critic could be unstinting in his praise of anything about the show it was the physical production. He insisted Singer was superior to Ziegfeld. Hough and Adams' plot was, indeed, slight. Princess Klioh of Egypt (Violet Dare) comes to America for a good time. She flirts with every handsome young man she meets, but finally succumbs to the charms of Jack Stuart (Harry Pilcer). (A Virginia Stuart was the heroine of *The Prince of Tonight.*)

November 1 presented competing openings in New York: **The Silver Star** with Adelaide Genee at the New Amsterdam; **Mr. Lode of Koal** with Bert Williams at the less centrally located Majestic. For *The Silver Star* Harry B. Smith sketched out something to pass for a plot, and a dozen hands contributed to manufacture a score. But it was Genee's dancing and Klaw and Erlanger's spectacle that drew the crowds. Genee danced in a military outfit, waving an American flag, and flitted under an iridescent grape arbor dressed as the "spirit of Champagne." The show never approached the popularity of *The Soul Kiss,* but it kept the New Amsterdam lit ten weeks.

Uptown at Columbus Circle Bert Williams, alone after paresis incapacitated George Walker, could keep *Mr. Lode of Koal* on the boards only half as long. Its plot was the sort of delicious minstrel nonsense Williams reveled in. Mr. Lode dreams he has been shipwrecked on an island. Revolutionists have kidnapped the real king, Big Smoke (Matt Housley), and since an old island legend promises a great ruler will one day come from the sea, Mr. Lode finds himself a reluctant king. He spends most of the remaining three acts futilely renouncing his throne and planning foredoomed escapes from the island. Just before curtain time Big Smoke returns, and Mr. Lode finds freedom by casting his lot with the audience. The best Negro talents of the day provided the material—J. A. Shipp, Alex Rogers, Rosamond Johnson, and Williams himself—but they provided nothing of lasting worth. Williams was responsible for what little appeal the show had. With this show he began to develop the droll monologues he used for the rest of his career.

The London success, **The Belle of Brittany** (11-8-09, Daly's), fared no better, achieving the same 40-performance run as *Mr. Lode of Koal*. In that short while audiences watched a marquis lose his estate to a miller, only to see it come back into his family after the miller's daughter marries the marquis' son.

Lew Fields and Victor Herbert, who collaborated so successfully to make a long-run delight of *It Happened in Nordland* (12-5-04), tried again with **Old Dutch** (11-22-09, Herald Square). Glen MacDonough was replaced by Edgar Smith, who adapted the libretto from a German comedy, and by George V. Hobart, who created the lyrics. Ludwig "Old Dutch" Streusand (Fields) flees to the Tyrol with his daughter, Lisa (Alice Dovey), to escape the attentions heaped on him after he becomes a successful inventor. He registers under the name of Leopold Mueller. While butterfly hunting he loses his wallet, with all his money and identification. A real Leopold Mueller (John E. Henshaw) discovers it, pretends he is Streusand, and basks in reflected glory, while Ludwig and Lisa do menial chores to pay their bill. The book was competent at best and Herbert's music no better. One joyous moment came early in the first act. Liza and her love interest, Alfred (William Raymond), sang a simple duet, "U, Dearie." When they finished, two ingratiating little tots solemnly pantomimed the lovers' movements, earning more encores for their bit than did the principals for theirs. The little boy mime disappeared from stage history; the little girl mime did not. Her name was Helen Hayes. Even Fields' fine production and clowning could not rescue the evening from the doldrums. The best that could be said for *Old Dutch* was that it gave a helping hand to a group of young performers such as Miss Dovey, Miss Hayes, and Vernon Castle.

Harry B. Smith and Raymond Hubbell suffered a humiliating failure when **The Air King** opened at Chicago's Colonial Theatre on November 28, received scathing notices, and was promptly withdrawn. Whether the show had its eye on New York is moot. Had it succeeded it would have popularized a story much like that employed by *The Aviator* and its musicalization *Going Up!* (12-25-17) nearly a decade later. Willy Ketchum (John Slavin) is a bellhop in Atlantic City. When a famous pilot fails to appear for a meet, Willy takes his place, although he has never flown before. Josephine Hall was featured as a character called Minerva Shine.

Exactly a month after Fields opened at the Herald Square, Weber's relit with Hough–Adams–Howard's **The Goddess of Liberty.** The date was December 22, making it 1909's last musical. The plot recalled *A Broken Idol.* Jack Wingate (Edward Abeles), an Englishman living from hand to mouth in America, comes into a title but no money. He decides to marry a rich, social-climbing American, Hope Butterworth (Frances Demarest). After the engagement he falls in love with Hope's cousin, Phyllis Crane (May De Sousa), and she with him. He sends a telegram announcing his brother has not died and is still lord. Hope breaks the engagement, allowing Jack and Phyllis to go off together. It was another Hough–Adams–Howard Chicago hit that found no favor in New York. Manhattan critics not only panned the writing, they came down heavily on the production, assailing what they felt were bad English accents (was Chicago trying to ridicule even English accents?) and deploring a wrestling match that "wasn't even a good fake." *The Goddess of Liberty* survived 29 performances.

Nora Bayes abandoned the *Follies* and returned to New York in **The Jolly Bachelors** (1-6-10, Broadway), a musical produced by Lew Fields with book and lyrics by Glen MacDonough and music by Raymond Hubbell. The book was claptrap and Hubbell's score a pleasant mediocrity. In the play Miss Bayes became Miss Vandergould, an heiress who takes a job as a cashier in a drug store. There she hopes to find romance among the less effete men of the middle class. When she mistakenly

gives a customer the wrong medicine, she and her beau scour the town to retrieve it. Their search takes them to a college campus (where Jack Norworth led students in a medley of college songs) and onto an ocean liner. The show's principal attractions were its fast pace and spectacular staging (including an airship sailing through the clouds), Miss Bayes, her excellent supporting cast, and one unforgettable interpolation, "Has Anybody Here Seen Kelly?" (C. W. Murphy and Will Letters). The *Times*' critic also called attention to the tastefulness of the drug-store set, done in various shades of brown instead of the gaudy rainbow of colors so common to the time. The set provided an attractive backdrop as Robert L. Dailey led twenty chorus boys in Ned Wayburn's clog dance for "We'uns From Dixie" and as Stella Mayhew sang Irving Berlin's "Stop Dat Rag."

Four nights later, January 10, **The Old Town** began a run of 171 performances at the brand new Globe Theatre. The *Dramatic Mirror* put its finger on the reason for the show's success, "The new musical scored a decided hit due less to the librettist and the composer than to the two comedians." The librettist was George Ade, the composer was Gustav Luders; the two comedians were Dave Montgomery and Fred Stone. Montgomery and Stone played two stranded circus performers, Henry Clay Baxter (Stone) and Archibald Hawkins (Montgomery), who encounter their old sweethearts, Caroline (Flo Hengler) and Diana (Mae Hengler). The girls' upstart Aunt Ernestine (Allene Crater) would have them marry "better" people. Ernestine's consternation is compounded when she discovers Baxter's father was a pirate. The boys find the pirate's loot, but Ernestine confiscates it and has them driven out of town. In California they help the girls' uncle (Claude Gillingwater) get elected senator. He rewards them with the girls and the treasure. The typescript reveals how flexible and compliant an established writer such as Ade felt he had to be when writing a vehicle for special stars. Montgomery and Stone's first entrance was to be a song called "Electric Signs." In the spot where the song would go Ade wrote, "as many verses as needed, all describing what happens to boys reared in the country towns when they get among the electric signs. Refrain music will lend itself to dance if the two wish to dance this early in the game. . . ." Stone did elect to dance later in the evening, jumping in and out of a lariat as he pranced. He also displayed his agility on a tightrope. Charles Dillingham was Ziegfeld's closest rival in taste and prodigality, so *The Old Town* was magnificently mounted. A remarkably beautiful chorus line paraded before Homer Emens' "exceedingly lovely back drop . . . with a far reach of glowing California landscape." The smaller, livelier "ponies" danced in kilts and played bagpipes, staged a precision drill dressed in sky-blue, and marched in tri-colors as suffragettes.

The King of Cadonia (1-10-10, Daly's) was imported from England the same night as *The Old Town* opened. It had a book by Frederick Lonsdale, who later wrote a number of good plays. His story followed a king as he goes in disguise among his people to see how they really live and what they really think of him. Marguerite Clark, William Norris, and Robert Dempster played the leads. The show boasted several Jerome Kern interpolations. But New York was not interested, and it was withdrawn after two weeks.

The Prince of Bohemia (1-13-10, Hackett), an American original, did little better, managing only two and a half weeks. Its book was by J. Hartley Manners, who had been represented earlier by *The Girl and the Wizard,* and who, like Lonsdale, later wrote successful straight plays. The story was elementary. Dick Conyers (Andrew Mack), rejected by his sweetheart's father, follows the girl and her parents to Europe where, disguised as an Irish servant, he eventually wins the father's approval. Christie MacDonald sang the sweetheart. The score was the first of three offered by A. Baldwin Sloane in the last half of the season. The disdain in which Sloane was held by the rest of the profession was reflected in a comment of the *Dramatic Mirror*'s reviewer, "a waltz number of superior texture which Mr. Baldwin Sloane presumably did not compose . . . stands out in bold relief against the medley of airs borrowed from Tosti and a dozen others which forms . . . Mr. Sloane's musical contributions." Sloane's second score was for **Tillie's Nightmare** (5-5-10, Herald Square). Like Lew Fields' earlier productions—*About Town* (8-30-06), *The Girl Behind The Counter* (10-1-07), *The Midnight Sons* (5-22-09), *The Jolly Bachelors* (1-6-10)—it was really a high-class vaudeville, enhanced with spectacular effects and held together by a flimsy story line. In this case, Tillie Blobbs, a drudge in her mother's boarding house, dreams of marvelous things that could happen to her: a rich marriage, a yacht trip, an "aeroplane" ride. But it's all a dream. Out of Sloane's score came the single song that promised to give him a classic, "Heaven Will Protect The Working Girl." But the song's vogue died with the advent of better conditions for the working girl. Marie Dressler sang the song at the very beginning of the evening, accompanying herself with

a comic lack of ability on the piano. She also had a hilarious scene on the yacht, tying on a hilarious jag as she attempted to assuage her seasickness with a magnum of champagne. Footwork by the "Original English Dancing Girls" enlivened the evening. Sloane's third score was heard in **The Summer Widowers** (6-4-10, Broadway), with which Fields hoped to repeat the popularity of the preceding season's *The Midnight Sons*. He almost did. It ran through the summer into the fall. Again it was another superior vaudeville with such sensational scenes as an entire apartment house with all its apartments, on several floors, revealed at once. If *The Jolly Bachelors* had a note-worthy airship scene, *The Summer Widowers* sent miniature airplanes buzzing over the audience's heads. The show's lighter-than-air plot recorded the misunderstandings that arise when a prima donna throws an innocent party for some men whose wives are away on vacation. Fields filled the cast with favorites from *Old Dutch* and his other shows: Maude Lambert, Alice Dovey, Vernon Castle, Ada Lewis, little Helen Hayes, and Fields himself. But Sloane's score added nothing of importance to the entertainment.

The lone English offering to win favor during the season was **The Arcadians** (1-17-10, Liberty), with its delightful Lionel Monckton and Howard Talbot score and its disarmingly fantastic story of unavailing efforts by denizens of utopian Arcady to teach the English their ways. Frank Moulan starred. The work played through the spring.

January's last musical, **The Young Turk** (1-31-10, New York), was a four-week failure. With inane dialogue it told how a banker named Oxenham steals the sultan's jewels and then dies, leaving a will stipulating that his wife must marry his partner, Howe Swift, Sr. But Mrs. Oxenham becomes engaged to Swift's son, while her young daughter is betrothed to the senior Smith. In the end the jewels are returned and the couples paired off more appropriately. The music of Max Hoffman, who had provided many of the songs for the old Rogers Brothers burlesques, was only a notch or two above the libretto. Max, the surviving Rogers brother starred, but Maud Raymond—singing, dancing, giving imitations, and burlesquing grand opera mannerisms—stole the show.

On January 31 Chicago's Princess Theatre raised its curtain on what proved to be the last of the musicals Hough, Adams, and Howard wrote together, **Miss Nobody from Starland.** As he had in *The Prince of Tonight* and *The Flirting Princess,* Howard permitted songs by other composers to be inserted, and when the show underwent revision during its ninth week he allowed additional interpolations. Hough and Adams' plot was as slight and loosely constructed as their last one had been. A chorus girl who dabbles in smuggling falls in with a pharmacist who is fleeing a charge of murder after he misfills a prescription. They wind up as performers in a Princess Theatre show. Bessie Wynn and Ralph Herz played the leads. *Miss Nobody from Starland* was no failure. No show by Hough, Adams, and Howard ever was. But it ran only 15 weeks, a short run as the series went. An increasingly critical climate, competition from other shows and other art forms, and possibly some backstage quarrel wrote "finis" to the partnership.

Blanche Ring and her interpolations accounted for much of the success of **The Yankee Girl** (2-10-10, Herald Square). Silvio Hein's music and George V. Hobart's book and lyrics had a certain professional competency, but little else. The demand for their services can be explained largely by their dependability. Both were more prolific than talented. The more demanding critics dismissed Hein much as they dismissed Sloane, "All the one-finger composers of musical comedies, since the halcyon days of Lederer, have grounds for action for petit larceny against Silvio Hein." There were equally unkind words for Hobart, "The book shares with the music the dullness of exhausted themes." Hobart's plot was slight. With the aid of her father (William Graham), his secretary, and the American consul, Jessie Gordon foils a series of villainous intrigues to deprive her father of his concession in Brilliatina. The villains include Brilliatina's President Castroaba (William Burress) and a Japanese called Oyama (Frederick Paulding). (Oyama remained a popular stage name for Japanese over the years. It was used as late as *La, La, Lucille* in 1919.) Impressed by Jessie's maneuvers, the consul proposes and is accepted. Miss Ring carried the show, and three of her interpolations were extremely profitable: "I've Got Rings On My Fingers" (brought over from *The Midnight Sons*), "Nora Malone" (Junie McCree/Albert Von Tilzer), and "The Glory Of The Yankee Navy" (Kenneth Clark/John Philip Sousa). *The Yankee Girl* had a successful pre-Broadway tour. It played New York for 12 weeks, beginning February 10, then continued a cross-country trek.

February's other musical was **Bright Eyes** (2-28-10, New York). Chicago's Favorites, Cecil Lean and Florence Holbrook, were starred. The show was a bitter disappointment for Dickson, Hauerbach, and Hoschna, who had hoped to repeat the success of *Three Twins* (6-15-08). The book was based on Grant Stewart's 1906 flop, *Mistakes Will Happen,* in which Dickson had played the lead. Dickson related a backstage yarn of an actress and a playwright who lose their jobs when their secret marriage is exposed. The two set about finding an angel to back a new show the husband has written, only to discover their rich supporter is the puritanical head of a ladies' seminary. His carefree wife helps extricate the young couple from their entanglement. Karl Hoschna's score was pleasant, especially the title song—though several critics complained the song was overplayed. But *Bright Eyes* ran a mere 40 performances, a far cry from the long run of *The Three Twins.*

No musical appeared in March.

A party of American tourists are aboard the *S. S. Pegasus* when the ship is battered by a violent storm. Neptune (Harrison Brockbank) appears and takes the Americans to Olympus, where "a very devil of a sport," Ruben Smith (John Slavin), flirts with Venus (Hazel Cox) and tries to elope with Juno (Clarice Vance). This was the plot of **A Skylark,** which followed *Bright Eyes* into the New York on April 4. A magnificent production offered "a beauty chorus such as is rarely seen" in gorgeous gowns and a scene change in which "shimmering gold and silver suddenly dissolves to reveal melting clouds of pinks and heliotropes and blues." Although the show was courteously received, including its score by the otherwise unheard-of Frank Dossert, it failed to catch on.

Four nights later Edwards' *Molly May* began its stay.

The beloved De Wolf Hopper closed out April with a "song play" based loosely on Molière's *Un Médecin malgré lui.* Medford Griffin, once **A Matinee Idol** (4-28-10, Daly's) but now down on his luck, comes to a boarding school expecting to be a teacher, finds the position filled and so claims to be a physician. His first case is the headmaster's son, Dick (Joseph Santley), who is pretending to be ill to avoid being separated from his sweetheart. Griffin handled the situation sympathetically and learns his long-lost flame is Dick's aunt. The show was clean family entertainment, something De Wolf Hopper's fans knew his presence assured. Hopper now and then stopped to talk with his audience, at one point confessing to feeling strange appearing in contemporary instead of period clothes. The much-married comedian didn't have to say a word to grab the biggest laugh of the evening by simply staring in dumb amazement at a young man who asked him if he knew what true love meant. Silvio Hein's score was merely another collection of undistinguished melodies. Hopper drew enough crowds to keep Daly's lit for 68 performances.

Three musicals opened in May. *Tillie's Nightmare* came on May 5; the other two competed for attention on the 30th. **The Merry Whirl,** a musical play verging on burlesque, gave the New York Theatre its fourth dud in a row, but at the Casino an all-star revival of *The Mikado* (Fritzi Scheff was Yum-Yum; Andrew Mack, Nanki-Poo; and Jefferson De Angelis, Ko-Ko) was well received and found public support.

The Summer Widowers and *Girlies* both arrived before the middle of June to end the season.

1910-1911

All three of the season's outstanding new American hits were operettas, regardless of what their authors called them. While all three added luster to the roster of great American musicals, not one had an American-born composer: Karl Hoschna was Bohemian; Ivan Caryll a Belgian with long experience in France and England; and Victor Herbert an Irishman. Hoschna and Caryll's score sounded thoroughly Viennese, while *Naughty Marietta,* if not Viennese, was distinctly in the grand European tradition. But all through the theatrical year there were hints of more American innovations to come.

Florenz Ziegfeld's **Follies of 1910** opened the season on June 20. The *Follies* were easing into a definitive pattern. They were also improving with each edition. Two newcomers were the major improvement this year—Fanny Brice and Bert Williams, probably the two finest performers Ziegfeld ever presented. Both had an almost incredible range, from hilarious ethnic travesty to broad human pathos. For Williams the debut signaled the acceptances of a major black artist in an important, otherwise white musical. Williams' numbers in his debut included "You're Gwine To Get Something What You Don't Expect," "That Minor Strain," and "I'll Lend You Everything I've Got Except My Wife" (Jean Havez/Harry Von Tilzer). In this last tune Williams made a generous offer to lend his audience anything he owned except his wife. After a pause he confided, "I'll make you a present of her."

. . .

Fanny Brice was born in the great melting pot of New York's Lower East Side on October 29, 1891, the daughter of saloon-keepers Charles and Rose Borach. Her first performances were warbling for pennies in her parents' saloon. At thirteen she won the amateur night contest at Keeney's Theatre in Brooklyn singing "When You're Not Forgotten By The Girl You Can't Forget." Three years later she was hired for the chorus of *The Talk of New York,* but she was fired by George M. Cohan while the show was still in rehearsal. Most students agree Cohan fired her because she couldn't dance, although a few writers have insisted her clownish antics cost her her job. She took work as a comic on the flourishing burlesque circuit, where Irving Berlin spotted her and gave her "Sadie Salome" to sing. It was her comic rendition of this song, sung in a Yiddish accent, that called her to Ziegfeld's attention. At this early date in her career she spelled her first name "Fannie," but in time she changed it and thereafter retained the new spelling.

. . .

Miss Brice went into dialect to introduce "Goodbye Becky Cohen" by another Follies first-timer, Irving Berlin, and stopped the show with a ragtime love song, "Lovie Joe" (Will Marion Cook/Joe Jordan). She is said to have received twelve encores on opening night. A rash of encores was commonplace at the time, but for once they were undoubtedly a spontaneous joy rather than a forced nuisance. The Ziegfeld beauties were there, too. Anna Held appeared briefly as a comet. Her appearance was all the more remarkable in that she herself was far away. Ziegfeld had filmed the entire sequence. Lillian Lorraine, flanked by some of Ziegfeld's loveliest girls, all on flower-bedecked swings, won applause with "Swing Me High—Swing Me Low" (Ballard MacDonald/Victor Hollaender).

Ziegfeld may have derived a special pleasure from mounting **The Girl in the Kimono** at Chicago's Ziegfeld Theatre five nights after he had unveiled his latest *Follies* in New York. The show had lyrics by Harold Atteridge and music by Phil Schwartz. In Helen Bagg's book a bride clad only in a kimono is locked out of her suite and forced to spend the night with a bachelor neighbor. But Ziegfeld's pleasure must have been dampened by the disheartening notices. He quickly closed the production.

July's sole entry was **Up and Down Broadway** (7-18-10, Casino), a revue that insisted on calling itself a musical comedy. There was a thin plot, since most contemporary revues had them. Apollo and the other gods have come to New York vowing to reform theatrical taste. Their janitor, Momus, tags along for laughs. In the end the gods conclude Broadway knows more about good entertainment than they do. Eddie Foy as Momus led an excellent cast which included two young composers, Irving Berlin and Ted Snyder, singing their own interpolations, "Sweet Italian Love" and "Oh, That Beautiful Rag." The principal score was by Jean Schwartz and from it emerged one hardy perennial, "Chinatown, My Chinatown," interpolated after the show opened to replace another Chinatown number, and sung by Ernest Hare (as a police officer) with the chorus. The show ran into the fall.

Young Deems Taylor tried his luck on Broadway, writing the score for **The Echo** (8-17-10, Globe). He quickly learned his calling lay elsewhere. William Le Baron's plot was standard musical comedy nonsense. Kate (Bessie McCoy), headwaitress at the Echo House, loves a boarder, Reggie (Joseph Herbert, Jr.). But Reggie's rich, widowed mother (Evelyn Carrington) disapproves. Kate and Reggie catch mama and a German soap manufacturer (John E. Hazzard) in a loving embrace and confront them with a photograph of the scene. Mama gives her consent. The show was most entertaining when it got to its feet. Dancing ranged from "old-fashioned clog to the latest Russian craze." Miss McCoy romped through a "French Fandango" and then led the "pony" chorus in a drummer routine which reminded the *Times* of her dance to "The Yama Yama Man." To bolster Taylor's fledgling score a large number of interpolations were added, including songs by Nat D. Ayer, John Golden, Karl Hoschna, and Jerome Kern. But *The Echo*, which opened on August 17, barely made it into October.

Chicago's two leading musical houses, the Princess and the La Salle, both had new musicals ready for their patrons in August. The Princess began the season on the 21st with **The Wife Tamers.** Its libretto and lyrics were by Oliver Herford and James Clarence Harvey; its music by R. H. Bowers. The plot revolved around the illusions two wives insist on retaining about their husbands' pasts. The naughty husband is imagined to have been a saint, while the good one is perceived as having been a devil. Claudine, an attractive milliner, comes on the scene and sets the record straight. *The Wife Tamers* received generally warm notices, but for some reason Chicagoans were not attracted to it. It went down on the records as a failure. On the other hand, **The Sweetest Girl in Paris,** which opened at the La Salle on August 29, was an immediate success with both the press and the public. Addison Burkhardt did the book; Collin Davis the lyrics; and Joe Howard the music. The sweet young miss in Paris is a girl with a nervous twitch that passes for a come-hither look. She rejects a number of Ameri-

cans before accepting a waiter in a café. He turns out to be a Pittsburgh millionaire. Burkhardt's dialogue was run-of-the-mill for the day. When a lady complains, "This noisy bustle annoys me," her escort responds, "Then why don't you take it off!" But the show's star, Trixie Friganza, and the staging and famous chorus line of Gus Sohlke helped keep the show at the La Salle into the new year.

In New York August's final two musical offerings appeared at the very end of the month. On the 29th the London hit, Ivan Caryll and Lionel Monckton's **Our Miss Gibbs,** augmented with a number of Kern interpolations, began a two-month run at the Knickerbocker. Miss Gibbs was another in a long line of London shop girls.

Madame Sherry (8-30-10, New Amsterdam) was the first of the season's three triumphs for the American Musical Theatre. Its success more than confirmed the promise of Otto Hauerbach and Karl Hoschna's *Three Twins* (6-15-08). For some curious reason the show was called a "French Vaudeville," even though it had a book—and a good one—as well as an irresistible score. Of course, Hauerbach based his work on Maurice Ordonneau's *Madame Sherry*. But Hauerbach made numerous changes in the story, while Hoschna's totally new score was far superior to the scores employed in London, Paris, and Brussels some years earlier. Edward Sherry's eccentric Uncle Theophilus (Ralph Herz), "a millionaire connoisseur of Greek Art," has set up his playboy nephew as head of The Sherry School of Aesthetic Dancing. Its pupils, all attired like young Isadora Duncans, are reminded of a basic rule of "aesthetic" dancing by their teacher Lulu (Frances Demarest), who is also Edward's sweetheart. She insists "Every Little Movement (Has A Meaning All Its Own)." Edward (Jack Gardner) arrives, upset that "Theophilus," on top of all his other demands, keeps insisting Edward write him about Edward's supposed family. Edward admits he is in no position to refuse:

Lulu: And your Uncle Theophilus has never suspected that he has been fooled?
Sherry: Never! In his letters he never fails to mention my dear wife Eusebia, my dear son Epaminondas and my daughter Scholastica.
Lulu: What crazy names!
Sherry: Chosen by my Uncle!
Lulu: And you get money for every child that's born?
Sherry: Exactly.
Lulu: If I'd been you, I'd have had a whole family.

Sherry: It's bad enough to keep track of the two he *thinks* I've got.

Lulu: But aren't you afraid that some day your uncle may take it into his head to pay you a visit?

Sherry: No danger. For the last twenty-five years he has been digging around in the ruins of Greece for the lost arms of Venus de Milo. Seems to have been the only arms he ever really cared for.

When Leonard Gomez (John Reinhard), the son of Venezuela's president, visits the school, Lulu repeats her instructions for him. But it is obvious "Every Little Movement" begins to have new meanings for the two of them. A third arrival is Yvonne (Lina Abarbanell). She is Theophilus' niece and has come to New York fresh from a convent school. She is intrigued by the glitter of the big city and would like to partake of it all, but, "Uncle Says I Mustn't, So I Won't." Still, she is not above comparing herself to "The Butterfly" about to emerge in all its finery. When Theophilus unexpectedly appears, Edward brazenly presents his housekeeper, Catherine (Elizabeth Murray), as his wife and two pupils as his children. Theophilus joyously assures them (and Lulu and Leonard) there is nothing like a wife's smile—"The Smile She Means For You." Soon Yvonne and Edward are left alone. Dancing together to the strains of "Every Little Movement" they, too, begin to fall in love. Theophilus has invited everyone to take a trip on his yacht, named for Yvonne. His motives are not completely selfless. From the start he has been skeptical of Edward's announced family. Catherine sings of a jilted bride begging for love ("Won't Someone Take Me Home"), while her real husband, Phillippe, tells Yvonne it is no good to teach a young girl the ways of the world, for when she learns them she runs off with "The Other Fellow." Tasting good life makes Yvonne giddy, though she insists, "I'm All Right." But then Edward kisses her and she cannot deny "The Birth Of Passion." Theophilus jolts his guests with an announcement. They will not return to land until he has discovered what everyone's real relationship is. By the time he learns, the relationships have changed from what they were when Edward first lied to him. Catherine and Phillippe admit they are married, Lulu and Leonard agree they will wed, and Theophilus happily consents to Edward's making Yvonne the true Madame Sherry.

Besides his marvelous book, Hauerbach gave Hoschna better than average lyrics. The words for "The Smile She Means For You" are remarkably similar to those of "Smiles" a few years later.

During the run comedienne Elizabeth Murray, who was praised for a drunk scene that never became offensive, was allowed to introduce several interpolations, the most famous of which was "Put Your Arms Around Me, Honey" (Junie McCree/Albert Von Tilzer). Because the songs she replaced were the weakest in the show the changes were for the better. By a curious coincidence, in all three of the season's major American hits the principal song was introduced early on and then repeated throughout the evening with different lyrics or in contexts that gave it novel nuances. As it was in most musicals of the era, dancing was a highlight of the production. In fact, the *Times* headed its review, "POLKA DOMINATES MADAME SHERRY—Very Little Waltzing." "Every Little Movement" was a "polka français," a term now rarely heard. The paper praised Miss Abarbanell's "exquisite" footwork, but went on to note that Dorothy Jardon, who had only a small part, was "the sensation of the evening when in the midst of a sort of Apache rag she turned herself into a human mummy—feet crossed and arms folded—and was tossed around." *Madame Sherry* ran into the spring and then toured, breaking house records in many of the cities it visited.

The Hippodrome's yearly extravaganza was unveiled September 3. It was actually a triple bill: *Ballet of Niagara, The Earthquake* (in which an earthquake upsets the plans of a South American general and frees the Indian girl he has kept as a slave), and the main part of the evening, **The International Cup.** The title hinted at an auto race, but with their customary generosity the Hippodrome management and R. H. Burnside gave audiences more. Roy Carewe (Ben Wainwright) does win the New York-to-Paris auto race after foiling villainy at the wireless station. A larger-than-life hero, he goes on to rescue a girl from a sinking yacht and win a yacht race as well. Manuel Klein supplied another competent score. But as always the imaginative effects were the thing. Two fully-rigged yachts sailed across the stage, elephants and lions romped, and an iridescent rainbow stretched from one side of the proscenium to the other. The effects kept playgoers gaping for 333 performances.

M. Louis Ganne's **Hans, The Flute Player** (9-20-10, Manhattan Opera House) was an imported comic opera with an eye on the children's market. Its variation of the Pied Piper tale entertained audiences for ten weeks.

He Came from Milwaukee (9-21-10, Casino) was another of those musical comedies in which an

American teaches Europeans a few tricks, but since Sam Bernard played in dialect there was an implication that even a short stay in the New World gave a man sharp, new perspectives. Bernard was Herman von Schellenvein, a successful immigrant, who persuades the Duke of Zurack to change places with him so the Duke can evade the clutches of a title-hunting American mother, Mrs. Matthew Harvey (Alice Gordon). Miss Harvey becomes engaged to the real duke in his disguise as Herman, and all ends well. Just as Bernard had, as a gem dealer in *The Girl and the Wizard* (9-27-09), enjoyed some of his best moments impersonating an excitable stage manager, so in *He Came from Milwaukee* the ersatz duke won many of his biggest laughs by turning into a wild animal to accommodate a lady lion-tamer. The score was by Ben Jerome, who had produced a Broadway score as early as 1903 and who wrote even more frequently for Chicago, and by Louis Hirsch, who until now had been represented only by intermittent interpolations. It was a pleasant score, its best numbers such as "Love Is Like A Red, Red Rose" more suggestive of the soft, sentimental material Jerome was writing for Chicago audiences than the lilting style Hirsch soon became known for. Broadway embraced Bernard for four months.

. . .

Louis Hirsch was born in New York City on November 28, 1887. Reputed to have taught himself the piano at an amazingly early age, he studied under a number of American teachers before becoming a pupil of Rafael Joseffy at the Stern Conservatory in Berlin. His first ambition was to be a concert pianist. But the need for immediate income prompted him to turn to popular composing. He worked for Gus Edwards and for Shapiro-Bernstein, and for a time wrote and arranged music for Dockstader's Minstrels. As early as 1907 his songs were interpolated into Broadway shows such as *The The Gay White Way* and *Miss Innocence*.

. . .

September's last musical was **Alma, Where Do You Live?**, an importation from France that proved one of the season's biggest hits, running 232 performances. Joe Weber's excellent mounting shared credit for the show's popularity with George V. Hobart's lively adaptation and Jean Briquet's captivating score. The story revolved around another musical comedy will. In this case the will requires the hero to refrain from marrying until he reaches a certain age. Just before the deadline his rivals plant the irresistible Alma in his path. A number of

critics, but notably the *Times,* praised Hobart and Weber for discarding all the suggestiveness they found in the original. Kitty Gordon, John Mc-Closkey, and Charles Bigelow led the cast.

October's first musical was also an importation. Unfortunately Leo Fall's **The Girl on the Train** (10-3-10, Globe) failed to live up to the great expectations the success of its tryout encouraged, and it was withdrawn after 40 performances. In its homeland the show was called *Die geschiedene Frau* (The Divorced Wife). The girl on the train was the lady the wife assumed was her husband's mistress. Vera Michelena and Melville Stewart were the principals.

Another failure came in the next night. **The Deacon and the Lady** (10-4-10, New York) described the efforts of Jim Gruff (Fletcher Norton) and Marie Trouville (Clara Palmer) to secure a valuable Montana property from Deacon Flood (Harry Kelly). There were some kind words for what proved to be Alfred E. Aarons' last Broadway score, but most critics agreed with the *Dramatic Mirror*'s assessment that "no effort seems to have been made to associate the story and the score." For many of those who saw the piece its chief attraction was the riotous antics of a young comedian named Ed Wynn. He earned some of his biggest laughs clowning with a "trained panama hat." But his Broadway debut was short-lived. The musical lasted just two weeks.

A more established entertainer, Marie Cahill, had slightly better luck with a vehicle called **Judy Forgot** (10-6-10, Broadway). Judy Evans is in a train wreck shortly after a big quarrel with her husband. As a result of the crash she loses both her luggage and her memory. She picks up the luggage of a Mrs. Stole (Truly Shattuck) and assumes her identity. The flabbergasted Mr. Stole (Joseph Santley) must go along with her to avoid antagonizing his rich uncle. A second accident, this time in an automobile, restores Judy's memory. There were serious reservations about the handling of the book and the quality of the music. One critic used his review to complain the American musical comedy composers were no longer "contributing anything fresh and splendid." Even the carefully drilled marching of the chorus girls as soldiers was seen to be old hat. Miss Cahill found excuses to impersonate a lady in an opera box and an ingenue misleading the press in an interview. The singing comedienne had sufficient following to rack up 44 performances.

Yet another importation, **Madame Troubadour** (10-10-10, Lyric), enjoyed a 10-week run. Grace

La Rue and Georgia Caine were featured in the story of scholar's wife who feels her husband cares more for medieval poetry than for her. A friend persuades her to flirt openly with another man. On the 24th, **The Girl in the Taxi** opened. It called itself a "musical play," but since it had only three songs it was really more of a straight piece.

Joe Howard had a second score ready for the Chicago season when **Lower Berth Thirteen** arrived at the Whitney Opera House on October 16. With his score for *The Sweetest Girl in Paris* helping to keep the La Salle lit, it might have been expected that the new work would play the Princess. But the Singer brothers, dismayed by the break-up of Howard's old partnership and unable to find an available musical when *The Wife Tamers* failed, had converted the house to straight dramatic fare. Only rarely thereafter did the Princess play host to a lyric work. Collin Davis and Arthur Gillespie created the plot which recounted the trials of a honeymoon couple on a train otherwise filled with a burlesque troupe. At one point the husband is mistaken for a horse thief. The show was only moderately successful.

Two musicals premiered in New York on the night of November 7. **The Bachelor Belles,** at the Globe, was a final vehicle for the fading star of Adelaide Genee. It related the story of the Bachelor Belles, an organization dedicated to celibacy. But when Charles Van Rensselaer (John Park) appears, Daphne Brooks (Eva Fallon) falls in love and breaks her vows. The other ladies admit they are secretly engaged. Genee was not Daphne. She spoke not a line and her dances had nothing to do with the plot. Nonetheless her allure was still such that the show ran a month.

The Bachelor Belles might have run even longer, but it vied for attention with four other openings, one of them **Naughty Marietta.** Though the new Herbert piece was far from being the runaway smash of the year, it was the finest show of the season. In fact, it was the American masterwork of the era. Interestingly, in a seven-year period given to an unconscious symmetry, it opened right in the middle of the epoch's central season. It was the fifteenth of the season's thirty-four musicals. Oscar Hammerstein had commissioned it as a showcase for the great singers of his troubled opera company, especially the diminutive soprano Emma Trentini. As Marietta, Miss Trentini scored the first of her two Broadway triumphs. Writing for such fine, thoroughly trained voices, Victor Herbert allowed himself a rare depth and range. His vocal lines were among his most operatic, his orchestrations far and away his most symphonic. Melodically the score was probably his most inventive and enthralling, with at least four of the songs taking their place among his finest, most popular classics. The conductor was Gaetano Merola, who later was instrumental in establishing the San Francisco Opera. The show was blessed from the start, and by the time it opened on November 7 at the New York Theatre, which Hammerstein had built and lost, and where he was now forced to display his presentation, its success was beyond doubt. Rida Johnson Young's libretto was set in 18th-century Louisiana. Captain Dick (sung by another Hammerstein luminary, Orville Harrold) and his rangers arrive singing their marching song, "Tramp! Tramp! Tramp!" They are seeking the pirate, Bras Prique. Marietta comes on the scene. She is a young lady of noble origin who has fled to America to escape an unhappy marriage. In the title song she mischievously describes herself as an impossibly capricious girl. She and Dick admit to a reciprocal fascination, but both profess, "It Never, Never Can Be Love." Adah (Marie Duchene), a quadroon slave belonging to Etienne Grandet (Edward Martindell), son of the Lieutenant Governor, appears. For a while Etienne has actually loved her, but his ardor has cooled. Still, Adah is hopeful. Love can rekindle, " 'Neath The Southern Moon." When Adah has left, Marietta longingly recalls her own youthful passion and fire in Naples with the "Italian Street Song," providing a striking contrast between the sultry slave girl and her own volatile personality. Etienne falls in love with Marietta and agrees to deny he knows her real history:

Marietta: Oh Monsieur I am glad you persuaded me to come. How I have laughed. How enjoyed!
Etienne: I have observed you, and Mademoiselle, I apologize for having disbelieved your statement that you were not the Contessa D'Altona.
Marietta: Eh?
Etienne: I have seen in you tonight the spirit of the people. No lady highly born could have entered as you have into our rustic festivity.

Eventually Dick is brought face to face with his own true feelings for Marietta, confessing, "I'm Falling In Love With Some One." The villainous buccaneer turns out to be none other than Etienne. Marietta is impressed by Dick's police work, but for years she has promised she will give herself only to the man who can finish a mysterious melody that haunts her dreams and that she has sung snatches of throughout the evening. Dick, in the operetta's soaring finale, does just that. Both rejoice: "Ah, Sweet Mystery Of Life" at last you have been found.

A legend has long circulated that this most popular of all Herbert songs was not in the original production. The legend is false. "Ah, Sweet Mystery Of Life" was in the operetta from the beginning. What gave the story currency was the fact that no one apparently guessed how popular the song would become. It was originally listed in the program solely as "finale" and was not published as a separate song in the initial printing of the show's music. Its immediate and phenomenal success changed matters swiftly.

The show ran 136 performances, including extra matinees added to satisfy the demand for seats. Herbert's superb biographer, Edward Waters, states the duration of the run was limited in advance by contractual commitments and that it could have remained in New York much longer.

The Girl and the Kaiser (11-22-10, Herald Square), another importation, began an eight-week engagement with Lulu Glaser starred as a girl whose fortuitous meeting with the Kaiser allows her to save her lover from execution. George Jarno composed the principal score.

The Spring Maid (12-26-10, Liberty), also foreign, was December's only musical. It was a smash hit, running into summer. No doubt Christie MacDonald's lovely singing of Heinrich Reinhardt's songs aided ticket sales. Although strictly speaking the show is not an important part of our record, one anecdote about it offers an enlightening insight into the age's theatrical morality on both sides of the footlights. The operetta's story related how a young lady stoops to conquer by becoming an attendant at Carlsbad Springs. According to Harry B. Smith, who adapted the show with his brother Robert, "Tom McNaughton, an English actor, was the leading comedian in 'The Spring Maid.' At rehearsal he asked to be allowed to interpolate a recitation called 'The Three Trees,' which he had given successfully in the London music halls. The recitation had absolutely nothing to do with 'The Spring Maid,' but McNaughton was so confident that it would be a hit that a way was found to introduce it. When it was rehearsed, accompanied by eccentric orchestral noises, the effect was so decidedly vaudevillian, that in order to account for its introduction in the operetta, a note was printed on the program stating that the fable of 'The Three Trees' was the legend of the original discovery of

Carlsbad Springs, and the authority given for this ingenious invention was 'Richter's Folk Lore of Germany,' of which, paraphrasing *Sary Gamp's* friend *Betsy,* I may say that 'I don't believe there's no sich a book.' However, my old friend, Mr. Krehbiel [critic for the *Tribune*], referred to the note in his review and seemed to know all about the mythical historical work."

Two musicals welcomed in 1911 on January 2. **Marriage à la Carte** at the Casino had a score by Ivan Caryll, who had decided to settle permanently in the United States, and a book by C. M. S. McLellan, with whom Caryll would collaborate on his next four shows.

. . .

Ivan Caryll was born Felix Tolken in Liège, Belgium, in 1861. The exact date may be still buried in some Belgian archives. He studied music both at Liège and Paris, settling in the French capital to compose operettas. However, he soon moved to England, where he helped adapt a number of French musicals to London's taste. In time he again started to compose his own works, many of which quickly graced American stages as well. The West End and Broadway both sang his songs for *The Shop Girl, The Circus Girl, A Runaway Girl, The Messenger Boy, The Toreador,* and a host of others.

. . .

McClellan's plot was slight. Mrs. Ponsonby de Coutts Wragge (Maria Davis) has divorced Napoleon Pettingill (Harry Conor) and is about to marry Lord Mirables (C. Morton Horne) when a train wreck deposits Pettingill on her doorstep. By the end of Act III she has decided to remarry Napoleon. Caryll's score was dashing and gay, but inconsequential. *Marriage à la Carte* lasted eight weeks, closing a few days before Caryll and McClellan's second effort opened.

The show competed for first-nighters with **The Slim Princess** at the Globe. Its star, Elsie Janis, played Princess Talora who cannot find a suitor because she is too slim. To make matters worse for her regal family her younger sister, Jeneka (Julia Frary), cannot marry until Talora does. When the Prince (Joseph C. Miron) learns that slim girls are stylish in America, he sends Talora to Washington. She falls in love and, after an initial reluctance, the Prince consents to her choice. Miss Janis, besides playing Talora, found excuses to impersonate Ethel Barrymore, Anna Held, Sarah Bernhardt, Sam Bernard, Eddie Foy, Harry Lauder, and George M. Cohan. When Miss Janis was not regaling patrons, Joseph Cawthorn was tickling their funny bones in another of his dialect roles, Louis von

Schloppenhauer. According to the program, the music was by Leslie Stuart. But in his research for his Victor Herbert biography, Edward Waters discovered that Herbert had a hand in part of the composition. None of the songs had any lasting value. The hit of the evening was "Let Me Live And Die In Dixie" (Elizabeth Brice and Charles King), a song its writers had already made popular in vaudeville and which was inserted into at least one other show during the season. *The Slim Princess* ran three months.

Planquette's **The Paradise of Mahomet** (1-17-11, Herald Square) was adapted by the Smith brothers. In its brief stay its story described the abduction of a supposed widow by a Turkish prince. He tries to persuade her she, too, has died, and that his harem is actually Paradise. George Leon Moore and Grace Van Studdiford starred.

As February began, the *Dramatic Mirror* reported that five of the twenty-one successes running on Broadway were musicals. February's first two musicals jumped the total to seven.

Lew Fields' "summer" shows had been so successful that he decided to offer one at the height of the season. **The Hen Pecks** (2-4-11, Broadway) told another homey story, elaborately mounted and stuffed with vaudeville turns. Henry Peck (Fields), fed up with married life, flees to Cranberry Cove. His wife Henrietta (Lillian Lee), his son Henderson (Stephen Maley), and his daughters Henoria (Gertrude Quinlan) and Henella (Blossom Seeley) follow him there and ultimately effect a reconciliation. Fields filled the evening with the "realistic" touches the era so loved. A farm boasted real chickens, ducks, geese, and pigs. A person could be seen dressing behind the curtain of a farmhouse window. For laughs, Fields and others hurled "missiles" through a pneumatic tube. Frank Whitman earned encores for playing his violin while he did a knock-about dance. The show had an ordinary A. Baldwin Sloane score, and a number of interpolations, including one by Jerome Kern and the same "Let Me Live And Die In Dixie" sung in *The Slim Princess*. The show ran until just about the time Fields would have been bringing in his hot weather production.

During the run of the piece, Fields made some startling statements in an interview. They suggested, at one and the same time, a condescension toward his audience and, since he was so successful, a sensitive appraisal of it. He felt that "the public want pretty much the same old thing from year to year, but they want little changes and little surprises hitched to the old situations and lines."

He attributed extremely short memories to his playgoers, concluding, "every entrance is, in effect, the actor's first appearance; because the three or four numbers intervening since his exit has made the audience forget just what he is doing." Equally surprising is his indifference to the integrity of the show itself. He announced his next show would be "the same sort" as *The Hen Pecks,* "except it has more of a story." He continued, "At least it has a story now, but I don't know what may happen to it after rehearsals begin. You see, an attraction of this kind can't get by on first rehearsal. Then the composer will complain that the numbers are not placed properly and the changes that suit him will probably interfere with the plot. Then the manager will find fault with the movement of the lyrics because they don't give him a chance to move the show girls around. . . . And so it goes. When it is all over, consistency of the narrative is a thing that was." As a parting shot, he added, "the author gets blamed for a lot of lines he was never guilty of."

In Chicago the La Salle's successor to *The Sweetest Girl in Paris* was a failure. **The Girl I Love,** which opened on February 5, had a libretto by C. V. Kerr and R. H. Burnside (Burnside also did the lyrics) and a score by J. S. Zamecnik and H. L. Sanford. In the slight plot Billy Phibbs is sent packing by his uncle for an imagined slight. But Billy proves his worth and wins the girl he loves, Jesslyn Bard.

Paul Rubens' **The Balkan Princess** (2-9-11, Herald Square), a London musical, ran 108 performances in New York. The title role of a princess who goes slumming was sung by Louise Gunning, but it was considered so arduous Christine Nielson replaced her for matinees.

A show possibly meant for New York, **Katie Did,** opened at the Colonial in Chicago on February 18. W. C. Duncan and Frank Smithson based their libretto on *My Friend from India,* in which a barber impersonating an Indian prince is invited by a drunken Charlie Underholt to the Underholts' party. The show received good notices, especially Karl Hoschna's score, but for some reason it was soon withdrawn.

Victor Moore returned to Broadway in **The Happiest Night of His Life** (2-20-11, Criterion). The book, by Junie McCree and Sydney Rosenfeld, began like one of George H. Cohan's librettos through which Moore had so often romped. Its denouement, however, was the sort of musical comedy absurdity Cohan would never have allowed. Tom (Jack Henderson) has stolen $500 from his Uncle Harry (Phil Ryley). To get it back before Uncle Harry discovers his loss, Dick Brennan (Moore) suggests charging Harry $500 for a tour of the Manhattan underworld. The "tour" takes place at Mrs. Rickett's, where Uncle meets the ladies of the "Chicago Protective Order of Young Widows." The music was by Tin Pan Alley's Albert Von Tilzer, a writer who never developed a truly identifiable style of his own and who, for this show, was not above consciously imitating Cohan, in such songs as, "Oh You Chicago, Oh You New York." The public sensed a bad imitation and *The Happiest Night of His Life* lasted only three weeks.

An even worse hodgepodge came in two weeks later and also ran three weeks. **Jumping Jupiter** (3-6-11, Criterion) was tailored to the talents of Richard Carle, a comedian with a large following, especially in Chicago and on the road. Carle wrote his own libretto in conjunction with Sydney Rosenfeld, who had collaborated on the Victor Moore book. Several of the songs were also credited to Carle. Robert Winthrop (Burrell Barbaretto) tires of his wife Connie (Edna Wallace Hopper) and offers her a large check if she will leave. She tears up the check. But, unknown to Winthrop, Connie has been posing as Professor Goodwillie's wife. When the real Mrs. Goodwillie (Jessie Cardownie) and the professor (Carle) arrive, Winthrop sees another way out.

During the run of *Marriage à la Carte* Ivan Caryll granted an interview, in which he presented his opinions of the American lyric stage: "American popular music overdoes ragtime, although in proper amount, syncopation is a legitimate device. This country, however, does not lack composers of merit. 'Robin Hood' is one of the best of its class. Besides De Koven you have Herbert . . . and Sousa. . . ." It was clear with what style of musical composition Caryll's sympathy lay. But, like so many of his contemporaries, he did not look on it as comic opera or operetta, for he added, "America has the best musical comedy soloists—Fritzi Scheff, Emma Trentini, and Emmy Wehlen—although the men do not outrank the English."

One young lady Caryll failed to mention was Hazel Dawn, although she was in no small measure responsible for giving Caryll and McLellan the season's biggest musical hit, when she opened in their "musical comedy," **The Pink Lady** (3-13-11, New Amsterdam). McClellan based his libretto on *Le Satyre* by Georges Berr and Marcel Guillemand. A satyr is loose in the Forest of Compiègne, stealing hugs and kisses from comely young passers-by. He is the talk of all the customers at Le Joli Coucou, a restaurant in the park—all the customers except the narcissistic Benevol (Fred Wright, Jr.), who arrives urging the crowd to "Bring Along The Camera," since everything he does is worth a photo. Lucien Garidel (William Elliott), whose marriage to Angele (Alice Dovey) has been announced, arrives, calculating, "I'm Single For Six Weeks More." Before his wedding he will have one last fling with his old flame, Claudine (Miss Dawn). He sees nothing wrong in this, but he is taken aback when Angele appears with another man to have dinner. Angele and her escort coyly agree "Love Is Divine." A third couple, Desiree (Ida M. Adams) and Bebe (John E. Young), concur that, once you've met a girl by the Seine, it becomes almost impossible to remain true to an old love "By The Saskatchewan." Claudine arrives and Lucien introduces her to the suspicious Angele as the wife of his friend, the antiques dealer, Dondidier (Frank Lalor). Knowing that Angele will seek to verify their story, Lucien and Claudine rush to the Rue St. Honoré, where they beg the baffled Dondidier to back them up. The Comtesse de Montavert (Louise Kelley) appears, but before she can transact her business she is kissed on the cheek. Though she did not see who did it she blames Dondidier and brands him the satyr. Sides are hastily chosen in "Donny Didn't, Donny Did." Claudine, while not the satyr, admits to an ample supply of kisses in "The Kiss Waltz."

Angele and her escort, Maurice, arrive. The four youngsters insist that in France you must fight for "The Right To Love." But the police have been summoned by the Countess, and they appear, "properly copperly" to arrest Dondidier. At the Restaurant of the Satyrs, Dondidier, released, and now confessedly the satyr, contemplates his new notoriety and concludes, "I Like It!" But Angele and Claudine decide men do not really know how to court women. The girls would do it to soft lights and sweet music, the same music in fact that Claudine has more flippantly sung as "The Kiss Waltz." But the words have changed, with the suitor professing his heart sighs as he raises his eyes to "My Beautiful Lady." Angele wins back Lucien, while Claudine, a member of the demimonde, goes on her way.

The gay confectionary of a book was perfectly matched by the dainty, melodious score. Miss Dawn walked away with honors not just for her acting, singing, and dancing, but for her violin playing as well. So well balanced was the show that two of its biggest hits—"By The Saskatchewan" and "Donny Didn't, Donny Did," a brilliantly staged number—were given to minor players. In its review, the *Times* suggested that the show achieved a goal that shows of the epoch are rarely credited with, insisting that the fun and songs "developed logically out of its situations." The paper also praised Julian Mitchell's fine direction, notably the "magnificent bustle" at the end of the first act, and it enjoyed a real blonde posing on the steps in front of the restaurant. *The Pink Lady* ran well into the 1911–12 season.

One week after *The Pink Lady*'s premiere, **La Belle Paree** opened the spanking new Winter Garden on March 20. The new theatre almost stole the show. The Shuberts had built it at Broadway between 50th and 51st Streets, far uptown from most theatres of the day. It was a spacious house with a disproportionately large number of its nearly 1600 seats on the orchestra level, assuring a handsome gross at capacity. Food and drink were served. The theatre was clearly to be the Shubert flagship. Before the main event of the evening the Shuberts unveiled Manuel Klein's one-act "Chinese" opera, *Bow Sing*. A small dose of culture was deemed desirable. The "Jumble of Jollity" that followed was little more than glorified vaudeville. It had an undistinguished score by Frank Tours and Jerome Kern, which included a song called "Paris Is A Paradise For Coons" sung late in the evening by a newcomer, Al Jolson. His appearance was so late in the overlong affair that all but one of the newspaper critics—and a fair part of the audience—had left. But the Shuberts, with their excellent theatrical instinct, had faith in him and promptly gave him an earlier spot on the program. He proved a sensation and was an important factor in the show's 104-performance run. Jolson and the Winter Garden would be virtually inseparable for the next fifteen years.

. . .

Al Jolson was born in Washington, D.C., on May 26, 1883. His real name was Asa Yoelson. Although the name sounds Scandinavian, Jolson was the son of a Jewish cantor. He ran away from home in his early teens, was returned, and shortly took off again. However, before he left he attended a vaudeville show at Washington's Bijou Theatre where Eddie Leonard was on the bill. Jolson, from his seat in the gallery, began singing along with Leonard. Leonard was so impressed he offered Jolson a job in his act, singing along from the balcony. But the new act did not last long, for Jolson did not like the obscurity of the balcony. His first New York appearance was in a mob scene in *The Children of the Ghetto* at the Herald Square on Oc-

tober 16, 1899. Thereafter he found employment with a circus, with Dockstader's Minstrels and, finally, in vaudeville.

. . .

Of course, Jolson was far from the whole show. The Hess Sisters did "whirlwind" Russian dances, Dazie toe-danced, and Yvette, like Frank Whitman earlier in the season, mixed footwork and fiddling. Kitty Gordon again displayed her celebrated back. Ragtime numbers were sparked by Stella Mayhew. In the finale, "cunning little" Mitzi Hajos delighted audiences by jumping from the stage to lead the orchestra. Shell pink and soft sea green dominated the sets, while abundant plumage, hobble skirts, and harem skirts bedecked parading show girls.

The Globe relit on April 3 for Nora Bayes and her husband, Jack Norworth, in **Little Miss Fixit.** Miss Bayes played Delia Wendell, who busies herself match-making and patching up problem marriages, and who doesn't get around to resolving her own marital difficulties until curtain time. Some small, felicitous touches pleased the critics. Miss Bayes eschewed the noisy first entrance so common at the time. Instead a lady, shielded behind a parasol, was seen sitting quietly through the first songs and opening dialogues. Only when she sedately lowered the umbrella was she discovered to be the star. Norworth and Miss Bayes appeared soaking wet for the first-act finale after supposedly suffering a canoe accident. Two other performers who delighted the critics apparently had no names. They were a pair of trained dancing dogs. On opening night there were eight songs in the show by various composers. The biggest hit of the evening was "Mister Moon-Man, Turn Off Your Light," which Bayes and Norworth wrote for themselves, apparently as a sort of sequel to their 1908 "Shine On, Harvest Moon." Nor was "Shine On, Harvest Moon" ignored—it opened the overture. In her customary fashion, Miss Bayes added and dropped interpolations during the seven-week Gotham stay and the long tour.

Two shows came into Chicago the first half of April. On the 3rd, Joe Howard offered a rewriting of his 1906 New York failure, *The District Leader.* As **Love and Politics** it failed again, even with Ned Wayburn's dynamic staging. On the 16th Sophie Tucker was starred in **Merry Mary.** The show received a critical drubbing, the critics looking on it as little more than a bad vaudeville. But the *Tribune*'s man did have a few grudging encomiums for Miss Tucker's "fleshy love songs."

In New York, a vaudeville called **London Follies**

(4-17-11, Weber's) was a quick flop, as was a second show that opened the same night. **Doctor De Luxe** (4-17-11, Knickerbocker) bore brief witness to the incessant little symmetries of the period. Its failure coming after its author's early season smash of *Madame Sherry* balanced the early failure and late season hit of Caryll and McLellan. Karl Hoschna and Otto Hauerbach wrote the show as a vehicle for Ralph Herz, who had served them so well as Theophilus in *Madame Sherry*. Herz was an engaging comedian with an unusual background —born into vast wealth derived from the construction of the Suez Canal, he turned to the stage when his family lost its fortune. The plot Hauerbach threw together for him was simple, reminding some of De Wolf Hopper's *A Matinee Idol* (4-28-10), the preceding year. John Truesdale, through mistaken identity, becomes a substitute for Dr. Melville. He prescribes nothing stronger than salt tablets and in the end marries Melville's daughter (Jeanette Childs). Whatever else its faults, the show offered some interesting staging. The evening began with a young boy (Albert Lamson) singing the show's hoped-for hit song, "For Every Boy That's Lonely There's A Girl That's Lonely Too." So engrossed is he in his song, he fails to hear the honking of an automobile, which knocks him down. Truesdale's rushing to his aid starts the complications. Dousings seemed popular during the year, so bare-legged chorus girls, attempting to scamper up trellises, were sprayed by a gardener. In return the girls smashed all the windows in a summer cottage. One critic suggested, "Stage realism can go no further." The score, with one interpolation by Edward Laska, offered no outstanding melodies, but was invariably pleasant.

A Certain Party (4-24-11, Wallack's) ran only three weeks although a number of commentators had kind words for its interesting book. Homer Caldwell (James Seeley), aspiring to a place on the reform ticket, finds he must ally himself with Jerry Fogarty (John T. Kelly), the ward boss. Since Caldwell's son George (Alfred Kappeler) had done a good turn for the brother of their maid Norah (Mabel Hite), Norah is asked to approach Fogarty. Sydney Finch (Harold Hartsell) tells Fogarty that years ago George signed his father's name to a gambling debt. But Norah prevails with the ward leader. The second act contained a highly praised burlesque of a political convention. The lateness of the season, the location of the house at the edge of the theatre area, and a weak score by Robert Hood Bowers stifled whatever chance the lively book had.

Another new theatre, the Follies Bergere, opened April 29. Located on 46th Street, just off Broadway, it was designed as a theatre-restaurant. Its first attraction was a triple bill. *Hell* opened the evening. Called "a profane burlesque" it was a loose vaudeville of gags about spinsters, nouveaux riches, promiscuous sailors, and others, presided over by the Devil and Mrs. Devil "forty-five seconds from Broadway." *Temptation,* a one-act ballet, and *Gaby,* a "satirical revuette" in three scenes, completed the bill. Ethel Levey, returning to Broadway after a protracted absence, played the title role, which purported to be a spoof of Gaby Deslys, a celebrated entertainer who had yet to make her Broadway debut. Her Gaby was represented as a Spanish dancer, but Arenera Duo's castanet-clicking dances stole her thunder. Show girls opened and closed the evening parading as "Beauties of All Nations."

Uptown at the Majestic on May 8 a black entertainment **His Honor, the Barber** became New York's last new musical of the stage year. Raspberry Snow's great ambition is to shave the President of the United States. Raspberry (S. H. Dudley) falls asleep on the White House steps, is chased away, wins a jackpot at the races so big the President hears of it and calls him in. Just as he is about to realize his ambition, he wakes up. He is still outside the White House. Special bits included a donkey brought on stage in blue overalls. Critics always displayed mixed feelings about Negro shows; they were often viewed as *sui generis* and a world apart. The *Times* lamented the actors in *His Honor, the Barber* made "too much effort to imitate white performers," adding it was a failing common to black shows. But the most discerning critics, even when they could not completely rid themselves of racial distinctions, were careful to appreciate the change of values. The Boston *Evening Transcript,* praising the music, had even more praise for the way it was handled: "The music of ragtime is one thing when the youngsters of Broadway scream it and another when Negro voices croon it or give it really the rhythm its name implied." *His Honor, the Barber* ran only two weeks on the Rialto, but it toured successfully for several years.

Two May arrivals ended the Chicago season. **Will o' the Wisp** premiered at the Studebaker on May 8. Alfred G. Robyn composed the score, while Walter Percival not only wrote the book but took the leading role as well. Percival played Forest Kidder, a well-meaning young man who is forever being caught in compromising positions by his sweetheart. Hough and Adams returned to the scene of earlier triumphs, the Princess, on May 30. The score for their latest offering, **The Heartbreakers,** was by Harold Orlob and Melville Gideon. Sallie Fisher starred as the leading student in a school for brides. Both shows were received with little enthusiasm; the reviews for *The Heartbreakers* were reduced to little but passing notices when space was required for extended obituaries of W. S. Gilbert.

Back in New York the season closed with a revival of *H.M.S. Pinafore,* with a cast that included De Wolf Hopper, Marie Cahill, and Louise Gunning, and a revival of the 1902 success, *A Country Girl.*

1911-1912

For the first time in its history, Broadway was to see over forty new musicals offered in a single season: forty-one or forty-two depending on how the double bill at the Follies Bergere was counted. But this encouraging jump in numbers coincided with a disastrous slump in quality. Not one new American show of lasting merit appeared; even superior tunes were few and far between. Three of the importations are sporadically revived on their native stages, although none was of the highest order. Throughout the year newspapers and trade journals commented forlornly on the sad state of the musical theatre. Bewailings of this sort have been perennial, but in 1911–12 they were justified.

The season's first presentation, **The Red Rose** (6-22-11, Bijou), set the tone for the months to come. It was at once professional and hackneyed. The Smith brothers' libretto was set in Paris, where Dick Lorrimer (Wallace McCutcheon), an art student, loves Lola (Valeska Suratt), a girl he believes to be a concierge's daughter, but who is in reality Baron Le Blanc's lost child. Dick's family is pleased when he and Lola have a falling out, for the family want Dick to marry Daisy Plant (Lillian Graham). However, Daisy has eyes only for an Englishman. Dick and Lola are reconciled and marry just in time to thwart the Baron's plan to wed Lola to one Mr. Du Pont (Henry Bergman). Another Paris setting, another unimaginative story, and more lackluster dialogue. The brothers' lyrics were no better, nor was R. H. Bowers' score. To first-nighters, the happiest moment of the evening was the dainty Miss Graham's toe dance; they awarded her three encores. One curious sidelight may well have been the most interesting thing about

the show: its costumes and sets were credited to its feminine lead, Miss Suratt. The show came in on June 22, and for all its weaknesses played through the hot weather.

Four nights later the **Ziegfeld Follies of 1911** (6-26-11, Jardin de Paris) opened. It was the first time the title officially included Ziegfeld's name. As if to honor the occasion he brought together a glamorous collection of old and new favorites: Bert Williams, Fanny Brice, Lillian Lorraine, Vera Maxwell, Bessie McCoy, and the Dolly Sisters—surrounding them with his increasingly legendary line of gorgeous girls. Still called "Anna Held Girls," their numbers had swollen to seventy-five. One important new addition to the roster was Leon Errol.

• • •

Leon Errol was born in Sydney, Australia, on July 3, 1881. He planned to become a doctor and originally performed in Australian vaudeville solely to earn enough money to pay his way through school. However, he was so successful on stage he soon abandoned his earlier ambition. He played in Shakespearean repertory, clowned with a circus, and took small parts in comic opera. Eager for broader opportunities he came to San Francisco, taking a job as a singer waiter while looking for more serious employment. His singing went largely unapplauded, but his eccentric, wobbly-kneed dancing landed him a job in American vaudeville. The San Francisco earthquake prompted his move to the East. A stint as a vaudeville-pantomimist failed. To provide employment for himself he wrote a play called *The Lilies.* The play apparently never reached New York. How Ziegfeld discovered the comedian is uncertain.

• • •

Maurice Levi and Raymond Hubbell produced the principal score for the new *Follies,* with Irving Berlin, Jerome Kern, James Blyler, and Sid Brown among those who provided additional melodies. By and large it was an undistinguished score, the best number being Berlin's "Woodman, Woodman, Spare That Tree"—a song perfectly atuned to Bert Williams' melancholy drollery. Its plea was not that of an alarmed nature-lover, but of a much put-upon husband fearful of losing his lone avenue of escape. Perhaps the evening's most famous comedy skit was a routine using only Williams and Errol, recounting the plight of a small, nervous tourist (Errol) arriving at Grand Central Station in the midst of new subway construction. To help the tourist safely across the girders, the tall, stolid redcap (Williams) joins himself and his customer with a rope. As a safety measure it comes none too soon, for the wobbly Errol, too intrigued by the work going on far below him, falls off a girder marked "160 Foot Drop." Using a laborious hand-over-hand pull, Williams dutifully brings the man back up. Just before he has a secure foothold, Errol asks Williams, "Porter, have you a match?" Obligingly, Williams searches his pockets as the tourist once again plummets down. Already exhausted from his first hauling, Williams must once again begin his hand-over-hand rescue. As he brings Errol to safety for a second time, Errol politely remarks, "Never mind the match, Porter, I broke my pipe." While they stand together catching their breaths, the tourist asks the porter about his private life:

—You have a wife and family, I suppose?

—Oh yes sir; I's married and I'se got three child'un.

—Is that so? Ah, that's very commendable.

—Yes sir, so it is.

—What are the names of your children?

—Well, I names 'em out de Bible. Dar's Hannah and den dar's Samuel and de las' I names "Iwilla."

—Iwilla? I dont remember that name in the Bible.

—Sure 'tis. Don't you 'member where it say IWILLA RISE?

The two climb to a higher girder to look for the right train. Since it hasn't arrived at the station, Williams sits down to have his lunch. He describes the simple food his wife prepares for him so temptingly that Errol approaches hastily to look at it, knocking the lunch pail off the girder in his excitement. Williams, his lunch irretrievably gone, sits slowly nodding his head, tapping his fingers and staring at Errol. Abashed, Errol promises the porter an especially big tip—five cents. Williams accepts the nickel with patent scorn. This so unnerves Errol that he once again falls off the girder—this higher one marked "288 Foot Drop." As the rope keeps running out of the porter's hand, indicating Errol is falling farther and farther, Williams stands and stares deadpan at the audience. When the rope stops uncoiling, Williams mutters "Five Cents!," unwinds the rope from his waist and lets it fall, then, as a sort of coup de grace, hurls the tourist's luggage down at him. An explosion from the construction site follows. Williams looking out into space tells the audience that Errol is a victim of the blast, "There he goes, now he's near the Metropolitan Tower. If he kin only grab that little gold ball on the top . . . 'um, he muffed it." He looks at the audience with an obviously hypocritical compassion.

Walter Browne's morality play *Everywoman* was spoofed as "Everywife" (with Williams playing a character listed as "Nobody"), and *The Pink Lady* was burlesqued in drag. A production number called "HMS Vaudeville" included in its cast of characters Sir Glassup Pilsener and Capt. Headliner. One medley of popular American songs was sung in literal German translations, a stunt used years before in *1492* (5-15-93). The revue played through the summer, then toured.

No shows opened in July, but three appeared in August. **The Girl of My Dreams** (8-7-11, Criterion) had been traveling around the country since 1910, while Otto Hauerbach (assisted on the book by Wilbur Nesbit) and Karl Hoschna strove to recapture the charm and success of *Three Twins* (6-15-08) and *Madame Sherry* (8-30-10). They failed, largely because Hauerbach could not put the book in order. His story line was too frail, his dialogue dreary. Hauerbach apparently designed his story around a saucer-eyed innocent Quaker miss that one of his stars, Leila McIntyre, had portrayed in a vaudeville act. In Hauerbach's book this young lady, now called Lucy Medders, reforms Harry Swifton. Harry seems to relapse into his former ways when Mrs. Blazes is found in his room. But he was only helping her after his car had knocked her down. If the story was trite, the staging was hackneyed. Some way was found to allow the "pony" chorus to stage yet one more drill as red-cheeked soldiers with snare drums. At other point the girls played follow-the-leader as they romped through "some pretty stiff gymnastic paces." Despite the presence of John Hyams and Miss McIntyre in a large, well-chosen cast, the musical ran only 40 performances. The short run was doubly sad. First, since Hoschna's score, as the title song suggests, was quite good, even if too many tunes had treacly titles such as "Dr. Tinkle Tinker" and "Oooh! Maybe He's A Robber!" Secondly, because it proved to be his last score Hoschna would hear performed. He died not quite five months later, December 23, 1911. He was only thirty-four years old and still at the height of his creative powers.

On August 19 Henry Harris and Jesse Lasky made one last attempt to keep alive their dinner-theatre, the Follies Bergère. A revue called **Hello, Paris** (to which, on September 22, they appended a short musical, *A La Broadway*) had some interesting staging by Ned Wayburn, songs by J. Rosamond Johnson, and the popular Harry Pilcer as the featured principal. But Harris and Lasky still could not sell their entertainments to the public. When

Hello, Paris was withdrawn at the end of the month, they transformed the house into a regular legitimate auditorium, staidly renaming it the Fulton.

August's last entry was **The Siren** (8-28-11, Knickerbocker), Leo Fall's attractive operetta, which Harry B. Smith translated from Stein and Willner's original. The story centered on a lovely young lady employed by the police to prove a handsome young marquis is writing satiric letters about the government. Donald Brian was starred, with up-and-coming Julia Sanderson as his leading lady, and Frank Moulan providing laughs. Charles Frohman gave it an elegant production, embellishing the score with Kern interpolations. It became the first show of the season to have an appreciable run.

. . .

Julia Sanderson (née Julia Sackett) was born into a family of actors in Springfield, Massachusetts, on August 20, 1887. As a child she played small roles with a Philadelphia stock company. Tiny, round-faced, and bright eyed, she made her New York debut at fifteen as a chorus girl in *A Chinese Honeymoon.* In the following year she graduated from the chorus of *Winsome Winnie* to the show's lead. Roles in *Wang, Fantana, The Tourists,* and *The Dairymaids* followed. Like so many great performers of the era, part of her apprenticeship was spent doing a stint in London musicals. When she returned to New York to play Frank Moulan's wife in *The Arcadians,* her excellent notices helped earn her the feminine lead in *The Siren.*

. . .

But the longest run of the season's musicals was, as indeed it was season after season, the Hippodrome's annual pageant—for 1911 called **Around the World.** The show came in on September 2 and with its unique two-a-day policy chalked up 445 performances. A skimpy plot about an eccentric millionaire who purchases a diamond against the warning of a mysterious Swami, finds the jewel stolen, and searches the world over to recover it, provided all the excuse necessary for a succession of spectacular scenes. These sets included the lawn of a Hudson River mansion, a yacht plowing through the water, and a grand finale with the theatre's huge tank in the foreground "backed by a grotto of mammoth rocks, over which rises a golden barge, on which a number of beautiful women are grouped. As the changing lights begin to play, the rocks at the rear of the stage become transparent, and in them are seen some exquisitely posed and draped groups of living statuary." Manuel Klein's

likable, if forgettable, score was exemplified by "It's A Long Lane That Has No Turning."

Although its halcyon days as a production center for musicals were ending, Chicago was still far from inactive. One of its biggest hits arrived at the La Salle on September 3, **Louisiana Lou.** Addison Burkhardt and Frederick Donaghey created the book and lyrics and Ben Jerome provided the score. The show starred Alexander Carr and featured Bernard Granville and Sophie Tucker (demoted from the preceding season's star billing). In her autobiography, Miss Tucker regarded the show as a forerunner of *Abie's Irish Rose.* Jacob Ladoffski (Carr), a rich New Orleans Jew, adopts a waif and raises her as his daughter Lou. A cheery man-about-town, Nixon Holmes (Granville), would marry her. (The *Tribune* couldn't resist advising its readers to translate the gay blade's name as "Nix-on-homes.") But Jacob has planned to marry Lou to Jack Konkarney, the son of a friendly Irish political boss. With the help of Lou's "chaperon," Jennie Wimp (Miss Tucker), love wins the day. Both Miss Tucker and Carr had show-stoppers. Carr won applause with the sentimental "My Rose Of The Ghetto," while Miss Tucker brought down the house each night with a foot-stomping spoof of underworld dancing, "The Puritan Prance." *Louisiana Lou* played joyously on at the La Salle well into the new year.

Bothwell Browne, a female impersonator from the vaudeville circuits, looked to cash in on Julian Eltinge's legitimate vogue with a vehicle entitled **Miss Jack** (9-4-11, Herald Square). Jack Hayward visits a girls' seminary to see his sweetheart and finds he must disguise himself as one of the girls to avoid some awkward situations. The book was so clumsily constructed that what little plot there was had been done away with by the end of the second act, leaving the whole third act to a series of Browne's vaudeville specialties, particularly his "Egyptian" dances. Two weeks and *Miss Jack* departed.

One reason for its swift exit may have been that Julian Eltinge himself arrived a week later in **The Fascinating Widow** (9-11-11, Liberty). Eltinge was probably the greatest of our female impersonators. His "women" were never offensive burlesques, never the blatant drag queens that Bert Savoy and his followers foisted on their audiences. Taste and restraint marked every Eltinge impersonation. In **The Fascinating Widow** Eltinge played Hal Blake, Margaret Leffingwell's suitor. When Oswald Wenworth (Cyril Chadwick), an effeminate fop, forces his attentions on Margaret (Winona Winter), Hal attacks him. To avoid repercussions Hal disguises himself as a "Mrs. Monte" and hides in a girls' dormitory. He is compelled to silence the Reverend Watts (Charles W. Butler) and Detective Bulger (James E. Sullivan) with compromising photographs after they discover Mrs. Monte smoking a pipe. He allows Wentworth to court him and then exposes him as a two-timer. *Theatre Arts* assured its readers, "The comedy is more consistent in *The Fascinating Widow* than is usual in musical plays." And there were kind words for Kerry Mills' lilting score. The show failed to equal the success it had enjoyed in Chicago and on the road, but its seven-week run was still considered satisfactory.

There seems to have been little that was satisfactory about **When Sweet Sixteen** (9-14-11, Daly's). The show was ill-fated from the start. Originally announced in 1908 as "a song play" called *Victoria*, then renamed *Sweet Sixteen*, the show was at one time or another optioned by several producers, one of whom, Lew Fields, even saw it through five weeks of rehearsal before dropping it in discouragement. Harry J. Everall and Samuel H. Wallach (operating as the Ever-Wall Co.) finally brought it to New York after a long road tour that might have been a total disaster but for a cordial reception and successful run in Chicago. There Percy Hammond noted the "Sweet Sixteen" of the title "must come from [the sixteen numbers in Victor] Herbert's score, since there was no other excuse for it." In George V. Hobart's book *nouveau-riche* Mrs. Hammond (Josie Intropidi), to secure herself a place in society, demands that her daughter, Victoria (Harriet Standon), marry the Laird of Loch Lomond. Mr. Hammond (Frank Belcher) wants Victoria to marry his old friend, Jefferson Todd (William Norris). Victoria seemingly goes along with her father—for she loves Todd's secretary, Stanley Morton (Roy Purviance). Stanley and Victoria win the day, and Todd settles for Mrs. Hammond's manicurist. Hammond hinted at the mediocrity of the libretto when later in his review he added, "Theatregoers, it seems, care not who composes the book of musical comedy so long as Victor Herbert writes the music." How like a grab bag of clichés the book was can be seen in the *Dramatic Mirror's* praise, "Josie Intropidi was a joy. Her 'nigger' laugh with the accompanying facial, manual and physical play, and her mimic trombone solo . . . and her drum major jugglery, were the funniest things in the play." Even Herbert was not above throwing in anything that might help the show catch on. At the Hammond's party in the

second act the company sang an extended medley of Herbert favorites, ranging as far back as *The Wizard of the Nile* (11-4-95). Unfortunately, nothing could save their star-crossed evening. *When Sweet Sixteen* ran a mere 12 performances. Among Herbert's works only *The Gold Bug* (9-21-96) had a shorter New York run.

Herbert had a more disheartening failure one month later when his fourth vehicle for Fritzi Scheff, **The Duchess** (10-16-11, Lyric), managed to survive only 24 performances. Like *When Sweet Sixteen*, the show had a long pre-Broadway tour the preceding season and a history of name changes, including *The Rose Shop, Rosita, Mlle. Rosita,* and *Mlle. Boutonière.* It told how foppish Count de Paravante (John E. Hazzard) wants to marry Rose, a florist's daughter, but is proscribed from marrying anyone below a marquise. So Rose agrees to wed an unknown marquis who is leaving for Africa, divorce him, and marry the count. But Rose and Phillipe (George Anderson), the marquis, fall in love, and the count is sent on his way. While the critics divided sharply on the merits of the book, most were in accord in rating Herbert's score pleasant but not outstanding. Its best number was a simple waltz, "Cupid, Tell Me Why." In the course of the evening Miss Scheff changed from the short skirts of the flower girl, to the long gown of the marquise, to a final appearance in a white riding habit. The set for this last scene was contrived to resemble an English hunting print, with "green turf, russet boles of trees, and huntsmen in hunting pink, to say nothing of huntresses in habits of brown and Lincoln green." On opening night Miss Scheff urgently pleaded for patronage, but when it was not forthcoming, the show was hastily returned to the road. There Miss Scheff's temperament created further problems, forcing the musical to close. Herbert was so annoyed that he never again wrote a musical for her.

Three nights after the premiere of *The Duchess*, a third Herbert opus appeared. It was his only successful work of the season. Even though a previous booking forced **The Enchantress** (10-19-11, New York) to close after only 72 performances, it spent three richly rewarding years on post-Broadway tour. Its book by Fred de Gresac (actually Mrs. Victor Maurel, wife of the great French baritone) was unalloyed Graustark. Only Graustark was now called Zergovia, whose minister of war, Ozir (Arthur Forrest), persuades the prima donna, Vivien Savary (Kitty Gordon), to seduce Prince Ivan (Hal Forde). If Ivan marries a commoner, he must abdicate, and Ozir will then govern the country.

Vivien succeeds, but falling in love with Ivan, she forces Ozir to give her the abdication papers, which she destroys. A timely discovery that Vivien has royal blood solves any remaining problem. The critics were happy with the book. They were happy with the star, Miss Gordon (an Englishwoman more famous for her beautiful back than her beautiful voice). They were happier with the sumptuous mounting (the production cost $60,000, although in keeping with a still common practice of the day it had only one set for each act). But they were happiest with Herbert's appropriately enchanting score. They especially praised two of the lovers' duets, "Rose, Lucky Rose," and "One Word From You"; Vivien and Ozir's "All Your Own Am I" (Champagne Song) and the show's loveliest melody, sung by Vivien on her first entrance, "The Land Of My Own Romance," a song still sometimes revived. While the music sounds to us like a typical Herbert score, Herbert himself issued the startling statement, "I believe that one reason why 'The Enchantress' has had so huge a success in New York, and wherever it has played, is that I determined, when I started its composition, to disregard absolutely every foreign impulse and to write in a frank, free American style." The critics agreed. The *Dramatic Mirror* felt the score "typifies American popular music, so far as we can be said to have any type. At least, it is far removed from the sprightly brilliance of the recent Viennese inundation." The *Herald* attempted something of a balance, insisting, "He has written waltzes that would be applauded, even in Vienna, and in addition he has snappy, truly American, dashing march numbers and some graceful dances." In one respect Herbert was unerringly prophetic when he added, "American musical taste has developed to a point where it demands something that is native." His judgment would be vindicated three years later.

Five other shows appeared in the period between the openings of *When Sweet Sixteen* and *The Enchantress*. A Viennese operetta, **The Kiss Waltz** (9-18-11, Casino), with more Kern interpolations, began an 11-week run. A fine cast led by Robert Warwick, Eva Davenport, William Pruette, and Adele Rowland played out the tale of a young Italian composer—creator of "The Kiss Waltz"—who precipitates complications by courting one lady to divert attention from a second, more fervent courtship.

One week later, George M. Cohan had a resounding hit with **The Little Millionaire** (9-25-11, Cohan). But if Cohan had managed to win over the public, he still had very few critics in his corner.

Theatre Magazine blasted it as "the usual Cohan music salad . . . hackneyed nonsense." The *Dramatic Mirror* labeled it, "A Cohan show. Everybody in the United States . . . will understand what that means." Certainly the equivocal statement was fairer to the show than was the magazine's "hackneyed." True, Cohan resorted to many by now familiar patterns—the racy, slangy dialogue; the jingoism; the intratheatrical devices. But by the same token Cohan was tirelessly innovative. For example he assigned the show's hit love song—"Oh, You Wonderful Girl"—to the villain's buddy. As in *Forty-five Minutes from Broadway* (1-1-06), the three-act musical farce had not a single song in its middle act. Sadly, the plot was trite. Henry Spooner (Jerry Cohan) and his son Robert (George) are both to be married in order to fulfill the conditions of the late Mrs. Spooner's will. Bill Costigan (Tom Lewis) and his crony, Roscoe Handover (Sidney Jarvis), unsuccessfully oppose Richard's marriage to Goldie Gray (Lila Rhodes). Henry marries Goldie's aunt, Mrs. Prescott (Nellie Cohan). Just as sad as the trite plot was Cohan's failure to introduce an outstanding song. The score was gay, but not memorable. Cohan compensated by filling the evening with lively dancing. Some, like a flag-waving military drill, were commonplaces both for the time and for Cohan. But he also created several happily "zippy" routines for himself. Most of all he staged the finale—the wedding ceremony—as a "capital pantomime dance." The best man tripped on, followed by the bridesmaids. Then came the bride and groom, "toeing it to the altar." Last, but not least, the jauntily stepping minister appeared. The knot tied, the ensemble celebrated with fervent footwork as the curtain fell. New Yorkers flocked to the Cohan Theatre for 192 performances, making *The Little Millionaire* the biggest American musical hit of the season (always excepting the Hippodrome show).

On September 27 the Shuberts presented **The Revue of Revues** at the Winter Garden. It was a hodgepodge significant only in that it marked the American debut of Gaby Deslys. Her principal moment came in an extended dance-skit "Les Débuts de Chicine," in which she portrayed a little Parisian waif willing to sell herself for stardom. Frank Tinney, in blackface, won many of the best notices for a long comic monologue. Also on the bill was a "Japanese Operetta."

Lew Fields' summer shows—*The Midnight Sons*, (5-22-09), *The Summer Widowers* (6-4-10), and the regular season's *The Hen Pecks* (2-4-11) that grew out of that series—were so successful it was inevitable that a new production would be mounted for 1911–12. **The Never Homes** (10-5-11, Broadway) had fun with the raging feminist movement. Lilydale has been taken over by its women. Young Jimmy Louder (Will Archie), neglected by his political mother, sets fire to his house. Since the firewomen are busy redecorating the firehouse, they have no time to respond to the alarm. "Besides it's sort of damp today, and it wouldn't be good for the horses to go out." All Lilydale burns down. The women are hauled into court, where they are placed in the custody of their children. The men resume running the city. *The Never Homes'* burlesque antecedents were honored by having hefty George W. Monroe play the mayoress. The music by Raymond Hubbell and A. Baldwin Sloane was mediocre, although "There's A Girl In Havana," encored until everybody in the house learned the tune, enjoyed some contemporary fame. The song was sung in the show by Jimmy and his little girl friend, Fannie Hicks—a role assumed by the young girl Fields had favored since she made her debut in his production of *Old Dutch* (11-22-09), Helen Hayes. While the sheet music credited others with its authorship, Irving Berlin is now known to have written the number. The drill work which so often in this period substituted for choreography was well received. But the most striking feature of the evening, as it was in Fields' earlier offerings, was the stunning staging. A real fire engine, its siren howling, darted across the stage. In the first-act finale, Lilydale burned in a stylized fire of gigantic tinsel ribbons waving in red and orange light. When the show ran 92 performances, far fewer than its predecessors, Fields' sensitive antennae should have warned him against continuing the series. Still, two more similar musicals followed. Both were quick failures.

The Duchess followed on the 16th. A cheaply produced version of Franz Lehar's fine **Gypsy Love** opened the next evening at the Globe, but bad reviews deprived it of a run. Marguerite Sylva was starred as Zorika, a wealthy young lady who dreams of marrying the gypsy half-brother of her fiancé, but, in a bittersweet ending, marries her fiancé after all. On the 19th, *The Enchantress* premiered.

Four nights later Lionel Monckton's delightful London musical **The Quaker Girl** (10-23-11, Park) won New York's heart and was awarded the longest run of the season (again ignoring the Hippodrome)—240 performances. *The Quaker Girl's* story flattered audiences in this country by allowing Prudence, its heroine, to be wooed and won by Tony, the dashing American diplomat who had taught her what fun high life can be. Before the final happy ending, Prudence is rejected by her fellow Quakers for drinking champagne and insulted by a jealous actress. Ina Claire and Clifton Crawford were the leads.

November's first entry, Lew Fields' mounting of **The Wife Hunters** (11-2-11, Herald Square), was a reworking of *Three Million Dollars*, which had toured at length the year before but never reached New York. The reworking was no help. A dreary book and weak score sank *The Wife Hunters* after only 36 performances. Its main plot revolved about Reginald Ogden Bruce's efforts to find a wife. Bruce (John Park) discovers that the daughter of his business rival would suit him perfectly. In a comic subplot Emma Carus as Mrs. Homer Van Pelt proves her many prosperous marriages have only enhanced her allure to the wife hunters. Some novel staging had hedges and parts of a log cabin descend from the flies, to be assembled by the chorus as it sang "Mammy Jinny."

About this time a musical version of a beloved comic strip, **Mutt and Jeff,** made some brief appearances at outlying theatres such as the Grand Opera House. In this mounting Mutt and Jeff take a trip to South America and help quell a revolution in Nicadoria. They become rich after Jeff, as a jockey, wins a big race. With their wealth, they help a young man defeat the chewing-gum trust which would seize his chicle plantation, and they briefly take turns as president of the republic. The show received pleasant notices but never braved the main stem. In 1912–13 six companies played one-night stands in small cities and neighborhood houses. Sequels followed, but they too carefully confined their routes to the hinterlands. Still, in 1914–15 five companies of *Mutt and Jeff in Mexico* were on tour.

The Red Widow (11-6-11, Astor), like so many of the season's musicals, came to New York only after an extensive tour that began the preceding season. Its story had Colonel Cicero Hannibal Butts (Raymond Hitchcock), a Yonkers corset-maker, allowing Anna Varvara (Sophie Bernard), would-be assassin of the czar, to use his wife's passport to cross into Russia. The real Mrs. Butts is arrested, and only when Anna falls in love with Captain Basil Romanoff (Theodore Martin) of the Imperial Bodyguard and renounces her old ways are the Butts' problems solved. The book never took itself too seriously, and it was helped immeasurably by the personable Raymond Hitchcock. He made a marvelously comic first entrance onto a stunningly conceived set. It depicted the foyer of a Parisian theatre. Doors leading to the various levels were slightly ajar, and through them one could see a performance on stage. Hitchcock arrived nattily dressed as a playgoer, but immediately dropped the story line to acknowledge his audience's applause with "fifty-nine varieties of smiles and smirks"— a take-off on the falsely humble gratitude of celebrities not unlike a spoof Beatrice Lillie would offer in *High Spirits* (4-7-64) a half-century later. The music, while commonplace, was unfailingly pleasing. The convenience of the Astor also stimulated sales. *The Red Widow* ran 128 performances.

About the time the show was premiering, the November issue of *Theatre Arts* appeared. It noted, "There was one period, not so very remote, when it seemed as if popular interest in comic opera and musical comedy was on the wane. Not so now. 'The Merry Widow' started a renascence." In its review of *The Red Widow* in its December issue, the magazine reiterated its conclusions: "The standard of musical comedy has been so raised of late that it has to be a very good show indeed to hold its own on Broadway." The review felt the new show didn't come up to the mark. Its opinion didn't affect the box office, but its generalizations suggested the increasingly thoughtful attention being given the musical stage. Although the magazine was correct in appreciating the higher senses of style and tone *The Merry Widow* (10-21-07) displayed for all who were ready to learn, it ignored the immediate debilitating effect it produced on native creativity. Not all publications were quite so insensitive to this point.

The Three Romeos (11-13-11, Globe) detailed the efforts of Dick Dawson (Alfred Kappeler), Bertie Montague (Edward Alfino), and Jack Willoughby (Fritz Williams) to find wives, when, for example, Jack loves Rosie Bellamy (Vivian Rushmore), but Rosie loves Bertie. R. H. Burnside (of the Hippodrome) was responsible for the book and lyrics, while Raymond Hubbell (later of the Hippodrome) did the music. Everything about the show was mediocre, and it lasted only 56 performances.

Vera Violetta, which the Shuberts brought into the Winter Garden on November 20, was the major offering on a three-part bill. A brief vaudeville preceded it, and *Undine,* a one-act vehicle by Manuel Klein for the swimmer-showgirl, Annette Kellerman, comprised the remaining item. As far as *Vera Violetta* was concerned, Harold Atteridge and Leonard Liebling were only minimally faithful to Louis Stein's original. The story recounted the hot water a professor's wife finds herself in after she flirts with the husband of the professor's old flame. Neither woman was Vera Violetta; that was the name of the professor's wife's irresistible perfume and of a waltz sung in its honor. Much of Edmund Eysler's music also gave way to domestic interpolations. The Shuberts breathed a sigh of relief when Gaby Deslys not only knew her lines but enunciated with something approaching clarity. Her difficulties with English had caused problems almost nightly in *The Revue of Revues.* She and Harry Pilcer stopped the show each evening with "The Gaby Glide," for which Louis Hirsch composed the air and Pilcer provided the words. José Collins also had a showstopper in "Ta-Ra-Ra-Boom-Der-E." The song had been made famous by her mother, Lottie Collins. Opening night, the young Miss Collins' nerves were so on edge, she couldn't remember the lyrics, so the conductor had to prompt her audibly. But the center of attention was Al Jolson. He portrayed a blackface waiter who burst into song at the slightest excuse. In *Vera Violetta* Jolson confirmed that the unique incandescence with which he had lit up the same house in *La Belle Paree* was no one-shot freak. The repeated encores he was called on to sing with "Rum Tum Tiddle" (Edward Madden/Jean Schwartz) and George M. Cohan's "That Haunting Melody" were the prelude to fifteen years as Broadway's biggest drawing card. With Jolson leading the way *Vera Violetta* recorded 112 showings.

Two importations followed. Henri Bereny's **Little Boy Blue** (11-27-11, Lyric) was a twenty-two week success; Leslie Stuart's **Peggy,** a quick failure. In the former a barmaid hears that a Scottish lord is seeking his lost heir, so she dresses up as a boy and stakes her claim. Gertrude Bryan played the barmaid, with Otis Harlan and Maude Odell sparking the comedy. Peggy also is a poor girl—a manicurist at a fashionable London hotel—who stumbles into marriage with a high-born Englishman. Renée Kelly, Farren Souter, and Harry Fisher played leading roles.

The critics found more to admire in **Betsy** (12-11-11, Herald Square) than did the public, who bought tickets in such small numbers the show was withdrawn after four weeks. Admittedly the plotline had been used before. Its story seemed a rewrite of *The Duchess* with a suggestion or two from *The Little Millionaire,* although it was actually based on an older play, Kitty Chambers' 1909 failure, *An American Widow.* By the terms of her husband's will, the widowed Mrs. Killigrew (Grace La Rue) will lose her inheritance if she remarries anyone but an American. She marries Jasper Mallory (Robert Dempster), intending to divorce him and marry a titled Englishman (Alfred Deery). But she falls in love with Jasper and sends the earl on his way. What most pleased reviewers was the sense of tone and balance the evening evidenced, "a little play with music when it is needed . . . and dancing when something in the action can be better expressed in that way." Such virtues were too subtle to have general appeal.

Reginald De Koven once more tried and failed, this time with **The Wedding Trip** (12-25-11, Knickerbocker). His music was not unlikable, but forever missed that indefinable extra touch that would allow it to soar above the ordinary. On opening night only one song—Aza's "Soldier's Song"—earned three encores. De Gresac and Smith, who had worked together with Herbert on *The Enchantress,* could not overcome the drawbacks in the score. In fact, without Herbert's melodic genius to gloss over the shortcomings, the book and lyrics seemed more leadenly Graustarkian than de Gresac and Smith's earlier effort. Fritzi (Christine Nielson) no sooner marries Felix (John McCloskey) than he must take the place of his twin brother, François, who has deserted the army. All of François' old flames pursue Felix, but he remains faithful. When he reveals the substitution he is condemned to be shot, until a kiss by the Gypsy, Aza (Dorothy Jardon), melts his stern commanding officer. *The Wedding Trip* was 1911's final musical. It barely survived into the new year.

Nor did 1912 get off to an auspicious start. Its first night saw Jean Gilbert's **Modest Suzanne** at the Liberty. The importation about a young lady from Tours who works her way up in Paris could not make it through the month.

But the tide turned one week later, when Eddie Foy romped in with **Over the River** (1-8-12, Globe). Although it was based on Souchet's 1897 hit, *The Man from Mexico,* little of the story was retained. The plot concerned the problems of a man who must serve time in jail. Too ashamed to confess the truth to his wife, he pretends he is going on a trip to Mexico. His spouse's charity work leads her to his cell. Essentially a glorified vaudeville by the time Dillingham and Ziegfeld mounted it, with Maud Lambert and Lillian Lorraine prominent among the performers, it advertised "Real Cabaret on Stage" and did somehow contrive to set much of the action at Louis Martin's (read Sherry's). On opening night Fritzi Scheff and Geraldine Farrar were discovered among the on-stage patrons, and thereafter actresses impersonating The Red Widow and The Pink Lady were seated conspicuously among the guests. Much of the evening was given to dancing that ranged from "Turkey Trot to Tango." Specialty dancers, "The Marvelous Millers," "whirl and whirl and whirl," while composer Jean Schwartz played the piano as Lillian Lorraine and the chorus pranced through his "Chop Stick Rag." The show delighted seekers of good, light entertainment for four months, then toured.

Two more shows arrived in January. Both opened on the 22nd, and both closed after three weeks. One was an American version of Berte's *Kroelenblut,* called **The Rose of Panama** at Daly's. In the American retelling a Central American president prefers his romance to his position, so arranges for a coup to oust him. The other was a home-grown piece at the New York entitled **The Pearl Maiden.** Its story was a model of a type just going out of style. Pinkerton Kerr (Jefferson De Angelis), U.S. Consul on Mona Island, sells the Sharpe brothers (Charles J. Stine and Richard Taber) a bogus pearl bed in exchange for a yacht on which he hopes to flee with Nadine (Flora Zabelle), the pearl maiden. In the end the Sharpes are forgiving. The critics complained that the plot, tattered to begin with, was pushed beyond recognition by all sorts of extraneous additions. Their kindest words were reserved for Harry Auracher's music. None of it proved enduring. A decade passed before the composer, his name Americanized to Archer, had his lone smash success.

For many the most emotional event of the season was Weber and Fields' Jubilee on February 8, reuniting the long-estranged clowns in a bill not unlike their lovingly remembered annuals. Their old, tiny music hall was gone, so the reunion was staged at the larger Broadway ten blocks north. Besides the stars, most of the old crew was present—William Collier, John T. Kelly, Frankie Bailey, Fay Templeton, and the still entrancing Lillian Russell. Missing were the witty, congenial Peter F. Dailey, dead three years since, and David Warfield, by 1912 Belasco's top dramatic actor and playing to packed houses in *The Return of Peter Grimm.* Warfield rushed through his evening's performance and made a tear-filled surprise appearance toward the end of the opening night. The evening was given a typically nonsensical Weber and Fields monicker, **Hokey-pokey.** In the slight plot, millionaire Jeremiah McCann (Kelly) brings his daughter (Helena Collier Garrick) to Paris to finish her education. Michael Dillpickle (Weber) and Meyer Bockheister (Fields) are there to provide complications. One routine found Meyer and Mike about to enter a bar with only a nickel between them. Meyer arranges with Mike to demur when he asks if Mike wants anything, but everytime they go to order Mike forgets and requests a nickel cigar. Meyer keeps dragging Mike out to explain the plan and Mike keeps forgetting. Lillian Russell made her first appearance of the evening in a bejeweled pink gown to revive "Come Down, Ma Evenin' Star." The year's sensational hit comedy, *Bunty Pulls the Strings,* was selected for the burlesque, and distorted, although not beyond recognition, as *Bunty, Bulls and Strings.* The entire overture was devoted to a John Stromberg medley. More old Stromberg tunes were sung in the course of the evening, supplemented by new tunes from A. Baldwin Sloane and W. T. Francis. The show was joyously received and had a profitable three-month run. It held out hope that a great tradition had not permanently disappeared.

Heuberger's exquisite **The Opera Ball** (2-12-12, Liberty) was February's only musical. While Sydney Rosenfeld and Clare Kummer, both clever redactors, provided the American version of the libretto, miscastings and a generally slipshod mounting confined the run to four weeks. Marie Cahill made a wild knock-about farce out of the principal role of a captivating widow determined to flirt with all the men at the ball. Harry Conor abetted her in her antics. It was funny, but wrong.

As soon as *Vera Violetta* closed, the Shuberts rushed Jolson, now obviously their top ticket-seller, into another Winter Garden bill on March 5. Opening the three-part evening was *A Night with the Pierrots.* A gigantic ramp led from the rear of the house to the stage, and the cast, mostly in white masks, made its entrance running from the back to the footlights. A similar entrance had been used two months before in Max Reinhardt's *Sumurun,* so one of the first businesses of the evening was a ragtime burlesque of that wordless play. The burlesque included a "Ragtime Sextet" (based on *Lucia di Lammermoor*) with Jolson and José Collins among the singers, and ended with Blossom Seeley inviting the rest of the cast to join in one by one, "Toddling The Todolo." The evening concluded with a pretentious "operatic mimodrama," *Sesostra.* In between, the main part of the evening was **Whirl of Society.** The show had a thread of a plot centering on a party that Mrs. Dean (Stella Mayhew) throws. As Mrs. Dean's blackface servant, Gus, Jolson made his first appearance as a character he would portray for most of his stage career. But despite its modest story line, *Whirl of Society* was basically a revue. Louis Hirsch's score and what became Jolson's inevitable interpolations were lively enough, but none became standards.

While superb entertainers filled the cast, everyone knew who was the star. The same month *Whirl of Society* opened, *Variety* proclaimed, "The Shuberts may run the Winter Garden, but Al Jolson owns it." He most certainly owned it the next four months.

An importation, Felix Albini's **Baron Trenck** (3-11-12, Casino) lasted five weeks. The baron is a daredevil soldier in the wars between Maria Teresa and Frederick the Great. He is ordered by the Empress to find a wife. The operetta was followed three nights later by the first of a batch of revivals which suggested both the inadequacy of the new domestic offerings and beginnings of an awareness of the possibilities of an American musical repertory. The initial revival was Cohan's six-year-old *Forty-five Minutes from Broadway* (1-1-06). The same *Dramatic Mirror* which earlier had dismissed *The Little Millionaire* with condescending evasions warmly embraced the musical, rejoicing it had "stood the test of revival so staunchly," adding, "It was good to hear the old songs again . . . for they belong to a very popular class of musical Americana."

Five new musicals, brought in with an eye to the warm weather business, followed. **The Man from Cook's,** which opened on March 25, had more Raymond Hubbell music, coupled this time to a Henry Blossom libretto. In it Prince Victor (Walter Percival) disguises himself as a Cook's agent to woo Marjorie Benton (Stella Hoban). Marjorie is betrothed to Lord Baffington, whom she has never seen, so Victor persuades Toto Soulard (Fred Walton) to impersonate the Lord, insult Marjorie's mother and allow Victor to come to her rescue. When the real Baffington (Leslie Kenyon) appears, Victor employs a second friend to impersonate an equally offensive Marjorie. Victor and Marjorie wed. What possibilities the book may have had in proper hands will never be known. By the time the musical reached New York, it had been largely displaced by a spate of interpolated specialties. These included a mandolin and guitar band and a long-legged, eccentric dancer, Eleanor Pendleton. It was this very sort of irresponsible slapdash that the *Dramatic Mirror* discussed a week later in an article examining how seriously film competition was hurting musical comedy. The problem was no the excellence of the new movies, but the tired ma terial and tacky productions presented to the pub lic: "The jokes are pretty musty; the stage Dutchman, Irishman and Jew have been used too long to be funny; the rag-time songs go stale with repetition, and so it is that this form of amusement is being backed off the boards in much the same fashion that melodramas were relegated to the junkpile." It also blamed composers like Hubbell, who poured out "trite forms of thrashed over melodies which run current in the decadent musical comedies on Broadway." The tradepaper further complained, "orchestras now consist, in most cities, of one or two violins, a viola, a flute, a clarinet, a cornet, a trombone, a piano, a double bass and a vast array of instruments of percussion. The sounds . . . are inexpressibly disagreeable."

Another plot got lost in **A Winsome Widow** (4-11-12, Moulin Rouge), a revision of Charles Hoyt's once popular *A Trip to Chinatown* (11-9-91). It, too, became little more than a series of vaudeville turns although, curiously, the part of Wilder Daly, eliminated in the original, was restored. What raised it above the level of ordinary hot weather fare was Ziegfeld's impeccable flair. The production was gorgeous. One number drew particular praise. Set in an ice palace, it had the Ziegfeld beauties skate in the bright sunlight, through the sunset, and finally out into a moonlit auditorium. Hubbell offered his second score in just over two weeks. It was another pastiche of trifling pleasantries. Several equally trifling, equally pleasant interpolations came from John Golden, Jerome Kern, Nat D. Ayer, Jean Schwartz, and a few minor names. One of these, "Be My Little Baby Bumble Bee" (Stanley Murphy/Henry I. Marshall) has retained sufficient appeal to enjoy occasional revivals. Ziegfeld filled the cast with sparkling, young talent: Emmy Wehlen, the Dolly Sisters, Elizabeth Brice, Charles King (who played the resurrected Daly), Frank Tinney, and Leon Errol. Mae West attracted the critics' attention for the first time. The show ran into September.

Four nights later Karl Hoschna's last score was introduced posthumously in **The Wall Street Girl** (4-15-12, Cohan). It was a good score, and gave the show's star, Blanche Ring, a song she would use for the rest of her career, "I Want A Regular Man." Ayer, Schwartz, and several others filled in the gaps Hoschna had left, but their material was patently inferior to Hoschna's. Miss Ring played Jamina Greene, a Wall Street "brokeress," who saves her father from financial ruin with the profits she earns from her half-interest in a controversial Nevada mine. She marries her partner, Dexter Barton (W. P. Carleton). Again, there was bright, up-and-coming talent in the supporting roles, with acclaim going to Charles Winninger and, especially, Will Rogers. His lariat act ("It's a pretty knot, is it not?"), surprisingly appropriate to the plot, stopped the show. Margaret Mayo and Edgar

Selwyn's book was more than competent. But the show was not a resounding hit, lasting only seven weeks.

Two importations followed in short order. **The Rose Maid** arrived at the Globe April 22. When his debts are called in just before his wedding, a Duke finds himself deserted by his friends and even his bride-to-be. Only a little flower girl remains loyal. A third-rate piece, beautifully done, it was a hit, running twenty-two weeks. The show's strong band of comedians joined Edward Gallagher and Al Shean for the first time. **Two Little Brides** (4-23-12, Casino) played 63 times. In a way, the evening was more a domestic than a foreign creation, since the original score was entirely discarded and a new one by Gustave Kerker (his last for Broadway) substituted. Similarly only the outline of the original story was retained. It provided a vehicle for James T. Powers. As Polycarp Ivanovitch, he and a friend are caught talking with two students at a ladies' seminary. A local law decrees that under such circumstances the men must marry the girls.

The same night *The Rose Maid* premiered in New York, Philadelphia welcomed what proved to be Willard Spenser's last musical. **The Wild Goose** of the show at that city's Lyric Theatre was actually Princess Violet (Ethel Jackson). Her unconventional behavior while exiled in America earned her the nickname. But when it came to romance she proved conventional indeed, choosing Dick (David Reese), a handsome yachtsman, over Turnips (Will Philbrick), a cornball farmer. Although *The Wild Goose* was not nearly as successful as Spenser's earlier efforts, running only one month, it sent Philadelphians out of the theatre singing "Moon! Moon! Mooney Spooney Moon!" and a waltz played as a motif throughout the evening, "Your Dream Love."

In May the parade of revivals began in earnest. William Brady and the Shuberts presented an all-star cast (De Wolf Hopper, Christine Nielson, and Eugene Cowles) in *Patience* on May 6. The same night *Robin Hood* relit the New Amsterdam. Its cast included one old Bostonian, George Frothingham. *Robin Hood* ran two months, *Patience* ran one month. The shorter run reflected no lack of popularity. Rather Brady had meanwhile prepared *The Pirates of Penzance,* with much the same cast. It opened at the Casino June 3 and, like *Patience,* had a limited engagement.

Only one new show appeared during this time, **Mama's Baby Boy** (5-25-12, Broadway). Junie McCree adapted it from David Edwyn and George

Fletcher's *Ma's New Husband* which, in turn, was little more than a hasty rehash of Pinero's *The Magistrate*. To effect a second marriage, a woman lies about her age and, as a result, must deny her full-grown son. He poses as a cook. This imposture allowed a second act "kitchen cabaret" in which the cast performed their vaudeville specialties. On opening night Lew Dockstader and Elizabeth Murray made guest appearances in this scene, and Al Jolson hurried down from the Winter Garden to sing songs from *Whirl of Society*. But a brief Jolson appearance was not enough to save a dismal evening. The show lasted one week.

The season brought to light the growing malaise in the world of musical comedy. At times this was manifest by a clear demand for new standards; at times by a confusion of standards. In a long article on the front page of its May 29 issue, the *Dramatic Mirror* attempted to analyze the problem. Although it missed completely the debilitating effects of our reliance on Vienna, and betrayed a certain illogicality, it nonetheless put a finger on some salient points:

"One lesson stands out with amazing clearness as a result of the season's record in musical comedy. Up to the brilliant revivals at the close of the season only two, possibly three, productions of this class can be set down as genuine Broadway successes, although one or two others were forced into respectable runs.

"The interesting point is that not a single operetta or musical comedy of the real Viennese style has amounted to much—possibly excepting the last one to be produced [*The Rose Maid*]. Further the success of the musical entertainments appears to have been in inverse ratio to the tampering and rearrangements to which they had been subjected by the American managers. Simplicity of effect, studied, perhaps, has hit the public fancy, as a natural reaction from garish ostentation.

"Beyond this, demand for eccentric comedy has largely been converted into a demand for adequate singing. The failure of the operetta [*Gypsy Love*] that had far and away the best score among the new productions is ascribed by every commentator to the superlatively inane comedy injected into it for the benefit of American patrons.

"If producers are as eager to learn from experiment as they assert, we ought to have a season of really artistic musical comedies next year. Simple, straightforward plot, capable singers, light, tasteful comedy and easy romance are the elements that have won favor lately. Long may they flourish!"

1912–1913

The poor showing of the 1911–12 season made producers doubly cautious. As a result they brought in fewer offerings (only two dozen new Americans mountings and eight new importations, but many of the pieces they did present showed a marked improvement in quality. They also relied heavily on revivals. *H.M.S. Pinafore* and *The Mikado* concluded the string of Gilbert and Sullivan revivals the Shuberts and William A. Brady had begun at the end of the preceding year. Although each was given only two performances, both were enthusiastically received by the press and the public, and both were returned for brief runs in the spring, when *Iolanthe* was performed as well.

The Shuberts offered the season's first new musical on July 22, **The Passing Show of 1912.** Apart from its title, it bore no connection with *The Passing Show* (5-12-94) George Lederer had produced at the Casino eighteen years before. But Broadway's smart money knew of another connection. The Shuberts were consummate businessmen. The risks of innovation were normally too prohibitive for them, but they were quick to follow trends and capitalize on them. They could not ignore the growing success and fame of the *Follies*. Nor, given their vindictive natures, could they forgive Ziegfeld's close ties with Klaw and Erlanger. Apart from this rivalry, a summer annual could assure the success of their flagship, the Winter Garden, while Jolson was on vacation. One lucky break helped in the series' inauguration. *A Winsome Widow* was so successful at the Moulin Rouge that Ziegfeld decided to leave it there for the summer and delay a new *Follies* until the fall. For the moment, then, the Shuberts had the field to themselves. *The Passing Show of 1912* was in two parts. The first was a "mime-dramatic ballet," "The Ballet of 1830." Mounted originally at London's Alhambra, it told of love among Paris artists. It wasn't particularly high-toned, but it had fun pretending it was. The real fun, the meat of the evening, came in the second part. From its inception *The Passing Show* remained closer to the old Weber and Fields tradition than the *Follies* did. Like the *Follies*—and like Weber and Fields, although it is often forgotten—there was always a line of beautiful girls in attractive, sometimes provocative, costumes. There were elegant sets, too, notably an ocean liner, a harem scene (filled with bathing girls), and an elaborate ragtime wedding scene. But unlike Ziegfeld's revues, the comedy in *The Passing Show* time and again came from burlesquing current shows. It was not the sustained spoof of a single Broadway hit in Weber and Fields' manner, but shorter parodies, of a sort later revues employed until they faded from the theatre scene. For their initial edition the brothers assembled an impressive array of young talent: Charlotte Greenwood (and her sometime partner, Sidney Grant), Anna Wheaton, Trixie Friganza, Jobyna Howland, Harry Fox, and Eugene and Willie Howard.

. . .

Willie and **Eugene Howard** were born in Germany, sons of a Jewish cantor. Their real family name was Levkowitz. The elder Levkowitzes emigrated from Germany in 1887, when Willie, the younger of the brothers, was a year old. Willie made his debut in vaudeville thirteen years later as a boy soprano. For a short while he was a song-plugger for Witmark. His entry into the legitimate theatre was to have been in an Anna Held show, but his voice changed while the show was in rehearsal and he was fired. In 1903 he joined his brother, always the better singer and thereafter usually the straight-man, in a vaudeville act. But the shorter, sad-faced Willie was always recognized as the better of the two.

. . .

When the cast of *The Passing Show* was not mocking *Bought and Paid For, Bunty Pulls the Strings, Officer 666, The Quaker Girl,* and *The Return of Peter Grimm,* it was singing songs from Louis Hirsch's score or interpolations by Earl Carroll, Harry Orlob, and Irving Berlin. A run of 136 performances was more than enough to convince the Shuberts their new entry could be a bona-fide annual.

As if to suggest there was some curious, inarticulated influence between the Shuberts and Weber and Fields, Lew Fields styled his latest entry "A Jumble of Jollification" (much as the first Winter Garden attraction had been called "A Jumble of Jollity"). The musical's title, **Hanky-Panky** (8-5-12, Broadway), connected it squarely with the old music hall tradition. But instead of Weber and Fields sparking the fun, Bobby North and Weber and Fields' old rival, Max Rogers, clowned as Herman Bierheister and Wilhelm Rausmitt in a series of misadventures that included another attempt—as in *Hurly-Burly* (9-8-98)—to resuscitate Cleopatra's mummy. A. Baldwin Sloane's score was never more than satisfactory. Interpolations included Ir-

ving Berlin's "Opera Burlesque," "Oh, You Circus Day" (Edith Maida Lessing/Jimmy Monaco), and the already popular "On The Mississippi" (Ballard MacDonald/Harry Carroll). The show ran three months.

The Girl from Montmartre opened at the Criterion the same night as *Hanky-Panky.* Harry B. Smith adapted it from *The Girl from Maxim's,* cutting it to fit the talents of Richard Carle and Hattie Williams. Carle as Dr. Pepyton initiates a series of comic misconstructions by allowing a show girl (Miss Williams) to sleep in his bed. Jerome Kern and Henry Bereny supplied it with a pleasing, inconsequential score, the best number of which was Kern's "Don't Turn My Picture To The Wall." At least one song from *The Arcadians* ("Half Past Two") was also added. The show ran eight weeks and toured.

Chicago's most popular musical comedy performers, Cecil Lean and Florence Holbrook, co-starred in a new musical at that city's Ziegfeld Theatre on August 11. Apparently unable to find satisfactory material elsewhere, Lean himself wrote the show. **The Military Girl** had a simple plot, virtually identical to one Hough and Adams employed for *The Golden Girl* (3-16-09). Its heroine, Ione Field, must choose between two cadets; a rich, fat one her parents favor and a poor, thin young man. Naturally by curtain time she selects "Slim." If Lean was not much of a librettist he was even less of a composer. He prudently supplemented his own material with songs from *Florodora* (11-12-00) and several George M. Cohan shows. Lean and Holbrook were popular enough to win the show a modest run for all its weaknesses.

Die Fledermaus, disguised as **The Merry Countess,** began a four-month run in New York on August 20. Besides praising the show, several critics commented happily on its steadfast refusal to allow encores. The incessant repetition of hit tunes, or of songs producers hoped would become hits, had long been a recurring irritant, and, unfortunately, the practice continued.

Two shows competed to close out August on the 31st. At the old Academy of Music a thrown-together revue called **The Girl from Brighton** ran until almost midnight. It pranced through its turns 49 times. At the Hippodrome **Under Many Flags** began a 445-performance run. Its frame-plot followed the flight of Captain Alan Strong from the White House lawn around the world. It filled the vast stage with the canals and tulip fields of Holland, Far Eastern temples, and a gigantic silver fountain. Manuel Klein's score had a somewhat greater contemporary vogue than Hippodrome scores customarily enjoyed, but nothing survived this short-lived popularity.

The Girl at the Gate, the biggest hit of Chicago's season, opened at the La Salle on September 1. Its success was such that while the first company was enjoying a six-month run, a second troupe was sent out to entertain the rest of the Midwest. Neither contingent ever got closer to New York than Philadelphia. The show's bucolic title was deceptive. Its story was one of treachery and international intrigue. Will M. Hough and Frederick Donaghey's book was set in the installations surrounding the new Panama Canal. Normal Beane was expelled from West Point after he covered up the cheating of Tiffany Price, the brother of his sweetheart, Madelaine. Tiffany becomes the captain of the Engineers in Panama while Normal roams the world in disgrace. The two meet again just as Tiffany carelessly allows a beautiful Japanese spy— a young lady he believes loves him—to steal the plans for the canal's fortifications. Beane retrieves the plans, restores everyone's good name and marries Madelaine. The show's dialogue betrayed many of the prejudices of the day:

Stawl: They're bright alright but they don't remain servants! There's only one thing worse than a Jap!
Tiffany: What's that?
Stawl: Another Jap.

At one point the stage directions call for a Japanese to be "Cringingly humble." Much of the dialogue fell back on old vaudeville material:

Guest: Where is that half portion of chicken I ordered?
Coyne: We're waiting for someone to order the other half. We can't kill half a bird.

The lovers' dialogue was often discouragingly stilted:

Normal: Miss Price, I'm compelled to ask a favor. I'm sure you'll grant it.
Madelaine: A man with nothing to lose is always an optimist.
Normal: I know that I couldn't present you with a drink of water in the Sahara Desert; but what I've got to ask is not to benefit me.

Ben Jerome's score was serviceable. *The Girl at the Gate* was virtually the last major musical written with Chicago in mind. A half-dozen or so appeared each season for the next few years, and every year one or two were considered good enough to bring

east. But most had very brief runs. Their failures dissuaded producers from considering Chicago as an independent production center.

A number of "made-in-Chicago" shows played that city's Colonial Theatre during the 1912–13 season. They were burlesques almost in the Weber and Fields tradition. For example, *Madame X* was mounted as *Madame Excuse Me*. It was followed by *The Merry Widow Remarried*.

Clifton Crawford wrote some of the songs for **My Best Girl** (9-12-12, Park), in which he starred in New York. Its plot was reminiscent of *The Wedding Trip* (12-25-11). Richard Venderfleet takes the place of an army deserter, serves the deserter's time, and finds a girl. The army background gave a certain legitimacy to the chorus' snappy military drills, while Crawford provided some interesting contrasts with his delightfully languid solos. Both the book and the score offered slim pickings, but Crawford was enough of an attraction to keep the show playing eight weeks.

On September 16 **The Count of Luxembourg** made its debut at the New Amsterdam, the same house at which *The Merry Widow* once had waltzed. *The Count of Luxembourg* was the first of three Franz Lehar operettas rushed in during the 1912–13 season. The operetta was the sole success of the trio. Its tale of a marriage of convenience that becomes a marriage of love was studded with memorable melodies, notably the waltz translated as "Say Not Love Is A Dream." Ann Swinburne and George L. Moore sang the lovers, while Frank Moulan clowned. **Eva,** famous only for a single waltz, followed at the same theatre on December 30. It was poorly received and lingered only three weeks. The evening featured Sallie Fisher as an apprentice in a glass factory, wooed and won by the factory's young heir. **The Man with Three Wives** opened at the new Weber and Fields Theatre on January 23 and fared just a bit better.

The season's longest regular run was 248 performances; the show was **Oh! Oh! Delphine** (9-30-12, Knickerbocker), C. M. S. McLellan's adaptation of the French farce *Villa Primrose*, with music by Ivan Caryll. Posterity has not concurred with the contemporary judgment of the show, which hailed it as a worthy successor to the team's *The Pink Lady* (3-13-11). The plot was much the same French froth; but it was beguilingly handled, with a tongue-in-cheek naughtiness. The action was set in Brest, at a hotel where reserve officers on their yearly tour of duty house their wives and mistresses. Victor Jobileau (Scott Welsh) arrives with so many girls he is suspected of being "the Mormon of the house." Victor is separated from his wife, Delphine (Grace Edmond). Their friends Alphonse (Frank McIntyre) and Simone Bouchette (Stella Hoban) have fallen out of love. While Bouchette has brought along a Persian girl as mistress, the four principals agree to change partners. When rich Uncle Noel (George A. Beane) appears, they are forced to resume their original pairing, lest he disinherit them. They find they like this old way best, after all. The book was filled with "cute" touches. Delphine takes her parrot wherever she goes. The parrot is forever speaking out the show's title as a warning to his lady—even injecting it into the title song. When Bouchette attempts to pass off the Persian, Bimboula (Octavia Broske), as his wife, he warns the French commander, "She speaks no English." McLellan's lyrics were often droll. Early in the evening Victor, an artist by profession, tells philistines that ladies supply his afflatus. He employs so arcane a word, he sings, "to scare 'em," adding the dolts construe it as "Latin for harem." If the book was as well written as *The Pink Lady,* the evening nonetheless lacked two magical ingredients of the earlier hit: Hazel Dawn and a great waltz. The best Caryll could do this time around was "The Venus Waltz." In the hopes of establishing it as another "My Beautiful Lady," it was played, as one critic rued, "ad nauseum." (How swiftly the lesson of *The Merry Countess* was forgotten!) But it was patently inferior.

Tantalizing Tommy (10-1-12, Criterion), which the captivating Marie Lohr had made into a London hit, told of a rich candy-manufacturer's daughter who learns she cannot buy love. Unfortunately Miss Lohr remained behind in England. Deprived of her talents, the musical floundered after 31 performances.

The following night another musical destined for quick oblivion came from the opposite direction. **The Charity Girl** (10-2-12, Globe) had opened in Chicago in July and promptly created a furor. It created an uproar, of somewhat smaller proportions, in New York. There were some who thought the story was not fit for musical treatment, relating, as it did, the story of a young heiress (Marie Flynn) who gives up her comforts to do charity work in the slums. But the story was treated frivolously, in the musical comedy fashion of the day, so that much of young Rosemary's adventures revolved around a comic clairvoyant (Ralph Herz). Some idea of the show's general attitude can be gauged from the joyously syncopated song and dance Blossom Seeley and Henry Fink did as "The Ghetto Glide." Victor Hollaender's score would have been unexceptional, but for a single number. And to that number not only many critics but the police in both Chicago and New York took strenuous exception. Although the period still flaunted its rugged individualism and ill-concealed contempt for people on the dole, its moral hypocrisy demanded an outcry against any lady of the streets who would sing "I'd Rather Be A Chippie Than A Charity Bum." But the song's notoriety was not sufficient to make an otherwise somewhat feeble show into a hit. *The Charity Girl* ran two and a half weeks.

Edmund Eysler's **The Woman Haters** (10-7-12, Astor) quickly closed. During its brief stay it followed the downfall of a German major who quarrels with a widow he is about to marry, swears off all women, and forms a woman haters' club. The widow has a club that holds its meetings at the same restaurant.

Two weeks later, on the 21st, the long delayed **Ziegfeld Follies of 1912** appeared at the Moulin Rouge. It is remembered today largely for one interpolation, "Row, Row, Row" (William Jerome/ Jimmy Monaco), sung by Lillian Lorraine. But first-nighters found much more to applaud. Foremost were the beautiful girls, lavishly bedecked. The *Times* reported that in "The Palace Of Beauties," "The audience gasped . . . at the first figure to enter—a harlequin in complete attire of black lace." Venus, Carmen, and Joan of Arc followed. A finale in a circus tent had the "pony" chorus racing around the ring in tarlatan ballet dresses, while Lillian Lorraine, representing the 20th-Century Girl, paraded in a lemon-colored dress with a flaming orange cape and a black headpiece. Leon Errol and Bert Williams again led the clowns. Williams introduced three sorrowfully comic songs, "My Landlady," "You're On The Right Road But You're Going The Wrong Way," and "Blackberrying Today." He combined with Errol in a hilarious taxicab number. The broken-down hack was one Williams reportedly found and bought from a Central Park driver. In the skit he played a forlorn cabbie caught between his impatient, nervous customer (Errol) and a stage horse that sat down, crossed its legs and refused to budge. Bernard Granville came over from the Shuberts to sing the straight tunes. The *Follies* were not, as some detractors have claimed, ponderous, slow-moving affairs whose comic numbers were inserted to allow the girls to change costumes. Harry B. Smith, who bid farewell to the show with this edition, observed,

"The Follies of 1912" began in what was then a rather novel fashion. Before the curtain rose, people in the audience started an argument, the subject of the dispute concerning the kind of entertainment those present expected and preferred. The disputants were actors in the cast placed in various parts of the auditorium. Harry Watson was a gallery god vociferously demanding the sort of show he liked. Charles Judels was a Frenchman who from his orchestra seat decried all American theatricals.

Next to *Oh! Oh! Delphine* **The Lady of the Slipper** (10-28-12, Globe) had the longest run of any regular American musical of the season: 232 performances. Oddly, although it gave Victor Herbert one of the longest Broadway stays of his career, it remains among his least remembered works. The fault was not Herbert's, for the score, while not one of his best, was delightful. The musical's fame and fortunes have ebbed because it was created as a vehicle for its stars, and without them the heavy-handed libretto might bring down the whole enterprise. When Charles Dillingham first announced his plans, he boasted the show would have one of the greatest all-star casts in history. Inevitably, temperaments clashed; both Joseph Cawthorn and Irene Castle withdrew during rehearsals. Vernon Castle left shortly after the New York opening. But Elsie Janis, Dave Montgomery, and Fred Stone alone would have been enough to ensure its success. It was another of those wide-eyed, innocent drolleries they and their public reveled in. This time, as the title suggests, they cavorted with Cinderella (Miss Janis). Montgomery played Punks and Stone played Spooks, two characters, as the program stated, "from the cornfield"—a cornfield all their fans knew was situated not far from Oz. Both employed much the same make-up they had used a decade before. Together the boys helped Cinderella get to the ball. They saw to it Crown Prince Maximilian (Douglas Stevenson) put the shoe on her foot in time to save his throne. In her fetchingly candid autobiography Miss Janis confessed the stars "were the least fitted to sing Victor Herbert's music. Fortunately, we could always go into our dance, and we did!" How Herbert solved his stars' problems can be seen in the two-part harmony of "A Little Girl At Home." For Cinderella he wrote a simple repetitive line, almost a monotone, allowing the better-voiced Prince to carry the engaging melody. Since much of Herbert's most beautiful writing was for descriptive sections and for the ballet numbers, no other song attained the popularity of "A Little Girl At Home." Dillingham gave the work a sumptuous mounting that included

a chariot with six ponies to race Cinderella to the palace.

Probably the season's most noteworthy failure was an antiwar comic opera with a score by Walter Damrosch. Entitled **The Dove of Peace** (11-4-12, Broadway), it was a fiasco, removed from the stage after a meager two weeks. Most of the blame lay with the book, which had an intriguing, if complicated, story, but which handled its material ineptly and leadenly. The story, much simplified, ran as follows: Shy Willie Perkins' grandmother (apparently something of a witch or demi-god) states in her will that if Willie (Frank Pollock) is kissed before he is twenty-five universal peace will encompass the world. But Willie is so afraid of women, he runs away to Guam, and the Spanish-American War breaks out as a result. In Guam, Terrance Donnybrook (Arthur Deagon), the peace commissioner, persuades Willie at the last moment to kiss Hildegarde Tyler (Alice Yorke). When he does, everyone lays down his arms. Not unexpectedly peace proves stultifying. "What! No more parades, brass bands, tall soldiers with brass buttons and all that sort of thing? Nay, Nay." Conveniently, a clause in the grandmother's will is interpreted to mean only men won't fight. Suffragettes see their opportunity and seize the Senate from its sleeping members. Only then is it realized that, since Willie was on Guam when he was kissed, the time difference hid the fact that he had actually passed his twenty-fifth birthday. Everyone avidly returns to battle. Damrosch's score was strikingly superior to the book. Critic after critic lavished kudos on it. Even so, Damrosch must bear some of the blame for the show's quick failure. He was not unrealistic. He tried to write a commercial score, but his artistry was inimical to Broadway requirements. As the *Herald* observed, the "music is too ambitious for the 'tired businessman' who wants his to tinkle merrily." For example, although the chorus of the title song began with an especially pleasant melody, it quickly developed into a more complicated and hardly "catchy" theme. The verse, too, was a more artful than attractive lead-in to the chorus. The production was praised for exceptionally fine singing by both principals and chorus, and for the excellent symphonic sounds emanating from the orchestra pit. Nor was the evening without its livelier moments. Deagon and Jessie Bradbury were reported as "convulsing the audience" with their dance for "The Caveman and the Cavewoman." It is doubtful if any European powers ever heard of the show. They were too busy preparing for the war to come.

Another interesting failure entered just over a week after the first showing of *The Dove of Peace*. For nearly a decade Jerome Kern had been adding attractive interpolations to several musicals each season. Now the Shuberts, who had called on him to do a substantial part of the music for the first Winter Garden production, allowed him to compose the whole score for a lyric version of Rida Johnson Young's 1911 flop, *Next,* rechristened for the musical stage, **The Red Petticoat** (11-13-12, Daly's). While hindsight allows us to hear hints of the future Kern in some of his songs for the evening, the score was undistinguished. It received a fittingly polite reception, but no more. One passing comment in the *Times'* review suggests a degree of artistry was expected and appreciated—a sort of artistry discounted or taken for granted today. In remarking on the presentation of one song, "Since The Days Of Grandmama," the paper made a point to praise a felicitous "flute and clarinet obbligato" in the orchestration. Miss Johnson did the book. As she had the year before, she told of Sophie Brush's adventures as a woman barber in a rough and tumble mining town. Sophie (Helen Lowell) delighted the *Dramatic Mirror:* "For a musical comedy the heroine of *The Red Petticoat* is a most decided novelty. She is dressed to look her homeliest; she is an old maid and a combatively amatory one." The trade sheet recorded how pleased first-nighters were when Sophie changed her make-up and dress, and won her man. But there were limits to the *Mirror*'s tolerance of novelty, and it insisted archly that Nevada was "the last place in the world to furnish local color for a musical play." However, most critics agreed with its appraisal: "an unconventional musical comedy which will not especially amuse or bore." Enough ticket buyers appeared at the box office to keep *The Red Petticoat* alive for 61 performances.

In their own small ways Damrosch and Kern's pieces were daring, hinting at the depth and breadth of many later Broadway musicals. **The Gypsy** (11-14-12, Park), which opened the night after *The Red Petticoat,* looked unabashedly backward. Its story reminded playgoers of the ten-twenty-thirty melodramas that silent movies had done to death. Several commentators looked on it as a watered down *Il Trovatore,* for it detailed the mix-up of children at a gypsy camp. In the last act the handsome young gypsy chief is proven to be the long-lost heir to the baronial hall painted on the act's backdrop. The show was removed after 12 showings. What especially disheartened many writers was the obvious deterioration it revealed in the talents of both Frank Pixley and Gustav Luders. Their days of inventiveness and success were receding fast. No one was more disheartened than Pixley. He retired from the stage to devote his few remaining years to writing for silent pictures. He died, at fifty-two, on December 31, 1919.

(From) Broadway to Paris, a revue built primarily around the abilities of the audacious Gertrude Hoffman, arrived at the Winter Garden on November 20. Miss Hoffman's appearances disclosed her in a variety of styles and moods "from Aubrey Beardsley poster effects, deep-shadowed, Carmen-lipped and auburn-hued, to a sunlit figure, flesh tinted and flaunting a mass of golden hair." Her skimpy costumes and wriggling dances kept the evening on the boards for ten weeks.

November's fifth musical turned out to be the last of the great Weber and Fields' burlesques. On the 21st, it opened the new Weber and Fields Music Hall which the Shuberts had built on 44th Street and followed the comedians' traditional two-part pattern. The first part was **Roly Poly,** a vaudeville tied together with a weak plot in which Tanzman (Fields) and Schmaltz (Weber) take the waters at Raatenbad. Bijou Fitzsimmons (Marie Dressler) pursues Schmaltz, and he is forced to play dead to escape. The act ended with the colossal Miss Dressler collapsing on tall, thin Fields. Besides the great clowns, the star-studded cast included Nora Bayes, who sang "When It's Apple Blossom Time In Normandy" (Mellor, Gifford, and Trevor), Bessie Clayton, Jack Norworth, and Frank Daniels. Miss Clayton received special kudos for her "art dance." The *corps de ballet* was also praised, especially for a "stunning stage picture," with the *corps* divided into three groups—one in white, one in green, and one in scarlet. A Weber and Fields show meant a gorgeous chorus line—and *Roly Poly,* happily, proved no exception. For their second-act travesty they presented, with not too straight faces, **Without the Law.** The characters in what had once been Bayard Veiller's gripping thriller *Within the Law* were instantly recognizable to knowledgeable theatregoers. Inspector Burke became Inspector Bunk, with Weber under the greasepaint, while Fields transformed the forger Joe Garson into Joke Arson. Again the public and critics rejoiced. But things were not well backstage. The principals were all aging, and the infamous feud was still smoldering. An eight-year hiatus had deprived the company of the chance to recruit younger talent gradually and carefully. Moreover Weber, and particularly Fields, had found easier, more lucrative opportunities elsewhere. The seven-and-a-half-week run was the only time Weber and Fields played together at the theatre named for them. Indeed, it was the last time the great comics played together for New York audiences. Shortly after the house opened the Shuberts hastily changed its name to the 44th Street Theatre.

One sign that all was not well between Weber and Fields could have been read nine nights later when Fields alone offered New York **The Sun Dodgers** (11-30-12, Broadway). Fields apparently loved night people. *The Sun Dodgers,* like *The Midnight Sons* (5-22-09), dealt with a society that rarely awoke before the crack of noon. Mrs. Honoria O'Day (George W. Monroe) would cater to these night owls by turning her farm into a lively resort, but her nephew, with the help of Praline Nutleigh (Bessie Wynn), wangles the land for a homestead. As always Fields gave the evening a superb mounting. The *Dramatic Mirror* called the chorus line the most beautiful Broadway had seen in years and praised the effects Fields achieved at one point by having the girls dance with tiny electric bulbs on their caps and shoes. But most New Yorkers found better entertainment elsewhere, so Fields removed this "Fanfare of Frivolity" after just 29 showings.

The Firefly (12-2-12, Lyric) was the season's most endearing and most enduring musical. Behind it lay a revealing tale of backstage sensitivities. When Victor Herbert signed to write what ultimately became *Naughty Marietta* for Hammerstein's company, and notably Emma Trentini, he agreed to follow it with a second work, if the first enjoyed sufficient success. In the beginning there were good feelings all around. But as the tour of *Marietta* progressed, repetition and fatigue eroded much of the good will. Trentini grew increasingly difficult. During the first week of April 1912 a gala performance was scheduled, in honor of the twenty-fifth anniversary of Oscar Hammerstein's first theatre. It was to take place at the West End Theatre in Harlem, and Herbert was persuaded to conduct. From all accounts it was a superb performance—until Herbert signaled Trentini to encore "Italian Street Song." When she refused, Herbert thought she misunderstood his movements. He signaled again and, seeing Miss Trentini looking directly at him, motioned the orchestra to begin. Trentini walked obstinately off into the wings, and Herbert, in a fury, stalked out. The next day he announced he would never again write so much as a note for his erstwhile star. Since *Naughty Marietta* was about to close and the new show had been promised to the public, a desperate search began for Herbert's replacement. With insight and courage

Hammerstein turned to a young immigrant—Rudolf Friml.

. . .

Rudolf Friml was born in Prague on December 7, 1879. Something of a child prodigy, he had his first composition, a "barcarolle," published when he was only ten years old. Friends and relatives combined to send him to the Prague Conservatory, at that time flourishing under Antonin Dvorak. Soon he was accompanying the young violinist, Jan Kubelik. Both with Kubelik and alone as a concert pianist, he made several tours of the United States, settling here in 1906. When Hammerstein approached him, apparently at the suggestion of Max Dreyfus and Rudolph Schirmer, he had begun to make a small reputation as a composer of light concert pieces. But his ability to write a commercial, theatrical score was untested.

. . .

The score he provided for *The Firefly* fully justified Hammerstein's gamble. It was one of Broadway's great scores, a worthy sequel to *Naughty Marietta.* Although it was thoroughly European in its sound, it was composed for a story, like *Naughty Marietta*'s, set in America. Unlike the earlier piece, it was not an America of a distant, romantic day, but rather of much the same world its audiences stepped out into on leaving the theatre. At a pier at the foot of 23rd Street the Van Dare yacht is preparing to sail for Bermuda. Geraldine Van Dare (Audrey Maple), the owner's niece, arrives with her fiancé, Jack Travers (Craig Campbell). They are quarreling. Geraldine, snobbish and bitchy, insists she has witnessed a flirtation between Jack and a little Italian street singer. After the two have boarded, the waif, Nina Corelli (Miss Trentini), appears. She spots an old friend in Suzette (Ruby Norton), Geraldine's maid. Prodded by Suzette she admits she did indeed wink at Jack, but, after all, what does it matter if "Love Is Like A Firefly." Her lightheartedness is a cover. At home her drunken guardian beats her. She would like to escape, and when she hears the yacht is heading for Bermuda, she inquires if Bermuda is farther away than Coney Island. Assured it is, she begs to come aboard. Suzette points out that the jealous Geraldine would never allow it, so Nina rushes home and changes into her brother's clothes. She returns, and with disarming naïveté she tells Suzette she is now Antonio Columbo, a neighborhood pickpocket. Tony sings a love song, "Giannina Mia." Another passenger, the musician Franz (Henry Vogel), believes this is the voice he has been seeking for his choir. He begs the Van Dares to allow the "boy" to accompany them. There is some reluctance. But Nina, seeing Corelli approach, runs aboard as the gangplank is raised. At the Van Dare's Bermuda estate everyone has fallen in love with the boy, except Geraldine, whom the boy reminds of the street singer. And the disguised Nina has fallen in love with Jack. She is overjoyed when she is offered a job by Jack:

Jack: How would you like to be my valet, Tony?
Nina [As Tony]: What is valet?
Franz: You have to take care of Jack's clothes and help dress him.
Nina: Dress him? He's old enough to dress himself! I don't think I do for that job.
Jack: Why not?
Nina: I'm not that kind of a boy.

Geraldine, feeling more and more isolated, sulks. Jack's uncle, John Thurston (Melville Stewart), alone offers her "Sympathy." But a thief is loose, and when the police connect the robbery with a pickpocket, Antonio Columbo, known to be on the island, Nina is forced to drop her masquerade. Amid the general consternation Franz agrees to adopt the waif, and the two go off together. The last act takes place in the Van Dare home in New York. Three years have passed. While Jack has been away his romance with Geraldine has cooled. But he comes to her house on a courtesy call just as Franz returns with his charge. Only now she is no longer Nina Corelli. Under Franz' careful tutelage she has become Giannina, a great prima donna. Jack realizes it is she he loves, and Giannina confesses she has never stopped loving him.

The characters were well drawn, if sometimes two-dimensional. For the most part, Otto Hauerbach's dialogue was satisfactory, despite occasional infelicities. Hauerbach's way with dialect suggested he did not have the most carefully attuned ear. Nina says of her early encounter with Geraldine, "She looks as if she would keel me when I smile at the young gen'man." Now and then the writing could be surprisingly stilted. The tongue-lashed little immigrant responds, "How dare you thus revile me?"

Apart from Trentini, what made the show were Friml's melodies, and with Trentini's lovely soprano so long silent, it remains Friml's score that keeps the piece alive. Rich and diverse, the music stays fresh with repeated hearing. Three of its best-loved pieces indicate its range from the lushly arioso "Giannina Mia" to the tender "Sympathy" to the bubbly "Love Is Like A Firefly."

If the comment in the *Times'* review of *The Red*

Petticoat about some of the orchestration disclosed a happily thoughtful side of the American Musical Theatre of this era, another comment in the *Times'* review of *The Firefly* exposed a more debatable facet—the persistent demand for and granting of encores. (After all, a dispute over an encore resulted in Friml writing *The Firefly*'s score instead of Herbert.) While the *Times* and other papers had long railed against the practice, in the case of the new work the paper could note, "for once it was possible to be patient with the encore fiends."

For various reasons, nine of the season's musicals ran as long or longer than *The Firefly*. Its 120 performances coincidently equaled the run of Lehar's *The Count of Luxembourg,* the best of the new imports. And they alone remain unquestionably stageable today.

Two musicals came in for Chicago's inspection one night apart just before Christmas. **Frivolous Geraldine** opened at the Olympic on December 22; **Exceeding the Speed Limit** at Cohan's Grand Opera House on the 23rd. Both were set in Paris; both were failures. *Frivolous Geraldine* told of a young lady who must choose between an "apache" and an American who is under a cloud of suspicion. She clears the American's name and marries him. The musical's book was by Theodore Stempfel, its songs were by Herbert Stothart and Joe Howard. The *Tribune,* complaining Howard's music was increasingly derivative, remarked nastily, "He cares not who writes his songs, so long as he remembers them." The show at the Opera House was a French work with music by Antony Mars, adopted as a vehicle for Carter De Haven and Elizabeth Murray.

In New York three more musicals offered themselves for approval in December. **Miss Princess** (12-23-12, Park), more American-made Graustark, lasted two weeks. Its star, Lina Abarbanell, played Princess Polonia, whom political considerations have decreed must marry Prince Alexis (Henri Leoni), though she loves a common soldier, Capt. Merton Raleigh (Robert Warwick). Her problems are solved when Alexis elopes with an actress. A way was somehow found in Graustark for two "Texas Tommy" dancers to rouse the audience "to a high pitch of enthusiasm."

Franz Lehar's *Eva* premiered on December 30. The same night Sam Bernard came into the Lyric with **All for the Ladies** and for more than three months added to Broadway's merriment, even if the show made no significant contribution to Broadway's art. Bernard played Leon von Laubenheimer, a dress designer, whose comic machinations save the house of Clemente and Panturel from the financial rocks. The couturier's studio allowed a dozen or so beautiful showgirls to model gowns of such high fashion that the audience audibly gasped. In keeping with so many American musical comedies, its setting was European. Its American music, by Alfred G. Robyn, was commonplace. But Robyn and his librettist, Henry Blossom, seemed to think Europe gave the songs an added cachet. The juxtaposition had worked for Robyn in *The Yankee Consul* (2-22-04) and *A Yankee Tourist* (8-12-07), it worked again with *All for the Ladies*.

Nearly a month passed before another musical arrived. **Somewhere Else** (1-20-13, Broadway) was an 8-performance failure with shakingly tragic consequences. The show had the second Gustav Luders score of the season, but following the breakup of his partnership with Frank Pixley, Luders worked with a new librettist, Avery Hopwood. In later years Hopwood became a playwright of some renown, but the book for this "musical fantasy" represented one of his first public efforts and underscored his inexperience. The story line struck many critics as a bad example of a type that had flourished a decade or more before and which, while still not totally out of style, was rapidly losing its freshness and appeal. To escape a nagging stepdaughter, widowed Billy Getaway (Taylor Holmes) of New York sails his yacht to the land of Somewhere Else. He and the queen (Cecil Cunningham) of Somewhere Else fall in love. But his stepdaughter, Hepzibah (Catherine Hayes), having stowed away on the boat, appears, bent on trouble. Since Billy has told the queen his only daughter was still an infant, he has Hepzibah hypnotized and made to believe she is three years old. He builds her a monstrous perambulator to reinforce the delusion. An accidental handclap brings the girl to reality, but love wins out not merely for Billy and the queen, but also for Hepzibah and the queen's stepuncle. The faults of the libretto were aggravated by the weakness of the score. Luders, who had just turned forty-eight, was either written out or in a prolonged slump, which one will never be known. Two days after the scathing reviews appeared, Luders was found dead, officially of "cerebral apoplexy." Broadway scuttlebutt rejected this explanation, preferring to believe the composer, who had harbored the highest hopes for his last piece, succumbed to the shock and distress brought on by its failure. The appraisals of his output in his obituaries were not flattering. The *Dramatic Mirror*

wrote, "Mr. Luders' work was variable and not especially inspired, much of it suggesting familiar strains from many well known sources." Such harsh judgments were unfair. True, Luders did not grow with experience, as many gifted composers did. From the beginning the range of his best work was restricted. His was a small, sweet, clear voice. When it sang a felicitous melody, it sang enchantingly.

The night of Luders' death Lehar's *The Man with Three Wives* (1-23-13, Weber and Fields) began a 52-performance run. Four evenings later, Chauncey Olcott opened in **The Isle o' Dreams** (1-27-13, Grand Opera House). It was a typical Olcott vehicle, more a romantic melodrama than a musical. It attracted a typical Olcott audience—an audience not unlike those once loyal to Harrigan and Hart. It was predominantly Irish, if a bit more refined than patrons of the 1880s. One reviewer reported, "the audience very soon became a prominent feature of the performance, insisting on manifesting its pleasure after almost every line, as is the joyful custom with Mr. Olcott's regular clientele, and fairly going mad after he sang a song. As a result it was within one or two minutes of 11 o'clock when the curtain went up on the fourth and last act." Set in 1799 at the time of Napoleon's threatened invasion of Ireland, *The Isle o' Dreams* followed the adventures and love affair of Ivor Kelway. Kelway is mistaken for a French spy. Much of the action took place in the pub run by his foster mother (Jennie Lamont) on a small island off the Irish coast. Both the pub and the islet were called "The Isle o' Dreams." Out of Ernest R. Ball's numbers for the evening came two of the most popular songs the American stage has ever produced, "When Irish Eyes Are Smiling" and "Mother Machree," both, of course, sung by Olcott. Although *The Isle o' Dreams* played a mere 32 performances at the Grand Opera House, it toured big cities and small towns across the country for years.

Only two musicals arrived in February. Both were hits. The first was a London success, Paul Rubens' **The Sunshine Girl** (2-3-13, Knickerbocker), graced in Frohman's American production by the beguiling Julia Sanderson, as a young lady prevented by another stage will from marrying the man of her choice. Irene and Vernon Castle—who had come to America's attention in 1912 after their success in Paris—won applause with their graceful ballroom dancing, although the biggest show-stopper was a tango Castle performed with Miss Sanderson. The Castles' popularity coupled with the new tangos and ragtime dances gave birth to the phenomenon known as "The Dancing Craze." Miss Sanderson made "Honeymoon Lane," an interpolation by Jerome Kern, one of the evening's hits. Joseph Cawthorn provided the comedy. The show ran into the warm weather.

Equally successful was **The Honeymoon Express** (2-6-13, Winter Garden), a rapid-paced "farce with music" that starred Al Jolson and Gaby Deslys. Miss Deslys wore a series of striking gowns, from a simple black-and-white affair for her entrance to a wildly bespangled dress for a flashy dance with Harry Pilcer. Dixon and Doyle did several turns, and dependable Ada Lewis portrayed another of her tough ladies. The cast included two up-and-coming youngsters, Harry Fox and Fanny Brice. The score was undistinguished, but Jolson's delivery was so sensational few noticed. No Jolson standards came out of the score, although "You Made Me Love You" (Joe McCarthy/Jimmy Monaco), which Jolson sang to the last, was sometimes interpolated. Later Jolson stopped the show when he added "Who Paid The Rent For Mrs. Rip Van Winkle?" (Alfred Bryan/Fred Fisher). Apart from Jolson the hit of the evening was a spectacular stage effect that reunited the parted honeymooners Henri Dubonet (Ernest Glendinning) and Yvonne (Miss Deslys) in time for the finale. It depicted a race between a train and an auto "from the first faint glimmer of distant lights way up on the mountain side, through the devious turns of the road and down to the valleys, on to the level stretch, into tunnels and out of them, and finally, right down to the footlights with a rush and a roar."

Before March's first entry premiered, an interesting article appeared in the *Dramatic Mirror*. It was an interview with Gustave Kerker, in the first decade of the century one of Broadway's most popular and prolific composers, who, with one brief exception, had not been heard from since 1907—the year of *The Merry Widow*. His comments illuminated both the endemic public confusions and his personal bitterness. He began by saying he wanted to talk about "light operas (musical comedies we call them now)." If a musician like Kerker did not distinguish between the two forms, who could expect the public to be clear in its mind? "Ever since *The Merry Widow*," Kerker continued, "managers have simply fallen all over themselves in their efforts to acquire operettas, written by Viennese composers." But it soon became apparent his real objection was not to this. After all, Kerker himself was German and could write—though without any great flair—in the Viennese manner. His real animosity was directed at producers for their lack of respect toward composers. He rued the lack of respect for the integrity of score and then, in a seeming about-face, he decried the lack of recognition afforded interpolators: "There is a certain musical comedy playing in town now that has the name of a famous Viennese composer in letters of fire on the outside of the theatre. As a matter of fact there are three numbers by this composer in the entire score of eighteen numbers." Kerker looked back longingly to the days when "the author had the principal voice in the interpretation of the piece." There was a certain justice in Kerker's remarks. But he naturally overlooked the fact that some of the disrespect had been earned. It was understandable for producers inundated with hack material to attempt to improve their shows by any means available. But producers recognized and respected quality. There was little or no tampering with the work of Ivan Caryll or Karl Hoschna or Victor Herbert.

March's first entry presented coincidentally the music of another composer long absent from Broadway. **The American Maid** (3-3-13, Broadway) had a score by John Philip Sousa, some of which he lifted from his unproduced 1893 work, *The Glass Blowers*. The plot, too, was a reworking of the old book by the original librettist, Leonard Liebling. Silas Pompton, a glass manufacturer, wants his daughter Geraldine (Louise Gunning) to marry a duke (Charles Brown), but Geraldine prefers Jack Bartlett (John Park). Some "modernisms" crept in. The hero of the 1913 version distinguishes himself in Spanish-American War combat, shown on motion pictures while old Sousa marches were played. The public was not receptive. The show was withdrawn after two weeks, and without any ado Sousa bid a final farewell to the Broadway scene, except for scattered songs and appearances. The old Broadway Theatre, converting to a movie house, also left the legitimate arena.

A vaudeville called **Marie Dressler's All Star Gambols** frolicked for a week beginning March 10 on the new stage meant for Weber and Fields. Charles E. Evans brought over his playlet "It's Up To You" from the two-a-day circuits. After Robert Drouet and Mme. Yorska presented a truncated version of *Camille*, Miss Dressler and Jefferson De Angelis offered their mock version. De Angelis and Miss Dressler led the ensemble in "The Evolution Of Dancing." When the show left, New York saw the start of the spring parade of revivals that for a few seasons threatened to supplant the traditional "summer musicals." Between late March and late May six old-timers were brought back for runs of

286

varying length: *The Beggar Student, The Geisha, The Mikado, H.M.S. Pinafore, Iolanthe,* and *Mlle. Modiste.*

One exceptional amateur production deserves notice. **The Lady of Luzon** opened for a week's run at Pittsburgh's Alvin Theatre on June 2. It advertised itself as "made-in-Pittsburgh," and the Pittsburgh *Dispatch* recorded, "No amateur production was ever given on a more elaborate scale." The boast may well have been true, for the Pittsburgh Athletic Association spent $20,000 on the production. Only the most sumptuous Broadway mountings of the day equaled that figure. Like *The Girl at the Gate,* the show reflected America's concern with "The Yellow Peril." Brigado Faustino Guillermo would force Olivia Benicia, the lady of Luzon, to marry Lt. Monroe of the Army Engineer Corps. Guillermo is fond of Monroe's mother and together they hope to wrest Olivia's land from her. But Olivia loves Rosendo Montijo. Montijo is an inventor, and Guillermo's treachery includes a plan to sell the design of a gun Montijo has invented to a Japanese spy. An American newspaperman, Warren Phyxit, arrives to set matters straight. The athletic association hired R.H. Burnside to direct the production, but it relied on local talent to write the show. Alfred W. Birdsall created the book. A local newspaperman, Marcus C. Connelly, provided lyrics for Zoel Parenteau's music. The *Dispatch* was especially happy with Parenteau's "style of his own," adding he "juggled harmony and counterpoint with daring." Parenteau was to go on to receive similar praise on Broadway, only to fade away. But for Marc Connelly the show inaugurated a distinguished career.

Only three new musicals opened in the final months of the season. **The Purple Road** (4-7-13, Liberty) told the bittersweet story of Wanda (Valli Valli) who comes with a petition to Napoleon (Harrison Brockbank) while he is in Austria. He is charmed by her and, disguised as a captain, woos her. The romance continues years later in Paris, but from an overheard conversation, Wanda realizes who her lover is and leaves. In an epilogue gaily attired rustics celebrate Napoleon's downfall while Wanda, clothed in black, sings a contrapuntal lament. The score by Heinrich Reinhardt and William Frederick Peters was gay and supple. Its best waltz, "The Mysterious Kiss," gave Peters, who ended his days as organist in the New York movie palaces, his only theatrical hit.

The Smith brothers adapted Oscar Straus' **My Little Friend** (5-19-13, New Amsterdam) for New World audiences, but somehow missed its Continental appeal. The story recounted how a poor count and a rich upstart try to force their children to wed. Fred Walton, Crawford Kent, William Pruette, Harry MacDonough, and Maude Gray were featured. The operetta lingered just three weeks.

Lew Fields kept the tradition of "summer" musicals alive when he brought in **All Aboard** on June 5. Ironically it played the Roof Garden at the 44th Street Theatre, once the Weber and Fields. Fields became Jan Van Haan, a sailor down on his luck, who goes to sleep on the dock and dreams of enough vaudeville turns to fill out the evening. In the prologue and in a suffragette skit Fields walked a narrow line between pathos and farce—a technique used by many great clowns, but rarely by Fields. George Monroe, in a woman's wig and a man's trousers, hewed a more steadfast comic line in the suffragette skit. Dancing ranged from neat little duets by the De Havens to a livelier pirate dance by Ralph Riggs and Kathryn Witchie to a chorus going through the paces of "Monkey Doodle" with real monkeys. A first-act finale ended with a Wild West shooting spree. The entertainment played through the summer months, folding just before the first cooler weather arrived.

1913-1914

The new season witnessed a further drop in the number of musical productions and, in spite of three works of lasting appeal, it proffered virtually nothing else of artistic or historic importance. One of the three jewels was an importation. In keeping with the chance symmetry of this seven-year period, this final season's importation established the reputation of the second of the two masters of Vienna's last golden age, Emmerich Kalman, just as the first had rocketed Franz Lehar to fame. Once more the major American hits, Victor Herbert's *Sweethearts* and Rudolf Friml's *High Jinks,* were operettas with a distinctly European bias. Indeed, in terms of native creativity, it was a doleful twelve months. Of the thirty-four musical entries, thirteen were foreign, two were revivals of older works, eight were revues, and only eleven were newly-minted American book musicals.

The year began on June 16 with the **Ziegfeld Follies of 1913**, the first *Follies* to play the magnificent New Amsterdam, where, with rare exceptions, all the remaining editions were unveiled. It was not one of the better *Follies*. But Ziegfeld's taste and imagination saw to it that it was superior to any other revue the season offered. The dimple-kneed dancer, Ann Pennington, began her long association with the show. Songwriters Gene Buck and Dave Stamper also appeared in the credits for the first time. Both remained with Ziegfeld until his death. And Frank Tinney joined rubber-legged Leon Errol to enliven the comic department. Errol's "Turkish Trot" (a takeoff on the "Turkey Trot," a dance rage of the day) was the show's big hit. Errol's pants kept falling down as he taught the entire cast the steps. Eventually the whole cast joined in, including a stage horse. Musically, the show was weak. José Collins made a short-lived hit out of the florid "Isle d'Amour" (Earl Carroll/ Leo Edwards). But the main Raymond Hubbell and Stamper score was so pallid, Ziegfeld quickly bought the rights to several already popular tunes —"A Little Love, A Little Kiss," "Peg O' My Heart," and "Rebecca Of Sunnybrook Farm"—for Miss Collins to sing. Cubist painters and after-hours shenanigans at Rectors (a famous restaurant of the day) came in for spoofing as well, while the suffragette movement was ridiculed—in ragtime. The show's finale was a spectacular salute to the newly opened Panama Canal.

The Passing Show of 1913 followed on July 24 at the Winter Garden. The "cultural" addendum of the preceding season was dropped and the entire evening devoted to more traditional revue material. As it usually would, *The Passing Show* remained closer to the old burlesque tradition than did most of the other revue-extravaganzas, relying heavily for its comedy on satires of contemporary Broadway hits. *The Sunshine Girl, Within the Law, Broadway Jones, Oh! Oh! Delphine,* even the eight-year-old *Wizard of Oz*, were made fun of. *Peg o' My Heart*, besides being parodied, provided the slender story line that was still a requirement for revues of the day. Peg sails to America to learn the Turkey Trot. She spends the evening seeing the town under the tutelage of a comic couple and falls in love with Broadway Jones. Jean Schwartz replaced Louis Hirsch as composer, but not a single hit came from his pen—nor from the numerous interpolations. The cast included a number of young performers heading for bigger and better things: Charlotte Greenwood, Charles and Mollie King, and John Charles Thomas. Ned Wayburn again staged the evening, finishing with a number that had the line of girls parading up and down the steps before the U.S. Capitol. A more important piece of mounting was a runway projected out into the auditorium. By bringing the chorus beauties within

arm's reach of the audience, the Shuberts helped change the nature of the chorus line. But this was not fully appreciated until the next edition.

On July 26 the Chicago *Tribune* ran an article that reflected on the Chicago musical scene. It recorded that Marc Klaw had announced European musicals were better than American shows. More importantly it noted that Mort Singer had just returned from Vienna, where he had secured the rights to two operettas. Singer, too, apparently despaired of finding good local material any more.

Philip Bartholomae and Silvio Hein built "a musical comedy of youth" around the talents of the no-longer-quite-juvenile Joseph Santley. They called it **When Dreams Come True** (8-18-13, Lyric). The dreams that came true were those of immigrants who saw America as a promised land as well as Kean Hedges' dream of marrying his sweetheart, Beth (Marie Flynn). Comedy was provided by May Vokes and Amelia Summerville, the latter as a middle-aged dowager. A good dancing chorus was displayed in "The OK Two-Step" and held up to the critics' ridicule in a pointless finale with everyone imitating horses and jockeys. The evening was well crafted, if unexceptional. It had a comfortable run of eight weeks.

The biggest "made-in-Chicago" hit of the season arrived at the La Salle on August 24 and seemed to confirm the pronouncements of decline the *Tribune* had made public the preceding month, for **A Trip to Washington** was Henry Blossom and Ben Jerome's musicalization of Hoyt's *A Texas Steer* (11-10-90), a show that had had music from its inception. The show ran to the end of November. A month later a musical called **September Morn** came into the La Salle, was panned and quickly shuttered. In September also Joe Howard had a fast flop with a revue called **Broadway Honeymoon**, while Joe Hyams and Leila McIntyre suffered the same fate with a sequel to *The Girl of My Dreams*, **When Love Is Young.** Slowly, without fanfare, the once-thriving Chicago musical theatre was fading away.

The Doll Girl (8-25-13, Globe) was the first of the year's many importations. Leo Fall's music was supplemented with a rash of interpolations, mostly by Jerome Kern. Some of these Kern pieces, such as "If We Were On Our Honeymoon" and "Will It All End In Smoke?" manifested his growing inventiveness, even if they were not memorably melodic. To suit the needs of the stars, Richard Carle and Hattie Williams, Harry B. Smith made substantial revisions in his adaptation of a story in which a marquis jealously pursues the little tobac-

288

conist his nephew hopes to marry. Some critics complained, but the public applauded for eleven weeks.

Critics and public alike embraced a second importation, Philipp and Briquet's **Adele** (8-28-13, Longacre). Georgia Caine, Natalie Alt, and Hal Forde interpreted the tale of a French girl in love with the son of her father's business rival. Although the piece is now neglected and practically forgotten, even on the Continent, it was the most successful of the season's foreign musicals, running 196 performances.

The annual Hippodrome extravaganza premiered August 30. In an era of burgeoning national achievement and joyous flag-waving it was entitled simply **America.** Its frame-plot, reminiscent of Chicago's *The Girl at the Gate* (9-1-12), told how plans to fortify our new Panama Canal are stolen and how Lt. Forsythe chases the thieves through a series of spectacular scenes that included a gigantic East Side fire. The chase was interrupted at times to present vignettes from American history. Manuel Klein's music was dull, but the public that flocked to see these extraordinary mountings remained generally indifferent to their scores. Still, despite good notices, *America* compiled only 360 performances, a sharp drop from preceding years.

A second Leo Fall operetta followed. It defied common practice by retaining its German title, **Lieber Augustin** (9-3-13, Casino). If this was a gimmick, meant to lure sophisticates, it failed. Augustin, a music teacher, helps a Thessalian princess after her father is bankrupted by a comic villain, Prince Nikola. The show played less than five weeks. It had better luck on the road when its star, De Wolf Hopper, persuaded the Shuberts to retitle it *Miss Caprice.* Nonetheless, as far as American audiences were concerned, Fall was fast on his way to becoming another one-show composer. And that show—*The Dollar Princess*—was not quite top drawer.

One truly top-drawer work, Herbert's **Sweethearts,** arrived at the New Amsterdam five nights later, September 8. Herbert wrote the score with Christie MacDonald in mind. Her fine voice allowed him to write with a range and depth often denied him. The show's magnificent title song (its best number) had a range just short of two octaves. The heroine and the chorus sang this description of idealized love and lovers. The diversity and richness of the other numbers was awesome, running from the radiant sanctity of "The Angelus," sung by the romantic leads, to the beguiling fluff of "Pretty As A Picture," sung by a minor figure and the chorus.

One critic exclaimed, "It is scarcely possible to enumerate the 'gems' of this work for the mere reason that practically every number could qualify as such." The critic for the *Tribune* agreed, adding a point that applied to most Herbert works and a few others in this musicianly era, "That he has written it con amore is proved by the delicate care he has bestowed upon his orchestration, which at times rises to the level of grand opera." The day of composer-orchestrated scores was rapidly waning. Unfortunately, Fred de Gresac and Harry B. Smith's book and Robert B. Smith's lyrics were musty. Many a commentator felt so fine a score deserved better writing, and the stodgy libretto may have helped shorten the run. Several inferior pieces stayed on the boards longer during the season.

Programs of the period often gave synopses of the plot. *Sweethearts'* program coupled its synopsis with its cast listings. It read, with slight emendations, "The story of the opera is founded on the adventures of Princess Jeanne, daughter of King René of Naples, who reigned in the fifteenth century. Time has been changed to the present, and the locale to the ancient city of Bruges, to which the little princess is carried for safety in time of war, and is given the name Sylvia (Christie MacDonald). As an infant she is found in the tulip garden one morning by Dame Paula (Ethel Du Fre Houston), who conducts the Laundry of the White Geese, and who is known as 'Mother Goose.' Sylvia is brought up as the daughter of Paula, although the latter has six daughters of her own. . . . Mikel Mikeloviz (Tom McNaughton) . . . disguised as a monk, left Sylvia when an infant in Dame Paula's care. Knowing that Sylvia is the Crown Princess of the little Kingdom of Zilania, Mikel is conspiring to restore her to the throne, which is about to be offered to Franz, the heir presumptive (Thomas Conkey), who, in traveling incognito, has fallen in love with Sylvia and who finds a rival in Lieutenant Karl (Edwin Wilson), a military Lothario, betrothed to Sylvia. Mikel's plans are endangered by the schemes of [three villains. Furthermore] Liane, a milliner (Hazel Kirke), has sought temporary employment in the Laundry of the White Geese, and is mistaken by Mikel . . . for the lost Princess." Of course it all ends happily with Franz and Sylvia marrying and swearing to rule together. The show played 136 performances and then resumed a national tour that had begun in March of 1913. Thirty-four years later a superb revival, sparked by the antics of Bobby Clark, nearly doubled the run of the original.

A revival of Reginald De Koven's *Rob Roy* (10-

29-94), featuring Jefferson De Angelis, opened seven nights after *Sweethearts* and lingered two weeks.

Despite its European origins, Victor Jacobi's **The Marriage Market** (9-22-13, Knickerbocker) was set rather fancifully in San Francisco, where, at an auction sale for brides, two girls offer themselves as a lark, and are bought by a cowboy and an English lord. Donald Brian was starred. The evening proved to be of more than passing interest because of one of Jerome Kern's interpolations, a lively two-step called "You're Here And I'm Here," that was added either late in the stay, or, more likely, during the post Broadway tour. In his *American Popular Song,* Alec Wilder singles out the song for special attention, noting, "It obviously seeks a native point of view, and though it hasn't the curious quality that makes for comparative permanence (the standard song), it is worthy of mention as another bar sawed away from the cage of imported culture." A simple tune, "a series of imitations of the initial phrase, the principal characteristic of which is a pronounced syncopation at the end of the third, seventh, nineteenth, and twenty-third measures," it gave Kern his biggest hit to date. Full-page advertisements for this "world-beater" extolled it as the "song hit of six different $2.00 a seat musical comedies." In his autobiography, Harry B. Smith names one of these shows as *The Laughing Husband,* stating it was for this show the song was actually written. *The Laughing Husband* came in much later and was less successful than *The Marriage Market,* so it remains the latter with which the song is generally associated. That a second bar may have been sawed away may be read in the *Dramatic Mirror*'s joyful remark, "At last we have the cowboy in comic opera [even if the comic opera is] a musical comedy by two Germans, to music made in Germany." The show had a modest success, running ten weeks and touring.

The revival of De Koven's *Rob Roy* was followed a month later by a new De Koven work, **Her Little Highness** (10-13-13, Liberty). Based on *Such a Little Queen* by Channing Pollock (the co-librettist), it told how a revolution interrupts the betrothal ceremonies of King Stephen (Wilmuth Merkyl) of Bosnia and Queen Anna of Herzegovina, forcing them to flee to New York. There they are helped by Adolph Lauman (Willard Louis), who has plans for marrying his own daughter to the king. Stephen works in a department store until he is summoned back to Bosnia. The summons demands that he return alone, and he complies, but before long he prevails upon his people to accept

Anna. Anna was played by a rising figure on the musical stage, Mitzi Hajos. Possibly because much of the action was set in America, the show offered an "exhilarating and effective display of the latest things in dance . . . the tango, trot, waltz, and Brazilian." Of course, given the freewheeling ways of the day, even a European setting would probably have furnished some excuse for a similar succession. The book was mediocre, and the score once more displayed De Koven's debility. It ran a mere two weeks. When it closed, De Koven faced up to the loss of his creativity and discreetly retired from the popular stage, closing a career that had begun a quarter of a century earlier when *The Begum* was first sung in November of 1888.

A Glimpse of the Great White Way (10-27-13, 44th St.), a vaudeville, coupled with a one-act "comedy with music," "The Modiste Shop," eked out a single week's run on a two-a-day policy, although it had a sound Lew Fields' production and Sam Bernard heading the cast. Actually "The Modiste Shop" was a cut-down version of Bernard's earlier vehicle, *All for the Ladies,* shortened to about three-quarters of an hour. Frances Demarest as Miss Manhattan acted as hostess for the vaudeville, introducing such acts as "The Human Spider," a contortionist who performed on a gigantic web that filled the proscenium; the Schwartz Brothers in a mirror dance in which one brother seemed to be miming into an invisible mirror while the other brother became his reflection; and a *Carmen* ballet.

Oh, I Say! (10-30-13, Casino) offered Jerome Kern's second complete score and a book based on a French bedroom farce. The actress Sidonie's maid, Claudine (Clara Palmer), in the mistaken belief her mistress has embarked on an extended trip, sublets Sidonie's apartment to a young couple on their honeymoon. Complications inevitably ensue when it becomes known the groom (Charles Meakins) was Sidonie's lover and when the bride's father engages Sidonie (Cecil Cunningham) to give the newlyweds a special performance. It was typical of the light, comic fluff so beloved by the era. It was well handled, but in no way out of the ordinary. Similarly, Kern wrote a thoroughly pleasing, varied score, running the gamut from rags ("Katydid") to waltzes ("The Old Clarinet," "Each Pearl A Thought") to polkas ("I Know And She Knows") to a standard love song ("A Wifie Of Your Own"). All the score lacked was the truly outstanding number that could have pulled the rest together and somehow imparted a little extra melody to every other song in the show. One interesting musical sidelight was "the effective use of saxophones in the orchestration at a time when the saxophones had not yet begun to dominate popular musical scoring." Although the saxophone was a European invention, it would be American street music that gave it its first importance. But the *avant-garde* sounds emanating from the pit were not enough to carry the show beyond 68 performances.

The Pleasure Seekers, another "Jumble of Jollification," danced into the Winter Garden on November 3. It was a well-mounted revue of otherwise little merit, although one interpolation, "He'd Have To Get Under–Get Out And Get Under" (Grant Clarke and Edgar Leslie/Maurice Abrahams), was brought over by Bobby North from his vaudeville act and has endured. North and Harry Cooper played two businessmen who decide to give friends sailing for Europe a send-off, and then decide to sail with them. The action moved from an elaborate re-creation of the new Ritz-Carlton Hotel to a finale that had the cast tobogganing down a Swiss mountain and throwing cotton snowballs at the audience. Max Rogers and Dorothy Jardon had one of the evening's highspots, singing a medley of old songs.

One of the season's biggest hits followed a week later when the curtain went up on **The Little Café** (11-10-13, New Amsterdam). Although called a musical comedy, the C. M. S. McLellan–Ivan Caryll piece by today's lights would be another operetta. The star was Hazel Dawn, who had served the pair so well in *The Pink Lady* (3-13-11). McLellan used yet another French farce as his source, this time Tristan Bernard's *Le Petit Café*. The plot told how Albert Loriflan (John E. Young) had for years been able to idle away his time "at the uncertain favor of a lord." When the lord turns against Albert he is forced to scratch out a living as a waiter —and a very bad waiter at that—in the Little Café. He is nearly tricked out of an inheritance, but ultimately settles down with Yvonne (Alma Francis), one of the many young ladies he had been courting. Surprisingly, Miss Dawn did not play Yvonne, but rather, as she had in *The Pink Lady*, another demi-mondaine. As such, the mores of the day demanded she be rejected in the end. Her character was called Gaby Gaufrette, a not altogether complimentary bow to Gaby Deslys. Originally it had been a small part, but it was enlarged and provided with a love interest when Miss Dawn was cast. A large measure of the show's popularity was attributable to the star, for the book was uneven, especially as a result of the rewriting necessary to expand Miss Dawn's part, and the score, run-of-the-mill. Its most popular tunes were "Thy Mouth Is A Rose," sung by Gaby and the chorus and "Just Because It's You," sung by Gaby, Albert, and the chorus.

Victor Herbert's **The Madcap Duchess** (11-11-13, Globe) gave every indication of surpassing the box office figures of both the Caryll operetta and Herbert's own September success, *Sweethearts*. Added to Herbert's renown was the fame of the co-librettist, Justin Huntly McCarthy, one of the most popular romantic novelists of the day. In fact, the new musical was a theatricalization of McCarthy's 1908 best-seller, *Seraphica*. Selected for the title role was Ann Swinburne, a rising leading lady who had scored triumphs in *The Count of Luxembourg* and the revival of *Robin Hood*. From its out-of-town opening to the morning-after reviews in New York, the piece was showered with praise, particularly Herbert's score. But theatregoers would not buy it, not in New York nor on the road. It would be unfair to blame the librettists. By now both critics and audiences had come to expect no more than an unobtrusive competency in librettos for Herbert's musicals. *The Madcap Duchess* was no exception. The book was stolid, but in no way seriously objectionable. It related how Seraphina (a one letter change for the sake of euphony), the madcap, teen-aged Duchess of Bapaume (Miss Swinburne), assumed various disguises in her unconventional but determined courtship of Renaud, Prince of St. Pol (Glenn Hall). Unfortunately for Seraphina, Renaud is passionately in love with Stephanie, the Marquise of Phalaris (Josephine Whittell). Renaud's ardor has provoked the Duke of Orleans (Francis K. Lieb), then Regent of France, to ban the young suitor from Paris on pain of imprisonment. To see Stephanie, Renaud masquerades as a strolling player at Watteau's Versailles theatre. Seraphina appears as a young man, a serving maid, and player, and in the end convinces Renaud that she would be the better mate for him. Critics found the show remarkable in several ways. The settings captured the light, airy grace of Watteau. Even more commendable in many eyes was the show's stringent adherence to a sense of time. Not a single anachronistic tango or turkey trot marred the period flavor. The show's failure and subsequent obscurity can only be blamed on Herbert's musicianly score. In his pursuit of art Herbert lost track of memorable melody. Edward Waters, in his biography, praises the score, but his descriptions betray the problem—"well-turned phrases," "unusual degree of dignity." He calls "Far Up The Hill" "a conversational duet," continuing, "The conversation in gavottelike phrases gives way to a strict two-part canon in the octave (eight measures) which in turn yields to eight more measures of part singing, four independent parts over an ostinato bass. So much musical science in such a short piece was probably lost on the audience. . . ." And there was the nub of the difficulty!

November's last entry was an importation, an English pantomime, **Hop o' My Thumb,** adapted for American tastes by Sydney Rosenfeld and Manuel Klein, and brought into the Manhattan Opera House on the 26th in time to capture the pre-Christmas children's trade. Hop saves his brothers and sisters from being lost in the woods by scattering crumbs to trace their path. He also restores King Mnemonica's memory by giving him a pair of seven-league boots that allow the king to visit the land of Lost Memories. De Wolf Hopper starred, his exceptional height contrasting to the Hop of the diminutive sixty-pound English actress, Iris Hawkins.

The season's biggest hit—excepting, as usual, the Hippodrome's attraction—arrived December 10 at the Lyric. In a sense, it, too, was just right for the season. A "musical jollity" (no "jumble" here) with the appropriately frivolous title of **High Jinks,** it delighted its audiences into the summer. For those ticket buyers who might hesitate to pay out good money for anything as loose as a "jollity," the producers were happy to refer to the piece as a "musical farce" or a "musical comedy." Its story (based on Leo Ditrichstein's 1905 hit, *Before and After*) was so slight and so padded with vaudeville turns that nobody quibbled over what terms advertisements branded the piece with. Dr. Gaston Thorne (Robert Pitkin), a Parisian nerve specialist, obtains a druglike perfume which produces the giddiest consequences when a little is sprayed near the ear. It also produces some Act I complications for the courtship of Dick Wayne (Burrell Barbaretto) and Sylvia Dale (Mana Zucca) which are not resolved until moments before the final curtain. However its own day saw it, *High Jinks* was yet another of those many pieces we would unhesitatingly call "operetta." Coming a year and a week after his brilliant debut with *The Firefly* (12-2-12), *High Jinks* elevated Rudolf Friml into the forefront of Broadway composers. It remains one of his finest scores. In keeping with the libretto his musical numbers have a little lighter texture than his songs for Emma Trentini, and they have not achieved

quite the lasting fame that some of *The Firefly's* songs enjoy. But they remain familiar enough. The hit of the evening, sung by Dick, so perfectly captured the spirit of the piece that it is often mistakenly thought of as the title song, although its actual title is "Something Seems Tingle-Ingleing." Friml filled the rest of the score with everything from exquisite waltzes such as Sylvia's "Love's Own Kiss" to the seductive syncopation of "Jim," sung by the soubrette, Adelaide. Since his contemporaries saw the piece as musical comedy, Friml apparently made no strenuous objection to an interpolation. Elizabeth Murray, who had performed so ably as the comedienne in *Madame Sherry* (8-30-10), took the song, "All Aboard For Dixie" (Jack Yellen/George L. Cobb), and made it into one of the reigning hits of the day. It was the only number some critics singled out, and it became popular enough for Victor to include it as one of the "Gems" on its recording of the show's music.

A pair of musicals arrived on the 29th of December (along with an "all-star" variety bill that included Anna Held in a miniature comic opera "Mlle. Baby," brought into the Casino for the holiday week). One was a German musical comedy called **The Girl on the Film** at the 44th Street. A cast imported from George Edwardes' Gaiety romped through the adventures of a general's daughter who runs away to work in films. The work ran eight weeks. A more interesting American piece, **Iole,** ran only three at the Longacre. It attempted to have much the same fun with Elbert Hubbard that *Patience* had with Oscar Wilde. Hubbard was a fascinating, if minor, figure on the late 19th- and early 20th-century American literary scene. A successful businessman, he retired at thirty-five to devote his time to writing and publishing. He founded the Roycroft Shops and brought out several "artistic" magazines. His most famous work was *A Message to Garcia*. Robert W. Chambers had originally written the satire as a novel and, with Ben Teal, adapted it for the stage. William Peters wrote the music. In the Chambers-Teal libretto Clarence Guilford (Frank Lalor) is a poet who has raised his eight daughters in sylvan isolation. The property is owned by George Wayne (Carl Gantvoort). (Note again how names have a vogue. Dick Wayne was the lover in *High Jinks.*) Wayne arrives to dispossess the Guilford clan, but falls in love with one of the daughters, Iole (Fern Rogers). Iole is engaged to marry a cubist painter, Lionel Frawley (Steward Baird), and he moves the family to his house. Coincidently, Wayne also owns Frawley's house. As the weddings of all eight daughters are about to take place, Wayne, disguised as an organ-grinder, and seven of his friends, in similar disguises, invade the house and win the girls. Guilford, Frawley, and the other bohemians are given Wayne's wooded estate to retire to. There were kudos all around for the book and for some superior lyrics, although the writing was not as deliciously Gilbertian as some more enthusiastic reviewers suggested. There was no praise for the score that gave Sullivan no competition whatsoever. Unfortunately the weak music and perhaps too esoteric book hurt what chances the piece otherwise might have had.

The Whirl of the World opened at the Winter Garden January 10. It was 1914's first musical and by way of a New Year's gift offered Broadway a new composer, Sigmund Romberg.

. . .

Sigmund Romberg was born July 29, 1887, in the Hungarian village of Nagy Kaniza. He began studying the violin as a young boy, but as he grew older planned to give up music for a career in engineering. However, he soon decided one career need not exclude the other. While furthering his engineering studies in Vienna he obtained a position as assistant manager at the Theater-an-der-Wien, the city's leading house for operetta. Finally realizing where his future lay, he moved first to London and then to New York. He accepted work as a pianist and soon became the orchestra leader at one of New York's leading restaurants, Bustanoby's. A few of his early songs were published by Joseph W. Stern and these came to the attention of J. J. Shubert.

. . .

No one was overwhelmed by Romberg's first score, for Romberg was not as fortunate as Friml in his debut. *The Whirl of the World* was a lively, elaborate Winter Garden revue with a fine cast that included the Howard brothers, Ralph Herz, Bernard Granville, Lillian Lorraine, and one Dolly sister, Rosie. The show was advertised as the "dernier cri in dance craze," and, fittingly, Herz opened the evening with a long song mocking all the dance rages from the Castle Walk to the Zulu Hop, with a bow to a few probably apocryphal steps such as the Rheumatism Dip. Dancing was clearly the strong point of the evening, ranging from a Maxixe performed by Lester Sheehan and Miss Dolly to Serge Litavkin and a *corps de ballet* in "Harlequin and the Bluebird." Herz played a marquis who bets

Jack Phillips (Granville) that he can't win thirty girls in thirty days, getting each to sign her name in his little red book as proof. The story excused not only the dancing, but all sorts of outlandish comedy. Willie Howard presented a series of imitations and combined with his brother, Eugene, to spoof grand opera. Much of their humor no longer seems funny. For example, when Eugene asked Willie, "What is worse than having the earache and the toothache at the same time?", Willie's reply was "Rheumatism and St. Vitus." The evening also offered one more spectacle of a ship sailing away from a pier. Clearly, the skits and musical numbers were an ocean away from the old world charm and grace that brought out the best in Romberg. It would be a while before Romberg would find himself, or, perhaps more accurately, Broadway would find Romberg. Nonetheless, while no memorable song was forthcoming, the music was pleasant enough, and with so many increasingly popular young performers to lure in trade, the show ran twenty weeks.

Another German musical comedy, **The Queen of the Movies** (1-12-14, Globe), caused some to confuse it with the earlier importation, *The Girl on the Film*. But it was in every way superior to its predecessor, and it ran three months. Its story had the attempts of a mad professor (Frank Moulan) to form a league for the suppression of movies thwarted when a clever actress (Valli Valli) maneuvers to compromise him. Among its lesser attractions was an added Irving Berlin tune, "Follow The Crowd."

The next evening, brought in Emmerich Kalman's early Viennese masterpiece, **Sari** (*Der Zigeunerprimas*) (1-13-14, Liberty). In its story of gypsy passions, an old violin virtuoso and his young son both love the same woman. Sari, the old man's daughter and the young man's sister, resolves the problem and wins herself a mate at the same time. Her performance and singing of the title role gained petite Mitzi Hajos stardom, a stardom she clung to for years, even after she shortened her professional name simply to Mitzi. The operetta's success and fame went far to compensate Kalman for his lamentable failure five years before with *The Gay Hussars*. His waltzes from *Sari* remain light concert favorites.

A third importation, **The Laughing Husband** (2-2-14, Knickerbocker), based its libretto on another musical comedy misunderstanding, this time when a husband threatens to divorce his novelist wife after misconstruing her meeting with a notorious count. If the show has any hold on our attention it must be solely as the show for which Jerome Kern wrote "You're Here And I'm Here," sung and danced by Venita Fitzhugh and Nigel Barrie.

Blanche Ring opened the same night in a specially tailored vehicle, **When Claudia Smiles** (2-2-14, 39th St.). She played Claudia Rogers, who divorces her husband, Johnny (Harry Hilliard), to further her career as an actress. The twists in the plot come from an innocent letter she sends one of her new suitors. His misreading of the letter breaks up a marriage and sends a man to jail. But before the evening is over Claudia sets everything right and winds up back in Johnny's arms. To bolster the weaker new numbers from various pens, Miss Ring interspersed some of her old favorites, such as "Bedelia" and "I've Got Rings On My Fingers." All in all it was sufficient to please her following for seven weeks in New York, plus the inevitable tour.

The Midnight Girl, an importation from France, was February's third and final musical offering. Set in Paris, the plot depicted the romance of a cabaret singer and a man she mistakes for a famous senator. It had music by Briquet and Philipp, and arrived at the 44th Street Theatre just as their earlier success, *Adele,* left for the road. While *The Midnight Girl* never matched *Adele*'s popularity, it nevertheless ran 104 performances with George MacFarlane, Eva Fallon, and Margaret Romaine in principal roles.

A second girl, **The Crinoline Girl,** opened at the Knickerbocker March 16, and since Julian Eltinge was the star there were doubting Thomases ready to assure you that the crinoline girl was no girl at all. The doubters were wrong. Richard Ainsley (Charles P. Morrison), hoping to discourage Tom Hale (Eltinge) from marrying his daughter Dorothy (Helen Luttrell), insists Tom must first earn $10,000 by his own wits. At the same time Ainsley is also offering a $25,000 reward for the capture of a jewel thief, the Crinoline Girl (Edna Whistler), and her accomplices. Tom captures the Crinoline Girl, dresses like her to nab her accomplices, and wins Dorothy. The music was by the popular Tin Pan Alley songwriter, Percy Wenrich, who wrote "Moonlight Bay," "Put On Your Old Gray Bonnet" and, in this same 1914, "You Wore A Tulip And I Wore A Big Red Rose." No comparable hit emerged from *The Crinoline Girl,* and what success the musical had must be credited to Eltinge. In New York at least that success was scant. Revealingly, the *Times* noted that Eltinge had always been more welcome on the lucrative road. In a

poignant curtain speech on opening night Eltinge expressed his hope that New York would hereafter be more receptive. His hopes were never realized, although he was looked on fondly and with respect.

More importations followed. **The Maids of Athens** (3-18-14, New Amsterdam), with a Franz Lehar score, lasted less than three weeks. In its American version it made its hero an American naval officer, who helps a princess break up a bandit ring. The bandit king turns out to be her brother. Elbert Fretwell, Albert Pellaton, Cecil Cunningham, and Leila Hughes led the cast. **The Belle from Bond Street** (3-30-14, Shubert), an updated version of *The Girl from Kay's* (11-2-03), ran only a little longer, in spite of an excellent cast headed by Sam Bernard (from the original) and Gaby Deslys. In the tolerant fashion of the period the show included "Who Paid The Rent For Mrs. Rip Van Winkle?" which Al Jolson had introduced in *The Honeymoon Express* and which he was still singing on its cross-country tour.

On April 9 a colossal mounting of *H.M.S. Pinafore* began an 89-performance run at the Hippodrome. The house made no exception to its two-a-day policy for Gilbert and Sullivan, but did allow separate casts for evenings and matinees. The nighttime crowds were treated to Fay Templeton as Little Buttercup.

Four nights later the last two American book musicals of this chapter arrived simultaneously. They exemplified the American musical comedy just before its great emancipation. They were musical, and they were comic. What remains moot is how American they were. Both were set in Europe, though in both American ingenuity overcomes foreign obstacles. Both had their share of waltzes and tangos, though this undoubtedly struck no one as unusual or alien. As so often happened, the more daring of the two was the less successful. It was a musical that began with a point of view as well as a plot. **The Red Canary** (4-13-14, Lyric) escapes from its cage in Paris and disturbs the lives of all who see it, until a cool-headed American, Hunter Upjohn (T. Roy Barnes), captures it and restores it to its cage. The point the book tried to make, however naïvely, was that color and emotion are inseparable. The canary's hot coloring excited feelings and led to irrational behavior. The point was not labored; and musical comedy clichés prevailed. For many the best thing about the evening was Harold Orlob's score, his first on Broadway. A few critics predicted a bright future for him, and, indeed, he was represented regularly for more than a decade thereafter. But his was a long career without an iota of distinction. What hardly anyone knew was that his one great number, "I Wonder Who's Kissing Her Now?", was enhancing the fame of Joe Howard—to whom he had signed away the rights. *The Red Canary* survived a mere two weeks.

The Beauty Shop (4-13-14, Astor) was more successful, even if its plot was creaky. Dr. Arbutus Budd is about to lose his beauty shop when he receives word from Corsica that he is an heir. But in Corsica his inheritance turns out to be an old revolver with which he is expected to continue an ancient vendetta. More diplomatic than brave, he offers to marry his enemy's daughter. When she turns out to be ugly he employs his beauty ointments, and the results so please the girl's father he drops the feud and gives Budd the money to save his shop. The book, by the same team who had written *Her Little Highness* earlier in the season, was claptrap, held together by its capable star, Raymond Hitchcock. Its score was largely by Charles Gebest, with a few interpolations by Silvio Hein. It was pleasant on the ear, but quickly forgettable, filled with sweet nothings of the day. The popular Hitchcock spent much of the second intermission, at least on opening night, chatting from the stage with the audience. He won a hearty round of applause for his tango with Marion Sunshine. On her own, Miss Sunshine performed some vibrant Spanish dances. Fifty gorgeous girls rested the eyes of tired businessmen.

After years of silence Ludwig Englander's music was heard again when **Madam Moselle** (5-23-14, Shubert) began a 9-performance run. The music, his last for Broadway, was undistinguished. Englander died soon afterwards. The plot, adapted by Edward Paulton from a French farce, told how both Nina and her mother love young Fred Corson. Ralph Herz, Josie Intropidi, and Diane O'Aubrey were featured. The only noteworthy thing about the evening was its intimacy. There was no male chorus and only eight girls in the ensemble.

Two spectacle revues—the only American genre to develop in this period—brought both the season and the period itself to an end. **The Ziegfeld Follies of 1914** premiered at the New Amsterdam June 1; **The Passing Show of 1914** relit the Winter Garden nine nights later. The *Follies* was the last before the truly great editions, but, along with the edition which had opened the season, it was better than anything else of its kind on Broadway. Bert Williams provided the high spot singing "Darktown Poker Club" and following it with his single-handed card game. He was the only player, and his free hand became a hilariously dexterous computer.

This skit generally has been considered his finest moment. Ed Wynn—in the first of his two *Follies* appearances—augmented the comic department. Errol danced an exaggerated tango with Stella Chatelaine. Errol, in fact, staged the evening after Ziegfeld battled with Julian Mitchell. Ann Pennington danced a buck and wing. A Palm Beach dance contest served as a finale for an evening that had begun in Hades with Vera Michelena as the Devil. The beauties and principals marching as soldiers, presented a stirring first-act finale that concluded with "The Star Spangled Banner," and that perhaps unwittingly foreshadowed a mood that World War I would make pervasive. No song from the score and no interpolation enjoyed more than a passing popularity.

Sigmund Romberg's score for the Shuberts (with Harry Carroll's four interpolations) was of the same modest order. Numerous take-offs on current hits confirmed that *The Passing Show* still held closer to the old burlesque tradition than did the *Follies,* although spectacle and show girls were not forgotten. Notable in the cast were Lillian Lorraine, José Collins, T. Roy Barnes, and Bernard Granville. Marilyn Miller made her first appearance in a legitimate New York show, although, curiously, her imitation of Julian Eltinge, elicited more comment than her beauty or dancing. One reason for this puzzling oversight may have been the attention gained by the show girls. Indeed, the real importance of the edition was the success of its line of slim chorus girls. The thinner queens of the new silent movies and the proximity that the new Winter Garden ramp offered conspired to end forever the reign of more buxom beauties. Not only was the new glamor paraded on the ramp, a first-act finale had them floating in an airship. In another spectacular scene for "The Sloping Path" they danced their way up into the flies.

And so seven lean years of native creativity came to an end, though they were not without interest or influence. The sweepingly gorgeous Viennese material accustomed Broadway to superior craftsmanship (sometimes badly manhandled in the adaptation) as well as to memorably melodic scores. As long as Vienna and the rest of Europe offered enough of this fine artistry, it was difficult for Americans to compete, especially when they persisted in their obsolescent ways. Significantly, the few composers who did succeed in writing masterpieces for our national stages—Victor Herbert, Karl Hoschna, Rudolf Friml—were immigrants whose music was clearly stamped "European." The "native American" music employed on Broadway during this period changed little—primarily marches, two-steps, and simple domestic waltzes. And while commercial ragtime numbers were interpolated in many American works, and often, jarringly, into foreign operettas and musical comedies, no major composer appeared capable of expanding the form into an exciting, cohesive score. It was beginning to seem that ragtime would pass on without leaving more than a superficial mark on the American Musical Theatre and that no other indisputably native musical form would emerge to replace it or the Viennese style.

The composers with the most native accent were confined to writing occasional tunes for revues—a form not wholly American in its origins but at this time displaying the healthiest American growth. Irving Berlin was the best of the lot. An exception was Jerome Kern, who by and large ignored revues, inserting his compositions in Viennese and London musicals. These shows, consciously or otherwise, modified his Americanisms, allowing his style to coalesce into a unique lyric language.

Even librettists felt the malaise. During an interview in the *Dramatic Mirror* just as this period was drawing to a close, Edgar Smith described the contemporary American musical as "a hybrid type . . . built upon no sure foundation of story or plot and constructed of a varied assortment of elements which cannot be expected to assimilate." American musicals for the most part, he lamented, were put together when a producer had several songs by one or more composers and possibly a star. But he prophesied that this sort of show would "fall of its own weight. From the ruins let us hope that a saner and better structure may be built." His hopes were realized with extraordinary speed.

6

ACT THREE
The Birth of
the Modern Musical
1914-1921

The seasons from mid-1914 to mid-1921 were possibly the most exciting in the history of the American Musical Theatre. These seven years saw the birth of the American Musical as it was to be known for at least the next half-century. They witnessed, as well, its astonishingly rapid maturity. From 1915 on, no year passed without one or more offerings of such enduring merit that they could not be included unhesitatingly in a permanent repertory. The great periods ahead produced more shows of higher quality, but never before or since was the joyous thrill of discovery and first achievement so pervasive.

There were two principal reasons for this sudden, glittering outpouring. The first was a disenchantment with Europe and things European; the second was our own new self-awareness and with it the onset of a genuine self-confidence.

In 1907 *The Merry Widow* had waltzed across America, cavalierly elbowing aside the bright promise of George M. Cohan, Hough–Adams–Howard, and other young native talents. A frantic rush of immigrants followed—rose maids, chocolate soldiers, dollar princesses—until an inevitable surfeit set in.

Circumstances outside the theatre contrived to hasten and deepen this rejection. A catastrophe such as the sinking of the unsinkable *Titanic* in 1912 pointed to the end of Europe's seeming invincibility. Increasingly heated rivalries between the Great Powers set one national group against another, until finally the assassinations at Sarajevo

in June 1914 led inevitably to a general European war. In the United States anti-German sentiment surfaced at theatre box offices and eventually extended to a palpable distaste for even the most harmless Austro-Hungarian operetta.

The old order on Broadway, most of it Central European in origin, passed on just before this sentiment erupted. Karl Hoschna (only 34 years old) died in 1911, Gustav Luders (just 49 years old) in 1913, and Ludwig Englander (at 56) in 1914. Gustave Kerker was in virtual retirement.

Happily for the American theatre, a group of young, highly talented composers was waiting, almost literally, in the wings. Talent was not the only thing they displayed. Equally important was the new musical language they spoke. It was a new American idiom—most often a patois called "ragtime."

Ragtime's origins in Sedalia, Missouri, and elsewhere in the Midwest and South were untheatrical. Ben Harney first brought the new rhythm to New York in 1896. His success was immediate. Ragtime spread with remarkable speed through the expanding vaudeville circuits, and before long singers were interpolating so-called ragtime into musical comedies and revues. In 1911 Irving Berlin's "Alexander's Ragtime Band" gave the form its widest, wildest vogue.

As its vogue crested, however, ragtime dried up at its sources. Pure, classical ragtime is generally considered to have faded away by 1917, the year of the death of its most celebrated master, Scott Joplin. Claiming ragtime's place was a freer, harder, more insistent music, emanating from the same black elements that had once nurtured rag. The new music was, of course, jazz. Its pushier, seemingly chaotic sound offended many. Its Negro origins further hindered easy acceptance at a time of hardening anti-Negro sentiment, and the crucial improvisatory nature of pure jazz prevented carefully prewritten commercial materials from being anything but a pallid reflection of the original article.

Moreover the term "jazz," like "rag" before it, spread more swiftly than did a clear understanding of its meaning. To many, jazz meant simply "fast," or "noisy," or "cacophonous"—or merely "new." It was not surprising that one critic saw nothing contradictory when he called the songs in *Love Birds* "jazz rags" (they were neither). Many scores that critics hastily labeled "jazz" during this period sound today as sedate as Victorian tea dance melodies—devoid not just of improvisation, but of the distinctive chordings, rhythms, and patterns that helped define the style. Several years passed before there was a more universal enlightenment and acceptance. A few young composers, notably Jerome Kern, rarely employed black styles, but wrote with a new clean-cut line that was unmistakably Yankee, whatever its influences.

Both new composers and older ones combined in 1914 to form ASCAP—the American Society of Composers, Authors, and Publishers. The original impulse behind the move was to halt the endemic evasion of royalty payment. ASCAP's start was rocky, and it would take the seven-year span of this chapter before it consolidated its gains. Once it was established, regular payments to members allowed them an artistic independence that challenged the producer's hegemony in controlling the musical idiom in shows.

The American Musical Theatre was not alone in its renaissance. The arts all across the nation were awakening. Harriet Monroe founded her *Poetry* magazine in 1912, bringing into household use names like E. A. Robinson, T. S. Eliot, and Robert Frost. In 1914 Edgar Lee Masters published his *Spoon River Anthology*. Novels were announced by new authors such as Sinclair Lewis and Willa Cather. Frank Crowninshield took over *Vanity Fair* in 1913, and a year later, H. L. Mencken and George Jean Nathan assumed the editorship of *The Smart Set*. The 1913 Armory Show alerted Americans to the power of modern painting. The Little Theatre Movement sprang up. Out of it came the Provincetown Playhouse and Eugene O'Neill, and the Washington Square Players who gave birth to the Theatre Guild. It was a heady era for the arts.

1914-1915

The European war was less than three weeks old when the season's first musical arrived. **The Dancing Duchess** (8-20-14, Casino) moved through two worlds—the frenetic, contemporary world of the dancing craze and the carefree, war-free world of a suddenly bygone Vienna and Budapest. The Duchess of Darmia (Laura Hamilton) runs away when the Duke bans all modern dancing. Under the name Celestine she becomes the rage of Vienna's Trocadero. The repentant Duke unmasks her in Budapest, where she and her men friends have gone to enter a tango contest. Both the show's dialogue and songs were turgid. In addition it was unable to make the best of its two worlds. Its American authors, working freely from a Continental original, made a few token bows to the musical modes of the day, especially in "The Tango Breakfast," its first number, and "The Ragtime Whirl," its last. For many of the dances and the greater part of the evening's lightest capers the producers hired John Hyams and Leila McIntyre, two performers more popular on the road and in vaudeville, where Miss McIntyre's Quaker act was a headliner. Hyams and Miss McIntyre imbued *The Dancing Duchess* with a bit of vitality and a touch of modernity. But most of it was ersatz operetta, persisting in the delusion "Everybody's Happy In Vienna." Devastated by even the most lenient critics, the duchess left the scene in two weeks' time.

The Girl from Utah (8-24-14, Knickerbocker) was one of four shows of the 1914–15 season that must be considered milestones in our musical theatre's history. Oddly enough, this Charles Frohman production was an importation. With a book by James T. Tanner, lyrics by Adrian Ross and Percy Greenbank, and a score by Paul Rubens and Sidney Jones, it had enjoyed a long London run with the American Ina Claire in the name role. Its plot made it a natural for Broadway. Una Trance (Julia Sanderson) of Utah arrives in London to escape an objectionable Mormon marriage. At Rumpelmeyers' she meets an actor, Sandy Blair (Donald Brian); a ludicrous butcher named Trimpel (Joseph Cawthorn) of Brixton Rest; and, to her dismay, her pursuing Mormon. The Mormon forces Una to go with him to Brixton Rest, but she leaves a trail for Blair and Trimpel to follow. At the Arts Ball (decorated in an Indian motif, with the Taj Mahal at the rear), the Mormon finally agrees that Sandy would be the better match for Una and decides to return home alone. Frohman astutely realized that, notwithstanding the excellence of the book, the show needed better songs than Rubens and Jones had provided. In what proved to be one last, inspired gesture he hired Jerome Kern to write additional numbers. Kern had interpolated tunes in Frohman's London shows as early as 1903 —a year before New York heard its first Kern melodies. Thereafter Kern songs had been added to numerous Frohman productions on both sides of the Atlantic. But never before were the songs of such significance. Kern's interpolations not only made the show a smash hit, they established Kern as a master of light, lyrical composition.

Kern and Frohman apparently felt that, in view of the international cataclysm, the show's story might seem unduly frivolous and old-fashioned. To assure the acceptance of its theatricality they framed the whole evening in one of Kern's most exquisitely fey melodies, "The Land Of 'Lets Pretend'." The show's three stars—Miss Sanderson, Brian, and Cawthorn—stepped out of character at the beginning and end of the story to sing Harry B. Smith's stilted but workable lyrics for the song, lyrics inviting audiences to "find folly a good friend." Six other Kern songs were added to the main story, most in the second half—the affectionate "We'll Take Care Of You All," the willowy "Alice In Wonderland," two vivacious fox-trots, "Same Sort Of Girl" and "You Never Can Tell" (in the pattern of the preceding season's "You're Here And I'm Here"), the foot-stomping "Why Don't They Dance The Polka Anymore?", and the hit of the show, "They Didn't Believe Me." A long line of musicians and scholars has devoted prolonged analysis to this magnificent melody. In his *American Popular Song,* Alec Wilder took nearly two pages to discuss it. He called the melodic line "as natural as walking," although "its form is not conventional even by the standards of the time." In his opinion the controversial triplet coupled with the words "cert-'n-ly am" was not a concession to the lyricist's needs and rightly observed it is usually sung " 'and I'm cert-'n-ly,' making of the 'n' the second note of the triplet." In the show the song was given first to Una, although its lyrics were really more suitable for a man; more often than not a

man sings it today. It remains one of Kern's finest achievements. For fifty years after it was written, until the rock and roll sound came to dominate popular music, there was not a time when it could not have seemed absolutely up-to-date.

Because Brian was fortunate enough to star in so many of the most melodic shows of the era, it is often forgotten that he was more of a dancer than a singer. But in these gay old song and dance shows, where dance and song entertained equally, most performers had to be doubly skillful. No one was surprised at Brian's lively polka or snappy tap routines, nor was there any amazement when Miss Sanderson joined him, notably at the costume ball finale, to glide gracefully arm in arm across the stage.

In the freewheeling ways of the day, other songs were interpolated into the score. Initially these included two of Herman Finck's English hits, "Gilbert The Filbert" and "Florrie The Flapper" (both with lyrics by Arthur Wimperis), as well as "At Our Tango Tea" (Worton David and Bert Lee) and "The Girl In The Clogs And Shawl" (Harry Castling and C. W. Murphy). A few less discerning critics singled these out for praise and ignored Kern's pieces. At some time during its tour "Balling The Jack" (Chris Smith and James Reese Europe) was inserted. And when *The Girl from Utah* announced a return engagement in the summer of 1915 it was noted that three new songs, none by Kern, were part of the score—"Molly Dear, It's You I'm After," "If I Can't Be Captain, I Don't Want To Play," and "Grown Up Children."

The annual Hippodrome show followed on September 5. It ran 229 performances. This was not a bad run considering the size of the house, but it was the least successful of the eighteen extravaganzas mounted there. Its forbidding, if timely, title, **Wars of the World,** may have discouraged potential patrons, even though the wars it presented included "The War of Sport" (with Harvard winning a regatta) and "The War of Pleasure" (an Italian carnival where the funmakers sang in the best Tin Pan Alley style of "Baby Eyes"). Even in the more serious "Wars for Religion" or "War of Brother against Brother," multicolored spectacle all but denied any horror. Other problems contributed to the slow box office. Over the years, a sameness had crept into the presentations and the novelty of their grandeur had worn thin. Worse, in the last season or two the movies had begun to provide spectacle beyond the facilities of even the Hippodrome's vast stage. Finally, by November it was obvious that the public, fascinated by the war but disturbed by the economic uncertainties it threatened, was staying away from theatres everywhere. The Shuberts announced they were withdrawing from the productions. A new producer had to be found.

Miss Daisy (9-9-14, Shubert) survived less than a month. Philip Bartholomae's story told of Daisy Hollister's taking a job as a maid in the Swigget's home in order to attract their guest, the Duke of Tormina (Joseph Lertora). Daisy (Florence Mackie) wins the Duke, and her brother (Donald MacDonald) wins Miss Swigget (Anna Wheaton). As usual, Silvio Hein's music was "agreeable without being distinctive."

A more interesting failure followed. **Pretty Mrs. Smith** (9-21-14, Casino) is about to be divorced from her third husband—all three have been named Smith. She goes to Palm Beach for rest and soul-searching. Instead, she finds all three Messrs. Smith there—a particularly nasty shock since she had believed the first two were dead. After some indecisive flirting she is reconciled with number three. Although the glamorous and popular Fritzi Scheff was starred, she found the show stolen from her by Charlotte Greenwood, a tall, slender, young girl with beautiful eyes and with long legs that seemed not to have any joints as the youngster did splits and unbelievable "flat footed" kicks. Miss Greenwood's "Long, Lean, Lanky Letty" was so well received that the show's producer, Oliver Morosco (for whom she had worked in other West Coast musicals), revised the show and retitled it *Long-Legged Letty*. It was the first of a series of musical comedies written around the comedienne's unique talents. "Letty" shows kept her busy on and off for a dozen years. *Pretty Mrs. Smith*, with Letitia Proudfoot removed, was made into a silent movie, Fritzi Scheff repeating her Broadway role.

A Winter Garden revue—billed as a musical spectacle—appeared on October 10. While it was called **Dancing Around**, its main attraction was the singing of Al Jolson. Unhappily, neither the Sigmund Romberg and Harry Carroll score nor Jolson's interpolations had special merit. "It's A Long Way To Tipperary" (Jack Judge and Harry Williams) was inserted briefly but never became associated with either Jolson or the show. Jolson's informality, projected so irresistibly across the footlights, was captured on his recording of another of the show's interpolations, "Sister Susie's Sewing Shirts For Soldiers." Jolson sang the song, then had a member of the audience sing it with him. Finally he reached out to the other patrons cajoling, "Now folks you've all heard the song a couple times. I

think we oughta all sing it together." Jolson also clowned in the evening's skits. He wiped away his blackface to play a mincing designer in a parody of *My Lady's Dress*, a play that shared the same opening night as *Dancing Around*. He also became the entire staff of a hectically under-manned Hotel Lavender. For spectacle the Shuberts offered a locomotive race and a gavotte performed in a setting out of Watteau. The revue was not yet free of the notion that some sort of story line was necessary. But in this case, as the *Dramatic Mirror* observed, "The plot, which concerned the search of a British army officer [Bernard Granville] for a prima donna [Cecil Cunningham] wearing a crescent of court plaster on her back, dropped into oblivion about half-past nine o'clock, and never again emerged." For all its inadequacies, *Dancing Around* ran 145 performances.

In the season's biggest success, **Chin-Chin** (10-20-14, Globe), Dave Montgomery and Fred Stone once again led the way to their unique never-neverland where the playthings of childhood come back to life in a strangely contemporary world. At a Pekin toyshop tin soldiers and painted dolls sing to each other of their love, and the ways of the world in which history heroes have hearts of gold—though they add that sometimes less than the whole truth is told. In a land such as this there is no reason not to meet Aladdin (Douglas Stevenson) and his aunt, Widow Twankey (Zelma Rawlston), who possesses "a golden lamp that looks like brass—perfectly straight, except where it's crooked, short the tall way, and tall the short way, with a little round knob on the top." The villainous Abanazar (Charles T. Aldrich), the toyshop's owner and Aladdin's employer, wants to buy the lamp and sell it to a rich American, Cornelius Bond (R. E. Graham). Bond's daughter Violet (Helen Falconer) falls in love with Aladdin, and he, in turn, falls in love with the "Yankee princess." But Bond will not hear of his daughter marrying anyone who is not a "bultibillionaire." Luckily, two Chinese mannequins, Chin Hop Hi (Stone) and Chin Hop Lo (Montgomery), who are also slaves of the lamp, bring the lamp to Aladdin. With two rubs Aladdin is rich and lastingly assured of Violet's love. The first act curtain falls while "Ev'ry chink goes just as dippy as a coon from Mis-si-si-pi" to the "Ragtime Temple Bells." But Abanazar manages to obtain the lamp and transports them all to a circus in Holland and a park in Paris where Hi, disguised as a ventriloquist (whose most common response is "Very Good, Eddie"), a gendarme, Paderewski, Mlle. Falloffski, and Lo, masquerading as another gendarme, a widow, a coolie, and a clown, always turn up and finally put things right.

Ching [the coolie]: Now you can go
Abanazar: Why?
Ching: Because you are the villain and we can't finish the story with you here!
Abanazar: And you can't start without me, so I will be here tomorrow night at eight-thirty. Matinees at two-fifteen.

One reviewer intimated that Hi and Lo's ultimate reward was to be turned white.

Older playgoers—or younger ones familiar with still lively English traditions—quickly recognized the source of the evening's drolleries—the children's pantomimes once so popular in America and even now a holiday favorite in England. Abanazar, the Widow Twankey, and several minor characters had appeared regularly in British retellings of the Aladdin story since the 18th century and, conceivably, even earlier.

Ivan Caryll's score and Anne Caldwell's lyrics were pleasant. Not all of the lyrics were Caldwell's. Aladdin's amazement at finding the love of his life, "Goodbye Girls, I'm Through" (with words by John Golden), was popular in its day. Hi and Lo's two original numbers, "A Chinese Honeymoon" and "Ragtime Temple Bells," had lyrics by Bryan and Williams, and James O'Dea respectively. Nor was all the music by Caryll. During the run three other songs were given to the stars, "Bally Mooney" (Terence Lowry), "Go Gar Sig Gong-Jue," and the already popular "It's A Long, Long Way To Tipperary."

Because Montgomery and Stone shows were so suitable for children, they benefited from an extra large audience. Yet, as we have shown, critics never thought they patronized their audiences and so considered their vehicles adult entertainment. References in *Chin-Chin* to the dancing craze, bridge, futurists, and cloisonné imply a knowing crowd. But something in Montgomery and Stone's style, now irretrievably lost, must have assisted in conveying a truly universal appeal. When a brutal box office slump hit in what should have been the height of the season, *Chin-Chin* alone of all Broadway shows continued to sell out.

George V. Hobart, the popular librettist, wrote *Experience,* for which Silvio Hein composed a few songs and Max Bendix proved background music. One of the hits of the year, it was not, however, a true musical. It was followed by **The Lilac Domino** (10-28-14, 44th St.), a European favorite by the Belgian composer, Charles Cuvillier. Three young

men have lost so heavily at cards they agree one must wed an heiress wealthy enough to keep them all in chips. The heiress was played by Eleanor Painter. America's heartfelt sympathy for Belgium's plight was not reflected at the box office, and the operetta was withdrawn after three weeks.

November 2 gave first-nighters a choice of two musicals **Papa's Darling** and **The Only Girl.** *Papa's Darling* was based on the French comedy *Le Fils Surnaturel* by Grenet d'Ancourt and Maurice Vaucaire. The young lady of the title does not exist. She is the fictitious daughter of a village professor (Frank Lalor), who uses her as an excuse for his Parisian flings. It was another Harry B. Smith adaptation (he had done *The Lilac Domino,* too), with Smith also supplying lyrics for the second Caryll score to be heard in two weeks. In his autobiography Smith wrote, "In telling the plot to Klaw and Erlanger, Caryll laughed more than any audience that ever attended the play. If we could have had him in the audience instead of in the conductor's chair, we might have had a success." *Papa's Darling* was a five-week failure at the New Amsterdam.

However, the small, unlucky 39th Street Theatre had one of its few successes with *The Only Girl.* Henry Blossom, working from Frank Mandel's *Our Wives,* retained the original's intimacy by keeping to two simple sets and a relatively small cast. Four bachelors—Alan "Kim" Kimbrough (Thurston Hall), Sylvester "Corksey" Martin (Richard Bartlett), John "Fresh" Ayre (Jed Prouty), and Andrew "Bunkie" McMurray (Ernest Torrence)—determine to stay single. Kim, in whose apartment the action takes place, hears someone in a neighboring flat play a beautiful love theme. The composer, Ruth (Wilda Bennett), proves to be as beautiful as her music, and Kim, who is a librettist, proposes they work together. Strictly business. "We both hate things sentimental. We are two machines. That's all!" Six weeks later Corksey, Fresh, and Bunkie have lapsed into matrimony. The three couples sing and dance a happy sextette, "Connubial Bliss," while offstage Ruth is heard singing her love theme. The men have second thoughts several hours later when their wives refuse to let them leave for a night on the town. But even their warning, "When You're Wearing The Ball And Chain," cannot save Kim. Ruth pleads, "You're The Only One For Me," and Kim is beyond resisting.

The love theme, which is initially heard (apart from the overture) offstage early in the first act and then is sung by Ruth moments later as "When

You're Away," was one of Victor Herbert's most beguiling melodies. But the whole score, while far from Herbert's best, was above Broadway's average. Blossom's lyrics, fustian in the more serious numbers ("Ah! When in sweet raptures of love you enfold me"), could be refreshingly colloquial in the lighter tunes ("She said, 'Dear, What do I hear? That ev'ry pretty little skirt within a mile you try to flirt with! I just won't stand for it! See!' "). These lighter tunes were given to Patsy La Montrose (Adele Rowland), the one important character besides the eight lovers. Her numbers were used to inject a contemporary immediacy into the show. Her first song, "The More I See Of Others, Dear, The Better I Like You," had an almost equally long subtitle, "An Imitation Of The Present Day Ragtime Song." Actually it was a standard Herbert melody cleverly set on top of rag-like base. Patsy and Kim sing the militaristic "Here's To The Land We Love, Boys," which acknowledged the three-month-old war and warned we would fight if we had to. In the last act she took the producers of the day to task in the delightful "You Have To Have A Part To Make A Hit." Assigning the comedienne biting or down-to-earth lyrics and more stylish music was a common practice of the time. It reflected the epoch's more decorous proprieties. But it often gave romantic leads an unworldly wholesomeness, sometimes even an irritatingly saccharine innocence. It was rare, before the twenties, to help create more fully dimensional characters by carefully distributing assignments of various types of songs.

An unsuccessful importation, **Suzi** (11-3-14, Casino), was the sole musical to appear between *The Only Girl* and Herbert's second entry, **The Debutante** (12-7-14, Knickerbocker). *Suzi,* with José Collins in the title role and a large company in support, depicted the love of an opera star for a hussar. A company of 100, including a "pony" chorus dressed nattily as middies, struggled to make *The Debutante* frolicsome. The book was by Harry B. Smith, so its readers fairly well knew what the *Dramatic Mirror* meant when it suggested, "It does not soar above the level of a Smith libretto, and does not fall below it." Smith's debutante, Elaine (Hazel Dawn), the daughter of Sir Francis Vane, is engaged to a rich young American, Philip Frazer (Wilmuth Merkyl). But Philip loves Irma (Zoe Barnett). Elaine arranges with the Marquis de Frontenac (Stewart Baird) to make Philip notice the Marquis' attentions to her. Later, at a ball, she outshines Irma, and Philip is won over. Harry's brother Robert wrote the lyrics. Herbert's music, praised by many of the critics, was not his most

inspired. Reviewers singled out Philip and Elaine's "The Golden Age" and "The Love Of The Lorelei" as well as the Marquis' "All For The Sake Of A Girl." Even with Miss Dawn as star, *The Debutante* lasted only six weeks.

Besides the show's weaknesses and the economic plight of the theatre, a third circumstance possibly shortened the operetta's run. It opened one night ahead of the season's most ballyhooed show, Irving Berlin's **Watch Your Step** (12-8-14, New Amsterdam).

. . .

Born Israel Baline in Temun, Russia, on May 11, 1888, **Irving Berlin** and his parents were driven to emigrate by a bloody pogrom. The family settled on New York City's Lower East Side. A few years later his father's death sent Berlin out on the streets to earn his living by accompanying a blind singer on his rounds of saloons. Berlin served as a youthful song plugger and as a singing waiter. In 1907 he wrote the lyrics for "Marie From Sunny Italy" (music by Nick Nicholson), and a year later wrote both words and music for "She Was A Dear Little Girl," which Marie Cahill interpolated into *The Boys and Betty*. 1909 brought his first substantial success, "Sadie Salome," and in 1911 "Alexander's Ragtime Band" made him famous.

. . .

The twenty-six-year-old Berlin had quickly caught on to the advantages of astute public relations. In a well-spaced series of interviews, both before the show opened and during its run, Berlin insisted his great ambition was to write a "ragtime opera." Ragtime to Berlin was simply syncopation, and while syncopation had always existed, American rag was distinguished by a "more graceful rhythm." Berlin, a musical illiterate, undoubtedly understood that composing an opera—even a ragtime opera—required more than his great melodic and rhythmic gifts would ever allow. But not since George M. Cohan's works, a decade before, had there been quite so determined an effort to produce an entire score using only native musical speech. Even the earlier Negro musicals, which, consciously or not, offered ragtime in their numbers, preferred to imitate foreign styles. The *Evening Sun*, with an appreciative sense of occasion, concluded the "work is ephemeral as art, but is permanent as a landmark."

Ballyhoo or no, the score was inventive and effervescent. Although only one of its songs became a Berlin standard, and that only after forty years of neglect, the entire score deserves study. The overture itself, wrapping a medley of the best numbers around the exhilarating "Syncopated Walk," promptly raised the highest expectations. The show's dancing emphasis was established in the cute but inane opening—one of the score's few weak spots—when the chorus complains it can't work all day if it's been dancing all night. The nation was in the throes of "the dancing craze," and the nation's stellar ballroom dancers, Irene and Vernon Castle, led the cast. The first regular number of the show, sung by its ingenue, Ernesta (Sallie Fisher), was a waltz—a seemingly most unragtime tempo. But if, as Berlin proposed, ragtime was merely syncopation, then he had written a startlingly rag-like waltz, "What Is Love?" "I'm A Dancing Teacher Now" had Vernon Castle kidding the dancing school explosion. It was followed by "The Minstrel Parade," "Let's Go Around The Town," and "They Always Follow Me Around." Irene Castle, who alone was not given a character to play and appeared on the program simply as Mrs. Vernon Castle, next had what was really the title song, though it was published and listed as "Show Us How To Do The Fox Trot." It was an irresistible invitation to the dance. "When I Discovered You," a fast-stepping love duet, was followed by the show's theme, "The Syncopated Walk." Berlin employed it as a frame for the overture, as the first act's principal production number and finale, as an entr'acte, and as the grand finale. Its lyric, proclaiming "ever since the dancing craze, Ev'rybody has a syncopated walk," suggested how thoroughly the new fad had spread. The second act centered upon the Metropolitan Opera, building to the musical's major production number, an "Opera Melody," ragging the most popular arias. This brings the Ghost of Verdi stalking to the old house, where he clashes with the modern boys and girls. The last entr'acte repeated "Settle Down In A One Horse," sung in the second act, and promptly followed with an orchestral piece called "Homecoming." Ernesta protests she is tired of the new music and begs to hear a "Simple Melody," while Algy in counterpoint insists he wants to listen to rag. (This is the song that was rediscovered after forty years and now is considered a great Berlin standard.) Rag triumphed with everyone ending the show again doing a "Syncopated Walk."

As usual, Berlin was his own lyricist. The dialogue was by the indefatigable Harry B. Smith—his fourth libretto in just over a month. But in this case it was moot if there was in fact a libretto. Smith himself, in the program and on the vocal score, accepted the credit "Book (if any)," and several aisle-sitters stated the show had no plot.

Actually there was the thinnest of story lines. Jabez Hardacre bequeaths a legacy to any male relative who has never loved, been engaged, or married. The effort to determine which of Jabez' two male survivors best fits the description provides the continuity. The cast of characters included such minor figures as Willie Steele, "a tango lawyer," Silas Flint, "a maxixe lawyer," and Estelle, "a hesitating typewriter." Estelle was played by a statuesque beauty Ziegfeld glorified, Justine Johnstone. Curiously, the ingenue's unusual full name, Ernesta Hardacre, was not new to Broadway. Augustin Daly had included a character by that name in his proto-revue, *Round the Clock* (11-25-72), a generation before. With "revues" still insisting on stories to hold them together and "musical comedies" still accepting the most meager excuses for plots, *Watch Your Step* demonstrates the confusion between the genres at the time: the theatrical sheets of the day discussing the "Rush of Revues" included the show (as well, sometimes, as *Chin-Chin*) in their articles. Robert Baral, in 1962, accepted it as a revue in his study of the genre. But before the month was out, another show began putting an end to the confusion thin plots created.

Dillingham's sumptuous mounting featured an elaborate, if necessarily scaled-down, re-creation of the old Metropolitan, with patrons in evening clothes filling both lower level boxes and the Diamond Horseshoe, and a simulated production on the "Met's" stage. Besides those already mentioned, performers included Elizabeth Murray and Charles King.

Christmas week brought in three musicals. **Tonight's the Night** (12-24-14, Shubert) was an English creation about love in not so high society. On the 25th, **Lady Luxury** at the Casino vied for attention with **Hello, Broadway** at the Astor. *Lady Luxury* starred the beautiful comedienne, Ina Claire, as Eloise Van Cuyler, the long-repressed ward of her uncle (Harry Conor). She comes of age fifteen minutes after the curtain goes up and throws a big party. Naturally the party allowed the evening to be stuffed with specialty acts. Francis Bryan and Emilie Lea as a pair of high-kicking Russian dancers won the greatest applause. At the end of the evening the guardian reappears from a secret panel behind which he has been watching the giddy cavortings.

Lady Luxury was a quick, insignificant failure; *Hello, Broadway* was an innovative George M. Cohan revue. It had a satisfactory run and a brief tour. But it was a far more important work than its modest success suggests. Cohan discarded the heavyweight opulence of the *Follies* and the Winter Garden shows. Instead he looked back to the Weber and Fields tradition of burlesque, out of which his costar, William Collier, came. All the skits satirized American institutions, although the emphasis was on the New York stage. To speed the action, sets were changed while audiences watched. Jurors and witnesses grabbed parts of a courtroom scene and ran off stage with them as players brought on the props they would require for the spoof of *My Lady's Dress* that followed. The pacing was quick by Ziegfeld or Shubert standards, even if sketches were longer than in later, still faster-paced revues. Nor was the later clear-cut separation of skits and musical numbers always evident. Numbers utilized the auditorium as well as the stage. "Down By The Erie Canal" was first sung by Louise Dresser and a chorus shaking tambourines. A boy in the gallery took up the song, followed by an old man in a box. Then the curtains parted to disclose "ladies and gentlemen dressed in heavy, purple velvet, rowing Venetian gondolas along a green-ribbon Erie Canal." If the music included an "Old Fashioned Cake Walk" it also had a "Jesse James Glide" and a "Barnum and Bailey Rag." The first-act finale was a generous Cohan tribute to his younger competitor, Berlin. Although the rapidly churning musical world soon left Cohan sadly behind, at least at this point Cohan embraced the changes. He offered a list off composers and shows that he proclaimed were "all through." His list included the Merry Widow and "Mr." Sousa. In another way Cohan helped establish the modern revue. He liberated it from any pretense of plot. Several performers remained in character throughout the evening, but they served essentially as extended compères. In the show's most famous bit, a hat box, purporting to contain a plot, was carried on stage at intervals. At the end three players meet:

McCluskey: Ah Ha! The hat box. Now to reveal the plot of the play. (Opens the box) Empty!
Babbit: What became of the plot?
George: There never was a plot.

From "plot (if any)" to "there never was a plot" in less than a month's time! Modern revue had arrived. Certainly theatregoers thought so, and they were obviously happy about it. Two weeks after *Hello, Broadway* appeared the *Dramatic Mirror*, under the heading "More Revues Coming," noted, "The revue, which for the last two years has been the most popular form of musical entertainment in London and Paris, is invading New York with the force and dispatch of the German Army. . . . The

musical revue seems to be what the public wants, judging from the attendance at 'Watch Your Step' and 'Hello, Broadway'." At the same time, on the front page of its January 16, 1915, issue, *Variety* published Cohan's hope that "the permanent policy of the Astor Theatre in the future will be for 'revues' along the lines of the old Weber and Fields music hall." Cohan added that the cast of *Hello, Broadway* might serve "as the nucleus of a stock company there."

After the Christmas rush, no musicals came to New York until the 25th of January 1915. That night's arrival at the Knickerbocker proved an especially poignant failure. **Ninety in the Shade** was set in the Philippines, where Willoughby Parker (Richard Carle) has settled down to enjoy his reputation as a ladies' man. What the ladies don't know is that Willoughby is engaged to Polly Bainbridge (Marie Cahill). Her unexpected appearance produces immediate complications which are resolved only when Bob Mandrake (Edward Martindell), a smuggler, woos and wins Polly, leaving Parker to pursue a lady known as "The Hot Tamale" (Jean Newcombe). Although some critics complained that Guy Bolton's book belonged to an obsolescent school, they nonetheless found much to praise in it and in Jerome Kern's lovely score. But there was a feeling that Miss Cahill and Carle were perhaps a bit too old for the principal roles. Except to tie wedding knots for secondary characters who would otherwise be left at loose ends, Broadway musicals were not yet prepared to deal with love interests beyond a young boy's meeting a young girl. Miss Cahill, whose dismissal from *It Happened in Nordland* (12-5-04) had taught her nothing, aggravated matters by insisting on her own interpolations, however inappropriate and jolting they might be. Kern was still not quite famous enough to protest effectively. The musical's incongruities, coupled with the generally bad business conditions, kept patronage down, and *Ninety in the Shade* closed abruptly and ignominiously when its unpaid actors refused to perform. Since the production was a low-budget affair, employing only eight chorus girls and eight chorus boys, the failure was doubly humiliating. For Carle and Cahill it was the virtual end of musical stardom. In the issue of the *Dramatic Mirror* that detailed the closing, another column advised, "A radical change of policy is impending at the Princess Theatre . . . F. Ray Comstock, manager of the Princess, has announced that in the near future he will present there a musical comedy, the book of which has been adapted from an English original." The adaptation was by *Ninety in the Shade*'s librettist, Bolton, and the songs were assigned to its composer, Kern. No one could foresee that Comstock, Bolton, and Kern were about to make American Musical Theatre history.

. . .

Guy Bolton was born in Broxbourne, Hertfordshire, England, on November 23, 1884. His parents were American, and his father a celebrated engineer. Young Bolton studied architecture in France. After moving to New York he helped design the Soldiers' and Sailors' Monument on Riverside Drive. His first attempts at playwriting went unproduced or folded out of town, but in 1914 his farce, *The Rule of Three,* realized a modest success. This same year saw some of his writings published in *The Smart Set* and also witnessed his first meeting with Jerome Kern.

. . .

Maid in America, the next Winter Garden revue, opened February 18 and played up to the growing patriotic fervor the European war was stimulating. Its cast of characters included a "Made-in-America French Actress" and a "Made-in-America English Lord." And while a cast of characters suggests a book, the Shuberts followed the trend and credited Atteridge solely and honestly with "Song Cues." Unfortunately Sigmund Romberg and Harry Carroll's songs were again commonplace. But the show had the customary Winter Garden glitter, unusual staging (the chorus girls flashed lights at the men in the audience as they sang of their search for "Someone's Heart"), and enough names—such as Nora Bayes, Charles Ross, Harry Fox—to give it a respectable run.

Another respectable run was recorded by an importation, **The Peasant Girl** (3-2-15, 44th St.), which starred Emma Trentini and for which Rudolf Friml wrote additional melodies. Miss Trentini played another waif who rises to heights in the opera world. She had to fight for her laurels this time, since Clifton Crawford's lithe dancing and gay comedy almost stole the show. It was the first of two March entries. The second, **Fads and Fancies** (3-8-15, Knickerbocker), by Glen MacDonough and Raymond Hubbell, survived for six weeks. The show was a lavish vaudeville tied together with a thin plot in which Professor Glum (Frank Moulan) enlists the aid of two detectives, Chase Clews (Tom McNaughton) and Hawkshaw Holmes (John Miller). Specialty acts included an Italian monologue by Leo Carrillo (as Giovanni Gasolini) and a blackface dialogue about beating the insurance companies conducted by Conroy and Lemaire.

In mid-April, William Brady mounted a repertory of Gilbert and Sullivan favorites: *The Yeomen of the Guard, The Mikado, The Sorcerer, Trial by Jury, H.M.S. Pinafore,* and *Iolanthe.* Brady offered the additional lure of two beloved clowns, De Wolf Hopper and Digby Bell.

Conceived by Elizabeth Marbury as a showcase for young playwrights and their one-act plays, the Princess Theatre was the smallest house in New York, seating only 299 people. Its location on the south side of West 39th Street, across from Maxine Elliott's jewel box auditorium, put it at the very edge of the theatrical map. When it announced a "radical change of policy" in March, it had been operating under its old policy for less than two years—the theatre opened on March 14, 1913. Not too surprisingly, the short plays had failed to attract sufficient audiences. Miss Marbury, an agent, and Comstock, the theatre's head, desperately needed another type of entertainment. They had commissioned Bolton and Kern to revise Paul Rubens' *Mr. Popple of Ippleton* for Broadway tastes. A private reading of the revisions proved disastrous, so they decided to limit their expenditures and produce the show as frugally as possible at the Princess. They gave their authors a freer hand but insisted that because of the house's limited capacity, there could be only one set for each act, few costume changes, and as small a cast as possible. A budget limit of $7,500 was set. The show was retitled **Nobody Home.** A preopening brochure promised the "Smartest musical offering of the New York season." Making virtues out of necessities, it continued, "It is said of 'Nobody Home' that there is a real story and a real plot, which does not get lost during the course of the entertainment . . . this particular offering seems especially appropriate to an intimate playhouse of the character of the Princess." A cleverly coordinated campaign before the April 20 premiere spread the word that something new was afoot.

The first act is set in the Hotel Blitz (New York's Ritz-Carlton, affectionately known as "the Ritz," was almost as new as the Princess, having opened in 1907). Vernon Popple (George Anderson) is in love with Violet (Alice Dovey), but before they can marry he must obtain the consent of her snobbish, domineering aunt (Maude Odell) and her aunt's ludicrous Italian husband (Charles Judels). The chances of the aunt's acquiescing are slim, for Vernon is a "society dancer" and has been seen around town with the Winter Garden star, Tony Miller (Adele Rowland). Vernon's Dundrearyish brother, Freddy (Lawrence Grossmith), arrives and unwittingly amuses Miss Miller. She discovers he has no place to stay and lets him use the apartment she has just purchased. She will not be inconvenienced, for she is about to take her show on tour and had planned to sublet the apartment anyway. The second act moves to the apartment, in and out of which a foppish decorator keeps running as he applies last-minute touches. Vernon arrives to visit his brother; Violet arrives to find Vernon; the aunt and uncle arrive to consider subletting; and Tony arrives to precipitate the confusion. When the inevitable mistaken relationships are explained, Vernon and Violet can marry. Surprisingly, Tony announces she will marry Freddy if he will have her. He will.

The writing was not always the most felicitous. There were lines that seem incredibly stilted, even for the period:

Vernon: I hope I shan't offend you if I say you are the loveliest thing my eyes have ever rested on?

Some of the humor was outrageous:

Aunt: Do you feel like a pot roast?
Uncle: I don't know how a pot roast feels.

And some not funny at all:

Uncle: I want to be sure that in case of fire nothing happens to me.
Hotel Manager: Excuse me. I am sure you have made a mistake. You mean that nothing should happen to your wife.
Uncle: No. I don't make mistakes. I mean me.

Some of the other writing seems hasty and clumsy. The uncle, an inveterate skirt-chaser, realizes he was wrong to bring his wife with him to New York. He sings his regrets, "You Don't Take A Sandwich To A Banquet," after this lead-in:

Uncle: Where did you say they [his and his wife's rooms] were?
Clerk: In opposite wings.
Uncle: That's the nearest I ever got to a chicken.

Similarly, late in the second act the stage is momentarily empty, and the typescript reads "(Dance Specialty)."

Kern's music, while not as consistently fine as his songs for *The Girl from Utah*, was still excellent—although Kern did not write as much of the score as the cover of the sheet music or the title page of the program would suggest. "Beautiful, Beautiful Bed" was by C. W. Murphy and Dan Lipton. The sandwich song was by Worton David and J. P. Long. The celebrated black bandmaster, James Reese Europe, and his associate Ford T. Dabney provided

the chorus of "At That San Francisco Fair" (Kern added an introduction). Otto Motzan composed the "Nobody Home Cake Walk." Motzan collaborated with Kern on "The Chaplin Walk" and "Any Old Night." Kern's outstanding numbers were "In Arcady"—sung in the show by a minor character—and Vernon and Violet's "Another Little Girl" (both with Herbert Reynolds lyrics), and Tony's "The Magic Melody" and Vernon and Violet's "You Know and I Know" (the two with Schuyler Greene words). The roster of songs changed occasionally and inexplicably. Neither "The Chaplin Walk" nor "You Know and I Know" was listed on the program of the road company that played Philadelphia in the 1915–16 season.

Although the critics were entertained, the pre-opening publicity seemed to have backfired. "What was supposed to be a reformation of musical farce took place last night in the delightful little auditorium of the Princess Theatre," the *Sun* observed, concluding, "very little . . . could have been called important from any point of view." The show ran 135 performances—enough to induce Marbury and Comstock to try again with a second Bolton-Kern effort.

More Kern music was heard in **A Modern Eve** (5-3-15, Casino), a German musical that was first "Americanized" for Chicago and further revised for New York. The story told how a wife's indiscreet action almost cost her husband his business.

On May 7 the horror of the *Lusitania* sinking was brought home to Broadway with the loss of its pre-eminent producer, Charles Frohman, and of one of its earliest librettists, Charles Klein.

The season's last production was **The Passing Show of 1915** (5-29-15, Winter Garden), considered by many the best edition of the series. Marilyn Miller, who was to reign over musical comedy for the next two decades, stole the show and began her quick climb to the top. She highlighted the first-act finale, a lavish Spring Ballet, and showed her versatility by dressing up as Clifton Crawford to imitate his taps and shuffles.

. . .

Marilyn Miller, the daughter of vaudevillians, was born in Evansville, Indiana, on September 1, 1898. She made her debut with her mother and stepfather in an act known as the Columbian Trio in 1904. Later in an expanded act called the Five Columbians she toured the world for nearly ten years. Lee Shubert discovered her while she was dancing at London's Lotus Club and promptly signed the petite, blonde dancer with a face of Dresden doll beauty for *The Passing Show of 1914*.

By then she had long dropped her real name, Mary Ellen Reynolds. For a time she spelled her stage name Marilynn until Florenz Ziegfeld persuaded her that the simpler spelling was more desirable.

. . .

The Howard brothers mocked Shakespeare, George du Maurier's novel *Trilby*, and lampooned the ill-starred matinee idol Lou Tellegen as Lou Tellegram. Willie Howard as Charlie Chaplin cavorted with Miss Miller's Mary Pickford. Most of the other skits also dealt with theatrical people and current shows, but, like so many 1915 entries, for additional inspiration it looked to the San Francisco fair ("Panama-Pacific Drag") and the hula rage ("My Hula Maid"). This hula fad, part of the dancing craze, had a side benefit for chorus lines, allowing an "easy, lush, exotic carnality" somehow less vulnerable to prudish condemnation than Latin or European choreography. Like *Nobody Home* and *Hello, Broadway*, the revue looked back a bit in time with a cakewalk number.

Only twenty-three musicals opened in the 1914–15 season, the lowest figure since 1901–02. But the small total belied the importance of the more significant shows. *The Girl from Utah; Watch Your Step; Hello, Broadway;* and *Nobody Home* marked historic beginnings for the American Musical. They established not just new, major names, but more urgently the validity of American styles and ideas. The *Dramatic Mirror,* cantankerous, wrongheaded, and moribund, pleaded in May of 1915 for a new school of Gilbert and Sullivan operetta, blind to the miracle it had just witnessed. From 1914 on, there was a slow, but essentially uninterrupted evolution of our musical style—an evolution governed almost entirely by domestic conditions. In the ensuing years Vienna, Paris, Berlin, and particularly London looked increasingly to New York for their shows or at least for their material and ideas. For the better part of the 20th century America dominated the musical theatre.

1915-1916

The aura of superiority that emanated from the Winter Garden was short-lived. On June 21, the **Ziegfeld Follies of 1915** came into the New Amsterdam and affirmed beyond any doubt Ziegfeld's preeminence in the field of elaborate revues. What overwhelmed the critics and audiences at this and subsequent productions was, sadly for posterity, the breathtaking but ephemeral settings of Joseph Urban.

. . .

Joseph Urban was born in Vienna on May 26, 1872. He graduated from the Art Academy and from the Polytechnicum, where he was a pupil of Baron Carl Hassauer who designed Vienna's Hofburg Theatre and Palais Lützow. After winning medals at several international expositions of the day, Urban was selected to design a palace for Count Esterhazy and the Czar Bridge over the Neva. He first came to America in 1901 to create an Austrian Pavilion for the 1904 St. Louis Fair. The Boston Opera Company brought him back to mount several of their productions. A fine illustrator as well as an architect, the busy Urban found time to provide attractive drawings for numerous children's books.

. . .

Ziegfeld sought Urban out after admiring his scenery for Edward Sheldon's failure, *Garden of Paradise*. Instead of the more or less haphazard mélange of sets, painted in a thoughtless pastiche of gaudy colors, long accepted even in better New York productions, Urban carefully designed and colored each mounting with the flow of the entire production in mind. The 1915 edition played with shades of blue, a favorite of both Urban and Ziegfeld. The show's opening, with its simulated underwater effects, and the "Gates of Elysium" flanked by water-spouting elephants elicited the greatest enthusiasm. Reviewer after reviewer was unstinting in his praise.

This edition added W.C. Fields to the program, and, for the first time, allowed the heretofore silent juggler to juggle lines as well. The skits included his quickly-to-be-famous billiard scene, turning the game into a frenetic tennis match as he became his own opponent. From the audience Ed Wynn directed a movie in which Bernard Granville and Mae Murray played the lovers and Leon Errol an inept villain. Bert Williams clowned as a put-upon house boy. George White, Carl Randall, and all the unforgettably beautiful girls, headed by Ina Claire and Ann Pennington, were in the superlative roster.

The score's best numbers were by Louis Hirsch. "Hold Me In Your Loving Arms" was the romantic hit when sung by Helen Rook and the chorus, while "A Girl For Each Month In The Year"—sung by Granville as part of a larger "Silver Forest" number—gave a theme to the expected parade of young ladies. But Hirsch's top tune was "Hello, Frisco!", celebrating not so much the San Francisco fair as the inauguration of transcontinental phone service.

Act Three: The Birth of the Modern Musical, 1914–1921

Miss Claire and Granville sang the song. A less escapist reference to the news of the day was a spectacular red, white, and blue production number, "America," with the principals representing the armed forces and one of Ziegfeld's loveliest girls, Justine Johnstone, bedecked as "Columbia." Granville welcomed "a hundred thousand refugees" with "We'll Build A Little Home In The U.S.A."

Sigmund Romberg songs were featured in the next two shows to arrive in the summer of 1915. **Hands Up** (7-22-15, 44th St.) was a typically thrown-together Shubert hodgepodge. Calling itself —coyly, but uncertainly—a "musico-comico-filmo-melo-drama," it presented a number of younger Broadway talents, with Will Rogers receiving the loudest applause. E. Ray Goetz collaborated with Romberg on the music, but neither offered anything exceptional. A composer new to Broadway, Cole Porter, interpolated one song, "Esmerelda."

The type of music Romberg had to supply for **The Blue Paradise** (8-5-15, Casino) was clearly more congenial to his Hungarian background, and the results were far more memorable. A Viennese creation, it told of a young European who leaves his sweetheart to make his fortune in America and returns to realize she is merely a shrew. It ran out the season. Only the Hippodrome spectacle had a longer run. The musical's book was adapted by Edgar Smith. Eight of Edmund Eysler's original songs were retained. Two songs were by Leo Edwards, and one Cecil Lean rag was included. But it was the eight new Romberg melodies, particularly the lovely "Auf Wiedersehn," which were hummed by departing playgoers. For reasons only the Shuberts could explain, they failed to grasp the excellence of their staff composer when given suitable material. Two more seasons passed before Romberg properly established himself, and even then the Shuberts, usually so quick to capitalize on a good thing, almost let him slip away. If *The Blue Paradise* failed to assure Romberg's future, it handsomely paved one young lady's way to success. Although Cecil Lean and Cleo Mayfield were the best known names in the cast, Vivienne Segal walked away with the loudest plaudits. Luckily for Miss Segal the lone song she was assigned was her duet with Lean to close Act I—"Auf Wiedersehn."

. . .

Vivienne Segal was born in Philadelphia on April 19, 1897. Her father was a well-to-do physician who sent his daughter to private schools and gave her private tutors. His generous support of cultural and theatrical enterprises allowed Miss Segal to start at the top. She made her debut in 1914, in Philadelphia, singing the title role in *Carmen,* and followed with Siebel in *Faust.* Her father helped underwrite the cost of *The Blue Paradise.* She was engaged to replace the original, unsatisfactory fiancée-turned-shrew.

. . .

One reason the Shuberts may have ignored Romberg's potential was increasing tensions the European war was producing, and the early evidence of anti-Austro-Hungarian feelings. But the *Dramatic Mirror* suggested that the war was not an unmitigated curse. In a July 28 article, "Comic Opera in the War," the paper thought fine musical subjects would come out of the holocaust: "The field for comic opera will be as expansive as the great deep out of which it will be born." This myopic, traditional publication failed to see that the side effects of the war would give us—indeed already were giving us—our new musical forms. The very term "comic opera" would be relegated to the shelves of history.

An importation from France, **The Girl Who Smiles** (8-9-15, Lyric), had a passing success and continued, for those who wanted to believe it, the illusion that the war was not really changing much. But **Cousin Lucy,** which arrived on August 29 at the Cohan and was one of those borderline pieces between a straight play and a musical, underscored the changes. The play's author was Charles Klein, who had gone down on the *Lusitania,* and one of its three Jerome Kern numbers, "Society," had some remarkable blues-like chords coloring the song's burthen.

Two Is Company (9-22-15, Lyric), a second musical by the team that wrote *The Girl Who Smiles,* was a quick failure. The next night, at the magnificent, ill-fated Century Theatre—built too far out of the way, on Central Park, to realize its builders' ambition to see it Manhattan's leading temple of drama—Ned Wayburn produced an elaborate revue, **Town Topics.** It was a lushly ornate mounting and gave its audience a certain value for its money, running, as it did, almost to midnight. But it could not compete with the more famous spectacles playing at more centrally situated houses. It lasted nine weeks and left nothing behind but its own statistics. For comedy the fast-rising Will Rogers appeared in evening dress to deliver his monologues, producing his lariat from his top hat. Spectacle included a ballet of the seasons, performed on a revolving stage. Mannequins in an elegant dress shop came to life to provide the expected parade of beauties.

Far more successful and enduring was **The Prin-**

308

cess Pat, which John Cort presented on September 29 at his small playhouse on 48th Street. In the style of so many musicals of the day, it had three acts, with only one set for each. Although the names of its characters were Continental its whole story unfolded on Long Island. Patrice O'Connor (Eleanor Painter) is an Irish beauty married to Prince Antonio di Montaldo (Joseph R. Lertora). Though she loves her husband deeply, she flirts with old Anthony Schmalz (Al Shean) to save her friend Grace Holbrook (Eva Fallon) from marrying him —and also to make the prince a trifle jealous. She pretends to elope; she and Schmalz are arrested; and the truth is out. Pat returns to the prince, and Grace finds a more suitable partner in Tony Schmalz, Jr. (Robert Ober). The critics were, for the most part, quite pleased with the show. Perhaps because the show was called a comic opera, the *Dramatic Mirror* permitted itself to wax especially ecstatic. It found Henry Blossom's libretto "a great improvement over the run of recent books." "In fact," it concluded, "the Blossom characters might really have existed." The lyrics, as Blossom's were wont, could be light and natural in the more frivolous numbers, but stiff and involuted in the serious pieces. The show's triumph was its Victor Herbert score. At least two numbers, "Love Is The Best Of All" (sung by Pat directly after her first-act entrance) and "Neapolitan Love Song" (sung by the prince early in Act II), have found places in the canon of Herbert standards. Miss Painter was one of the many multi-talented actresses who graced the lyric stage of her generation. In later years she enjoyed modest success in a number of straight plays. In *Princess Pat* audiences enjoyed her singing as well as the delightful bonus of her graceful waltzing.

When the open-handed Dillingham took over the Hippodrome from the penny-pinching Shuberts, he renovated the entire theatre, gave the ushers smart new uniforms, printed handsome new programs, and rethought the whole production set-up. Spectacle remained. The house was built for it and could not survive without it. But "personalities" were brought in. However tiny they might seem to those in the last row of the balcony, they nonetheless had their allure. R. H. Burnside was now completely responsible for assembling the company and providing what dialogue was deemed necessary. For the music, Dillingham replaced Manuel Klein, a hack, with Raymond Hubbell, another hack. Isadore Witmark, the music publisher, has written, "on account of its size, the Hippodrome was hardly the place in which to introduce song successes." Per-

haps Dillingham reasoned along similar lines. But though Klein's melodies enjoyed some modest popularity and Hubbell wrote "Poor Butterfly," the one still popular song to emerge from these extravaganzas, the fallacy of this theory, and the loss to the Hippodrome, was not shown until twenty years later, when a great composer, Richard Rodgers, filled the huge house with memorable music.

Dillingham unveiled his initial presentation on September 30. The first big name to appear was John Philip Sousa. Besides Sousa's band, theatregoers watched skiers "slide down the mountain side and leap a seemingly impassable chasm," the wedding of Jack and Jill, and New York by night from a rooftop. Patriotic bunting was unfurled, and along with Hubbell's "For The Honor Of The Flag," Marc Connelly and Zoel Parenteau offered "My Land, My Flag," the hit song from their Pittsburgh show, *The Lady of Luzon* (6-2-13). Dillingham, who had produced the preceding season's two major smashes, *Watch Your Step* and *Chin-Chin*, had Seymour Brown write a production number advertising the latter, then on tour. Whatever the show's shortcomings, it became the most successful Hippodrome spectacle up to its day and justified its cheery title, **Hip–Hip Hooray.**

Miss Information (10-5-15, Cohan) was billed as a comedy with music, although its sheet music called it "a little comedy with a little music." Many critics ignored its music, even if Elsie Janis, its star, was customarily considered a songstress. Its book described how Mrs. Calwalder (Annie Esmond) has her son Jack (Howard Estabrook) hide her jewelry so she can enjoy the publicity a theft will bring. The plan misfires, and the jewels are stolen by a gang of crooks. A telephone girl, Dot from Nowhere (Miss Janis), in a series of disguises, solves everything and wins Jack. The music the critics ignored was by Jerome Kern. Most of it was not particularly good, but one tune, "Some Sort Of Somebody," was whisked away and reused several months later, at which time it was not overlooked. An interpolation, "Two Big Eyes," marked the second Cole Porter song heard on a Broadway stage.

Alone at Last (10-14-15, Shubert), by Franz Lehar, ran until the spring. Its biggest hit, however, was the uproarious "Some Little Bug Is Going To Find You" (Benjamin Hapgood Burt and Roy Atwell/Silvio Hein), an American look at the germ menace. For the moment, with this and *The Blue Paradise*, the Central Powers' forces were beating the Allies in the battle of the importations.

A World of Pleasure, which also premiered on

the 14th, was a predictable Winter Garden show. It had only the thread of a plot. Rich Tony Van-Schuyler (Clifton Crawford) courts an heiress (Venita Fitzhugh) and wins her at 11:30. The plot did little more than offer situations for vaudeville turns and production numbers the public came to see. Romberg's score was the pleasantly workaday material he had offered before *The Blue Paradise,* and many of the critics regretted his reversion to this patently crass style, typified by "I Could Go Home With A Girlie Like You." Only one interpolation outlived the show, "Pretty Baby" (Gus Kahn/Tony Jackson and Egbert Van Alstyne), also worked into a second Shubert show at the Winter Garden the following season.

Around the Map (11-1-15, New Amsterdam) provided an interesting case of missed opportunities. It advertised itself as "a musical globe trot," implying it was the latest in stylish revues. Essentially, it was. But the story that tied its various turns together told a curiously unpleasant tale. The dressmaker Impikoff (William Norris), to win the hand of Madame Kapinski (Hazel Cox), bets her he can turn the ugly sock-mender, Jacqueline "Tootsi" Bonheur (Else Adler), into a great beauty and make the Count de Gai (Robert Pitkin) fall in love with her. If he succeeds Madame agrees to marry him. The count gets wind of the machinations and wagers he will be able to reject "Tootsi," no matter how attractive she becomes. Kapinski brings a rival for the count's affections into the picture. But Impikoff, in various disguises, prevails. Several critics saw in this plot the possibilities for a tough, sardonic musical comedy. But the book minimized the vicious, cynical undertones of the story, casting aside the chance to introduce a fresh approach to librettos. The lyrics were better, hinting at the mordant possibilities. "Here Comes Tootsi" may sound like the name of a hearty rag, and for all its use of minor key, its chorus is not unlike the welcome of "Hello, Dolly!" But its poignant verse is the wail of a lonely, gauche waif, the butt of inevitable cruelties. Herman Finck's music, unvaryingly routine, seemed totally unaware of the dark possibilities in the lyrics and dialogue. The show's attractions were enhanced by striking Urban sets that transported the audience to Berlin's Unter den Linden, a Wagnerian Dream Garden, a Japanese Jockey Club, the San Francisco Exposition, and a finale done brazenly in torrid crimson, depicting the "Red Hot Stove Cabaret."

Almost two months elapsed between the arrival of *Around the Map* and the next new musicals. Then in Christmas week three shows came in—two

on the 23rd and one on the 25th. All three were smash hits. They constituted the first such cluster of successful openings in the history of American musicals. In their quality, their diversity, and their striking acceptance they attested to the coming of age of an American art form.

Admittedly the first of these looked backward—or at least overseas. **Katinka** (12-23-15, 44th St.) was first and simply a Continental operetta. But immigrant composers had settled here and been accepted before, and now Rudolf Friml, fulfilling the promise of *The Firefly* and *High Jinks* with another enchantingly melodic score, become a lasting part of the Broadway scene. For the next fifteen years, as long as unabashedly European musical styles remained salable to New York, he vied with Romberg for honors in the field, although his masterworks came in a four-year period that lay ten years away. Out of a sense of duty, Katinka (May Naudain) has married Boris Strogoff (Count Lorrie Grimaldi), the Russian ambassador to Austria. Her real love is Ivan Dimitri (Samuel Ash), an attaché. Ivan's American friend Thaddeus Hopper (Franklin Arcade) helps Katinka escape and hides her in his house. When Mrs. Hopper (Adele Rowland) becomes suspicious and angry, Hopper pays Arif Bey (Edward Durand) to conceal Katinka in his harem. By error Mrs. Hopper is placed in the harem. At a Viennese café the principals are all gathered. When a lady named Olga (Edith Decker) announces she is Boris' lawful wife, a happy ending follows. The story, however preposterous, was professionally handled. The music was gorgeous. "Allah's Holiday" (one of Olga's three second-act numbers) swiftly established itself as a classic. "Tis The End," "Rackety Coo," and the beautifully arioso "My Paradise" were all far above Broadway's norm. The public responded wholeheartedly, and *Katinka* ran seven months.

The same night the incontestably American **Very Good Eddie** opened at the Princess. Some early announcements proclaimed it as the Marbury-Comstock Company's "annual Princess Theatre production." Just as *Katinka* confirmed the promise of *The Firefly* and *High Jinks, Very Good Eddie* even more emphatically and more importantly fulfilled the promise of *Nobody Home.* The Hudson River Day Line's *Catskill* stops for 15 minutes at Poughkeepsie. Dick Rivers (Oscar Shaw) comes aboard. He has fallen in love with Elsie Lilly (Ann Orr), Madame Matroppo's pupil. To be alone with Elsie he begs Madame Matroppo (Ada Lewis) to let him interview the girl for a magazine article.

She agrees. Elsie is not easily wooed. She has known Rivers and suggests he is always in love with "Some Sort Of Somebody." Newlyweds Eddie and Georgina Kettle (Ernest Truex and Helen Raymond) board the boat. It is obvious from her incessant barking of commands that Georgina is determined to wear the pants in the family—though little Eddie's trousers are probably several sizes too small for her. They are followed by two more honeymooners, Percy and Elsie Darling (John Willard and Alice Dovey). The Darlings and the Kettles meet, and Eddie and Percy turn out to be old schoolmates. All four rejoice, "Isn't It Great To Be Married?" Georgina and Percy leave the boat—the one to send a telegram, the other to find some missing baggage—and the vessel sails without them. Eddie and Elsie, alone, discover they haven't even enough money for one meal. Rivers appears, and Eddie, who knows him, is forced to pretend Elsie is his bride. Rivers lends Eddie the money he will need. He also tells Eddie that Eddie's old flame Elsie Lilly is on the boat. Eddie and his "Mrs." sit down not just to dinner but to cocktails as well. Rivers returns and introduces Madame Matroppo to "Mr. and Mrs. Kettle." On top of his martinis, Eddie orders champagne for everyone. They celebrate with "Wedding Bells Are Calling Me."

At the Rip Van Winkle Inn, Rivers and Elsie Lilly dream of the joys "On The Shore At Le Lei Wi." Eddie and his Elsie, increasingly nervous at their masquerade, now discover there won't be a return boat—or a train—until the next day. There is nothing for them to do but remain overnight. To the astonishment of the desk clerk, they request separate rooms. Once they have signed the register, Eddie carefully spills ink over it to conceal his presence. Rivers is as puzzled as anybody by Eddie's behavior, insisting he'd act differently "If I Find The Girl." (The typescript gives five encores for this.) Madame Matroppo catches Eddie slinking off to eat dinner alone and orders him back upstairs to dine with his "wife." Eddie regrets he is so small he must wear a "Size Thirteen Collar." Georgina and Percy arrive, but with the register ruined cannot be sure they have come to the right hotel. Madame Matroppo, who can never remember names correctly, assures them the only honeymooners are named "Fish." Since it is late, they also take two rooms and head for bed. Georgina, learning that Darling's wife is named Elsie, goes upstairs with the uneasy feeling she is the same Elsie that Eddie loved long ago. A mouse scares Elsie Darling out of her room, and when she knocks on Eddie's door he comforts her, advising her to be as brave as the "Babes In The Wood." The next morning Percy and Georgina meet Rivers, who tells them Eddie Kettle and his wife are at the Inn. But it is a changed Eddie who comes downstairs. He has learned how to handle himself, and when he orders Georgina to sit down, she does.

Guy Bolton and Philip Bartholomae's book was based on Bartholomae's *Over Night* (earlier announcements credited only Bartholomae with the book and Schuyler Greene with the lyrics). It was a tightly written book. The strained humor and awkward gaps of *Nobody Home* were gone. The fun flowed directly from the legitimate characterizations. On boarding, Georgina noisily issues commands about baggage and tips:

Steward: Say, boss
Mr. Kettle [Eddie]: Are you speaking to me?
Steward: I was speaking to *her*.

But Georgina's pushiness masks her naïveté:

Mrs. Kettle: So this is the Hudson, is it? When do we get out of sight of land?
Mr. Kettle: This is a river.

There is a clever running gag on Madame Matroppo's inability to remember Rivers' name. It comes out as "Lake" or "Brooks" and ultimately is made to bear on the story when she also confuses the Kettles' name. In *Nobody Home* the title was used several times in the dialogue. In *Very Good Eddie, Oh Boy!,* and *Oh, Lady! Lady!!* Bolton used the titles for curtain lines. In this case, when Eddie, in his new-found strength, orders Georgina to sit down, the delighted clerk shouts admiringly, "Very Good, Eddie." The title came from Fred Stone's popular line in *Chin-Chin.*

Once again, accomplished as the book was, the music was better. The songs, even when not written for the show, seemed to fit naturally into place in the story. The down-to-earth nature of the characters allowed a refreshing distribution of songs. The cynical Rivers was given the optimistic "If I Find The Girl"; he and Elsie Lilly sing romantically of far-off Hawaii. But the closest thing to a pure love song, the show's hit "Babes In The Wood" (for which Kern collaborated with Greene on the lyrics), was given to two honeymooners who are not married to each other and who go their separate ways at the end of the evening. For many who saw the original its most precious memory was Ernest Truex' singing of "Size Thirteen Collar." To list the other excellent tunes would be to list almost the entire program. It is interesting how good and how surprisingly appropriate the lyrics by diverse hands proved—"Old Bill Baker" (Ring Lardner), "Some Sort of Somebody" (Elsie Janis), "Wedding Bells Are Calling Me" (H.B. Smith), "If I Find The Girl" (John E. Hazzard and Herbert Reynolds), "I'd Like To Have A Million In The Bank" and "On The Shore At Le Lei Wi" (both Reynolds). But Kern and Bolton were not content, and for their next Princess show they recruited a friend who brilliantly complemented and augmented them.

Very Good Eddie ran just under a year and toured to big profits. More than any other piece it formed the mold out of which poured a half-century of American Musical Comedy. Its people were everyday people—neither cartooned clowns nor cardboard lovers. Its situations were plausible—however unlikely. Its easily singable songs helped the story flow but were lovely and natural away from the stage.

The last of the Christmas week triumvirate was the Dillingham production of Irving Berlin's **Stop! Look! Listen!** (12-25-15, Globe). This time Harry B. Smith did have a recognizable plot, and a well written one at that. When Owen Coyne's leading lady, Mary Singer (Justine Johnstone), marries Gideon Gay (Frank Lalor) and leaves for a honeymoon in Japan, Violette (Marion Sunshine) steps forward and offers to perform the lead. The chorus girl is laughed away. Coyne's authors give him three months to find a suitable star. Together they set out around the world seeking her. They finally hire an actress who impresses them as the heroine of a "ragtime melodrama" that is the second-act finale. By the end of the third act Coyne (Harland Dixon) is convinced he has seen the girl somewhere before. Of course, she is Violette, who has been coached by Abel Connor (Harry Fox), a man who saw promise in her all the time. Her curtain line to Coyne is, "And I lived right next door to your theatre." The fun was broader than in *Very Good Eddie*. The girls in the show had names such as Iona Carr, Gladys Canby, and Nora Marks. A philanthropist called Van Courtland Parke (Joseph Santley) tells the audience, "I'm looking for poor and deserving children to whom I can do some good with my money. Little girls over eighteen preferred; no objection to good lookers." Gideon and Abel meet in the Pacific:

Gideon: Do you understand Sandwich?
Connor: Do I? All the dialects—ham, tongue—all of 'em.

At one point Coyne expresses what must have remained many customers' philosophy of an eve-

ning well spent, "I have to find some new way to undress the chorus . . . costumes make the show. Leave me my ponies and my clotheshorses, and musical comedy will still go on!" The theatrical setting allowed some celebrated turns to be inserted. Dixon combined with his partner, James Doyle, for comic bits and dances, while Gaby Deslys and Harry Pilcer performed ballroom specialties and ragtime stepping.

Again the music was the most durable feature of the show. Two of Berlin's best came out of this score, "The Girl On The Magazine Cover" and "I Love A Piano" (played on six pianos). Harry Fox introduced both songs. Berlin was constantly experimenting. While concerted pieces were by no means new, Berlin's contemporary American musical forms made them seem innovative. The opening was rhymed dialogue set to ragtime (using rhymes such as "nervous" and "observe us" Berlin reemployed in *Mr. President*, his last musical fifty years later).

The rest of the songs were not as well integrated into the piece as were Kern's songs at the Princess, but the music was solidly diverting, up-to-the-minute, and American all the way.

Romberg's incidental songs for *Ruggles of Red Gap*, which arrived the same night as *Stop! Look! Listen!*, were not nearly as interesting as Kern's for *Cousin Lucy* and *Miss Information*. More than either of these, the Harrison Rhodes' play was straight comedy rather than musical. In any case, it was a quick flop.

January's only new musical was **Sybil** (1-10-16, Liberty), an importation in which a prima donna poses as a duchess to save her beloved hussar. It reunited the three stars of *The Girl from Utah* (8-24-14)—Julia Sanderson, Donald Brian, and Joseph Cawthorn. They helped it to run for 168 performances.

George M. Cohan attempted to keep his promise of a permanent revue at the Astor when he brought in **The Cohan Revue of 1916** on February 9. But the Weber and Fields of *Hello, Broadway* (12-25-14), William Collier, and Cohan himself were missing, and only John Hendricks' name was in both cast lists. Nonetheless, the show's sharp burlesque of the prominent people and creations of the time did continue the tradition Cohan so admired. War fervor, professional fundamentalism, and Shaw's *Major Barbara* were all spoofed when Andrew Overdraft kills the bartending-evangelist Billy Holliday after Holliday opposes arming our troops. The take-off of the season's sensational *Common Clay* was the show's high spot. In Cleves Kinhead's drama a reformed slut is brutally tongue-lashed by an unforgiving judge, who then discovers the girl in his daughter. In Cohan's court the swearing-in was on a telephone book and the witness appealed for help to 42nd Street's gods, "K. and E." and "Jake and Lee." The girl's name turns out to be not Clay, but Mud. And Judge Oliver Mud is her father:

Judge: Is there a scar on your left hand ear?
Jane: Yes, on my left hand ear, you can see it right here.
Judge: My dear!
Jane: What?
Judge: I'm here.
Jane: Who?
Judge: Your dad.
Jane: You're mad.
Mother: No. No, it's so, I can tell by the sty on his left hand eye. Oliver!
Judge: Maud!

Jane and her lawyer, Steve, listen as Oliver and Maud Mud also remember their little boy who disappeared:

Judge: I'll find him sure as sin—I can tell him by the scar on his left hand chin.
Steve: Excuse me, please, if I butt in—but I've got a scar on my left hand chin.
Jane: Where?
Steve: There!
Jane: Is it true—it is you?
Steve: Sister!
Jane: Brother!
Mother: Father!
Judge: Mother!

Even more than in *Stop! Look! Listen!* much of the dialogue was rhymed and much of the rhyme set to a ragtime beat.

Cohan's songs, none distinguished, included the inevitable (for Cohan especially) Irish number, a necessary (for 1915–16) San Francisco tune, a generous tribute to Ziegfeld, and a song, "Julia, Donald And Joe," which, in the fashion of that more leisurely era, had five long verses and choruses ready should audiences demand them. There was a patriotic "Young America" and, in an apparent change of heart, "Sousa Melodies." Better economic conditions and the beginning of a series momentum allowed this edition to outrun *Hello, Broadway*.

Michael Freedland, in his biography of the great jazz singer, correctly stated **Robinson Crusoe, Jr.** (2-17-16, Winter Garden) "was the nearest Jolson

had yet come to a show with a real plot," but his governing phrase lay in his subordinate clause, "although from opening night on, it was quite plain that the story was not going to interfere with his domination on stage." The "real plot" told how Hiram Westbury, exhausted from chasing moviemakers off his Long Island estate, falls asleep and dreams he is Robinson Crusoe, Jr. His chauffeur Gus (Al Jolson) becomes his Friday. They have a series of slapdash adventures with pirates and with a Spanish dancer. Trees come alive and sway to the music. Gus-Friday-Jolson has comic scenes with a goat and a crocodile, and at one point masquerades as Fatima. In these Winter Garden mountings, Sigmund Romberg's score was insignificant, and was pushed further and further aside as Jolson played with his interpolations. There were Negro spirituals, a Stephen Foster song, and, among the newer comings and goings, three tunes which Jolson used the rest of his life—"Where The Black-eyed Susans Grow" (Dave Redford/Richard Whiting), "Yaka Hula Hickey Dula" (E. Ray Goetz, Joe Young, and Pete Wendling), and "Where Did Robinson Crusoe Go With Friday On Saturday Night?" (Sam M. Lewis and Joe Young/ George W. Meyer).

Anne Caldwell used the outline of another Austro-Hungarian operetta as the start of her book for **Pom-Pom** (2-28-16, Cohan). Her story centered on another prima donna, this time one who is kidnapped and lives for a while as a pickpocket. Hugo Felix provided the score. With Mitzi Hajos, recently of *Sari*, as its star, it held the public's affection for four months, then toured.

There were two March entries: one at the very beginning of the month, the other at the end. **The Road to Mandalay** (3-1-16, Park) had music by Oreste Vessella. Though he is now forgotten, Vessella was then a popular bandmaster. He had tried before to write for Broadway, and, although his music had won praise from the tryout critics, book trouble prevented it from being heard in New York. This time his luck was little better. Twenty-one performances, and *The Road to Mandalay* was withdrawn. The show wasn't set in Mandalay nor did the region have anything to do with it. Kipling's cry "come you back" provided the germ of the off-again, on-again love affair of Lt. Jack Poindexter (Frank Pollock) and Lily Montgomery (Leola Lucy). Bad luck plagued even Vessella's opening night. Miss Lucy, hurt shortly before in an accident, played the heroine from a wheelchair.

The other March entry failed to run even as long as *The Road to Mandalay*. But **See America First**

(3-28-16, Maxine Elliott) was historically far more important. For its less-than-two-full weeks of life a New York program carried a new credit—score by Cole Porter.

. . .

Cole Porter was born into great wealth in Peru, Indiana, on June 9, 1891. His mother, to whom he was closely attached until her death just a few years before his own, began his musical training at an early age. By the time he was eleven he had published his musical writings. Sent to Yale to prepare to study law, he spent much of his time composing music for collegiate shows, for the glee club, and merely for the entertainment of his classmates. His football songs "Bull Dog" and "Eli" remain in use to this day in New Haven. By the time he reached Harvard Law School he knew composing was to be his life. Despite family objections he transferred to the School of Music. Broadway first heard his tunes earlier in the season when *Hands Up* and *Miss Information* each presented Porter interpolations.

. . .

See America First was advertised as "a comic opera." Produced by the enterprising Elizabeth Marbury at the Maxine Elliott, across the street from the Princess, it had Senator Higgens (Sam Edwards) leaving the effete East so his daughter can find a red-blooded American husband in the West. However, Polly Higgens (Dorothie Bigelow) has fallen in love with an Englishman, Cecil, Duke of Pendragon (John Goldsworthy). By coincidence they meet again while Cecil is vacationing as a cowboy. Polly and Cecil, Senator Higgens and Polly's headmistress, Sarah (Clara Palmer), are paired at the final curtain. The show lacked professional polish. But even the unyielding *Dramatic Mirror* could see that Porter and his coauthor T. Lawrason Riggs showed "promise of writing something wholly meritorious." Riggs rejected the theatre in favor of the church. And even Porter temporarily fled, leaving behind only one minor gem, "I've A Shooting Box In Scotland." One of the principals was another young man, Clifton Webb.

April's only arrival was also a quick failure. An arid book, a lackluster score, and yet another Parisian setting left the critics and playgoers indifferent to **Come to Bohemia** (4-27-16, Maxine Elliott). On critic did suggest, "A glorious opportunity awaits a librettist with a keen sense of the ironic in the pseudo-Bohemianism of Greenwich Village." It was shamefully long before producers and authors took the hint.

Two May musicals, neither particularly successful, were nonetheless interesting. They suggest "nostalgia" has a perennial pull. **Molly O'** (5-20-16, Cort) was the American wife (Katherine Galloway) of Count Walter von Walden (Albert Parr), who leaves her because she makes him feel bought. He goes to Vienna. At an art students' auction there he pays $20,000 for a mysterious model. The unveiling reveals the model is Molly, who has pursued the Count because she genuinely loves him. Now he has "bought" her, thereby giving their marriage some sort of reasonable equilibrium. The show, for which the inexhaustible Smith brothers did the book and lyrics, lasted only five and a half weeks. What intrigued a few ticket buyers was the title, which harked back to a decade before, when Blanche Ring interpolated "My Irish Molly O" in *Sergeant Brue* (4-24-05), when a younger Jerome Kern wrote "Molly O'Halleron" as "Edna May's Irish Song" for *The Catch of the Season* (8-28-05), and when Eddie Foy was singing the virtues of his Molly in *Mr. Hamlet of Broadway* (12-23-08). (Older playgoers with longer memories undoubtedly recalled W.J. Scanlan's "Molly O." in *Mavourneen* [9-28-91].) Ten years are as long or as short a time as circumstances dictate. But to the discerning playgoers of 1916 the last two seasons made 1905 seem light years away.

The other May production, **Step This Way** (5-29-16, Shubert), helped reinforce this sense of change. A revised version of Lew Fields' beloved *The Girl Behind the Counter* (10-1-07), with new songs by E. Ray Goetz and Bert Grant (plus Berlin's painfully funny "I've Got A Sweet Tooth Bothering Me") and with Lew Fields himself again as star, it attracted audiences for eleven hot summer weeks.

The season ended as it began, with a new edition of the **Ziegfeld Follies** (6-12-16, New Amsterdam). Pince-nezed Ned Wayburn, who had impressed Ziegfeld with his short-lived *Town Topics*, began a seven-year stint as stager. Urban was back, his mountings dazzling as ever. Lucille (Lady Duff Gordon) created the girls' gowns. Will Rogers was added to the growing roster of regulars. The 1916 edition had a Shakespearean theme. Bert Williams spoofed Othello, Bernard Granville and Ina Claire were Romeo and Juliet. Urban's sphinx for Antony and Cleopatra elicited awed approval. Spoofing other fields, Fanny Brice appeared in a tutu to sing about "Nijinsky" and his ballet, which Miss Brice, of course, pronounced "belly." Miss Claire mimicked Geraldine Farrar, Jane Cowl, and Irene Castle. The war inevitably made its way into the revue with Urban's North Sea naval battle. No song as popular as the previous year's "Hello, Frisco!" emerged, but Louis Hirsch, Jerome Kern, and Irving Berlin joined the dependable Dave Stamper to provide a solid, diversified score. Kern's "Have A Heart" was the best number, despite its weak ending. His "When The Lights Are Low" and Hirsch's nostalgic "Bachelor Days" were also attractive and popular.

There were twenty-seven musicals in 1915–16, up just four from the preceding year. But the excellence and maturity of its best shows—particularly *Very Good Eddie*—mark it as a banner year in the history of the American Musical Theatre.

1916-1917

The 1916–17 season saw a small increase in the number of musicals and a slightly more discernible drop in quality, although the season did produce the first indisputable masterpiece of our modern lyric stage. But tumultuous events here and abroad claimed prime attention. At home an urgent presidential election drew near. As the first shows of the new season were finishing their rehearsals and beginning their tryouts, the Republicans met in Chicago and nominated Charles Evans Hughes to run on a platform of avowed neutrality, a notable victory for the German-American element of the party. Five days later, June 15, the Democrats renominated President Wilson. Pacifist sentiment was strong, and the party rallied (ironic in the light of events) to the cry, "He kept us out of war." The close results were dramatic—with Hughes going to bed on election night believing he had defeated Wilson. Yet despite pleas for peace, the awful truth remained, there was probably no way of staving off American intervention. The sickening carnage was making both sides desperate, the Central Powers fatally so. On March 1, the President gave the Associated Press the infamous Zimmermann telegram, which disclosed that the German ambassador in Washington was offering American territory to Mexico. On March 18 U-boats sank three American ships without warning and with a high loss of life. On April 7 we were at war.

A fourth of the musicals to open were importations from the belligerents—one from France, one from England, the rest from Vienna. The French and English shows were reasonably faithful to their originals, and failed or succeeded on their own merits. But the others encountered growing resis-

tance. Two days after the Zimmermann telegram was made public, the *Dramatic Mirror* acknowledged that since the opening of the season there had been a "reaction in the theatrical world against Viennese musical plays" which, as a result, had to be "so largely Americanized . . . that they lost most of their Viennese atmosphere." The two works the article mentioned as most drastically revised, *Miss Springtime* and *Her Soldier Boy*, were the only genuinely successful of the Austro-Hungarian arrivals, though *Flora Bella* had a modest run.

As usual, one of the annual extravaganzas opened the season. This year it was **The Passing Show**'s turn on June 22. The success of Cohan's revues and the excitement on front pages of the dailies convinced the Shuberts that more topicality would pay. Hughes, Wilson, the warmongering Teddy Roosevelt, and Pancho Villa were all satirized. When Roosevelt boasted that if he were still in the White House the war would be over, Wilson replied, "Over here!" Ed Wynn, lured from the *Follies*, sparked the clowns. Audiences first caught sight of him sitting in a box, shouting "The show's terrible!" Inviting himself on stage, he proceeded to improve matters. A patriotic spectacle number offered an effective twist for an old device. Whereas races had been depicted with horses running on a treadmill that moved from one side of the stage to the other, a treadmill moving front to back allowed a troop of horses and their riders to simulate a cavalry charge. Musically, the show had more than its customary fleeting interest. One song from this edition remains popular. It was the interpolation, "Pretty Baby" (Gus Kahn/Tony Jackson and Egbert Van Alstyne), which the Shuberts had also inserted into *A World of Pleasure*. The main Romberg-Motzan score was neither better nor worse than the other scores Romberg and his associates churned out two or three times a year for these Winter Garden productions, but one of its otherwise ordinary numbers, "The Making Of A Girl," coupled Romberg's name with one new to Broadway—George Gershwin.

· · ·

George Gershwin (Jacob Gershvin) was not quite eighteen when the show opened. He was born in Brooklyn on September 26, 1898. His love of music came very early, and his childhood friendship with his classmate the violinist Max Rosen reinforced the love. When the Gershwins purchased a piano so his older brother Ira could learn to play a musical instrument, it was young George, then twelve, who monopolized it. Two years later, in 1912, he began lessons with the man who most influenced his musical life, Charles Hambitzer, a composer and pianist of broad and enlightened musical tastes. From Hambitzer, George received a thorough classical training. Gershwin was aware of the native musical ferment around him, but he found most popular compositions trite. At the wedding of an aunt he heard an orchestra play several tunes that captured his attention. They were soaringly superior to the run-of-the-mill numbers bands of the day offered. When he discovered that all the songs were from the same Broadway show, he was determined to write musical comedy material, and set about studying the works of the songs' composer. The musical was *The Girl from Utah* (8-24-14), and the songs were Jerome Kern's interpolations. Kern remained a Gershwin idol, although their music rarely followed similar paths.

. . .

The first August entry was **Yvette** (8-10-16, 39th St.), of which no trace seems to survive. If the notices are to be believed, it must have been atrocious, with its leading lady screeching off key. The public obviously read and accepted the reviews, for *Yvette* could muster only four performances.

Broadway and Buttermilk (8-15-16, Maxine Elliott) was a Blanche Ring vehicle that toured as *Jane O'Day of Broadway*. Neither title gave away the story line. Mary Denby's spoiled daughter, Ruth, loves wastrel Franklyn Abbot. Jane O'Day, calling herself Madame Nadine, shows Franklyn is really decent and responsible. She brings Ruth down to earth and even finds a mate for Mother Denby. The songs, which included old Blanche Ring favorites, were by various hands. Like several of the preceding year's offerings this was more a "comedy with songs," as the program stated, than a musical comedy.

The season's first importation was **The Girl from Brazil** (8-30-16, 44th St.). Sigmund Romberg supplemented the score with songs in the best Winter Garden mode, but even they weren't good enough to keep the show on the boards beyond October.

The Big Show at the Hippodrome opened on August 31st. For the audiences that came to see it during its 425 performances, the main attraction was almost certainly the great ballerina, Anna Pavlova, dancing an abbreviated version of Tchaikovsky's "Sleeping Beauty" (with Leon Bakst scenery). Charlotte skated on ice, elephants played ball, and the ensemble participated in a gigantic minstrel show. The edition also contained the one song to become a popular standard out of all the music the Shuberts and Dillingham introduced at the house. "Poor Butterfly" was, moreover, the

prolific Raymond Hubbell's single claim to lasting fame. Its lyrics were by John Golden, who in a few years became one of New York's most successful and best-loved producers. This lament for Madame Butterfly was written when Dillingham thought he had secured the services of a then famous Japanese soprano, Tamaki Miura. The arrangements fell through. On opening night a Chinese-American vaudevillian introduced the song, but she was so bad she was hastily replaced.

The earliest September offerings were both imports. **Pierrot the Prodigal** (9-6-16, Booth) was a French pantomime with music, retelling the Prodigal Son tale. It ran twenty weeks. But neither Lina Abarbanell, Charles Cuvillier and Milton Schwarzwald's delightful music, nor a more than adequate book could propel **Flora Bella** (9-11-16, Casino) beyond fifteen weeks. Abarbanell played a princess who poses as her nonexistent twin sister to rekindle her husband's ardor.

The next September entry was **The Amber Empress** (9-19-16, Globe). Although it lasted only 45 performances, it was in many ways an interesting show. "The Amber Empress" is the name of a movie a group of Americans are filming in Italy. The company runs out of money, and the Americans are stranded in Europe. Luckily, rich Percival Hopkins (Frank Lalor) comes to the rescue. The author of the libretto was Marc Connelly in his first Broadway effort, but the wit and compassion that distinguished his later writings were well hidden in this instance, and the pastiche of jokes that passed for a book help cut short the show's chances. This was especially sad, since the show also marked the debut of Zoel Parenteau, a composer with a uniquely expressive melodic gift and with whom Connelly had collaborated in amateur productions. Several critics hailed Parenteau as a major discovery, and he was compared to Rudolf Friml and Victor Herbert, even if his musical line was far more contemporary than theirs. It was closer, if anything, to Jerome Kern's best style. Parenteau only did one other full score, and once again he was unsuccessful. Later he wrote two songs for Belasco's *Kiki* and then disappeared from the musical comedy scene.

For a second time in less than a month two importations arrived back to back. Both were given choice houses, but only the first, **Miss Springtime** (9-25-16, New Amsterdam), chalked up a run. Looked at today the libretto seems hardly "Americanized." Its story is pure Old World. Rudolfo Marta, Pilota's sole claim to fame, refuses to return to the village for a festival in his honor. Robin gets Varady to pose as Marta. Rosita is under Marta's spell, though she has never met him. Paul, who loves Rosita, must expose the impostor to bring Rosita back into his arms. "Americanization" seems to have consisted solely of offhand references to things American, such as Robin's remark to Varady, "Oh, you Mormon you. Maybe I didn't let you in for a nice soft job, when I hired you to play Marta." In no way was Emmerich Kalman's score Americanized. It was not of an order with his best, but it was still delightful and hummable. The show's hit was its opening number, "Throw Me A Rose," and it was used effectively throughout the evening. Three Kern songs were used. Gorgeously mounted by Joseph Urban and excellently cast (its feminine lead was Sari Petrass, prima donna of Budapest's Kiraly Theatre), it attracted audiences into the spring. However, *Miss Springtime*'s happiest claim to fame was its introducing Americans to a new lyricist, P.G. Wodehouse.

. . .

Pelham Grenville Wodehouse was born at Guildford, Surrey, England, on October 15, 1881. He was educated at Dulwich College and planned on entering the financial world, but soon turned to writing. Some of his very first lyrics were set to music by a young American come to write songs for Charles Frohman's London shows—Kern, of course. Their first success saluted a then famous politician, "Mr. Chamberlain." From 1903 to 1909 Wodehouse served as a columnist on the London *Globe*. A year after he left the post, the first of his Psmith novels, *Psmith in the City*, was published. The popularity of these books earned him a trip to America, where he wrote articles for the *Saturday Evening Post* and served as drama critic for *Vanity Fair*. While covering the opening of *Very Good Eddie*, his old collaborator, Kern, approached him about working together again.

. . .

Paul Rubens' **Betty** (10-3-16, Globe), the story of a serving girl who marries an earl, was less fortunate. Even with Raymond Hitchcock, Ivy Sawyer, and Joseph Santley as principals, it survived only eight weeks.

If Betty failed to win favor, Letty succeeded. Letty, of course, meant loose-jointed, high-kicking Charlotte Greenwood, who had rocketed to fame as Letitia Proudfoot in *Pretty Mrs. Smith* (9-21-14). Now Morosco brought her back in **So Long, Letty** (10-23-16, Shubert), with Letty as one of two wives who agree to change partners. They quickly realize they are no happier with their new spouses than they were with the old ones. After a week they are back with their original mates. The score was by Earl Carroll, who, like John Golden, soon gave up writing for producing. The title song was the show's best number. The run of 96 performances is deceptive. *So Long, Letty* opened in 1915, starting, as did all Letty shows, in Morosco's home base of California. By the time it reached New York, Carroll had rewritten much of the score, adding one more hit, "When You Hear Jackson Moan On His Saxophone." After the show left Broadway and resumed its tour, additional numbers were added as late as 1917 by young composers such as Harry Tierney and Walter Donaldson. Although not one of the Letty shows played much time on Broadway, their long tours amounted to longer runs than most shows achieved. They were remembered with a particular affection by the generation that saw them.

When Ray Comstock insisted that the next Princess Theatre show should be an updated, fully musicalized version of Charles Hoyt's *A Milk White Flag* (10-8-94), his regulars—Jerome Kern and Guy Bolton—and newly signed P.G. Wodehouse disagreed. They argued the show could never have the charm they deemed so fundamental to the theatre's earlier hits. Comstock refused to heed their warnings and signed John Golden, John Hazzard, and Anne Caldwell to do the modernization. The result was **Go To It** (10-24-16, Princess). Although a solid cast led by Emma Janvier, Percival Knight, and Will Deming did their best to spark the old tale of a fake funeral and its effects on several romances, one critic assailed the evening as "deadly dull." After three weeks Comstock took the play on the road, where its reception was no better. He promptly announced that Kern, Bolton, and Wodehouse were working full speed on a new musical.

On October 26, **The Show of Wonders** gave the Shuberts and the Winter Garden one more successful extravaganza. Although the score, mostly by Romberg, was weaker than usual, the production was lavish and the cast strong. Walter C. Kelly (brother of George and uncle of Grace) moved over from vaudeville to do his already popular "A Virginia Court Room"; McIntyre and Heath did their blackface routines and Willie and Eugene Howard their dialect bits. Willie also impersonated a sour elevator operator at the Giltmore Hotel with Eugene his pretentiously dapper passenger. Willie's imitations included Jack Norworth, while Eugene did a turn on a "ukalale." Dancers included sharp little Sammy White and, best of all, Marilyn Miller, who shone in an exotic "Burmese Ballet" that opened the second act.

New York's two finest producers of musicals, Charles Dillingham and Florenz Ziegfeld, combined their impressive talents to mount an opulent revue at the Century Theatre on November 6 and called it, appropriately, **The Century Girl.** A star-studded cast featured Hazel Dawn, Leon Errol, Elsie Janis, and Van and Schenck. Urban outdid himself creating breathtaking sets—including a staircase that became Ziegfeld's trademark. Apparently the two top producers reasoned they needed two top composers. Irving Berlin and Victor Herbert were recruited to collaborate on the score. In a witty musical scene an actor portraying Herbert played "Kiss Me Again," while an actor pretending to be Berlin offered a ragtime countermelody. The approaching war clouds prompted "When Uncle Sam Is Ruler Of The Sea" and "Uncle Sam's Chilren." Unfortunately none of the songs represented the composers at their best. The show left nothing except its own legend. But it unwittingly participated in the demise of tradition—a tradition growing out of the fame, if not the legend, of certain theatres. For many years musical comedy houses, especially those which offered shows famous for their beautiful chorus lines, sooner or later found themselves in the title of successful attractions—*A Gaiety Girl, The Casino Girl. The Century Girl* was the last, at least for American musicals. New movie palaces rising across the land quickly seized the fame and affection legitimate auditoriums sometimes had gained.

On November 29 the Shuberts brought Ziegfeld's ex-wife, Anna Held, to the Casino in **Follow Me.** Based on a German show, discreetly unmentioned, it credited Romberg with the score, even though most of the songs were by Harry Tierney. These included one final Held success, "Oh, I Want To Be Good But My Eyes Won't Let Me." The single tune still revived was not sung by Miss Held, but by Henry Lewis. It was "Oh Johnny, Oh Johnny, Oh!" (Ed Rose/Abe Olman). Because the plot centered on the romance of Clair La Tour, star of Paris' Theatre Varieties, the Shuberts had a ready-made excuse to bring on a procession of "Junoesque show girls" and vaudeville turns such as the dancing Cansinos.

December, which usually offered a batch of musicals, brought in only one in 1916, **Her Soldier Boy** (12-6-16, Astor). Its success held out hope that Kalman, who had written the music for September's *Miss Springtime* and who, with Romberg, wrote the new show's score, somehow might ride above international animosities. As the title suggested the musical dealt with the war head on. It

was the first to do so, although not without a romantic bent. It told how a soldier (John Charles Thomas) pretends to be his dead buddy so the buddy's family will be spared the painful truth. There is a doubly happy ending, for the soldier marries the buddy's sister (Beth Lydy) and the supposedly dead boy (Frank Ridge) turns up among the missing. Neither Romberg's nor Kalman's music caught on, anymore than did interpolations by Clifton Crawford or the show's conductor, Augustus Barrett. But another insert, the English war song, "Pack Up Your Troubles In Your Old Kit Bag And Smile, Smile, Smile" (George Asaf/Felix Powell), outlived both the show and the war. The song was rousingly delivered by Adele Rowland, playing the pal of a comic reporter. In turn, the reporter was played by Clifton Crawford, who several times won hearty rounds of applause soft-shoeing "drowsily."

The new year brought a happy upturn in the quality of its new musicals. Regrettably the public did not always respond. Jerome Kern, who, except for a few interpolations in the *Follies* and *Miss Springtime,* had not been heard from since 1915, wrote the scores for both January entries. 1917 was Kern's most prolific year. He had a third score ready in February and two more in the fall. **Have a Heart** (1-11-17, Liberty) was not a hit, although it deserved to be. Originally slated for the Princess, it had a good Guy Bolton-P.G. Wodehouse book, marvelous Wodehouse lyrics, and ingratiating Kern music. The plot was frivolous, but frivolity was a musical comedy tradition, and, in the worrisome days of early 1917, not unwelcome. Besides, in the hands of Bolton and Wodehouse the frivolity was literate and witty. Rutherford "Rudy" Schoonmaker (Thurston Hall) and his wife Peggy (Eileen Van Biene) decide to elope on the eve of their divorce. They hide away at a seaside resort, but their plans for a second honeymoon run into all sorts of complications, especially in the form of Dolly Barbizon (Louise Dresser), Schoonmaker's former shop girl and now a movie star. Schoonmaker's trusted elevator boy, Henry (Billy B. Van), arrives to save the day. Wodehouse's lyrics could be literate and witty, too, as in "They All Look Alike." Or they could have just the right touch of sentimentality—as in "Honeymoon Inn" with which Rudy persuades Peggy to elope, telling her they'll survive "on bread and cheese and kisses," and insisting "this is the thing to do." Most of all, Kern's music was a delight. The song hit—sung by several minor charaders—was "You Said Something," direct and memorable. But the most remarkable number was a forgotten gem, Rudy and Peggy's "And I Am All Alone." Clearly Kern and the producer wanted it to be the real hit, for it was long featured as a sample on the back of much of Kern's other sheet music. Its harmonics were striking for the day, but even more fascinating was its beautiful emotional development building up to a pause and a last melancholy phrase. Kern experimented all through this imaginative score.

Considering the number of favorable reviews *Have a Heart* received, its poor showing is a puzzle. Perhaps some confusion was created by using for its title the title of the still new and popular Kern song from the *Follies*. Whatever the reason, failure and obscurity were undeserved.

Four nights later Kern's second show premiered. **Love o' Mike** (1-15-17, Shubert) had a book by Thomas Sydney and lyrics by Harry B. Smith. Thomas Sydney was a pseudonym for the real librettists, Augustus Thomas Jr., and Harry's son, Sydney. Their plot was inane. The girls at Mrs. Marvin's house party all fall in love with Lord Michael Kildare (Lawrence Grossmith), but he has eyes only for Vivian (Vivian Wessell). The fun at the party is marred when the butler (a sometime second-story man) steals one young lady's money. Then, for reasons never explained, Mike takes credit for rescuing some people from a local tenement fire. His bravery further mars the fun of the men—as they watch their girls' adulation of Mike go out of control. With the butler (George Hassell) the boys plot a phony rescue to counter Mike's heroics. But the two-faced butler tells Mike and the girls of their plans. The dialogue was as inane as the story, often sounding like a satire on itself. Kildare discusses a genuine war wound with his man, Stafford:

Stafford: Wounded arm troubling?
Kildare: Just a bit. Soon be as right as rain.
Stafford: Have a drink, old scout.
Kildare: Thanks, help yourself.

The lyrics, perhaps under the spell of Kern's magic, were above Smith's norm. His idea of how a European might write the lyrics for a "coon" song is still amusing: he told of a girl named Susquehana who lives in Dixie or the banks of the Catskill. But the best lyric was by Herbert Reynolds, and it was for the best song of the show, "It Wasn't My Fault." As with most Kern scores there was hardly a weak number in the show. Good dancing helped put over the songs. The dancing ranged from the suave routines of Quentin Todd to the exuberant stepping of Gloria Goodwin and Clifton Webb. While the

better *Have a Heart* flopped, *Love o' Mike* ran six months.

A few days after *Love o' Mike* opened, the major Broadway producers were asked to comment on the season's musicals. Their remarks suggested their opinions were governed more by their account books than by any overriding vision. John Cort, who had only middling luck with the operetta *Flora Bella*, insisted the season was "strictly a musical comedy one," but Lee Shubert, his coffers piled high with profits from *The Passing Show, Show of Wonders, Follow Me, Her Soldier Boy*, and now *Love o' Mike*, stressed its quality rather than its type and unequivocally hailed 1916–17 as "the best musical comedy season of recent years."

The same team that brought *So Long Letty* from California in October brought a second show east February 5. **Canary Cottage** (2-5-17, Morosco) had even less plot than *Love o' Mike*. At another house party, a group of men are entertaining "young ladies" when the men's wives and sweethearts arrive. By curtain time everyone is properly paired. Although several of the critics were unusually sharp in their denunciations, branding the evening "vulgar" and "low," and although none of Earl Carroll's score was more than superficially pleasing, *Canary Cottage* had a respectable stay.

You're in Love (2-6-17, Casino) was more successful. Just as *Canary Cottage*'s plot bore some resemblance to *Love o' Mike*, so *You're in Love*, portraying another troubled honeymoon, recalled *Have a Heart*. In this case the young couple had to contend with a busybody aunt-in-law. The book by Otto Hauerbach and Edward Clark was conventional. Much of the success was due to Rudolf Friml's fetching score, particularly the show's title song. If the music is no longer familiar, Friml himself is to blame. His great scores have overshadowed this charming, inconsequential material. But the show also was given an imaginative mounting. The second act was set on a realistically recreated ship. The heroine (Marie Flynn) was a sleepwalker, and her nightly rambles took her onto a cargo boom. As soon as she was on it, the boom swung dramatically out over the audience. At the opening one uninhibited first-nighter removed her pink slipper and tickled her feet as she walked over him.

Oh, Boy! opened at the Princess two weeks later, on February 20. The critics and public immediately knew they were witnessing a consummate triumph. The *Times* rejoiced, "You might call this as good as they make them if it were not palpably much better," while the *Sun* exulted, "If there be such things as masterpieces of musical comedy, one reached the Princess last night." Along with a sense of achievement came a sense of occasion. It was realized that the Princess Theatre and its band-box shows were establishing an important American tradition.

Like *Very Good Eddie* (12-23-15), *Oh, Boy!* has fun with mistaken relationships. It begins at George Budd's apartment when Briggs (Carl Lyle), his valet, answers the door to accept a telegram. While Briggs is at the door, George's playboy friend Jim (Hal Forde) and Jim's girls enter through the window, looking for George (Tom Powers). Not finding him in the living room, they disappear into the rest of the apartment to search for him. George arrives with his new bride, Lou Ellen (Marie Carroll). They are madly in love with each other and can't imagine how they muddled through when "You Never Knew About Me." The telegram is from Aunt Penelope (Edna May Oliver), George's Quaker guardian. She has learned he is contemplating marriage and is coming to talk to him. George fears she will cut off his allowance if she discovers he is already married. Lou Ellen decides it might be prudent for her to go home until Aunt Penelope leaves. She will do whatever George suggests, since she wants only to be "An Old-Fashioned Wife." Their cry, as George escorts her out, "Just Think. . . parted like this on our bridal night," could have come from the Kettles or the Darlings. Jim returns. Jackie (Anna Wheaton), a buxom, attractive young lady in handsome evening dress, arrives, as Jim and friends did earlier, through the window. She is fleeing from a policeman whom she hit in the eye during a rumpus that began when an old gentleman known as Tootles persisted in giving her lingering looks at the Cherrytree Inn. Jim tells her he is enchanted to meet "A Pal Like You." He persuades Jackie to stay, and to claim she is Mrs. Budd if anyone comes. Meanwhile he will find Tootles. Jackie puts on Lou Ellen's pajamas just as George returns. She explains her predicament in the nick of time, for the policeman she hit is knocking at the door. George shows the policeman the wedding license, and the officer allows he has made a mistake. Before he departs he admires her pajamas, and "Mrs. Budd" offers to obtain the pattern for him. With the policeman gone, Jackie prepares to leave. But it has started to rain and she and George agree she will have to stay "Till The Clouds Roll By." Judge Carter, Lou Ellen's father, drops in to meet his new son-in-law, but George hurries him out, while Jackie hides in the bedroom.

Lou Ellen and her mother arrive. When they confront Jackie, George introduces her as his Aunt Penelope. Lou Ellen had imagined a different sort of aunt. But her surprise is nothing compared to Jackie's when Judge Carter reappears. Jackie sees that the judge is Tootles. At the Meadow Country Club Jim and Jackie dream of "Nesting Time In Flatbush." Jackie must continue her masquerade as Aunt Penelope, but she is not above ordering a couple of stiff drinks:

Jackie: Hast thou been enjoying thyself?
Lou Ellen: Not a bit. Mother won't let me speak to George.
Jackie: What have they got against the gink?
Lou Ellen: Gink?
Jackie: (*George pokes Jackie*) A Quaker word . . . poor lad I should say . . .
Policeman: How about the pajama pattern?
George: It's coming . . . it's coming.
Lou Ellen: Pajama pattern?
Jackie: Thee shall have it, good man, I promise thee.
Policeman: How's that?
Jackie: I will even give thy good wife mine if thee will only beat it.

The real Aunt Penelope arrives, and the policeman points out George and "his wife" to her. Before she can protest, she is served a spiked lemonade Jackie has ordered. In no time she is tipsy and forgiving.

The book was fast moving, its characters well drawn and its humor, as the excerpt indicates, flowed logically from the characters and situations. Song assignments proved how stunningly Bolton and Wodehouse had advanced. The wryly comic "You Never Knew About Me" was given to the principal lovers, while the cozy "Nesting Time In Flatbush" was sung by the comic leads, and the show's top tune, "Till The Clouds Roll By," was sung by the hero and the comedienne. Wodehouse's lyrics were little short of miraculous. Again they were literate and natural, with a precisely right balance of wit and sentiment. Lou Ellen laments not knowing George when they were children:

> I was often kissed 'neath the mistletoe
> By small boys excited with tea.
> If I'd known that you existed,
> I'd have scratch'd them and resisted, Dear!

But as usual it was Jerome Kern's music that capped the evening. Once more there was hardly a weak number. The show was done as *Oh, Joy!* in England. More than almost any other important

American musical, *Oh, Boy!* has slipped undeservedly into limbo.

Another fine musical arrived one month later. But though **Eileen** (3-19-17, Shubert) had one of Victor Herbert's finest scores and remained Herbert's personal favorite among all his works, it ran only eight weeks. Its ill-timed opening undoubtedly hurt, coming as it did one day after U-boats had sunk the *City of Memphis,* the *Illinois,* and the *Vigilancia,* and our ultimate, headlong plunge into war had begun. The reviewers' raves were overlooked in the headlines' compelling excitement. Moreover, war was the theme of the operetta, and even romanticized war is terrifying on the brink of real battle. Barry O'Day (Walter Scanlan), an Irish revolutionist, is about to be arrested for treason when his high-born sweetheart, Eileen Mulvaney (Grace Breen), disguised as a maid, helps him escape. He is recaptured and is on the verge of being shot when a pardon arrives. The book was well written but in no way exceptional. On the other hand the score had a magnificent Irish flavor, and three Herbert classics have come out of it: "The Irish Have A Great Day To-night," "Thine Alone," and the title song.

It was almost the end of April before another musical opened—the season's second **Passing Show** (4-26-17, Winter Garden), coming in far ahead of its customary time. Its single memento, reflecting the new war fervor, was "Goodbye Broadway, Hello France!" (C. Francis Reisner, Benny Davis/ Billy Bashette). De Wolf Hopper and Jefferson De Angelis, both stars of a bygone day, joined the ranks, to compete for laughs with Chic Sale and Ray Dooley. The consensus was that the comedy was weak. Spectacle included a harem scene featuring not only girls but soft, flickering lights reflected in tiny mirrors. As one slightly weary-of-it-all critic noted, the girls themselves were "seriously affected by the new custom of dressing chorus girls, if at all, in things that are not so much gowns as structures." The "things" included fans, drinks, and fully-set tables. In the finale the girls became college students at the Yale Bowl. Clowns, beauties, and a basic Sigmund Romberg score all combined to keep the show at the Winter Garden into the fall.

His Little Widows (4-30-17, 44th St.) was another instance of critics and public going opposite ways. Favorably received, it played only nine weeks. William Schroeder's lame score did nothing to help the show win favor. However, its story was just the sort of fluff ticket seekers looking for distraction should have flocked to. Jack Grayson's Mormon uncle dies. To inherit his uncle's fortune Jack (Robert Emmett Keane) must marry the dead man's eleven wives. The least desirable widow begins to pursue him. But he succeeds in avoiding all except the loveliest of the group. The show was filled with vaudeville turns. Frank Lalor repeated bits he had performed in *The Pink Lady,* Carter De Haven sang and did a soft shoe, but a jazzy quartet, the Haley Sisters, won the biggest round of applause, largely thanks to one of its girls. She had a "voice like a moose" and performed acrobatic dances on a par with Fred Stone and Charlotte Greenwood.

Two revivals, Reginald De Koven's *The Highwayman* (12-13-97) and Julian Edwards' *When Johnny Comes Marching Home* (12-16-02), were the only openings in May. Both were quickly gone, although the Edwards work's six-week run was not a bad showing. It opened at the New Amsterdam, and when it had to make way for the *Follies* was still considered strong enough to be moved to the Manhattan Opera House for three more weeks. Curiously, De Koven's work had a far better, more celebrated cast that included John Charles Thomas and Jefferson De Angelis.

June ended the season with a pair of revues. The first was Raymond Hitchcock's **Hitchy-Koo** (6-7-17, Cohan and Harris). In an interview, Hitchcock, who had heretofore worked primarily with book shows, observed, "Restlessness of American life has brought a demand for speed and the quality best described as 'Zippiness' in stage productions, and the revue is the type of entertainment in which these qualities are best expressed." He predicted the demise of the book musical, "in which the naval lieutenant rescued the irritatingly ingenuous heroine from an impossible situation, while the chief comedian acted as a sort of deus ex machina." Hitchcock was correct in sensing the faster pace that Broadway audiences sought. Shows that went on till 11:30 or 11:45 became rarer with each season. But he was wrong in thinking only the revue cleared the path for fast action. He brought to his own production some of the new pace, and a feeling for personal intimacy unknown till then. Like George M. Cohan and Will Rogers he made fun of even the most sacrosanct figures—Billy Sunday being dismissed as "the P.T. Barnum of the hymnbook." Hitchcock was careful to surround himself with other sterling talent. In this edition he employed Leon Errol, the baby-talking Frances White, Grace La Rue, and Irene Bordoni. Errol garnered more than his fair share of laughs, not merely for his expected drunk act, but for his routine as a cockney waiter defending his pet lobster. Spectacle included a first-act finale in which couples walked out of wedding album pictures. Each couple took the audience back a generation further and sang or danced an appropriate period piece. E. Ray Goetz, who coproduced the evening, did most of the songs. As happened so many times, an interpolation was the hit of the show. "I May Be Gone For A Long, Long, Time" (Lew Brown/Albert Von Tilzer) sang another war song to a now accepting nation. Some of Goetz' songs were actually better, but none so good as to demand rehearing. The show delighted audiences for seven months, and three more editions followed.

The Ziegfeld Follies of 1917 (6-12-17, New Amsterdam), which closed the season, had an all-star cast—Fanny Brice, Will Rogers, W.C. Fields, Bert Williams, and, for the first time, Eddie Cantor. The stunning Dolores became the center of all eyes in a ravishing "Episode in Chiffon." Fields revived his billiard scene, calling the shots so unerringly that the *Times* wondered how he could do it night after night. Rogers twirled his rope in time with his hilarious anecdotes, which were taking on an increasingly political slant. He found Congress strange, noting, "A man gets up to speak and says nothing. Nobody listens. Then everybody disagrees." Fanny Brice vamped as an Egyptian odalisque. Cantor, in blackface, played the college-educated son of a porter (Williams), intolerant of his father's illitteracy. But he really called attention to himself singing "That's The Kind Of Baby For Me." (Alfred Harrison and Jack Egan). Again in blackface as he sang, he rolled his eyes and jumped up and down, clapping his hands and excitedly waving a handkerchief.

. . .

Eddie Cantor was born on New York's Lower East Side on January 31, 1892. His name was Isidore Itzkowitz or Iskowitz. His family was musical, with his father often earning money as a violinist. When young Isidore was fourteen he won first prize at an amateur night at Miner's Bowery. A year later he made his vaudeville debut at the Clinton Music Hall, and thereafter alternated between two-a-day and jobs as a singing waiter. His first legitimate appearance was in London, in a revue called *Not Likely*. A young lady named Beatrice Lillie was also in the cast. After

playing a while in English music halls, he returned to America, where he was cast for a role in *Canary Cottage*.

. . .

As always Joseph Urban created magical effects on stage and off. He presented a stunning roof-top view of New York and a scene of Lower Manhattan flanked by "fruit festooned" parapets. A set simulating Chinese lacquer had fifty Ziegfeld beauties scampering up and down red and gold ladders against a black background. Girls as flowers sprang from trap doors, and an opalescent curtain of beads parted to reveal Venuses in a gigantic bubble. A Ben Ali Haggin tableau portrayed Paul Revere riding a white horse (on a treadmill). When an actor impersonating President Wilson came to review girls dressed in red, white, and blue, the orchestra began "The Star Spangled Banner," and, as the audience rose, a tremendous flag unfurled to cover the ceiling. Raymond Hubbell and Dave Stamper's music was pleasantly adequate. Besides the necessary parade numbers such as "In The Beautiful Garden Of Girls," it included the topical "I'll Be Somewhere In France" and, somewhat bafflingly, a number advertising a forthcoming show that was not Ziegfeld's, *Chu Chin Chow*. Victor Herbert wrote a "patriotic finale," "Can't You Hear Our Country Calling?" But Ziegfeld could not find a top-flight interpolation. Still, Ziegfeld's touch was so sure and Ziegfeld's name so potent the show played fifteen weeks to good houses and then toured.

It was altogether a good season. Not one of the best, but one that did leave behind a number of good tunes, *Eileen, Have a Heart, Love o' Mike* and, most of all, *Oh, Boy!*

1917-1918

War-born prosperity and an urge to escape the daily unpleasantness of the news stimulated box office sales. As a result thirty-eight musicals were offered on Broadway—almost half again as many as the old season had seen. With theatre construction halted for the duration, a temporary theatre shortage developed. Shows that would have normally been allowed a few extra weeks to find an audience or to add a small sum to their profits were hurried off onto the road or to Cain's fabled warehouse. Therefore, despite the huge jump in the number of new musicals, there was no in-

crease in the number playing over 100 performances—fourteen both years. However, there was
a marked improvement in quality, of which perspicacious writers and audiences were gratefully
aware.

At the beginning of the season there must have
been playgoers who wondered if a musical could
make its way to New York without something in
it by Sigmund Romberg. No less than six of the
preceding season's scores were in large or small
part by him. This dependence on an apparent
hack undoubtedly perplexed more demanding
ticket buyers. Apart from the few winning melodies he inserted into *The Blue Paradise*, his songs
were never more than what his kindest critics
labeled "tinkly." Now another outpouring of lilting mediocrity seemed in store. The first two announcements for the coming season listed Romberg's name among the credits, and the Shuberts
admitted he would be composing for several more
unspecified productions. The season's opener did
nothing to enhance Romberg's reputation. **My
Lady's Glove** (6-18-17, Lyric), for which he wrote
some additional music, was an importation using
the old folklore motif of The Fair Unknown for
its story. Oscar Straus had composed the original
score. Anti-German sentiment, coupled with the
show's banality, made it one of the fastest flops of
the year. It was gone after 16 performances. Quite
possibly the Shuberts suspected they might have
trouble with the work. To fend off resentment
they changed the scene to France, had chorus girls
distribute free chocolates as they sang "Oo, Buy
Some Candy, Sir" and gave the leads to Vivienne
Segal and Charles Purcell. When the show nonetheless folded abruptly, they hustled Purcell into
their very next show.

The fate of Romberg's second entry was markedly different. Romberg had threatened to leave
the Shuberts if more congenial material to work
with was not found. J. J. Shubert, fearing to lose
Romberg's services, brought a Viennese story to
Rida Johnson Young with instructions to turn it
into a piece for which Romberg could write an
entire score in his own style. Mrs. Young, assisted
by Cyrus Wood, reset the story to span over sixty
years of New York life. So adroit was Mrs.
Young's "Americanization" and, as the Shuberts
had learned with *My Lady's Glove*, so virulent the
anti-German emotions, that the source of the story
(*Wie Einst im Mai*) was never mentioned on the
work's programs or sheet music. The book, though
its dialogue was occasionally stiff, had great
appeal. **Maytime** (8-16-17, Shubert), in 1840

New York, was not only a time for resuming
outdoor work, it was a time for love. A group of
apprentices, led by youthful and handsome Richard Wayne (Charles Purcell), are busy on sundry
jobs at Colonel Van Zandt's home in Washington
Square. The colonel's daughter, Ottillie (Peggy
Wood), is engaged to her cousin Claude (Douglas J. Wood), but she has fallen in love with
Richard, and Richard with her. Alone together
they dream of a life "In Our Little Home, Sweet
Home." Neighbors and friends arrive, along with
a gypsy band, and Ottillie leaves Richard to help
as hostess. When the crowd is gone, Ottillie and
Richard meet again. Richard's father, once well-
to-do, had lost his money and to repay some of
his debts had given Van Zandt the deed for the
Wayne house. As Richard and Ottillie are talking,
the deed falls from the Colonel's window. Thinking it an unimportant piece of paper, Richard
writes a love poem on it and they bury it in the
garden, asking each other if they will always remember this day in May. They are interrupted by
Claude and the Colonel (Carl Stall):

Claude: What's this? How dare you?
Richard: What business is it of yours?
Claude: My affianced bride in the arms of a low
    apprentice!
Ottillie: I'm nothing of the kind. I'll never marry
    you! I love Dick!
Colonel: What's this? What is all this?
Claude: This fellow, this dependent—she was in
    his arms!
Dick: Yes, in my arms, where I intend to keep
    her!
Colonel: You forget yourself, Dick! Let my
    daughter go at once!
Dick: She loves me, Sir!
Colonel: You are discharged. Take your things
    and leave at once!
Ottillie: No! No! Father!
Dick: You may send me away sir, but I'll come
    back; and when I do it will be to claim her!
Colonel: Begone! Out of my sight!

Fifteen years later, in Mme. Delphine's Night Club,
the rage of New York is "Jump Jim Crow," "a
dance that's rather shocking." By chance Ottillie,
now married to Claude, and Richard meet there.
They admit they still love each other and confess
their loneliness on "The Road To Paradise." A
quarter of a century later Claude dies, leaving
Ottillie penniless. Her house and its contents are
put up for auction. Richard, now wealthy, comes
to the auction and buys the property back for

Ottillie. About thirty more years pass. Richard and Ottillie are both dead, Ottillie's granddaughter and namesake (Miss Wood) has converted the parlor into a dress shop. Dicky Wayne (Purcell), Richard's grandson, appears to court the young lady. The love story comes full circle, but with a happy ending when the old deed is unearthed and its value appreciated.

Several devices were used to tie the epochs together. William Norris, playing Ottillie's carefree brother Matthew, lived long enough to appear in all four acts, marrying a different heiress in each of the first three acts and, as a very ancient dodderer, flirting gamely with chorus girls in the last. In the first act the lovers plant a young apple tree. The tree is shown blooming in the second, dying in the third, and dead in the fourth. "Will You Remember?" was employed as a leitmotif throughout.

Maytime was the year's overwhelming hit. Its bittersweet tale and exquisite songs struck some responsive chord in troops embarking for overseas. Among departing soldiers it quickly became the ticket most requested. The demand for tickets was so great a second company had to be opened across the street from the original. (This, incidentally, justified the Shuberts advertising both companies on their tours as "entire N.Y. cast"—always a boost to sales.) More important than its immediate success was *Maytime*'s keeping the vogue for operetta alive during the height of the war. Equally significant was the vindication of Romberg's gifts. Although he still had to battle the Shuberts for proper material, his ordeal as a staff writer was virtually behind him. America's last great composer of classical operetta had come to the fore.

The score was among Romberg's best. While clearly not 100 percent American—except possibly for the ragtime songs that give contemporary flavor to the fourth act—the score was not flagrantly Viennese. Romberg was now a Hungarian-American, and even his waltzes would show a certain intangible softening away from the sweep of the pure Continental style. "Will You Remember?" was, more than "Auf Wiedersehn," Romberg's first real classic.

Cheer Up arrived on August 23 at the Hippodrome. Even though the costly spring offensives were several months away, the news was nevertheless unsettling. A happy title and Dillingham's masterful showmanship packed the big house for 456 performances, even if Raymond Hubbell's score was routine. Spectacles included horses div-

ing into the theatre's tank, a full-sized locomotive filled with hoboes, and a cornfield turned into a field of poppies.

Another hit, the third, bounced in six nights later. **Leave It to Jane** (8-28-17, Longacre) was based on George Ade's *The College Widow*, a comedy that had opened at the old Garden Theatre the night after Jerome Kern's first Broadway effort, *Mr. Wix of Wickham*, premiered (9-19-04). It is interesting to speculate whether Kern, to celebrate his first New York production or to console himself after its dreadful reviews, had attended the first night. In any case, he combined with Bolton and Wodehouse to write what was essentially another Princess Theatre show, although the continuing popularity of *Oh, Boy!* at the small house and other commitments brought the new work to a bigger uptown auditorium. Ade's plot was faithfully retained. Jane (Edith Hallor), the college widow, is the daughter of President Witherspoon of "Good Old Atwater." While her philosophy is "Wait Till Tomorrow," students all know that if there is a serious problem, the answer is to "Leave It To Jane." A serious problem quickly develops for the football-mad school. Billy Bolton (Robert G. Pitkin), a super athlete, threatens to play for archrival Bingham. Jane is recruited to lure Billy to Atwater with her "Siren's Song." She succeeds, and Billy agrees to play for Atwater under an assumed name. "The Sun Shines Brighter" for almost everyone after the victory—everyone except Billy, who feels he may have been duped. But Jane and the sirens and the crickets who warn "be glad while you may" prove irresistible. Billy wins Jane as well as the game. Much of the comedy was provided by Oscar Shaw as Stubby and Georgia O'Ramey as Flora. Miss O'Ramey mugged, let herself be hurled through the air, and stopped the show with her comic Egyptian dance for "Cleopatterer."

Bolton's solid book and Wodehouse's free-flowing lyrics were enhanced by Kern's exuberant score. "The Crickets Are Calling" and "The Siren's Song" are Kern at his winsome best, and many a show would have been grateful for so catchy a title song. When *Leave It to Jane* was revived at a house no bigger than the Princess in 1959, it ran for two years, testifying to its ageless charm.

September's initial offering was a Chicago success hoping to make good in the East. It failed. Called **Good Night, Paul** (9-3-17, Hudson), its silly plot had eccentric Uncle Paul (Frank Lalor) visiting the home of an unmarried nephew (Ralph

Herz). The nephew lives with his business partner and the partner's wife (Burrell Barbaretto and Elizabeth Murray). The youngsters are on the verge of bankruptcy. Uncle Paul agrees to make them solvent again if the bachelor nephew changes places with his married partner. Along with the claptrap book came a third-rate score. Paul and his family left town after five weeks.

Two pleasant operettas followed in short order. Both were well received, and both missed being successful, possibly because the public associated them with Vienna. The first was **Rambler Rose** (9-10-17, Empire), with a book by Harry B. Smith and songs by Victor Jacobi (by 1917 an American citizen). The rose of the story is Rosamond Lee (Julia Sanderson), an American girl who is the niece, ward, and pupil of Lady Cloverdale (Kate Sergeantson). Lady Cloverdale runs an ultramodern girls' school where books are frowned upon and the curriculum includes make-up, smoking, ragtime, and "a special course in talking at the opera." Bashful Joseph Guppy (Joseph Cawthorn) loves Rosamond, but she has eyes only for the handsome art teacher, Gerald Morgan (John Goldsworthy). When he leaves the school to return to Paris, Rosamond follows him, and he is forced to put her up at his apartment. Guppy arrives in hot pursuit. His motives are not entirely pure, for if he fails to marry before his next birthday his rich uncle will disinherit him. Guppy prevails on Gerald's friend, Marcel (Stewart Baird), to help in a ruse. Marcel is to create a statue and allow Guppy to present it as his own masterwork. Guppy hopes the money and prestige from its sale will win Rosamond. Marcel, of course, does not realize Guppy wants to marry Rosamond. The millionaire who buys the statue turns out to be Guppy's rich uncle. The uncle not only takes home the statue, he woos and wins Gerald's old flame, leaving Gerald and Rosamond free to wed. Guppy goes "back to bashfulness, it's cheaper." The plot and the dialogue contained not a hint of the war. It seemed just the sort of escapist diversion an audience would crave. But even Miss Sanderson and Cawthorn could not keep the musical on the boards beyond nine weeks.

Ten weeks was all **The Riviera Girl** (9-24-17, New Amsterdam), which arrived seven nights later, could achieve. Here was a show that did begin life in Vienna, Emmerich Kalman's *Czardasfürstin*. Guy Bolton created a not quite completely fresh book for New York, telling of the love of a count (Louis Cassavant) for a vaudeville singer (Wilda Bennett), and Jerome Kern wrote some new songs, including the popular, lively "Bungalow in Quogue." This song elicited amused comments from a critic who wondered if the European characters singing it had ever heard of Long Island, let alone Quogue. Gorgeous Urban settings "all keyed to the velvet, impenetrable blue of a Mediterranean sky" were "of monumental stateliness and a rich simplicity in color." Urban allowed the costumes to provide the variety and punctuation. All the fine American additions, coupled with Kalman's lovely score, could not save the show. Not even Kalman, it turned out, could overcome international enmity.

When Edward Clark's comedy *Coat Tales* had but a 32-performance run in 1916 some reviewers suggested it would have been better as a musical. Arthur Hammerstein, who produced the play, took their advice and brought it back as **Furs and Frills** (10-9-17, Casino), with a Clark book, Clark lyrics, and Silvio Hein music. The critics wondered about the soundness of their own advice. However, those who liked it compared it to "those 'operettas *intimes*' with which the Princess Theatre of late years has been restoring the lost art of Gilbert and Sullivan." The story could have easily come from Bolton instead of Clark. The extravagant Mrs. Macey (Beatrice Allen) brings home a $5,000 fur coat, but before she tells her husband of the purchase, her scapegrace brother steals it and pawns it. Mr. Macey (George Anderson) unwittingly reclaims it and, not knowing its history, gives it to his partner's wife. The fur flies. If Clark was almost a Bolton, Hein was woefully short of being a Kern. A weak-voiced chorus attempted to gloss over its inadequacies by playing violins in one number. The show ran exactly as long as its source—32 performances.

After the death in the spring of his partner, Dave Montgomery, Fred Stone determined to continue alone. His first solo venture confirmed that he needed no help to pack an enthralled house. **Jack o' Lantern** (10-16-17, Globe), created by much the same team that had written and produced *Chin-Chin* for him—Ivan Caryll, Anne Caldwell, R.H. Burnside, and Charles Dillingham —once again placed Stone in his unique world halfway between reality and toyland. This time it was called Appledale Farm and run by mean, old Uncle George (Oscar Ragland), who stands to inherit a lot of money should anything happen to his young wards. He hires a man to kill them. Since he has never seen the man, he arranges for a password to identify him. When John Obadiah

Lantern, who is called Jack o' Lantern because he is light in the head, inadvertently mentions the password, he is mistaken for the would-be assassin. Catching on to the uncle's wicked plans, Jack kidnaps the children. But not without a chase: "Jack jumps off [the] haywagon, landing on the end of the see saw, which is at the side of the haywagon. As he lands he throws a policeman, who has been standing on the other end of the see saw up in the air. The policeman does a somersault—landing on the top of the haywagon." Although Jack has proclaimed, "I'm a socialist—Got nothing and believe in sharing it with everybody," he takes the children to his mansion, where a staff attends to their wishes. From there they are transported to a "Cave of Dreams," in which all sorts of adventures befall. At one point they are in the army and Jack is the mail censor. He "censors" six letters, all in the same fashion:

Jack: This letter must be from a married man
 (*reading:*
 "My mother-in-law is a kind woman. She sent me a bottle of Old Crow."
 (*musing*
 That doesn't sound natural—
 (*drawing pencil thro' part of letter*
 That's better.
 (*reading*
 My mother-in-law is an Old Crow.

Jack and the children finish at an Ice Palace, where Jack, dressed as Charlotte Russe, puts on a skating show. Uncle George inexplicably mends his ways in the last lines of the show, and everybody is happy.

Caryll's score was melodic and carefree. The appropriately bucolic "(Won't You) Wait Till The Cows Come Home?" remained a favorite long after Urban's magnificent sets had disappeared and Stone himself had departed to yet another world.

But while Alan Dale in the *Sun* professed to see *Jack o' Lantern* setting "a standard for the musical show," by and large it was Urban, whose "continued presence in the Broadway theatre endows it with a splendor it has never before possessed," and the inimitable Stone who were responsible for the box office bonanza. Urban did not design all the sets. Some were by Homer Ewens and Ernest Albert. Still, Urban's scenary received all the praise, especially an apple orchard, stylized like drawings in a child's book, and a pink, pale green, white, and silver candyland peopled with a chorus of "gayly colored barber poles of candy, tooth-

some jujubes, and lingering, delectable all-day-suckers." When Stone finished his extensive tour with the piece, Doyle and Dixon took it out to the one-night stands, using the original version written before Montgomery's death.

Doing Our Bit came into the Winter Garden on October 18. It had the requisite patriotic trimmings, including a troopship number in which the entire chorus, men and women, were dressed as soldiers. It had Ed Wynn, Frank Tinney, and even former heavyweight boxing champion James J. Corbett. It had a score of no special interest by Romberg and Herman Timberg. It also had a warning from critics that the day of the slapdash extravaganza was waning, the *World* lambasting it as "bankrupt in talent" and "threadbare," while the *Evening Post,* affecting a blasé boredom, concluded, "the new Winter Garden show is very like all the other Winter Garden shows, though experienced first-nighters were able to note certain differences in costume detail." It had, lastly, a satisfactory run of 130 performances.

Four nights later, F. Ray Comstock and his associates, who had been instrumental in establishing the vogue for the Princess Theatre's small-scaled shows, went to the other extreme by importing the spectacular London rage, **Chu Chin Chow** (10-22-17, Manhattan Opera House). It lavishly recounted Abu Hassan's exotic and fatal machinations while disguised as the Chinese merchant, Chu Chin Chow, at Kasim Baba's palace. Kasim's brother is the famous Ali Baba, and the forty thieves figure prominently in the evening's intrigue. The extravaganza broke all London records for longevity and its record was not surpassed for decades. The American production had a stellar cast. Tyrone Power (the fine, old dramatic actor) was Abu Hassan, the seemingly forgotten Henry Dixey was Ali Baba, while Tessa Kosta and Florence Reed played the female leads. *Chu Chin Chow*'s American reception was disappointing, although its run of 208 performances at the large Manhattan Opera House was by no means negligible.

An importation inaugurated November's offerings. It was a Havana revue, **The Land of Joy** (11-1-17, Park). In a book rewritten for New York, audiences watched a group of Americans take a tour to Spain. The show's composer Joaquin Valverde, was hailed as a Spanish Victor Herbert, while the set designers, the Tarazona Brothers, were compared favorably with Urban. A dancer named L'Argentina stopped the show with a heel dance, a table dance, and an impassioned tango. However, before the show finished an eleven-week run she was replaced by another dancer, Violeta.

On paper **Miss 1917** (11-5-17, Century) was one of those shows that had almost everything. Conceived by Dillingham and Ziegfeld as a successor to *The Century Girl*, it had music by Herbert and Kern, lyrics and sketches by P. G. Wodehouse, splendid Urban sets, and a cast of old and new favorites including Lew Fields, Bessie McCoy Davis, Van and Schenck, Brice and King, Irene Castle, Bert Savoy, and Vivienne Segal. Its failure is even more astonishing when the generally rave reviews are considered. But the Century was out of the way, and the material, however good, represented no one's best—although the lovely "The Land Where The Good Songs Go" (originally composed for *Oh, Boy!*) was used by Hollywood nearly thirty years later in its supposedly biographical movie on Kern. One false legend connected with the song and the show makes a telling comment on the still vaudeville-like freewheeling that went into assembling these revues. Kern's number was used to introduce a medley of old favorites, particularly with Bessie McCoy returning to sing them after a protracted absence. Vivienne Segal was also to sing an older tune. Kern wanted her to do "They Didn't Believe Me," but Dillingham and Herbert reached farther back for "Kiss Me Again," and Miss Segal sided with them. Kern, depending on who tells the story, never forgave her and never spoke to her again. If the story has any truth at all, it is certainly not in any enduring anger on Kern's part. When *Miss 1917* folded after six weeks, Kern rushed Miss Segal into the starring role of his very next show. While *Miss 1917* remained on the boards, Irene Castle waltzed in a blue, moonlit dreamland. Miss Davis introduced "I'm The Old Man In The Moon" and revived "The Yama Yama Man." Fields clowned as a farmer who raises pickles in a spoof of *Turn to the Right*. Urban employed his revolving stage to depict a grove of trees losing their leaves as autumn gives way to winter.

The next opening also witnessed the return of an old favorite, Alice Nielsen, who found fame in the earliest Victor Herbert operettas at the end of the 19th century and who then left the light opera stage for grand opera. She returned to sing the principal role in **Kitty Darlin'** (11-7-17, Casino), the Otto Harbach-Rudolf Friml adaptation of David Belasco's *Sweet Kitty Bellairs*. The book was "violently faithful to the original," rehearsing

how Kitty, the flirtatious young lady from Bath, decides to play coquette with Lord Verney. Kitty hides under his bed at the sound of feminine footsteps. It is Lady Standish, who also hides when voices are heard approaching. The room is about to be searched when Kitty comes out of hiding, thereby halting the search and sparing Lady Standish. The book, however faithful, was uninspired. Critics seemed more fascinated by the change in the spelling of the librettist's name. "Up to last night he was Otto Hauerbach," the *World* noted. The old spelling was a war casualty. But neither a new spelling nor an old favorite could save *Kitty Darlin'* from a quick death.

Victor Herbert's **Her Regiment** (11-12-17, Broadhurst) fared little better. Although it had pleasant music and the popular Donald Brian as star, it survived only 40 performances. Again critics were more than kind. Possibly the public was kept away in the mistaken assumption the military title announced a war story. The show, in fact, told a romantic tale, set in Normandy just before the war erupted. Love and disguise, not hate and battle, were the themes. André de Courcy (Brian), a wealthy aristocrat, pretends to be a common soldier. Estelle Durvernay (Audrey Maple), another wealthy aristocrat, pretends to be a lady's maid. The maid and the soldier fall in love. As always, Brian's graceful dancing was as much or more of an attraction than his singing. His second-act ballroom turn with Cissie Sewell won special plaudits. Frank Moulan was also on hand to provide comic relief.

Odds and Ends of 1917 (11-19-17, Bijou) was another intimate revue. One of its producers, Jack Norworth, preferred the word "chummy," and this drew amused comment. Critics compared the evening to *Hitchy-Koo*. Its idea of humor was a first-act finale honoring famous couples of history, Anthony and Cleopatra, Elizabeth and Essex, and the Smith Brothers of cough drop fame. The music was ordinary. One song, "Fancy You Fancying Me," received considerable advance build-up. Its mediocrity left playgoers shaking their heads. But uneven as *Odds and Ends* was, it managed a four-month stay.

The Franz Lehar operetta which followed was the fastest flop of the season. **The Star Gazer** (11-26-17, Plymouth) was withdrawn after only 8 performances. More than merely bad Lehar, it was an Austro-Hungarian composition. Its fiasco finally drove home a lesson to Broadway's producers. No more Viennese operettas were attempted until the Armistice was several months old. As they had with *My Lady's Glove*, the Shuberts attempted to avoid possible disaster by switching the setting from Austria, this time to 1830 New England. They attempted to economize by eliminating any chorus. John Charles Thomas was the star, but on opening night an understudy had to replace the original leading lady. Her fine acting and singing catapulted Carolyn Thomson into the limelight.

Over the Top was designed as a vehicle for the ravishing Justine Johnstone. It was originally called *Oh, Justine!* Brought in on December 1 to the 44th Street Roof, it was a miniature Winter Garden revue, and that meant another largely Romberg score. The show purported to be Miss Johnstone's dream of a trip to visit her lover (Colin Campbell). T. Roy Barnes made intermittent appearances as "The Plot" to create problems and then arbitrarily resolve them. Between spectacles such as "The Land of Frocks and Frills" and a German trench attacked by American planes, specialities enlivened the proceedings. Harry and Emma Sharrock were droll mind readers, announcing inscriptions on watches, masonic badges, and Yiddish coins belonging to the audience. A pair of brightly agile young dancers made an appealing debut—Fred and Adele Astaire.

The Grass Widow (12-3-17, Liberty) was, in view of the casualty lists appearing in the papers, perhaps a bit thoughtless as a title. Based on Bisson and Albin's *The Yellow Peril*, it described how the hot-headed Denise (Natalie Alt), angered at the seeming slights of Jacques, Count of Cluny (Howard Marsh), marries Anatol Pivert (George Marion), an old restaurateur. Jacques enters as the ceremony is ending and carries Denise away to Paris. Anatol follows them, but young love wins the day. It was a clean show, with a good cast, but it failed to catch on. In the hopes of surviving until an audience could be found, it took the unusual step of moving from the standard size Liberty Theatre on 42nd Street to the small Princess three blocks south. The hoped-for business never materialized, and after a total of six weeks the show was closed. For Louis Hirsch, its composer, it was the first of three major scores he would offer in a single season and the only unsuccessful one.

Hirsch's next complete score was heard three weeks later, on Christmas night, when **Going Up** flew into the same Liberty Theatre. The show was based on James Montgomery's *The Aviator*, a well-thought-of comedy that had failed to meet expec-

tations. This time both Hirsch and Montgomery (who collaborated with Otto Harbach on the book) knew the outcome was different. While the braggart who was its central character is universal, there was something apple pie American about *Going Up*'s hero. Robert Street (Frank Craven) writes a best seller on flying and boasts of his aeronautic skills. Actually he has never been in a plane. Street is challenged to an air race, and he must win the race to win the girl he loves, Grace Douglas (Edith Day). He wins. The book was laughter all the way, and the jaunty score was topped by a title number which promised to leave the ground any minute and by a universally praised dance number, "Tickle Toe." One showstopping effect was Street's flying through the night air in a full-scale biplane late in the second act.

Hirsch's score for **The Rainbow Girl** (4-1-18, New Amsterdam) was even better. A few critics, like the gentleman from the *American,* disagreed. But then on balance he was willing to allow "Excepting for 'The Chocolate Soldier' and 'The Only Girl' there has seldom been a musical comedy with a more interesting story." His fellow reviewers were less rash, contenting themselves with "tells a simple story simply" or falling back on "a real plot." The story was based on Jerome K. Jerome's *The New Lady Bantok*. What no critic noted was that each libretto for which Hirsch wrote the music honored a different one of the Allies. *The Grass Widow* was set in France, *Going Up*, in the U.S.A. On April 1, *The Rainbow Girl* took audiences to England, where Mollie Murdock (Beth Lydy), "The Rainbow Girl" of the Frivolity Theatre in London, marries Robert Dudley (Harry Benham), unaware he is Lord Wetherell. Arriving at his ancestral estate, she receives a second shock, for she is related to all his serving staff. Mollie, it seems, had run away from a serving-class family to try her luck on stage. Love levels ranks, and everyone joins the marriage celebration. Hirsch provided another vibrant title song. "I'll Think Of You" had a droll, tongue-in-cheek poignancy. It was sung in the show by the second leads, Harry Delf and Lenora Novasio. Despite rave reviews, *The Rainbow Girl* ran twenty weeks, considerably less than the all-American *Going Up*. Its late arrival and all the fine competition hurt. It remains among the season's very best newcomers.

Three other shows opened in December between *The Grass Widow* and *Going Up*. A second Valverde revue, **A Night in Spain** on December 6 at the Century Roof, failed to equal even the limited success of his *The Land of Joy*, even though Raymond Hitchcock served as compère.

Flo-Flo (12-20-17, Cort) had a solid, if elementary book, which enmeshed Flo-Flo (Vera Michelena), daughter of a bankrupt social climber, and a pseudo-Spanish nobleman (George Renavent). It also had another listenable, forgettable Silvio Hein score. Its 220-performance run was the longest any Hein show managed. Isadore Witmark referred to Hein as "gentle and revered," insisting he wrote "Songs the whole nation sang." It sang none for long. "The Small Town Girl" and "Good Bye Happy Days" typify his output and suggest the perpetually likable quality of even Broadway's minor creations during this period. The evening was largely a succession of vaudeville turns. Thomas Handers and Arthur Mills juggled as they danced, while Oscar Figman and Leon Leonard indulged in Yiddish banter. Since the first act was set in a lingerie shop chorus girls weren't weighed down with clothes; but the second act—a wedding rehearsal—allowed them to parade in lavish gowns.

For **Words and Music** (12-24-17, Fulton) Richard Carle was on hand with some slightly off-color jokes and a running gag that had him breaking dishes all night long. If anyone believed the program, the words were by William Shakespeare and the music by Ludwig Beethoven (no "von"), two names not heretofore familiar to the revue field. But since Raymond Hitchcock and E. Ray Goetz were the evening's producers, more knowledgeable playgoers suspected they had lent a helping hand. Their help was not enough to keep the show alive more than three weeks.

December's final show, **The Cohan Revue of 1918**, followed *Going Up* by a week, opening at the New Amsterdam as part of the New Year's Eve festivities. Even though Cohan asked Berlin to write the songs with him, something went wrong. The score was dreary and the skits lacked the originality, snap, and wit of Cohan's earlier revues. His 1916 skit "Common Clay" had already become a minor classic. Critics generally lamented a decline in quality, although many singled out "Polly of the Follies," which managed to spoof at one and the same time the *Follies*, Belasco ("My name is not Dave Morosco, but Oliver Belasco"), and his *Polly with a Past*. Imitations proved a high spot of the evening with Charles Winninger aping Leo Ditrichstein and Nora Bayes mimicking Ina Claire and Florence Reed. Cohan was not given to sulking over failures and would probably have

bounced back in a year or two with a new edition. But the animosities that grew out of the 1919 actors' strike, when Cohan sided with the producers and theatre owners, put an end to his dreams of establishing another Weber and Fields tradition.

Almost a month elapsed before 1918's first musical danced across the boards. **Girl o' Mine** premiered at the little Bijou on January 28. Its book was by Philip Bartholomae, who had collaborated on the initial Princess smash, *Very Good Eddie* (12-23-15). And the book was quite good. Betty (Dorothy Dickson) comes to Paris seeking an uncle she has never met. She is assisted in her search by a prizefighter and his wife who have opened an American bar after running out of money on their honeymoon. All Elizabeth Marbury and the Shuberts, who produced the show, lacked was a second Jerome Kern. Frank Tours did the weak score. Its weakness contributed to the show's short run. Miss Dickson, who in a few years went on to become a London favorite, was praised for her captivatingly airy dances, while Frank Fay and Marie Nordstrom won kudos for their singing of satiric songs.

Kern himself may have contributed to *Girl o' Mine*'s failure when four nights later on February 1 he gave New York and the Princess another lyrical hit, **Oh, Lady! Lady!!** As prolific at this time as Hirsch and Romberg, but infinitely more inventive, Kern produced three scores in four months. *Oh, Lady! Lady!!* is best remembered as the show that did not include "Bill." How the song's elimination affected our musical history will never be known, but it did not alter the show's charm or success. The *Times* called it "virtually flawless," and many other critics, with a growing sense of occasion, compared it gleefully to the earlier Princess shows, especially "the enduring *Oh, Boy!*" As Willoughby "Bill" Finch (Carl Randall) and Mollie Farrington (Vivienne Segal) are about to be married, Willoughby is confronted by Fanny Weld (Florence Shirley), who claims to be his boyhood friend. She is really the girl friend of Willoughby's man, Spike (Edward Abeles), a reformed criminal, and she is after the Farrington jewels. She steals them, but Spike extricates his master from the embarrassing and suspicious situation by recovering the jewels. Mollie is free to marry her Bill. The only song from the show to remain steadfastly favored is the discarded "Bill." Originally it was placed at the beginning of the first act when Mollie attempts to explain her infatuation to her mystified mother. Even after it was dropped, the first-act finale retained several bars of it. Kern, who was particularly fond of the song, kept trying to find a place for it in later musicals. Marilyn Miller tried it and rejected it for *Sally*. Ten years passed before it received recognition. Most of the remaining songs still await recognition. Tops in the superb score are Mollie's sly "Not Yet," her haunting "When The Ships Come Home," the gay title song that Bill and the chorus girls sang, and the lush but strangely disconnected chorus number "Moon Song." In keeping with the practice of the day, almost every song was accompanied by a dance, and the principals, notably Randall, were praised for their light footwork. Even Miss Segal was singled out for her elegant waltzing. The show's second-act set, depicting a Greenwich Village rooftop, also elicited kind comments.

Directly after the show opened, Bolton in an interview discussed "The Improvement in Musical Comedy Standards." The librettist insisted, "Our musical comedies . . . depend as much upon plot and the development of their characters for success as upon their music, and because they deal with subjects and peoples near to the audiences." Two points were stressed. First, "In the development of our plot . . . we endeavor to make everything count. Every line, funny or serious, is supposed to help the plot continue to hold." Secondly, "if the songs are going to count at all in any plot, the plot has to build more or less around, or at least, with them." Similar statements were forthcoming at the start of each great era of the American Musical Theatre. At this early day these standards were not a little utopian. For years after, good scores kept weak librettos on the boards long after they deserved to be forgotten. But this in no way gainsays Bolton. His foresight, his high aims, and his skills almost singlehandedly pioneered the modern book show.

Kern's two other scores were for **Toot-Toot!** (3-11-18, Cohan) and **Rock-a-Bye Baby** (5-22-18, Astor). Although *Toot-Toot!*, based on Rupert Hughes' 1911 hit, *Excuse Me*, was a 40-performance failure, one tune had a tremendous vogue. Ironically, it was not by Kern. "The Last Long Mile" was a hastily inserted soldiers' marching song by Emil Breitenfeld that served as a stirring first-act finale. A war song was not out of place in a plot that described how Lt. Harry Malloy (Donald MacDonald), on receiving his orders, decides to marry Marjorie Newton (Louise Allen)

at once. Since no minister can be located, they chance finding one on the train taking Malloy to his base. There is a young minister on board with his wife; however, the plot requires that he conceal his identity. His calling is discovered in time for a happy ending. The book was good enough, but Kern's score, with the exception of "If," was below his standard. However, their vivacious singing of "If" launched both Louise Groody and Billy (later William) Kent on their way to prominence. Several critics mentioned that the costume designer had an easy time of it, since all the men were in khaki. The women's costumes and the sets were largely ignored in the reviews.

If on one hand, *Rock-a-Bye Baby*, based on Margaret Mayo's *Baby Mine*, had a varied, tuneful score, it also had a serious problem. Its authors, Miss Mayo and Edgar Allan Woolf, had not read Bolton's interview. The *Times*, which reflected the prevailing sentiment, thought "the adaptor selected too good a farce to work upon . . . too good a tale to stand idly by while the principals and the friends of the principals sing pleasant little melodies which have nothing to do with the case." Typically, the joyful "There's No Better Use For Time Than Kissing" was sung by "persons totally unconnected with the plot, who just happen to enter the lady's boudoir." The lady in question is Zoie Hardy (Edna Hibbard), who is stranded at the Rock-a-Bye Baby Inn when a new auto she is test-driving with Mr. Jenks (Walter Jones) breaks down. Business brings her husband (Frank Morgan) to the inn, and he misconstrues the situation. To reclaim her husband Zoie announces she is about to have a baby. Helpful Mr. Jenks sets out to find a baby and brings back three. When their parents come to take the babies home, everything is explained, and Mr. Hardy, realizing the lengths his wife will go to keep him, is mollified. The "pasted hit or miss" songs were luminous, the best having a loving, nurserylike warmth. The slapdash nature of construction was disclosed further when Dorothy Dickson was rushed in to dance. She was not even assigned a character part, but apparently appeared solely as herself. (However, later programs call her character Dorothy Manners.) Oblivious to the show's faults, one first-nighter wrote, "I don't know any musical comedy that has appealed to me more." The praise, not intended for publication, was recorded in his diary by twenty-one-year-old Ira Gershwin. If more people had been as pleased, *Rock-a-Bye Baby* would have played longer than eleven weeks.

The Love Mill (2-7-18, 48th St.), which opened six nights after *Oh, Lady! Lady!!,* came from Chicago. The mill operated at the Mt. Vernon, New York, home of Mrs. Thompson (Jeanette Lowrie), a matron living a high life on a low income. She is determined to marry off her three daughters. All of them give her problems, especially fat Millie (Carrie McManus), whom she forces to drink vinegar to lose weight. By curtain time she has found mates for all three. Earl Carroll's book and lyrics and Alfred Francis' score left much to be desired. *The Love Mill* employed only eight chorus girls, and cutely assigned them names, from Laura to Lauretta, whose first letters spelled the title. As sometimes happens, the reviews of a failure are more fascinating than the show itself. Several critics took the opportunity to discuss musicals in general and the season in particular. The often curmudgeonly *Dramatic Mirror* concluded it was in the middle of "a season in which the musical productions have attained a higher standard than in recent years." But then the sheet was in the minority praising the show. Heywood Broun, panning the show in the *Tribune*, reported, "The show begins with a song called 'opening chorus,' which is led by six 'Tennis Boys,' armed with three-ounce racquets. After they have committed a few foot-faults there is a joke about Haig and Haig, and presently the fat comedienne says: 'I could live on onions alone,' only to meet the response: 'If you do, you will.' The leader of Tennis Boys, by the way, is down on the programme as Joe Miller." In broader terms Broun posed a question that could still be asked, "Why is it that the book of 'The Love Mill,' like most musical comedies, is full of cynicism about marriage while the lyrics by the identical author approach the self-same institution with reverence, truth and sweetness?"

Sinbad appeared on February 14. It was the quintessential Jolson show. The story opened at a Long Island dog show, but soon found itself in exotic settings—Cabin of the Good Ship Whale, Grotto of the Valley of Diamonds, Island of Eternal Youth. Romberg's score was no different from any other score he had supplied for the Winter Garden. Only Jolson's interpolations remain, including three of his most popular songs —"Rock-A-Bye Your Baby To A Dixie Melody" (Joe Young, Sam Lewis, and Jean Schwartz), "My Mammy" (Irving Caesar/Walter Donaldson), and "Swanee" (Irving Caesar/George Gershwin). "My Mammy" was introduced late in the run, and "Swanee," which made Gershwin famous over-

night, was not brought in until the road tour was under way. The Shuberts had installed a ramp from the stage far out into the audience, and Jolson, in blackface and white gloves, and down on one knee, generally sang "Mammy" and other selected tunes within arm's reach of his admirers. "Hello, Central, Give Me No Man's Land" (also by Young, Lewis, and Schwartz) was popular at the time, as was "Chloe," which Jolson is purported to have worked on with Buddy De Sylva.

Zoel Parenteau made a second attempt to succeed on Broadway with his music for **Follow the Girl** (3-2-18, 44th St. Roof). Henry Blossom supplied the book and lyrics. The action took place at a Maine summer hotel, where Mrs. Niles (Jobyna Howland) attempts to find a wealthy husband for her daughter, Gladys (Eileen Van Biene). Gladys needs no help. She finds Alfred Vanderveer (Harry Fender) on her own. One line in the dialogue tickled a number of critics, who reported that Walter Catlett, spying Jobyna Howland in a low-backed gown, announced he would follow "the trail of the lonesome spine." The war presented a problem for the German dialect comedian, who now had to be clearly identified as Swiss. As in *The Love Mill,* the chorus made its first appearance in tennis clothes. One of the girls seemed outstanding and before long she had a solo. Her name was Dorothy Godfrey, a contortionist. But the book was not very good, and some of Parenteau's best music, such as "Don't Lose Your Way," was from the preceding season's *The Amber Princess.* Parenteau, except for his two songs in *Kiki,* spent the rest of his life—he died in 1972—working as musical director in various American cities.

One of the most affectionately remembered of shows, **Oh, Look!** opened the intimate Vanderbilt Theatre on March 7. It was based on another James Montgomery farce, *Ready Money.* Long Island, which seemed to be the only proper locale for smart, intimate plots, is the site of the Welch estate, where a smart, intimate weekend is in progress. Should anyone doubt young Welch's credentials he was quickly, if stiffly, disabused:

Welch: You know my father's very wealthy
Turner: Yes
Welch: I'll get all that someday, but I want to be a success by my own endeavor. He's done everything for me. He gives me all the money I want and more. See here—a check for $10,000—a present from my father.

But it develops that Welch (Clarence Nordstrom)

is not to be the protagonist. Stephen Baird (Harry Fox), a young man on the verge of bankruptcy, commands our attention. His friend, Jackson Ives (Frederick Burton), provides him with money until Baird's gold mine can begin to produce. The new money brings as assortment of new friends. But they all desert him when the money is found to be counterfeit. Only his girl, Grace Tyler (Louise Cox), remains loyal. Luckily the mine proves a bonanza. Stephen and Grace sing the final duet knowing they will be genuinely rich.

Harry Carroll's music, with one exception, was of the same crude order as the book. The evening's big production number, repeated as the finale, was "Typical Topical Tunes." "Topical" was suitably alliterative, but meaningless. Night after night the handsome Fox stopped the show with "I'm Always Chasing Rainbows," adapted from Chopin's Fantasy Impromptu. Though the musical could not satisfactorily fill even the new bandbox playhouse for more than 67 performances, it was revamped for the road with the Dolly sisters as stars and played to packed houses around the country.

Advertised as "a costless, castless, careless revue," **Let's Go** (3-9-18, Fulton) lived up to its billing. It lurked around for three weeks and went away, but not before singing longingly of "The Land Of Yesterday" and looking with a jaundiced eye on an army run by women.

Toot-Toot! and *The Rainbow Girl* followed.

Fancy Free (4-11-18, Astor) was a serviceable romp, set in Palm Beach, where there is a mix-up about who is married to whom. "The songs," the *Globe* reflected, "have very little to do with it, being more or less irrelevant." What was relevant was one young lady who stole the show and the notices. Broun, expressing himself with his customary felicity, summed up the general feeling, "Fancy Free gets up on its toes early in the evening and stays there. The ten best toes belong to Marilynn Miller."

Another young lady, the comely Fay Bainter, was responsible for what success **The Kiss Burglar** (5-9-18, Cohan) enjoyed. The "burglar" (Armand Kalisz) indeed steals only a kiss when he finds himself in the boudoir of a grand duchess while fleeing from a dishonest but titled gambler. The war forces the duchess to take refuge in America. For a second time, the young man, who is American, finds himself in her apartment. When he steals his second kiss they both realize they are in love. Glen MacDonough's book and Raymond Hubbell's music were never much more than

competent. Nonetheless the show chalked up 100 performances and then toured.

Biff! Bang! (5-30-18, Century) was a vaudeville mounted by sailors from the Pelham Naval Training Station and brought in as a curiosity for two weeks. Among its "stevedore" show girls was Lew Fields' son, Joe.

With the coming of June it was time for the summer revues. **Hitchy-Koo of 1918** (6-6-18, Globe) led off. Hitchcock informed his audience the evening was "drammed jammed with hokum and jazz." The material, mostly by MacDonough and Hubbell, was no better than what they had offered in *The Kiss Burglar*. Hubbell's music contained nothing of the promised "jazz." But the cast was strong enough to put any mediocrity across. Besides Hitchcock it included Leon Errol, Irene Bordoni, and Florence O'Denishawn. Baby-talking Ray Dooley replaced the last year's baby-talking Frances White. It stayed nine weeks and it, too, went on tour.

1918-1919

As the new season opened, the war news became less bleak. The submarine offensive, probably the greatest remaining threat, was obviously collapsing. Its diminution allowed 600,000 American troops to be transported safely to France in May, June, and July. It was increasingly apparent the war would be over soon. The feeling of imminent victory brought into the open cries for change in all aspects of American life. Suffragettes, prohibitionists, League of Nation supporters, isolationists, and Ku Klux Klansmen made public their disparate plans for a postwar world. For the country as a whole what loomed beyond the armistice remained a large, unarticulated question. This malaise of uncertainties and adjustments affected Broadway as well. Though the public packed the theatres in search of escape (and more than half the season's musicals ran over 100 performances), no truly first-rate show was presented and no smash hit of *Maytime*'s proportion emerged. The names of the season's musicals are at best only vaguely familiar. But the season was far from uninteresting. The quality of the preceding sessions often masked their creative turmoil. Now the ferment stood revealed.

The Ziegfeld Follies of 1918 (6-18-18, New Amsterdam), which inaugurated the season, subtly and unwittingly exposed the new uncertainties, although those who didn't wish to see them were not compelled to leave the theatre concerned. Joseph Urban's sets were as luxurious as ever (particularly a gigantic re-creation of a miniature bonsai with cherry tree and bridge); the girls and their gowns resplendent. Will Rogers, Eddie Cantor, W. C. Fields, and Ann Pennington headed the cast. Rogers joked about American politics and the Irish demand for home rule, but also appeared in musical numbers, lassoing Ann Pennington as she danced, and strutting in white tie and tails with Lillian Lorraine. Cantor, without blackface for the first time, appeared as a client in a patent attorney's office and as an enlistee taking a physical. He returned to burnt cork to sing "But After The Ball Was Over." Fields put aside his billiard green to wreak havoc on a putting green. Marilyn Miller—a name new to Ziegfeld's ranks —won many of the raves, while one of the first girls ever glorified by Ziegfeld, the beautiful but star-crossed Lillian Lorraine, performed for the last time in a *Follies*. Louis Hirsch and Dave Stamper, who composed most of the score (with Gene Buck for lyricist), also seemed to look both ways at once. They gave their songs up-to-the-minute titles but their music was in a dated style. Stamper provided one of the big production numbers, "I Want To Jazz Dance" (virtually the earliest use of the term in a Broadway song), while Hirsch composed a second production number, "When I Hear A Syncopated Tune." But Stamper's "jazz" caught none of the newer rhythms that soon pushed the old syncopation aside. It was not even the transitional shimmy. Both songs were simple commercial ragtime. The war prompted tunes such as "I'm Gonna Pin A Medal On The Girl I Left Behind" and "You Keep Sending 'Em Over And We'll Keep Knocking 'Em Down." Since the show ended its Broadway run just as the war ended, the program was revamped for the peacetime tour.

While over the years the Ziegfeld extravaganzas produced better songs than the Shubert Winter Garden revues, **The Passing Show of 1918** (7-25-18, Winter Garden), in the day's topsy-turvy way, came up with the season's biggest hit, "Smiles" (J. Will Callahan and Lee S. Roberts). The main Romberg and Jean Schwartz score reflected the same ambivalence as the *Follies* program, ranging from "The Galli-Curci Rag" to "Trombone Jazz." "Jazz" here meant the transitional "shimmy." Frank Fay, backed by a line of baby-talking chorus girls, hit pay dirt with "My

Baby-Talk Lady!," so the Shuberts rushed in a second "Baby" (Gus Kahn and Egbert Van Alstine). A lavish "Birdland" number included the young Astaires singing and dancing dressed as chickens.

In May a thrown-together vaudeville by sailors had had a 16-performance run at the Century. On August 19 a somewhat less hastily thrown-together revue, this time by soldiers from Camp Upton, opened at the same house. It ran 32 performances and most likely would have passed as quickly into obscurity had it not been for one thing. Irving Berlin wrote the score. Called **Yip Yip Yaphank**, it presented pictures of rookie life in its songs and sketches, including a burlesque of a *Follies* visit to the camp. It even offered a boxing match by world lightweight champion Benny Leonard, then an instructor at Upton. But the show was raised to a prominent place in our musical history by its tunes—particularly the second most popular of World War I songs, "Oh, How I Hate To Get Up In The Morning." Berlin himself sang the song, playing a private who has been asked to get up sometime before noon to attend the morning roll call. A second fine number, "Mandy," was not immediately popular, but Ziegfeld, catching the show, grabbed it for his next *Follies*. Berlin unintentionally demonstrated how much the war had gnawed away at audiences' acceptance of excessive sentimentality. "I Can Always Find A Little Sunshine At The Y.M.C.A." was laughed off the stage for lines such as "You can picture me at the close of the day," which asked "mother darling" not to worry, in a letter being written in the Y.M.C.A.

George Broadhurst, hoping to create a hit for his Broadhurst Theatre, wrote his own book and lyrics for his August 20 presentation, **He Didn't Want To Do It.** The critics wished he hadn't. The dismal book revolved about a scheme whereby some fake emeralds are stolen so insurance can be collected. Silvio Hein wrote the score, which was not much better than the libretto. In three weeks' time the Broadhurst was looking for a new tenant.

If Dillingham's Hippodrome extravaganza didn't have **Everything** as its title proclaimed on August 22, it had enough to thrill audiences for 461 performances. There were songs by John Philip Sousa and Irving Berlin, among others. De Wolf Hopper was the star. Berlin's numbers included "The Circus Is Coming To Town." Hopper was announced as John Jingling, and a circus spectacle followed. Even though the critics were all favorable, most notices were unusually brief, a sign that Hippodrome annuals—like Winter Garden productions—were taken less seriously than they once had been.

The circus was also a prominent part of **Head Over Heels** (8-29-18, Cohan). Edgar Allan Woolf and Jerome Kern wrote it as a vehicle for petite Mitzi, basing it on Lee Arthur's dramatization of Nalbro Bartley's *Shadows.* Mitzi played a European acrobat who falls in love with an American. She follows him to New York, and, when she realizes he can never be faithful, she settles for his business partner. Because she was no gymnast, Mitzi's acrobatics were "performed" off-stage and recounted to audiences in the manner of classic Greek and French drama. Woolf's book was hackneyed, and although Kern was incapable of writing a bad score, this was among his least interesting. Mitzi carried the show for 100 performances.

Kern had a better score, but not much better success, at the end of the season, when he did **She's a Good Fellow** (5-5-19, Globe) with Anne Caldwell. Her book must have reminded Kern of his shows with female impersonator Julian Eltinge. Young Robert McLane (Joseph Santley) has married Jacqueline Fay (Ivy Sawyer) against the wishes of her guardian. Since she is under age she is taken back to school. Before he can convince her guardians he is worthy of Jacqueline, Robert spends a substantial part of the evening disguised as a Spanish lady. In the first act Santley sported a black dress and black wig; in the second his wig and dress were red. At one point in the story, Olin Howland as a country bumpkin and Santley, still in drag, did a show-stopping burlesque of the era's high-kicking dances. The Duncan Sisters somehow found a place to insert their vaudeville songs and dances. The book was gay and the score catchy. The show's hit, "The First Rose Of Summer," was given an added boost when John McCormack recorded it. Unfortunately, the show never recovered from the actors' strike.

Fiddlers Three (9-3-18, Cort) ran eleven weeks in the face of generally indifferent notices, which wrote off the piece as "old-fashioned" and "Absolutely Victorian." The fiddlers were violin makers in Cremona. A young lady (Tavie Belge) arrives just as a contest to see who can make the best violin is about to take place. She wins the youngest and handsomest of the craftsmen (Thomas Conkey). The principals found the show stolen from them by the lively Louise Groody as she "smiled and moved and rollicked her way into the audience's heart." Her fast-stepping dances

with Hal Skelly received much of the evening's loudest applause.

A major disappointment for many was the quick failure of **The Maid of the Mountains** (9-11-18, Casino), which José Collins, once of the *Follies,* was then singing for 1,352 performances in London. The maid, Teresa (Sidonie Espero), and her mountain brigands had no appeal to New Yorkers. The Broadway run fell 1,315 showings short of the musical's London mark.

The Girl Behind the Gun (9-16-18, New Amsterdam) was a suitably martial title for a nation still at war. But the title had little to do with the show's plot. Playwright Robert Lambrissac (Donald Brian), on leave from Paris, visits his godmother instead of his wife. This pleases the godmother (Ada Meade), who would make her husband jealous, but it angers Robert's wife (Wilda Bennett), and she begins to flirt with a colonel. The critics raved about Guy Bolton and P.G. Wodehouse's book, but could muster little enthusiasm for Ivan Caryll's score. But with Miss Bennett's lovely voice and Brian's dancing to make the songs seem better than they were, ticket buyers ignored the flaws, and the girl was shouldering her gun long after the war was over.

A bad show once more prompted interesting reviews when the critics sat down to write about **Some Night** (9-23-18, Harris). Charles Darnton of the *Evening World* shrugged off the evening as "A bad dream." Other recent achievements allowed him to conclude that, despite duds, "New York sets the pace for musical comedy. London is no longer in the running, Vienna is on its last legs and Paris has lagged behind the procession for years...." As recently as four years earlier, no critic could have conceived of this pronouncement. No one could foresee that the statement would hold true for a half-century. *Some Night,* which ran only three weeks, told how Dorothy Wayne (Roma June) "steals" money which is rightfully hers from her tightfisted guardian. She goes to stay with John Hardy (Louis Simon), a rich young man. All ends well.

Fortunately for Rida Johnson Young and Rudolf Friml, ticket buyers didn't confuse **Sometime** (10-4-18, Shubert) with *Some Night. Sometime* was one of the biggest hits of the season. The great 1918 flu epidemic was raging, and one critic praised the show as "catchy as the grip and likely to last longer." It lasted into the summer heat. Why it was so enthusiastically received is not easy to see. The novelty of the book, which was one of the earliest uses of flashback, may have intrigued audiences. Enid Vaughn (Francine Larrimore) has caught her fiancé Henry (Harrison Brockbank) in a compromising situation and has refused to see him for five years. The scene flashes back to depict the incident that caused the split, and then proceeds to move between the present and the past. In the end it develops that a vamp named Mayme using "Theda Bara tricks" had planned the incident. Henry is shown to be innocent. Enid and Henry are reunited. Mayme, left without "a single soul to vamp," pleads, "If the boob can walk, He don't have to talk: Send me any kind of man." Mayme was played by Mae West. Ed Wynn was the star (he also wrote some of the lyrics), and much of *Sometime*'s popularity probably must be attributed to him. Popping in and out on the feeblest excuses in his character of Loney, he won laughs with his lisping delivery of lines such as, "What is a man to do in wartime when he can't make both ends meat?—Make one end vegetables!"

. . .

Ed Wynn's real name was Edwin Leopold. He was born in Philadelphia, on November 9, 1886. In 1902, he joined a local repertory company to play small comic parts, but after a year switched to playing sketches in vaudeville. Two-a-day gave him eight years in which to develop his art before he made his legitimate debut in 1910 in *The Deacon and the Lady*. Stints in the *Follies* and Shubert revues followed. His lisp, his fluttering hands, and his outlandish puns and costumes soon became trademarks. His preposterous inventions were a later addition to his legitimate act, although he had employed them in vaudeville.

. . .

Friml's music was charming enough, but between *Katinka* and *Rose-Marie* his songs had no real distinction. At times he seemed to be repeating himself and others. "The Tune You Can't Forget" has been forgotten, largely because it sounded too much like his own hit from *High Jinks*, Kern's "Little Tune, Go Away," and Hirsch's "Tickle Toe."

Friml's second October show was **Glorianna** (10-28-18, Liberty). It was October's lone failure, although not by much. It missed by only four nights the 100-performance mark which at this period often indicated a return on investment. Based on Catherine Chisholm Cushing's 1913 *Widow by Proxy*, a title which revealed much of the plot, it found Glorianna Grey (Eleanor Painter) pretending she is a widow to help a friend (Dorothy South) obtain the legacy of the friend's husband. When the husband (Joseph Lertora) turns up alive, there is momentary confusion, but everything is quickly straightened out. Once more Friml's music was pleasant, but it offered nothing memorable. Even the presence of Miss Painter could not edge the show over the 100-mark. Indeed, she may have been partly responsible for the musical's poor New York record. Some critics, while praising her fine singing, suggested she was too sedate. Memories of the rambunctious May Irwin in the original straight play were still vivid and dear to many. When Fritzi Scheff replaced Miss Painter for the tour, results were happier.

Late in March, Friml's third and final offering of the season, **Tumble In** (3-24-19, Selwyn), made it over the 100-performance line. It might have run longer but for the Equity strike. Retaining the flimsy story line of its source, Mary Roberts Rinehart and Avery Hopwood's 1909 smash, *Seven Days*, it made a whole evening out of a house party quarantined for a week. Friml's music was on a level with his other two scores; nothing from *Tumble In* has gone into his standard canon. But the evening's inadequacies were not wholly creative. They were conceptual as well. The *Globe*'s review affirmed that however far American musicals had recently advanced there was room for improvement: "To weave the songs into a musical affair has never been an art of proportions, and it is done here in the approved and without reason fashion. That they seem less of interruptions indicates only that the story, as such, didn't particularly matter." In staging and dancing, the show was more imaginative and lively. Good shimmying sparked the stepping, while one novel scene had all the principals hanging precariously over the edge of a roof as they sang "Won't You Help Me Out?"

Apart from the Hippodrome show, the season's longest run for a musical was achieved by an importation, **The Better 'Ole**. Based on Bruce Bairnsfather's cartoon and starring Charles Colburn, it opened on October 19 at the small, out-of-the-way Greenwich Village Theatre; yet not even the Armistice, which came three weeks after its opening and destroyed its immediacy, affected its popularity. Its success was so great that in a month it was playing to packed houses at the larger, uptown Cort. While the program credited Herman Darewski and Percival Knight with the score, most of the tunes were established favorites brought in to fill out the evening. Its story probably needed filling out. "Old Bill" captures a spy's plans to trap a French regiment by blowing up a bridge after the regiment has crossed. Bill blows up the bridge before they can cross. His action is misunderstood, and he is arrested. But after explaining his reasons he is vindicated.

Ladies First (10-24-18, Broadhurst) gave Broadway three musical hits in a row. The musical looked to the growing woman's suffrage movement for its story. Betty Burt, at the instigation of "Aunt Jim" (Florence Morrison), an old suffragette, runs for mayor of her small town against her sweetheart, Benny (Irving Fisher). She really cares for Benny and doesn't mind when she loses. The deep-voiced, full-bosomed Miss Morrison was abetted in her comedy by William Kent, who played her small, brow-beaten husband. The show was based on Hoyt's *A Contented Woman* and produced as a vehicle for Nora Bayes. Its score was by A. Baldwin Sloane, who had not been heard from in five years, and the book was by Harry B. Smith, who had. Coincidentally, two reviewers struck on the same gimmick to convey their boredom with the librettist's style. Both the *Times* and the *Dramatic Mirror* referred to the adaptation as "harrybsmithed." One interpolation, "Just Like A Gypsy" (which Nora Bayes purportedly wrote with Seymour B. Simons), remained one of her favorites. Two early Gershwin numbers were introduced, "Some Wonderful Sort Of Someone" (lyrics by Schuyler Greene) and "The Real American Folk Song," for which Ira wrote the words. The latter was not inserted until the post-Broadway tour. Other numbers came and went as circumstances suggested. And circumstances must have suggested changes with some frequency. A random comparison of programs for the week of April 21, 1919 (at the Riviera in upper Manhattan) and for the week of November 13, 1919 (at the Saxon Auditorium in Toledo) discloses only two songs in common.

Friml's *Glorianna* followed *Ladies First* and was October's last show.

A second show with a Smith libretto soon came in for appraisal. Even though **The Canary** (11-4-18, Globe) ran 152 performances, Smith considered it a failure. His recounting of the show's inception reveals his heavy-handed style and his hack willingness. "Caryll's purchase of French farces were not always good bargains. A year or two before the composer's death, Charles Dillingham sent for me and said, 'I want you to get right to work on the funniest farce I ever heard.' Chuckling and trying to keep from laughing, he informed me that the story concerned a comedy

character who accidently swallowed a diamond. The humor, it appeared, consisted in the pursuit of the comedian to recover the jewel. My own risible faculties were not violently jarred by this brilliant comic idea and my comment was that it seemed rather physiological in its humor." Caryll must have come around to Smith's view and lost interest. Less than half the completed score was his. Others, including Irving Berlin, Jerome Kern, and Harry Tierney, filled in. But inspiration failed, and no one produced a topflight number. Julia Sanderson and Joseph Cawthorn were starred, but critics distributed praise to many supporting players. Harland Dixon and James Doyle were liked for their grostesque dances in their roles as two crooks, while homely, hefty Maude Eburne waddled hilariously around the stage in pursuit of Cawthorn.

Little Simplicity (11-4-18, Astor) opened the same night as *The Canary*. Its story line was as simple as its heroine, Veronique (Carolyn Thomson), an Algerian flower girl who falls in love with an American (Carl Gantvoort), loses him, and five years later at the Y.M.C.A. rediscovers and wins him. She also won 112 performances.

One week later the war was over.

The great Princess Theatre shows had all opened while the war was raging. On November 27, with peace not three weeks old, a new Princess musical appeared, **Oh, My Dear!** It had another likeable Bolton book in which an assortment of New York oddities descend on Dr. Rockett's Health Farm, although not for the good doctor's ministrations. There is boozy Broadway Willie (Roy Atwell) fleeing his alimony-hungry ex-wife; handsome young Bruce Allenby (Joseph Santley), of Allenby Umbrellas, fleeing trust busters; and a bevy of road company chorus girls stranded when their show folded. The girls are old friends of Willie and hope he will lend them train fare home. A Rolls-Royce drives up. Willie fears it is his ex and runs away. But it is only Mrs. Rockett (Georgia Caine). She is angry because earlier in the day she saw Dr. Rockett (Frederick Graham) downtown, holding an umbrella for a pretty young lady, and she has put the worst possible construction on it. Seeing him surrounded by chorus girls only increases her wrath. The doctor insists they are all looking for Willie, but with Willie gone he could have a difficult time proving it. So Bruce is made to pretend he is Willie. This might have quieted Mrs. Rockett had not Willie's ex suddenly arrived. Not only can she not recognize her supposed husband, but both the doctor and his spouse realize she is the lady for whom he held the umbrella. By curtain time everything is explained, and Bruce wins the hand of the Rocketts' lovely daughter, Hilda (Ivy Sawyer). Wodehouse's lyrics were equally funny. Wodehouse made Willie's delirium tremens hilarious and colorful with pink and green spiders "fox-trotting over the floor." Wodehouse also played with variant forms of "father" in "Ask Daddy," finally rhyming "dadda" with "had a." However, there was one major change. For reasons now lost, Jerome Kern had left the series. Louis Hirsch was called in to do the music, but his score was so obviously deficient that for the first time since *Nobody Home* interpolations were permitted. They were by Jean Schwartz, and they were no help at all. The critics were satisfied, although almost to a man they agreed it was not one of the better evenings at the small house. The *Sun* could not see the sad implications of its seemingly kind remark, "The Princess Theatre is by way of becoming an historical institution." *Oh, My Dear!* ran a respectable six months and sent out two touring companies. But it was appreciated that without Kern, or someone of Kern's caliber, there was no point in continuing, for there could be no totally achieved piece. And so the most important series in the history of the American Musical Theatre was finished. It was just four-and-a-half-years old, and (if one includes *Have a Heart* and *Leave It to Jane*) had produced just seven shows.

A month passed before another musical opened. Then, on December 23, three arrived on the same night. **Atta Boy** at the Lexington was another all-soldier show. Captain Frank Tinney headed the performers, who mocked army life and often dressed as women, as their counterparts had in earlier service shows. Coming nearly two months after the war had ended, its time had clearly passed. Three weeks and it was gone.

The other two openings were *Listen Lester* at the Knickerbocker and *Somebody's Sweetheart* at the Central. Both were hits. **Listen Lester** even managed to survive the August Equity strike and continue into fall. Set in a Florida hotel, where Lester Lite (Hansford Wilson) works, it told of Colonel Dodge's attempts to retrieve embarrassing letters he had written to a lady with the unlikely name of Arbutus Quilty (Gertrude Vanderbilt). Billy Penn (Johnny Dooley) and Lester help retrieve them. Then the colonel (Eddie Garvie) is free to marry Tillie Mumm (Ada Lewis). The

love interest, Mary Dodge (Ada Mae Weeks) and Jack Griffin (Clifton Webb), can also marry. The book was incessantly flippant:

Lester: Good Afternoon
Arbutus: I can't help that. I want a room and bath.
Lester: I can give you the room, lady.
Arbutus: What exposure?
Lester: None, if you pull down the shades . . .

Harold Orlob's music was equally vapid. Playing with the title, the headlines of reviews warned "Not Much For Listeners" or "More Dancing Than Listening." One critic felt the show would have been happier called "Dance, Mary." He was probably right. Webb and Miss Weeks glided gracefully across the boards, while Dooley and Wilson combined for more grotesque stepping. The chorus tapped and kicked in unison.

The gypsy Zaida (Nonette) was **Somebody's Sweetheart.** But whose? Harry Edwards (Walter Scanlan) is about to wed Helen Williams (Eva Fallon), daughter of the U.S. Consul at Seville. Harry had once loved Zaida, and to avoid awkwardness at the wedding he claims her old lover was his best man, Sam Benton (William Kent). Since Sam loves Helen's sister Bessie (Louise Allen), he has to do some fast explaining. Kent's antics were a highlight of the evening, notably at the wedding, where he determines to be a very inconspicuous best man, hiding behind taller ushers and peeking out from a bridal train under which he has crept. Still another pleasant but forgettable score and more good dancing, especially by Veronica, an "oriental dancer with occidental restraint," kept the show on the boards until the summer.

Many critics hailed the plot of **The Melting of Molly** (12-30-18, Broadhurst). As in Maria Thompson Davies' novel of the same name, Molly Carter (Isabelle Lowe) has grown fat waiting for her diplomat lover, Albert, to marry her. He cables from London that he will return in three months and insists she wear a particularly "Dear Old Gown" as her wedding dress. With the help of Dr. Moore (Charles Purcell) she reduces enough to fit into it. But when Albert enters, he is so fat she decides to marry Dr. Moore instead. Romberg's score was unattractive. His "Jazz, How I Love To Hear It" and "Jazz All Your Troubles Away" betrayed how uncomfortable he was outside his natural style. The new, harder jazz coming in was far more inimical to him than even the gentler ragtime. The show was taken off after eleven weeks, although "Dear Old Gown" had a second chance under peculiar circumstances several years later.

No musicals arrived in January. More important matters preoccupied the nation. On January 29, 1919, the Secretary of State announced that, with the ratification by a 36th state on January 16, Prohibition was to be the law of the land. The last legal drink would go down the hatch a second or so before the year ended. Broadway's immediate response was a rash of interpolated songs and gags. Nora Bayes, for example, added "Prohibition Blues" (Ring Lardner and Miss Bayes) to her touring *Ladies First*. But these changes were superficial. More lasting influences could not be foretold.

A Victor Herbert show opened the new year. **The Velvet Lady** (2-3-19, New Amsterdam) ran seventeen weeks and left us one of Herbert's most endearing songs, "Life And Love." The rest of his score was not on the same level, and one critic saw the piece "preeminently a dancing show"— a comment unheard of when Herbert was writing the music. Henry Blossom's book, based on a Frederick Jackson farce, unfolded without enough laughs to suit many in the audience. George Howell (Ray Raymond) must go to Boston to retrieve embarrassing letters that his sister's fiancé, Ned Pembroke (Alfred Gerrard), once wrote to a nightclub singer, the Velvet Lady (Fay Marbe). Coming back the train is wrecked, and George mistakenly picks up a bag containing stolen jewels. His bride (Marie Flynn) discovers the jewels and jumps to the wrong conclusion. But the Velvet Lady appears to explain everything. Since the Velvet Lady didn't appear until the last fifteen minutes, she was clearly not the center of attraction, but then neither were the lovers. For most critics the evening's happiest moments came from Georgia O'Ramey as the Howells' maid, Susie. Her vivacious clowning and even more vivacious dancing compensated for many a lesser moment.

Good Morning, Judge (2-6-19, Shubert), an English show with music by Monckton and Talbot, boasted two George Gershwin interpolations, "I Was So Young" and "There's More To The Kiss Than XXX." The word boasted is not premature. A week or so earlier Jolson, touring in *Sinbad*, had introduced "Swanee." It was so sensationally received it was recorded the same weekend. It made Gershwin a name to be reckoned with.

On February 12, Sigmund Romberg and Jean Schwartz were back at the Winter Garden with what sounded like a Jolson vehicle but wasn't, **Monte Cristo, Jr.** A young man named Monte, who just read the Dumas book, falls asleep and dreams he and his friends are characters from the novel. Done tongue-in-cheek, with a flock of vaudeville turns thrown in, it was the antithesis of the romance on which Romberg thrived. The score was typical of his Winter Garden material. Well mounted, and with names like Charles Purcell, Ralph Herz, and Chic Sale to draw the patrons, the extravaganza compiled a fine 254 performances.

Even more antiromantic was **The Royal Vagabond** (2-17-19, Cohan and Harris), which George M. Cohan had written from a faltering operetta, *Cherry Blossoms*. In this "Cohanized Opera Comique," Stephan (Frederick Santley), Crown Prince of Bargravia, is assigned to subdue a revolutionary movement. When he falls in love with Anitza (Tessa Kosta), an innkeeper's daughter, he is converted to the revolution and becomes its leader. He triumphs—buying off his mother's troops—and a new era dawns for Bargravia. The lyrics of the opening chorus set the tone, with the villagers singing tra la la because "In every comic opera it's got to be sung." And the dialogue continued the fun:

Prince: Doesn't that sound like a horseman approaching?
Tutor: Not exactly. But it's a good effect.

Anselm Goetzl's score was correctly "Schmalzy," but Cohan and Irving Berlin threw in additional tunes to spark the gaiety. The rising Dorothy Dickson enlivened the evening and called further attention to herself with her airy dancing in the small role of Charlotte.

Both *Monte Cristo, Jr.* and *The Royal Vagabond* revealed a growing reaction to the fustian melodrama and operetta of a passing age. In a few years Sigmund Romberg helped revive the vogue, but only briefly. But for Cohan, who first led the way to modern American Musical Comedy, then pioneered in the modern revue, *The Royal Vagabond* could only be a one-time lark. What his future contributions would have been will never be known. More than anyone else he was thrown off balance by the divisions and enmities arising out of the actors' strike.

Friml's *Tumble In* followed.

Take It from Me (3-31-19, 44th St.) arrived

a week later with a cute idea. Tom Eggett (Jack McGowan) inherits a department store and has a good time ruining it rather than let it fall into the hands of a scheming director. Unfortunately, the book by cartoonist Will B. Johnstone was clumsily written. Nor could the public find the "breath of freshness" in the Will R. Anderson score that made music publisher Isidore Witmark single it out years later as one of his favorites. The evening was filled with vaudeville turns, such as an old man in a comic roller-skating bit.

Come Along (4-8-19, Nora Bayes) came along at least a year too late. Its story of a nurse (Regina Richards) who goes to France and finds she must care for her wounded lover (Paul Frawley) had lost its appeal. The evening's problems were exacerbated by the drabness of its costumes, with all the men in khaki and most of the women in Red Cross or Salvation Army uniforms. A comic secondary plot attempted to redress matters. Private Barker (Allen Kearns) has a falling out with his childhood friend (Charles Stanton) when that friend, now a lieutenant, attempts to pull rank. A sly mess sergeant (Harry Tighe) resolves matters. All the principals find themselves at the Statue of Liberty in time for a finale. Nothing in *Come Along*'s score could overcome the public's antipathy to more war stories. The musical survived for six weeks.

Two nights after Jerome Kern's *She's a Good Fellow* lit up the Globe on May 5, the lights were turned on again at the Princess. But again Kern's name was not on the marquee. **Toot Sweet** had music by Richard Whiting, who had made his reputation with "It's Tulip Time In Holland," "Mammy's Little Coal Black Rose," and "Where The Black-Eyed Susans Grow"—the last used by Jolson in *Robinson Crusoe, Jr.* (2-17-16). This was his first complete score. The music failed not only on its own, but because its lyrics, like the show's sketches, were war-oriented—reflecting the revue's beginnings as an overseas troop entertainment. Much of the evening was a show within a show, a vaudeville presented to a "doughboy" chorus. Will Morrissey served as compère, introducing singers, mimics, comics, and a highly praised team of eccentric dancers, Miller and Ward.

Kern was credited with one interpolation in **The Lady in Red** (5-12-19, Lyric). The musical dealt with the love of an artist and his dream girl, and their relations with a comic soap-manufacturer. (The *Times* noted that in these modern, antiseptic days soap makers had replaced turn-of-the-century pickle kings.) But the show needed more

than a Kern tune to save it. It stayed 48 performances.

La, La, Lucille (5-26-19, Henry Miller) was the first complete Broadway score by George Gershwin. Yet though "Swanee" was by now a top hit, the critics gave Gershwin no special attention. Burns Mantle noted in the *Evening Mail*, "of the recent musical plays, *La, La, Lucille* is much the best." But he was looking at the show as a whole. He picked out "Tee-Oodle-Um-Bum-Bo" for praise, mentioning without further comment that Gershwin was the show's composer. The *Times* viewed the musical as "the incarnation of jazz"— a form to which Gershwin would be forever tied —but failed to mention Gershwin at all. The *Globe,* in a puzzling comment, felt, "The songs by a new young composer, George Gershwin, are tuneful if in many instances negative, but they retard the action." The action begins with a chorus line of bill collectors attempting to get John Smith (Jack Hazzard), a young dentist, to pay his overdue accounts. A lawyer arrives advising John his Aunt Roberta has died and willed him two million dollars, provided he divorce his wife, Lucille (Janet Velie). The aunt objects to the marriage, for Lucille comes from a family of jugglers. Since John won't lose the money if he remarries Lucille, they decide to get the divorce and rewed. John takes their janitress, Fanny (Eleanor Daniels), who will act as co-respondent, to a hotel. Before they can be properly "caught," Fanny's husband, unaware of the plan, comes after his wife. A honeymoon couple in the next room get dragged into the melee when John hides Fanny and insists the young bride is the co-respondent. Everything is resolved when the "dead" aunt enters and reveals she was only been testing John and Lucille. She feels they have passed the test. The show's dialogue also passed the test—but just barely. The lawyer, Blackwood (J. Clarence Harvey), convinces Lucille and John to go through with the staged hotel scene. Once Blackwood gets Lucille and John to agree, they must convince Fanny to play along:

Fanny: . . . if I risk it all, it'll have to cost you something.
Lucille: Of course! We're quite willi. to pay— anything within reason.
Blackwood: How much do you want?
Fanny: Well—there's my reputation—and risk I run with Oyama [her husband]—a the chances I take with him.
Lucille: Chances?

Fanny: I've got to figger, ma'am, in case anything
    should go wrong!
John: Nothing will go wrong.
Fanny: I couldn't do it for less than—$5.

Arthur Jackson and Buddy DeSylva's lyrics were
not as brilliant as George's brother Ira later provided for him, but they were acceptable. And
though no song from *La, La, Lucille* has entered
the canon of Gershwin classics, they are very
attractive. Listening to "The Best Of Everything"
and "Nobody But You" one can still hear Kern's
influence on the young New Yorker, but unmistakable Gershwin touches are there as well.
Like so many of the season's musicals, *La La
Lucille* became a casualty of the Equity strike.

A week after *La, La, Lucille*'s debut, another
new name—one Gershwin would long be associated with—made its first Broadway appearance.
The **Scandals of 1919** danced onto 42nd Street.
Dancing was the word for it, as it was for many
of the season's musicals. George White—who
would not add his name to the title until later—
was born George Weitz on the East Side and
worked his way from a Bowery hoofer to a *Ziegfeld Follies* spot. With his *Follies* associate, Ann
Pennington, he paced the stepping for the first
edition. Their shimmying and tapping earned them
encores, but while they were catching their breath
other dancers, particularly a contortionist named
La Sylphe, kept audiences occupied. The music
by Richard Whiting (recently of *Toot Sweet*) and
the lyrics of Arthur Jackson (of the competing
La, La, Lucille) were pedestrian. White learned his
lesson quickly. Future *Scandals* had some of the
best songs ever to come out of Broadway's revues.
Sketches by Jackson and White himself also left
something to be desired. Skits spoofed bedroom
farces, courtroom dramas, overcrowded hotels,
and, with Prohibition just around the corner, life on
a rum-running houseboat. But if the comedy too
frequently misfired, the beautiful girls and giddy
dancing caught New York's fancy. Another great
revue series was launched.

The season's last musical, **A Lonely Romeo** (6-
10-19, Shubert) was a vehicle for Lew Fields,
utilizing a book by Fields himself in partnership
with Harry B. Smith. Harry's brother Robert supplied the lyrics for Malvin Franklin's and Robert
Hood Bower's melodies. A light summer entertainment, it watched Augustus Tripper, a hatter
by day and a "cabaret fiend" by night, get in and
out of trouble when his wife discovers where he
spends his evenings. There were two interpola-

tions. One was "I Guess I'm More Like Mother
Than Like Father" (Richard Egan/Richard Whiting). The second was added just before the actors'
strike closed the show. Called "Any Old Place
With You," it confronted Broadway playgoers
with two more new names—Lorenz Hart and
Richard Rodgers. Those with an alert ear might
well have caught Rodgers' promise in his pleasant
melody, but Hart was already more fulfilling than
promising. In the song he brazenly rhymed Virginia with Abyssinia, and went on to proclaim,
"I'd go to hell for ya,/Or Philadelphia." For all
the brief display of Hart's wit and for all Fields'
clowning, most critics considered the evening, as
they did so many musicals, a dancing entertainment. The first-act finale brought the entire cast
on, a few at a time, in a rousing crescendo of
ensemble dance that had Fields himself doing flip
flops as the curtain fell.

1918–19 was qualitatively the leanest season in
this period. Coming after three high-flying sessions
it may seem leaner than it was. But it pointed to
new directions and saw Broadway settle, not
always comfortably, into the track it rolled on for
the next four or five decades. It was the first
season anything approaching commercial jazz
played a prominent part on the musical stage,
and while jazz was not yet always clearly defined
or understood, the most progressive of the season's
new lyric pieces mirrored its excited tempos and
steely texture, pronouncing the future of American musical comedy. Only seven out-and-out
revues appeared—a similar foreshadowing, but
this time auguring decline and demise. Ridicule of
old world operettas gave voice to a growing intellectual rejection of the form—although, as we
have noted, it was to have one brief, luminous
renaissance.

1919-1920

Florenz Ziegfeld gave the season the grandest
possible start. **The Ziegfeld Follies of 1919** (6-
16-19, New Amsterdam) is generally regarded as
the high point of the series. Certainly the press
thought so. The *American* headed its review,
"1919 'Follies' Surpasses All Others." The *Herald*'s banner echoed the sentiment, "Thirteenth
'Ziegfeld Follies' Eclipses Predecessors in Beauty,
Color and Action." Ultimate laurels were awarded
by the *Evening Sun*, "Ziegfeld Outziegfelds Zieg-

feld." From this edition came the consummate girlie revue song, Irving Berlin's "A Pretty Girl Is Like A Melody," which the greatest of revue tenors, John Steel, sang, as Ziegfeld beauties promenaded by, representing the "Barcarolle," "Elegy," "Humoresque," and other semiclassics. Berlin also gave Bert Williams his wry Prohibition protest, "You Cannot Make Your Shimmy Shake On Tea." For Eddie Cantor he composed "You'd Be Surprised," so successful a song it was soon being sung in other shows. In the first-act finale, "The Follies Minstrels," Williams and Cantor combined to sing another Berlin number, "I Want To See A Minstrel Show." As part of the same scene, Van and Schenck popularized "Mandy," which Ziegfeld had taken over from *Yip Yip Yaphank* (8-19-18). Ray Dooley impersonated Mandy, while Marilyn Miller appeared as George Primrose. Two songs not by Berlin also had a brief vogue—"Tulip Time" (Gene Buck/Dave Stamper) and "My Baby's Arms" (Joseph McCarthy/Harry Tierney). Cantor had the best comedy of the evening as a nervous patient at "The Osteopath's Office." For Williams and Marilyn Miller, this edition marked their last *Follies* appearances. Joseph Urban's sets, particularly his harem scene, and his flower-filled urns for Miss Miller's "Sweet Sixteen" number, elicited the customary gasps of approval.

Down in the modern-day Bohemia below Washington Square, John Murray Anderson put together a new revue initially entitled *Greenwich Village Nights,* but quickly changed to **Greenwich Village Follies** (7-15-19, Greenwich Village Theatre). Ziegfeld was not pleased, but, since a "Follies" had been produced in New York before he launched his own series, he had no legal recourse. The new annual, and it became just that, gave him serious competition. "Next to Ziegfeld," Robert Baral notes in his study, *Revue,* "these revues were the most exciting annuals on Broadway." Anderson combined with Philip Bartholomae to do the sketches and lyrics. For the first score he tapped A. Baldwin Sloane. This was Sloane's second show after a protracted absence, but his work was as pallid as for *Ladies First.* One song, "I Want A Daddy Who Will Rock Me To Sleep," had a fleeting success, but as so often happened to Sloane an interpolation outshined all of his material. Ted Lewis introduced "When My Baby Smiles At Me" (Andrew Sterline, Ted Lewis, and Bill Munro) and retained it as his theme song throughout his long career. Like Ziegfeld's uptown revue, Greenwich Village could not ignore Prohibition. Bessie McCoy Davis ridiculed the upcoming nonsense with "I'm The Hostess Of A Bum Cabaret." Memorable production numbers included one with the cast as marionettes, a Javanese scene, and a stage strewn with red roses. After six weeks in which favorable word of mouth confirmed the critics' judgments, the show was moved uptown.

Two nights after the *Greenwich Village Follies* previewed, the **Shubert Gaieties of 1919** (7-17-19, 44th St.) gave the season its third revue. Its best number was "You'd Be Surprised," which was being better done at the New Amsterdam. Besides Henry Lewis, who sang it, the evening offered Gilda Gray, the shimmy queen. A quickly-thrown-together affair, it was able to reassemble hastily after the actors' strike (with George Jessel replacing Henry Lewis). It ran until superior entertainment came along.

Oh, What a Girl! opened across the street at the Shubert on July 28. The exclamation came from both Jack Rushton (Sam Ash) and his uncle, Deacon Amos Titmouse (Harry Kelly), who love Margot Merrivale (Hazel Kirke), a cabaret singer. Jack wins Margot only after exposing his uncle's philandering. The best song in the show was an interpolation—Irving Berlin's "You'd Be Surprised."

A week after *Oh, What a Girl!* opened, the Actors' Equity strike began. Actors, tired of years of abuses—being stranded out of town, poor pay, no rehearsal pay—demanded recognition and certain concessions. Producers refused. On August 7 the actors closed twelve shows. One by one additional houses went dark. On August 13 Eddie Cantor, Ray Dooley, John Steel, and Van and Schenck refused to perform, so the *Follies* shut down. By August 21, twenty-four productions in New York alone had been halted. The *Greenwich Village Follies,* non-Equity, was one of the few attractions to keep going. It cleaned up. Caught in the middle was George M. Cohan. Both an actor and a producer he tried at first to be conciliatory, only to meet with vilification from the union. The response embittered him and turned him actively against the union. Many better established actors ignored Equity and formed the Actors Fidelity League, a group more sympathetic to the producers. But numbers, not quality, told.

Only a single musical production opened during the strike. The Hippodrome, with its gift for cheery but ironic titles, brought in **Happy Days** on August 23. Another typical Hippodrome extravaganza, it had no artistic distinction. One set was done almost entirely in gold, another took audiences to Fairyland, while a third, like a set in the *Greenwich Village Follies,* filled the stage with roses. Acrobats, jugglers, ballerinas, and trained animals cavorted on the gigantic stage. But *Happy Days* earned itself a dubious place in theatrical history, for, when its cast walked out on the 28th in sympathy with other Broadway performers, producers decided to recognize the union and end the five-week strike. One immediate effect of the strike was an increase in the cost of production and a consequent rise in ticket prices. The war and its aftermath had brought about a small inflation. But it had not seriously affected Broadway or its patrons. *The Ziegfeld Follies* had cost $88,000 to mount in 1917 (when an average musical cost $20,000 to $30,000). One year later, the *Follies* cost $120,000, and the new edition, brought in just before the actors' demands were met, represented a $170,000 investment. Ticket prices had risen accordingly. The 1917 top of $2.00 had given way to $3.00 in 1918 and $3.50 in 1919. Of course few other shows dealt in what seemed at the time astronomical figures. And a good part of the *Follies'* higher costs reflected Ziegfeld's increasingly extravagant demands. If an ordinary Broadway musical could no longer be put on for $20,000, the figure was not too much higher. Nonetheless during the new season almost all musicals raised their best seats to $2.50 or $3.00. The $1.50–$2.00 top which had prevailed virtually since the Civil War was gone forever.

The strike had cancelled rehearsals and tryouts for sixty shows. As a result no new musical appeared until September 23, when **See Saw** opened at the Cohan. Cynthia Meyrick (Dorothea McKaye) must choose between English Lord Harrowby (Charlie Brown) and American Richard Minot (Frank Carter). Minot is the Lloyd's of London American agent, and Lord Harrowby has insured with Lloyd's against Cynthia's refusal. The book was adequate, but Louis Hirsch's score failed to provide the necessary uplift. Several reviewers mentioned the many encores for "When Two Hearts Discover" (a dozen repeats according to the *World*), but the consensus found the music "reminiscent." *See Saw* ran eleven weeks.

Roly-Boly Eyes (9-25-19, Knickerbocker) did slightly better. A showcase for Eddie Leonard's blackface talents, it ran 100 performances. Leonard played Billy Emerson, who runs away from home after being wrongly accused of a crime and joins a minstrel troupe. He later returns home, is vindicated, and extols his loyal sweetheart

(Queenie Smith) as, "Ida, Sweet As Apple Cider." The song, which later became an Eddie Cantor standby, was written by Leonard. The minstrel troupe was never shown, although it might have made the show more colorful and lively. Instead all the action was set in the garden and on the sleeping porch of Ida's home.

Hitchy-Koo, 1919 appeared at the Liberty on October 6. As always, Raymond Hitchcock served as the genial, slightly cracker-barrel, compère. Florence O'Denishawn performed her elegant, balletlike dances. For novelty, two American Indians, Chief Eagle Horse, and Princess White Deer, sang and danced. "Old Fashioned Garden," a sentimental ballad from the revue was an instant success. The song hardly suggested the sophisticated material the world came to expect from its author, Cole Porter. But that might have been there too had not Hitchcock cut "That Black And White Baby Of Mine." The show's limited success discouraged Porter, and it was another five years before a new Cole Porter score was heard on a Broadway stage.

Hello, Alexander (10-7-19, 4th St.), a reworking for McIntyre and Heath of *The Ham Tree,* came in the following night and stayed seven weeks. Between minstrel numbers Alexander (McIntyre), induced by Henry Clay Jones (Heath) to leave a good job, pretends he is an important dignitary. A costume ball allowed for a gaudy, peppy finale, filled with typical vaudeville turns.

A second show opened the same night. It was **Apple Blossoms** (10-7-19, Globe), one of the season's commercial and creative triumphs. Its success was especially noteworthy in view of problems it imposed on itself. *Apple Blossoms* was an undisguised operetta, a form that, except for *Maytime* (9-16-17), seemed to have lost broad appeal, and, as the preceding season had shown, was fair game for parody. Moreover, half the score of the new piece was by Fritz Kreisler, an Austrian and the leading violin virtuoso of his generation. No Austro-Hungarian works had braved New York since *The Star Gazer* (11-26-17) was so ignominiously hustled away during the war. The show confirmed what *Maytime* had suggested: that, given a truly fine operetta, there would still be a vast public clamoring for seats. It also demonstrated how rapidly war-born animosities had faded. But there were other problems. Was the show in three acts or a prologue and two acts? The working typescripts had it both ways, while the published program, which lists a prologue and two acts, contradicted the published text, which divided the evening into three acts. The problem is the length and richness of the prologue, or, if you will, the shortness of the first act. It takes too long to set up the basic situation. The hero does not make his appearance until well into the second act; this may have been a compelling reason for calling it Act I. Conversely, the denouement is too swift to be fully justified. Nancy Dodge (Wilda Bennett) thinks she loves Dickie Stewart (Percival Knight), the wastrel brother of her classmate, Polly, but her Uncle George (Harrison Brockbank) insists she marry Philip Campbell (John Charles Thomas). Philip is in love with a young widow, Anne Merton (Florence Shirley). Philip and Nancy capitulate and are married, but they agree that each is free to go his or her own way. They resume their old flirtations, but in the confusion of a masked ball discover they really love each other. Dickie and Anne, old flames, leave hand in hand. Even if there were faults of proportion, William Le Baron's characters and dialogue were far above operetta standards. Dickie has marvelously witty and suitable lines. He complains that at Nancy's school, "they won't let you see a girl in her room even if she isn't studying," and after the wedding confesses to the bride, "I was afraid you might think that when you were married I would want to break our engagement." Nancy, obviously determined to block out her marriage, returns from the ceremony alone:

Julie [the maid]: But where is Mr. Campbell?
Nancy: Who?
Julie: Your husband.
Nancy: Oh—Oh—isn't he here?—I guess I jumped into the wrong car, or else he did—or perhaps he isn't coming—I don't know—My brain is in a whirl anyway.
Julie: And this is your wedding day. Oh, Miss Nancy, it ain't right—you're starting out where most of them finish.

Philip is equally well drawn. He enters with the rousing, if slightly Merry Widow-like "Little Girls, Goodbye," but he is no cardboard ladies' man. He is alert and humorous. He quickly realizes Dickie is Nancy's boyfriend and naughtily contrives an awkward meeting for them. But as good as the libretto was, the show might have been lackluster without its scintillating score. Embarrassingly for Kreisler, who garnered most of the preopening attention, it was Victor Jacobi who wrote the hit, "You Are Free," a duet for Nancy and Philip. The song had oddly Victorian lyrics for its 20th-

century message. Jacobi was responsible as well for "Little Girls, Goodbye." Time helped redress the imbalance. Nancy's first act waltz, "Who Can Tell?", which Kreisler composed, was given new lyrics and new life in 1936 as "Stars In Your Eyes." Besides two top singers, Thomas and Miss Bennett, the show featured two personable young dancers, Fred and Adele Astaire. The *Times* alerted readers to watch for "the vastly entertaining dances by the two Adaires [*sic*], in particular for the incredibly nimble and lackadaisical Adaire named Fred. He is one of those extraordinary persons whose senses of rhythm and humor have all been mixed up, whose very muscles, of which he seems to have an extra supply, are downright facetious." One of their dances was done to Kreisler's "Tambourin Chinois," the other—to Jacobi's music—began when Fred playfully retrieved a ball of yarn Adele had dropped. Although the paper was careless in its spelling, it was also perspicacious. All during the twenties Adele was awarded the lion's share of praise for the team. Not until Fred was forced to perform alone did most critics and audiences fully appreciate his brilliance. *Apple Blossoms* had the added allure of three sumptuous Urban sets, re-creating a garden at a girl's school, an elegant Fifth Avenue study, and a spacious ballroom. The operetta played into May, then toured successfully.

Another hit, **The Little Whopper** (10-13-19, Casino), followed. To facilitate her elopement, Kitty Wentworth tells her school proprietress she is going to Philadelphia to meet family friends. She winds up in the wrong hotel room, and as one complication piles on top another, fib piles on fib. Rudolf Friml's score was second-rate, but adequate. It leaned, as Friml's next score did, toward contemporary musical comedy and away from Friml's native bent. With Vivienne Segal as star, the show ran over six months. An omen of things to come might have seen in the source of the book, *Miss George Washington, Jr.*—a silent screenplay!

Nothing but Love (10-14-19, Lyric) was a quick flop about a young man (Andrew Tombes) who can't remember rescuing his sweetheart (Ruby Norton) until an understanding doctor (Donald Meek) jolts his recollections. The musical was sandwiched in between the procession of hits which continued with **The Passing Show of 1919** (10-23-19, Winter Garden). The Shubert mentality could not compete with Ziegfeld or Anderson's taste. J. J.'s inevitable response was to bring on more girls. It was an answer that pleased many a tired businessman, who probably left the theatre humming the show's hit, one more interpolation, "I'm Forever Blowing Bubbles" (Jean Kenbrovin and John W. Kellette). The revue offered the Avon Comedy Four doing their famous skit, "The Doctor's Office," which the group's two long-lived survivors, Smith and Dale, continued to play for years as a wise-cracking duel between a doctor and a patient. The rest of the cast—none with the big names Ziegfeld so generously paid for—included Olga Cook (later of *Blossom Time*), Walter Woolf (later of *Countess Maritza*), James Barton, Charles Winninger, and Mary Eaton: youthful and talented performers who soon left for bigger salaries which the increasingly tight-fisted Shuberts refused to pay.

Buddies (10-27-19, Selwyn) was another hit. Just as Kreisler's reception indicated the end of ill-feelings, so *Buddies* meant war stories, of a sort, were acceptable once more. Actually the story unfolds in Normandy a few days after the Armistice. A group of soldiers are billeted with Madame Benoit (Camile Dalberg) and her daughter Julie (Peggy Wood). One doughboy, Babe (Roland Young), falls in love with Julie but is too shy to court her. Fond of Babe and hoping to make him jealous enough to speak up, Julie flirts with his buddy, Sonnie (Donald Brian). Her ruse works. The music (including one song partially by Cole Porter) was flavorless, the lyrics drab. But in singing, "There is a world of fairy tales, wherein we love to dwell," or, "Good-bye, trenches; Farewell, Frenchies," they commented perceptively on the mental frame of the audiences. One stage picture elicited special praise. The soldiers were housed in an old French barn. When taps was sounded from an off-stage village, the soldiers crawl into bed, candles are extinguished and the silent barn lit only by moonlight. Such sentimental, rustic touches appeared throughout the evening. That the show was so fondly remembered was probably to the credit of its stars, Brian, Young, and Miss Wood. Brian's lithe stepping and Miss Wood's lovely singing (despite the *Times* insisting her voice was "unruly") undoubtedly were taken for granted. But some theatregoers may have been startled by Young's "manneristic and talented" dances.

With four hits in five tries, it was too much to expect the run of success to continue. Two other musicals opened the same night as *Buddies*; both closed in five weeks' time. **Fifty-Fifty, Ltd.** (10-27-19, Comedy) turned William Gillette's *All the Comforts of Home* into a jazzy vaudeville. The old plot of a home rented to a collection of boarders was a natural, since all the guests could and did have specialty acts. Even the chorus, which apparently slept en masse in the attic, was said to be from the "Midnight Scrambles." Herbert Corthell walked away with the evening's honors for his portrayal of a henpecked husband.

In October 27th's third opening, the trio responsible for *Listen Lester* tried to repeat its success at the same Cort Theatre with **Just a Minute**, proffering an even sillier book and weaker score than *Listen Lester* got by on. For its composer, Harry Orlob, it was his second fast flop of the year. He had composed the slightly better music for *Nothing but Love*. In five years' time Orlob wrote five scores without a single hit tune. Although his work was the grossest hack writing, he was still enough in demand to be asked to write two more scores in the twenties. Sadly, it took thirty-odd years for him to receive credit for his lone great melody, "I Wonder Who's Kissing Her Now?", attributed to Joe Howard when it was sung in *The Prince of Tonight* (3-9-09). What little *Just a Minute* had to recommend it came largely from its bare-legged dancing chorus, whose sprightly synchronized steps won several rounds of applause.

The Little Blue Devil (11-3-19, Central) was also a flop, even though it had any number of good things going for it. It had two Ziegfeld favorites, Bernard Granville and Lillian Lorraine, as stars; a likable Harry Carroll score; and Clyde Fitch's *The Blue Mouse* as source. Harold Atteridge's adaptation may not have been the most cerebral, but the story was no more farfetched than many of the librettos attracting applause. Augustus Rollett passes off Paulette Divine, the Little Blue Devil, as his wife in order to win a promotion from his roving-eyed boss. He wins the promotion, but he's left with a lot of explaining to do to the real Mrs. Rollett.

It was November 11 before Sigmund Romberg's name appeared on a season's program, and when it did Romberg was listed as coproducer as well as composer. After *Maytime* the Shuberts continued to press Romberg to grind out Winter Garden scores, offering no attractive libretto to compensate. In despair, Romberg broke with them and established a producing company with Max Wilner. For their first production, **The Magic Melody**, Romberg picked the predictably bittersweet type of tale he always was to favor. Beppo Corsini, his opera rejected, his wife seemingly unfaithful, leaves home, taking his young son with him. Twenty years later, Beppo is long dead and his son has become a handsome captain. He is reunited with his long-lost mother when he sings excerpts from his father's opera. His mother is able to prove she was never untrue to Beppo, making the reunion a happy one. The dialogue and the lyrics were stodgy, and, considering all the show must have meant to Romberg, the score was annoyingly weak and derivative. The show's best number, a pleasant waltz called "Once Upon A Time," unwisely began, "Once upon a time in May,/How can you forget, dear?" This echo of *Maytime* (9-16-17) was reinforced by that show's star, Charles Purcell, playing both Beppo and his son, just as he had played both Richard and his grandson in 1918. The rest of the score sounded sometimes like Jerome Kern, sometimes like Irving Berlin and most often like more Winter Garden dross. The show ran 143 performances at the Shubert, but was generally recorded as a failure.

Irene (11-18-19, Vanderbilt) immediately became the season's runaway hit. It showed the work of the Princess pioneers had not been in vain. A believable plot told about believable people who sang lovely songs brought naturally into the story. If this time there was more sentimentality than wit, no one cared. It remains one of the most cherished of American musicals. Irene O'Dare (Edith Day), a poor shop girl, is sent on an errand to the Marshalls' Long Island estate. The Marshalls' son, Donald (Walter Regan), promptly falls in love with her and finds her a job as a model in a couturier's shop run by a gentleman known as Madam Lucy (Bobbie Watson). When Irene walks off with everyone's heart at J. P. Bowden's party, both Mrs. O'Dare (Dorothy Walters) and Mrs. Marshall (Florence Hills) put aside their prejudices, allowing Donald and Irene to marry. The solid book moved tellingly back and forth between the rags of the O'Dares' tenement and the riches of the Long Island estate. A set depicting a fire escape outside the O'Dares' flat became one of the most celebrated of the day. The show's great hit, "Alice Blue Gown," was Irene's first number; it effectively won over any audience. The remaining tunes were almost as good, especially the infectious title song and the joyous "The Last Part Of Every Party." They were incorporated for the first time into a successful Cinderella formula that was employed by musical after musical until, like Irene's gown, it wilted. Wisely, the best of the imitations never used the little cheat Joseph McCarthy and Harry Tierney resorted to, sneaking in a Chopin theme for Irene's "Castle Of Dreams." One may have been neces-

sary to prop up a weak *Oh, Look!* score, but Tierney's material for *Irene* could have stood on its own feet. A 1973 revival, while successful, made so many changes it hardly deserved to retain the name.

Charlotte Greenwood and her Letitia Proudfoot came back to New York in **Linger Longer Letty** (11-20-19, Fulton). A paper-thin plot portrayed Letty as her family's ugly duckling who finds love and happiness with a neighbor, Jim (Olin Howland). No one cared that there was barely enough plot to make it to 11:00 P.M. Miss Greenwood kicked high, joined Howland for several eccentric dance duets, and sang "Oh, By Jingo," so all was right with the world. But Broadway was never Letty's first home. She lingered only nine weeks and returned to the long road before her.

When F. Ray Comstock, Guy Bolton, and P.G. Wodehouse delivered another Kern-less musical, they suffered another flop, at least as far as Broadway was concerned. **The Rose of China** (11-25-19, Lyric) had music by the Hotel Ritz' fashionable orchestra leader, Armand Vecsey. He did his house no credit. The story, which in outline does not sound like the expected Bolton material, has Tommy Telford (Oscar Shaw) forced to marry Ling Tao (Jane Richardson) when he becomes the first man to see her with her face exposed. Since he loves her, his only problem is disposing of his American fiancée, Grace (Cynthia Perot), and her grim-visaged mother (Edna May Oliver). Bolton had trouble cutting this simple story down to size. On opening night there was still one whole act to come at 11:00 P.M. At least Wodehouse could take a little heart in the *Times'* calling his rhyming of "Los Angeles" and "man jealous," "probably the greatest single achievement of its kind this season." Six weeks and *The Rose of China* moved to Chicago, where it was an "instantaneous smash," retasting the tremendous popularity it had enjoyed on its pre-Broadway tryout.

A second F. Ray Comstock and Morris Gest production was more successful. **Aphrodite** (11-24-19, Century) was a Hippodrome-like spectacle whose book, never properly credited, and handful of songs took second place to its pageantry. The famous ballet choreographer Michel Fokine did the dances.

Five musicals opened in December. **Elsie Janis and Her Gang** (12-1-19, Cohan) led the parade. Miss Janis had spent the war months entertaining the troops at the front lines. To the doughboys she had become "The Sweetheart of the AEF."

Dressed in smart military uniforms or at least sporting a soldier's helmet, she offered Broadway the sketches and specialty acts she had put together for France. Eva Le Gallienne, who later won fame in more serious enterprises, had a small part. The Gang remained in New York seven weeks as part of a national tour.

R. H. Burnside and Raymond Hubbell, who had been creating the colossal entertainments at the Hippodrome, did a turnabout and brought their **Miss Millions** into the petite Punch and Judy Theater on December 9. It employed the rags-to-riches plot that was to overrun Broadway musicals in the wake of *Irene*. Jack Honeydew's uncle (Rayley Holmes) suspects Jack's fiancée, the tea-shop waitress Mary Hope (Valli Valli), of loving Jack (Vinton Freedley) less than she loves Jack's money. The uncle arranges for Mary to believe she has come into a large inheritance and that Jack has lost all his wealth. Mary remains true until she learns she is being used. She runs away to a farm in New Jersey, where Jack pursues her and wins her back. Without the Hippodrome's pyrotechnics to divert theatregoers' attention from the hack material, *Miss Millions'* weaknesses were all too visible. Even at its tiny playhouse, six weeks was all the show could hold on.

Monsieur Beaucaire (12-11-19, New Amsterdam) was an Allied effort that enjoyed a five-month run. Based on a short story by American Booth Tarkington, with a score by French André Messager and libretto and lyrics by English Adrian Ross, it had been a European success before coming to America. The plot told of the adventures of the Duc d'Orleans (Marion Greene), disguised as Beaucaire, a barber in Bath, England.

Above the classic splendor of *Aphrodite*, **Morris Gest's Midnight Whirl** (12-27-19, Century Roof) gave late-nighters more up-to-date diversion. Gershwin's music was pleasant but his best song, "Poppyland" was no more typical of his style than "Old Fashioned Garden" had been of Cole Porter's. Bernard Granville and Bessie McCoy Davis headed the cast.

Just before the teens slipped away, **Angel Face** (12-29-19, Knickerbocker) appeared. Even though Victor Herbert and the Smith brothers belonged squarely in the era that was fast receding, they tried to be as modern as possible. Harry B. Smith's plot grew out of the latest medical rage, Voronoff's contention that monkey gland grafts could rejuvenate the old and feeble. But Smith had learned little from the Princess Theatre shows.

His book was weak and turgid. A vial is left carelessly at Tom Larkin and Arthur Griffin's bachelor apartment. The elixir's effect on various people who sample it in the course of three acts provided the evening's fun. Between specialty turns such as Jack Donahue's supple tap and soft-shoe routines, angel-faced Betty (Marguerite Zender) wangles Arthur (Tyler Brooke) away from her older sister, Vera (Minerva Grey), while Tom (John E. Young)—who is also composer of the successful musical comedy, "The Lemon Girl" —woos and wins Tessie (Emilie Lea). Brother Robert's lyrics tugged at both worlds with lines such as, "Ere the world is awake, You and I will take an aeroplane." Herbert, also trying to keep in the swing of things, wrote fewer waltzes. But, with one exception, his tunes were inferior. The exception was "I Might Be Your 'Once-in-a-While'," its light, easy grace catching the more gentle charm of a passing day. It remains a Herbert standard. The song alone was not sufficient to save the show. *Angel Face* smiled for only 57 performances, then a booking jam forced it to leave while it still had respectable grosses.

A less interesting, but more successful Herbert show followed a little over a month later. **My Golden Girl** (2-2-20, Nora Bayes) had a hand-me-down Herbert score and a book by Frederic Arnold Kummer that seemed like a rewrite of *Apple Blossoms*. Peggy and Arthur Mitchell (Marie Caroll and Victor Morely) have each found extramarital love interests. They agree to a divorce. But they soon realize they still love each other. For all its lack of originality, *My Golden Girl* ran three months, helped by the cavorting of Edna May Oliver as yet another battle-axe mother, and Ned Sparks as a young, sourpuss lawyer.

The new year was five days old when **Always You** arrived at the Central. It was the first Broadway musical to have a book and lyrics by Oscar Hammerstein II.

. . .

Oscar Hammerstein II was born in New York on July 12, 1895. His grandfather, the first Oscar, was a leading impresario whose Manhattan Opera House briefly rivaled the Metropolitan. His uncle was a leading Broadway producer and his father was manager of the Victoria Theatre. Young Hammerstein attended Columbia, where he wrote and acted in varsity shows. He took a degree in law, but quickly forsook it for the stage when his uncle made him assistant manager for *You're in*

Love. After a drama he wrote folded hastily out of town, he turned his hand to musicals.

. . .

Because of his famous name, Hammerstein's contributions received closer scrutiny than they might have otherwise. Some critics were happier with his lyrics than with his book. But by and large they were gratified to find a genuine new talent in the family. Hammerstein wrote of Bruce Nash (Walter Scanlan), who wavers between the girl he fell in love with while serving in France (Helen Ford) and his American sweetheart (Julia Kelety). As in *The Rose of China*, the American girl loses. For the umpteenth time many critics saved their happiest encomiums for the show's peppy chorus and the specialty dancing, in this case by Cortez and Peggy. Kind words were also reserved for the genial clowning of Ralph Herz and of Edouard Ciannelli, the latter of whom went on to become one of Hollywood's most sought-after villains.

Frivolities of 1920 (1-8-20, 44th St.), a revue of no merit, came and went quickly. During its brief stay, Henry Lewis and Irene Delroy sang and joked about celebrated sites from the old Waldorf's Peacock Alley to the sands of Araby.

As You Were (1-27-20, Central) sent Sam Bernard (with peace once more a "German" comedian) as Wolfie Wafflestein back through the ages to prove to him that the great beauties of history were every bit as impossible as his wife. With Irene Bordoni as the wife and beauties, and Clifton Webb as all her lovers, this Paris original repeated its European success. Although it called itself a revue—and Baral treats it as such—it had sufficient plot and consistent characterization to qualify as a musical comedy. Herman Darewski and E. Ray Goetz' tunes were unimaginative. But for 143 performances Miss Bordoni made sure you didn't notice.

A superb all-American entry competed with Herbert's *My Golden Girl* for attention. Charles Dillingham offered Anne Caldwell and Jerome Kern's **The Night Boat** (2-2-20, Liberty), a lively romp about Bob White (John E. Hazzard), who pretends to be the captain of a Hudson River boat to Albany so that he can have a fling away from home. When Mrs. Maxim (Ada Lewis), his mother-in-law, becomes suspicious and decides to sail with him, White wangles the uniform of the captain, who luckily is named Robert White (Ernest Torrence). But his luck doesn't hold out.

Some hastily contrived explanations bring a reluctant forgiving—and a promise to behave. There was as much fun in the music as in the book. The fast-stepping "Whose Baby Are You?" and the evening's hit, "Left All Alone Again Blues," topped a score filled with gay, woefully neglected melodies. Once again, as they had in *Fiddlers Three*, Louise Groody and Hal Skelly stole the show from its principals. Their infectious charm, exuberant singing and dancing, especially in a reprise of "Whose Baby Are You?," were highlights of the evening.

February's only other musical was a vanity production by Herman Timberg of his own material, unveiled on the 23rd. He called his revue **Tick-Tack-Toe** and tried to entertain with "Hoppy Poppy Girl," "Chinese-American Rag," and "Take Me Back To Philadelphia, Pa." With songs like that it was fortunate to record 32 performances at the tiny Princess. Actually reviews for *Tick-Tack-Toe* were not bad—the critic for the *World* professing to enjoy and understand the differences that separated the "jazz, rag and shimmy" numbers in the score. More interesting than the show itself or its notices was Timberg's determination to tour it. Theatrical economics remained such that this was not only feasible but common. After all, *Irene*, which cost $41,000 to bring in and grossed less than $20,000 a week at capacity, had paid off its entire nut and banked $20,000 surplus after just six weeks at the small Vanderbilt. It quickly sent out four more companies. There was such a demand for plays to fill houses across the country that during 1919–20 there were still on tour two companies each of *Oh, Boy!* (2-20-17), *Oh, Lady! Lady!!* (2-1-18), and the previous year's disappointing *Oh, My Dear* (11-27-18). *Listen Lester* (12-23-18) continued to have three troupes dancing across the land, and Fritzi Scheff was still singing *Glorianna* (10-28-18). These were only a few of the older vehicles still touring. But even musicals that failed on Broadway, such as *The Rose of China*, made huge profits on subsequent road tours. *Frivolities of 1920* betook itself to Philadelphia and points south after its quick demise in New York. *Gaieties of 1920, Hello Alexander, Hitchy-Koo,* and *Always You* were all listed by *Variety* as recent Broadway flops that paid off handsomely on the road. So it was not too unreasonable for Timberg to try to salvage both his investment and his good name. He hired Sophie Tucker to star and reopened in Far Rockaway on April 24. But even the hinterlands would not buy the revue, and after a few weeks Timberg threw in the towel.

March had two new offerings. Both ran eleven weeks. The first probably deserved no more, the second surely should have enjoyed a longer stay. **Look Who's Here** (3-2-20, 44th St.) starred Cleo Mayfield and Cecil Lean, both then at the height of their popularity. It had another tinkly Silvio Hein score and an adequate Frank Mandel libretto about a number of husbands and wives who meet at the same hotel when they are all supposed to be elsewhere. In every way it was run-of-the-mill, and Broadway treated it accordingly.

In his study of revues, Robert Baral calls **What's in a Name** (3-19-20, Maxine Elliott) "a brilliant gem . . . way ahead of its time." He adds, "This revue is credited with spearheading the parade of artistic musicals which came on Broadway right after World War I's Broadway renaissance." It is clear, however, from his discussion and from contemporary notices that what awed and moved playgoers was not the show's sketches or music but the glowingly beautiful sets and costumes of a young artist, James Reynolds. Carefully restrained color combinations, scenery projected delicately on screens, subtle, gradual changes of sets evoked delighted bravos. Joseph Urban had a rival. The show's most famous setting—dancers in 18th-century clothes posing like Dresden china figurines on a gigantic music box—looks ludicrous on the show's sheet music, a parody of a girls' school amateur production. But for its time—before the more substantial sets of the cinema and television—it was a pace setter.

A totally different sort of revue followed. **The Ed Wynn Carnival** (4-5-20, New Amsterdam) was built around its star's talents. If the scenery and costumes were not a matter of indifference, no one lost sleep over them. The music, to use a future Wynn title, was a grab bag. Wynn wrote some of it himself; one interpolation was by George Gershwin, the rest by various hands. It was all undistinguished. Even the dancing chorus was dismissed as substandard. Wynn's unique, zany clowning—with his ridiculous clothes, preposterous inventions, and lispy, somewhat effeminate delivery—were the hilarious be-all and end-all of the evening. Wynn demonstrated an absurd lightning calculator, fouled up a violin solo, and deposited cigar ashes in the pit's piano. In their laughter most people forgot that Wynn was producing his own show because the established producing fraternity would not forgive him for being a leader in the Equity strike.

Two other musicals opened the same night as the *Carnival*. The Shuberts mounted a revival of *Florodora* at the Century, stirring enough happy memories to keep the sextette singing into the hot weather. Its statistics underscored the inflationary pattern on Broadway. The original, twenty years earlier, had grossed $10,000 a week at capacity. The revival needed over $16,000 to break even—and capacity at the large Century was $35,000. There were some complaints, notably from Alexander Woollcott in the *Times*, that the book had been unnecessarily refurbished with topical jokes and that songs not from the original, but from the musical's era, were added to supplement the original melodies. Eleanor Painter, Christie MacDonald, George Hassell, and the rising young Walter Woolf were featured.

"A comedy with music," **Three Showers** (4-5-20, Harris), completed the evening's arrivals. William Cary Duncan's book was based on an old adage that, if you make a wish on a day with three showers, your wish will come true. Roberta Lee "Bob" White (Anna Wheaton) wishes for Peter Fitzhugh (Paul Frawley) and gets him. The show conveyed Broadway's idea of 1920 rusticity in a number that found Miss Wheaton dressed as a "farmerette" in pink and white checked trousers and a bright red sash, and had her pushed around the stage in a wheelbarrow. The score by two blacks, Turner Layton and Henry Creamer, was lively, but not memorable. *Three Showers* departed after six weeks.

Catherine Chisholm Cushing's *Kitty MacKaye* had been one of the hits of the 1913–14 season. She converted it into a musical with Hugo Felix providing the music. As **Lassie** the show came into the Nora Bayes on April 6, giving New Yorkers four new musicals in two successive nights. The story remained the same: Kitty MacKaye (Tessa Kosta) was abandoned as a baby in Scotland in the 1840s. Now grown, she is returned to her wealthy London family. She falls in love with her half-brother (Roland Bottomley), and, knowing she cannot marry him, returns to her poor Scottish home. He comes after her, and when she discovers that as an infant she was substituted for a child who had died, they arrange to wed. Besides lauding the fine singing of the beautiful Miss Kosta, critics recommended the flowing footwork of Carl Hyson and Dorothy Dickson. For Miss Dickson, *Lassie* marked her last American appearance before sailing for London, where in the following year her interpretation of Marilyn Miller's role as *Sally* made her a reigning West

End favorite. Although some critics and theatregoers considered *Lassie* one of the top musicals of the season, not enough agreed to make it a major success. It did run through the summer and attempted a post-Broadway tour but was closed when it proved "too high class for popular trade."

All the appeal and skill of Charles Dillingham and Frank Craven couldn't make a hit of **The Girl from Home** (5-3-20, Globe), a musical version of Richard Harding Davis' *The Dictator*. Craven himself played the old William Collier role of Brook Travers, who flees New York, believing he will be arrested for punching a cab driver, and lands in mythical San Manana in time for the latest revolution. He further complicates his own life by pretending to be the American consul and calling in the American navy. In the end his boyish derring-do wins him Lucy Sheridan (Gladys Caldwell). It was precisely the sort of cracker-barrel fun Craven excelled at. One refreshing novelty was nine of its chorus girls, garbed as nuns, singing "Nine Little Missionaries." But its late arrival and another feeble Silvio Hein score deprived *The Girl from Home* of the popularity it might otherwise have won. The backstage bickering between Craven and the producer over what improvements were required hastened its closing.

On the other hand, a melodic, vivacious score augmented by a strong book and a clever production gave **Honey Girl** (5-3-20, Cohan and Harris) a well-earned reward. Like *Lassie* and *The Girl from Home*, it used an old play for a start, in this case, Henry Blossom's *Checkers*. And like the horses and races it so amusingly dealt with, *Honey Girl* got off to an uncertain start. Originally produced as *What's the Odds* with the book adapted by Edgar Allan Woolf (who had worked on a silent movie version the same year), it was taken over by Sam Harris, who put in a new version of the book—this time by Edward Clark—remounted and rechristened the piece. All he wisely retained was Albert Von Tilzer's marvelous score, with its less than marvelous Neville Fleeson lyrics. "Checkers" is the nickname given David Graham (Lynne Overman), a young man unable to stay away from race tracks. He falls in love with Honey Parker (Edna Bates), daughter of Parkertown's banker. But Honey's father (Dodson Mitchell) will not hear of their marrying until Checkers is worth $25,000. Checkers leaves to make his fortune, first promising Honey he will never again go near a horse race. When he spots a nag named "Honey Girl" running at odds of 25 to 1, he pledges his fiancée's ring and puts a thousand dollars on the horse to win. Of course, the horse wins, and Checkers wins Honey. The book was exceptionally well written, and the songs, for the most part, in no way held up the action. The lovely "Close To Your Heart" was the standout, but it was by no means unique. Von Tilzer composed a fine, old-fashioned waltz, "I'm Losing My Heart To Someone"; two jaunty, up-to-the-minute fox-trots, the one appropriately exclaiming "I Love To Fox Trot," the other "Small Town Girl." As was often still the case, these two more voguish melodies were sung in the show by the principal comedienne, Honey's friend, Lucy (Louise Meyers), leaving the sweeter sentiments to the lovers. There was also an irresistible chorus number in the galloping "Racing Blues." The production was elaborate. A race was run on stage, with horses on a treadmill. For no good reason other than to insert a spectacle, a lovely Bluebird Ballet was added. *Honey Girl* ran well into the next season. Its neglect is saddening, and probably can be attributed to the small name Von Tilzer created for himself in the theatre. Interestingly, the Fleeson-Von Tilzer classic, "I'll Be With You In Apple Blossom Time," written in the same year, remains a barbershop quartet favorite.

The season's last musical comedy, **Betty Be Good** (5-4-20, Casino) advertised itself as "a smart comedy with smart music." Unfortunately, it wasn't smart enough. Supposedly based on "a French vaudeville by Scribe," the plot seemed little more than a twist on the preceding season's *Somebody's Sweetheart*, with a hint of *Nobody Home* (4-20-15) for good measure. Betty Lee (Josephine Whittell), whom the title admonished without the fashionable exclamation point, is a touring actress who sublets her New York apartment to a man she doesn't know. At the Bon Ton Hotel in Lenox, Massachusetts, she meets her old flame, Sam Kirby (Frank Crumit). He is about to be married, but he lies to Betty, claiming he is merely the best man. The real best man is the unknown renter of Betty's flat, and he has given it to Sam and his bride for their honeymoon. When Betty returns unexpectedly, the inevitable musical comedy complications set in. Although Harry B. Smith was coming under increasing attack for the obsolescent "Joe Miller" joke material that he palmed off as librettos, his book of *Betty Be Good* suggested he didn't care. His lyrics were a little fresher. In "I'd Like To Take You Away" Smith tried, not successfully, to have the words of the chorus comprise a dialogue. But Smith was just as easily content to title a principal love song "Keep The Love Lamps Burning In The Windows Of Your Eyes." Hugo Riesenfeld, the composer, also tried to escape commonplace patterns in songs such as "Same Old Stars, Same Old Moon," where the show's chorus sang a counterpart to Sam's main theme. It was evident he lacked the melodic gift to create another "Simple Melody."

The **Scandals of 1920** (6-7-20, Globe), the first of the annual revues to arrive, announced the coming summer and closed the theatrical year. Dancing once again dominated George White's show, but this time Ann Pennington and White had Gershwin music to tap, soft shoe, and shimmy to. The score was not strikingly good. Critics and historians have lauded "Idle Dreams," but the truth is the great Gershwin still lay ahead. One song, "Tum On And Tiss Me," points to the baby-talk craze, which seems to have been not so much an urge to revert to infantile ways as a reaction against the last generation's persistent retention of childhood themes (best exemplified by Fred Stone's appeal). Even the show's comedy routines on Prohibition (set in an airship), profiteering, and politics suggested the new decade would have a tougher outlook on things.

The old decade was patently over, and with it went several eras—a wartime era, a ragtime era, an era of easy grace and elegance. New ideas and new standards were noisily on the way. There was a new music called jazz; there was a new optimism tempered by a light, tongue-in-cheek cynicism. They would make the seemingly modern approaches and still contemporary music of the season's best shows—*Apple Blossoms, Irene, The Night Boat,* or *Honey Girl*—seem abruptly dated to faddists. Even George Gershwin's early "Swanee" would be put down as not real jazz. Nonetheless, the songs and the shows have remained viable and loved.

1920-1921

At four in the morning of August 26, 1920, Tennessee's ratification of the 19th Amendment was delivered to the Secretary of State. Women would shortly have the vote. Broadway could only guess at the vast implications. Undeniably, it would bring changes, but not overnight. Certainly they would not be as rapid as the changes brought by ASCAP's and Equity's new-found strengths, both of which were bent toward immediate and meaningful theatrical reforms. Broadway's first reaction was its typical reaction to such upheavals—interpolated jokes and songs.

Broadway admittedly wasn't too concerned with social significance. Broadway was booming. New theatres were opening in every direction to offer stages for the explosion of new productions. Almost fifty new musicals vied for patronage in the 1920–21 season, up 10 percent from the preceding year, and more than double the number presented at the beginning of the period.

The very first offering, **The Ziegfeld Follies of 1920** (6-22-20, New Amsterdam) affirmed the forthcoming Constitutional amendment would bring no swift alterations. Ziegfeld continued to "glorify" the American girl. Of course rows of ravishing young ladies were only a part of his evening. They posed and paraded before more sumptuous Joseph Urban décor, while John Steel sang topflight Irving Berlin songs such as "Tell Me, Little Gypsy" and "The Girls Of My Dreams." Ben Ali Haggin framed the girls in a lush Venetian tableau for Victor Herbert's "The Love Boat." Harry Tierney and others contributed additional songs. For comedy, W.C. Fields (with baby-talking Ray Dooley to assist) attempted to repair "The Family Ford." Fanny Brice had three riotous showstoppers, "I'm A Vamp From East Broadway" (Berlin, with Bert Kalmar and Harry Ruby), "I Was A Florodora Baby" (Ballard MacDonald and Harry Carroll), and "I'm An Indian" (Blanche Merrill/Leo Edwards). Moran and Mack clowned in blackface, while Van and Schenck delighted with their high-styled duets. Young Jack Donahue advanced his dancing fame. Ziegfeld built the year's finale around his *Midnight Frolic*, the cabaret-cum-revue playing upstairs on the New Amsterdam's roof.

Two more summer revues followed. **Cinderella on Broadway,** which opened on June 24, was a typical Winter Garden show. It originally was to have been *The Passing Show of 1920*. But the Shuberts were conscious of a growing indifference to their annuals, although officially they professed fear that out-of-towners who kept the box office busy might somehow confuse the new edition with several older ones still treking from city to city. The brothers announced their new show would be known as *Rip Van Winkle, Jr.*—a title that picked up another Winter Garden tradition. Just before the opening the title was inexplicably changed. The frame of Cinderella's search for Prince Charming demonstrated war-nurtured cynicisms had not completely routed an older, benign infantilism. Harold Atteridge continued to provide sketches and lyrics, while Al Goodman, later a distinguished orchestra leader, and Bert Grant replaced Sigmund Romberg as composer. There was less of Vienna and ragtime in their music, but it offered nothing outstanding. No then important names were in the cast, although Al Shean and Georgie Price soon became well known. Cinderella searched for her prince eight times a week until well into the fall.

Buzzin' Around (7-6-20, Casino), a mediocre vaudeville, lingered less than three weeks. Magic acts, jugglers, a Chinese wedding spectacle, and a travesty of *The Mikado* were performed by a cast that included Elizabeth Brice and the evening's co-producer and director, Will Morrissey.

The Girl in the Spotlight (7-12-20, Knickerbocker) was the season's first book musical. It played seven weeks. The backstage story was produced by an old theatrical hand, George Lederer, and set to music by another old hand, Victor Herbert. This time their experience failed them, even though the book by "Richard Bruce" (actually two more old hands, the Smith brothers) was competent enough. In it Frank Marvin (Ben Forbes), a composer, lives at the boarding house where Molly Shannon (Mary Milburn) works. Hearing him rehearse his compositions, she learns them by heart. When the leading lady of Marvin's opera refuses to perform, Molly goes on in her place. She becomes a star and Mrs. Marvin. The backstage settings led to a number of specialty turns. Hal Skelly appeared briefly as a dance director, Watchem Tripp, to perform his own eccentric routines. Johnny Dooley also displayed some fancy footwork. The last act included an elaborate garden set, supposedly a scene from the opera in which Molly sang. For Lederer, *The Girl in the Spotlight* represented the last of his nearly two-score productions, that had begun with *Princess Nicotine* (10-24-93) and included the first indisputable revue, *The Passing Show* (5-12-94). Coincidentally, his erstwhile rival at the Casino, Rudolf Aronson, had died in February. Lederer himself survived in retirement until 1938.

If Ziegfeld could plug his *Midnight Frolics* in his *Follies,* the Shuberts could go him one better. On July 12, the same night *The Girl in the Spot-*

light premiered downtown at the old Knickerbocker, they opened two revues uptown at the Century. **The Century Revue** had a regular curtain. When it was over the audience could remain to see **The Midnight Rounders** on the theatre's roof. Like the *Midnight Frolics,* it was really a cabaret. *The Century Revue* displayed its line of beauties in bottles, while *The Midnight Rounders* showered them with roses. Many of the principals of the earlier show followed audiences upstairs: Walter Woolf, Madelon La Verre, Green and Blyer, and Vivian Oakland.

Silks and Satins (7-15-20, Cohan) added one more revue to the growing tally. After 53 performances, it was also added to the season's list of failures. In that short while it offered theatregoers another rose number, took them into China, rejoiced at "That Colored Jazzboray," and made fun of *Macbeth.*

Poor Little Ritz Girl (7-28-20, Central) was produced by Lew Fields, who in 1918–19 had given Richard Rodgers and Lorenz Hart a chance to interpolate one song in his *A Lonely Romeo.* Now he let them write a whole score. But the youthful songwriters were stunned on attending the opening to find some of the songs weren't theirs. No one had told them eight of their numbers had been dropped during the tryout and replaced by Sigmund Romberg and Alex Gerber music. They were left to draw what consolation they could from the more discerning critics, who singled out their songs to praise. How values were changing was seen in the *Globe*'s Kenneth MacGowan's saluting their work as "hard, brisk tunes." George Campbell's libretto made *Poor Little Ritz Girl* the third book show in a row about theatre people. It was a variation of *Betty Be Good*'s (5-4-20) apartment problem. Annie Farrell (Florence Webber), a chorus girl rehearsing "Poor Little Ritz Girl" at the Frivolity Theatre, subleases rich, handsome William Pembroke's Riverside Drive apartment. Pembroke (Charles Purcell), a bachelor, had not intended for the apartment to be sublet and returns to use it himself. Annie persuades him to let her remain until the show opens. Pembroke agrees to take a room at his club until then. By opening night they have fallen in love. It was not the best of books, although it had a good cast to gloss over its weak spots. Andrew Tombes and Lulu McConnell provided much of the evening's laughs. By putting its sets on rollers and changing them rapidly in full view of the audience, *Poor Little Ritz Girl* gave the audiences a glimpse of advanced technique. The show ran 119 performances—not enough to make Rodgers and Hart the talk of the town. Five years had to pass before New Yorkers took proper notice of the talented team.

August's first entry on the 9th was the Hippodrome's annual spectacle. The title, **Good Times,** was again ironic in light of the economic and artistic problems just ahead. To standard Raymond Hubbell tunes, the public that flocked to the big house was whisked away to "The Valley Of Dreams," "Colorland," and "The Wedding Of The Dancing Doll." *Good Times* amassed 456 performances.

Tickle Me (8-17-20, Selwyn) was the first of two shows presented during the season by Arthur Hammerstein that had book and lyrics by Otto Harbach, Oscar Hammerstein II, and Frank Mandel, and music by Herbert Stothart. The second, *Jimmie*, was the better of the two.

Tickle Me was a vehicle for Frank Tinney, who played the part of Frank Tinney. When the stage Tinney writes a scenario that Poisson Pictures believes to be a masterpiece, a backer is found to send the company on location in Tibet. In "The Veil Of Mystery" and "The Bower Of Temptation" all variety of musical comedy complications await the budding genius. By the time the company is homeward bound on the *S.S. Tickle Me,* even a love interest is happily resolved. The best of Stothart's score was "If A Wish Could Make It So." When the swirling, kicking chorus or dance specialists such as Olga and Mishka, and Frances Grant and Ted Wing were not delaying the plot, Tinney resorted to his old practice of stopping the action to chat with his audience. His personal following helped keep *Tickle Me* running for six months.

Its tauter book and superior score should have helped **Jimmie** (11-17-20, Apollo) match that run, but the show lasted only 71 performances. The best of the baby-talkers, Frances White, was the star, impersonating Jimmie, the long-lost daughter of Jacob Blum (Ben Welch). Vincenzo Carlotti (Paul Porcasi), knowing Jimmie stands to inherit vast wealth, tries to substitute his own daughter for her, but his ruse fails. Jimmie and Jacob are reunited, and Jimmie is assured of her fortune. Meanwhile, she will more than earn her keep as a cabaret star. Stothart's score was the best he ever did for Broadway. Unfortunately, it was too little, too late. *Mary* had opened a month earlier, and the overwhelming success of "The Love Nest" momentarily stifled any chance for the show's

hoped-for hit to become popular. "Cute Little Two By Four," while outclassed by Louis Hirsch's ballad, was still catchy and memorable. The lovely, wispy "Baby Dreams" also seemed a bit frayed, recalling earlier Kern pieces. But the happy-go-lucky title song and the jaunty "Rickety Crickety" both received some passing attention.

The new **Greenwich Village Follies of 1920** (8-30-20, Greenwich Village) was quickly so much in demand it was rushed uptown. Opulent James Reynolds sets and complementary Robert Locher costumes transported audiences to 14th-century Russia, an Oriental perfumerie, and an Empire-style carnival. Bert Savoy, who had replaced the more subtle Julian Eltinge as New York's reigning female impersonator, swished about, spoofing the real beauties of the more traditional numbers. Phil Baker accompanied his comic monologues with his accordion playing. The songs, mostly A. Baldwin Sloane's customarily humdrum material, were handled by Frank Crumit and by Howard Marsh, who soon gained recognition in *Blossom Time* and went on to sing the leads in *The Student Prince* and *Show Boat. The Greenwich Village Follies* was always to have a blind spot—or a deaf ear—in the song department. But it had enough other attractions to run twenty-four weeks before touring.

August's last arrival was **The Sweetheart Shop** (8-31-20, Knickerbocker). It had enjoyed an unprecedented engagement in Chicago. In April *Variety*'s Chicago man noted that not since *Madame Sherry* had "A musical premiere been such an instantaneous, unanimous and vigorous success." By the end of May he called the show "the biggest musical comedy money-maker in America." But on Broadway it was a seven-week failure. Anne Caldwell's book, depicting the romance of Natalie Blythe (Helen Ford) and an artist, Julian Lorimer (Joseph Lertora), was dismissed as "infantile" and Hugo Felix' score as little better. The show remains of interest because one of the Gershwin interpolations, "Waiting For The Sun To Come Out," was the first published coupling of George's music with his brother Ira's lyrics. Still unknown and not wanting to ride George's coattails, Ira took his other brother's and his sister's first names and called himself Arthur Francis.

. . .

Born on December 6, 1896, **Ira Gershwin** (Israel Gershvin) was the oldest of the Gershwin children, two years older than George. The shy scholar of the family, Ira took occasional courses at City College but never earned a degree. His first piece, a satire entitled "The Shrine," was accepted by *The Smart Set*. He served a brief stint as a vaudeville critic on *The Clipper*. By this time he had turned his hand to lyrics.

. . .

The lines to "Waiting For The Sun To Come Out" gave no hint of the clever, manipulating word-master Ira shortly became. But George's music distinctly sounded his new note.

Little Miss Charity (9-2-20, Belmont) had a cute twist for the rags-to-riches theme. It made Angel Butterfield (Juanita Fletcher), its heroine, rich—so rich she advertises for help in giving away her wealth. Three shady characters— "Dickey" Foster (Frederick Raymond, Jr.), "Fingers" Clay (Frank Moulan), and Amy Shirley (Marjorie Gateson)—appear, intending to trick Angel out of her fortune. But Angel's enthusiasm for her plan to build a model village to accommodate poor rent-strikers wins them over. By reforming and by marrying Angel, "Dickey," the hero, goes from poverty to riches. Edward Clark's dialogue was on a par with his popular *Honey Girl* libretto. But the score was weak. And the cast's only two names—the fading Moulan and Miss Gateson—were not sufficient draws. *Little Miss Charity* threw in the towel after nine weeks.

Four nights later the long-heralded Efrem Zimbalist musical opened. Zimbalist, a distinguished violinist, had read Joseph Herbert's *The Scourge of the Sea*, a satire on the old Spanish romantic drama, and thought it would make an excellent operetta. The piece opened with a long, rhymed prologue, outlining the play, recited by the vagabond, El Remandodo. As the vagabond tells it, Pedro and Serafin both love Manuela. Manuela picks Pedro. But necessity drives Pedro into piracy, and Serafin uses this treacherously to win away Manuela. Pedro is caught and conscripted as punishment while Manuela is compelled to accept Serafin. Herbert, and probably Zimbalist, did not expect the story to be taken seriously. The producers wouldn't take the text at all. Somewhere between the show's inception and the show's arrival at the Casino, they threw away the old text. Herbert produced a new libretto based on *Les Surprises de divorce*. By the time the high-minded *Scourge of the Sea* settled down on 39th Street, it had become the simpleminded **Honeydew** (9-6-20, Casino). The basic plot told of complications that arise when the father-in-law of a newly remarried man takes the man's first wife for his own bride. Honeydew's appropriately simple-

minded hero, Henry Honeydew—the name had also been used in *Miss Millions* (12-9-19)—composes cantatas on the love-life of insects. His father-in-law, a prominent exterminator, convinces him to turn one motif into a pop tune, "The June Bug," which can be used by termite-killers as a premium. Hal Forde clowned in the title role. The critics praised the show, extolling Zimbalist's music. "Sunshine Of Love," a waltz, and "Drop Me A Line," a fox trot, are good examples of Zimbalist's style. Although the show was one of the year's biggest hits, the truth is that the music was little better than the book. Had it not come to town with Zimbalist's name attached to it, critics probably would have given it far less attention and praise. Zimbalist may have realized this, or he may have been disgusted with the whole affair. Whatever his reasons, he never again wrote a score for the musical theatre. And the rumor, current at the opening of *Honeydew*, that Misha Elman would follow Kreisler and Zimbalist in writing for Broadway, never materialized.

On September 17 *Variety* reported that business on the road had started off poorly. Figures all across the country were disappointing. But for the moment Broadway trade was still satisfactory.

On the 24th, putting ill-feelings aside, George M. Cohan gamely announced he intended to continue his revue series. Moreover, he had succeeded in reuniting Weber and Fields, and they would star in the new edition. The reunion never took place, and the new Cohan revue never went into rehearsal. Whether the falling out of the great comedians was beyond repair will never be known. For publication, Cohan explained that he could not secure female principals of the caliber of his two old masters.

Pitter Patter (9-28-20, Longacre) was a musical version of William Collier and Grant Stewart's 1906 *Caught in the Rain*. The musical retelling stayed fourteen weeks. As he did fourteen years before, Dick Crawford (William Kent), a disinherited scion, takes work as a soda jerk, falls in love with Muriel Mason (Jane Richardson), fights the villain in a downpour, and saves Mr. Mason (Hugh Chilvers) from financial ruin. The adaptation was by Will M. Hough (who had spent most of his career writing musicals for Chicago). William Friedlander did the music, and the two collaborated on the lyrics. Although most of the action took place in Colorado, one song honored "Baghdad On The Subway," but a finale moved the action to Cuba allowing the cast occasion for "Jazzing Up In Havana."

Act Three: The Birth of the Modern Musical, 1914–1921

George LeMaire lured Eddie Cantor and Bert Williams away from Ziegfeld and presented them on September 29 at the Shuberts' Winter Garden. He called his offering **Broadway Brevities of 1920,** hinting it was the beginning of yet one more series. Although he employed two of the greatest entertainers of the day, and while the music included three George Gershwin interpolations and one Irving Berlin song, Le Maire could not quite put the thing together. Cantor and Williams helped keep the review alive thirteen weeks. Cantor for the moment had left Ziegfeld, both still clinging bitterly to their positions about the Equity strike. Hoping to effect a reconciliation, Cantor had made a surprise appearance in the *Follies* during its first week, but left insisting Ziegfeld would not give him suitable material. In the 1919 *Follies* Cantor did a popular skit called "The Osteopath's Office." With minimal alteration it appeared in the *Brevities* as "The Dentist's Office." Ziegfeld sued and won. The sketch was dropped. Two fine Williams' numbers came out of this evening, "The Moon Shines On The Moonshine" (Francis De Witt and Robert Hood Bowers) and "I Want To Know Where Tosti Went (When He Said Goodbye)" (Chris Smith). No one could guess that this would be Williams' last important New York appearance. Eighteen months later he caught cold while on tour and within a few days he was dead—only forty-nine years old.

F. Ray Comstock and Morris Gest, looking to repeat their preceding year's success of *Aphrodite,* brought **Mecca** into the Century on October 4 with elaborate fanfares. Its authors were English, and much was made of its being offered to Broadway before London saw it. It was another Arabian Nights tale, extravagantly mounted. Fokine choreographed. It pleased the Hippodrome–Radio City Music Hall mentality, and ran five months.

The Corts and Orlob having gone their separate ways, James Hanley was called in to provide the score for the Corts' next show, **Jim Jam Jems** (10-4-20, Cort). The show's music was no better than in the earlier Cort-Orlob shows, and neither was the book. Cyrus Ward (Stanley Forde) keeps his niece, June (Ada May Weeks), carefully away from all society, but Johnny Case (Frank Fay), a newspaper reporter hoping to sniff out a scandal, takes her on the town. Luckily Cort hired a band of brilliant young comedians—Joe E. Miller, Joe E. Brown, Ned Sparks, and Fay. Together they made the book seem funnier than it was. Miss Weeks' attractive dancing also helped. *Jim Jam*

Jems ran 105 performances and toured, changing its name to *Hello, Lester!* to capitalize on *Listen, Lester*'s popularity.

For all the changes the war had produced there was still plenty of room for old-time innocence and humor. The frame of *Cinderella on Broadway* had suggested as much. Fred Stone proved it hands down when he came in with **Tip Top** (10-5-20, Globe) and ran out the season. His success was all the more remarkable in view of the show's weaknesses. Anne Caldwell and R.H. Burnside's book was several notches below the material they had provided for *Jack o' Lantern* and *Chin-Chin*. It so lacked direction, the meager story line often got lost. Some critics looked on the evening as a revue. It almost was. The curtain rose on the trial of Miss Puff (Helen Rich), a cat, presided over by Judge Tiger (Oscar Ragland). Miss Puff had been a fairy, but she had been turned into a cat for failing to tie wedding knots for Alice (Gladys Caldwell) and Dick (Scott Welsh) and Jinia (Teresa Valerio) and Tip Top. Alice is the daughter of Jonas Barker (Ragland), a shopkeeper, and Dick, her boyfriend, is an employee. Jinia is the girl who sweeps the shop, while Tip Top is its not very handyman. An explosion propels Tip Top on stage. Sitting up, he notices a lady in the shop. Apologetically he explains:

Tip Top: I put in one raisin too many.
Adele: What on earth were you doing?
Tip Top: Making the hard liquor to put in the soft drink.
Adele: I'd like to know you better—Who are you?
Tip Top: I'm Tip Top
Adele: I didn't say how are you, I said, who are you?
Tip Top: I'm Tip Top
Adele: I'm glad you are—but what's your name?
Tip Top: Tip Top—it used to be Tipton Topping, but things go so fast nowdays, folks ain't got time to say it, so they call me Tip Top.

A shyster lawyer, I. Skinnem (Gus Minton), visits the store and informs Barker that Dick has inherited $5,000,000. The two conspire to keep Dick from learning about his wealth, concealing the letter Skinnem should have delivered. They hope to find a way to share the money themselves. But Tip Top discovers the letter and shows it to Dick. The résumé makes the plot seem more important than it effectively was. It was frequently sidetracked by the specialties of Stone and the Duncan Sisters (who portrayed the Terrible Twins, Bad and Worse). Stone disguised himself at one time or another as a fortune teller, a burglar, and a cigar store Indian. He fell off a horse and "walked" on his shoulder and ear. He also danced with tiny Violet Zell "clinging to his insteps." The Duncan Sisters sang and danced demurely, while sixteen "London Palace Girls," directed by John Tiller, displayed their precision movements. Six saxophonists known as the Brown Brothers played and clowned, with much clowning by a particularly lugubrious brother. The authors were aware how slipshod the writing was. The finale harked back to *Hello, Broadway* (12-25-14):

Barker: What on earth have you fellows been searching for?
Sharpe: We've been looking for the plot of the show.
Smart: And we can't find a sign of it.
Dick: Here it is (*points to Tip Top*)
Tip Top: Ain't I awful.

Another weakness was Ivan Caryll's score, which offered nothing as good as "Wait Till The Cows Come Home." Two interpolations for the Duncan Sisters enjoyed the most success—"Humming" (Louis Breau and Ray Henderson) and "Feather Your Nest" (Kendis and Brockman, and Howard Johnson).

A second Caryll score was played six nights later in **Kissing Time** (10-11-20, Lyric). While Caryll's songs sang of "Mimi Jazz" and "Keep A Fox Trot For Me," his heart clearly belonged to an earlier day and his melodies were no longer strikingly memorable. George V. Hobart's book was based on a French-style comedy by Adolf Phillip and Edward A. Paulton. Robert Perronet (Paul Frawley) has Clarice (Edith Taliaferro) pose as his wife when his employer tells him only married men rise in business. The employer falls in love with Clarice and so does Robert. Robert wins when it develops Clarice is the girl his family has planned for him to marry. The show ran nine weeks.

When **Mary** (10-18-20, Knickerbocker) opened in Washington the preceding spring it had been *The House That Jack Built*. But with George M. Cohan at the helm no one was too startled by the change of title. One of the best loved and best remembered of the decade's shows, it was not as great a Broadway success as it is commonly supposed. Five of the season's musicals ran longer, including the more or less forgotten *Good Times, Honeydew,* and *Tip Top*. Undoubtedly its long

pre-Broadway tour and its four road companies (one of which was on the boards before the main company reached New York) cut into sales at the Knickerbocker. But its critical reception by the New York press didn't help. The consensus was that the book bogged down too often. Though it was no leap forward in libretto writing, its central position was, luckily for the twenties, ahead of its time. The authors could not foresee the blight trailers and mobile homes would cause someday. Still, Jack Keene (Jack McGowan) is convinced he can make a fortune with Gaston Marceau's suggestion that he build "portable houses" to sell for $1,300 apiece. Madeline (Florrie Millership), a divorcée with eyes for Jack, and Tommy (Alfred Gerrard), a playboy, with eyes for Madeline, look at the model and reject it, even though they concede "That Might Have Satisfied Grandma." But Jack finds support from his mother's secretary, Mary (Janet Velie). Both recall wistfully, "That Farm Out In Kansas." Tommy proposes to Madeline, promising to do "Anything You Want To Do, Dear." But Madeline is not prepared to say yes. Gaston (Charles Judels) enters. He claims to be an incorrigible womanizer, falling in love "Every Time I Meet A Lady." He, too, falls for Madeline. To get his mind off the situation, Tommy offers to teach the neighborhood girls how to "Tom Tom Toddle." When he and his companions dance off onto the veranda, Jack and Mary find themselves alone. It is obvious to everyone but Jack that Mary is in love with him. He thoughtlessly adds to her unhappiness when he caressingly details his plans for "The Love Nest" that will make him rich and fails to find room for her there. He announces he is going to Kansas to start building the houses. Six months later Mary is courted on every side, but she spurns all the young men's attention. Finally, misinterpreting a suggestion of Mrs. Keene's, she consents to marry Gaston. Jack returns. Oil has been found on his land, and he will soon be rich. He realizes he loves Mary, but assumes the realization has come too late. However, Mrs. Keene (Georgia Caine), who has determined to marry Gaston herself, prevails on Mary to break her engagement. Tom and Madeline, assuring everyone, "We'll Have A Wonderful Party," announce they will marry. Mary and Jack join the other couples in proclaiming, "Better than a palace with a gilded dome is a love nest you can call home." What made the show was Louis Hirsch's finest score and Cohan's staging. Anytime the book faltered Cohan sent his dancers spinning and tapping across the stage. Because of the show's long tryout its hit song, "The Love Nest," preceded it into town. By the time *Mary* opened the tune had swept the country. But it was merely the top number in a scintillating score. Legend has it the title song was meant to be the show's hit. During the tryout it was moved to several spots in an attempt to promote it. It ended, amusingly, with Mary herself singing it to the men's chorus as the plaint of a too much wooed young lady. The other songs included all the types that a 1920 musical hereafter could be expected to have and that were ridiculed so accurately years later in such musicals as *Lend an Ear* (12-16-48) and *The Boy Friend* (9-30-54). There was a dance number, "Tom Tom Toddle"; a chorus of celebration, "We'll Have A Wonderful Party"; an exchange of emotions, "Anything You Want To Do, Dear" (with a lyric that promised whenever Madeline is blue, Tom would feel melancholy, too; whenever she feels like feeling gay "all you have to do is say, dear, That you'd like to have me happy and snappy for you"). The show made its audiences happy for 219 performances.

Raymond Hitchcock and Julia Sanderson led the cast of **Hitchy-Koo 1920** (10-19-20, New Amsterdam), which also included a young singer, Grace Moore. It was almost aggressively old-fashioned, extolling "the little New York we used to know." Jerome Kern's music was strangely elementary and drab. The titles gave away the mood—"Chick! Chick! Chick!," "Ding Dong It's Kissing Time," "Buggy Riding" and "The Old Town." The public applauded for two months, then the show went on the road.

Joseph Cawthorn, Edna May Oliver, Oscar Shaw, Joseph Santley, and Ivy Sawyer—an all star line-up—couldn't save **The Half Moon** (11-1-20, Liberty). William Le Baron's plot was almost too simple. It was riches-to-riches. Rich Henry Hobson (Cawthorn) threatens to disinherit his son, Charlie (Santley), when he falls in love with a rich, seemingly snobbish Boston Brahmin. But Miss Bolton (Miss Sawyer) turns out not to be a snob, so papa Hobson relents. Le Baron's lyrics may have alienated an important part of the audience. For Hobson asks what the matter is with women now: "They're crazy to vote, but don't know how." Victor Jacobi's music was dull. Six weeks, and *The Half Moon* sailed away.

In one respect Hobson was wrong. Only 35 percent of the newly enfranchised women bothered to vote. Their ballots seemingly made no difference. Warren Gamaliel Harding was elected to replace

Wilson with a majority of over seven million votes. His total was double that of his opponent, James Cox. One politician concluded, "It wasn't a landslide, it was an earthquake." Broadway felt a few tremors of its own. The theatre was no longer booming. On election week *Variety* recorded that some Broadway shows had begun to lower ticket prices. Nonetheless the onslaught of musicals continued.

Alice Delysia, the rage of London and Paris, brought in her Continental hit, **Afgar** (11-8-20, Central), and for five months theatregoers bought tickets to watch Miss Delysia form a union for harem odalisques and provide a husband for every girl. The European score was supplemented by James Monaco's "Caresses" and several McCarthy and Tierney tunes, the best of which was "Why Don't You?"

Jimmie, the Harbach-Hammerstein-Mandel-Stothart musical, followed.

Impoverished British aristocrats who opened their castles to the public after World War II would sympathize with Countess Antonia-Celestina-Elizabeth-Selana-Wilhelmina of Pardove (alias Lady Billy) who poses as her gardener's son when she shows tourists her palace. John Smith (Boyd Marshall), visiting Pardove, suggests the "young man" go to America as a boy soprano. Lady Billy falls in love with Smith and takes his advice. Ultimately, she abandons her trouser role and marries John. Zelda Sears, who wrote the book, was a Jill of several trades. An actress and a director as well, she wrote a number of solidly professional librettos, but almost always to inferior music. **Lady Billy** (12-14-20, Liberty) was no exception. Harold Levey's score was leaden. But the show's star, Mitzi, had enough following to allow the musical to run out the season.

Sally (12-21-20, New Amsterdam), one of the most magical of all American musicals, was the year's biggest hit, running 570 performances. The *World* called it "nothing less than idealized musical comedy." The show had everything. As producer, it had Florenz Ziegfeld, who knew "a little more than any of his competitors the secret of bringing beauty to his stage." It had Joseph Urban mountings. It had Leon Errol and Walter Catlett for comedy. It had the entrancing Marilyn Miller as Sally. (With this show she became Broadway's undisputed queen of musical comedy.) It had a fine Guy Bolton book. It had ballet music by Victor Herbert. And most of all it had an incandescent Jerome Kern score. The *Times* was not alone in suggesting Ziegfeld wanted his people to "put together a pretty little piece after the pattern and in the modest manner of 'Irene!' " They did better, though the resemblances were there. Wealthy Mrs. Ten Broek (played in the original by Ziegfeld's magnificent mannequin, Dolores) brings a group of poor girls looking for work to the Elm Tree Alley Inn in Greenwich Village. A dishwasher is needed, so Sally is selected. A fellow employee is "Connie," the exiled Duke Constantine of Czechogovinia (Errol). Blair Farquar (Irving Fisher), scion of the Long Island Farquars, arrives to book a party. He is captivated by Sally and urges her never to be dismayed but rather to "Look For The Silver Lining." Sally dances for joy, further impressing Blair and Connie. Connie, as Duke, is to attend a gala at the Farquars'. A theatrical agent, Otis Hooper (Catlett), who was to supply the principal entertainment for the soirée arrives and confesses his prima ballerina has backed out. Hooper also has noticed Sally dance and decides to pass her off as his leading lady. At the gala Sally is nervous, insisting to the guests she is just a "Wild Rose." Blair and Sally, whom Blair at first fails to recognize, recall the happiness of their first encounter, "Whip-poor-will." When she teases Blair, he angrily berates her. Thoroughly nonplused she drops her disguise. Otis, however, promptly produces a silver lining by disclosing he has arranged for Sally to dance in the Ziegfeld Follies. She triumphs in the Butterfly Ballet. Hooper and his girl friend; Connie and Mrs. Ten Broek; and Sally and Blair all head for the Little Church Around the Corner for a triple nuptial.

The resemblances to *Irene* were somewhat coincidental. Wodehouse and Bolton had planned a Princess Theatre show with a working title, *The Little Thing*, about a girl who dreams of stardom as she washes dishes. Ziegfeld was quick to see the possibilities of a part for Marilyn Miller and chance to promote the *Follies* in a musical just as he had plugged his cabaret in the *Follies*. Commitments kept Wodehouse from helping with the rewrite. Bolton did the job alone. Though Leon Errol was costarred, his part of Connie was a last-minute addition. Ziegfeld had promised George M. Cohan that Errol would be free for Cohan's revue. When Cohan's show failed to materialize, Ziegfeld, appreciating Errol's value as both a comedian and a director, had the role hastily inserted.

Curiously, much of the score, brilliant as it was, was not written for the show. Sally's opener, "You Can't Keep A Good Girl Down," and the closing "The Church Around The Corner" had been blocked out for *The Little Thing*. Two of the best songs, "Whip-poor-will" and "Look For The Silver Lining," were brought over from a fiasco called *Zip Goes a Million*. "The Lorelei" had been dropped from a Kern-Caldwell show. "Bill," discarded from *Oh, Lady! Lady!*, would have been in it if Kern had had his way, but he had to agree Miss Miller's voice could not properly project it. Of the show's better numbers, only the pulsating opening and the haunting "Wild Rose" were composed with *Sally* in mind. If Urban had little leeway with the finale at the Church Around the Corner, he could give freer rein to his imagination in designing the Elm Tree Inn, a Long Island garden, and backstage settings, while no restraints, but his good taste, bridled his ideas for the Butterfly Ballet. The show was revived in 1948 at the height of Broadway's serious pretensions. Brought in as the hot weather approached, without Ziegfeld or Urban or Miller, it had no chance at all.

Nora Bayes returned to please the loyal Bayes' following for three months with **Her Family Tree** (12-27-20, Lyric). It reminded many of *As You Were* (1-27-20). The action begins "at a party at the home of Nora Bayes, overlooking New Jersey, but not overlooking it altogether." A ouija board and a crystal ball hurtle the hostess and her guests back through the ages to see if Miss Bayes "might have been a goldfish or a bluebird, or a bluefish or a Goldberg." Knowledgeable theatre-goers remembered that Miss Bayes' real name was Dora Goldberg.

Just before the year faded away, the Shuberts produced **The Passing Show of 1921** (12-29-20, Winter Garden). They had skipped a 1920 edition—an ominous indication in itself—and then brought their customary summer attraction in at the dead of winter—a further sign all was not what it once had been for the big annuals. Little effort was made to buck the advances of the *Follies*. Instead, the 1921 edition was a throwback to the Shuberts' very first version. Willie and Eugene Howard were brought back for comedy, most of which burlesqued current Broadway offerings. Just as a good part of the 1912 version had been devoted to "The Ballet of 1830," so "Dream Fantasies" occupied much of the new edition's second act. Jean Schwartz' score was weak, but "My Sunny Tennessee" (Bert Kalmar and Harry Ruby) received some play. Although cast changes were frequent (Marie Dressler opened but did not remain long), the show was enough in demand to keep the Winter Garden lit for six months.

1921 arrived and with it the promise of the soon-to-be inaugurated Harding of a return to "normalcy." An agricultural depression had darkened 1920 for farmers, and now it was spreading throughout the whole nation. Broadway was not to like "normalcy."

But the year began pleasantly with a well-received revival of *Erminie* (5-10-86). The old show, January's only musical, proved still viable when it opened at the Park on the 3rd. Old timers could rejoice that Francis Wilson was still around to re-create his original role of Cadeaux, while De Wolf Hopper played Ravennes.

The Shuberts and Ziegfeld brought more cabaret entertainments to town at the beginning of February. It was soon obvious that Prohibition was hurting these roof "dinner-theatres." Their days were numbered, and the numbers were few indeed. Thanks largely to Eddie Cantor, normally a Ziegfeld star, the Shuberts had a modest success, but Ziegfeld, Urban, and a cast that included Oscar Shaw, Anna Wheaton, the Fairbanks Twins, and the pianist Edythe Baker could not make a go of their evening.

February also saw two regular musicals appear. Both were a little old-fashioned, but the more backward of the two was the more popular. Mignon Latour, **The Rose Girl** (Mabel Withee), flees to Paris to escape having to marry a plant foreman. Victor, the Marquis de la Roche (Charles Purcell), runs after her, woos her, and wins her. The music was as unoriginal and unimaginative as the plot. Nonetheless the show, which opened on the 11th, played fourteen weeks at the spanking new Ambassador Theatre, aided by the light-hearted performing of Marjorie Gateson and some light-footed gypsy dancing.

Lew Fields and Mollie King could not make a go of **Blue Eyes** (2-21-21, Casino). The beautiful eyes belong to Dorothy Manners (Miss King), who knocks down a struggling writer, Bobby Brett (Ray Raymond), with her automobile. When she visits him while he is convalescing, they fall in love. Both pretend to high stations in life, but in the end both are content simply to have each other. As had happened with *The Rose Girl* and many other shows, the clowning of a secondary performer—this time the dependable Andrew Tombes as Bobby's studio mate—and lively dancing won many of the best notices.

Sigmund Romberg had less luck with **Love Birds** (3-15-21, Apollo) than with *The Magic Melody* (11-11-19). Edgar Allan Woolf's book recounted how Allene Charteris (Elizabeth Hines), forbidden to marry Hal Sterling (Barrett Greenwood), and refusing to marry her parents' selection, runs away to the Emir Duckin's Persian harem, where Hal comes to rescue her. Although Romberg again coproduced the show and assuredly picked the story himself, he received no inspiration from it. The score could have been transferred to a Winter Garden revue without anyone's noticing. The show garnered 105 performances. Its failure was the last straw for Wilner and Romberg. They had not succeeded with either Romberg's own musicals or with straight plays they had produced. For the time being Romberg was forced to swallow his pride and return to the Shubert fold as a staff writer. When the show left New York it was not sent to Cain's Warehouse, instead Pat Rooney and Marian Bent, who had played secondary roles that allowed them to bring their popular soft shoe and light comic routines from vaudeville, bought the rights to the show, rewrote it to emphasize their parts, and toured it with a modicum of success.

The Right Girl (3-15-21, Times Square) opened the same night as *Love Birds*, and played a week less. The Right Girl was Dera Darcy (Carolyn Thomson) who loves a gilded youth, Henry Watkins (Robert Woolsey), even when he loses his money, and keeps on loving him when he becomes rich once more. The score was by Percy Wenrich, whose Broadway material never rivaled his Tin Pan Alley successes.

It's Up to You (3-24-21, Casino) used songs by the Hippodrome's late Manuel Klein to fill out a skimpy and dull J. L. McManus score. It also used some devices *Mary* and *Blue Eyes* had employed to fill out its plot. Ned (Charles King) and Dick (Douglas Leavitt) pretend to be rich in order to win Mrs. Van Lando Hollistar's consent to marry her daughters, Harriet (Betty Pierce) and Ethel (Ruth Mary Lockwood). A wild real estate scheme makes them genuinely rich in time for the curtain. Each of the three acts was given a name —"Laying the Foundation," "Building," and "The House Warming." But audiences weren't amused. *It's Up to You* collapsed after three weeks.

Rudolf Friml had a flop with April's only musical, **June Love,** which followed *Mary* into the Knickerbocker on the 25th. June Love (Else Adler) is a pretty widow determined to make Jack Garrison (W.B. Davidson) her next husband. He thinks she is married and only when he discovers she is not does he propose. Friml's score, about his worst, was so dreary only four songs were published.

Although the season was growing late, two more big hits were to come. May 3 welcomed one of them at the Cohan, Abe Erlanger's production of **Two Little Girls in Blue**. The little girls were the Sartoris twins, Dolly and Polly (played in the show by the Fairbanks Twins), who would like to sail to India to claim an inheritance. Since they have only enough money for one passage, they take turns making appearances on deck and in the public rooms. When the girls fall in love with Robert Barker (Oscar Shaw) and Jerry Lloyd (Fred Santley), the confusion is compounded, since the men, unaware they are courting twins, often pursue the wrong girl. By the end of the voyage, the girls and their men are engaged, and the extra fare taken care of. The best numbers were by Vincent Youmans, his first Broadway musical; and all the lyrics were by Ira Gershwin (still writing as Arthur Francis), his first complete show. George Gershwin had obtained jobs for both of them, and the two managed to come up with solid material, even though the director, Ned Wayburn, would only tell them the type of song he wanted with no details of how it would fit into the story. As David Ewen quotes Ira, "Obviously to Wayburn neither the play nor the numbers were the thing—only tempo mattered."

. . .

Vincent Youmans was born in New York September 27, 1898—one day after George Gershwin—into a family of well-to-do hat-store owners. Educated at private schools and given piano lessons from boyhood, he rejected an engineering career his family had planned for him and took a job on Wall Street. His nine-to-five routine permitted him to spend his evenings composing. In World War I he served at the Great Lakes Naval Station, where the bandleader encouraged the young sailor. One piece he wrote at the time was featured by John Philip Sousa. After the war Youmans tucked it away, to use it a decade later as "Hallelujah." More than any of his contemporaries Youmans made constant reuse of a limited number of melodies. A song that failed in one show was revised for a later show. As a result, the body of published songs he left behind is startlingly small.

. . .

Two Youmans numbers were the cream of the score, "Dolly" (sung in the show by the men to whichever girl they were pursuing at the moment) and the titillating "Oh Me, Oh My" (a duet of Robert and Dolly). Ira's lyrics, freer than his earlier material, were still not vintage Gershwin. But the music—angular, simple, repetitive phrases with changing harmonies—was pure Youmans. *Two Little Girls in Blue* played through the summer and went on tour.

All the publicity the soldier-composer Gitz Rice received during the war was little help when he and B.C. Hilliam—of *Buddies* (10-27-19)—combined to write a score to go with Hilliam and L.A. Browne's trite book for **Princess Virtue** (5-4-21, Central). The story described Liane Damerest's search for happiness in Paris. Liane (Tessa Kosta) finds it with Bruce Crawford (Bradford Kirkbride), her childhood sweetheart from back home. Two meager weeks was all the show managed.

Biff! Bing! Bang! (5-9-21, Ambassador), a soldier revue that had been prepared for Canadian troops overseas, came in as part of a cross-country tour. Like every other service show before it, it leaned heavily on burlesques of army life, and routines with soldiers dressed as girls.

The same night saw **Phoebe of Quality Street** (5-9-21, Shubert), a musical version of the James Barrie play. Barrie's charm proved elusive. The *Evening Post* lamented the musical "lacks action—and Quality." It was quickly withdrawn.

Oscar Straus' **The Last Waltz** (5-10-21, Century) danced in with its libretto adapted to give it an American naval officer as hero. Its score assured its success. Walter Woolf and Eleanor Painter starred.

On May 19, the Southern Light Opera Company brought its homegrown operetta version of **The Three Musketeers** to the Manhattan Opera House, where it failed to elicit any interest.

Nor was there much interest at first in **Shuffle Along** (5-23-21, 63rd St.). The show had been put together after a chance meeting in Philadelphia by two black teams, Noble Sissle and Eubie Blake (for lyrics and music) and Flournoy Miller and Aubrey Lyles (for libretto). An angel was found and a limited amount of money made available. For costumes they purchased clothes from a folded show (*Roly-Boly Eyes*). The scenery was minimal. By hook or crook the company managed a series of one-night stands in New Jersey and Pennsylvania, always a step or two ahead of foreclosure, until it was felt the show was ready for New York. Although blacks had performed on Broadway and all-Negro shows had played in principal houses, in some respects there was more discrimination since the war. All the show could book was a dilapidated theatre, far from the main Broadway crowds. First-nighters were probably reminded by the plot of old Williams and Walker, and Cole and Johnson shows. Steve Jenkins (Miller) and Sam Peck (Lyles), partners in a Jimtown grocery store, are rivals for the mayoralty—though each has assured the other he will be the winner's chief of police. Jenkins, helped by a sharper of a campaign manager, wins. True to his word, he appoints Peck chief of police. But Peck soon realizes he has nothing to do, and the two fall out. Their corruption and inefficiency, topped off now by their noisy squabbling, are too much even for lackadaisical Jimtown. Harry Walton (Roger Matthews) announces he is a reform candidate, and every citizen responds, "I'm Just Wild About Harry." Jenkins and Peck are given the boot. The book represented no step forward for the musical theatre, but the music certainly did. Blake's was a foot-stomping score. Its rhythms provoked an orgy of giddy dancing that had audiences shouting for more tap routines, soft shoes, buck and wing, and precision numbers. The hit, of course, was "I'm Just Wild About Harry." Originally conceived as a waltz, it was much more at home as a fast-moving fox trot. Romberg and Friml tried the same trick for several years, but so innate was the waltz to their thinking that nothing productive resulted. But for Blake the waltz was alien, and his native rhythms, just coming to be understood by the more advanced critics and public, offered the more logical frame for his melodies. Though "I'm Just Wild About Harry" alone is remembered, the score was first class all the way. Whether in a stunning, ahead-of-its-time love ballad like "Love Will Find A Way" (sung by Matthews and Lottie Gee as his girl, Jessie) or in the racy festivity of "Bandana Days" (essentially a chorus number), Blake's melodic gift and taste were unfailing. The brighter critics hailed the show, and the public slowly began to find its way uptown. Then midnight performances were added on Wednesdays. Theatre and society people caught these late shows and spread the word. Suddenly *Shuffle Along* was a smash. By the time it was through it had reached 504 performances on Broadway alone. The show launched a flock of great names—Florence Mills, Josephine Baker, Hall Johnson. Singlehandedly, *Shuffle Along* made black shows voguish, or at least, acceptable. A 1951–52 "revival" with new music and a different plot lasted half a week.

Three more revues followed. Fanchon and Marco, a dancing team, brought **Sunkist** (5-23-21, Globe) from California. It had fun with the movies and the whole Hollywood scene, but it

failed to please the public as much as it delighted the critics.

On the other hand, **Snapshots of 1921** (6-2-21, Selwyn)—with Nora Bayes, Lew Fields, De Wolf Hopper, Lulu McConnell, and Gilda Gray—gave the public just the high-class vaudeville it sought. Songs saluted reigning hits. One proclaimed, "Every Girlie Wants To Be A Sally," while "Irene Rosensteen" noted "My little Yiddle, Irene [doesn't] live in a palace/or wear blue gowns of Alice." E. Ray Goetz and George Gershwin combined to look back "On The Brim Of Her Old-fashioned Bonnet" and ahead with a "Futuristic Melody." A spectacle number advertised "Beautiful Feathers Make Beautiful Birds." *Snapshots* played six weeks.

The Broadway Whirl (6-8-21, Times Square) and **The Whirl of New York** (6-13-21, Winter Garden) were the last shows of the theatrical year. Their titles may have created some confusion, and neither show did a land-office business. *The Broadway Whirl*, a revue, had old and new favorites contributing bits and pieces. Richard Carle (no longer quite the star he once was), Blanche Ring (still big box-office), and Charles Winninger (on the way up) headed the cast. Harry Tierney composed most of the music. *The Whirl of New York* was "an expanded version" of *The Belle of New York* (9-28-97). Expansion consisted of updating ("Sherrie's Tiffin Shop" replaced "Smyler's" just as the real Sherry's had outlasted Byler's), new interpolations by Al Goodman and Lew Pollack, and a series of vaudeville turns.

It was a memorable season.

In fact, it was a memorable seven years. While Europe warred, while old idols fell and new gods arose, Broadway danced merrily to an eloquent group of pipers. In seven years these masters of the American Musical Theatre had shaped the new American musical. It was a musical endearingly simple, honest, and direct. It told a believable story about everyday people. Its songs fitted in smoothly on stage and almost hummed themselves outside the theatre. Of course there were still composers and singers of the old arioso school. And there were still producers and directors of another old school willing to throw in anything as long as it worked—and mood and logic be hanged. But Broadway remained expansive enough to accommodate these schools as well.

Yet, without warning, something went awry. Not only had the country slipped into an economic depression, it seemed stymied emotionally and intellectually as well. "Normalcy" looked like a euphemism for stagnation. Postwar exhaustion and a concurrent ferment of changing values left audiences uncertain what to applaud. It was as if just at this point the great pipers asked to be paid in the very applause and understanding Broadway could not give. The pipers had nowhere else to ply their trade. But, unrewarded, they played an indifferent tune.

Broadway took three years to find itself, to sweep out the cobwebs and rearrange its house. Almost paralleling the Wilson and Harding administrations, seven years of feast gave way to three seasons of relative famine.

7

INTERMISSION
The Cinderella Era
1921-1924

A baffling and abrupt creative slump began at the opening of the 1921–22 season and was over just as suddenly with the onset of 1924–25 theatrical year. Reasons for previous spurts of creativity and for previous declines—financial panics, booms, wars, migrations—were more or less apparent. None adequately explained these three years of treading water. World War I had receded far enough into the past not to matter any longer (though audiences had tired of war stories), and the post-war recession was not especially severe. Theatregoers remained, ethnically and socially, the same pleasure-seekers who had been lining up at box office for the last decade. Those who had abandoned live theatre for movies had done so some years back, and sound would not come to movies to lure away more patrons until the twenties were almost over. Radio, while growing rapidly, could not present similar competition, and was, in any case, more likely to take away audiences from films than from the living theatre.

An upheaval in musical fashions might be part of the explanation. Commercial ragtime was dying; commercial jazz had not yet found itself—nor, as we shall see, had most critics yet found jazz. But the musical theatre was never completely dependent on any one lyric language, so the transition could hardly have been convulsive. True, Reginald De Koven, representing more traditional composition, had died a year before, but he had long ceased to be an active or important figure. Ivan Caryll and Gustave Kerker, both written out, were to die in

1921 and 1923 respectively; while Victor Herbert, his creativity not quite exhausted, as *Orange Blossoms* was to show, would die in May 1924. Regrettably, two younger composers, Victor Jacobi and Louis Hirsch, were also dead by the time these three years had passed—Jacobi almost at the start and Hirsch two weeks before Herbert. But Jerome Kern, Irving Berlin, Rudolf Friml, and Sigmund Romberg, all in their mid-thirties to early forties, could be expected to continue providing the fine material Broadway was growing accustomed to. Best of all, exciting newcomers were appearing from every corner.

Yet something clearly went wrong. Perhaps Elizabeth Marbury had foreseen the problem in a 1917 interview. At that time she suggested that Kern, who then had five successful musicals competing against each other, would no longer be fresh or original in five or six years. Happily, Kern and other leading contemporaries had resiliencies beyond Miss Marbury's furthest hopes. But it did seem that these writers, practically to a man, had stopped to catch their breath.

The best material offered the public for the next three years would be for the most part from an occasional importation, or, more likely, from a revue—a form less dependent on sustained creativity. Since 1919 "the deluge of revues" had overwhelmed Broadway. Indeed, revues seemed all our musical stage cared about. It was, though, the last hurrah of extravagant revues.

One point ought to be made before examining

these three seasons. Most critics reacted favorably to almost every musical put before them. Even Alexander Woollcott, Percy Hammond, and Alan Dale, probably the best and toughest of the lot, were easily seduced. In fact, Woollcott confessed to a double standard that judged musical offerings with a conscious leniency. Considering the tone of many reviews, there should have been more smash hits. But a close reading of these columns shows that quite often critics were careful to separate the immediate entertainment value of a piece from any lasting artistic merit. Time and again praise was actually bestowed on the interpreters or, just as often, on other ephemeral aspects of a production—scenery, costumes, or choreography.

1921-1922

Appropriately, in this last hurrah for the spectacular revue, the **Ziegfeld Follies of 1921** (6-21-21, Globe) opened the season. Many a critic, insisting the *Follies* were still improving every year, hailed this edition the "Best of them All." It was an expensive production—the first to cost Ziegfeld over a quarter of a million dollars. By the standards of the day, when an ordinary musical could still be sumptuously mounted for $50,000, it was a mammoth sum. But Joseph Urban's sets and the costumes of James Reynolds—new to the *Follies*—justified the outlay. Two stage pictures were especially praised. One portrayed a 12th-century Persian court in which Florence O'Denishawn was seen as a dancing odalisque. For the other, the entire cast assembled at the opening of the second act to re-create the royal gardens of Versailles in all their splendor. As always, the parade of beautiful girls was enthralling and the comics (in this edition Raymond Hitchcock, W. C. Fields, Ray Dooley, and Fanny Brice) as funny as ever. Charles O'Donnell attempted to tune a recalcitrant piano. Miss Brice and Miss Dooley exchanged blows in one of the era's funnier prizefight skits. Fields introduced "The Professor," a character and a skit he would go on to develop later in vaudeville. But the comic highlight of the evening was "the Barrymores" in *Camille*. Since the Barrymores were busy elsewhere, their understudies assumed their roles for the entire run. Miss Brice graciously took on the title role, Hitchcock played her lover, and Fields became his father—a father patently ill-at-ease with the virtuous precepts he was advocating. Only in its songs

did the *Follies of 1921* betray any falling off of standards. Though Herbert and Friml joined Gene Buck and Dave Stamper to compose the score, the only durable numbers were two interpolations: "Second Hand Rose" (Grant Clarke/James Hanley) and the French "Mon Homme" (Channing Pollock/Maurice Yvain). Both were introduced by Fanny Brice, the latter as "My Man." Both injected a note of poignancy and suggested a facet of Miss Brice's talent not obvious before. Both, moreover, were basically intimate numbers that could have been performed to advantage in scaled-down productions at smaller theatres. It was a point not immediately understood. Unwittingly, Ziegfeld was foretelling the future.

George White's Scandals (7-11-21, Liberty) opened less than a month later. For the second year in a row George Gershwin wrote the score. While Gershwin's unique idiom was clearly heard, none of his songs was exceptional. Nonetheless "South Sea Isles" and "Drifting Along With The Tide" were singled out for some praise. Both were optioned by Charles Cochran for London. White and agile Ann Pennington led the dancers, assisted this year by Lester Allen's clownish stepping. Comedy took a back seat to spectacle, song, and dance. Skits in the *Scandals* customarily were shorter and more broadly comic than those in the *Follies*. Some of the better 1921 sketches recounted the story of Samson and Delilah in slapstick pantomime, covered the mock divorce of Sillyman vs. Sillyman, and had fun with Trotsky's discomfort in the czarist luxury of the Winter Palace. Though the *Scandals* were looked on as snappier and more up-to-date than the *Follies*, they had yet to win the older show's extensive audience. While the *Follies* ran four months (and could have run longer) at the large Globe, the *Scandals* had virtually exhausted its lure when it closed at the smaller Liberty after a three-month stay.

One of the season's two hugely successful American musical comedies, **Tangerine** (8-9-21, Casino), told of three men who have been jailed for not paying alimony. A brawl lands their friend, Dick Owens (Frank Crumit), in the same jail, where he is visited by the girl he loves, Shirley Dalton (Julia Sanderson). To aggravate a bad time for Dick, Shirley has decided not to marry him until his jailed comrades are once more happily back with their former wives. Dick transports them all to the South Sea isle of Tangerine, where an expatriate American, King Home-Brew (John E. Hazzard), rules a society in which women do all the work. The men soon rebel at sitting home, and the girls quickly appreciate the drudgery of the men's world. The marriages are mended; Dick and Shirley are united. Only the poor king is excluded from the happy ending. He loses his entire chorus line of wives.

Although the critics obviously enjoyed the evening, many of them noted it was a reversion to a far earlier kind of show. The *Globe* remarked that it "reminds you of *King Dodo* without a twinge of regret," while the *Times,* lauding the work as "high above the musical comedy average," added it "savors just a bit of the early Frank Moulan period." The book was indeed good, for it was by Guy Bolton and Philip Bartholomae, two Princess Theatre librettists in top form. There was no opening number. The curtain rose on a funny, expository jail scene, and from there on the action never faltered. The closest it came to joke-book writing was in scenes with the king. Yet even here the dialogue was appropriate and amusing:

King: [*crawling out of his hut in the morning*] All night I dreamed I was talking to my first wife.
Clarence: Oh, no, your majesty—for hours and hours you didn't utter a sound.
King: That's the time she was talking to me. Clarence how do I look?
Clarence: You look great.
King: That's strange. I feel terrible. How's the wife this morning?
Girls: Very well, thank you.
King: I see you have your new shredded wheat dresses on . . . It's tough for the moths and great for the mosquitos. Does the wife kiss me this morning?
Girls: Of course we do.
King: Attention. Position. Present mouths. Osculate. That's very refreshing. Now how do I look Clarence?
Clarence: Terrible.
King: That's funny. I feel great.

Had the score been as good as the book, *Tangerine* would have been an outstanding show. The hit tune, "Sweet Lady" (an interpolation with music by David Zoob and Frank Crumit), and the best of Carlo and Sanders' regular score, "Listen To Me"—both sung by the lovers—depended heavily on successions of semitones. They were pleasant but forgettable. The rest of the tunes were, at best, tinkly.

A third revue, **The Mimic World** (8-15-21, Century Roof), came and went quickly. The musical was one of the few during the season to receive genuinely bad notices. An ill-omened affair from its inception, it suffered a major blow when its star walked out on the opening. James Barton, then appearing in another show, was called in for double duty, a possibility since *The Mimic World* was performed after the regular theatres had let out. Heavyweight boxer Jack Dempsey's arrival just after the show started overshadowed anything on stage, and the applause was so persistent Dempsey was called before the footlights to say a few words. The rest of the evening was an anticlimax.

Sonny (8-16-21, Cort) recited much the same story *Her Soldier Boy* (12-6-16) had told five years earlier. A look-alike takes the place of a dead war buddy to spare the dead man's family anguish. The victim's mother (Emma Dunn) in this instance is blind, and she brings about a happy ending when she reveals the impostor as a long-lost twin brother. Both brothers were played by Ernest Glendinning except at a hospital encounter in which the dying man was so swathed in bandages a second actor could easily portray him. The show, considered by some as a sequel to *Buddies,* was poorly timed. The public had put the war out of its mind and seemed determined not to have it brought back. Even the highly praised drama, *The Hero,* which opened less than a month later, had to be withdrawn for lack of patronage after 80 performances. *Sonny*'s farfetched ending, besides weakening any claim to seriousness the "melody play" may have made, undoubtedly also hurt its acceptance.

The last August musical was the **Greenwich Village Follies.** This year it didn't play the Village at all. Instead, it opened on August 31 at the large Shubert Theatre, just off Broadway. A number of critics rued a loss of intimacy, but the show was a hit, leaving behind the series' most memorable tune, "Three O'Clock In The Morning"—a waltz by an Englishwoman, Dorothy Terris, and Julian Robeldo, used as the finale. The song was first sung and then danced to in front of a simple blue set. Restrained use of color marked the evening. Robert Locher employed only black and white for a handsome number that had overtones of the decadence of Aubrey Beardsley. The number began with two performers dressed as black peacocks. Alone on the stage at first, they were soon part of an opulent art nouveau tableau. Throughout the evening Venetian blinds were used in place of stage curtains, allowing imaginative lighting effects. Much of this edition's comedy was placed in the hands of a team brought over from vaudeville, Brown and Watts. Their rowdy slapstick was at its best in "A Dying Duck in a Thunderstorm." James Watts soon disappeared from the theatrical scene, but big-mouthed Joe E. Brown went on to lifelong popularity. Ted Lewis and his small jazz band provided the music, some of which was sung by the vaudeville favorite, Irene Franklin, and some by Al Herman, a black-face singer who never quite made it to the top.

The annual Hippodrome spectacle, **Get Together,** opened on September 3 with a "motion picture prelude." Significantly, the Hippodrome had been given over to motion pictures all summer. The main attraction of the evening was the dancing of ballet choreographer Fokine and his wife, Fokina. For this mounting he created an extended, serious ballet, *The Thunderbird.* Critics admired Fokine's dancing, but many felt his choreography was imitative, a pale reflection of the dynamism of his own work for Stravinsky's *The Firebird.* Another "ballet," done on ice, ended the evening. Its star was the famous skater, Charlotte, who had appeared years before at the Hippodrome and whom Fred Stone had spoofed in *Jack o' Lantern* (10-16-17). Between ballets elephants roamed the stage. Bulldogs and Jocko, the crow, did their juggling acts.

On September 5, Henry Savage revived *The Merry Widow* (10-21-07) at the Knickerbocker. Lydia Lipkowska and Reginald Pasch sang Sonia and Danilo, while Jefferson De Angelis provided the comedy. The opening of the original production fourteen years before had inaugurated a new chapter in the American Musical Theatre—an unhappy one for native American art. The 1921 opening came at the start of another disappointing period. But this time *The Merry Widow* was not to blame. The revival's opening passed without any extraordinary notice.

On September 22, Broadway saw for the first time a new, exquisitely beautiful theatre, The Music Box, and the initial edition of a new revue series, **The Music Box Revue 1921–1922.** The two were the creations of Irving Berlin (working with George M. Cohan's old partner, Sam Harris). The shows were opulent, but the smallness of the house did not demand broad clowning nor strong musical projection, and so allowed for some intellectualization of the sketches and a softer-toned immediacy between singer and audience. A more relaxed, urbane style became possible. As a result the *Music Box Revues* helped build a bridge between the open-handed lavishness of the *Follies*-type revue and the more thoughtful intimacy of the revues of the thirties. Berlin's first score was good, including as it did the song that would become the series' theme, "Say It With Music." The number, given a relatively simple mounting, was sung by Wilda Bennett and Paul Frawley. On the other hand the Brox Sisters' clarion call of "Everybody Step" summoned the entire chorus to a floor-shaking stomp. This

very sort of dancing and the sillier aspects of the still raging dancing craze—absurdities such as dancing marathons—were joshed when Sam Bernard and Rene Riano came front and center with "They Call It Dancing." Their contortions and pratfalls were nothing, however, compared with the knot Miss Riano twisted herself into while singing "I'm A Dumbbell." The revue cost $187,613, with much of that money lavished on three production numbers. In "Dining Out" chorus beauties appeared as the food and the place settings of a regal banquet. In "Eight Notes" eight of the loveliest ladies became the notes of the scale and accompanied Berlin himself on stage. While Miss Bennett sang "The Legend Of The Pearls," girls bedecked in radiant pearls paraded against a black velvet background. Apart from the comedy in some of the musical numbers, humor was the weak point of the evening. William Collier wandered in and out as a part-time compère noting, when laughs didn't come in expected places, that the show might have to be retitled "The Harris and Berlin Worries of 1922." A few critics singled out Florence Moore's lampoon of bedroom farces as the best skit of the evening. Since at its premiere the show ran from 8:25 to midnight, a number of the lesser comic pieces were quickly dropped. Berlin was a perfectionist. Later editions of the series would have some of the best comedy to come out of revues.

The season's biggest hit, **Blossom Time** (9-29-21, Ambassador), was one of two shows of the theatrical year to run over 500 performances. Both were importations. *Blossom Time* purported to be a musical biography of Franz Schubert, employing the composer's melodies as the source of its songs. Originally a Viennese work with a musical adaptations by Heinrich Berté, *Das Dreimäderlhaus,* it was an instant international success. London knew it as *Lilac Time;* Paris as *Chanson d'Amour.* The American version was drastically rewritten by Dorothy Donnelly and Sigmund Romberg. Romberg discarded most of Berté's adaptations, selecting different Schubert themes and reworking them more facilely and more theatrically than Berté had done with his choices. The evening's hit was "Song Of Love," taken from the *Unfinished Symphony*'s first movement. Two exceptionally fine singers, Bertram Peacock and Olga Cook, played Schubert and his beloved Mitzi. But it fell to another excellent vocalist, Howard Marsh, to stop the show with Schubert's "Serenade." Alone of the season's shows the operetta was revived and toured constantly over the next quarter of a century, in increasingly cheap productions, until "a road company of *Blossom*

Time" became synonomous with the shabbiest theatrical commercialism.

The next entry, **The O'Brien Girl** (10-3-21, Liberty), typified the hand-me-down nature of this interval's hits. It told the rags-to-riches story of Humphrey Drexel's sweet little Irish stenographer, Alice O'Brien (Elisabeth Hines), who receives an $800 windfall and decides to spend it all on one giddy vacation in the Adirondacks. Unfortunately, Mr. Drexel (Robinson Newbold) and his jealous wife (Georgia Caine) happen to be staying at the same hotel. But love, in the person of rich and handsome Larry Patten (Truman Stanley), is a hotel guest, too. By the evening's end Alice and Larry have decided the hotel might serve as well for a honeymoon as for a vacation. For the most part critics endorsed the show, though these same critics looked back longingly to successes of preceding seasons. The plot recalled *Irene* (11-18-19) and *Sally* (12-21-20), while the Hirsch-Harbach-Mandel-Cohan team responsible for the evening suggested *Mary* (10-18-20). These three musicals were mentioned not only in many reviews of *The O'Brien Girl,* but in notices of musical after musical for the next three years—notices which generally conceded the new shows were diverting but insisted they fell short of the quality that was making the older productions legends in their own day. While several critics mentioned "Learn To Smile" as the outstanding song, the consensus was that the score was not as fetching as earlier Hirsch scores. No song approached his preceding year's "Love Nest" in popularity or durability.

If Cohan and his authors failed to create another *Mary,* at least they enjoyed a modest success. Charles Dillingham was not so fortunate. For **The Love Letter** (10-4-21, Globe), he reunited William Le Baron and Victor Jacobi, who, with Fritz Kreisler, had given him *Apple Blossoms* (10-7-19). He also brought back one of the principals, the strong-voiced baritone, John Charles Thomas, and two young dancers who had received brilliant notices in minor roles—Fred and Adele Astaire. Though Le Baron had Molnar's *The Phantom Rival* to work from, though Dillingham bedecked the piece with sets and costumes reflecting the baroque splendor of Middle Europe, and though the critics, with the exception of the scathing *Sun,* were not unkind, the show lasted a mere four weeks. By changing the plot from the heroine's need to pick between husband and lover to a need simply to pick a husband, Le Baron may have made his tale seem trivial. Still, he was writing in an era when triviality in musicals

was no offense. In his reworking, Madame Charlot (Katherine Stewart) selects a rich but unattractive man to marry her daughter, Miriam (Carolyn Thomson). Miriam takes refuge in fantasies in which her former suitor, Philip Delma (Thomas), returns to court her as a dashing soldier, a glamorous statesman, and a romantic artist. The flesh and blood Philip appears. He is a mundane businessman, but successful enough to permit Madame Charlot to reconsider her choice. One highly praised Joseph Urban set was a ballroom done all in maroon (as were the men's uniforms). Because the ballroom was seen in a dream, Urban subtly and humorously distorted chandeliers, chairs, and other features of the set. Possibly Jacobi's peculiar score was partly to blame for the short run. The musical's most touted number, "My Heart Beats For You," was almost an Irish air, belonging more to a Chauncey Olcott or a Cohan production than to an operetta set in Hungary. While the rest of the songs were more of the order Jacobi's admirers might expect, none proved another "You Are Free." Jacobi died a few weeks after the show folded. He was only thirty-seven years old, and like Gustav Luders before him, was said to have died from the shock of his show's failure.

Bombo disappointed no one—at least no one who knew and loved Al Jolson extravaganzas. The production, which premiered October 6, was housed in a new theatre the Shuberts had built just below Central Park and had named for Jolson. There was the merest hint of a plot, with Jolson playing his blackface-servant-boy Gus—this time as Bombo, serving none other than Christopher Columbus. The official Romberg score was unimportant. The hits were the interpolations. In *Bombo,* Jolson introduced three of his greatest songs—"April Showers" (B. G. DeSylva/Louis Silvers), "Toot, Toot, Tootsie!" (Gus Kahn, Ernie Erdman, Dan Russo), and "California, Here I Come" (DeSylva, Jolson/Joseph Meyer). These interpolations illustrate the freewheeling ways still current at the time. "California, Here I Come" was not added until the show left New York and went on tour. "April Showers," which grabbed most of the opening night applause, was, as one critic noted, not even on the program. Another critic begrudged the expenditures the Shuberts lavished on the sets and costumes, insisting the money would have been better spent on a superior supporting cast. But he also revealed why, in a way, even sumptuous sets were unnecessary when Jolson was on stage. Jolson, he reported, "sang with his old-time knee-slapping, breast-beating, eye-rolling ardor, sang with a faith that moved mountains and audiences. You should have heard them cheer."

Love Dreams (10-10-21, Times Square), with a book by Anne Nichols, who later in the season would find fame and wealth with *Abie's Irish Rose,* was a quick failure. It remains of interest, if at all, because it exemplifies the pitiful groping for new musical forms or new names to dress old forms in. It called itself a "Melody Drama," which the *Daily News* interpreted for its readers as "plusquam-perfect musical comedy." The *Globe* accepted only the first half of the author's new coinage, referring to it as a "melody play." The *Journal,* taking the left-over half, made it into a "musical drama." Renee d'Albret (Vera Michelena) is a musical comedy star whose notoriety is largely the work of her press agent. She allows herself her scandalous reputation because she supports an ailing sister with the extra money it brings. Renee becomes engaged to Larry Pell (Tom Powers), but gives him up when she realizes he prefers her sister. Her goodness is rewarded when Larry's brother, Dr. Duncan Pell (Orrin Johnson), cures her sister and falls in love with Renee. If the book attempted a more serious, somewhat soap-opera-like story, Werner Janssen's music clearly looked backward. Today *Love Dreams* would unquestionably be labeled "operetta."

Good Morning, Dearie (11-1-21, Globe) remains, with the equally successful *Tangerine,* the best of the season's plotted shows. Its superiority to *Tangerine* lies in its lovely Jerome Kern music. Because it once more told of a modern-day Cinderella, critics were again drawn back to *Sally* and *Irene.* But so beguiling were the songs and so solid the book that the critics, this time, were kind in their comparisons. The story was not unusual. Society's Billy Van Cortlandt (Oscar Shaw) is engaged to Ruby Manners (Peggy Kurton), but he has fallen in love with a couturiere's assistant he has seen from the window of his tailor's. The girl in question, Rose-Marie (Louise Groody), had once been the pet of a crook, Chesty Costello (Harland Dixon)—an attachment she would dearly like to forget. Chesty, just out of prison, hopes to steal Mrs. Greyson Parks' jewels while Mrs. Parks is busy with a large party, but Billy and Rose-Marie foil the robbery and let Chesty escape on condition that he give up his old girl friend. Ruby finds a fiancé in Bill's cousin George (John Price Jones), leaving Billy and Rose-Marie free to head for Niagara Falls. The dialogue was probably meant to sound tough

and to titillate a 1921 audience. Madame Bompard (Ada Lewis), Rose-Marie's employer, has written to warn the girl Chesty was free. Rose-Marie has misplaced the note and fears someone who knows Chesty will find it and show it to him:

Rose-Marie: Gee, remember what you wrote on it?
Mme. B.: Not exactly.
Rose-Marie: You wrote "Costello's time is up and he's coming out—you oughter get a pal with weight behind his wallop to put the big brute to sleep."
Mme. B.: My very words.
Rose-Marie: Gee, if Chesty ever got hold of that— I'd get a wallop with his weight behind it.

Later, when Chesty senses Rose-Marie is not happy to see him, he threatens her, "You better be glad— or you'll be sorry." What might make *Good Morning, Dearie* dated now are its racial attitudes and its often impossible lyrics. "Chink" and "Wop" are used unconcernedly throughout the dialogue. In fact, one of the directions in the typescript reads, *"Steve enters as Chink Waiter."* Sadly, some of Kern's most engaging melodic phrases are wasted on lyrics such as "with your true love happy may you be." Only "Ka-lu-a" has remained a standard, though the two-part harmony of "Blue Danube Blues" made it a big hit in its day. But "Didn't You Believe?" (sung by Billy and the girls' chorus), Chesty and Rose-Marie's "Way Down Town," and the title song (sung by Rose-Marie and the men's chorus) have been undeservedly neglected, while "My Lady's Dress" cut, unfortunately, during try-out would reward study as an example of Kern's musicianship.

Though Ed Wynn announced at the start of **The Perfect Fool** (11-7-21, Cohan) that there was a plot about a newly married man who falls in love with a second woman, no one took the news seriously. It was simply one of the great Wynn-dominated revues—featuring his outlandish costumes and his absurd inventions. His master stroke this time around was a "non-eye-destroying spoon for ice tea." The spoon bent over the rim of the glass whenever the drink was raised. Wynn allowed a bit of Ziegfeld-like spectacle to entertain the audience while he changed costumes. In one scene chorus girls became typing-bars on a larger-than-life typewriter.

Ziegfeld's Midnight Frolic, with several of his Follies stars, came in November 17 and kept the New Amsterdam Roof busy all winter. All during the heyday of roof gardens Ziegfeld's shows on the New Amsterdam roof were style-setters. Ziegfeld often used the entertainments to try out new performers or to allow his *Follies'* stars to test fresh material. But these roof shows were more nearly vaudeville or cabaret than legitimate theatre.

Suzette (11-24-21, Princess), a musical of no distinction whatsoever, struggled through 4 performances. Suzette (Marie Astrova) is a Montmartre flower girl who captivates the American millionaire Paul Huntley (James R. Marshall) and wins a proposal of marriage from him after she hastily pinchhits for a temperamental prima donna. A somewhat ghoulish importation, the Spanish music drama **The Wildcat** (11-26-21, Park), had only a slightly better reception, though its somber, driving plot approached the more serious musical plays of later years. A second foreign show—a revival of *The Chocolate Soldier* (12-13-09)—followed, and closed out the year at the Century. The fine-voiced Tessa Kosta and Donald Brian starred, while Detmar Poppen provided the comedy.

To open 1922, Tom and Will B. Johnstone continued their futile search for success with **Above the Clouds** (1-9-22, Lyric), a musical with a motion picture background. The Hollywood movie star, Jean Jones (Grace Moore), returns east to expose J. Herbert Blake's disreputable school, which has been using her name without permission, and to encourage a war hero, Archie Dawson (Hal Van Rensselaer), with his patriotic screenwriting ambitions. Archie and Jean end by singing love duets.

The second musical of 1922 was an inferior Rudolf Friml piece, **The Blue Kitten** (1-13-22, Selwyn). It managed a modest run. *The Blue Kitten* must have reminded many patrons of *The Little Café* (11-10-13). It, too, was adopted from a French farce, in this case *Le Chasseur de Chez Maxim's.* In both *The Blue Kitten* and *The Little Café,* a waiter who comes into an inheritance was a central figure. The newly rich Theodore Vanderpop's problem is to make his daughter's fiancé, a former patron, believe Vanderpop is not his old waiter. As in *The Little Whopper* (10-13-19), Friml seems to have been trying to speak with an American vocabulary. But his European accent betrayed him. Although "Cutie" and "Smoke Rings," probably the best numbers in the show, were written in 4/4 and "Cutie" called for a "slow fox trot time," the world of the waltz was not too distant to go unheard. In this instance Friml did not even have *Whopper*'s American setting to help him. A number of fading

performers—Joseph Cawthorn (Vanderpop), Lillian Lorraine—could not help, either.

Elsie Janis and Her Gang (1-16-22, Gaiety) came in for two months as a vaudeville-cum-revue. Miss Janis had learned while entertaining troops in France that she didn't need scenery to win applause. Ahead of her time, she used only the barest drapes and props. But Alexander Woollcott in the *Times* felt she went too far. Her curtains seemed to him like old blankets Miss Janis had sewn together herself. Nonetheless the material was good, and Woollcott suggested her rendition of "Mon Homme" was the equal of Fanny Brice's singing it as "My Man." Other performers were handed equally worthy bits. Arriving as it did in the middle of the postwar recession, "The Bonus Blues" stopped the show. It was sung by a group of ex-soldiers in the waiting room of an employment office.

In their reviews of **Marjolaine** (1-24-22, Broadhurst), several critics suggested that the show on which it was based, *Pomander Walk,* practically begged at its inception to be made into a musical. They lavished an intriguing amount of affection on Louis Parker's now all-but-forgotten play. The story told of Marjolaine Lachesnais' (Peggy Wood) troubled romance with Lieutenant Jack Sayle (Irving Beebe). The difficulty stems from Jack's father having jilted Marjolaine's mother years before. There is a doubly happy ending. The young lovers are united and the parents, both widowed, resume their old romance. Unfortunately, the music was assigned to a hack, Hugo Felix, so that despite an indulgent reception and Peggy Wood's drawing power, *Marjolaine* ran only seventeen weeks. Burns Mantle, writing in the *Evening Mail,* offered an interesting sidelight. His complaint of unnecessary encores acknowledged that all the editorializing and campaigning against a surfeit of reprises were still not universally heeded.

An English revue, **Pins and Needles** (2-1-22, Shubert), failed to cause a stir. But a revue conceived in Russia, revived in Paris, and brought to the 49th Street Theatre three days after *Pins and Needles* proved a sensation. It was **Chauve Souris**, and its "Parade Of The Wooden Soldiers" remains a delight. Because few of its performers spoke English, the show was largely a succession of beautifully staged songs and pantomimes. Its creator, spherical, sly Nikita Balieff, acted as compère, explaining in drolly broken English whatever he thought audiences might not otherwise understand. His delightful little monologues helped propel the show to a run of over 500 performances. *Chauve Souris* was another of the faster paced, more intimate revues sounding the death knell for the ponderous Ziegfeldian offerings. All during the 1920s it returned to Broadway in "revised" editions that nevertheless retained the best original material.

Two nights later, February 6, **The Blushing Bride** and **Frank Fay's Fables** competed for the attention of the critics. Fay's was a revue of no special interest apart from the personalities of some of its performers—dependable old hands such as Bernard Granville and Fay himself (as droll and sly a compère as Balieff). It lasted 32 showings at the Park. On the other hand, *The Blushing Bride* at the Astor was generally well received and even its inferior Romberg score praised. But its plot, really an excuse for a series of specialty acts, was described by the *Tribune* as "a tinge of vaudeville, a shade of revue, a color of burlesque, a hue of musical comedy, a suggestion of concert." Lulu Love is a chorus girl turned hat-check girl at Paul Kominski's cabaret. Colley Collins, her suitor, hires himself out as a public chaperon whose presence disguises the fact that the couple he is with should not be together. Between assignments, propositions, and vaudeville turns Lulu and Colley pursue their courtship. Cecil Lean and Cleo Mayfield, always more popular on the road than in Manhattan, were the principals.

Although it was only late February, the excitement of the season was fast draining away. Nevertheless, **For Goodness Sake** (2-20-22, Lyric) sent ecstatic critics running to their typewriters. Many of them found nice things to say about the show, but their joyous kudos were for the Astaires, who according to the *Evening Telegram,* elicited "storm after storm of applause."

• • •

Fred and **Adele Astaire** were born in Omaha, Nebraska; Adele in 1898, Fred just under a year later on May 10, 1899. Their family name was Austerlitz. Adele was enrolled in Chambers' Dancing Academy in 1902. The family moved east and, after Fred received lessons from his sister, Fred and Adele obtained work on the Keith vaudeville circuit in 1906. A year later they enjoyed further private tutelage from Ned Wayburn. The young Astaires worked steadily in vaudeville for ten years, leaving it to make their legitimate debut in *Over the Top* (12-1-17). Though his later solo career would make him far more famous than his sister, Fred was generally looked on as the lesser of the

two during the early years of their partnership. Both had what can loosely be called "style" or "class." They danced with a remarkable grace and ease, creating routines that were not only inventive but often enhanced with a subtle wit. One of their most famous bits was first displayed in *For Goodness Sake.* For a number called "Upside Down," British-born choreographer Edward "Teddy" Royce had the Astaires run around the stage like circus horses in the ring. Fred and Adele described ever widening arcs until, before their audiences realized it, they had danced themselves off the stage. As Fred Astaire's biographer, Michael Freedland, notes, "It sounds simple, almost childish. But it established an Astaire trademark." Neither Fred nor Adele had noteworthy voices, but both, nonetheless, could "put over" a song.

• • •

It was solely because of the Astaires that *For Goodness Sake* played fourteen weeks. Except for two pleasant, if unexceptional, George Gershwin songs, the music was as ordinary as the book. In the latter, Vivian Reynolds (Marjorie Gateson) sees her husband remove a cinder from a pretty young girl's eye. She misunderstands the action and places the worst construction on it. Vengefully, she plans a fling of her own. To win back his wife's attention, Perry Reynolds (John E. Hazzard) decides to disappear and make his disappearance seem like suicide. Vivian overhears his plot and confounds her husband with her indifference to his supposed death. By curtain time the misunderstandings are resolved. Not only are the Reynoldses hand in hand, but so are the secondary lovers, Teddy Lawrence and Susan Hayden, the parts the Astaires played.

Leo Fall's **The Rose of Stamboul** (3-7-22, Century), with Romberg interpolations, had a three-month run. More than one critic compared Romberg's raggy additions and Fall's original material and asked why the new ones were included. The critical assault on inappropriate interpolations continued as unavailing as the critical attack on excessive encores. Tessa Kosta starred as a pasha's daughter in love with a poet, but ordered to marry a man whose name she does not recognize. The poet and the stranger prove one and the same.

Guy Bolton, forever fascinated with the workings of thieves, almost had a hit in **The Hotel Mouse** (3-13-22, Shubert), adapting the story from a French farce. The thief in this instance is the gamin, baby-talking Mauricette (Frances White). When she makes the mistake of trying to rob Wally Gordon's suite, Wally (Taylor Holmes) shields her from the police, reforms her, and then marries her. The score was lame and probably responsible for the show's disappointing eleven-week run. It was Ivan Caryll's last work. He had died in November, not living to see his piece performed.

Just Because (3-22-22, Earl Carroll) ran only half as long as *The Hotel Mouse* despite the presence in its cast of such fine talents as Frank Moulan and Queenie Smith. It described how a young lady pretends to be an orphan so that she can win a proposal of marriage from the director of an orphan asylum.

Charlotte Greenwood was even less lucky with a musical version of Charles Klein's *Maggie Pepper*. Of course, Miss Greenwood altered the character's first name to Letty. Her Letty begins life as a change clerk in Colby's department store. Letty's ambition arouses the ire of her superviser, who fires her. Letty tells her woes to a stranger, who turns out to be Mr. Colby (Ray Raymond). He appoints her a buyer. Her success wins her a promotion and the love of Mr. Colby. The reviews, which called the show "unmusical comedy" and "nursery stuff," were among the harshest of the season. Even Miss Greenwood's eccentric, loose-jointed dances couldn't override the glaring inadequacies. Morosco quickly sent **Letty Pepper** (4-10-22, Vanderbilt) to the safety of the hinterlands.

Make It Snappy, a Winter Garden revue starring Eddie Cantor instead of Jolson, opened April 13 and was virtually the last bright spot of the dying year. Cantor performed one of his most famous comedy parts—Max, the Tailor, a little man harassed by a customer who insists he wants a coat with a belt in the back. The belt the exasperated Cantor finally gave his customer was not the one the customer had in mind. Cantor also played a taxi driver and an all too timid candidate for the police academy. No Cantor standards emerged from the show, but his distinctive style of presenting songs—skipping back and forth, his hands gyrating, his eyes rolling—made the numbers festive if not memorable. When Cantor was off stage the vacuum was filled by a band of tumblers (Eight Blue Devils), the Cleveland Bonner Ballet, and chorus spectacles such as one with all the girls dressed to look like pink roses.

R. H. Burnside and "De Wolf Hopper's Funmakers" put together a revue they called **Some Party** (4-15-22, Jolson's). The funmakers, both before the footlights and behind the scenes, were oldtimers. The *Times* critic exaggerated only slightly when he observed, "the three leading comedians were in show business when Lillian Russell was a babe in arms." He referred to Hopper, Jefferson De Angelis, and Lew Dockstader. Silvio Hein, Percy Wenrich, and Gustave Kerker composed what new music the show required. The revue's simple mounting was a conscious protest against the increasingly elaborate spectacles cascading onto Broadway. The *Times* continued, "not in ten years has a revue been put forward in this pampered city with quite so stern and fine a Puritan disregard for mere good looks." In this sense the simple production was as avant-garde as it was retrogressive. The show advertised a "chorus of genuine debutantes," which probably meant nothing more than that most of the chorus girls were making their Broadway debuts. The revue's idea of humor was a parody of Mascagni operas, its heroine christened "Rustic Anna." This slow, gentle humor of another era was, unfortunately, no longer welcome.

Go Easy, Mabel (5-8-22, Longacre), an amateurish botch of a musical comedy, came and disappeared in less time than *Some Party*. Its three acts unfolded the complications that ensue when Ted and Mabel Sparks (Will J. Deming and Estelle Winwood), bored with their marriage, try some extramarital flirting. Their flings convince them of the worth of their own marriage.

The last musical comedy of the season was **Red Pepper** (5-29-22, Shubert), a McIntyre and Heath vehicle, with the two blackface comedians in their typical routines. The Red Pepper of the title was a racing horse whose career moves the action with little motivation, other than the desire for a change of scenery, from Havana to Arizona to Georgia. Following the horse, hoping to get rich quick from his winnings, are Jimpson Weed (Heath) and his hard-luck buddy, Juniper Berry (McIntyre). The show enjoyed only a modest success, but one of its appraisals contained a fascinating example of how unprepared even professional critics were for the latest changes in musical fashion. The *Post,* commenting on the show, exclaimed: "there's nothing in the piece that is real music. Jazz, yes. Any amount of it, but jazz isn't music. Not by a long shot." Music or jazz, the score by Albert Gumble and Owen Murphy followed the scenery to oblivion.

The Ziegfeld Follies of 1922 (6-5-22, New Amsterdam) opened a little earlier than customary, so that Broadway had the unusual appearance of two editions within the same season. This 1922 production is generally looked on as the last great edition, although most of the big names had left. Only Will Rogers remained, with Gilda Gray and Mary Eaton contributing their glamour. Miss Gray did her inevitable wriggling shimmy, while Miss Eaton, whom

Ziegfeld hoped to groom as a second Marilyn Miller, danced more aesthetically. The spectacle was magnificent. Two of the most memorable sets were conceived for Fokine ballets. "Farlanjandio" unfolded in a Sicilian gypsy encampment; "Frolicking Gods" in a museum where Greek statues come to life. But this was the year in which Ziegfeld introduced his famous slogan, "Glorifying the American Girl," and he reserved the two most eye-filling mountings for his line of beauties. In "Lace Land" the ladies paraded before lace draperies coated with luminous paint. The first-act finale had the girls on a golden staircase, marching through golden gates. Ring Lardner was credited with the sketches and lyrics; Victor Herbert, Louis Hirsch, and Dave Stamper provided the basic score. But if any tune from the version remains popular it is the comic "Mr. Gallagher And Mr. Shean," which the clownish pair wrote for themselves. Their brand of smiling humor is out of vogue today. For example, Shean describes a game played on the links. People knock a ball with a stick while a caddie "thinks and thinks." Shean guesses the game is croquet, but Gallagher assures him it's lawn tennis. After the second-act finale Ziegfeld introduced a novel curtain call. The curtain rose on a set simulating the New Amsterdam's stage door. The performers came past one by one waving to the audience as they seemingly left the theatre.

The popular Raymond Hitchcock, tiring of *Hitchy-Koo*, ended the season with a revue called **Pinwheel** (also called **Pinwheel Revel**). Like *Elsie Janis and Her Gang*, the show used little scenery, although this time it was attractively done. Like *Chauve Souris*, much of it was in pantomime. Surprisingly, since Hitchcock was in charge, there was little comedy in the show. It was an evening of dance, but not the ballroom-derived dancing filling most shows. The celebrated choreographer Michio Itow offered instead Japanese, Hindu, Spanish, Gypsy, and Greek dances, mostly to music of such masters as Brahms and Debussy. The little humor in the evening came from the two compères, Frank Fay and Hitchcock. *Pinwheel* (6-15-22, Earl Carroll) was the seventeenth revue out of thirty-seven musical productions. The statistic is revealing in itself, and it represents the highwater mark in the popularity of the genre. Ephemeral revues so engulfed the year that only one below-average American book show, two at most, remain to represent the season. The next season saw a sharp drop in the proportion of revues to traditional musicals. In 1923–24 the number rose again, but it was a last gasp.

1922-1923

Burns Mantle, in his annual year book of *Best Plays*, wrote that 1922–23 was "the first theatrical season in a generation that has not been described as 'the worst in years.'" Of course, Mantle was speaking of the season as a whole, taking into account new American plays (*Icebound, You and I, The Fool, The Old Soak*), importations (*R.U.R., Loyalties*), revivals (*Romeo and Juliet, Hamlet*), and such special events as the Moscow Art Theatre's visit. He makes no mention of the musical scene, and for good reason. It was bleak. The 1922–23 season conceivably represents the worst twelve months for the musical theatre in the seasons between the early teens and the middle thirties. An appallingly high number of offerings tried brazenly to cash in on the popularity of older hits, but their material was not only derivative, it was usually lackluster, often banal. Little more than half a dozen songs from all the forty-one shows that opened during the season have survived as standards, a depressing figure in view of many great shows, before and since, that each produced four or five memorable songs. Of the major book shows, the best score was coupled with a weak libretto, while better books had pedestrian scores.

Strut Miss Lizzie (6-19-22, Times Square) began the season. It was the first of many black revues hoping to follow in *Shuffle Along*'s glory. Its authors, Henry Creamer and Turner Layton, opened the show by phoning each other from opposite sides of the stage. What followed purported to be their affectionate recollections of gay times they had enjoyed. They joined forces at the end of the evening for a bit in the style of Van and Schenck, with composer Layton at the piano and lyricist Creamer standing alongside. The *Times* had serious reservations about the evening, concluding it was "happiest when its people sing and dance." The high-stepping dancing was described, not unkindly, as "raucous." *Strut Miss Lizzie* folded after four weeks.

The more conventional **Spice of 1922** (7-6-22, Winter Garden) ran just over twice as long. The two shows were connected in a curious fashion. *Spice of 1922* introduced an American classic, "Way Down Yonder In New Orleans" (Henry Creamer/Turner Layton). The song was an interpolation, used after it was discarded from the Creamer-Layton score for *Strut Miss Lizzie*. George Gershwin was also represented by a song,

"Yankee Doodle Blues," with lyrics by Irving Caesar and Buddy DeSylva. One show-stopper was "An Old-Fashioned Cake Walk," with the entire ensemble dressed in bright reds. Nudity crept into the spectacle although there was little complaint about the scene, set as it was in an artist's studio and done in silhouette. But some critics suggested the producer was testing the limits of public tolerance in "The Garden of Eden" number. The show's idea of comedy was a travesty of *Tosca*.

Sue, Dear (7-10-22, Times Square), the season's first book musical, ran through the hot weather, only to succumb to a rash of more popular shows brought in during late August and early September. Its Cinderella plot recounted how Suzanne Milliken (Olga Steck), a salesgirl in a jewelry store, is hired to impersonate a bride who has telegraphed that she will be unable to attend her own wedding. Sue does not conquer the groom, but captivates and wins Phillip (Bradford Kirkbride), a heretofore woman-hating publisher.

A second black entry, **Plantation Revue** (7-17-22, 48th St.), fared little better than *Strut Miss Lizzie* despite the presence in the cast of composer Shelton Brooks (who wrote no music for the piece), the captivating Florence Mills, and Will Vodery. Only a small part of the evening used plantation settings. New Orleans and New York were also depicted—as they had been in *Strut Miss Lizzie*. But the name did invite the public to another evening of spirited black dancing—buck and wing, lively tap routines, and cake walks.

Guy Bolton, working with young Oscar Hammerstein II, provided the book for the "musigirl" comedy **Daffy Dill** (8-22-22, Apollo), for which Hammerstein also supplied lyrics to the Herbert Stothart score. The show teetered dangerously on the brink of vaudeville, but its star, Frank Tinney, kept it going nine weeks. Tinney played himself, performing his standard routines in each of the twelve scenes. At one time or another he appeared as a Chinese magician, a coachman, and a black porter. Now and then he would halt the action and, with an "air of stuttering impromptu," talk to the orchestra leader. What little plot *Daffy Dill* possessed told yet another Cinderella story in which poor Lucy Brown (Irene Olsen) gains the love of rich Kenneth Hobson (Guy Robertson).

George White's Scandals of 1922 and **The Gingham Girl** opened on the same night, August 28. Though the *Scandals* ran only eleven weeks at the Globe while *The Gingham Girl* ran out the season at the Earl Carroll, the *Scandals* was of more interest, for it had songs by George Gershwin, including his early and remarkable "I'll Build A Stairway To Paradise." The song served as the first-act finale, and White gave it a brilliant setting that presaged the Art Deco rage about to burst on the scene. While a Paul Whiteman orchestra played in the pit, girls dressed in black patent leather marched up a shimmering white staircase. The second act originally opened with Gershwin's *Blue Monday Blues*, a twenty-five-minute tragic jazz opera, to a text by Buddy DeSylva. Commercial considerations hustled the opera away after opening night, but it was ultimately revised and presented in concert as *135th St.* White was undoubtedly wrong to consider using the piece in a "tired-businessman's" entertainment such as *Scandals*. That he included it in the first place hints at the creative ferment on Broadway. Regrettably these daring ventures often were perceived merely as new dissonances, new stridencies. The show opened with a Garden of Eden number apparently less offensive to critics than that in *Spice of 1922*. One can only guess at the feelings of Whiteman's fine jazz musicians as they accompanied the scene—playing "In The Shade Of The Old Apple Tree." For this edition White succeeded in luring W. C. Fields away from Ziegfeld. Fields appeared in a skit satirizing primitive radio and in a bit about baseball. He wrote the latter himself. But the consensus was that the material was far from Fields' best.

Its homey title suggests how different *The Gingham Girl* was. Once more critics were reminded of not-long-gone shows, *Irene* coming to mind most often. But if the critics had reservations, they willingly laid them aside. The *World* praised *The Gingham Girl*'s "book of simple charm," concluding it would have a long run, "if there is a place left on Broadway for a musical comedy of sweetness." There was. John Cousins (Eddie Buzzell) leaves Crossville Corners, New Hampshire, and gingham-garbed girl, Mary Thompson (Helen Ford), to make his way in New York. Mary, afraid to lose him, follows. She sets herself up in the cookie business, and, when John tires of chasing chorus girls, she is waiting for him with a money-making enterprise. The music by Albert Von Tilzer and the lyrics by Neville Fleeson seemed inferior to their lilting *Honey Girl* work. But the hit of the score, "Just As Long As You Have Me," was bucolically appropriate, an excellent example of all but the most advanced writing of the day.

Molly Darling (9-1-22, Liberty) just missed being a hit. It was interesting on two accounts. First, the story told of a good melody that failed to win public favor until it was played as jazz; and second, because important action took place at a radio station. The new music and the new medium were becoming commonplaces, and Broadway would not ignore them, as the *Scandals* had already demonstrated. The young man who helped the heroine reap her $75,000 jackpot for her song was played by an up-and-coming dancer, Jack Donahue.

If *Molly Darling* offered a glimpse of the future, **Better Times,** an ironic title, all things considered, opened at the Hippodrome the next night to present one final souvenir of a special past. This was the eighteenth and last of the mammoth theatre's extravaganzas. Little had changed from the opening production. In one number the chorus formed a gigantic fan. Another number was done entirely in silhouette. A ballet with the huge ensemble all in white was danced against a black background. A second "ballet" was performed by twenty horses. The elephants were back, as was Jocko, the juggling crow. The evening ended with the house's bathing beauties disappearing into its famous tank. Although *Better Times* ran as long as its predecessors, no producer could be found to continue the mountings when Charles Dillingham bowed out. Gorgeous, but inane, the Hippodrome productions were lumbering theatrical dinosaurs, whose day was coming to a close. What demand there was for such spectacles would be met by stage shows accompanying motion pictures at great movie palaces—or by movies themselves. The greatest of all these accompanying stage presentations would be offered years later by the Radio City Music Hall, a few blocks north of the Hippodrome site.

In the most blatant of all attempts to capitalize on the afterglow of recent seasons, the ever-opportunistic Shuberts presented **Sally, Irene and Mary** (9-4-22, Casino). The show had begun life as a satirical Eddie Dowling sketch in Winter Garden vaudeville. Dowling soon expanded it and brought it back to New York as a three-and-a-half-hour mélange of satire and sentiment, mostly sentiment. Sally (Jean Brown), Irene (Kitty Flynn), and Mary (Edna Morn) are growing up in a tenement district. So is Jimmie Dugan (Dowling). They are visited by their rich landlady, Mrs. Jones (Winifred Harris), and her son Rodman (Hal Van Rensselaer). Years pass. Mary has been courted successfully by Rodman. But Jimmie Dugan is on his way up politically, and at the last moment he talks Mary into marrying him instead. They go off to be wed at the same time as Sally and Irene and their beaux. Vestiges of Dowling's original spoof remained. Irene was Irene O'Dare, and the opening tenement scene reminded many of the older show's famous set.

Mary's last line was, "They're waiting for us at the Little Church Around the Corner"—an unmistakable allusion to *Sally*. In between was a long-winded, humorless book interspersed with a hodgepodge of songs—including "Dear Old Gown" from *The Melting Of Molly* (12-30-18). Though critics ignored the score and some had serious reservations about the book and the casting, the public bought tickets, and the musical ran into June.

A moderately successful revue, **A Fantastic Fricasee,** opened at the Greenwich Village Theatre on September 11, one night before the *Greenwich Village Follies* opened at the Shubert. The smallness of the Village house allowed the show to employ marionettes to good effect, notably in a scene in which Orlando Furioso slays a dragon. There was a soldier ballet a bit too reminiscent of "The Parade of the Wooden Soldiers." A number of critics singled out the lyrics of Robert Edwards and foresaw a bright future for the writer. Edwards' lyrics were indeed witty, at least as far as excerpts from reviews suggest. For example, he winked at "Greenwich Village flappers in their dirty batik wrappers," thereby putting on record how little Bohemia changes. Although Edwards did not go far, one young singer in the show did. She was Jeanette MacDonald.

Audiences arriving at the Shubert for the **Greenwich Village Follies** were confronted by a startling show curtain. The drop was painted by the distinguished American artist, Reginald Marsh. A panoramic mural on canvas, it depicted dozens of Village celebrities going about their business. Knowledgeable playgoers could identify Sinclair Lewis, Eugene O'Neill, Zelda Fitzgerald, and a host of other figures, most now forgotten. Two important additions were made to the series. John Murray Anderson introduced the first of the "Ballet Ballads" that would remain a feature of succeeding editions. His initial offering was based on Oscar Wilde's poem, "The Nightingale and the Rose," sung to a melody by Louis Hirsch, then danced to Chopin airs. The edition also marked the debut of Bert Savoy, the successor to Julian Eltinge's mantle—or stole—as Broadway's reigning female impersonator. The two men were worlds apart in style. Whereas Eltinge was elegant and discreet, Savoy swished and leered his way across a stage. Robert Baral in his history of the genre, *Revue*, contends that Mae West's exaggerated mannerisms were derived from Savoy's flamboyant technique and that her famous "Come-up-and-see-me-sometime" reflects Savoy's "You musssst come over!" Savoy was abetted by his partner Jay Brennan, to whom he passed on all the latest scuttlebutt about a scandalous friend named Margie. Savoy's reign was brief. He was killed by lightning just after the show closed. When audiences were not laughing at Savoy and Brennan they would be amused by skits, such as the one parodying Eugene O'Neill's stark tragedies. John Hazzard milked laughs from a spoof of sentimental old ballads, "Goodbye To Dear Alaska." Hirsch's regular score was unexceptional. The two most popular songs of the evening were interpolations. Yvonne George offered her version of "Mon Homme" to compete with Fanny Brice's "My Man" and Elsie Janis' rendition of the original; while Ted Lewis and his band made a small hit out of "Georgette" (B. G. DeSylva/Ray Henderson).

Orange Blossoms, the last Victor Herbert show done in his lifetime, opened on September 19 at the Fulton. The libretto was by Fred de Gresac (Mrs. Victor Maurel), one of Herbert's favorite collaborators, and was based on the play *La Passerelle,* which she had coauthored. Her plot was a variant of *Betsy* (12-11-11) and Victor Herbert's *The Duchess* (10-16-11). In de Gresac's story, Kitty agrees to marry and divorce the Baron Roger Belmont in order to override a clause in his aunt's will which disinherits him if he first marries a Brazilian dancer, Helene de Vasquez. Kitty makes the marriage so pleasant the Baron decides to forget about the dancer. It was not one of Herbert's best scores. Some of the songs—"The Lonely Nest," "A Dream Of Orange Blossoms"—appeared to be waltz themes wrenched into 4/4 time. Herbert had the same problem that Rudolf Friml had. How Herbert resolved it was seen after his death in his music for *The Dream Girl* (8-20-24). But with "A Kiss In The Dark" he left behind one final waltz classic. The song was sung in the show by Kitty, not to Roger, but to her handsome godfather, Brossac, the lawyer responsible for the arrangement between Kitty and the Baron. The original Irene, Edith Day, starred as Kitty. Her husband, Pat Somerset, played Brossac, while Robert Michaels was Roger.

The next night **The Passing Show of 1922** came to the Winter Garden, its gift to posterity one Gus Kahn–Walter Donaldson interpolation, "Carolina In The Morning." The song was introduced by the Howard brothers, who also sang "My Coal Black Mammy." Fred Allen was a newcomer to the series. His dry humor and gravelly voice were displayed in an extended monologue, "The Old Joke Cemetery." Ethel Shutta brought down the house in a musical spoof of Eugene O'Neill's *The Hairy Ape.*

Emmerich Kalman's lovely *Die Bajadere* was brought to New York as **The Yankee Princess** (10-2-22, Knickerbocker) and failed despite the presence of Vivienne Segal in the title role of the American actress who wins the love of an Indian rajah. But on the same night, another importation was a solid hit at the Ambassador. **The Lady in Ermine** had American interpolations by Al Goodman and one number, the show's hit, "When Hearts Are Young," by Sigmund Romberg. The story told of a conquerer (Walter Woolf) conquered by the lady (Wilda Bennett) of the castle in which he is billeted. Three nights later a Russian vaudeville called **Revue Russe** came into the Booth. Unfavorably compared to *Chauve Souris,* it beat a hasty retreat.

A vehicle for Nora Bayes called **Queen o'Hearts** (10-10-22, Cohan) allowed the youthful Oscar Hammerstein II to continue his apprenticeship. Miss Bayes played Elizabeth Bennett, the head of a matrimonial agency, whose efforts to marry off her sister nearly come to nothing when the drunken antics of a friend's husband are misconstrued by the sister's suitor. While Lewis Gensler wrote the body of the score, Miss Bayes followed her customary practice of interpolating a number of other songs, some of which she wrote herself. The *Times* review is indicative of the tolerance of the day. Though the critic saw it as "a thoroughly conventional musical comedy, equipped with a story whose complications manage to be even sillier than those things usually are," he nonetheless recommended the show as enjoyable. The public didn't concur. Thirty-nine performances were all Miss Bayes could achieve.

The second edition of the **Music Box Revue 1922–23** (10-23-22, Music Box) came next, bringing with it a pair of riotous comedians new to Broadway, McCullough and Clark.

. . .

Bobby Clark was born in the rectory of the First Episcopal Church of Springfield, Ohio, on July 16, 1888. His grandfather was the church's sexton, and Clark's first public performances were as a member of the church choir. At the age of four he met a neighbor, eight-year-old Paul McCullough, and the two began a friendship and partnership that endured until McCullough's suicide. The boys taught themselves tumbling and bugling, and McCullough later often used a toy bugle as part of their routine. They toured as a teen-age minstrel act, switching briefly to circus clowning after their minstrel show folded and stranded them in Florida. In 1912 they entered vaudeville. Ten years later they made their legitimate debut in a London revue, *Chuckles of 1922.* When it closed they came back to America to appear in the Music Box entertainment. McCullough, slightly taller than Clark, mustached, and pudgy-faced, was the stooge of the act, who vacillated between childish glee and puerile pouting. The livelier Clark scampered across the stage wearing a passionate leer and painted-on eyeglasses, his hands forever occupied with his stubby cane and his usually burnt-out cigar.

. . .

Abetting McCullough and Clark in dispensing the evening's nonsense was wide-eyed, long-legged Charlotte Greenwood. The best comic bit of the evening fell to her. This was a humorous staging of Berlin's "Pack Up Your Sins [And Go To The Devil]" with Miss Greenwood in the devil's scarlet sending jazz musicians of the moment to their just damnation. Performers impersonating Gilda Gray, Ted Lewis, and others were hurtled into a steaming abyss. The greatest of the revue tenors, Irish-brogued John Steel, was given the hit of the evening—the song that for years afterwards Irving Berlin insisted was his personal favorite, "Lady Of The Evening." Steel sang the song in front of a simple setting of moonlit rooftops. The show's spectacle numbers were superb, if not always original. Twice in one evening the show used a similar device. In "Diamond Horseshoe" the train of Grace LaRue's Thais costume grew until it covered the stage and again, as Miss LaRue sang "Crinoline Days," a stage elevator lifted her higher and higher, while her hoop-skirt extended until it almost touched both sides of the proscenium. Hassard Short's setting for "Porcelain Maid" was perhaps more dazzlingly lavish than delicate, but his finale was more dazzling yet. It played upon the audience's perception of depth. Done all in gold, each time it seemed the rear wall of the stage had been reached another curtain parted to reveal more people and more of the set.

Springtime of Youth (10-26-22, Broadhurst), adapted from the German, was October's last entry. Its story was the Enoch Arden legend. In this version, set in 1812 New Hampshire, Arden was called Roger Hathaway (George MacFarlane) and the heroine, Priscilla Alden (Olga Steck). In his autobiography Harry B. Smith claimed credit for the adaptation, although the program and sheet music omitted his name. He wrote: "The most remarkable thing about this operetta was that the critics urged the public to hear it and the public obstinately refused to take the expert advice." Smith missed the point that the growing trend to reset European musicals in American surroundings often created absurd inconsistencies of tones. In this case, imagine an 1812 New Englander singing florid Viennese waltzes. Sometimes the public was apparently more sensitive to such incongruities than were the critics.

Up She Goes (11-6-22, Playhouse) was hailed as a delight, and this time the public did respond. The *Telegram* rejoiced, "One of the best musical shows seen in this city in many moons," and to drive its point home continued, "It is better than *Irene*." Since the score was by *Irene*'s Joseph McCarthy and Harry Tierney, the comparison was not farfetched. But the music, while pleasant, had no standouts. At best, "Journey's End" was hummable in the "Love Nest"–"Cottage Small" tradition. The book was better. Frank Craven adapted it from his own *Too Many Cooks,* and it still reads entertainingly. Of course, Craven's Cooks were not chefs but members of the Cook family, whose unsolicited visits and advice nearly wreck the plans Alice Cook (Gloria Foy) and Albert Bennett (Donald Brian) have to marry and to build a bungalow. Playgoers watched as act by act the house took shape.

One of the season's saddest and most instructive failures opened November 7, the night after *Up She Goes.* Though it played the minuscule Punch and Judy Theatre, **The 49ers** survived only two weeks. Its title stemmed not from its authors' expectations of striking gold, but simply the fact the theatre was on 49th Street. The authors, all on their way to renown, were largely from the Algonquin's Round Table. George S. Kaufman and Marc Connelly were apparently the prime movers, with Ring Lardner, Heywood Broun, Franklin P. Adams, and Robert Benchley assisting. What they attempted was a revue that eschewed spectacle and vaudeville vulgarity. Some of the best of the old burlesque tradition was kept, though the evening was more intimate, more literate, and more bitingly witty. Benchley and Dorothy Parker ridiculed fustian historical dramas. Their imaginary playwright got some chronology confused, forcing Richelieu, Queen Victoria, and Robert E. Lee to mix uncomfortably. Kaufman constructed a glimpse of American home-life with dialogue borrowed almost entirely from advertising slogans of the day. Broun rewrote Hans Christian Andersen's "The King's New Suit of Clothes," giving it a Pirandelloish bent by suggesting pretense becomes reality. When the royal tailor is exposed and condemned, he hangs himself with an invisible sash. Adams' contribution turned the routine of business into a musical comedy—product loses customer, product wins customer. "The Love Call" ridiculed contemporary operettas. As Burns Mantle noted, "the multitude sniffed and would have none of it." *The 49ers* went the way of *Blue Monday Blues,* without the consolation of revival.

If these up and coming writers were too advanced for their public, one oldtimer was not. George M. Cohan saw his **Little Nellie Kelly** (11-13-22, Liberty) run out the season. The critics, though they couldn't agree on what made the play entertaining, agreed it was an evening well spent. Cohan told another of the homey Irish stories he had come to depend on, this time coupled with a satire on the mystery plays so popular at the moment. Nellie (Elizabeth Hines), daughter of Police Captain Kelly (Arthur Deagon), works at Devere's Department Store. To court her, the wealthy Jack Lloyd (Barrett Greenwood) throws a party for all the Devere girls at his aunt's mansion. Jerry Conroy (Charles King), another suitor, crashes the party; and when the aunt's jewels disappear, he is suspected. Eventually he is cleared, and Nellie decides she prefers his simple, wise-cracking Irish ways to Jack's world. In the glittering twenties, when prosperity made material acquisitions more readily obtainable and clever advertising made them universally desired, Cohan often held to the earlier American dream that love outweighed riches. Curiously, the same philosophy would seem to apply at the close of Eddie Dowling's *Sally, Irene and Mary* —a departure from the ending of all three shows he was spoofing. Writing, as both Irishmen were, for heavily Irish or working-class audiences, they were undoubtedly responding to some hard-nosed inner reality these playgoers retained. But Cohan's dialogue was spunky, and his music, while not up to the best of his early masterpieces, was better than anything he had done in years. The song "Nellie Kelly, I Love You" came near to becoming standard, and "You Remind Me Of My Mother" is still sung occasionally.

In **Liza** (11-27-22, Daly's) the critics discovered what many felt was a worthwhile successor to *Shuffle Along* (5-23-21). Audiences were transported back to Jimtown, where an effort is being made to erect a monument to the town's deceased mayor. The town's dandies grow rich pocketing the funds. There was much praise for Maceo Pinkard's music. But, as had become the custom in reviewing black shows, the highest praise was reserved for the dancing. Words like "joyous," "zesty," "vital" filled the morning-after columns. Yet *Liza,* while enjoying a twenty-one-week run, never approached *Shuffle Along's* raging popularity, and Pinkard's score is totally forgotten. For all his luck outside the theatre—and he composed such standards as

"Sweet Georgia Brown"—Pinkard never found success on Broadway.

The night after *Liza* opened uptown, **The Bunch and Judy** arrived at the Globe in the heart of Times Square. With the freshly acclaimed Astaires, now virtual stars, singing and dancing Jerome Kern's latest score, the run of only 63 performances was plainly disappointing. But Kern's lovely score contained no exceptional melody, and the book was a mess. The *Call* looked on the show simply as a "succession of variety acts." The *Times* complained, "Caldwell's play attempts nothing like [a plot]" and rationalized, "It is the scenario of the scheme— stage, moorland and cabaret." What little plot there was told of a musical comedy star who deserts the stage to marry a Scottish lord, curiously foreshadowing Adele Astaire's own decision ten years later. But in the case of Judy Jordan, she is snubbed by Lord Kinloch's friends, and returns to America to make a happier second marriage with her former leading man, Gerald Lane.

Gershwin's name appeared briefly on the programs of the Bayes Theatre, where **Our Nell** (12-4-22, Bayes), a burlesque its creators referred to as a "musical mellowdrayma," languished for five weeks. Its plot had Nell pursued by a city slicker and saved by a wholesome country boy.

The Clinging Vine was Henry Savage's Christmas gift to Broadway at the Knickerbocker. It probably would have been received more gratefully if its score had been as good as its Zelda Sears' book. The *Times* extolled it for "a novel plot and a most appealing character," and the *American,* calling it "a capital story," felt it exemplified the best in "musical comedy—or, if you prefer it, the play with music which should be rational, humorous, simple and, if possible witty . . . It should be of today and the more so the better." The show related the adventures of Antoinette Allen, a young lady who runs the family paint business in Omaha. When she visits her Connecticut grandmother, the old woman forces her to play "the clinging vine" to win a husband. She not only wins a slew of suitors, but she bests them in a real estate deal. Then she announces she has had a fiancé waiting for her back home all the while and, money in hand, leaves for Omaha. With Peggy Wood as Antoinette, the show ran nearly six months despite its weak score.

Glory (12-25-22, Vanderbilt), a James Montgomery musical comedy for which his old *Irene* partners, Joseph McCarthy and Harry Tierney, were called in to provide part of the score, was a quick failure. The "Glory" of the title was another young lady (Patti Harrold) who goes from rags to riches. She is the daughter of the village ne'er-do-well, Abner Moore (Peter Lang). When William Harriman (Walter Regan), a villager who has made good in the big town, returns for a visit he falls in love with Glory, helps her win a popularity contest, and marries her. Some of the critics, tiring of the theme even faster than the public, were abrasive in their inevitable comparisons.

Lady Butterfly (1-22-23, Globe) used the old device of a luggage mix-up for its thin plot. Albert Hopper, a clownish wastrel, discovering he has mistakenly acquired the suitcase and papers of Enid Crawford's expected groom, decides to pretend he is the partner-to-be, whom Enid has never seen. Florenz Ames and Marjorie Gateson, two excellent performers, headed the cast. Werner Janssen wrote the score. However, most critics passed over the book and music, viewing the evening as a dancing show, praising soft shoe and ballroom routines as well as some comic tap dancing. They felt much the same way about a more appropriately titled piece, **The Dancing Girl.** The musical, which premiered January 24, was a typical Winter Garden revue, strung together with a vestigal plot of a ship-to-shore romance in which first-class passenger Bruce Chattfield falls in love with a steerage-class dancer, Anna. The evening's best dancing was provided by Trini, with her heel-clicking Spanish numbers. But the variety of passengers allowed almost any sort of vaudeville to be inserted. Benny Leonard, a real boxing champion, fought mock bouts, while Marie Dressler came on late in the evening to twit the season's biggest straight play hit, the Somerset Maugham story that John Colton and Clemence Randolph had turned into *Rain*. Both shows found audiences and both chalked up three-month runs.

Caroline (1-31-23, Ambassador), the melodic Kunneke operetta, *Der Vetter aus Dingsda,* was reset in Civil War Virginia for American theatre-goers and had a fair stay with Tessa Kosta in the title role, while an inept **Sun Showers** (2-5-23, Astor) managed five weeks. Its plot pictured the attempt by a poet and a prizefighter to help a band of schoolteachers win a raise. The Sun Showers of the title was the name of one of the poet's works.

The *Evening Mail,* singing a now familiar refrain, lamented the season's biggest hit, **Wildflower** (2-7-23, Casino), was not as good as *Irene* (11-18-19). The *Times* man regretted the book was "never funny, and now and then a little dull," but he lost his head over the music and approached

good old-fashioned raving. "The most tuneful score that Rudolf Friml has written," he began, following with a whole paragraph of ardent praise in which "Bambalina" was singled out. He opened his next paragraph reiterating his kudos for Friml. His embarrassment must have been acute when he learned Friml wrote not one note of the score. The error was not entirely absurd. Half the music was written by Herbert Stothart, who worked with Friml and whose compositions had an operettaish flavor. Furthermore, "Bambalina" could remind a hearer of, say, "Something Seems Tingle-Ingleing." In his study of our popular songs, Alec Wilder argues it has no distinctively American sound to it.

In any case, it was the songs by the composer of "Bambalina," Vincent Youmans, that made the show and established him as a major figure. The promise of *Two Little Girls in Blue* (5-3-21) was fulfilled, and his simple linear phrasing with changing harmony became a rapidly identifiable musical trademark. The critics who lambasted the libretto were not unjust. Though the experienced Otto Harbach worked with the increasingly active Oscar Hammerstein on it, it was a lame-brain affair—the sort that continued to give musical comedy books a bad name for years to come. Fiery Nina Benedetto (Edith Day) is willed a small fortune, provided she can keep her temper for six months. In spite of all sorts of nasty provocations from her cousin Bianca (Evelyn Cavanaugh), she succeeds, winning not only her inheritance but her lover Guido (Guy Robertson) as well. Several years after the show closed, Hammerstein attempted to rationalize the use of the story. His rationalization was not especially convincing, but it did suggest that, regardless of the name Hammerstein would give to his style of writing, he was, at heart, a fabricator of operetta. Hammerstein wrote, "*Wildflower* was a 'feeler,' a timid attempt to bring back the operetta, but still keeping enough of Cinderella and her dancing chorus to compromise with the public who demanded those elements." Hammerstein wrote these words after the opening of *Rose-Marie* (9-2-24). By that time he was already searching for a term to replace the unstylish "operetta." He decided on "musical play," a name often employed for operettas ashamed of their genre. For Edith Day, *Wildflower* was her last major Broadway appearance. She left to become one of London's favorite musical stars.

Go-Go (3-12-23, Daly's), a musical comedy based on a confusion of twins, had a competent book and a competent score, with one slightly better than average number, "Rosetime And You." The twins are Isabel and Florabell Parker (both played by Josephine Stevens). During the war Jack Locksmith (Bernard Granville) met Isabel, who was a nurse in France. Setting out to find her again, Jack stumbles on Florence, a singer at "The Pink Poodle." But Isabel turns up in time for a happy ending. It was another in the line of solid but undistinguished shows that John Cort kept giving New York and of which *Listen, Lester* (12-23-18) remained the best received.

Jack and Jill (3-22-23, Globe) was another revue with musical comedy pretensions. The nouveau-riche Mrs. Malone (Georgia O'Ramey) buys a chair made from wood of the cherry tree George Washington chopped down. Anyone sitting in the chair is compelled to tell the truth. The confessions help Jill Malone (Virginia O'Brien) win Jack Andrews (Donald MacDonald) rather than the man her mother would have her marry, Jimmy Eustace. The show came in with the spring and lasted out the season thanks largely to the dancing of stylish Clifton Webb as Jimmy and the more unrestrained Ann Pennington as Jimmy's "pal," Gloria Wayne.

Neither Carlo and Sanders (of *Tangerine*) nor Sissle and Blake (of *Shuffle Along*) could save **Elsie** (4-2-23, Vanderbilt). And Friml, who really did write this score, could do no more the next night for **Cinders** (4-3-23, Dresden). Both shows employed the period's favorite story. *Elsie* unfolded the trials of a young actress in winning the acceptance of Harry Hammond's rich, snobbish family. Their ideas are far behind the times, and they do not take easily to a girl or her friends who proclaim "Everybody's Struttin' Now" and who are thrilled by "Thunderstorm Jazz." The plot was loose enough to allow for a number of vaudeville specialties. Harry was portrayed by Vinton Freedley, who soon found more congenial employment as one of Broadway's leading producers. *Cinders,* as its title suggests, took the obvious course in this era of rags-to-riches plots by simply retelling the Cinderella story in a modern setting. Cinders (Nancy Welford) is a waif who was discovered in an ash can and who has grown up dreaming of being a jazz-age Cinderella. Assigned to deliver a gown to a rich Mrs. Horatio Winthrop, she appropriates the dress and takes herself to a charity ball. There she meets Mrs. Winthrop's son, John (Walter Regan), and the two fall in love. Cinders is accused of stealing jewels at the party, but clears herself in time for a happy finale.

The critics simply shrugged their shoulders at

How Come? (4-16-23, Apollo), another attempt at copying *Shuffle Along* (5-23-21). Billed as "a girly musical darkomedy," its high-stepping black dancing was tied together with a shoestring plot in which Rastus Skunton Lime (Eddie Hunter) endeavors to embezzle funds from the Mobile Chicken Trust Corporation. The evening's best comic scene was Rastus' attempted jail break. Concluding subtlety would fail, he makes his attempt as noisy and visible as possible, only to discover the jailer is deaf and virtually blind.

Dew Drop Inn (5-17-23, Astor), with Friml interpolations, was praised largely for James Barton's clowning, including Barton's famous drunk act. A tenuous plot revolved around a young heir's determination to make good on his own and on his fiancée's refusal to leave him for a bribe of $20,000.

Adrienne (5-28-23, Cohan) similarly had to rely on its principals to overcome an undistinguished Albert Von Tilzer score and a plot that harked back to Marie Cahill's heyday. It used the perennially popular motif of a jewel robbery, or at least an attempted theft, as the basis for its story. Adrienne Grey believes in reincarnation. A band of jewel thieves persuades her to wear her precious stones and they lure her to a temple with the story that she will meet the spirit of a prince who loved her in a former life. Her present-day lover gets wind of the plot and helps foil the gang. Vivienne Segal played the title role, while Billy B. Van and Marie Cahill's onetime costar, Richard Carle, led the comedians.

Just as booking quirks in 1921–22 produced two editions of the *Ziegfeld Follies* in one season, 1922–23 presented two **Passing Shows.** The 1923 edition, which opened at the Winter Garden on June 14, betrayed a distressing slippage in quality: no good songs and feeble comedy. These weaknesses were doubly sad because the handsome, full-voiced Walter Woolf was on hand to sing and young George Jessel replaced the Howards as master of comedy. Jessel wrote his own monologues and a skit "Upper Box at a French Comedy." Spectacle and largely undressed girls were all that maintained the old standards. In one scene three gigantic chandeliers were formed by the ladies of the chorus. The girls also came on stage in costumes suggesting the popular best-sellers of the day, two of which were "The Beautiful and Damned" and just plain "Damned." The show ended the season on an appropriately commonplace note.

378

1923-1924

The big revue made a comeback in 1923–24. Twelve of the season's first nineteen musical offerings were revues of one sort or another, and, somewhat surprisingly, eight achieved some degree of success. Of course, four were time-tested series that now claimed a certain loyal clientele and had established so broad a national name for themselves that they were a likely choice for tourists. If *The Passing Show*, which technically ended the previous season, is included, all the major annuals were accounted for. This year even Burns Mantle could not ignore the general musical decline. Judging the general season better than the last, he attributed part of its superiority to "fewer of those musical entertainments of which kindly disposed reviewers are wont to write that the librettos were terrible but the music good."

Even the music was not that good in the season's first entry, **George White's Scandals of 1923** (6-18-23, Globe). Baral in his study, *Revue,* rightly gives the show short shrift, noting merely that, while Gershwin's score "sounded bright in overture, no real hit emerged. The whole show was several grades lower than the preceding edition." Winnie Lightner attempted to put over the songs. Tom Patricola danced, played the ukulele, and acted in a travesty of *Romeo and Juliet*. Lester Allen clowned in his acrobatic dances. White arranged his girls in rows one atop the other to create a "living curtain"; he paraded them bedecked as rare jewels, and turned them all into roses. Good or bad, its public supported the revue for twenty-one weeks.

One interesting book show interrupted the procession of revues. **Helen of Troy, New York** (6-19-23, Selwyn) had a George S. Kaufman and Marc Connelly libretto, Bert Kalmar and Harry Ruby songs. The score was the team's first, and they were not yet in full stride. Aisle-sitters found it no more than "so-so" (*Tribune*), "fairly good" (*World*), or "well-made" (*Times*). Again, not a single hit tune emerged. But the very same critics greeted the book with huzzahs—the *Tribune* hailing it as "a bright travesty" and the *World*, welcoming "the business satire of *To The Ladies* into the musical comedy field," added prophetically that Kaufman and Connelly had determined "a musical show should be taught new tricks." The story told of Helen McGuffey (Helen Ford)—even here there

would be a poor Irish heroine—who loses her stenographer's job at a collar factory when the president learns his son loves the office girl. She invents an improved, softer collar, which she sells to a rival house. Her former company is forced to merge and she wins the heir apparent. However stale the plot line, the mordant Kaufman and Connelly wit distinguished the show. For example, the head of the vast manufacturing enterprise can never remember his own collar size. He has to refer sheepishly to his notebook to find it. There were even some very private jokes only a handful of the audience might really understand. One character was a mincing male model who posed for the collar ads. Insiders knew he was drawn after a model used by J. C. Leyendecker, the man who created the famous Arrow collar drawings.

Kaufman and Connelly came from somewhat similar backgrounds.

• • •

George S. Kaufman was born in Pittsburgh on November 16, 1889. Because his parents had lost a son shortly before George was born, George was given a pampered upbringing, kept away from games and sports that might prove harmful. He became an avid reader. He entered the newspaper field, obtaining work with the Washington *Star*. Fired by the paper's owner when he discovered George was a Jew, he moved to New York and got a job with the *Evening Mail*. In 1915 he became drama critic for the *Tribune* and shortly thereafter for the *Times*. He gave up criticism to handle the paper's theatrical news and to try his own hand at playwriting. His first effort folded out of town.

• • •

Marc Connelly was born just over a year after Kaufman, on December 13, 1890, in McKeesport, a steel town not far from Pittsburgh. He, too, took quickly to journalism, first locally and after 1916 in New York. While still in Pittsburgh he wrote the lyrics for a local 1913 production, *The Lady of Luzon*. His first professional theatrical plunge was helping to revise the libretto of *Erminie* for the 1921 revival. That same year he teamed with Kaufman to write *Dulcy,* a smash hit. One year later the pair had a second hit on their hands, *To the Ladies*.

• • •

July and August brought three more revues. Only the Earl Carroll **Vanities of 1923** (7-5-23, Earl Carroll) succeeded. It was a new series, bankrolled by a Texas oilman, that would be produced erratically over the next decade. It was more interested in its girls than in what they wore—a hint sensationalism might stimulate ticket sales. Less clothing also meant less expense; and higher costs were helping to bring down the curtain on the older series. But the *Vanities'* songs and sketches were never of a high order. Nothing of permanent value was presented in any of its editions. The 1923 version opened with "The Birth of a New Revue," in which the loveliest girls were brought forth to represent the *Follies,* the *Scandals,* and the other annuals. The last girl to appear represented the *Vanities.* The first-act finale put each girl in a different fur, with the radiant Peggy Hopkins Joyce promenading in chinchilla. The inevitable staircase was also present, but Carroll found a novel use for it. Renoff (of Renoff and Renova) finished his dance by dramatically plunging down all the steps. More dainty toe dancing was performed by petite Gertie Lemmon. Bernard Granville was on hand to sing the songs, but they were undistinguished and bore titles typical of this genre, "Girls Were Made For Dancing," "A Girl Is Like Sunshine," and "My Cretonne Girl." The comedy was largely in the hands of Joe Cook, who brought his "One Man Vaudeville" over from the two-a-day circuits.

A trio of old hands on stage and behind the scenes—Arnold Daly, Harry B. Smith, Ted Snyder—tried and failed with **Fashions of 1924** (7-18-23, Lyceum). The critics looked on it as an elaborate, poorly assembled fashion show. Nor was its comedy original or good, falling back on overworked bits such as a comic prize fight skit.

The Newcomers (8-8-23, Ambassador) attempted unsuccessfully an idea Leonard Sillman would revive with happier results eleven years later—a revue assembled as a showcase for new talent. To some extent *The Newcomers* was a vanity production. Will Morrisey wrote the work, produced it, and served as its compère. He perched himself down by the footlights to introduce each act and provided some commentary. The acts were largely vaudevillian, including a male impersonator and a ventriloquist.

The season's biggest hit, **Little Jessie James,** opened at the modest-sized Longacre on August 15. The critics, while not unhappy, showed no special enthusiasm. Mantle awarded it only passing mention in his review of the year. That old theatrical shibboleth "the audience show" apparently applied here. *Little Jessie James* was not a western. All the action takes place in an apartment overlooking Central Park, where Jessie Jamieson (Nan Halperin) pursues Paul Revere (Jay Velie) and does not let bedroom farce misunderstandings prevent her winning him. Miriam Hopkins and Allen Kearns called

attention to themselves in supporting roles. "I Love You" was the most successful song to come out of a musical during the season, and its great vogue undoubtedly lengthened the box office lines. Harry Archer's score—played in the theatre by a Paul Whiteman band—was otherwise mediocre, and Archer never again had so solid a hit. A further aid in lengthening the show's run was its low initial and operating costs. There was only one set, and at a time when forty or more people comprised an ordinary chorus, *Little Jessie James* frugally employed only eight chorus girls. A 1953–54 revival foundered quickly.

The Shuberts, always quick to sense and follow trends, established a Carroll-like revue, **Artists and Models** (8-20-23, Shubert), just as years earlier they had offered *The Passing Show* to compete with Ziegfeld. Even more than the *Vanities,* the new series depended on nudity to entice theatregoers. Like the *Vanities* it appeared erratically, and left nothing to posterity. Frank Fay, considered by many the drollest of compères, performed the task in this edition.

A late August arrival, **Little Miss Bluebeard** (8-28-23, Lyceum), though listed on its sheet music as a "gay song-play," was a comedy for which E. Ray Goetz and George Gershwin wrote a handful of tunes for Irene Bordoni. It straddled the fence between straight play and musical.

Poppy (9-3-23, Apollo) was one more rags-to-riches tale. Two of its songs, "What Do You Do Sundays, Mary?" and "Alibi Baby" (Howard Dietz/Arthur Samuels), were well received and had a contemporary popularity. Madge Kennedy, playing the title role of the circus waif who discovers she's an heiress, collected handsome notices. But the main attraction of *Poppy* was W. C. Fields as Eustace McGargle, the girl's preposterously unconventional guardian. The show ran the whole season.

Two more annuals followed: *The Greenwich Village Follies* ("Strong on beauty, but somewhat dull otherwise") and *The Music Box Revue.* **The Greenwich Village Follies** (9-20-23, Winter Garden) displayed another Reginald Marsh show curtain, this time depicting an old, turn-of-the-century village. Lavish production numbers included "Moonlight Kisses" (in which great ladies of legend and history passed briefly across the stage) and a Spanish fiesta number designed by James Reynolds in the style of a Velásquez painting. There were two "Ballet Ballads." The first, based on Poe's "The Raven," was a dud and quickly withdrawn. But "The Garden of Kama," telling a tragic tale of love in India, was praised. Martha Graham danced in both the latter and in the fiesta scene, dances far removed from the modern dance style she later popularized. A new female impersonator, Karyl Norman, was called in to replace the late Bert Savoy. Norman's style was closer to the dignified Julian Eltinge's than to the rowdy Savoy's. Tom Howard presented his country bumpkin humor. The diminutive twosome, Sammy White and Eva Puck, offered their brand of light comedy and dancing. The show's principal weakness was its score.

The score of **The Music Box Revue 1923–1924,** which premiered September 22, also proved so weak that Irving Berlin hurriedly interpolated his own "What'll I Do?," which was not written for the show. Another song, "An Orange Grove In California," was given a striking mounting. The song was first sung by John Steel and by Grace Moore (whom Berlin had given "What'll I Do?") walking together in an orange grove. Slowly the grove melted away into a kaleidoscope of shimmering orange lights and the audience found itself sprayed with orange perfume. A silver and gold mesh curtain, reputed to have cost $50,000, was featured in another scene. Two extraordinary sketches for this edition have managed to survive and enjoy lives of their own. The first was Benchley's "Treasurer's Report"; the second, Kaufman's hilarious masterpiece, "If Men Played Cards as Women Do." Benchley purported to be an officer of a choral society and was offering its members his latest accounting. With embarrassed little coughs and tugs at his collar he acknowledged gaps and discrepancies. But after all, other pressing matters—such as his sister's wedding—necessitated his omitting a month here and there. In the Kaufman sketch four men (played in the show by Joseph Santley, Hugh Cameron, Solly Ward, and Phil Baker) sit down to a friendly game of bridge. John, the host, and Bob, the first player to arrive, gush over a new hat band on Bob's year-old Knox. The two men talk cattily about George, only to do a smiling about-face when George appears. Their backbiting then shifts to absent friends. The fourth player, Marc, stops the game briefly to preen himself, placing a pocket mirror on the card table, shaving a rough spot on his carefully examined chin, and slicking down his hair with two military brushes. The skit ends with the startling revelation that one of the men's friends, somebody named Sid, will become a father in April—though he only married in January! In its original performance the skit's humor was heightened by the players eschewing all traces of effeminacy. The skit was played, as Kaufman demanded, "in forthright and manly fashion."

Charles Dillingham assembled a superb cast for **Nifties of 1923** (9-25-23, Fulton). The producer poured most of his money into this cast, giving the evening a tasteful but relatively simple mounting. Some critics viewed it as little more than stylish vaudeville. With Ziegfeld now advertising that he was glorifying the American Girl, *Nifties* boasted in turn that it was "glorifying clean American humor." The material was written by the show's stars, Sam Bernard and William Collier. They appeared together as quarreling neighbors in a skit called "Keep Off the Grass." Curiously, none of the other performers were given star billing or even mentioned in the regular advertisements, though many had recently been top names. Hazel Dawn played her violin and gave her interpretation of Jeanne Eagels in *Rain.* Frank Crumit lead the Elm City Four in barber shop favorites. Others in the excellent company were Van and Schenk, Florence Ames, Ray Dooley, Helen Broderick, the toe-dancing Lina Basquette, and the Twelve Tiller Girls, precision dancers. If Dillingham contemplated another series, he arrived on the scene with it much too late in the day, and a number of his best names were also beyond their brightest years.

Zelda Sears and Harold Levey could not re-create their success of *The Clinging Vine* (12-25-22) in **The Magic Ring** (10-1-23, Liberty). The show was a vehicle for Mitzi. She played a ragamuffin organ-grinder whose discovery of a magic ring brings her wealth and romance. In short, the musical was another rags-to-riches tale, with Oriental trappings. It ran 96 performances, almost reaching that 100 mark, which in the twenties, suggested a probable return on investment.

Three nights later Arthur Hammerstein at the Century Roof failed with an imported English entertainment he rechristened **Hammerstein's 9 O'Clock Revue.** But an Americanized English musical, with a prizefight theme, **Battling Buttler** (10-8-23, Selwyn), delighted both the critics and its audiences. The *Times* rejoiced, "musical comedies are really getting better."

They grew worse abruptly with **Ginger** (10-16-23, Daly's), a Harold Orlob offering that couldn't manage five full weeks. Originally titled *Take a Chance,* it spent the evening searching for someone to test a new-style parachute. The dialogue was the *Listen, Lester* (12-23-18) variety:

—Are you a reactionary?
—I haven't been examined yet.

—Well, do you like conventions?

—I've only attended one.

Even the **Ziegfeld Follies of 1923** (10-20-23, New Amsterdam) was obviously a step down. Ziegfeld's stars were fast leaving him for book shows, vaudeville, and movies. Of his greatest performers, only Fanny Brice remained, and she was so displeased with the weak material given her that she, too, bid adieu to the revue when this edition closed. James Reynolds also left after this production, but unlike Miss Brice, he went out with a flourish. He set "The Legend Of The Drums" in Napoleonic times and ended the scene with a spectacular effect that simulated the burning of captured war drums. Another dazzling bit was a "Maid of Gold" number, for which the exotic dancer Muriel Stryker painted her body with special gold paint. Costumes were designed by the rage of fashionable Paris, Erté, and the scene set to music by Rudolf Friml. It did not remain in the show for long—at least not in its original form. The dancer's physician warned her that the paint would endanger her life. A gold lamé dress replaced the gold paint. As a rule, the *Follies* no longer elicited composers' best works. However, "Chansonette," a Friml melody from his background music for the show, was made into "The Donkey Serenade" a dozen or so years later. Audiences at the show went home singing "Take, Oh Take Those Lips Away" (Joseph McCarthy/Harry Tierney). Though it fell far short of the best McCarthy and Tierney songs, Ziegfeld marshaled his best forces for the number. The song was sung by the boyishly handsome Brooke Johns, whom Ziegfeld hoped to groom as John Steel's replacement, much as he hoped to find a second Marilyn Miller in Mary Eaton. Johns lacked the radiant Irish tenor of Steel, but he could play the banjo and he had no drinking problem. Unfortunately, he was no actor, and with revues fading there would be little room for him in book shows. The lips Johns bid be taken away were the cupid bows of Ann Pennington. Paul Whiteman's orchestra accompanied the performers. Because rising costs discouraged Ziegfeld from taking the show on the road, it was able to remain in New York as long as the public wanted it. Before it closed it compiled an usually long run for a *Follies,* 333 performances.

Some real life jumped back into the season with **Runnin' Wild** (10-29-23, Colonial), the closest any black musical comedy of the era came to repeating *Shuffle Along*'s success. It presented the usual flimsy plot principaled by the sharper and dolt that Bert Williams and George Walker had established as a formula for Negro shows almost a quarter of century before, and which Flournoy Miller and Aubrey Lyles had perpetuated with *Shuffle Along* (5-23-21). Miller and Lyles were the show's librettists and were also back on stage to portray Steve Jenkins and Sam Peck again. Naturally the setting was once more Jimtown. Sam and Steve jump their board bill but return to Jimtown disguised as mediums. Typical of the humor was Sam's blaming their bad business luck on "de ducks." His elaboration on his analysis shows he "de ducks" $10 for everything he can get away with. There were the customary racial comedy scenes; for example, the timid Negro confronted with a ghost. But what the public really enjoyed was what the *Tribune* termed "rhythm . . . and risible dental display." Virtually all the reviewers, employing such words as "dark" and "dusky," still implied these shows were not to be considered in the theatrical mainstream, but something *sui generis*. It may not be coincidental that the most successful of these were usually presented either at the Colonial or at Daly's, both north of 57th Street, and away from the center of the theatrical district. But in this instance the critics turned out to be remarkably myopic, for there was one number in the show, a dance that ultimately expressed and symbolized the whole gaudy era about to explode. It pronounced the beat for the "lost generation" and liberated the whole jazz movement. The dance song was, of course, "The Charleston." The dance typified the black-inspired high-stepping of the era. It was gawky, zesty, and, obviously, irresistible.

Just as Jerome Kern's *The Bunch and Judy* (11-28-22) at the Globe followed *Liza*'s uptown opening, so Kern's **Stepping Stones** at the same house on November 6 brought the critics back downtown after *Runnin' Wild*. What interested the reviewers and the public was the debut as star of Dorothy Stone, Fred's daughter, and much publicity was given to her name being put up in lights alongside his while the first-night audience was applauding her. Kern also came in for high praise. And his score was beautiful. The virtually forgotten "Once In A Blue Moon" and "In Love With Love" rank with all but his greatest melodies. However, this musicalized version of Little Red Riding Hood, in which Rougette Hood (Dorothy Stone) is pursued by the villainous Otto De Wolfe (Oscar Ragland) and is rescued "in song dance and acrobatic comedy by one Peter Plug" (Fred Stone), demanded specialized lyrics that undoubtedly kept some of the melodies from general currency. Rougette, her mother (Allene Stone) and the girls' chorus sang "Little Red Riding Hood." Plug sang and danced to "Pie," while Rougette and Prince Silvio (Roy Hoyer) sang the love song.

Topics of 1923 (11-20-23, Broadhurst) was a revue written by many old Winter Garden hands for the ballyhooed Alice Delysia, who had come to Broadway two years before in *Afgar*. Neither Miss Delysia nor the show found favor. A few critics praised the gowns, and the *Times* noted that an acrobatic dancer, Nat Nazzaro, gathered more applause than the star. The revue headed quickly for Cain's warehouse, and the star returned to Europe.

Two nights later, November 22, the group that had presented *Go-Go* (4-12-28) the preceding season with a modicum of success tried again with **Sharlee** at Daly's. Sharlee Saunders (Juliette Day) is a nightclub singer aching to find love and a home in the country. She succeeds, but nobody on the other side of the footlights seemed to care. The show was gone before the new year arrived.

On the 27th, Dillingham brought in a French musical, *Ta Bouche,* with a score by Maurice Yvain, who composed "Mon Homme." Called **One Kiss** here, the show ran 95 performances at the Fulton. The story told how young love triumphs over parental objections. The cast of *One Kiss* was a remarkable roster of old and new favorites—Ada Lewis, John E. Hazzard, Louise Groody, Oscar Shaw, and John Price Jones. Dillingham, like Ziegfeld, never did things by halves.

Three memorable and noteworthy musicals closed 1923. The first two arrived on Christmas, the third on New Year's Eve. The Christmas presents were **Mary Jane McKane** at the new Imperial and **The Rise of Rosie O'Reilly** at the Liberty. The credits for *Mary Jane McKane* read almost like those of *Wildflower,* only Otto Harbach had given place to William Le Baron. The plot was old hat. Mary (Mary Hay), another poor Irish secretary, loses her job when her boss's son, Andrew Dunn, Jr. (Stanley Ridges), shows interest in her. She returns in a drab disguise and later goes into business with the son when his father fires him. By 11 o'clock she is Mary Dunn, with even the elder Dunn approving. To a man the critics could find nothing exciting in the plot, or in the music. The *Times* critic did, however, give Vincent Youmans proper credit this time. At most, the show was adjudged professional and diverting, while the real praise was awarded its star, Miss Hay. It ran 151 performances. In some of his better numbers—"Toodle-oo," "Flannel Petticoat Gal"—Youmans' peculiar technique of small repeated phrases varied har-

monically was again immediately identifiable. Since the sale of the show's sheet music was small and complete score recordings (at least in America) were twenty years in the future, Youmans was able to put two of the show's songs away for reuse: a waltz called "My Boy And I" and "Come On And Pet Me." With new lyrics and with the former's waltz tempo dropped, they would re-emerge in *No! No! Nanette!* (9-16-25) and *Hit the Deck* (4-25-27) respectively.

The critics did not have to reach back three or four years to find a musical to compare with *The Rise of Rosie O'Reilly*. Though most of them greeted George M. Cohan's new work affectionately, it was simply too much like *Little Nellie Kelly* (11-13-22). *Theatre Arts* observed: "Rosie O'Reilly looked like all her little sisters who have gone before." Rosie (Virginia O'Brien), who sells flowers beneath the Brooklyn Bridge, meets Bob Morgan (Jack McGowan), a wealthy man-about-town. They fall in love, but Bob is disinherited and goes to work at a florist's. Eventually the elder Morgan relents. Bob and Rosie are married, though Rosie clearly would have taken Bob even if he had never been restored to his fortune. This could represent a compromise with the Cinderella ending Cohan had heretofore avoided. But nothing else was markedly different, and the score was several notches below Cohan's compositions in *Nellie Kelly*. The show ran eleven weeks before it went on tour. Cohan began slipping back to the short New York runs and long national tours of his early shows. But in his youth he had been a pathmaker, bursting with enthralling melody. By the twenties he was old fashioned, unable to compose little more than hand-me-down tunes, which often seemed an inferior rehash of his older songs.

Ziegfeld celebrated New Year's Eve by offering Broadway **Kid Boots** at the Earl Carroll, with Eddie Cantor as star and Mary Eaton as the principal beauty. William Anthony McGuire and Otto Harbach did the book, which had fun with the popular craze for golf, a sport formerly restricted to the upper classes, and bootlegging. Cantor, in white-face for most of the show, played a less than honest caddy who sells crooked balls and booze. The plot thickens when the club champion, his friend, inadvertently uses one of the balls to play the match of the year. A romantic subplot gave the show's costar, Mary Eaton, several chances to do her light, breezy dances. George Olsen and his jazz orchestra were on hand to play the new Joseph McCarthy-Harry Tierney score, but even Cantor could not put over the mediocre music. Only an interpolation,

Harry Akst's "Dinah," caught on. "Dinah," Cantor, Miss Eaton, and the Ziegfeld magic kept *Kid Boots* going for months.

One of the finest of all revues, **Charlot's Revue** (1-9-24, Times Square) came from London. And it came as a revelation to American theatregoers. In a way (and a number of critics saw this) comparison with American shows was unfair, for André Charlot had culled his material from several of his London successes. The evening could have been called "The Best from Charlot's Revues." But this in no way gainsaid the quality of its material or the talent of its performers. Charlot made the evening seem to move at a lightning-like pace by flying in the face of Broadway practice and steadfastly refusing to allow encores. The show made the American reputation of three great English performers. The first and least was suave Jack Buchanan, a performer equally adept at singing, dancing, and light comedy. Though the show revealed Gertrude Lawrence's gift for putting across a song (and she sang the show's hit, "Limehouse Blues"), it gave her little opportunity to display her comic and acting abilities. Most of all, the show brought America Beatrice Lillie, England's greatest comedienne.

. . .

Though her career kept her largely in London or New York, **Beatrice Lillie** was born in Toronto, Canada, on May 12, 1898 (possibly 1894). She made her debut at the Chatham Music Hall in 1914. A stint in vaudeville quickly gave way to increasingly important appearances in London revues with snappy titles such as *Samples, Some, Cheep, Tabs,* and *A to Z.* In 1919 she interrupted this chain of revues to take the principal comedienne's role (Jackie) in the London version of the Princess Theatre hit *Oh, Boy!,* known on the West End as *Oh, Joy!*

. . .

In one number Miss Lillie played an aging soubrette clinging desperately to the songs of her youth. But her greatest moment came in "March With Me," in which she attempted to lead a cadre, only to move left when they moved right, hopelessly scrambling ranks and creating further chaos by trying to set things in order. Miss Lillie would reduce an audience to nearly helpless laughter by some bit of absurdity and then devastate it completely by glowering at it in outrage for laughing at her in the first place. *Charlot's Revue* helped point the way to the more intimate, literate and fast-paced revues that later dominated Broadway. In after years the show would be looked back on as a mile-

stone. Yet it is necessary to remember that the show did not start an immediate rush to a new style. It took several years before this newer type of revue caught on.

Lollipop (1-21-24, Knickerbocker) holds a quirky interest. It was Vincent Youmans' first complete score, to a book by Zelda Sears, who had been supplying strong librettos to limp composers. This time the situation was reversed. Miss Sears let Youmans down with a book the *Times* dismissed as "weakly Cinderella-ish." Laura "Lollipop" Lamb (Ada May Weeks), an orphan, is adopted by the well-to-do Mrs. Garrity (Miss Sears). Laura clears herself of the charge she has stolen her benefactor's purse, finds love, and ultimately throws a big costume ball. The score was not all bad, including as it did the still familiar "Tie A Little String Around Your Finger" as well as "Take A Little One Step," which Youmans would reuse in *No! No! Nanette!* (9-16-25). *Lollipop* ran 152 performances, one more than *Mary Jane McKane.*

George Gershwin was also on the eve of finding himself, having left the *Scandals* to concentrate on book shows. He pleased the critics on the same January 21 with **Sweet Little Devil** (one of the last shows to play the desirable Astor before it became a movie house), but his songs have long since been pushed aside by greater Gershwin works that followed. The critics disagreed on the merits of the book. The *World* extolled the "novel plot," while the *Post* complained, "the plot is almost completely missing." As Frank Mandel and Laurence Schwab conceived it, *Sweet Little Devil* related Tom Nesbitt's (Irving Beebe) astonishment when Joyce West (Marjorie Gateson), the sweet Follies beauty he has been corresponding with, proves a callous money-grabber. It develops her roommate, the little devil Virginia Culpepper (Constance Binney), has really been doing the corresponding. Tom settles for Virginia and a life in Peru. It was, in fact, a good contemporary book, catching the smart talk of the times: "He's so mad about me," Joyce gloats, "I could kick him in the nose, and he'd say it's being done this season." *Sweet Little Devil* enjoyed a fair run of fifteen weeks.

Moonlight (1-30-24, Longacre), a highly touted show, with music by Con Conrad and a book by William Le Baron based on his own farce, *I Love You,* had an eighteen-week stay. Like many of the period's musicals, it was a one-set, basically intimate piece—a comedy with music, although in this instance sixteen songs were published. Several of them, for example, "On Such A Night," are still pleasantly hummable. They exemplify the constant melodic appeal of even the second-string songs of the period. Conrad was a fine composer, though his best work, notably "Margie" and "Memory Lane," was done outside the theatre. No poor girl makes good in *Moonlight.* Jimmie Farnsworth (Louis Simon) bets George Van Horne (Glen Dale) that given the proper setting anyone will fall in love. He wins his bet, but only after some unexpected matches are untangled. *Moonlight,* like *Lollipop* and *Sweet Little Devil,* ran up to the warm weather.

In mid-February Eleanor Painter, most famous as Herbert's Princess Pat, came back to sing Carlo and Sanders' score for **The Chiffon Girl** (2-19-24, Lyric). The plot was operetta with a jazz age twist. It may have recalled *Suzette* (11-24-21) to the few who saw that flop. A beautiful Italian fruit vendor is sent to Italy to study voice. She returns four years later a great prima donna. However, she does not marry her benefactor but her old boy friend—now a bootlegger. The Carlo-Sanders score was no better than any of their other efforts. Nonetheless, *The Chiffon Girl* ran three months.

No musical arrived on Broadway for the next month and a half. With hot evenings approaching, the Shuberts broke the lull by offering **Vogues of 1924** (3-27-24, Shubert). It had a fine cast and ran into the summer. Some of its numbers may have reminded playgoers of *Nifties of 1924.* Where Hazel Dawn had played her violin in the earlier show, Odette Myrtil played hers in the new entertainment. Miss Dawn had twitted *Rain*'s Sadie Thompson, so did the new show. But *Vogues* did it with a vengeance, with six Sadies and six Rev. Davidsons singing a Florodora-like sextette. Jimmy Savo and Fred Allen also accounted for much of the laughter. The best bit of the evening fell to Allen, in a monologue not too far removed from Benchley's "Treasurer's Report." Allen took it upon himself to teach the audience his brand of algebra, insisting, "Let X equal my father's signature."

Paradise Alley (3-31-24, Casino), a musical with a *Sally*-like plot, had a brief spring stay. It recorded the rise of Bonnie Brown (Helen Shipman) from an alley urchin to the rage of London's musical comedy stage. Courted by a number of Englishmen, she rejects them all for Jack Harriman (Charles Derickson), an American boxer.

Sitting Pretty came April 8 to remain until July. But *Sitting Pretty* should have run longer. Though done at the Fulton, a band-box house just off Times Square, it was a Princess Theatre show. F. Ray Comstock and Morris Gest were once again the producers. More importantly, Guy Bolton, P. G.

Wodehouse, and Jerome Kern were again the authors. Following the old pattern of two acts with one set for each, it portrayed the troubles of Horace (Dwight Frye), a small-time crook (how Bolton loved crooks!), who has been robbing rich men's homes. His plan to rob the Penningtons is thwarted when he falls in love with May Tolliver (Gertrude Bryan) at the Penningtons' house. May and her sister Dixie (Queenie Smith) reform Horace. Dixie's reward is the Pennington heir (Rudolf Cameron). The critics, recognizing its provenance, were delighted. The *Sun* called it "a charming and likeable sequel to the miniature musical comedies . . . at the Princess before the war." Kern received most of the laurels, though very kind words were also saved for Wodehouse's marvelous lyrics. Some critics had a reservation or two about the book, Percy Hammond in the *Tribune* going so far as to suggest, cantankerously and shortsightedly, that Bolton would find more rewarding employment in "smart revues" than in "the mawkish vapidities of musical comedy." The book, however, is still eminently playable, and the Kern-Wodehouse songs exquisite. The lovely title song, sung by Harold and Dixie, seems a full ten years ahead of its time in its chromatics. More of their own epoch, "A Year From Today," "The Enchanted Train," and "All You Need Is A Girl" (all three sung by May and Bill Pennington) are graceful gems, well worth replaying, while Wodehouse's "Bongo On The Congo" lyrics (sung by Horace and his cronies) would probably stop a show even today. In the Congo, he assured playgoers, they present a visitor with a dozen wives when he arrives. A man with fewer than two dozen wives is considered a bachelor.

May 5 saw what augured to be an interesting evening at the Jolson—a musical version of *Peg o' My Heart,* only slightly rechristened **Peg o' My Dreams.** As she had in the original, Margaret O'Connell (Suzanne Keener) wins the hand of Sir Gerald (Roy Royston), who loves her even though she is an heiress. But Hugo Felix' score was even drearier than his *Marjolaine* (1-24-22) material, and, with no Laurette Taylor or Peggy Wood to help, the show barely survived the month.

Another Cinderella version entered the arena as **Plain Jane** (5-12-24, New Amsterdam). Jane Lee (Lorraine Manville), another tenement waif, enters her rag doll in a contest. She fails to win, but the son of the doll manufacturer who sponsored the contest falls in love with her. He has an argument with his father over Jane, quits his job, and wins enough money in a prize fight to set himself and Jane up in a competitive company. A superbly staged fight scene seems to have been its main claim to fame, for the book was drab and the music of Tom Johnstone, who seemed to be eyeing A. Baldwin Sloane's dubious mantle, was merely the music of Tom Johnstone.

Another Johnstone score was heard on Broadway exactly a week later. It was heard, that is, if the constant laughter that filled the house didn't mercifully drown it out. For the show was **I'll Say She Is!** (5-19-24, Casino) one of the hits of the season and the main stem's introduction to the Marx brothers.

The births of the four **Marx brothers** who composed the act during its legitimate career spanned ten years. **Leonard (Chico)** was born in New York on March 26, 1891. **Adolph (Harpo)** was born there on November 21, 1893. **Julius (Groucho)** followed on October 2, 1895, while **Herbert (Zeppo)** came on the scene nearly six years later, February 25, 1901. A fifth brother, **Milton,** appeared with the boys briefly during their early vaudeville days. He used the name **Gummo.** The brothers belonged to a theatrical family. Their maternal grandparents had been performers in Germany; their maternal uncle was Al Shean of Gallagher and Shean. From the beginning they were encouraged in their own theatrical ambitions by their mother Minnie, who in time came to personify the pushy, conniving parent determined that her talented offspring would reach the top of the show business ladder. Years after her death, she was made the comic heroine of a Broadway musical, *Minnie's Boys* (3-26-70). In varying combinations (often in association with outsiders) the boys appeared in a number of vaudeville acts, beginning in 1909 with one called "The Three Nightingales." The acts blended singing, simple dance steps, and broad comedy. In 1912 Minnie persuaded her brother Al to wrote an extended skit for Gummo, Groucho, Harpo, and several other performers. Shean wrote a schoolroom sketch on the order of those made popular by Gus Edwards. The skit was called "Fun in Hi Skool." Groucho played the professor. One of his pupils was played by his Aunt Hannah, and sometimes even by his mother. Beginning in 1915, the brothers played top vaudeville in a 45-minute musical, "Home Again," written and staged for them by Shean and using songs, such as "Sweet Kentucky Lady," plucked from Broadway shows or Tin Pan Alley. The boys early on established the characterizations they would employ for the rest of their careers. Chico became the high-strung, fast-dealing Sicilian immigrant. Harpo, forever mute, scampered across the stage in a red wig and battered hat, gleefully chasing girls and pilfering everything in sight. Out of his oversized topcoat came any absurdity the action required. The smart-aleck Groucho dressed more often than not in an ill-fitting mourning suit. He walked with a deep-kneed crouch, flourished his cigar and displayed a painted-on box moustache with boxy eyebrows to match. Zeppo, the youngest and handsomest, played straight man.

I'll Say She Is! billed itself as a musical comedy revue, acknowledging the tenuous thread of a storyline Will B. Johnstone created for the boys and at the same time accepting the havoc the boys wreaked on the plot. In Johnstone's original typescript the brothers are introduced by having them apply one by one at a talent agency. Each brother offers his idea of how Gallagher and Shean's act should be revised. The action begins when the boys meet a young lady known on the program and in the script solely as Beauty (Carlotta Miles). The show's title was probably a contraction of the popular exclamation, "I'll say she's a beauty." Carlotta Miles underwent a similar contraction to Lotta Miles. Both contractions undoubtedly seemed titillatingly suggestive to the period. Beauty was a young woman desperately determined to "search for a thrill." Her search takes her to a Chinatown opium den, where she is accused of murder. Groucho advises her, "You are charged with murder and if you are convicted you will be charged with electricity." Nor can he offer her much hope:

Groucho: You are going to be convicted of murder.
Beauty: What makes you so confident?
Groucho: I'm going to be your lawyer.

The trial approaches mayhem, with Chico, for example, trying to inveigle the judge into a poker game. After she is acquitted, Beauty attempts to continue her search for a thrill by allowing herself to be hypnotized. Her trance sends her back to Napoleon's times where she is transformed into Josephine. Groucho appears as a mustached Napoleon and dismisses the courtiers, "Begone peasants! Take French leave." He tells Josephine he must go to meet his Waterloo, but he assures her, "I shall not fight until I see the whites of their eggs. That's a good yolk." He departs, pretending not to notice his brothers, who, as Josephine's lovers, are hiding conspicuously under tables and chairs. Chico performed some of his nimble piano playing and Harpo followed with his tour de force on the harp as part of the Napoleon scene. The evening continued in a similar vein until 11 o'clock. At one point Groucho appeared as Cinderella, despite his mustache and (at least in the show's publicity stills) a pipe. The public and the critics were overwhelmed by the team's wild nonsense. Indeed, they soon became something of a cult. Apart from the clowning the hit of the evening was a French-style apache dance done by D'Andrea and Walters in the opium den scene.

Four revues, opening on three successive May nights, all but brought the season to a close. **Innocent Eyes** (5-20-24, Winter Garden) was mounted to showcase the famous French cabaret entertainer Mistinguett. It was a major disappointment. Mistinguett made her entrance in a dress trailed by a twelve-foot train of ostrich feathers. In her most applauded scene she portrayed a French maid sold by her callous father to a brutish Parisian apache. He throws her in the river (out of which she emerges dripping wet). She kills him and runs off with the barge man she loves. Cleo Mayfield and Cecil Lean headed the supporting cast. Unfortunately, Mistinguett had no better luck than Delysia, and she too was soon aboard an eastbound liner.

The Grand Street Follies quickly proved the most forward-looking of the new revue series, relying for effect solely on the skill of its small band of entertainers and the wit of its writers, and in a way accomplished what *The 49ers* failed to do. These *Follies* came to New Yorkers' attention under peculiar circumstances. Situated at 466 Grand Street, far from the bustling theatre district, the Neighborhood Playhouse had for several years offered a group of loyal subscribers a program of classic and popular drama. It had promised its followers that for its final presentation during the 1921–22 season it would unveil some yet untried work. When the selection committee rejected all the efforts submitted for consideration it was decided to close the season with an intimate revue that would burlesque reigning Broadway successes of the day. The first edition of *The Grand Street Follies,* which the program branded "A low brow show for high grade morons," premiered with two subscription performances on June 13 and 14, 1922, and then played three additional nonsubscription performances. The curtain rose on a skit called, appropriately, "In the Beginning," depicting the world's earliest drama critic, Adam Stale and his wife Eve, and from there went on to twit theatrical luminaries such as Doris Keane, Laurette Taylor, David Belasco, and John Barrymore. For this first edition the music was credited to "Great Composers, arranged mostly by Lily M. Hyland," though special note was made

that Albert Carroll wrote his own words and music for "Personality." From the series' inception, Carroll and Dorothy Sands were the *Follies'* comic pillars. Their cavorting allowed audiences to overlook indifferent music that was to be characteristic of the series. After a season's hiatus, *The Grand Street Follies* went public with its second edition on May 20, 1924. As with the earlier mounting the entertainment concentrated on spoofing plays and players, especially shows the company had staged during the year such as *Blanco Posnet* and *The Player Queen*. Carroll walked away with the heartiest applause for his mimicry of John Barrymore, Elsie Janis, and Jeanne Eagels.

Round the Town (5-21-24, Century Roof), an almost instant dropout, took its title from a column one of its writers, S. Jay Kaufman, wrote for the New York *Telegram*. Most of its contributors were newsmen, with Kaufman and Herman Mankiewicz providing the bulk of the material. The show's most talked about skit, however, was by George S. Kaufman and Marc Connelly, who offered a tongue-in-cheek version of their own play, *Beggar on Horseback*. Naturally the title was changed slightly to "Beggars off Horseback."

Keep Kool's (5-22-24, Morosco) title reflected the popular slogan of the presidential campaign getting under way, "Keep Cool with Coolidge!" But if its title was the last word, the cast consisted not of top stars but of names on the way up (Charles King) or on the way down (Hazel Dawn). The revue was advertised as "a musical revelation in 24 scenes," but the best it could reveal was a modestly funny skit showing how Eugene O'Neill, Avery Hopwood, and George M. Cohan would have handled the same basic story.

A dimwit affair called **Flossie** (6-3-24, Lyric) arrived to give the season and the period the dreariest possible curtain. For her uncle's benefit Flossie (Doris Duncan) pretends to be married to Archie (Sydney Grant). Archie hadn't time to tell his fiancée, Bessie (Alice Cavanaugh), of the ruse and she arrives to misconstrue Archie's behavior. Explanations follow, allowing Archie and Bessie, and Flossie and Chummy to go off happily hand in hand.

Three seasons, 120 musicals, and so little to show for it. But as suddenly as the dreariness began, it ended. The American Musical Theatre was at the threshold of one of its great epochs.

8

ACT FOUR
The Golden Age
of the American Musical
1924-1937

The national rage for jazz polarized the musical stage. From this period on, America's lyric works were, with rare exceptions outside of revues, clearly either up-to-date musical comedies or operettas from an older tradition. Supported by a muscle-flexing ASCAP, composers increasingly demanded and won the right to be responsible for whole scores, to do what a later generation would call "their own thing." As a result they no longer felt compelled to distort their natural idioms or to compromise them. The disturbing hodgepodge of styles that had so often debased the musical integrity of past shows vanished seemingly overnight. Coupled with this clarification of theatrical forms was a standardization of popular musical forms. The dominance of the AABA pattern in popular music began during this same period. The thirty-two-bar song became the accepted musical housing. It took a principal eight-bar melody, repeated it, inserted a secondary eight-bar melody known as a bridge, and then concluded by returning to the original eight-bar theme. Not all songs employed the pattern, nor certainly did all composers. Most of the better songwriters were frequently willing to explore other possibilities. But the formula did free composers from at least one concern—the shape of their songs, even though at the same time it imprisoned them in a repetitive convention. By the same token, this very convention provided a challenge, demanding of songwriters that they conceive eight-bar phrases of sufficient originality and strength to sustain constant replaying.

The new breed of composers rose to the challenge handsomely. Significantly, two of the supreme mediocrities of the old school passed from the scene about this time. A. Baldwin Sloane tried to retire in 1921 and died, still young, in 1925; Raymond Hubbell composed his last score in 1928, though he survived through a quarter of a century in retirement. The onslaught of great new talent was too much for such hacks. And onslaught it was. The most notable achievement of the following thirteen-season period —1924–25 to 1936–37—was the enthralling outpouring of magnificent melody. In the number and greatness of its scores no other era approaches it. In its musical comedies its superb songs were often accompanied by the most brilliant lyrics the American Musical Theatre has ever known. Three men in particular—Ira Gershwin, Lorenz Hart, and Cole Porter—gave a new, unique sophistication to their rhymes. In his own way each made as original and lasting a contribution to his art as W. S. Gilbert had done, and yet almost all their most exciting work was done in this single period. Only in librettos was there little innovation. But the best of the librettists, and there were a number of them, exhibited such solidly professional craftsmanship that it was often easy to overlook their lack of inspiration.

In terms of "acts" this period shares with the second and fifth acts a division into two "scenes." The first five seasons, roughly paralleling Coolidge's term, were the happiest and most fruitful. 1929 brought the depression and the first real competition from Hollywood musicals. Those who didn't abandon Broadway and rush west found themselves confronting a changed world and a changed audience. Alert and able, they quickly, subtly but perceptibly altered their own ways of writing. There was no revolution in the musical theatre, but there was an undeniable change of tone.

Scene One
SONGWRITERS' SHOWS AS PURE ENTERTAINMENT 1924-1929

1924-1925

Things were looking up all across the nation in the summer of 1924, and with Coolidge obviously about to be elected in November there was little reason for concern and some good reason to relax. As he did so frequently, Florenz Ziegfeld presented the first offering to please the tired businessman. **The Ziegfeld Follies of 1924** (6-24-24, New Amsterdam) compiled 401 performances, the longest run any of Ziegfeld's revues ever enjoyed. Yet it was not a critical or artistic success. Oddly, many aficionados remember it best for the beautiful cover Albert Vargas created for its sheet music, a single smiling brunette invitingly fingering a necklace. When the show opened, it included Will Rogers and Ann Pennington (both in their final *Follies*) as well as Vivienne Segal. It also displayed a line of precision dancers, the Tiller Girls. To keep things humming at the box office, Ziegfeld announced seasonally revised "editions," bringing in W. C. Fields, Ray Dooley, and Ethel Shutta for the "winter" and "spring" line-ups. Miss Shutta did her bit in between her chores in *Louie the 14th*. A police escort helped clear her path from theatre to theatre. One of the numbers Miss Shutta belted out was "Eddie, Be Good." She sang it to twenty-four Ziegfeld beauties, all made up to resemble Eddie Cantor. Harry

Tierney score's had no memorable numbers, though "Adoring You" received some play. Nor was there any superior material in the supplementary songs by Raymond Hubbell, Dave Stamper, James Hanley, or Victor Herbert (who had died the previous May while working on his melodies for the show). Herbert's music provided the background for a major production number in which Peggy Fears portrayed a sleeping prince surrounded by wooden soldiers—an obvious reference to the wooden soldiers of *Chauve Souris* (2-4-22). Even George Olsen and his band could not make the tunes sound better than they were. Fields' entry into the show was prompted by the out-of-town failure of a vehicle Ziegfeld had mounted for him, *The Comic Supplement*. Two of the skits from this fiasco were salvaged for the *Follies*. In one Fields was frustrated in his attempt to take a short nap; in the other he was set upon by his nagging wife. Apart from the number in which Miss Fears played the sleeping prince, the evening's most lauded spectacle was probably its finale, "Fine Feathers Make Fine Birds," with Ziegfeld's girls bedecked in more than their customary allotment of feathers. Interestingly, a number with a similar title had been offered in *Snapshots of 1921* (6-2-21). The *Follies* was the first of the season's many revues. Their number was impressive, but, as the season will show, their vogue was indisputably waning.

George White's Scandals of 1924 (6-30-24, Apollo) was far less successful than the *Follies,* running 192 times. However, it left behind one Gershwin classic, rich in new jazz-age harmonies, "Somebody Loves Me." A cozy, intimate song, it was nevertheless given the gimmicky staging that was a White trademark. As she sang it, Winnie Lightner found herself wooed by past and contemporary heroes—Mark Antony, Romeo, Harold Lloyd, and William S. Hart. Gershwin was earning $125 a week, plus royalties from the show. When he asked White for a raise, White demurred, so Gershwin left the series. Many of the revue's musical numbers incorporated burlesques. Will Mahoney spoofed Jolson's rendition of "My Mammy," while Lester Allen and Tom Patricola kidded Ann Pennington and Brooke Johns, with Allen's knees conspicuously dimpled for the occasion. The skits were at times as gimmicky as the musical staging. In one sketch the dialogue consisted solely of variously delivered "Ahs." Allen and Miss Lightner were the principals in a comic take-off of *Abie's Irish Rose*. White's spectacles for this edition included a number in which his girls formed parts of larger-than-life handbags.

The season's first book musical, **Marjorie** (8-11-24, Shubert), detailed how brash, young Marjorie Daw (the evening was originally given her full name) passes off her brother's play as her own and persuades Brian Valcourt (Roy Royston) to produce it. Marjorie (Elizabeth Hines) also persuades Brian she would make an ideal wife for him. A large group of well-known and unknown artists all had a hand in the show, with the result that it had no distinctive style. The *Sun* complained it was "like a hundred others in the same pattern." Anything went. Much of the critics' praise was awarded to the show's comedians, Andrew Tombes (who played a curiously taciturn press agent) and Skeet Gallagher (as Marjorie's brash play-writing brother). The dances ranged from a flapper chorus doing the Charleston to the eccentric stepping of Edward Hopper. Hopper appeared briefly as a bellhop in the second act with a routine utilizing the luggage he was carrying. *Marjorie* was no triumph, but it kept a theatre lit into 1925.

Two lesser-known songwriters, Bert Kalmar and Harry Ruby, soon to be much more famous, provided the tunes for Aaron Hoffman's book to **No Other Girl** (8-13-24, Morosco). It was a lamebrain affair about the efforts of Ananias Jones (Eddie Buzzell) to build an advertisement-lined concrete highway to Quakertown so that his fellow citizens can learn what's happening in the big, wonderful world out yonder. With the encouragement of steadfast Hope Franklin (Helen Ford) he prevails by curtain time. A number of critics applauded the pathos Eddie Buzzell managed to mix with his customary sassiness; but for at least one reviewer the best part of the evening was the oversized model of the highway with its billboards that was lugged on stage. The Kalmar-Ruby score was not memorably melodic. If much of the music had a contemporary jazz sound, one number steadfastly insisted "I Would Rather Dance A Waltz." *No Other Girl* survived seven weeks.

Victor Herbert's last score was presented posthumously in **The Dream Girl** (8-20-24, Ambassador). Not one of his best accomplishments, it was nonetheless pleasant and in its title song offered one final addition to Herbert's canon. The song served as Herbert's answer to changing fashions. Though several critics all too hastily branded it a waltz, it was actually a thoroughly up-to-date fox trot. With Herbert unable to supply last-minute changes, the Shuberts discreetly added uncredited Sigmund Romberg interpolations. Rida Johnson Young and Harold Atteridge based their libretto on *The Road to Yesterday*, a 1906 play by Beulah Marie Dix and

Evelyn Greenleaf Sutherland. Elspeth, fatigued from a day of hunting for antiques, falls asleep and dreams she is in the 15th century. She is kidnapped by a handsome ruffian. When she awakes she realizes the ruffian was Jack Warren, who has been posing as a bandit for her painter-friend, Will Levison. She and Jack decide that since they have loved each other for 500 years they might as well marry. The story toyed with the possibilities of reincarnation, allowing everyone Elspeth met in one century to behave similarly in another. But it was solely a romantic touch, not a philosophic exploration. Much of the comedy was in the hands of Billy Van. Van managed to sneak a radio into the 15th century and collected laughs with lines such as "The trouble in the Garden of Eden was not caused by an apple; it was caused by a green pair." Fay Bainter brought her wistful charm to the role of Elspeth. Her voice was pleasant, but small. It fell to a better singer, the handsome Walter Woolf, to play Jack and to sing the title song. *The Dream Girl* ran fifteen weeks, then toured.

The season's first fiasco, **Bye, Bye, Barbara** (8-25-24, National), lasted a bare two weeks. It recorded the devices and disguises the Great Karloff, a balloonist and parachutist, must use to escape his alimony-seeking ex-wife, as well as Barbara Palmer's (Janet Velie) need to procure $50,000 for her actor-lover so her father will consent to their marriage. The dialogue ran to such drivel as:

Paulette [Lillian Fitzgerald]: Are you a Russian?
Karloff [Jack Hazzard]: Yes, I'm rushin' to get away.

The plot fell to pieces in the second half, and the evening was reduced to a series of specialty acts. For Carlo and Sanders it represented another futile effort to repeat their success in *Tangerine* (8-9-21).

Golf, a favorite pastime of the era, and a rich boy's making good on his own, a favorite theme of the period, were combined with moderately happy results in **Top-Hole** (9-1-24, Fulton). When the young golfer-playboy, Robert Corcoran (Ernest Glendinning), is ordered out of the house by his father, Judge Corcoran (Walter Walker), and told not to return until he can earn $1,000 on his own, he becomes a golf instructor and wins a tournament with the encouragement of loyal Marcia Willoughby (Clare Stratton). The show kept its weekly running costs down by employing a chorus line far fewer in numbers than was the practice of the era. There were only twelve girls. However, they made up in quality what they lacked in ranks. The *Times* joyously reported they harked back to "a real Weber and Fields dancing chorus." Inviting audiences to "Dance Your Way To Paradise" they made the low-budget musical frisky enough to keep the small Fulton occupied for 104 performances.

Though **The Chocolate Dandies** (9-1-24, Colonial) was lavishly mounted, excellently cast, polished by six months on the road, and well received, it failed to give Noble Sissle and Eubie Blake another *Shuffle Along* (5-23-21). In their study of the song writers, Robert Kimball and William Bolcom attribute the failure to the production's "unnecessary extravagance." Figures do indeed suggest they are right. Salaries alone were double those of *Shuffle Along*: $7,500 a week against $3,700. The relative opulence and slickness of the production disconcerted a number of critics. *Shuffle Along*'s hand-me-down simplicity inadvertently had set a standard by which the twenties insisted on judging black musicals. Time and again critics—and not only in New York—seemed to resent a black musical that strove to emulate costly white mountings. Ashton Stevens' comment in the Chicago *Herald and Examiner* typified this sentiment. Stevens bemoaned, "the show seems to suffer from too much white man." Blake felt the score was his best, telling Kimball and Bolcom, "there is nothing in *Shuffle Along* anywhere near the melodies of 'Dixie Moon' or 'Jassamine Lane.'" Most critics preferred "The Slave Of Love." The show was originally known as *In Bamville*. Kimball and Bolcom explain "Bamville" as "a Negro folk expression" for a place name roughly equivalent to "Podunk." Mose Washington (Lew Payton), who owns a race horse named Dumb Luck, falls asleep before the race and dreams his horse has won him a small fortune. He becomes president of Bamville's bank, only to have a run on the bank start. He wakes up to discover Dumb Luck has not won. The big money has gone to Dan Jackson's Rarin'-to-Go, and with his winnings Dan (Ivan H. Browning) has also won the hand of Angeline Brown (Lottie Gee). The race was shown on stage, using three horses on a treadmill. But nothing would rekindle the interest theatregoers had shown for *Shuffle Along*. *The Chocolate Dandies* recorded a disappointing 96 performances.

Rose-Marie (9-2-24, Imperial) was not only the biggest hit of the season, it was the biggest grosser of the decade. In fact, nothing surpassed its multimillion dollar take until *Oklahoma!*, over twenty years later. The story was a variant of the plot of *Naughty Marietta* (11-7-10), a tale that would be used again for *Rio Rita* (2-2-27). A heroine, in a romantic North American setting, wins her love (who is usually associated with a colorful arm of the law) only after exposing a villain not immediately obvious to the characters in the play. Rose-Marie Le Flamme (Mary Ellis) is a singer at Lady Jane's, a small hotel in the splendor of the Canadian Rockies. She loves Jim Kenyon (Dennis King). But Ed Hawley (Frank Greene), whose love for Rose-Marie is in no way reciprocated, throws suspicion on Jim for the murder of Black Eagle (Arthur Ludwig). Jim had come to Black Eagle's cabin after Black Eagle had accused him of taking gold off Black Eagle's land. Kenyon brought with him maps that showed he was working his own property, not the Indian's. But when Kenyon arrived at the cabin only Black Eagle's wife Wanda (Pearl Regay) seemed to be present. Actually Hawley was there, too, but hearing Kenyon's approach, he had been hidden by Wanda, who loves him. Black Eagle returned after Kenyon had departed and discovered Hawley and his wife embracing. He started to throttle Hawley, whereupon Wanda stabbed him. Convinced that her beloved Jim is a murderer, Rose-Marie reluctantly agrees to marry Hawley. The comic, but clever trader, Hard-Boiled Herman (William Kent), wheedles the truth from Wanda, allowing Sergeant Malone (Arthur Deagon) of the Mounties to make the proper arrest. Rose-Marie and Jim are reunited in the woods, where he has been hiding. The book, by Otto Harbach and Oscar Hammerstein II was never dull, but never exceptional. Its attempt to convey an Indian accent was no more farfetched than Harbach's attempt to convey an Italian accent in his first collaboration with Friml, *The Firefly* (2-2-12). The part-Indian Rose-Marie's first line is, "I am take sleigh ride with Jeem." But the development in the dialogue is reasonably fresh and colloquial. Here is Herman attempting to force a confession from Wanda:

Herman: Going so soon?
Wanda: You don't think I stay to see Hawley marry another woman, do you?
Herman: Well, it's your own fault.
Wanda: How you mean my own fault?
Herman: Rose-Marie wouldn't be marrying him if you'd kept your promise to Jim.
Wanda: I no promise nothing.
Herman: You said you'd tell who killed Black Eagle.

The principal reason for the operetta's success was its great Friml score. It was not only glowingly melodic, it was refreshingly different. It suggested how far the Viennese tradition could be "Americanized." The musical line of the title song (sung, of course, by Jim) employed shorter phrases than was Friml wont, reflecting the easy lilt of American speech. Clearly band leaders and arrangers of the time thought so, emphasizing its immediacy by giving a tango effect—then the rage—to the ninth to fourteenth bars. The unusual chromatics of Rose-Marie and Jim's "Indian Love Call," while not truly Indian, were an ocean away from Vienna. "The Song Of The Mounties" was a rouser for Malone and his officers that recalled *Naughty Marietta*'s "Tramp, Tramp, Tramp" and that started a vogue for such crowd stirrers in succeeding operettas. All three of the show's biggest hits came— virtually together—early in the first act, where they did little to advance the action but effectively delineated the characters of Rose-Marie, Jim, and Sergeant Malone. The incessant beat in "Totem Tom Tom," while again not legitimately Indian, undoubtedly conveyed red-skin images to the audience. This number was given the show's most memorable staging. Row after row of chorus girls dressed as totem poles marched and danced to the song's compelling beat. Few playgoers or critics probably recalled a similar show-stopping staging in *The Alaskan* (8-12-07). Only the "Door Of Her Dreams" had an unmistakable Austro-Hungarian flavor. Friml had great hopes for it, insisting it be given a striking production number and seeing it was placed first in the sheet music listings. But the public failed to respond. It was Friml's tragedy that he could never be completely objective and gauge the temper of the times. This failing ultimately removed him from the Broadway scene.

The songs were not listed separately in the program. In what may have been an early example of Hammerstein's pretensions a program note read, "The musical numbers of this play are such an integral part of the action that we do not think we should list them as separate episodes." This was no more true than it had been a dozen of fine shows before. It announced a high ambition rather than a practical achievement. Writing in *Theater Magazine* in May 1925, when *Rose-Marie* was still the reigning hit on Broadway, Hammerstein attempted further to rationalize and intellectualize the show's triumphant success. Ignoring Friml's contributions, he suggested, "the revolution in musical comedy which *Rose-Marie* has wrought was not accidental. It was a carefully directed attack at the Cinderella show in favor of operatic musical comedy." Moving from the specific to the general, he continued, "The history of musical comedy has passed through a variety of phases, but the type that persists, that shows the signs of ultimate victory, is the operetta— the musical play with music and plot welded to-

gether in skillful cohesion." At the end of his article he asked, "Is there a form of musical play tucked away somewhere . . . which could attain the heights of grand opera and still keep sufficiently human to be entertaining?" He himself later provided an answer, though by that time he would be loath to admit the direct descent of his "musical play" from operetta. The show's original Rose-Marie, Mary Ellis, was brought over from the Metropolitan Opera. She found nightly performances taxing, and her Broadway career was short, though she did become a popular London star in the thirties. On the other hand, Dennis King discovered in Jim the sort of role that would keep him busy for the rest of the decade and it launched his career as one of Broadway's great leading men.

• • •

Dennis King was born in Coventry, England, on November 2, 1897. He began his apprenticeship as a call boy with the Birmingham Repertory. He soon worked his way to the stage, at which time he dropped his family name of Pratt and adopted his mother's maiden name. By the late teens King was playing important roles in everything from Sophocles to Shakespeare to Somerset Maugham. His London debut was in Booth Tarkington's *Monsieur Beaucaire* in 1919. Two years later the Barrymores brought him to New York for *Clair de Lune*. Jane Cowl brought him back to America in 1923 to play Mercutio to her Juliet. *Rose-Marie* taught King that musicals would give him steadier employment and bigger salaries, but he always took pride that he had been an accomplished actor first, a singer second.

• • •

Mounted with a "prodigal magnificence" and gorgeously sung, *Rose-Marie* ran 557 performances. Four road companies satisfied the demand for seats across the country. In London the musical was even more triumphant than in New York, with 851 showing. It established a Paris long-run record of 1,250 showings, and played successfully in Berlin, Stockholm, and Moscow.

With **The Passing Show Of 1924** (9-3-24, Winter Garden), the waning series called it a day. Only the 1922 edition had a shorter run. James Barton and Lulu McConnell led the comedians through the inevitable skits about Prohibition, flappers, Coolidge, gangsters, and mahjongg. Indeed some felt there was too much Barton. In two of his better pieces he played a lost Paul Revere and a more contemporary citizen learning the art of getting into a phone booth gracefully. The chorus line, cut by the economizing Shuberts to forty-five, arranged itself in row above row to compose the expected living curtain. It also celebrated the beauties of "A Beaded Bag." Dances included a number that could almost be called an Irish Charleston, "Dublinola." However, nothing from Sigmund Romberg and Jean Schwartz' score became popular outside the theatre. The show was a mediocrity, gone after 93 performances.

Ninety-three performances was also the total achieved by **Be Yourself** (9-3-24, Harris), for which George S. Kaufman and Marc Connelly created the book. In its original version, it represented Kaufman and Connelly's first collaboration. The pair had written it in 1917 as *Miss Moonshine*, a vehicle for Irene Franklin. When no production was forthcoming, the script was shelved. The revised book had music by Lewis Gensler and Milton Schwarzwald. Ira Gershwin supplied some of the lyrics (as did Kaufman and Connelly). A Hatfield-McCoy feud—this time between the Brennans and the McLeans—comes to a boil when Matt McLean (Jack Donahue) innocently trespasses on Brennan property in the Tennessee mountains. Kaufman and Connelly reduced the feud to a collegiate rivalry with team letters awarded for every opponent shot. Intentionally or not, the production also spoofed the spectacles of the day, when the rising Queenie Smith sauntered on stage garbed as "The Spirit of Bituminous Coal." Georgia Caine, who years earlier helped make Jerome Kern's first Broadway songs popular, was now cast as Grandma Brennan, and William Collier, another star of an earlier era, directed.

Three revues followed in fast succession. **Earl Carroll's Vanities** (9-10-24, Music Box)—Carroll added his name to the title with this edition—proclaimed it was "exalting the human form." Everyone understood Carroll meant the female form. Carroll ingeniously circumvented the rule that nudes must not move by placing one undressed young lady on a giant pendulum. However, he prudently minimized the chance of an outcry by having her swing back and forth behind an only partially revealing lace curtain. Little else was properly displayed. The clowns, headed by Joe Cook, had only second-rate material. Cook's best skit was one he had done in vaudeville, "The Electrical Factory." It afforded Cook an opportunity to display Rube Goldberg type inventions. The singers, led by Sophie Tucker, fared no better. Miss Tucker put across a few rags with slightly off-color lyrics. She hit her peak, literally at least, when she appeared as the "High Priestess of Pep" atop a "Pyramid of Dance." Luckily for Carroll his girls were alluring enough to revitalize the tired businessman for 133 showings.

The **Greenwich Village Follies of 1924** and **Hassard Short's Ritz Revue** opened back to back. The *Follies* (9-16-24, Shubert) had one Cole Porter tune, "I'm In Love Again," which enjoyed a vogue twenty years later. But no song proved a hit at the time, and the alarmed producers rushed in additional ditties by Owen Murphy and Jay Gorney. The new tunes had no more success than the original ones. The stars of the show were the flamboyant Dolly Sisters, who probably did not belong in the relatively intellectualized atmosphere of the series. One number they did was "The Dollies and the Collies," in which the girls' movements were mimicked by trained dogs. The edition's Ballet Ballad was based on Oscar Wilde's tale, "The Happy Prince." Many of the critics singled out the blackface team of Moran and Mack for special praise. Heywood Broun even quoted his favorite bit from their material. His excerpt suggests how transient are ideas of humor. Moran advised Mack that he had bought a pig for four dollars in April and sold it for four dollars in August. Mack pointed out that Moran hadn't made any money on the deal. After a deliberative pause Moran replied, "Yes, we found that out." With Vincent Lopez and his orchestra supplying the evening's music, the show lingered for 127 performances before heading for its national tour. Substantial cast changes were made for the road, and Rodgers and Hart's "Manhattan" and "Sentimental Me" were apparently added. Thus, an exceptional amount of the material New York firstnighters saw had been eliminated. The show on the road ran only until eleven o'clock; on opening night in New York the first act didn't end until eleven.

By contrast, the *Ritz Revue* (9-17-24, Ritz) was beautifully paced and programed from the onset. Hassard Short's evening promised to begin a new series, but didn't. Raymond Hitchcock, who had abandoned his own series, was costarred with Charlotte Greenwood. Hitchcock had little to do but serve as compère. The best comic material was handed to Miss Greenwood. "Her Morning Bath" found the lanky comedienne prevented from bathing by visits of friends, clothiers, and the neighborhood iceman. When the iceman dropped his block of ice, Miss Greenwood was able to perform an abbreviated, comic version of her famous doublejointed dance as she attempted to avoid the broken ice. Short's spectacles were excellent. In "The Red Ladies," scarlet women of the past—from Salome to Camille—paraded across the stage; while "Crystal Wedding Day" lit the stage with translucent shimmerings. The music, all ordinary, was by almost a dozen different hands. Short's evening was attractive enough to keep the band-box Ritz lit for 109 performances.

One more book show interrupted the parade of revues. **Dear Sir** (9-23-24, Times Square) had a libretto by Edgar Selwyn and music by Jerome Kern. It also had lyrics by a newcomer, Howard Dietz. Dietz' contributions were not all that promising, including as they did lines such as "Marriages that never fade/Always are in heaven made." Some of the lyrics from unpublished numbers were better. "If I Could Lead A Merry Mormon Life" offered first rate comedy, asserting bigamy and polygamy could "make a pig o' me." "A Houseboat On The Harlem," stuck in the muck, exposed some peculiar horrors of urban life with grace and wit. Dietz could not have received much inspiration from the Selwyn libretto. Laddie Munn (Oscar Shaw), a man about town, is publicly rebuffed at Sherry's by Dorothy Fair (Genevieve Tobin). At a Park Avenue charity auction he wins her services for one week. By the time the week is over he has won her affection and her hand. Dietz could find no more excitement in Kern's score than he could in the libretto. Kern's music fell lightly on the ear, but it was far less attractive than his unappreciated *Sitting Pretty* music. The show was withdrawn after an embarrassing two weeks.

The Grab Bag (10-6-24, Globe) was another delightful bit of Ed Wynn lunacy. Its score was culled from various sources, with Wynn himself taking credit for several of the tunes. Though Janet Velie sang and Marion Fairbanks (half of the Fairbanks Twins) danced, the evening was dominated by the great, lisping clown. Wynn made his entrance wearing a ludicrous travesty of a homburg and a kilt. He announced that a Russian Octette would sing Cossack folk-songs, beginning with, "He Eats French Dressing Every Night So He Can Wake Up Oily In The Morning." Another song he promised was, "She Might Have Been A School Teacher, But She Hadn't Any Class." Among his inventions was a typewriter-like contraption for eating corn, allowing the diner's hands to stay cool and clean.

Nudity—even if the nudes had to hold statuesque poses—was the lure that kept the Shuberts' **Artists and Models of 1924** (10-15-24, Astor) on the boards for nearly eight months. The brothers resorted to an antiquated practice by framing the evening with a thin story. Perhaps more accurately, the show began with a plot that took an innocent young lady from her New Hampshire home to explore the wonders of Greenwich Village. The plot quickly disappeared in a welter of spectacle and specialties, "a dazzling succession of golds and blacks and

grays . . . rose numbers, color numbers, jazz numbers." A visit to an Italian restaurant in the village suddenly evolved into a colorful panorama of "Mediterranean Nights." The scene gave Trini an opportunity to perform her fiery Spanish dances. Closer to home came high-stepping Charlestons and a number that proclaimed, "I Love To Dance When I Hear A March." As was the case with *The Passing Show,* the score (by Sigmund Romberg and Fred Coots) gave audiences nothing to take home. Weakest of all was the show's lame, anemic comedy.

Dixie to Broadway (10-29-24, Broadhurst), a black revue, is remembered wistfully as enchanting Florence Mills' last major New York appearance before her untimely death. Her singing, dancing, and "native grotesqueries" stopped the show in "Jungle Nights in Dixieland." The black performers gave imitations of white favorites such as George M. Cohan, Gallagher and Shean, and Eva Tanguay. *Chauve Souris* (2-4-22) was saluted with a march of black wooden soldiers. Typical of the evening's humor was the comedian who refused a ten-dollar bill, claiming, "That's tainted money! 'Tain't yours and 'tain't mine." The expected black vitality kept the show on the boards eight weeks.

Ziegfeld brought in a musical version of Clare Kummer's hit of eight seasons back, *Good Gracious, Annabelle.* It was produced as a vehicle for his current wife, Billie Burke. Since Miss Kummer off and on had interpolated songs in musicals, it was not surprising that she wrote a number of the tunes for this musicalization, rechristened **Annie Dear** (11-4-24, Times Square). But Ziegfeld was never content to do things by halves. Sigmund Romberg and Harry Tierney were called in to embellish the score. Miss Kummer's libretto remained faithful to her original story. Annie Leigh has run away from her rough, bearded Western groom (Marion Green) on the day of the wedding and taken a job as a servant on the Long Island estate of the bibulous copper magnate, George Wimbleton (Ernest Truex). When her groom appears, minus his beard, she fails to recognize him, so he has time to ingratiate himself and effect a reconciliation. The lavish garden setting of the last act gave Ziegfeld an excuse to stop the story while he treated his customers to a "brilliant, luxurious" ballet, "Little Boy Blue's Search for the Crock of Gold at the End of the Rainbow." Miss Burke became the little boy. The ballet, at first only in blues and grays, recounted the boy's meeting Cloud, Moon, Rain, Wind, and other figures as he seeks the crock of gold. Only at the end did the stage blaze forth in an appropriate rainbow of colors. But Ziegfeld's traditional largess was wasted on *Annie Dear*. The music was inferior, and the fights between Ziegfeld, who wanted to make more changes, and Miss Kummer, who wanted to restore the original material Ziegfeld had cut, finally so exasperated the producer he threw up his hands and closed the show, after 103 performances.

Miss Kummer had an even more unhappy experience when she provided the American adaptation of Leo Fall's **Mme. Pompadour** (11-11-24, Martin Beck). The rage for Viennese operetta was long over. *Mme. Pompadour*, which told of a romance that blossoms when its heroine (Wilda Bennett) goes slumming incognito, opened a week after *Annie Dear* and was long departed before *Annie Dear* terminated its own short run.

Another team that had reaped success a season or so back tried again and met with disappointment, though not with failure. Harlan Thompson and Harry Archer of *Little Jessie James* (8-15-23) offered what they termed "a smart musical farce," **My Girl** (11-24-24, Vanderbilt). The story told of the Whites (Jane Taylor and Russell Mack) throwing a fancy, if dry, party in order to win acceptance at the Rainbow Club. A bootlegger, desperately trying to hide his illegal stock, mixes his more potent drinks with the innocent stuff the Whites are serving. The complications that follow are resolved happily when the Whites win the desired acceptance. Nothing from the evening approached the popularity of *Little Jessie James'* "I Love You." Still, because of tunes on the order of "You And I," "all the feet in the auditorium were set tapping." The six-month run was not unrewarding, but it was a far cry from the authors' earlier bonanza.

A fourth lady entered the theatrical scene the next night. **The Magnolia Lady** (11-25-24, Shubert) was a musical version of A. E. Thomas and Alice Duer Miller's 1916 hit *Come Out of the Kitchen*. The score was by Harold Levey. But Levey had split with Zelda Sears, collaborating instead with another popular woman—librettist and lyricist, Anne Caldwell. Her book was set at "The Magnolias," the Ravenel mansion in Virginia horse country. The Ravenels have come upon hard times. To help pay for their father's surgery they rent their estate to an Englishman, Kenneth Craig (Ralph Forbes). When to their surprise he insists on white servants they agree to fill the positions. Before the final curtain Craig has fallen in love with and proposed to Lily-Lou Ravenel (Ruth Chatterton). The show required more urgent surgery than did Mr. Ravenel (Skeet Gallagher). Miss Caldwell

could no more inspire Levey to write vital, exciting music than could Miss Sears. Some potential customers may have been put off by the casting of Forbes and Miss Chatterton, better known for their work in straight plays. One critic felt the leading lady's small, sweet voice was "a shade studied." Whatever the reason, *The Magnolia Lady* folded after six weeks.

The distaff side was also featured in the titles of two of the three musicals that raised their curtains on the same night, December 1. The book of one was a throwback to the poor-Irish-girl-makes-good plots of the preceding period. Society's polished Roger Utley (Nathaniel Wagner) loves April Daly (Tessa Kosta), the daughter of an uncouth upstart, Patrick Daly (Harry Allen). He calls her his **Princess April** (12-1-24, Ambassador). But Roger's snobbish sister, Kathryn (Audrey Maple), objects to their marrying. Only when April gallantly claims to own a beaded bag found in a compromising situation, a bag everyone knows really belongs to Kathryn, does Roger's sister fall in line. More than one critic complained that Miss Kosta's lovely, clarion voice was wasted on Carlo and Sanders' tinny musical comedy jingles. The unoriginal book, weak score, and unfortunate miscasting all contributed to making *Princess April* a three-week flop.

The girl in the second title was unnamed, but she was admonished **Lady, Be Good!** (12-1-24, Liberty). Though it was not the biggest smash of the season, it may well have been its most important musical. For with this show the rhythms, tensions, and color of stage jazz were defined; the gutsy Negro creation was given a cerebral white reinterpretation. Gershwin had demonstrated the grammar of the style in "Somebody Loves Me" and a few other, earlier, songs. Now he supplied an entire, consistent score in the idiom. Coupled with his brother Ira's fresh, colloquial, and often sassy lyrics, a new tone was introduced to the American musical stage. It was an abrupt contrast to the arioso style of operetta. These songs could almost be spoken; indeed, they often were. It may have been this the *Times* meant when it predicted the show had "a number of tunes the unmusical . . . will find hard to get rid of." Attempting to get to the essentials of this style, Alec Wilder in his *American Popular Song* has suggested, "The melody should be spare, containing a minimal number of notes, and the harmony should be similarly uncluttered, almost skeletal." To Wilder four songs from the show were intriguing enough to deserve special attention—"Fascinating Rhythm," "Little Jazz Bird," "The Man I Love" (dropped from the show during its tryout), and the title song. He describes "Oh, Lady, Be Good!" as "a strict A-A-B-A song, very spare in its use of harmony and without syncopation," insisting, "Its special trademark is the quarter note triplet." The unusual beat of "Fascinating Rhythm" made it an immediate attention grabber. Not all the songs were so patently "jazzy." One of the loveliest and most popular tunes from the piece was the simple, echoing "So Am I." The pianistic texture of Gershwin's music was underscored by his use of the dual pianists, Arden and Ohman, as a prominent part of the pit band.

The story was not especially complicated. When Dick Trevor (Fred Astaire) rebuffs Josephine Vanderwater (Jayne Auburn), she has Dick and his sister, Susie (Adele Astaire), evicted from the house she owns. Brother and sister set up housekeeping on the sidewalk, hanging their "God Bless Our Home" sign on the lamppost. A passerby named Jack Robinson (Alan Edwards) has such a torn suit that Susie momentarily forgets her own problems and mends Jack's tattered jacket. "Watty" Watkins (Walter Catlett), a clownish, garrulous lawyer who in good musical comedy fashion represents both the impecunious Trevors and the rich Vanderwaters, attempts to effect a reconciliation at the Vanderwaters' party. His fee is oddball. Watty has been threatened by a Mexican whose sister has been jailed for biting a man's ear. The Mexican insists Watty arrange his sister's release so she can collect the estate of her late husband. If Watty succeeds, the Mexican will pay him $100,000. Watty prevails on Susie to impersonate the Mexican's sister and help collect the money. Susie agrees only when she realizes that the money will help get Josephine off Dick's back. It develops that the Mexican lady's husband is not dead. He is, in fact, the very Jack Robinson whose clothes Susie sewed. He proves that the Mexican marriage was forced and illegal, convinces his uncle, who had disinherited him, that he is worthwhile and proposes to Susie. Aided by Jack's restored fortune, Dick gives Josephine the boot and is free to marry the girl he truly loves, Shirley Vernon (Kathlene Martyn). Contemporary critics and later commentators, such as Robert Kimball and Alfred Simon, dismissed the book as a collection of "shopworn musical-comedy formulas." Perhaps Guy Bolton and Fred Thompson's outline was just that. But Bolton was too sure and witty a librettist; he rarely released anything that was not at least a notch or two above the run-

of-the-mill. Not all of the dialogue was on a high, cerebral plane:

Jack: I'm just a poor hobo!
Susie: Then I must be in Hoboken.

But much of it was slangy, with a clipped, natural sound, and with a casual use of expletive a step or two removed from the underlined or coy employment such expletives had heretofore generally suffered. At the Vanderwater party two minor figures engage in the following colloquy:

Daisey: And you said you wanted me to help you reform.
Bertie: I do—Duckie—I do. But I don't want to reform too darned fast. It might make you lose interest if there wasn't something about me for you to pick on.

The lead-in to "The Half Of It, Dearie, Blues" runs:

Dick: I'm so gosh darn blue.
Shirley: Blue? Why?
Dick: Because you're going to marry someone else and I've got to marry someone else, and oh it's hell!

Not all the songs had quite so well motivated lead-ins. Old formulas still applied here as well as to some of the jokes. Cliff (Ukulele Ike) Edwards' walking on stage in the middle of an argument between Susie and Dick was all the cue given for "Fascinating Rhythm"; and the poignancy of "So Am I" was lessened when it was sung by Susie and Jack parting until they meet the next day for breakfast. The title song was a bit more cleverly and unusually placed. It is not sung by Dick or Jack to his girl, but by Watty as an inducement to Susie to cooperate in the masquerade. Ira Gershwin's lyrics displayed something of the same ambivalence. The Vanderwater soiree begins with the chorus singing "Oh, What A Lovely Party," the sort of song and conventional lyrics heard in show after show during the era. But the innovative, distinctive Ira Gershwin was also present, and not merely in the outstanding tunes of the evening. He opened the second act with a lyric that had recourse to the old inversions and stilted rhetoric, but which made them painless and contemporary by his diversionary, startling rhymes such as "adjectives are spilt more" and "Biltmore." No critic of the day fully sensed the importance of *Lady, Be Good!*, though some, such as the man on the *World*, hailed it as the "best musical in town." What praise the show received was largely for its immediate values as entertainment. Gershwin's music was lauded, but most of the applause went to the Astaires and to Norman Bel Geddes' brightly colored, slightly stylized sets, stylizations reflecting the growing popularity of art déco. One critic felt Bel Geddes went on a "well-earned spree after the penitential severity of [Max Reinhardt's] 'The Miracle.'" Color, comedy, melody, and the Astaires kept *Lady, Be Good!* in New York for 330 performances.

The third December 1 opening signaled the end of another revue series. **The Music Box Revue 1924-1925** reverted to what for these big extravaganzas had become an obsolescent tradition by having a compère for the evening—in this case Rip Van Winkle awakened from one more long sleep. What he heard was a hand-me-down Irving Berlin score into which Berlin felt it necessary to inject his already popular "All Alone." Grace Moore and Oscar Shaw, spotlit and holding telephones, sang the song from opposite sides of an otherwise dark stage. Miss Moore also sang "Call Of The South" and "Rock-a-bye Baby." McCullough and Clark and Fanny Brice provided the laughs. In her "Don't Send Me Back [To Petrograd]" she pleaded, "I'll even wash the sheets for the Ku Klux Klan, but don't send me back." She donned one of her favorite costumes, a tutu, for "I Want To Be A Ballet Dancer," done with Bobby Clark. It wasn't Miss Brice's fault if she looked silly in the outfit or if, in her Russian-Yiddish accent, she made "ballet dancer" sound like "belly dancer." Miss Brice and Clark also had fun playing Adam and Eve. Clark became a boxer in one of the era's many prizefight skits, "The Kid's First and Last Fight." He and McCullough appeared as "A Couple of Senseless Censors." The production numbers sped the audience to Tokyo, to old New York, to Alice's Wonderland, shaded them beneath a gigantic weeping willow, and even sprayed them with perfume as was done in 1923. John Murray Anderson and James Reynolds designed the spectacles. The evening survived 186 showings, but Berlin and his partner Sam H. Harris read the temper of times and turned the Music Box over to general bookings.

One night after this trio appeared, **The Student Prince** (12-2-24, Jolson) was sung for the first time in New York. Dorothy Donnelly took her story from *Old Heidelberg,* a play in which Richard Mansfield had appeared for years on end. In fact, this musical version was originally announced with the fuller title of *The Student Prince in Heidelberg.* It retold its old tale quite faithfully. Prince Karl Franz (Howard Marsh) is about to leave for Heidelberg with his tutor Dr. Engel (Greek Evans).

Engel looks back on his own student life as his "Golden Days," assuring the prince, "we remember them all else above." They arrive incognito at the Inn of the Three Golden Apples. There they find their wish for anonymity abetted by the clownish Lutz (George Hassell), who has been dropping hints all over the place that he is the important person the students and beer girls have been waiting for. The "Students' Marching Song" heralds the arrival of the prince's future classmates. They join in a "Drinking Song," saluting in particular their favorite waitress, Kathie (Ilse Marvenga). The prince's presence is finally acknowledged, and he is invited to join the Saxon Corps. He accepts. Kathie and Karl Franz fall in love at first sight, and they swear eternal allegiance "Deep In My Heart, Dear." The prince further swears his eternal vow in an impassioned "Serenade." But Karl Franz' grandfather, the king, is taken ill, and not expected to live. Karl must return home. For important reasons of state, he must also marry Princess Margaret (Roberta Beatty), though both candidly admit their loves lie elsewhere. Margaret and her Captain Tarnitz (John Coast) ruefully wish the world were only for "Just We Two," while the prince in turn laments that he will see his beloved Kathie "Nevermore." But echoes of the past are too strong, and Karl returns to Heidelberg for one farewell with Kathie. Realizing they must go their own ways, they again promise that deep in their hearts they will remember their love forever.

Sigmund Romberg's score for this bittersweet story was his finest achievement. It was finally obvious to everyone, even the Shuberts, that Romberg was no hack. The music was Viennese-American: more sentimental and strong-fibered than Austro-Hungarian material but less grandly sweeping and less saccharine. The success of the show was phenomenal. Its original run was 608 performances, and in its heyday required nine companies to satisfy the nation-wide demand for seats. It toured virtually without cessation for a quarter of a century, until a road company of *The Student Prince,* like a road company of *Blossom Time,* became synonymous with theatrical shabbiness. Amazingly, there almost was no *Student Prince.* The Shuberts were aghast at what they considered Romberg's operatic music, appalled at the unhappy ending, and utterly bewildered by Romberg's demand for a large, strong voiced male chorus rather than a long line of feminine beauties. They threatened to throw out both Romberg and his score. Luckily, Romberg and his lawyer won the day. The Shuberts profited from the lesson not just by watching their coffers fill. The reception awarded the fine male ensemble (36 men in the original production) prompted them to insert similar groups into many of the operettas they later mounted, and these male choruses became almost a Shubert trademark.

Four musicals came in at the end of the month. The Duncan Sisters arrived in a musical version of *Uncle Tom's Cabin* called **Topsy and Eva** (12-23-24, Harris). The sisters claimed to have written all their songs themselves. They also sang them, with Vivian in golden curls and Rosetta in blackface and pigtails. The songs presented the same sentimental, idealized picture of the old South Al Jolson and Eddie Cantor often portrayed. These new numbers included "Moon Am Shinin'," "The Land Of Long Ago," and the hit of the show, "Rememb'ring." The sisters, aided by the appeal of the old story and new songs, kept the show in town for twenty weeks. However, this was less than half of the forty-three weeks the musical had compiled earlier in Chicago.

Betty Lee (12-25-24, 44th St.) was only slightly less successful, playing fourteen weeks. A musical version of Paul Armstrong and Rex Beach's 1909 *Going Some,* it recounted the adventures of Wallingford Speed (Hal Skelly) and Lawrence Glass (Joe E. Brown), who arrive broke at the Chapin estate and, hearing a famous racer and his trainer are expected, pretend to be the pair. A race is arranged, and Speed is threatened with dire consequences if he loses. Cheered on by Betty Lee (Gloria Foy), he manages to win. The show offered posthumously the last Louis Hirsch songs Broadway would hear. Con Conrad filled in the gaps Hirsch had left. But no superior melodies emerged, though the songs were bouncy enough to spark the evening. Skelly and Brown as the two impostors had a large share in the show's popularity. Many who remember the wide-mouthed, impish-looking Brown only as a comedian will be surprised to learn that a number of reviewers praised him not only for his fun-making but for several "eccentric dances," including the mock soft-shoe routine he performed in the course of the evening.

A revival of Gilbert and Sullivan's *Patience* began a three-month stay at the Provincetown Playhouse beginning December 29. On the same night another Russian revue hoping to equal the rage of *Chauve Souris* appeared at the Frolic. Called either **Seeniaya Ptitza** or **The Blue Bird,** it drew middling attendance for eight weeks.

The first musical for 1925 was **Big Boy,** with which Jolson returned to the Winter Garden on January 7. Once again Jolson was Gus, and this time Gus was a stable boy at the Bedfords. For years

he had ridden the Bedford entry in the Derby, but a group of sharpers connive to replace Gus with a famous English jockey. Their plan is foiled, and Gus wins the Derby riding Big Boy. The show used the same device musicals such as *Honey Girl* and *The Chocolate Dandies* had already employed to good effect: the race was run with real horses moving on treadmills. Percy Hammond in the *Herald-Tribune* exclaimed the race in *Big Boy* made " 'Ben Hur' look like a country affair." Apart from such gimmicks, the evening was a claptrap affair, and many a night Jolson repeated his old trick of dismissing the cast midway through the performance and singing for the audience the rest of the evening. Some of the songs he introduced in *Big Boy* became Jolson standards and perennial favorites: "California, Here I Come" (actually first sung during the road tour of the 1921 *Bombo*) and "Keep Smiling At Trouble" (Jolson, DeSylva/Lewis Gensler). At one point he tested "If You Knew Susie," but dropped it and gave it to Eddie Cantor. The show should have been a smash hit with a long run, but after six weeks Jolson became too ill to continue. The scenery was stored in the hope of reviving the show when Jolson recovered.

When the Shuberts imported **The Love Song** (1-13-25, Century), Edward Kunneke's operetta based on the life and music of Offenbach, the brothers expected another *Blossom Time.* Instead the new work moved on after just four months.

Charles Dillingham, John Cort, and Martin Beck combined forces to mount an A. Baldwin Sloane operetta, **China Rose** (1-19-25, Martin Beck). It detailed the efforts of Cha Ming (J. Harold Murray), the Prince of Manchuria, to win the virgin, Ro See (Olga Steck). He sends a pair of ludicrous muddlers to escort her to the palace, then disguises himself as a bandit on the road. His persistence prevails, and the diffident Ro See is won over. The show had sumptuous settings. It also offered some unusual dancing. In one "Chinese" dance the leading artist startled many in the audience by bending backwards until her head touched the floor. *China Rose* opened January 19. Just over a month later Sloane, who had attempted to return from retirement with this show, died at the age of fifty-two. His last score marked no advance over his first, or any of the many he composed in between. *China Rose* played for three months before fading.

Elsie Janis romped in with a revue called **Puzzles of 1925** (2-2-25, Fulton). She mounted the show as austerely as she had *Elsie Janis and Her Gang* (12-1-19). She even took credit for several of the songs, including one with the fetching title "Do-I-

Or-Don't-I Blues." For most of the evening Miss Janis acted as commère to a parade of knockabout comics, ballroom dancers, and other vaudeville acts. Only just before the final curtain did she herself come front and center to sing many of the songs she had sung for the troops in France and to imitate Lenore Ulric, Bea Lillie, and John Barrymore. Her popularity was still broad enough to keep the show on the boards fourteen weeks.

Aging, and surrounded by cleverer competitors, Harry B. Smith was less and less active. He had worked on *The Love Song,* and now, with Karl Hajos adapting Tschaikowsky melodies for him, Smith fashioned the book and lyrics for an operetta he called **Natja** (2-16-25, Knickerbocker). Because Prince Potemkin (George Reimherr) does not fairly represent her Crimean homeland, Natja (Madeline Collins) disguises herself as a young man to win the ear of Catherine the Great and get justice for her neighbors. She also wins Lt. Vladimir Strogonoff (Warren Proctor). It was typical Smith hackwork, and the public would not buy it. The show was hurried away after four weeks.

If *Natja* presented an obsolescent form of operetta, **Sky High** (3-2-25, Shubert) was clearly a throwback to the old producer-assemblages. The Shuberts put it all together as a vehicle for Willie Howard (with Willie's brother and erstwhile partner, Eugene, listed as coproducer). Using a Berlin and West End success (*Whirled into Happiness*) for a start, they planted the sad-faced, put-upon Willie as Sammy Myers at the Majestic Music Hall in London. There he gives up his befuddling job as an attendant to become a valet. But his master is a fake, passing himself off as a lord to make a good marriage. Sammy innocently bungles into exposing his master. The original piece was first translated by Harry Graham, then "adapted" by Harold Atteridge. At least a dozen writers helped on the songs. A Victor Herbert song, "Give Your Heart In June," was advertised as "His Last Waltz." Howard won applause not only for his clowning but for his dead-on-target imitation of Al Jolson. If he received little assistance from a tired book and score, he was able to leave the stage at intervals knowing the show's excellent dancers were ready to delight with their kicks and taps. The well-liked Howard helped keep the show going into the summer.

Another great comedian, Leon Errol, opened the following night, March 3, in **Louie the 14th.** For the occasion, Florenz Ziegfeld and Joseph Urban completely refurbished the old Majestic, by then called the Cosmopolitan. Errol played Louie Ket-

chup, an army cook with the A.E.F. who elects to remain in France. When rich Paul Trapman (J. W. Doyle) discovers there will be thirteen at the table for his grand dinner, he hastily enlists Louie as a fourteenth guest. Louie's gaucheries provide the fun and complications. Inevitably, since Errol and Louie were one and the same, a drunk scene ensued. There was, the *World* insisted, "nothing more comical than his old act of falling down horribly and humilitively every so often." The show was elaborately mounted by Ziegfeld. The dinner was served on a real gold dinner service that had once belonged to the Russian Imperial family and now was the property of the Ziegfelds. A chef in the wings prepared a real meal. Unhappily, Romberg's score was a major letdown after the richness and depth of *The Student Prince.* The show's berth up at the somewhat distant Columbus Circle may have hurt attendance. *Louie the 14th* ran until it could begin a fall tour, but the tour was cut short when Errol was hurt in an accident.

George McManus' popular comic strip *Bringing Up Father* provided the inspiration and title for a musical version (4-6-25, Lyric) of the battles between the stern-eyed Maggie, rolling pin in hand, and the dapper, hen-pecked Jiggs. A series of **Bringing Up Father** shows had been popular in the hinterlands for nearly a decade. They included *Bringing Up Father in Florida, Bringing Up Father on Broadway, Bringing Up Father in Ireland* (shades of Emmet's Fritz!) and *Bringing Up Father at the Seashore.* This particular production was rushed in from the road to fill a vacant theatre. In this version Maggie follows a fleeing Jiggs from Ireland to a yacht headed for Spain. The story was halted frequently for vaudeville specialties. One performer, Mary Marlowe, did a series of imitations early in the evening and came on later to perform a "Legmania Dance." Neither the music nor the comedy was inspired enough to attract Maggie and Jiggs' followers away from their papers. The show lasted three weeks.

Princess Ida and *The Mikado* were revived two days apart at theatres directly across the street from one another. Unlike the simple staging of *Patience* earlier in the season, both shows were given relatively elaborate productions and both had important artists in their casts, most notably Tessa Kosta as Ida; *The Mikado* was the more successful of the two newcomers. Three Gilbert and Sullivan revivals in a matter of months attested to a reawakening interest in the great English masters.

Two other musicals vied with *Princess Ida* for opening nighters. **Tell Me More** (4-13-25, Gaiety) gave Broadway its second Gershwin score to a book show in five months. Just as Romberg's material for *Louie the 14th* disappointed after his work for *The Student Prince,* Gershwin's score was a letdown after *Lady, Be Good!* No Gershwin standards emerged. Nor was the book particularly strong. Its straightforward story of Kenneth Dennison's (Alexander Gray) courting of Peggy Van De Leur (Phyllis Cleveland) at a masked ball in New York and a vacation retreat in New Hampshire barely had enough twists to see it through to eleven o'clock. At one point Peggy poses as a shop girl to test the seemingly snobbish Kenneth's ardor. Lou Holtz' clowning concealed many of the dull spots. He played poor Monty Sipkin, the beau of the comic subplot's rich Jane Wallace (Esther Howard). Besides performing his low-dialect comedy Holtz was allowed to add one of his own songs just before the final curtain, a number he had been doing in vaudeville, "Oh, So La Mi." But even more of the dull spots were glossed over by the favorite cure-all of 1920's musical comedy—dancing. Sammy Lee's chorus girls were described as "comely, tireless and thoroughly expert in all the acrobatics to which modern dancing has come to bend the knee." They brought down the house with their high-stepping to Gershwin's "Kickin' The Clouds Away." As if so agile a line were not enough, three specialty dancers—Dorothy Wilson, Mary Jane, and Vivian Glenn—were seen to "reduce to absurdity the doctrine of speed, and particularly of touching the back of the head with the toes." *Tell Me More* was light and bubbly enough to register 100 performances. Interestingly, its original title was to have been *My Fair Lady,* but that was dropped as not sufficiently commercial.

Mercenary Mary (4-13-25, Longacre), which rounded out the trio of openings, had a plot reminiscent of an earlier Gershwin show, *La, La, Lucille* (5-26-19), though it was actually based on Herbert Hall Winslow and Emil Nyitray's 1923 farce, *What's Your Wife Doing?* Chris and Mary Skinner (Louis Simon and Winnie Baldwin) have married over the objections of Chris' grandfather. They fear he will disinherit them. So they decide to stage a divorce, get back in the will, and then quietly remarry. Chris' friend, Jerry (Allen Kearns), agrees for a fee to play co-respondent in his apartment. Mary is so nervous she drinks too much and almost spoils everything, but the uncle relents and all ends well. William B. Friedlander, who coauthored the book with Isabel Leighton, and staged the piece, collaborated with Con Conrad on the songs. Their "Honey, I'm In Love With You" exemplifies the

lesser tunes that filled the more commonplace musicals of the season. While a band known as the "Jazz Ambassadors" played the score, a "star and garter" chorus kicked its shapely, well-exposed legs in unison, and "Nellie Breen's amazing twinkling toes [touched] the ground only for the sake of bouncing off it." When New York proved indifferent, the show was hustled off to London, where it enjoyed a huge success.

The first half of June delivered three new musicals. **Lucky Sambo** (6-6-25, Colonial), produced, as so many black shows had to be, at a somewhat declassé house, watched Rufus Johnson (Joe Boyd) and Sambo Jenkins (Tim Moore) tricked into a dubious oil-drilling scheme by Jim Nightengale (Clarence Robinson). But the tricksters are themselves duped, and Rufus and Sambo do strike oil. It was all—book, lyrics, and music—by Porter Grainger and Fred Johnson. The critics responded to their efforts the way they responded to all black shows of the period. One reviewer wrote, "These negro musical shows vary in titles and principals but they all have one glorious feature in common— a genuine and spontaneous hilarity which can't be surpassed by the most elaborate troupe on the other side of the cotton line." Grainger and Johnson knowingly included all the stereotypes the critics and public expected. The show opened in front of Aunt Jemima's cabin, where the chorus demonstrated "the violent convulsions of the Charleston." The chorus also sang spiritual-like songs such as "I'm Comin' Home." Bit parts included a slow-moving, bug-eyed, comic porter.

On May 17 the "Junior members" of the Theatre Guild staged a matinee and evening performance of a revue they had completed to help purchase tapestries for the new theatre the Guild was guilding. Because the performances were to be at the Garrick, the evening was christened **The Garrick Gaieties.** The revue was small-scaled, relying for its appeal on its wit, its melody, and the skill of its young performers. Since these youngsters included Romney Brent, Sterling Holloway, and Philip Loeb, the skills were impressive. The critics hailed the skits, which bit the hand they were trying to feed by satirizing such Guild productions as *The Guardsman* and *They Knew What They Wanted* (rephrased by the players as "They Didn't Know What They Were Getting"). In "The Theatre Guild Enters Heaven," Brent appeared as St. Peter, rendering judgment on the acceptability of the heroines in recent Guild plays. The sole political spoof was "Mr. and Mrs.," in which the Coolidges' idea of an enjoyable evening was seen to be listening silently to the radio and going to sleep by ten. The Scopes "Monkey Trial" was staged with a jury in monkey suits. The three musketeers, New York's police, and subway manners were all twitted. The evening's lone bow to "spectacle" was the opening of the second act. "Rancho Mexicana" was danced by Rose Rolando in a multi-colored set designed by her husband, the distinguished artist, Miguel Covarrubias. Music for the scene was by their friend, Tatanacho. As far as the rest of the production went, one critic estimated it included "about $3 worth of scenery." The most lasting part of the evening proved to be the songs, seven of which were written by Richard Rodgers and Larry Hart.

. . .

Lorenz Hart, the older of the pair, was born in New York City on May 2, 1895. He claimed he was distantly related to the German poet, Heinrich Heine, though the claim is open to suspicion. From the time he saw his first play at the age of seven he was an inveterate theatregoer. His early education was in select private schools. He entered Columbia College, where he began majoring in journalism and writing material for varsity shows. He even appeared in one as a female impersonator. Hart never finished his schooling, leaving Columbia to translate plays for the Shuberts. Extremely short, a heavy drinker from boyhood, the mercurial Hart was in many ways the perfect foil to his sober, business-like partner.

. . .

Richard Rodgers was born in New York, seven years after Hart, on June 28, 1902. His mother was a pianist, and his father, a doctor, was a good singer. Rodgers began to learn the piano at the age of six. In his early teens he fell in love with musical comedy, and Jerome Kern became his idol. He entered Columbia, and like Hart before him, joined the varsity shows. Together they wrote the school's 1920 production, *Fly with Me.* Songs from this show, with new Hart lyrics, were sung in *Poor Little Ritz Girl* (7-27-20). Rodgers continued to pursue his serious musical studies even after his disappointment with his 1920 Broadway debut. But by 1925 he was sufficiently discouraged to consider dropping music and entering business. The reception accorded *The Garrick Gaieties* removed any doubts about his future.

. . .

Hart's almost pyrotechnical ingenuity was revealed in the lyrics to their opening song, "Guilding The Guild." While hailing competitors like the Neighborhood Playhouse that "shine below the Macy-Gimbel line" he welcomed the greater variety

and daring of the Guild which one night served "a mild dish of folklore quaintly childish" and then turned "Oscar Wildish" the next evening. And together Rodgers and Hart made unforgettable words and music with "Manhattan." The song was sung by sad-voiced, tousled-hair Holloway and pert June Cochrane. Its mounting was the utmost in simplicity. Holloway and Miss Cochrane sang on an undecorated stage before the plain show curtain. Rodgers and Hart's main contribution was meant to be the first-act finale—their "jazz opera" "The Joy Spreader." The opera told of a sales-girl and a clerk (Betty Starbuck and Brent) accidently locked overnight in a department store. The next morning the puritanical owner refuses to believe they were not up to some mischief. The "opera" suffered the same fate as Gershwin's "Blue Monday Blues" in the George White *Scandals* (8-28-22). It was hastily dropped. But its removal left space for a new Rodgers and Hart song, "Sentimental Me," which Holloway and Miss Cochrane were awarded for the excellent rendition of "Manhattan." After a few additional special performances, the show became the regular attraction at the Garrick on June 8 and compiled an impressive 211 performances before it was through. *The Garrick Gaieties,* as much as *Charlot's Revue* (1-9-24), announced that small, literate revues were the wave of the future and that the death knell of the great extravaganzas was tolling for all to hear.

Kosher Kitty Kelly (6-15-25, Times Square), with music by Leon De Costa, hoped to attract the same Irish and Jewish elements that had long been a strong bulwark to the New York theatre and were at that very moment helping *Abie's Irish Rose* achieve the longest run until that time in Broadway's history. It failed, though it took a tack most Irish and Jews probably liked better than the mixed marriage of Anne Nichols' farce. Kitty Kelly (Helen Shipman) dates Morris Rosen (Basil Loughrane), but she finally selects Patrick O'Reilly (Fred Santley), while Morris seems happy with Rosie Feinbaum (Beatrice Allen).

1925-1926

There was a slight, unimportant drop in the number of new musicals during 1925–26, but no slackening of excitement or of quality. However, a real if not apparent drop in the number of revues occurred, though booking quirks brought two editions of the *George White Scandals* and the *Grand Street Follies.*

The season opened and closed with **The Grand Street Follies.** The series' spotlight remained focused on its bright travesties and impersonations, minimizing any musical originality. The earlier of the season's two editions (6-18-25, Neighborhood Playhouse) offered a skit called "They Knew What They Wanted Under the Elms." The set recalled Robert Edmond Jones' multi-storied set for O'Neill's play. A different Broadway hit was burlesqued in each of the four rooms. Actually almost all the show's material related to recent Broadway seasons. *The Guardsman* was spoofed, with Lynn Fontanne's role assumed by the company's master impersonator, Albert Carroll. *Abie's Irish Rose* was transformed into an Italian opera, "L'Irlandesa Rose dell'Abie," while the tough-talking (for the era) *What Price Glory?* was cleansed and daintified, its foul-mouthed Sergeant Quirk "fragrant and fairy-like in lavender pyjamas."

Gilbert's Engaged (6-18-25, 52nd St.), a freakish affair, was a musical version of W. S. Gilbert's old play, *Engaged.* It utilized songs of the play's era with new words and occasional new melodies by Brian Hooker. The show met with little success and did nothing but momentarily interrupt the progression of summer revues.

The **Scandals** returned four nights later with a 1925 edition (6-22-25, Apollo). Its cast included Harry Fox, Helen Morgan, and Tom Patricola. Strumming on his ukulele and backed by sixty of George White's fast-stepping chorus girls, Patricola provided the night's show-stoppers in his Charleston-like dances. Albertina Rasch Girls, "supremely charming and unmechanically graceful," provided more ballet-like moments. One of the evening's capital numbers was White's good-humored bow to his competitor, Irving Berlin. Gordon Dooley impersonated the composer-producer. As he lamented he was all alone White's beauties flitted around him "twining in and out over his body." With Gershwin gone, White hired Buddy DeSylva, Lew Brown, and Ray Henderson to do the score. Though they soon established one of the nation's best song mills, the team's efforts for this edition were unavailing. Their initial offerings are well represented by "What A World This Would Be." Neither the public nor White was unduly disturbed by the music's lack of distinction. Theatregoers flocked to the *Scandals* for 171 performances, and White signed the boys for the 1926 version.

Both **Artists and Models** (6-24-25, Winter Garden) and **Earl Carroll Vanities** (7-6-25, Earl Carroll) had even less of merit to offer than did the *Scandals.* Both featured their celebrated nudes. And both had quickly garnered such large regular followings that each ran out the entire season despite all the critical harrumphs. The girls were not the only attraction in *Artists and Models.* Phil Baker played the concertina, while his stooge, Sid Silvers, planted in a stage box, harassed him. When Silvers complained, "I have no home," Baker, playing merrily on, promised, "I'll dig you one." "Jazz à la Russe" demonstrated how American music might be handled in *Chauve Souris.* A dance called "The Promenade Walk" was awarded "eight honestly earned encores." Hawaiian dancing was featured in "Poi Ball." Later the hula dancers became flappers, doing a fast-stepping Charleston. The Grace Hoffman Girls performed precision dancing that equaled the best the Tiller Girls were doing elsewhere. A ballet entitled "The Lily Pool" had two sets of dancers, one set pretending to be the reflection of the other. Unfortunately, Sigmund Romberg and Fred Coots' songs once again sent few playgoers whistling out of the playhouse.

For his *Vanities,* Carroll extended the stage around the front of the orchestra pit and placed tables on the extension to give a cabaret effect. He was so generous in filling his offering that at midnight the show was still not in sight of its finale. Carroll's spectacles included a bird ballet and a color ballet, while his dancers stomped as they spelled out "C-H-A-R-L-E-S-T-O-N." Comedy interludes between the lavish production numbers were generally in the hands of Ted Healy.

J. Fred Coots, who did some of the music for *Artists and Models,* did most of the score for **June Days** (8-6-25, Astor), a musical version of Alice Duer Miller and Robert Milton's *The Charm School.* Cyrus Wood's book tampered only lightly with the original story of a young man, Austin Bevins (Roy Royston), who inherits a girls' school, decides that the only important thing to teach is charm and is himself charmed into marriage by one of his students, Miss Curtis (Millie James). Jerome Kern had written incidental songs for the original play. His sweet, flowing style was undoubtedly correct for the tone of the piece, though his music was not among his best. Coots' music for "Why Is Love," "Remembering You" or the title tune was more obviously a product of Tin Pan Alley. Much of the evening's comedy came from Jay C. Flippen. Performing in blackface, he played a gardener whose lady friend is so cheap she tries to send a night letter during an eclipse. The tired businessman, for whom the era insisted this sort of musical was often written, was no doubt pleased when a dormitory scene allowed chorus girls to wear noticeably sheer pajamas. The show found a limited audience and stayed eleven weeks.

Still more Coots music was heard twelve nights later when the Shuberts, with Rufus La Maire, assembled a revue called **Gay Paree** (8-18-25, Shubert). Not a single song dealt with Paris or France, and the comedy rarely touched on either. Most of the comedy fell to Chic Sale. He offered a series of monologues, vignettes of characters from an imaginary Hickville. These home-folks included a weak-minded farm boy, a deacon, and a tottering Civil War veteran. In one skit Sales helped educate Winnie Lightner:

Sales: Do you know why Peggy Hopkins Joyce didn't marry Santa Claus?
Lightner: No.
Sales: She didn't marry Santa Claus because there is no Santa Claus.

Lavish production numbers had the chorus beauties parading in "Glory of Morning Sunshine" and "Venetian Nights." A tableau called "Dixie" celebrated sentimentalized plantation days. Dancing girls shimmied to "Florida Mammy," singing as they danced, "My old-fashioned Mammy owns half of Miami." Shenanigans of this sort kept ticket sales brisk for six months.

August's last musical was the return of *Big Boy*. With Al Jolson in better health the show chalked up another 120 performances before taking to the road.

Clyde Fitch's 1901 success, *Captain Jinks of the Horse Marines,* which had launched Ethel Barrymore on her road to stardom, was brought up to date and set to music by Frank Mandel and Laurence Schwab (libretto), B. G. DeSyla (lyrics), and Lewis E. Gensler and Stephen Jones (tunes). It once again recounted the tempestuous romance of Capt. Robert Jinks (J. Harold Murray) and Suzanne Trentoni (Louise Brown), formerly of Trenton, N.J., and now a world-famous dancer. The updating made no effort at elaboration. The production retained the single sets used in each act: A New York pier in Act I (allowing Trentoni to make a sweeping entrance down a gangplank), and a town house drawing room in the second act. One addition to the musical was the role of a comic hackdriver, written in to afford Joe E. Brown another chance to display his rowdy comedy and eccentric dances. Unfortunately, his material was not top quality, forcing Brown to mug where words failed him. Another good Sammy Lee chorus diverted attention with its snappy dancing. The songs were nondescript. But with its title shortened to simply **Captain Jinks** (9-8-25, Martin Beck), the musical still found enough favor to last twenty-one weeks.

Thursday, September 16, 1925, began what may have been the most remarkable seven days in the history of the American Musical Theatre. *No! No! Nanette!* opened on that evening, followed by *Dearest Enemy* on September 18, *The Vagabond King* on the 21st, and *Sunny* on the 22nd. If *Rose-Marie* was the biggest musical success of this era, **No! No! Nanette!** was the most successful musical comedy. Its relatively short Broadway run of 321 performances is generally attributed to the fact that the show had already run a year in Chicago and had sent out road companies in advance of its New York opening. Oddly, the show almost died aborning at its Detroit premiere, and only its producer's determination kept it alive. No sooner had the discouraging Detroit reviews appeared than H. H. Frazee set about completely recasting his production. He also goaded his song writers for new material. Two of the additions they gave him proved to be the hits of the show: "Tea For Two" and "I Want To Be Happy." *No, No, Nanette*'s story was typical 1920 frippery, a musical version of *His Lady Friends* in which Clifton Crawford had starred and for which he wrote incidental songs in 1919. Nanette (Louise Groody) is the unconventional flapper daughter of Billy Early (Wellington Cross). Early, a prosperous publisher of Bibles, is himself not a little unconventional. He has a weakness for sharing some of his wealth with pretty young ladies whose careers need financial encouragement. But he is more openhanded than openminded—at least where Nanette is concerned. Nor is Nanette's boyfriend Tom (Jack Barker) completely in sympathy with Nanette's free ways. He is particularly taken aback by the interest Nanette and Jimmy Smith (Charles Winninger), Early's friend and lawyer, display toward each other. The older Jimmy has advised Nanette he won't be happy till he makes her happy too. Misunderstandings come to a head in Atlantic City. At first even Tom's glowing picture of a love nest where he and Nanette won't have it known they own a telephone fails to help matters. Mrs. Early arrives, disposes of her husband's lady friends, puts Jimmy in his place, sees that Tom and Nanette are paired and that a good deal more of Mr. Early's generosity will thereafter be directed toward her. Vincent Youmans' score was his best, catchy and endearing for all his stylistic limitations. Several of the songs were brought over in one form or another from earlier shows. "Take A Little One-

Step" was taken whole from *Lollipop*, while the title song was a clever rewriting of "My Boy And I" from *Mary Jane McKane*. "I Want To Be Happy" and "Tea For Two," the belatedly added hits, were numbers of striking simplicity. The open sentimentality of "Tea For Two," coupled with the easy directness of both its main theme and an almost similar bridge, made the song the most popular of all American standards for years afterwards. The original production was tasteful and essentially intimate. The living room set of the third act, for example, displayed homey wicker furniture, and the second-act lawn was a cozy, flower-strewn, trellised retreat. While *No, No, Nanette* played the large Globe Theatre in New York, many of the houses it booked on the road were among the smallest in their respective cities. The show was revived in an overblown production, but with a fair degree of faithfulness, in 1971. It was a smash all over again.

The subtlety, inventiveness, and sophistication of **Dearest Enemy** (9-18-25, Knickerbocker) stood in direct contrast to the slap-on-the-back obviousness of *No! No! Nanette!* The primary colorings of Youmans' music and of Irving Caesar and Otto Harbach's lyrics gave way to the nuances and offbeat shadings of Rodgers and Hart's material. It was practically impossible not to predict the next note or turn of phrase in *Nanette*'s songs. *Dearest Enemy*'s tunes titillated their audience with delicious and unexpected surprises. Moreover, in their range the melodies occasionally touched briefly on arioso effects. "Here In My Arms" stretches to an octave and fifth in the nineteenth bar of its chorus, still pleasantly and easily singable, but a departure from the tightly knit melodies of most popular musical comedy song. Both "Here In My Arms" and "Bye And Bye" were shortly hummed everywhere and are still popular half a century later. With his lyrics for this show Hart made public once and for all his unique, bittersweet cynicism. It was a view of the world he retained, only slightly altered, to the end of his career, and it gave his body of rhymes a philosophic backbone not found in any other major lyricists. Shouting "War Is War," his ladies rejoice in the collapse of morality, "Hurray, we're going to be compromised!" The same change of climate was conveyed more quietly and suavely in "I Beg Your Pardon" where the hero begged to kiss a heroine so "divinely radiant" as long as her "lady aunt" was not around to see.

In rhymes that harked back to *Patience* and *Iolanthe*, Hart captured the polite but insistent sexual give and take of the show's 18th-century subject matter. The contrast between the soft expressions and determined feelings was one that Hart would often return to with good-natured, knowing amusement. It is easy to see why the quality of the songs led the *Times* to compare the material to Gilbert and Sullivan and why more than one critic commented favorably on the operatic excellence of the work. Lew Fields' son, Herbert, wrote the libretto.

* * *

Herbert Fields was born in New York City on July 26, 1897. He was the son of Lew Fields and the brother of Dorothy Fields. After leaving Columbia, he tried his luck at acting, often appearing in dialect roles not very different from those his father had performed. He early on became friends with Rodgers and Hart, and they helped persuade him to try his hand at writing. Together the three wrote a musical, *Winkle Town*, for which they could find no producer. But Lew Fields did mount a straight play the trio wrote. *The Melody Man* told of an old immigrant's dismay on hearing his serious music played as jazz. Though Rodgers and Hart inserted a few of their earliest songs, the play was offered as the work of Herbert Richard Lorenz. Not even fine acting by Lew Fields and a young actor named Fredric March could save the evening. Shortly after the show folded the boys turned their efforts to *Dearest Enemy*.

* * *

If the book was not on a par with the music, it was still better than average. Fields along with Rodgers and Hart got his inspiration from a plaque they stumbled upon on 37th Street. It read,

> [General] Howe, with Clinton, Tryon, and a few others, went to the house of Robert Murray, on Murray Hill, for refreshment and rest. With pleasant conversation and a profusion of cake and wine, the good Whig lady detained the gallant Britons almost two hours. Quite long enough for the bulk of Putnam's division of four thousand men to leave the city and escape to the heights of Harlem by Bloomingdale Road, with the loss of only a few soldiers.

That was the plot, though in sound and contemporary fashion Fields added some musical comedy touches. He inserted a love interest between Mrs. Murray's niece, Betsy Burke (Helen Ford), and Capt. Sir John Copeland (Charles Purcell). In keeping with the vogue he made Betsy an Irish leading lady. And at a time when in the first gleanings of sexual freedom nudes were being seen on stage, Fields allowed her to make her entrance in nothing but a barrel. The established producers all rejected the work. Only when the *Garrick Gaieties* had made Rodgers and Hart names to be reckoned with did George Ford gamble with it—and then only because his wife Helen was starred as Betsy. Helen, in fact, obtained the backer who made the production possible. Actually the show did not have to cost much since, like *No! No! Nanette!* and so many other shows of the day, it used just three sets —one for each act. *Dearest Enemy* ran out the New York season, but on the road it was far less profitable than *Nanette*.

The Vagabond King (9-21-25, Casino) swept theatregoers into the world of pure operetta. Rudolf Friml dropped the unusual chordings and rhythms that gave a suggestion of American flavor to *Rose-Marie.* His score was full-blooded and glowingly, throbbingly romantic as befitted a musical version of Justin Huntly McCarthy's *If I Were King.* Its original production had made a star of E. H. Sothern in 1901, the same year *Captain Jinks of the Horse Marines* catapulted Ethel Barrymore to fame. For 511 performances Louis XI (Max Figman) again made the irresistibly smooth-tongued poet and scoundrel, François Villon (Dennis King), "king for a day." In that one day he must woo and win Katherine de Vaucelles (Carolyn Thomson), or lose his head. He serves his king better than his king serves him. Villon rouses the Parisian rabble and routs the Burgundians—thereby saving Louis' kingdom. When Hugette (Jane Carroll), a prostitute who had hoped to marry Villon, realizes that she stands in the way of his advancement, she commits suicide. Louis in turn realizes none of his citizens would make so great a sacrifice for him and allows the poet and Katherine to wed. W. H. Post and Brian Hooker's dialogue and Hooker's lyrics were journeyman. Happily, the score was the best Friml ever wrote. It varied from the moving beauty of its love songs—Villon and Katherine's "Only A Rose" and Katherine's "Some Day"—to the poignant "Hugette Waltz," to Villon and Katherine's tremulous "Love Me To-Night," to Hugette's torrid, but heartbreaking "Love For Sale," to Villon's rousing "Song Of The Vagabonds"—the last two numbers sung with the chorus. Surprisingly, though the show confirmed Dennis King's claim to stardom, his swashbuckling playing and fine singing were almost taken for granted. The lush mounting practically stole the evening. The production was as rich and overflowing as the music. In many notices James Reynolds' sets were accorded as much praise as Friml's score. Louis XI's medieval Paris was depicted "ablaze with autumn coloring." The blaze of fall colors gave way to a "riot" of

every conceivable hue in **Sunny** (9-22-25, New Amsterdam). Its curtain rose on an extravagantly colorful circus set filled with freaks, snake charmers, barkers, and roustabouts. As the evening progressed, the circus was supplanted by a brilliant hunting scene (probably with autumn colors and certainly with bright red riding habits), an ocean liner, and an elegant ballroom (with George Olsen's jazz musicians on stage to supplement the pit orchestra). *Sunny* happily reunited Marilyn Miller and Jerome Kern. But they were only the most prominent names in a splendid array of talent. This time Charles Dillingham, the closest thing to a rival Ziegfeld had, mounted the piece. Miss Miller's co-players included Jack Donahue, Clifton Webb, Cliff "Ukulele Ike" Edwards, Mary Hay, and the fading Joseph Cawthorn. Otto Harbach and Oscar Hammerstein II, who had collaborated so handsomely on *Rose-Marie,* combined their efforts for book and lyrics. (*Sunny* was the first Hammerstein and Kern collaboration.) Theatrical imperatives made absurd demands on the writers. Edwards' contract called for him to do his speciality between precisely ten and ten fifteen each night. But somehow they threw everything together in a workable if uninspired plot. Basically it dealt with the romance between Sunny Peters (Miss Miller) and Tom Warren (Paul Frawley). Sunny is a circus rider come to perform in England, while Tom is an American working there. When Tom has to return to the States, Sunny finds she lacks the funds to follow him. The circus owner, her ex-husband (Donahue), suggests they remarry, sail back and get another divorce. But Sunny suspects his plans. She stows away instead. She is caught and has to marry Tom's best friend to avoid the brig. But by curtain time she and Tom are arm in arm. The ending is so last minute that in London, where Tom was not so important a player, Sunny was given in marriage to someone else merely by changing the final lines.

Kern's music was a delight: flowing, graceful, and imaginative. It was worlds beyond the simplistic jinglings, however catchy, of so much of the day's musical comedies. Even minor numbers were noteworthy. "Sunshine" has a curiously flexible melody and drive; of a sort that would not be disturbed by the rhythmic distortion of later orchestral fashions. The touching "D'ya Love Me?" was equally pliant, played both as a waltz and as a fox-trot in the show. The lilting title song became an immediate hit, its fine melody coupled with such colloquial yet inventive lines as "Smiling all the while, Tomboy/where'd you get your smile from boy." Lines such as these were probably the brain child of the fast-developing Hammerstein. The lyrics to the show's runaway hit, "Who?", were known to be his, and Kern often insisted the success of the song was the result of Hammerstein's coupling the sustained opening note of the chorus—sustained for two and a quarter measures and repeated five times—with the word "who." In "Two Little Bluebirds" Webb and Miss Hay provided the evening's best eccentric dancing. Still, it was Marilyn Miller's light tap dancing and graceful ballet-like pirouettes the public came to see. Miss Miller's voice was not big— and there were occasional complaints she could not be heard in the far reaches of the house. But her airy footwork, her beauty, and her indefinable magnetism were more than enough compensation. The show was the most popular ticket of the season and afterwards on the road. But unlike *Nanette,* which reaped profits from several companies, *Sunny* was felt to need the presence of its stars.

Harlan Thompson and Harry Archer, still hoping to write a second *Little Jessie James* (8-15-23), offered the public their latest collaboration, **Merry, Merry** (9-24-25, Vanderbilt). Another backstage yarn, it traced the history of Eve Walters (Marie Saxon) from her arrival in New York, an innocent young lady with plans to be a chorus girl, to her acceptance of everyday Adam Winslow (Harry Puck) as her husband and her abandonment of her theatrical ambitions. What changes Eve's thinking is the greedy, dishonest attempt of her roommate and fellow chorine, Sadi La Salle (Sacha Beaumont), to extort money from a stage-door Johnny. Thompson and Archer may have suspected from the start that *Merry, Merry* lacked the appeal of *Little Jessie James.* In any case, they dropped the single set simplicity of their earlier work, moving the action from a subway to an apartment to the stage of the very Vanderbilt where the show played. Though the sets lacked the magnificence of those in *The Vagabond King* or *Sunny,* they did apparently divert audiences from the musical's lack of distinction. *Merry, Merry* had a satisfactory five-month run.

Tom Johnstone's forlorn quest for Broadway acclaim continued with his score for **When You Smile** (10-5-25, National). But his score was as drab as a Johnstone score was expected to be. Nor did the book help matters. The title gave no clue to the plot, a musical revamping of the 1923 play, *Extra.* John W. King (John Maurice Sullivan), the publisher, decides to wreck his film weekly, *The Movie News,* so that he may buy its outstanding stock at a bargain price. King can think of no better way to wreck

it than to put his ne'er-do-well son, Wally (Ray Raymond), in charge. But Wally and his drunken buddy, Larry Patton (Jack Whiting), turn the sheet into a gold mine. King's only consolation is that he has gained a daughter-in-law in June Willard (Carol Joyce). *When You Smile* was a quick flop.

Another quick flop was a production of **Polly,** John Gay's sequel to *The Beggar's Opera.* The show was produced on October 10 at the Cherry Lane Playhouse, far from Broadway, with an unexceptional cast. An even quicker closing befell **Holka Polka** (also known as *Spring in Autumn*) (10-14-25, Lyric), an importation that starred Orville Harrold (the aging leading man of *Naughty Marietta*) and his daughter, Patti. They played father and daughter in the show, with papa leading his daughter into a happy marriage.

Charles Dillingham followed with a second Jerome Kern musical, **The City Chap** (10-26-25, Liberty), a musical version of Winchell Smith's *The Fortune Hunter.* James Montgomery devised the book and Anne Caldwell handled the lyrics. Their story had down-and-out Nat Duncan (Skeet Gallagher) arrive in the small town of Radford to court a rich man's daughter. But a visit to Graham's drugstore changes his plans. He falls in love with Betty Graham (Phyllis Cleveland) and gives up seeking the pot of gold. Kern's score was weak; so weak only three songs were published. Its best number "No One Knows" was a reversion to the plain but charming two-steps he offered in the teens. Minor roles were filled by Betty Compton (Mayor Jimmy Walker's mistress), Irene Dunne, and George Raft. Raft did a brief tap dance in one scene. *The City Chap* was a nine-week disappointment. It was the fourth and final October musical: all failures.

Artistically, November showed little improvement, though several of its entries rolled up appreciable runs for the time. Two musicals arrived hand in hand on November 2. **Florida Girl** at the Lyric had a comic-thriller plot. Unknown to Daphne (Vivienne Segal), smuggled diamonds have been hidden in her shoe. The shoe is stolen off her foot as she detrains in Coral Gables. For the rest of the evening Daphne, her boy friend, Henry (Irving Beebe), the smugglers, and the police race to recover the shoe. Milton Suskind's sole Broadway score was commonplace, and failed to find a public, though it touched all the popular topics of the day: the Florida land boom ("Oranges"), campus capers ("The Collegians"), and the contemporary dance rage ("Chinky China Charleston"). Earl Carroll as producer brought all his notorious talents to "bare" on the piece. The costumes he gave his chorus girls were described as "diaphanous," though in one number they dressed as sailors wearing blue taffeta silk coats, navy caps, and tight-fitting bell-bottom trousers. Some of the comedy was in the hands of the Ritz brothers as three clowning gangsters— Aristotle, Plato, and Socrates. Like so many comics of the era, they were also agile dancers, and their dance routines earned them as much commendation as their comedy. Another comic who doubled as an eccentric dancer was Lester Allen. He played the part of a detective, resorting to disguises much like those the famous Prohibition agents Izzy and Moe were using at the time to grab bootleggers and headlines. The show employed at least one intriguing sight gag—a black toupee that turned white when its wearer was frightened. Unfortunately, nothing seemed to help. *Florida Girl* had to be withdrawn after five weeks.

Sigmund Romberg and the Shuberts undoubtedly hoped to match Friml's record of two smash hits in two consecutive seasons by following *The Student Prince* with **Princess Flavia** (11-2-25, Century), a lyric recounting of Anthony Hope's *The Prisoner of Zenda*. Instead, as it had with Kern and Gershwin, triumph gave way to failure—or something close to it. Romberg and the Shuberts overlooked the bold departures *The Vagabond King* had shown from *Rose-Marie* in story and musical style. Everything about *Princess Flavia*, including the royal rank in the title, seemed purposefully to recall *The Student Prince*. The plot again told of unfulfilled love. On a visit to Zenda, Rudolph Rassendyl (Harry Welchman) is mistaken for Rudolf, Crown Prince of Ruritania. When the real prince becomes incapacitated, Rassendyl is prevailed to act as a substitute at the coronation. Princess Flavia (Evelyn Herbert) falls in love with him and he with her. But they both understand such a match would be impolitic. As Karl Franz and Kathie did before them, Rassendyl and Flavia go their separate ways. To underscore the similarities, much of the music seemed almost a parody. The hit of the evening was meant to be "I Dare Not Love You." It was an extended waltz number with several melodies in the manner of "Deep In My Heart, Dear" leading up to a principal theme that was all but a parody of the same song. Romberg and his producers had learned nothing from the imitative *Melody*'s failure to recapture the appeal of *Maytime*. At best Romberg had taught the Shuberts the advantages of filling the stage with fine singers. Several critics applauded the large male chorus—the same sort of chorus Romberg had fought to get for *The Student Prince*.

Harry Welchman moved on to become one of London's most popular leading men. Most important, Evelyn Herbert was finally allotted her place in the sun. It is generally conceded that Miss Herbert had the finest voice of any of the 1920s' major prima donnas. Broadway often welcomed volume before refinement. Miss Herbert's voice was big, but it was also warm and superbly modulated. *Princess Flavia* managed to run nineteen weeks before moving to Chicago.

Naughty Cinderella (11-9-25, Lyceum), billed in its program as "a farce" and on its sheet music as "a song-farce," was really a straight play with incidental songs for its star, Irene Bordoni. Miss Bordoni played the role of an attractive French girl who wins her sweetheart away from the married woman he dotes on.

The following night saw the arrival of **Charlot's Revue of 1926** (11-10-25, Selwyn). The new material included a popular American interpolation, "A Cup Of Coffee, A Sandwich And You" (Billy Rose, Al Dubin/Joseph Meyer). Three things that hadn't changed were its top performers, Beatrice Lillie, Gertrude Lawrence, and Jack Buchanan. They brightened Broadway for 138 additional performances.

Arthur Richman's *Not So Long Ago* was turned into an operetta for the Shuberts by Clifford Grey and Edward Kunneke. Like a *Princess Flavia* it seemed determined to echo past hits. The Shuberts, possibly still recalling two companies of *Maytime* playing across the street from each other, called the evening **Mayflowers** (11-24-25, Forrest). The title had really no pertinence to the plot. When the little seamstress, Elsie Dover (Ivy Sawyer), pretends to have a lover, her father demands the boy's name. Nonplused, she can only think of the name of her employer's son, Billy Ballard (Joseph Santley). Mr. Dover confronts Billy. Billy grasps the situation and plays along. Before he knows it, he has fallen genuinely in love with Elsie. Kunneke's music had a Continental flavor. J. Fred Coots interpolated a number of songs with a more American style. In another echo, the title of one of Coots' tunes, "Mayflower, I Love You," probably reminded some theatregoers of the opening lyrics to "Wildflower." The musical barely made it into the New Year. In its failure it exemplifies the shows of the period that received generally favorable notices from tolerant critics but were shunned by a less tolerant public. The word that pervaded the morning-after notices was "charm." At least one reviewer singled out the "bustled chorus" as a relief from the skimpily clad lines of many "up-to-date" book shows.

Carlo and Sanders had another score ready for **Oh! Oh! Oh! Nurse** (12-7-25, Cosmopolitan). Marion Gay (Rebekah Cauble) is a nurse who can inherit her aunt's estate only after she buries her first husband. She loves Dr. Sidney Killmore (John Price Jones) too much to kill him so he persuades I. Dye (Don Barclay), a patient of Killmore's who is supposedly dying, to become a groom before he expires. But the marriage ceremony proves tonic, and I. Dye recovers overnight. Only then is it revealed the aunt's will is a bad joke. There were many who thought the whole evening a bad joke. The chorus numbers were stupefyingly inane. At one point "the line of girls simulate a train with red and white lights"—this in a hospital corridor. Patients and nurses alike gathered for another presentation with candles in hand. *Oh! Oh! Oh! Nurse* managed 32 showings. For Carlo and Sanders it was virtually the final straw. With two exceptions years later, they never again wrote Broadway musicals.

Jokes of a different sort regaled the audience at the Lyric the night after *Oh! Oh! Oh! Nurse* opened. The occasion was the premiere of **The Cocoanuts** (12-8-25, Lyric), two and a half hours of nonsense Irving Berlin and George S. Kaufman (aided, without public credit, by Morrie Ryskind) provided for the Marx Brothers. Perhaps two and a half hours is an understatement. Opening night in New York the show was far from over at 11:30. Kaufman's book had fun at the expense of the Florida real estate boom, with Groucho as a rapacious, unethical Florida hotel owner and real estate developer, Henry W. Schlemmer. He was abetted in his schemes by Willie the Wop (Chico), Silent Sam (Harpo), and to a lesser extent by Jamison (Zeppo). Complications rear their comic head when Harvey Yates (Henry Whittemore) and Penelope Martyn (Janet Velie) steal the jewels of a rich hotel guest, Mrs. Potter (played by Groucho's incomparable foil, Margaret Dumont). The thieves throw suspicion on Robert Adams (Jack Barker), the fiancé of Mrs. Potter's niece, Polly (Mabel Withee). With the brothers' help Adams is cleared by the end of the last act. How much of what finally appeared on stage was Kaufman and how much Marxian ad-libs remains moot. Almost every critic excerpted an absurdity or two for his readers. Alexander Woollcott was tickled by Groucho's announcement, "The next number on the program will be a piccolo solo which we will omit." Percy Hammond enjoyed Groucho's praise of a young lady's eyes that shone "like the pants of a blue serge suit," and Chico's identifying a blue print as an oyster. All during the run the brothers added and

dropped stage business. One night Harpo decided to throw Groucho off balance. In the middle of one of Groucho's scenes a chorus girl ran across the stage followed by a leering, horn-honking Harpo. Groucho refused to be disconcerted. He remarked "The nine-twenty's right on time" and resumed the regular action. It was generally conceded that the evening was not as zany as *I'll Say She Is* (5-19-24), but given such a feast of wild hilarity no one complained. Most critics were indifferent to Berlin's score, and the public seemed to agree with them. This indifference is lamentable because song after song was engaging and lilting. Berlin caught the period's infectious free-flowing gaiety in numbers like "Florida By The Sea," "Lucky Boy," "A Little Bungalow," and "The Monkey Doodle-Doo." If they didn't stop the show, they at least propelled it happily from scene to scene. Substantial additions and changes during the summer were introduced. The show ran into the following season, then moved out to spread its laughter around the country.

The night before Christmas the latest edition of the **Greenwich Village Follies** premiered at the 46th Street Theatre. The edition's most lauded number was "Lady of the Snow." Jack Frost, human snowballs and snowflakes filled the stage, only to "melt" at the end of the scene. Chorus girls also appeared as flower pots and as an apple pie. Florence Moore was in charge of the comedy. Recent hits such as *The Vortex* and *Cradle Snatchers* were spoofed. But the consensus deemed the material inferior. Kendall Capps did soft-shoe routines, while Myrio supplied gymnastic ballet. No song hits developed, and it was acknowledged the series had run its course. Though it played 180 performances, the 1925 edition was the last in the regular series, excepting one attempt at resuscitation in 1928.

The producers (Alex A. Aarons and Vinton Freedley) and writers (Guy Bolton and Fred Thompson) of *Lady Be Good!* (12-1-24) repeated with a second hit, **Tip-Toes** (12-28-25, Liberty). It had another of the Florida settings so popular at the time. And it had a plot as simple as it was simple-minded. "The Three K's" are a vaudeville trio stranded in Palm Beach. Al and Hen (Andrew Tombes and Harry Watson, Jr.), the two men in the group, are the brother and uncle of its girl, "Tip-Toes" (Queenie Smith). They wangle a thousand dollars from one of "Tip-Toes'" many admirers, dress her in style, and set her on the trail of Steve Burton (Allen Kearns), the glue magnate. By the end of the evening "Tip-Toes" and Steve have fallen in love. With *Tip-Toes* Ira Gershwin's lyric writing hit full stride. He could be outrageous, as in "These Charming People" (the title, by the way, of a Michael Arlen comedy then on Broadway), where he coupled "million dollars blokes pass" with "faux pas" Or delightfully witty, in the same song when he told of a Mr. Smythe-Smythe who was childless until twenty-seven children appeared for the reading of the will. Or, in phrases at once clipped and flowing from "That Certain Feeling," uncloyingly sentimental. Nor was it to hard to fall in love with—or to—George Gershwin's music for the heroine's "Looking For A Boy." The words and melodies went together impeccably. And when the entire cast stamped its feet and blared its trombones to "Sweet And Low Down," the audience stomped along. Mounted in stylishly art-déco fashion, *Tip-Toes* played merrily for 192 performances.

By the Way (12-28-25, Gaiety), a London revue, arrived, bringing with it such bright young people as Jack Hulburt and Cicely Courtneidge. Miss Courtneidge dressed for the occasion in white tie, top hat, and tails. Though the material was branded less original than Charlot's, *By the Way* found a receptive public for five months.

Gershwin's name was on another marquee two nights after the opening of *Tip-Toes*. Some New Yorkers, seeing it there, may have done a double-take, for **Song of the Flame** (12-30-25, 44th), listed as a "romantic opera," was unalloyed, flamboyant operetta. Actually Gershwin only composed a part of the score. An old operetta hand, Herbert Stothart, supplied the rest. But it is generally acknowledged that the stirring title song, the best number in the show, was Gershwin's. It suggests an unusual coupling of his clipped, clean-cut musical line with central European harmonies. Harbach and Hammerstein, having moved deftly from operetta to musical comedy, moved back again to do both the book and lyrics. Their plot recalled *The Red Feather* (11-9-03). Though she is a noble, Aniuta (Tessa Kosta) incites the peasants of Russia to revolt against oppression. She is known as "The Flame" because of the scarlet dress she wears. Prince Volodyn (Guy Robertson) falls in love with her, not suspecting her double identity. After the revolution they meet again in Paris, where they accept each other for what they truly are. The producer, Arthur Hammerstein, wisely refused to rely solely on his principals to put over the material. An extra large orchestra give unusual body to the accompaniments, while on stage a "Russian Art Choir" added its voices to the regular chorus. Nor was spectacle ignored. A symbolic ballet recorded the change of Russian seasons, beginning all in win-

try white and blossoming in full color as spring arrived. At an elegant palace festooned with Slavic motifs a wardrobe master removed bejeweled gown after bejeweled gown out of a seemingly bottomless trunk, and a tsarist fashion parade ensued. Hammerstein's skill and largess were awarded with a run of over six months.

Having done so well at the box office with *Gay Paree* earlier in the season, the Shuberts packaged another revue and called it **A Night in Paris** (1-6-26, Casino de Paris), 1926's first musical. They filled the show with bright low-paid youngsters on the way up, and with serviceable J. Fred Coots songs. Norma Terris sang some of the songs. Jack Pearl amused with his German dialect comedy. Gertrude Hoffman Girls danced and paraded as African savages, flowers, powder puffs and lipsticks, and gold and silver coins. The evening had the empty glitter of so many Shubert assemblages. But the Shuberts knew what the public wanted, at least that not unsizable section of the public they considered theirs. And they were right. *A Night in Paris* ran through the season. It was the sixth successive commercial hit. Not one ran less than five months.

Hello, Lola (1-12-26, Eltinge) brought the winning streak to an abrupt halt. A musical version of Booth Tarkington's *Seventeen*, it faithfully retold the familiar story of the troubled puppy-love affair between baby-talking Lola Pratt (Edythe Baker) and Willie Baxter (Richard Keene). Willie steals his father's dress suit to impress his young lady. Dorothy Donnelly's book was competent but not good enough to overcome William Kernell's flaccid score.

Tin Pan Alley's popular Walter Donaldson collaborated with Joseph Meyer on the tunes for **Sweetheart Time** (1-19-26, Imperial), but failed to come up with anything to equal the songs he was writing outside the theatre. A run-of-the-mill Harry B. Smith libretto (based on William Collier's *Never Say Die*) may have stifled his inspiration. It was not a little like *Oh! Oh! Oh! Nurse*. Violet Stevenson (Mary Milburn), desperate for money, is about to marry Lord Raybrook (Fred Leslie) for his. Dion Woodbury (Eddie Buzzell) appears and, falling in love with Violet, suggests she marry him instead. He tells her he is rich and dying. He promises that he will leave immediately after the wedding, and within a year she will be advised she has become a wealthy widow. She accepts. But a year later Dion returns in the pink. Violet's realization that she loves him allows for a conveniently happy ending. Smith's humor had not changed much over the years. He had one character command, "Bring me a book on livers by Bacon!" Collier staged the piece, including such stunts as a cocktail song in which the cast rattled cocktail shakers in time with the music. The hit of the evening was an interpolation by Jay Gorney, "A Girl In Your Arms." Far from top drawer, the show nevertheless thrived on a booming Broadway for 143 performances.

But even the good times could not save **The Matinee Girl** (2-1-26, Forrest) from a three-week debacle. Its plot reminded some of *The Firefly* (12-2-12). "Bubbles" Peters (Olga Steck) disguises herself as a cabin boy on the yacht of matinee idol, Jack Sterling (James Hamilton). They sail for Cuba. When they disembark, she reveals her masquerade. Before long Jack is won over. The score by Frank Grey was no better than the one he had written for *Sue Dear* (7-10-22). Nor was the show's humor better than that of *Sweetheart Time,* one character promising, "When we cross the Gulf Stream, I'll wear my golf suit."

Bunk of 1926 (2-16-26, Heckscher) was another of the many one-shot revues that began to appear in the wake of the dying annuals. Housed first far uptown, it moved to the centrally located Broadhurst late in April. Gene Lockhart, who later became a much-loved movie actor, wrote most of it and was its principal entertainer. A caustic critic in the *Telegram* recalled that Lockhart had recently performed the part of a feeble-minded boy in *Sun-Up* and suggested that Lockhart was still under the role's influence when he created the revue. Typical of the show's skits was a travesty of English drawing-room drama, "Good Old Smill, or Faithful to the End." For all its lack of brilliance, the show was sufficiently frothy and diverting to last fourteen weeks.

In August, Zelda Sears had written and produced a quick flop called *A Lucky Break.* It was withdrawn after 23 performances. But Walter De Leon took the story and with Miss Sears' erstwhile collaborator, Harold Levey, and with Owen Murphy, turned it into a musical. As was so frequently the case, their title had little to do with the plot. **Rainbow Rose** (3-16-26, Forrest) merely combined two voguish titular words. Sears and De Leon told of John Bruce's returning home after twenty years' absence. In the interval Bruce (Jack Squire) has become wealthy. But wanting to separate his real from his fair weather friends he suggests he has lost his fortune. He finds almost everyone is a true friend, especially one young lady, Rose Haven (Shirley Sherman). Undistinguished music joined to a play that hadn't been satisfactory in the first place told against the show. Only the show's excel-

lent dancing received general commendation. *Rainbow Rose* lasted just a little longer than its source.

But practically everyone embraced the next night's arrival, **The Girl Friend** (3-17-26, Vanderbilt). Its creators were the trio responsible for *Dearest Enemy* (9-18-25): Herbert Fields, Lorenz Hart, and Richard Rodgers. After the success of their first work they had little trouble in persuading Lew Fields to be their producer. And the authors knew this time Fields would not resort to interpolations, as he had with *Poor Little Ritz Girl* (7-27-20). The plot was thin and trite, written around the talents of the diminutive dancers, Sammy White and Eva Puck. It recounted how Leonard Silver (White) trains for a bicycle race by hitching his wheel to a churn in the backyard of his family's dairy farm. His coach is his sweetheart, Mollie Farrell (Miss Puck), the daughter of a professional cyclist. After a shady promoter picks Silver for a big race, gamblers attempt to keep him out of it. As if these troubles are not enough, aristocratic Wynn Spencer (Evelyn Cavanaugh) attempts to woo him away from his betrothed. But Leonard wins both the race and Mollie. Whatever the weaknesses in the story line, Fields told it amusingly. Some of the jokes clearly showed their vaudeville origins, but Fields had clearly selected the least outrageous and the most literate to transpose to the legitimate stage. When a guest at the Spencer party learns Leonard has hurt his ankle he inquires with due concern, "Is it broken?":

Leonard: I says to the doctor, I says, "It ain't broken, doctor"
Guest: And what did the doctor say?
Leonard: You mustn't say ain't.

Rodgers' score had two knockouts, the title song and "The Blue Room," both sung by the romantic leads. The Charleston rhythm of the first made it as danceable as it was singable. Hart's seemingly inexhaustible stock of striking word plays is perhaps even more apparent in the too often neglected verse, where, for example, a boy proclaims he wants to keep "steady company" with a girl who'll let him "bump a knee" in the Charleston. But "The Blue Room" has remained the enduring hit which Alec Wilder in his book on American popular song calls "the first wholly distinctive Rodgers song," adding, it "is a strong, uncluttered, direct statement. In it is the first instance of a Rodgers stylistic device which he continues to use throughout his career, that of returning to a series of notes, usually two, while building a design with other notes." It is an endearing love song, enhanced by Hart's seemingly simple rhymes. Several critics placed a third song on a par with the show's two hits. "The Damsel Who Done All The Dirt" was a comic number, given to Miss Puck as a solo. When *The Girl Friend* failed to catch on at first, Rodgers and Hart waived their royalties to keep the work on the boards. Their sacrifice was justified. Word of mouth was favorable, and soon the show was selling out. Broadway supported *The Girl Friend* for nine months. It was beginning to look as if Broadway had found logical successors to the Princess Theatre's triumvirate.

April brought revivals of *H.M.S. Pinafore* and *Iolanthe*. *Pinafore* lured Fay Templeton out of retirement to play Buttercup. John Hazzard impersonated Sir Joseph Porter, while the fine tenor, Tom Burke, was Ralph. The resurgence of interest in Gilbert and Sullivan prompted Winthrop Ames to begin a policy of annual revivals with his mounting of *Iolanthe*. *Iolanthe*'s 66 performances were ten more than *Pinafore* achieved. Nonetheless Ames felt encouraged and determined to stick to his announced plans.

Another one-shot revue, **Bad Habits of 1926** (4-30-26, Greenwich Village), tried to bury the Charleston prematurely and also to ridicule operetta into oblivion in "The Student Robin Hood of Pilsen." *The 49ers* (11-7-22) had introduced a spoof of operettas, and, ten nights after *Bad Habits* opened, *The Garrick Gaieties* would offer another. Unfortunately just about every attempt at humor in *Bad Habits* misfired. The show received some of the worst notices of the year. It was *Bad Habits* itself which hurried on to oblivion after one of the shortest runs of the season, 19 performances.

Three musicals arrived in May. **Kitty's Kisses** (5-6-26, Playhouse) told a complicated story of Kitty Brown's losing a handbag with all her money in it. Kitty (Dorothey Dilley) is refused a room at the Hotel Wendel, only to be rushed upstairs moments later when she is mistaken for a woman who has rented the bridal suite. The next morning she learns she has shared the suite with a man, Mr. Dennison (Mark Smith), whose wife is looking for an excuse to divorce him. The wife's lawyer appears. He turns out to be a young man she met on the train the previous morning. His name is Robert Mason (John Boles); he has found Kitty's handbag and has fallen in love with her. The show was in competent hands. Philip Bartholomae and Otto Harbach did the book, Gus Kahn the lyrics, and Con Conrad the music. If it wasn't one of the season's more inspired evenings, it was still lighthearted fun. Brooks Atkinson, just then beginning his distinguished career as the *Times*' drama critic,

put his finger on the source of this gaiety, confirming how necessary dancing was to the era's musicals. Atkinson noted "the chief distinction of *Kitty's Kisses* is the rough-and-tumble of dancing men and women, individually and in chorus, at a pace that exhilarates while it kills. As soon as the first curtain goes up the chorus begins dancing ecstatically between the railroad tracks, and from then on it glides, pops, swoops, careens, and Charlestons through hotel lobbies, bedrooms, and gardens indiscriminately." Even the leading lady, Atkinson observed, "dances on the tips of her toes upon the slightest occasion."

May 10 brought the first of five revues that wound up the theatrical year, the **Garrick Gaieties of 1926.** The show had many of the same principals of the first editions; it also had much of the same format. It spoofed the current Guild offerings (*Arms and the Man*, *Androcles and the Lion*) and made fun of the other arts. Ballet as done by the great Nijinsky was given rough treatment in "L'Après midi d'un Papillon." The sporting world was cut down to size in a transvestite tennis match (Romney Brent becoming Helen Wills; Edith Meiser, Bill Tilden). Even the musical theatre of the day was parodied in "Rose of Arizona," which David Ewen later labeled "the grandmother of *Little Mary Sunshine*." Operettas had come under attack earlier; ten days before *Bad Habits* had parodied them. Rodgers and Hart's spoof seemed directed not at the older comic opera or Viennese schools so much as at *Rose-Marie* and its antecedent, *Naughty Marietta*. Its heroine Gloria Van Dyke loves Capt. Allan Sterling, chief of police of Rose Raisa, Arizona, but her father wants her to wed Gerald Slades. The bandit, Caramba, kidnaps Gloria, but Allan rescues her just as her father is about to pay the ransom. Like *Little Mary Sunshine* years later, "Rose of Arizona" was not especially scrupulous in sticking to a single target. It went to a number of places in search of mirth. The old *Sally* tradition was gently mocked in "It May Rain," assuring audiences that it would probably rain "when the sun stops shining" and "when the sky is gray." Even opera, or at least one of the great prima donnas of the day, was appropriated to give the setting its outlandish name. But much of the spoof was unerringly on its mark. Still, the fun was harmless, and operetta emerged unscathed. Rodgers and Hart must have had a good laugh when in the very next season *Rio Rita* (2-2-27) delighted Broadway. The show's authors, Harry Tierney and Joseph McCarthy, rather than be put off by the ridicule of its genre, seem to have complacently borrowed from the spoof. In "Back

To Nature" Rodgers and Hart extolled the "Hootin', scootin' land of Arizona"; *Rio Rita* had its Texas Rangers salute "rootin' pals, hootin' pals, scootin' pals, shootin' pals." Happily Rodgers and Hart had a worthy successor to "Manhattan" in "Mountain Greenery," with its aggressive but irresistible repetition of its first three notes. Sterling Holloway again had the honor of introducing a hit—this time with Bobbie Perkins, since June Cochrane had a small role in *The Girl Friend*. Though this *Gaieties* had nearly a half-year run, the budding series was also discontinued, with only one later attempt to revive it.

Great Temptations, another Shubert revue, came into the Winter Garden on May 18. The cast was filled with rising and falling stars: Hazel Dawn, Miller and Lyles, J. C. Flippen, and Jack Benny. As usual Harold Atteridge was responsible for whatever dialogue the performers themselves did not provide. Maurice Rubens did the music. He was a hack who would provide a number of Broadway scores in the last half of the twenties without ever offering a single outstanding tune. One interpolation from *Great Temptations*, however, has remained popular for over fifty years: Jose Padilla's "Valencia." Miss Dawn introduced the song. She also participated in a burlesque of *The Shanghai Gesture*. She was assisted by Billy Van, who announced, "I like Chinese brothels because Chinese broth is so good." Miller and Lyles proved to their own satisfaction that thirteen is one-seventh of twenty-eight. Jack Benny boasted he had driven from Atlantic City to New York in four hours and five subpoenas. The Foster Girls toe-danced, and the chorus compared 1925 flappers to the ladies in Koster and Bial's 1896 line.

More Maurice Rubens music was heard in a second Shubert revue, **The Merry World** (6-8-26, Imperial). J. Fred Coots and a number of lesser known figures also contributed. The show was an importation from London, dismissed by one critic as "something between Charlot and Messrs. Ringling."

The second **Scandals** of the season (6-14-26, Apollo) was vastly superior to the edition that George White had presented late the previous June. In fact, it was at one and the same time the most successful and the best of the entire series. Its run of 424 performances almost doubled the series' second longest stay. A healthy economy accounted for part of its longevity, but most of the evening's success must be attributed to its merits. The cast was the finest White had ever assembled. Ann Pennington led the dancers, Eugene and Willie Howard

headed the clowns, and Harry Richman and Frances Williams were in charge of the songs. Tom Patricola was back. The McCarthy Sisters also returned, and were joined by the Fairbanks Twins at the forefront of the eye-filling chorus line. The chic Erté conceived the costumes. But the sensation of the evening was DeSylva, Brown, and Henderson's score, undoubtedly the finest score to come out of any of the great annuals. The trio more than justified White's faith in them and silenced skeptics who could not forget their lackluster efforts in the preceding edition.

George Gard DeSylva (better known as **"Buddy"** or **B.G. DeSylva)** was born in New York City on January 27, 1895. His father had been a vaudevillian but gave up the theatre to raise a family. An early attempt by the DeSylvas to make a child performer of George was thwarted by his grandfather. While a student at the University of Southern California, Buddy helped with college shows, earned extra money by playing ukulele in a Hawaiian band, and, most significantly, began writing lyrics. His lyrics came to the attention of Al Jolson, who had them set to music and used some of them in *Sinbad* (2-14-18). In short order DeSylva was writing words for Gershwin, Herbert, and Kern. His rhymes were used in *La, La, Lucille* (5-26-19), *Sally* (12-21-20), *Bombo* (10-6-21), and *Orange Blossoms* (9-19-22), as well as in several revues.

. . .

Louis Brownstein was born in Odessa, Russia, on December 10, 1893. His family settled first in New Haven, but soon moved to New York. After quitting high school he found work with Albert Von Tilzer. Two of his earliest hits were "I May Be Gone For A Long, Long Time" (*Hitchy-Koo of 1917*) and "Oh, By Jingo" (*Linger Longer Letty*). In 1922 he wrote words to Henderson's music for "Georgette" (*Greenwich Village Follies*).

. . .

Ray Henderson—né Raymond Brost—was the composer of the group. He was born on December 1, 1896, in Buffalo where his mother, herself an excellent pianist, supervised his early musical training. He later enrolled in the Chicago Conservatory of Music. His ambitions to be a serious musician soon succumbed to the enticements of jazz. He played the piano briefly in vaudeville and then became a song plugger for Leo Feist. Before long he transferred his allegiances to Shapiro-Bernstein, where Louis Bernstein introduced him to Brown.

. . .

The show's songs were as diverse as they were

memorable. They perfectly exemplified the range of the period's popular writing. There was an ingratiating love song "The Girl Is You And The Boy Is Me" (sung by Harry Richman and Frances Williams) and a rousingly joyous "Lucky Day" (sung by Richman and the chorus). The team also created the most popular of all variations on the Charleston with their "Black Bottom"—danced wildly by Miss Pennington. But the most durable hit was "The Birth Of The Blues," rich with the most advanced popular harmonies. By later standards, the song was overmounted in the show. It would seem to need little except a piano, a good singer, and a spotlight. But the twenties and White would tolerate no such austerity. There was the inevitable revue staircase flanked for this number by chorus girls dressed as angels. As Richman sang the song, a battle raged between contemporary blues and the classics. The McCarthy Sisters wore gowns suggesting "The Memphis Blues" and the "St. Louis Blues," while the Fairbanks Twins opposed them in costumes symbolizing Schubert and Schumann songs. In the still fashionable practice of the day, a number of the songs were tied closely to the subjects in the skits. For example, the song "David And Lenore" was part of a skit twitting David Belasco and his reigning star Lenore Ulric. Another skit found Otto Kahn and J.P. Morgan sitting down to examine the financial scene. Irving Berlin's marriage to Ellin Mackay was the subject of "A Western Union." The title reminded audiences that Miss Mackay's father, who vigorously opposed the marriage, headed large telegraph interests.

The next night the **Grand Street Follies** (6-15-26, Neighborhood) wrapped up the season. Like the *Scandals,* it was the second edition in what was technically the same season. The series' most talented principals, Albert Carroll and Dorothy Sands, were on hand again with their impersonations and their satire. Carroll impersonated the famous clown, Toto, and Joseph Santley. Miss Sands starred in the show's take-off of *The Shanghai Gesture,* appearing not as Mother Goddam but as Mother Goshdarn. Modern theatrical design and interpretation were mocked in a new version of *Uncle Tom's Cabin,* offered "in a constructivist setting—an example of sympathetic elastic theatre." As the virtuous characters of the piece died, an Otis elevator took them to heaven, where angels greeted them with handshakes. Not letting go of a good thing, the company also presented *Jack and Jill* as the Theatre Guild, in its symbolic phase, might have done it. Musically the evening offered nothing approaching the brilliance of the new *Scandals* or *Gaieties.* But there were two interesting names among the composing credits. A few of the songs were by Randall Thompson, who shortly went on to headier musical heights. Further melodies bore the signature of Arthur Schwartz.

1926-1927

Forty-eight new musicals came before the footlights in the 1926–27 season. High quality, coupled with the continuing national prosperity, pushed almost half beyond the 100-performance mark. In fact, thirteen ran over 200 or 300 showings, while *The Desert Song* and *Rio Rita* each played nearly 500 times. As expected the summer entries were primarily revues. Six appeared at the beginning of the season; three more opened as the warm weather returned. However, only three revues competed with the book musicals that arrived in the fall and winter. Four of the early revues were in varying degrees successful, though their overall achievements were disappointing.

The first of these should have been the *Ziegfeld Follies of 1926,* but it wasn't. The new revue was created to open a new theatre Florenz Ziegfeld and Joseph Urban helped build in Palm Beach. Though the popularity of the annuals continued to wane and though for one reason or another Ziegfeld announced at intervals he was abandoning the *Follies,* he still hoped to open the new house with another edition of his great series. Legal entanglements, stemming from a dispute with Abe Erlanger, dealt him a bitter blow. Erlanger had bank-rolled the first Follies and retained an important piece of the revue. Ziegfeld found himself enjoined from using the name he had made famous. As a result, the new show was premiered with the obviously temporary but not inappropriate title *Ziegfeld's Palm Beach Girl.* The name didn't last. On the way to New York it became **Ziegfeld's American Revue** (6-24-26, Globe). Ziegfeld mounted it with his customary flare. A large ball made up of glittering mirrors opened to reveal a lavishly befeathered dancer. More feathers were in evidence later when a line of chorus girls, supposedly just out of the ocean, entered in feathered headpieces that reached the floor and were meant to suggest foam. Though a number of the chorus girls, such as Paulette Goddard, went on to fame, it was not a truly first-rate cast. Charles King was no longer youthful, James Barton, though fine, was no match for a Fields or a Williams. Still, Barton and Ray Dooley had two riotously funny skits. In a railroad car that stretched across the stage Barton appeared as a battered conductor desperately trying to wheedle a ticket from Miss Dooley in her role of an "incorrigibly cute" brat. Barton chased Miss Dooley over seats, passengers, and luggage from one side of the stage to the other. Later Barton played a stern, slave-driving Latin lover, slashing a whip as he sang, while Miss Dooley meekly and worshipfully attempted a fandango. Among the female principals Claire Luce and Peggy Fears were the beauties. For music Ziegfeld called on both Rudolf Friml and James F. Hanley. It was Hanley who came up with a winner. "No Foolin' " quickly became so popular Ziegfeld made the song title the show title. It was a jaunty theme perfectly in tune with the time. Buck's closing line was a cute play on the expression's other meaning, "after we're wed—No Foolin'." Unfortunately this was Buck's last association with Ziegfeld. The show's run was a discouraging 108 performances. Even more disheartening to Ziegfeld must have been the pasted-together affair touring backwaters as the *Ziegfeld Follies*. A bottom-rung producer named George Wintz had managed to secure the rights to the name, and, though he also managed to secure the services of Ruth St. Denis and Ted Shawn, leading modern dance exponents, he surrounded them by an evening "closer to Minsky's" than to Ziegfeld. Ziegfeld persisted in the courts, and by the time his show reached Chicago he was able to rechristen the evening once more and at last offer it as the *Ziegfeld Follies of 1926*.

An all-black revue, **My Magnolia** (7-8-26, Mansfield), managed to get closer to the heart of Times Square than many Negro shows of the era. But even the convenience of the Mansfield could not help it. It opened on a Thursday night and closed the following Saturday. The evening's bright spot was an ensemble that "performed Charlestons, taps, and other convolutions with frenzied expertness." For the luckless C. Luckyeth Roberts it was apparently the last straw. The score was his third in three years to be given short shrift. He disappeared from the Broadway scene.

Another minor figure, Leon De Costa, had better, if no more deserved, luck with his score for **The Blonde Sinner** (7-14-26, Cort). He received royalties on his run-of-the-mill score for the twenty-two weeks it played New York, plus its time on tour. The story was fitting for its July opening. The Hemmingworths (Ralph Bunker and Enid Markey) rent a Long Island summer home that is well beyond

their means. To balance their budget they take in boarders. But before long Mrs. Hemmingworth is accused of being a co-respondent in a divorce. The show was really a straight play with the boarders performing "three of four specialties in each act." So intimate was the mounting that only four girls —all blondes—comprised the chorus that performed the requisite Charlestons. A small part of the musical's popularity may have derived from its being the only book musical in a rash of revues. Four more revues appeared in short order.

Bare Facts of 1926 (7-16-26, Triangle) opened at midnight two evenings later, its title hinting at the tenor of much of its material. It offered one of the decade's many jungle numbers, done this time in silhouette while a lady recited Vachel Lindsay's "The Congo." For comedy the show kidded reigning hits of the day such as *Lulu Belle* and *The Great God Brown*. In another skit Chopin, Liszt, and Mendelssohn complained Tin Pan Alley was stealing all their best melodies. The revue provided nothing of merit, but it did provide the sort of entertainment that segments of the theatregoing public would pay for. They paid for 107 performances.

A more interesting evening premiered at the tiny Belmont Theatre ten nights later, July 26. Called **Americana,** it touched lightly on then current foibles and fashions in its skits and in songs such as "Riverside Bus," "Kosher Kleagle," and "That Lost Barber Shop Chord." This last was a pleasant if not top-drawer number by the Gershwins that several critics nevertheless singled out as a high point of the evening. Ira also put some of his stylish verbal shorthand to a tune by Phil Charig. The result was "Sunny Disposish." Actually, while almost all of the show was intelligently assembled, nothing was outstanding or durable. No small part of *Americana*'s success—and it ran 224 performances—was a result of the effectiveness of some bright young talent in their truly intimate surroundings. Charles Butterworth went on to become a well-known screen and radio figure, especially as a shy, defenseless gentleman. Butterworth had the best moment of the evening, delivering a halting, painful after-dinner speech to a group of Rotarians. His listeners, seated in elegant, high-backed chairs on both sides of him, failed to respond to anything he said. They couldn't. They were all dummies. Helen Morgan sang while sitting on the top of an upright piano. It is said that Jerome Kern recalled her plaintive rendition of "Nobody Wants Me" (Morrie Ryskind/Henry Souvaine) when he was casting about for a Julie for *Show Boat*. And Mayor Jimmy Walker's inamorata, Betty Compton, shortly made the front pages of the "Tabloid Papers" the show sang about. Two more editions of *Americana* followed in later years.

A pair of minor songsmiths, Gitz Rice and Werner Janssen, did most of the music for **Nic Nax of 1926** (8-2-26, Cort). Rice was also one of the performers, as was the sketch writer, Roger Gray. Songs saluted the obviously growing Negro influence in both popular music and dance with "Everything Is High Yellow Now," but none of the contributions was striking or memorable. The show was condemned as "amateurish." It was also obviously trouble-plagued. Its opening had to be delayed several times. On the first night nearly a third of the numbers mentioned on the program were not included. Lights failed; scenery could not be gotten in place. Only the fancy footwork of Nat Nazzaro was acclaimed. However, the *Times'* notice did suggest that the increasing number of shows was taxing Broadway's resources when it observed, "Half of the chorus is, by count, fairly good looking. This is a high average." Rice faded from the scene, and Janssen, the son of a famous New York restaurateur, successfully set his sights higher in the musical field. He wrote one more score three years later, then confined himself to serious composing and conducting.

With the great annuals dying, Earl Carroll momentarily found himself with less serious revue competition than he had had before. Given so open a market, he brazenly charged $100 a ticket for opening-night orchestra seats. In return he was prodigal with his entertainment. The show was only three-quarters over by eleven o'clock. Carroll even festooned his auditorium with Spanish decorations to give the suggestion of an Iberian fiesta. Although he enlisted some fresh song-writing talent, nothing distinguished emerged from his latest **Vanities** (8-24-26, Carroll). His comic line-up included Moran and Mack, Smith and Dale, and Julius Tannen. Moran and Mack delighted theatregoers with an argument over a dog's paternity and with an attempt to break out of jail. Smith and Dale played two firemen who answer calls only when the whim strikes them—shades of *The Never Homes* (10-5-11). Spectacles included a sumptuous Russian scene, a number using mosaic glass and sparkling mirrors, and a set composed largely of ladders. But Carroll's scantily clad girls remained the major lure. With their help this edition compiled over 300 performances.

The arrival of book musicals began in earnest after Labor Day. Raymond Peck and Percy Wenrich, who had not been wildly successful with *The Right Girl* (3-15-21), nonetheless tried again with **Castles in the Air** (9-6-26, Selwyn). Theatrical acclaim continued to elude Wenrich, one of Tin Pan Alley's most prolific and famous composers. Peck's book was neither novel nor exceptional. His humor ran to one-liners such as "Perhaps there's a Methodist in my madness" and to repartee on the order of:

—Are you traveling incognito?
—No, in a Ford.

The musical was a Chicago production that had been running for nearly a year in that city when the company was split, with some staying with the original troupe and others assisting in the road unit. For New York, Vivienne Segal, J. Harold Murray, and Bernard Granville were added to the cast. In *Castles in the Air* two college graduates, Monty Blair (Granville) and John Brown (Murray), arrive at Evelyn's 21 Club, an exclusive Westchester resort they have mistaken for an inn. They quickly catch on, and Monty introduces John as a Latvian prince. Evelyn (Miss Segal) is something of a social climber, so her uncle Philip decides to teach her a lesson by taking her and her friends to Latvia, intending to expose John. The plan backfires when it is learned that John is indeed a prince. Chicago hits rarely repeated their Chicago runs on Broadway. *Castles in the Air* was no exception. Nonetheless, its five-month stay put the show squarely in the hit column.

A summer-long tryout in Philadelphia had allowed "Cross Your Heart," the hit of **Queen High** (9-8-26, Ambassador), to sweep New York far in advance of the show's arrival. But Broadway welcomed the story, too, especially with Charles Ruggles' clowning. T. Boggs Johns (Ruggles) and George Nettleton (Frank McIntyre), partners in the Eureka Novelty Co., have fallen out. They decide a poker game will determine who runs the business. The loser, moreover, must serve as the winner's butler. Johns loses. His gaucheries as a servant worsen the rifts between the old friends, but their children, Richard Johns (Clarence Nordstrom) and Polly Nettleton (Mary Lawlor), fall in love and help bring about a reconciliation. Laurence Schwab, the producer, collaborated with Buddy DeSylva on the book, while DeSylva also did the lyrics for Lewis Gensler's score. Though "Cross Your Heart"—sung by Polly and Richard —was far and away the most popular tune, the whole score had an infectious, rippling gaiety. It included a salute to Anita Loos' popular book *Gentlemen Prefer Blondes* (a stage version opened twenty nights after *Queen High*) as well as unnecessary interpolations by James Hanley. *Queen High* ran just short of 400 performances. It was the first in a series of musicals from this season that are remembered today largely for one outstanding song in each.

The old warrior, Harry B. Smith, made his first appearance on the season's credits as adapter of **Naughty Riquette** (9-13-26, Cosmopolitan), which the Shuberts imported and mounted for the aging Mitzi. Smith's story of a telephone operator whose marriage of convenience develops into a love-match elicited neither loud applause nor unhappy head-shaking. It ran eleven weeks.

But five nights later Smith and the Shuberts again combined forces; this time with stunning success. **Countess Maritza** (9-18-26, Shubert) remains Emmerich Kalman's masterpiece, an unsurpassed example of the poignant Hungarian side of Austro-Hungarian operetta. For this story of an aristocratic lady reluctant to love her handsome caretaker lest he prove a fortune hunter, Kalman composed sweeping waltzes, whirling czardas, and his most beloved song, "Play Gypsies—Dance Gypsies," sung by Walter Woolf in the Broadway production. Once again the Shuberts tampered with their material. Al Goodman and Sigmund Romberg were called in to interpolate. But the interpolations were overwhelmed by the rich, high colorings of Kalman's melodies. Even the lackluster dialogue and lyrics Smith offered could not hurt. Happily, the Shuberts gave the work a fine cast headed by Woolf, Yvonne D'Arle, Odette Myrtil, Carl Randall, and George Hassell. *Countess Maritza* ran out the season.

The Ramblers (9-20-26, Lyric), too, ran out the season. A musical romp by Harry Ruby and Bert Kalmar (with Guy Bolton assisting them on the libretto), it starred the uproarious Bobby Clark and Paul McCullough as a roving spiritualist medium, Professor Cunningham, and his patsy, Sparrow. They stumble on a unit filming a movie in Tia Juana for the Fanny Furst Film Company and help rescue its heroine, Ruth Chester (Marie Saxon), when she is kidnapped by the villainous Black Pedro (William E. Browning). For McCullough and Clark (with his painted-on glasses and his cocky cigar) it was the first time they saw their names above the title. But their antics proved they deserved their stardom. Somewhat surprisingly, the funniest scene of the evening fell not to Clark but to McCullough. When he is persuaded to play the heavy in Fanny's movie, his make-up turns him into Black Pedro's double. Black Pedro appears on the set, and a chase

ensues, filled with Keystone Cops confusion. Though the entire score of *The Ramblers* was bouncy and melodic, it is remembered, like *Queen High*'s, for one song, "All Alone Monday," sung by the romantic leads, Miss Saxon and Jack Whiting.

The same night, September 20, **Honeymoon Lane** raised its curtain down Broadway at the Knickerbocker. It was the third musical in a row to play through the season and, like *The Ramblers* and *Queen High*, it too, left one noteworthy tune behind. Eddie Dowling and James F. Hanley's book, lyrics, and music suggested once again George M. Cohan's slant on the poor-Irish-secretary-makes-good motif was a pathblazer. Dowling, of course, had employed a similar theme in *Sally, Irene and Mary*. Tim Murphy (Dowling) buys a cottage on romantically named Honeymoon Lane in unromantic Canningville, Pa. Tim hopes he will soon place his bride-to-be, Mary Brown (Pauline Mason), in the cottage's kitchen. Tim and Mary both work at the W.H. Kleinze Pickle Factory, and young Ted Kleinze (Al Sexton) induces Mary to try her luck on Broadway. Tim pursues her to New York, where it seems he will have a hard time competing with the big town's enticements. Their experience turns out to be a bad dream, and Tim takes Mary's hand as they walk down the lane. There was nothing original or particularly brilliant about Dowling and Hanley's material. Dowling always tended to be a bit heavy-handed and obvious. Still, a large public, substantially Irish, remained receptive to this pleasant escapism. Furthermore, Dowling and Hanley contrived another popular "love nest" song with "The Little White House (At The End Of Honeymoon Lane)" that Dowling sang in the show. A second song, "Half A Moon (Is Better Than No Moon)" had a passing vogue. When the homey, vine-covered exterior of Mary's house and the relatively somber colors of the pickle factory gave way to the theatre scenes that comprised the second act, the show erupted in a kaleidoscope of colors. But as the colors broke out, the book broke down. Most 1920s book musicals stopped their action now and then for an irrelevant specialty. But when a story moved characters into a theatre, no 1920s producer could resist a spate of vaudeville turns. In *Honeymoon Lane* these specialties included the "exquisite" dancing of Florence O'Denishawn (who played herself) and the Broadway debut of a "coon-shouting 'blues' singer," Kate Smith (who played Tiny Little—a name that did anything but describe the expansive Miss Smith).

September's last musical broke the string of successes. Ironically called **Happy Go Lucky** (9-30-

26, Liberty), it told how the family and friends of curmudgeony Chester Chapin (Taylor Holmes) attempt to change him with kindness. They do, until he catches on to their scheme. He almost reverts to his old ways, but he finally admits being agreeable is nicer. Most of the score was by Lucien Denni, his sole Broadway effort. But there were several interpolations by the ubiquitous Hanley. Playgoers who saw the show during its 52 performances may have pondered the sad fickleness of theatrical fame. Lina Abarbanell, who years earlier had captured New York's heart in *Madame Sherry* (8-30-10), played what was a secondary role, although she did sing three songs.

Another failure followed. But **Deep River** (10-4-26, Imperial) was a far more important work, a "native opera" lost in a Broadway jungle of slapstick clowns, high-kicking choruses, and snappy jazz tunes. Arthur Hopkins, one of New York's most daring producers, yet a name rarely associated with the musical theatre, presented the work. The book and lyrics were by Laurence Stallings, a generally serious playwright best remembered as co-author of *What Price Glory?* Stallings placed his story in 1835 New Orleans, days before Mr. Hercule's Quadroon Ball. At the ball the elite Creole men of the area pick the most attractive dancers and set them up as mistresses. An aged quadroon, Octavie (Rose McClendon), who is sort of duenna to the younger girls, warns them, "Unless you catch your true love at your first quadroon ball; you will never know true love at all." Brusard (Luis Aberni), one of the leading Creoles, has his eye on Mugette (Lottice Howell), an especially beautiful quadroon. He is anxious to find a new girl, since just the previous night he threw his unfaithful mistress out, after administering a public whipping to her lover. Brusard is a dangerous man, responsible for more than mere whippings. As one character notes, "dat charm of his . . . it has killed three men." Two visiting Kentuckians, Colonel Streatfeld (Frederick Burton) and his brother Hazard (Roberto Ardelli), also are attracted to Mugette. When the colonel insults Brusard, a duel ensues. The colonel is killed. Mugette runs off to a voodoo séance in the Place Congo, praying to her dark spirits for Hazard's love. But Hazard, too, finds himself obliged to fight a duel with Brusard; this time Brusard is fatally wounded. Hazard cannot remain in New Orleans and, unable to take Mugette home with him, leaves the stunned girl in Octavie's hands. Mugette must dance at the ball knowing she will never find a satisfactory suitor.

Deep River had no compromising humorous in-

tervals. The brooding story moved inexorably to its tragic end. The second act, at the voodoo ceremony, had virtually no dialogue; the building tensions of the rites, performed to a choral background, propelled the story. Some of the dialogue in the surrounding acts contained pompous passages, but these merely reflected the more formal, latinate speech of 19th-century Louisiana. Southern settings, Negro life, and the relations between the black and white worlds have provided all or part of the plot of many of the earliest innovative musicals: *When Johnny Comes Marching Home* (12-16-02), this work, *Show Boat* (12-27-27) in the next season, and eventually *Porgy and Bess* (10-10-35). The score represented Franke Harling's sole Broadway effort. Harling was a fascinating minor figure, striving for fame in both the popular and more serious worlds of music. The year before *Deep River* was produced, the Chicago Opera had staged his full-length version of Keats' "The Eve of St. Agnes" entitled *A Light from St. Agnes*. Several years later, the man-in-the-street might well have been whistling Harling's melody for "Beyond The Blue Horizon." For *Deep River* Harling persuaded Hopkins to hire a thirty-piece orchestra—oversized by Broadway standards of the day. He also prevailed on the producer to employ Jules Bledsoe, the black who walked away with the evening's singing honors. Bledsoe had only a minor role, and his songs served more to create atmosphere than to advance the story. Harling's music was beautiful and, like the book, reasonably uncompromising. But the show was ahead of its time. Even *Show Boat*, a year later, bowed to commercial imperatives. *Deep River* ran only four weeks. Burns Mantle, decrying the loss of such "a lovely thing," ruefully observed "the opera-going public would not come down to it, nor could the theatre public rise to it."

It is worthwhile quoting Mantle's summary of the plot of the season's next musical, **Criss Cross** (10-12-26, Globe). "Christopher Cross, being a resourceful aviator, manages to help Captain Carleton save Dolly Day from the designing schemes of Benani, who would rob her of her birthright and a considerable fortune." Mantle makes it sound like the outline of a more or less routine musical comedy. He neglects to mention that the evening began in the "Town Hollow in Fable-land" and proceeded to the south of France, Algiers, a bazaar, "The Jar of Ali Baba," a palace garden, and ended in "The Diamond Palace." The first and last setting in particular would tell musical comedy fans of the era that this was not quite another routine affair, but a trip to the special world of Fred Stone. Stone, of course, was Cross; his daughter, Dorothy, followed her auspicious debut in *Stepping Stones* (11-6-23) by playing Dolly Day. Though it was a quarter of a century since the acrobatic Stone first somersaulted onto the Broadway stage, the intervening years had apparently done little to diminish his energies. He did a tumbling act, burlesqued a harem dance, performed with a two-man stage camel, and for a finale arrived on a flying trapeze to rescue Dolly. When he and his cast were not having fun with Otto Harbach and Anne Caldwell's dialogue, they were delighting their patrons with Jerome Kern's latest tunes. The songs were not on a par with Kern's music to *Sally* or *Sunny,* but they were a discernible improvement over *The City Chap.* The best was probably "You Will—Won't You?" Stone's fantasy world allowed James Reynolds to splash his sets with an unaccustomed gaudiness. The show was not the top hit of the year, as old Stone vehicles often had been in the past, but it ran profitably for six months, then toured.

A Shubert-imported operetta, **Katja** (10-18-26, 44th St.), began a four-month run telling one more tale of a princess who stoops to conquer her conqueror. The inevitable Shubert interpolations included songs by a name new to Manhattan, Vernon Duke.

Rudolf Friml suffered his second disappointment of the still young season when he and his associates from *Rose-Marie* (9-2-24), Otto Harbach and Oscar Hammerstein II, offered **The Wild Rose** (10-20-26, Martin Beck). It tallied a meager 61 showings. The story line was relatively uncluttered. American Monty Travers (Joseph Santley) breaks the bank at Monte Carlo, so he and his beloved Princess Elise of Borovina (Desiree Ellinger) can outwit the capitalistic oil promoters and bolshevist malcontents who beset Elise's father. One song, "A Little Kingdom Of Our Own," received some play, but nothing entered the Friml canon of standards. The show seemed to be one of those ill-starred affairs plagued with troubles from beginning to end. Lew Fields was to have been its principal comedian, but just before opening night he took ill and William Collier was rushed in at the last minute. Arthur Hammerstein hired Joseph Urban to do the sets, but Urban's efforts for this production displeased his usually overwhelmed admirers. Most critics dismissed the sets with faint praise, while the *World* stated bluntly that only the opening of the second act (a palace scene) revealed Urban's customary taste and imagination.

Oh, Kay (11-8-26, Imperial) joined the wordsmiths of the Princess Theatre shows, Guy Bolton

and P. G. Wodehouse, to the steely jazz idiom of the Gershwin brothers. Puzzlingly, when Ira took sick during the writing of the show, Howard Dietz, not Wodehouse, lent a helping hand. According to Dietz, this was done at George's insistence, so that Ira would be able to receive as much credit as possible. The new combination clicked beautifully. The incomparable Victor Moore contributed his unique, tough wistfulness. In the hands of Broadway's newest star, Gertrude Lawrence, the material took on an added glow.

. . .

Gertrude Lawrence (née Gertrud Klasen) was born in London on July 4, 1898. Convent-educated, she moved out into the world as a child dancer in a 1908 Christmas pantomime. To advance her career she studied acting and elocution with Italia Conti and dancing with Mme. Espinosa. At Mme. Espinosa's she began a lifelong friendship with another young pupil, Noel Coward. Miss Lawrence first came to America with the original *Charlot's Revue.* Like her co-performer in that entertainment, Bea Lillie, Miss Lawrence's pre-Broadway appearances were in London revues such as *Cheep, Tabs, Buzz-Buzz, A to Z,* and *Rats.* So seductive were her fragile elegance and beauty that most composers and audiences overlooked a slight off-tone in her singing.

. . .

The story had a good time with Prohibition and bootlegging. An impoverished Duke (Gerald Oliver Smith) has turned to rum-running to keep in pocket money. With the help of his sister, Kay (Miss Lawrence), and a sometime butler, "Shorty" McGee (Moore), he caches his stock on the Long Island estate of a young playboy, Jimmy Winter (Oscar Shaw). This is normally no problem, for Winter is frequently away. But when Winter returns unexpectedly, their scheme is jeopardized. Fortunately, the susceptible Winter falls in love with Kay, a girl he had once rescued from drowning. He helps them guy the revenue boys and renounces all his previous marital commitments— and they were legion—to marry Kay. The dialogue was charming, typified by a much quoted line, "Don't criticize a bootlegger's English if his Scotch is all right." But the show's greatest joy was the superb hit-filled Gershwin score. At least four Gershwin standards were first sung in *Oh, Kay,* "Maybe," "Do-Do-Do" (both sung by Miss Lawrence and Shaw), "Clap Yo' Hands (a revival-type number sung by the cast), and "Someone To Watch Over Me." The staging of this last song was memorable. Kay is pretending to be a maid. She has put on an apron and cap. Left alone on stage, she huddles in the corner of a sofa and croons her plaint to a doll. (The doll had been purchased by George Gershwin for Miss Lawrence during the Philadelphia tryout.) Since the rest of the tunes were almost as good, departing playgoers had a wide choice of melodies to whistle. *Oh, Kay* had an eight-month run.

The next night the Shuberts delivered "the new 1926 edition" of **Gay Paree** (11-9-26, Winter Garden), threatening to initiate a new annual. A number of the original cast were back, as were some of the old songs and sketches. But there was substantial fresh material as well. In "The Gold Plaque" Helen Wehrle posed covered with burnished gold. Chic Sale portrayed an announcer at a church social and, on an unaccustomed serious note, read "Lincolniana." Muckraking Ida Tarbell was herself raked over. Though the show again proved popular, registering 175 performances, the Shuberts quietly let the series die with this second version.

Harry Archer and Harlan Thompson made one last attempt to repeat the success of their *Little Jessie James.* (8-15-23). But Archer's score for **Twinkle Twinkle** (11-16-26, Liberty) was so weak Bert Kalmar and Harry Ruby were called in for additional numbers. Harlan Thompson's libretto watched Hollywood's Alice James (Ona Munson) give up her lucrative movie career to settle as an anonymous waitress in Pleasantville, Kansas. She falls in love with Richard Grey (Alan Edwards). A comic detective, "Peachy" Robinson (Joe E. Brown), appears and, between laughs, almost scuttles Alice's matrimonial plans by revealing who she is. The show was excellently mounted with ultra-realistic sets, notably the first scene, which showed a private railroad car. A garden set in the second act sported a real tree. Still, if one reason for the show's twenty-one week run can be singled out, it would probably be Brown's cutting-up. The *World,* for example, professed to be awed by "Joe E. Brown doing incredible things with a mouth like a subway kiosk." His humor was brash. Asked if some oysters are fresh, he retorted, "They're almost impertinent!"

Sacha Guitry and Reynaldo Hahn's comedy with music, **Mozart,** received two New York mountings during the season. The first, in English, starred Irene Bordoni and appeared at the Music Box on November 22; the second, with Guitry and Yvonne Printemps, was done in French at the 46th Street Theatre for five weeks beginning December 27.

From 1921 to 1926 a Berber chieftain named Abd-el-Krim amazed the world with his battles against the Spanish and French in the Riff revolt. Only when the French succeeded in bribing some of his tribes and he was confronted with the prospect of Moroccans slaying Moroccans, did he surrender. He was sent into exile. Out of this front page news came one of the most romantic and beloved of all operettas, **The Desert Song** (11-30-26, Casino). Its coproducer, Frank Mandel, collaborated with Otto Harbach and Oscar Hammerstein on the book, and Sigmund Romberg supplied the ravishing score. For reasons that can only be guessed at, they made their hero a Frenchman, who, costumed in flaming red, with a red mask hiding his face, leads the Moroccan Riffs against his fellow French. His dress has given him his name, The Red Shadow (Robert Halliday). He travels with impunity between the two camps. At the French garrison he is Pierre Birabeau, the dim-witted son of the commanding general. Pierre loves Margot Bonvalet (Vivienne Segal) and in his swashbuckling disguise brazenly abducts her to the Riff encampment. But a treacherous maiden betrays the Red Shadow's hiding place. General Birabeau (Edmund Elton) arrives, challenging the Riff leader to a duel. Rather than fight his own father, the disguised Pierre lays down his sword. The chagrined Riffs strip him of leadership and he walks off into the desert. The French pursue him, but find only Pierre, and assume he has slain the outlaw. News of the Red Shadow's death stuns Margot, for she has fallen in love with her kidnaper. But while her back is turned Pierre dons his mask. The two swear to be eternally true, heartened by the prospect of a Riff-French reconciliation.

Romberg's lushly melodic score was the triumph of the evening. From the stirring "Riff Song" in the opening scene to the haunting title song (with which the Red Shadow invited Margot to come away with him) to the rapturous "One Alone," which the lovers reprise as a finale, it was filled with rich, unforgettable melodies. In its contemporaneity *The Desert Song* was firmly in the tradition of the great Viennese operettas. Romberg took full advantage of the 1926 setting. Side by side with the arioso melodies given to Halliday and Miss Segal were up-to-the-minute pieces such as "It," which Eddie Buzzell danced and clowned through. "It" made knowing references to Clara Bow, Elinor Glyn, and other voguish figures of the day. *The Desert Song* compiled 471 performances, just short of the season's long run of *Rio Rita.*

In his review of *The Desert Song,* Richard Watts, Jr., writing in the *Herald Tribune,* observed snidely, "the lyrics gave indication that W.S. Gilbert had lived and died in vain." As if to prove the point, a revival of *The Pirates of Penzance* headed December's entries. The production was the second in a series of Gilbert and Sullivan mountings Winthrop Ames began with *Iolanthe* in the preceding year and which he hoped to make an annual affair. It chalked up an encouraging 128 performances, double the stay of its predecessor.

Oh, Please (12-17-26, Fulton) had a Vincent Youmans' score and a book by Otto Harbach and Anne Caldwell based on a French farce by Hennequin and Veber. Three top comic talents—Beatrice Lillie, Charles Winninger, and Helen Broderick—headed the cast. Charles Purcell helped with the singing. The story detailed the troubles that plague Nicodemus Bliss (Winninger), who is suspected by his wife, Emma (Miss Broderick), of flirting with an actress named Lily Valli (Miss Lillie). For all the talents involved the show failed to catch fire. It had a disappointing New York run and not much better luck elsewhere. Part of the problem was that Miss Lillie seemed conspicuously ill-at-ease in her straight, romantic scenes with Purcell. But her comic moments remained delicious. At one point she lampooned modern Broadway musicals, playing not only the principals but the chorus and audience as well. She wrapped herself in a convenient table cloth to sing the lugubrious "Love Me," assuming all sorts of preposterous attitudes, trying all the chairs and sofas in the room and peeking behind screens. As her own audience she applauded so wildly she forced herself to take bow after bow. One Youmans song from the piece has survived, the lively "I Know That You Know," sung by Miss Lillie and Purcell. It was another of the readily identifiable Youmans pieces with a simple repeated series of notes saved from monotony by the insistent chord changes.

Rodgers and Hart, and their librettist, Herbert Fields, scored another hit with **Peggy-Ann** (12-27-26, Vanderbilt). Old timers who didn't read their programs carefully may have had a feeling of *déjà vu.* For the show was a reworking of Marie Dressler's musical vehicle, *Tillie's Nightmare* (5-5-10). The story was essentially the same, with the names changed. Tillie became Peggy-Ann (Helen Ford), a boarding house drudge who dreams of partaking in the exciting worlds beyond her reach and wakes up to confront the fact that her pleasures are, indeed, only a dream. But while the story was the same, the tone was drastically altered. The broad, rough-and-tumble musical hall fun of the earlier

show gave way to finely turned words and music and to a plot that incorporated the latest Freudian thinking about dreams. Fields had fun with the meaningful distortions of the night: animals spoke, people had pink hair, small objects grew to outlandish size. Nocturnal embarrassments crop up when Peggy-Ann arrives at her wedding practically undressed. At one point, recalling Cohan's spoof of *Common Clay,* Peggy-Ann is required to take an oath on the telephone book. Fields was as daring in his construction as in his content. There was no raucous musical opening, nor any songs until the story was well under way. And the finale was a quiet dance on a dim stage. Though *Tillie's Nightmare* had given Sloane his one more or less durable hit in "Heaven Will Protect The Working Girl," no Rodgers and Hart classics emerged from *Peggy-Ann.* Nonetheless their words and music kept the show moving for 333 performances.

The night after *Peggy-Ann* opened, Rodgers and Hart had a second set of songs ready for **Betsy** (12-28-26, New Amsterdam). It was the first time in a while the pair had not worked with Herbert Fields, and they must have quickly come to regret it. Their producer, Ziegfeld, hated the show from the beginning, according to his biographer. Nonetheless, the *Times* insisted he mounted it with his "customary opulence and unimpeachable taste." At heart it was a vehicle for the popular vaudevillian, Belle Baker. In Irving Caesar and David Freeman's book she played a girl whose Jewish mother will not let her other children marry until Betsy has found a husband. When her brothers corral a pigeon-fancier named Archie (Allen Kearns), he imprudently falls in love with Betsy's younger sister. But Betsy is able to win him over. The book had none of the sophistication or relative subtlety of *Peggy-Ann.* It did, however, offer a hilarious new monicker when Al Shean (once of Gallagher and Shean) appeared as Stonewall Moscowitz. The quick failure of the piece—it ran just 39 times—dragged down with it one of Rodgers and Hart's best tunes, a bittersweet gem, "This Funny World," that has only lately been revived. In his book on American popular song Alec Wilder gives it appreciable space, concluding: "It could easily have been written in a minor key. But Rodgers achieves his atmosphere of loneliness within the confines of a major scale. And this couldn't have been easy." Even in their less subtle shows Rodgers and Hart maintained their independent, high standards.

Miss Baker also introduced Irving Berlin's "Blue Skies," which the program stated was "specially written" for her. Ziegfeld's "unimpeachable taste" didn't stop him from injecting a number of extraneous specialties. The morning-after notices recorded that the biggest applause of the evening was garnered not by Miss Baker, but by Borrah Minnevitch and his Harmonica Orchestra. (Their antics while they played later caused the troupe to be renamed the Harmonica Rascals.) They added another famous name to the credits, for their principal number was an abbreviated version of Gershwin's "Rhapsody In Blue."

The first musical of 1927 reunited Guy Bolton, P.G. Wodehouse, and Armand Vecsey, who had pleased the road, if not New York, eight years earlier with *The Rose of China* (11-25-19). Classified as "a musical romance" with a plot reminiscent of Edward Sheldon's old play, *Romance*, it gave the real Jenny Lind a fictitious, star-crossed love affair with Capt. Rex Gurnee (Glen Dale) of West Point. Much to Barnum's relief Jenny concludes her way of life would hinder the captain's army career. Not only Barnum (Tom Wise) and Lind, but Robert E. Lee and Cornelius Vanderbilt were brought back to life on the Jolson's stage. (Both Lee and Vanderbilt were portrayed by the same actor, Victor Bozardt.) Out of a less distant past Eleanor Painter, beyond her prime, but still beautiful, returned to star as Jenny. It was all competent; no more. Some critics were unhappy with Stanley Lupino's anachronistic jokes about radio, near beer, and flappers—a device Billy Van had used in *The Dream Girl* (8-20-24). Called **The Nightingale** (1-3-27, Jolson), the musical left after twelve weeks.

Creoles, quadroons, and New Orleans reappeared one evening later in **The Lace Petticoat** (1-4-27, Forrest). But its approach was far more traditional than *Deep River*'s. A rich Creole, Raymond de la Lange (Gerald Moore), coveting the beautiful Renita (Vivian Hart) and jealous of her open affection for Paul Joscelyn (Tom Burke), tells the girl she is a quadroon. Renita is tempted to run away, but the truth comes out in time to bring the lovers together for the Mardi Gras. All the hands responsible for the work were relatively inexperienced, and it is telling that one of the composers had also to be the show's producer. No one thought much of the effort, and it was withdrawn after two weeks.

Piggy, which arrived on January 11 to open the new Royale Theatre, was a jazzed-up version of *The Rich Mr. Hoggenheimer* (10-22-06). The story line remained and, most happily, Sam Bernard was back in the title role. Monocled and blustering, Bernard had fun turning "minister plenipotentiary"

into "minister in a penitentiary." The abbreviated, informal title characterizes the changes that were made. Ludwig Englander songs such as "Five O'Clock Tea," "Be Demure," and "Cupid's Auction Sale" were replaced by Cliff Friend tunes (to Lew Brown lyrics), with up-to-date titles such as "It's Easy To Say Hello" and "Oh, Baby." But the adapters lacked the imagination, skill, and panache that Fields, Rodgers, and Hart had brought to their reworking of *Tillie's Nightmare*. Though the show was mounted with brilliantly colored sets and costumes, and often brought to life by forty dancers of the "clippety, cloppity school of hoppers," Bernard's skill and popularity really kept it going eleven weeks. Sadly, just after the show closed, Bernard died.

Bye, Bye Bonnie (1-13-27, Ritz) also harked back, but not as far. The show was another of the poor-Irish-secretary-makes-good line that had so dominated Broadway just a few seasons before. Bonnie Quinlin (Dorothy Burgess) is the secretary to Noah Shrivell (Louis Simon) of Shrivell Soft Soap. When teetotaling Mr. Shrivell is sent to jail for buying booze for his customers, Bonnie not only spearheads the maneuvers to free him but helps elect him to Congress on an anti-Prohibition platform. In one of the few twists in the plot she does not marry Shrivell but her old flame, the newly prosperous Ted Williams (Rudolf Cameron). The show was beset by problems. Fritzi Scheff and Frances White were to have been the stars, but both dropped out during the tryout. Albert Von Tilzer's score was tinkly, though below the quality of *Honey Girl* (5-3-20) and *The Gingham Girl* (8-28-22). At least one critic objected strenuously to the many "unmerited encores," particularly those taken by the specialties inserted into the show. The critic cited as notable offenders the Tampico Tappers, a dance troupe that performed the appropriately titled "Tampico Tap." A footnote should probably record that the colibrettist was the same Louis Simon who played Shrivell. Faults and virtues, the show ran four months.

In January Leon Errol came in as the main attraction of **Yours Truly** (1-25-27, Shubert). The plot was more than usually silly and complicated. A group of crooks hope to obtain a large sum of money from sweet Mary Stillwell's rich father. Shuffling Bill (Jack Squires) would seem to be among the wickedest of the lot, but he proves to be a detective, and he keeps both Mary (Marion Harris) and her father from harm. The *Herald-Tribune* hailed Errol as "the inebriate deluxe." His role of

Truly had little to do with the plot, but gave him several drunk scenes. The best was his flailing attempt to get out of a taxi. When the story and Errol were not occupying the audience, its attention was given to another band of Tiller Girls, who "wind themselves up into rhythmic knots, fall on their backs without spoiling the formation, rise again just as skillfully, kick and swing, and continue their gymnastics." Raymond Hubbell's music sounded distinctly dated; "Someone Else," for example, falling on the ear as a not very creative re-tinkering of Victor Herbert's "I Might Be Your Once In A While." But Errol and good times kept *Yours Truly* going through 129 showings.

The season's most heralded musical opening took place on February 2, 1927. It was a double-barreled event. Not only was the season's biggest musical hit unveiled, but the finest musical playhouse ever constructed in America was revealed to the public. The theatre was the Ziegfeld; the show was **Rio Rita.** Bankrolled by William Randolph Hearst, the Joseph Urban-designed house was a masterpiece of art déco. The auditorium was egg shaped. Seated in a gold-upholstered orchestra seat a spectator could feel engulfed by the burnished colors of Urban's stylized mural which swept without interruptions or sharp corners from one side of the house to the other. There were no boxes to destroy the simplicity of design. The proscenium was austere. It was gold with subtle bas-relief interrupted only by a door on either side. No mouldings or other frills cluttered the arch. The lobbies and even the lavatories were spacious beyond anything New York had seen.

The show that Ziegfeld elected to open the house was a somewhat backward-looking swashbuckler. Though it was branded a musical comedy and its creators (Guy Bolton and Fred Thompson on the book, Harry Tierney and Joe McCarthy for the songs) were identified with lighthearted contemporary pieces, the show was in reality an operetta. Certainly Tierney had never before written so full-blooded and romantic a score. *Rio Rita*'s story line and its songs put it squarely in the tradition of *Naughty Marietta* (11-7-10) and *Rose-Marie* (9-2-24). The Texas Rangers are hunting a notorious bandit known only as the Kinkajou. The rangers are lead by a handsome hulk of a man, Jim (J. Harold Murray). Jim loves Rio Rita (Ethelind Terry), but General Esteban (Vincent Serrano), who also loves her, persuades Rita that Jim courts her because he believes her brother is the man they are looking for. Only when Jim arrests Esteban as the real villain can he and Rita hope for happiness. The comedy was provided by Bert Wheeler and Robert

Woolsey, making their first appearance as a team. The book was well crafted; the music was something more. All the standard song types of the genre were present and happily inspired. There was the two-fisted men's chorus, "The Rangers' Song," the caressing waltz, "When You're In Love You Waltz," the direct appeal of the title song, and the production dance number, "The Kinkajou." For many, however, the glory of the evening was Ziegfeld's breathtaking production. The *American* observed, "Urban sublimates scenery" with an art "unblemished by vulgarity." According to the *Times*, Urban brought to the Ziegfeld's stage the "limitless space of the Mexican outdoors and the evening warmth of a patio; and fine tapestries [woven with Indian designs, stylized cacti and motifs from Spanish shawls—all glowing with rhythmic color patterns] that masked the stage during scene changes." Ziegfeld filled empty spaces with 100 of his most beautiful women (counting the toe-dancing Albertina Rasch Girls). In the first act Ziegfeld, Urban, and Miss Rasch moved away from both the story and the rich colorings to present a ballet done entirely in black and white. Its beauty and elegance compensated for its inappropriateness in an essentially swashbuckling evening. *Rio Rita* ran over a year, closing one week short of reaching the 500 performance mark.

A string of flops followed. The first was a near miss. **Judy** (2-7-27, Royale) was a musical version of the 1924 farce *Judy Drops In*. It featured Queenie Smith, late of *Tip-Toes,* and Charles Purcell, who had left *Oh, Please.* A single set was employed for the whole evening, giving the musical the intimacy of a straight play. Having been locked out of her home by a mean stepfather, Judy is taken into the bachelor digs of a group of young men in Greenwich Village. It is all quite innocent, and Judy is carefully watched over by Mrs. Maguire (Lida Kane), the janitress. The score was by Charles Rosoff, another in the long line of aspiring composers who reached the big time once and then disappeared from the scene.

Edmund Joseph was also a member of this forlorn group. He did most of the score for a three-week failure, **Polly of Hollywood** (2-21-27, Cohan). Will Morrissey contributed a bit of the music, as well as all the book, the lyrics, and the staging. The slight story had Polly (Midge Miller) try her luck in the movies and in the movie colony only to decide she prefers small town ways.

A revue entitled **The New Yorkers** (3-10-27, Edith Totten) achieved a short run. The title had been used before, in 1901, and would shortly be used again. Edgar Fairchild and Charles M. Schwab wrote half the score, the remaining half being supplied by Arthur Schwartz. Schwartz' great period lay just ahead, and nothing outstanding appeared at the moment. Much of the show's humor misfired. Typical was a late-in-the-day spoof of *Chauve Souris* (2-4-22) entitled "Café Habima." A skit meant to mock the health faddist Bernarr MacFadden was more salacious than funny. It portrayed the celebrity in a brightly striped bathing suit as he interviewed potential secretaries simply by taking chest measurements. When the revue could not sustain its theme of life in Manhattan ("brown stone fronts that were famous once," etc.), it thought nothing of bringing on Benn Trivers and his harmonica for an interlude of "Song Of India."

Lucky (3-22-27, New Amsterdam) was a major disappointment. It was created by the combined talents of Otto Harbach, Jerome Kern, Bert Kalmar, and Harry Ruby. The capable Charles Dillingham produced it. He mounted it with a multi-set lavishness. One scene depicted "jade temples and henna ships against the ardent blues of an Indian sea." Mary Eaton, Skeets Gallagher, Ivy Sawyer, Joseph Santley, Walter Catlett, and Ruby Keeler led the impressive cast, while Paul Whiteman and his orchestra made a brief late evening appearance on stage. But the pieces would not come together properly. The story told how Jack Mansfield (Santley) opens the eyes of the innocent pearl diver, Lucky (Miss Eaton), to the treacheries of her supposed father. Its best number was a Kalmar and Ruby contribution, the toe-tapping "Dancing The Devil Away." All the good efforts could not induce ticket purchasers to stop by the New Amsterdam box office. *Lucky* departed after 71 showings.

Two openings vied for attention on March 28; both closed on the same night seven weeks later. **Rufus Le Maire's Affairs** was the first attraction at the new Majestic Theatre on 44th Street. It was a revue with a solid cast including Charlotte Greenwood, Ted Lewis, Peggy Fears, and John Price Jones. Miss Greenwood regaled audiences with her high-kicking dances and played Lorelei Lee in a burlesque of *Gentlemen Prefer Blondes*. Lewis, wearing his battered top hat and singing with his tongue-in-cheek melancholy, led his jazz band through "Land Of Broken Dreams" and "The Prisoner's Song." Albertina Rasch rounded up another bevy of toe-dancers and put them through their paces. The revue even had something approaching a song hit in "I Can't Get Over A Girl Like You (Loving A Boy Like Me)." Its composer, Martin Broones, became still another name in the growing list of writers with only a single score to their credit.

Sigmund Romberg was anything but a one-shot composer, while Harry B. Smith had long since lost count of the shows for which he provided the book and lyrics. But neither had better luck than Broones when they offered **Cherry Blossoms** (3-28-27, 44th St.), their musical version of Benrimo and Harrison Rhodes' *The Willow Tree*. It was a cross between *Madame Butterfly* and *Pygmalion,* with a bittersweet ending so dear to Romberg. On a world tour to forget an unhappy love affair, Ned Hamilton arrives in Japan. At a curio shop he buys a statue of a maiden carved from the heart of a willow tree. According to legend, if the soul of a woman caught in a mirror is placed before the image, the statue will come to life. When Ned follows these instructions, the canny curio salesman replaces the statue with the beautiful and quite real Yo-San. The two fall in love, but when Yo-San learns that Ned still has a girl friend at home, she concludes the races will not mix and that Ned will be happier with his American sweetheart. She behaves disloyally in public so that he can have an excuse for leaving her. Years later Ned returns to Japan. He learns Yo-San is dead, but their daughter has grown to become the image of her mother. Romberg's score was anemic and Smith's lyrics cumbersomely out-of-date. The show was sumptuously mounted, the willow-filled garden of its second act winning critical kudos. Costumes were stylized, listed curiously as "French variations" of traditional Chinese dress. Neither Howard Marsh (the original Student Prince) nor Desiree Ellinger (who a year before had dramatically flown from Boston to replace an ailing Mary Ellis in *Rose-Marie*) could infuse any life into the work.

Almost a month passed before another musical appeared. Like the two shows that came immediately before it, **Lady Do** (4-18-27, Liberty) ran just seven weeks. Billed as "a surprising musical comedy," it offered little anyone familiar with Julian Eltinge's female impersonation shows could not predict. Its plot told how Buddy Rose (Karyl Norman) follows Dorothy Walthal (Nancy Welford) from Paris to her family's Long Island estate to woo and wed her. In the process he frequently has to disguise himself as a girl. For Abel Baer *Lady Do* was his lone Broadway score. His songs, such as the title tune, characterized the minor writing of the day.

A second double opening occurred on April 25 when *Hit the Deck* and *The Circus Princess* both premiered. Together they broke the chain of failures. **The Circus Princess,** at the Winter Garden, was a Shubert importation, the last of Emmerich Kalman's great operetta successes. Oddly its plot centered upon a disinherited prince who joins a circus. The princess was merely the girl he marries.

Hit the Deck (4-25-27, Belasco) was produced by Lew Fields. His son, Herbert, wrote the book and Vincent Youmans did the score. Louise Groody, Youmans' original Nanette, played Loulou, the owner of a Newport coffee house. She falls in love with Bilge (Charles King), one of the many sailors who patronize her eatery whenever they're in port. But Bilge is reluctant to consider marriage. So Loulou takes a small fortune she has come into and follows Bilge, attempting to change his mind. She follows him all the way to China. When she finally seems to have won her point, Bilge discovers she is wealthy. He demurs. Loulou wins this round by agreeing to sign away her money to their first child. The musical offered a variety of dancing—precision chorus work, black bottoms, Charlestons, and a "knee-twisting" solo ballet by Madeline Cameron. No small factor, however, in *Hit the Deck*'s 352-performance run was Youmans' effervescent score. Two Youmans classics came out of it. "Hallelujah" ("strutted rather than sung" by Stella Mayhew) and "Sometimes I'm Happy" (Bilge and Loulou's love song). Neither of these hits was written for the show. "Hallelujah" had been composed in Youmans' World War I navy days, while "Sometimes I'm Happy" was first written as "Come On And Pet Me" for *Mary Jane McKane* (12-25-23). Recourse to old materials was a perennial trick of all composers, but especially of Youmans. Curiously, his great hits to come were generally written for the shows or films they were a part of. And though several of these were as durable as anything he wrote earlier, as far as Broadway was concerned, Youmans was never again to work them into a hit show.

The second shortest musical run of the season, eight performances, was the lot of **The Seventh Heart** (5-2-27, Mayfair), an amateurish botch of a musical comedy. A vanity production (reputedly paid for by the loving sons of the authoress), it prompted one critic to suggest shows of its ilk should not be allowed in professional houses. It was followed on the next evening by another of the Shubert "A Night In" revue series, **A Night in Spain** (5-3-27, 44th St.). As usual Harold Atteridge provided the sketches. Jean Schwartz did the music. Because the vogue for Spanish material was at its height, the show constantly resorted to Spanish

themes in numbers such as "My Rose Of Spain" and "A Spanish Shawl." But it also encompassed broader horizons, moving on to "Argentina" and dancing to an "International Vamp." Inevitably it returned home for the Charleston of "Hot Hot Honey." For comedy Phil Baker and his stooge in the box, Sid Silvers, continued to trade insults. Ted and Betty Healy added to the merriment, while petite, baby-voiced Helen Kane, not yet a full-fledged star, helped sing the songs. The bright youngsters sparked the show for seven months.

A voice out of the past, Robert Hood Bowers returned to Broadway after an absence of sixteen years with his score for **Oh, Ernest!** (5-9-27, Royale). It was a musical version of Wilde's *The Importance of Being Ernest,* which needed no music, especially Bowers' mundane material. The show clung desperately to much of the original dialogue, but resolved everything in the second-act garden without ever moving everyone into the manor house, as Wilde had done for his third act. *Oh, Ernest!* left after seven weeks.

The Grand Street Follies brought in a new edition to the Neighborhood Theatre on May 19. This time the music was by a newcomer, Max Ewing. There was nothing noteworthy about his songs, but the series was never particularly strong in its musical department. The cavorting of Albert Carroll, Dorothy Sands, and the rest of the regulars promoted the annual trek of loyalists to the small, downtown house. Carroll impersonated Mrs. Fiske and both Ethel and John Barrymore, while Miss Sands masqueraded as Jane Cowl and Laura Hope Crews. The evening's funniest skit, "Hurray For Us," found "Cautious Cal" Coolidge giving away no information at a collegiate press conference. This year's version chalked up a 148-performance run.

The White Sister, an opera, was performed at the old Wallack's on May 17. Its place in this record is questionable. Based on a Marion Crawford novel, it was set to music by Clement Giglio. It related the dilemma of a girl who has taken her vows after hearing of her sweetheart's death and now discovers he is alive and still in love with her. She chooses to remain in the nunnery.

Two Gilbert and Sullivan companies opened three days apart bringing *Ruddigore* into the Cosmopolitan on the 20th and *Patience* into the Masque on the 23rd. The revivals further attested to the sudden, new interest in Savoyard musicals.

In **Tales of Rigo** (5-30-27, Lyric), an operetta passing itself off somewhat pretentiously as a "music drama," Zita (Mira Nirska) is a member of Rigo's camp of gypsies. When she falls in love with a rich society figure, Ralph Clark (Warren Sterling), she is told that he is really her half brother. She is about to leave when she learns her informant was mistaken. The score was by another one-timer, Ben Schwartz.

A promising combination of rising young theatrical luminaries and popular oldsters had a middling success with a summer revue, **Merry-Go-Round** (5-31-27, Klaw). It was the eighth May musical (not counting *The White Sister*). Newer faces included the authors, Morrie Ryskind and Howard Dietz on the words and sketches, and Henry Souvaine and Jay Gorney for the music. Youngsters in the cast included Philip Loeb, Leonard Sillman, and Libby Holman. William Collier and Marie Cahill led the veterans. Collier stepped in at the last moment (as he had the year before in *The Wild Rose*). His entry was so late that, according to one reviewer, he wasn't even mentioned in the program. The comedy twitted querulous customs officials, added a third story (and towel service) to New York's double-decker buses, and followed the ambulance-chasing of four lawyers named Moskowitz, Gogeloch, Babblekroit, and Svonk. Walter Kuhn, soon to be recognized as a distinguished American artist, created not the sets but the ballets and pantomimes. However, Miss Holman made the hit of the show singing Gorney's "Hogan's Alley." *Merry-Go-Round* ran until the fall.

Talk About Girls (6-14-27, Waldorf) finished the season. It was a lyric version of a vehicle John Hunter Booth had written for James Gleason, *Like a King*. The plot utilized a theme that in one variation or another had been tried unsuccessfully in several shows the preceding season: *The City Chap, Rainbow Rose, A Lucky Break.* The story had Philip Alsen (Russell Mack) returning to his home town of Lower Falls, Massachusetts, in the middle of a town celebration. Since he arrives in a Rolls-Royce, it is presumed he is rich, and he is hailed as a local hero. The truth is Philip is down-and-out and the car belongs to a chance acquaintance. Luckily, he puts through a major deal for a local power plant before he can be exposed. He also wins the hand of Sue Weston (Jane Taylor). The Rolls was the real thing, pushed, not driven, on from the wings. Its funereal chauffeur was played by Andrew Tombes, who grabbed most of the evening's laughs and much of the critics' commendations. Stephen Jones—who had done most of the music

for *Poppy* (9-3-23)—and Harold Orlob contributed the music. A tired score, a mediocre book and the heat conspired to close the show after just 13 showings. It was an unfitting end to a generally superb year.

1927-1928

The musical theatre, growing more exciting and more productive for three consecutive seasons, peaked in 1927-28. The number of new lyric pieces reached an all-time high: fifty-one according to the theatre chronicler Burns Mantle, fifty-three by *Variety*'s count. Neither figure was ever approached again. The quality of the works was equally astounding; the hits including *Good News, My Maryland, A Connecticut Yankee, The Three Musketeers, Blackbirds of 1928, Rosalie,* and, best of all, *Show Boat.* The musical stage was not alone in the magnificence of its outpouring. Among the plays Broadway hailed in this halcyon year were *Marco Millions, Strange Interlude, The Royal Family, Porgy, Paris Bound, Behold the Bridegroom, Burlesque, Coquette,* and *The Trial of Mary Dugan.* In fact, though the musical theatre had never been healthier, artistically or commercially, its share of Broadway openings was somewhat smaller than before or since. A record 270 plays (Mantle's figure, *Variety* lists 264) reached New York. This meant just 20 percent of the new attractions were musicals, compared with 28 percent a quarter of a century before (twenty-seven out of ninty-eight plays in 1902–03) and the nearly 30 percent in 1960–61 (fifteen out of forty-eight productions.)

Of the eleven musicals to open in late June, July, and August, eight were revues. But, with the exception of a rather unusual edition of the *Ziegfeld Follies,* the old annuals were missing. Three of the summer shows were black. Indeed, the 1927–28 season marks the first year in which a number of both straight plays and musicals were filled with blacks. **Bottomland** opened the season June 27 down at the tiny Princess Theatre. May Mandy Lee (Eva Taylor) is an ambitious and starry-eyed resident of Bottomland, a Negro slum. Hearing that her old friend, Sally (Olive Otiz), has met with success in New York, she decides to follow in her steps. But when she finds Sally disillusioned and alcoholic in a Harlem cabaret she returns home. It was a thrown together piece written and produced by Clarence

Williams, who tripled in brass by playing the piano in the theatre's orchestra. Performers whose specialties could not be worked into the plot as part of their character were simply listed as specialty acts. Catering to the white public's idea of Bottomland residents, the evening peopled its slum and Harlem with names such as Rastus, Shiftless Sam, and Mammy Chloe. At least in pandering to white expectations Williams knew what he was doing. But when he attempted some "white" ballet and ballroom dancing he brought down the ire of the critics. The *Times* assailed the evening's "slavish imitation of Caucasian song and dance," while the *Post* expounded at length, "To what avail is negro musical comedy entertainment if it puts behind it all the racial naiveté, the lugubrious humor, the vital rhythm of its own natural self, and proceeds to ape the mincing manners of Caucasian carnivals. Pickaninnies are not ladies of the ensemble." Perhaps because of such notices the public wouldn't buy the piece and it left after less than three weeks.

Bare Facts of 1927 (6-29-27, Triangle) attracted much the same crowd the 1926 version did, but in smaller numbers. Several critics could see little difference in the two versions.

The Shuberts attempted to capitalize on the notoriety of the Wales Padlock Act which allowed New York's district attorney to close for a year any theatre offering salacious plays. They called their offering **Padlocks of 1927** (7-5-27, Shubert). A few ticket buyers may have been titillated by the title, but most came to see Texas Guinan, the great night club hostess of the twenties, famous for greeting her patrons as "suckers." There was little she would not do for effect, and in *Padlocks* her antics included riding a horse around the stage. When she spotted celebrities in her audience, she departed from her text to ad lib a few well-chosen barbs at them, and on opening night she even inveigled a censor to come on stage to tell a clean joke. Some fine, young talent assisted the flamboyant Texas— Lillian Roth, J.C. Flippen, and George Raft (then a hoofer). Billy Rose wrote most of the lyrics to music by an assortment of minor composers. Thanks mainly to Miss Guinan, the show ran out the summer.

Two black revues followed: **Africana** (7-11-27, Daly), **Rang Tang** (7-12-27, Royale). Neither Donald Heywood's nor Ford Dabney's scores produced anything that became a major hit, though both contained the sort of incisively rhythmic tunes people came to enjoy in black musicals: "Everybody Shout," "Africana Stomp," "In Monkeyland," and "The Cake Walk Strut." *Africana* was in remarkable trim for opening night. It was long since over by eleven. While it bubbled along it turned its spotlight on an important new entertainer, Ethel Waters. Performers of this era often had to double in brass. The vibrant Miss Waters was no exception. Though she is best remembered for her singing and, late in her career, for her surprisingly warm dramatic acting, a number of reviewers were especially taken by her eccentric, loose-limbed dancing. The *Times* was sufficiently impressed with her stepping to hail her as a "dusky Charlotte Greenwood." The *Times* also fell into line by giving special praise to the dancing in *Rang Tang*. "First rate dancing is a concomitant of all negro shows," it proclaimed for anyone who by this time didn't know what was expected of black revues. The paper waxed ecstatic about the jungle choreography of "Monkeyland." Another number that pleased the critics found the entire chorus strumming banjos as they danced. But the paper did imply that, like *Bottomland*, the show foolishly attempted to imitate white practices—in this case by dividing its ensemble into show girls, ponies, and ballet dancers. *Rang Tang* was the more successful of the two. Helped by the presence of Miller and Lyles (of *Shuffle Along*), it sneaked past the 100-performance barrier.

A lamebrain affair called **Kiss Me** (7-18-27, Lyric) lasted 32 showings. It told how Tom Warren (Ralph Whitehead) pretends to marry Doris Dodo (Desiree Ellinger) in order to enter Prince Hussein's (Joseph Macaulay) harem and paint the prince's favorite. Inevitably Tom and Doris' mock marriage turns into the real thing.

August's first offering was **Allez-Oop** (8-2-27, Earl Carroll), a revue with an excellent cast headed by Victor Moore and Charles Butterworth. Moore participated in a spoof of silent movies, while Butterworth drew applause with a variation of his already famous Rotary speech from the last season's *Americana*. The similarity was underscored by the fact that both speeches had been written by the man responsible for the bulk of the material in this and the earlier revue, J.P. McEvoy. Many found the evening most entertaining when "50 Dancing, Dashing Alley-Oopers" went ape "Doin' The Gorilla." All in all, the mixture of song, dance, and comedy was good enough for a fifteen-week stay.

Another revue, arriving from Greenwich Village, **The Manhatters** (8-3-27, Selwyn) survived for eight and a half weeks without offering anything of special merit. Though it was a white musical, its big production number offered playgoers the era's umpteenth jungle dance. One skit belittled the self-important pomp of the ushers at the great movie palaces. The imaginary theatre in the skit saluted two of New York's great new auditoriums by calling itself the Roxymount. An offhand remark in a review of the shows hints at the overall quality frequently displayed by so many of these offerings that began in the Village. Observing that the evening often lacked a firm touch and professional competence, the critic insisted such failings made it seem "like most 'intimate' revues with similar geneses."

To give the **Ziegfeld Follies of 1927** (8-16-27, New Amsterdam) its customary opulence, Ziegfeld spent $289,000, a staggering sum for a show at the time. Joseph Urban accounted for a substantial part of the expenditures, creating a show curtain composed of Ziegfeld's beauties, a lush jungle scene alive with human-sized cobras, tigers, and flamingos, a bamboo forest, and a rainbow of colored lights. A live ostrich with a bejeweled collar carried Claire Luce across the jungle setting. And as the Brox sisters sang "It's Up To The Band," the curtains opened to reveal nineteen young ladies called The Ingenues dressed in white and playing on a collection of white pianos and other instruments, while the regular Ziegfeld beauties made music with kazoos. In one major respect this edition was a departure for the producer. A single star, Eddie Cantor, dominated the proceedings. "In blackface again after Kid Boots, clapping his white [gloved] hands and strutting breathlessly across the stage," he sang three Irving Berlin songs, and interpolated a "revival" of the not very old Walter Donaldson favorite, "My Blue Heaven." Cantor also impersonated flamboyant Mayor Jimmy Walker, a pet shop owner with a forlorn mutt to sell, and a New York taxi driver. In a skit not unlike the tailor routine he had performed for the Shuberts in *Make It Snappy* (4-13-22), Cantor became so exasperated with a customer in a hat shop he crowned the man with a straw hat. Asked in another scene why he changed his name from Levy to Ginsburg, he responded that back home in Mississippi levees were being blown up. Ziegfeld's reliance on Cantor proved the show's undoing. Cantor felt he deserved more for shouldering so much of the evening, and, when Ziegfeld didn't agree, Cantor announced he was too exhausted to continue. Ziegfeld was forced to close the still-booming revue after 167 performances. The producer hauled his reluctant star before Equity, and Equity sided with Ziegfeld. But that was small consolation. Besides his three songs for Cantor, Berlin wrote most of the songs Cantor didn't sing. Unfortunately Berlin was in a low period. No great tunes were heard, though Ruth Etting did her best with "Shaking The Blues Away."

A la Carte (8-17-27, Martin Beck), the last of the summer revues, came in the night after the *Follies,* and left shortly thereafter. Its sole claim to distinction were skits by the Pulitzer Prize playwright George Kelly, who took a jaundiced view of women's golfing manners, Atlantic City hotels, and backstage gossip.

A la Carte was followed two nights later by the last of the hot weather book musicals, which fared no better. Called **Footlights** (8-19-27, Lyric), it told how George Weston (J. Kent Thurber) is bamboozled into backing a Broadway musical by Jacob Perlstein (Louis Sorin) and Violet Wilding (Ruth White), a burlesque star. George loses his $20,000, but he falls in love with Hazel Deane (Ellalee Ruby), who has a small part in the show. He takes her back with him to his hometown. The original score was by Harry Denny, but by opening night it was laden with interpolations. For about half the evening the story was halted while second-rate specialties ("the crudest form of burlesque," "cheap vaudeville") attempted to divert the audience. *Footlights'* backstage plot made such interpolations almost inevitable, if it didn't excuse their dire lack of quality. At one point in the show Jacob Perlstein was heard to bemoan, "Such a terrible flop I never saw in my life." The critics shook their heads in sad agreement.

Three weeks went by before another musical arrived. The season began in earnest and in style with **Good News** (9-6-27, 46th St.). *Good News* was probably the quintessential musical comedy of the "era of wonderful nonsense." The decade's jazzy sounds, its assertive, explosive beat, its sophomoric high jinks were joyously mirrored in a hilarious, melody-packed evening. To emphasize the show's collegiate background, the ushers of the theatre wore collegiate jerseys, while George Olsen and his band, themselves exemplars of the twenties, shouted college cheers as they ran down the aisle and into the orchestra pit. Above them, on stage, the scene depicted Tait College. Tait, like *Leave It to Jane*'s Atwater, is football-mad. But Tom Marlowe (John Price Jones), the team's star, may not play if he can't pass his astronomy exam. Luckily, Tait is coeducational, and one of the prettiest of the coeds, Connie Lane (Mary Lawlor), tutors Tom sufficiently so that he manages to get through. Connie has fallen in love with Tom but believes he's engaged to Patricia Bingham—a name out of *Leave It to Jane* (8-28-17). Tom almost loses the game with a fumble, but the clownish Bobby Randall (Gus Shy) recovers, saving the game, Tait, and Tom. When Connie learns that Tom is not committed to Patricia

(Shirley Vernon), she and Tom freely acknowledge their feelings for one another. The hilarity of the book and the exuberance of the production were matched, exceeded in fact, by the brilliance of De-Sylva, Brown, and Henderson's score. Five songs became standards: "Lucky In Love," "Just Imagine," "The Best Things In Life Are Free," the title song, and "The Varsity Drag." This final number accounted for the last popular variation to appear in the period's Charleston craze. While the principal romantic leads were given the love songs, "Good News" and "The Varsity Drag" were assigned to a young lady who portrayed the secondary comic role of Flo, high-kicking, doll-faced Zelma O'Neal. Mirth and music combined to keep *Good News* alive for 557 performances in New York alone.

My Maryland (9-12-27) arrived in New York after a record-breaking forty-week Philadelphia tryout. Its music was by Sigmund Romberg; its book and lyrics by Dorothy Donnelly, who had worked with Romberg on *Blossom Time* (9-29-21) and *The Student Prince* (12-2-24). *My Maryland* proved her last successful effort, for she died shortly after the show opened. The operetta was a romantic reworking of the Barbara Frietchie legend, based on a Clyde Fitch play which had transformed Miss Frietchie into a young, beautiful woman caught in the sundering hatreds of the Civil War. Barbara (Evelyn Herbert) is courted by Confederate Jack Negly (Warren Hull) and Yankee Captain Trumbull (Nathaniel Wagner). When she chooses Trumbull and defends the American flag, Negly's colonel father (Louis Cassavant) would have her shot, but Stonewall Jackson (Arthur Cunningham), impressed by her youthful bravery, saves her. Romberg provided another masterful score. Negly courted Barbara with the pleading "Won't You Marry Me?"; Trumbull countered with "Silver Moon"; Barbara touched heartstrings with a prayer for guidance to her "Mother"; and the entire cast joined in the stirring "Your Land And My Land." Not everyone was enthralled with *My Maryland*'s libretto; and some critics expressed reservations about Civil War uniforms that looked suspiciously Middle European. (Had the frugal Shuberts simply refurbished costumes from an earlier failure?) But praise was almost universally accorded the singing of "the large and inevitable Shubert male chorus" and, most of all, the era's finest soprano, Miss Herbert. Critics' kudos, coupled with prosperous times, allowed *My Maryland* to repeat its Philadelphia success and to run through the season.

A one-week flop opened the same night as *My Maryland*. **Half a Widow** (9-12-27, Waldorf) reached back ten years to World War I for its story. Bob Everett (Halfred Young), convinced he will be killed in the fighting, marries Babette (Gertrude Lang), a French girl he is fond of. As his widow she will be financially secure for life, and can marry the Frenchman her father has selected for her. But when Everett returns unscathed, Babette chooses to remain his wife. Like so many weaker shows of the era, its authors fell back on vaudeville specialties whenever they ran out of conversation. In *Half a Widow* a team of grotesque acrobats "Three Must-Get-Theirs" and a troupe of Spanish dancers won the biggest applause. The Spaniards tangoed and clicked their heels. All the excuse needed to bring them on stage was one character's observing that a Red Cross nurse reminded him of a girl he had met in Spain. The music was by yet another of the numerous one-score composers, Shep Camp, with one interpolation by Geoffrey O'Hara, who had written "K-K-K-Katy" back when the war was real, and who took a small part in the play.

A revival of *The Mikado* found a fair-size audience. The revival was the third in the series Winthrop Ames was turning into an annual event. Later in the season *Iolanthe* and *The Pirates of Penzance* were brought back, and the three comic operas played briefly in repertory.

The ranks of one-score writers were enlarged by a woman named Ida Hoyt Chamberlain, whose **Enchanted Isle** (9-19-27, Lyric) failed to impart its magic to either the critics or the public. Miss Chamberlain also did the book and lyrics. Her story recounted a troubled love affair between an eastern society figure and a rugged forest ranger. Even the sleazy Count Romeo De Spagino cannot keep them apart for long. The *Sun* dismissed the writing as "doggerel" and complained that no one associated with the show understood that some lively dancing might have dispelled the evening's languors. The critic recorded with some amazement that one chorus number consisted solely of deathly still girls slowly nodding their heads.

Five hit shows opened on the night of September 26. Three were straight plays: Somerset Maugham's *The Letter* (with Katharine Cornell); *The Shannons of Broadway,* and *Jimmie's Women*. The musical successes were *Manhattan Mary* and *The Merry Malones*. **Manhattan Mary** was an Ed Wynn vehicle, more carefully plotted than usual. George White produced it and collaborated on the book. DeSylva, Brown, and Henderson came up with their second full score in three weeks. Wynn played Crickets, a waiter who helps Mary Brennan (Ona Munson) get a job in the *Scandals* after her mother's bad investments force her family to give up their restaurant in Greenwich Village. Verisimilitude was achieved by housing the show at the Apollo, where the *Scandals* generally played; by George White portraying himself on stage and by Harry Old-ridge's fine impersonation of New York's leading stage-door Johnny, Mayor Jimmy Walker. At one point in rehearsals, when White felt overwhelmed by book problems—exacerbated by Wynn's inabil-ity to project narrative dialogue—he considered coverting the evening into a 1927 *Scandals*. Most likely Wynn would have been just as content. His best bits had no real connection with the unfolding story. For example, he cast aside the plot to tell the audience about his uncle. His uncle had once been mayor. Well, not exactly mayor. More like a friend of the mayor. Anyway the mayor had given him a good job in City Hall. In City Hall? Actually, out-side. By the time he was finished Wynn had con-fessed that his uncle had been a street cleaner. When White started to hoof in the last act, Wynn ran down into the pit, shooed away the conductor, and began frenetically leading the musicians. Scene stealer that he was, at the end of the number Wynn asked the audience, "Wasn't I good?" But for all Wynn's extraneous antics, the libretto proved to be quite serviceable by the standards of the day. The disappointment of the evening was the music. But it was too much to ask the writers to repeat the richness of *Good News* regularly. Actually, the score was not bad. It was hummable and rhythmic, but not memorable. The show's good points over-rode its weaknesses, and the musical delighted New Yorkers for eight months.

George M. Cohan's **The Merry Malones** (9-26-27) ran almost as long: six months. A.L. Erlanger honored the great song-and-dance man by allowing *The Merry Malones* to open a new house Erlanger named after himself. Cohan's story used a motif from the preceding season's *Hit the Deck* and from Cohan's own *Forty-five Minutes from Broadway* (1-1-06). Rich Joe Westcott (Alan Edwards) must find a way of disinheriting himself, or Molly Malone (Polly Walker) won't have him. He finds a way, but his father cannily maneuvers Molly into accepting the money. The show contained all the expected Cohan devices: the intratheatrical comments kid-ding the show itself, a mystery subplot and Cohan's inevitable detective. Cohan was, as his biographer suggested, on a treadmill. But it was a pleasant treadmill, made to seem less work-a-day by superb mounting. One set was a painstakingly realistic re-creation of a New York subway car, complete with all the latest advertisements. The chorus, seated

boy-girl, boy-girl, occupied the entire length of the car with a few, center stage, as straphangers. The boys were as colorfully garbed as the girls, wearing brightly hued, checked berets and matching vests. No doubt audiences were unaware, as possibly Cohan was himself, that his performance as Molly's father would be the last time he would ever sing and dance in one of his own musicals.

Two musicals opened on October 3. **Sidewalks of New York,** at the Knickerbocker, was by Eddie Dowling and James Hanley, the team responsible for the preceding year's *Honeymoon Lane*. Its 112-performance run was respectable, but far short of *Honeymoon Lane*'s. The plot told how Mickey O'Brien (Dick Keene) wins a $25,000 prize for a tenement design, based on a layout his friend Gertie (Ray Dooley) has dreamed of. When the philanthropist who gives the prize decides to adopt Mickey, it seems Gertie will lose him, but she doesn't. Because the action spanned several years, Miss Dooley was afforded a rare, if somewhat con-trived, opportunity to display acting dimensions her followers might not have known she possessed. She began the evening playing her familiar shrill, ob-streperous *enfant terrible*. By the final curtain she had evolved into a warm, affectionate young lady, capable of eliciting moments of pathos from her viewers. Some of the bit players were of special in-terest. Smith and Dale discovered ways to include parts of their vaudeville act, while Ruby Keeler led a long line of attractive tapdancers. Elizabeth Mur-ray, who had been featured in *Madame Sherry* and other pre-World War I hits, was Mickey's mother. But producer Charles Dillingham went even farther back in theatrical history to reintroduce "Three Old Timers": Barney Fagan, the old minstrel who wrote "My Gal's A High Born Lady"; James Thornton, the vaudevillian-composer of "When You Were Sweet Sixteen"; and Josephine Sabel, who years be-fore helped make a hit of "Hot Time In The Old Town Tonight."

Yes, Yes, Yvette (10-3-27, Harris) came in the same night from Chicago. Its producer, H.H. Fra-zee, had hoped it would follow in the footsteps of his earlier, *No! No! Nanette!* (9-16-25). The new piece had been a modest hit in Chicago; it became a quick flop in New York. Its book was based on James Montgomery's 1916 farce, *Nothing but the Truth*. At a Washington's Birthday celebration its hero, Richard Bennett, bets $30,000 that he can tell the truth for twenty-four hours regardless of costs. The costs turn out to be high indeed. He almost loses his fiancée, Yvette, and nearly wrecks his own business. The book was good, but Frazee failed to enlist Youmans or another major composer for the songs. *Nanette*'s lyricist, Irving Caesar, tried his hand at composing, abetted by Phil Charig and Ben Jerome. The best song, Caesar's "I'm A Little Bit Fonder Of You," couldn't compare with *Nanette*'s better numbers. Charles Winninger was back, as Yvette's father; the Mask and Wig's attractive graduate, Jack Whiting, was Bennett, and Yvette was sung by Jeanette MacDonald. Winninger stopped the show singing a comic paternal lament, "Woe Is Me." With no microphones to distort or deceive, most critics insisted Whiting and Miss MacDonald were better as dancers than as singers. The *Times* politely added that was the way things ought to be in "an up-to-date musical." Sammy Lee's chorus provided more up-to-date hoofing, winning accolades for its interpretation of the Black Bottom.

Sigmund Romberg had two more operettas ready for October. Both failed. The more humiliating fiasco was the first, **My Princess** (10-6-27, Shubert). Written with his *My Maryland* partner, Dorothy Donnelly, who based her libretto on an Edward Sheldon play, it told of the attempt by a social-climbing oil heiress (Hope Hampton) to break into society by palming off a poor Italian immigrant (Leonard Ceeley) as her princely husband. She makes the mistake of marrying him, and, when her endeavors at moving up in society fail, he forces her to live with him in his Little Italy tenement. She grows to love him. In the true, undemocratic fashion of operetta, he turns out to be a real prince. No one accused the Shuberts of stinting on this production. Indeed a lack of restraint marked every aspect. Miss Hampton overacted, resorting to that school of emoting that expresses grief by pressing a fist against the forehead. A Cherry Street block party prompted a bit of "savage" Italian folk dancing, while Amerique and Neville found a spot in the last scene for a "flaming tango." Everyone seemed carried away. As the *Times* noted, "Written for the liveliest sort of expression, the music is played by an unthrottled orchestra, sung in full voice by a chorus of healthy fellows and danced by a troupe of Albertina Rasch girls with an expert hop, skip, and jump."

At the end of the month, Romberg had only slightly better luck with **The Love Call** (10-24-27, Majestic). Edward Locke adapted it from one of the Shubert's first straight-play hits, Augustus Thomas' *Arizona*. Some papers, such as the *Sun*, wondered out loud whether it was really necessary to keep turning old straight-play favorites into musicals. Looking into his crystal ball, the paper's critic

predicted that in the 1950s young Oscar Hammerstein IV would be turning Somerset Maugham's *The Letter* into a lyric evening and advertising it as "A Musical Play of Magic Malay." But Malay and 1950 were worlds away from old Arizona. As they did in 1900, Lieutenant Denton (John Barker) and his Rangers rescue trapped ranchers from an attempted Indian massacre, precipitated by the villainous Captain Hodgman (Richard Lee). Through all the terror a romance flourishes between Lena Keller (Jane Egbert) and Tony Mustano (Joseph Macaulay). Though Romberg and the Shuberts enjoyed their greatest triumphs when they struck out into relatively fresh territory, they persisted in trying to imitate their own and others' successes. The very title of the piece harked back to *Rose-Marie,* while "The Rangers' Song" reused a title employed so happily the year before in *Rio Rita*. But the song's lyrics minimized the camaraderie of Joseph McCarthy's words, recalling instead the determined warnings in "The Song Of The Mounties"! Smith urged "Horse thieves run, for a chance you've none." The operetta's principal love song, "I Live, I Die For You," contained pomposities so typical of Harry B. Smith such as "Awake, from dreams arise."

A more important opening occurred October 6, 1927, the same night *My Princess* premiered. *The Jazz Singer,* the first full-length movie in which the human voice was heard had its first public showing to wild ballyhoo. No one can calculate the effects it and the sound movies that followed had on the American Musical Theatre. But after October 6 the eyes of every Broadway artist were turned westward. Before long, many great names and a larger number of the second-stringers were riding the tracks, bound for Hollywood.

Four nights after *My Princess* opened, Mary Eaton and Oscar Shaw raised the curtain on **The 5 O'Clock Girl** (10-10-27, 44th St.). It had a thin plot, reminiscent of the poor-little-girl-makes-good stories. Every day at five Patricia Brown (Miss Eaton) leaves her job at the Snow Flake Cleaners' Shop and calls a young man whose number she has come across. He turns out to be wealthy Gerald Brooks (Shaw). When they finally meet, she is forced to play the rich society girl. Her ruse is exposed, but with the help of Gerald's valet, Hudgins (Louis John Bartels), who loves Patricia's co-worker, Susan Snow (Pert Kelton), a happy ending is manipulated. The show was written and produced by the team who had offered *The Ramblers* (9-20-26). The book was by Guy Bolton (joined this time by Fred Thompson). Their humor generally eschewed the puns employed by the era's hack librettists. Instead they drew laughs from situations implicit in the text or in the social structure of the day:

Hudgins: When we get married we'll go and live with your parents.
Susan: It can't be done.
Hudgins: Why not?
Susan: Because they're still living with their folks.

The songs were by Bert Kalmar and Harry Ruby. As they had for their earlier work, the songwriters came up with one topflight number, "Thinking Of You," sung by Eaton and Shaw. Norman Bel Geddes designed the show's *avant-garde* sets, modernistic fantasies that established just the right tone for this "fairy tale in modern dress."

Three failures followed. **White Lights** (10-11-27, Ritz) was another backstage story, embellished with a mediocre J. Fred Coots score. It lasted less than a month. Each night for that short spell a society girl named Polly Page (Gertrude Lang)—how many Pollys there were in this era!—triumphed over parental objections and managerial villainy to achieve stardom as a nightclub performer and to win the love of Danny Miles (Sam Ash). The plot was largely an excuse for variety turns—seven of the show's sixteen numbers were listed merely as "specialties." Unsophisticated playgoers may have found some novelty in the actors' walking up and down the theatre aisles during rehearsal scenes, but even less knowing tourists must have winced at one-liners such as, "You may have been bred in old Kentucky, but you're only a crumb here."

A musical version of A.E. Thomas' *Just Suppose*, **Just Fancy** (10-11-27, Casino) recounted in flashback the bittersweet love affair between Edward, the Prince of Wales (Joseph Santley), and Linda Lee Stafford, an American girl (Ivy Sawyer). Linda was not as fortunate as a later American lady; Linda's Edward preferred his throne. Curiously, while Santley played both the youthful prince in the main story and the aging king in the frame, Miss Sawyer portrayed only young Linda. The distinguished, beloved old actress, Mrs. Thomas Whiffen, came out of retirement to play the gray-haired Linda. Raymond Hitchcock, once a star of the first magnitude, was reduced to a single appearance as a dinner speaker during a reception for the prince. Mme. Marguerite attempted to re-create the Spanish dances Chiquita had performed in Niblo's hey-day—the era of the main story. For audiences requiring more modern stepping, the Chester Hale Girls did a polo ballet. Joseph Meyer and Phil Charig's score, with Leo Robins lyrics, was never more than competent. Only the somewhat tattered popularity of its stars kept *Just Fancy* on the boards for ten weeks.

All six of November's new musicals were hits, even if some were not so successful as their creators had hoped. Rodgers and Hart and Herbert Fields were in top form when they unveiled **A Connecticut Yankee** (11-3-27, Vanderbilt). They had fun adapting Mark Twain's story, and their New York audiences had even more fun watching their version for a full year. At his bachelor supper Martin (William Gaxton) flirts with Alice Carter (Constance Carpenter) to the chagrin of his bride-to-be, Fay Morgan (Nana Bryant). In a jealous pique Fay breaks a champagne bottle over his head, knocking him out. The unconscious Martin dreams he is back in Camelot, where his bachelor friends are fellow knights of the Round Table, Fay Morgan is metamorphosed into Morgan Le Fay, and Alice appears as Alisande La Carteloise. The courtiers are convinced the stranger is dangerous. They prepare to burn him at the stake. But Martin conveniently recalls his astronomic history and correctly predicts an eclipse of the sun. The awed knights release him. In gratitude Martin proceeds to modernize Camelot. Telephones, radios, and every conceivable modern device suddenly grace King Arthur's court. All might have been well had not Morgan Le Fay been bent on making trouble. Martin only escapes by waking from his dream. Back at the Hartford hotel he reconsiders his marriage plans, deciding to marry the girl he really loves. Two Rodgers classics came out of the show: "Thou Swell" and "My Heart Stood Still." The latter had first been used in the 1927 London revue, *One Dam Thing After Another*. Rodgers and Hart had to buy the rights back from a London producer. Hart's lyrics were brilliant. Two of the best songs in the show, "On A Desert Island With Thee" and "I Feel At Home With You," were given to a second pair of lovers, Evelyn La Belle-Ans (June Cochrane) and Galahad (Jack Thompson). They agreed they deserved each other because they were not particularly bright. The show was mounted with gaudy, witty sets and costumes by John F. Hawkins, Jr. His Camelot became a land of "topless, tottering towers of the expressionist pattern. Towers of many colors. . . ." In fact, there were too many colors for some, leading the *World* to complain of the production's "seed-catalog floridity." Busby Berkeley's dancers won their share of accolades as their routines sent them prancing over tables, over sofas, over anything between them and the other side of the stage. An interesting revival was offered in the 1943–44 season.

The Shuberts introduced their latest edition of **Artists and Models** (11-15-27, Winter Garden) and were satisfied to see it run nineteen weeks. Probably the majority of ticket buyers came to see the "100-Winter Garden Girls-100" (there were also 25 chorus boys). When the girls weren't forming a bracelet of nudes or posing in a living tableau of Reins [sic] Cathedral, other entertainers had their chance. Jack Pearl told dialect stories about his experiences as a deck hand on a submarine or of playing hookey from correspondence school. Florence Moore played an unsmiling, strong-armed nurse. In a more lyric vein, Ted Lewis led his little band of musicians and sang his cheerily forlorn songs. While the run was profitable, it was noticeably shorter than the earlier editions. The Shuberts put the series to bed for a number of years.

Another musical gem opened November 22, **Funny Face.** For its producers, Alex Aarons and Vinton Freedley, it was a doubly proud moment. They brought their show into their brand new Alvin Theatre, the name derived by combining the initial syllables of their first names. Fred Thompson and Robert Benchley had originally written the book, when the show was called *Smarty*. But Benchley was roasted for offering the same stolen-jewels plot he had so often ridiculed in his capacity as critic for *Life*. Benchley withdrew and was replaced by Paul Gerard Smith. The Gershwins, who created the songs, and their producers re-employed favorite performers from their earlier shows: Fred and Adele Astaire, Victor Moore, and Allen Kearns. Moore was brought in at the eleventh hour in a hastily devised role. Even with Benchley gone, the stolen jewels story remained. Jimmie Reeve (Astaire) is Frankie's unbending guardian. He has locked her pearls in his safe and adamantly insists they will remain there. Frankie (Miss Astaire) cajoles her boyfriend Peter Thurston (Kearns) to help her steal them. But they are not alone in their desire to put their hands on the jewels. Two comic burglars, Herbert (Moore) and Dugsie (William Kent), are also after them. Of course Frankie wins, winning Peter in the bargain. The haste with which Thompson and Smith wrote in Moore's part may have explained their frequent recourse to the very sort of puns Thompson had generally avoided in

The Five O'Clock Girl. The puns were particularly noticeable in Moore's material:

Dugsie: I'm an artist. I etch.
Herbert: Then why don't you scratch yourself?

Even in their settings the librettists tinkered with verbal inflations. Atlantic City's Traymore Hotel became the Paymore, while the Million Dollar Pier grew into the Two Million Dollar Pier. (The settings themselves were attractive but unexceptional.) The top Gershwin tune, made even more memorable by Ira's clever shorthand, was " 'S Wonderful," sung by the lovers. Ira's lyrics for "The Babbitt And The Bromide"—a last-minute addition—were singled out for anthologizing years later. The song's verse recounted the scattered meetings over the years of two bourgeois, "sub-sti-an-tial men," played by the Astaires. Its chorus detailed a collection of driveling, unvarying commonplaces that comprised their conversations—"Hello! How are You?/Howza Folks? What's New?" Not even their final meeting in heaven inspired any change of clichés. Their dance for the number allowed the Astaires a chance to offer their celebrated "run-around" step just before the final curtain. One show-stopping number provided Fred Astaire with what became a virtual trademark in later years. For "High Hat" he donned a tuxedo, and, with his hands in his pockets, tapped away while a chorus of two dozen men in black tie echoed his stamping feet. Other memorable Gershwin songs were the title song (sung by the Astaires), "He Loves And She Loves" (sung by the lovers), and "My One And Only" (sung and tap-danced by Astaire, Gertrude McDonald, and Betty Compton).

Another show opened the same night as *Funny Face*. **Take the Air** (11-22-27, Waldorf) has long been forgotten. But it was almost as successful in its day as the Gershwin work. It ran 206 performances, despite an almost nonexistent plot and a commonplace score. Gene Buck, now split from Ziegfeld, produced the show and co-authored it with Anne Caldwell. Another old *Follies* regular, Dave Stamper, did the score. The story related how Carmela Cortez (Trini) flies all the way from Spain to the Texas-Mexican border to help Happy Hokum (Will Mahoney) court Lillian Bond (Dorothy Dilley). Carmela plans a little smuggling on the side. She also helps Captain Haliday (Greek Evans) of the U.S. Army Aviation Border Patrol. Then they all fly to the Bond estate at Sands Point, Long Island, to celebrate the Hokum-Bond nuptuals. Trini and Mahoney turned the affair into another dancing evening, though the dancing was a far cry from the elegant grace the Astaires brought to *Funny Face.* Trini emphasized her exotic Spanish routines, while Mahoney did "taps with the force of a pile driver," taps punctuated with comic pratfalls.

The popular Harry Delmar assembled an excellent group of performers for **Delmar's Revels** (11-28-27, Shubert): Frank Fay, Winnie Lightner, Patsy Kelly, and one name not yet famous, Bert Lahr. The comedians clowned in a burlesque of English manners and spoofed theatrical groups such as the Provincetown Players and the Theatre Guild in "The Straganota Players." Critic after critic showered praise on one spectacular number, a "deepwater" ballet, "Under the Sea," in which the dancers glided along as jelly fish, octopuses, and other creatures of the ocean depths. Miss Lightner sang "I Love A Man In Uniform," while the Chester Hale Girls danced in precision. The revue had music by a number of composers. Delmar's hodgepodge was pleasant enough to run fourteen weeks.

A third new musical house opened November 30. The new theatre was Hammerstein's, built by Arthur Hammerstein in memory of his father, the first Oscar. Its opening attraction, **Golden Dawn,** was something of a family affair. Arthur produced it; Oscar II was co-librettist and Reginald Hammerstein co-director. Otto Harbach again collaborated with Oscar on the book, while Emmerich Kalman, Herbert Stothart, and Robert Stolz created the music. Somewhat pretentiously they labeled their effort a "music drama." It was an odd piece to open a new American musical house, an operetta with a distinctly Viennese flavor set in Africa with white members of the cast in blackface seriously portraying Negroes. A blonde native beauty named Dawn (Louise Hunter) has been reared to believe she is an African princess. She meets Steve Allen (Paul Gregory), who is being held as a prisoner of war by the German colonials. They fall in love. The heartless black overseer, Shep Keyes (Robert Chisholm), would keep them apart, and keep Dawn for himself. To bring this about he engineers her "marriage" to the tribal god. A drought destroys the village's crops, prompting a native uprising. When Dawn still rebuffs Keyes' advances, Keyes turns the revolt against Dawn by persuading his fellow Africans she is to blame for their troubles. Her problems end only after the chief confesses Dawn is actually a white woman. Kalman's score was by no means his best, but Robert Chisholm as Keyes electrified audiences with his singing of "The Whip." A hint that something was amiss came in the re-

views. Though the *Daily Mirror* lauded Joseph Urban's sets as "breathtaking," most of the other critics didn't even mention them. The show had a profitable run of 184 performances, but it was a disappointing, though prophetic, opener for the ill-fated house.

Frank Grey had tried and failed to win Broadway acclaim with *Sue Dear* (7-10-22) and *The Matinee Girl* (2-1-26). He made a third effort with his score for **Happy** (12-5-27, Earl Carroll). When he failed this third time he called it quits. With its collegiate background and affirmative title, *Happy* seemed to be trying to become another *Good News.* Fortune rather than football was the theme. Siggy Sigler (Percy Helton) must earn $100,000 on his own to inherit his family wealth. With his classmates' help, he does. He, in turn, helps untangle three love affairs, the most important of which finds Jack Gaynor (Fred Santley) writing love lyrics to Lorelei Lynn (Madeleine Fairbanks). As was the case with so many musicals of the period, the show was best when it was on its feet. Long-legged Gen Collins and Bill Brown won encores with their eccentric dancing, while the chorus started hands clapping with a rousing second-act tap dance done to the music of Carleton Kelsey's jazz band.

Eleven new shows opened on the night of December 26. **The White Eagle,** at the Casino, was the lone musical in the batch. A lyric version of Edwin Milton Royle's *The Squaw Man* (a 1905 hit and a famous early movie), it had book and lyrics by Brian Hooker and W.H. Post, and music by Rudolf Friml. The old story was faithfully retained. When the Earl of Kerhill (Fred Tilden) steals money from his regiment, his brother James (Allen Prior) publicly takes the blame, then flees to America. Under the name Jim Carson he becomes a successful rancher and marries an Indian girl called Silverwing (Marion Keeler). On his brother's death he stands to inherit the title. But Silverwing feels her presence will hinder him and kills herself. The old play, like *Arizona* earlier in the season, seemed ready made for a thumping, romantic operetta. (Its Indian heroine may have led Friml to hope he was working on another *Rose-Marie.*) But like *The Love Call,* it was a quick flop. In this case it was a pity, for it dragged down with it one of Friml's loveliest melodies, "Give Me One Hour"—although the atrociously clumsy Hooker lyrics might have killed the song in any case. Some critics complained that the bright colors used in the sets and costumes were not correct for Indian motifs, while others could see no use in inserting a dream ballet with "corn-flower-blue and gold shepherdesses." But there was general approval for the rousing War Dance that ended the show.

Only two plays came in the following night, December 27. But one was Philip Barry's literate and knowing comedy *Paris Bound;* the other was *Show Boat.* **Show Boat,** at the Ziegfeld, was the outstanding commercial success and artistic triumph of the 1927–28 season, and it has survived as one of the masterpieces of our lyric stage. Based on Edna Ferber's novel—for which, thinking it unsuitable for a musical show, she gave her very reluctant consent—it had book and lyrics by Oscar Hammerstein II and music by Jerome Kern. For Kern, and, arguably, for Hammerstein it remained the high points of their careers.

In the 1880s, the heyday of the traveling showboats, the *Cotton Blossom* docks in Natchez. The townsfolk welcome it, hailing it by name. Cap'n Andy (Charles Winninger) appears to greet the crowds and tell them of all the marvelous attractions he has for them. The enticements include the sultry Julie La Verne (Helen Morgan). The captain is assisted by his wife, Parthy Ann (Edna May Oliver), and their daughter, Magnolia (Norma Terris). In the crowd is a dashing, riverboat gambler, Gaylord Ravenal (Howard Marsh). He falls in love with Magnolia at first sight, and she with him. They cannot admit their feelings, but profess a willingness to "Make Believe." Their reverie is shattered when the sheriff warns Ravenal his likes are not wanted in town and he would be wise to move on. Magnolia encounters Joe (Jules Bledsoe), a black workhand on the levee. She presses him for information of Gaylord, but if he knows anything he is loath to reveal it. He suggests if anyone can give her answers it would be "Ol' Man River." On the *Cotton Blossom* Julie laments that for all his faults she "Can't Help Lovin' Dat Man" of hers, Steve (Charles Ellis). But when Magnolia tells her she, too, has found a man, Julie warns her to be cautious. The Sheriff arrives. He informs the showboat that Julie is part Negro, and, since Steve is white, they are guilty of miscegenation. Steve cuts Julie's finger and sucks in some of her blood, claiming that makes his blood part Negro, too. But Steve and Julie leave the ship to spare the others any problems. Magnolia is assigned Julie's parts. Seeing his chance to get out of town and also to be with Magnolia, Gaylord volunteers to assume Steve's duties. Before long Magnolia and Gaylord tell each other "You Are Love" and agree to marry.

Time passes. It is 1893, and the Chicago World's Fair is in progress. Gaylord and Magnolia visit the exposition. Joyful and amazed that their love is still so strong, they ask one another "Why Do I Love You?" Secretly Gaylord has continued to gamble, and his debts become so great he deserts Magnolia, leaving her with a young daughter. Magnolia learns the manager of the Trocadero is having trouble with his alcoholic singer and wants a replacement. The boozy songstress is none other than Julie, and just before Magnolia's arrival she rehearses her evening's number, "Bill." Magnolia does not recognize Julie, but Julie recognizes her and, understanding Magnolia's plight, sacrifices what is left of her own faltering career by walking out on the night club so that Magnolia can have her job. After an awkward start, Magnolia makes a hit, singing Charles K. Harris' "After The Ball." But she realizes this cannot be a life for her and is easily persuaded to return to the *Cotton Blossom.* More years pass. By the 1920s Magnolia's daughter, Kim, is a young lady. An old man appears at the entrance to the showboat. He is, of course, Gaylord Revenal. He spots Magnolia, also aged. But he insists to her "You Are Love" as always. They head hand in hand into the ship.

Hammerstein's changes from the original Ferber story are intriguing. A slew of minor figures inevitably were dropped. Julie's ultimate degradation as a lady of the streets went unmentioned. Though at the end of the novel many of the principals were dead or had drifted far away, Hammerstein contrived to reunite all of them except Julie. His ending may have been less realistic than Miss Ferber's, but it did tie together the loose ends of the history in a theatrically happy fashion. Furthermore Hammerstein managed to create a heroine whose character develops and matures; he also confronted black-white relations head-on.

Ziegfeld mounted the piece with his usual lavishness and taste. Joseph Urban's settings were among the finest he had ever done. Neither the imaginative stylizations he devised for the *Follies,* nor the Graustarkian baroque of his designs for some operettas, *Show Boat*'s sets filled the stage with a colorful, slightly heightened *verismo.* The opening of the first act was a bustling levee enlivened by the arrival of Cap'n Andy's floating auditorium. Later Urban revealed the auditorium itself, its main floor and balconies crowded with spectators engrossed in the drama playing on the boat's stage. The opening of the second act brought back the splendor of the 1893 Chicago fair. John Harkrider's costumes matched Urban's sets for flair and color. Ziegfeld's cast was near perfection, though only Helen Morgan went on to real stardom. (Indeed, Howard

Marsh's career began to fade after *Show Boat*. While Bledsoe helped make "Ol' Man River" an instant classic, he quickly faded from the scene.) The show was not the sort usually associated with the producer, but then the show was not the sort Broadway had ever seen before. For Ziegfeld the show may have brought back a swell of memories, recalling the same 1893 World's Fair where he first came to the public's attention.

For 1927 audiences, apart from whatever memories it evoked, it presented possibly the most important breakthrough in the history of our musical stage. Neither a Viennese operetta nor an American musical comedy, it was the first real "musical play": a lyric piece with a relatively serious romantic story about essentially everyday people set to music neither as clipped as typical musical comedy writing nor as fully arioso as operetta, although leaning toward the latter. It could be called American operetta, if only "operetta" could lose its pejorative connotations. Once again the matter of integration arises. Given the exigencies of the commercial theatre the aim of a subtle, seemingly inevitable blend of dialogue, song, and dance is a probably unattainable goal: at least in its purest form. But if inevitability is replaced by reasonableness a number of our best shows certainly attain it. And *Show Boat* is high among the best. Though "Bill" was written for a Princess Theatre show ten years earlier and though "After The Ball" was an extraneous piece incorporated for period effect, everything seemed comfortably in place. A number of the splendid musicals from the 1927–28 season have been given important revivals at different times. None so often nor so gratifyingly as *Show Boat*.

1927's final musical opened two nights after *Show Boat*. **Lovely Lady** (12-29-27, Harris) used the French farce, *Dejeuner de Soleil,* as its source. It had a score by Harold Levey and Dave Stamper. The plot recounted how a young lady named Folly Watteau (Edna Leedom) induces Paul de Morlaix (Guy Robertson) to pretend he is her husband. Before long the pretense becomes reality. Much of the show's dancing was performed by yet another group of Chester Hale Girls. The sameness of the "precision and counter-point routines" in musical after musical finally drove the *Times* to urge "there must be other dance patterns." Like Stamper's *Take the Air* earlier in the season, *Lovely Lady* was a small hit, running twenty-one weeks. And, like *Take the Air,* it left nothing memorable behind. For both Stamper and Levey, who had long been secondary figures on the Broadway scene, the musical represented their last major effort to play New York.

1928's first new musical, **She's My Baby** (1-3-28, Globe) was one of those surprising failures that on paper seems to have everything. Bert Kalmar and Harry Ruby took a vacation from songwriting to provide the book, leaving the music and lyrics to Rodgers and Hart. The cast included Beatrice Lillie, Clifton Webb, Jack Whiting, and Irene Dunne. The story had the comfortable feel of an old hat. In a way it was a reversal of *Lovely Lady*'s plot. Bob Martin (Whiting) must pretend he's married and a father so that he can borrow several hundred thousand dollars from his uncle. He selects his maid, Tillie (Miss Lillie), to play his wife, and they borrow the neighbors' baby. Rodgers failed to come up with a top tune, and Hart, experimenting with the limits of colloquialism in lyrics, momentarily became too colloquial and not sufficiently bright or witty. For example Hart purposely injected the pointless, all too ubiquitous "I mean" in sentence after sentence of "You're What I Need." It was Miss Lillie who was largely to credit for the show's surviving nine weeks. Her Tillie ate nothing but vegetables with Vitaphones, and when Webb proposed, "Let us ensconce ourselves upon the sofa," her reply was a terse, "No, I prefer to sit down." She stopped the show singing "A Baby's Best Friend Is His Mother." Webb and Ula Sharon also had a much-applauded number, "A Little House In Soho." As they sang, the house of their dreams took shape behind them, and, when it was ready, chorus girls dressed as flowers provided it with an instant garden. Eight Tiller Girls—called for this occasion "Lillie Cocktails"—performed the expected precision stepping.

For **Rosalie** (1-10-28, New Amsterdam), Ziegfeld corralled an impressive array of talent. Guy Bolton and William Anthony McGuire wrote the book; P.G. Wodehouse and Ira Gershwin wrote the words for George Gershwin and Sigmund Romberg's music. The queen of musical comedy found herself playing a princess. The *World* described her entrance. Violins tremble; trumpets blare: "Fifty beautiful girls in simple peasant costumes of satin and chiffon rush pellmell onto the stage, all squealing simple peasant outcries of 'Here she comes!' Fifty hussars in a fatigue uniform of ivory white and tomato bisque march on in a column of fours and kneel to express an emotion too strong for words. The lights swing to the gateway at the back and settle there. The house holds its breath. And on walks Marilyn Miller." Princess Rosalie falls in love with a West Pointer, Lieutenant Richard Fay (Oliver McLennan). He pulls a Lindbergh, flying the Atlantic to be with her; then she and her family reciprocate by visiting America. But Rosalie cannot marry a commoner unless her father abdicates. He does just that, joining the ex-kings of Portugal, Bulgaria, Prussia, Greece, Bavaria, and Turkey in celebration. Frank Morgan was the comic king. Romberg produced no standouts, but Gershwin gave the show a solid hit, "Oh, Gee! Oh, Joy!" Another fine Gershwin number, "How Long Has This Been Going On?," discarded during the *Funny Face* tryout, was used but failed to cause a stir. The title song associated with the piece was not in the stage version but was supplied later by Cole Porter for the movie version. A Ziegfeld production meant Urban sets. *Rosalie* was no exception. His opening set was all in brown: a brown arch framing a brown village rising to a bluish-brown sea. Several scenes were played against a scarlet and silver show curtain. Urban's lavish ballroom in the finale gave Miss Miller perfect surroundings for an elegant ballet. *Rosalie* danced on for ten months.

A cheerily titled flop, **The Optimists** (1-30-28, Casino de Paris), was something of a vanity production. Its producer, composer, and star was Melville Gideon. An American ragtime pianist who had long lived in England, Gideon had first offered the entertainment to London as *The Co-Optimists* where it had played in ever-changing editions for five years. The revue did have some good people in its cast, especially Luella Gear and the young dancer who would one day be Hollywood's Rosalie, Eleanor Powell. Its idea of humor was a "Song Of The Vulgar Boatman."

January's last musical, **The Madcap** (1-31-28, Royale), just made it over the 100-performance mark—103. The piece was adapted from a French farce with a plot not unlike *The Magistrate*, except that the sex of the protagonist has been changed. Claire Valmont (Ethel Intropodi), hoping to wheedle a proposal of marriage from Lord Clarence Steeple (Sydney Greenstreet), claims she is only twenty-nine. This presents a problem for her twenty-year-old daughter, Chibi, who must now admit to only twelve years. In turn, the lie complicates Chibi's romance with Lord Clarence's son, Harry (Harry Puck). Third-act confessions clear up everything. Arthur Treacher had a minor role, but the star of the evening was Mitzi, no longer young, and fading as an attraction. She was egregiously miscast as Chibi. The music was by Maurice Rubens, who contributed a number of Broadway scores in the late twenties: six between 1926 and 1929. His style was typical of the crisp, bouncy writing of the day, but he never produced anything memorable. His catchiest tune in *The Madcap* was "Odle-De-

O," to Clifford Grey's nonsense lyric evoking the old yodeling songs.

Sunny Days (2-8-28, Imperial) was another musical based on a French farce and, like *The Madcap,* just made it across the 100-performance line. Leon Dorsay (Frank McIntyre) tires of his young mistress, Ginette (Jeanette MacDonald), and decides to devote his time to his wife. However, his childless wife has another plan. She has decided to adopt a young girl and, of course, selects Ginette. But Ginette finally prefers a more mature liaison with Paul Morel (Carl Randall). It was the sort of plot Ivan Caryll and his generation decorated with trippingly appropriate music. In fact, an old-timer, Jean Schwartz, did the score. But the music was dishearteningly lackluster and a little out of date. Schwartz joined the composers who were abandoning Broadway for greener pastures elsewhere. To a large extent the show relied on its comedy and its dancing to attract pleasure seekers. The blimp-like McIntyre milked laughs with a pair of ill-fitting trousers, while Billy Van stumbled through a drunk scene shouting "pa-leese, pa-leese." The *Times,* resigned to its inability to change dancing styles, noted "choruses of 'Sunny Days' buck and wing and cavort and stamp and clap their hands in unison." A glimmer of respect shown through the critic's report on *Sunny Days*' "Premier Dancer," Charlotte Ayre. According to the reviewer, to impress audiences she "pivots on tip-toe and steps out in the fast tango of the music and hurdles across the stage with Carl Randall."

One of the season's biggest musical hits opened the next night. **Rain or Shine** (2-9-28, Cohan) had a brash, undistinguished book by James Gleason and Maurice Marks, and commonplace if serviceable songs by Jack Yellen (lyrics), Milton Ager and Owen Murphy (music). Its prime attraction was Joe Cook, who had been working his way to stardom in vaudeville and the *Vanities.* Cook played Smiley Johnson, who finds himself in charge of the Wheeler Circus, since Mary Wheeler (Nancy Welford), the show's young heiress, spends her time chasing a handsome roustabout, Jack Wayne (Warren Hull). Johnson thwarts the machinations of Jesse Dalton (Joe Lyons), who would take the show away from Mary. When the star of the show refuses to perform, Smiley takes his place, becoming almost a one-man circus. Cook juggled Indian clubs, performed a knife-throwing act, pranced on a high-wire, and walked on a ball. Even a banjo-strumming leopard couldn't steal the star's thunder. Cook also found time to unveil some of his Rube Goldberg-like inventions. One enabled him to

make music from the opposite side of the stage. A whirling saw approached a man holding a siphon. The man became so frightened he squirted the siphon, startling a second man standing in the crank of a Ferris wheel. Each carriage of the wheel held a violinist, and, as the wheel revolved, the freely swung violin bows hit a third man, on a pedestal, holding a hammer. The hammer struck an iron ring. Voilà, music!

Rain or Shine competed with **Parisiana** (2-9-28, Edyth Totten) for the attention of first-nighters. *Parisiana,* a mediocre revue, disappeared after 28 performances.

Keep Shufflin' (2-27-28, Daly's) was an attempt by Flournoy Miller and Aubrey Lyles to reconstruct the exciting Jimtown of *Shuffle Along* (5-23-21). Miller and Lyles were again Steve Jenkins and Sam Peck. They form the Equal Got League and plan to promote their new equality by blowing up the local bank and redistributing the cash. (The nonsense of one era becomes the horror of another.) Of course, the boys intend to see that they are a bit more equal than others. As they had been earlier, they were up at Daly's out-of-the-way house. Eubie Blake was gone from the pit. In his place, at one piano, was Thomas "Fats" Waller, who composed the score along with Jimmy Johnson (at the other piano) and Clarence Todd. Henry Creamer and Andy Razaf set words to the tunes. The show's best number was a Razaf and Waller song, "Willow Tree," a blues tune they labeled "a musical misery." *Keep Shufflin'*s reviews were the sort white critics had been writing for black musicals ever since *Shuffle Along*. Black dancing remained the yardstick by which such evenings were rated. In the case of *Keep Shufflin'* at least one paper thought the dancing went overboard. The *World* observed that the chorus "danced with such ardor and such grotesquerie last night as to knock the show out of drawing." Not all critics were so taken. Indeed the *Herald-Tribune* complained the show was not Negro enough. Only "delightfully un-Nordic" touches such as the "beaming pianist" redeemed the evening. Indeed Waller must have been far more enjoyable to watch than much of the action on stage, for a number of other critics marked him out for attention. Considering the stiff competition *Keep Shufflin'* found and the show's distance from the heart of the theatre district, its run of 104 performances was not too disappointing. Obviously it nevertheless fell far short of *Shuffle Along*.

The Three Musketeers (3-13-28, Lyric) was a musical version of Alexandre Dumas' story, adapted for the stage by William Anthony Mc-Guire and set to music by Rudolf Friml. P.G. Wodehouse and Clifford Grey supplied the lyrics. D'Artagnan (Dennis King) comes to Paris, where he soon joins the happy band of Athos (Douglass R. Dumbrille), Porthos (Detmar Poppen), and Aramis (Joseph Macaulay). He falls in love with Constance Bonacieux (Vivienne Segal). When the Duke of Buckingham (John Clarke) takes the French queen's jewels, D'Artagnan and his companions steal off to England to recover them before their loss embarrasses the queen. For the third time in a row Dennis King found success singing Friml's glorious music. For Ziegfeld it was his third hit of the season. He was coming increasingly to depend on William Anthony McGuire as a replacement for the departed Gene Buck, and McGuire staged the work as well as taking responsibility for the libretto. But Friml's score proved the evening's most durable offering. Not quite on a par with *Rose-Marie* (9-2-24) or *The Vagabond King* (9-20-25), it still was a richly textured, varied, and melodic achievement. Four songs stood out: "Ma Belle," "My Sword," "Your Eyes," and the "March Of The Musketeers."

"Unfailing Urban" once more provided Ziegfeld with eye-filling sets. The stage was framed in a Gothic-arched proscenium displaying the king's and the cardinal's escutcheons and bordered in gilt with grotesque figures. The show curtain was flat-tinted and thin-lined to resemble the drawings in primitive illuminations (a slight anachronism). The Tuileries were seen through a great circle of shrubbery; a city on a hill was silhouetted in burnt-red and buff; the queen's pavilion glistened in white, blue, and crystal. John Harkrider's plumed, multi-colored costumes added to the luster of the production. Sixteen Tiller Girls somehow found a way to do their precision movements in old France, while the Albertina Rasch Girls offered ballet-like dances. All the excellences combined to make the musical a success—but not an overwhelming success. The show ran 318 performances, a substantial falling away from the runs of Friml's other hits. But tastes were changing and new attitudes were soon to dominate the musical world. Though Friml continued to write, *The Three Musketeers* was to be his last success.

The Beggar's Opera (3-28-28, 48th St.), with contemporary music added, failed to find an audience.

The Greenwich Village Follies returned on April 9, signaling that the warm weather and the end of the season were both near. Oddly (and significantly), when it opened it was the only revue on

Broadway. The cast was high in talent: Dr. Rockwell, Benny Fields, Bobby Watson, Grace La Rue, and Blossom Seeley. Unfortunately their material was hackneyed. Travesties on plays such as *The Command To Love, The Trial of Mary Dugan* and *The Silent House* all seemed to miss the mark. And too many patrons had already seen Rockwell in vaudeville, using a banana stalk to illustrate the spinal column in his anatomy lesson. Grace La Rue, in a sequined gown, won applause with "Every Little Heart That's Lonely." Sixteen more Chester Hale Girls competed for encores with Ralph Reader Girls. In short, the evening was overdone. At best, Broadway heard what was probably its first taste of Calypso in this edition. Blame for a slackening in quality most likely lies with the Shuberts, who were now calling the shots. They brought the show into their Winter Garden; their dependable Harold Atteridge did most of sketches, while Ray Perkins and Maurice Rubens did the songs. Though it ran a satisfactory 155 performances, the Shuberts were astute enough to realize the day of the annual, like the day of the operetta, was ending. When the final curtain fell on this edition, the *Greenwich Village Follies* became part of history.

Rodgers and Hart and Herbert Fields had their second hit of the season when they introduced **Present Arms** (4-26-28, Mansfield). Charles King, who had been the shy but demanding sailor in *Hit the Deck,* was transformed into a tough, uncouth marine, Chick Evans. He is anything but shy in his courtship of Lady Delphine (Flora Le Breton). Fearing he will lose her to a rich German, Ludwig Von Richter (Anthony Knilling), he promotes himself to the rank of captain. When his imposture is exposed, he loses both his job and his would-be bride. But his heroism in a yacht disaster restores both his rank and esteem. In some respects the musical side of the show was peculiar. Though the piece was set in Hawaii, the songs that might have supplied local color—"Hawaii," "Kohala Welcome," and to a lesser extent "Blue Ocean Blues" —were not played until the very end. And the hit of the show "You Took Advantage Of Me" was not given to the principals. The Rodgers-Hart-Fields team was seldom anything less than daring. The song was sung in the show by Joyce Barber and Busby Berkeley. Berkeley, doing double duty, created the evening's dances as well. His routines had his dancers off their feet so often one critic dubbed them "aerial formations." *Present Arms* fell short of repeating *A Connecticut Yankee*'s success, but it ran through the summer. Rodgers attributes part of the short run to the show's similarity—including its star—to *Hit the Deck* (4-25-27).

Though it contained one of the best and most enduring jazz numbers of the epoch, **Here's Howe** (5-1-28, Broadhurst) was not a hit. It was produced by Alex A. Aarons and Vinton Freedley, who had brought so much of the best Gershwin to New York. They employed their *Funny Face* librettists (Paul Gerard Smith and Fred Thompson) to flesh out a rather venturesome, free-thinking story with a novel twist on the old poor-secretary-makes-good theme. Joyce Baxter (Irene Delroy) is a stenographer at the Tredwell Motor Company, where her boyfriend, Billy Howe (Allen Kearns), works as a mechanic. In their spare time they dream together of building a combination tearoom and gas station on the Boston Post Road. But her boss offers Joyce a trip around the world, ostensibly as his secretary. When Joyce demurs, Billy insists she not give up so rare an opportunity. Billy and Joyce meet months later in Havana, where Billy has become rich by gambling. But easy come, easy go. The finale finds the two of them standing on the Boston Post Road, poor again, but hopeful. Roger Wolfe Kahn, son of the banker and Metropolitan Opera benefactor, Otto Kahn, wrote the score with Joseph Meyer. Irving Caesar did the lyrics. One tune that stopped the show nightly was the best in a livelier than average score, "Crazy Rhythm." It was sung by Ben Bernie, Peggy Chamberlain, and June O'Dea. The song wasn't expected to be the show's hit. Hopes ran higher for a song called "Imagination," a number played again and again throughout the evening. Much of the music was played on stage by Bernie and his orchestra. And Bernie, "bending his knees and waving his violin to keep time [while he] patters innocuously," walked away with some of the best notices. One dance novelty elicited bravos. Miss Chamberlain and Ross Hines reversed roles in their apache number, with Miss Chamberlain throwing Hines roughly around the stage. But all its attractions were not enough to push *Here's Howe* past the July heat.

This was one season that never slackened. May 9 brought in another smash hit at the Liberty. The show was **Blackbirds of 1928,** an all-white creation for an all-black cast. The songwriters were new to Broadway. Dorothy Fields did the lyrics and Jimmy McHugh composed the music. Together they put a lot of old-timers to shame.

. . .

Dorothy Fields was clearly a child of the theatre. She was the daughter of Lew and sister of Herbert. Born in Allenhurst, New Jersey, on July 15, 1905, she was educated in New York City schools, where she performed in some of the fledgling efforts of the still unknown Rodgers and Hart. She toyed with poetry and lyric writing while teaching school until a fortuitous meeting with Jimmy McHugh at Mills Music brought her together with the composer for whom almost all her early professional work would be done.

. . .

Jimmy McHugh was eleven years older than Miss Fields, having been born in Boston on July 10, 1894. His mother was his first piano teacher. Preferring the practical experience offered as rehearsal pianist for the Boston Opera Company, he turned down a scholarship that would have allowed him to attend the New England Conservatory. He supplemented his income by serving as a Boston song plugger for Irving Berlin's publishing house. Moving on to New York, he composed songs for the famous Harlem night club of the day, The Cotton Club. His first hit, "When My Sugar Walks Down The Street," came from one of the nightspot's revues.

. . .

The McHugh-Fields score was filled with riches. Two songs—"I Can't Give You Anything But Love" and "Diga Diga Do"—have both retained their popularity. "I Can't Give You Anything But Love" (originally called "I Can't Give You Anything But Love, Lindy") was sung first by Aida Ward and then by Lois Deppe and Adelaide Hall. Miss Hall belted out "Diga Diga Do" in another 1920 jungle setting. In this case the setting was not elaborate, for the *Times* noted, "As to production [the revue] is nearly nil, drapes constituting the principal stage dress. 'Blackbirds' depends on its players and numbers." The player and number that drew the most applause seems to have been Bill Robinson, snazzily stepping his way through "Doin' The New Low Down." Amazingly, it was his only solo in the show. Sketches were routine for the black shows of the day. One more imaginative skit presented a black version of Elinor Glyn's "It." Wisely, these comic moments were held down. They took a back seat whenever the orchestra began to play. In New York the orchestra found itself playing the score 518 times. A decade elapsed before another revue ran as long.

The season ended with the latest edition of the **Grand Street Follies** (5-28-28, Booth). Albert Carroll, Dorothy Sands, and Marc Loebell were back to head a cast that included a young dancer named James Cagney. As always impersonations and spoofs of current Broadway plays highlighted these

Follies. Carroll fell back on two stand-bys, Ethel Barrymore and Mrs. Fiske. Miss Sands was a bit more original, impersonating Mae West as she might have done Juliet in a Max Reinhardt version on the steps of the New York Public Library. The famous scene in *Strange Interlude,* in which Nina sits down at a table with all the men in her life, was re-created in "The Strange Inner Feud" when Columbia sits down at a table with Calvin (Coolidge), Al (Smith), and Herbert (Lehman). *Coquette* was done as a miniature musical comedy. A pleasant, unexceptional show, it compiled 155 showings.

1928-1929

Burns Mantle bewailed that "the legitimate theatre came a cropper" in the "rotten season" of 1928–29. The season was not really all that bad, although in retrospect there was clearly a tapering off. If the fall presidential elections diverted some energies, more important forces also exerted a debilitating influence. Inevitably the rush of screen musicals that began in earnest in 1929, coupled with the first rumblings of the approaching economic debacle, had unnerving, enduring effects. Moreover, tastes in musicals were changing. Somehow this time playwrights and songsters were not thrown off balance, as they had been before, by earlier upheavals. In fact a number of the better creative talents took bold innovative strides, though the failure of *Chee-Chee, Treasure Girl* and, to a lesser extent, *Rainbow,* taught them painful lessons about the public tolerance of novelty. However, there was a noticeable drop in the number of new musicals, from over fifty to just over forty—a drop of 20 percent. The drop was far sharper than the drop in straight plays. The high quality that prevaded preceding seasons was also in shorter supply. As a result the number of long runs dropped. Four musicals from the magnificent 1927–28 season had run over a year; one from the new season did, *The New Moon. Hold Everything* ran exactly a year; and *Follow Thru* chalked up fifty weeks.

A Baltimore revival of *Patience* opened the season on June 25. It ran three weeks, as did the season's first new musical, **Say When** (6-26-28, Morosco). The show was coproduced by Elizabeth Marbury, who had been so instrumental in initiating the Princess Theatre series a dozen years back. She advertised it as "an intimate musical comedy," sensing correctly the reaction to overblown, gaudy productions of the day. Theatrical intimacy would soon be the thing in musical productions. All that Miss Marbury misjudged was the quality of her offering. It recounted problems Diana Wynne (Dorothy Fitsgibbons) brings on herself when in a moment of weakness she accepts Count Scippio Varelli's (Joseph Lertora) proposal. She finally worms her way out of her predicament and into the arms of her real fiancé, Gregory Farnham (Bartlett Simmons). Calvin Brown based his libretto on Amelie Rives and Gilbert Emery's *Love in a Mist*. For music Miss Marbury culled songs from various writers. One tune, "Cheerio," boasted lyrics ("You'll find smiling worthwhile") by the mayor of New York, Jimmy Walker. Assignments and settings for some of the songs were so curious as to raise eyebrows. "Cheerio," for example, was given to the fiery count, while the Oriental-sounding "In My Love Boat" was sung under the magnolias of a southern garden.

July and August each had only one new musical; both were the latest editions of the surviving annuals, and both ran six months. **George White's Scandals** (7-2-28, Apollo) had a stellar cast: the Howard Brothers, Harry Richman, Tom Patricola, Ann Pennington, and Frances Williams. The hoofers still monopolized much of the attention. The *Times* saluted Miss Pennington as the "most petite of the shake and quiver dancers" and even lauded Patricola, though it couldn't resist a slight dig at his "elephantine grace." This edition also had the last score DeSylva, Brown, and Henderson created for the series. A pale shadow of their great material for the previous edition, its opening number proclaimed correctly "Not As Good As Last Year." "I'm On The Crest Of A Wave" and "American Tune" received some play, though "Pickin' Cotton," which its authors hoped would be another "Black Bottom," got nowhere. The sketches, serviceable at best, attacked such obvious targets as Prohibition and *Strange Interlude*. One skit had all the citizens of gangster-infested Chicago wearing bullet-proof clothing and armed to the teeth. A spoof of the newfangled talking movies hid actors behind a screen to shout out the dialogue. When they lose their places, the handsome matinee idol is seen to speak with a squeaky voice, while the glamorous heroine has suddenly turned baritone.

The **Earl Carroll Vanities** (8-6-28, Earl Carroll) had a better than average cast for the series. W.C. Fields, Ray Dooley, and Joe Frisco were the top bananas, while Lillian Roth belted out the songs. The scantiest-clad chorus girls on the main stem

were a big draw as always. Though over a dozen lyricists and tunesmiths combined their talents to fill out the score, nothing worth mentioning emerged. But Carroll's customers never expected much in the music department. Even the titles stayed comfortably in the expected girlie show patterns—"Say It With Girls," "Getting The Beautiful Girls," "Pretty Girl," and "Painting A Vanities' Girl." The rainbow of colors that exploded over this last number gave way to more restraint in the revue's most highly praised moment, a stage bathed entirely in blue for "Blue Shadows." If Carroll's customers cared little for the music he offered, a number of them were probably even indifferent to the great clowns. Almost all the best comic material fell to Fields—or at least he made it seem so. Fields impersonated Dr. Pain, the dentist; a progression of railroad officials in "The Caledonian Express"; and Brigham Young about to take on a chorus line of brides in "The Mormon's Prayers."

Good Boy (9-5-28, Hammerstein) opened the post-Labor Day rush of musicals. Its title may have been meant to recall the preceding year's smash opener, *Good News*. The show's surprisingly cynical libretto by Otto Harbach, Oscar Hammerstein II, and Henry Meyers was certainly as solid. But its score, by the curious combination of Herbert Stothart, Bert Kalmar, and Harry Ruby, was patently inferior. Its one memorable number was made a hit by the unique, squeaky delivery of the "boop-boop-a-doop" girl, Helen Kane—"I Wanna Be Loved By You." Miss Kane's part of Pansy McManus was not a central figure in the show. The principal character was Walter Meakin, who comes with his brother, Cicero, from their Arkansas home to try their luck in New York. Walter meets an attractive chorus girl, Betty Summers, and she wangles him a job as a chorus boy. But the ambitious Betty soon decides Walter is going no place and leaves him for the stage manager. Only when Walter starts to reap a fortune from a doll he has devised does Betty return. For many critics Arthur Hammerstein's imaginative mounting was the best part of the evening. The sights and sounds of New York were vividly re-created, climaxing in a first-act finale in which an apartment opened up to reveal a balcony with a breathtaking panorama of Central Park's skyline. Besides Miss Kane the better known players included Eddie Buzzell as Walter, Charles Butterworth as Cicero, Barbara Newberry as Betty, and Dan Healy as the tap-dancing Bobby D'Arnell. The show's eight-month run was a happier affair for the Hammersteins and their new theatre than *Golden Dawn* had been, but

440

the runaway hit the family had dreamed of for its house was always to elude it.

The Shuberts continued their futile search for another *Blossom Time* (9-29-21), bringing in **White Lilacs** (9-10-28, Shubert), a fictionalized biography of Chopin that had met with some success in Europe. Perhaps dreaming of the very bonanza *Blossom Time* remained for them the brothers gave the importation a loving mounting. For the interior of a chateau, they painstakingly re-created Fragonard paintings for all the walls. The cast was as carefully selected as the designs. Guy Robertson and Odette Myrtil portrayed Chopin and George Sand, while a name from a fast receding past, De Wolf Hopper, handled the main comedy. In Harry B. Smith's version *White Lilacs* ran eighteen weeks.

What had originally been *Un Bon Garçon,* a French piece with music by Maurice Yvain, came in September 15 as **Luckee Girl** (9-15-28, Casino). It was another Shubert importation, and by the time it raised its curtain in New York only three or four of Yvain's songs remained. A staff of writers provided the interpolations. But nothing they added could prod the show beyond ten weeks. *Luckee Girl*'s sole claim to fame may be that it provided Irene Dunne with her first leading role on Broadway. She impersonated a saucy French lady, Arlette, who determinedly wins her heart-throb away from the girl he was slated to marry.

Cross My Heart (9-17-28, Knickerbocker) survived only eight weeks. Daniel Kusell's book provided a variation on Molière. The upstart Mrs. T. Montgomery Gobble (Lulu McConnell) is determined her daughter, Elsie (Doris Eaton), will marry a title. So Elsie's real love, Charlie Graham (Bobby Watson), goes to the Slave Ship Café in Greenwich Village and hires a distressed Maharajah to go through a ridiculous ceremony. Mrs. Gobble is brought to her limited senses, and the lovers do marry. A subplot followed the romance of Sally Blake (Mary Lawlor) and Richard Todd (Harry Evans). The Harry Tierney-Joe McCarthy score was their last for Broadway. The best they could come up with was "Right Out Of Heaven," which faltered after an attractive start. If the dancing of "The Ten Little Tappers" (all girls) never faltered, neither did it win any wild applause. When *Cross My Heart* closed, Tierney joined the exodus to Hollywood. But his scores there were unsuccessful, and when he attempted to write shows again none ever got past a tryout.

The New Moon (9-19-28, Imperial) was the only show of the season to run over 500 performances. Yet only an act of faith got it to Broadway. Though its original tryout was not disastrous, the show was quickly closed. Both the producers, Frank Mandel and Laurence Schwab, and the writers, Oscar Hammerstein II (with Mandel), and composer Sigmund Romberg felt they had the makings of a better work. The show was rewritten, recast, and reopened. The major additions were in Romberg's score. All but one of the show's hits were introduced during these revisions. The plot remained involved and farfetched. Robert Misson (Robert Halliday), a French nobleman turned revolutionary, is hiding in New Orleans in the guise of a servant to a rich shipowner, Monsieur Beaunoir (Pacie Ripple). Robert falls in love with Beaunoir's daughter, Marianne (Evelyn Herbert). Beaunoir's ship "The New Moon" under Captain Paul Duval (Edward Nell, Jr.) arrives, bringing as a passenger the Vicomte Ribaud (Max Figman). Ribaud had been charged by the king with finding Misson and returning him to France. At a tavern Robert's friend Phillippe (William O'Neal) cautions him that, while love steals in, "Softly, As In A Morning Sunrise," its vows are always betrayed. But Robert ignores the warning. Given a band of "Stout-Hearted Men" both liberty and love will triumph. Back at Beaunoir's Marianne prepares for a ball. She acknowledges, "To be really in the fashion today, You must have a dozen beaux in your sway," but insists her dream is to have just one man. And for that man she saves her "One Kiss." Robert and Marianne admit their longing for each other, "Wanting You." But Duval, who has fallen in love with Marianne, recognizes Robert and has him seized. The vicious Ribaud tells Robert that Marianne betrayed him. Robert is to be returned home on "The New Moon." Feigning a desire to be with Duval, Marianne sails with the ship. To her dismay Robert will have nothing to do with her. She pleads, "Lover, Come Back To Me." But Robert is mainly interested in stirring up a mutiny. He succeeds. The crew lands on an island, where they set up a free government. A ship brings news of the French Revolution. At the same time, Robert learns of Marianne's innocence.

Of the great songs in the revised show, only "Stout-Hearted Men" was in the original version (called in the program "Shoulder To Shoulder"), though the delightful production number "Try Her Out At Dances" was also included from the start. Apart from Romberg's melodious material, the glory of the original production was its singing. (The sets were sumptuous, but unexceptional.) Either at Romberg's insistence or because they had profited from the Shuberts' experiences, Mandel and Schwab enlisted a large, fine-voiced male chorus. Miss Herbert's supremely beautiful notes glorified Romberg's music to the farthest reaches of the auditorium. While Romberg was to remain an active writer, apart from a freakish affair nearly two decades later, *The New Moon* was his last great hit. The day of the Viennese-American operetta was over. Its incredibly melodious heyday encompassed a mere five seasons. They were the same five seasons that saw the coming of age of the sassy, cynical jazz musical comedy.

It was just such a sassy, cynical jazz musical comedy the daring trio of Rodgers, Hart, and Fields offered with **Chee-Chee** (9-25-28, Mansfield). In his autobiography Richard Rodgers complains, "There was an appalling monotony of subject matter in even the best musical shows of the twenties." His complaint cannot apply to *Chee-Chee*. Its setting was one operetta had appropriated as its almost exclusive domain in recent years: an exotic Oriental court. No occidentals arrive to set up a comic contrast, as they did in the turn-of-the-century musical comedies. The story (based on Charles Petit's novel, *The Son of the Grand Eunuch*) told of the successful attempt of Li-Pi Tchou (William Williams) to inherit his father's position as Grand Eunuch without paying the usual price. He and his wife, Chee-Chee (Helen Ford), suffer banishment in a forest before they reach their happy ending by arranging for a friend first to kidnap and then substitute for the surgeon. They play dominoes while the operation is supposedly in progress.

Rodgers and Hart attempted to integrate the songs firmly into the story. In fact, there were only six full-fledged songs in the show. In a purposeful effort to keep the story moving, the other musical "numbers" ranged from sixteen bars (the chorus of an ordinary song contains thirty-two) down to an almost unheard of four bars. A program note similar to one *Rose-Marie* (9-2-24) had offered was inserted into *Chee-Chee*'s playbill: "The musical numbers, some of them very short, are so interwoven with the story that it would be confusing for the audience to peruse a complete list." In a way Rodgers and Hart were too successful, for the public could take none of the songs out of the theatre. Hart's lyrics were as brilliant as ever and Rodgers' melodies gave a clearer foretaste of the even more subtle musical lines and chromatics he would employ in the thirties. Rodgers was not above a few erudite, almost private, jokes in the score. He was delighted when a handful of the audience each night recognized the bars from Tchaikovsky's *Nutcracker Suite* inserted into the

march with which Li-Pi-Tchou is led off to his supposed emasculation. Herbert Fields' beloved father Lew mounted the show with opulence and, perhaps, wit. Certainly a few critics were amused at the girls' Chinese dresses that seemed more like multicolored pajamas and at the Chinese warriors in Tartar uniforms brandishing harmless, little tin swords. Unfortunately, *Chee-Chee*, lacking Rodgers, Hart, and Fields' customary theatricality, could not find a public. It departed after four weeks.

October witnessed the end of another tradition when Broadway's first great song-and-dance man, George M. Cohan, brought in his last musical comedy. **Billie** (10-1-28, Erlanger) was a musical version of Cohan's own 1912 play, *Broadway Jones*. Once again Jackson Jones' secretary, Billie (Cohan's favorite leading lady, Polly Walker), talks him out of merging his chewing-gum factory with bigger interests and thus keeps him independent. To override the musical's obviously hand-me-down nature, Cohan filled the evening with superb dancing. Everybody danced. Cohan even allowed his villain to win the audience's affection with some amusingly eccentric dance routines. Despite the diverting footwork, most critics commented on how old-fashioned Cohan's evening was. The days when Cohan was looked on as a noisy upstart were long gone, and critics generally found some kind things to say. Good notices or no, the public would not come. At least not in the numbers it once did to a Cohan work. *Billie* ran for just 112 performances. Cohan came to admit his musicals were relics of a gentler age. As his biographer McCabe said, "the Cohanic musical play had no chance to remain in a world whose innocence and optimisms it no longer mirrored." There was something poignantly existential in the song Cohan hoped be the hit of the show. "Where Were You–Where Was I" had the subtitle "Exactly Where We Are." The title song had Billie describing how much she loved her name, even though her parents had given her a boy's name, after her father.

Paris (10-8-28, Music Box) was as succinct, sophisticated, and naughty as its title and star could make it. Its star, Irene Bordini, was wickedly abetted in her plot to entertain by Cole Porter, who provided most of the songs. His style and wit finally became evident to the world at large with his first characteristic hit, "Let's Do It." The slight story followed Miss Bordoni as Vivienne Roland, a worldly, free-thinking young lady, in her pursuit of Andrew Sabot (Eric Kalkhurst), scion of the proper New England Sabots. She gets her man. The whole affair was playfully intimate, confined to a single set (a lavish hotel suite) and with no regular chorus. However, space was found in the suite for Irving Aaronson and his ten jazz musicians, the Commanders. Since the men not only played their instruments but sang and danced as well, they constituted an *ad hoc* chorus. A harbinger of the chic musicals Porter and his followers would hereafter provide, *Paris* ran for six months.

Two other musicals opened the same night as *Paris*. Neither *Just a Minute* nor *Ups-a-Daisy* was as snappy as their titles, and both were soon gone. Harry Archer did most of the music, his last Broadway score, for **Just a Minute** (10-8-28, Ambassador). Little more than a vaudeville tied together with a flimsy story, it told of two songwriters who persuade one of their girlfriends to date a Broadway producer so the girl can interest him in the composers' songs. The plan backfires when the producer and the girl take a genuine liking to each other. *Just a Minute*'s showbusiness background allowed the entertainment to be filled with specialty dancers: Walker and Thompson, the Ebony Steppers, and sixteen Russell Markert Girls. They danced to the music of the pretentious-sounding pit band, Count Berni Vici and his Symphonic Girls, and to the jazzy on-stage playing of Peek-a-boo Jimmie and his band.

Lewis Gensler, still searching for another *Queen High* (9-8-26), did the songs for **Ups-a-Daisy** (10-8-28, Shubert). He had more of a story to work with. Ethel Billings (Luella Gear), annoyed at her husband's pretensions, demands he and his friends go mountain-climbing in the Alps to prove he really wrote a book on the subject. Of course, Billings isn't the real author. Young Roy Lindbrooke (Roy Royston) is. By the end of their adventure Billings (William Kent) is reasonably deflated, and the Billings' niece, Polly (Marie Saxon), is engaged to Roy. Even two top comedians, Miss Gear and Kent, couldn't put the material across, though they were assisted by another up-and-coming comic, Bob Hope, who played the butler, Screeves.

If DeSylva, Brown, and Henderson had disappointed their admirers with their indifferent score for the *Scandals*, they partially compensated by providing better than average scores for two of the season's book musicals. Their music for these shows was not as hit-packed as their *Good News* (9-6-27) or *Scandals of 1926* (6-14-26) material,

but each show provided at least one knockout number. And part from *The New Moon*, the two musicals were the major hits of the year. Knockout is perhaps a more appropriate word for the first of the two, **Hold Everything** (10-10-28, Broadhurst), which unfolded a tale of the world of prize fighting. The sport had exploded as one of the rages of the theatrical year. Two straight plays, *Ringside* and *The Big Fight,* had already appeared, although without much success. In the new musical, "Sonny Jim" Brooks (Jack Whiting), a welterweight champion, loves Sue Burke (Ona Munson). She leaves in a huff when he refuses to think seriously about a charity boxing exhibition. Her temper is not improved when she watches flashy Norine Lloyd (Betty Compton) try to fill her shoes. But when Brooks' opponent slaps Sue, Brooks gets fighting mad. The show had a fine cast that also included Victor Moore. However, it was Bert Lahr as the punch-drunk Gink Schiner who walked away with the best notices. Lahr staggered around the stage, crinkling his face, crossing his eyes, and gargling a nasal outcry something like "gnong, gnong, gnong." Demonstrating his ring prowess he landed a knockout punch—on his own jaw. The morning after the opening he found himself a star.

. . .

Bert Lahr was born in New York City on August 13, 1895. His given name was Irving Lahrheim. He entered show business at the age of fifteen. Lahr gained his experience in both burlesque and vaudeville, initially as a single and then as a team with his first wife. Broadway applauded him briefly in *Delmar's Revels.* But *Hold Everything* represented his big break.

. . .

The score for the musical included a clever twist on a title song, this one warning "Don't Hold Everything." Only one tune from the show remains alive, displaying DeSylva, Brown, and Henderson's razzle-dazzle at its best: "You're The Cream In My Coffee" (sung by Whiting).

Three Cheers (10-15-28, Globe) had been created by the faithful R.H. Burnside and Anne Caldwell as a vehicle for the seemingly timeless Fred Stone and his daughter, Dorothy. But time did begin to catch up with Stone, who was too ill to consider a Broadway effort. Will Rogers was called in as a replacement, changing the tenor of the antics slightly. Stone's acrobatic comedy gave way to Rogers' more verbal wit. Into King Pompanola's serene wonderland of Itza a Hollywood movie crew descends for background shots.

The usual misunderstandings occur, but at least Princess Sylvia has time for a romance with the director, Harry Vance (Alan Edwards). If the end of the trail was ineluctably approaching for Stone, it arrived abruptly for Raymond Hubbell. A prolific if uninspired composer of the prewar era, he saw his music becoming hopelessly out of date. Hubbell, though still reasonably young, retired to Florida, where he lived another twenty-five years. DeSylva, Brown, and Henderson were called in for additional, more contemporary tunes, and Miss Caldwell put new words to some of Leslie Sarony's English melodies. Even with its modest score, *Three Cheers* was attractive enough to run six months.

Had Stone been in *Three Cheers*, his smiling, innocent fun would have made a sharp contrast to the leering and brash clowning of the Marx Brothers in **Animal Crackers** (10-23-28, 44th St.). Everything—the George S. Kaufman–Morrie Ryskind book, the Bert Kalmar–Harry Ruby songs—took a back seat to the clowning of Zeppo, Harpo, Chico, and, maddest of all, Groucho. The action took place on the estate of Mrs. Rittenhouse, played by the brothers' matchless straight lady, Margaret Dumont. A picture is stolen, and Mrs. Rittenhouse's honored guest, the famous explorer, Captain Spalding (Groucho), sets about to retrieve it. The humor at times was so outlandish that someone never seeing the Marx Brothers in action would wonder if it was humor at all:

Spalding: Say, I used to know a fellow that looked exactly like you by the name of Emanuel Ravelli. Are you his brother?
Ravelli [Chico]: I am Emanuel Ravelli.
Spalding: You're Emanuel Ravelli.
Ravelli: I am Emanuel Ravelli.
Spalding: Well, no wonder you look like him. But, I still insist there's a resemblance.

Groucho spoofed the "asides" of *Strange Interlude* and used another famous play of the era for one of his outrageous puns. Asked if he had seen a habeas corpus, he replied, "No, but I've seen Habeas Irish Rose." Groucho's first entrance—on a litter borne by native bearers and with his joining the chorus to sing "Hooray For Captain Spalding" —became a classic, the song itself forever after associated with him. The nonsense kept Broadway laughing just short of six months and then set out to tickle the nation.

An attempt to resuscitate **Americana** (10-30-28, Fields'), the well-thought-of revue from 1926–

27, met with instant failure. Roger Wolfe Kahn wrote most of the music, and his orchestra was in the pit. But as far as Broadway was concerned, Kahn was destined to be a one-hit-song ("Crazy Rhythm") composer. The cast had two curiosities. The Gershwins' only sister, Frances, tried her wings as a singer, and the aging Rosamond Johnson, so prominent in earlier black musicals, returned. Indeed one novelty was the show's use of two choruses, the first white, the second black. The revue seemed to go to the same pump for its skits that the *Scandals* had primed. Like the *Scandals* it satirized talking movies, gangster-ridden Chicago (whose last honest policeman hides in a kindergarten), and *Strange Interlude* (satirizing the easy O'Neill target seemed the rage of the season). In *Americana*'s version the play was accelerated by having all the players on roller skates. One original number reflected the new law that required the city's taxi drivers to hang their pictures in their cabs. The cast sang "Remember The Face Of Your Driver," peeking through the holes in a curtain composed of oversized identification cards.

Richard Myers tried for a third time to offer Broadway an acceptable score. His "Rah!! Rah!! Rah!!" collegiate musical **Hello Yourself** (10-30-28, Casino) ran eleven weeks, helped no doubt by the presence of Fred Waring and his popular singing group, The Pennsylvanians. The score was filled with typical period pleasantries—"He-Man," "You've Got A Way With You," and "I Want The World To Know." The book succeeded in combining two popular stage worlds, with some of the action set in the theatre as well as in academia. Bobby Short (Al Sexton) is expelled from Westley University. A happy ending follows only after the president's niece, Dale Hartley (Ruth Sennott), arranges for her producer-father to mount a play Bobby has written.

November's first musical was an importation, Noel Coward's witty, melodic revue, **This Year of Grace** (11-7-28, Selwyn). A good deal of the grace, and fun, came from Coward himself in the cast and from the incomparable Bea Lillie. Out of the show came three Coward classics—"A Room With A View," "Dance, Little Lady," and "World Weary." This last song was sung by Miss Lillie, sitting on a stool, munching an apple.

The Gershwins and their loyal producers found themselves with a decided failure on their hands after **Treasure Girl** (11-8-28, Alvin) opened. Looking back, Ira was inclined to blame the book, suggesting it made its star, Gertrude Lawrence, so bitchy and grasping that it poisoned the whole evening. Miss Lawrence played the clothes-conscious, money-hungry Ann Wainwright, who is not above stepping on the toes of her would-be fiancé, Neil Forrester (Paul Frawley), to get at the $100,000 treasure Mortimer Grimes (Ferris Hartman) has hidden for his "Pirate's Party" treasure hunt. Neil brings Ann to earth when they are stranded on an island. He swims to shore, leaving her deserted. Room was found in the show for more lighthearted diversions. Clifton Webb and Mary Hay again charmed with their eccentric dancing, while Walter Catlett grabbed a reasonable number of laughs with his brash humor. The show was beautifully mounted, its show curtain welcoming audiences with an explosion of brightly colored, stylized tropical flowers. It should have set the tone for the whole evening, but, alas, it didn't. The failure of the show dragged down with it some of Ira's best lyrics and some of George's most vivacious music. Ira, for example, came up with clever, telling rhymes such as "A B C" and "incompatibility" for "I Don't Think I'll Fall In Love Today." George's striking melody for "Feeling I'm Falling" also got lost in the wreckage. One song that became a Gershwin standard, "I've Got A Crush On You," was introduced by Clifton Webb and Mary Hay.

An equally interesting and off-beat show, **Rainbow** (11-21-28, Gallo), suffered an even worse failure. Called "a romantic musical play," it attempted to portray seriously a bit of bygone Americana, embellishing it with songs that strove to combine lean jazz with arioso passages. Surprisingly, the composer was Vincent Youmans. Not so surprisingly, the librettists were Laurence Stallings, who had tried something similar before with *Deep River* (10-4-26) and failed, and Oscar Hammerstein II, who had tried something similar with *Show Boat* (12-27-27) and triumphed. Their story was set during the Gold Rush of 1849. Having killed a man in a fight over a woman, Captain Stanton (Allan Prior) poses as a parson in the rough-and-tumble army of the time. He falls in love with Virginia Brown (Louise Brown), the daughter of his colonel, marrying and supporting her in some style by gambling winnings. The ubiquitous Lotta (Libby Holman) persists in trying to win him away from his bride. In the end he is cleared of wrongdoing and restored to his regular post.

There are some intriguing parallels with the *Show Boat* story. Stanton like Ravenal is given to gambling. Charles Ruggles played "Nasty," a muleteer as colorful in his own way as Cap'n Andy. And Libby Holman's role of Lotta was not unlike Julie. Youmans produced a startlingly virile, melodic score, noticeably less angular than was his custom. In his study of American popular song Alec Wilder claims the best song in the show, "The One Girl," failed largely because lyrics such as "cheers me when I go out to fight, boys" were uncommercial. But the words fall comfortably into place when the whole song is sung. The melody does resemble Rodgers' "Blue Room," but remains original enough to stand on its own. Lotta was given a fine torch song, "I Want A Man," and Hammerstein created some of his drollest lyrics for "I Like You As You Are." *Chee-Chee* and *Treasure Girl* had failed because they went a little too far within the accepted forms of the day, but *Rainbow* failed to a large extent because it was ahead of its time. Nonetheless a number of the best critics praised the show, calling it "gorgeously different," "stirring," and "absorbing." Only the sort of score Kern gave *Show Boat* could, possibly, have made it palatable to its own age. A disastrous opening night, plagued with mechanical failures, also hurt.

December's initial offering was a five-week failure. The Shuberts called it "a comedy with music," though its songs had operetta overtones. Jeanette MacDonald played the title role of **Angela** (12-3-28, Ambassador)—her full name was Princess Alestine Victorine Angela—and she was the daughter of Arcacia's King Louis VII (Eric Blore). For reasons of state her father insists she marry a prince. But Angela has her heart set on Count Bernadine (Roy Hoyer). Fortunately the count turns out to be a prince as well. Everything about the show seemed wrong. The *Times* noted condescendingly, "It strove to create comedy by putting a tall man and a short man together and letting a superannuated detective in a uniform cape snoop across the stage." The stilted dialogue ran to lines such as, "Hearts are not fashioned of clay." Complaints were registered about the tired routines of the Chester Hale Girls. The *World* lamented even the lighting effects were "abominably done."

One of the season's best remembered hits came in when Eddie Cantor and Florenz Ziegfeld reconciled their differences once again and together made **Whoopee** (12-4-28, New Amsterdam). The still dependable William Anthony McGuire adapted it from Owen Davis' *The Nervous Wreck*; Walter Donaldson provided the score. Donaldson was one of Tin Pan Alley's most successful composers, but his only other score for Broadway, a partial one at that, had been for *Sweetheart Time* (1-9-26). Before he realizes what's happening to him, Henry Williams (Cantor), a shy hypochondriac, is induced to elope with Sally Morgan (Frances Upton). As far as Sally is concerned, the elopement is simply a delaying action. She is being pressed to marry the local sheriff, Bob Wells (Jack Rutherford), while her only heart-throb is Wanenis (Paul Gregory), apparently a half-breed Indian. The sheriff pursues the elopers to an Indian reservation, where it is revealed that Wanenis has no Indian blood. But Henry is not abandoned; his faithful nurse, Mary (Ethel Shutta), is ready to take over where Sally left off. The book's strong, well-motivated story is especially remarkable when it is realized how much of the writing was done with particular performers and not the plot in mind. For example, though Cantor played a seemingly white Anglo-Saxon Protestant, he could indulge in the following dialogue:

Wanenis: I studied the ways of your race—I went to your schools!
Henry: An Indian in a Hebrew school? Tell me, how did you get along?

But nowhere is the nature of construction more apparent than in the role performed by the show's featured player, Ruth Etting. She played a movie star called Leslie Daws. The role has no function in the plot. It simply gave Miss Etting a name. As often as not she merely came on stage to sing a song without the smallest lead-in, then walked off. All the characterization she was awarded suggested several times that she loved an irresponsible, tough guy who failed to reciprocate her affections. The man never appears. Cantor had one of his all-time favorites in "Makin' Whoopee," in which he warns of the dangers of married life. But the show also had a standout ballad, "Love Me Or Leave Me," sung not by Sally but by Ruth Etting in her role of Leslie Daws. (The song would forever be identified with her. When her biography was filmed nearly a quarter century later, the song became the title of the film.) Donaldson's score was superior all the way through, but he was not oriented towards the theatre and never again did another score. *Whoopee*'s Wild West locale thrilled Ziegfeld. No doubt he recalled all the times he played hookey as a boy to watch Buffalo Bill's entourage. Ziegfeld bedecked his beauties in feather luxurious beyond an Indian's most colorful fantasies and then he brought the

girls on stage riding real horses. (He also hired a real cow for further verisimilitude.) He gave Joseph Urban free rein, and Urban created a series of brilliant sets, notably a re-creation in reds and rusts of the Grand Canyon. The show ran into the 1929–30 season, when financial reverses forced Ziegfeld to sell the rights to Sam Goldwyn, who promptly closed the piece so that he could make a movie version with Cantor.

With *The New Moon* turning them away at the box office, it was not yet obvious that the old-school operetta had seen its day. The Shuberts probably helped disguise the change in taste when they brought in a very second-rate piece and saw it run twenty-one weeks. **The Red Robe** (12-25-28, Shubert) was a swashbuckler laid in Cardinal Richelieu's France. Gil de Berault (Walter Woolf) is relieved by the cardinal (Jose Ruben) of serving a prison sentence for dueling. In gratitude de Berault agrees to capture the cardinal's enemy, Henri, Count de Cocheforet (S. Herbert Bragiotti). But the Count has a beautiful daughter, and, seeing her, de Berault allows the Count to escape. Jean Gilbert's songs for this American work differed not at all from his European material, and Harry B. Smith's lyrics were of a predictable quality. Their best number was "You And I Are Passersby." Walter Woolf, who had acquitted himself so well in *Countess Maritza*, walked off with most of the best notices. The evening's heroine was played by Helen Gilliland, another of the many London ladies who illuminated the stages of the era. Her career, however, was far shorter than those of other fresh British faces—Gertrude Lawrence or Beatrice Lillie. Not all of the entertainment was given over to arioso singing and swashbuckling dialogue. Periods of roughhouse comedy relief were provided by towheaded Violet Carlson and another London favorite, Barry Lupino. A contingent of Chester Hale Girls danced in split-second precision, most notably in a show-stopping drum dance.

The Fields family joined forces with Jimmy McHugh and came up with a six-month hit, **Hello Daddy** (12-26-28, Fields'). Herbert Fields wrote the book, sister Dorothy wrote the lyrics, and Lew Fields starred and produced the show. For years three old friends—Henry Block (Fields), Anthony Bennett (Wilfred Clark), and Edward Hauser (George Hassell)—have been paying the same young lady support for what each has been told is his child. The racket is no sooner exposed than the young man appears. He turns out to be something of an idiot. But he also turns out to be as fraudulent as his mother's claims. The hit of the show was a comedy number, "In A Great Big Way," sung by the not-very-bright Noel (Billy Taylor) to a fiancée (Betty Starbuck) with an equally low I.Q. It was a hilariously lugubrious description of love among the lower mental orders. A subplot romance between Connie Block (Mary Lawlor), Henry's daughter, and Lawrence Tucker (Allen Kearns) allowed for standard love ballads. Herbert Fields based his libretto on *The High Cost of Loving* and filled it with the sort of one-liners his father had always employed, especially word plays such as "a wolf in cheap clothing." McHugh's score was effective and entertaining in the theatre but seemed made of less solid stuff in the light of day. The show was 1928's last musical.

The first musical of the new year arrived two weeks later. **Deep Harlem** (1-7-29, Biltmore) opened on Monday and folded on Saturday. It was a Negro revue with a tenuous story line holding the material together. The evening began in the Kingdom of the Cushites. A black tribe, they are defeated in war and sent into slavery. From there the story followed the slaves' descendants from a southern plantation to 1929 Harlem. Everything about the show seemed wrong. What the *Times* called "an abundance of flappy canvas scenery," the *Post* viewed as a *Grand Street Follies* spoof of *Aïda*. Even the dancing was spanked—unheard of for a black show. The day after the show closed, the *Herald-Tribune* ran a long article prompted by its dismay with both the show's failure and with New York critics. The paper felt the show was striving to be a little different from other black entertainments. The article went on to suggest New York would never let black shows be different, that all the local critics would permit in a black musical was "meaningless whirling and fizzing with 'pep'." Unfortunately the idea that black musicals should be allowed into the mainstream and should then be judged by the same standards was some years too advanced. *Deep Harlem* was written by and filled with largely unknown names who remained unknown after the show closed.

Polly (1-8-29, Lyric) did better. It ran two weeks. A musical version of Belasco's *Polly with a Past*, it was put together by a number of experienced hands, including Guy Bolton, Irving Caesar, and Arthur Hammerstein. The story recounted how Polly Shannon (June) agrees to impersonate a French actress and flirt with Southampton's Rex Van Zile (John Hundley) in order to make Myrtle Grant (Lucy Monroe) take an interest in Rex. Of course, Polly also loves Rex, and she gets him by the final curtain. Though yet another attractive English leading lady, June, was prominently featured, the bright spot of the evening was the clowning of Fred Allen as the gravel-voiced, wise-cracking reporter for the backwater Sag Harbour *Bee*. Apart from Allen, the show was as commonplace as its Phil Charig music, which always seemed to be a note or two away from the correct melody.

The next night brought one of the season's smash hits. Having struck paydirt with a musical about one sport—prizefighting—DeSylva, Brown, and Henderson (with Laurence Schwab, one of their producers, as co-librettist) went after a second sport, golfing, and came back with a winner. **Follow Thru** (1-9-29, 46th St.) punningly called itself "a musical slice of country club life." Its main plot followed the rivalry between Lora Moore (Irene Delroy) and Ruth Van Horn (Madeline Cameron) for the Bound Brook Country Club's women's championship and for handsome Jerry Downs (John Barker) as well. Lora wins both. But much of the fun and drive of the show came from a subplot in which a determined Angie Howard (Zelma O'Neal) pursues the shy, slightly odd Jack Martin (Jack Haley), son of a chain store executive. Jack tries to teach a friend the game, only to throw his hands up in exasperation, "The trouble with your game is that you stand too close to the ball—after you've hit it." Later Jack and his friend invade the ladies' dressing room in the guise of plumbers. Jerry Downs had the musical's best ballad, "My Lucky Star," while he and Laura sang "You Wouldn't Fool Me, Would You?" But Jack and Angie had the real show-stopper, a perfect swatch of early 1929 esprit, "Button Up Your Overcoat." The evening was filled with superb, lively dancing not only by a thoroughly drilled chorus, but by a young lady in the very minor role of Molly, Eleanor Powell. Her scintillating tap numbers earned her several encores every night. Though it was only early January, *Follow Thru* proved to be the season's last major hit but one.

Ned Wayburn's Gambols (1-15-29, Knickerbocker) was a minor revue that lasted a mere 31 performances but at least gave Libby Holman another step up toward stardom. Her sultry-voiced renditions of "Salt Of My Tears" and "Mothers O' Men" won her applause and good notices. Most of the other good notices were reserved for the show's dances—and the entertainment was largely occupied with choreography of one sort or another. Gypsy dances, Oriental dances, and Indian dances filled the stage. At one point "two nearly nude gentlemen tossed a nearly nude lady back and forth in the air for several minutes." Some of the best stepping was in the show's tap routines (the *Enciclopedia Dello Spettacolo* credits Wayburn with originating the tap as opposed to the older clog dance). The *Gambols'* totally forgotten score was by another of the many one-timers, Walter G. Samuels, but Arthur Schwartz, who would soon work so closely with Miss Holman, took credit for two interpolations.

Two more musicals arrived to round out the month. Jeanette MacDonald continued to move from the lead in one flop to the lead in another. In the prologue of **Boom Boom** (1-28-29, Casino), one of the pointlessly alliterative titles the decade adored, Jean has a brief shipboard romance with Tony Smith (Stanley Ridges). Later she marries Worthington Smith (Frank McIntyre), a man much older than herself and, it develops, Tony's father. But the marriage is annulled so that she can make a more suitable marriage with Tony. Miss MacDonald had worked with McIntyre the year before in *Sunny Days* (2-8-28). The hefty comedian was once again cast as a dirty old man, one who had just spent six months in the hospital. A friend solicitously asks if the long stay meant he was "pretty sick." To which McIntyre replied, "No. Pretty nurse." More comedy was provided by Henry Welsh as a head waiter. His suggestion of soup declined, he tells his customer, "Well, it's soup to you." The dancing was more varied. Jack Donahue and John Boyle each provided a contingent of fast-stepping girls (one band known as the "Lightning Dancers"). Kendall Capps entertained with his stunt dancing, while Cortez and Peggy danced a Spanish number. This musical version of Louis Verneuil's *Mlle. Ma Mère* had another nondescript score by Werner Jannsen, his last Broadway effort before he left for the more rewarding fields of serious composing and conducting.

In December a musicalized version of one Owen Davis play had become *Whoopee*. The last day of January saw Eddie Buzzell adapt Davis' *Easy Come, Easy Go* for his own uses. He called it **Lady Fingers** (1-31-29, Vanderbilt), and it had a score by Joseph Meyer. Buzzell played a sociable bank robber, Jim Bailey, who, in gratitude to rich, dashing but innocent Dick Tain (John Price Jones) for nursing him through a fever, involves Tain in his latest heist. They are forced to hide out at Dr. Jasper's Health Farm, where they en-counter Mortimer Quayle (Herbert Waterous), the very banker they have just robbed. Since Dick comes from a prominent family and since he and Hope Quayle (Louise Brown) are in love, there is really very little problem setting everything right. Buzzell was no Cantor, but he was clever enough and funny enough to keep audiences coming and the show going for 132 performances.

In a startling departure for him, Earl Carroll tried his hand at operetta. Carroll worked on the book, as well as producing and staging **Fioretta** (2-5-29, Earl Carroll). The show was so clean several critics sat up and took notice. But they also noted the desperately old-fashioned story. The wicked Duke of Venice plans to marry Fioretta (Dorothy Knapp) to the outlawed Count Di Rovani (George Houston), slay Rovani, and have the girl to himself. But with her father's help, Fioretta and the Count escape. The show had a vapid score by George Bagby and G. Romilli, featuring numbers such as "Dream Boat." Carroll's name and particular flair helped keep the show on the boards for weeks, as did the clowning of two former Ziegfeld regulars, Leon Errol (as an inebriated gondolier) and Fanny Brice (as a courtier with a ghetto accent). Carroll humored Errol's famous penchant for falling down drunk by dressing the comedian in a suit of armor, giving him a crate full of oranges to tote, and then sending him flying down a grand staircase. Errol had another drunk scene in which he jumped onto a table to give a slurred, confused after-dinner speech, concluding by falling into his listeners' laps. Miss Brice took advantage of *Fioretta*'s Italian setting to twit the overblown mannerisms of grand opera singers and then stopped the show singing "Old Wicked Willage Of Wenice." When the story was not unfolding or the clowns cavorting, Carroll brought in "acres and battalions of girls . . . in spangles, trailing skirts and ostrich plumes." He even inserted a dance—which at least one critic branded as tasteless—that found the Duke's dead ancestors stepping lively in their tomb. The show could probably have run longer than 111 performances had not Carroll quarreled with his backer. The dispute revealed that the money for the show had come from a rich aunt of composer Bagby.

Pleasure Bound (2-18-29, Majestic), a Shubert revue that was almost pure vaudeville, nevertheless had a seventeen-week run. The show had begun life as a musical version of *Potash and Perlmutter* called *Well, Well, Well*. By the time it reached Broadway the plot had been jettisoned. The dutiful Harold Atteridge provided the dialogue, while a number of writers contributed the songs. One of the composers was featured in the show, the comedian-accordionist Phil Baker. Baker had a new stooge harassing him from an upper box, John Muldowney. Muldowney complained he was leg weary, not from standing, but from watching the long line of Busby Berkeley high-kickers. More clowning came from "excitable" Jack Pearl. Pearl's guttural German dialect burlesque caused the *Times* to sit back and realize that such dialect comedy had "almost vanished from the legitimate stage." The heyday of Weber and Fields, Sam Bernard, and their ilk was part of an ever more distant history. Pearl performed in various guises, appearing, for example, as a dress designer and later as an orchestra leader. Besides her Spanish dances, Pepita tip-toed across a line of band boxes. Aileen Stanley did her best to put across inconsequential music, such as a Baker and Maurice Rubens tune, "Just Suppose," with lyrics by Sid Silvers and Joe Jaffe.

A novelty, **Trois Jeunes Filles Nues,** a musical comedy from Paris given entirely in French, opened on March 4 and played 40 performances uptown at the Jolson.

Spring Is Here (3-11-29, Alvin) arrived a few days prematurely. For Owen Davis it must have seemed like his special season. First, two of his older works had been turned into musicals, then, with *Spring Is Here*, an original Owen Davis libretto was unveiled. It was not remarkably original. Davis derived the story from his own play, *Shot-Gun Wedding*, which had never reached New York. Betty Braley (Lillian Taiz) thinks she loves Stacy Haydon (John Hundley), and only when their elopement is foiled by her father does she come to understand she was meant for Terry Clayton. If she hadn't seen the light, her sister, Mary Jane (Inez Courtney), would have been happy to become Mrs. Clayton. The Rodgers and Hart score was a dandy. To 1929 audiences it may have even sounded vaguely like a Gershwin score, since the orchestra featured Gershwin's favorite duo pianists, Victor Arden and Phil Ohman. But an oddity developed during rehearsals when Glenn Hunter was cast as Terry. Though a fine actor, he had no singing voice at all. The evening's best love songs had to be shared by Betty and her losing suitor, Stacy. Rarely has a young man been given such a lovely melody as "With A Song In My Heart" and not the girl. "Baby's Awake Now" had lyrics showing Hart's cynical charm. Once again Rodgers and Hart's

willingness to be a little different probably cost them trade. The show left before the spring did, a disappointing 104 performances to its account.

Another premature title announced **Music in May** (4-1-29, Casino). It was another Shubert importation, substantially revised and with virtually a new score by Maurice Rubens. Its story told how Prince Stephan falls in love with a simple village girl, Vita. But it seems there is no way he can marry a commoner. So he hits on the ingenious scheme of first making Vita a baroness and then marrying her. The show ran ten weeks.

A black revue called **Messin' Around** (4-22-29, Hudson) advertised itself as "a musical novelty," but neither the public nor the critics found it novel—or entertaining. A thin plot line followed two comedians to a southern carnival and back to a Harlem nightclub. One of the turns featured a boxing match between two girls. The girls went at their business with abandon, clouting each other so lustily they brought down the house. However, at least two other bits also started hands clapping. One was a stunt dance performed by Bamboo McCarver on roller skates; the other a wild African strut by Cora La Redd. These bright spots weren't enough to save the evening. Richard Watts, Jr., writing in the *Herald-Tribune*, alluded to the double standard his paper had complained critics used in reviewing black shows. He noted that *Messin' Around* would have been "inexcusable if white" and therefore insisted it wasn't really any better because it was black. The revue folded after four weeks.

On the other hand theatregoers found novelty, entertainment, and no little theatrical art in April's last lyric offering, a revue known as **The Little Show** (4-30-29, Music Box). A number of names became famous with the show. The songwriting team of Arthur Schwartz and Howard Dietz came to the public's attention with this, their first joint effort.

· · ·

Howard Dietz was born in New York City on September 8, 1896. While attending Columbia at the same time as Hart and Hammerstein, he contributed light verse and comic pieces to the college publications, to Don Marquis' column, and to Franklin P. Adams' popular "The Conning Tower" in the *World*. After serving in the navy during World War I, he began a brief, but prosperous career as an advertising executive. He brought himself to Hollywood's attention when he created the roaring lion trademark for Goldwyn Pictures and in 1924 became advertising director for the young M-G-M. But his duties failed to keep him from lyric writing. He had written the lyrics for "Alibi Baby," which was interpolated into *Poppy* (9-3-23). With *Dear Sir* (9-23-24) Dietz became a full-fledged wordsmith.

. . .

Arthur Schwartz was born in Brooklyn on November 25, 1900. Though he was destined to be a lawyer and had no formal musical education, he composed songs from a very early date. While working for his bachelor's degree at New York University, he wrote several football songs. He continued his academic studies, obtaining a Master's in literature at Columbia and then taking up law. He was admitted to the bar in 1924. His law practice was still active and successful when his first songs were heard in small downtown revues.

. . .

Schwartz and Dietz' best number in *The Little Show* was "I Guess I'll Have To Change My Plan." Schwartz had originally written the melody to early Lorenz Hart lyrics and entitled the tune "I Love To Lie Awake In Bed." Even with Dietz' superior lines, the song was not an immediate hit. It only became popular and entered the standard repertory when it was brought back from England several years after the show had closed. The songs that appealed most to the patrons were not by Schwartz, and only one had Dietz lyrics. "Can't We Be Friends?" was written by the New York banker James Warburg, under the name Paul James, and his wife Kay Swift. And a stunning applause-getter "Moanin' Low" had music by Ralph Rainger. The show also made stars of Clifton Webb, Libby Holman, and Fred Allen. The debonair Webb had been prominent in musicals for over a decade but had never until *The Little Show* secured a firm hold on the top rung of the profession.

. . .

Clifton Webb was born in Indianapolis, Indiana, on November 9, 1896, and christened Webb Parmalee Hollenbeck. While still an infant his stage-struck, domineering mother took him to New York and saw to it he made his debut at the age of three in *The Brownies*. He was enrolled in dancing school and at seven in Malcolm Douglas' Children's Theatre. In his early teens Webb's interests grew more elevated. Art lessons led to a one-man show of his paintings in 1914, while instruction with Victor Maurel earned him roles in provincial grand opera. His first legitimate roles were small parts in *The Purple Road* (4-7-13) and *See America First* (3-28-16). Within a few years he was prominently featured in such musicals as *Listen, Lester!* (12-23-18) and *Sunny* (9-21-25). Tall, slim, dapper, and suave, Webb was often mistaken for an Englishman.

. . .

Miss Holman's rise was far more meteoric, starting with *Merry-Go-Round* (5-31-27), and including two flops in the current season. Fred Allen, like Webb, had been around a while but without ever achieving prominence. His stardom in the revue came practically out of nowhere. Ably assisting were such fine talents as Romney Brent, Bettina Hall, and Portland Hoffa (Mrs. Allen). Webb introduced "I Guess I'll Have To Change My Plan." Miss Holman sang "Can't We Be Friends?" while the two combined for a roughhouse staging of "Moanin' Low." The best of the sketches was a George S. Kaufman gem. "The Still Alarm" found two men (Romney Brent and Clifton Webb) in a burning hotel calmly debating what is the proper dress to wear on a fire escape. The firemen (Fred Allen and Harold Moffet) arrive. They are deferential and as unconcerned as the guests. One fire-fighter has even brought his violin (he never gets a chance to practice at home). In the end, "The Second Fireman takes Center of stage, with all the manner of a concert violinist. He goes into 'Keep The Home Fires Burning.' Bob, Ed [the two guests], and First Fireman wipe brow as curtain falls slowly." Nonsense of this sort, beautifully done, kept the show running for ten months.

The Grand Street Follies (5-1-29, Booth), one of the very series that prompted intimate revues such as *The Little Show*, brought in a final edition the evening after *The Little Show*'s premiere. The faithful regulars were on stage again. Albert Carroll impersonated Harpo Marx, Bea Lillie, Constance Collier, and the first Queen Elizabeth, while Dorothy Sands appeared as Lenore Ulric and Irene Bordoni. The sketches mixed history and show business. The siege of Troy was restaged as Belasco might have done it; the Marx Brothers landed on Plymouth Rock; and Paul Revere's ride was chronicled by the sassy, irreverent reporters from *The Front Page*. Arthur Schwartz had more songs ready to contribute to the score. But Schwartz' best efforts were being played in *The Little Show* at the Music Box across the street, and the old stand-by performers had worn out their material and, perhaps, their welcome. The *Sun* observed that, while the

450

evening often "brightened in anticipation," the hopes were never fulfilled. Substantial revisions in July failed to turn the corner.

Pansy (5-14-29, Belmont), a Negro collegiate musical, could manage only 3 performances at the tiny Belmont theatre, though blues singer Bessie Smith, famous but not yet legendary, made an appearance as herself. The college setting was almost incidental; what skimpy plot there was related how Pansy Green (Pearl McCormack) won the hand of Bob (Billy Andrews), though her father Ulysses Grant Green (Speedy Wilson) preferred she marry Bill (Alfred Chester), the "Proposition Kid." *Pansy*'s composer, Maceo Pinkard, had not been heard from with a full score since *Liza* (11-27-22). He got his score played this time by producing the show on his own. But the normally kind Brooks Atkinson branded it "the worst show of all time." Several critics recorded that the audience hissed the performers.

To close the season, the Shuberts brought the last of their "A Night in" series, **A Night in Venice** (5-21-29, Shubert). Ted Healy led the comedians, even wrestling a trained bear for laughs. Two acrobatic sailors did somersaults, and a xylophone ensemble made tinkly music. One more contingent of Chester Hale Girls competed with sixteen Allen K. Forster Girls. Tableaux whisked audiences to a moonlight Paris and a snow-covered Venice. The score was mostly by Maurice Rubens, though several others chipped in. Vincent Youmans salvaged "The One Girl" from *Rainbow*, but it still failed to click. Shubert's know-how rather than any overriding merit kept the show's not too demanding customers pleased into the fall.

Scene Two
DEPRESSION AND "TALKIES"— BROADWAY'S ANSWER
1929-1937

1929-1930

The onslaught of film musicals jolted Broadway, and the October stock market crash gave the American Musical Theater a further blow. The musical stage recovered, but it was never the same. The wildly extroverted jazz and florid romance of the twenties gave way to both the subdued, introspective material and strident muckraking of the early thirties. The great annuals were dead, though a few straggling editions come forth at irregular intervals. Viennese-American operetta was also gone. True, Noel Coward's superb *Bitter Sweet* had its American premiere in this season, but it failed to find a large public. On the other hand, in a seeming effort to cling to the past a rash of revivals were mounted with surprising success. In the midst of such change and uncertainty enough momentum and enough talent remained on Broadway to allow this great act to continue. But in theatrical terms the 1929–30 season represents the lowering of the curtain or of the lights to effect a scene change. The remainder of the act was played in a different setting.

For the second year in a row the number of new musicals dropped precipitously, to thirty-two —the lowest figure in eleven seasons. And nine of these came in the summer, before the main season had gotten under way. A Negro night club revue, revised for Broadway, opened the season. **Hot Chocolates** (6-20-29, Hudson) was principally by Andy Razaf and "Fats" Waller. The two had come to Broadway's attention two years before with their work for *Keep Shufflin'* (2-27-28). Their material for their new offering was even better, including, as it did, the enduring "Ain't Misbehavin'." The plaintive undertones of the song hint at the stylings of much of the music that would come out of Broadway for the next few years. A young orchestra member was Louis Armstrong, who was called from the pit to present a trumpet solo. For Armstrong it was the beginning of forty years at the top of his profession. Skits made fun of traffic in Harlem, photographing a prizefighter, and an animal wedding. Young ladies of the chorus were listed in the program as "Hot Chocolate Drops" and chorus boys as "Bon Bon Buddies," suggesting that either the verse to the Black Bottom had given currency to some new expressions or that both shows were recording fashionable clichés of the day. *Hot Chocolate* caught on quickly and ran over six months.

Two flops followed. Will Morrissey and Jimmy Duffy were largely responsible for a revue called **Keep It Clean** (6-24-29, Selwyn). They wrote much of it, were the featured players, and Morrissey helped stage it. He also opened the show walking on stage in a battered top hat and launching into a long monologue filled with backstage references understood only by the initiated. Duffy offered an off-color song about the Lindbergh-Morrow marriage. Their helpers included Midge Miller, giving an impersonation of Bea Lillie, and Douglas Stanbury, solemnly singing of "Marching Home." Such efforts earned them only 16 performances.

A Negro book musical, **Bamboola** (6-26-29, Royale), told of the attempts to take a home-grown show to New York. Dancing was the highlight of the show, as it was for most black musicals. A salute to Bill Robinson found twenty of the show's top hoofers mimicking Robinson's famous routine tapping his way up and down a staircase. The evening's funniest sketch portrayed a Harlem rent party. Rigidly preconceived notions of what a black entertainment should be inevitably led one critic or another to see unwarranted attempts to imitate white musicals. The *Evening Journal* reflected the continuing insistence of most New York reviewers that black revues should be distinctively black in their vitality, tackiness, and naiveté. The paper proclaimed, "the Negro IS funny. He's very funny when he's allowed to be funny in his own way." This band of Negroes had their own way for a mere four weeks.

The season's biggest musical hit was **Earl Carroll's Sketch Book** (7-1-29, Earl Carroll).

There was no edition of the *Vanities* this season, but a number of critics suggested the *Sketch Book* was merely the *Vanities* by another name. Having taken Leon Errol and Fanny Brice away from Ziegfeld for *Fioretta*, Carroll advertised noisily that Eddie Cantor was now in his corner. And Cantor did contribute some sketches. But anyone coming to see Cantor saw only a brief, sound film in which Cantor and Carroll dickered over Cantor's price. Since Ziegfeld gave Cantor a gold watch, Carroll gives him a grandfather clock. Performers in the flesh were led by Will Mahoney, with William Demarest and Patsy Kelly assisting. The funniest skit of the evening had Miss Kelly trying to take a bath while her bathroom suddenly has more traffic than Times Square. How many in the audience remembered Charlotte Greenwood's taking "Her Morning Bath" in *The Ritz Revue* (9-17-24)? Movies were not the only technical device used. The show opened with a partly raised curtain revealing a line of beautiful "Legs, Legs, Legs," but when the curtain was fully raised it was shown the legs were merely the legs of phonographs. Jay Gorney did much of the score, with E.Y. Harburg writing the lyrics. Billy Rose, Harry and Charles Tobias, Benny Davis, Ted Snyder, and Vincent Rose all lent a hand without creating any long-lasting melodies. On the strength of its comedy and its production numbers the show ran fifty weeks.

Ziegfeld was less successful, though he assembled a magnificent line-up for **Show Girl** (7-2-29, Ziegfeld). He had William Anthony McGuire adapt J. P. McEvoy's novel and hired George Gershwin to set it to music. His cast featured Ruby Keeler in the lead; Clayton, Jackson, and Durante; Eddie Foy, Jr.; Harriet Hoctor; and, playing the music, Duke Ellington. *Show Girl* was, in a way, a jazzy version of *Sally* (12-21-20). Like *Sally* it followed a pretty unknown in her climb to Ziegfeld stardom. In keeping with its jazzier tone, Dixie Dugan was a harder, pushier young lady. But she makes it. Eddie Foy, Jr., was a salesman whose cigarette lighter kept exploding and whose gifts triggered alarms when they were opened. Jimmy Durante played a property man. He supplied his own songs, probably much to Gershwin's relief, since Ziegfeld had given Gershwin only two weeks to write a score. Ira Gershwin was also relieved when Ziegfeld asked if he would allow Gus Kahn to aid with the lyrics. The two-week deadline was no more attractive to Ira than to George. But the best lyrics were unmistakably Ira's. The incorrigible, wide-eyed hypocrisy of a young-lady-about-town is unerringly and hilariously captured in "I Must Be Home By Twelve O'Clock." At 3 a.m. she is still protesting she must be home by midnight. But the hit that has so long outlived the show was "Liza." Written for a second-act minstrel number with "one hundred beautiful girls seated on steps that cover the entire stage," it was to be led by Ruby Keeler. In one of the Broadway's most famous incidents, Al Jolson appeared on several nights singing the song from the audience to calm Miss Keeler, who had just become Mrs. Jolson. The show also included a sumptuously mounted and blazingly choreographed ballet by Albertina Rasch to music from Gershwin's "An American In Paris." But for all its attractions the show seemed heavy and slow. Miss Keeler left before *Show Girl* ran its course of 111 performances.

Busby Berkeley helped stage **Broadway Nights** (7-15-29, 44th St.), a revue that included Dr. Rockwell, Laura Lee, and Odette Myrtil in its cast. Rockwell delivered a hilarious lecture in which he proved to his own satisfaction that popcorn causes dandruff. Maurice Rubens did most of the score (his last major appearance on New York programs), and old Edgar Smith devised most of the sketches. King, King and King offered some hot tap-dancing. Chorus girls danced through a routine bouncing rubber balls. When they finished they hurled the balls out into the auditorium. Later they assembled to form a train, prompting the *Times* to hail the "Big Railroad Year" in musicals. Not all the music was by Rubens—Johann Strauss and Rimsky-Korsakov provided backgrounds for ballets. But the material couldn't strike a responsive chord in theatregoers. Five weeks and it was gone.

A month went by before another musical—another revue—arrived. It, too, had an imposing array of talent and failed. **Murray Anderson's Almanac** (8-14-29, Erlanger)—Anderson had dropped the John from his name, at least as far as this title was concerned—had sketches by Noel Coward, Rube Goldberg, and Peter Arno, among others. Its songs were by Milton Ager and Henry Sullivan. The evening used the frame-device of thumbing through a magazine to survey the past, present, and future. Young Jimmy Savo and no-longer young Trixie Friganza were starred. Reginald Marsh created the show curtain. But something went wrong. Oscar Wilde's "The Young King" performed as a ballet ballad of the sort Anderson had used in the *Greenwich Village Follies* went largely unapplauded. Skits that made

fun of everything from Whistler's mother to the latest talking pictures weren't sufficiently amusing, and most of the score was no more than serviceable. The sole surviving melody, sung strangely enough as a spoof of sentimental duets by the two stars, was "I May Be Wrong."

A Noble Rogue (8-19-29, Gansevoort), a one-week disaster, was an operetta describing the romance of a New Orleans belle, Virginia Mulford (Marguerite Zender), and the dashing buccaneer, Jean Lafitte (Robert Rhodes). Performed at a small Greenwich Village theatre, the musical was lambasted as "stupefying" and "deadening"—a work devoid of flair, wit, or melody.

Flair, wit, and melody were abundantly evident in Broadway's next lyric entry. Oscar Hammerstein II and Jerome Kern combined to write "a musical romance of the gay nineties," centering their story on a role built for Helen Morgan. (Kern and Hammerstein even indulged in private jokes with Miss Morgan, naming one character after her mother.) They called their show **Sweet Adeline** (9-3-29, Hammerstein). The title, of course, harked back to a song and a singer of the turn of the century. But the musical's Addie Schmidt was no great opera star. She sang her songs in her father's Hoboken beer garden in the days of the Spanish-American War. Hers is an unhappy life. She loves Tom Martin (Max Hoffman, Jr.), but loses him to her sister, Nellie (Caryl Bergman). She leaves Hoboken, and starts her rise to Broadway stardom in a Bowery theatre. Her climb is helped by James Day (Robert Chisholm), and, in time, she falls in love with him. Comedy relief was provided by Charles Butterworth in the role of Ruppert Day, a hick drama-lover. His outlandish awe at the rehearsal of a cheap burlesque show became the hilarious highlight of the performance. The Kern score was not as rich, diversified, or hit-filled as *Show Boat*, but it was unfailingly lovely. It included one remarkable concerted number for the principal men, "A Girl Is On Your Mind," that used blues colorings for its languid soliloquies.

If the score had a fault it may be that the songs assigned to Miss Morgan all dwelled on the same poignant note of hope and despair. But she made hits of them, especially, "Why Was I Born?" This song and another tearful ballad, "Here Am I," were ever after identified with her; in the show she also sang " 'Twas Not So Long Ago" (reprised by the chorus at the end of the show) and "Don't Ever Leave Me." In a novel departure, Kern's songs were not played in the overture. Instead, to create some period verisimilitude, the overture consisted of a medley of songs from the 1890s. To speed the action within the play itself, no encores were allowed. *Sweet Adeline* was presented by Arthur Hammerstein and staged by Reginald at their family theatre. It immediately began playing to standees. At first it seemed as if it would run as long as *Show Boat*, but the stock market crash brought a sickening halt to its ticket sales, and by April it was gone. All shows were hurt by the slump, but brainlessly cheery affairs like *Earl Carroll's Sketch Book* seemed a little less damaged than pieces with serious pretensions such as *Sweet Adeline* or *Bitter Sweet*.

Kern granted an interview to the *Times* shortly after *Sweet Adeline* opened. The interview was largely a paean of praise for Oscar Hammerstein, whom the composer hailed as the "ideal collaborator." Kern was especially delighted with what he saw as Hammerstein's daring and realism. He mentioned especially a drunk scene written for Miss Morgan, noting it was not one of the era's overdone comic bits but a serious attempt to portray an unfortunate weakness in a heroine. Years later Richard Rodgers was to applaud the same virtues in Hammerstein. How curious and revealing that two of the American Musical Theatre's greatest composers—two men who had worked with brilliantly literate and witty lyricists —clearly preferred their more solemn, sentimental associate.

Like *Show Girl* and *Sweet Adeline*, **The Street Singer** (9-17-29, Shubert) recorded the rise of a young lady to stardom. But not in a Ziegfeld show or even an ordinary Broadway musical. Set in Paris, it recorded how suave, rich George (Guy Robertson) helps an attractive flower girl (Queenie Smith) to become a shining light of the Folies Bergère. He almost loses her in the process, but they end happily in each other's arms. The music and lyrics were by a number of minor figures, but all of it was pleasant, if determinedly backward-glancing. It had all the standard types of the better, second-string twenties shows: for example a rippling waltz in "You Might Have Known I Loved You" and a lively dance creation in "Jumping Jimminy." Because Busby Berkeley was co-producer (with the Shuberts), the mounting was assured of fine dancing. Yet, oddly enough, Berkeley and Miss Smith, both proponents of flashy tapping, scored the evening's biggest hit with a charming ballet set in the Folies' greenroom. No doubt most theatregoers were unaware Miss Smith began her career as a ballerina at the

Metropolitan Opera. *The Street Singer* helped keep troubled minds diverted for six months, but nothing from it was strong enough to survive.

A revue originally put together at the Cape Cod Playhouse and appropriately called **The Cape Cod Follies** (9-18-29, Bijou) arrived fresh from its summer success. The New Englanders sang hymns to hooked rugs, cranberries, and Puritans (they insisted the Puritans really landed at Cape Cod). They also offered Broadway's umpteenth travesty of Eugene O'Neill. Peter Joray won the highest commendations for his impersonation of Queen Victoria, while six Cape Cod Belles elicited somewhat quieter applause with their tap dancing. The revue looked a lot less fresh far from home, so it packed its bags and headed back north after 30 performances.

The Shuberts decided to revive Victor Herbert's *Sweethearts*. It was a decision stemming from their need to occupy the Jolson Theatre for a few weeks. But the reception was so overwhelming that before the theatrical year was through they had revived *Mlle. Modiste, Naughty Marietta, The Fortune Teller, Robin Hood, The Merry Widow, Babes in Toyland, The Prince of Pilsen, The Chocolate Soldier, The Count of Luxembourg,* and *The Serenade.* Fritzi Scheff sang *Mlle. Modiste*, while Tessa Kosta, Olga Steck, Ilse Marvenga, Al Shean, and Greek Evans appeared in one or more mountings. The eleven shows kept the Jolson lit for seven months.

George White's Scandals of 1929 (9-23-29, Apollo) was the only one of the major old annuals to make an appearance during the year. It wasn't very good. White himself wrote some of the songs as well as creating some of the sketches and dancing in the show. Cliff Friend and Irving Caesar helped with the songs. Besides White the cast included Eugene and Willie Howard and Frances Williams. The show opened with a number honoring the dancers and dances of the earlier *Scandals,* culminating in a rousing Black Bottom. Later on the Abbott Specialty Dancers did some fancy stepping and Marietta did a contortion dance. In the comedy routines Willie Howard was driven to mayhem by a radio that talked back to him. Spectacles included a "Parade of All Nations" and a finale set at the Café Lido in Paris, which allowed the chorus girls and other members of the cast to disappear into a tank not unlike the one the old Hippodrome once boasted. There were enough loyal fans to keep the show at the Apollo for twenty weeks, but when the show departed it left nothing permanent behind.

Vincent Youmans had made his name with bright, contemporary musical comedies. Now, for the second time in a row, he met failure with a rough, romantic bit of old Americana. Youmans produced the show himself, thereby aggravating his loss. **Great Day** (10-17-29, Cosmopolitan) was set in the ever popular New Orleans of long ago. The Randolph Plantation is located just outside the town. Pretty Emma Lou Randolph (Mayo Methot) is forced to sell it to the shifty Carlos Zarega (John Haynes). Her circumstances are so reduced that she is forced to go to work for Zarega. But a young engineer, Jim Brent (Allan Prior), comes along, disposes of Zarega by hurling him into the river, and restores the old homestead to Emma Lou, who consents to become Mrs. Brent. The story was a little looser and less well wrought than *Rainbow* (11-21-28). Its looseness allowed Miller and Lyles to caper through some of comedy bits and Walter C. Kelly, famous for his judge role in vaudeville, to play a not too dissimilar judge here. But if William Cary Duncan and John Wells were not as adept as Stallings and Hammerstein had been in *Rainbow,* Youmans was in top form. Three of his finest numbers survived the grueling four-month tryout: Emma Lou's "More Than You Know," "Without A Song," and "Great Day"—the last two sung by Lijah (baritone Lois Deppe) and the plantation hands. But all the hirings and firings that Youmans as producer resorted to during the out-of-town ordeal could not shape the musical into something salable. Moreover, twelve days after the show opened the economic world collapsed. *Great Day* folded after just 36 performances.

Delighted with the success of their Jolson Theatre revivals, the Shuberts brought an elaborate version of *Die Fledermaus* to town. They called this revival **A Wonderful Night** (10-31-29, Majestic) and brought it in two days after the Wall Street crash. The show had been done in 1912 as *The Merry Countess* and would be done again under different titles in the 1930s and 1940s. The part of Max was played by Archie Leach, who later changed his name to Cary Grant. An indestructible perennial, the show racked up 125 performances.

The finest, most cohesive work of the season, Noel Coward's **Bitter Sweet** (11-5-29, Ziegfeld), was given a typically thorough and elaborate Ziegfeld mounting. In Coward's flashback tale a grandmother recalls her own marriage for love to help her granddaughter decide which young man to marry. The great English favorite Evelyn Laye (star of the original London productions of *Mary* and *The New Moon*) helped acquaint Americans with one of Coward's masterpieces, "I'll See You Again." But the times were against *Bitter Sweet*, and its New York run of twenty weeks fell far short of its earlier London success.

Six nights later, Rodgers and Hart, assisted by John McGowan and Paul Gerard Smith on the book, saw their **Heads Up** (11-11-29, Alvin) begin a modest run of 144 showings. The musical had originally been called *Me for You* and had sported a libretto by Owen Davis, in which the heroine threw over a district attorney to marry a law-breaker and in which Victor Moore played a not very comic villain. Such unpleasant changes were too much for tryout audiences. Perhaps Rodgers and Hart also recalled the bad luck that pursued the Gershwins when they gave Gertrude Lawrence a nasty disposition in *Treasure Girl* (11-8-28). Using the same cast and scenery, the new story had fun with rum-running. Since Victor Moore was the principal fun-maker, a number of theatregoers found themselves recalling Moore and a similar plot in another Gershwin–Lawrence opus, *Oh, Kay* (11-8-26). Lieutenant Jack Mason (Jack Whiting) of the Coast Guard is convinced Mrs. Trumbell's yacht, *Silver Lady*, is rum-running. He's right; but Mrs. Trumbell (Janet Velie) is innocent. Her own captain (Robert Gleckler) is doing it on the side, without her consent. The captain burns the yacht rather than let its telltale cargo fall into government hands. But Jack is not left empty-handed. He wins Mrs. Trumbell's daughter, Mary (Barbara Newberry). Rodgers, like Kern, was virtually incapable of writing a bad score, but *Heads Up* contributed little to the standard Rodgers cannon. Though a number of singers and musicians have singled out "A Ship Without A Sail" for praise, only "Why Do You Suppose" still enjoys something approaching popularity.

While the public began to allow more masterful, serious pieces to languish, it still embraced good, lighthearted musical comedies. Two of them came in during the last week of November. The first, **Sons o' Guns** (11-26-29, Imperial), imposed a slight handicap on itself by taking up a war theme. But it did so with such a frivolous, devil-may-care pose that no one minded. Its story was slightly reminiscent of one of the most popular musical hits of "the great war," *The Better 'Ole* (10-19-18). Playboy Jimmy Canfield (Jack Donahue) finds himself in the army, with his former valet, Hobson (William Frawley), as his top sergeant. Things go from bad to worse for the bumbling Jim, culminating with his arrest for spying. But Jimmy escapes, bumbles into some heroic acts and wins a pretty French miss, Yvonne (Lily Damita). Miss Damita, who had made her name in Hollywood, surprised Broadway with her talent and vitality. No one was surprised by Donahue's likable human comedy or, even more, by his supple "ankle and knee gyrations." Albertina Rasch girls provided ballet-like chorus numbers. A particularly attractive feature of the evening was Joseph Urban's magnificent scenery, re-creating a huge Arc de Triomphe, a French village, and a red, white, and blue victory ball. The score was the last Broadway offering for another of the better, second-level composers of the day, J. Fred Coots. Coots' top numbers in *Sons o' Guns* were "Why?" and "Cross Your Fingers." A run of 295 performances gave *Sons o' Guns* the third longest stay of any 1929–30 musical.

Fifty Million Frenchmen (11-27-29, Lyric) was almost as popular. Like *Sons o' Guns,* it had a playboy for its central figure. And, like that show, it was set in France. Only this time the setting was gay, up-to-the-minute Paris. The impetuous Peter Forbes (William Gaxton) falls in love with Looloo Carroll (Genevieve Tobin) on first sight. He bets his friend Michael Cummins (Jack Thompson) $25,000 that he can win Looloo without flaunting his money. Taking a job as a guide he pursues his new heart-throb and wins her away from the Grand Duke Ivan Ivanovitch of Russia (Mannart Kippen), whom Looloo's social-climbing parents had slated for her. His performance as Peter sealed Gaxton's reputation and established him as a top impersonator of suave, but tough-fibered leading men.

. . .

William Gaxton was born in San Francisco on December 2, 1893. His Italian parents named him Arturo Gaxiola. A stint at Boone's Military Academy instilled in him the manly bearing he brought to all his roles. After furthering his education at the University of California he entered vaudeville, first in a song-and-patter act with Anna Laughlin and subsequently as a single in a skit called "A Regular Business Man." He appeared briefly in the *Music Box Revue* in 1922, then took to the road in *Betty Lee, All for You,* and *Miss Happiness.* His first important Broadway appearance was as Martin in the 1927 hit, *A Connecticut Yankee* (11-3-27).

. . .

In supporting roles, Evelyn Hoey, as May

De Vere, brought down the house singing "Find Me A Primitive Man"; Helen Broderick was an American tourist, Violet Hildegarde, buying copies of James Joyce's *Ulysses* to send home to the kids; while Thurston Hall, who had played romantic leads in musicals like *The Only Girl* (11-2-14), was now old enough to asume the minor role of Looloo's father. The show boasted impressive sets by Norman Bel Geddes. They turned out to be too large to fit on the stage, so the show's out-of-town opening had to be delayed while they were cut down to size. Even in reduced versions Bell Geddes' Ritz Bar, American Express Office, and Eiffel Tower were stunners. The show's dances included one more number done all in black and white. Best of all, the show had a good Cole Porter score, coupled with some of his most brilliant lyrics. Since refrains had to be simple his best lines were often in the verse; one rhymes sacrifices, Isis, and vices, while a second joined day, play, straight away, and croupier. Besides Peter's "I Worship You" and May's "I'm Unlucky At Gambling," from which these excerpts are taken, the Porter flair was evident in "Where Would You Get Your Coat?," and "Tale Of An Oyster" (both sung by Violet). But the public, however much it laughed at Porter's wit in the theatre, went out into the night singing "You've Got That Thing" sung by Michael and Joyce (Betty Compton) and Peter and Looloo's "You Do Something To Me." For all the evening's attractions the critics were not overwhelmed. Irving Berlin, who was originally to have produced the show, took out a large ad praising it. In a short time word of mouth built the piece into a hit.

A musical that no word of mouth could save opened the same night. **The Silver Swan** (11-27-29, Martin Beck) told of Capt. Richard Von Orten's switch in allegiance from Hortense (Alice MacKenzie), leading lady at the opera, to Gabrielle (Vivian Hart), a new bit player. Not even the machinations of Princess Von Auen (Lina Abarbanell) can win Van Orten (Edward Nell, Jr.) away afterwards. The score was dreary, and not even another old-time star, Miss Abarbanell in the relatively minor role of the Princess, could breathe life into the piece.

Top Speed (12-25-29, 46th St.) arrived a season or so too late. Its tale of flashy, carefree high life was the sort the twenties adored. But with the stock market crash just two months old the show was not a very welcome Christmas present. At a posh resort in the Thousand Islands two impecunious broker's clerks, Gerry Brooks (Paul Frawley) and Elmer Peters (Lester Allen), pose as millionaires to court two very rich young ladies, Babs Green and Virginia Rollins (Irene Delroy). When Gerry is caught fishing at the fish hatchery they are almost exposed. By the time the truth does come out, love makes everyone indifferent. The show was written and produced by Guy Bolton, Bert Kalmar, and Harry Ruby. Not only were they ill-timed, they were none in top form. Indeed the best form of the evening seems to have been displayed by the exuberant girl who stole the show as Babs, Ginger Rogers. *Top Speed*'s dancers clearly took heed of the show's title. The *World* recorded that the "chorus beats out its rhythms in an increasing crescendo of high spirits." Two or three years earlier such snappiness would have probably been rewarded by a run of more than thirteen weeks.

The same night **Woof, Woof** (12-25-29, Royale) came in to begin a six-week stay. It was another retelling of the season's favorite plot: a poor girl's rise to stardom. This time the ending was not unlike *Merry, Merry* (9-24-25). Susie Yates (Louise Brown) has her chance for the big time if she will become the mistress of the popular band leader, Tommy Clair (Jack Squires). With fame and fortune so close at hand, she has second thoughts. She decides she prefers the small time with loving Monty Fleming (Al Sexton), a dancer. Their future is made easier when they win big on a dog race. Even Leonide Massine's staging— which included two whippets racing on a treadmill —failed to interest most playgoers.

More Cole Porter music, including his evergreen "What Is This Thing Called Love?" (sung by Frances Shelley and danced by Tilly Losch and others), was heard in an English revue, **Wake Up and Dream** (12-30-29, Selwyn). An attractive cast including European favorites Jack Buchanan, Jessie Matthews, and Miss Losch brought in ticket buyers for eighteen weeks.

The season's most innovative musical, **Strike Up the Band,** opened at the Times Square on January 14, 1930—the first musical of the new year and, more significantly, the first of the thirties. The Gershwins and George S. Kaufman had originally written it and watched it die during a 1927 Philadelphia tryout. At that time it was an uncompromising satire on war, big business, and international politics. It was the very sort of thing Gilbert and Sullivan might have contrived had they been children of the jazz age. In the original version the Swiss protest an American tariff on

their cheese. An American cheese manufacturer, Horace J. Fletcher, suggests the United States go to war over the matter. He will finance the battle so long as it goes down in the history books as the Horace J. Fletcher Memorial War. However, when his daughter's fiancé, Jim Townsend, threatens to expose Fletcher's use of Grade B milk in his products, Fletcher does an abrupt about-face, becoming an ardent pacifist. Unfortunately, his change of heart comes too late; the war fever is uncontrollable. After Fletcher is discovered wearing a Swiss watch, he himself comes under suspicion. The war delights everyone, including Swiss hotel owners who house idle American troops at inflated rates. The conflict ends when secret Swiss yodeling signals are decoded. But the war has been such fun that when a tariff is imposed on caviar, the U.S. and Russia gaily prepare to fight matters out. This first *Strike Up the Band* met with a refreshingly enthusiastic critical reception, but the public refused to respond. It preferred the farcical fripperies and pseudo-serious romance of the twenties' lyric stage. But in the troubled world of 1930 there seemed some hope that the musical's biting edge might prove tonic, especially if the worst of the bite were removed.

For the new version, Morrie Ryskind revised and softened the original book. The story became a dream, from which Fletcher awakes thoroughly reformed. Even the basic Swiss cheese was changed to more frivolous Swiss chocolate. George Gershwin's score introduced a number of songs that quickly became standards: "Soon," "Strike Up The Band," and "I've Got A Crush On You." "Strike Up The Band," the first-act finale, was sung by Townsend and the company.

Some of the best material was in comic numbers such as "A Typical Self-Made American," in which Colonel Holmes (patterned after Colonel House of the Wilson administration) tells how he got to the top. Ira's American counterpart to Sir Joseph Porter boasts, "I made mother my ideal, and never watched the clock." In its pertinence and impertinence; in its willingness to face important social issues *Strike Up the Band* broadcast a new era in stage musicals. And though its score had the electric drive and energy of all Gershwin compositions it broke with the elementary staccato rhythms that had pervaded the preceding decade. Considering its daring and the bad times, its six-month run was acceptable. There are two interesting sidelights to the show. George had tried to use "The Man I Love" in the score. The song was to him what "Bill" had been to Kern. But

Gershwin was never to find the right show for it as Kern did for his song. Bobby Clark played Colonel Holmes to Dudley Clements' Fletcher. Paul McCullough clowned as Holmes' sidekick Gideon, while Margaret Schilling and Jerry Goff handled the romantic leads. And the sad parade of passing luminaries continued. The once popular star Blanche Ring had a small part.

If *Strike Up the Band* provided a glimpse of the American Musical Theatre to come, the next two offerings gave Broadway a chance to reflect on long-gone glories. Mitzi, about to write "finis" to her career, returned briefly in a revival of the show that had made her a star sixteen years before, *Sari* (1-13-14). An even more popular and beloved figure of this earlier era followed in Mitzi's footsteps. Fred Stone was sufficiently recovered from the effects of an air crash to return to Broadway. Along with his wife (now listed simply as Mrs. Fred Stone) and his daughter, Dorothy, he introduced for public approval another daughter, Paula. For years Stone's shows had been reigning hits of the seasons in which they were produced, and if by some chance they turned out not to be the number-one hit, they were invariably close to it. Now Stone was to suffer a Broadway affliction he had never been bothered by, failure. In **Ripples** (2-11-30, New Amsterdam) Stone played Rip Van Winkle, the great-great-grandson of the original. Stone, for all his age and injuries, made another of his dramatic, acrobatic entrances flying through a barn door (horses' hoof prints on his coattails) and landing in a tulip bed. Rip is the town ne'er-do-well, a liar and a drunk. When he wakes from a drunken binge he finds himself surrounded by dwarfs. They turn out to be bootleggers, running from a comic state policeman, Corporal Jack Sterling (Eddie Foy, Jr.). Rip hopes his daughter, Ripples (Dorothy Stone), will marry Jack; but Ripples prefers rich Richard Willoughby (Charles Collins) and lands him. Charles Dillingham was once again Stone's producer; but he enlisted the support of a new roster of writers: William Anthony McGuire for the book, Irving Caesar and John Graham for the lyrics, and Oscar Levant and Albert Sirmay for the music. Caesar revived "I'm A Little Bit Fonder Of You" from *Yes, Yes Yvette*. Jerome Kern and Fred Coots each interpolated a song, as did the newly celebrated team of Arthur Schwartz and Howard Dietz. With John Tiller dead, his assistant Mary Read trained a new group of Mary Read Tiller girls to dance in unison and counterpoint. But neither the star, his writers, nor his supporting cast

could recapture the elusive magic that had served Stone for so long. The show left after a disheartening seven weeks.

Another flop opened the same night, the **9:15 Revue** (2-11-30, Cohan). It lasted only one week. Though it had songs by the Gershwins, Rudolf Friml, Vincent Youmans, and Roger Wolfe Kahn, its most attractive numbers were by relative newcomers. The Harburgs, writing as Paul James and Kay Swift, offered "Up Among The Chimney Pots," while Ted Koehler set words to Harold Arlen's music and came up with a tune that remains popular long after the evening has been forgotten, "Get Happy." The song was introduced in the first-act finale by Ruth Etting. A Victor Herbert waltz, "The World Of Dreams" was danced in a Degas-like setting. For comedy Anita Loos wrote a modern-day version of *East Lynn*, while Paul Gerard Smith drew a picture of a Chicago gangster very much not the boss in his own home. And for variety the popular magician Fred Keating entertained with his deceptions. When the show closed abruptly, most of the performers found themselves out of work with little prospect of new employment. But Ruth Etting, lucky for once in her unhappy life, found herself hustled into the very next musical to reach Broadway.

Since Ziegfeld employed more experienced or dependable hands for this Ed Wynn vehicle, **Simple Simon** (2-18-30, Ziegfeld), the results were happier than those Dillingham had produced for Stone. Wynn and Guy Bolton tailored the book to the comedian's special talents, while Rodgers and Hart created the songs. Joseph Urban's magnificent sets took everyone from Coney Island to King Cole's Palace and even up to the clouds. Oddly the book employed the very sort of story Stone had always done so well. Simon is a newspaper vendor who refuses to read the bad news of the day. He spends his time on fairy tales. When he's not reading them, he dreams about them—of course with himself figuring prominently in their stories. Brandishing a sword as big as himself, Simon rescues Cinderella. He wheels around making music on a piano built onto a bicycle. Lost with a picnic basket in a lovely Urban forest, he exults, "I love the woodth! Ah, how I love the woodth!" He loves them even after a giant frog appears (a frog played by contortionist William J. Ferry). Wynn and the frog share the picnic. No Wynn opus was complete without his absurd inventions. In *Simple Simon* he brought forth a mousetrap with no entrance so the poor little mice couldn't be hurt. Ziegfeld played havoc with the score. He cavalierly discarded "Dancing On The Ceiling" during the tryout, though it would have allowed him an imaginative production number. "Send For Me," rewritten from *Chee-Chee*'s "I Must Love You," was the show's most popular ballad. But it was Ruth Etting's singing of "Ten Cents A Dance" that proved the musical highlight of the show. In gratitude Ziegfeld revived "Love Me Or Leave Me," the song Miss Etting had sung in his *Whoopee* (12-2-28), and inserted it in the show though it impinged on Rodgers and Hart's material.

The International Revue (2-25-30, Majestic) cost over $200,000 to mount, a high figure at the time, and offered a seemingly irresistible line-up of talents. The cast included Gertrude Lawrence, Harry Richman, Jack Pearl, Anton Dolin, and the much-publicized dancer, Argentinita. The Spanish lady bombed so badly she was out of the cast after the first week. The songs were by Dorothy Fields and Jimmy McHugh. It was a melodic match for their fine work in *The Blackbirds* two seasons before. The best tunes from the striking score were "Exactly Like You" and "On The Sunny Side Of The Street" (both introduced by Richman). Lew Leslie, the show's producer, gave the show a lavish if not particularly tasteful mounting. An elaborate Montmartre set served as a background for a "Russianized" apache dance. The dance began when its heroine jumped from a second-story window to escape her violent lover. Not only people, but a dog, a donkey, and a goat crowded the scene. Reviews of the show were devastating. The *World* called it "long [the second act began at eleven o'clock] and dirty and dull," while the more tactful *Times* complained the "humor is anatomical." Because most of *The International Revue*'s material was not up to its music, the excellent cast seemed at times conspicuously empty-handed. The show ran twelve weeks.

In the late twenties Charles Lindbergh, Amelia Earhart, Admiral Byrd, and other gutsy fliers had made exciting headlines out of their flying escapades. They made it imperative that Broadway take up flying, too. George White presented what became DeSylva, Brown, and Henderson's last New York show when he opened **Flying High** (3-3-30, Apollo). It was the biggest musical comedy hit of the season, surpassed in longevity only by *Earl Carroll's Sketch Book*. Yet if Broadway legend can be believed, the book, apart from a vague outline, was not written until rehearsals began. In reality there were two loosely connected

stories. One told of a love affair that grows between lonely Eileen Cassidy (Grace Brinkley) and a flashy mail pilot, Tod Addison (Oscar Shaw), after Addison parachutes down on her New York City roof. The other told how Addison's mechanic, "Rusty" Krause (Bert Lahr), establishes an all-time endurance record in the air simply because he cannot figure how to land a plane. There were a few innovative touches in the book. The show opened quietly with Eileen on the roof; chorus girls came in much later. But the consensus was that *Flying High* was a conventional, somewhat old-style musical made hilarious by Lahr's antics. The show's most famous scene was a physical given to Rusty. He pours scotch into the specimen vial and when asked his nationality replies, with a unique consistency, "Scotch, by absorption." De-Sylva, Brown, and Henderson's score was a letdown. The trio's musical style was still firmly rooted in the twenties. Kate Smith's driving rendition made a show-stopper out of "Red Hot Chicago," though if any tune from the show has endured it is probably "Thank Your Father," sung by the romantic leads.

Maurice Chevalier, Eleanor Powell, and Duke Ellington and his Cotton Club orchestra each were given a full act to entertain in, in what was essentially a vaudeville that Charles Dillingham mounted at the Fulton on March 30. The evening was mounted with little but draperies, virtually all Dillingham—the first major producer hit by the depression—could afford.

Moss Hart and Dorothy Heyward provided a rather curious story for **Jonica** (4-7-30, Craig). Jonica (Nell Roy) leaves her convent school to attend a friend's wedding. On the train she meets some Broadway types also going to the wedding, and at the wedding she meets her old flame, Don Milan (Jerry Norris). Complications set in when a a gun the young heroine is carrying for self-protection accidentally discharges. Happily Jonica's wild bullet does no harm. Don and Jonica conclude they were fated for each other. It was not the sort of piece capable of making either of its librettists as famous as they would later become. Nor was Joseph Meyer's stolid score a help. *Jonica* left New York just five weeks after her arrival. Hart in after years insisted the work, which he had adapted at the urging of the producer from Mrs. Heyward's unproduced *Have a Good Time, Jonica*, was later completely rewritten by a third, anonymous hand.

The Shuberts brought in a European operetta called **Three Little Girls** (4-14-30, Shubert). It told a story not unlike *Maytime* (8-16-17) of a love thwarted in one generation fulfilled by the lovers' descendants a generation or two later. Beate-Marie (Natalie Hall) and Hendrik (Charles Hedley) would marry, but Beate-Marie is forced to marry the Count von Rambow (John Goldsworthy) instead. The same fate seems about to befall Beate-Marie's daughter and Hendrik's son, but love prevails. Though the whole evening belonged to a dying tradition, it appealed to enough old-timers to run 104 performances.

One brief, odd-ball entry was **Kilpatrick's Old-Time Minstrels** (4-19-30, Royale), a full-fledged minstrel entertainment of the sort Broadway hadn't seen for decades. The interlocutor, the end men, the sentimental old songs were all back. Only the compelling magic of yesteryear was missing. Tambourines and bones were quickly packed away, and the great old minstrel tradition went back into hibernation.

No musicals appeared in May, but two arrived the first week in June. One was a third and final edition of the **Garrick Gaieties** (6-4-30, Guild). Sterling Holloway and Philip Loeb of the original version were back; Albert Carroll moved over from the defunct *Grand Street Follies*; and some of the mirth was provided by a winsome young lady with the unlikely name of Imogene Coca. Unfortunately, Rodgers and Hart did not compose the songs. They were missed. None of the new songs captured the public's fancy the way "Mountain Greenery" or "Manhattan" had. But the new songs did at least give a leg up to several promising composers and lyricists. E.Y. Harburg and Vernon Duke had three songs on the program, the best of which, "I'm Only Human After All," had Ira Gershwin as colyricist. Harburg collaborated with Richard Myers in a song whose lyrics mimicked the unique patois of columnist Walter Winchell, "Ankle Up The Altar With Me." Marc Blitzstein contributed music for another burlesque of operetta. Johnny Mercer supplied words for "Out Of Breath And Scared To Death Of You." Happily, the skits were as incisive and hilarious as before. Plays such as *The Last Mile* and *Strange Interlude* were spoofed, with several of the Theatre Guild's most dependable playwrights— O'Neill, Molnar, and Shaw—getting mixed up in the proceedings. The ex-police commissioner, Grover Whalen, had just returned to his job at Wanamaker's Department Store. This, coupled with the announced Wanamaker policy of taking anything back, provided meat for an uproarious sketch with the dapper Whalen referred to as "the

gardenia of the law." To a chorus of thanksgiving in the background Whalen institutes traffic controls and the latest police methods to the staid, old store. The show ran through the summer, and just before it left on its tour a revised version, incorporating gems from the earlier editions was placed on the boards. "Rose of Arizona," for example, replaced the Blitzstein travesty.

Prohibition still seemed material for mirth to the authors of the black musical, **Change Your Luck** (6-6-30, Cohan). Broadway didn't agree. Nor did it see much original in the typical Negro stage names of the day—Hot Stuff Jackson, Romeo Green, Rat Row Sadie, or the almost inevitable Charleston Sam. And the lyricist wore threadbare the device of dropping the "g" to indicate a vowel change—"Ain't Puttin' Over Nothin'," "Waistin' Away," "Percolatin'," and "Travelin'." So Evergreen Peppers (Leigh Whipper), the bootlegging undertaker, packed his equipment and stole away after a mere two weeks.

The season's last show started life in London as a book musical called *Dear Love*. By the time the Shuberts were finished revamping it, it arrived in New York as **Artists and Models** (6-10-30, Majestic): the last in that dull series. Spectacle numbers paraded the girls as beauties of the past (Cleopatra, Thais), as guests in diaphanous gowns at a nobleman's wedding and, most appropriately for this revue, as models in an artist's studio. The Rath Brothers' acrobatic dances contrasted with the graceful toe-dancing of a small *corps de ballet*. Aileen Stanley and Phil Baker led the cast. Baker was again harassed by Mr. Muldowney. Regrettably, Baker's humor was not only often unfunny, but just as often smutty. The Shuberts withdrew the piece after seven weeks.

1930-1931

The theatrical year was sometimes brilliant; more often sad, even tragic. The number of original musicals continued to drop, though the decline was not as sharp as it had been in the last two sessions. Changes in theatregoers' tastes were also becoming evident. Yet here again the swings were not always too pronounced. While operetta was so moribund as to be for all practical purposes dead, the more intimate, thoughtful revue was obviously here to stay for a while. Uncertain which way to turn, lighter book musicals looked both backward and forward—some hits offering the latest in innovations and sophistication; some remaining contentedly lamebrain and irresponsible.

One surprising but incontestable change was a hardening of critical standards. Musicals were suddenly deprived of the easy-going, favored treatment they had so long received. Whether critics were concerned lest readers waste hard-to-come-by dollars, or whether they felt that they had to be more critical to retain their own jobs is difficult to judge. But the old-time tolerance vanished forever.

Much of the sadness was felt as Broadway bid adieu to a number of artists who had served it long and well. A few, like J. J. McNally and Sydney Rosenfeld, had been inactive for so many years that their importance to an earlier theatrical world was not universally appreciated. A number of performers, luminaries of earlier nights far gone, took their final bows as well, some heading hopefully to Hollywood, some retiring, some dying. More tragic was the plight of the producers. All the great theatrical empires fell. Men such as Arthur Hammerstein and Charles Dillingham fell first, never again to know the power and glamor that had been theirs. During the following season even the Shuberts submitted to the bankruptcy courts—although their action was questioned by some. They quickly retrieved all their important houses, and, though they thereafter operated on a smaller scale, they actually owned a larger percentage of working theatres than ever before.

The season's opener was a disaster. **Mystery Moon** (6-23-30, Royale) had one performance. The libretto dealt with the plight of a musical comedy road company when it books a Portal, North Dakota, theatre run by a gang of dope peddlers. One of the young ladies is even abducted by the son of the theatre owner. The songs were by the persistent Carlo and Sanders. Stanley Green, in his delightful survey of the decade's musicals, suggests one reason for the show's short run was the team's lyrics, filled with drivel, such as "smother me with kisses, for it's all O.K." Seventeen years passed before Carlo and Sanders recovered sufficiently to try again.

On July 1, changing times and crisis conditions allowed Earl Carroll to bring his 1930 **Vanities** into the New Amsterdam, once the flagship of his old Erlanger opposition. Jimmy Savo, Jack Benny, and Patsy Kelly were among the clowns. The show had trouble with the police. A swimming scene, with large mirrors revealing the action in a stage tank, had a man chasing several girls and catching one just as the lights went out. But more objec-

tionable was a show girl's fan dance and the coarseness of some of the sketches. In one skit that really raised eyebrows Jimmy Savo played a window-dresser changing mannequins' clothes. Carroll made the requested changes. No records suggest the police objected to the first-act finale, which made a prolonged, colorful protest against Prohibition. Though E. Y. Harburg, Harold Arlen, Burton Lane, and Jay Gorney put words and music together for the show, the songs were undistinguished. Ray Noble's "Good Night Sweetheart," not written for the evening, was interpolated for a time. With ticket sales hyped by all the publicity the police gave the show, Carroll was able to keep this edition of the *Vanities* on the boards into the first weeks of 1931.

Broadway and bad luck continued to go hand-in-hand for Percy Wenrich, the popular Tin Pan Alley figure. Wenrich wrote the songs for a revue called **Who Cares?** (7-8-30, 46th St.). It was a dangerous title, and the unemployed actors at the Lambs Club who put the piece together got their answer swiftly. The show left after one month. Yet not all the entertainment deserved brusque dismissal. One riotous skit, "What's Wrong with the Theatre," compared a patron's reception at a film palace and at a legitimate house. At the cinema four nattily dressed ushers welcome him rapturously, carry him to his seat, serve him tea and biscuits, and even do handstands for him until the movie begins. At the legitimate house the same patron is snarled at, ignored, shoved, and robbed. In a remarkable glimpse into the future, "So This Is Television" broadcast the Dumbell Department Store Hour. Less imaginative was still one more New York dig at criminal Chicago—with society dolled up in its furs, gowns, and guns. There was also a maudlin war scene, dancing condemned as "undistinguished," and songs written off as "dismal."

A black revue managed a slightly longer stay. **Hot Rhythm** (8-21-30, Times Square) lingered eight and a half weeks on 42nd Street. Attempting to pass itself off alternately as "A Sepia-Tinted Little Show" and "The Little Black Show," *Hot Rhythm* was nothing but a pastiche of typical black show material of the day—"rent party scenes, jungle scenes . . . even a beauty parade." The prison sketch that figured in so many black revues was a "lamentable burlesque of *The Last Mile*," the melodrama that had skyrocketed Spencer Tracy to fame. Whatever merit the show may have had must have been crammed into its opening numbers. The *Sun* noted that the first half-hour was the best, while the *World* admonished its readers, "leave at nine." Even with a Eubie Blake interpolation to bolster Donald Heywood and Porter Grainger's score, the show failed to generate much excitement. Soon after *Hot Rhythm* closed, the Times Square Theatre was converted into a movie house, and the inexorable decline of New York's greatest theatrical street began.

Hot Rhythm might not have been so anxious to associate itself with *The Little Show* if it had seen what **The Second Little Show** (9-2-30, Royale) was to offer. The show's producers had unwisely decided not to rehire the stars of the first edition. According to Howard Dietz, they "wanted the title *The Little Show* to be the star." As a result Schwartz and Dietz found they were writing the songs for two revues. *The Second Little Show* and a revue for the players from the first version. Their best material went into the latter. An interpolation by Herman Hupfeld, "Sing Something Simple" was the outstanding number of *The Second Little Show*. The principal entertainer was Al Trahan, a vaudevillian famous for his comic piano playing (he played his piano in the show, too). Trahan had the title role in the evening's only good sketch, "The Guest." This miniature Marc Connelly gem had first appeared as a small piece in *The New Yorker*. Connelly's guest made the mistake of checking into a modern hotel, where all the service is governed by pushbuttons. By some horrendous error the buttons have been miswired. Mayhem ensues. The guest's breakfast is pressed, and his suit served sunny side up. Other sketches were humdrum, and the cast patently inferior. *The Second Little Show* called it a run after eight weeks.

The two masters of Viennese-American operetta, Rudolf Friml and Sigmund Romberg, brought in their latest efforts back to back. Friml's piece was a fiasco. **Luana** (9-17-30, Hammerstein) was a $200,000 musical version of Richard Walton Tully's *The Bird of Paradise*. Written originally as a film musical, it was adapted for the stage when its filming was scrapped. Its producer, Arthur Hammerstein, perhaps sensing the drift away from operetta, billed it as a musical play. But a number of operettas had done that before, so no one was deceived. Luana (Ruth Altman) is a South Sea Island princess who renounces her prerogatives to marry an American, Paul Wilson (Joseph Macaulay). When Wilson deserts her, she commits suicide by jumping into a volcano. Neither Howard Emmett Rogers, who did the adaptation, nor J. Keirn Brennan, who wrote the

lyrics, was especially clever or original. Worse, Friml's score lacked the color and fire—and the memorable melodies—that this story called for and that he had so often injected into his earlier works. Hammerstein withdrew the show after 21 performances.

Romberg and the Shuberts had somewhat better luck with their "musical play," **Nina Rosa** (9-20-30, Majestic). First of all they had Otto Harbach to do the libretto and Irving Caesar for the lyrics. Secondly, they had Florenz Ziegfeld's ravishing Rio Rita, Ethelind Terry, for their lead. The story was set in the Peruvian Andes, where Jack Haines (Guy Robertson), a mining engineer, falls in love with Nina Rosa and has to fight to win her away from the hate-filled Pablo (Leonard Ceeley). Romberg's score was pretty, but a little thin-blooded. Still, it was a sufficiently pleasant evening to run 137 performances and to be accounted a modest success. In 1932 the show enjoyed a long vogue in Paris.

Three nights later Broadway applauded a solid hit, titled appropriately, **Fine and Dandy** (9-23-30, Erlanger). With the passage of time its most laudable asset would seem to be its vivacious Kay Swift score (with lyrics by Paul James), her only complete score ever sung in New York. The title song was one of the first public pronouncements of facile optimism that became so prevalent in the depression. There was also an exquisite romantic ballad, "Can This Be Love?" But the principal attraction for most of its 1930 audience was unquestionably Joe Cook's clowning. Cook was several comedians rolled into one. He was almost as acrobatic as Fred Stone (in *Fine and Dandy* he impersonated a whole team of German acrobats); he could juggle as comically as W. C. Fields (this time Cook juggled cigarettes); his crazy Rube Goldberg inventions put him in a class with Ed Wynn (one contraption punctured balloons, cracked nuts, and punched people at the same time), while Cook's dialogue often ranked with that of the Marx Brothers. Compare the excerpt from *Animal Crackers* (10-23-28) with this *Fine and Dandy* routine:

Joe: Are you his mother?
Mrs. Fordyce: No.
Joe: His father?
Mrs. Fordyce: No.
Joe: Well, then, how are you related to him?
Mrs. Fordyce: I'm not related to him at all.
Joe: Neither am I. Now there's a coincidence.

Joe is Joe Squibb, an employee of the Fordyce

Drop Forge and Tool Company, and Mrs. Fordyce (Dora Maughan) is the founder's widow and heir. The old gal finds Joe attractive enough to promote him to general manager. Joe is not above courting her a bit to get the post. He also courts pretty young Nancy Ellis (Alice Boulden). That leaves him little time for his wife and children. A prime attraction, apart from Cook's clowning, was the vivacious tap dancing of Eleanor Powell.

Performers were also a main attraction at October's first show, **Brown Buddies** (10-7-30, Liberty), a Negro musical comedy that featured Bill Robinson and his unique stepping, as well as the singing of Adelaide Hall. The story followed Sam Wilson and his girl friends from East St. Louis to the front in World War I and home again. Unfortunately Joe Jordan's score, with interpolations by Porter Grainger and Victor Young, was not on a par with Bojangles' tapping or Miss Hall's singing. Nonetheless the evening achieved 111 showings; not bad, all things considered.

On October 13 Evelyn Herbert, Robert Halliday, George Grossmith, and Victor Moore combined their talents in vain to put across **Princess Charming** (10-13-30, Imperial), an imported operetta bedecked in sumptuous Urban sets. The story told of a princess who prefers a sea captain to a king.

The season's best musical and biggest hit opened the next night. For the Gershwins, **Girl Crazy** (10-14-30, Alvin) represented a retreat from the adventuresome *Strike Up the Band*. It was strictly a formula show. But it had an electrifying Gershwin score sung, in part, by an electrifying singing discovery. The newcomer was Ethel Merman, soon to be Broadway's leading musical comedy star.

. . .

Ethel Merman (née Zimmerman) belted out her first notes in Astoria, New York on January 16, 1909. Her background was untheatrical, and her first paychecks were earned as a stenographer. She began singing in small night clubs in 1928. One year later she appeared in vaudeville with Clayton, Jackson, and Durante. Freedley discovered her singing on a bill at the Brooklyn Paramount. Hers was a style in direct contrast with her real predecessor, Marilyn Miller. Miss Miller was a dancer, Miss Merman was not; Miss Miller had a dainty, fine-featured beauty, Miss Merman could be termed handsome; Miss Miller had a small voice, Miss Merman had a bigger one. In fact, it was her "big voice" which was usually mentioned as her chief asset. Actually there were a number of singers with bigger and better voices. What Miss

Merman really had was impeccable diction and superb projection. In a sense she was closer to the Blanche Rings and Marie Cahills of an earlier era.

. . .

In *Girl Crazy* her brassy delivery stopped the show with "Sam and Delilah" and "I Got Rhythm." But she was not the only fine talent in the cast. There was the popular leading man, Allen Kearns, the rising Ginger Rogers, and the always funny Willie Howard. Howard was a last-minute substitution for Bert Lahr, still busy with *Flying High*. There was also a number of as yet unrecognized talents in the pit: Benny Goodman, Gene Krupa, and Glenn Miller. In Guy Bolton and John McGowan's book a New York playboy, Danny Churchill (Kearns), is sent by his father to Custerville, Arizona, where there are supposedly no night clubs, no gambling casinos, and no women. Danny's way of getting there is unusual. He hires Gieber Goldfarb's taxi to take him. But Danny is not one to sit around like some of the locals biding his time. He transforms a dude ranch into a club with a gaming room and lots of girls. He even succeeds in making a sheriff of Goldfarb (Howard), who talks to the Indians in Yiddish. Danny also succeeds in finding a wife in the town postmistress, Molly Gray (Miss Rogers). Miss Merman was Kate Fothergill, the daughter of the town's saloon keeper, played in the show by another funny man, William Kent. Gershwin's masterful score included half a dozen standards. Besides "I Got Rhythm," "Sam And Delilah," and "Bidin' My Time" there were "But Not For Me," "Boy, What Love Has Done To Me," and "Could You Use Me?" From the musical version of *East Is West*, which Ziegfeld dropped to do *Show Girl* (8-2-29), Gershwin brought over "Embraceable You." *Girl Crazy* ran out the season.

So did a revue which opened the following night. **Three's a Crowd** (10-15-30, Selwyn) reunited the stars of *The Little Show* (Fred Allen, Clifton Webb, and Libby Holman) with its songwriters (Arthur Schwartz and Howard Dietz). Burton Lane, Vernon Duke, Phil Charig, and others interpolated their songs. Max Gordon, the producer, added a song already popular in England, "Body And Soul" with music by Johnny Green and words by Edward Heyman, Robert Sour, and Frank Eyton. This number, and Schwartz and Dietz' "Something To Remember You By" were the evening's hits. Curiously, "Something To Remember You By" was also first made public in England, where it was a fast fox trot, "I Have No Words" in *Little Tommy Tucker*.

Its tempo was slowed for the new lyrics, and Libby Holman introduced it as well as "Body And Soul." These songs helped establish the long, brooding musical line that grew so popular in the thirties. Social protest crept into the program with "Yaller," which bemoaned the plight of a mulatto, unloved by the white world. The show began with a bedroom skit in which a wife's lover hides under the bed when the husband returns unexpectedly. But the skit was halted by Fred Allen, who promised there would be nothing of that sort in the entertainment. The promise wasn't kept. In a later skit Clifton Webb was interrupted in his bath by Tamara Geva, who recognizes him only when he pulls out the plug and she peers over the rim. The show's comic highspot was an Allen monologue—written by Corey Ford—in which Allen played a Byrd-like explorer lecturing on his experiences at the pole. He suggested the nation's unemployment could be solved by shoveling away all the snow at the pole. He inadvertently enforces his argument when he attempts to show slides. All that appears on the screen is white snow. Albertina Rasch, Broadway's leading choreographer at the time, staged the ballets. The lighting was especially innovative, discarding the use of footlights and hanging additional lights from the balcony. For his technical departures, Hassard Short received an award from General Electric.

The 1930 edition of **Lew Leslie's Blackbirds** (10-22-30, Royale) advertised itself as "the world's funniest and fastest revue" dedicated to "Glorifying the American Negro." It was so elaborate a production that Leslie attached a program warning: "subject to change owing to magnitude of production." Exactly how American Negroes were glorified by another eye-popping jungle number is debatable. "Mozambique" offered seventeen scantily dressed girls (in brightly colored wigs and sporting luxurious feather tails) stomping against a gaudy, stylized setting filled with lush tropical plants and native carvings. If some of the carvings the American girls danced in front of seemed more Micronesian than African, hadn't Lew Leslie been the producer of the *International Revue*? Perhaps he was momentarily confused. Leslie assembled a fine cast including Ethel Waters, Flournoy Miller (appearing without Lyles), and Buck and Bubbles. The show spoofed the Broadway hit *The Green Pastures*, smiling Aunt Jemima's imaginary marital troubles, and black honeymoons. Whereas the score for the 1928 version had been by whites, blacks did the songs for the new edition. Most of the music was

by Eubie Blake and most of the lyrics by Andy Razaf. Blake provided a musicianly score with numbers such as "Memories Of You," "You're Lucky To Me," and "That Lindy Hop." But nothing caught fire as the tunes from the earlier edition had—though "Memories Of You" slowly developed into a standard. This song, with its span of an octave and a fifth, was written especially for Minto Cato to introduce in the show. Her unusual range allowed her to sing it with ease. Latecomers, however, may have missed it, for Miss Cato sang it at the end of the opening scene, sitting in front of a slave's cabin, wearing an 1850 dress and a bandanna. The show left after seven weeks.

Lew Fields joined the ranks of revue producers with **The Vanderbilt Revue** (11-5-30, Vanderbilt). A number of the brightest young talents of the day contributed material: Dorothy Fields, Jimmy McHugh, E. Y. Harburg, and Kenyon Nicholson. Husky-voiced Lulu McConnell was in charge of most of the evening's comedy. She portrayed a dowager searching in not so quiet desperation for a gigolo, a meddling tourist at customs, and a gabber who ruins "A Quiet Game of Bridge." The morning-after notices were not kind, and the public stayed away. Fields closed the show at the end of its second week. Ruefully concluding he no longer understood changing tastes, Fields announced he was retiring. Unlike so many Broadway figures, he was true to his word. One more theatrical giant was gone from the scene.

The Vanderbilt Revue's thirteen performances were five more than an operetta entitled **The Well of Romance** (11-7-30, Craig) received. The book for the operetta was by the witty Preston Sturges, flush with the profits from his *Strictly Dishonorable*. Reading the story or the character names one wonders if Sturges wasn't having a private joke—at his own expense, since he obviously never collected royalties. The Princess of Magnesia is ordered to marry the Baron von Sprudelwasser (Max Figman), though everyone knows he is something of a villain. The Princess is told to drink from a well whose waters induce undying love. She drinks, but so does a poet who is there at the same moment. They fall helplessly in love, and only when the poet turns out to be a king is there a happy ending. Norma Terris and Howard Marsh, the Magnolia and Ravenal of *Show Boat*, were the princess and the poet, while Lina Abarbanell had a secondary role. The music was by H. Maurice Jacquet.

Ten days later the Shuberts brought in **Hello,**

Paris (11-15-30, Shubert), a loosely plotted musical comedy based on Homer Croy's novel *They Had To See Paris*. Filled as it was with specialities, it had something of the flavor of an old Shubert revue. One erstwhile star of the Shuberts' own Winter Garden revues, Chic Sale, played the lead. Sale was Pike Peters, an Oklahoman, newly rich on oil, who takes his family on the grand tour. Whenever an excuse offered itself, Sale went into a cracker-barrel monologue about guzzling, tobacco-chewing, or sea-sickness. More than one critic felt Sale had long since lost his audience appeal. Brooks Atkinson in the *Times* speculated that Sale's problem was his lack of real perception or depth. All his characterizations were "external portraits" relying more on costume (such as steel-rimmed glasses) and make-up than on any profound insights. Sale wasn't helped by Edgar Smith's adaptation or Russell Tarbox and Michael Cleary's score, both commonplace. *Hello, Paris* said "good-bye" after 33 showings.

Two nights later Billy Rose, a songwriter turned producer, offered Sweet and Low (11-17-30, 46th St.). The cast included George Jessel, James Barton, Arthur Treacher, and Rose's wife, Fanny Brice. Miss Brice and Jessel were featured in the evening's best skit, "Strictly Unbearable," a spoof of the preceding season's *Strictly Dishonorable*. Some of the songs were at a level to make even Earl Carroll wince, "When A Pansy Was A Flower," "Ten Minutes In Bed." But Rose was co-lyricist on two clean, melodic Harry Warren numbers that have survived. With Ira Gershwin he wrote "Cheerful Little Earful" and with Mort Dixon he provided rhymes for "Would You Like To Take A Walk?" Rose also collaborated with Charlotte Kent to put words to Louis Alter's "Overnight." Two songs kidded the growing Latin vogue. Both were listed slyly under "Customary Spanish Number." *Sweet and Low* played 184 performances.

Smiles (11-18-30, Ziegfeld) ran just half as long. But on paper it was the sort of show that should have been a smash. It had a book by William Anthony McGuire from a story suggested by Noel Coward. It had a Vincent Youmans score. The stars were Marilyn Miller and Fred and Adele Astaire. Ziegfeld produced it with magnificent Joseph Urban settings that depicted a 1918 French Village and 1930 Paris and New York. (Critics were beginning to take Urban for granted. Only the *Brooklyn Eagle* gave his sets more than passing notice.) The story told of a French waif adopted by three American doughboys during the war and afterwards brought to America. She grows up to be an attractive young lady, joins the Salvation Army, flirts with high society, and finally decides to marry one of the soldiers who adopted her. Book trouble developed early. Perhaps Coward, in giving the plot to someone else to develop, understood the difficulties of a successful dramatization. Worse, McGuire was becoming an alcoholic. His drinking and arguments became insufferable to Ziegfeld, who replaced him with a battery of writers, including Ring Lardner, though McGuire retained sole public credit. There were excellent scenes. The Astaires as society's Bob and Dot Hastings had fun trying to mix a complicated cocktail for a party at their Southampton home. Fred Astaire brought down the house with his dancing to Youmans' "Say, Young Man Of Manhattan." Tapping away dressed in top hat, white tie, and tails, he shot down a long line of similarly dressed chorus boys with his walking stick. But the succession of scenes never created a satisfactory theatrical tension. Youmans' score was solidly crafted. Still, the one Youmans classic to come from *Smiles*, "Time On My Hands," didn't become popular until long after the show closed. Like so many of the best of the early sophisticated melodies from the era it received its first real attention in England. In the show it was sung by the heroine and Dick (Paul Gregory), one of the young men who adopt her.

On the other hand, the brittle, bitter sophistication of The New Yorkers (12-8-30, Broadway) had an immediate appeal. Like Morrie Ryskind, the year before, Herbert Fields softened the harshness of his attitudes a bit by making his whole tale a dream in which Alice Wentworth falls in love with the murderous bootlegger, Al Spanish. Miss Wentworth is from Park Avenue where, in the show's most famous line, "bad women walk good dogs." The Avenue is an altogether unpleasant place. Alice's father, Dr. Wentworth, is not above flaunting his mistress, Lola McGee, in front of his wife. But then, Mrs. Wentworth makes no bones about her gigolo. Together this crowd heads for Miami, where Al finally runs afoul of the law, not for his illegal booze or his numerous killings, but for parking too close to a fire hydrant. The show was superbly cast. Hope Williams was Alice, Charles King was Al, Ann Pennington was Lola, Richard Carle was Dr. Wentworth, and Marie Cahill Mrs. Wentworth. For Carle and Miss Cahill the evening marked their Broadway farewells. Jimmy Durante, and Fred Waring and his Pennsylvanians were also prominent. Durante, as another gangster, had an hilarious first-act finale, singing one of his own songs, "Wood," and cluttering up the stage with every conceivable wood product. Apart from Durante's material and a few of Waring's songs, the score was by Cole Porter. His best song of the evening wasn't heard for years on radio, his words to "Love For Sale" were considered a little too wicked for general broadcasting. It was sung in the show by a minor figure, May (Kathryn Crawford), assisted by "The Three Girl Friends." More publicly witty Porter material was heard in songs such as "The Great Indoors," sung by another girl relatively unimportant to the main plot, Mona Low (Frances Williams), and the ensemble. "Let's Fly Away" (sung by Mona and Al) has since become a standard, while "I Happen To Like New York," sung by a comic hood, Mildew (Oscar Ragland), remains almost the epitome of songs praising Manhattan. At $5.50 top in the huge Broadway Theatre, *The New Yorkers* should have been a goldmine. But three days after the show opened the Bank of the United States closed and we were in the depths of the depression. Price cuts and salary cuts were to no avail. The show closed after twenty weeks of a forced, unprofitable run.

The second revival of *Babes in Toyland* in two years played a month during the Christmas season. The Shuberts took the occasion to announce their hope that this or some other children's favorite would be mounted every year thereafter as the theatre's holiday gift to the youngsters.

Arthur Hammerstein's bad luck pursued him and the losses from his production of **Ballyhoo** (12-22-30, Hammerstein) drove him to bankruptcy and cost him his beloved theatre. The show was a vehicle for W. C. Fields, who as Q. Q. Quale promotes a "bunion derby" to help unemployed actors get from New York to Hollywood. In Arizona he runs into his inevitable troubles with the law. He flimflams his way out of his difficulties and manages to get his crew to the Colossal Studios in California. After a grand entrance riding a steam calliope, Fields juggled cigar boxes (Cook had merely juggled cigarettes earlier in the season), played a big bass viol (patting it affectionately to make it respond), and lost his temper trying to repair a miniature car, much as he had years before repairing his Ford. Fields' opportunistic morality came to the fore when he changed his mind about robbing a man he discovers is armed—"A thing like that wouldn't be honest." When Hammerstein failed, Fields attempted unsuccessfully to run the show as a cooperative venture with the others in the cast. Unfortunately the book was lame and Louis Alter's score (part of which had lyrics by Oscar Hammerstein) had nothing to match his "Overnight" from *Sweet and Low*. Fields took Q. Q. Quale's hint and went west, never to return to Broadway.

The year's last show was a German importation, **Meet My Sister** (12-30-30, Shubert)—another operetta about a noble lady who stoops to conquer. Thanks to Benatsky's gay music and the cavorting of Walter Slezak, the Shubert production ran twenty-one weeks.

January 1931 saw only one new musical presented. Good times or bad, college musicals retained their vogue. Even a mediocre one like **You Said It** (1-19-31, 46th St.) offered enough fun to run twenty-one weeks. Not centering on football, as most college musicals had, Jack Yellen and Sid Silvers' libretto recounted how ambitious, immoral Pinkie Pincus (Lou Holtz) spends his freshman year organizing a series of rackets at Kenton College. Everything from the laundry to the commissary comes under his control. But Pinkie, being a musical comedy hero, has a heart of gold. When pretty Helen Holloway (Mary Lawlor), the dean's daughter, tries her hand at a little, harmless bootlegging, Pinkie steals the evidence which could wreck her budding romance. If Holtz was over-age for his part, his followers didn't care. Holtz' dialect bits and cocky comedy appealed to a large number of New York theatregoers. They seemed particularly taken with his Jewish burlesque of a "la-de-dah" Englishman. *You Said It* allowed theatregoers to hear Harold Arlen's first full score.

. . .

Harold Arlen was born in Buffalo, New York, on February 15, 1905. His original name was Hyman Arluck. Arlen's father was a cantor; his mother a pianist. Each hoped the boy would follow in his or her footsteps. But Arlen preferred popular songs to classical or liturgical music and by the time he was fifteen he was playing the piano in small Buffalo night spots and on lake steamers. He established a jazz orchestra good enough to warrant a New York engagement. From that stay he moved on to the orchestra for the *Scandals* and then to become Youmans' rehearsal pianist in *Great Day*. Gershwin offered him encouragement after hearing "Get Happy," and before long he was writing songs for the Cotton Club as well as Broadway.

. . .

Broadway was not overwhelmed by this first effort. The most impressive number in *You Said It,* one that Alec Wilder gives special attention to in reviewing Arlen's work, was "Sweet And Hot," "a truly swinging song." It was sung in the show with a fetching Slavic accent by Lyda Roberti.

Ever since their original successes, *The Student Prince* and *Blossom Time* had been on the road. In most major American cities their visits had become (and for years remained) annual affairs. Now, with the depression creating more and more empty theatres in New York, the Shuberts brought both works in off the road to keep Manhattan houses lit. *The Student Prince* arrived at the Majestic on January 29 and stayed five weeks. Just before it closed, *Blossom Time* returned to the Ambassador, the house where it had originally played, and chalked up an additional three and a half weeks. Neither production offered major names in the cast.

Rodgers and Hart reunited with Herbert Fields for **America's Sweetheart** (2-10-31, Broadhurst). When Geraldine March (Harriette Lake) becomes the rage of the silent movies, she seems to lose interest in her old beau, Michael Perry (Jack Whiting). Michael continues as a struggling actor. But the talkies reveal that Geraldine has a lisp, and her star fades. At the same time Michael's popularity skyrockets. Forgivingly, he escorts Geraldine to the premiere of his latest movie, at Grauman's Chinese Theatre. Fields' wit punctured the crassness and ignorance of much of Hollywood's top echelons. In a variation of his famous line from *The New Yorkers*, he referred to Hollywood as a place where good plays are turned into bad movies. The score was not prime Rodgers and Hart, but it was pleasant. "I've Got Five Dollars," a proposal of marriage commenting acidly on depression conditions, was the most sung number from the piece. A few years after *America's Sweetheart* ended its seventeen-week run, Miss Lake moved on to Hollywood, where the studio bigwigs changed her name to Ann Sothern.

Though composer Lewis Gensler had Russel Crouse, Oscar Hammerstein II, and Morrie Ryskind for librettists, he and his associates seemed unable to whip **The Gang's All Here** (2-18-31, Imperial) into shape. Several critics suggested the musical was so loose-jointed it should have been a revue. A war between rival gangs of bootleggers in Atlantic City provided the impetus for the story. Baby Face Martini (Jack McCauley) enlists Dr. Indian Ike Kelley (Ted Healy) to help push Horace Winterbottom (Tom Howard) out of his control of the resort's rackets. But Ike has a daughter, Peggy (Ruth Tester), and Horace, a son, Hector (John Gallaudet). They fall in love, befuddling all of Baby Face's carefully laid plans. One song had the title "By Special Permission Of The Copyright Owner (I Love You)." Special permission was only required for three weeks.

Perhaps its authors thought a name like **The Venetian Glass Nephew** (2-23-31, Vanderbilt) would intrigue. They were wrong. The title scared away patrons, and the show folded after one week. Terming it "a light opera" didn't help sales either. And the story based on an Elinor Wylie novel was odd, to say the least. It was a romantic fantasy, far out of date. Cardinal Bon (Dodd Mehan), wanting a nephew, persuades the magician, Chevalier de Chastelneuf (George Houston), to make him one of venetian glass. Rosabla (Mary Silveira) falls in love with the statue and has herself turned into porcelain so she can remain with it.

On March 17 Al Jolson returned briefly from his newfound home in Hollywood to star in **The Wonder Bar.** The show was an unusual affair for Jolson, accustomed as he was to having vehicles tailored to his special talents. *Wunderbar* had been a German hit that also enjoyed a long London run. The Shuberts converted the Nora Bayes (the roof theatre atop the 44th St.) into a cabaret, while on its open stage Jolson portrayed Monsieur Al, the proprietor of a similar establishment in Paris known as The Wonder Bar. Paris was not exactly a novel place for Jolson, who had opened the Winter Garden in *La Belle Paree* (3-20-11) singing "Paris Is A Paradise For Coons." But now Jolson played it straight, and in white face. He was anything but his old clownish Gus as he attempted a deal with the thieving, philandering male partner of his star dance act. Most of the original Robert Katscher score was retained, though Jolson took credit for several interpolations. But none of the numbers became Jolson classics, and there was something incongruous about the great Mammy singer crooning "Ma Mère." Even with Patsy Kelly, Arthur Treacher, Rex O'Malley, and Trini to assist, Jolson could not draw the expected crowds. The show ran less than ten weeks, after which Jolson packed his bags to return to movieland.

April saw no musicals appear; but May was sufficiently active to compensate. The first two musicals entered together on May 4. One was a revival of *The Mikado* at the Erlanger, with the all but forgotten Frank Moulan as Ko-Ko and Howard Marsh as Nanki-Poo. A Civic Light Opera mounting, it inaugurated a series of Gilbert and

Sullivan presentations. *H.M.S. Pinafore* sailed in on May 18. Howard Marsh was again the principal tenor, and another old-timer, Fay Templeton, returned to sing a role she had done so often, Buttercup. Like *The Mikado*, *Pinafore* stayed two weeks. *The Gondoliers* and *Patience* followed, both with Marsh and Moulan, but without Miss Templeton.

Having suffered a costly failure in October with his lavish *Blackbirds*, Lew Leslie mounted a budget-conscious entertainment he christened **Rhapsody in Black** (5-4-31, Harris). There was no chorus, and no fancy scenery. There were also no comedy numbers. It was a sort of singing vaudeville led by Ethel Waters and the Cecil Mack Choir. But the new songs the show relied on—including one by Fields and McHugh—were workaday. Better old numbers included "St. Louis Blues" and the Hebrew "Eli, Eli." Only *Rhapsody in Black*'s austere economies allowed it to continue for ten weeks.

Billy Rose presented **Crazy Quilt** (5-19-31, 44th St.), using much of the material that had served *Sweet and Low* so well all season. Fanny Brice was back, of course. And she had a new "Rose" number to add to her repertory, "Rest Room Rose," by Rodgers and Hart. But the hit of the new edition was a song she sang (in top hat and tails) with her new costars, Ted Healy and Phil Baker, "I Found A Million Dollar Baby—In A Five-And-Ten Cent Store." With Miss Brice's clowning and Baker's sassing everyone in sight, the evening provided light fun for ten weeks.

Noel Coward, S. J. Perelman, Marc Connelly, and Burton Lane were a few of the names that graced the credits of **The Third Little Show** (6-1-31, Music Box), but it was one of its stars, Beatrice Lillie (the other star was Ernest Truex), who was largely responsible for what success the show enjoyed. Miss Lillie, sporting a pith helmet and sitting in a rickshaw, introduced America to Coward's "Mad Dogs And Englishmen" and advised her audiences "There Are Fairies At The Bottom Of My Garden" (Rose Fyleman/Liza Lehmann). Walter O'Keefe treated patrons to Herman Hupfeld's "When Yuba Played The Tuba Down In Cuba," and two older musical-comedy favorites, Constance Carpenter and Carl Randall, sang "You Forgot Your Gloves" (Edward Eliscu/Ned Lehak). But most theatregoers forgot the melodies as soon as the evening was over. Miss Lilie's finest comic moment was her take-off of the celebrated monologuist, Ruth Draper—a performer given to appearing alone in the simplest

clothes on stages set only with bare draperies. Miss Lillie introduced herself and instructed her listeners, "In this little sketch I want you to imagine far too much." When the show closed after 136 performances, its producers decided to end the series.

If the season had begun disastrously, it ended gloriously when **The Band Wagon** opened on June 3. Arthur Schwartz and Howard Dietz, who had been so vital to the success of the first *Little Show*, gave *The Band Wagon* what is probably the greatest of all revue scores. Perhaps only the 1926 *Scandals* (6-14-26) and *This Is the Army* (7-4-42) were so filled with brilliant melodies. Out of this single evening came the jaunty "I Love Louisa," the effervescent "New Sun In The Sky" (singing of the hope so necessary to a dismal time), the lovely "High And Low," and, most of all, the incomparable "Dancing In The Dark." This show tune, perhaps more than any other, established the longer more thoughtful musical line of much of the thirties' best songs. The sketches were entirely by Dietz and Kaufman (who had also contributed to *The Little Show*). They had the curtain up when the audience entered—a device used earlier in the season at *The Wonder Bar*. As Dietz tells it:

> On stage the company took seats—a reflection, as if in a mirror, of the audience arriving. The ushers on stage wore costumes identical to the ushers in the aisles below ... as the lights were dimming, the company sang in strict unison "It Better Be Good."

Dietz' lyrics, though never on a par with Porter's or Wodehouse's best, were often witty and colloquial. In the show's most lauded sketch, "The Pride of the Claghornes," an aristocratic old southern family's pride is shattered and the marriage of the daughter jeopardized when it is discovered she is still a virgin. The staging was remarkably inventive. "Dancing In The Dark" was sung by John Barker as Tilly Losch danced on raked, mirrored floors with constantly changing lighting. Revolving stages were used imaginatively by the show's designer, Albert Johnson. As a beggar at a stage door dreams of the beautiful ballerina (Miss Losch) the stage swings around and he performs with her in the ballet. The dance done, he is back at his lonely post outside the house. A Parisian park revolved as children played "Hoops." And in the evening's most memorable set, a Bavarian merry-go-round turned as the cast sang "I Love Louisa." Hassard Short was responsible for much of the physical brilliance of the show and Albertina Rasch for its stunning dances. The Astaires, Tilly Losch, Helen Broderick, and Frank Morgan starred. The variety of roles each star took is a testimony to their versatility and professionalism. Fred Astaire, for example, was a French brat in "Hoops," the beggar, the suitor of Miss Claghorne, an accordion player and dancer in "Sweet Music (To Worry The Wolf Away)," and a dapper man-about-town for "New Sun In The Sky." Welcomed by virtually all the critics, the show ran 260 performances—good for the times. But when the show closed, Adele Astaire's career ended with it. Leaving to marry, she also left her brother to perform alone.

1931-1932

Times were dismal; it was the nadir of the depression. On Broadway many of the best talents were preparing to leave for Hollywood, if they were not already there. For those who remained, especially the great old-line producers, enforced idleness or bankruptcy loomed. Producers who had lived from production to production, men like Florenz Ziegfeld, Charles Dillingham, and Arthur Hammerstein, were the hardest hit. But even the massive Shubert empire was tottering. Nonetheless, for the first time in several years the drop in the number of new musicals was slight. If the new theatrical session lacked the overall quality of the last few seasons, it nonetheless witnessed the presentation of several musical gems.

The first lyric offering to arrive was *The Pirates of Penzance*. The production was the latest in a series the Civic Light Opera had begun the preceding season. *Iolanthe, Ruddigore,* and returns of *Pinafore* and *The Mikado* followed. When attendance waned, the company mounted a revival of *The Merry Widow*, bringing back Donald Brian to re-create the role of Danilo that had made him famous a quarter of a century before. An all-star staging of *The Chocolate Soldier* was offered next with Vivienne Segal, Charles Purcell, and Detmar Poppen in the leads. Growing more daring, the troupe presented Jones' *The Geisha* and Planquette's *The Chimes of Normandy*. Before the company left early in 1932 *Naughty Marietta, The Firefly,* and *Robin Hood* joined the repertory.

The season really opened on July 1, as seasons regularly had a decade or so back, with the

Ziegfeld Follies. The 1931 edition would be the last Ziegfeld himself would ever mount. The show was not at the New Amsterdam, busy with the more up-to-date *The Band Wagon* and soon to be given over to films, but at Ziegfeld's own, equally magnificent house. Like the early *Follies*, it used a theme to tie its sketches together: this time a weighing of the old and the new. Gene Buck and Dave Stamper returned to the Ziegfeld fold and created "Broadway Reverie," a threnody insisting, "It's not the place it used to be." Ruth Etting impersonated Nora Bayes and revived "Shine On Harvest Moon," the first hit to come from a *Follies*. Harry Richman and Jack Pearl mimicked past greats who had never played the *Follies* and sang songs no *Follies* ever heard. Richman was Al Jolson crooning "You Made Me Love You," while Pearl did Sam Bernard's "Who Paid The Rent For Mrs. Rip Van Winkle When Rip Van Winkle Was Away?" (a song Jolson also sang). Old, elegant Rectors was compared with a speakeasy then on its site. Returning to the world of 1931 Ruth Etting sang a sleazy cabaret girl's "Cigarettes, Cigars"; Richman offered the expected call for optimism with "Help Yourself To Happiness" (both by the show's principal song writers, Harry Revel and Mack Gordon), while Helen Morgan bemoaned the plight of Noel Coward's "Half-Caste Woman." "Doin' The New York" had everyone join in the requisite high-stepping. Ziegfeld's girls were as beautiful as ever and Joseph Urban's sets dramatic and gorgeous. For a South Sea number Ziegfeld imported a big-breasted dancer he had seen in Robert Flaherty's film, *Tabu*. The girl, called only Reri, could not really sing or dance and soon left the show. A lavish jungle scene employed large papier-mâché elephants, while another spectacular set celebrated the opening of the Empire State Building as the world's tallest structure. The *Follies* ran only 165 performances, but the depression was not solely responsible for the relatively short run. Elaborate annuals had begun to seem dated even in the affluent heyday of the twenties. A faster pace of life, as reflected in other entertainments, and an undeniable, if not general, rising of intellectual standards in musicals foredoomed them.

Heywood Broun, the celebrated newspaper columnist, produced a revue called **Shoot the Works** (7-21-31, Cohan) to make employment for over 100 of his actor friends. Its list of credits was as imposing as Ziegfeld's list, including as it did Broun, Dorothy Parker, Nunnally Johnson, Dorothy Fields, Ira Gershwin, and Irving Berlin. But in contrast to the expensive *Follies* the show was brought in on a shoestring budget of $6,000. There were no big names in the cast, though George Murphy and Imogene Coca would go on to stardom. The *Times* suggested the work's artlessness was its saving grace. It began on a bare stage with a chorus being "selected" and ended with Broun telling the critics what to write in their reviews; he even supplied the headline, "A Swell Show." In between the acts ran from Al Norman's fancy tap dancing "in the Hal Le Roy manner" to Harry Hirschfield's cartooning. But the material proved indifferent, and in the summer heat the show never got off the ground.

The 278-performance run of the latest **Earl Carroll Vanities** (8-27-31, Earl Carroll) far outshone the great Ziegfeld's *Follies*. Part of the show's attraction was the new, art déco Earl Carroll Theatre—an advanced, streamlined house seating 3,000 spectators. Instead of a box office cubbyhole, the lobby boasted a modern counter manned by tuxedoed ticket-vendors; free checking and free soft drinks were available. Regretfully, it soon became evident the house was too large for live entertainment, and within a few years the premises became a Woolworth's. The 1931 *Vanities* featured vaudeville's Will Mahoney, tough William Demarest, and Lillian Roth. The best numbers in the show had been heard elsewhere before. They included Ravel's "Bolero" (which provided the background for another mindless parade of beautiful, befeathered girls) and Ray Noble's "Good Night, Sweetheart." A major production number was "Parasols on Parade" with Carroll's lovely showgirls appearing as Parasol Rose et Noir, Parasol san Gene, and even Parasol Pistachio. Most critics were unkind, especially towards the evening's limp comedy. Considering the poor quality of the material, the hard times and the critical drubbing, the *Vanities'* run was remarkable. Carroll clearly had a loyal following.

For Oscar Hammerstein II, its co-librettist, the season's first new book musical, **Free for All** (9-8-31, Manhattan), must have been a doubly painful experience. The show was a 15-performance dud and played at a theatre until recently the Hammerstein. Schwab and Hammerstein's story was a little like *Girl Crazy* (10-14-30). When Steve Potter (Jack Haley), a rich man's son, gets mixed up in radical politics, his father sends him out west to run the family copper mine and stay out of trouble. Love and success follow in a place fittingly called "New Leaf Corners." The score was by Richard Whiting, another creative Tin Pan

Alley figure who never seemed able to do his best work for the theatre. Benny Goodman's band (with Glenn Miller one of its musicians) played the melodies. The show, like several of the season's musicals, employed no chorus, though it is moot whether fiscal or esthetic considerations prevailed in this case.

The Thomashefskys, well-respected in the fading Yiddish theatre, tried their luck with a Yiddish-style musical comedy presented in the best, Broadway vernacular. **The Singing Rabbi** (9-10-31, Selwyn) told of the rise of the Sheindels. Three sons have left their widowed mother in Galicia and made their way to separate parts of the world. When one son, Gidalia (Boris Thomashefsky), makes good in New York he persuades his mother and two brothers to emigrate. The show had run for many months downtown in the Yiddish theatre district and had apparently exhausted its potential audience. It failed to run a full week in its new version. When it closed at the Selwyn, the house went over to motion pictures, adding to the disheartening change on 42nd Street. Between new Minsky burlesques and grind movies the street was patently finished as the heart of the legitimate theatre.

A third of the old annuals made an appearance when **George White's Scandals** opened on September 14 at one of the remaining 42nd Street houses, White's favored Apollo. One sign of the changing times was that Joseph Urban did the sets for this *Follies* rival. As he had for Ziegfeld's production, he designed a set to welcome the Empire State Building. As they had the preceding season, the critics gave Urban far less attention than they once had showered on him. While the *Brooklyn Eagle* acknowledged Urban had conceived "pretty sets here and there," most critics, like Gilbert Gabriel in the *American*, were content to note in passing "the scenery is Urban's." Willie and Eugene Howard were in charge of the laughs. Together they did their famous "Pay the Two Dollars" skit, in which a lawyer's insistence his client not pay a two-dollar fine leads to higher and higher courts and bigger and bigger penalties. The diminutive Willie also appeared as a fearsome big-game hunter. Having announced he bagged a lion, he then confessed, "I bagged him and I bagged him—but he wouldn't go away." The songs were danced by Ray Bolger and sung by Rudy Vallee, Everett Marshall, and Ethel Merman. With Buddy De-Sylva in Hollywood, White's once great trio of songwriters was reduced to the twosome of Lew Brown for the lyrics and Ray Henderson for the music. But their excellent showing suggested DeSylva was not missed. Miss Merman sang the hit of the evening, another bit of depression philosophy, "Life Is Just A Bowl Of Cherries." Marshall in blackface led the first-act finale. It was not quite a typical blackface number. There was growing concern, especially among the liberal elements who comprised so large a part of show business, about how blacks were being treated in America. It had been hinted at earlier in numbers such as "Yaller" in *Three's a Crowd* (10-15-30). Brown was explicit. In "That's Why Darkies Were Born" he said they were the folk who "had to laugh at trouble" and "be contented with any old thing." Marshall also sang one of the best numbers, "The Thrill Is Gone," while Vallee sang two popular tunes, "This Is The Mrs." and (with Merman) "My Song." Easily the best of the better-known revues to come out during the season, the show was rewarded with a six-month run.

An all-black revue that opened the next night was another one-week flop. Its title, **Fast and Furious** (9-15-31, New Yorker), was not only inaccurate, it was somewhat out of date. As Brooks Atkinson noted in the *Times*, "grinning toothsome exuberance" was no longer enough to save a show. To its credit the revue tried to move away from the stereotyped dancing black shows had offered ever since *Shuffle Along*. Cuban and Oriental dances found niches alongside a number honoring a new dance craze, "Rhumbatism." In its comedy the entertainment was less original, falling back on a courtroom scene and on a boxing match between two girls not unlike that recently performed in *Messin' Around* (4-22-29). Most of the music was by Harry Revel, who had contributed the lion's share of the *Follies* score, but J. Rosamond Johnson and Joe Jordan were also credited with tunes.

One of 42nd Street's remaining theatres, the Liberty, housed another black show, **Singin' the Blues** (9-16-31, Liberty). This was "a negro-melodrama" by the sometime librettist, Jack McGowan. It did not have a score as such, but Eubie Blake led an orchestra that played popular tunes of the day and "incidental" songs by Dorothy Fields and Jimmy McHugh. The busy musical comedy choreographer Sammy Lee staged a number of dances. Negro speciality acts larded the story.

Nikki (9-29-31, Martin Beck) was based on a character created by John Monk Saunders, who worked her way from his short stories into a novel and then a film. In this musical version Nikki (Fay Wray) is the friend of three young members of the lost generation, all once aviators and all now at loose ends in Paris. Their boozy, brawling existence kills all of them before the final curtain in Lisbon, leaving Nikki to go off with a new-found friend. The show was not tightly knit and a number of speciality acts (ballroom dancers, tap dancers) were easily inserted. But the story was all wrong for the time, and Phil Charig's flat score, his last for some time, offered no inducement to attend. The show collapsed after five weeks.

The Shuberts' plodding Harold Atteridge adapted Frances Goodrich and Albert Hackett's *Up Pops the Devil* for musical purposes. The show was called **Everybody's Welcome** (10-13-31, Shubert) and had music by Sammy Fain. Its story told of a young unmarried couple in Greenwich Village. Steve (Oscar Shaw) is a writer whose creative inspiration has run dry, so Ann (Harriette Lake) volunteers to find a job while Steve does the housework. Steve rebels until he discovers Ann is going to have a baby. Besides Shaw and Miss Lake, the cast featured the Ritz Brothers and Ann Pennington. The brothers clowned and performed a bit of eccentric dancing, while Miss Pennington danced with her customary abandon and attempted some clowning. At the end of the story the cast all went to the Roxy (called Proxy's in the show) for a spectacular production number that twitted the stage and screen offerings at the film palace. Jimmy Dorsey led the pit band. One of the tunes they played asked the question, "Is Rhythm Necessary?" Fain remained one of several talented composers who never seemed to do things right on Broadway; his great successes all came after he left for Hollywood. But one Herman Hupfeld interpolation is still popular, though its real vogue came from the movie *Casablanca* years later: "As Time Goes By." Heavily discounted tickets permitted *Everybody's Welcome* to chalk up 139 performances.

The disappointing run of *Sweet Adeline* probably nipped in the bud the development of a new style of American musical play. When Jerome Kern returned to New York, it was not with Oscar Hammerstein II but in collaboration with Otto Harbach. They called **The Cat and the Fiddle** (10-15-31, Globe) "a musical love story." Actually it was closer in style and flavor to European operettas of the day, but with its musical lines toned down to American tastes. They were apparently Kern's real tastes, too, for he had always pursued something of a lone course, composing in an unusual, unique blend of American

471

and Continental sounds. Kern's score, filled with memorable melodies, was exceptionally rich and complete. It had recitatives and sung continuities, even regular numbers were led into with special care. The Continental aspects of Kern's writing were underscored by the play's Brussels setting. His modernity was reinforced by making the setting contemporary. A young composer named Victor Florescu (George Metaxa) has written an opera called "The Passionate Pilgrim." Victor is admired by another young composer, an American girl, Shirley Sheridan (Bettina Hall). But any love for her on his part is cooled when he suspects she would interpolate her material into his work. Happily, it is all a mistake. His brother had heard Shirley, who lives next door to Victor (shades of *The Only Girl*), playing one of her own tunes and thought the melody attractive. As it turns out, Victor has more trouble with the opera's prima donna, Odette (Odette Myrtil), than with Shirley. By the end of the evening Victor and Shirley are indeed deeply in love. There was again virtually no chorus, and the musical background of the play implies this was an economy measure rationalized. But the small cast was select. Interestingly the musician hero was given none of the unforgettable melodies that helped the show to its 395-performance run. "The Night Was Made For Love" and "She Didn't Say 'Yes' " were introduced by a strolling guitarist, Pompineau (George Meader), promoting the romance. Shirley joined Pompineau in the latter—both songs follow directly after the opening—and late in the last act Shirley alone sang the tearful "Try To Forget."

If Kern continued to strike out for new territory, the usually daring Hammerstein reverted to well-covered ground when he supplied the book and lyrics for a new Sigmund Romberg operetta, **East Wind** (10-27-31, Manhattan). About the only original thing in the show was its specific locale, Saigon. But its love affair between a French girl and a French boy could just as readily have been set in Paris. Claudette Fortier (Charlotte Lansing) marries Rene Beauvais (William Williams), who quickly deserts her. But Rene's brother, Paul (J. Harold Murray), has long loved Claudette. He seeks her out and marries her. Like Rudolf Friml's music for *Luana* (with its similar setting), there was a sad lifelessness to Romberg's songs. While panning the musical itself, a number of critics found kind words for the production, especially Donald Oenslager's "racy, realistic sets" which the *Times* termed "Indo-Chinese baroque."

The best of these scenes was for the first-act finale—a Saigon waterfront that exploded into a mass of lush tropical colors when a flower boat arrived. Charles LeMaire's costumes ran heavily to gold. A Hawaiian dancer, Ahi, earned loud applause for a hula she performed, even though she was supposed to represent a Chinese girl in Southeast Asia. When the show folded after 23 performances, its producers, Frank Mandel and Laurence Schwab, dissolved their partnership. Together they had brought to New York some of the twenties' best musicals: among them, *The Desert Song, The New Moon, Queen High*, and *Good News*.

Another Ed Wynn carnival, **The Laugh Parade** (11-2-31, Imperial), brought the perfect fool back to Broadway on November 2 with a grab bag of sketches and songs. The show had almost been a disaster. Its tryout had gone so badly and its advance sale had been so small that Wynn gave away seats on the first few nights to dispel the contagious gloom of an empty house. Happily he and his material were so good that the show quickly caught on. He had his customary zany inventions, including a miniature bed to catch bedbugs and a hat with a removable brim that allowed its wearer to tip it in the winter without risking a cold. Juggling with several balls at one time, he came up with one of his most often quoted lines when he instructed the orchestra leader to "play something in a jugular vein." Harry Warren followed up on his successful songs for *Sweet and Low* (11-17-30) and *Crazy Quilt* (5-19-31) with two solid hits, "Ooh, That Kiss" and "You're My Everything." The growing strain on Broadway as a result of competition from newer sources of entertainment was poignantly manifested during the run of *The Laugh Parade*. So that Wynn could broadcast his weekly Texaco "Fire Chief" series, Tuesday night performances were omitted.

Here Goes the Bride (11-3-31, 46th St.) was produced by the well-known cartoonist and theatrical dabbler, Peter Arno. He also wrote the book which, up to a point, reflected the beginnings of a more universal acceptance of divorce. June and Tony Doyle (Victoria—later Vicki—Cummings and Paul Frawley) have fallen out of love. They take their new loves with them to Reno while they get a divorce. They also take two riotous valets. The valets were played by McCullough and Clark. Actually Clark was Doyle's valet, B. Hives, and McCullough was the valet's valet.

But neither the comics nor composers, Johnny Green and Richard Myers, could inject the necessary vitality into the piece. Only Arno's imaginative sets won universal praise. He brought some of his graphic humor and style over from *The New Yorker* to create with "fetching craziness" (*Brooklyn Eagle*) "grotesque and nervous rooms" (the *Times*) at once "bold and witty" (the *American*). Arno's show curtain was a blown-up scandal sheet that actually served to set the exposition in motion. But such delicious sets couldn't save the show. One week, and it was gone.

The adventures of *Shuffle Along*'s Steve Jenkins and Sam Peck were continued in **Sugar Hill** (12-25-31, Forrest). This time the boys got themselves involved in Harlem bootlegging. The show's plot twists were ominous and ugly. This, plus the use of a single set depicting the front of a Harlem brownstone, led several critics to view it as a musicalized, black *Street Scene*. Gyp Penrose (Broadway Jones), a gangster attempting to kill a rival, kills a little girl instead. Peck, playing detective, sets up his girl friend, Cleo (Edna Moten), as a decoy and lures Gyp into a trap. In a further similarity to *Street Scene* a number of minor plots were woven into the main story. But there was no consistency of tone, and musical comedy trappings were legion. Penrose, for example, led the chorus in "Hot Harlem." Flournoy Miller and Aubrey Lyles again played their beloved comic pair, but they did not write most of their material; nor did they have anyone of the caliber of Eubie Blake or Fats Waller do the score. Though one of the songs was honest enough to express a sentiment dear to all the Jenkinses and Pecks in Harlem, "I Don't Want Any Labor In My Job," it said little to the few theatregoers who sat through the 11 performances and then shuffled on out.

But the following evening, December 26, 1931, witnessed the arrival at the Music Box of one of the greatest of all American musicals: **Of Thee I Sing.** The title seems an obvious one considering the plot, but there may have been something in the *Zeitgeist* of the time, now forgotten, that prompted it. *Here Goes the Bride* also used "My Country 'Tis Of Thee" as a source for the title of what it hoped would be its song hit, "My Sweetheart, 'Tis Of Thee." The new show took a barbed, witty look at American political institutions. It was never malicious and never stooped to personal attacks, though some critics felt the principal character was made to look and sound a little like New York's troubled Mayor Walker. If so, it was probably a trick of director George S. Kaufman, for co-librettist George S. Kaufman was above such pettiness.

The show opens with a campaign parade. Signs the marchers carry display an un-American political candor: "Turn the Reformers Out," "Vote for Prosperity and See What You Get," "A Vote for Wintergreen Is a Vote for Wintergreen." As they parade they chant "Wintergreen For President." The scene changes to a hotel bedroom where party bigwigs are assembled. Two things are bothering them: their campaign is not proceeding as smoothly as they hoped, and not one of them can recall the name of the vice-presidential candidate. There's a minor added irritant. A man named Throttle-something-or-other keeps phoning the room. The distinguished newspaper tycoon, Matthew Arnold Fulton (Dudley Clements), tries to reassure his associates, "The people of this country demand John P. Wintergreen for President, and they're going to get him whether they like it or not." The caller appears, shyly announcing he is Alexander Throttlebottom (Victor Moore), their candidate for the vice-presidency. (Precisely who wrote what in the libretto will never be known. But it is likely Morrie Ryskind gave the principal characters their names. A major figure in *The Gang's All Here* (2-18-31), on which he collaborated in the preceding season, was Horace Winterbottom.) The politicians all welcome their new candidate, though they are still not certain they can remember his name. But Throttlebottom comes bringing bad news. He wants to resign; the thought that her son is Vice President might prove too shameful for his mother to bear. He is talked out of quitting just as Wintergreen (William Gaxton) arrives. Wintergreen also can't remember who his running mate is, but he's more concerned with ominous reports from the grass roots. These reports all agree Wintergreen needs an issue. Fulton asks a chambermaid who happens into the room what she cares about most. When she replies apart from money it's love, the committee has its platform. Wintergreen will run on love! To strengthen his chances the party will hold a beauty contest in Atlantic City to select a Mrs. Wintergreen for the President to love. At the seashore the contestants sing of their import to the nation, explaining one of them will be "Mrs. Prexy" (if she's "sexy"). The photographers become the girls' allies, asserting the girls have nothing to worry about, even if they lose "Because, Because, Because . . . I could fall for you myself." To his colleagues' dismay, Wintergreen is not so ready to fall. He confides to Mary Turner (Lois Moran), who is acting as secretary for the contest, his fears that when he leaves the White House he'll discover his bride can't even cook. Mary suggests any girl can learn to cook. She adds she can "bake the best darned corn muffins you ever ate"—corn muffins that have no corn in them. Wintergreen is impressed. He's especially fond of corn muffins. The judges announce their decision. The winner is a loquacious southern belle, Diana Devereaux (Grace Brinkley). But Wintergreen demurs. He has decided he will marry Mary, and her muffins. Miss Devereaux stalks off demanding justice, while Mary and Wintergreen head for New York. Outside Madison Square Garden the excitement mounts, and the youngsters in the crowd agree, "Love Is Sweeping The Country." Inside the Garden speeches are interrupted by commercial messages on the loud-speaker. In the turmoil, a still unrecognized Throttlebottom barely misses being ejected from the hall. As election night begins returns are flashed on a screen. The photographs, interspersed with unrelated pictures and items, show that Wintergreen voted at least twice, that he won in Landslide, Nebraska, by 12,538 to 1 and lost in Rome, Italy, with 0 votes to Mussolini's 828,638. Wintergreen appears, thrilling the crowd by singing his campaign song, "Of Thee I Sing." But Diana arrives at the inauguration, halting the proceedings with her demand for a fair deal. For the moment she is unsuccessful. The scene switches to the White House, where a guided tour is passing through. One of the tourists is Alexander Throttlebottom. The White House guide can't tell him who the Vice President is or where the Vice President lives, but thumbing through his guides' manual he learns the Vice President is supposed to preside over the Senate. Throttlebottom decides that's better than nothing and rushes to the Capitol. The President and Mrs. Wintergreen share the oval office, with the first lady in charge of domestic and household matters. The atmosphere is tense because a movement sympathetic to Miss Devereaux is growing around the nation. Wintergreen shrugs it off, insisting "Who Cares?" The French obviously care. They send their ambassador (Florenz Ames) to the White House to protest, since a dishonor to Miss Devereaux is a dishonor to the whole French nation. Miss Devereaux, it seems, is "the illegitimate daughter of an illegitimate son of an illegitimate nephew of Napoleon!" Talk of impeachment spreads, worrying party

bosses who still can't recall the name of the Vice President. But it is this very Throttlebottom who must now preside over the impeachment. He calls the roll of the Senate, rhyming those states that will rhyme and excusing the rest. All that saves Wintergreen is the news that he will soon be a father. The Senators rejoice, "Posterity is just around the corner." The French demand the baby or war. But after the Supreme Court announces that the President's wife has had twins, a solution is found. Wintergreen points out that, according to the constitution, "When the President of The United States is unable to fulfill his duties, his obligations are assumed by —" by the Vice President, of course! Gleefully clapping his hands, Throttlebottom walks away with Miss Devereaux.

Like *The Cat and the Fiddle, Of Thee I Sing* had extended passages of rhymed recitative and continuity. The tone was naturally and fittingly different, but these recitatives further signaled an advance in the musical stage's ambitions. There is, however, a slight tendency to exaggerate the importance of this advance. Many old comic operas had long passages of rhymed dialogue set to music. But in both new musicals the passages were more frequent and more thoughtfully wrought, with more important melodic lines than in most of the older works.

For its authors—the Gershwins, Kaufman, and Ryskind—the show marked the perfecting of ideas first tried in *Strike Up the Band*. To their amazement their efforts earned them the first Pulitzer prize ever awarded to a musical. Ironically, since the award was a literary one, George was excluded. *Of Thee I Sing* also became the first musical published as a hardback book. The show's inherent brilliance, the critical kudos and the award all contrived to give it a run of 441 performances. Gaxton and Moore proved so excellent a team that they were called on to do several shows together afterwards. Moreover, despite the depression, a road company toured with Oscar Shaw and Donald Meek in the Gaxton and Moore parts. By coincidence that January 11 revival of *The Gondoliers* mentioned earlier gave a number of people who were calling the Gershwins the jazz Gilbert and Sullivan a chance for comparison.

Queenie Smith opened in the first new musical of 1932, **A Little Racketeer** (1-18-32, 44th St.), after a disastrous tryout which witnessed several changes in composers, principals, and director. But nothing helped. Miss Smith played Dixie, a street urchin who pretends to fall asleep in fashionable cars hoping their owners out of pity will give her a few dollars. When handsome young Dick Barrison (John Garrick) finds her in his car, he takes her to his apartment. Learning of her little racket and of her ambition to become a mobster, he pretends to be a society burglar. They soon fall in love, and Dixie is assured of a big car all her own. Even with a supporting cast that included Carl Randall, William Kent, and Barbara Newberry, the show could muster only 48 performances.

Vincent Youmans called his musical version of *Smilin' Through,* **Through the Years** (1-28-32, Manhattan). Youmans had been moving away from the staccato playfulness of his earlier songs ever since *Rainbow* (11-21-28). With his new show he also moved away from the *Show Boat* (12-27-27) or *Rainbow* variety of still unacceptable musical play (though "musical play" is precisely what he called *Through The Years*), leaning surprisingly toward Kern-like operetta. Several times in his last active years, Youmans seemed to follow the trails blazed by Kern. The romantic story leaped back and forth across the decades. In its forty-five-year time span and in its use of its principals in dual roles, the show recalled operettas such as *Maytime* (8-16-17) and, coincidentally or not, was set in the same periods. By what may have been a further coincidence, both shows had principals surnamed Wayne. In 1914 Kathleen and Kenneth announce their plans to marry. But Kathleen's guardian, John Carteret (Reginald Owen), objects. He cannot forgive Kenneth's uncle, Jeremiah Wayne, for killing John's bride-to-be, Moonyeen, forty years earlier. John's thoughts send him back to those days; in his reveries Moonyeen convinces him to let the young lovers have their way. Natalie Hall played Kathleen and Moonyeen, while Michael Bartlett was both Kenneth and Jeremiah. Two Youmans' classics came out of the show, though they were not universally appreciated in first hearing, Moonyeen's "Through The Years" and John's "Drums In My Heart." By and large the critics were unkind—to some extent because of their preconceived notions of a Youmans score. Nor was there an immediate public response. As a result the production was withdrawn after two and a half weeks.

On February 9 Charles Dillingham presented Maurice Chevalier at the Fulton in a one-man show, singing popular French and American songs.

If the critics were unhappy with Youmans, they were delighted with Irving Berlin. He had been in a rut for several years and only now showed signs of coming out of it. His excellent score for **Face the Music** (2-17-32, New Amsterdam) not only suggested his uninspired period was over but it nicely illustrated a major Berlin characteristic. His songs for the show are as unlike his 1920 music as his 1920 work was from his 1910 style. More than any other major American composer, Berlin's music mirrored the age in which it was written. Much of his greatness was his remarkable ability to adapt to and excel in the prevailing styles of any period. The longer lines and subtle, plaintive chordings and more subdued gaiety of the thirties are all evident in his *Face the Music* score. The show's hits, the glibly optimistic "Let's Have Another Cup Of Coffee" and the haunting "Soft Lights And Sweet Music," are standards, but they are exemplary period pieces as well. To many the show itself seemed a localized *Of Thee I Sing.* The fact that Sam Harris produced both and that George S. Kaufman directed the two undoubtedly served to underscore the similarities. But the cohesive intermixing of book and music so successful in *Of Thee I Sing* was missing here. Berlin's songs fit nicely into the story, yet they remained individual numbers that gained or lost nothing outside the theatre. Nor was Berlin's wit as literate or as rapierlike as Ira's. The essential warmth of both his lyrics and his melodies contrasted sharply with Moss Hart's biting satirical barbs.

• • •

Moss Hart was born in New York on October 24, 1904, and was educated in its public schools. While Hart was working for Augustus Pitou, the producer mounted the young writer's melodrama, *The Holdup Man.* But the show folded on the road. Besides his job with Pitou he worked on theatricals at Jewish resorts. His comedy, *Once in a Lifetime,* put into shape for Broadway by George S. Kaufman, was an immediate hit, establishing Hart as a name to be reckoned with. The libretto for *Face the Music* was his second experience in the lyric theatre. His first, *Jonica* (4-7-30), had been a quick failure.

• • •

In Hart's story Broadway producer Hal Reisman (Andrew Tombes) enters the Automat, where the Astors and Vanderbilts have taken to eating during the depression (it was here in the Automat that the aristocrats in morning suits and evening gowns sang "Let's Have Another Cup Of Coffee"). Reisman comes hoping to find a backer for his new show. In walks bejeweled and befurred Mrs. Martin Van Buren Meshbesher (Mary Boland). She is "lousy with money," though her money is a little newer than that of the aristocrats around her. Her husband is a policeman, and the source of their wealth is graft. But her husband and his fellow officers will be happy to have their money laundered in a musical show. With the Meshbesher cash Reisman puts on a Ziegfeldian "Rhinestones of 1932." The show is an apparent flop. However, the police and city hall have come under investigation (as indeed Tammany and Mayor Walker had), and the boys need all the money they can get. Mrs. Meshbesher barges into the investigation astride a papier-mâché elephant that could have been left over from the last *Ziegfeld Follies*. Matters take a turn for the better after the policemen persuade Reisman to add some titillating smut to their revue. The cast of *Face the Music* was fine, although it lacked the inspired assignments of *Of Thee I Sing*. Hassard Short designed the evening, again making stunning use of mirrors, and Albertina Rasch was in charge of the choreography. *Face the Music* was not the smash hit its quality deserved, but it ran a satisfactory 165 performances.

The Shuberts had another fiasco when they brought in a German operetta, *Hotel Stadt-Lemberg*, under the title **Marching By** (3-3-32, 46th St.). The old war-horse Harry B. Smith was responsible for most of the adaptation, while Mack Gordon and Harry Revel interpolated a number of songs not completely in keeping with the play's period. For Smith, who in fifty active years had made himself the most prolific librettist and lyricist Broadway was ever to know, the evening represented a disheartening farewell. His days of glory, which began far back with *The Begum* (11-21-88), were long gone; his years of retirement were to be unrewardingly few.

The ailing Florenz Ziegfeld suffered a major disappointment with a musical labeled **Hot-Cha** (3-8-32, Ziegfeld). The creators of *Face the Music* must have had a private laugh when they discovered that the money for the show came largely from two gangsters, Waxey Gordon and Dutch Schultz, who had tried to force Ziegfeld to call it leeringly *Laid in Mexico* (Ziegfeld reluctantly retained it as a subtitle). But Lew Brown got back, in part, with a couplet that kidded the more advanced shows of the season, referring to them as "Park Avenue librettos by children of the ghettos," though Brown had been a ghetto child himself. The libretto which Brown wrote with Ray Henderson and Mark Hellinger was anything but Park Avenue. It was really a loosely strung-together piece designed to provide a vehicle for Bert Lahr, ignoring to some extent the fact that Ziegfeld originally

conceived the evening as a showcase for Lahr's glamorous co-star, Lupe Velez. Lahr played Alky Schmidt, a speakeasy waiter, who finds himself in Mexico after he flees a raid on the nightclub. A promoter picks him up and advertises him as a great bullfighter. Bullfighting loses. Lahr's hilarious mannerisms—his nervous repetition to make a point, his crossing his eyes, his nasal "gnong, gnong, gnong"—helped cover the weaknesses in the book. So did Joseph Urban's "superlatively beautiful," "shimmering" sets. The *Times* advised its readers they would especially enjoy "public squares under a vast empyrean, and for a finale . . . a Ziegfeld fiesta." Brown and Henderson's songs included no standouts, but "You Can Make A Bed Of Roses" (which may have sounded like a remake of their "Life Is Just A Bowl Of Cherries") had a pleasing tune with a surprising turn of musical phrase. Faced with so much stronger competition, the show was lucky to survive for fifteen weeks.

April's lone American musical was a Negro revue patently attempting to cash in on the fame of the *Blackbirds*. Critics complained that the show's dancing lacked the "traditional abandon" and that the sketches resorted to such tired war-horses as Harlem rent skits and prison skits. A wary, dollar-conscious public wasn't fooled, and **Blackberries of 1932** (4-4-32, Liberty) beat a retreat after three weeks.

A Russian revue, **The Blue Bird** (4-21-32, Cort), was offered by Sol Hurok. Its reception was icy, and it tallied even fewer shows than had the black revue.

One-week flops were not uncommon in the depression. **There You Are** joined the list by opening at the Cohan May 16 and closing May 21. It told a *Rio Rita*-like story without that beloved show's singable melodies or magnificent settings. Carolita (Ilse Marvenga) agrees to marry the cynical Governor Jose Gomez (Joseph Lertora) rather than see her true love, Lloyd Emerson (Roy Cropper), jailed as the bandit, El Diable. The real El Diable (Hyman Adler), a south-of-the-border Robin Hood, appears. He gives the governor his comeuppance and unites the lovers.

Three nights later, May 19, Ziegfeld returned *Show Boat* (12-27-27) to New York, bringing it into the Casino. But the Casino was not the famous old musical house. It had been demolished in 1930. The new Casino had only recently been the Earl Carroll. When Carroll's financial problems deprived him of his house, Ziegfeld grabbed it, and rather cruelly obliterated every reference to

Carroll in the building. Yet Ziegfeld's vindictive pleasure was short-lived. He died just two months after the opening: July 22, 1932. However, *Show Boat* was a huge success with all the original principals except Howard Marsh and Jules Bledsoe returning. Dennis King and Paul Robeson replaced them.

Two revues finished the season. A black show, unattractively called **Yeah Man** (5-26-32, Park Lane), managed four performances at the end of May despite notices that branded it as "uncommonly bad" and "a new low." For comedy it attempted to find humor in an insane asylum. Marcus Slayter's Sixteen Black Hurricanes danced their way from a Mississippi levee at the opening of the show to a closing scene in Harlem.

Frank Morgan, most recently of *The Band Wagon* (6-3-31), starred in **Hey Nonny Nonny!** (6-6-32, Shubert)—a catch phrase he used throughout his career. A good part of the material was off-color. There was a song about a "Nude Ranch" and an examination of what might happen if Minsky, the girlie-burlesque king, took over the Metropolitan Opera as he had 42nd Street. The suggestive material proved no lure, apparently refuting the worldly-wise police of *Face the Music*, and the show closed quickly.

1932-1933

In a way, the death of Florenz Ziegfeld at the very beginning of the season—before the first musical offering arrived—was the most significant milestone of the theatrical year. Creative talents and responsible producers would continue to appear in the American Musical Theatre, but none would be (or ever had been before) so active for so long a time and none would ever possess Ziegfeld's expensive tastes or elegant panache. His death ended an era; he left a void that was never to be completely filled. To no small extent, commercial considerations have protected his uniqueness. In Ziegfeld's heyday the living theatre had been unchallenged and supreme. In his very last years sound movies came to offer more to please the eye than the richest Ziegfeld extravaganza could hope to match. They forced a new microphoned style of singing and therefore of song that was essentially inimical to the stage. Successes such as the incisively satiric *Of Thee I Sing* (12-26-31) and the romantically American

Show Boat (12-27-27) should have suggested to both writers and producers that the lyric stage could still create forms able to keep it reasonably competitive and alive. Instead, running scared, Broadway would not prove really venturesome (with few notable exceptions) until good times returned. Luckily, enough great talent was left in New York so that the next few seasons proffered a good deal of ongoing excellence, if on a smaller scale.

One week short of three months elapsed between the opening of *Hey Nonny Nonny!* and the first show of the 1932-33 season. On August 30 Fred Stone and his daughter, Dorothy, raised the curtain on their **Smiling Faces** (8-30-32, Shubert). The basic plot was the old one of a girl who marries one man to attain sufficient social standing to marry a second and then decides she prefers the first man. The story had been used before in *Betty* (12-11-11), *The Duchess* (10-16-11), and *Orange Blossoms* (9-19-22). In *Smiling Faces* the girl was motion picture actress Peggy Post, on Long Island to make a movie. The director of the picture group is Monument Spleen, a sometimes cantankerous, sometimes elfish old man. Such a tale was even more in the real world than Stone's previous *Ripples*, with its hints of Rip Van Winkle, had been. Certainly it was not the make-believe land in which Stone had always thrived. Moreover, Stone's age and illnesses had made him less able to perform the nonsensical acrobatics his fans so adored. The show came to Broadway after a lengthy, not always successful, road tour. Fred's other daughter, Paula, had been the original Peggy and was replaced by her older sister for New York. But Gotham was even less receptive than the rest of the country. The show stayed only four weeks. It was the second failure in a row for Stone, who had known only the most tremendous success heretofore. Sensing the changing times, this once-beloved comedian quietly retired from the musical stage. Mack Gordon and Harry Revel created the songs. They were the last of the many fine songwriters Stone employed; unlike the others, they failed to come up with hits.

Ballyhoo of 1932 (9-6-32, 44th St.) had no connection with W. C. Fields' vehicle of two years before. It was produced by Norman Anthony and his associates. Anthony was the editor of the popular magazine *Ballyhoo* and meant the show to be an in-the-flesh version of its barbed pages. On stage most of the barbs were hurled by Willie and Eugene Howard and, in his first important Broadway assignment, by Bob Hope. They were assisted by Lulu McConnell and Paul Hartman. Spoofs assailed Greta Garbo (as Margreta Garbitch), revolutionaries (with Howard crying "Rewolt") and Negro evangelists (with Willie in blackface). However, the evening's comic high point was the Howard version of the *Rigoletto* quartet with little Willie's eyes glued on the bosom of the prima donna. Even the serious numbers by E. Y. Harburg and Lewis E. Gensler were sometimes pricked with a pin. The torchy "Thrill Me" ended when the man being sung to lit up a sign advertising Ex-Lax. For Gensler the show was the final chapter in his Broadway career, remembered today solely for "Cross Your Heart" from *Queen High* (9-8-26). Yet, though none of his songs from this show became standards, they were included in the general critical praise for the evening. Regrettably the public response was halfhearted, and the show compiled a middling 95 showings.

Labor Day week usually saw the first of the September musicals, but in this troubled season it was the middle of the month before a new offering appeared. **Flying Colors** (9-15-32, Imperial) was "the fourth generation" in the revue series that had begun with *The Little Show* (4-20-29) and then sired *Three's a Crowd* (10-15-30) and *The Band Wagon* (6-3-31). A number of critics and scholars have pointed out how the series was settling into an imitative pattern, especially in its songs by Arthur Schwartz and Howard Dietz. "Alone Together" was not unlike the brooding "Dancing In The Dark," the Germanisms of "Meine Kleine Akrobat" were an extension of those in "I Love Louisa," and the requisite depression hopefulness was doled out by the delightful "A Shine On Your Shoes" instead of "Sweet Music." This last number, sung by Monette Moore, was danced in the show by Buddy and Vilma Ebsen to Larry Adler's harmonica accompaniment. Perhaps the most original melody in the evening was "Louisiana Hayride," a joyous re-creation of old Negro gospel songs with lyrics in fitting Negro dialect. Started by Clifton Webb and Tamara Geva but then sung by the whole ensemble, it served as the show's rousing first-act finale.

Dietz himself considered "Fatal Fascination" one of the better numbers. It was a song in which a man responds with spoken comments as his girl tells him of his mysterious appeal to her. His replies are actually reveries of his past life and seem directed at some inner reflections rather than his girl's remarks. Another number, "Smokin' Reefers," described the influence of marijuana in Harlem. Sketches made fun of friends and relatives seeing somone off to Europe, and of an accommodating hotel catering to clients driven to suicide by the depression. The rooms on the top floor cost more. Webb (retained from *The Little Show* and *Three's a Crowd*) and Patsy Kelly were the solicitous hotel-keepers, while Charles Butterworth was the guest. Just as Fred Allen's riotous explorer monologue was the comic high point of *Three's a Crowd*, so Butterworth's delivery of "Harvey Woofter's Five Point Plan" was the most praised bit of fun in *Flying Colors*. To obtain shorter working hours Harvey would allow each hour only 40 minutes. "Everything would be reduced in proportion. The minute would be 40 seconds, a second would go in a jiffy, and the jiffy would hardly be worth mentioning." The dollar would be strengthened by renaming it, and since so many European currencies like the Frank and the Mark are named, according to Harvey, after men, he suggests renaming the dollar the Harvey. Agnes de Mille did the original choreography, but disputes with the show's producer Max Gordon and its librettist, Dietz, forced her to turn over her assignment to Albertina Rasch. Webb and Tamara Geva (also from *Three's a Crowd*) were given some of the best choreography of the evening, particularly an elegant, sinuous dance for "Alone Together." They danced on a specially devised stage that slowly receded into the darkness. The stage was the creation of Norman Bel Geddes, whose "crisp, modernistic" settings were no small part of the show's critical success or of its high cost— $125,000 depression dollars. When attendance at $4.40 top proved disappointing, the best seats were reduced to $2.20. As a result the show made only the barest profit on its 188-performance run.

A "Vaudeville revue" that had Sam Bernard II as one of its authors and producers opened under the title **Belmont Varieties** (9-26-32, Belmont). So much was thrown together so hastily that on opening night the show played far too long. A ballet based on a Degas painting drew some kind notices, but most of the bill was minor specialty acts. For example, Lilyan Astaire (Sam Bernard's niece) impersonated Bert Lahr and Bea Lillie, Ray Benson entertained with feats of magic. The revue closed after one week; then reopened at the end of October, first as the *Cosmo Vanities* and then as the *Manhattan Vanities*. The rapid name changes were unavailing, and the show shortly disappeared.

The more famous **Earl Carroll Vanities** (9-27-32, Broadway) was a more streamlined edition than his earlier annuals, noteworthy for the imaginative staging of young Vincente Minnelli. Besides more traditional effects—such as girls representing a garden of gardenias or a locomotive or embellishing a luminous Maypole—Minnelli had the girls in glass tubes that lit up to display a variety of color and design. The cast included Helen Broderick, Harriet Hoctor, and young Milton Berle. Berle's funniest moment came when he played a coarse gangster who finds his wife entertaining a cultured Englishman in her bedroom. Round, red-faced little Will Fyffe amused audiences with his droll Scottish monologues. The evening offered an especially fine Harold Arlen melody that went largely unnoticed by critics, who applauded such forgotten songs as "Love You Are My Inspiration" (Ted Koehler/Andre Renaud), "My Darling" (Ed Hyman/Richard Myers), and "Along Came Love" (Charles and Henry Tobias). Arlen's "I Gotta Right To Sing The Blues," with lyrics by Ted Koehler, sung by Lillian Shade, remains popular to this day. For all its improvements—and the show was a slightly better than average edition—theatregoers indicated their indifference by staying away. The show closed after 87 performances, effectively ending the series, though one tentative effort was made to revive it eight years later.

A more interesting, sadder failure was the third and last in J.P. McEvoy's **Americana** (10-5-32, Shubert) series. Musically it introduced the song which for many became the theme of the depression era, "Brother Can You Spare A Dime?" (E. Y. Harburg/Jay Gorney). Rex Weber, a comedian, sang the number straight. Harburg and Gorney also contributed the attractive "Five Minutes Of Spring," while Harburg and Vernon Duke combined to write a rather bitter farewell to Jimmy Walker, "Let Me Match My Private Life With Yours," using Walker's tart statement, "I can match my private life with any man's," as a start. Harold Arlen, Herman Hupfeld, Johnny Mercer, and Burton Lane all supplied words or music as well. But for many the show's allure was its dancing by the Charles Weidman Dancers and the Doris Humphrey Dance Group. José Limon was in the former company. Their modern dance material included a stylized prizefight and a Shaker meeting. One oddity for a show with this title was the inclusion of Alfredo Rode's Tzigane Orchestra —playing Viennese waltzes. The comedy was weak or old hat or both. Skits made fun of movie moguls, breadline racketeers, and Walker (an easy, pathetic target at this date). Albert Carroll,

long a mainstay of the *Grand Street Follies,* could find nothing more novel to do than an impersonation of Lynn Fontanne, a great actress he had mimicked often before. But modern dance was apparently either too somber or too advanced for Broadway's pleasure-seekers and *Americana*'s comedy too lame. The show survived less than ten weeks.

Tell Her the Truth (10-28-32, Cort) was the second attempt in five years to convert the 1916 hit, *Nothing but the Truth,* into a successful musical. It was less skillful and less enduring than *Yes, Yes, Yvette* (10-3-27), managing to run only a week and a half, though the show had been a hit in England.

While the perennially pessimistic Burns Mantle insisted there were "precious few" outstanding musicals during the 1932-33 season, there were three major book shows and two revues that had both merit and success. Several other shows had merit or at least interest but failed to generate any popular response. It was not a bad showing, considering the times. The hit book musical that prompted Mantle's lament was **Music in the Air** (11-8-32, Alvin). Jerome Kern reunited with Oscar Hammerstein II for an evening that was closer in spirit to his previous collaboration with Otto Harbach, *The Cat and the Fiddle* (10-15-31), than to the works Kern and Hammerstein had written together. As in *The Cat and the Fiddle,* the setting was present-day Europe rather than bygone America. And again the story used the musical world as its milieu. In Edendorf, a small Bavarian village, the old music teacher, Dr. Walther Lessing (Al Shean), has worked with young Karl Reder (Walter Slezak) to write a song called "I've Told Ev'ry Little Star." They decide to go to Munich to have it published. Accompanying them are Karl's sweetheart, Sieglinde (Katherine Carrington), and the Edendorf Walking Club. The distance does not deter them anymore than does the chance that "There's A Hill Beyond A Hill." In Munich Karl finds himself pursued by the prima donna Frieda Hatzfeld (Natalie Hall), while the composer Bruno Mahler (Tulio Carminati) is so taken with Sieglinde he writes an operetta for her and includes a part for "A man about my age and wicked like me." He is put out when she prefers to play on a swing rather than listen to his new waltz, "One More Dance." But Sieglinde is happiest "When Spring Is In The Air." She cannot bring herself to be a thorough professional, even when Bruno insists that she is his inspiration and that no matter what song he writes,

"The Song Is You." The villagers prefer their sleepy hamlet to the dubious charms of the big city. Sieglinde and all the others return to Edendorf agreeing, "We Belong Together."

The show contained some of Hammerstein's most felicitous writing. But it also betrayed evidences of his recurring pretensions. In this case every scene of the "musical adventure" was given the name of a musical style or device, starting with "Leit Motif" and running from "Etude" through "Nocturne" and "Caprice" to "Rondo." Joseph Urban designed the sets. Critical reaction to them suggested either Urban was slipping, or else standards were either changing or becoming more demanding. While Robert Garland writing in the *World-Telegram* extolled the "lovely Urban mountains," Richard Lockridge of the *Post* felt "Joseph Urban's settings are pretty and not much more." Most critics kept their opinions to themselves by not even mentioning the sets. Primarily it was Kern's captivating score that accounted for the run of over seven months.

The morning of the reviews the front pages of all the papers announced that Franklin D. Roosevelt had been elected President.

Grace Moore proved the drawing card for a revival of Millöcker's *The DuBarry* in which Howard Marsh was her leading man. The show ran 87 performances. This represented two more weeks than the run achieved by **George White's Music Hall Varieties** (11-22-32, Casino). Financial difficulties prevented White from mounting a lavish *Scandals*. The stripped-down, retitled revue was his answer. White followed Carroll and Ziegfeld into the huge Casino in the hope that at $2.20 top playgoers would flock to the house. They didn't. Some of the material was old, like the Howards' "Pay the Two Dollars" skit. Bert Lahr was refreshingly restrained in his lampoon of Clifton Webb, whom he caricatured as Clifton Duckfeet. Several of the best numbers were songs Harold Arlen had written for the Cotton Club, the popular Negro night spot. One of these was the first-act finale, "I Love A Parade," which Harry Richman sang. Eleanor Powell's scintillating tap routines added to the audience's enjoyment.

All three of the season's hit book musicals arrived in November. *Music in the Air* opened the month, while *Take a Chance* and *Gay Divorce* came in three nights apart at its end. The success of **Take a Chance** (11-26-32, Apollo) was a surprise. It had begun life in September as a one-week flop in Pittsburgh called *Humpty Dumpty*. But co-producer Laurence Schwab had closed at

least one other show on the road (*The New Moon*), rewritten it, and watched it become a smash (9-19-28). With his associate Buddy DeSylva, he again gambled on revisions, and won. *Humpty Dumpty*'s original story of an attempt to produce a revue satirizing events in American history was retained with a love interest built around it. Kenneth Raleigh (Jack Whiting), a handsome Harvard graduate, decides to produce the revue. His backers include two not very honest young men, Duke Stanley (Jack Haley) and Louie Webb (Sid Silvers), and their attractive, honest girl friend, Toni Ray (June Knight). Kenneth falls in love with Toni, but when he realizes Duke and Louie have not been forthright in their dealings he suspects Toni is party to their schemes. Toni helps iron out everything and goes on to star in the revue. Oddly enough the star of the show, Ethel Merman, played the relatively minor role of Wanda Brill, but she dominated the evening by the force of her personality and the fact that she had all the hit songs to sing. The original score had been by Richard Whiting and Nacio Herb Brown, with Vincent Youmans called in for interpolations. To a chorus line of girls dressed as sailors, Miss Merman wailed a dirge for a departed bordello operator, "Eadie Was A Lady," with Jack Haley she offered, "You're An Old Smoothie," and from the Youmans' contributions stopped the show with another depression uplifter, "Rise 'n Shine." Youmans' songs were his last efforts on Broadway. For most of his final years he was too ill to compose. Stanley Green, in his study of 1930s musicals, offers the interesting note that a song called "Poppy Smoke" was to have been in the show but was dropped when "Smokin' Reefers" got to Broadway first in *Flying Colors*. The show played through the season but suffered a major change in tone just before it folded when the zany team of Olsen and Johnson, who had bought an interest, took over the parts of Duke and Louie.

Gay Divorce (11-29-32, Barrymore) also got off to an uncertain start. The critics didn't care for it. They were uncomfortable watching Fred without Adele Astaire. She had always been considered the major partner. But Astaire, excellently supported by Claire Luce, Luella Gear, Eric Blore, and Erik Rhodes, quickly proved he could go it alone. The show's hit tune, written to stay within his very limited range, soon became the nation's number-one hit. Cole Porter said he was inspired to write "Night And Day" after hearing Mohammedan calls to prayer in Morocco and that the "drip, drip, drip" of the verse was suggested by a comment of a hostess annoyed by the sounds coming from a broken eaves spout. The show abounded in comic numbers. A song about cynical social-climbing, "Mister And Missus Fitch," stemmed from a series of hoax letters Porter and his friends had written to a paper and signed with the names of various members of the imaginary Fitch family. Blore, the perfect waiter, bemoaned, "What Will Become Of Our England?" while Miss Gear detailed amusingly the reasons "I Still Love The Red, White And Blue." The story on which these songs were hung was little better than a French bedroom farce. Mimi Pratt (Miss Luce) seeks to give her husband grounds for divorce by letting herself be caught with a paid co-respondent. Guy (Astaire), who has fallen in love with her, substitutes for the co-respondent and pesters Mimi into loving him. The sophisticated, intimate nature of the story was mirrored in the elegant, intimate sets Jo Mielziner created for the production. Eschewing the plethora of sets most depression musicals offered (probably in hopes of competing with films), *Gay Divorce* reverted to the old practice of one set for each act. The first act unfolded in a hotel lobby; the second in Mimi's suite. True, there was a prologue that took place in Guy's home and a brief scene in a hotel corridor in Act Two—but they were minor excrescences. The show witnessed another Broadway farewell. With *Gay Divorce* Fred Astaire bid the legitimate theatre a permanent goodbye.

A number of great clowns who remained loyal to the musical stage to the end of their careers romped in a week later with **Walk a Little Faster** (12-7-32; St. James). Beatrice Lillie appeared in an S. J. Perelman sketch "Scamp of the Campus" (as a 1906 co-ed with the unlikely name of Penelope Goldfarb); as Frisco Fanny, a Gold Rush queen; and as a French "chantootsy." In one of her most famous bits, after making a staid announcement dressed in a conservative evening gown, she picked up her skirt and roller-skated off stage. In another Perelman skit Bobby Clark played the Russian dictator, Josef Stalin. He also played a sourdough to Miss Lillie's Fanny. Clark's long-time partner Paul McCullough remained his complacent stooge. The songs for the show were Vernon Duke's first complete Broadway score, although his songs had been interpolated into other productions and he had written *The Yellow Mask* for London.

. . .

Vernon Duke was born Vladimir Dukelsky in Pskov, Russia on October 10, 1903. Something of

a child prodigy, he composed a full ballet score at the age of eight. He studied under Reinhold Glière at the Kiev Conservatory, but was forced to flee Russia during the revolution. He eventually emigrated to America, where he met George Gershwin, who encouraged him to write popular music. Unable to support himself with his popular compositions, he returned to Europe and to serious music, but he soon found himself in London writing show tunes.

. . .

Out of *Walk a Little Faster* came Duke's classic "April In Paris." In his study of American popular song, Alec Wilder unashamedly calls it "a perfect theatre song" and uses a page and a half to analyze it. The song caused no stir among either the critics or first-nighters—possibly because Evelyn Hoey, who sang it, was suffering from laryngitis. It became another of the many songs that achieved fame only after the show it was written for had long closed (as did "I Gotta Right To Sing The Blues" in this same season). But even the show's minor, forgotten numbers such as "Where Have We Met Before?" have an appealing sweetness. Coming in directly behind two strong competitors and so close to *Music in the Air*, the new revue found its ticket sales were hurt. It left after sixteen weeks.

Shuffle Along of 1932 (12-26-32, Mansfield) was 1932's last regular musical. It reunited the three surviving creators of the original show, after Aubrey Lyles' death. Flournoy Miller was again Steve Jenkins of Jimtown, now trying to get rich quick with U-Eat-Em Molasses. A northern slicker and his Harlem cutie attempt to fleece Jenkins and Jimtown, but fail. Eubie Blake and Noble Sissle combined to write a totally new score, but nothing from it caught the public's fancy. Possibly because the evening was set in Jimtown instead of Harlem, and had none of the violent undertones of *Sugar Hill*, the critics, almost to a man, reverted to the customary appraisal of a Negro show, minimizing the value of the book and expending most of their time and praise on the dancing. The hard times of 1932 demanded something more. Even with a meager chorus of fourteen low-paid tappers, *Shuffle Along of 1932* could not make it past its 17th performance. Shortened into a "tab show" to accompany motion pictures, bad luck would not let it alone. The survivors were stranded in Los Angeles.

On December 27, 1932, the night after the new *Shuffle Along* debuted, Radio City Music Hall opened its doors. Conceived as a mammoth

481

vaudeville house, it was soon converted to a policy of first-run motion pictures coupled with elaborate, mindless spectacles of a kind once so popular at the long-darkened Hippodrome down the street.

The first show of 1933, **Pardon My English** (1-20-33, Majestic), was another of those musicals that looked infallible on paper. Instead it was the first in a dismaying parade of flops that continued until September—one of the most disastrous stretches in the history of the American Musical Theatre. *Pardon My English* had a book by Herbert Fields and songs by the Gershwins. It was produced by the usually lucky Alex Aarons and Vinton Freedley. Troubles began at the beginning. Aarons had intended to mount the show alone, but skyrocketing costs compelled him to call in Freedley. The extended tryout was traumatic. New writers and new directors were engaged, the original star (Jack Buchanan) left and a muddle ensued. What New York finally saw was a disjointed book in which Jack Pearl (the famous prevaricating Baron Munchausen) played a Dresden police commissioner who arrests a couple of innocent Americans, mistaking them for crooks. He also discovers his daughter is in love with a suave thief. Down the drain with the show went several lovely Gershwin numbers, including "Isn't It A Pity?", "Lorelei," and "My Cousin In Milwaukee." The show's German setting was disturbing to many regular theatregoers. Shortly before the show opened Hitler had assumed power in Germany, and the night *Pardon My English* closed, Berlin's Reichstag burned.

At the end of their careers almost all the producers of the annual girl shows turned to operetta at a time when its day was clearly done. Florenz Ziegfeld had mounted *Bitter Sweet* (11-5-29). Earl Carroll had tried *Fioretta* (2-6-29), and of course the Shuberts continued a policy that was as old as their revues. Now George White tried his hand at it, bringing in Sigmund Romberg's **Melody** (2-14-33, Casino). He hired Joseph Urban for the sets and assembled a stellar cast including Evelyn Herbert, Everett Marshall, Walter Woolf, and Hal Skelly. Edward Childs Carpenter's libretto told essentially another of the bitterweet, generation-bridging love stories Romberg was inordinately fond of but which he used succesfully only in *Maytime* (8-16-17). A number of theatregoers undoubtedly recalled a similar Romberg piece with a similar title, *The Magic Melody* (11-11-19). Andree De Nemours (Miss Herbert) is forced to marry the Vicompte De Laurier (George Houston) instead of her Tristan (Marshall). Tristan is killed in battle. Years later Andree's granddaughter, Paula (Miss Herbert), marries George Richards (Walter Woolf), the nephew of Tristan's friend. The story does not quite come full circle and somehow seems wanting because of this. In a like manner, Romberg's songs were reminiscent and pleasant, but lacked some final touch. Surprisingly some of New York's toughest and most up-to-date critics welcomed *Melody* as a nostalgic escape from 1933's harsh realities. One thing they did not welcome was Urban's sets. Almost to a man the critics merely mentioned them in passing or ignored them totally. This neglect was especially sad, for Urban's work for *Melody* was his last for Broadway. *Melody* witnessed another departure. Expenses at the large Casino, that coupled with a relative indifference on the part of the New York playgoers had doomed the show, doomed the theatre as well. When the operetta closed after its 79th showing, the virtually brand new Casino disappeared from the legitimate fold.

The closest this dismal period came to having a hit was **Strike Me Pink** (3-4-33, Majestic), which Lew Brown and Ray Henderson wrote and produced. It agonized through a bedeviled tryout, much like those several other of the season's shows endured. Its ultimate reception fell somewhere between the eventual success of *Take a Chance* and the glum failure of *Pardon My English*. A number of the problems on the road were caused by Waxey Gordon, one of the two underworld figures who had so pestered Ziegfeld in his effort to save *Hot-Cha* (3-8-32). Gordon had originally bankrolled *Strike Me Pink* when it was known as *Forward March* and slated to be a liberal-oriented revue showcasing new talent. When the road was cold to its charms, Gordon pumped money into it and used his influence to pressure Brown and Henderson into hiring names. By the time is reached New York Lupe Velez and Jimmy Durante were a bigger lure than the show itself. Much of the more strident left-wing material had been discarded, though "Home To Harlem" attempted to elicit some sympathy for a black criminal's longing for New York. The song was sung against Henry Dreyfuss' moving cyclorama that depicted episodes in the black man's progress—a cottonfield cabin, a prison chain gang, a Harlem nightclub. None of the show's tunes surged to the top of the popularity lists, but three songs, all somewhat more subdued than Henderson's material of old, enjoyed a contemporary vogue: "Let's Call It A Day," "It's Great To Be Alive," (taken over from *Hot-Cha*), and the title song. Durante made his first entrance down the theatre's aisle, fighting with an usher for the right to go on stage. Once behind the footlights he and Miss Velez had fun in a skit in which they both portrayed "children of nature" frolicking in Central Park. Late in the evening he reminisced about his cabaret days with Clayton and Jackson—both of whom joined in to sing their old songs, at least on opening night. Other entertainers included Hal Le Roy (who walked off with some of the best notices for his fancy tap dancing), Eddie Garr (who did a hilarious impersonation of Ed Wynn), and mannish Hope Williams (who seemed to be looking for something to do).

April's two musicals were both fast flops, and the contrasts between the two are revealing. **Humming Sam** (4-8-33, New Yorker) reached back to Charles Dazey's once-popular old melodrama, *In Old Kentucky*, as a source for its plot. An even older tradition was revived by having the principal male part played by a woman as a "trouser role." Once again a jockey (Gertrude "Baby" Cox) is torn between winning the Kentucky Derby to please his sweetheart (Madeline Belt) or losing to enrich himself and some crooked hangers-on. The horse and love win. *Humming Sam* was designed as pure, entertaining hokum. Murderously reviewed, the black musical never got past its first night.

Bertolt Brecht and Kurt Weill's **The 3-Penny Opera** (4-13-33, Empire) reached still farther back to John Gay's 18th-century *The Beggar's Opera* and turned it into a radical comment on modern life. Although the critics were only slightly less unreceptive, they seemingly enjoyed their first exposure to Kurt Weill's unique musical style. Gilbert Gabriel of the *American* called the book "a dreary enigma"; John Mason Brown of the *Evening Post* labeled it "appallingly stupid"; while Richard Lockridge of the morning *Post*, responding to its political colorings, assailed it as "sugar-coated communism." The show was put away after after a week and a half to await a more welcoming day.

No shows arrived in May, and the season concluded with a single June entry. **Tattle Tales** (6-1-33, Broadhurst) had begun life as a Hollywood revue assembled by the witty compère, Frank Fay. It had moved across the country after its Hollywood run and for New York, Fay's wife, Barbara Stanwyck, rejoined the show. Fay made his first appearance dressed as Louis XIV. Serving as master of ceremonies (the voguish night clubs of the twenties saw to it that the term replaced the older "compère"), Fay announced he had appointed Ray Mayer to be the evening's "Official Mr. 'Eh' 'Eh'." Mayer was to come out from the wings and say "Eh Eh" whenever the going got dull. Miss Stanwyck appeared in two scenes adapted from her current motion pictures, *The Miracle Woman* and *Ladies of Leisure*. *Tattle Tales* had suffered through a troubled career even in Los Angeles with both Fay and Miss Stanwyck out of the cast at times for various reasons. It offered New York nothing it had not seen better done and, with the hottest summer recorded until then beginning to make itself noticed, the show discreetly departed after a month.

1933-1934

For the first time since the beginning of the century the number of new musicals dropped below twenty. In fact the number dropped all the way to thirteen (though there were nearly a dozen revivals as well). Only once again in the ensuing years would the count of new lyric pieces ever reach twenty.

In certain respects the 1933–34 season could be looked on as the conclusion of this long, brilliant act. Certainly it witnessed the sad but definite end of several of the most promising trends in the musical theatre. On the other hand it also gave quick, inviting glimpses of the future. Promising new faces were beheld in a show of the same name and elsewhere; though many of them soon left for more lucrative situations in Hollywood. But the three seasons that followed 1933–34 saw several fine, traditional musicals by loyal old hands, and so the curtain will not come down on this act for a while.

Only one new piece braved the hot weather. **Shady Lady** (7-5-33, Shubert) told of Richard Brandt's attempt to paint murals for the "Shady Lady" night club using an ex-reformatory girl, Millie Mack, as a model. She is cold and cynical, but Richard's natural warmth melts her reserve. Richard was played by Charles Purcell and Millie, surprisingly, by the former squeaker of baby talk, Helen Kane. Both the night club, never shown, and Millie were suggested by the real-life Texas Guinan, and, should anyone miss the connection, one song was "Hiya, Sucker," an unmistakable reference to Texas' famous greeting. But the heat and the show's mediocrity soon told. *Shady Lady* lasted four weeks.

Milton Aborn continued the revivals his Civic Light Opera had been offering the last few seasons, bringing in *The Bohemian Girl, The Pirates of Penzance,* and *The Yeomen of the Guard.*

With the era of the great annuals over, Earl Carroll thought he had discovered a way to have his cake and eat it too. He combined with Rufus King to write a book musical about a **Murder at the Vanities** (9-8-33, New Amsterdam). Both Florenz Ziegfeld and George White had presented book shows in which their great revues were a part of the story. In *Sally* (12-21-20) and *Manhattan Mary* (9-26-27), the heroine rose to become a part of the *Follies* or the *Scandals* in the last act. But Carroll seemingly went one better. All the action took place during a performance of the *Vanities,* allowing Carroll to stage numbers from a typical *Vanities* production and, in effect, producing a virtual new edition tied together by the story of a chorus girl who is murdered by the wardrobe mistress so that her daughter can be a replacement. Special production numbers included a fan scene "with four rows of blonde chorus girls tossing uneasily to languorous rhythms." The opening scene was done entirely in yellow. Not all of the show was lavish or imaginative. Carroll apparently ran into difficulty with the designers' union while the entertainment was being put together. When his staff deserted him, he settled for performing several of the scenes against simple "sable hangings." At least nine songsmiths worked on the score. They included Victor Young, Herman Hupfeld, Richard Myers, and Johnny Green. Green, with Edward Heyman, came up with a characteristic ballad of the period, "Weep No More My Baby." In a small way Carroll got back at Ziegfeld for erasing his name from his new theatre. Carroll brought the show into Ziegfeld's old berth, the gorgeous New Amsterdam, where it played just over six months.

Like *Murder at the Vanities,* **Hold Your Horses** (9-25-33, Winter Garden) had a host of composers and lyricists working on the score, and like the Carroll piece no real hit emerged. But then *Hold Your Horses* itself was no hit. Joe Cook starred as another Joe, Broadway Joe, the driver of an old horse-driven cab. In typical Cook fashion the cab was loaded with wildly devised conveniences, including a kitchenette, a bath, and an elevator. Crooked politicians nominate Joe for mayor so that

the apparent opposition, whom they actually favor, will be a shoo-in. But Joe campaigns for his opponent, costing his hapless foe so many votes Joe wins. As mayor, Joe vetoes a projected subway construction to assure his fellow hack drivers a livelihood. The sets took old-timers back to Rectors, Nigger Mike's, and the original Casino Theatre. Diamond Jim Brady, Lillian Russell, and Anna Held paraded across the stage. But oldsters who remembered that era were not generally attuned to Cook's roughhouse clowning, and younger theatregoers asked for something more than just Joe Cook. In the face of such general dissatisfaction *Hold Your Horses* was lucky to survive eleven weeks.

Sketches for **As Thousands Cheer** (9-30-33, Music Box) were by Moss Hart, its songs by Irving Berlin. It gave its authors a melody-filled, laugh-laden successor to their *Face the Music.* The cast included Clifton Webb, Helen Broderick, Ethel Waters, and Marilyn Miller in her last stage appearance before her untimely death. Using the clever device of having each scene preceded by an appropriate newspaper headline, its skits sent their barbs far and wide: the Hoovers leaving the White House, with the President giving his cabinet a Bronx cheer; John D. Rockefeller refusing to accept Radio City as a birthday gift; commercials interrupting the singing during a Metropolitan Opera broadcast; a hotel staff falling under the influence of Noel Coward; and a Supreme Court decision that says musicals cannot end with reprises, resulting in a new number, "Not For All The Rice In China" as a finale. Berlin filled the score with top tunes. Besides "Supper Time," a Negro's lament for her lynched husband, and "Harlem On My Mind," in which a Josephine-Baker type of expatriate longs for her old home (her lips start to whisper "Mon Cheri," but her heart keeps singing "Hi-di-ho"), Ethel Waters introduced the sizzling "Heat Wave." Marilyn Miller and Clifton Webb stepped out of a sepia-tinted photo in the rotogravure section to enjoy the "Easter Parade." Berlin had written this song during World War I, when its lyrics began "Smile and show your dimple." The show was a triumph, running a year and making a handsome profit—a rarity during depression days.

In what was becoming a once-a-decade attempt to offer *Die Fledermaus* to Broadway in a new guise, **Champagne, Sec** (10-14-33, Morosco) was uncorked with Peggy Wood as Rosalinde and Kitty Carlisle as Prince Orlofsky. The evening revived a happier Vienna for 113 performances.

For one brief moment, 1933–34 looked to be

producer Sam Harris' season, but he was in for a major disappointment. At the end of September he had acquitted himself handsomely with *As Thousands Cheer*. Near the end of October he brought in a sequel to *Of Thee I Sing* (12-26-31) called **Let 'Em Eat Cake** (10-21-33, Imperial). Like *Of Thee I Sing*, it had a libretto by George S. Kaufman and Morrie Ryskind, and songs by the Gershwins. It also offered Victor Moore, William Gaxton, and Lois Moran re-creating the same characters they had portrayed two years before. A number of minor characters were also back, while Florenz Ames retired as the French Ambassador to play General Snookfield. But the horrors of the depression and of the fascist movements in Italy and Germany had thrown both the authors and the audience slightly off balance. The smiling satire of the original gave way to what the *Times'* Brooks Atkinson termed a "bitter, hysterical mood." Wintergreen and Throttlebottom in their bid for reelection have been defeated by John P. Tweedledee. Taking their cues from fascist powers, Wintergreen and his fellow politicians, abetted by the muddled pundits of Union Square, decide to overthrow the government:

Wintergreen: Italy—black shirts! Germany—brown shirts! America—blue shirts! By God, if the American people want a revolution we can give it to them! We've got the shirts for it!
Fulton: He's right!
Wintergreen: You bet I'm right! Do you know what we'll do? We'll put a Maryblue shirt on every man in the country! And we'll guarantee a revolution or your money back.

The army, promised all the war debts, quickly takes his side. Finally it is agreed that any still festering differences will be settled by a baseball game between the Supreme Court and members of the League of Nations. Throttlebottom is made the umpire. His decisions prove controversial. In fact, Throttlebottom's calls are so unpopular that he is sentenced to the guillotine. But Mary, who had earlier provided all the blue shirts, now unites the women of America, and a happy ending prevails. Ira Gershwin, writing years later, may have touched on a second reason for the show's failure: Its targets were too widespread. "If *Strike Up the Band* was a satire on War, and *Of Thee I Sing* one on Politics, *Let 'Em Eat Cake* was a satire on Practically Everything." Still, there were felicitous touches. For example, the "maryblue" shirts recalled not just the fascist dress but the Alice blue of an earlier White House. And Ira's lyrics were

brilliant. Brother George's music again was used not just for songs, but in long, clever extended passages. Only one tune became popular, the Wintergreens' "Mine," in which one melody is set in counterpoint against another.

Perhaps there was a third problem as well. *Let 'Em Eat Cake* came too soon. *Of Thee I Sing* played through an election year, and the authors might have been wiser to wait until the next election made the new show's material more immediate. The elapsed time also might have served to moderate some of its excesses. As it was, the show had little appeal. It left after less than twelve full weeks. It was the last work approaching musical comedy that George Gershwin composed for the stage. Though he was yet to give Broadway his masterful *Porgy and Bess* (10-10-35), he died before he could return to his more traditional stage material. With him apparently died the impetus to develop this style of satirical musical. Only Frank Loesser and Abe Burrows, twenty years later, succeeded at something in any way similar.

Jerome Kern was also approaching the end of his Broadway career. No composer in the history of the American Musical Theatre ever associated himself with so many innovative works. His Princess Theatre shows had helped define and establish the basic American musical comedy form; *Show Boat* (12-27-27) had pioneered the American musical play; and his recent shows had pointed the way toward full-fledged American operetta. With **Roberta** (11-18-33, New Amsterdam) he stepped back in the direction of more traditional musical comedy, though his basic melodic line remained more florid and romantic than most writers in the field. Kern's great score for *Roberta* may have saved the show. Though Max Gordon gave it an eye-filling presentation (its $115,000 cost was about average for the better musical mountings of the era) and cast it superbly, Otto Harbach provided a book and lyrics that were disappointingly turgid. Harbach based his story on Alice Duer Miller's novel, *Gowns by Roberta*. Except for a prologue set in the States, all the action took place in contemporary Paris. It was a background not too far removed from Harbach's setting for *The Cat and the Fiddle* (10-15-31). Unfortunately, he bungled it. John Kent (Ray Middleton), an all-American fullback at Haverhill College, learns he has inherited a dress shop run by his Aunt Minnie (Fay Templeton). But the shop is in Paris, where his aunt trades under the name of Roberta. Her assistant is a young lady named Stephanie (Tamara), and John proposes that she run the shop as his partner. She agrees. A budding romance between the two almost comes to naught when Sophie (Helen Gray), John's old college flame, appears. But he knows that Sophie has run off once before and suspects she'd do it again. Only as they are about to be married does Stephanie reveal she is a Russian princess. The ending suggests some of the ineptitudes in the libretto. Revelations of royal blood were stock conclusions in the operettas of previous decades. But with the heroine having no hope of returning to Russia as a princess the revelation is meaningless and gratuitous.

Bob Hope provided most of *Roberta*'s few comic moments. Happily, Carl Robinson, the set designer, and Kiviette, the costumer, working under Hassard Short's supervision, created a mounting of such visual beauty that many of the libretto's languors were handsomely glossed over. Quite naturally a fashion show, "Shadows of Silver," provided the evening's spectacular highlight. While an on-stage band played appropriate music, the ten gentlemen of the chorus and a handful of the twenty-eight chorus girls sat stylishly accoutered as buyers. Before them the remaining chorus girls paraded in elegant but simple gowns, the seven most expensive shimmeringly spangled with sequins. José Limon created a stunning dance for the seven mannequins. *Roberta*'s other major dance number was a wedding scene which found "supple, Polish-accented, blond" Lyda Roberti and her bridesmaids cavorting in the evening's most uninhibited number. One striking set represented an American bar in Paris. The bar's rear wall was composed of a thousand real bottles neatly aligned on shelves. Miss Templeton had only one number to sing, but it was Kern's lovely "Yesterdays." The sensuous score also included "The Touch Of Your Hand," "You're Devastating" and the incomparable "Smoke Gets In Your Eyes." Tamara accompanied herself on a guitar while singing this favorite in the American bar. The songs became popular though Kern continued to be daring and innovative (witness the curiously truncated structure of "The Touch Of Your Hand") and though Harbach affixed arcane and almost unsingable lyrics such as "So I chaffed them and I gaily laughed." With the songs stimulating box-office sales, *Roberta* ran nine months. During the show's New York stand *Fortune* magazine gave a fascinating breakdown on the production's financial picture. *Roberta*'s weekly nut was $20,000. At $3.30 for the best seats the weekly capacity gross would be $29,000. Had the show played consistently to full houses, it would have paid off its backers in three months. But the faults of the evening and tepid notices prevented the show from ever reaching the top figure. Nonetheless, with only *Murder at the Vanities* and *As Thousands Cheer* (both at $4.40 top) offering *Roberta* serious competition, *Fortune* predicted the show would be in black by the time it closed. Unfortunately for Broadway, Kern found the California sunshine congenial and except for one brief return spent the rest of his life writing for Hollywood.

Lew Leslie persisted in trying to recapture the élan and popularity of his original **Blackbirds** (5-9-28), and even when his 1933 edition (12-2-33, Apollo) folded after three weeks he refused to abandon his efforts. Several hands provided the songs, whose musical styles were adopted to the sounds of the day but whose lyrics still clung to the expected material of the old Negro shows ("Doin' The Shim Sham," "Great Gettin' Up Mornin' "). The best thing about the short-lived revue was Bill Robinson's joyous tap dancing.

As the old year disappeared, one thing seemed fairly certain: there would be no more Prohibition jokes on Broadway. Prohibition was gone. Utah had cast the decisive vote. Whiskey and wine could flow again.

There was no wine but plenty of women and song in 1934's first musical. More happily there was also lots of delicious comedy. The **Ziegfeld Follies** opened January 4, bankrolled by the Shuberts and playing their Winter Garden. Mrs. Florenz Ziegfeld was billed as producer, but Billie Burke's only real interest in the show was the possible profits that might help pay her late husband's debts. The show lacked the Ziegfeld look. With both Ziegfeld and Urban gone, that was inevitable. The *Brooklyn Eagle* complained the show was "too carelessly arranged to be Ziegfeld's"; the *American* acquiesced, finding the spectacle "not up to original snuff." In the *Times* Brooks Atkinson rued that Ziegfeld Follies had become a mere trade name. He lamented that the new mounting "lacks the grandee's unifying touch" and went on to slam specific scenes as "tawdry." Only one number done all in ivory and gold elicited some grudging praise from him. Still, the new *Follies* had enough glitter and frills to make a passable imitation. It also had three durable song hits: more than most of the old *Follies* ever had in a single edition. From the regular Vernon Duke score (with E. Y. Harburg lyrics) came "What Is There To Say?", while two interpolations, "The Last Round-Up" (Billy Hill), and "Wagon Wheels" (Hill and Peter De Rose), gave an unexpected western flavor to the show. Willie Howard and Fanny Brice sparked the clowning. Miss Brice mocked Aimee Semple McPherson in

"Soul-Saving Sadie"; harked back to another of her Sadies, "Sadie Salome," when she did "Countess Dubinsky" ("now she strips for Minsky"); and spoofed nudists in "Sunshine Sarah." She also introduced the character of Baby Snooks, the precocious, troublesome brat, whom she would play for years on radio. In her debut the not always truthful Snooks listened skeptically to the story of Washington and the cherry tree. With Howard, Miss Brice did a parody of the hit *Sailor Beware*. Howard did a hilarious reprise of "The Last Round-Up" with a Yiddish accent. The diminutive comedian was also both the outgoing and incoming presidents in a Cuban revolution, proclaiming a New Raw Deal. Jane Froman sang Duke's number, while Everett Marshall sang the interpolations. Marshall further sounded an increasingly fashionable note of social protest with "To The Beat Of The Heart" (Harburg/Samuel Pokrass) when, to a background of dying soldiers, he asked, "why, why, why did we die, die, die in vain?" All in all a solid evening's entertainment, this Ziegfeldless *Follies* ran nearly six months.

Old theatregoers may well have been reminded by **All the King's Horses** (1-30-34, Shubert) of a musical that predated the first *Follies*. The new show told a story not unlike Victor Herbert's *It Happened in Nordland* (12-5-04). If playgoers had long forgotten Herbert's piece the obituaries of Marie Cahill in August must have brought memories of it rushing back. Of course, the plot was also reminiscent of Sigmund Romberg's *Princess Flavia* (11-2-25). *All the King's Horses* called itself "a romantic musical comedy" but its story and the flavor of its music prompted several critics to call it an operetta. When it is discovered that the famous movie star, Donald McArthur (Guy Robertson), looks enough like King Rudolf of Langenstein to be his double, Rudolf persuades Donald to take his place while he goes to Paris for a fling. Donald's passionate crooning on the radio during a speech to "his" subjects brings the long estranged Queen Erna (Nancy McCord) eagerly back to his side. They, too, have a fling until the real Rudolf returns and Donald heads back to Hollywood. The score by Edward Horan (his only Broadway effort) was no match for the delightful old Herbert melodies. But the farfetched story and simple music had an appealing remoteness to many harassed playgoers, and they gave the show a passable run.

Four Saints in Three Acts (2-20-34, 44th St.) was the most talked-about musical of the season, but far from its most popular. Of course, controversy and its librettist, Gertrude Stein, went hand in hand. Miss Stein often professed to be more interested in the sounds of words than in their sense, and there were few indeed who could make head or tail of her "story." As best as could be determined it dealt principally with two saints, St. Ignatius Loyola and St. Teresa of Avila, as well as with Teresa's male alter-ego. There were random scenes from the saints' lives but no development. The first act took place in Avila and presented a pageant of incidents from Teresa's history. The second act, "Might It Be Mountains If It Were Not Barcelona," seemed to have even less point. In the third act St. Ignatius sees the Holy Ghost and disciplines his disciples. In the fourth act (to be expected of Miss Stein after she announced only three) a choir recapitulates the saintliness of the saints. The absurdities were underscored by having all the Spaniards played by Negroes and by the extensive use of cellophane for the sets. Miss Stein in a characteristic tautology referred to the work as "An opera to be sung." And indeed it was Virgil Thomson's precious but beautiful music that was the evening's chief delight. It had a simple, folk-like quality and drew its inspiration strongly from the church hymns of Thomson's southern background. But the piece was obviously not part of any on-going Broadway tradition and patently unlikely to initiate one. All that survives in common currency are a few of Miss Stein's curious rhymes: "Pigeons on the grass alas" and "When this you see remember me."

Leonard Sillman's **New Faces** (3-15-34, Fulton) was far more traditional and successful, and yet somehow innovative. Sillman achieved what Brown and Henderson had hoped to do with *Forward March* before it became *Strike Me Pink* (3-4-33), or what earlier shows such as *The Newcomers* (8-8-23) had attempted unavailingly. The revue was a showcase for aspiring stars. Though the entertainment had first seen the footlights as *Low and Behold* at the Pasadena Playhouse, Broadway had watched some of the performers before—in chorus lines or walk-ons, but never in any significant assignments. Now in lighthearted skits and pleasant but undistinguished songs they could be seen and heard to advantage. Only two, Imogene Coca and Henry Fonda, went to the top of the acting world, though Sillman and Nancy Hamilton made their marks as producers. The best of the material was by Miss Hamilton. In "The Disney Influence" she suggested how three current hits—*Ah! Wilderness, The Green Bay Tree*, and *Tobacco Road*—might seem in the hands of the Three Little Pigs. She herself performed a parody of Katharine Hepburn in *The Little Woman*. Imogene Coca spent most of the evening in a large top-coat, at one point sauntering across the stage in it, carrying a small feather and announcing she was doing her fan dance. The tunes were collected from a number of sources. None was top-drawer, though "Lamplight" (James Shelton) and "My Last Affair" (Haven Johnson) enjoyed a momentary vogue. The show carried Charles Dillingham's name as producer for the last time. But it was purely a courtesy. Dillingham was destitute and dying. Elsie Janis, another old name, sometimes associated with Dillingham, was credited as director. For her, too, it was a farewell to the New York stage.

S. M. Chartok revived a series of Gilbert and Sullivan works in April: *The Mikado, The Pirates of Penzance, H.M.S. Pinafore, Trial by Jury,* and *Iolanthe.* In May Charles Purcell and Donald Brian revived *The Chocolate Soldier* in an effort to make work for themselves, and the Shuberts brought back *Bitter Sweet* (with Evelyn Herbert and Allan Jones), hoping to find the audience it missed in 1929. The brothers also mounted a revival of *The Only Girl* (11-2-14). The revival had originated on the West Coast and in what was to become a dismaying practice in later revivals, indiscriminately culled popular Herbert favorites from his other shows and used them in place of weaker numbers from the original score.

Another operetta calling itself "a romantic musical comedy" closed the season. **Caviar** (6-7-34, Forrest) was a 20-performance dud. Its story was similar to *The Count of Luxembourg,* in which a couple are joined together sight unseen in a marriage of convenience and then fall in love with each other not knowing they are already married. In *Caviar* the lovers are Elena (Nanette Guilford), an American opera singer, and Dmitri (George Houston), an impoverished Russian prince. They woo in Venice and wed in Constantinople. The score was by another one-time composer, Harden Church.

1934-1935

For the first time in years there was a rise in the number of new musicals offered to Broadway. But the increase was slight, reflecting perhaps the small turn around in the economy. As so often happened when the number of shows rose, the quality dropped. Only one new show could be called superior, though several others maintained a reasonably high level. Nothing startlingly original appeared; if anything, it was a season when the musical theatre kept looking back over its shoulder to a happier past.

The season's very first show inaugurated this regressive tendency. While it called itself **Gypsy Blonde** (6-25-34, Lyric), it was admittedly merely an up-dated version of *The Bohemian Girl.* Balfe's score was retained faithfully, but the original story was reset in contemporary Westchester. The heroine (Isabel Henderson) is lured by the gypsies away from her wealthy home and the prospects of an uninteresting marriage. In the gypsy camp she falls in love with an escaped ex-convict (George Trabert). Inevitably the modern setting and the modern dialogue clashed with the century-old melodies. The show left after three weeks.

No more new musicals appeared until the end of August when three premiered in swift succession. **Keep Moving** (8-23-34, Forrest) was a mediocre revue by and with relative unknowns. The biggest "name" on the roster was crotchety Tom Howard, who warned audiences not to laugh or applaud lest they wake the critics. Singers' Midgets gave a third dimension to all the celebrated Walt Disney cartoon characters. And Clyde Hagan evoked enough laughs and clapping to wake reviewers with his take-off of a fast-talking carnival pitchman selling potato peelers. His peelings may have even landed on a critic if the reviewer happened to be in the first row. But such shenanigans were not enough to please an increasingly demanding Broadway. The unknowns remained unknown when the show left two and a half weeks after it arrived.

But four nights later a band of top professionals, all in good form, presented Broadway with a first-class revue, **Life Begins at 8:40** (8-27-34, Winter Garden). John Murray Anderson, James Reynolds, and Albert Johnson presided over the spectacle. Harold Arlen wrote music to words by E. Y. Harburg and Ira Gershwin. Bert Lahr, Luella Gear, Ray Bolger, and Frances Williams headed the excellent cast.

. . .

Raymond Wallace Bolger was born in Dorchester, Massachusetts, on January 10, 1904. He made his first public appearance at the age of eighteen in a serious dance recital, but quickly moved over to the vaudeville circuits. Broadway first saw the "nimble, rubber-legged" dancer in *The Merry World.* More vaudeville followed until Bolger returned to Broadway for *Heads Up* and *George White's Scandals.*

. . .

The show had originally been conceived as

another edition of the *Ziegfeld Follies,* and early announcements suggested the entire evening would be done daringly all in white. The title and the color scheme were changed—the former to reflect Walter Pitkin's bestseller, *Life Begins at Forty*—but the changes in no way lessened the show's attraction. Lahr performed his stage Englishman, a suicidal Frenchman, a gullible Wall Street client, and a pompous tea-concert singer gushing at the "utter, utter, utter loveliness of things" and getting as a reward a pie in his face. Miss Gear sang of "My Paramount-Publix-Roxy Rose" and bewailed that, though she dutifully bought everything in the all-promising ads, "I Couldn't Hold My Man." The rhumba beat that had begun to come to the nation's attention with "Siboney" came to Broadway with the curiously titled "Shoein' The Mare." Ray Bolger and Dixie Dubar boosted each other's ego with "You're A Builder-Upper." Bolger also offered his interpretation of the Max Baer—Primo Carnera fight, and took his work home in "The Window Dresser Goes To Bed." All the principals reassembled for the finale "Life Begins at City Hall," in which the new mayor Fiorello La Guardia (Lahr) awaits the arrival of Eleanor Roosevelt (Gear) to launch a gondola to Staten Island. Ex-Mayor Walker and his wife (Bolger and Williams) are found to be stowaways in the boat. Beautiful show girls twirled as untamed Cubans and posed as Doric columns and spring flowers. Even when they were still, they were in motion, for Albert Johnson placed his handsome sets on a revolving stage that turned to change scenes or because whim moved the director. John Mason Brown, writing in the *Evening Post,* complained this sort of "lazy susan" staging was so overdone it gave him vertigo. Audiences apparently disagreed. Life and fun began at 8:40 for seven months.

Saluta (8-28-34, Imperial) was advertised as a "musical comedy satire," professing to continue where *Let 'Em Eat Cake* (10-21-33) left off. But its authors were virtually talentless, and the only noticeable similarity was that both aimed to have fun at Mussolini's black shirts. *Saluta* went a step further, impersonating Il Duce on stage. Milton Berle played the leading role of "Windy" Walker, an "M.C." at a sleazy New York night spot who is persuaded by his gangster cohorts to sail to Italy and stage an opera in competition with the fascists' official productions. A rich American (Dudley Clements) adds his funds to the enterprise after he is promised his daughter Elinore (Ann Barrie) will be the prima donna. Il Duce represses the whole operation, but his anger does not extend to Windy

or Elinore and her boyfriend. The Americans sail gaily back on the *Rex.* The score was Frank D'Armond's lone New York exposure. Some of his lyrics were by his star, Berle. But Berle was not enough to override his writers' faults and *Saluta* quickly disappeared.

The D'Oyly Carte Company came from London on September 3 for a fifteen-week engagement that offered ten Gilbert and Sullivan masterpieces as well as *Cox and Box.* The visit was the troupe's first in fifty years—when it had come offering New York its original mountings. The resurgence of interest that Winthrop Ames and others had sparked in the Savoyard comic operas during the late twenties made the company doubly welcome.

A spectacularly mounted operetta, **The Great Waltz** (9-22-34, Center), proved so surprising a success it was forced to close while still profitable because a road trip had been booked before the extent of its popularity could be accurately judged. Hassard Short had suggested the show to Max Gordon after Short had produced a similar piece called *Waltzes from Vienna* in London. *Waltzes* in turn had been based on a Viennese hit. Both shows presented fictitious biographies of the Johann Strausses, father and son, and both used Strauss melodies for their songs. Moss Hart wrote the American libretto. It was not typical Hart, but it was typical operetta. In Hart's version the elder Strauss (H. Reeves-Smith) refuses to allow his son's music to be played. Countess Olga (Marie Burke) contrives to keep the father from the Dommayer's Garden's opening, thereby allowing the younger Strauss (Guy Robertson) to lead the band in his own melodies. The melodies were known and liked, but the principal attraction of *The Great Waltz* was undoubtedly its elaborate production. Mounted at the huge Center Theatre in the Rockefeller complex, it placed nearly 200 performers on the large, mechanically advanced stage. The settings and costumes had cost nearly $250,000, only one of few such expenditures between the heyday of Ziegfeld and the arrival of Mike Todd. In the evening's most magnificent moment Dommayer's Garden was transformed while the audience watched into a gigantic, sumptuous ballroom, with the entire orchestra of fifty raised from the pit in front of the stage to a balcony at the rear of the set. For some it called to mind the old Hippodrome extravaganzas that had played a few blocks down Sixth Avenue.

A vaudeville-revue, **Continental Varieties** (10-3-34, Little), cast entirely with European talent such as Lucienne Boyer and Nikita Balieff (late of *Chauve Souris*), began a ten-week stay. Balieff served as master of ceremonies. Miss Boyer sang her Parisian hits such as "Parlez-moi d'Amour." Vicente Escudero stamped out Spanish dances, and a magician named De Roze poured all manner of drinks from a single pitcher. The entertainment was presented by Arch Selwyn and Harold B. Franklin. At the other end of the month—October 23—these same gentlemen imported Noel Coward's **Conversation Piece,** housing it at the 44th Street Theatre, next door to the Little. Pierre Fresnay and Yvonne Printemps were starred. The show was about the love of a guardian and his ward, and not to the public's taste, but it left behind it one of Coward's loveliest songs, "I'll Follow My Secret Heart."

Composer Ray Henderson and librettist Jack McGowan combined to produce their own musical **Say When** (11-8-34, Imperial). With Buddy De-Sylva in Hollywood and Lew Brown striking out on his own, Henderson worked with lyricist Ted Koehler on the songs. McGowan's story began on a transatlantic liner where two entertainers, Bob Breese (Harry Richman) and Jimmy Blake (Bob Hope), fall in with Betty and Jane Palmer (Betty Dell and Linda Watkins), the daughters of a rich banker. Romances quickly blossom. But the girls' father opposes having show people in the family. Only when Bob and Jimmy discover Mr. Palmer (Taylor Holmes) is having an affair are they able to obtain the family's blessing. The show opened to rave notices. But the public proved bafflingly fickle, and the show ran just ten weeks, despite singable Henderson ditties such as "Don't Tell Me It's Bad."

Anything Goes (11-21-34, Alvin), the season's biggest musical hit, was more than just the runaway smash of the year. More, too, than merely a well-wrought, hilarious show, filled with unforgettable melodies and sophisticated lyrics, it was "the quintessential musical comedy of the thirties." If it was not as original or cohesive as, say, *Of Thee I Sing* (12-26-31) or *Porgy and Bess* (10-10-35), it never pretended to aim as high. Designed to be pure entertainment, and never losing sight of its intention, it succeeded sterlingly. That it seemed all of a piece and not the slapdash assemblage its title suggested undoubtedly amazed those who knew its history. For the show was already in rehearsal with a Guy Bolton and P. G. Wodehouse libretto that recounted the adventures of a group of shipwrecked passengers when the cruise liner *Morro Castle* burned off Asbury Park, killing 125. A new story had to be worked around the songs, sets, and principals. With both Bolton and Wodehouse unavail-

able, producer Vinton Freedley introduced the show's director, Howard Lindsay, to Russel Crouse, a Theatre Guild press agent, and prevailed on them to supply the new book. It was the beginning of one of the most profitable collaborations in theatrical records.

. . .

Howard Lindsay was born in Waterford, New York, on March 29, 1889. His family moved to Boston where he attended Boston Latin School and Harvard. Slated for the ministry, he abandoned his studies and enrolled in the American Academy of Dramatic Arts. After graduation he was active as a performer and director in vaudeville, burlesque, and silent films as well as the legitimate stage.

. . .

Russel Crouse was Lindsay's junior by four years, having been born in Findlay, Ohio, on February 20, 1893. After graduating from Toledo's public school system he spent his early years in journalism. His first acting job came in 1928 in an appropriate play, *Gentlemen of the Press*. His name first appeared as a co-librettist when *The Gang's All Here* (2-18-31) premiered. Lindsay and Crouse's long, successful career included *Life with Father*, which held the record as the longest-running show in Broadway's history when it closed and whose 3,224 performances make it still the longest-running straight play of the New York stage.

. . .

The story the neophytes concocted remained on the high seas for most of the evening, although it opened at a New York bar where the hostess, Reno Sweeney (Ethel Merman), a former evangelist, confesses she gets a kick out of Billy Crocker (William Gaxton). Reno is about to sail for England on the same ship as Hope Harcourt (Bettina Hall), the young lady Crocker fancies. Crocker goes to see Hope off, and on the spur of the moment decides to stow away so that he can remain with her. He is forced to adopt a number of disguises, at one point even clipping a dog for its hair. He finally wangles a legitimate ticket and a not quite legitimate passport from the Reverend Dr. Moon (Victor Moore), a wistful bit of a man who has been branded "Public Enemy #13." With a reverend and an erstwhile evangelist aboard, the captain distracts his depression clientele with a rousing revival meeting. Even Reno is so moved she belts out a paean to the archangel Gabriel. But for Crocker the distraction can only be momentary. When the ship lands, his beloved Hope will marry Sir Evelyn Oakleigh (Leslie Barrie). It is to be a marriage of convenience, but it is made suddenly unnecessary when Hope's business is sold for a handsome sum. Hope and Crocker go off together, while Sir Evelyn turns his attention to Reno. A cable from Washington announces that Moon has been adjudged harmless and is no longer wanted. His ambition to rise to "Public Enemy #1" frustrated, Moon departs after adding his name to the anti-Hooverites.

Donald Oenslager's stylishly contemporary sets included a triple-tiered view of the liner's decks, allowing an excellent exposure for bathing-suited chorus girls as they tapped away to Cole Porter's tunes. Though its scenery, tone, and allusions made *Anything Goes* up-to-the-minute, its refusal to allow its demi-monde heroine win her man hints that the same morality that governed *The Pink Lady* (3-13-11) and its day still obtained. But Porter's songs betrayed no such qualms. Melodically, they ran the gamut of the period's most popular tunes: from the revival fervor of "Blow, Gabriel, Blow" to the Latin undercurrents of the sultry "All Through The Night" (sung by Billy to Hope) and "I Get A Kick Out Of You," to the jumpy "You're The Top" (in which Billy and Reno flattered each other in catalogue fashion), to Reno's hard-riding title song. The songs Ethel Merman sang would forever after be closely associated with her. Lyrically, the songs displayed Porter's erudite wit (in "You're The Top" he paired Russia with Roxy usher) and civilized look at romance. Horrors in the news forced Porter, as well as his librettists, to make changes. Before the Lindbergh kidnaping "You're The Top" included a line that went "I shouldn't care for those nights in the air/That the fair Mrs. Lindbergh goes through." But for all the changes, the score was Porter's best up to the time and, except for *Kiss Me, Kate,* one he never again matched.

Donald Heywood's all-black operetta, **Africana,** premiered at the Venice on November 26. Heywood had written a score for a revue with the same name that ran for nine weeks in the summer of 1927. In 1932 his music for *Blackberries* failed to survive the show's three-week run. Heywood, something of a scholar, went to Africa to study native composition before setting his own story to music. His plot recounted the return of King Yafouba's eldest son, Prince Soyonga, from school at Oxford. Soyanga is filled with ideas for reform and modernization, but goes too far when he falls in love with a maiden who is taboo because she is half-white. Heywood himself conducted the open-

ing. During the performance he was attacked by a man who claimed Heywood had stolen his melodies. The man was removed and the performance finished. The *Times, Daily News, Sun,* and *World-Telegram* all remarked that the attack was the most theatrically satisfying part of the evening. *Africana* folded after three performances, but Heywood remained on the Broadway scene.

By Broadway's crassest commercial test **Revenge with Music** (11-28-34, New Amsterdam) was a hit. It made money, showing a $45,000 profit on a $120,000 investment. And it left behind some of Arthur Schwartz' more beguiling melodies, including "You And The Night And The Music" and "If There Is Someone Lovelier Than You." Still this first effort by Schwartz and Dietz at a book show never quite came together. Dietz lays part of the blame on Libby Holman, who costarred with Georges Metaxa and Charles Winninger. He contends that singing lessons had both spoiled the natural sultriness of her voice and ruined her enunciation. This may be true. But another problem could also be that Dietz considered the work an operetta. Admittedly its simple story and setting lent itself to the genre. In Spain, provincial governor Don Emilio (Winninger) attempts unsuccessfully to woo away Maria (Miss Holman) on her wedding night. In revenge Maria's husband, Carlos (Metaxa), has a fleeting romance with Don Emilio's wife, Isabella (Ilka Chase), wooing her, as he has his wife, by insisting if there is someone lovelier he doesn't know her. While, ten years before, Rudolf Friml or Sigmund Romberg might have filled just such a tale with rich, arioso passages, Schwartz was of a different school. True, his melodic line was longer and more graceful than that of most of his competitors, but his chromatics were strictly of the decade and his range within a song carefully restricted. At best he approached Jerome Kern in Kern's latest efforts to re-create the obsolete operetta in modern, native terms. If Dietz' book was at least adequate, his lyrics were disappointingly uneven. Within Maria and Carlos' "You And The Night And The Music" he could poetically capture a mood and incorporate a startling, yet fitting, metaphor ("Our hearts will be throbbing guitars"), while elsewhere sound as hackneyed as Harry B. Smith at his worst ("Make the most of time ere it has flown"). Seventeen colorful Spanish settings passed from one to another quickly on the season's second major revolving stage. This time no one seemed to become dizzy. Not coincidentally, the sets were the work of the same artist who had earlier mounted his spectacle on a turning platform, Albert Johnson. Even with a critical drubbing, *Revenge with Music* managed to survive for twenty weeks.

Given the declining number of live playhouses and the relative health of films, the conversion of the Hollywood Theatre from motion pictures to a legitimate auditorium must have seemed at once puzzling and heartening. The show honored to open the theatre in its new form on December 13 was **Calling All Stars.** Lew Brown did the lyrics and a number of the sketches. Harry Akst did the music. Even the title of their "I'd Like To Dunk You In My Coffee" suggests a certain come-down from the days when Brown created "You're The Cream In My Coffee" with Buddy DeSylva and Ray Henderson. Moreover Brown's continued insertion of left-wing pleas assuredly offended many in the audience. In "Straw Hat In The Rain" Brown addressed the "high hat" as "high and dry hat." For a lavish production number the producers could devise nothing more original than another jungle dance. Lou Holtz and Phil Baker handled the comedy, which the *Times* condemned as "dressing room jokes and smug obscenities." Holtz kidded late arrivals and offered his audience three kinds of gin— nitrogen, oxygen, and hydrogen. Later he ran up into a box to play stooge to Baker. While Baker made music on his concertina, he and Holtz traded insults. Everett Marshall, Jack Whiting, and Gertrude Niesen did what they could with Akst's inferior melodies.

A second December revue fared even less well. Leonard Sillman compiled it, using some of the talent (especially Imogene Coca) from *New Faces* (3-15-34). But **Fools Rush In** (12-25-34, Playhouse) rushed out before anyone knew it was there. In its short stay it celebrated the birth of the Dionne quintuplets and recorded an imaginary meeting between Mrs. Roosevelt and Mrs. Hoover. It also sang tunes by Will Irwin and Richard Lewine that few remembered outside the theatre.

Two more musicals arrived together on December 27. One was an eleven-performance fiasco, the other a twenty-week disappointment. The twenty-week run was all **Thumbs Up** could muster at the St. James, though it was gorgeously mounted by John Murray Anderson, James Reynolds, and Raoul Pène Du Bois; riotously performed by Clark and McCullough, Ray Dooley, and others; and blessed as "the birthplace of two important songs." James Hanley assured his admirers he had not lost his touch and could adapt to the smoother rhythms of the thirties with "Zing Went The Strings Of My

Heart" (sung and danced by Hal Le Roy and Eunice Healey), while Vernon Duke added "Autumn In New York" to his portfolio of classics. This was sung by J. Harold Murray before a background of moving screens showing pictures of Manhattan. Arthur Schwartz contributed several numbers, but none to equal the show's hits or his own best tunes from *Revenge with Music*. The comedy offered Miss Dooley climbing a human pyramid in "My Arab Complex" and Clark as a microphone-hogging judge at a broadcast trial. Spectacles presented a bit of Currier and Ives Americana in the opening and, since Eddie Dowling was producer as well as co-star, an elaborate Irish number, "Eileen Avourneen."

The dud that opened the same night was an operetta with a book by Brian Hooker and Russell Janney based on a novel and play by Justin Huntly McCarthy. To that extent it resembled *The Vagabond King* (9-20-25). Its story was just as swashbuckling, recounting the exploits of Flynn O'Flynn (George Houston) during the wars between William of Orange and James II in which O'Flynn still finds time to court and win Lady Benedetta (Lucy Monroe). However, the music for **The O'Flynn** (12-27-34, Broadway) was not by Friml, but by Franklin Hauser. It lacked the high-colored romance and imperishable melodies that Friml had provided.

By chance, Rudolf Friml was the composer for the very next lyric attraction. **Music Hath Charms** (12-29-34, Majestic) opened two nights later, the fourth musical of the week and the last of 1934. It was also the last new Friml score Broadway was to hear. The show had begun on the road some months before under a different name and filled with bright hope. At that time the hoardings proclaimed, "Messrs Shubert Have The Honor Of Presenting Maria Jeritza in the Rudolf Friml operetta 'Annina'." Playing opposite the great opera star and receiving meager publicity was the rising young Allan Jones. But it soon became obvious the show was not another Friml masterpiece. Miss Jeritza was replaced by Natalie Hall and young Jones by the older Robert Halliday. Once again an operetta told a story of similar loves in separate generations, though in *Music Hath Charms* the story leaps back over a century and a half as Maria, Marchese Del Monte Nee Di Orsano, reluctantly changes her mind about her American suitor after her grandfather narrates the love story of her great-grandmother. Miss Hall played the heroines of both epochs just as she had done in *Three Little Girls* (4-14-30). There may have been a certain charm in Friml's music, but it was pale in comparison to his scores of the teens and twenties. The show was sumptuously if garishly mounted. For some critics its chief attraction was its excellent dancing—not dancing of the kind common on Broadway, but gavottes, polkas, and tarantellas.

The plight of the depression's musical stage was brought home by the great gap of time between the December crush of new offerings and the appearance of the next musical. Five months elapsed—January through May—before **Parade** (5-20-35, Guild) arrived. It was the first of only ten musicals to open in 1935. And though several of these shows ran six months or more, not a single one repaid its investment. By Broadway commercial terms the year was a washout. *Parade* was a blatantly leftist tract that featured Jimmy Savo. Its much-discussed opening had the police ignoring radio reports of violent crimes but rushing to break up a parade of poor people. It saw fascists in every government seat and villains in every executive office. Not surprisingly the score was brassier and more martial than most, and the closest thing to the expected love song exclaimed, "I'm All Washed Up With Love" (Albert Silverman/Kay Swift). Marc Blitzstein and Will Irwin contributed interpolations to what was primarily a Jerome Moross score. Bad reviews and word-of-mouth closed the show after five weeks.

Earl Carroll displayed his latest **Sketch Book** (6-4-35, Winter Garden) to close out the season. With cries for social significance in the air, Carroll labeled his production a "Hysterical Historical Revue" and broadcast that it presented a chorus girl's perception of American history. This "Lorelei Lee" of the footlights had some strange ideas of the past. For her the Mexican War was a torrid dance done by a gaudily dressed line of "Gringolettes." Great figures from Washington to Lincoln to Bea Lillie were lampooned, with Charlotte Arren's take-off of Jenny Lind winning the most applause. Somehow reason was found to bring in an act of juggling animals, an eye-filling production number in honor of Carroll's (as well as Ziegfeld and Urban's) favorite color, "A Blue Paradise," and Mlle. Nirska's butterfly dance, with its billowing silks shimmering in soft pink lights. Cheerful, bustling Ken Murray, a cigar hanging from his mouth, presided. The music was undistinguished although obviously in touch with the times in songs such as "Let's Swing It." However absurd the whole conglomeration seems forty years later, the revue attracted enough patrons to record 207 performances.

1935-1936

The usually dissatisfied Burns Mantle had a brief change of heart while reviewing the 1935–36 season. "It is quite generally admitted," he rejoiced, "that this theatrical season has been the most exciting and most satisfying of any New York has enjoyed since . . . the crash of '29." It would be hard to gainsay a year that gave the stage *Jubilee, On Your Toes, Jumbo, At Home Abroad,* and *Porgy and Bess,* or that poured into the repertory of long-lived favorites the fine songs 1935–36 first sang. But it must also be remembered that, at least as far as the musical stage was concerned, only twelve new creations appeared (*Variety* listed fourteen by including two vaudeville bills). This represented a meager 10 percent of the season's productions, the smallest portion since musicals became a regular part of the New York theatrical scene in the late 19th century. To add insult to injury, only a single musical, *On Your Toes,* realized a decent profit. Seven of the shows were revues. A mere five were book musicals. Of these one relied heavily on spectacle, one was virtually an opera, while a third marked a return to old-fashioned operetta. Only two were standard, contemporary pieces.

Three nights before the first new musical arrived, one major event took place in American popular music that found Broadway reacting with a somewhat surprising indifference. Most students agree that "the swing era" officially opened with the wild acclaim Benny Goodman's band received on August 21, 1935, at the Palomar Ballroom in Los Angeles. Though "swing" tunes and arrangements had already infiltrated the American Musical Theatre—witness "Let's Swing It" in Earl Carroll's *Sketchbook* (6-4-35)—Broadway never responded with the enthusiasm or imagination it had brought to ragtime and jazz. At least two reasons probably account for this cool reception. Swing was, to no small extent, unmelodic and untheatrical. Its insistent, driving rhythms and strictly coordinated ensemble sounds were designed for what became known as "the big bands." The seeming improvisation, individuality, and intimacy of jazz were shunted aside. Though jazz, of course, originated far from theatrical footlights, its personal qualities allowed it to be adapted, however impurely, to theatrical purposes. But swing without its big bands was not as malleable, and big bands would have been lost in theatre orchestra pits. (To their credit, swing band recordings often helped popularize the era's show tunes.) Yet, even if swing had been more readily transferable, there is some cause to doubt its welcome would have been much heartier. Broadway was growing old. The word "youngster" seems slightly out of place in 1935 theatrical terms. Bright juveniles were still appearing on the stage each season, but with rare exceptions New York had become for them merely a way station on the road to Hollywood. Though no precise statistics exist, it is safe to suggest that the average age of Broadway's principal creators and stars was markedly higher than it had been twenty or forty years before.

A series of Gilbert and Sullivan revivals opened at the Adelphi on July 15 and ran until early September. The troupe returned in April for a second stand. Its slate included *The Mikado, The Pirates of Penzance, The Yeomen of the Guard, The Gondoliers, Trial by Jury,* and *H.M.S. Pinafore.* Howard Marsh, Bertram Peacock (the Schubert of the original *Blossom Time*), and Margaret Daum were the principal singers, while New York's original 1902 Sultan of Sulu, Frank Moulan, played the main comic role.

It was an unhappy year for the great funny men of old. Two of the earliest clowns of the musical stage died in the fall: De Wolf Hopper in September and Francis Wilson in October. In March of 1936 Paul McCullough committed suicide. The more conventional Cecil Lean died in July; Will Rogers was killed in a plane crash in August.

The end of August saw the season's first new work, a revue asking its patrons to **Smile at Me** (8-23-35, Fulton). They didn't—not at a begrimed parody of *Tobacco Road* called "Tobacco Juice," not at a slipshod South Sea Island ballet, nor at the feverish hosting and clowning of Jack Osterman. The revue was quickly gone, taking with it Gerald Dolin's only Broadway score.

The procession of unprofitable "hits" began with **At Home Abroad** (9-19-35, Winter Garden). Reverting to a favorite device of the earlier revues, the show used a tenuous story line to connect songs and sketches. In this case it relived the world cruise of Otis and Henrietta Hatrick. The natives they met in various countries kept bearing remarkable resemblances to Beatrice Lillie, Ethel Waters, and Eleanor Powell, not to mention Reginald Gardiner and Eddie Foy, Jr. Miss Lillie was a geisha girl (insisting, "It's better with your shoes off"), a Russian ballerina, the wife of an alpine guide, and an English lady trying to make a simple purchase of "a dozen double damask dinner napkins." Miss

Powell was a high-hatted, toe-tapping Eton boy and a Samoan beauty. A torchy lament, subtly leavened with humor, "Thief In The Night" fell to Miss Waters' capable voice. She also reigned as "The Hottentot Potentate," giving her subjects the benefit of her years in Harlem: both her "hotcha" and her "Je ne sais quoitcha." Actually, neither Howard Dietz' lyrics nor Arthur Schwartz' music was on a par with their best. Besides choreographing such fine dance interludes as "Farewell, My Lovely" and "Love Is A Dancing Thing," Paul Haakon brought the house down each night portraying the matador in a bullfight ballet. Vincente Minnelli created a magnificent gilt baroque setting for the show's finale and earlier in the evening won approval with a papier-mâché Matterhorn in a paper snowstorm. For the most part Minnelli's cheerful palette dripped with light colors. Thanks largely to Minnelli and the performers *At Home Abroad* survived six months.

Since **Porgy and Bess** (10-10-35, Alvin), the season's masterpiece, called itself, honestly and accurately, "An American Folk Opera," it may seem surprising to find it at a commercial Broadway house. But the truth is it had no place else to go. New York offered no institution to compare with Vienna's Volksoper or Paris' Opéra Comique. There was nothing for the Gershwins and their associates to do but raise the artistic standards of the Great White Way. Though Norman Nadel in his *Pictorial History of the Theatre Guild* suggests a different version, it is generally agreed that Gershwin became interested in making an opera of DuBose Heyward's novel, *Porgy,* soon after its publication in 1925. His plans were thwarted when he learned Heyward and his wife Dorothy had signed to do a dramatization of the work for the Theatre Guild. It became part of the Guild's magnificent 1927–28 season. Afterwards, ignoring Gershwin, the Guild began seeking for someone to make a light musical of the piece as a vehicle for Al Jolson. Their prime candidate was Jerome Kern. But Heyward, reminded of Gershwin's more serious ambitions, held out. He prevailed on Gershwin to spend time both in Charleston's Cabbage Row slum and on Folly Beach off the Carolina coast studying Negroes and their music first-hand. Later Heyward and Gershwin continued to develop their project by mail, bringing Ira into the picture at the same time. In a virtually unheard-of move at this late date, Gershwin orchestrated all of the score himself.

At the end of a hot summer day a Catfish Row mother (Abbie Mitchell) attempts to lull her baby to sleep with "Summertime." When she fails, the child's father (Edward Matthews) tries by singing cynically of a widespread and earthy sentiment, "A Woman Is A Sometime Thing." The baby finally falls asleep, but the courtyard of the slum is dangerously awake. Its men are drinking and gambling away their small hoards of cash. Porgy (Todd Duncan), a cripple who rides around in a goat cart, enters. The men tease Porgy about his love for Crown's girl, Bess (Anne Brown). Unconvincingly, Porgy denies any interest in her. The women who are standing nearby applaud Porgy's disclaimer, for they hold with Serena (Ruby Elzy), "That gal Bess ain't fit for Gawd fearin' ladies to 'sociate with." But Serena is more troubled by her husband Robbins' gambling with the others, especially with Crown (Warren Coleman). Her fears are justified, for when the men get to quarreling Crown kills Robbins (Henry Davis). At the funeral the neighbors take up a collection as Serena wails, "My Man's Gone Now." With Crown having fled to avoid jail, Porgy can be more open in his sentiments about Bess. He is happy in his small world, unashamed to cry, "I Got Plenty O' Nuttin'."

Porgy has gotten the unethical but accommodating lawyer Frazier to arrange to divorce Crown and Bess. The matter out of the way, he joyfully announces, "Bess, You Is My Woman Now." They join the restless slum folk in heading for a picnic. By chance, the island on which the picnic is held turns out to be the very place Crown is hiding. He appears long enough to warn Bess that she is still his. Before long he will be back to claim her. The festivities are enlivened by Sportin' Life (John W. Bubbles), a drug peddler, who gives his own version of things biblical, insisting, "It Ain't Necessarily So." Back in Catfish Row, Bess sings, "I Loves You, Porgy." Crown then appears, and in a fight with Porgy, he is killed when Porgy turns Crown's own knife on him. The police come and take Porgy to jail. Sportin' Life, seeing a chance for a fling, tells Bess that Porgy will never be set free. He lets her try some of his drugs, and she soon agrees to accompany him since "There's A Boat Dat's Leavin' Soon For New York." When Porgy is released he returns with a new dress for Bess. With pained reluctance the neighbors tell him what has happened. Porgy is undaunted. Though he has no idea where New York is, he sets out in his goat cart to go there and find Bess, crying "I'm On My Way."

The opera was mounted with a stunning realism, most notably in the grim, pathetic courtyard where so much of the action takes place. It was staged and performed with scenes of haunting fervor—the depthless grief of the deaths, the electrifying terror of blacks caught in a ramshackle house during a hurricane, or the innocent, uninhibited gaiety of a picnic. The major New York newspapers sent both their drama and music critics to the opening. The drama critics were far more enthusiastic than the music commentators. Unfortunately, only a small audience was willing to listen to other people's woes in the depression. As a result, the original production ran just 124 performances and, even with a Guild-sponsored post-Broadway tour, failed to retrieve its $50,000 investment. There was a wistful footnote to this original production. The small part of the lawyer was played by J. Rosamond Johnson, who a generation earlier had himself tried with little success to advance the cause of both black performers in general and the musical stage as a whole. Most sadly of all, this masterpiece marked the last major writing by George Gershwin for that same musical stage.

Two nights after the opening of *Porgy and Bess*, a third excellent but unprofitable musical appeared. **Jubilee** (10-12-35, Imperial) was a conventional book musical—one of only two the season brought forth. Stories of the British royal family's Silver Jubilee gave Moss Hart and Cole Porter the suggestion for the show. Together they took a leisurely world cruise with their friends while working on it. The result was lighthearted, escapist fun. Another royal family is about to celebrate its jubilee. But the King (Melville Cooper) and Queen (Mary Boland) and their children are fed up with their constrained if luxurious life. When a left-wing outbreak led by a rebellious nephew prompts their advisers to order them into seclusion they decide to have a fling as commoners instead. The Queen flirts briefly with Charles Rausmiller (Mark Plant), the ape man Mowgli of the movies (a takeoff on Johnny Weissmuller's Tarzan). Her daughter (Margaret Adams) has a brief romance with a celebrated writer (Derek Williams), while the Prince (Charles Walters) takes the famous dancer, Karen O'Kane (June Knight), to the Café Martinique, where they "Begin The Beguine." As for the King he can spend all his waking hours playing his beloved parlor games. Of course, they are finally recognized and forced to return to a more regal life.

By and large the critics enjoyed the show, though they had some reservations about the music. Apparently so did Porter, his producers, and his publishers. When the songs were first issued, two that became Porter classics were not included, "Begin The Beguine" and "Just One Of Those Things" (also sung by Karen and the Prince). In fact it was several years before the latter achieved its ultimate popularity. Another Porter classic, "Why Shouldn't I?", was sung by the princess. The show's high level of sophistication as well as its large number of private jokes and allusions undoubtedly hurt at the box office. The majority of the show's audience was not intrigued by references to George Gershwin's inevitable playing of his own music at posh parties or to Clifton Webb's domineering mother. When the popular Miss Boland left to return to Hollywood, ticket sales slumped to the point where the show had to be withdrawn after just twenty-one weeks.

The **Provincetown Follies** arrived November 3 to begin a two-month stay at the small, out-of-the-way Provincetown Playhouse in Greenwich Village. For all its Village origins the revue spoke with a markedly British accent. Its master of ceremonies was a favorite of London and Paris night spots, Barry Oliver, while many of the evening's loudest laughs were grabbed by Cyril Smith, especially with his monologue about a cockney lion tamer. Beatrice Kay won some good notices for her burlesque of a torch singer. The dances were staged by John Tiller's protégé, Mary Read. Dave Stamper, who had provided so many of the songs for the *Ziegfeld Follies* in their heyday, contributed several of the tunes, while two unknowns, Frederick Herendeen and Sylvan Green, rushed in a timely "Poor Porgy." But nothing caught the public's fancy nor survived the final curtain.

The old Hippodrome was returned to the legitimate fold for one last time when Billy Rose mounted his noisily ballyhooed production of **Jumbo** on November 16. Actually it was not quite the Hippodrome its regulars might have remembered, for Rose made substantial renovations to house his production properly. The orchestra level was gutted and rearranged to make it resemble a circus tent. This prompted a few skeptical playgoers to remark that the original auditorium seemed more than adequate for the opening spectacles at the turn of the century, the first two of which had circus themes. After extended rehearsals and numerous delays in the announced opening, the show was brought in at the staggering cost of $340,000. Ben Hecht and Charles MacArthur's book was sufficiently loose to allow for a large number of circus acts. In fact, Actor's Equity declared the work a circus instead of a musical. Two circus proprietors, Matthew Mulligan (W. J. McCarthy) and John A. Considine (Arthur Sinclair), have long been at loggerheads. They are not made any happier when

Matt Jr. (Donald Novis) falls in love with Considine's daughter, Mickey (Gloria Grafton). Considine's drinking problem grows worse, and he faces bankruptcy until his press agent, Claudius B. Bowers, burns down Considine's house, allowing him to collect the insurance. In the end the lovers succeed in bringing the rival fathers together amicably. The songs were by Rodgers and Hart, their first for the theatre since 1931. It gave the lie to the Broadway superstition that great songs could not come out of the Hippodrome. Three Rodgers and Hart classics emerged: Mickey and Matt's driving waltz, "The Most Beautiful Girl In The World," the wispy "Little Girl Blue" (the first-act finale in which Mickey dreams she is a child again, being entertained by circus folk) and the lovers' assertive "My Romance."

The show's star was Jimmy Durante, playing the resourceful Bowers. But for many theatregoers the main attraction was the spectacle. Paul Whiteman, after making his entrance on a large white horse, led his orchestra, while hundreds of animals, acrobats, clowns, and other circus standbys cavorted in the great, old house. Unfortunately not enough theatregoers were attracted. Although the show ran over seven months, its gigantic initial outlay and its abnormally high weekly running costs prevented it from recouping more than about half of its investment.

May Wine (12-5-35, St. James), another operetta calling itself a musical play, had a book by Frank Mandel, based on Eric von Stroheim and Wallace Smith's novel *The Happy Alienist*. The show's music was by Sigmund Romberg, its lyrics by Oscar Hammerstein II. In an attempt to fall in with more or less recent fashions the musical omitted the chorus. And the curtain rose without an overture or an opening number, to give the impression of an intimate straight play. It also, as the title of its source hints, used a very 20th-century figure as the center of its 19th-century plot. The cynical Baron Kuno (Walter Woolf King) encourages Marie, the Baroness Von Schlewitz (Nancy McCord), to accept the proposal of Professor Johann Volk (Walter Slezak), a psychoanalyst. He hopes to blackmail the professor. But after the wedding Marie finds herself falling in love with Johann. Johann learns of Marie's original intentions, and, not knowing of her new feelings, determines to kill her. Luckily he misses, shooting merely the dummy he had made and to which the shy Johann had confessed the depths of his ardor. Mandel's libretto was claptrap. But Romberg's score, while lightweight, was appealing. Out of it came his only show hit of the decade, "I Built A Dream One Day." 1935 was a relatively good year for Romberg. His "When I Grow Too Old To Dream" from the movie *The Night Is Young* was even more popular than his song hit from *May Wine*. But these were the last successes he would enjoy until *Up in Central Park* (1-27-45).

The old Hippodrome relit, a Romberg operetta running six months—the past seemed to be reasserting itself. As if to underline the return to the good old days, **George White's Scandals of 1936** (12-25-35, New Amsterdam) came in one week before the new year of its title. Willie and Eugene Howard were on hand with Bert Lahr to head the comic section. Rudy Vallee sang the best tunes. A dance team known as Sam, Ted, and Ray did the fastest stepping. Much of the material was old hat. The Howards got their *Rigoletto* costumes out of the mothballs, and Willie went on to teach still more French lessons. Bert Lahr played a renowned cook who managed to throw even his wig in his soup. Ray Henderson again composed the songs, using still another new lyricist, Jack Yellen. But the fire had gone out of Henderson, as had the gift for readily hummable tunes. The songs often had pleasant phrases, but in the end seem to go nowhere. Henderson joined the swelling ranks who were abandoning Broadway. He returned only once, in the early forties. And the current edition joined the growing ranks of musicals that couldn't realize a return on their investment, though in the case of the *Scandals* its 110-performance run probably precluded that anyway.

On January 1, 1936, the musical stage mourned the loss of the man who will probably never be surpassed as its most prolific librettist and lyricist. Harry B. Smith died at the age of seventy-five. He was credited with writing, in part or alone, the books for over 300 shows and the words for over 6,000 songs. But it would take an acute, and possibly imaginative, observer to see any progression from his stilted if competent early writing to his stilted if competent final pieces. Yet in his own day he was thought of highly enough to be the first American lyricist to have his works published without the music in a hardback book.

The new year got off to an unpromising start with a five-performance fiasco called **The Illustrators' Show** (1-22-36, 48th St.). The show had called itself to the public's attention when police raided and closed it while it was being performed uptown earlier in the year. It was originally presented by the Society of Illustrators more to put their own works before the public than as a showcase for theatrical talent. Several famous artists of the period made personal appearances. Almost without exception the critics pounced on Otto Soglow, who impersonated "the Little King" he had drawn for *The New Yorker* and for syndication. The reviewers took strong exception to the off-color sketch in which Soglow placed his lovable, rotund monarch. Two of the most successful figures of a later Broadway had a hand in the evening. Most of the lyrics were by Frank Loesser, who quickly displayed his penchant for off-beat verbal rhythms in "Bang—The Bell Rang," while Frederick Loewe, in collaboration with Earle Crooker, inserted "A Waltz Was Born In Vienna."

As she had been in 1933, Mrs. Florenz Ziegfeld was listed as the producer of the latest edition of the **Ziegfeld Follies** (1-30-36, Winter Garden), and as they had been in 1933, the Shuberts were the real producers. Vernon Duke and Ira Gershwin were again the songsmiths, John Murray Anderson was once more in charge of the staging, and Fanny Brice returned to lead the list of funny people in the show. But there were new, added performers. Bob Hope had important bits, including the show's hit tune. Gertrude Niesen was on hand to sing the more sultry numbers. Eve Arden provided more restrained comic moments and Judy Canova offered more low-brow fun, when Miss Brice was off stage. The almost legendary Josephine Baker came home from Paris to parade her talents. Miss Brice had a field day kidding her own classic "My Man" in "He Hasn't A Thing Except Me," desperately tried to reclaim a winning sweepstakes ticket she has inadvertently given away, and played Baby Snooks in Hollywood and on "Major Bones" amateur hour. Miss Niesen and Miss Baker shared a big production number, "Island In The West Indies," which suggested that melodically and lyrically these spectacle numbers had not advanced much in a quarter of a century. But Hope and Miss Arden dramatized the evolution of the love ballad when they sang "I Can't Get Started."

The cynical flippancy of the staging underscored the changes. Hope sang the song to Miss Arden and, when she finally responded, walked away indifferently. The most important new name on the program was George Balanchine, who worked with Robert Alton on the dances. His sensual choreography for "Five A.M." gave audiences a hint of his future prowess; a power he more decidedly displayed in his next assignment, two months later. The extent to which the show depended on Fanny Brice was made apparent to Broadway when her illness forced the show to close after 115 performances. Everything was stashed away until the fall when she was well enough to return. But by that time all her associates had found work elsewhere, and a new cast was assembled headed by Bobby Clark in his first solo appearance.

In a year laden with noteworthy theatrical deaths none diminished the glitter of Broadway as much as the passing of Marilyn Miller on April 7.

The book for the season's biggest hit, **On Your Toes** (4-11-36, Imperial), was primarily by George Abbott, with help from Rodgers and Hart, who had thought up the plot in the first place. Its story was complicated and not always well motivated, but serviceable. Junior Dolan is the son of old vaudevillians who have educated him beyond his desires. He has become a professor of music, though he would prefer to be a simple hoofer. Dolan helps a struggling Russian ballet company restore its sagging finances by mounting a jazz ballet and even takes the lead himself when the head male dancer fails to appear. He then realizes his love for the prima ballerina is as absurd as his parents' plan for him had been. He settles for simple Frankie Frayne (Doris Carson), his old flame who saved his life by warning him that gangsters, mistaking him for the original dancer, were out to kill him. Two triumphs were the principal reasons for the show's success. The first was the lovely Rodgers and Hart score coupled with Rodgers' impressive music for the ballet "Slaughter on Tenth Avenue." After being away for so long, this was their second fine achievement in a matter of months. They gave every promise of recapturing their incredible fecundity. The most played song from the show was unquestionably Junior and Frankie's caressing "There's A Small Hotel" written originally for *Jumbo*. But the tunes ranged from the jaunty title song—sung by Junior, Frankie, and Sydney Cohen (David Morris)—to Frankie and Sydney's sweetly forlorn "Glad To Be Unhappy." Hart's comic lines were never better than in his hilarious roasting of the excesses of the rich (supper clubs where people are close as sardines in a can), "Too Good For The Average Man," sung by snobbish Peggy Porterfield (Luella Gear) and the equally snobbish émigré, Sergei Alexandrovitch (Monty Woolley). The main theme from the "Slaughter on Tenth Avenue" ballet became one of the few wordless excerpts from the Broadway stage to achieve independent vogue. The second great asset was, obviously, George Balanchine's superb ballets, brilliantly danced by the show's Junior Dolan, Ray Bolger, and Tamara Geva.

. . .

George Balanchine (Gyorgi Balanchivadze) was born in St. Petersburg, Russia, on January 9, 1904. As a boy he trained at the Russian Imperial School. In the late twenties he worked with Diaghilev and in the early thirties with Colonel de Basil. Coming to New York in 1934 he founded, with Lincoln Kirstein, the School of American Ballet.

. . .

The first ballet, "Princess Zenobia," was a satire on classic offerings. Bolger danced the part of a blackface native, discovering too late he had forgotten to paint the rest of his body. But it was the second-act ballet, "Slaughter on Tenth Avenue," that was the high point of the evening. It took place in a sleazy West Side bar, where a hoofer pays the owner to let him spend some time with the stripper. The owner becomes jealous, shoots the girl, and the hoofer shoots him. The ballet was worked in loosely to the plot both front and back by first having Junior substitute for the male lead and then having the gangsters aim at him thinking he is the same absconding dancer. The connection was clever but hardly more germane than, say, the late Marilyn Miller's Butterfly dance in *Sally* (12-21-20), which convinced her admirers that she should be in the *Follies*. Truly integrated dance, where the ballet takes over and advances the story when the actors leave off, had to wait for *Oklahoma!* (3-31-43) or, if that is ruled out because it was merely a dream, the opening pantomime of *Carousel* (4-19-45). Innovation had not been popular on Broadway in recent seasons. But the originality and daring of *On Your Toes*—aided by Abbott's brisk staging—was clothed in such colorful raiment, audiences cheered for nearly ten months.

. . .

George Abbott was born in Forestville, New York, on January 25, 1887. His formal education included time at the Kearney Military Academy, the University of Rochester, and George Pierce Baker's famous "47 Workshop" at Harvard. Abbott's early years in the theatre were spent acting in plays such as *Dulcy, Hell-Bent fer Heaven,* and *Processional*. In the mid-twenties he turned to writing and directing plays; first fast-moving melodramas and later even faster-moving farces. Among the plays on which he served as collaborator, director, or both were *Broadway, Chicago, Twentieth Century, Boy Meets Girl, Room Service,* and *Three Men on a Horse*. He assisted John Murray Anderson with the direction of *Jumbo*, his first musical. Abbott's background in fast-moving plays (and probably his military school training) led him to place his unique stamp on those musicals he worked with. His direction was almost always to be marked by a special tautness and lively pacing.

· · ·

Old-timer Gus Edwards assembled another vaudeville, **Broadway Sho-Window** (4-12-36, Broadway), with a cast that included Joe Cook, Jr. and Mark Plant. But Broadway wasn't interested.

Another, "sho-window," **New Faces of 1936** (5-19-36, Vanderbilt), arrived five weeks later on May 19 to close the season. This time Broadway was more receptive. Not all the faces were new. Imogene Coca was back, seemingly in the same coat she had worn all through the first edition. She also played a Cinderella who begged her fairy godmother to let her be a stripper. Mrs. Roosevelt and Mrs. Hoover were kidded again, as were the Girl Scouts. Dorothy Parker, an easy target, was knocked in "Lottie Of The Literati" with the snide couplet, "No matter who said it, Dorothy Parker gets credit." Musically the evening was uneventful. Its best numbers were probably "My Last Affair" (Haven Johnson) and "You'd Better Go Now" (Bickley Reichner/Irvin Graham). When business fell, two anything-but-new faces, the Duncan Sisters, were rushed in with some of their material from *Topsy and Eva*. But old faces or new, the show drew crowds for only six months.

1936-1937

No new musicals appeared between the arrival of *New Faces of 1936* at the end of May and opening of **The White Horse Inn** on October 1. But the D'Oyly Carte played twenty weeks beginning August 20. *The White Horse Inn* was adapted from Ralph Benatzky's melodious Berlin operetta, *Im Weissen Rossl*. Mounted at the mammoth Center Theatre with even greater opulence than *The Great Waltz,* it ran 223 performances. William Gaxton, Kitty Carlisle, and Robert Halliday were the stars— though it is doubtful if anyone could see their features or even hear them clearly from the back of the balcony.

At the end of the month—on October 29—three more stars, Jimmy Durante, Ethel Merman, and Bob Hope could be better seen and heard at the more sensibly sized Alvin. Their vehicle, **Red, Hot and Blue!,** was written and produced by the team that created the preceding season's *Anything Goes:* Cole Porter for the songs, Howard Lindsay and Russel Crouse for the book, and Vinton Freedley behind the scenes. Originally it had been designed for all three stars of *Anything Goes*. But Gaxton preferred the offer he received for *The White Horse Inn* and Moore was busy elsewhere. Perhaps because they had Gaxton and Moore in mind at first, the librettists came up with a story that reminded many in the audience of *Of Thee I Sing* (12-26-31). In both cases the hero's mate is to be chosen in a contest, in both the hero rejects the winner, in both the White House is a prominent setting, and in both the Supreme Court's decision is significant. "Nails" O'Reilly Duquesne (Miss Merman), a new millionairess, decides to hold a lottery for charity. Even the Senate buys tickets, hoping to make a dent in the national debt. The winner will be the person who discovers the whereabouts of Bob Hale's childhood sweetheart. She shouldn't be too hard to find, for she carries a distinctive mark. As a child she sat on a hot waffle iron and the imprint is still there. To assist in the search, "Nails" arranges the parole of several inmates at the swank Lark's Nest Prison. The leader of the parolees, "Policy" Pinkle (Durante), resents his release, since he has risen to captain of the prison polo team. The girl is found, but Hale (Hope) can't understand what he once saw in her. However, he is not obligated to marry her, since the Supreme Court declares that any lottery benefiting the American people is unconstitutional. Bob jumps at the chance to marry "Nails." The book, however entertaining, lacked the sharpness and tonal consistency so evident in *Of Thee I Sing*. Porter's songs, while excellent, were far more conventional than the Gershwin brothers' material. The most widely played song was "It's De-Lovely," which, in its stage version, had Bob and "Nails" recount a romance from the lovers' first encounter to their grown son's social success. Porter's literate wit leavened the pain of the young lady "Down In The Depths" on the 90th floor—another song since associated with Merman. The melody of Nails' vivacious "Ridin' High" became popular, even if the words didn't. An equally lively title song received some attention, but the lovely, minor-keyed "Good-bye, Little Dream, Good-bye" was dropped during the tryout. The comic numbers were superb. In "A Little Skipper From Heaven" Durante announced to his surprised cohorts, "I'm about to become a mother," and in a spoof on country music, "The Ozarks Are Callin' Me Home," he noted that while he was busy in the kitchen fryin' chicken, he could hear Paw givin' Maw her daily lickin'. For all its merits the show was a disappointment at the box office, compiling a good, but in no way overwhelming, 183 performances.

The first of three November openings was Sigmund Romberg and Otto Harbach's operetta—they called it "a musical romance"—**Forbidden Melody** (11-2-36, New Amsterdam). Romberg and his associates were apparently not concerned that the public would confuse the title with Romberg's earlier failures, *Melody* (2-14-33) and *The Magic Melody* (11-11-19). Their lack of concern was justified. The show was bad enough to flop on its own. Rumor gave out that the story had been based on an actual incident in the life of King Carol of Roumania. In Bucharest Gregor Fiorescu (Carl Brisson) is photographed in a hotel room with the wife (Ruth Weston) of a prominent politician, Colonel Geza (Arthur Vinton). To avoid difficulties he persuades an actress friend to claim it was really she with whom he was meeting. But when Gregor finds himself falling in love with Elene (Ruby Mercer), he also finds he has a jealous and vengeful Mme. Geza on his hands. Romberg's music was pretty, but as out of date as Harbach's lyrics. Even the slightly more contemporary sound of "You Are All I've Wanted" lacked an additional something extra to put it across. When the show closed at the end of the month, the New Amsterdam Theatre, in which it had played, went over to movies. The magnificent theatre had been the last holdout on 42nd Street. With its changeover, a glittering era, actually gone for five years, was unmistakably over.

On November 3 Roosevelt was elected to a second term, thereby assuring at least the temporary continuation of state-supported theatre projects and an increasingly left-wing tone to their presentation. This new slant was bound to spill over into more commercial enterprises.

As if to underscore this irresistible drift, the leftish Group Theatre mounted Paul Green's play with music, **Johnny Johnson** (11-19-36, 44th St.). The songs and background music were by Kurt Weill, a refugee whose only other Broadway exposure had come with an unsuccessful adaptation of his German *Die Dreigroschenoper*.

. . .

Kurt Weill was born in Dessau, Germany, on March 2, 1900. After some early musical training at the hands of his parents, he studied at the Berlin High School of Music and privately under Ferrucio Busoni. An advocate of the Zeitkunst school, he began composing operas larded with styles borrowed from contemporary popular music, especially those employing American jazz idioms. His early operas, generally well-received by German operagoers, included *Der Protagonist* and *Royal Palace*. He soon joined forces with the leftish Bertolt Brecht to create two outstanding successes for the popular German theatre of the time, *Die Dreigroschenoper* and *Aufstieg und Fall der Stadt Mahagonny*. But Nazi persecution drove Weill, his wife Lotta Lenya, and Brecht to Paris. A short while later the Weills accompanied Max Reinhardt and Franz Werfel to America to assist in a mounting of *The Eternal Road*.

. . .

Green's somewhat confused parable ventured into fantasy and almost into allegory as it followed the history of a benign, pacifist stonecutter (Russell Collins)—the play opens with the dedication of his monument to Peace—as he is inexorably sucked into World War I, is wounded, momentarily disrupts the war by spraying the Allied High Command with laughing gas, is committed to a mental institution, where he and his fellow inmates assume the mantles of the world statesman and establish the League of World Republics, is finally released, and goes home to peddle nonmartial toys to a war-happy village. Weill's music gained little popular currency, but it displayed the quick, nervous lines and sardonic harmonies that would become his trademark. Though the left-wing writers insisted they spoke for the masses, the masses had long since abandoned the theatre. So stark, if touching, an antiwar piece could muster only 68 performances.

Like *Johnny Johnson,* Noel Coward's **Tonight at 8:30** (12-24-36, National) was a play with music, or, more accurately, nine one-act plays, three of which had songs. "Red Peppers," for example, depicted the battle between a small time vaudeville act and the band leader. The show, with Coward and Gertrude Lawrence in the leads, repeated its London success.

Three failures had not discouraged Donald Heywood from trying his luck again. Writing the book and songs, co-directing the production, and conducting the orchestra, Heywood was unable to achieve more than six performances for his **Black Rhythm** (11-19-36, Comedy). Heywood's story was a backstage yarn recounting the efforts of a young hopeful named Jenny (Jeni Le Gon) to break into the big time. For the most part the evening consisted of a series of specialty acts—such as a plantation hilly-billy band that made music with combs, jugs, and washboards. At the opening of his last show Heywood had been assaulted by an irate patron. At the opening of *Black Rhythm* two stink bombs exploded in the theatre. Since there was apparently no racial prejudice behind either incident, Heywood took the hint and finally gave up trying to please Broadway.

December's only other musical was the revue, **The Show Is On** (12-25-36, Winter Garden). It was the last show of 1936. It was also the last of the bright, brittle, tune-filled escapist revues that Americans had thrown together so knowingly since the late twenties. More good revues would follow, but they invariably seemed somewhat wanting in one department or another, especially in their music. For *The Show Is On* the music was "mostly by" Vernon Duke with lyrics "mostly by" Ted Fetter. But their songs were not as catchy as the show's charming hit "Little Old Lady" (Hoagy Carmichael and Stanley Adams), sung and danced by Mitzi Mayfair and Charles Walters. Carmichael was one of the most popular song writers of the thirties, creating one of the era's great standards, "Stardust." But he never found time until 1940 to sit down and compose an entire score. The Gershwin brothers contributed an uncharacteristic salute to the Viennese waltz in "By Strauss" (sung by Gracie Barrie and Robert Shafer, while Mitzi Mayfair danced), their last offering to Broadway. Rodgers and Hart wrote "Rhythm," in which Bea Lillie devastated the singers of the day, and, for a time, resuscitated "I've Got Five Dollars,"—originally from *America's Sweetheart* (2-10-31). Harburg and Arlen threw in "Josephine Waters" and Bert Lahr's showstopper "Song Of The Woodman." And Herman Hupfeld gave Miss Lillie a riotous take-off on all the old "moon" numbers, "Buy Yourself A Balloon," in which Miss Lillie swung out over the audience while sitting on a stage moon and threw garters at the men in the house.

The show, like its predecessor, *At Home Abroad,* used a theme to tie its material together. This theme was an old and natural favorite, show business. Reginald Gardiner was Shakespeare rewriting his material to suit 20th-century tastes; Bert Lahr played a Hollywood idol sent to lure away a Baltimore matron from a king who would give up his throne for her, and Miss Lillie as a great lady of the theatre attended "The Reading Of The Play" which, when she is told it "is about a man and a woman," she cavalierly rejects for "too much plot." Both John Gielgud and Leslie Howard were offering Hamlets to New York. In the show's most hilarious bit Gardiner played Gielgud playing Hamlet while Miss Lillie was a noisy latecomer. When Gardiner-Gielgud offered to buy her a ticket to Howard's Hamlet if she will only leave, Miss Lillie declines,

saying Howard paid for her ticket to Gielgud. The show was lavishly and tastefully staged by Vincente Minnelli. His production numbers included "Parade Night," filled with the "soft, nostalgic coloring of bygone days." Another critic saluted Minnelli's "subtle, witty" designs. The show remained on into the hot weather.

In his survey of 1930s musicals, Stanley Green is quite right when he says of 1937, "More sharply than did any other year, it pitted the old versus the new." Just how decisive the result was remained uncertain at the time. It was January 23 before the first musical hit of 1937 arrived. **Naughty Naught** (**'00**) was produced by the Krimsky Brothers at their American Music Hall. Jerrold Krimsky, writing as John Van Antwerp, supplied the book, while Ted Fetter set words to Richard Lewine's music. The American Musical Hall was a name new to Broadway. It had been a church. Now the Krimsky Brothers converted it into as genuine a replica of the old Rialto musical halls as the time and safety codes would allow. The *double entendre* of the show's title fetchingly caught the period flavor. The story dealt with a turn-of-the-century regatta in which the villainous P. De Quincy Devereux (Alexander Clark) attempts to undermine Yale's great stroke, Frank Plover (Bartlett Robinson), by plying him with spiked lemonades and having a lady of questionable repute vamp him in front of his betrothed. Virtue triumphs. Though the music didn't try too hard to have appropriate period flavor, the show pleased its happily guzzling patrons for the rest of the season, and inaugurated a short, insignificant series.

A more genuine turn-of-the-century sound was evoked in **Frederika** (2-4-37, Imperial), but not tongue-in-cheek. The Messrs. Shubert presented Dennis King, Helen Gleason, and Ernest Truex in Franz Lehar's 1928 hit. Its story told of a foredoomed love affair between the poet Goethe and the beautiful Frederika. While the sets and costumes were 18th century, the music was typical Lehar. Though the book was adequate and the music pleasant, the show was not strong enough to overcome changing tastes, the poor economy, and an under-current of resentment against Lehar, who had tacitly embraced the new Nazi regime. In that respect the situation was not unlike the reaction Lehar had encountered twenty years before during World War I. The show closed after twelve weeks.

Two and a half months went by before the next musical, **Babes In Arms** (4-14-37, Shubert), appeared. But it represented a complete turnabout from the musicals that preceded it. It sang out with a youthful, contemporary vitality. It was in its own way a sort of "new faces," filled with young, relatively unknown performers. Its story was simple. To avoid being sent to a work farm, the children of traveling vaudevillians pool their talents to present a show called "Lee Calhoun's Follies." The show fails, at least financially, and the kids are hustled off to the farm. They are rescued when a French aviator, on a transatlantic flight, makes an emergency landing on the field and befriends them. The show within a show allowed for ample displays of the performers' diverse talents. And great talents many of them were! Out of this show came Alfred Drake, Mitzi Green, Ray Heatherton, Robert Rounseville, Dan Dailey, and Wynn Murray. The flexible nature of the story allowed for a dream ballet in which the would-be stars meet the magical names of Hollywood. George Balanchine did the choreography, and Rodgers and Hart created their own book. But it was their songs that were quickly recognized as the show's finest, most enduring feature. Four Rodgers and Hart standards were first heard in *Babes in Arms.* They ranged from the off-beat, romantic opening "Where Or When" (sung by Miss Green and Heatherton) to the flashy, witty "The Lady Is A Tramp" to the wistful "My Funny Valentine" (the last two both sung by Miss Green) to the vibrant "Johnny One Note" (sung by Miss Murray). "My Funny Valentine" illustrates Hart's resourcefulness. Though the song is especially popular around Valentine's Day with lyrics that could pass for a bemused holiday paean, in the show it was sung to a boy named Valentine. As with most Rodgers and Hart scores, even the less-known songs had style and melody. The rousing title song and the mockingly cynical "I Wish I Were In Love Again" (sung by Grace McDonald and Rolly Pickert) typify the unfailingly intelligent blend of words and music. Produced for a mere $55,000, the show ran nine months and became a goldmine.

Two May musicals, both flops, ended the season.

Orchids Preferred (5-11-37, Imperial) told how two bar girls persuade the innocent Marion Brown (Vicki Cummings) to join their racket. But she manages to fall in love with her first supposed victim, Richard Hope (John Donaldson). When her friends see how serious the romance is becoming, they tell Richard of their trade. Marion tries to run away but Richard, understanding her better nature, runs after her. In the emergency exit of the posh Waldmore Hotel they agree to be Mr. and Mrs. The songs were by Dave Stamper and Frederick Herendeen, who had turned out the score for the previous season's *Provincetown Follies.* Their bad luck still held. One week and the show folded.

Sea Legs (5-18-37, Mansfield) did a little better. It ran two weeks. Based on the play, *The Cat Came Back,* it had a book and lyrics by Arthur Swanstrom and music by Michael H. Cleary. The evening was mounted as a vehicle for Dorothy Stone and her husband, Charles Collins. It was one of the few musicals written since the twenties that used a single set for each act. In fact, it used the same set —the deck of a yacht—for both acts. Barbara Deeds (Miss Stone) is a guest on the widowed Alice Wytcherly's yacht "Pixie." Barbara's suitor, Bill Halliday (Charles Collins), stows away on the boat to be near her. When he is discovered he claims to be a veterinary hired to treat Mrs. Wytcherly's cat. But Mrs. Wytcherly's admirer, George Tuttle (Walter N. Greaza), resentful of her attention to her cat and suspecting Halliday is also pursuing Mrs. Wytcherly (Mary Sargeant), pays the steward to kill the cat. The steward tries, but this cat clearly has more than one life. Before its ninth life is snuffed out, the misunderstandings are cleared up and Barbara and Bill make plans to marry. The music was on a par with the rest of the show, filled with pleasant tunes typical of the lesser writing of the period. Given better times, it was the sort of low-budget affair that might have realized a small return on its investment.

9

INTERMISSION
Broadway's Response
to the Swing Era

By the summer of 1937 the swing era was at its peak. The jazz era, which had reigned through the gay, gaudy years of the twenties and, with a subdued, modified tone, continued through the somber years of the early thirties, had drifted incontestably into history. George Gershwin's death on July 11, 1937, underscored its passing. In theatrical terms, Gershwin had been the most articulate and memorable of the modernists, the personification of his high-kicking epoch. No similar figure emerged to give comparable theatrical definition to swing. To some extent this was predictable, because swing, as has been noted, was a less theatrical musical idiom than jazz or ragtime had been, and because, as an expression of popular musical speech, it was more likely to be appropriated by and developed in Hollywood than on a stage catering to an increasingly older audience. Unfortunately Broadway's most gifted melodists, men such as Richard Rodgers, Irving Berlin, and Cole Porter, while complaining about the harsh treatment their songs received at the hands of swing arrangers, actually abetted the trend toward exaggeratedly rhythmic presentation by falling into creative slumps during this period. Good songs were fewer; songs that proved lastingly popular, fewer still. National and international turmoil—the persistent depression, the Nazi terror, the onset of World War II—undoubtedly had a debilitating influence. Librettists as well as composers were affected. Books became trite, satire less bitingly satiric, romance less flamboyantly romantic. Only toward the end of this five-

year lull did two daringly pioneering works present genuine possibilities. Yet, as it turned out, neither pointed precisely in the direction that ultimately led the American Musical Theatre out of its doldrums.

1937-1938

This intermission opened with an eerie, uncomfortable season. The depression, which had seemed to be lifting, suddenly took a turn for the worse, and the number of shows produced on Broadway fell to the lowest figure in thirty years. Almost defiantly, the number of new musicals rose slightly. Yet even here a feeling of uneasy change prevailed. Productions came from unaccustomed sources. The WPA Federal Theatre Project mounted several. The Mercury Theatre, a repertory company heretofore devoted to the classics, helped stage one of the most controversial, and a labor union offered what became the long-run hit of the year. These organizations naturally influenced the tenor of the pieces. Social and political outlook became as important as entertainment value. Harsh, provocative words claimed priority over sweet, singable melodies. A malaise affected even the more conventional commercial productions. There were few outstanding songs, and most of those were subdued ballads. Lyricists and librettists fared a bit better, but two of the biggest hits of the season, for all their success, represented unhappy matings of stars and authors.

The Federal Theatre Project opened the season in the middle of summer with a black musical comedy, **Swing It** (7-22-37, Adelphi). Its story line followed the down-at-the-heels crew and entertainers of a rickety Mississippi show boat in their effort to find a better lot in Harlem. The show was really "a potpourri of minstrelsy, singing, dancing, mugging, clowning, spirituals, jazz, swing, tapping and the carrying of Harlem's throaty torch." Henry Jines and James Green sparked the comedy, playing two characters with Tweedledum-Tweedledee names, Rusty and Dusty. Herbie Brown's dancing waiter served up flashy tap routines between courses. Romantic interests, so carefully muted in early Negro shows, crept in, allowing Sherman Dickson and Frances Everett to smooth their path to the altar with "Ain't We Got Love." Although the strongly rhythmic, sometimes antimelodic, sounds of swing were coming to dominate the world of popular music, Eubie Blake's score was "muted, more pastel in color." His biographers attribute this to his catching the spirit of his new partner, Milton Reddie. But a look at the season's musicals will show he was in the spirit of the times as well. When neither the show nor the new Blake style appealed to the public, *Swing It* left after nine weeks.

Seeking a successor to *The Great Waltz* and *The White Horse Inn* for their behemoth Center Theatre, the Rockefellers commissioned a musical about colonial Williamsburg, which the family had begun to restore. Called **Virginia,** the show opened on September 2. It was overwhelmed by the house. The Center, like the Hippodrome or the Earl Carroll, was adequate for spectacle, but intimate spoken dialogue and the low-ranged, croonable melodies of the American Musical were lost in its vastness. With proper spectacle the more broad-stroked, highly colored Viennese operetta could pass, but it was really the spectacle that counted. From the American repertory only a musical play on the order of *Show Boat* (12-27-27) might have made a success. Apparently this is what the Rockefellers had in mind. Their choice of Laurence Stallings as librettist was enlightened, if a bit risky. Stallings was a gifted, intelligent playwright who nonetheless had only one real success to his credit, his collaboration with Maxwell Anderson on *What Price Glory?* His two produced efforts at musical books, *Deep River* (10-4-26) and *Rainbow* (11-21-28), had failed as much because they were ahead of their time as for any other reason. Stallings hit upon a story for *Virginia* that had the necessary sweep and

pageantry required by the house, but something went wrong. Even while the work was in rehearsal Owen Davis was called in to sharpen it. When Fortesque (Gene Lockhart) of Drury Lane comes to America in 1775 with a company of London actors, he also brings with him a letter for General Washington. The loyalists attempt to prevent the letter's delivery, but Fortesque quietly passes it to his leading lady, Sylvia Laurence (Anne Booth), who in turn passes it on to Colonel Richard Fairfax (Ronald Graham), her American admirer. Although the British seize Fairfax, he manages to get the letter through.

In selecting Arthur Schwartz to write the songs, the management made a major error. Schwartz had a long, romantic musical line, much like Jerome Kern's at his most intimate, but he was not given to the more full-bodied melodies the large house required. His martial title song approached what was needed, but the better numbers—and he composed a fine score—were small-scaled and tender. Radio, not the show, made a hit of "You And I Know" (sung by Sylvia and Richard). Three other Schwartz songs—"An Old Flame Never Dies" (Sylvia's solo), "If You Were Someone Else" (Richard's solo), and "Goodbye, Jonah" (sung and tapped by Buck and Bubbles)—can still be heard on rare occasions. Albert Stillman's slightly fustian lyrics were more in keeping with the show's requirements than with Schwartz' music. *Virginia,* like *Swing It,* ran 60 performances.

The WPA again headed the credits as producer when **A Hero Is Born** followed *Swing It* into the Adelphi on October 1. In spite of its stirringly militant title, a type of title so beloved by the age, the musical told an innocent, childlike tale. At his christening Prince Prigio of Pantouflia (Ben Starkie) is lavishly favored by the fairies. His mother (Margaret Wycherly) has no time for such unworldly creatures and their equally unworldly gifts, so the presents are never shown to the young boy. He grows up to be an intellectual snob. One day he stumbles on the long-hidden treasures. He finds a magic cap that makes its wearer invisible, one that grants its wearer any wish, a magic carpet, and a host of other wonders. Aided by these marvels he also finds a becoming modesty and a beautiful princess, Rosalind (Drue Leyton). This surprisingly apolitical book was adapted from an Andrew Lang fairy tale by Theresa Helburn, of the faltering Theatre Guild. A. Lehman Engel, who, simply as Lehman Engel, soon became the musical theatre's leading conductor, wrote the score. The show was mounted with "circus dimensions," its scenes filled not just with a cast of nearly 100 but with "props and magic machines" of every sort. But the public was not attracted. In part the show's problem was that it was not sufficiently political for the loyal hardcore of the WPA audience, while WPA productions were automatically anathema to a large group who might have found this piece enchanting.

Broadway has generally believed that if at first you do succeed, try and try again. Certainly the Krimskys and their associates (Ted Fetter and Richard Lewine) held to the dictum. Fast on the vogue of *Naughty Naught ('00)*, they relit their American Musical Hall on October 9 with **The Fireman's Flame.** It was another first-class spoof of bygone melodramas, and it, too, could have been called *A Hero Is Born*. The Red Heart Hose Boys cannot see the heroic qualities in Harry Howard (Ben Cutler). Rejected by the brigade, he joins the less desirable Bluebird Hose Company. His rescue of the rich Adolphus Vanderpool (Philip Bourneuf) and his foster daughter Daphne (Cynthia Rogers) reflects unfavorably on the Red Heart Boys. They try to besmirch Harry's good name, coupling it with the scarlet Vera Violet (Grace Coppin). But the grateful Vanderpool foils the nefarious machinations. Harry turns out to be Vanderpool's son. By curtain time Daphne is slated to be Harry's wife and Harry is made fire chief. The songs sometimes mocked the speech patterns of the earlier days ("Do My Eyes Deceive Me?"), sometimes accepted their declarative directness ("It's A Lovely Night On The Hudson River"), and sometimes wryly combined the old and the new ("Doin' The Waltz"). "Do My Eyes Deceive Me?" and "It's A Lovely Night On The Hudson River" were love songs sung by Harry and Daphne, while Vera was awarded "Doin' The Waltz." Both the exaggerated gestures of the performers and such devices as simulated gas lamps for footlights affected proper 19th-century stage conventions. Theatregoers found it hard to resist such good fun. *The Fireman's Flame* surpassed the run of *Naughty Naught '00*, playing 204 performances.

The American Musical Theatre came back to the world of 1937 with its next two musicals. Nonetheless, in treating their own unhappy times these shows were poles apart. **I'd Rather Be Right** (11-2-37, Alvin) was a warm-hearted jab at the Roosevelt administration. Presidents had been portrayed on the musical stage before, especially in revue skits. But *I'd Rather Be Right* made Roosevelt the first incumbent President to become the central figure of a book musical. Since George S. Kaufman and Moss Hart wrote the book, expectations were high.

And the humor in the show was every bit as biting and to the point as the fun-making in *Of Thee I Sing* (12-26-31) or *Face the Music* (2-17-32). Unfortunately, the book turned out to be a collection of witty lines without any interesting turns of plot. The locale is Central Park in New York and the time July 4. Peggy Jones (Joy Hodges) and Phil Barker (Austin Marshall) would like to marry but feel they must wait for a pay raise that will come only when Roosevelt balances the budget. Phil falls asleep in the park and dreams he meets Roosevelt (George M. Cohan). The President proves sympathetic to Phil's problem and sets out immediately to see what he can do to aid the lovers. But every suggestion—taxing government property, hundred-dollar postage stamps—is rejected on some ground or other. And the idea that the treasury should hire pickpockets to relieve the nation of its money painlessly is thwarted by a vengeful Supreme Court, still smarting from Roosevelt's attempt the previous January to "pack" it with additional members. Roosevelt resorts to a fireside speech, begging American woman to eschew cosmetics for a year and donate the savings to the government. The women are not receptive. FDR's presidential rival, Alf Landon (Joseph Allen), reduced to a White House butler, is no help. Neither is Eleanor Roosevelt, who is away on a trip and unable to get back for Phil's dream. In the end Roosevelt suggests the youngsters ought to marry anyway. It's the right thing to do, and Roosevelt would rather be right than President. The lovers agree. Almost all the important political figures of the day except Eleanor Roosevelt were impersonated, while dozens of prominent Americans from Walter Lippmann to John L. Lewis came in for jibes. The dialogue was rib-tickling, such as the uproarious bit between the Postmaster General and the President:

Farley: This fellow is Chairman of the Fourth Assembly District in Seattle. He wants to be Collector of the Port of New York.
Roosevelt: But we've got a Collector of the Port of New York.
Farley: Not in Seattle.

Many of the best laughs fell to Farley. In discussing the postal rates he suggests all letters be required to carry airmail stamps, even if they are only being sent from the Bronx to Brooklyn. Roosevelt professes to be shocked:

Roosevelt: No, no, Jim. That wouldn't be honest.
Farley: Oh! I thought you were talking about taxes.

Later, after Roosevelt proposes to dispose of national encumbrances, Farley inquires, "Do we need Baltimore?" In some respects the show had an old musical comedy flavor. Touches of vaudeville were interspersed throughout the evening. When Roosevelt asks to see the Wagner Act, the act turns out to be not a law but a pair of acrobats. And as soon as a crowd assembles a Federal Theater troupe rushes in to sing "Spring In Vienna." The show, like *Sea Legs* a few months earlier, was one of the last to use a single set for the entire evening. (When FDR needed some place to deliver a fireside chat, a fireplace was wheeled on stage.)

The most endearing touch of an older era was the show's star, George M. Cohan. It was a perfect role in many ways for the great showman. He could be brash, vital, chauvinistic, and preachy. Regrettably, there were problems for him and his audience. First of all, Cohan hated Roosevelt. At one point during the Boston tryout he inserted his own anti-Roosevelt lyrics until Rodgers and Hart read him the riot act. But even more urgently, Rodgers let Cohan down. The score was one of Rodgers' weakest. Furthermore, Rodgers' subtle, contemporary style was not only alien to Cohan, it was anathema. Behind the scenes Cohan referred to his song writers as Gilbert and Sullivan—and he didn't mean the comparison to be complimentary. Even if he were right about Rodgers' music, Cohan was blind to the merits of Hart's lyrics—the equal of Ira Gershwin's for *Of Thee I Sing*. The cabinet enters and sings a chorus that belies their subsequent quarreling. They insist they are such a "homogeneous cabinet," unable to be told apart, that you'd swear that they had toured with Rupert D'Oyly Carte. Each secretary follows with a personal plaint. The lone woman in the entourage, Frances Perkins (Bijou Fernandez), the Secretary of Labor, remarks that she barely has time to powder her nose. She adds that for all the good she achieves, she might as well resign and go on powdering her nose. Even in the lyrics much of the fun continued to center on Farley. In "Off The Record" Roosevelt recounts their first meeting, recalling Farley talked until Roosevelt was in such a stupor that Farley had no trouble selling him the works of James Fenimore Cooper. Regrettably, except for Peggy and Phil's love song, "Have You Met Miss Jones?", Rodgers' melodies, while filled with interesting, sophisticated phrases, never added up to memorable tunes. Although *I'd Rather Be Right* enjoyed a healthy advance sale, business was further helped by the amazing, if poignant, fact that, for the first three and a half weeks of its nine-month run, only one other musical was competing with it on Broad-

way—another Rodgers and Hart hit, *Babes in Arms*.

There were virtually no advance sales for **Pins and Needles.** No advertisements were placed in the major dailies, and in return no major critic attended the show's opening night. Sponsored by the International Ladies' Garment Workers Union, the evening was unveiled on November 27 at what once had been the Princess Theatre and now was given the more aggressive name, the Labor Stage. The cast was recruited entirely from the rank and file of union members—cutters, weavers, machinists. So small were the union's expectations that initially only weekend performances were scheduled, thereby allowing the cast to do their regular work from Monday through Friday. The aggressive new name for the house reflected the aggressive, if honest, tone of the revue. Its most famous number insisted: "Sing Me A Song Of Social Significance," adding that unless the song is "packed with social fact" no love will follow. This sort of militancy led to some regrettable extremism—with the unionists seeing fascists and other villains in every person who deigned to disagree with them, much as many rightwingers of the day saw anarchists and communists in every member of the opposing camp. One dance number was the vitriolic "Doin' The Reactionary" ("Close your eyes to where you're bound"), a far cry from the insouciant "Doin' The Waltz" being sung uptown. In so charged an atmosphere even love became a distorted image of the group's social and political thinking, with, for example, extramarital flirting branded as "scabbing." Undoubtedly the polarization of political stances created in the ferment of the depression and New Deal endeavors to deal with it were accurately, if unfortunately, reflected.

Happily, the show found time to leave such cares behind. In a song that may have reminded inveterate theatregoers of Luella Gear's plaint, "I Couldn't Hold My Man" in *Life Begins at 8:40* (8-27-34), a young dressmaker named Millie Weitz rued that for all her dutiful adherence to advertising injunctions, "Nobody Makes A Pass At Me." International wrongdoing was chided in "Four Little Angels Of Peace." The number presented Hitler attempting to justify the Austrian Anschluss, Mussolini excusing his invasion of Ethiopia, an unidentified Japanese rationalizing the attack on China, and, somewhat unfairly, Anthony Eden singing of supposed English injustice to South Africa, India, and Ireland. The revue's low budget kept *Pins and Needles* going for 1,108 performances—first at the 299-seat Labor Stage, later at the 849-seat Windsor. While in no way gainsaying the show's incontestable popularity, it should be remembered that even the Windsor was only about half the size of the average Broadway musical house. Had *Pins and Needles* been presented with a professional cast in a theatre of average size, its run might well have been markedly shorter.

Curiously, the show's long run helped perpetuate itself. Fans could and did make repeated visits, since sketches and musical numbers were constantly changed to keep abreast of national and international developments. For example, even before Munich Eden was replaced by a figure more deserving of ridicule, Neville Chamberlain. When the Daughters of the American Revolution refused the Negro singer, Marian Anderson, permission to give a concert in their Washington auditorium, a spoof of *The Hot Mikado* (3-23-39) and *The Swing Mikado* (3-1-39) suddenly found three little maids singing, "Three little DARs are we/ Full to the brim with bigotry." During the show's long run it also underwent several minor title changes, being called at one time or another *New Pins and Needles, Pins and Needles of 1938,* and *Pins and Needles of 1939.* Perhaps the show's most enduring legacy was its gift to Broadway of a new composer-lyricist, Harold Rome.

. . .

Harold Rome was born in Hartford, Connecticut, on May 27, 1908. He attended Trinity College and Yale, receiving his B.A. from the latter in 1929 and a degree in architecture in 1934. Unable to find work in his chosen profession he turned to writing music. Rome had studied piano as a boy and helped pay his own way through college by playing in jazz bands and the Yale orchestra. He came to the attention of the International Ladies' Garment Workers Union while he was writing revues for a summer camp in the Adirondacks.

. . .

If Cohan had been ill at ease with the songs Rodgers and Hart had written for him, Ed Wynn was equally uncomfortable with E. Y. Harburg, Howard Lindsay, and Russel Crouse's book for **Hooray for What!** (12-1-37, Winter Garden). By stages he turned what had begun as a satire of the armaments race into another lunatic carnival. Gone by the time the show reached New York was the taut, hard-driving book, much of Agnes de Mille's antiwar ballet, and a number of the original leads. Wynn had to dominate his shows. But he wisely allowed enough of the story and malicious fun to remain to satisfy both the critics and his loyal following.

Chuckles is a zany scientist who invents a gas to kill appleworms. When the world powers discover it kills humans with equal efficacy, they trip over one another trying to steal it. Chuckles is invited to the League of Nations. At the Grand Hotel de l'Espionage one Mata Hari type copies his formula with the aid of a mirror, thereby getting it backwards and producing a laughing gas. The show was filled with Wynn witticisms, delivered with his exaggerated lisp: "Generally speaking diplomats are generally speaking"; "The trouble with Europe is Italy's in Ethiopia, Japan's in China, Russia's in Spain—nobody's home"; "Don't you fellows know that if you miss two more payments, America will own the last war outright?" E. Y. Harburg and Harold Arlen's score was less vulnerable to Wynn's revision than the book. The songs were pleasant, if not particularly distinguished; certainly not in keeping with the high satiric aim of the original libretto. Its best numbers were "Down With Love," "I've Gone Romantic On You," and "God's Country." The last included the rather startling phrase "every man is his own dictator." June Clyde, Vivian Vance, Jack Whiting, and the fine dancer, Paul Haakon, were featured. Whiting introduced all three of the songs mentioned, accompanied by Miss Vance in "I've Gone Romantic On You" and by Miss Vance and Miss Clyde in "Down With Love." Despite the havoc Wynn created, *Hooray For What!* ran for six months.

Looking back after forty years on **Between the Devil** (12-22-37, Imperial) its librettist and lyricist, Howard Dietz, concluded it was "almost a good show," failing primarily because he "didn't make it hilarious enough." He is probably too harsh on himself. This kind of drawing room musical comedy, really old French bedroom farce streamlined for modern consumption, was nearing the end of its vogue. Brooks Atkinson of the *Times* begrudged having to sit through the sort of "imbecilities that were risqué in 1917, piquant in 1927, and only a pain in the first and second acts today. . . ." In Dietz' plot Peter Anthony (Jack Buchanan), believing his first wife dead in a shipwreck, remarries. He no sooner settles in with the second Mrs. Anthony (Evelyn Laye), than his first wife (Adele Dixon), reappears. In a novel departure, the ending was left up to the audience. During the show's tryout Anthony was aware his first wife was still alive when he married for the second time. Howls of outrage and threats to close the show for indecency forced Dietz to modify the libretto. However troublesome the play proved for Dietz, for Arthur Schwartz it was a return to the more intimate surroundings in which he belonged. Another Schwartz standard, "I

See Your Face Before Me" (sung first by Miss Laye, later by Miss Dixon and Buchanan) came from the show. It used effectively a device Schwartz generally ignored, the repeated note. Even "By Myself" (a Buchanan solo), another fine and unusual number from the show, restricted itself to a limited range but came up with a richly textured melody, helped by Schwartz' striking harmonies. Dietz' lyrics were not quite equal to his partner's music. Dietz was a fine lyricist but not really on a level with the best. His lines invariably seem to lack that exquisite choice of word or phrase that would make them masterful. For example, there is something a trifle contrived in the fourth line of "I See Your Face Before Me" ("You are my only theme"). The lyrics for "Triplets," of which he is especially fond, and which was sung as an incidental number in the show by a specialty act, are not particularly smart or witty. ("She admits Lane Bryant thought they were measuring a giant" is the description of the woman pregnant with the triplets.) They clearly need a clever production to put them over. With so many lines delivered in Buchanan and the ladies' English accents, the evening must have sounded especially high-hat to playgoers who saw any of *Between the Devil*'s 93 performances.

If the story of *Between the Devil* appeared to be going out of fashion, all of **Three Waltzes** (12-25-37, Majestic) was a museum piece. Perhaps the fact that the Shuberts were the producers of both shows had something to do with this eagerness to retrace theatrical steps. (Even Ed Wynn's emasculating the satire in their production of *Hooray for What!* probably struck them as no more than a regression to the old star-dominated assemblages that had once kept their box offices busy.) *Three Waltzes* was an adaptation of a Viennese hit, *Drei Wälzer*, using melodies from three composers (Johann Strauss, Sr., Johann Strauss, Jr., and Oscar Straus) to tell in three acts three love stories of three related generations. It would be convenient to add that the show ran three months, but it ran closer to four. It might have run even longer had it been given a more extravagant mounting at the Center. At the Majestic it looked dowdy and old hat, despite the youthful charm of Kitty Carlisle, Michael Bartlett, and the fine supporting acting of Glenn Anders.

Had the activity in 1938's first week been indicative, the new year would have seen a happy revitalizing of the musical theatre. Three musical evenings premiered, one on January 3 and two on the 4th. One of these was actually a repertory of 17th- and 18th-century English operas that included works by Purcell and Arne. More pertinent to 1938 America

was **The Cradle Will Rock.** It had a bizarre history. It had been dropped as a WPA project in Washington and was about to be done in New York in June, with John Houseman in charge, when an injunction prevented the actors from performing. Houseman and Orson Welles hired the empty Venice Theatre and marched the cast and patrons twenty blocks north. Since the musicians union would not go along with the arrangement, the show's creator, Marc Blitzstein, played his score from a piano on stage. The actors, to overcome the technicality of the injunction, bought tickets, sat with the audience and performed from their seats. The play was repeated 19 times at the Venice, then at the Mercury on Sunday nights, and finally began a regular run at the Windsor right on January 3. It was a hate-warped tract which sadly saw everything in black and white. Steeltown is run by Mr. Mister (Will Geer) and his family for the benefit of Mr. Mister and his family—and a few selected cohorts. Forthright Larry Foreman (Howard da Silva) organizes the workers at a steel plant to fight for union recognition. Prostitutes such as Moll (Olive Stanton) support the union cause. Blitzstein's songs were skillfully wrought, but as strident and cantankerous as the plot. The show drew few of the regular musical theatregoers (a number of better dressed first-nighters walked out early in act one), but with $1.65 the top price at the tiny Windsor it attracted enough patrons to run 108 performances.

Blitzstein probably never meant his songs to have popular currency. But Sammy Fain, who wrote many of the tunes for **Right This Way** (1-4-38, 46th St.), did. Considering that both "I Can Dream, Can't I?" and "I'll Be Seeing You" were from this score, the show's run was dismayingly short: 15 performances. The short run is even more puzzling when it is remembered that the stars were Guy Robertson, Tamara (who introduced both of the show's best songs), and, in his Broadway debut, Joe E. Lewis. Blanche Ring also had a small part. A little of the surprise at the short run disappears on reading the book. The story is not especially novel or complex. Jeff Doane (Robertson) and Mimi Chester (Tamara) have been living happily without the benefit of clergy in Paris. When Jeff's newspaper reassigns him to America, he insists they must marry to accommodate back-home mores. But wedded life is not wedded bliss, and Mimi soon returns to her Paris apartment. Jeff follows, and so does a reconciliation. For most critics the evening belonged to Lewis. He introduced much of his night club patter and cared so little for the integrity of the piece that on several occasions he parodied the show's songs after they had been sung. Small as her part was, Miss Ring pleased her old fans by inserting "I've Got Rings On My Fingers."

Two months passed before the next musical was unveiled and it, too, had an ignominiously short run. **Who's Who** (3-1-38, Hudson) ran just 23 performances, and the recriminations over who was to blame may have been more entertaining than the revue itself. Leonard Sillman assembled it and named the famous party-giver Elsa Maxwell as producer in return for her promised financial assistance and her plush first-night crowd. The financial assistance was never forthcoming; the first-night crowd arrived late and talked all through the show. But New York critics had long learned to pay no heed to the rudeness of the first-nighters. Nevertheless, they were not impressed with the revue. It was patently more sophisticated than Sillman's earlier efforts—if sophistication means elegant dress and talk about society's interests. Its skits included a turnabout on all the left-wing rantings in the WPA and the Group Theatre. "Forgive Us Odets" had the rich planning a revolt. Sillman's favorite, Imogene Coca, performed a whole Billy Rose saturnalia singlehandedly in the austere style of *Our Town.* A popular burlesque knock-about clown, Rags Ragland, with several of his teeth conspicuously missing, appeared in a sentimental travesty of small-time burlesque and as a performer attempting to entertain from a raft during a storm at sea. Musically, Sillman's shows were always weak, and *Who's Who* was no exception. To make matters worse the dancing was dismissed as "graceless," the singing as "voiceless."

The last two musicals of the season didn't arrive until May, but the first of these was **I Married an Angel** (5-11-38, Shubert). Another suave, literate Rodgers and Hart contribution to the betterment of the American Musical Theatre, it had originally, like *On Your Toes* (11-29-36), been envisioned for the screen. Based on an Hungarian play by John Vaszary, the story had as its hero a banker and ladies' man, Willie Palaffi (Dennis King). Willie's bank is in trouble, and so is his courtship of a "Benny Goodman jitterbug," Anna (Audrey Christie). In a rash moment Willie breaks off his affair and swears to marry no one but an angel. When the gods wish to punish us they answer our prayers, and an angel (Vera Zorina) flies into Willie's rooms. He marries her and promptly clips her wings. But the gods above are snickering. Her open, angelic ways cause endless embarrassment until Willie's sister, the Countess Palaffi (Vivienne Segal), indoctrinates her brother's angel in the ways

of the world. A vengeful Anna spreads tales about the bank's problems. But Willie's backer, Harry Szigetti (Walter Slezak), arrives to save the day. Even his arrival would have been too late had not the Countess again stepped in to help. She bribes the cab drivers who are bringing the creditors to drive so slowly that the creditors appear only after Harry and Willie have come to terms. Two distinguished Rodgers standards were first sung in the show: the title song and "Spring Is Here" (a different number from the title song for their 1929 show). Miss Segal joined King to sing the latter. But the songs, in a sense, were only one manifestation of the excellent, innovative material Rodgers and Hart created for the show. The partners also adapted the book, but Hart's drinking was becoming a problem, so Joshua Logan was called in to assist. There were two musical interludes—one in each act—in which the dialogue was rhymed and sung; and two ballets, again one in each act. The interludes were "The Modiste," in which the Angel is fitted for her wardrobe, and "Angel Without Wings." The first-act ballet was straightforward, a Honeymoon Ballet. But the second, like "The Princess Zenobia" in *On Your Toes,* was satiric. "The Dream of Roxy's Music Hall" mocked both the size of the house and its lavish stage productions. Balanchine allowed Miss Segal and Miss Christie to represent the entire long line of Rockettes. Miss Zorina slithered out of a green cheesecloth sea to dance with a "headless" partner, while Slezak romped about with elephantine grace as an underwater monster. In an accompanying song, Hart was at his mischievous best. He described a typical spectacle (where acrobats performing on their "digits" seem as small as "midgets") and the audience reaction in the balcony ("so high you get the fidgets"). Who cares if "Any week you go, it's the same old show." In their autobiographies, both Rodgers and Logan looked back with special affection and amusement on the number. Rodgers can still not remember how so lavish a salute to a New York institution found its way into a musical set in Hungary. Logan added, the number provided "an astounding lesson for me. When you have no reason for putting something in a musical show, then for Christ's sake, don't give a reason. Just do it." Another novel feature was the rhymed dialogue with musical background that led into several of the songs. When the principals discuss going to the Music Hall, each has a comment. These were not verses in the customary sense, but pertinent dialogue metamorphosing into lyrics. Operatic ambitions continued to creep into musical comedy. Neither the show's novel departures nor its inconsistencies alarmed patrons. *I Married an Angel* kept Broadway applauding for ten months.

The season's closing show was an importation from London. **The Two Bouquets** (5-31-38, Windsor) had enjoyed a nine-month run at that city's minuscule Ambassador. Now at the not much larger house, where *The Cradle Will Rock* had recently been brandishing its sword, it met with a cool reception. In spite of a cast that included Viola Roche, Leo G. Carroll, Enid Markey, Robert Chisholm, and the not yet famous Alfred Drake and Patricia Morison (as two of the four principal lovers whose lives are complicated when flowers are delivered to the wrong recipients), the show lasted only seven weeks. Nosegays in the summer were even less alluring than bile in the cold weather.

1938-1939

Over the unproductive summer the turmoil of the preceding season subsided. In its aftermath Broadway quickly reverted to more conventional ways. But the ferment had taken its toll. The American Musical Theatre seemed pallid and limp, virtually exhausted. Even though the number of new musicals increased ever so slightly, there seemed to be only two completely achieved shows, just two works in which literate, witty dialogue; fine, memorable melodies; and choice casting and careful production joined forces. And one of these works was an importation. Several other pieces had bright moments and a good song or two, but not enough to add up to a totally satisfactory evening. The hit of the season was not in any of these categories. It was a freakish, coarse-grained, raucous affair out of the theatrical mainstream.

The season began with three shows that opened during the week of September 18. Ruefully they demonstrated the near bankruptcy of creativity. **You Never Know** (9-21-38, Winter Garden) led off. Like *Between the Devil* (12-22-37), it was another dated drawing-room musical comedy. Once a play by Siegfried Geyer (Gertrude Lawrence and Leslie Howard had performed it as *Candle Light* in a 1929 P.G. Wodehouse translation), it had been transformed into a Viennese musical, *Bei Kerzenlicht*. In the story the Baron Ferdinand de Romer (Rex O'Malley) exchanges places with his man, Gaston (Clifton Webb), so that he may more conveniently woo Mme. Henri Baltin (Libby Holman).

Maria (Lupe Velez), Mme. Baltin's maid, takes to wearing her mistress' clothing, and before long a second romance ensues between her and Gaston, whom she mistakes for the baron. The Shuberts retained only two of the original songs, entrusting most of the new material to Cole Porter. Porter was recovering from a riding accident which had cost him the use of one leg. It had been a long, painful recovery, and undoubtedly deprived Porter of more than just physical strength. His score was in no way up to snuff. Porter himself in later years generally referred to *You Never Know* as his worst show. Porter's way with words suffered less than his music. The lyrics for the show's best ballad, "At Long Last Love" (sung by Gaston), were good, and the rhymes for the cheerful number Gaston and Maria sang, "From Alpha To Omega," even better. A still better example of his wit and clever in-rhyming came in "What Shall I Do?" where Maria must decide between two heart throbs. Confessing her "itch to," she rues she can't choose "which to hitch to." To aggravate the show's shortcomings, what could have been a saving intimacy was discarded in favor of a lavish production at the huge Winter Garden. Some of the action was moved to a night club, where Shubert show girls paraded lumberingly and battalions of dancers tapped and whirled away. These big production numbers inflated the musical's running costs and helped close it after just 78 performances.

On the other hand **Hellzapoppin** (9-22-38, 46th St.) was rushed into the highly suitable Winter Garden when the Porter piece folded, and it remained there till it ended its run of 1,404 performances. When *Hellzapoppin* closed it held the long-run record for a musical on Broadway. Like the equally long-running *Pins and Needles* (11-27-37), it frequently added and dropped new material. At one point, near the end of its run, it even changed its title slightly to *The New Hellzapoppin*. But unlike *Pins and Needles* its humor was zany, happy, and irrelevant. Olsen and Johnson, two old-time vaudevillians who had never made the big time, sparked the antics. A filmed sequence that opened the evening offered praise for the revue from Hitler (speaking with a Yiddish accent), Mussolini (ranting in a Negro dialect), and Roosevelt (talking gibberish). "Workmen" lumbered through the rows of seats with large ladders, forcing patrons to get up and out of their way; in the middle of the performance a woman screamed she had left her baby at the automat and rushed out of the theatre; a man walked up and down the aisles attempting to give a lady a plant she had ordered, the plant grew bigger with each appearance, and by the end of the evening departing crowds could see the man sitting in the lobby with a small tree and still forlornly calling out the lady's name. Sirens, firecrackers, and guns were going off incessantly. In a show such as this there was little use for good music. Sammy Fain and Charles Tobias did journeymen's labor but came up with no winners. The show's deliriously puerile escapism was called to the nation's attention by the influential columnist, Walter Winchell. After the fence-straddling reviews of the show he never missed a chance to plug it in his columns or on his radio show. He often took credit for making the show the great bonanza it turned out to be. No one disputed him.

Sing Out the News (9-24-38, Music Box) had no such benefactor. And though it enjoyed better reviews than *Hellzapoppin* it ran only 105 performances. It represented an interesting merging of the talents of the liberal George S. Kaufman and Moss Hart with the leftish Harold Rome and Charles Friedman. Kaufman and Hart assumed the sketch-writing chores Friedman had originally been slated for, leaving Friedman solely with credit for conceiving and directing the show. The fun was still at the expense of the successful, but, being successes themselves, Kaufman and Hart knew how to temper their wit. The show's best skit was at once a deft parody of *I Married an Angel* and a dig at the GOP. In "I Married a Republican" the leaders of the party despair of finding a candidate when a male angel (played by the revue's drollest clown, Hiram Sherman) flies in through a window. They select him to oppose Roosevelt. To their horror he is all for the New Deal, but they persuade him to their point of view, causing him to lose his wings in the change-about. In other skits Roosevelt was blamed for the weather; a young boy trying to reconcile groups of rich and poor children was arrested for disturbing the peace; and a Hollywood epic about Marie Antoinette was disrupted when the movie mogul realized the picture ended with an effective revolution. A congressional minstrel show closed the first act. The evening's ballet showed peace cruelly manhandled by the world's diplomats.

Happily, success had also come to Harold Rome and the difference was obvious in his songs. For example, "My Heart Is Unemployed" (sung in the show by Mary Jane Walsh and Michael Loring) mixed romance and the economic picture much as "One Big Union For Two" had, but its tone was noticeably cheerier. And "Franklin D. Roosevelt Jones," the show's rousing hit, celebrating the birth of a black baby into a world of hope, became a na-

tional hit. (The song—sung in the show by **Rex Ingram** and the chorus—in its sheet music is called simply "F.D.R. Jones.")

Knights of Song (10-17-38, 51st St.) gave Arthur Sullivan (John Moore) a fictitious romance with a married American (Natalie Hall). She mediates his battles with Gilbert (Nigel Bruce) and helps him win the favor of Queen Victoria (Molly Pearson). Famous figures who paraded across the stage included the Prince of Wales (Monty Woolley), Oscar Wilde (Robert Chisholm), and George Bernard Shaw (Winston O'Keefe). Though Laurence Schwab produced the mounting and Oscar Hammerstein staged it, the piece was written by relatively untested hands. Much the best parts of the evening were the beloved old songs Gilbert and Sullivan wrote for the English musical stage. But they could not keep the show on the boards beyond its second week.

One of the most beloved of all American show standards, "September Song," came out of the next musical to premiere, **Knickerbocker Holiday** (10-19-38, Barrymore). It was sung in the show by the much-admired Walter Huston, making an unusual appearance on the lyric stage. As a result the evening often has been looked back on in an afterglow of longing and affection. Its admirers forget that the show was neither a financial nor a critical success. (Many forget as well that the much-loved Huston was considered in some quarters too likable to be a believable villain.) Despite its low initial cost it was never able to recoup its investment during its 21-week run. And despite its festive title and charming, off-beat setting, it was a rather heavy-handed anti-fascist tract, that, wittingly or no, also protested growing governmental interference from Washington.

The lyrics and libretto were by one of the most distinguished and high-principled American playwrights, Maxwell Anderson. His play begins in 1809 with Washington Irving (Ray Middleton) deciding to write a history of old New York. Irving extricates himself from his own day and enters 17th-century New Amsterdam, commenting on the action, sometimes participating in it, and in the end becoming a sort of *deus ex machina* to give his tale a happy ending. In Irving's old town the council awaits the arrival of a new governor, Peter Stuyvesant. The council is made up of the best names in the village—Vanderbilt, Van Cortlandt, De Peyster, and, among others, Roosevelt. But this Roosevelt speaks not in the cultured tones of a fireside chat but with the pronounced "Dutch" accent that had only recently been the stock in trade of certain

511

stage comedians: "I vould not be silent! I vould vant to know who done something!" The council does indeed need to know "who done something," for it is hanging day and the council has no one to hang. Arbitrarily, the councilmen select an independent-minded, troublesome knife-sharpener, Brom Broeck (Richard Kollmar). He is condemned on the exaggerated charge that he forgot to get a license. Brom, who loves Tina (Jeanne Madden), the daughter of councilman Tienhoven (Mark Smith), prefers to live. He is temporarily saved from the gallows by the arrival of Stuyvesant (Huston). But it is a mixed blessing, for Tina's father offers his daughter in marriage to the new governor, and Stuyvesant, liking the girl and understanding he is in the autumn of days, suggests they brook no delay. Stuyvesant's methods are high-handed and dictatorial. After the governor abolishes all the freedoms the town had enjoyed, even the councilmen mourn the loss of "Our Ancient Liberties." When Brom protests he is jailed. Just as Tina and Stuyvesant's wedding is about to take place, Indians attack. Brom escapes from jail, joins the fighting, and becomes its hero. When Brom accuses the governor of conspiring with the Indians, Stuyvesant reimposes the sentence of hanging. Irving steps into the picture and reminds the governor he must think of how posterity will remember him. Stuyvesant prefers a good name in history and lets the lovers go off together. Stuyvesant asks Irving if he could be considered an American:

Stuyvesant: Maybe I could qualify. I was never able to take orders.
Irving: That's how you tell an American!

Much of Kurt Weill's music for Anderson's book and lyrics was not at all traditional Broadway material. Weill's score was free in form, shaped within the requirements of the scene and lyrics, but too sprawling to be extracted and given a separate life. Moreover even in expressive numbers such as "It Never Was Anywhere You" use of Dutch constructions in the principal lyrics hindered easy acceptance. However, "September Song" was written in the customary AABA pattern and within the limited range of Huston's voice.

Knickerbocker Holiday was one of two October offerings. The second was the Krimskys' **The Girl from Wyoming** (10-29-38, American Music Hall), with Ted Fetter and Richard Lewine again writing the songs. But good luck did not come a third time. The novelty of their musical hall spoofs had worn thin. In a *Whoopee* (12-4-28) or *Girl Crazy* (10-14-30) sort of tale, Harvard's dapper Ben Long-

wood (Philip Huston) heads west for freedom and refreshment. Instead his life is complicated by all the wrong western types. He is spared in the end thanks to the charm of the young lady of the title (June Walker). Longwood best expressed his feelings in "Stay East, Young Man." When attendance faltered, the Krimskys brought *Naughty Naught ('00)* (1-23-37) back in repertory with the new piece, but it failed to revive flagging interest in the ersatz beer hall.

The second Cole Porter score of the season was heard in **Leave It to Me** (11-9-38, Imperial). It suggested that following his accident Porter was having a serious problem marshaling his musical forces, although his gift for lyrics remained intact. His best ballad was "Get Out Of Town," sung by Tamara in the show. It employed the elementary device of a repeated note, but its torrid lyrics gave it a welcome bite. The show's biggest hit was "My Heart Belongs To Daddy," which had no real relevance to the plot but which nonetheless rocketed Mary Martin to stardom. (She sang it wrapped in furs, sitting on a trunk at a Siberian whistle-stop and slowly doffing her garments.)

. . .

Mary Martin was born in Weatherford, Texas, on December 1, 1913, and made her stage debut at the age of five, singing at a Firemen's Ball. She came to Broadway following a brief fling singing in night clubs and the break-up of her first marriage. Radiating wholesomeness, she could employ her small, clear soprano to deliver a straight, sentimental ballad. But she just as magically could bring to her numbers a fragile wispiness or a coy impishness. It was the latter which helped her first make her mark on Broadway.

. . .

In his lyrics for the song Porter had more fun with the word "daddy" than anyone since P. G. Wodehouse in *Oh, My Dear* (11-27-18). Porter rhymed "Daddy" with everything from "caddie" to "finnan haddie," and then turned "daddy" into a series of "dada-das." Having presented a not too faithful young lady, Porter offered the other side of the coin, more or less, with "Most Gentlemen Don't Like Love" (sung by Sophie Tucker and the chorus), insisting "they just like to kick it around."

The plot on which these love and anti-love songs were hung concerned the adventures of meek, domestic Alonzo "Stinky" Goodhue (Victor Moore), who is made ambassador to Russia after his ambitious wife (Sophie Tucker) contributes generously to Roosevelt's re-election campaign. To get himself recalled, Alonzo kicks the Nazi ambassador and shoots a political figure in Red Square (hitting a counterrevolutionary by mistake). Somehow all his mischief rebounds to his credit. Only when he begins to enjoy his work and proposes a plan for world peace do the great powers become up in arms. In a romantic subplot, Moore's partner, William Gaxton, played a brash newspaperman, working for a publisher who had coveted the ambassadorial post, and attempting to embarrass Goodhue. Tamara played Gaxton's girl, Colette. Sam and Bella Spewack adapted the story from their own play, *Clear All Wires*. Their libretto lacked the slashing satire of recent thirties' shows, and its targets appeared increasingly riddled, at least on stage. Since America and, in particular, its large liberal segments were still on good terms with Russia, *Leave It to Me*'s first-act finale was set in Red Square. The communist anthem, "The Internationale," was sung and a friendly Joe Stalin (Walter Armin) condescended to do a little dance. By the time the show embarked on a national tour during the next season, Stalin and Hitler had signed their pact. Stalin was eliminated as a character in the show and a warning was added to the program insisting the evening bore no relation to current events.

The season's best musical, though not its biggest hit, was November's other entry. George Abbott took Shakespeare's *Comedy of Errors,* modernized Shakespeare's dialogue and handed it over to Rodgers and Hart for words and music. The three came up with a joyous romp, **The Boys from Syracuse** (11-23-38, Alvin). The play retained the story of the twin Antipholuses, separated by accident shortly after birth, and their twin servants, both named Dromio. The confusions that arise when the pair from Syracuse find themselves in Ephesus, where the other master and servant reside, are only straightened out when their father appears with his explanation. In an inspired bit of casting, Teddy Hart (Larry's brother) and Jimmy Savo were assigned the parts of the two Dromios. Not only did the two diminutive comedians impart the same air of boyish innocence and pathos, but they looked so much alike they could almost have passed for twins. The evening's most famous moment fell to Savo. When a seeress pronounced, "The venom clamours of a jealous woman poisons more deadly than a mad dog's tooth"—the only line Abbott retained from the original play—Savo jumped from the wings and joyously cried, "Shakespeare!" Eddie Albert and Ronald Graham portrayed the two Antipholuses. Rodgers provided a rich, varied score, and Hart, giving no sign of his drinking problems, wrote

brilliantly appropriate lyrics. Both the fetching, bittersweet waltz, "Falling In Love With Love"—sung by Adriana (Muriel Angelus)—and the effervescent "This Can't Be Love"—introduced by Antipholus (Albert) and Luciana (Marcy Wescott)—became immensely popular. But Hart (and Rodgers) was equally adept in the scathingly comic "What Can You Do With A Man?" ("He eats me out of house and home/But doesn't like my cooking!"), which Dromio and Luce (Wynn Murray) sang, and the moodily poetic "You Have Cast Your Shadow On The Sea," assigned to Luciana and the 1st Antipholus. There were also the lovely ballads, "The Shortest Day Of The Year," sung by the second Antipholus (Graham) and "Sing For Your Supper," a women's trio (Luce, Adriana, and Luciana) that nightly stopped the show. *The Boys from Syracuse* brought the ancient world alive for seven months. A fine, if minor, off-Broadway revival in 1963 confirmed that the show had lost none of its sparkle.

Only one musical appeared in December and that one, **Great Lady** (12-1-38, Majestic), was a quick flop. It told an incredibly complicated plot that kept jumping back and forth in time between the French Revolution and 1939, and back and forth in place between France and America. Based loosely on the story of Eliza Bowen, a girl of somewhat dubious reputation who had several love affairs and marriages ending with her marriage in middle age to the seventy-eight-year-old Aaron Burr, it starred three gracious ladies of an earlier musical stage: Norma Terris (as Eliza), Irene Bordoni, and Helen Ford. When it folded after 20 performances, it took with it the first full Broadway score by young Frederick Loewe.

A revival of *Blossom Time* closed out the old year. The show was brought in from the road where it had been touring, virtually without a halt, since its first traveling company had been sent out seventeen years before. Everett Marshall was its Schubert, a role he continued to sing until he closed his career.

The last year of the decade began with importations. The D'Oyly Carte arrived January 5 for a brief season of Gilbert and Sullivan. The Savoyards were followed by **Set to Music** (1-18-39, Music Box), a revue Noel Coward designed around the talents of Beatrice Lillie. Most of its material came from his London production *Words and Music,* but he culled songs from other of his shows and wrote new numbers as well. As far as American audiences were concerned, *Set to Music* was their introduction to "Mad About The Boy," "The Party's Over," and

"The Stately Homes Of England," only the first sung by Miss Lillie. It played for 129 showings.

The first new American offering of 1939 was not unveiled until February. It, too, was a revue. And it, too, was aimed at the knowing, well-heeled crowds that supported Coward. **One for the Money** (2-4-39, Booth) was conceived, produced, and, except for the music, written by Nancy Hamilton. Miss Hamilton was no newcomer to revues. She had been a significant factor in the success of the early Leonard Sillman revues. Like Sillman she appeared relatively indifferent to the music in her productions. At least no more major songs ever emerged from her shows than did from Sillman's. Certainly Morgan Lewis' songs were not the talk of the town. Miss Hamilton's emphasis was on her skits, and even more on her bright, young performers. In her cast, besides herself, were Brenda Forbes, Philip Bourneuf, Ruth Matteson, Keenan Wynn, Gene Kelly, and Alfred Drake. The mood of the show was quickly established when a handsome-looking family in proper evening attire was served champagne by their maid and announced, "We think that right is right and wrong is left." Drake was assigned one of the evening's most delicious bits—an affectionate dig at Orson Welles. Drake's Welles boasted he knew Shakespeare backward at two, forward at three, and personally at four. The show playfully teased modern art, Wagner, Eleanor Roosevelt, and parlor games of the idle rich. The rich were apparently neither idle enough nor rich enough to support the show for very long, but a satisfactory run of 132 performances determined Miss Hamilton to try again.

The following week brought in two shows. Both were disappointments. Ethel Merman and Jimmy Durante were partnered again, this time in **Stars in Your Eyes** (2-9-39, Majestic). The show had a book by J. P. McEvoy. It had music by Arthur Schwartz, but Schwartz was working with a new lyricist, Dorothy Fields. So glittering an array of talent gave every promise of bringing in a hit. But troubles began early on. The musical had originally been intended as a satire on leftist influence in Hollywood, but the producer concluded the line had been overplayed. As a result much of McEvoy's original plot was left behind in rehearsals and on the road. What survived was largely a trite love story. The great Hollywood star, Jeanette Adair (Miss Merman), loves John Blake (originally a leftist screenwriter), but John (Richard Carlson) loves Tata (Tamara Toumanova). Jeanette's pursuit of John is abetted, and sometimes complicated, by the movie studio idea man and troubleshooter,

Bill (Durante). (In the original script Bill was a union organizer.) Jeanette gets her man. On top of the book trouble, the score was not among Schwartz' best, and the hit of the evening, "It's All Yours," was made not on the strength of the song, but on Miss Merman and Durante's horseplay. Each tried to throw the other off balance with outrageous ad-libs and anything else that came to mind. It was to its stars and Joshua Logan's fluid direction that the show owed its run of 127 performances.

Lew Leslie tried for a fifth time to recapture the magic of the original *Blackbirds* (6-9-28) with **Blackbirds of 1939** (2-11-39, Hudson). A number of first-rate writers helped with the material: Johnny Mercer, Mitchell Parish, and Sammy Fain. Ferde Grofé did the orchestrations and J. Rosamond Johnson the vocal arrangements. "When A Blackbird Is Blue" (Parish/Fain) led into a choral version of Gershwin's "Rhapsody In Blue." Ralph Brown provided the evening's best dancing, dressed up as a pirate king. For comedy the revue milked laughs from a Harlem bridge game. But even with promising newcomers such as Lena Horne to present the songs, the evening found no takers. It closed after nine performances. For Leslie it was the last straw. He never again attempted a *Blackbirds*. Actually, although no one could realize it at the time, his original *Blackbirds* was the last in the brief, select line of jazzy Negro revues that had begun with what was really a book show, *Shuffle Along* (5-23-21). Leslie himself was responsible for mounting half the black shows of the thirties. They were all either flops or barely successful.

Two freakish Negro shows followed; both were jazz versions of *The Mikado*. The first to arrive was **The Swing Mikado** (3-1-39, New Yorker). It had been the sensational success of the Federal Theatre in Chicago, compiling a remarkable run of twenty-two weeks. Mike Todd had offered to bring it to New York, and when his overtures were rebuffed he mounted his own, more lavish version with Bill Robinson in the title role and called it **The Hot Mikado** (3-23-39, Broadhurst). While the cast of the Federal Theatre production performed in costumes and sets that resembled Africa far more than old Japan, Todd's performers went a step farther from the original. Robinson strutted in a gold suit, gold shoes, with a gold derby and gold cane. Todd's chorus girls tapped away bedecked nattily in slacks on a stage filled with stylized, modern decor. For a brief time in May the two Mikados played across the street from each other. Neither was a runaway success on Broadway. The Chicago original ran 86 performances; Todd's one less. But Todd astutely avoided losing money on his production by moving it lock, stock, and barrel to the World's Fair in Flushing.

The Federal Theatre, about to be disbanded, was also the producer of the final show of the theatrical year, **Sing for Your Supper** (4-24-39, Adelphi). By and large it reserved its satire for foreign matters, particularly the Nazi take-over of Austria. "The Blue Danube" under Hitler's glowering watch was transformed into the goose-stepping "Horst Wessel-lied," Sketches had fun at the expense of naval war games, *The Cradle Will Rock* school of sceneryless opera, and New York's official greeter, Grover Whalen. On the domestic front the show's songs took a far more optimistic view as their titles suggest: "Oh, Boy Can We Deduct," "Bonnie Banks," and "Lucky." One uplifting ensemble number celebrated the news that "Papa's Got A Job." Papa was fortunate, since he was about to be evicted for not paying his rent. The enthusiasm of his neighbors congregating in an alley canopied with fully hung clothes lines was so moving that Brooks Atkinson in the *Times* hailed the scene as "modern theatre at its best." But in the long haul the evening's most successful number was its finale, called in the show "The Ballad Of Uncle Sam," and led by Gordon Clarke and the chorus. It was an extended, discursive paean by Earl Robinson to lyrics by John La-touche. The word poem extolled the richness and diversity of America in a hymn of hope for the future. When the war broke out, the song was re-done by Paul Robeson as "Ballad For Americans" and proved a popular instrument of wholesome propaganda.

1939-1940

The New York World's Fair provided a timely diversion for New Yorkers and visitors during the summer months of the new season. Unfortunately, the exposition's slightly unworldly euphoria was shattered in September when many of exhibiting nations found themselves engulfed in the opening battles of World War II, just a month over twenty-five years since the guns that initiated World War I had fired away. Broadway's first response was not surprising. It ignored the war. For the musical theatre, keeping the conflict at arm's length was easier than it had been at the outbreak of World War I. At that time, the musical stage depended heavily on Vienna and to a lesser extent on London and Paris for much of its entertainments. But the Great War had made Broadway self-sufficient. It was a self-sufficiency the American Musical Theatre never afterwards lost. The new war made itself felt in two ways. For one, there was a draining away of young talent to serve in the forces, thereby further thinning theatrical ranks already depleted by Hollywood. But this came later. The initial reaction was to change the emphasis of the librettos. Real war was the topic of the day, and real war was no joking matter. Topicality largely disappeared from the books of new Broadway musicals.

For the most part the new offerings remained steadfastly contemporary, but with equal purpose they carefully eschewed the political, economic, and social implications in the headlines. Left-wing propagandizing suffered the severest setback, especially during the period of Soviet-Nazi détente. Some residual philosophizing was tolerated partly in the spirit of a necessary patriotic ecumenism and partly because so many of both the audience and the creators held to their liberal views. In time—after two or three seasons passed by—a new interest and a new style of musical appeared. It inaugurated a major new chapter in the history of the lyric theatre.

The season opened when the Shuberts in association with Olsen and Johnson presented **The Streets of Paris** (6-19-39, Broadhurst). The producing credits warned what sort of revue Broadway could expect. Two old New York favorites were in the cast: Luella Gear and Bobby Clark. But the roster of performers also included a number of not-so-well-known names soon to become more familiar on the Broadway stage or elsewhere: Bud Abbott, Lou Costello, Carmen Miranda, Jean Sablon, Ramon Vinay, and Gower Champion. There was little, apart from Sablon and one or two other artists, that was truly French, though Jimmy Mc-Hugh's songs sang of "Rendezvous Time In Paree," "Thanks For The Franks," and the titular "The Streets Of Paris." Harold Rome contributed one number with a Gallic reference, "The French Have A Word For It." Miss Miranda, decked out in an outlandish headdress, offered the show's hit in the first-act finale when she pointed not across the Atlantic but below the border in "The South American Way." It caught the Latin flavor that was sweeping the country. One of the show's few allusions to current international problems was the satiric dance number "Doin' The Chamberlain." Mustached, somber-suited chorus boys stepped out gingerly with their umbrellas. More typical of the show's humor were the Clark, and Abbott and Costello sketches. One of Clark's routines had him playing four characters in the same sketch—its belly laughs coming not so much from its lines as from Clark's increasingly frantic costume changes. Costello mistook a mental institution for a hotel and didn't seem to notice his error even when a swami who asked him if he wanted his palm read dabbed Costello's hand with red paint. One sign of the improving economic picture was the show's ability to hike its price from $3.30 to $4.40 as soon as success was determined.

Europe's turmoil was brought home the night after *The Streets of Paris* premiered when **From Vienna** (6-20-39, Music Box), a revue by and with refugees from Hitler's persecutions, presented its wares. The group of Austrians and Germans were talented, but not attuned to Broadway. They lingered through the summer.

July's only entry was the season's first book musical, **Yokel Boy** (7-6-39, Majestic). Lew Brown, who produced and directed the piece, was responsible for its story and shared credit for its tunes with Charles Tobias and Sam H. Stept. The first act finale, "Uncle Sam's Lullaby," injected a bit of vestigial topicality into the evening, assuring the audience that we were strong enough to protect ourselves if war broke out. An entire chorus marching determinedly in soldiers' uniforms seemed to Brooks Atkinson "like the thumping epics of '17." Otherwise, Brown's plot appeared to be merely a variation on the story of *America's Sweetheart* (2-10-31). Elmer Whipple (Buddy Ebsen), the son of a once-famous dancer, and Mary Hawkins (Lois January) have been fond of each other since childhood. When a chance to become a Hollywood star takes Mary away from her Lexington, Massachusetts, farm, Elmer follows her. Mary's career fails to live up to its initial promise, but by a fluke Elmer gets a part and becomes an overnight success. Success brings him no happiness, especially as he watches a budding romance between Mary and a matinee idol. His persistence and charm finally scotch the romance. Mary and Elmer decide they prefer a New England farm to the glamor of Hollywood. Judy Canova added to the merriment with her hillbilly rendition of three songs only loosely connected with the plot, "Catherine The Great," "Jukin'," and "Comes Love." In August changes were made to tighten the narrative and bolster the humdrum score. "The Beer Barrel Polka" (Brown/ Jaromir Vejvoda) was interpolated in the process. But a lion's share of credit for *Yokel Boy*'s six-month run had to be given to its principal enter-

tainers; plus a young comic in a minor role who made critics take note, Phil Silvers.

The **George White Scandals of 1939–40** (8-28-39, Alvin) proved to be the last in the series. The tradition of the great annuals had long since withered away; their fervor, excitement, and grandeur were only memories. But this farewell edition was not without its high moments. Ann Miller capably filled the shoes once worn by Ann Pennington. Ray Middleton was as good a singer as the *Scandals* had ever employed, although he left the cast shortly after the opening. And Ella Logan was a lively heir to the tradition of Frances Williams. The Howard brothers, the Three Stooges, and Ben Blue were more than capable of handling comedy. Some of their original comic material was so off-color it brought down the wrath of Boston censors and was eliminated. The World's Fair was kidded, with Willie and Eugene playing Sam Trylon and Max Perisphere; unions were spoofed when a union husband was prevented from kissing his nonunion wife; Willie Howard played a French poodle "saluting" a German dachshund in a slightly vulgar but popular joke. There was even a skit about a machine that allows viewers to watch people in another room for a small price. Willie Howard used it to spy on his wife. The machine was called "Tell-u-vision." The Three Stooges splattered each other in a free-for-all pie-throwing melee, while Ben Blue provided more subtle humor with his airy pantomimes. Sammy Fain's score (with Jack Yellen lyrics) was pert and attractive. The songsmiths took account of the craze for Latin rhythms in "The Mexiconga" but came up with their best number in a hedonistic bit, of the sort that had been voguish in the now-receding depression, "Are You Havin' Any Fun?" (sung in her Scottish brogue by Miss Logan, dressed as a sailor). It was a score that ranked with all but the very best of the old *Scandals* scores. The "Mexiconga" number, filled with swirling senoritas led by Ann Miller dancing against a flamboyant south-of-the-border setting, and a South Sea hula spectacle offered touches on the old time lavishness, while a first-act finale wistfully recalled a happier past by saluting the great show tunes of the twenties. Yet for all its goodies, *The Scandals* could only run up a record of 120 showings.

The only new musical to arrive during September was **The Straw Hat Revue** (9-29-39, Ambassador). As its name announced, it had been a summer circuit attraction and was brought to the big town for a mere $8,000. The show threw stones at a corpse by mocking operettas with "The Grand Chandelier" and kidded the best number of *The Streets of Paris* with "Soused American Way" (in which Imogene Coca impersonated Carmen Miranda). No hits emerged from Sylvia Fine and James Shelton's score, but a number of young talents beside Miss Coca continued their climb to the top: Danny Kaye, Alfred Drake, and Jerome Robbins. What looked so fresh in the Pennsylvania mountains seemed less attractive in an aging, ugly Broadway house. The show lasted ten weeks.

In the middle of October Rodgers and Hart came up with another hit, if not another gem. **Too Many Girls** (10-18-39, Imperial) restored collegiate life and football to the musical stage, where Pottawatomie College joined the league that included Bingham and Tait. In some ways it was a backward institution, playing its football games on Friday because it didn't know any better. But it was far ahead of its time in insisting that freshman coeds wear beanies colored to let the boys know whether or not the girls were virgins. When Harvey Casey sends his sometimes wild daughter Consuelo (Marcy Wescott) there, he discreetly sends four football players as bodyguards. She falls in love with one of them, Clint Kelley (Richard Kollmar), only to discover his real job on the day of the big game with Texas Gentile. Consuelo announces she is heading back east immediately. Since Clint and his associates must remain with her, they will not be able to play. Common sense and love prevail for the happy ending. Two of the other fullbacks were Eddie Bracken, who provided much of the lighthearted comedy, and Hal Le Roy, who did more fancy stepping on the boards than on the grid. The solidly professional George Marion, Jr., book provided cues for an equally professional score. Like almost everyone else during the season, Rodgers and Hart fell into the Latin beat with "All Dressed Up (Spic and Spanish)" and more obviously with "She Could Shake The Maracas." The Latin numbers were sparked by the fourth fullback, Desi Arnaz. (These Latin influences probably provided excuses for Jo Mielziner's sun-splashed sets and Raoul Pène du Bois' colorful costumes, both of which sometimes smacked more of old Mexico than of New Mexico.) In "I Like To Recognize The Tune" Rodgers and Hart protested against "the musical distortions then so much a part of pop music because of the swingband influence." Hart had a lyric field day with "Give It Back To The Indians." On those occasions when Hart was too drunk to write, Rodgers was forced to supply his own words. He proved he was a match for his irresponsible partner. Rodgers'

lyrics for the opening number found the football players lamenting they were no longer Saturday's heroes when the season is finished, "Spring is the winter of our discontent." But only once did Rodgers and Hart hit upon the magical mixture of words and music that make a standard. "I Didn't Know What Time It Was" has aged far less than the lovers (Consuelo and Clint) who sang it.

One seemingly timeless song is all that **Very Warm for May** (11-17-39, Alvin) also left behind. The show promised to be one of the major hits of the season, reuniting Jerome Kern, Oscar Hammerstein II, and Max Gordon. Its disastrously short run of 59 performances was generally attributed to a lifeless, laughless book. Whether Hammerstein was to blame, or whether the onus belonged on the revisions Gordon and his director, Vincente Minnelli, demanded during the tryout will never be known. But as the *Times'* Brooks Atkinson concluded, the libretto presented on the first night made "a singularly haphazard appreciation of Mr. Kern's music almost a challenge." The story was not unlike *Babes in Arms* (4-14-37). May Graham (Grace McDonald) is the daughter of an old theatrical family. They want her to go to college, but she prefers to continue the family's stage tradition. When she runs away to take a job at Winnie's Barn, a summer theatre, they chase after her. But May lands a part in the musical Ogdon Quiller's Progressive Playshop is mounting at the theatre, and she also lands Winnie Spofford's son (Richard Quine). Hammerstein's lyrics were uneven, often inferior; but they disclosed that at this early date, three years before he began working with Richard Rodgers, the style and mannerisms of his final years were coming to the fore. "May Tells All," in which May describes an imaginary elopement, revealed his penchant for American hyperbole (Hammerstein would use "world famous" to better effect in *South Pacific*), his perennial discomfort with in-rhyming, his heavy-handed verbal wit ("squirt" coupled with "Detroit"), his repetition (four "alls" in eight lines, and only the last two "alls" necessary or well employed), and his striving for simple, honest poetic images ("a moon, all misty and gray"). Although Hammerstein's lyrics were not among his best, most critics and the public rose to the challenge of appreciating Kern's lovely score. "All The Things You Are" became an immediate Kern classic, even though Kern himself is said to have felt its key and tempo changes would militate against success. The song, used in the show as part of the play within the play, was as sweet and thoughtfully conceived in its verse as in its chorus (or, as Kern always insisted, burthen). It was sung by Quiller (Hiram Sherman) and several members of the Progressive Players. The rest of the score, including the enchanting "Heaven In My Arms," was excellent, although it went with the scenery to Cain's warehouse.

The failure of *Very Warm for May* was doubly sad. Besides depriving most of the score of a chance to be heard, it closed the Broadway career of Kern on an unhappy note. Kern returned to Hollywood. He continued to produce fine songs for films. In 1945 he came back to New York to write additional material for a revival of *Show Boat* (12-27-27) and to begin work on a new show. But he died suddenly before any real progress had been made on the new piece.

In a small footnote, Donald Brian was one of the principals, May's father. He had played the leads in *The Merry Widow* (10-21-07) and *The Girl from Utah* (8-24-14), thereby participating in the opening of two important acts in the American Musical Theatre. Now he closed his career at the same time as Kern. Others in the cast included Jack Whiting and Eve Arden (as Winnie).

The success of the jazzed *Mikados* (3-1 and 23-39) and *The Boys from Syracuse* (11-23-38) prompted the mammoth Center Theatre to mount a similar enterprise on November 29 in hopes of reviving its faltering fortunes. *A Midsummer Night's Dream* was reset in 1890 Louisiana and retitled **Swingin' the Dream.** Jimmy Van Heusen's score was sung by a predominantly Negro cast that included the famous jazz trumpeter Louis Armstrong as Bottom, Butterfly McQueen as Puck, and Jackie "Moms" Mabley as Quince. One minor standard, "Darn That Dream," came from the show. Settings based on Walt Disney drawings gave the production a curious cartoonlike air. Benny Goodman and his Sextet added a stylish note to the jitterbugging and ballad singing. But the lindy-hop and other modern touches, such as Puck drugging the lovers by using a flit gun, dispelled the Shakespearean magic. The show was a sumptuous 13-performance fiasco. Its failure determined the Rockefellers to look for some other form of entertainment to keep the house open.

December's first musical was **DuBarry Was a Lady** (12-6-39, 46th St.). Like several other major hits of the decade, it was originally developed with the films in mind and turned into a stage piece only after it had been rejected by Hollywood. The female lead was said to have been tailored at first for Mae West, but by the time it was slated for Broadway Ethel Merman had signed to head the cast and, as a

result, Cole Porter agreed to create the songs, continuing his successful partnership with Broadway's leading musical comedy star. Bert Lahr was Miss Merman's associate, and actually had the pivotal role.

The story begins in New York's Club Petite, where Louis Blore (Lahr) is a washroom attendant and May Daley (Miss Merman) graces the floor show. Blore nurtures a forlorn crush on Miss Daley. When he wins $75,000 in the Irish Sweepstakes, he sees his opportunity to pursue the romance openly. But May loves a married newspaper columnist, Alex Barton (Ronald Graham). To break up the romance Blore decides to slip Alex knock-out drops. By mistake he drinks the potion himself. Unconscious, he dreams he is Louis XV and May is Madame Du Barry, "mistress in name only." Just as he is about to consummate his love affair, the dim-witted dauphin shoots an arrow into his derriere. Blore awakens to realize the hopelessness of his passion. He gives Alex enough money to procure a divorce, pays the rest to the government in taxes, and resumes cleaning washbasins. The Buddy DeSylva—Herbert Fields book was a noisy, guffaw-filled caper, but Porter's music was not his best. Like almost every other major composer working on Broadway, Porter found himself in something of a creative slump. Only one minor standard appeared in the show, Alex and May's ballad "Do I Love You?", with its poignantly undertoned melody and deceptively natural lyrics. Most of the score was lively, if not memorable. "Katie Went To Haiti" benefited from a lavish night club setting in which Ethel Merman was assisted by a line of chorus girls decked out in Caribbean styles and toting baskets of fruit on their heads. "Well, Did You Evah?" introduced Betty Grable to Broadway. And the hillbilly-like "Friendship" ("a perfect blendship") allowed Louis and May to part amicably. If the night club setting excused the insertion of songs with no bearing on the plot, the 18th-century milieu of the dream permitted Porter to set his smart, off-color rhymes to a stately minuet for Louis and May, "But In The Morning, No." Indeed, it was Porter's unfailing gift for superior lyrics and outrageous couplets that continued to lift him through his musical doldrums. Raoul Pène du Bois' sets and costumes depicted both the 18th and 20th centuries with a flamboyant elegance. *Du Barry Was a Lady* was the last full-length musical of the decade and ran almost to the close of 1940.

Christmas night at the Broadway saw one more musical entry, an abbreviated French vaudeville that called itself rather unfairly **Folies Bergère.** It was short enough to be performed twice nightly as well as on matinees. A limited audience, some undoubtedly lured by the deceptive title, kept it running for 121 showings.

Like the *Scandals* earlier in the season, the **Earl Carroll Vanities** (1-13-40, St. James) came in for one last visit. Carroll had moved his show to his Hollywood dinner-theatre, where it had thrived for several years. On January 13, 1940, he braved Broadway with inferior material and, apart from his line of beautiful girls, a mediocre cast—all in a form Broadway had tired of. Jerry Lester, the edition's principal comic, burlesqued burlesque dancing. Ygor and Tanya performed a more serious adagio, while the Four Hot Shots stepped lively in "Harlem style." "Professor" Lamberti offered musical interludes on his xylophone. Carroll, once given to imaginative mountings, discovered his scenery was rejected this time as an "antique model." After 25 performances the company headed back west. If it left anything of value behind it was the brief popularity of the Latin beat in "I Want My Mama" (Albert Stillman/Jararaca and Vicente Paiva). However, Carroll did leave behind another legacy, one that has had irreparable effects on the American Musical Theatre. In a disastrous innovation, the producer brought microphones onto the legitimate stage. Responsible critics such as Richard Watts, Jr., and Brooks Atkinson quickly called him to account, but their far-sighted, high-principled outcries were to go largely unheeded.

There still remained some demand for small, bright revues; Nancy Hamilton proved that when she brought in a successor to her *One for the Money*. No one was very surprised when the entertainment was called **Two for the Show** (2-8-40, Booth). It affected the same debonair stance as the first edition, although it moderated its former anti-left militancy. Alfred Drake, Keenan Wynn, and Brenda Forbes were retained from the original cast. They were joined by Betty Hutton, Richard Haydn, and a number of other lively youngsters. Miss Hutton stopped the show with a wild jitterbug routine. But the musical hit of the evening was "How High The Moon"—the only enduring song to come from the Morgan Lewis tunes for the series. Its intriguing passage from G major through ten other major and minor chords before it returned to G made the song the delight of a generation of progressive jazz artists. The song was sung by Alfred Drake and Frances Comstock against the background of a wartime blackout in London.

The next show was also a revue. **Reunion in New York** (2-21-40, Little) was created and performed by many of the same refugees who had offered *From Vienna* earlier in the session. In fact, it used much of the first evening's material. The revision was hardly more successful than the original, lasting eleven weeks.

No musicals opened in March, but April brought in the second Rodgers and Hart offering in less than six months. **Higher and Higher** (4-4-40, Shubert) was an even less satisfying work than *Too Many Girls*. In contrast to the October entry, it was a relatively quick flop. Initially not a single top-drawer Rodgers melody emerged, although in later years singers such as Mabel Mercer and Frank Sinatra turned "It Never Entered My Mind" into a standard. Alec Wilder in his *American Popular Song* speaks highly of "Ev'ry Sunday Afternoon" and comments in amazed tones on the contrast between its romantic melodic line and the brusque colloquialisms of Hart's lyrics, such as "Were you that dumb? She loves the bum."

The Gladys Hurlbut–Joshua Logan book was a contrived affair relating how a group of servants, threatened with unemployment in the face of their master's bankruptcy, combined efforts to marry one of their number to a rich man. Originally written with Vera Zorina in mind, it was rashly, and according to Rodgers, fatally changed when she was not available to star in it. Marta Eggerth was enlisted as a replacement. The Hungarian actress was a fine singer, but she was no dancer and, more importantly, she lacked Miss Zorina's slightly exotic glamor. She and her excellent associates (Jack Haley, Robert Chisholm, and Shirley Ross) must have been aghast when the evening's biggest applause was won by a trained seal. As Rodgers ruefully concluded, "If a trained seal steals your show, you don't have a show."

The Shuberts brought in a talent-packed revue, **Keep Off the Grass** (5-23-40, Broadhurst)—among the performers, Jimmy Durante, Ray Bolger, José Limon, Larry Adler, Jane Froman, and Ilka Chase. Jimmy McHugh wrote the score. Balanchine did the choreography. The show was a 44-performance dud. Howard Dietz had been called in during the tryout, but left after a battle with the explosive Lee Shubert. Other show doctors came and went, but the sketches and songs were too weak for mere hasty repairs. Durante tried his best to garner laughs as an uncouth man about town in top hat, white tie, and tails. Virginia O'Brien succeeded a little better with her dead-pan, motionless rendition of a wild jitterbug number. Hapless Ilka Chase tried to make something funny out of a monologue on love-making among fish. Bolger portrayed a superannuated jitterbug and later displayed a more serious side to his art in a "Raffles Ballet."

Like Kern, Irving Berlin had been away mining gold in the hills of Hollywood. He returned to Broadway at the end of May to provide songs for **Louisiana Purchase** (5-28-40, Imperial). His score was a far cry from the musicianly, exquisite melodies of *Very Warm for May,* but he was luckier than Kern in his associates. Thanks to a good book by Morrie Ryskind and a stellar cast, the show was the biggest hit of the season. On the surface Ryskind's book seemed topical, a commentary on the recently assassinated Huey Long and the Long family's domination of Louisiana politics. But the material was only lightly satiric, getting most of its laughs from the antics of Victor Moore and stock musical comedy blackouts. Moore was cast as Senator Oliver P. Loganberry, who is sent to investigate the high-handed, corrupt power of the Louisiana Purchase Company. Its attorney, Jim Taylor (William Gaxton), attempts to compromise the Senator with the sultry Marina Van Linden (Vera Zorina) and with the more coquettish Madame Bordelaise (Irene Bordoni). But Loganberry comes through unscathed. Like so many of great composers' scores during the year, Berlin's music was far from his best. It had variety, leaning toward the era's most popular beat in "Latins Know How" (sung with Gallic know-how by Mme. Bordelaise), then turning from a Negro spiritual in "The Lord Done Fixed Up My Soul" to the lively title song (sung by beautiful, young Carol Bruce, in the small role of Beatrice, and a male chorus). Marina and Loganberry helped get another fine song, "You're Lonely And I'm Lonely," off to a proper start. At the time the show was running, "It's A Lovely Day Tomorrow" (also sung by Mme. Bordelaise) received considerable play, but it never found a secure niche in Berlin's canon. Nonetheless, the show ran well over a year.

The season's last musical gave the Shuberts their second major flop in two weeks. It must have irritated the brothers to see Buddy DeSylva, with whom they could rarely work harmoniously, producing the season's two biggest hits: *DuBarry Was a Lady* and *Louisiana Purchase.* The new Shubert money-loser was called **Walk with Music** (6-4-40, Barrymore), although it had begun life as *Three after Three.* The original title had nothing to do with time but with three New Hampshire farm girls—Pamela (Kitty Carlisle), Rhoda (Mitzi Green), and Carrie Gibson (Betty Lawford)—who set out for Palm Beach to marry into wealth. Their plan is to let Pamela pose as a rich girl, while Rhoda pretends

to be her maid and Carrie acts as chaperone. But Pamela fouls up the plan by falling in love with a poor boy, Wing D'Hautville (Jack Whiting). Luckily, rich Steve Harrington (Art Jarrett) falls in love with Rhoda, and by the time the girls arrive in Havana, Carrie has hooked Henry Trowbridge (Lee Sullivan), a night club owner. The night club scenes allowed the Shuberts to fall back on a device they so often used to mask a show's dullness; parades of beautiful, outlandishly-garbed show girls. Such parades had often saved shows in the happier twenties, but by 1940 they were obsolete and ineffective. Guy Bolton worked with Parke Levy and Alan Lipscott on the book, while Johnny Mercer wrote lyrics for Hoagy Carmichael's songs. The show encountered difficulties from the moment it opened on the road. Two of the three original Gibson girls—Simone Simon and Mary Brian—were replaced by Miss Carlisle and Miss Lawford. The Shuberts threw interpolations into the score and just as quickly threw them out. By the time the show arrived at the Ethel Barrymore the score was wholly Carmichael's again. Some of his music was inventive. "The Rhumba Jumps" had a pronounced Latin beat in its verse and a solid, swinging chorus. Only "Way Back In 1939 A.D." enjoyed some appeal, but not enough to save the show.

1940-1941

This was a strange season. All its musical openings were packed together between the middle of September and the end of January. The number of new lyric shows plunged and for the most part what did appear was mediocre to blatantly horrendous. But the season also brought forth two of the most innovative musicals of the American stage. Both were well received and successful. These two gems aside, theatregoers' attention was often more readily diverted by the news of the war, the impassioned election campaign, with Roosevelt running for an unprecedented third term, as well as by other pleasures.

Hold on to Your Hats, the season's first new musical, waited until September 11 to raise its curtain at the Shubert. It also raised high hopes for the season, for the show brought with it the long-absent Al Jolson, once Broadway's reigning musical star. Jolson had made a second career in pictures, but when his star began to fade in Hollywood he was persuaded to try a new Broadway vehicle. His new show reflected changes that had taken place since Jolson had left the stage. Guy Bolton, Matty Brooks, and Eddie Davis' book was more cohesive than the old librettos Jolson had been accustomed to. Nor was the score studded with interpolations. All *Hold on to Your Hats'* songs were by Burton Lane, with E. Y. Harburg lyrics. And in a third departure from tradition Jolson was not the only star. Martha Raye, Jack Whiting, and Bert Gordon all had their names above the title with Jolson's. The implications were that the aging Jolson needed all the help he could get and that, even if this were not so, the days of a vehicle tailored to the demands of a single all-powerful performer were waning. Nonetheless, as he had in his heyday, Jolson still toyed with his material and sometimes discarded it altogether to talk directly to his audience. Jolson played "The Lone Rider," a popular radio cowboy, and obviously a take-off on the Lone Ranger. He finds listeners can't separate the actor from the character, and he is called upon to pursue a real-life villain, Fernando (Arnold Moss). Lane's score was good workaday material with one outstanding number, "There's A Great Day Coming Mañana." Miss Raye, grinning from ear to ear, helped make the evening cheery with her raucous singing of "Life Was Pie For The Pioneer" and "She Came, She Saw, She Can-canned," while Bert Gordon (the "Mad Russian" on Eddie Cantor's radio program) added to the merriment by playing Concho (read "Tonto") with his Russian accent. Everything conspired to make a hit of the evening, except that Jolson was unhappy in New York, claiming he could no longer stand the cold weather. The show closed after 20 weeks, although it could have run at least several more months.

The Lyric Opera Company, an American group, arrived on the 30th and spent three weeks offering Gilbert and Sullivan works. *The Gondoliers, The Mikado, Trial by Jury,* and *The Pirates of Penzance* were mounted—without exceptional staging, important names, or D'Oyly Carte authenticity.

On the next night Ed Wynn brought in **Boys and Girls Together** (10-1-40, Broadhurst). Since he himself produced it and since it was a revue with no plot to hamper his loose-jointed antics, Wynn was able to dominate the evening, as was his wont, with his customary puns, inventions, and "one crack-brained costume after another." In a memorable scene Wynn entered paddling a boat; he put his oars aside to check his road map, and, satisfied he was where he wanted to be, called for an anchor—which promptly dropped from the flies. Wynn also got himself enmeshed in the acrobatic efforts of the La Varres. The more he attempted to untangle the knot the more he found himself locked in. Distinguished talents such as choreographer Albertina Rasch and composer Sammy Fain were employed, but it was Wynn who kept audiences coming for 191 performances.

Another outrageous clown, who like Wynn was famous for his nonsensical inventions, arrived nine days later. Joe Cook was ostensibly the star of **It Happens on Ice** (10-10-40, Center). For the occasion he carted cartloads of his wacky inventions onto the ice. But in truth the show was little more than another attempt to make the Center Theatre a legitimate playhouse. Over the summer the house had been rebuilt so that the stage could accommodate ice-skating spectacles, of which this was to be the first. Vernon Duke was among those called in to compose the score, but neither he nor his collaborators were particularly inspired. It soon became evident that the spectacle was sufficient. Attempts to pass for more legitimate attractions were abandoned, and the house embarked on a decade of successful ice extravaganzas. Norman Bel Geddes designed shimmering silver sets for this production, combining with Leon Leonidoff to mount eye-filling scenes such as "The Legend of the Lake."

A musical fantasy concocted by Lynn Root proved much more inspiring to Duke, and he came up with a solid score for **Cabin in the Sky** (10-25-40, Martin Beck). Root's libretto drew a charming, unworldly picture of the Negro South. Devout Petunia Jackson (Ethel Waters) prays to the Good Lord that he spare the life of her no-good husband, "Little Joe" (Dooley Wilson). The Good Lord agrees, giving Joe six months in which to redeem himself. The Lord's General (Todd Duncan) is sent to assist, but from the nether regions comes Lucifer, Jr. (Rex Ingram), just as determined to claim what he believes is his. It looks as if Joe will succeed, but he gets into an argument with Petunia at John Henry's Café and shoots her. When they arrive at the Pearly Gates the Good Lord's stern heart melts at the entreaties of the ever-forgiving Petunia, and Little Joe is admitted along with her. Duke's tunes ranged from the jivey up-to-the-minute "Boogy-Woogy" to the wry "Honey In The Honeycomb." With his title song and "Taking A Chance On Love," Duke composed his last Broadway melodies to have popular appeal. Miss Waters' affectionate rendering of "Taking A Chance On Love" was a highlight of the show and of her career. In after years Duke looked back on *Cabin in the Sky* as his "all-time high." J. Rosamond Johnson, besides taking a small role, trained the singing chorus. Katherine Dunham led her dancers through their slithering paces, assisted in the choreography by George Balanchine. Wisely, everyone involved in the show rejected the easy excesses and crassness so many musicals resorted to. Certainly they avoided turning the evening into a black minstrel show. Throughout the production a tasteful restraint, a sense of what was appropriate to the story, was maintained. This rare display of integrity made *Cabin in the Sky* an attractive enough evening to keep ticket buyers coming for 20 weeks.

A brainless revue called **'Tis Of Thee** (10-26-40, Maxine Elliott) opened and closed the next night. Like the earlier *Straw Hat Revue* (9-29-39), the show was a product of the summer camps. The cast was damned as "untalented," their material as "poor." At best a pair of ballroom dancers, Cappella and Beatrice, and a comic, George Lloyd, who offered "turns in Neurasthenia," elicited some good notices. However, Lloyd and the dancers were professionals brought in to bolster the sagging entertainment.

The busy month ended more festively when Buddy DeSylva, Herbert Fields, Cole Porter, and Ethel Merman again combined their awesome talents to put across **Panama Hattie** (10-30-40, 46th St.)—a smash hit, but not a very good show. It was the sort of splashy, sassy affair that in this interim period substituted for generally better material. Still, the improving economic picture helped it become the first book show since the twenties to run over 500 performances. Hattie Maloney (Miss Merman)—obviously first cousin to May Daley of *DuBarry Was a Lady*—is a bar girl in the Panama Canal Zone, where she meets Nick Bullett (James Dunn), scion of an old Philadelphia family. When Nick proposes marriage, she agrees, provided Nick's young daughter by his first wife accepts her. At first little Geraldine (Jean Carroll) is difficult, but by the end of the evening she and Hattie agree "Let's Be Buddies." For many, Miss Merman's duet with little Miss Carroll—a remarkably touching, sentimental digression for Porter—became the high spot of *Panama Hattie*. Much of the evening's best comedy game from the knock-about antics of three girl-seeking sailors, Pat Harrington, Frank Hyers, and, most of all, Rags Ragland. For the craftsmanlike book Porter supplied what was at best a competent collection of tunes. Only one number from the show achieved anything more than passing popularity, "Make It Another Old Fashioned, Please." Again Porter's lyrics outclassed his melodies. "I'm Throwing A Ball Tonight" became the

latest in his growing portfolio of "laundry list" tunes whose rhymes were essentially lists of people or places hilariously juxtaposed. His fresh uses of clichés, clever in-rhymes, and brazen inversions were displayed in top form in the verse to Hattie's "I've Still Got My Health," "where alabaster, Missus Astor, and oil castor" were rhymed. As he had for *DuBarry Was a Lady,* Raoul Pène du Bois created colorfully flamboyant costumes and scenery that often made the evening seem better than it really was.

No new musicals opened in November and none in December until two appeared on Christmas night. **Meet the People** (12-25-40, Mansfield) had originally been produced on the West Coast one year earlier, then wended its way across the country. Some of its creators, like composer Jay Gorney and skit writer Edward Eliscu, had once been minor figures on Broadway. Others were new to the living theatre. In some respects their work was in tune with the latest fads, with, for example, the Latin beat of "In Chi Chi Castenango" (also listed as "In Chichicastenango"). In others, such as "Union Label," it displayed a certain fading left-wing militancy. One comic song, designed to devastate the sentimental paeans Jolson and Cantor once sang to Dixie, brought Eddie Johnson and Jack Albertson on stage to sing about "The Same Old South." Dorothy Roberts and Ted Arkin whirled to a snappy jitterbug. Sad-faced Jack Gilford delivered a monologue on the joys and pains of being a movie fan at a double feature—with trailers. Making her debut was an attractive young lady listed in the program as Nanette Fabares. In later years she made a slight change in the spelling of her last name and went on to become one of Broadway's brightest leading ladies. The revue was generally fast paced and professional but also unexceptional. It found enough of an audience to run twenty weeks. It might have run even longer if it had not elected to compete for opening night attention with *Pal Joey*.

Pal Joey (12-25-40, Barrymore) was something different—a cynical, snarling yet sentimentally lyrical examination of bought love. Gigolos were not new to the musical stage. Until now they had been secondary figures, French comic characters, or coy mentionables in a Cole Porter lyric. But here in *Pal Joey* was a musical with a hollow, self-serving, two-timing little twerp as its hero and an equally self-serving, hard, past-her-prime matron as his vis-à-vis. There were almost certainly no writers of significance on Broadway in 1940 but Rodgers and Hart who would have attempted to put something of this sort into musical form and assuredly no one else who could have pulled it off so handsomely. The evening had its genesis in John O'Hara stories from the *New Yorker,* and O'Hara carefully adapted his own pieces. His literate, adult book follows the rise of a cheap, handsome night-club hoofer named Joey Evans (Gene Kelly). Joey is at the beginning of a romance with a sweet, relatively innocent girl named Linda English (Leila Ernst). His line is smooth and irresistible, as he announces "I Could Write A Book" telling of how she would "walk and whisper and look." But he soon finds it to his advantage to court Vera Simpson (Vivienne Segal), a much older and knowing lady-about-town. While she is not inexperienced at the game, she professes to be overwhelmed; not merely wild, beguiled, and turned into a simpering whimpering child, but completely "Bewitched, Bothered and Bewildered." In return for Joey's favors, Vera sets him up in a posh apartment and even helps him open his own night club, Chez Joey. But Joey's fundamental selfishness soon begins to tell on Vera. Matters come to a head in Joey's apartment where Linda discloses that she has overheard a plan to blackmail Vera by threatening to tell Vera's husband of her relation with Joey. Vera assumes this is Linda's way of scaring her out of the picture. But Linda assures Vera her ardor for Joey has cooled; in her own simple way she has seen through him. And Linda's new perceptions help Vera clarify hers. Each woman begs the other "Take Him"; one refusing to "put a price on him," the other offering no more encouragement than "Pajamas look nice on him." Joey, realizing he has lost everything, walks off into the night. On the street he meets another young lady who, he tells her, could inspire him to wrote a book.

Because so much of the action took place in night clubs it was all too easy for Rodgers and Hart to insert several extraneous cabaret numbers, songs such as "That Terrific Rainbow" and "The Flower Garden Of My Heart." But in Joey's similar numbers, such as "You Musn't Kick It Around," "Plant You Now, Dig You Later," and "Do It The Hard Way," the songs skillfully reflected the attitude of the principals in seemingly incidental ditties. At one point Hart had devastating fun with the intellectual pretensions of the famous burlesque stripper, Gypsy Rose Lee. In "Zip" his stripper (Jean Casto), as she relieves herself of her garments, bemoans that Walter Lippmann wasn't brilliant today, wonders if Saroyan will ever write a great play, but puzzles over the identity of someone named Sally Rand. Yet *Pal Joey*'s meatiest songs were those sung by Vera, Joey, and Linda, bearing directly on the plot.

Here more than anywhere else in their career Rodgers and Hart's songs are a unique, curiously satisfying blend of Rodgers' warm lyricism and Hart's street urchin toughness. The melodies of "Bewitched, Bothered and Bewildered" and "Take Him" are characteristic. The evolution of stage dialogue is vividly illustrated by comparing the tinselly toughness of the scene between Rose-Marie and Mme. Bompard in *Good Morning, Dearie* (11-1-21), written not quite twenty years earlier, with the steely, contained cruelty of a typical scene between Joey and Vera. At the end of the play, disturbed by the blackmail attempt and tired of Joey, Vera decides to break the relationship. She cuts short Joey's braggadocio.

Vera: Some other time, Beauty. Right now I have some questions to bother you with. How are you fixed, financially?

Joey: I got rid of a lot of dough, recently. Why? You want some back?

Vera: No, but I've been thinking. What if I were called away to California, or dropped dead, or something—would you be all right? I mean, for instance, would you eat?

Joey: Honey Sug, somehow, I always eat. But what's on your mind?

Vera: Well, I think I'm going to be called away to California, or maybe drop dead.

Joey: Come on, say it. This is the brush-off. Those punks gave you a scare, and you're walking out.

Vera: A slightly brutal though accurate way of putting it. You can keep the club. . . .

Joey foolishly turns petulant and nasty . . .

Vera: I have a temper, Beauty, and I want to say a few things before I lose it.

Joey: Lose it. It's all you got left to lose.

Vera's reply to this vicious retort is to call the bank and close Joey's private account. Even though Kelly's smiling warmth mitigated some of Joey's harshness, not every critic could stomach so honest an approach. In a question to which he would revise his answer a dozen years later, Brooks Atkinson in the *Times* asked, "can you draw sweet water from a foul well?" Several of his fellow aisle-sitters answered firmly "no." On the other hand, critics such as Wolcott Gibbs in *The New Yorker* hailed the musical for putting "three-dimensional" human beings on the musical stage. The public was not discouraged by the critics' divisions and *Pal Joey* ran 374 performances. When it was revived in 1952, a changed moral climate and more relaxed theatre standards made it wildly successful.

Leonard Sillman put together another revue, called **All in Fun,** opened it at the Majestic Friday, December 27, and closed it Saturday, December 28. From the moment of his first entrance dressed in a white sailor suit and tapping joyously away, Bill Robinson was the bright spot of the evening. Later he donned top hat, white tie, and tails for another show-stopper. Brooks Atkinson insisted, "even when he is standing still you feel he is dancing." Sillman's favorite comedienne, Imogene Coca, was back, but she was handed some of the show's weakest material. The Latin beat of "Macumba" failed to scintillate, as did the drolleries of "April In Harrisburg" (an ur-"Boston Beguine" that spoofed the then popular "April In Paris").

The Shuberts had no better luck with a Robert Stolz operetta based on the 1930 hit *Tonight or Never*. **Night of Love** (1-7-41, Hudson) retained the story of a frigid prima donna (Helen Gleason) who finally finds love with a handsome but vaguely identified young man. The man (John Lodge) turns out to be a scout for the Metropolitan Opera. With the vogue of operetta at its nadir, the piece was able to survive just one week.

It looked at first as if one week was all **Crazy with the Heat** (1-14-41, 44th St.) would last. Although the cast included old favorites Willie Howard (without his brother), Luella Gear, and Carl Randall (back in front of an audience after years of creating the dances for Broadway musicals), the revue posted its closing notice immediately after opening. However, Ed Sullivan, the newspaper columnist, liked it enough to attempt to save it. He enlisted Lew Brown to enliven the staging, added a number of South American-type singers and some first-class dancers and reopened the show after a brief hiatus. Miss Gear, besides acting as "M.C.," smoked three cigars simultaneously in an effort to draw laughs. Willie Howard, trapped in sketches "with pointless dialogue and flat endings," encased his bony legs in tights to portray a ballet master. Informed he had killed a relative, he asked, "What have I done? Murdered my own fish and blood." One more attractive number was a serious ballet set in Toulouse-Lautrec's Paris. But the material still was not really strong enough to afford a fully entertaining evening. *Crazy with the Heat* ran an additional 92 performances before folding.

Although the calendar indicated that the season was little more than half over, January 23 at the Alvin witnessed the last musical premiere of the season. But it was the most imaginative, intelligent and cohesive work of the theatrical year—**Lady in the Dark.** Dreams had long been employed as a

theatrical device, but their psychoanalytic implications had been largely ignored. There had been occasional jokes, and *Peggy Ann* (12-27-26) flirted with the matter, but it took Moss Hart to write a libretto bearing down squarely and seriously on the subject. His dialogue was far more literate than that of the run-of-the-mill Broadway musical book. His characters not only spoke grammatically correct and complete sentences, they often spoke complete paragraphs. Yet his touch was so light, stylish, and sure that he dispelled the artificiality and turgidness of the old comic-opera librettos—where years before characters also spoke whole paragraphs. A leavening influence was undoubtedly Kurt Weill's now gossamer, now brittle score and Ira Gershwin's clever, tonically jolting lyrics. Hart's plot was slight. His central figure was austere, severely tailored Liza Elliott (Gertrude Lawrence), editor of a successful fashion magazine. Although she has fought her way to the top in a man's world, she recognizes she is sufficiently unhappy to warrant a visit to a psychoanalyst's office. She has been bothered by "confused, fantastic dreams. I knew the people—they were the people I see every day—and yet they were not the people I knew at all." Primarily "They" were four men: Kendall Nesbitt (Bert Lytell), her married lover and benefactor, the man instrumental in helping her rise to her position; Randy Curtis (Victor Mature), a glamorous, shallow Hollywood idol; Randall Paxton (Danny Kaye), the magazine's photographer; and, most important of all although she fails to realize it, Charlie Johnson (Macdonald Carey), her crusty, unbowed advertising manager. In her dreams she has heard wisps of a melody that haunt her, but which she cannot identify. The four dreams she relates to her psychoanalyst finally bring her to understand that her childhood rejection by her father and his prediction she would never possess her mother's beauty have shaped her every adult move. She breaks with Kendall, rejects Curtis and Paxton, and, singing the nursery song she at last remembers, dances off with Charlie. With one exception all the work's songs were offered in the dream sequences. These were elaborate, extended production numbers that moved from one facet of a dream to another on four revolving stages. In the "Glamour Dream," done mostly in Ziegfeldian blues, Liza sees herself as "The World's Inamorata" until a portrait presented to her limns the real Liza. A "Wedding Dream" also ends unhappily when Charlie in the guise of the minister asks if anyone can show cause why he shouldn't proceed and the chorus responds, "This woman knows she does not love this man." A gaudy

"Circus Dream" finds Liza accepting the fact that, like a lady named Jenny, she has brought problems on herself by making up her mind. Full enlightenment (and the denouement) comes in the brief "Childhood Dream." Weill's most memorable melody was saved appropriately for the song that haunts Liza, "My Ship." Elsewhere his pleasant tunes often played second fiddle to Gershwin's ingenious lyrics. Gershwin's readily identifiable shorthand was heard in songs such as "One Life To Live," where he announced "gloom can jump in the riv'!" For Danny Kaye he composed the least relevant song of the work, a terrifying, tongue-twisting list of Russian composers headed by "Tschaikowsky." Many of Gershwin's drollest lines were given to Liza in "The Saga Of Jenny," the story of a determined young lady whose plans always backfire. Fine writing, superb casting—especially the authority and grace Miss Lawrence brought to Liza— and brilliant mounting helped Liza and her ship to sail smoothly for 467 performances.

Neither *Lady in the Dark* nor *Pal Joey* seemed to have much effect on the American Musical Theatre other than to fill the coffers at their respective houses. When both shows closed, their influence seemed nil. It would be years later, looking back, that they would be recognized as isolated beacons in an otherwise dark period illuminating ways to the future. Broadway quickly returned to the easier *Panama Hattie* type of musical.

1941-1942

The year was dominated by the war, which in the middle of the season engulfed America. Daily recountings of battlefront horrors and agonies turned theatregoers away from more serious, innovative efforts. Light, escapist material was not merely acceptable, it was encouraged. Even among straight plays, comedies such as *Blithe Spirit, Junior Miss,* and *Jason* and thrillers such as *Angel Street* and *Uncle Harry* were far more in demand than plays with timely, thoughtful statements. The exciting possibilities of *Pal Joey* and *Lady in the Dark* were shunted aside. The public wanted conventional musicals, and, to paraphrase *Of Thee I Sing* (12-26-31), it got them, whether it liked them or not. By and large it didn't, for the season's musicals were not only conventional, they were uninspired or insipid.

The first new show of the season arrived at the Barrymore on October 1, over eight months after the last musical premiere. With **Best Foot Forward** Winsocki joined the ranks of other imaginary stage schools, Pottawatomie, Tait, and Bingham. Readers can deduce what they choose from the fact that the older schools had Anglo-Saxon names, the later colleges Indian ones. The visit to Winsocki, unlike the earlier trips, occurs not at the height of the football craze, but at prom time. As a lark Bud Hooper (Gil Stratton, Jr.) invites the Hollywood starlet Gale Joy (Rosemary Lane) to be his prom date, never seriously expecting her to accept. However, Gale's press agent, Jack Haggerty (Marty May), sees excellent promotional possibilities in the stunt and gets Gale to accept. Bud's girl friend, Helen Schlessinger (Maureen Cannon), is so furious that she rips off part of Gale's gown, signaling a wild tearing and stripping session in which Helen's classmates claw for souvenirs. Avoiding scandal, Gale agrees to return quietly to Hollywood while Bud and Helen are reunited. The book was by John Cecil Holm. The music by Hugh Martin and Ralph Blane. Only one song became nationally popular, "Buckle Down Winsocki." When the war broke out the song had a second vogue with revised lyrics, as "Buckle Down Buck Private." Both Martin and Blane did most of their best work in Hollywood (including *Meet Me in St. Louis* three years later). Martin did the words and music for several later Broadway shows, but his clever way with words served him better than his facile melodic gifts. The show's ten-month run started a number of bright young performers on the road to stardom, especially Nancy Walker, the most original and consistently hilarious comedienne since Beatrice Lillie. She played Winsocki's ever-available, ever-rejected "Blind Date" and won applause delivering the wistfully worldly wise "A Little Joint With A Juke Box." Even when the material occasionally let the cast down, George Abbott's lively staging glossed over its flaws.

A lamebrained piece called **Viva O'Brien** (10-9-41, Majestic) managed to survive for 20 performances. It followed a band of J. Forster Adams' cocktail party guests on a colorful tour of Mexico and their search for a legendary wishing stone. The show employed a nine-foot-deep swimming pool that allowed a diving scene just before the finale. More water was splashed on the stage from an elaborate waterfall, part of a jungle scene that necessitated a ritual dance calling to mind the jungle numbers of the twenties' spectacles. Since Chester Hale was the choreographer as well as one of the producers, he saw to it his chorus girls also did some high stepping.

Things improved when **Let's Face It** (10-29-41, Imperial) premiered. Thanks to Herbert and Dorothy Fields' adaptation of the 1925 hit *The Cradle Snatchers* and to Cole Porter's songs, the evening was tightly professional. Thanks to the clowning of Danny Kaye it was sometimes uproarious. But the truth is that *Let's Face It* depended on its creators' know-how to put it across. It was, for all this know-how, a second-rate show. Cole Porter's melodic genius continued to elude him, although his unfailingly excellent lyrics continued to pull him through. Songs such as "Farming," "Let's Not Talk About Love," "Ace In The Hole," and "Everything I Love" represented lesser achievements. Perhaps sensing this, he even allowed interpolations, with Kaye's wife, Sylvia Fine, writing much of Kaye's material. Kaye stopped the show, as he had *Lady in the Dark,* with a "jabberwocky of song, dance, illustration, and double-talk" called "Melody In Four F." The Fields' story, in keeping with the period's contemporary, but not topical bent, made the three gigolos of the original show three young soldiers. They are recruited by three wives, who have become convinced their husbands are cheating on them. The husbands' unexpected return could have proved embarrassing had not the husbands coincidentally taken up with the soldiers' girls. Feigned outrage, preposterous excuses, and some brazen half-truths offer everyone a way out. Harry Horner, the set designer, had an easy time turning farms and country estates into bright-colored sets. John Harkrider, the costume designer, wasn't so lucky. Most of his men had to be dressed in drab khakis. To compensate he gave his fashionable ladies exaggeratedly hued and contrived wardrobes. Besides Kaye the cast included Eve Arden, Vivian Vance, Mary Jane Walsh, Benny Baker, and, in a small role, Nanette Fabray (formerly Fabares). They sparkled gaily enough to allow theatregoers to overlook the lackluster music. Aside from the *sui generis Sons o' Fun, Let's Face It* became the long-run winner of the season, compiling 547 performances. Its run was as much an indication of the new war-born prosperity as of any overriding merit.

A group of old Broadway and vaudeville favorites pooled their talents and prestige to mount **High Kickers** (10-31-41, Broadhurst); George Jessel conceived the work. He wrote the book in collaboration with his songwriters, Bert Kalmar and Harry Ruby, and he costarred with his old pal, Sophie Tucker. Carl Randall did the suitably old-fashioned dances. The prologue was set in 1910 at Piner's Burlesque, where George M. Krause (Jessel) and his "High Kickers" troupe are appearing. Young George, Jr. (Dick Monahan), is with the company. But the action quickly advances to 1941. George, Sr., is dead and his son (now played by Jessel) is running the company. The troupe is arrested in Chamberville, Ohio. They are released when Sophie Tucker, who is traveling with them, reminds the mayor his wife once had been a member of the troupe. Miss Tucker, playing herself, was undoubtedly meant to give the piece a certain verisimilitude. But the librettists also resorted to distortions (Piner's for what was most likely meant to be Miner's) and in-jokes (one character was S. Kaufman Hart). Besides the confused approach the authors were burdened by a lack of anything fresh to say. In another reversion to old-fashioned ways, specialty acts and parading show girls were enlisted to liven the proceedings. The score was Ruby and Kalmar's last for Broadway, but it was merely a feeble echo of their earlier vitality. Still, the old names had a following, so the show recorded a 22-week run.

The spurt of October openings was followed by a void in the November calendar. But on December 1 at the Winter Garden the Shuberts reunited with Olsen and Johnson to provide Broadway with a successor to their zany *Hellzapoppin.* **Sons o' Fun** repeated the same formula (or lack of it) of outrageous nonsense. Patrons were intentionally escorted to the wrong seats, and those unlucky enough to have bought boxes had to reach them by climbing ladders. Once the show began, audience members were invited on stage to participate, and chorus girls came down the aisles to dance with theatregoers. The few formal skits burlesqued *Panama Hattie* and *Charlie's Aunt,* and in a brush with topicality, included a madcap version of the army's basic training. Ella Logan and Carmen Miranda were in charge of interpreting the Sammy Fain and Will Irwin songs (with lyrics mostly by Jack Yellen). Miss Logan sang "Happy In Love" and "It's A New Kind Of Thing," while Miss Miranda handled the Latin items such as "Thank You, South America." War clouds prompted the insertion of patriot pieces such as "It's A Mighty Fine Country We Have Here." The tunes weren't much; they were there because the show was a musical and because even zaniness must rest. It was Olsen and Johnson's unique brand of comic mayhem that pleased New Yorkers and their guests for two years.

Sunny River (12-4-41, St. James) was set along the banks of the old man river that its librettist, Oscar Hammerstein II, had dealt with so poetically before. But the story was not actually a bit of Americana. Instead, it was a tale of foredoomed love that could as easily have been set in the Hungary of its composer, Sigmund Romberg. Indeed it was the very sort of story Romberg loved best, but that, apart from *Maytime* (8-16-17) and *The Student Prince* (12-2-24), had never inspired his most memorable compositions. In this instance a young café singer, Marie Sauvinet (Muriel Angelus), falls in love with the highborn Jean Gervais (Robert Lawrence). When she is told that Jean has long been in love with Cecilie Marshall (Helen Claire), she runs away to Paris, returning years later as a great prima donna. Once again romance blossoms between Marie and Jean, but once again Jean's obvious affection for Cecilie causes Marie to leave. It was a pedestrian book with equally pedestrian, if sweet, music. *Sunny River* folded after five weeks.

Three days later, December 7, 1941, Japan bombed Pearl Harbor, and the United States was caught up in World War II.

The first musical to arrive in wartime New York was **Banjo Eyes** (12-25-41, Hollywood). It made a hasty concession to the situation when during its Philadelphia tryout it inserted the uplifting "We Did It Before (We'll Do It Again)" (Charles Tobias and Cliff Friend). But aside from this token flag-waving, it was a gaudy, escapist musical version of John Cecil Holm and George Abbott's *Three Men on a Horse*. Neither Holm (who had done the book for *Best Foot Forward*) nor Abbott participated in the adaptation, which was by Joe Quillan and Izzy Elinson, two radio script writers, for the show's star, Eddie Cantor. Holm and Abbott's original piece was so well constructed that no damage was done. The songs were by Vernon Duke, with lyrics by John Latouche and Harold Adamson. But the real attraction of the show and its principal prop was Cantor, in his first Broadway appearance since *Whoopee*. Cantor played Erwin Trowbridge, a greeting card salesman, who talks to horses in his dreams. This might not be so unusual if the horses didn't give him tips that always win. Of course, there's a catch. The horses insist Trowbridge never bet money on the races. A gang of crooks hears of his phenomenal pickings and attempts to make him work for them. But when they force him to put money on a race, his dream horses suddenly refuse to reveal anything. Duke's score, like most of the season's scores, was serviceable without being exceptional. Apart from the rousing interpolation, the hit of the evening was "We're Having A Baby (My Baby And Me),"

which Trowbridge and his wife sang. Somehow it never became a Cantor standby, although it was the last good number Cantor introduced on the Broadway stage. Late in the evening Cantor dropped his role of Erwin and came on in blackface to bring down the house with an extended medley of his old favorites. Cantor, like Jolson before him, had become enamored of the milder California weather. When the winter rigors proved too much for him, *Banjo Eyes* was forced to close in its sixteenth week, even though it was still going strong.

More Vernon Duke music and more John Latouche lyrics were heard two weeks later when **The Lady Comes Across** (1-9-42, 44th St.) arrived as the first musical of 1942. The show had Fred Thompson, an old hand at librettos, collaborating with Dawn Powell on the book. George Balanchine created the choreography, while the suave Romney Brent directed a cast that included Evelyn Wyckoff, Joe E. Lewis, Mischa Auer, Wynn Murray, Ronald Graham, and Gower Champion. The impressive roster of talent belied the show's sometimes slapdash nature. For example, it re-employed the scenery left behind by *She Had To Say Yes*, a musical that had failed to reach Broadway the preceding season. The plot, however timely, seemed frail enough even to its authors to impel them to use the frame device of a dream. The sleeping heroine (Miss Wyckoff) sees herself meeting an FBI agent, and together they capture a spy operating a Fifth Avenue dress shop. The evening's weaknesses became apparent to its original stars, Ray Bolger and Jessie Matthews, both of whom resigned their roles before the show opened. Their foresight didn't deprive them of much work. *The Lady Comes Across* folded after a humiliating run of 3 performances.

On January 21 the Boston Comic Opera and the Jooss Ballet Dance Theatre combined their resources to bring in a curious repertory of modern dance and Gilbert and Sullivan operettas. For example, *H.M.S. Pinafore* was on a double bill with a ballet, *The Green Table*. In *The Mikado,* which was presented along with two ballets—*The Big City* and *A Ball in Old Vienna*—the producers felt compelled to change "gentlemen of Japan" to "gangsters of Japan." The public came anyway.

The next night Cheryl Crawford revived Gershwin's *Porgy and Bess* at the Majestic with many of the original principals (notably Todd Duncan, Anne Brown, and J. Rosamond Johnson). Time had popularized the great Gershwin melodies from the work, allowing audiences to accept it as an old friend instead of a forbiddingly daring and serious new effort. The resurgent prosperity also helped sell tickets. To ensure its acceptability to a larger audience, Miss Crawford wrenched the work more into the Broadway mainstream by removing recitative passages and by shortening it through the elimination of several musical numbers. Her tactics worked. With this production, which ran 35 weeks in New York and toured successfully, *Porgy and Bess* comfortably became a welcome classic of the American Musical Theatre.

A semiprofessional revue originally mounted in the fall as *V for Victory* was polished for Broadway by Alexander Cohen and presented on February 11 as **Of V We Sing** (2-11-42, Concert). Its performers included names that would soon make a bigger mark in the theatre: Betty Garrett, Phil Leeds, and Curt Conway. The show dug for laughs at the expense of unions, the Brooklyn Dodgers, and Mother's Day ("Don't kill your mother on Mother's Day"). Excellent jitterbugging highlighted the evening. The songsmiths didn't fare so well, but they offered a range of suitable patriotic material—"You Can't Fool The People," "Red, Whites And Blues," a title song, and returned to Flatbush for the "Brooklyn Cantata."

With so many younger performers being drafted and with the public clamoring for diverting entertainment, Clifford C. Fischer, a nightclub impresario, who had given Broadway the illegitimate *Folies Bergère* (12-25-39), convinced the Shuberts that vaudeville and old vaudevillians would help light their dark theatres. Their first offering, **Priorities of '42** (3-12-42, 46th St.) seemed to vindicate Fischer. Willie Howard, Lou Holtz, Phil Baker, Paul Draper, and Hazel Scott were the headliners. To a great extent the performers used their own material. There were no sketches. For the most part simple draperies and old drops from the Shubert warehouse provided backgrounds. With $1.00 top at matinees and $2.00 at night, the response at the 46th Street Theatre was so hearty that in a little over a month a second assemblage was offered two blocks south. **Keep 'Em Laughing** (4-24-42, 44th St.) presented William Gaxton and Victor Moore, Hildegarde, Paul and Grace Hartman, Jack Cole and his dancers, and a young Zero Mostel. While most critics thought this an even more impressive and diverting bill than the first, it failed to receive the same attention. After 77 times, it was revised and retitled **Top-Notchers** (5-29-42, 44th St.). Gaxton and Moore were gone, as well as Hildegarde, but Gracie Fields was an attractive addition. None-

theless the bill refused to catch on. After a further 48 showings the affair was dropped.

In the meantime Ed Sullivan and Noble Sissle quickly brought together a company of Negro artists including Sissle's associate of yore, Flournoy Miller. They hoped to offer Broadway a black *Priorities*. But it was becoming manifest that the first Fischer-Schubert bill was a freak success. **Harlem Cavalcade** (5-1-42, Ritz) quickly departed.

The season's last new show, **By Jupiter** (6-3-42, Shubert), was its best. In Broadway's heyday the slapped-together, frivolous "summer musical" had been an annual event. But *By Jupiter,* though it was lighthearted, was not lightweight. This lyric version of Katharine Hepburn's 1932 vehicle, *The Warrior's Husband,* was a firmly constructed, intelligently wrought, adult musical comedy. It was also, sadly, Rodgers and Hart's final collaboration. Hart's drinking and instability were becoming too much for Rodgers, and Rodgers discreetly made overtures elsewhere. In a sense the overtures came none too soon, for Hart died, only forty-seven, in November 1943. But the public knew none of this. All it saw was a glittering, melodic romp set in ancient Pontus. Queen Hippolyta (Benay Venuta) and her women rule over their milksop husbands, a hegemony they will hold as long as Hippolyta can wear her magic, strength-endowing girdle. A band of Greeks led by Theseus (Ronald Graham) and Hercules (Ralph Dumke) invade Pontus, hoping to capture the girdle and restore the men to rightful place. Where their swords fail their sexual wiles conquer. King Sapiens (Ray Bolger) assumes the throne his wife has held, and Theseus is rewarded with Hippolyta's attractive sister, Antiope (Constance Moore). The score was musically and finely nuanced, but only one number immediately caught the fancy of the public outside the theatre. The man in the street who whistled or sang Bolger's number, "Ev'rything I've Got," was most likely unaware that the cheerful, clever commercial lyrics were matched on stage by the snarling, barbed rhymes of Hippolyta and Sapiens' duet. With time, Theseus' "Wait Till You See Her" joined the ranks of Rodgers and Hart classics. However, in the theatre, Bolger's biggest show-stopper was a minor number, "Nobody's Heart." Young Bolger was partnered in his hilarious yet affectionate dance for the song with sixty-year-old Bertha Belmore. Curiously, Miss Belmore had played the same role (Sapiens' mother) in *The Warrior's Husband.* By Jupiter ran well over a year and might have run longer had not Bolger left to entertain the troops overseas.

10

ACT FIVE
The American Musical
as a Conscious Art Form

The last act in this history of the American Musical Theatre was long, approximately as long as the first, three-quarters of a century before. Like that opening act it was not consistently exciting. But if at times a whole season passed without producing an outstanding addition to the repertory, the masterworks of this era were such towering achievements they more than compensated for dry spells.

Both the beginning and the end of the era found America at war. The act began when World War II was a year old. In theatrical terms the great conflict was relatively insignificant. The coming of World War I had instantly liberated the American Musical Theatre from Viennese thralldom. 1914 exposed the ferment overflowing behind the scenes and the brilliant group of young American composers, lyricists, and librettists who were waiting to display their talents. On the other hand 1942 found most young talent either in Hollywood or fighting the war. Equally discouraging, new movements in American music were far less vital, if indeed concerted new movements existed at all. The coming fire had to be sparked by older Broadway hands—one of whom, Irving Berlin, had been instrumental in the earlier resurgence. Because they were older, because they had seen that the "war to end all wars" ended nothing, because they had suffered through the depression, these writers and composers had become less optimistic, less flashy. They led the American Musical Theatre into a more sober, sentimental era. While war-born prosperity gave the theatre a momentarily healthy glow,

it was the escapist turnback to real or exaggerated joys of a bygone Americana that became the war's impressive and lasting contribution to the lyric stage. Curiously, the lesser of the two wars, the Korean War at the close of the epoch, forcefully affected the musical scene. The inflation it engendered, coupled with the competitive drain from richer media, hurtled theatrical economics into a frightening purgatory. Nor did national unrest that developed help the theatre in any way.

Variety records that 320 new musicals premiered during this twenty-three-year period, compared with 426 that opened in the thirteen years of the preceding act and 139 that appeared in the seven years of Act III. The strikingly long runs attained by the masterworks of this final era were largely deserved, but they should not cause the works to be overrated. The lessening of competition within the theatre and the dwindling number of road companies concentrated attention on the best shows during their New York runs. If an accurate count could be made of all the theatregoers who saw, say, *The Merry Widow* (10-21-07) or *Rose-Marie* (9-2-24) in their original productions and touring companies, it would most likely demonstrate they represented an equal, possibly greater, proportion of the population than did the theatregoers who flocked to *Kiss Me, Kate* (12-30-48) or *South Pacific* (4-7-49). On their own terms, the older shows were every bit as good as the new ones. Melodically they were often more tuneful and offered a greater range of musical languages, from

George Gershwin's steely American jazz to Rudolf Friml's full-blooded Austro-Hungarian romanticism. By comparison the new act sometimes seemed musically constrained and monotonous. Nonetheless, between *Oklahoma!* (3-31-43) and *Fiddler on the Roof* (9-22-64), the American Musical Theatre witnessed a sustained seriousness of approach unknown before on the lyric stage. It achieved this with a remarkably small number of inspired creators.

Scene One
AMERICANA AMID A NEW SERIOUSNESS
1942-1951

1942-1943

The war news had been bad all during the preceding season. It continued unpleasant off and on during the new theatrical year, but there were indications that the tide was turning in favor of the Allies. Since the war was far away and promised to stay far away, Broadway could look happily on a side benefit. Business was booming. Of eighty offerings presented in Manhattan, twenty-four could be classified as musicals: an abnormally high percentage. Yet the figure was deceptive. The ice show that was clearly becoming an annual and a Yiddish-English musical belonged outside Broadway's mainstream. Seven were revivals. Even among the remaining eighteen presentations eleven were revues, and most of these were vaudeville-assemblages of the sort that began the past season with *Priorities* (3-12-42). There were only five new book musicals, and only two of these were hits.

The season began without promise. Ed Wynn brought in the first of the vaudeville-assemblages, **Laugh, Town, Laugh** (6-22-42, Alvin). Wynn's outrageous inventions and preposterous costumes

were laid away, and the great comedian was reduced to serving as an amiable master of ceremonies—so amiable that, at least on opening night, he ambled among the audience during intermission, talking with playgoers and the band leader, Emil Coleman. Wynn was slightly handicapped. Una, a donkey in a trained animal act, had kicked him during a rehearsal, breaking his hand. Turns included Smith and Dale in their ancient "Dr. Kronkeit" routine, Senor Wences' sleight-of-mouth ventriloquism, and Jane Froman singing popular songs of the day. For all the talent, the pastiche didn't even make it through July. It would take Broadway producers the rest of the season to realize these cheaply gathered together affairs were really not to theatregoers' likings.

The Chocolate Soldier, Oscar Straus' 1909 operetta, had even harder going despite a fine cast headed by Allan Jones, Helen Gleason, and Detmar Poppen, and sought no extension of its original three-week engagement. The new type of musical play that came into vogue this season made such lovely old operettas subject to particularly vehement scorn. But this was something the producers, who brought the offering into Carnegie Hall instead of a regular house, could not foresee. The producers offered a second revival in Carnegie Hall on July 15. Their production of *The Merry Widow,* with Wilbur Evans and Miss Gleason, ran 39 times. It was followed on August 18 by their revival of *The New Moon* (9-19-28), with Evans and Ruby Mercer, which, like *The Chocolate Soldier,* gave 24 performances.

The night after the Straus revival the season's first hit arrived, a "burlesque revue" called **Star and Garter** (6-24-42, Music Box). It was a Mike Todd production that to some degree capitalized on the closing of New York's burlesque houses after the once-great burlesque tradition had degenerated into a tawdry strip show. The doyenne of the burlesque wheel, the beautiful, intellectual Gypsy Rose Lee, led a parade of well-proportioned ladies that also included Georgia Sothern. Miss Lee's costar was Bobby Clark. In his first chance for solid clowning in several years, he portrayed a spitball-hurling judge, repeated his "Robert the Roué" from *The Streets of Paris* (6-19-39), and played a modern-day Falstaff in "That Merry Wife of Windsor." Musical credits listed Irving Berlin, Harold Rome, and Harold Arlen among others, but their songs were culled from their already standard material. The newer tunes were thoroughly mediocre. But New Yorkers, who during Prohibition had obligingly drunk their whiskey in tea cups, for a year and a half gleefully flocked to enjoy their burlesque at the elegant little Music Box.

Stars on Ice, billed simply as an ice-skating revue, began its long run at the Center on July 2. Its incidental songs had music by Paul McGrane, Paul Van Loane, and Irvin Graham, and lyrics by Albert Stillman. Their titles—"Little Jack Frost," "The World Waltzes"—conveyed an idea of the production numbers they accompanied. However, in "Juke Box Saturday Night" the spectacle had the sole hit to emerge from the series. The song was a sure-fire boogie, a popular form customarily ignored by more conventional Broadway musicals. Its inclusion in *Stars on Ice* reflected the different audience the show was appealing to. Broadway's aging, more self-contained regular theatregoers no longer capitulated to the latest musical fads. What few boogie-woogie numbers were included in more traditional shows were there almost incidentally, to produce a contemporary flavor rather than a hit song.

The first of the season's two major hits opened two nights after *Stars on Ice*. **This Is the Army** patriotically selected July 4 as its premiere date. It ran only 113 performances at the large Broadway Theatre, but every performance was sold out to the limit of standees. The show was conceived and its songs written by a theatrical figure listed in its program as "Sgt. Irving Berlin (1917)." The erstwhile sergeant was a member of the cast as well, stopping the show nightly with his singing of a number he had performed in *Yip Yip Yaphank* (8-19-18) almost a quarter of a century before: "Oh, How I Hate To Get Up In The Morning." Berlin and a handful of the old show's veterans, all dressed in 1917 uniforms, performed the number much as they had twenty-five years before. *Yip Yip Yaphank*'s "Mandy" was also revived. The rest of the score was new. In fact it covered an exemplary range of then contemporary song styles. There were three crowd stirrers, "American Eagles" ("America's strong just as long as they fly"), "With My Head In The Clouds" ("How I yearn to return to the one I love on the ground"), and the title song (technically, "This Is The Army, Mr. Jones"). Two poignantly expressive ballads, "I'm Getting Tired So I Can Sleep" ("I want to dream so I can be with you"), sung by Stuart Churchill in the barracks scene, and the show's hit, "I Left My Heart At The Stage Door Canteen," sung by Earl Oxford, recorded a soldier's loneliness far from home. "What The Well-Dressed Man In Harlem Will Wear" caught the snappy Negro musical idiom of the day. There was nothing innovative this time about Berlin's music. The day when Berlin led the popular *avant-garde* was long over. Though a few critics, such as Richard Watts, Jr., in the *Herald-Tribune,* hailed the revue as "a great and historic show," the importance of *This Is the Army* score was generally overlooked. It was a hit-packed, unforgettably melodic work that roused the American Musical Theatre from its lethargy. For the first time in years patrons could leave the theatre with a number of melodies to whistle or hum. The show was given an eye-filling mounting (soldiers across the giant wing of a plane) and a vigorous staging. An all-soldier cast included at one time or another Ezra Stone, Burl Ives, Gary Merrill, Julie Oshins, and Joe Cook, Jr. In the celebrated Stage Door Canteen number that opened the second act young Cook impersonated his more famous father, while other men appeared as Gypsy Rose Lee, Jane Cowl, Lynn Fontanne, Alfred Lunt, and Noel Coward. There were sketches by James McColl, but they were relatively insignificant. The show toured until late 1945, its great Berlin score announcing throughout the land that Broadway was bursting with song again.

All in all, it was a singularly busy summer—the busiest the American Musical Theatre had enjoyed in many a season, and a justifiably hopeful augury.

All three of September's offerings were vaudeville-assemblages. The first and least successful was **New Priorities of 1943** (9-15-42, 46th St.) by the same Clifford C. Fischer who had begun the short-lived fad. Despite the presence of Harry Richman, Bert Wheeler, Hank Ladd, Henny Youngman, and Carol Bruce, it recorded only 54 showings. On the other hand, **Show Time** (9-16-42, Broadhurst), which opened the next night, ran through the season. Its main attractions were George Jessel and Jack Haley in old routines, Ella Logan singing her songs, and the ballroom dancing of the De Marcos. The Shuberts hoped to resuscitate the dying vogue and cash in on the success of *Star and Garter* as well by calling **Wine, Women and Song** (9-28-42, Ambassador) a "revue-vaudeville-burlesque show." There is no record of the Shuberts giving away wine, but they offered music and girls performing "quivers, bumps and lethargic strip tease." Margie Hart led the strippers. Jimmy Savo headed the comic department, winning applause for his rendition of "River, Stay Away From My Door." Unfortunately Savo and Miss Hart were not in a class with Bobby Clark and Gypsy Rose

Lee. At 16 performances a week the show lasted seven weeks.

Let Freedom Sing (10-5-42; Longacre) was a more traditionally shaped revue. Harold Rome's songs were fittingly patriotic—"It's Fun To Be Free," "I Did It For Defense," "Be Calm," "Little Miss Victory Jones," "Johnny Is A Hoarder." Numerous interpolations followed along the same line. Ostensibly, Mitzi Green, fresh from Hollywood, was the principal performer. She lent her husky voice to Rome's "The Lady Is A WAC" and Marc Blitzstein's "Fraught," besides portraying a young lady stood up by her soldier sweetheart. But Betty Garrett won even more acclaim singing Rome's lively Latin melody, "Give Us A Viva" and his jivey "History Eight To The Bar." Comedy was in the hands of Berni Gould and Phil Leeds. Together they fought battles as armchair strategists and confused everyone with their directions to Gramercy Square. Little of the material was meritorious. The show waved its flag for one week and departed.

A loosely-structured musical comedy, **Count Me In** (10-8-42, Barrymore), fared only slightly better, achieving a 61-performance run. Originally mounted at Catholic University, its authors included Nancy Hamilton and a young man destined for fame as a fine critic, Walter Kerr. Their thin story recorded the attempts of father (Charles Butterworth) to do at least as much for the war effort as mother (Luella Gear) and the children. He succeeds when he sells phony maps to Japanese spies. So slapdash was the show, a number of critics were reminded of the worst contrivances of earlier decades. For much of its entertainment it relied on specialty acts such as the Rhythmaires and the Ross Sisters. Like so many of the old pastiches it was best when it was on its feet. Hal Le Roy supplied some glittering tap routines while Gower and Jeanne swirled in more elegant ballroom numbers. Gower, of course, was Gower Champion. The urbane John Mason Brown, reviewing the show for the *World-Telegram*, could not resist insisting "count me out."

On October 12 the old Jolson Theatre, lately the Venice, was renamed the Molly Picon and raised its curtain on a musical biography of the celebrated star of the Yiddish Theatre. With Miss Picon playing herself, **Oy Is Dus a Leben!** recounted her rise from her early experiences at Philadelphia's Arch Street Theatre in 1912, to her marriage to Jacob Kalich and her trips in Europe to improve her art and her Yiddish, and her climb to stardom. Joseph Rumshinsky, who provided scores for Yiddish musicals on Second Avenue and thereabouts, cre-

ated appropriate songs. Miss Picon's loyal following had her relive her life 139 times.

A loud, jivey musical that paid little heed to the warring world outside opened two nights later. George Abbott produced, directed, and coauthored the book with George Marion, Jr. Johnny Green returned from a long stay in Hollywood to write the score. **Beat the Band** (10-14-42, 46th St.) told how Querida (Susan Miller) comes to New York to find her godfather. But her godfather's apartment had been sublet to a popular band leader, Damon Dillingham (Jack Whiting). Misunderstandings and detectives complicate a budding romance between the two until a happy ending ensues in the boiler room of the Savoy-Perkins Hotel. Though Marion's titles make Green's songs sound lively—"Let's Comb Beaches," "I'm Physical, You're Cultured," "The Steam Is On The Beam," "Keep It Casual," "Break It Up"—the music was a far cry from the memorably sultry beauty of some of Green's earlier numbers. After eight weeks Abbott admitted he had erred and withdrew the show.

The most baffling revival in years came next. The Hough-Adams-Howard Chicago hit *The Time, the Place and the Girl* (8-5-07) was pulled from the shelf and given a renewed life on October 21 at the Mansfield with slightly rewritten book and lyrics. The fascinating old piece had never been welcome in New York when it was fresh and contemporary, though it had established a Chicago long-run record in its day. A program note advised audiences: "The authors have not attempted to make it into a modern musical comedy. While all the padding and all of the bromides of the gas-lit era have been deleted the play is, nevertheless, presented as of that period. . . ." A popular burlesque comedian, "Red" Marshall, and pert Vicki Cummings sparked the performers. Joe Howard even made an appearance as himself. Their labors were to no avail. New York again dismissed *The Time, the Place and the Girl* with a condescending wave of the hand.

But another old work was made most welcome. *Die Fledermaus* returned in what continued to be an unintentional pattern of once-a-decade revivals. As *The Merry Countess* it attempted to cash in on the vogue of *The Merry Widow* and succeeded in running for 135 performances in 1912. As *A Wonderful Night* it played for 125 showings in 1929. And as *Champagne, Sec* it chalked up 113 performances in 1933. Now as **Rosalinda** (10-28-42, 44th St.) it ran for a whopping 521 times, with Dorothy Sarnoff in the title role and the amusing refugee Oscar Karlweis as Prince Orlofsky. An authentic *Mittel-europa* flair was imparted by several other distinguished exiles. Gottfried Reinhardt was on hand to see that some of the touches his father Max had used in a 1929 Berlin revival were recreated. In the orchestra pit, the famous composer Erich Wolfgang Korngold conducted.

Two weeks after the unsuccessful revival of Joe Howard's old musical and a week after Strauss' operetta settled in for a long run, George M. Cohan died, on November 7, 1942. Cohan, more than any other man, had sparked the second great act in the American Musical Theatre. Howard had been a rival who generally kept a safe distance in Chicago. But the heirs of Strauss had driven Cohan's style of art from the stage. Cohan never fully recovered from the changes they wrought, and it is doubtful if he would have appreciated the renaissance about to dawn.

Still another old musical piece followed. In a way finding it in a Broadway house was as surprising and unlikely as the revival of the Hough-Adam-Howard show, for **Once Over Lightly** (11-19-42, Alvin) was simply an "Americanized" version of Rossini's *The Barber of Seville*. Broadway felt Rossini was better served at the Met, and the show lasted less than one full week.

Just before Christmas, Leonard Sillman presented another edition of his erratic **New Faces** (12-22-42, Ritz). Mr. Sillman, far from a new face, appeared in the show besides serving as both producer and director. John Lund also doubled in brass, writing the show's skits and cavorting nightly behind the footlights. Irwin Corey and Alice Pearce were cast members who went on to make names for themselves. Curiously, the performer who pleased critics the most faded from the theatre scene. Tony Farrar was a dancing pantomimist who won loud cheers and considerable space in the morning-after notices for his imitation of Fanny Brice imitating Paul Draper and for a dance depicting a bullfighter who has lost his glasses. Skits included "Quiet Zone," set in a shirt hospital where doctors and nurses solemnly operate on cuffs, collars, and seams, and a piece making fun of tourists at the Radio City Music Hall. Orson Welles was shot down in "Welles of Loneliness," while Hamlet was made to suffer the slings and arrows of outrageous recapitulation in Corey's monologue. The material itself was not particularly memorable and the 1942 (called 1943 in the title) edition's run of 94 performances was the shortest in the series to date.

Eddie Cantor, George Jessel, Walter Winchell,

the Marx Brothers, Georgie Price, and Hildegarde all appeared in **You'll See Stars** (12-29-42, Maxine Elliott). Only it wasn't the real-life greats audiences saw; rather young actors impersonating them, for *You'll See Stars* purported to be a retelling of Gus Edwards' career as a star-maker. The show had been conceived by Herman Timberg, who had written songs for the Shuberts in the halcyon days of the late teens and twenties, and who at that time had tried unsuccessfully to enter the producing ranks. The music was credited to another name out of the past, Leo Edwards. But the show was tackily put together; it played at the out-of-the-way Maxine Elliott; and, most damaging of all, it was assailed by Gus Edwards himself as inaccurate and unauthorized. It beat a retreat after 4 showings.

The season's first truly successful book musical was more commercial than artistic. **Something for the Boys** (1-7-43, Alvin) was a splashy Mike Todd mounting that once again had Ethel Merman singing Cole Porter songs. Herbert Fields, who had collaborated with Buddy DeSylva on the two preceding Merman-Porter shows, did the book with his sister Dorothy. Their story was a rambling affair—contemporary but not truly topical—that begins when three cousins learn they have jointly inherited a large Texas ranch. Chiquita Hart (Paula Laurence) is a night-club entertainer; Harry Hart (Allen Jenkins), a sidewalk pitchman, and Blossom Hart, the central figure, a chorus girl turned defense worker. Their new ranch house turns out to be as ramshackle as the plot. Worse, the army has appropriated the building for maneuvers, since it lies close to an army base. Blossom promptly falls for the officer in charge, Sergeant Rocky Fulton (Bill Johnson). When the army moves out, Blossom and her cousins renovate the house and open it up to servicemen's wives. Just when things seem rosy, Blossom's rival for Rocky's attentions, Melanie Walker (Frances Mercer), tells the commanding officer that the girls are loose women, and when he makes a surprise visit circumstances suggest the accusation is just. Blossom's house becomes off-limits. Out of a blue sky Blossom discovers that carborundum in her fillings allows her to be a human radio. After she proves her efficacy by using her built-in communications system to save a distressed plane, all is forgiven, and Blossom and Rocky are paired. Though Cole Porter's tunes sounded bright in the theatre, especially when Miss Merman was belting them out, they represented the weakest body of songs Porter had composed for any show, except, perhaps, *You Never Know*. Todd tried to familiarize audiences with them by the novel stunt of allowing chorus boys to sing some from the orchestra pit during the overture. "Could It Be You?" and "Hey, Good Lookin' " were the best numbers of the evening, while Miss Merman and Miss Laurence brought down the house with a comic plaint of two squaws married to the same brave, "By The Mississiniwah." Miss Merman, Todd's lavish, garish production, and the generally good times kept the show on the boards for over a year.

February saw the 11-performance run of **For Your Pleasure** (2-5-43, Mansfield), a "dance vaudeville" featuring the self-advertised "Lunts of the Dancing World," Veloz and Yolanda.

Only one musical appeared in March and that on the very last day. But it was one of the milestones of the American Musical Theatre: **Oklahoma!** (3-31-43, St. James). The show changed fashions in musicals for two decades. It rejected the topical and even the contemporary and instead embraced a sentimental look at bygone Americana. For the most part it also rejected wit and patently polished sophistication for a certain earnestness and directness. It was, in a way, a reversion to the standards of long-departed comic opera. Of course the new school's settings were generally native, characters mostly everyday people, the music less arioso and occasionally reflective of modern chromatics and dissonances. But the more light-hearted fun of American musical comedies or even of Viennese operettas was discarded with a certain trumpeted contempt.

It is hard to say if Rodgers and Hammerstein consciously planned so dramatic a turnabout, although they clearly understood they were attempting something uncommon. The fact that they opened in tryout with the title *Away We Go* suggests they were not espousing a revolution. However, praise accorded the show and its phenomenal success tended to concentrate attention on the changes that made *Oklahoma!* unique rather than on its place in an ongoing tradition. Its innovations were so ballyhooed that they came to dominate the thinking not only of Rodgers and Hammerstein in their future works but of the creators and critics of the American Musical Theatre as a whole.

The curtain rises to reveal Laurey's farm. Aunt Eller (Betty Garde) is alone, churning. From the distance comes the sound of a young man's voice: He apostrophizes, "Oh, What A Beautiful Mornin'." The singing young man is Curly (Alfred Drake), and he has come to court Laurey (Joan Roberts), although he won't admit as much at first, since he and Laurey have been quarreling. Laurey

pays no attention to him when she enters, but Curly is soon describing the joys of accompanying him to the box social in "The Surrey With The Fringe On Top." Laurey's excitement wanes perceptibly when Curly admits he doesn't own any such wonderful carriage. Will Parker (Lee Dixon) arrives extolling up-to-date pleasures in "Kansas City" and especially happy that fifty dollars he won there in a steer-roping contest will allow him to meet Mr. Carnes' conditions for marrying Carnes' daughter, Ado Annie (Celeste Holm). Curly returns and asks Aunt Eller if there is anybody else Laurey is seriously interested in. Aunt Eller names a few of the more attractive young men of the area and then reluctantly adds Jud Fry (Howard da Silva), their farm hand, to the list. To Curly, Jud is a "bullet-colored, growly man" and not to be trusted. Curly is dismayed to learn that Laurey has in fact consented to allow Jud to drive her to the social. Ado Annie arrives. She is torn between her desire to marry the exotic Persian peddler, Ali Hakim (Joseph Buloff), whom she believes has proposed to her, and her equally strong urge to marry Will Parker, who has finally met her father's requirements. She would be happy to accept both. Indeed there is no boy she would not be happy to accept, for as she herself acknowledges, "I Cain't Say No." Although Laurey has not considered that she might hurt Curly by accepting Jud's invitation, she is put out when she learns Curly will take a pretty lass named Gertie to the party. She poutingly protests that "Many A New Day" will dawn before she lets a man upset her. Ado Annie reappears, with her father and his shotgun. When old man Carnes (Ralph Riggs) learns that Ali invited Ado Annie to a hotel he suggests, shotgun pointing at the peddler, that there had better be a proposal of marriage. Ali agrees. He can do little else except bemoan "It's A Scandal! It's A Outrage!" Curly reminds Laurey that people are talking about them, and Laurey replies in that case the wisest thing for her to do is to be seen with Jud. She suggests Curly not display his obvious admiration for her, since if he does, "People Will Say We're In Love." Curly visits Jud in the hovel of a smokehouse where he lives. He warns Jud to let Laurey alone, but his advice is so indirect that at first Jud does not comprehend. Curly's trick is to tell the loveless Jud how many girls would mourn if for one reason or another news got around that "Pore Jud Is Daid." But when Jud finally realizes what Curly is actually saying he grows surly and menacing. After Curly leaves he decries his lonely life and his "Lonely Room." Laurey's girl friends are puzzled that Laurey would prefer Jud to Curly. She herself would like to have the answer to her choice come "Out Of My Dreams." As soon as the girls depart she does indeed drift off into a dream. In "The Dream Ballet" Laurey sees herself about to be married to Curly when Jud appears. In a fight Jud knocks Curly unconscious and carries off Laurey. She awakens from the dream with her fear of Jud brought home to her. She goes off silently with him as the curtain falls. At the box social there is general agreement "The Farmer And The Cowman" should be friends. But there is little friendship between Curly and Jud as they bid for Laurey's box supper. Jud offers all the money he has in the world, and Curly is forced to sell his gun and horse to outbid Jud. Jud stalks off. Relations are happier between Ado and Will, who have set the date for their marriage, though Will warns Ado Annie its got to be "All Er Nuthin!" Annie agrees, but says it's all for Will and nothing for her. Still, she finds she can accept his terms—on her terms. As the party continues, Jud dances Laurey around to the back porch. His advances rejected, he leaves her, but not without some threats. Curly appears to comfort her, and they agree to marry. The wedding crowd exults in the beauty and richness of "Oklahoma," which is soon to be a state. Just as the ceremonies begin, Jud appears and in a fight Curly kills Jud with Jud's own knife. (Much as Porgy had killed Crown in *Porgy and Bess*.) Luckily, the local judge is present. He holds a quick trial and acquits Curly. The happy couple ride off in a surrey with a fringe. It is, indeed, a beautiful morning.

Hammerstein's libretto was based on Lynn Riggs' 1931 play, *Green Grow the Lilacs*. Hammerstein was faithful to its essentials and to many of its details, even lifting stretches of dialogue. The changes Hammerstein made are enlightening. In the original Curly was allowed to marry but detained for his trial. The decision was never announced, though given the circumstances there was little doubt of what it would be. And the original Ado Annie was left without a promise of marriage. Hammerstein created the character of Will Parker from a remark of Curly's to the villain of Riggs' play, Jeeter. In short Hammerstein was largely tying up loose ends and expanding comic scenes. But he made one unfortunate change. In the smokehouse confrontation, "Pore Jud Is Daid" and Jud's bawling reaction to the song came perilously close to a lesser order of stage comedy. It is a scene that falls apart in all but the most professional hands. Hammerstein's lyrics were straightforward. His use of repetition, which became an annoying Hammer-

stein trait, could be justified in this instance since it nicely mirrored the repetition of folk lyrics used in Riggs' original. But some of Hammerstein's attempts at poetry or at least at romantic statement sounded, even in this early collaboration with Rodgers, distressingly like the fustian nonsense of Harry B. Smith and his era—"Out of your dreams and into his arms you long to fly." Nonetheless, for the most part, Hammerstein's lyrics for *Oklahoma!* had an affecting simplicity.

Rodgers' music marked a change from suave, brash musical lines he had turned out when he was working with Hart. In its directness and apparent flatness was hidden a sophistication as knowing and intelligent as his earlier works. It is sometimes hard to realize that "Oh, What A Beautiful Mornin' " is a waltz. The melody of "The Surrey With The Fringe On Top" unerringly captures the clippety-clop of a horse pulling the vehicle. Rodgers' long-sustained opening note of his title song coupled with the driving melody that follows was one of the freshest inventions of the sort since "Who?" And the impeccable mating of words and music in "People Will Say We're In Love" justifiably made it the most popular song of the year. Much ballyhoo ensued over how well the songs and plot were integrated. They were. But such integration was neither unique nor original. Hammerstein in *Rose-Marie* (9-2-24) and Rodgers in *Chee-Chee* (9-25-28) had professed to offer similarly integrated works. In the teens Guy Bolton had suggested the later Princess Theatre shows aimed for something close to a natural meshing of songs and story. Even in the 19th century integration was sought after and sometimes achieved in better comic operas. But if the ballyhoo was overdone, that in no way gainsaid the excellent totality of *Oklahoma!* The show's musical director, Jay Blackton, appreciating the work's nature, discarded the common musical comedy practice of having the entire chorus sing only songs' melodies. Instead, he reverted to the tradition of operetta and comic opera by dividing his singers and assigning them various parts, not always the principal melodic line. Lemuel Ayers' scenery, essentially realistic sets placed before slightly stylized backdrops, captured the feeling of wide-open spaces and of homey goodness.

Virtually every critic sang the show's praises, even if few could foresee its stunning effect on the musicals to follow. Howard Barnes, writing in the *Herald-Tribune*, labeled it "superb," while *PM*'s Louis Kronenberger thought it offered "just enough to add something special to Broadway's musical life." In the *Times*, Lewis Nichols attempted to assess *Oklahoma!*'s nature as well as its worth. He concluded accurately, "Possibly in addition to being called a musical play, 'Oklahoma!' could be called a folk operetta; whatever it is, it is very good." *Oklahoma!* became more than the hit of the season. Mounted for just over $75,000, its multimillion dollar gross allowed it to surpass *Rose-Marie*'s long-held record. Its 2,248 performances in New York and the record-breaking runs of its road companies gave it one of the largest audiences in American musical history. Some of its records were later surpassed, but *Oklahoma!*'s importance in opening a new era in the American Musical Theatre will never be challenged.

Several young artists were catapulted to fame by *Oklahoma!*, notably Celeste Holm, Alfred Drake, and Agnes de Mille. Much of Miss Holm's later career was largely outside the American Musical Theatre, but Drake and Miss de Mille went on to become significant luminaries on our lyric stage.

. . .

The darkly handsome **Alfred Drake** was born Alfred Capurro in New York City on October 7, 1914. After studying voice with Clytie Mundy, he made his debut in 1935 as a chorus boy in Gilbert and Sullivan operettas. A stint in Atlantic City with the Steel Pier Opera Company followed. Drake understudied William Gaxton in *White Horse Inn* and then increasingly called attention to his fine baritone and his natural acting gifts in *Babes in Arms, The Two Bouquets, One for the Money,* and *Two for the Show.*

. . .

Agnes de Mille was a member of a notable theatrical family. Her grandfather was the famous 19th-century playwright, Henry de Mille; her uncle was also a playwright, but more justly renowned as Hollywood's great epic-maker, Cecil B. de Mille. Miss de Mille was born in the first decade of the 20th century in New York City. She graduated from U.C.L.A., cum laude. Her early ballet instruction and experience came with a large number of major and minor figures, of whom Anthony Tudor was the name most familiar to the general public. She appeared as a dancer in the 1928 edition of the *Greenwich Village Follies*. Her first theatrical choreography was for London shows— *Nymph Errant* and *Why Not Tonight?* Stints as choreographer for *Hooray for What!* (12-1-37) and *Swingin' the Dream* (11-24-39) brought her more heartache than fame. Less than six months before *Oklahoma!* opened, her ballet, *Rodeo,* to Aaron Copland's music, had been first presented by

The Ballet Russe de Monte Carlo. Its cowboy tunes and square dances made it an immediate hit and prepared the way for the *Oklahoma!* dances. Her abilities to express moods and feelings, rather than to devise formally traditional excercises, made her eminently suitable for the new sort of storied dancing that her ballets for *Oklahoma!* made the rage.

. . .

A vestige of an earlier era opened the night after *Oklahoma!* Kronenberger headed his *PM* review, "A Famous Name Is Taken In Vain," and he went on to report a possibly imaginary conversation in the lobby before the show began. According to the critic, Moss Hart gushed, "Who'd have thought that we'd see another *Follies?*," only to have Lillian Hellman respond, "What makes you think we will?" It was moot if they did. What was called the **Ziegfeld Follies of 1943** (4-1-43, Winter Garden) featured Milton Berle, Ilona Massey, Arthur Treacher, Sue Ryan, and Jack Cole among the performers. There wasn't even the pretense of Mrs. Florenz Ziegfeld's association; the Shuberts were the principal producers. Much of the score was by Ray Henderson, his last for Broadway. But apart from his nervous "Hold That Smile," no song managed to get any attention. Burton Rascoe in the *World-Telegram* condemned the music as "raucous and unrhythmical; it is largely scored for percussion instruments." Far more shocking was Rascoe's remark that the "scenery looks as though it came from Cain's storehouse without much retouching." Nor could the critics find many kind words for the comedy. After sneaking on stage as part of a line of kicking chorus boys, Milton Berle treated the show as something of his personal property, interrupting other acts whenever the whim prompted. His best bit may have been his role as J. Pierswift Armour, a butcher flanked by tommy-gun-toting bodyguards, who draws his war-scarce steaks from a safe-deposit box. Arthur Treacher played a butler in several skits, one of which was a spoof of *Private Lives* that degenerated into *Hellzapoppin* mayhem. Much of what praise the critics could dole out was reserved for Cole's dances—his jivey "Wedding of the Solid Sender" and his arcane "Hindu Serenade." Despite the critics' carping, the show chalked up 553 performances—a longer stay than any of Ziegfeld's annuals ever enjoyed.

A revival of a show of Ziegfeld's era closed the season. The Shuberts brought in a road company of *The Student Prince* (12-2-24) from the backwaters. Though Everett Marshall and Ann Pennington were in the cast, the mounting displayed the famed Shubert shabbiness at its worst. Moreover with *Oklahoma!* all the rage, Romberg's old war-horse was dismissed by faddists as beyond reclaim. Nonetheless, *The Student Prince* ran, with some forcing, through the summer and achieved 153 performances.

1943-1944

Although it became obvious soon after *Oklahoma!* opened that a new era was under way, it took time for the show's effects to be manifest. Broadway could not react as quickly as it once did. Its great creative talents were getting old, many were elsewhere, and huge taxation on success militated against more prolific writers creating two or three shows a year as they once had done. While awaiting the renaissance, Broadway spent most of the season fervently recalling old glories. Yet one exceptional and one very hopeful work pranced into town.

The season began with a number of determinedly old-fashioned works. The very first effort, **Early to Bed** (6-17-43, Broadhurst), was a moderately good example of the gaudy, contemporary musical comedies that had entertained Broadway the past few seasons. It was spiced with a touch of the modern burlesque that *Star and Garter* (6-24-42) had shown could be so profitable. Set largely in and around a Martinique bordello, "The Angry Pigeon," run by a former schoolmarm named Madame Rowena (Muriel Angelus), it recounted the adventures that ensue when a famous bullfighter, El Magnifico (Richard Kollmar), and his son (George Zoritch) come to visit. El Magnifico remembers Rowena from her school days. The stay is complicated by the arrival of a track team that hopes to use the place for a training quarters. Almost everybody, it seems, is blind to the real business of the house. *Early to Bed*'s score was by "Fats" Waller, with lyrics by George Marion, Jr. Both the melodies and the lyrics tended to be flaccid. Only one comic song, a tribute to "The Ladies Who Sing With The Band," proved a show-stopper when Mary Small, Jane Deering, Jane Kean, and Miss Angelus joined forces to sing it. To compensate for the lackluster score, George Jenkins filled the stage with "prismatic and opalescent" colors, while to minimize the drag of the sluggard, double-entendre-packed book Jenkins kept his scenery in motion all evening long. The *Post*'s Wilella Waldorf announced the scenery was "the biggest hit of the show." The bawdy yarn appealed to a large segment of the theatregoing crowd, and *Early to Bed* ran out the season.

Of an even older school was *The Vagabond King* (9-20-25), which arrived at the end of June with John Brownlee singing Dennis King's role. It failed to find the market the preceding season's revival of *The Student Prince* apparently had satisfied and closed after seven weeks.

However, a lavish revival of *The Merry Widow* (10-21-07) reached back still farther, to the days of the second Viennese school's glory, and with a fine cast headed by Marta Eggerth, Jan Kiepura, and Melville Cooper played into the spring. Just as one distinguished refugee composer had led the orchestra for the previous season's *Rosalinda,* so another, Robert Stolz, conducted for *The Merry Widow.* Sitting prominently in the first-night audience on August 4 at the Majestic was the Sonia of the principal 1907 road company, Lina Abarbanell.

Still another old name appeared on August 12 at the Royale when **Chauve-Souris 1943** premiered. "The Parade Of The Wooden Soldiers" was back, as were several other minor songs from the original. With Balieff gone, Leon Greanin served as master of ceremonies. A number of critics professed to be delighted that Greanin was more articulate than his predecessor. Contemporary additions included a duet between a Russian sniper and an American WAC. For all its revisions the show had long since worn out its welcome. It lasted less than two weeks.

The success of *The Student Prince* prompted the Shuberts to pull *Blossom Time* (9-29-21) from the road as well, but New York would not support three operettas simultaneously, and after six weeks the show returned to its perennial touring. Opening, as it did on September 4, it failed to provide a sparkling or original send-off for the main fall season.

Laugh Time (9-8-43, Shubert) didn't help matters when it premiered four nights later. The vaudeville was the third in a series of West Coast productions, the first of which, *Show Time* (9-16-42), had enjoyed a long run on Broadway the preceding season. Its sequel, *Big Time,* never made it to New York. *Laugh Time*'s 126 performances fell between its predecessors in drawing power. To many it should have stayed longer, for its bill included such attractive entertainers as Ethel Waters, Frank Fay, Bert Wheeler, and Buck and Bubbles.

Nor could attractive old favorites save **My Dear Public** (9-9-43, 46th St.), which some critics looked on as a revue and some as a book musical. To the latter its construction resembled many of the musicals of two and three decades before when a weak plot served as an excuse for a number of specialty acts. Other critics suggested it marked a return to the revue that employed a thin story line to hold it together. Book musical or revue, its slim plot told how Daphne Short (Ethel Shutta), with the connivance of the swishy Byron Burns (Eric Brotherson), persuades her husband Barney (Willie Howard), the zipper king, to back a musical in which she has been promised the role of a harem queen. The resulting auditions and rehearsals occupied much of the evening and gave specialty acts their moment. Typical of the specialties was Al Kelly's celebrated double-talk routine. Howard revived his old revolutionary soap-box speech, varying it for the occasion by mixing a Scottish burr with his Yiddish. In "If You Want To Deal with Russia" he solved a major international problem. The credits did not distinguish between lyricists and composers. Irving Caesar, Sam Lerner, and Gerald Marks were lumped together as the songsmiths, perhaps in the hope that it would offer a small refuge from specific blame. The songs were quite bad. Caesar was also the producer and colibrettist. Even Howard and Miss Shutta couldn't overcome such material.

An admitted revue, that did indeed have a thin story line, came in three nights later. The plot of **Bright Lights of 1944** (9-16-43, Forrest) was almost identical to the plot that had served *My Dear Public* so inadequately—only this time two Sardi waiters decide to put on the show. Smith and Dale played the would-be producers. Somehow they found a way of running through their "Dr. Kronkeit" skit in case theatregoers had missed it the year before in *Laugh, Town, Laugh* or in any of its other numerous reincarnations. The talent they auditioned included James Barton and Frances Williams. Barton also resorted to a turn theatregoers must have come to know by heart, his drunk act. As a bonus, he added a spoof of a character he had successfully portrayed for several years, Jeeter Lester of *Tobacco Road*. Miss Williams offered a straightforward rendition of "Frankie And Johnny." The new songs the cast sang were by Jerry Livingston. But they didn't sing them for long. *Bright Lights of 1944* closed after four performances, still 16 weeks away from the year in its title.

A more off-beat, successful entertainment followed two days after *Bright Lights,* when Sol Hurok presented Katherine Dunham and her dancers in **A Tropical Revue** (9-19-43, Martin Beck).

An evening of sizzlingly brilliant black choreography and interpretation, the show gave audiences a taste of Negro rhythms the world over in numbers such as "Darktown Strutters' Ball," "Rhumba Suite," "Rites de Passage," "Br'er Rabbit," "Woman With A Cigar," and "Bahiana." The revue stayed two months, toured profitably, and returned the following season.

Harold Orlob was yet another old timer, but one whose name had long been missing from Broadway credits. He had hung on tenaciously in the teens, twenties, and thirties without ever surpassing the limited success of *Listen, Lester* (12-23-18). Now, after changing waves of style had left him far behind, he attempted a musical farce of the old school, even to re-employing the custom of a single set for the whole evening. Orlob wrote both book and music for **Hairpin Harmony** (10-1-43, National). His plot described Howard Swift's search for a radio program to push his baby food. He settles on an all-girl orchestra with a baby-talking announcer. Devastated by the critics, the show collasped after three performances, and Orlob bid a final farewell to the musical stage.

By this time theatregoers understandably could have begun to wonder if *Oklahoma!* (3-31-43), instead of signaling an advance, had driven Broadway into a headlong retreat. But **One Touch of Venus** (10-7-43, Imperial) cast away any doubts. Superficially it was just another of the recent musical comedies with an innocuous plot and a contemporary setting. It bore a discernible resemblance to *I Married an Angel* (5-11-38). Of course the story of an unnatural or preternatural figure enjoying a brief mortality had been popular in the American Musical Theatre as far back as *Adonis* (9-4-84). What elevated *One Touch of Venus* above recent run-of-the-mill offerings and placed it firmly in the advance guard was its intelligence and cohesiveness. S. J. Perelman and Ogden Nash based their plot on F. Anstey's *The Tinted Venus.* Their new musical told its tale with an unfailing sense of style and literate wit, never stopping to introduce extraneous bits of froth nor stooping to inject currently voguish elements of stripper burlesque. In keeping with the classic elegance of its heroine, its story was attractively simple. Whitelaw Savory (John Boles) has unearthed a long-lost statue of Venus of Anatolia and puts it on display at his museum. One early visitor to the museum is Rodney Hatch (Kenny Baker), a rather naïve young barber about to become engaged. Determined to prove that his fiancée's hand has a Hellenic grace, Rodney places the engagement ring he is taking to her on the statue's finger. By some feat of magic the marble is turned to life in a blinding flash. The living, breathing Venus (Mary Martin) relishes her new existence. Almost at once she sets about winning Rodney away from his mother-dominated sweetheart, Gloria (Ruth Bond). Venus has virtually ensnared Rodney when a dream warns her of the excruciatingly humdrum life she will lead in bourgeois Ozone Heights. She realizes that once a goddess, always a goddess. In another blinding flash she is transformed back into stone. The forlorn Rodney is left standing alone in the museum. A young lady enters. Her appearance is so remarkably like the statue's that she might very well pass for Venus' country cousin:

Girl: Oh—excuse me. Can you tell me where I register for the Art Course?
Rodney: (*Looks at the statue—then at the Girl*) Why—sure . . . Where do you come from?
Girl: Ozone Heights.
Rodney: Do you like it there?
Girl: I wouldn't think of living any place else.
Rodney: My name is Rodney Hatch.
Girl: Mine is . . .
Rodney: (*Going quickly to her*) You don't have to tell me. I know.

Nash's lyrics in *One Touch of Venus* rank with the best ever created by P. G. Wodehouse, Lorenz Hart, Cole Porter, or Ira Gershwin. His romantic lines flowed easily and naturally, yet remained incontestably warm. But, as might be expected from Nash, his comic lines were even better. Hatch, Savory, and two other men seek to analyze "The Trouble With Women" and conclude "The trouble with women is men." Much of the best material fell to Savory's secretary, played in the original by lean, angular, wry Paula Laurence. In the title song she notes that Venus, a goddess in a world dominated by gods, had only to open her bodice to equalize the odds. Later she consoles Savory by assuring him that, like so many of the "Very, Very, Very" rich, "You huddle with your memoirs, and boy! what memoirs them was." Kurt Weill's score was lovely and appropriate, if largely unexceptional. Although at the time the show opened much publicity was given to a song Mary Martin sang from a chair pulled close to the footlights, "That's Him," the only song to win enduring popularity has been Rodney and Venus' "Speak Low," an almost Porterish beguine that echoed the popular Latin rhythms of the day. Two triumphs of the original

production were Agnes de Mille's ballets. The first, "Forty Minutes for Lunch," wittily depicted Venus tasting her new-found freedom in the mindless hustle and bustle of noon hour at Rockefeller Center. The ex-goddess flirts with a sailor and cavorts in a shop window. The second act "dream ballet," "Venus in Ozone Heights," was more like a pagan rite. The ballets coming just a season after *Oklahoma!* confirmed that Agnes de Mille had replaced George Balanchine as Broadway's leading choreographer. The dream ballet, less fortunately, suggested that such pieces from there on were de rigueur in fully realized musicals. One attractive young ballerina emerged from the evening, Sono Osato. The designer, Mainbocher, devised lovely Grecian draperies and gowns for Miss Martin. Everything on the stage of the Imperial fell together with such impeccable style that *One Touch of Venus* had 567 performances before it went on tour.

The movement to advance the art of the musical theatre took some giant steps backwards when **Artists and Models** (11-5-43, Broadway) returned after a thirteen-year lapse. Night-club impresario Lou Walters brought the show in and determined its tone. Walters employed only fifteen show girls, a far cry from forty to sixty Ziegfeld and his rivals regularly presented. To open the show the girls paraded about as bottles of perfume, advertising then popular essences such as Velvet Night, Bridal Blush, and My Sin. The revue's idea of contemporary humor was revealed in songs such as "Swing Low, Sweet Harriet," done as part of a minstrel show entitled "Way Up North In Dixieland." The cast featured Jane Froman and the rising Jackie Gleason. But their material was thin and the public indifferent.

A partnership that would eventually be one of the glories of the American Musical Theatre began inauspiciously with **What's Up?** (11-11-43, National). It marked the first public collaboration of Alan Jay Lerner and Frederick Loewe (with Arthur Pierson assisting on the book).

• • •

Frederick Loewe was born into a theatrical family in Berlin, Germany, on June 10, 1904. His father played Prince Danilo in the original Berlin production of *The Merry Widow*. A child prodigy on the piano, Frederick became the youngest soloist ever to appear with the Berlin Philharmonic. Two of his early instructors were also famous composers, Ferruccio Busoni and Eugene d'Albert. Early Loewe songs were heard in *Petticoat Fever* (a straight play starring Dennis King) and the *Illustrators' Show* (1-22-36). His first score was for a failure, *Great Lady* (12-1-38). Loewe met Lerner when he was looking for someone to revise *Great Lady* for a 1942 Detroit production.

· · ·

Alan Jay Lerner was born in New York on August 31, 1918. His family owned the Lerner Shops, a chain specializing in popular-priced women's wear. Lerner's early education was at select private schools in England and at home, after which he took a Bachelor of Science degree at Harvard. While there he helped write material for two Hasty Pudding shows. Lerner had settled down to write radio scripts when his meeting with Loewe redirected his energies into the legitimate theatre.

· · ·

The story was an interesting reversal of the old *Sultan of Sulu* (12-29-02) type plot—and one wonders why no one tried it when that sort of theme was all the rage. Instead of Americans visiting a potentate in some exotic land, the bigwig comes to the States. (Reflecting the growth of modern technology, the air force, not the once ubiquitous navy, is involved.) But the plane carrying the Rawa of Tanglinia crashes at Miss Langley's School for Girls, allowing everyone to have a seemingly naughty, but actually harmless, good time. Jimmy Savo forsook his customary baggy trousers to play the Rawa in a snappy morning suit, supplemented by a "lorgnette" and a fez. Balanchine, working with a smaller than usual corps de ballet, probably found himself compelled to insert a voguish "dream ballet." But he used the opportunity to give Savo one of the evening's most delightful moments with the forlorn, little comedian pursuing an Amazonian ballerina. Yet something about the nature of the book was so irresistibly old-fashioned that the best dancing of the evening came not in the new-fangled ballets but in Don Weissmuller's show-stopping tap routines. Boris Aronson housed the entertainment in scenery with a Valentine card frilliness. Lerner and Loewe's songs, while bright, were not overwhelming, while the book revealed that Lerner had a lot to learn about writing librettos. His story was largely humorless and ill-proportioned. *What's Up?* survived eight weeks.

A revival of *A Connecticut Yankee* (11-3-27) began a disappointing run of 135 performances at the Martin Beck on November 17. Vivienne Segal as Morgan Le Fay and Dick Foran as Martin sang the leads. The prologue was brought up to date, making Martin a navy lieutenant. But the original body of the story was faithfully retained. Rodgers

and Hart added several new numbers. The brilliant lyrics for Morgan Le Fay's catalogue of murders in "To Keep My Love Alive" demonstrated that Hart, for all his problems, had lost not a jot of his genius:

Sir Roger played the harp; I cussed the thing.
I crowned him with his harp to bust the thing
And now he plays where harps are just the thing.

But these were the last new Hart lyrics Broadway would ever hear. Five nights after the opening Lorenz Hart was dead.

Moss Hart's play about Air Force life, *Winged Victory,* included a number of songs, mostly by David Rose. But the piece was essentially a straight play-chronicle.

Oscar Hammerstein tried something novel when he jazzed up *Carmen* for an all-black cast. **Carmen Jones** (12-2-43, Broadway) became a worker in a parachute factory and similar changes brought everything up to date, although Mérimée's story and Bizet's score were retained. However, song titles now ran to "Beat Out Dat Rhythm On A Drum." Since the principal roles remained uncompromisingly strenuous, singers alternated in main roles. Both Muriel Smith and Muriel Rahn sang the title part. A patently more serious effort than the thirties' tinkering with *The Mikado, Carmen Jones* ran a surprising 503 performances, helped extensively by producer Billy Rose's astute publicity. It was the last musical offering of 1943.

A month and a half passed before another musical arrived. The preceding season Vernon Duke and Howard Dietz had done tunes for a Mary Martin musical, *Dancing in the Streets,* which folded on its tryout. Their luck with **Jackpot** (1-13-44, Alvin) wasn't much better. The show struggled along for 69 performances before throwing in the towel. Duke's music wasn't to blame, for he came up with lively, instantly hummable songs such as "Sugarfoot." In fact neither Dietz' lyrics nor Guy Bolton, Sidney Sheldon, and Ben Roberts' book was truly culpable. Rather the era of purposefulness on the musical stage was at hand, so *Jackpot* was harshly received. Its innocuous, old-fashioned plot told how Sally Madison (Nanette Fabray) is put up as first prize in a bond-selling rally. Three marines—Hank Trimble (Allan Jones), Jerry Finch (Jerry Lester), and Winkie Cotter (Benny Baker)—win her with lucky 7777777. But since they can't share her affections Jerry and Winkie settle for Nancy Parker (Mary Wickes) and WAC Sgt. Maguire (Betty Garrett).

Equally old-fashioned, but eagerly welcomed

was **Mexican Hayride** (1-28-44, Winter Garden). Mike Todd gave it the most lavish, expensive mounting a musical had had in years, adding more than a touch of burlesque. Herbert and Dorothy Fields wrote the book and Cole Porter the songs. Bobby Clark was the show's roustabout star, portraying Joe Bascom, a fugitive from American justice. His hayride begins when an American girl bullfighter, Montana (June Havoc), throws him the bull's ear. When he catches it, tradition makes him the guest of the Mexican government. This gives him time to establish an illegal lottery with a newfound crony, Lombo Campos (George Givot). The Mexican government tracks them down and informs the American chargé d'affaires, David Winthrop (Wilbur Evans). Winthrop has been fond of Montana, but now suspects she is in league with Bascom. To prove her innocence she goes with Winthrop to the flower-strewn, floating gardens at Xochimilco, where American tourists spend Sunday reading the comics and where Joe and Lombo are posing as mariachi players. Realizing the law is on their scent, Joe and Lombo flee, reappearing soon after as tortilla vendors. But their plight is hopeless. The crooks are turned over to their respective governments, while Winthrop and Montana proceed with their wedding plans. Fields' book was serviceable and in the hands of so many fine fun-makers exceptionally diverting. Todd, as he had learned to do in *Star and Garter* (6-24-42), provided an attractive chorus line whose costumes offered tantalizing glimpses as they moved about. But for many the best news of the evening was the Cole Porter score. It was not a great one. But it gave an unmistakable indication that he was coming out of his doldrums. The hit of the evening was another beguine, "I Love You" (sung by David). But other memorable pieces were the jolly "laundry list" of Montana's "There Must Be Someone For Me," the passionate "Carlotta"—sung by a minor character, Lolita (Corinna Mura), with the ensemble—and Montana, Joe and Lombo's comic "Count Your Blessings." *Mexican Hayride* was added to the list of 1943–44 shows that ran over 500 performances.

R. H. Burnside, who decades before had mounted the Hippodrome extravaganzas, brought a Gilbert and Sullivan repertory into the small Ambassador for a total of 54 performances. The bill included *The Mikado, Trial by Jury, H.M.S. Pinafore, Cox and Box, The Pirates of Penzance, The Gondoliers, Iolanthe, Patience, Ruddigore,* and *The Yeomen of the Guard.*

Another smash hit, **Follow the Girls** (4-8-44, Century), was one more in the dying line of rowdy, modern musicals that were sometimes called "glorified burlesque." The popular night club star, Gertrude Niesen, did in fact play Bubbles La Marr, a burlesque queen who takes over a servicemen's canteen as her contribution to the war effort. This inadvertently excludes her 4-F suitor, Goofy Gale (Jackie Gleason), who is obliged to steal a Wave's uniform to gain entrance. Dependable Guy Bolton and Fred Thompson combined with Eddie Davis to create the book, while Phil Charig did the music, assisted by Dan Shapiro and Milton Pascal on the words. The suggestive words to one song, "I Wanna Get Married," allowed Miss Niesen to stop the show nightly. Like several musicals of the season, it used its plot as a frame for vaudeville specialties such as the dancing of the Di Gatanos. With its eye-filling chorus line and entertaining specialties *Follow the Girls* ran over two years, far longer than the merits of its basic material justified. No doubt soldiers using New York as a major leave town or embarkation point eagerly sought out this sort of girlie show, thereby lengthening its run.

There was little merit to **Allah Be Praised!** (4-20-44, Adelphi) and even less public interest. The show, with a book and lyrics by George Marion, Jr., and music by Don Walker and Baldwin Bergersen, told a confused tale of the search for a missing American in the postwar harems of Sultanbad. The American, Tex O'Carroll (Edward Roecker), is discovered to be none other than the Sultan. The show sought laughs from the same device employed earlier in *What's Up?*, by pitting little Joey Faye against tall Jayne Manners. One imaginative bit that went down with all the claptrap was Jack Cole's ballet depicting a softball game in slow motion. During its tryout Ned Sparks had brought down the house reliving in song his pleasant stay at Dannemora prison, but by the time the show got to New York Sparks had left the cast, though the song remained. At least it remained as long as the lavish show stayed, but that was a mere two and a half weeks.

A modern version of Offenbach's *La Belle Hélène* was offered on April 24 as **Helen Goes to Troy** (4-24-44, Alvin). The show, like *Rosalinda* before it, was based on an earlier Max Reinhardt staging. Erich Wolfgang Korngold was again on hand to conduct, but this time he was also credited with adapting the music and adding a few minor songs of his own. He was not above using other Offenbach material, such as the "Barcarolle" from *The Tales of Hoffmann* to stimulate interest. Jarmila Novotna, William Horne, and Ernest Truex were featured, although Miss Novotna (of the Metropolitan Opera) and Horne didn't sing at matinees. Despite generally favorable notices, the public wouldn't come; the show died with the hot weather.

Harem sets returned in **Dream with Music** (5-18-44, Majestic). Since the author of *Allah Be Praised* was George Marion, Jr., and the producer of the new entry Richard Kollmar, there is the possibility they had discussed some sort of Arabian Nights theme when they had worked together on *Early to Bed*. Perhaps both came to wish they had dropped the matter, for *Dream with Music* survived only a week longer than *Allah Be Praised*. Dorothy Kilgallen, Sidney Sheldon, and Ben Roberts' book recounted the adventures of a soap-opera authoress, Dinah (Vera Zorina), when she dreams she is Scheherazade. Clay Warnick's music and Edward Eager's lyrics were livelier and more imaginative than *Allah*'s. Some critics found amusement in the show's use of one old song not by Warnick. A genie's appearance was underscored by "Jeannie With The Light Brown Hair." By the time *Dream with Music* arrived, dream ballets had become requisite. Balanchine dutifully provided one, though his heart and his art were clearly not in it. As one reviewer noted, Ronald Graham as Aladdin "clomps around in oversized wedgies, while Miss [Joy] Hodges is generally buried in a group of not too seductively undressed chorines."

In the 19th century opera had been close to a commonplace in regular Broadway houses, but in recent decades it had been limited to the Metropolitan and a few other special auditoriums. So it is probably worth noting that two performances of Pergolesi's *The Maid as Mistress* (*La Serva Padrona*) and Wolf-Ferrari's *The Secret of Suzanne* were mounted at the Alvin on May 14 and 21. Meanwhile at the New York City Center, where a great new opera company was in the making, a revival of *The New Moon* (9-19-28) was displayed from May 17 until June 24. Dorothy Kirsten and Earl Wrightson sang the leads.

The season ended drearily with yet another vaudeville, **Take a Bow** (6-15-44, Broadhurst). The evening gave New Yorkers a last chance to see at least one of the Marx Brothers, Chico. Dressed in his familiar green hat and coat, he made his first entrance from a box trying to coax a neighbor to laugh. Before his last appearance, playing the piano in the orchestra pit, he revived a poker game routine from *Cocoanuts* (12-8-25). Others on the bill included Pat Rooney in his popular soft-shoe

routine, and "Think-a-Drink" Hoffman, magically pouring a variety of concoctions from a single pitcher. The vaudeville bubble had long since burst, so *Take a Bow* bowed out after a mere 12 showings.

1944-1945

Outside the theatre it was a tumultuous year. Roosevelt was elected to the only fourth term in American history and shortly after taking office became the eighth American President to die in office. The war with Germany ended May 7, and the war with Japan just weeks after the theatrical season closed. And a good theatrical season it was! Both on stage and at the box office it outshone any session in years. The diversity of the straight play successes can be gauged by the mention merely of *Harvey, The Glass Menagerie, Anna Lucasta, Ten Little Indians,* and *Soldier's Wife,* as well as a number of useful dramatizations of popular books. The American Musical Theatre proved equally diverse, equally rich, and equally successful.

Hats Off to Ice (6-22-44, Center), the annual "icetravaganza," with songs by James Littlefield and John Fortis, got the season off to a flying start. It ran through all of 1944–45 and then through all of 1945–46. Songs such as "Isle Of The Midnight Rainbow," and "Headin' West" suggest the nature of the spectacle.

The first conventional musical appeared two months later. **Song of Norway** (8-21-44, Imperial) was a fictionalized, romanticized stage biography of Edvard Grieg using his music as the source of its songs. An unabashed operetta, it continued the tradition most successfully represented by *Blossom Time* (9-29-21). Grieg (Lawrence Brooks) is lured away from his Nina (Helena Bliss) and from his beloved mountains and fiords by the dashing prima donna, Louisa Giovanni (Irra Petina). She takes him to Italy with her. But the voices of Nina and his dead friend Rikard (Robert Shafer) and the voice of Norway itself are too strong to ignore. Grieg returns home. The libretto and lyrics were adequate, if at times a bit stilted or heavily showy. What made Edwin Lester's West Coast production a two-year favorite in New York was lovely Grieg music, fine mounting, and superb singing. At a time when the war and Hollywood had deprived the stage of its better voices, *Song of Norway* offered the radiant singing of not only of its principals but of such minor players as the aged Ivy

Scott. Unfortunately, this brief renaissance of operetta ended quickly, and these artists never again had as fine an opportunity to display their voices. The hit of the evening was "Strange Music" (sung by Grieg and Nina), with its principal theme taken from Grieg's "Wedding Day In Troldhaugen."

Star Time (9-12-44, Majestic), another in the waning series of inexpensive and quickly assembled vaudevilles, stayed for 120 showings. Lou Holtz, Benny Fields, and the De Marcos led the bill.

A third musical that ran through two seasons was **Bloomer Girl** (10-5-44, Shubert). Its advance notices hinted that it was another *Oklahoma!* (3-31-43). It, too, used a bit of early Americana for its story; it, too, had Agnes de Mille ballets; and it, too, offered *Oklahoma!*'s unforgettable Ado Annie, Celeste Holm, in the lead role, along with the hit of *Oklahoma!*'s ballet, Joan McCracken, as its principal dancer. What first-nighters saw and heard instead was an attractively mounted production (by *Oklahoma!*'s Lemuel Ayers and Miles White) of a superficial and somewhat silly, if entertaining, book and a singable, though not well-sung, score by Harold Arlen (with E. Y. Harburg lyrics). *Bloomer Girl* had little of *Oklahoma!*'s seriousness of purpose or artistic cohesiveness. However, it did contribute one additional element to the new musical vogue. In going back to "the good old days" it resuscitated historical figures. This device intrigued librettists frequently during the rest of the season, and often thereafter. Set during the Civil War, the story recounted the rebellion of Evelina Applegate (Miss Holm), daughter of a Cicero Falls, New York, hoopskirt manufacturer. Not only does she refuse to marry the man her father has in mind for her, but she actively supports the campaign of her aunt, Dolly Bloomer (Margaret Douglass), to replace her father's profitable hoopskirts with the more comfortable garment that soon carried her aunt's name. Evelina's independence is manifest in more dangerous ways, for, while she is an abolitionist, she falls in love and ultimately consents to wed a southern slaveholder, Jeff Calhoun (David Brooks). Miss de Mille's Civil War ballet did not really have much pertinence to the plot, although it did to the period of the piece. With World War II still raging, it also had a certain thinly-disguised timeliness. It poignantly depicted the grief of wives and mothers whose loved-ones will never return. None of Arlen's fine songs became standards, though Evelina and Jeff's duet "Right As The Rain" is still occasionally heard. But three songs stood out in the evening. Besides "Right As The Rain," a beautiful, intense ballad that eschews the easy AABA formula, there was Jeff's happy, curiously rhythmed "Evelina" and the impassioned, tuneful plea for racial understanding, "The Eagle And Me," sung by black Pompey (Dooley Wilson) and a mixed chorus.

For the next musical offering R. H. Burnside reached back even beyond the years when he was an active theatrical figure to revive Reginald De Koven's *Robin Hood* (9-28-91) at the Adelphi on November 7. But New Yorkers preferred the 19th century as seen through 20th-century eyes to the 19th-century's view of the past. Two weeks and the old comic opera was gone. One week later the City Center brought back *The Gypsy Baron* for 11 performances, following it with brief revivals of *La Vie Parisienne* in January and *Carmen Jones* (5-2-45) in May.

A musical version of Jeanne Eagels' great hit, *Rain*, was planned around the talents of Ethel Merman. But Miss Merman and the authors became disenchanted with each other during rehearsals (when Miss Merman demanded that her husband provide lyrics), so June Havoc was called in to play the title role in **Sadie Thompson** (11-16-44, Alvin). The shock of the original version had long since worn away, leaving Howard Dietz and Rouben Mamoulian with a rather harsh story that didn't lend itself to conventional musical treatment. Sadie was still the sharp-tongued lady of the streets exposing the hypocrisy of the Reverend Davidson (Lansing Hatfield) on sultry Pago Pago. Unfortunately, Vernon Duke's pleasant melodies and Dietz' commonplace lyrics lacked the bite and drive that might have moved the story forward. Sadie was almost apologetic as she sang "The Love I Long For" ("I've no right to demand"). More than one reviewer felt the physical production outshone the text and cast. Boris Aronson drenched the stage in realistic rain and dramatically flew Trader Joe's Hotel up into the flies so that he could reveal a lush jungle set. Dismayingly, the jungle set was largely an excuse for the sort of orgiastic, pagan dance that had gone out of fashion with the old extravaganzas. The dance only served to underline the musical's debt to the 1920s and, given the inclination of the forties to treat almost anything from the twenties as hopelessly outdated, helped foredoom the show.

Broadway turned a deaf ear when a new operetta, **Rhapsody** (11-22-44, Century), appealed for patronage. The music Broadway refused to heed was by Fritz Kreisler, who twenty-five years before had written half the score for fondly remembered

Apple Blossoms (10-7-19). Kreisler even worked old favorites such as "Caprice Viennois" and "The Old Refrain" into his new score. The book, which dealt with court intrigues in the Vienna of Francis I (George Young) and Maria Theresa (Annamary Dickey) and which included a comic Casanova (Eddie Mayehoff), was by the relatively unknown Leonard Louis Levinson and Arnold Sundgaard. The authors attempted a pure, old-school piece and thereby undoubtedly engineered their own downfall. New Yorkers might flock to a sumptuous revival of a genuine masterwork such as *The Merry Widow* or clamor for tickets to old forms resuscitated with modern amenities such as *Song of Norway* or, later in the season, *Up in Central Park*. But an uncompromising, and admittedly somewhat weak, effort to exhibit the style of a bygone era met with no approval.

Three revues followed. They were as unlike one another as Broadway could imagine. The first was the most conventional. **The Seven Lively Arts** (12-7-44, Ziegfeld) had been given the extensive ballyhoo that attended any Billy Rose production. Pre-opening publicity boasted of its Cole Porter songs, its Igor Stravinsky ballet music, its sketches and monologues by, among others, Moss Hart, George S. Kaufman, and Ben Hecht. At carefully selected intervals announcements added names to a cast that ultimately included Beatrice Lillie, Bert Lahr, Benny Goodman, Alicia Markova, Anton Dolin, Doc Rockwell, Albert Carroll, and Dolores Gray. For many the most joyous news was that Rose had purchased the magnificent Ziegfeld and was returning it to the legitimate fold after a dozen years as a grind movie house. But the advance cheering backfired. *The Seven Lively Arts* disappointed both critics and public. Cole Porter had one bittersweet ballad, sung by Nan Wynn, that has remained popular, "Ev'ry Time We Say Goodbye." But Stravinsky's music, "Scene du Ballet"—and the Dolin-Markova dances—seemed too arty to Gotham playgoers and too condescending to serious critics. The comic material was especially weak. Bert Lahr had no good numbers, although Miss Lillie got some laughs with a tropical dance routine subtitled "Let's End The Beguine," as an English lady attempting to talk like an American soldier, and as a ballet fan who wants to buy a seat but can't remember the name of the ballet and so dances the piece for the startled ticket seller. Benny Goodman led his combo in some swing renditions. Show girls—only twelve—paraded in front of not especially attractive Norman Bel Geddes sets. But for all its advertised lavishness and despite its huge (for the time) advance sale of over $350,000, word about the show spread quickly, and it closed after just over 20 weeks.

Olsen and Johnson offered the third of their loony vehicles, **Laffing Room Only** (12-23-44, Winter Garden). It was filled with much of the same demented zaniness that had made their earlier shows so popular. But the novelty had worn off, and, further, the comedians were competing in the richest musical season Broadway had enjoyed in years. As a result *Laffing Room Only* closed after 233 performances—a good run but far from the lengthy stays of *Sons o' Fun* (12-1-41) or *Hellzapoppin* (9-22-38). The show left behind one song, not particularly popular at the inception, but which later became a favorite on radio, the hillbilly take-off that Pat Brewster sang, "Feudin' and Fightin'" (Al Dubin/Burton Lane).

More hillbilly music was heard four nights after the opening of *Laffing Room Only* when the Theatre Guild brought in **Sing Out Sweet Land** (12-27-44, International), a "Salute to American Folk and Popular Music" compiled by Walter Kerr. Alfred Drake and Burl Ives led the singing of native American tunes from the first Puritan days to World War II. For all the new interest in Americana and folklore, the show proved a bit esoteric for commercial purposes. It played 13 weeks.

The next night saw the opening of another of the season's long-run hits, **On the Town** (12-28-44, Adelphi). The musical comedy had a score by the young darling of the serious music world, Leonard Bernstein. Its book, by Betty Comden and Adolph Green, was derived from Jerome Robbins' popular ballet, *Fancy Free*. Robbins remained to attend to the new ballets the evening required. His two free-wheeling, concerted ballets "Miss Turnstiles" and "Gaby in the Playground of the Rich" were not only lively in themselves but forcefully propelled the story.

• • •

Jerome Robbins was born in New York on October 11, 1918. His real patronymic was Rabinowitz. In 1940 Robbins joined the Ballet Theatre as a dancer, and in the following year called attention to himself in Agnes de Mille's *Three Virgins and a Devil*. Important roles in *Petrouchka* and *Pillar of Fire* followed. But it was his initial creative effort, *Fancy Free*, in 1944 that firmly established his reputation.

• • •

When Robbins was not keeping the players in

motion, George Abbott kept them less literally on their toes. Three sailors embark on a twenty-four-hour leave in New York. They are the romantic Gaby (John Battles), the clownish Ozzie (Green), and the more earthbound Chip (Cris Alexander). On the subway Gaby falls in love with a picture of the month's "Miss Turnstiles" (Sono Osato), and the three pals set out to find her. In a search that takes them as far uptown as the Museum of Natural History and as far out of Manhattan as Coney Island, Chip and Ozzie find romance of a sort, respectively, in Hildy (Nancy Walker), a cab driver, and Claire de Loon (Miss Comden), an anthropology student. Hildy, besides hacking it, proudly announces, "I Can Cook, Too," though her strenuous labors in the kitchen achieve nothing more than a peeled banana. With a dinosaur casting an empty eye on them, Claire and Ozzie confess, "I Get Carried Away." It remains for Gaby to find "Miss Turnstiles" himself. And he does. Bernstein's score was intelligent, lively, and uncompromisingly contemporary. At times it suggested the path Gershwin might have pursued had he lived. But the songs lacked the sweet melodic catchiness that Gershwin so often presented. Still, Gaby's love ballad, "Lucky To Be Me," is heard intermittently while the opening measures of the sailors' trio, "New York, New York," are often used as a background or lead-in for scenes of Manhattan.

. . .

Leonard Bernstein was born in Lawrence, Massachusetts, on August 25, 1918. While still in grade school he began studying piano under Helen Coates. At Harvard he pursued his studies under Heinrich Gebhard and Walter Piston. After leaving college, he enrolled at the Curtis Institute in Philadelphia to study conducting under Fritz Reiner. In time he became the protégé of Serge Koussevitsky. He called himself to public attention dramatically when he substituted for an indisposed Bruno Walter at a concert of the New York Philharmonic on November 13, 1943.

. . .

Though **Betty Comden** and **Adolph Green** have proved the most durable writing team in the American Musical Theatre, their paths crossed long before the opening of *On the Town*. Indeed their histories are strikingly parallel. Both were born in New York City in 1915—Miss Comden on May 3, Green on December 2. They attended New York University together. Both joined the Washington Square Players. In the thirties they were part of a night-club act, the Revuers, an act that also included young Judy Holliday.

. . .

Gershwin's name came up again with the arrival of 1945's first musical, for part of the score was by George's brother Arthur. The show's story sent a navy lieutenant Anthony Caufield (Arthur Maxwell) back to 16th-century Venice and China to establish his virility. Once he does, he wins the hand of the attractive Ghisella. Hollywood's attractive Carole Landis as Ghisella and Sue Ryan as the saucy Licetta were the pillars of the production. Miss Ryan stopped the show with a Will Morrissey interpolation, "Brooklyn, U.S.A." Noel Coward had recently made some disparaging remarks about soldiers from Flatbush, and Miss Ryan assured the audience that a nicely flowered grave awaited the Englishman in the borough. The musical's title was **A Lady Says Yes** (1-10-45, Broadhurst), but the public responded with a firm no. The Shuberts kept it on the boards 11 weeks before calling it quits.

January's other musical was a smash hit. **Up in Central Park** (1-27-45, Century) was a colorful Mike Todd production with a book by Herbert and Dorothy Fields and a score by Sigmund Romberg —his first success in years. Actually both the book and songs were several steps removed from what their authors had once produced—steps down. The brittle, innovative Herbert Fields of the twenties had given way to a librettist willing to write hackneyed, fustian dialogue for a shallow, melodramatic plot. Romberg's tinkly melodies rarely had more than a fragile appeal. Though it called itself a "musical play," it was like so many "musical plays" of ten and twenty years before, essentially an operetta, cleverly minimizing the fact by emphasizing the voguish Americana of its setting, its plot, and its "Currier and Ives Ballet." The ballet, an exquisitely wrought skating scene in Central Park choreographed by Helen Tamaris, was the high point of the evening. Fields' book recounted the exposure and wrecking of the notorious Tweed political clan by the dogged efforts of a *New York Times* reporter, John Matthews (Wilbur Evans). His rewards include the hand of Rosie Moore (Maureen Cannon), the daughter of one of the politicians he attacked. But this marriage takes place only after Rosie annuls a marriage made in pique because of John's attacks on her father. Fortunately for John, Rosie had married a married man. Although Romberg generally avoided the three-quarter time so identified with operetta, his songs were strictly of the genre. A thumping "The Big Back Yard" (Central Park) recalled his earlier marches, while the delicate and sweet "April Snow" reminded oldsters of songs such as "In Our Little Home Sweet Home" from *Maytime* (8-16-17). The hit of the evening was Romberg's attempt to combine contemporary ballad with his arioso style. The result was John and Rosie's interesting, if overblown, love song, "Close As Pages In A Book."

There were no musicals in February. March's lone entry was a failure, albeit a fascinating failure that probably deserved a better hearing. Ira Gershwin and Edwin Justus Mayer adapted Mr. Mayer's 1924 hit *The Firebrand,* calling it **The Firebrand of Florence** (3-22-45, Alvin), and embellishing it was a rich Kurt Weill score. The plot remained the same. Benvenuto Cellini (Earl Wrightson) wins the hand of Angela (Beverly Tyler) after convincing his Duke (Melville Cooper) that he had no share in a conspiracy. Though Max Gordon bestowed a thoughtfully lavish mounting on the work, it folded after 43 performances.

For many, Rodgers and Hammerstein's **Carousel** (4-19-45, Majestic) was the season's triumph. For others, it was the beginning of an era of pretentious solemnity in the American Musical Theatre, an era that attempted to replace the marquee with a steeple. *Carousel* was adapted from Ferenc Molnar's 1921 success *Liliom*. Hammerstein transposed the story to 1873 New England, where Billy Bigelow (John Raitt) is a hard, mean carnival barker at an amusement park carousel. In Agnes de Mille's ballet-pantomime which opened the work and which was her first show ballet that truly moved the plot forward, Billy spots the lovely Julie Jordan (Jan Clayton) and proposes a rendezvous, while Billy's employer, Mrs. Mullin (Jean Casto), watches gloweringly. Julie is attracted to the handsome barker, but she is nonetheless uncertain. Finally she acquiesces. Julie conveys her uncertainty to her friend, Carrie Pipperidge (Jean Darling). Carrie responds, "You're A Queer One, Julie Jordan," and goes on to tell Julie of her ambitious hopes, "When I Marry Mr. Snow." When Billy appears, he is discovered to be unexpectedly shy. He can only talk of his feelings by indirection, letting Julie know how he would act "If I Loved You." By the time "June Is Bustin' Out All Over," Julie and Billy are married. With spring everything seems to be in love. Carrie and Mr. Snow (Eric Mattson) contemplate a glowingly sentimental evening "When The Children Are Asleep." Only the villainous Jigger Craigin (Murvyn Vye) fails to share the happy

reveries. The sailor complains in "Blow High, Blow Low" that he is misunderstood. Billy learns he is about to be a father. At first he is dismayed, but his second thoughts are different. If the child is a boy he will make him into a barker like himself—"Of course, it takes talent to do that well"—if it is a girl, well, he will steal and even die to see that she is supported properly. Carrie warns Julie of the company Billy is keeping, especially Jigger. But Julie can only reply, "What's The Use Of Wond'-rin'." To get money for the expected child Jigger and Billy stage a hold-up, and Billy kills himself when he realizes he will be caught. Julie is comforted by Nettie Fowler (Christine Johnson), who assures her, "You'll Never Walk Alone." In purgatory, Billy demands to be judged by "The Highest Judge Of All," and he is allowed to return to earth to redeem himself and see his now-grown daughter (Bambi Linn). He sees her snubbed on the beach and when she refuses to accept a star he has pilfered vents his fury on himself and the others by slapping her. For this he is returned to purgatory. But he has lingered long enough to witness his daughter's graduation and understand the hope for a future without him both she and Julie hold. The evening had beautifully evocative sets by Jo Mielziner and costumes by Miles White that knowingly re-created a 19th-century New England fishing village. Theatregoers heard better singing than in any show except *Song of Norway*. But the greatness of the evening lay in Richard Rodgers' impressively deep and varied music. Rodgers himself considered his score "more satisfying than any I've ever written"—doubly satisfying because he was aware both Gershwin and Puccini rejected the opportunity to bring *Liliom* onto the lyric stage. Eschewing an overture, the show opened with some startling dissonances in the "Carousel Waltz"—a trick Rodgers hereafter moved from his ballet music to his regular songs—but swiftly proceeded to the thoughtful, elongated musical lines of such diverse hits as "If I Loved You" and "June Is Bustin' Out All Over." Although the show had more music and less spoken dialogue than any lyric offering in years, including an eight-minute soliloquy by Billy, there was no such pretentious announcement as in *Rose-Marie* (9-2-24) or *Chee-Chee* (9-25-28). Songs were listed on the program by title. What few complaints there were about the evening were generally directed at Hammerstein. Both his lyrics and his dialogue were thoroughly professional, but a certain sententiousness was creeping in. In retrospect, hints of the heavy-handed repetition and preachiness of some of his later offerings are easily discerned. His solemnity and sentimentality, coupled with Rodgers' broader new style, suggest that what the new American musical play really had suddenly become was the mid-20th-century native answer to the Continental operetta, the same answer Hammerstein and Kern had hit upon with *Show Boat,* but never properly pursued. If this is true, it might also partially explain the appeal of operettas and operettas disguised as musical plays running so successfully at the time on Broadway. But operetta or no, drawbacks or no, the totality mesmerized most audiences into overlooking the faults.

April, like February, brought in no new shows. But three musicals were ushered in during the last two weeks of May. The first was **Blue Holiday** (5-21-45, Belasco), a Negro variety show starring Ethel Waters, the Hall Johnson Choir, and the Katherine Dunham dancers. Duke Ellington and E. Y. Harburg were among those who supplied interpolations to bolster Al Moritz' uninteresting music. But the performers were not strong enough to fight both their lackluster material and the strong competition around them. The show left after one week.

Then, just as two jazz *Mikados* had appeared almost back to back during the 1939–40 season, two musicals derived from *H.M.S. Pinafore* came in a week apart to close out the month. But, unlike the earlier duplication which, since one show had consciously copied the other, produced two similar pieces, the new shows took quite different tacks. About all they had in common, other than their source, was that they were both flops.

The first to arrive was **Memphis Bound!** (5-24-45, Broadway). It wrapped its excerpts from Gilbert and Sullivan's work in a sentimental bit of 19th-century Americana. A contingent of black performers boards the *Calliboga Queen* bound for Memphis. The boat hits a sandbar, and the actors start a performance of *Pinafore* to earn money to pay for the ship's release. But the performers are jailed for not having a license. A trial and acquittal follow. Besides using much of *Pinafore*'s material, the show offered extensive excerpts from *Trial by Jury,* since, as one performer noted, " 'Trial by Jury' is always on the same program with 'Pinafore.' " Don Walker and Clay Warnick's songs, when not lifted intact, still utilized *Pinafore* melodies with original, if consciously old-fashioned, words. For example, "The Nightingale, The Moon And I" recalled the "tale" songs of Pixley and Luders, and other allegorical ditties of their contemporaries. Of course, the production's "boogie-woogie accents" were new to Gilbert and Sullivan. As was so often the case with earlier black shows, dancing was its forte. In this case the dancing was especially good, with sixty-seven-year-old Bill Robinson tapping his way up and down flights of stairs, spelled by the more sinewy, soft-shoe routines of a lavender-garbed Avon Long. But the fine stepping was no lure in a season of such strong competition. *Memphis Bound!* folded after 36 showings.

Hollywood Pinafore (5-31-45, Alvin), with William Gaxton and Victor Moore as its stars, outran its rival by only 17 performances. Its approach was precisely the opposite of *Memphis Bound!* It was contemporary and satirical, with George S. Kaufman providing the book and lyrics for his former *Of Thee I Sing* associates. In Kaufman's new version Joseph W. Porter (Moore) lords it over the Pinafore Studios in Hollywood where the hack writers, led by Ralph Rackstraw (Gilbert Russell), dress in prison stripes and Dick Live-Eye (Gaxton) is an agent interested solely in his percentage. Recognizable Hollywood names such as Louhedda Hopsons (a combination of the two leading gossip columnists, Hedda Hopper and Louella Parsons, played by Shirley Booth) rubbed elbows with the original Gilbertian figures. Some of Kaufman's material was superb. His version of Buttercup's song contained delicious references to the Orson Welles–Rita Hayworth marriage and to Welles' feud with William Randolph Hearst that followed the release of *Citizen Kane.* They were as witty as Gilbert's allusions to the figures of his day and also caught the unctuousness of then contemporary columnists (revealing why Kaufman's character was sometimes called Butter Up):

Poor Rita's divorcin' that awful man Orson
(I'm making that up to please Hearst);
And Alice Faye may be expecting a baby
A year from next October first.

Even the dialogue reflected a certain Gilbertian formality:

Ralph: For you will be my father-in-law, and in accordance with an old studio custom I now sign you for *twice* your old salary or twenty times what you are worth.

Regrettably, too many of Kaufman's darts apparently missed their mark. Max Gordon gave it an excellent mounting, including an Anthony Tudor ballet depicting the rise of a Hollywood starlet. Called "Success Story," it used melodies from a number of Sullivan works, but none from *Pinafore.* Viola Essen danced the central figure. The ballet was highly praised, even though it ran against the satiric intent of the rest of the evening. Like *Memphis Bound!*, *Hollywood Pinafore* was not sufficiently strong in all its points to compete with better offerings occupying so many Broadway stages. It succumbed to its inadequacies and the heat.

Concert Varieties (6-1-45, Ziegfeld) was another vaudeville, assembled this time by Billy Rose when he realized *Seven Lively Arts* would not make it through the spring. It was better than most, but still not strong enough to buck the competition and the heat. Deems Taylor served as master of ceremonies, announcing such acts as Imogene Coca in a demonstration of how to wear fur coats, Zero Mostel giving a political speech, and Eddie Mayehoff mimicking famous actors. The Salici Puppets offered a variety show within a variety show, while Jerome Robbins created a ballet, "Interplay," to Morton Gould's music. When *Concert Varieties* closed, it ended the string of vaudevilles that had kept theatres lit intermittently over the preceding three seasons.

1945-1946

More or less inevitably, both the number of shows and their quality fell slightly in the first postwar season. The astonishing number of long runs held over from the preceding year deprived incoming musicals of choice houses. Few of the theatres converted to movies or radio had owners who would willingly reconvert them to legitimate offerings. The vast adjustments demanded by the change from war to peace threw both writers and their audiences off-balance, so that just as a pattern seemed discernible something happened to make it seem no pattern at all.

Two operettas began the season. Neither seemed anxious to be considered an operetta though one did acknowledge it on its sheet music—in very small type. **Marinka** (7-18-45, Winter Garden) came first. George Marion, Jr., and Karl Farkas' book was the latest in the countless retellings of the Mayerling mystery. The score was by Emmerich Kalman, of recent years a refugee in America. Kalman apparently made some efforts to compose in contemporary modes. Because "Cab Song" suggested "The Surrey With The Fringe On Top," a few playgoers waggishly branded the show a Viennese *Oklahoma!* (3-31-43). But most of Kalman's score retained his old three-quarter-

time sweep, even if melodies such as "One Last Love Song" were not transparently Middle European. Comparison with *Oklahoma!* was unavoidable with Joan Roberts (the original Laurey) playing the title role and Harry Stockwell (Curly in a road company) as Crown Prince Rudolph. Neither of these attractive youngsters garnered the kudos won by Luba Malina for her performance as the Archduke's discarded mistress. A veteran of the Mayerling era, Ethel Levey, appeared briefly in the cameo role of Madame Sacher, doyenne of Vienna's famous hotel. Critics also praised the peasant costumes Mary Grant designed for Albertina Rasch's lively Hungarian dances. If the evening seemed largely "old hat," it was nonetheless pleasant enough to earn a modest run of 21 weeks.

Mr. Strauss Goes to Boston (9-6-45, Century) followed nearly two months later. It told of the waltz king's (George Rigaud) visit to Boston in 1872, of his flirtation with Mrs. Brook Whitney (Virginia MacWatters), and of Frau Strauss' (Ruth Matteson) winning him back with the aid of President Grant (Norman Roland). The plot was reminiscent of the still-popular *Song of Norway* (8-21-44), while the Strauss family had been on stage before in *The Great Waltz* (9-22-34). Besides the fine singing and spectacle these earlier mountings had offered, both used the cherished melodies of the composers they depicted. *Mr. Strauss Goes to Boston* relied instead on a lame score by Robert Stolz. Stolz had been a popular Viennese figure, and, like Kalman, was a refugee, but he had never enjoyed an extended vogue on this side of the Atlantic. His new score was no help. Though Miss MacWatters' glittering coloratura interpretation of the "Laughing Waltz" brought down the house and though several critics were heartily amused by Strauss' worshipful admirers screaming and swooning much as bobbysoxers were doing for Frank Sinatra, these better moments could not compensate for a general inadequacy. The show folded after a week and a half.

At the end of the month **Carib Song** (9-27-45, Adelphi) attempted to provide a vehicle for Katherine Dunham and her dancers. It told a serious, tragic story of an unfaithful woman, her fisherman lover, and her husband's revenge. There was an element of pretension in the attempted universality of the characters. They were not given names but were identified simply as "The Woman," "The Fisherman," "The Husband" or "The Boy Possessed by a Snake." Nor was the setting more specific than a "Small West Indian Village." The dancing was excellent, while Jo Mielziner's sets and Motley's costumes seemed appropriately lush. The cast of top Negro entertainers included Avon Long as the villain. But the book was indifferent, Baldwin Bergersen's score much better, yet the whole affair stranded at a never popular, out-of-the-way theatre. *Carib Song* languished for 36 performances.

On October 6 two more operettas appeared. One was a revival of *The Gypsy Baron* as part of the City Center opera season. The other, **Polonaise** (10-6-45, Alvin), recounted Kosciuszko's experience both in the American Revolution and in an uprising he finds when he returns to Poland. He also finds time to woo the lovely Marisha. The story jumped back and forth between the United States and Poland, injecting a slightly confused, frenetic tone into the telling. The music was attractive and familiar. It was all by Chopin, adapted with lyrics by John Latouche. Chopin's polonaises became the source of the show's ballet music. The evening received a critical drubbing, and much of the head-shaking was prompted by Jan Kiepura's atrocious acting. Robert Garland headed his *Journal American* notice "Ham and Eggerth." But Kiepura and Marta Eggerth (Mrs. Kiepura) had won a host of admirers in their recent revival of *The Merry Widow*. This loyal following helped *Polonaise* achieve 113 performances, despite the critical rejection.

On the other hand critical kudos and long lines at the box office greeted *The Red Mill* (9-24-06) after its October 16 bow at the Ziegfeld. Herbert and his generation had considered the work a musical comedy, but the increasing simplicity and shortened musical phrases of modern melodies—plus the musical's age—caused most commentators to look on it as operetta. Paula Stone, the daughter of its original costar Fred Stone, was coproducer. And Stone's more celebrated daughter, Dorothy, was in the cast as Tina, along with Michael O'Shea (Con), Eddie Foy, Jr. (Kid), and Odette Myrtil (Madame La Fleur, a role not in the original). There were some minor, harmless revisions, mostly to keep the dialogue from sounding dated. A few new lyrics were added, some characters were also added, and some character roles were expanded, while Gretchen's lover was now Captain Hendrik Van Damn instead of Captain Doris Van Damn. But for the most part, the story, score, and tone of the original were faithfully retained and lovingly revived. The show ran 531 performances, falling just 27 performances short of doubling the 1906-07 run. A long, highly successful tour followed.

November was active and uneven. Its first premiere was a dim-witted affair called **The Girl from Nantucket** (11-8-45, Adelphi) which struggled through a 12-performance stay. Walella Waldorf, writing in the *Post,* summed up the critical consensus when she noted, "It lacks everything." The book depicted the confusion that ensued when a house painter is mistakenly selected to create a mural at a museum. The score was by Jacques Belasco, his only big-time effort.

More talented, more experienced hands collaborated to create **Are You With It?** (11-10-45, Century) They succeeded, almost in spite of themselves. Sam Perrin and George Balzer's book was adapted from George Malcolm-Smith's novel, *Slightly Imperfect.* It told the kind of story that set the show several years behind the times. Wilbur Haskins (Johnny Downs) is fired from his insurance company job after he misplaces a decimal point. A carnival barker known as "Goldie" (Lew Parker) persuades him to join the carnival. Wilbur is a nervous, literal, serious-minded young man who unself-consciously orders a glass of milk at Joe's Bar Room. After he falls in love with Vivian Reilly (Joan Roberts), he calms down. The show's idea of humor was to have a character in one train compartment misconstrue instructions for taking a photograph ("move over," "get it all in") being offered in the next compartment. One clever, if appropriately obsolete, device was the use of silhouettes to open the show. An entire boarding house was seen getting out of bed, getting dressed and ready for work. The suggestive glimpses of nudity led into a song packed with double entendres, "Five Minutes More In Bed," with which a minor character, Marge (Jane Dulo), and a fast-stepping ensemble launched the evening. The score was the last one Harry Revel produced for Broadway. Although his Hollywood hits included "Did You Ever See A Dream Walking?", the best he could do for New York was a song such as "Here I Go Again." With no other good, fresh shows in sight, *Are You With It?* got off to a flying start and ran through the season.

In his review of the next musical to open, Louis Kronenberger of *PM* noted that, "Most musicals this season have been exercises in torture." In a small way, the new arrival improved matters. **The Day Before Spring** (11-22-45, National) was an innovative, melodic musical that didn't quite work and didn't quite make it. It reunited Alan Jay Lerner and Frederick Loewe, of *What's Up?* (11-

11-43), and furthered what soon became one of the most fruitful of lyric partnerships. Although Lerner approached his book thoughtfully and maturely, his story, at least in outline, could, like the plot of *Are You With It?*, have been the plot of a 1920s musical. Moreover in execution Lerner still manifested a clumsy, heavy hand. The Peter Townsends return to Harrison University for their tenth reunion. There Katherine Townsend falls in love again with Alex Maitland and decides to run away with him as she had tried to a decade before. Their car broke down then and breaks down again on this second elopement. But all is forgiven, or at least understood. To tell some of the story Lerner allowed Anthony Tudor to conceive a ballet for each of the principal characters, retelling significant incidents from different points of view. The device, which seemed clever on paper, proved repetitious and tedious on stage. The happiest aspect of *The Day Before Spring* was its wide-ranging, infectious collection of songs: the sober considerations of the title song and "You Haven't Changed At All," the bubbly gaiety of "I Love You This Morning," the simple joys of "A Loaf Of Bread, A Jug Of Wine And Thou, Baby," and the then still popular Latin undercurrents of "God's Green World." The show had a first-rate cast headed by Hollywood's Irene Manning as Katherine and Broadway's Bill Johnson as Alex. But the show's faults ultimately told, and it closed after 21 weeks.

Betty Comden and Adolph Green, who had worked so profitably with Leonard Bernstein on the thoroughly contemporary *On the Town* (12-28-44), now sat down with Morton Gould to produce a brash and not altogether feeling or faithful look at the bygone twenties. That the era was completely out of fashion at the moment didn't help the show's reception. Somehow even the title **Billion Dollar Baby** (12-21-45, Alvin) suggested World War II figures rather than the millions the twenties talked about. And the songs were completely contemporary, with only the tiniest hints of the real tempos and chromatics of the period. The plot recorded the desperate rise of pushy, calculating Maribelle Jones (Joan McCracken), who ditches her sweet boyfriend for a dangerous gangster on the run, soon finds herself attending a lavish gangster funeral and finally settles for a rich tycoon just before the 1929 crash. The show touched on all the favorite stereotypes of the era: the underworld, the bull market, and the great annuals (here called the "Jollities"). Much of the action took place around "Chez Georgia," where the twenties' wild hostess, Texas Guinan, lived again in Mitzi Green's impersonation of Georgia Motley. It was ersatz twenties in a day that rejected even the real thing. Still, with little real new competition in sight, *Billion Dollar Baby* was able to hold on for nearly seven months.

But in fact, there was something from the twenties the forties could embrace, and that was *Show Boat* (12-27-27). Hammerstein gave it a sumptuous revival at the Ziegfeld on January 5, 1946. Both critics and theatregoers rejoiced. The revival confirmed what had, since *Oklahoma!* (3-31-43) and *Carousel* (4-19-45), seemed likely: that, fifteen years ahead of its time, *Show Boat* had determined the basic form and inaugurated the era of great American musical plays. With a fine cast headed by Jan Clayton (Magnolia), Charles Fredericks (Ravenal), Kenneth Spencer (Joe), and Carol Bruce (Julie), the revival played for a full year. Joy at the success of the revival was tempered somewhat by the sudden death of Jerome Kern two months before, on November 11, 1945. He had come to New York to aid in the production and to write the songs for a new musical Rodgers and Hammerstein were to produce for him. For this revival he provided Broadway with one final song, "Nobody Else But Me."

Show Boat excepted, as far as the rest of the twenties, the public wanted little of it. A good revival of *The Desert Song* (11-30-26) at the City Center three nights after *Show Boat* caused no great stir, although Walter Cassel was present to bring his fine voice to the part of "The Red Shadow." Between these two openings Bobby Clark tried unsuccessfully to make a modern musical comedy of Molière's *Le Bourgeois Gentilhomme*, **The Would-Be Gentleman** (1-9-46, Booth), using Lully's music.

A popular star of the twenties, Eddie Cantor, returned to Broadway on January 21, but only as a producer. In keeping with the current fascination for Americana, he presented a musical built around the adventures of **Nellie Bly** (1-21-46, Adelphi). When *The World* assigns Miss Bly (Joy Hodges) the task of beating Phileas Fogg's fictitious eighty-day circumnavigation of the globe, *The Herald* hires Phineas T. Fogarty (Victor Moore) to thwart her. Frank Jordan (William Gaxton), the *Herald*'s managing editor, decides to accompany Fogarty. Miss Bly not only makes good, she makes Jordan fall in love with her. The book was by the relatively inexperienced Joseph Quillan, but the tunes were in the hands of the competent Johnny Burke (words) and James Van Heusen (music). The dances were snappy, if patently old-fashioned; the best were tapped out by an all-male specialty act, The Debonairs. Besides the stars, Benay Venuta was on hand with a capital performance as an aging "toughie," Battle Annie. But the mixture failed to jell. *Nellie Bly* gave up in far less time than it took its heroine to make her trip.

Having returned to Broadway two seasons before in the brilliant *One Touch of Venus* (10-7-43), Mary Martin heightened her reputation by appearing in a fine, off-beat "love story with music," **Lute Song** (2-6-46, Plymouth). Based on a 14th-century Chinese play, *Pi-Pa-Ki*, by a writer known either as Kao-Tong-Kia or Tse-Tching, it had been worked into an American play in the late twenties by the distinguished dramatist Sidney Howard and Will Irwin. It could find no commercial takers for a number of years. The producer, Michael Meyerberg, engaged Raymond Scott to provide the songs. As the prologue announces, "It is a venerable tale of the time when the gods walked upon earth and wrought their magic in the sight of men." The scholarly Tsai-Young has refused to take the examinations at court, preferring to remain at home with his beautiful wife. But she and his parents prevail on him to go. His wife comforts him with her vow to remain loyal: "Mountain High—Valley Low." He does so well in the examinations he is appointed Chief Magistrate. As a result he is forced to marry the daughter of Prince Nieou Chi. His attempts to communicate with his family are blocked. His mother and father die of starvation and his wife is reduced to beggary. She treks across the country and appears at his house. The Princess recognizes her. Sympathetic and knowing, she arranges for the wife to be reunited with her pining husband. Even the harsh Prince is touched by their obvious love and agrees to annul the second marriage: "What the Voice of Jade has ordained; the Voice of Jade may revoke." If Ward Morehouse in the *Sun* found Robert Edmond Jones designs filled with "unearthly beauty," in the *Times* Lewis Nichols went so far as to insist, "Mr. Jones' settings, costumes and lighting are the heroes of the evening." Jones achieved many of his effects through stylization and simplicity, often relying on shadings of a single hue to color a set. Unfortunately, *Lute Song* was too esoteric for mass appeal. Even at an intimate theatre, it ran only 142 times.

A lavish, brassy, conventional musical comedy followed a week later. In **The Duchess Misbehaves** (2-13-46, Adelphi), Woonsocket faints and dreams he is Goya cavorting with the Duchess of Alba. Jackie Gleason started in the part of Woonsocket, but, realizing how hopeless the show was, left during the tryout. Joey Faye and Audrey Christie performed the main parts during all of the show's five New York performances.

Nancy Hamilton resurrected her intermittent revue series when **Three To Make Ready** followed the duchess into the Adelphi on March 7. The cast featured Brenda Forbes, Gordon MacRae, Harold Lang, Bibi Osterwald, Meg Mundy, Carleton Carpenter, and Arthur Godfrey—almost all names on the way up. But its star was Ray Bolger, and his dancing brightened an otherwise ordinary evening. "The Old Soft Shoe," Bolger's solo in straw hat, striped blazer, white pants, and cane stopped the show. Bolger also displayed his comic talents in such skits as "Kenosha Canoe," a spoof on the new-style musical play, purporting to show how Rodgers and Hammerstein might adapt Dreiser's *An American Tragedy*. Morgan Lewis was back to write the songs with Miss Hamilton, but songs on the order of "A Lovely, Lazy Kind Of Day" had little power outside the theatre.

St. Louis Woman (3-30-46, Martin Beck) was another interesting show that failed to make a big splash. It told of the loves of Della Green (Ruby Hill), a leading Negro beauty in turn-of-the-century St. Louis. Actually there was little reason for the show to be set in the period, but the suggestion of another slice of Americana didn't hurt among the faddists. Della is fickle. She's Biglow Brown's girl until the jockey, Little Augie (Harold Nicholas), has a winning streak that makes him the talk of the town. The vengeful Brown (Rex Ingram) beats Della, and Augie in turn promises to even the score. But before he can, Brown is shot by a woman he rejected. He curses Augie. Unnerved, the jockey starts losing races, and when he does he loses Della. But when his good luck returns Della is back to help him celebrate. The book by Countee Cullen and Arna Bontemps, from Bontemps' novel *God Sends Sunday*, left something to be desired. But the score by two solid professionals, Harold Arlen and Johnny Mercer, often helped it through the weak spots. Arlen created one of his classics for this show, Augie and Della's "Come Rain Or Come Shine," and Mercer gave Pearl Bailey, in a comic-relief role, show-stopping lyrics for "Legalize My Name." Harold Nicholas and his brother Fayard did the show's brightest hoofing. Rouben Mamoulian gave the evening a dramatic staging. His crowd scenes at the end of each act reminded playgoers of his stunning ensembles for *Porgy and Bess*. The first-act finale was a rousing cakewalk; the second act concluded with a funeral, while the last curtain fell on a mob watching a race from the wrong side of the fence.

Just as the City Center mounted *The Gypsy Baron* at the same time *Polonaise* was being presented, and then brought back *The Desert Song* when Hammerstein was offering *Show Boat*, its revival of an older black show, *Carmen Jones* (12-2-43), followed *St. Louis Woman* by one week.

Call Me Mister (4-18-46, National) was the first original musical of the season that could be unhesitatingly labeled a smash hit. It had fun with the mustering-out process and with its not always kind looks back at army life. Its ex-soldiers imagined the problems Paul Revere might have had, had he tried to procure his horse through modern army red tape; they discerned Noel Coward influences in the air force; and in "South Wind" they depicted the snail's progress in enlightening three southern senators. The veterans also stopped for a reverent moment of respect to their former commander-in-chief with "Face On A Dime." But the runaway hit of the show had little to do with the armed forces. Betty Garrett as a canteen hostess, exhausted from the rhumbas and congas her partners danced, pleaded, "South America, Take It Away!" Although the song was the only number in Harold Rome's score to achieve national prominence, it helped *Call Me Mister* to a run of over 700 performances.

On May 12 the City Center opera added *The Pirates of Penzance* to its repertory.

Four nights later, the biggest hit of the season arrived. **Annie Get Your Gun** (5-16-46, Imperial) was the Rodgers and Hammerstein production that Jerome Kern had been slated to write the songs for. With Kern's death, Irving Berlin was called in and during the short interval between then and the rehearsals composed what was immediately recognized as his greatest score. Like most of the shows of the day, *Annie Get Your Gun* was set in 19th-century America. But it made no pretense of being a serious musical or advancing the art of the "musical play." *Annie* set out solely to entertain. It entertained so well because it was far more artful than some of its more aggressively noble competitors. And it entertained so well it ran 1,147 performances in New York; a road company had Mary Martin as star and the show was a four-year smash in London. Annie Oakley (Ethel Merman) is a poor but happy country girl—happy to proclaim "I Got The Sun In The Morning." She and her family have made do on native intelligence, "Doin' What Comes Natur'lly." Her sharpshooting soon makes her the rage of Buffalo Bill's Wild West Show. Sharpshooting is her life, but being of a susceptible age she finds herself falling in love with her costar Frank Butler (Ray Middleton). But Butler's ideal for "The Girl That I Marry" is a far different woman from the tough, outspoken Annie. Annie can only despair, "You Can't Get A Man With A Gun." But she has one consolation: she is a member of the greatest profession on earth. She and her cohorts agree, "There's No Business Like Show Business." And to top it all off she's initiated into an Indian tribe and can exult, "I'm An Indian, Too." She and Frank agree at least part way about romances, "They Say It's Wonderful." But Frank is especially jealous of Annie's superior marksmanship. He knows it in his heart, though he maintains a brave front as they argue, "Anything You Can Do (I Can Do Better)." Only on one point is it a draw—neither can bake a pie! They remain at odds until Chief Sitting Bull (Harry Bellaver) takes Annie aside and makes her realize that only by intentionally, but discreetly, losing a match to Frank can she win him. She does just that. The Herbert and Dorothy Fields book was well crafted. The exposition was particularly fine, quickly drawing principal characters amusingly, yet poignantly. Annie first appears shooting a bird that turns out to be a decoration on a lady's hat. The incident occurs in front of a small-town hostelry that Annie hopes to supply with game so she can support her young sisters and brothers. Annie presents the proprietor with another example of her shootings:

Annie: Look it over, Mister. Look it over keerful. Lift up his wings. See? No buckshot in that bird. Jes' one little hole in his head.
Wilson: Mighty pretty shooting!
Annie: Mighty pretty eatin', too. Fer evvy one I get ye, ye gotta give me two nickels and a dime.
Wilson: Can't hurt to try them. I'll take two dozen.
Annie: How many is that?
Wilson: Twenty-four.
Annie: [*to her brothers and sisters*] Who do we know kin count up to twenty-four?

Fine as the Fields' libretto was, Berlin's songs really raised *Annie* to its heights. They ranged from the solid ballad melody of "They Say It's Wonderful" to the openhanded joy of "I Got The Sun In The Morning." "There's No Business Like

Show Business" has become something of a professional anthem in the years since its debut. Rodgers and Hammerstein gave the show a stunning staging. And Ethel Merman established herself beyond any recall as the leading musical comedy star of her generation. Ray Middleton, who had been struggling on the sidelines since *Roberta,* was a virile, believable Frank.

No one thought that Orson Welles was anyone but Orson Welles when he arrived two weeks later to close the season as the villainous Dick Fix with his adaptation of Jules Verne's novel, the title abbreviated to **Around the World** (5-31-46, Adelphi). Welles appeared in all sorts of disguises, and even performed a magic show. He filled the stage with circus performers and animals and staged a miniature train wreck. Cole Porter provided the words and music, which were generally mediocre. His one good number, "Should I Tell You I Love You?", sung by Mary Healey, was lost in the mayhem. The critics were unkind, but the show ran 75 performances and might have made a modest go of it had not its late arrival forced it into the hot weather. In the August heat the show's scenery joined the ashes of *Nellie Bly.*

1946-1947

It was a curious season. Fine dramas and comedies were abundant and diversified. Better straight plays included *The Iceman Cometh, All My Sons, Joan of Lorraine, Another Part of the Forest, Years Ago, John Loves Mary, Present Laughter,* and *Happy Birthday.* Up at Columbus Circle, the American Repertory Theatre emerged to offer the bright, if short-lived, hope of a permanent dramatic company. As far as musicals were concerned, the season saw the new, more sober, intellectualized approach to lyric theatre settle in comfortably. A superficial survey of the season's musicals might suggest "sober" was an ill-chosen word. All through the theatrical year, angels, fairies, leprechauns, and evil spirits reveled in song and dance. The season's most successful lyric work was set in a miraculous village. Happily, the quality of the fantasy was noteworthy. In the best works, it was employed with intelligence, imagination, a respect for tone, and a sense of style. It made a concerted attempt to replace Americana as the reigning vogue. When it failed or petered out, the *Show Boat–Oklahoma!* school was assured a

prolonged hegemony. But for this single season attempts to confront hard-nosed reality, regardless of approach, met with disappointment. The commercial debacle of the most seriously considered, genuinely artful of the season's musicals warned Broadway of the public's still-limited tolerance, even for these new "musical plays." The count of new musicals held relatively steady, but it wasn't until the very end of 1946 that the first interesting new piece appeared. The first smash hit of the season didn't arrive until January 1947.

The perennial ice revue opened the season. The latest edition was called **Icetime** (6-20-46, Center). It introduced its audience to Mary, Mary, Quite Contrary; Old King Cole, and the Candy Fairy as well as talking it to Sherwood Forest and back to the Good Old Days. Faithful followers of the series rewarded it by flocking to Sixth Avenue for a full year.

Icetime's only summer competition was **Tidbits of 1946** (7-8-46, Plymouth), a revue which a number of young professionals derived from a Youth Theatre revue. Their cast was more experienced, a number of them refugees from the preceding season's failures. For example, The Debonairs escaped the wreckage of *Nellie Bly* to dance again, while Joey Faye, without his misbehaving duchess, brought over his "Flugle Street" number from vaudeville. Joseph Marais and Miranda's South American rhythms contrasted with Muriel Gaines' black songs. However, nothing was original or inviting enough to buck the heat, so the revue folded after one week.

Two months elapsed before the main season began with **Yours Is My Heart** (9-5-46, Shubert). This American version of Lehar's last major operetta, *The Land of Smiles,* brought prewar Vienna's great matinee idol, Richard Tauber, to the New York stage to re-create the story of a Chinese prince's foredoomed romance with a Paris opera star. Tauber was no longer in his prime, and when throat trouble began to plague him the show was forced to close after only a month's run.

A second operetta followed twelve nights later. **Gypsy Lady** (9-17-46, Century) was a pastiche of Victor Herbert melodies from five of his earliest works—primarily *The Fortune Teller* (9-26-98) and *The Serenade* (3-16-97)—set to a new book by Henry Myers. Myers' story was a half-serious, half-tongue-in-cheek reconstruction of a typical turn-of-the-century comic-opera plot. André (Gilbert Russell), the marquis of Roncevalle, proposes to Musetta (Helena Bliss), a gypsy princess, believing she was a princess royal in disguise. She is also beloved by the dashing Alvarado (John Tyers) and a strong strapping gypsy Sandor (George Britton), each of whom has an appropriate song with which to beguile her. In the end, blood proves stronger than wine. The show was originally done on the West Coast by Edwin Lester's excellent organization, the same group that had brought *Song of Norway* (8-21-44) east two seasons before. It was given a sumptuous production, fine comedians (headed by Jack Goode), and superb singers. But Broadway had succumbed to its adulation of the new musical plays, and *Gypsy Lady* was patently old-fashioned—a conspicuously vulnerable target. Unkindly received, it left after ten weeks.

October's only musical was the unlikely revival of *Naughty Naught ('00)*, a novelty first offered New York January 23, 1937. But what had seemed good, harmless fun ten years back no longer appealed. The show came to naught, with only 17 performances.

November's two musical offerings were both disappointments. Much had been hoped for from Max Gordon's production of **Park Avenue** (11-4-46, Shubert). After all, it had a book by Nunnally Johnson (so successful in Hollywood) and George S. Kaufman, lyrics by Ira Gershwin, and music by Arthur Schwartz. The story centered upon Mrs. Sybil Bennett (Leonora Corbett), a New York socialite. She is the sort of charity worker who during the past war had busied herself with gathering "Bundles for Britain" and, now that the war is over, heads a group trying to get the bundles back. However, her real passion seems to be darting in and out of marriages—so many marriages she cannot keep the facts and figures straight. Sybil's confused family tree almost discourages a gentlemanly young southerner, Ned Scott (Ray McDonald), from marrying her daughter, Madge (Martha Stewart). To everyone's dismay, the book proved heavy-handed, relatively humorless, and lacked enough plot twists to sustain it for two and a half hours; Schwartz' music sounded humdrum. The quality of the show's lyrics may be judged by the absence of a single excerpt in Kimball and Simon's fascinating collection of Gershwin material, though in his *Lyrics on Several Occasions* Ira included five examples that show flashes of his former pyrotechnic—at least on paper. *Park Avenue* made a brave nine-week bid for business. When it took its leave of Broadway, so did Ira Gershwin. Old age, death, and Hollywood continued depleting the ranks of those who had made the last great era so bright and fun-loving.

Katherine Dunham and her fine Negro ensemble thought they had a successor to *A Tropical Revue* with a second entertainment based on black dancing from around the world, **Bal Negre** (11-7-46, Belasco). Broadway didn't agree, at least not in sufficient numbers to keep the show running beyond two months.

The ever-popular Cinderella story was the basis of **If the Shoe Fits** (12-5-46, Century), which tried to combine a sometimes off-color musical comedy book (the godmother became Cinderella's sporty rival) with all the primary colors of childhood. The result, in the "Fabulous Kingdom of Nicely," was often more a clash than a blend. Ingenious sets that popped out like the illustrations in some children's books were one uniquely attractive feature. Lacking the excellent casting and tinkly tunes of *The Lady of the Slipper* (10-28-12, Century), the show, booked way uptown, could find no audience.

Nor could **Toplitzky of Notre Dame** (12-26-46, Century), which was quickly rushed into the same house three weeks later. The angels so admire Toplitzky's (J. Edward Bromberg) nonsectarian passion for Notre Dame's football team they send a fellow angel (Warde Donovan), who was a former football star, down to Toplitzky's Tavern and allow the angel to help Notre Dame beat Army. When the angel, christened Angelo, falls in love with Toplitzky's daughter, his cohorts above also allow him to stay on earth happily ever after. Although both the Irish and the Jews were staunch theatregoers and the musical obviously hoped to draw support from both groups, neither appeared especially interested. When the show folded it took with it some pleasant Sammy Fain music (with words by Jack Barnett) such as "Love Is A Random Thing."

On the same night that *Toplitzky* opened, **Beggar's Holiday** (12-26-46, Broadway), John Latouche and Duke Ellington's updating of *The Beggar's Opera*, premiered. In the new version Macheath became an American gangster. With the leading role played by Alfred Drake, so recently *Oklahoma!*'s Curly, the audience could muse over whether the stage gangster wasn't simply a nasty first cousin to the stage cowboy. Latouche retained the strange amalgam of the original: its viciousness, its cynicism, and its likability. It was an eminently theatrical combination. Regrettably, the tone would prove inimical to the subtle, untheatrical harmonies of Ellington's essentially intimate music. Much of Latouche's sting and Ellington's intimacy was lost in the cavernous auditorium of the large, inconvenient Broadway Theatre. As far as the public was concerned, the whole piece didn't quite come off. It survived a far from satisfactory 14 weeks.

Bloomer Girl returned for a brief, popular-priced stay at the burgeoning City Center on January 6, 1947. (In May the Center also revived *Up in Central Park.*) But the year's first new musical waited until three nights later to raise its curtain. **Street Scene** (1-9-47, Adelphi) was a faithful, largely uncompromising adaptation by Elmer Rice of his 1929 dramatic hit. The poet Langston Hughes composed the lyrics, and Kurt Weill created the score. Rice retained his original story, which dealt principally with the short-lived, star-crossed romance of Sam Kaplan (Brian Sullivan) and Rose Maurrant (Anne Jeffreys), and with the fatal consequences of the infidelity of Rose's mother (Polyna Stoska). These stark, poignant themes were played out on a single set depicting a seedy row of brownstones and with a number of character vignettes as a basso ostinato. Characters included Sam's communist father, the impoverished, improvident Mrs. Hildebrand and her children who are about to be dispossessed, a happy Italian music teacher and his German wife, and the screams of a woman in delivery. The honesty and power of the book came as no surprise, but the excellence of Hughes' lyrics undoubtedly startled those Broadway types unfamiliar with him. The naturalness and directness of his lines were close to the ideal Hammerstein had been crusading for. Only when he attempted to revive the old "Love Nest" motif did Hughes go astray. In grasping for fresh images he overreached. The simple home for two was carried off in flights of fancy. Weill's score reflected his propensity for jittery, abbreviated musical lines and for startling, noncommercial harmonies. The music was thoughtful and appropriate, but not readily salable. Only the atypical "Moon Faced, Starry Eyed," sung and danced by two minor characters, Mae (Sheila Bond) and Dick (Danny Daniels), received some attention outside the theatre. *Street Scene*'s fundamental somberness discouraged all but the most dedicated playgoers. The Shuberts aggravated matters, as was their wont, by giving the off-beat evening an off-the-beat theatre. *Street Scene* compiled only a modest run of 148 performances, though it soon drifted into the repertory of the New York City Opera.

The next evening a splendidly theatrical musical danced and sang its way onto the stage at the convenient 46th Street Theatre. **Finian's Rainbow** (1-10-47, 46th St.) succeeded where *If the Shoe Fits* and *Toplitzky of Notre Dame* had failed, by making fantasy a popular alternative to the rage for Americana. No doubt this unworldliness represented as much an escape from postwar turmoil as did flight to an earlier era. But period costumes were easy to design, while workable fantasy proved tricky to sustain. As a result the vogue for fantasy persisted for just one season, although attempts to keep it alive continued with markedly less success for several ensuing seasons. Superficially, *Finian's Rainbow* resembled the early and mid-thirties musicals in its left-wing leanings as well as in its somewhat topical and satirical bent. But its politics was tempered by wit, melody, and, most of all, by a fundamentally sunny, compassionate disposition toward even those it was laughing at. On the other hand, its more or less unhappy, sentimental ending suggested a certain earnestness of purpose that seemed quite contemporary.

Finian McLonergan (Albert Sharpe) arrives in America from Glocca Morra, Ireland, with his daughter Sharon (Ella Logan) and with a crock of gold he has stolen from the leprechauns. He hopes to plant the gold at Fort Knox and watch it grow. He is pursued by Og (David Wayne), a mischievous leprechaun. They find themselves in Rainbow Valley, Missitucky, where Sharon falls in love with handsome Will Mahoney (Donald Richards). Their romance is complicated by Og, who has fallen for Sharon. Og is particularly nervous because he seems to become more and more a mortal with each passing day. But he still retains enough magic to turn the Negro-hating, xenophobic Senator Billboard Rawkins white after Sharon has inadvertently turned him black by making a wish in the presence of the crock. Rawkins (Robert Pitkin), a parody of the very real Mississippi Senator Bilbo and Representative John Rankin, complains, "My whole family's been havin' trouble with immigrants ever since we *came* to this country." Og also gives the power of speech to mute Susan Mahoney (Anita Alvarez), a young lady who finds expression in dance. When Og realizes the futility of his passion for Sharon, he settles for Susan, admitting, "When I'm not near the girl I love, I love the girl I'm near." Will also discovers his love for Sharon can never be fully reciprocated. Sharon confesses that Finian has no pot of gold and that his beloved Glocca Morra exists only in his mind. But it remains a lovely place nonetheless, and as she and her father head off to continue their wanderings, she expresses the hope, "may we meet in Glocca Morra some fine day."

E. Y. Harburg and Fred Saidy's lyrics were a delight. To Og they gave an inventive speech and two delicious songs, "Something Sort Of Grandish" and "When I'm Not Near The Girl I Love." His heart was "in a pickle" and "not too partickle." A Negro trio singing "The Begat" could note that when the begetting got under par they gave birth to the ladies of the D.A.R. There were zesty Burton Lane love songs such as Woody's "If This Isn't Love"; romantic reveries such as Sharon's "Look To The Rainbow." However, the hit of the evening—the biggest hit to come from Broadway during the season—was "How Are Things In Glocca Morra?" That it was sung in the show by Scottish Miss Logan and that the stream it mentioned would have had to cover half of Ireland to touch all the towns it supposedly lapped bothered no one. The show ran out the rest of the season and all through the following one.

While Broadway gladly capitulated to fantasy all season long, only once did it allow itself the pleasure of nostalgia. The producers who had so succesfully resuscitated *The Red Mill*, closed January with a second Victor Herbert revival, *Sweethearts* (9-8-13), at the Shubert. Herbert's score was faithfully retained, as was most of the original libretto, although again the dialogue was heavily doctored. The principal change was the enlargement of the part of Mikel Mikeloviz, to serve as a vehicle for the show's star, Bobby Clark. Clark fought battles with his shortened cane, while he and his cigar wreaked havoc on Zilania's laundry. The integrity of the show was in no way compromised, but its hilarity was enhanced inestimably. Mark Dawson, Gloria Story, and Robert Shackleton sang the romantic leads.

No musicals appeared in February, but three arrived in the space of four nights in March. The first was merely a one-man show, but the one man was Maurice Chevalier, and even if his actions during the war had cast a shadow on his good name, his reputation as an entertainer was unsullied. He packed the small Henry Miller for 46 performances.

A fine revival of Oscar Straus' 1909 hit, *The Chocolate Soldier*, bowed two nights later, March 12. Despite the excellent singing of Frances McCann as Nadina and the presence of the genial Hollywood clown Billy Gilbert and his catalogue of sneezes as Popoff, the public failed to respond. Once again part of the problem may have been

that the evening was housed at the out-of-the-way Century, across from Central Park. A second part of the problem was that respect for old operettas was at its nadir, while a third reason was undoubtedly that one operetta had already bucked the disdain and captured the market, thanks as much to Bobby Clark's drawing power as to its own merits.

But the almost equally inconvenient Ziegfeld welcomed the season's biggest hit the next evening. Like *Finian's Rainbow*, **Brigadoon** (3-13-47, Ziegfeld) told an unworldly tale. An offstage chorus set the scene, describing how two hunters lost their way one night on a murky brae. The hunters were two postwar Americans, Tommy Albright (David Brooks) and Jeff Douglass (George Keane). Something eerie pervades the woods in which they are lost—"Something," as Tommy says, "about this forest that gives me the feeling of being in a cathedral." Suddenly distant voices are heard, singing of a valley filled with love. Just as suddenly Tommy and Jeff see a village they hadn't noticed moments before. They arrive in the quaint village in the midst of a fair. In fact it is a sort of double celebration, for two of the villagers, Jean MacLaren (Virginia Bosler) and Charlie Dalrymple (Lee Sullivan), are shortly to be married. Jean's older sister Fiona (Marion Bell) should have married first, but Fiona has not found the right man and insists she is willing to spend her remaining days "Waitin' For My Dearie." Jeff is quickly taken in hand by the brash Meg Brockie (Pamela Britton), while Tommy and Fiona strike up a friendship. Charlie arrives. He "used to be a rovin' lad" but promises hereafter "I'll Go Home With Bonnie Jean." Tommy offers to go walking with Fiona through "The Heather On The Hill," but a storm prevents them. Meanwhile Meg has lured Jeff to a shed, where she confesses how many men have been "The Love Of My Life." Unfortunately she has not been the love of theirs. Still, she is willing to try again. At the MacLaren house Charlie arrives to sign the family Bible, and, although he knows tradition prohibits him from seeing his bride until the wedding, he begs Jean, "Come To Me, Bend To Me." Tommy, who has left an unhappy love affair in New York, is exhilarated by the charming Fiona. He feels "Almost Like Being In Love." But he is also a bit troubled. Brigadoon and the villagers are odd. They have refused to accept American money; they have never heard of telephones. When he discovers that Charlie has signed the Bible with the date "1746," he can no longer restrain himself. He demands Fiona tell him why Brigadoon is so odd. She takes him to the village schoolmaster, Mr. Lundie (William Hansen), who reveals that their minister was disturbed by encroaching outside influences and so took himself off one night to a hill beyond the town:

There in the hush of a sleepin' world, he asked God that night to make Brigadoon an' all the people in it vanish into the Highland mist. Vanish, but not for always. It would all return jus' as it was for one day every hundred years. The people would go on leadin' their customary lives; but each day when they awakened it would be a hundred years later. An' when we awoke the next day, it was a hundred years later.

There is a catch, Mr. Lundie adds. None of the villagers may leave or the spell will be broken. But that is precisely what seems about to happen, for the churlish Harry Beaton (James Mitchell), who had hoped to marry Jean himself, threatens to depart and destroy the miracle. In a forest chase Harry is killed when Tommy inadvertently trips him. Although Tommy feels he will be lost without Fiona and tells her of his love in "There But For You Go I," and "From This Day On," he is so upset by the killing he determines to return to New York. There his nagging girl friend makes life unbearable. Before long Tommy and Jeff are again seated in the Scottish woods, with Tommy wondering if there is some way to make Brigadoon reappear. Once more they hear the townspeople singing of Brigadoon, and Mr. Lundie appears. As he leads Tommy away he remarks, "when ye love someone deeply anythin' is possible."

Although the show established Alan Jay Lerner and Frederick Loewe in the front ranks of the American Musical Theatre, it was not faultless. The second act sagged a bit and had a jarring change of tone in the New York scene. Moreover the involutions of "There But For You Go I" and the pretentious solemnity of "From This Day On" were too heavy for so light and romantic a piece. But the freshness of the setting and the story counterbalanced some of the shortcomings. In having the hero kill the villain and in the rich Agnes de Mille chase-ballet, it successfully subscribed to the new stage conventions of the day. Moreover, it reminded some of *Oklahoma!* (3-31-43) in its Ado-Annie-like Meg. The lovely score helped popularize the work. "The Heather On The Hill" and "Almost Like Being In Love" were instant commercial hits, while Al Jolson, on his radio appearances, gave "Come To Me, Bend To Me" national recognition.

The new fashion in musical plays militated against the old collegiate musical. Nonetheless George Abbott courageously brought in **Barefoot Boy with Cheek** (4-3-47, Martin Beck). The gag-filled Max Shulman libretto—on a par with his best-selling comic novels—described the riotous attempts of Yetta Samovar (Nancy Walker), a campus "pink," to convert all of the University of Minnesota (and especially the Alpha Cholera Fraternity) to her political thinking. She would also like to win the heart of Asa Hearthrug (Billy Redfield), but loses him to Clothilde Pfefferkorn (Ellen Hanley). Precisely why Shulman set such oddball people with oddball names on a legitimate campus is uncertain. But the brilliant clowning of Nancy Walker kept such questions from being explored.

. . .

Nancy Walker was born into a theatrical family in Philadelphia on May 10, 1921, and christened Anna Myrtle Swoyer. Her father was a vaudevillian who used the stage name Dewey Barto. Trained at the Professional Children's School in New York, the comedienne made her debut in *Best Foot Forward*. Following a brief stint in films, she returned to Broadway in *On the Town*. Short, and cynical-miened, Miss Walker excelled at wise-cracking overreachers whose pretensions are quickly punctured. One critic observed that, whenever she struck an attitude, the attitude struck back.

. . .

The show's glaring weakness was its songs, Sidney Lippman's only Broadway score. The fun on stage would have been enough to secure *Barefoot Boy with Cheek* a respectable run five or six years earlier. But changing tastes and the summer heat took their toll.

A double bill of contemporary operas got off to an uncertain start but soon met with astonishing success. Gian Carlo Menotti's **The Telephone** and **The Medium** (5-1-47, Barrymore) were intimate pieces ideally suited to a small legitimate playhouse. They were written in a musical idiom that was at once contemporary and readily acceptable. Although the writing was popular by serious standards, it was serious by popular measurement. Menotti kept studiously away from *avant-garde* composition. Moreover he told two good stories.

The Telephone was little more than an old vaudeville sketch with only two singers. When the constant ringing of Lucy's phone prevents Ben (Frank Rogier) from proposing, he leaves, goes to a pay-phone and proposes to Lucy (Marilyn Cotlow) from there. *The Medium* recounted the last agonies of the charlatan Madam Flora (Marie Powers). She goes mad and determines to kill the evil spirit she believes has beset her. Instead she accidently kills her deaf-mute assistant. None of the arias enjoyed a commercial vogue. But good notices, good word-of-mouth and the appeal of something different allowed the bill to achieve 212 showings.

The season ended, as it began, with a new ice show. Actually much of **Icetime of 1948** (5-28-47, Center) was held over from the previous edition. No one cared. Like its predecessor it ran a full year.

1947-1948

There were half a dozen highly entertaining musicals to cheer theatregoers during the season, even if all were flawed, none truly first-class. Every one of these hits gave the man in the street a song he liked to whistle; some even produced two hit songs. Yet there was an inadequacy about the scores. The hit tunes, like the shows they came from, were not the best their creators had offered. Constant propagandizing about the artfulness of the new musical play did, nonetheless, have certain interesting effects. By and large, even in the lightest popular musical comedies some additional effort was made to relate songs to plot, to give a feeling of cohesiveness and a pervasive unity of tone. However, the most obvious influence of the school of *Show Boat* and *Oklahoma!* was the setting of more and more pieces in an earlier America.

The season's first offering confirmed the vogue. **Louisiana Lady** (6-2-47, Century) was a four performance fiasco with a score by Monte Carlo and Alma Sanders. Carlo and Sanders had been absent from the New York scene since they suffered an even worse debacle with the single-performance run of their *Mystery Moon* (6-23-30). They had spent most of the twenties trying to repeat the success of their *Tangerine* (8-9-21), apparently forgetting that show owed most of its popularity to its star and an interpolation. The failure of

Louisiana Lady may well have brought such painful truths home to them, for they never again wrote for Broadway. "When You Are Close To Me" typified the dullness of their last work. A musical version of Samuel Shipman and Kenneth Perkins' 1927 *Creoles*, *Louisiana Lady*'s setting resembled that of *Early to Bed* (6-17-43). Convent-trained Marie-Louise (Edith Fellows) leaves Miss Browne's Finishing School to visit her mother, Madame Corday (Monica Moore), who runs a fashionable bordello in 1830 New Orleans. Madame Corday had been forced into the trade by the villainous Merluche (George Baxter), but she and her girls and customers go to great lengths to make her house seem like a home to Marie-Louise. Merluche appears, hoping to court Marie-Louise, and her life takes an ominous turn until she is rescued by a good-natured pirate.

Four months passed between the opening of *Louisiana Lady* and the premiere of the next lyric piece, **Music in My Heart** (10-2-47, Adelphi). This "romantic musical play" was another operetta in the *Blossom Time* (9-29-21) tradition, this time using Tchaikovsky melodies to embellish a story of his purported romance with the French singer, Desirée Artot. The show made its concession to the new ballet rage right at the start, opening with a comparatively classic-style ballet entitled "The Storm," but apart from setting the mood of old St. Petersburg it had little relation to the story. A fine cast headed by Robert Carroll (Tchaikovsky), Martha Wright (Desirée), Vivienne Segal, and Charles Fredericks was the evening's pillar of strength. They supported it through its four-month run.

Under the Counter (10-3-47, Shubert), an importation from London, could generate no interest and folded after 27 showings despite the presence in the cast of Cicely Courtneidge (as a black-marketeering actress) and Wilfrid Hyde-White.

The season's biggest musical hit, **High Button Shoes** (10-9-47, Century), dressed its conventional musical comedy book in modish period costumes. It allowed its bungling small time con-man, Harrison Floy (Phil Silvers), to return to 1913 New Brunswick, New Jersey, and be greeted by his innocent old neighbors as an up-and-coming tycoon. He and his crony, Mr. Pontdue (Joey Faye), are embraced with special warmth by the Longstreets (Jack McCauley and Nanette Fabray). Harrison switches from selling not-quite right automobiles to selling land. But when the townspeople discover the land is useless swamp, Floy is forced to flee. He takes the money, Pontdue, and Mrs. Longstreet's sister, Fran (Lois Lee), to Atlantic City. A wild Keystone Cop chase ensues. Fran returns to New Brunswick and to her boy friend, the Rutgers football player, Hubert Ogglethorpe (Mark Dawson). Floy also reappears, promising to make amends. To get enough ready cash, he bets on Princeton in the forthcoming game with Rutgers, tries to get Rutgers' team to throw the match, and when Rutgers wins finds himself on the run again. The book, which Stephen Longstreet based on his semi-autobiographical novel, *The Sisters Liked Them Handsome,* was not especially witty, but Phil Silvers' rough-and-tumble clowning kept audiences laughing. Miss Fabray and Jack McCauley stopped the show twice with Jule Styne's best melodies, the foot-stomping polka, "Papa, Won't You Dance With Me?" and the sentimental soft-shoe "I Still Get Jealous."

. . .

Jule Styne (originally Julius Stein) was born in London on December 31, 1905. His family moved to America when he was eight, settling in Chicago. His musical parents began his piano lessons at an early date, and, to their delight, the youngster proved a prodigy, making appearances with symphony orchestras in Chicago and Detroit. After attending Chicago Musical College, he renounced serious composing and established his own dance band. His work brought him to Hollywood's attention, where he soon teamed with lyricist Sammy Cahn. Their hits included "I've Heard That Song Before," "It's Been A Long, Long Time," "I'll Walk Alone," and "Five Minutes More." He and Cahn went their separate ways shortly after the opening of *High Button Shoes,* Cahn remaining in Hollywood, while Styne returned only intermittently.

. . .

Good as Styne's score was, the highlight of the evening was Jerome Robbins' uproarious Mack Sennett Ballet, in which Floy and Pontdue are chased by the villagers, bathers, Keystone Cops, and a bear. The chase ends in a jumbled pyramid of bodies capped by a flag-waving cop.

What promised to be an even bigger hit opened the next evening. **Allegro** (10-10-47, Majestic) was Rodgers and Hammerstein's third collaboration, and the first which Hammerstein did not adapt from an older work. Instead of revising an existing, tightly-knit plot, Hammerstein composed a loose, rambling chronicle recounting the life of an ordinary upper-middle-class professional. He planted a Greek-like chorus at the side of the stage to set the scenes and comment on the action. The chorus' costumes announce it is again the turn of the century—1905 in fact. The singers inform their listeners that the woman in the bed is Joseph Taylor's wife, Marjorie. Marjorie (Annamary Dickey) has just given birth to a son, Joe, Jr. Joe's father (William Ching) already has plans for him to be a doctor, but Marjorie refuses to think so far ahead. Grandma assures them both that time will handle the child in its own way. We start out "foolishly small," but we're soon adult. Grandma (Muriel O'Malley) has seen it happen before, and she knows it will happen again. When Joe takes his first step the chorus exhorts him to move first one foot out, then the other foot, first foot, second foot, first foot, second foot. Now the chorus exults that the whole world belongs to Joe. Time passes. Joe (John Battles) is ready for college. He is still a little shy and naïve with girls, but everything will come naturally in due course, After all, Dr. Taylor assures his wife, "A Fellow Needs A Girl." Joe overhears and thinks to himself, "They're funny when they're by themselves—not like a mother and a father. A fellow and a girl—like Jenny and me—almost." And all the while he is away at school he remains faithful to Jenny (Roberta Jonay), writing her "You Are Never Away." Jenny is not completely happy waiting for Joe to get his feet on the ground, and her ambitious father is no help. Meanwhile, at school Joe halfheartedly courts other girls. His line to them in his flings is to insist they hardly know each other "So Far." In the end Jenny waits, and when Joe finishes college they marry. The chorus chants repeated good wishes to the couple. More time passes. It is the depression, and Jenny's father has lost his business. Life is hard for a small-town doctor, and Jenny would push Joe on to bigger things. He finally acquiesces, though he knows it will sadden his parents. Joe is successful in Chicago, almost too successful. Social and professional pressures mount. To the despair of his nurse Emily (Lisa Kirk), Joe is blind to Jenny's cheating on him. Affectionately Emily complains, "The Gentleman Is A Dope." Just as he is about to accept an important new appointment, Joe finally learns that Jenny is unfaithful. Voices from his past sing out to him, and Joe declines the new post to return to his small town. Although the characterizations were reasonably good, the book and lyrics were assertively sentimental, rarely humorous, and filled with the drabness and repetition of everyday speech. Agnes de Mille was again Rodgers and Hammerstein's choreographer, but the rambling story failed to inspire any fine ballet. "So Far" and "A Fellow Needs A Girl" did become independently popular, and their success played no small part in the 315-performance run of *Allegro.*

On October 30 Edith Piaf brought a Continental vaudeville into the Playhouse for 44 showings beginning the end of October. After her premiere, over a month elapsed before the next musical appeared. **Caribbean Carnival** (12-5-47, International) was a black revue filled with the lusty, exotic rhythms of Africa and Latin America. Pearl Primus paced the dancers. But Katherine Dunham had demonstrated that Broadway would rarely support an entire evening of such relentless vitality. The show survived for only 11 performances.

Six nights later a more conventional intimate revue met with immediate acclaim and inaugurated a spate of relatively successful examples of this once-popular type. For a brief time it looked as if revues might stage a comeback. But television's fast-paced, star-studded variety shows soon overwhelmed these more modest entertainments, whose quality, in any case, fell below the great offerings of bygone seasons. **Angel in the Wings** (12-11-47, Coronet) featured the dancing and clowning of Paul and Grace Hartman, the droll monologues of Hank Ladd, and the singing of Elaine Stritch. The Hartmans, who had been seen primarily in vaudeville and night clubs, made themselves at home in the intimate Coronet. Their sketches included a hilarious cooking demonstration in which a husband grew increasingly queasy as his wife detailed each step for frying snails in yoghurt. Ladd wore a rowboat as he toured the St. Lawrence looking for Florence, whom he had lost on one of the Thousand Islands. Miss Stritch had the hit of the evening in "Civilization," in which she renounced the uncertain joys of the modern world, and insisted, "Bongo, Bongo, Bongo, I don't want to leave the Congo." The song had not been written for the show, but was hastily added when it became a runaway success on the air. Its authors were the men who had written most of the score, Carl Sigman and Bob Hilliard.

A revival of *The Cradle Will Rock* (6-16-37) played briefly over the holidays. The critics were not as harsh on the work as many of them once had been. Nevertheless, good times and the Christmas spirit made Marc Blitzstein's "angry, theatrical prank" seem especially dated. A fine cast led by Alfred Drake performed earnestly, but to no avail.

The year ended with the first postwar visit of the D'Oyly Carte Opera Company, who embarked on an 18-week stay December 29, proffering such old favorites as *The Mikado, Trial by Jury, The Pirates of Penzance, Iolanthe, Cox and Box, H.M.S. Pinafore, The Gondoliers, The Yeomen of the Guard,* and *Patience.*

1948's first musical was the season's second revue hit. **Make Mine Manhattan** (1-15-48, Broadhurst) had sketches and lyrics by Arnold B. Horwitt and music by Richard Lewine, whose only other complete scores had been written for the Krimsky's American Music Hall pieces in the thirties. One pleasant, unexceptional number, an urban hoe-down that served as the first-act finale, "Saturday Night In Central Park" enjoyed a passing vogue. But the evening's principal joys were its comedians, Joshua Shelley, David Burns, and Sid Caesar. In "Subway Song" Shelley sang a hilarious plaint of a young man who lives at one end of the subway system and whose girl lives at the other end. The marshmallowy dishes and bird-size portions served by restaurants such as Schrafft's were spoofed in "Trafts," where you can eat all night and not affect your appetite. In the show's best sketch Sid Caesar played a cocky, wasp-named Hollywood director, come to make a film in New York. He assures the mayor that once the film is released New York will become world famous. But most of his time is spent arguing with a bystander (Burns) who would tell him how to shoot the film. The director doesn't get angry until the man makes a suggestion about the gloves a performer is wearing. At that point the director not only loses his temper, he loses his English accent as well, for if there's one thing he really knows it's the glove business. Theatregoers remembered that at least one major Hollywood mogul had once been a glovemaker. Colorfully mounted by Hassard Short, well sung, peppily danced, and superbly clowned, *Make Mine Manhattan* ran over a year.

A brassy, contemporary musical called **Look, Ma, I'm Dancin'** (1-29-48, Adelphi) bounced in next. Jerome Robbins and George Abbott had conceived the evening as a vehicle for Nancy Walker. Miss Walker played Lily Malloy, a brewery heiress, who underwrites a ballet company, travels with it, and ultimately dances with it and modernizes it. Jerome Lawrence and Robert E. Lee's dialogue was commonplace and Hugh

Martin's score facile. One song did slip away to earn some national prominence, "Shauny O'Shay," sung in the show by a lesser character, Suzy (Sandra Deel) and the chorus. Most of the other songs were jazzy and momentarily clever, but not memorable. What lifted the show above its material was Abbott and Robbins' fast-paced staging, Robbins' dances (with Harold Lang in the main parts), and Miss Walker's inspired lunacy. At the end of the first-act finale Miss Walker fought off a stage full of dancers, grabbing a floral arrangement that an usher had brought down the aisle. She felt she was entitled to it, since she had paid for it and sent it to herself. Miss Walker and her troupe danced merrily on for just short of six months.

Beginning February 20 Gertrude Lawrence and Graham Payn sang those songs featured in Noel Coward's *Tonight at 8:30,* which was revived for a short stay, while nine nights later Maurice Chevalier returned for a second consecutive season with a one-man show.

March and April went by without producing any new musicals until the very last day of April. Then the season's third major revue, **Inside U.S.A.** (4-30-48, Century), raised its curtain. The show was the most elaborate of the three and, on paper, promised to be the most exciting. John Gunther's best seller of the same name had provided the inspiration. Beatrice Lillie and Jack Haley were returning to Broadway to be its stars and with them came the feline dancer Valerie Bettis, handsome, strong-voiced John Tyers, and the bumptious Hoosier monologist, Herb Shriner. Moss Hart, Arnold Auerbach, and Arnold B. Horwitt (of *Make Mine Manhattan*) wrote the sketches, while Howard Dietz and Arthur Schwartz were reunited to provide the songs. It became apparent as soon as the show began its tryout that its material fell short of everyone's high hopes. The lone hit to emerge from the score was the somewhat stiff, overblown "Haunted Heart," sung in the show by Tyers. Actually the lighter numbers were better. In a laundry list song Haley enumerated, sometimes seriously, sometimes not, the main attraction of each state, concluding "Rhode Island Is Famous For You," while in the first-act finale, "First Prize At The Fair" (which Dietz considered the best song in the show), the whole cast sang of a boy who lost all the contests but nonetheless won a girl's affection. Haley and Miss Lillie as two Indians adamantly informed palefaces, "We Won't Take It Back." Haley taught waiters how to be rude to customers, while Miss Lillie played a bitch whose snide, throw-away remarks ruin an actress' first night (she also used the actress' hair brush to clean her shoes). The comedienne became a gay Mardi-Gras participant ("cherchez la femme they were playing/I was the femme they were cherchezing"); and the leader of a choral group singing an ode to Pittsburgh (where smoke gets in your eyes). Miss Bettis danced the part of a Chicago gun moll. If *Inside U.S.A.* was a disappointment, the quality of competitive revues was no better, so the show was able to run a year.

One outside event which conceivably prevented more tunes for the show from becoming popular was the ASCAP strike. Composers and lyricists withdrew radio and recording privileges, until their demands for better terms were met. As a result the airwaves—long the principal method of popularizing a song—played largely uncopyrighted music, so new shows whose music was written after the strike began went temporarily or permanently unrecorded. *Inside U.S.A.* recorded its "original cast" album just before the deadline. But since it had to be produced in advance of the opening it was in the unique position of including a song cut during its tryout.

Three musicals closed out the season during the start of May. Another contemporary collegiate musical attempted to buck the trend and failed. **Hold It!** (5-5-48, National) was the work of several young unseasoned musical hands and showed it. The claptrap book was by Matt Brooks and Art Arthur. Their escapade begins when a picture of Bobby Manville (Johnny Downs), dressed as a girl for his part in a Mask and Pudding show, is submitted to a Hollywood beauty contest. Naturally, Bobby wins and has to spend the rest of the evening explaining away his victory. In the end, his girl Jessica (Jet McDonald) goes to Hollywood in his stead. Sam Lerner did journeyman lyrics for Gerald Marks' pleasant, inconsequential tunes, the best of which was "Always You."

The following night, May 6, a masterwork by some old, experienced hands was revived at the Martin Beck, but by 1948 the twenties and its shows were considered frivolous and obsolete. In fact it was probably this very season, just before *Lend An Ear* (12-16-48) came to make theatregoers reconsider, that the disdain for the era of wonderful nonsense was at its most rampant. As a result *Sally* (12-21-20) would have probably failed under all but the most miraculous circumstances.

Bambi Linn and Willie Howard were good in the roles Marilyn Miller and Leon Errol had originated but they could not perform wonders. Worse, the producers hurt the integrity of the show by "modernizing" the book (though retaining the essentials of the original story) and by interpolating songs from other Kern shows. This new *Sally* ran a mere 36 times compared to 570 performances for Ziegfeld's production.

The Experimental Theatre, operating at the old Maxine Elliott, presented a triple bill on May 9 under the title **Ballet Ballads.** It was so well received it was rushed up to the Music Box. All three one-act plays had music by Jerome Moross and lyrics by John Latouche; each had a different choreographer. In each show a singer and a dancer shared the principal roles. *Susanna and the Elders* depicted the legend as retold by a parson at a revival meeting. *Willie the Weeper* was essentially a two-character piece (considering the singer and dancer who played Willie as one), in which Willie runs the gamut of drug-induced moods in his "Untidy Mind." Two songs, "Willie, The Weeper" and "Cocaine L'll," provided the idea for the sequence. *The Eccentricities of Davy Crockett* sang and danced a series of Davy's tall tales: his marriage to a mermaid, his saving his country from Haley's comet. The excitement generated by the opening and the fine reviews dissipated with the summer heat. *Ballet Ballads* folded July 10, providing a slightly downbeat ending for the season.

1948-1949

This was one of the greatest seasons in Broadway history. Just why so many fine shows appeared so suddenly was baffling, but Broadway was too grateful to ask questions. Although *Variety* listed only 76 productions, the quality and diversity of the season made it the best since the heyday of the 1920s. John Chapman, selecting the ten top works for the *Burns Mantle Best Plays* series, awarded places to *Death of a Salesman; Anne of the Thousand Days; The Madwoman of Chaillot; Detective Story; Edward, My Son; Life with Mother; Goodbye, My Fancy; Light Up the Sky; The Silver Whistle;* and *Two Blind Mice.* He could find no room for two of the American Musical Theatre's masterpieces, *Kiss Me, Kate* and *South Pacific,* not

to mention other innovative, gorgeously melodic works that abounded in this theatrical year.

The season began inauspiciously on June 3 with an inept musical version of the Ichabod Crane legend called **Sleepy Hollow.** It came into the St. James, which had been occupied happily for six years with *Oklahoma!* The house found itself looking for a new tenant after just a week and a half.

The annual ice revue, **Howdy, Mr. Ice!** (6-24-48, Center), had songs by Al Stillman and Alan Moran, but they were no different from the numbers Littlefield and Fortis had composed for the earlier ice shows. The public couldn't have cared less. It came to see the shimmering spectacle and got it. The skaters took the audience to Trinidad, to an African safari, to the Himalayas, and introduced it to Little Bo-Peep. Patrons kept the box office happy for 406 performances.

September brought a rerun of the 1946 revival of *Show Boat,* this time at the City Center's popular prices. The same low prices prevailed when the house revived *The Medium* and *The Telephone* in December and *Carousel* in late January.

Comedian Morey Amsterdam led the bill in a revue named **Hilarities** (9-9-48, Adelphi). The evening was little more than glorified vaudeville, although much of Amsterdam's humor would have been too bawdy for B. F. Keith. Other acts included Al Kelly in his time-tested double-talk routine and the popular radio and night club singer, Connie Stevens. Ballroom dancers and acrobats helped fill the bill. No one found it very satisfying; *Hilarities* lasted less than two weeks.

A far more stylish, traditional revue opened six nights later. **Small Wonder** (9-15-48, Coronet) featured a number of entertainers who would shortly receive prominence: Tom Ewell, Alice Pearce, Jack Cassidy, Mary McCarty, and Joan Diener. Some of its sketch material was by George Axelrod (who would soon write Ewell's big hit, *The Seven Year Itch*), and the dances were by Gower Champion. Unfortunately the producer went for his music to Albert Selden and to Baldwin Bergersen, who had a record of failures to his discredit and with this show departed from the Broadway scene. Their contributions were lackluster. Their best number brought Mary McCarty on stage in a cloche and a betasseled dress to sing with tongue-in-cheek longing of the "Flaming Youth" of the twenties. The song was a harbinger of a revival of interest in the decade which *Lend an Ear* shortly would stimulate. In a fetching monologue Ewell demonstrated the superiority of the Model T Ford to the human body (perhaps unconsciously furthering affection for the twenties). The talented youngsters kept the show running for 134 performances and might have had a greater success had not the higher prices postwar production costs forced on the show necessitated a relatively steep ticket charge, and had not so much better competition come along demanding its share of that dollar.

Rising production costs were such that the next two musicals lost $650,000 between them—a frightful sum for its day. There was little sympathy for the losses incurred by **Heaven on Earth** (9-16-48, New Century), a dim-witted, banal, and unmelodic affair that ran 12 performances. It tried to be another *Finian's Rainbow*, but lacked that show's redeeming charms. James Aloysius McCarthy (Peter Lind Hayes), a Central Park horse-hack driver, befriends a young couple who are so poor they live in a tree. With the help of a pixy named Friday (Dorothy Jarnac), he sets them up in a model house. The outraged, blustering builder (David Burns) has the whole gang arrested, but McCarthy's imitation of Hollywood stars convinces the builder to let the nuts go. The score was by Jay Gorney, who was almost at the end of his career. John Murray Anderson directed it (with an uncredited assist from Eddie Dowling), and Raoul Pène du Bois designed the sets and costumes. For many, du Bois' sets were the saving grace of the evening, notably in a magnificent re-creation of Central Park and in a comic, push-button-bedeviled "Hutton Home Of Tomorrow." His efforts were futile; the show seemed beyond anyone's help.

Far more deserving of hearing was **Magdalena** (9-20-48, Ziegfeld), a production by Edwin Lester's California-based group that had offered *Song of Norway* and *Gypsy Lady*. Unfortunately, all most New Yorkers heard were arguments over the show's merit. It was indisputably the most controversial musical in several seasons. Those who admired it, praised its intense, colorful score by Heitor Villa-Lobos, the distinguished Brazilian composer, its Ziegfeld-like opulence (at the Ziegfeld, appropriately), and its cast of fine singers. Its detractors decried its stolid book, the lack of obvious commercial appeal in the score, and the seemingly unnecessary lushness of its staging. The musical's principal story, set in the tropical richness of Colombia, recounted the efforts of simple, devout Maria (Dorothy Sarnoff) to convert her

cocky, bus-driving fiancé Pedro (John Raitt) to Christianity. A subplot described a revolt in an emerald mine, a general (Hugo Haas) sent to restore order, and the mistress (Irra Petina) he brings along. Villa-Lobos made no concessions to popular taste, discarding the conventional AABA formula in favor of free-flowing melodies. Robert Wright and George Forrest saddled the songs with too strivingly poetic lyrics. For example, the title song, saluting the great river, announced the river's "mother is the snow" and her "love is the sea." The public hesitated, then decided to wait for more surefire entertainment. *Magdalena* closed after 11 weeks.

The public did not have long to wait for a more patently commercial offering. **Love Life** (10-7-48, 46th St.) fell easily into the consciously artful patterns now in vogue. It was innovative and purposeful. Like the preceding season's *Allegro* (10-10-47), it was essentially a chronicle, but it added an element of fantasy or allegory by following the vicissitudes of a single marriage through 150 years of American history. Instead of a Greek chorus to propel and comment on the action, simulated vaudeville turns performed "on one" between meatier scenes. The couple in question are Sam and Susan Cooper. In 1791 they are reasonably happily married, with two attractive children. As they moved from 1821 to 1857 to 1890 the stresses and strain of staying together begin to tell. By the 1920s cynicism and infidelity are apparent. The second act is set entirely in the present, and the marriage is on the rocks. But a stylized minstrel show offers hope that things can be set right again. The show's philosophy was summed up in a song which kept arguing, "That's good economics, but awful bad for love." If Alan Jay Lerner's libretto was as uneven as it was loose-jointed, the show had several compelling assets. Nanette Fabray and Ray Middleton, both at top form, were the stars. And the score—not by Lerner's customary partner, Loewe, but by Kurt Weill—was delightful. The prolonged ASCAP strike deprived it of some of its deserved recognition. Still, the Coopers' caressing "Here I'll Stay" and Susan's jaunty "Green-Up Time" enjoyed some circulation, despite Lerner's still occasionally uneasy lyrics. The show displayed gaudy scenery and had the requisite ballets. Both were good, although unexceptional. The mixed critical reaction to *Love Life*'s novelty, the waning appeal of fantasy and the stunning competition that appeared all through the season took its toll. *Love*

Life's 252-performance run would have seemed excellent ten or twenty years before, yet in a day of rising costs it meant a disappointment.

Where's Charley? (10-11-48, St. James), a musical version of *Charley's Aunt,* was noticeably more conventional than *Love Life.* George Abbott provided the serviceable, if surprisingly leisurely adaptation, and directed the show as well. George Balanchine devised the choreography. The critics, while receptive, were not overwhelmed, and the show got off to, at best, a respectable start. There was little indication that it would run over two years. Three virtues most likely contributed to its surprising durability. Most conspicuous was its star, Ray Bolger, in the best role he ever had. His transvestite clowning was innocent good fun, and his soft-shoe routines (one performed partly atop a piano) enchanting. He was supported by a sterling cast that included Byron Palmer (Jack Chesney), Doretta Morrow (Kitty Verdun), and Allyn Ann McLerie (Amy Pettigue). Secondly, word soon spread that *Where's Charley?* was not only good fun; it was good clean fun. As a result the show began to profit from a youth market that Broadway had rarely tapped in recent years. With time Frank Loesser's brilliant score overrode the obstacles of the ASCAP strike.

. . .

Frank Loesser was born in New York on June 29, 1910. Although he came from a musical family—his father taught piano—he was given no formal musical education because of an early lack of interest on his part. In his first efforts at songwriting he was content to write lyrics to other men's music. His clever way with words was immediately appreciated, and from the beginning he set rhymes to melodies by topflight composers such as Burton Lane, Jimmy McHugh, Hoagy Carmichael, Arthur Schwartz, and Jule Styne. During World War II he tried his hand at both words and music, creating two memorable successes: "Praise The Lord And Pass The Ammunition" and "[The Ballad Of] Rodger Young." Like Jule Styne before him, he left a profitable Hollywood career to try his luck on Broadway.

. . .

One fine ensemble number, "The New Ashmolean Marching Society And Students' Conservatory Band," showed fresh, tongue-in-cheek iconoclasm, just as off-beat counterpoints in Charlie and Amy's duet "Make A Miracle" similarly announced the arrival of an exciting new talent. Jack and Kitty's love song, "My Darling, My Darling,"

became one of the season's most popular ballads. In the long run, "Once In Love With Amy" has proved the enduring favorite. It was a second-act show stopper which Bolger put over, alone in front of the show curtain, with his droll delivery and incomparable dancing. When the song became generally known, Bolger cajoled his audiences into singing along.

October's last musical was a Sigmund Romberg operetta with another of his beloved plots of thwarted love. **My Romance** (10-19-48, Shubert) was a musical version of Edward Sheldon's 1913 hit, *Romance.* To the most likable melodies Romberg had written in a long while—they were far more in his natural style than his songs for *Up in Central Park*—the great prima donna Cavallini once again fell in love with Reverend Armstrong, and once again ran off to a life of song and celibacy rather than hinder his chances for advancement in the church. The principal roles were superbly sung by the dashing Lawrence Brooks and the ravishingly beautiful Anne Jeffreys. The Shuberts gave *My Romance* a surprisingly loving and careful mounting. In keeping with an old operetta tradition, each of the three acts employed only a single set. But reaction against the favorite forms of an earlier era was at its height. Not only did the public and critics fail to respond, but rumors were circulated suggesting one of the Shubert brothers had actually composed some of the melodies attributed to Romberg. Romberg and the Shuberts had worked together for nearly forty years, but by a sad coincidence *My Romance* was the last Romberg score heard in his lifetime and the last show to carry the banner "The Messrs Shubert present." The musical struggled through an unhappy run of three months.

A joyous, uninhibitedly old-fashioned musical followed and met with a livelier reception, thanks to a brightly colored Mike Todd production, the side-splitting antics of Bobby Clark and, to a lesser extent because of the ASCAP strike, a superior Jimmy McHugh score. Coming in an election year the show's plot could be considered topical, though it was set four years in the future, just after the 1952 election. **As the Girls Go** (11-13-48, Winter Garden) imagined what would happen with the election of the first woman President, Lucille Thompson Wellington (Irene Rich). But though the show occasionally touched on politics and changes a woman would bring about (there are now Secret Service Women attending her), it was largely a burlesque romp in which her husband, Waldo (Clark), the First Gentleman, cavorts with all the beautiful, scantily-clad girls in sight, and helps and hinders his son Kenny's (Bill Callahan) romance with Kathy Robinson (Betty Jane Watson). One of its biggest laughs came from a topical sight gag when Waldo, sitting in a barber's chair, is asked if a visitor who has always wanted to see the inside of the White House might look at the room. When the visitor arrived he proved to be an actor impersonating Thomas Dewey, who had just suffered the most stunning upset in American history in his second bid for election. More than any other musical score of the season Jimmy McHugh's excellent tunes (with lively Harold Adamson lyrics) were caught up in and hurt by the ASCAP strike. By the time the strike was settled and recordings could come out again, there were newer and equally good or better songs for artists to work with. McHugh's material was the best he had done since the original *Blackbirds* (5-9-28). It went from solid ballads such as Kenny's "You Say The Nicest Things, Baby" and his "I Got Lucky In The Rain" to the lusty title song, sung by Clark and the chorus. Clark also helped put over a show-stopping comic number in "It Takes A Woman To Take A Man." Adamson and McHugh even gave a hint of things to come with "Rock, Rock, Rock!" In another way the show forewarned of an ominous turn. It cost $340,000 to mount, forcing Todd to ask a then-unheard-of $7.20 top price. Though it ran nearly a year, it failed to pay off. The years of a kind Broadway economy were gone.

A consistently funny revue that had originated in Pittsburgh, **Lend an Ear** (12-16-48, National), made stars of Yvonne Adair, Gene Nelson, William Eythe, and, most of all, a towering amazon of a girl with big, wide-open eyes, Carol Channing. The show aimed its darts at every kind of absurdity and always struck dead-center. Two prominent celebrities who live by what columnists say about them are forced to book the next plane when they read they are going on vacation. When a second newspaper announces they are expecting a baby, they have to take a later flight. An opera was performed without its music. But the highlight of the evening was a devastating spoof of a 1926-style musical comedy. It was, according to the compère, the real thing, since "The Gladiola Girl" had sent out a number of road companies and one of them had never come back. Now that road company, its performers not looking a day older than when they began, had been located and was offered as the first-act finale. The songs included

all the requisite types once a stock-in-trade of musical comedy—"Where Is The She For Me?," "In Our Teeny Little Weeny Nest" and "Doin' The Old Yahoo Step." The parody was riotous, but somehow also managed to convey the fun and zest of the old shows. Its success marked the beginning of a turn-about in feelings toward shows of the preceding generation. Interestingly, in this American burlesque the boy and girl are both poor but pretend to be rich. When the British travesty *The Boy Friend* (9-30-54) arrived several years later, the lovers were lordly, but pretending to be poor. Gower Champion staged the dancing. The show's only weak spot was its commonplace score, typified by "Who Hit Me?" Audiences lent an ear to its mirth, and the revue ran a year on its gales of laughter.

December 29 brought Benjamin Britten's opera **The Rape of Lucretia** to the Ziegfeld. In the days before operetta or musical comedy as we know it, operas were often performed at regular Broadway houses as well as at the opera house of the period. But with grand opera largely a museum piece and with commercial audiences attuned to lighter entertainment, operas rarely trod the legitimate boards anymore. Menotti operas had been notable exceptions, but Britten's work was not welcomed by Broadway.

Some of the wildest welcomes of the season were extended to the next evening's opening, **Kiss Me, Kate** (12-30-48, New Century). This musical built around Shakespeare's *The Taming of the Shrew* was Cole Porter's masterwork, although the excellent libretto of Bella and Samuel Spewack played a large part in its success. So, for that matter, did coproducer Lemuel Ayers' gay sets and an impeccable cast led by Alfred Drake, Patricia Morison, Lisa Kirk, and Harold Lang. The action begins on the stage of Ford's Theatre in Baltimore where Fred Graham (Drake) has just finished a run-through of his musical production of *The Taming of the Shrew*. Opening night is only hours away and nerves are on edge. Fred is feuding with his costar and ex-wife, Lilli Vanessi (Miss Morison), while Lois Lane (Miss Kirk) is unhappy about the progress of her romance with her fellow player, Bill Calhoun (Lang). Lilli's maid Hattie (Annabelle Hill) has seen it all before and knows what it's like, "Another Op'nin', Another Show." When Bill appears, he confesses to Lois he has been gambling. Not only has he lost all his money, he has signed Graham's name to an IOU. All Lois can ask is, "Why Can't You Behave?" Meanwhile in Lilli's dressing room Fred and Lilli are fighting over each other's supposed rudeness. They are both still in love with each other, but neither will admit it. Lilli, in fact, has gone so far as to become engaged to Harrison Howell (Denis Green), a wealthy, influential Washington figure:

Lilli: Did I show you the star sapphire Harrison sent me? It was his mother's engagement ring.
Fred: His mother must have worn it on her big toe.
Lilli: And now it's mine!
Fred: Congratulations!
Lilli: Do you know what day this is, Fred? Our anniversary, and you forgot.
Fred: What anniversary?
Lilli: The first anniversary of our divorce.

This sets them reminiscing, and they remember their first show together, an impossible operetta in which they were both part of the chorus. There was a waltz in it, "Wunderbar," and they find themselves singing and dancing the song. Two surprisingly benevolent-looking gunmen enter Fred's dressing room. They have come to collect on his IOU. Fred cannot recall signing any. The men are understanding. They will give him time to refresh his memory and come back later. In Lilli's dressing room she is presented with flowers, which she recognizes as her wedding bouquet. Joyful that Fred has not forgotten, she confesses privately she remains "So In Love" with him. But Fred had meant the flowers for Lois. He arrives in time to prevent Lilli from reading the card but not from her stashing it away in her costume. The play within a play begins. In "We Open In Venice" Katharine, Petruchio, Bianca, and Lucentio (Lilli, Fred, Lois, and Bill) proclaim they are merely strolling players, not film stars like Louis B. Mayer's. Their itinerary takes them from Venice around the map of Italy and back to Venice. Petruchio arrives to seek the hand of Katharine, knowing full well her reputation. She in no way hides her feeling, insisting, "I Hate Men." Petruchio woos her with, "Were Thine That Special Face." But Katharine is unmoved. Lilli, however, is. She has had a moment to pull out the card and read it. She and Fred use the roughhouse action of the play to indulge in a real slugging match, ending with Fred's giving her a solid spanking. Offstage Lilli announces she is leaving the show at once. Fred seems unable to force her to stay, until the hoods return. Seeing his chance, he acknowledges the baffling IOU, but tells the gunmen he will have to renege if Lilli walks out and the

show closes, Lilli stays, at gunpoint. During intermission the actors and their dressers head for the alley to escape the heat. Some of them would like to go off on dates tonight, but they recognize it's "Too Darn Hot," even for that. Back on stage, all is not going well for Petruchio and he sighs, "Where Is The Life That Late I Led?" He longs for the women in his past. Harrison Howell appears in answer to an urgent distress call from Lilli. Before he can see her, he mets Lois. It seems they have met before, although at that time he told her his name was Harold:

Lois: Harold, don't you remember? In front of the Harvard Club. I had something in my eye, and you took me to Atlantic City to take it out?

But Lois understands the situation and promises to be discreet. Bill, on the other hand, has overheard and wonders aloud what kind of girl he's going with. Lois reassures him that she's "Always True To You In My Fashion." Harrison tells Lilli he will take her away from all this hubbub and indignity. As he details their future life together, it becomes clear he will take her so far away from everything she will die of boredom. When he falls asleep in the midst of drawing his picture of the future, Lilli and Fred sneak out. They meet the gunmen, who tell them their boss has been done away with and the IOU is no longer binding. Before they leave, the hoods, confessing they have become fascinated by the bard, urge "Brush Up Your Shakespeare." They suggest if you quote "Othella" your girl "will think you're a helluva fella." The performance resumes. Katharine admits "I Am Ashamed That Women Are So Simple" and bids all women be humble, upon which Petruchio happily bids her "Kiss Me, Kate."

In *Kiss Me, Kate* the ideals that musical plays had been striving for were triumphantly realized. Here was a book with remarkably lifelike, believable protagonists, with every character having a sensible and important bearing on the plot, with every song perfectly related to the action and more often than not advancing it. Here were lyrics and dialogue that never cheapened themselves for effect, that remained literate and witty or touching throughout. The day after the show opened, long lines formed at the out-of-the-way Century (then called New Century), and the show romped merrily through 1,070 performances.

Two revues appeared in January 1949. Both missed the mark, even if both had runs that a decade or two before would have been considered satisfactory. **Along Fifth Avenue** (1-13-49, Broadhurst) enlisted the aid of Nancy Walker, Jackie Gleason, Carol Bruce, Hank Ladd, and several other excellent featured performers, then failed to give any of them first-class material. Miss Walker had one of the better comic numbers, which allowed her to tell Sigmund Freud where to go "If This Is Glamour!" and Carol Bruce was assigned the most memorable of Gordon Jenkins' ballads, "The Best Time Of Day." But the rest of Jenkins' songs—and Jenkins was a leading arranger and composer of "semiclassic" pieces—were run of the mill. The cast did the best it could, and its best was good enough to keep the show on the boards into the summer.

Paul and Grace Hartman scuttled the intimacy which has been so meaningful a part of their success with *Angel in the Wings* and helped Anthony Brady Farrell fill his large converted motion picture theatre with an elaborate, cumbersome revue, **All for Love** (1-22-49, Mark Hellinger). Max Shulman was listed as "editor" of the sketches, but he could come up with nothing funnier than the skit in which the stars brought to life two gigantic mannequins that graced a large Times Square advertisement at the time. Nothing in the musical department approached the songs for the Hartmans' first show. Farrell forced the run in hopes the revue would catch on. When it didn't, he withdrew it after 141 performances.

The season's most eagerly awaited musical was virtually its last. **South Pacific** (4-7-49, Majestic) was based on two of the stories from James A. Michener's Pulitzer-Prize-winning book, *Tales of the South Pacific*. The book was adapted by Oscar Hammerstein II and Joshua Logan, while Hammerstein supplied lyrics for Richard Rodgers' music. The stars were Mary Martin and the Metropolitan Opera's great basso, Ezio Pinza. Despite the general disappointment with Rodgers and Hammerstein's previous musical, *Allegro* (10-10-47), the new show opened to the largest advance sale in Broadway history, and despite some easily assailable shortcomings, it proved a glorious musical romance and was received with open arms. Logan and Hammerstein based their material on "Our Heroine," which told of the romance of Emile de Becque and an American nurse, Nellie Forbush, and "Fo' Dolla," which recounted the love affair between an American lieutenant and a native girl. The two tales were tied together by having de Becque and the lieutenant undertake a wartime mission together. As the curtain rises, de Becque's two Eurasian children are singing a French children's ditty. De Becque (Pinza) is pre-

paring to entertain an American nurse he has met and whom he has taken a liking to, although they are obviously worlds apart in more ways than nationality. Nellie (Miss Martin) describes herself as "A Cockeyed Optimist." She is optimistic even though she is still single and not getting any younger. But de Becque knows she has no reason for concern; she will meet her man "Some Enchanted Evening." For the boys who are fighting the war, things are not as simple nor as promising. Yet, at times the war doesn't seem as bothersome as the absence of the girls they have left at home. Jokingly, they pin their affection on an elderly, rough-talking harridan from a neighboring island, "Bloody Mary." Such playfulness doesn't assuage their real loneliness, and they are forced to admit, "There Is Nothin' Like a Dame." Bloody Mary (Juanita Hall) would like to marry her daughter, Liat (Betta St. John), to one of the Americans, especially Lt. Joseph Cable (William Tabbert). To entice the boys she extols the mysterious magic of her island home, "Bali Ha'i." For the moment a more urgent matter demands attention. A secret base must be established on a nearby enemy-held island. Cable is to lead the attempt, but he would like de Becque, who has lived on the island for years, to assist. De Becque demurs. He is growing fond of Nellie and would prefer to be with her. But Nellie is uncertain. In her shower she sings, "I'm Gonna Wash That Man Right Outa My Hair." However, a brief meeting with de Becque changes her thoughts completely, and she acknowledges her revised feelings, rejoicing, "I'm In Love With A Wonderful Guy." With the mission postponed, Cable finds time to meet Liat. When the language barrier makes conversation all but impossible, he conveys his emotions in song, telling Liat, who can comprehend the gist of his statements, that she is "Younger Than Springtime." Racial and national differences emerge when Bloody Mary presses the two young lovers to pursue their affair. Cable confesses he could not marry an Asian. Bloody Mary stalks off in a fury, taking Liat with her. Cable is shaken. He receives a further jolt when he overhears Nellie explain to Emile why she cannot continue to see him:

Nellie: It means that I can't marry you. Do you understand? I can't marry you.
Emile: Nellie—Because of my children?
Nellie: Not because of your children. They're sweet.
Emile: It is their Polynesian mother then—their mother and I.

Nellie: . . . Yes. I can't help it. It isn't as if I could give you a good reason. There is no reason. This is emotional. This is something that is born in me.

Cable concludes prejudices are not natural, "You've Got To Be Carefully Taught." Emile takes it all more philosophically, ruing in "This Nearly Was Mine" the paradise that has slipped through his fingers. With Nellie apparently out of his life, de Becque agrees to participate in the mission. Cable is killed. But on returning Emile finds Nellie has reconsidered. They sit down to discuss their future as the little French ditty that opened the evening closes it.

The faults in the evening were obvious, and, by and large, they were Hammerstein's. While he invented such felicitous phrases as "corny as Kansas in August," which enjoyed universal acclaim, many of the lyrics strove too hard, resulting in an affected simplicity. There was more than the usual repetition of lines. To some extent Hammerstein's old argument for the integrity of the whole suffered some setbacks when it was learned that "Younger Than Springtime" had been written for *Allegro* and interpolated in the new work, where, it must be admitted, it fit quite well. Nor was there really a place or need in a romantic work for the preaching of "Carefully Taught." Hammerstein's preachments got the show into trouble when it toured the South. It could also be argued that *South Pacific*, more than the earlier Rodgers and Hammerstein pieces, demonstrated that the new genre really presented the natural contemporary American evolution of the older European operetta. Although almost all the characters were Americans, three principals were not. And the setting was distinctly exotic. The rousing men's choruses were the best that had been offered since the days of Teutonic drinking songs, while "I'm In Love With A Wonderful Guy," with its beat repeated and emphasized, suggested much the same style. Because most popular singers could not properly handle the fully arioso melodies of the older works, Rodgers had to temper his love songs. Yet here and there a suggestion of the older melodic line remained evident. None of this detracts from the overriding excellence of the work.

There were two unforgettable performances in the show. Pinza brought to de Becque a manly, yet graceful authority. If his great basso voice was no longer equal to Mozart, it was nevertheless far and away superior to anything else heard on Broadway. His falsetto high note at the end of "Some Enchanted Evening" brought storms of applause. Miss Martin's Nellie was apple-pie American, yet she kept Nellie's prejudices from seeming mean or parochial. The zest with which she imbued Nellie was mirrored in Logan's fluid staging and Jo Mielziner's clever deployment of sets, which allowed each scene to blend into the next without any pause.

Rodgers' richly textured, enthrallingly melodic songs made the show's score the most popular in years. Several million copies of its sheet music were sold. One technological development increased substantially the raging popularity of both the work and its music. *South Pacific*'s arrival more or less coincided with the advent of LP records, allowing buyers to take home on a single disc original casts singing virtually all of a show's songs. *South Pacific*'s album has been described as a "blockbuster." Actually Americans had been buying original-cast albums with some regularity ever since Decca's *Oklahoma!* Moreover the English—so often leading the way in the musical theatre—had been dutifully putting original London casts on record since the turn of the century. This resulted in the odd situation of a number of great American musicals recorded for posterity not in their homeland with their original Broadway casts, but in England with West End players. But all these older 78s were breakable and cumbersome. The new plastic 33s opened a whole new prospect of easy preservation and easier listening.

The show ran just short of 2,000 performances in New York, while its road company and London company played long runs as well. When, in the following season, the Pulitzer Prize judges could find no play of outstanding merit, they resorted to a technicality in their calendar and awarded the prize to *South Pacific*. It was only the second musical to win the award.

The very last offering of the season was **Howdy, Mr. Ice of 1950** (5-26-49, Center). One spectacle number was done all in pink. A red, white, and blue number saluted "The Forty-Eight States," while a gaudy set took spectators to jazzy New Orleans. The show proved to be the very last offering of the Center Theatre. Although the show ran 430 performances, increasing costs were making it less attractive to its producers and the house. The series was discontinued and the auditorium converted into additional offices for Rockefeller Center.

1949-1950

Only an incorrigible optimist of Nellie Forbush's stripe could have hoped for another season as brilliant as the preceding one. In the twenties such a hope might have been reasonable, but, as the theatre entered the fifties, sustained achievement was too much to expect. Production costs were soaring, and chances to recoup these higher costs were hurt by increasing competition, especially from television. Once a viewer had paid for his set, he could sit comfortably at home and watch a variety of entertainments at virtually no expense. Moreover, television and movies continued to drain away talent from the living theatre, especially vital, young talent with new styles and fresh approaches. The remaining talent continued to be beset by higher taxes on their success, discouraging the creativity of an earlier day.

Still, the season was interesting. There were three fascinating attempts to nudge the American Musical Theatre into the realm of higher art. None was fully realized artistically, and all three proved commercial disappointments. Indeed, there was only one solid box office hit, and that was a patently old-fashioned musical comedy glossed over with some modern sounds.

The season opened with a Spanish revue, **Cabalgata** (7-7-49, Broadway), that arrived in Manhattan after an extensive tour of Latin America. Its material was culled largely from the folk songs and dances of Spain. With the growing interest in folklore of all sorts, the show was able to run to the beginning of September.

The season's opener should have been **Miss Liberty** (7-15-49, Imperial), which was scheduled to open patriotically on July 4, three nights before *Cabalgata*. It had been announced months earlier and gave every promise of becoming another bright light in the glowing Broadway scene. Its score was by Irving Berlin, whose *This Is the Army* (7-4-42) had opened on an earlier July 4. Its book was by two of America's most intelligent and resourceful playwrights, Robert Sherwood and Moss Hart. The cast included the popular Eddie Albert, as well as two of the most promising young ladies available: Mary McCarty, a comedienne who had called attention to herself in *Small Wonder* (9-15-48), and *Where's Charley?*'s (10-11-48) fine ballerina, Allyn McLerie. The

musical built a fictitious romance around the presentation of the Statue of Liberty to America by France. A circulation war between Bennett's *Herald* and Pulitzer's *World* provided further color. Horace Miller (Albert) is a bungling newspaper photographer who is fired from his job after he takes the wrong photographs at the ceremony where Pulitzer presents a check for the base of "The Most Expensive Statue In The World." Horace decides he is "A Little Fish In A Big Pond" who would do better at home. His girl friend, Maisie Dell (Miss McCarty), suggests he go to France instead and find the model for the statue. Horace agrees, but when he arrives in Paris he mistakes another model, Monique Dupont (Miss McLerie), for the one Bartholdi actually used. He befriends her by suggesting, "Let's Take An Old-Fashioned Walk." Back in the states, Maisie makes plans for the sweet domesticity of "Homework," unaware Horace is finding Monique increasingly attractive. He attempts to overcome the language barrier by professing there is "Just One Way To Say I Love You." Maisie persuades Bennett to underwrite a tour for Monique. Only when Monique arrives in New York to unexpected fanfare and hoopla does she perceive there has been a mistake. When she tells Horace and Maisie, they decide they must bluff it through. Bartholdi arrives, and the error is in danger of being exposed. Bennett would have Horace, Maisie, and Monique arrested, but Pulitzer proves more understanding. He bails Horace out of jail and offers him a job. At the dedication of the statue, all the voices are raised in song, singing a musical hymn based on Emma Lazarus' poem that began, "Give Me Your Tired, Your Poor."

Berlin's score moved from one pleasantry to another, including a lovely production waltz, "Paris Wakes Up And Smiles." The veteran Ethel Griffies stopped the show nightly with her raffish "Only For Americans," which argued, "the price that's more is only for Americans from the U.S.A." But the public embraced none of the songs, and, worse, perceived the book as seriously flawed. It was surprisingly humorless and heavy-handed, and, most surprisingly of all, clumsy. The characters of both leading women were sympathetically drawn, and yet, with only one hero, one girl had to be left out in the cold. That the girl turned out to be the American homebody seemed particularly unpalatable to many in the audience. When *Miss Liberty* finally made its delayed opening on July 15, expressions of disappointment were universal.

Only its large advance sale, coupled with a lack of competition, allowed it to run until April.

A good many New Yorkers also may have had great expectations for Ken Murray's **Blackouts of 1949** (9-6-49, Ziegfeld). It had run for years at the El Capitan in Hollywood and looked forward to a reasonably long New York stay. But what the Coast has viewed as good, not always clean, fun Broadway frowned on as cheap, hackneyed vaudeville. Besides a standard assortment of turns that included ballroom dancers, knockabout clowns, and a monologist (who impersonated all the characters in his retelling of *Oliver Twist*), Murray presented a small band of show girls he labeled "glamourlovelies." Some not so young or shapely "elderlovelies" revived old songs such as "Silver Threads Among The Gold" and "Put On Your Old Gray Bonnet." Murray even staged a Tarzan jungle fantasy reminiscent of the twenties' jungle scenes. When Broadway showed its disdain, the show headed back west after 51 performances.

S.M. Chartock met with a similar disappointment when he attempted to establish a permanent Gilbert and Sullivan repertory company on this side of the Atlantic. Although the four shows— *The Mikado, The Pirates of Penzance, Trial by Jury,* and *H.M.S. Pinafore*—were tastefully mounted and beautifully sung, the critics bewailed the absence of a proper flair and style. Mr. Chartock withdrew his players after three fruitless weeks.

Touch and Go (10-13-49, Broadhurst) was a pleasant revue that had first seen the footlights at Catholic University in Washington, D.C. The show had attractive music by Jay Gorney, particularly the plaintive ballad, "Things Will Be Alright In A Hundred Years," and the ingratiatingly childlike "Funny Little Old World." Lyrics and sketches were by the husband and wife team of Walter and Jean Kerr. Mrs. Kerr went on to write several successful comedies, and Mr. Kerr became New York's leading drama critic. Their efforts in the revue were generally frothy and fun, culminating in an uproarious spoof of the haggard, bedraggled heroines so voguish at the moment on the screen. Three supposed queens of the silver screen, dressed like skid-row derelicts, proclaimed the secret to success was to "Be A Mess." In "Great Dane a-Comin' " *Hamlet* was staged as a Rodgers and Hammerstein musical, with real Rodgers melodies sung to revised lyrics on the order of, "You're A Queer One, Dear Ophelia." A Tennessee Williams-style Cinderella, hidden from the prince by her wicked stepsisters, disclosed her

whereabouts by flushing a toilet. Unfortunately, the resurgence in the popularity of the revue form had begun to wane. *Touch and Go* compiled a not altogether satisfactory run of 176 performances.

The last two nights of October witnessed the unveiling of two of the most daring, uncompromising musicals of the season. **Lost in the Stars** (10-30-49, Music Box) was a musical version of Alan Paton's poetic and popular novel, *Cry, the Beloved Country*, adapted for the stage by the distinguished playwright Maxwell Anderson, with music by Kurt Weill. Together they told and sang a tragic tale. A black South African preacher, Stephen Kumalo (Todd Duncan), and his wife, Grace (Gertrude Jeanette), grow concerned when they receive no letters from their son, Absalom (Julian Mayfield), who has gone to Johannesburg. They decide to go to the big city to seek him out. But they cannot find him, for Absalom is living with his pregnant girl friend and keeping bad company in a rough part of town. To get money for himself and his girl, Absalom participates in a holdup and kills young, white, liberal Arthur Jarvis. Alone with the news that his son has been arrested, the minister broods on our insignificance and unhappiness, on his realization that we are all "Lost In The Stars." The preacher returns to Johannesburg to see his son. He also meets Absalom's girl, Irina (Inez Matthews). When he overhears her singing "Stay Well," his sympathies for her are enlisted. He agrees to marry them in prison. In the courtroom Absalom's confederates lie about their own guilt and are acquitted. Absalom will not lie, and he is sentenced to be hanged. The minister takes Irina with him back to the village. A quarter of an hour before Absalom is to die, James Jarvis (Leslie Banks) appears at the minister's house. He has not approved his son's liberal racial views, but he is not without compassion. He, too, has lost a son and can understand Stephen's feelings. Moreover he was touched by Absalom's rigid honesty in court:

Stephen: You think well of my son?
Jarvis: I tried not to. But you and I have never had to face what Absalom faced there. A man can hardly do better than he did when he stood before the judge. Stay in Ndotsheni, Stephen, stay with those who cried out to you in the chapel. You have something to give them that nobody else can give them. And you can be proud of Absalom.
Stephen: And he is forgiven, and I am forgiven?
Jarvis: Let us forgive each other.

Stephen: Umnumzana-umnumzana!
Jarvis: Let us be neighbors. Let us be friends.

Unfortunately the show had its problems. Much of the action or commentary on it was provided by a Greek-like chorus, very like the one employed in *Allegro* (10-10-47). This gave a static quality to what should have been a compelling drive. The florid richness of South African speech as conveyed by both Paton and Anderson sometimes seemed unnatural and stilted. Furthermore, there was the unyielding starkness of the story itself. All argued against commercial acceptance, and while *Lost in the Stars* ran until July 1 it was not considered a commercial success. There are three footnotes. The title song, which fit so beautifully into the work, was actually written several years before. And Weill returned to a practice that had been largely neglected on Broadway for forty years or so. He orchestrated his own work. Sadly, it was the last new Weill work heard on Broadway. He died suddenly during the run of the show on April 3.

An even more uncompromising musical opened the following night. **Regina** (10-31-49, 46th St.) was an operatic rendering of Lillian Hellman's saga of interfamily struggle, *The Little Foxes*. Both the libretto and the score were by Marc Blitzstein. A superb cast featured Brenda Lewis (Birdie), Jane Pickens (Regina), George Lipton (Ben), Russell Nype (Leo), Priscilla Gillette (Alexandra), and William Warfield (Cal). As they had for *Porgy and Bess*, many newspapers sent both their drama and music critics to opening night. By and large the music critics found more to enjoy than the drama critics. To some extent this judgment was vindicated. The show struggled along for 56 performances. It was later added to the repertory of the New York City Opera, and enjoyed a limited popularity. Had the piece been better, it might have had a longer, possibly even a successful, Broadway run. Its failure was not a reflection on the limits of acceptance so much as a reflection of *Regina*'s own inadequacies. Curiously, *Lost in the Stars* also found its way into the New York City Opera's repertory, but its long stretches of dialogue were better served in the intimacy of a legitimate playhouse. Its failure to survive—as a highly praised revival revealed—again was due largely to its own shortcomings.

Anthony Brady Farrell, still determined to mount a success at his Mark Hellinger, brought in **Texas, Li'l Darlin'** (11-25-49, Hellinger) just before Thanksgiving. He lured Kenny Dalmar, who

hit the height of his popularity as the blustering Senator Claghorn on Fred Allen's radio show, to star, and got the popular musician, Robert Emmett Dolan, to set Johnny Mercer's words to song. John Whedon and Sam Moore did the book. Their story followed the adventures of Hominy Smith, a psalm-singing, grass-roots Texas politician whose cushy berth is jeopardized by a crusading veteran and who looks at the possibility of kicking himself upstairs to the presidency. It was a conventional evening—too conventional for many. Oddly enough its one song to achieve even a passing popularity had an unconventional 16 bar chorus and depended for much of its interest, as so many songs had two generations back, on the lyrics of its verse. The song was a revival meeting hymn called "The Big Movie Show In The Sky."

The season's runaway hit was 1949s last musical. It, too, was conventional, but it was conventional with a flair. **Gentlemen Prefer Blondes** (12-8-49, Ziegfeld) was a musical version of Anita Loos' best-selling novel of more than two decades before. The twenties had started to come back in vogue with the affectionate travesty, "The Gladiola Girl," in the preceding year's *Lend an Ear*. Two of the principals from that revue were signed for the leading female roles. Carol Channing attained a stardom she was never to lose as Lorelei Lee, and Yvonne Adair played her friend Dorothy Shaw.

. . .

Carol Channing was born in Seattle, Washington, on January 31, 1921. Her early Broadway appearances included *No for an Answer* and *Proof through the Night*. She served as Eve Arden's understudy in *Let's Face It*. A statuesque, wide-eyed blonde with a voice that could change abruptly from a babyish squeak to a baritone growl, Miss Channing's wildly gyrating flapper chorus-girl in *Lend an Ear* assured her a special niche in Broadway's pantheon.

. . .

Lorelei leaves her doting button manufacturer, Gus Esmond (Jack McCauley), to sail for Europe with Dorothy. Dorothy finds a stable love affair with Philadelphia's stuffy Henry Spofford (Eric Brotherson). Meanwhile Lorelei's coquetry wangles a tiara from the dithering Sir Francis Beekman (Rex Evans) and gets her into romantic complications with a zipper mogul, Josephus Gage (George S. Irving). Gus learns of all her playing around and is about to throw her over, but Lorelei is resourceful enough not only to go on to a successful nightclub act but to win back Gus' affection. From the opening scene recording the wildly festive mayhem as the *Ile de France* is about to sail from the French Line pier, through the scenes depicting the highspots of Paris, to a glittering finale at the Central Park Casino, the show was splashily mounted, which helped conceal the mediocrity of the book. Jule Styne's music was brasher and colder than his *High Button Shoes* score. He did not attempt to recapture faithfully the tones and beats of the twenties, but rather to hint at them in a thoroughly contemporary collection of songs. The show's hit ballad, "Bye, Bye, Baby," sung by Gus, quietly underscored an essentially lively melody with a touch of nostalgia. The real hits of the evening were Lorelei's two comic numbers. Lorelei recounted her rise from humble beginnings into the lap of luxury as "A Little Girl From Little Rock." As she noted, in New York, unlike Arkansas, the man a girl calls daddy ain't her "paw." She expressed her philosophy in "Diamonds Are A Girl's Best Friend," concluding that even in old age when a woman is bent over or plagued with stiff knees, she can still "stand straight at Tiffany's." Miss Channing's Lorelei was a far cry from the diminutive, shy-seeming girl of Miss Loos' book, but no one cared. She regaled audiences at the Ziegfeld for 740 performances.

January 1950 brought in three musicals; all flops. The first was the most off-beat and had the shortest run. **Happy as Larry** (1-6-50, Coronet) starred Burgess Meredith as an Irish tailor who is allowed to return to his grandfather's time to learn which of his grandfather's two wives was really the better one. *Heaven on Earth* (9-16-48) had suggested that *Finian's Rainbow* (1-10-47) had exhausted the demand for whimsical Irish tales. *Happy as Larry* confirmed it. It was gone after just three showings.

Two revues attested to the waning interest in that genre, though both were admittedly inferior, and neither would have probably been more than a modest success a few seasons back. **Alive and Kicking** (1-17-50, Winter Garden) was fittingly strong in the dance department. Jack Cole devised the choreography, and his young dancers included two names soon to be celebrated, Bobby Van and Gwen Verdon. Cole's bizarrely conceived ballets, eclectically mixing classical, African, Hindu, and other movements, were "Abou Ben Adhem," "Calypso Celebration," "Propinquity," and "Cole Scuttle Blues." Cole himself was the principal dancer, performing with an "unearthly fire and flickering motion—his fingers dance as wildly as his feet." For comedy, Jack Gilford gave up cigarettes only to spend his day inhaling his neighbors' smoke; David Burns became a grandiloquent speaker at a literary lunch; while Leonore Lonergan made free with her tears and her handkerchief in a spoof of Edith Piaf. The skits by popular writers and comedians such as Henry Morgan, Jerome Chodorov, and Joseph Stein, and the songs by such composers as Sammy Fain and Harold Rome were lackluster and readily forgettable. The show ran eight weeks.

Dance Me a Song (1-20-50, Royale) could not survive even that long. While it, too, offered some fine dancing by Joan McCracken and Bob Fosse, it was neither its dances nor its songs that won most critics' kudos. The drily humorous monologues of shy Wally Cox stole the show. Cox dissected the not very bright mind of a soda jerk and documented the history of a hopelessly inept juvenile delinquent. Unfortunately, he was not well enough known to prop up the evening singlehandedly.

The faltering Theatre Guild and Anthony Brady Farrell tried to change their luck with a musical version of an old Guild success, *The Pursuit of Happiness*. The original play had been written by two of the Guild's top executives, Lawrence Langner and Armina Marshall. Herbert and Dorothy Fields and Rouben Mamoulian collaborated on the adaptation. As she had in the straight-play version, Jo Kirkland (Nanette Fabray) dons trousers and takes up arms after she is driven from her home by redcoats during the Revolution. She even uncovers a spy. By the end of the evening, she and a Hessian named Franz (Georges Guetary), who was originally thought to be the spy, are fondly embracing. Miss Fields did the lyrics for the songs by Morton Gould, a respected arranger and composer in other fields. The book was cumbersome, and Miss Fields' straight lyrics often startlingly naïve and inept. She saluted the entrance of Washington with, "Mr. Washington, Uncle George," and allowed Franz to suggest, in what was meant to be the evening's hit love song, that all he wanted in life was "A Cow And A Plow And A Frau." (Guetary's French accent broke through as incongrously as Ella Logan's Scottish burr had in *Finian's Rainbow*.) Nanette Fabray was able to enhance the lilt of "That's My Fella," a song not unlike, "I'm In Love With A Wonderful Guy." What little real success the evening enjoyed came from Pearl Bailey's clowning as a servant named Connecticut and her singing of two songs. She expressed her outlook on life in general with some felicitous Fields rhymes in "Nothin' For Nothin' " and stopped the show with her feelings on romance in "There Must Be Somethin' Better Than Love" (where she wondered out loud, even if there was, would anyone want it). Even with its attractive cast and a Guild subscription to bolster its early weeks, **Arms and the Girl** (2-2-50, 46th St.) was added to the list of the season's failures after a 134-performance try.

The cold war in all its brutality was brought home by Gian-Carlo Menotti in his opera, **The Consul** (3-15-50, Barrymore). Although none of its music had popular appeal outside the theatre and although its tale was rank topical melodrama, it was the most cohesive, fully achieved of the season's more serious offerings, and the most successful. It narrated Magda Sorel's attempt to get visas that would allow her persecuted family to flee from an unnamed Iron Curtain Country. Thwarted by red tape, she commits suicide. The evening was superbly sung by a cast of fine artists, several of whom went on to renown at the Metropolitan, the New York City Opera, or Broadway. These included Cornell MacNeil, Patricia Neway (Magda), Marie Powers, Gloria Lane, and George Jongeyans, who soon changed his name to George Gaynes. *The Consul* was voted the best musical of the season by the New York Drama critics and ran eight months.

A weak musical that tried to make a whole evening out of a single joke premiered eight nights later. Vivienne Segal and Stuart Erwin were the stars of **Great To Be Alive** (3-23-50, Winter Garden), which featured a fine cast including Bambi Linn, Rod Alexander, Valerie Bettis, and Mark Dawson. The plot told of how Mrs. Leslie Butterfield buys an old mansion from Woodrow Twigg. Woodrow has lived there happily among ghosts who will show themselves and will speak only to virgins. The ghosts—who danced the evening's ballets—and Woodrow are on the best of terms. He and Mrs. Butterfield strike up a friendship. By the end of the evening Woodrow can no longer see or hear the ghosts. The material, by inexperienced writers, was humdrum; the cast was helpless, and the musical left after 52 showings.

Katherine Dunham brought a titleless dance revue into the Broadway Theatre on April 19 under Sol Hurok's aegis and pleased her admirers for 37 performances.

The season's last new revue was another Paul and Grace Hartman creation. The Hartmans came before the footlights at the opening to explain the title, **Tickets Please** (4-27-50, Coronet). It seems they hadn't been able to devise what they felt would be an appealing name. When they attended a performance of *South Pacific,* they heard a crush of people in the lobby crying, "tickets, please," and decided since the expression seemed to be on everyone's tongue it would make a voguish title. They also decided that if they insulted the critics, the aisle-sitters would be too embarrassed to pan the show. So they promptly insulted the newsmen and proceeded confidently with the rest of the entertainment. The Hartmans had wisely returned to the intimacy of *Angel in the Wings* (12-11-47). Insults or no, their drollery was appealing, and the show ran until Thanksgiving. Its success suggested that an occasional revue, even one such as this with no music of any merit, could find an audience.

May came in hand in hand with a popularly-priced return of *Brigadoon* at the City Center.

The season ended with the failure of another interesting attempt at something novel, a musical version of Goldoni's **The Liar** (5-18-50, Broadhurst). Alfred Drake collaborated on the book and staged the evening, with an excellent ensemble that included William Eythe, Joshua Shelly, Russell Collins, Paula Laurence, and Melville Cooper. Lelio (Eythe) is an amorous 16th-century rake whose romances have forced him to flee from Rome to Venice. There he leads the Venetians to believe he is the King of Sicily. His lies and loves keep him in hot water all night. John Mundy did the music, and the colibrettist, Edward Eager, did the lyrics. The elements wouldn't hold together and *The Liar* folded on May 27.

1950-1951

So many good musicals opened during the 1950–51 season, Broadway couldn't handle the crush. With rising prices and alternate sources of diversion, potential patrons became increasingly choosy. To a large extent they chose wisely. The most fully realized shows were the biggest hits. On the other hand, several better-than-average shows, while still faulty, were not able to run long enough to pay off their investments. The season also seemed to suggest that the appeal of Americana had dwindled. The one good show to turn back the clock to an earlier America was one of the better works that failed. For an instant the season may have also suggested that the revue had more life in it than local Cassandras would believe, although the Cassandras turned out to be right. Revues were moribund, even if Americana was not. One further point of interest was ominous in its implications. All the better shows were by older figures. The youngest, Frank Loesser, had just turned forty.

The very first show of the season, **Michael**

Todd's Peep Show (6-28-50, Winter Garden), was the revue that won the longest run. It was a confused affair. At times it was lavish in its mountings; at times tawdry. Strippers were headed by a long-legged New Orleans favorite, Christine. Skits made no pretense at high-minded wit or satire; they were strictly gag-filled pieces brought over from the dying burlesque wheels. Most of the clowns who performed them were drafted from the same circuits. They included such nonlegitimate comics as "Peanuts" Mann, "Bozo" Snyder, and "Red" Marshall. For his songs Todd went to Sammy Fain, Jule Styne, Harold Rome, and the king of Thailand. The King's contribution was "Blue Night," but the only song to appeal to the public was Styne's "Stay With The Happy People." After the opening, Todd was forced to modify some strip-tease and off-color material, but he was still correct in thinking there would be an audience for even such mildly censored shenanigans.

The musical theatre jumped from the ridiculous to the serious with a revival at the Arena (where the audience surrounded the performers) of Menotti's double-bill *The Medium* and *The Telephone* (5-1-47). The works proved as effective in the new house as on a proscenium stage, and they added 110 performances to their record.

No musicals arrived in August or September, but two came in a week apart in the first half of October. **Pardon Our French** (10-5-50, Broadway) was another Olsen and Johnson revue, graced with music by the distinguished Victor Young. Regrettably, Young's melodic gifts eluded him for the moment. The public had had enough of Olsen and Johnson's peculiar brand of zaniness, although the whole evening aimed a bit higher than their earlier efforts. The comedians went so far as to let a ballet, "Venezia and Her Three Lovers," finish without a comic interruption. Theatregoers were not interested and the show was withdrawn after 100 performances.

One reason the public may not have been all that interested was the imminent opening of **Call Me Madam** (10-12-50, Imperial). News from the tryout indicated that Irving Berlin had come up with another smash score for Ethel Merman and that Howard Lindsay and Russel Crouse had given her a first-class libretto. In a way *Call Me Madam* was a reversion to the topical musicals of the thirties, for there was no secret that its heroine was patterned after Pearl Mesta, the Washington hostess. President Truman had appointed Mrs.

Mesta minister to Luxembourg. Nonetheless, Lindsay and Crouse insisted in the program that the show was "laid in two mythical countries. One is called Lichtenburg, the other is the United States of America." In Washington, Sally Adams has just been appointed Ambassador, largely, as she confesses, because she is "The Hostess With The Mostes' On The Ball." Otherwise, her credentials are meager. She is amazed, for example, that the landscape is not the same color as it is on the map. Even her efforts at a simple curtsey are ludicrous. Such gaucheries fail to faze her, for she knows she has large sums of money to distribute, and she's not above donating them freely once she falls in love with Lichtenburg's Prime Minister, Cosmo Constantin (Paul Lukas). Of course, she will not buy his affections, since she subscribes to that old-fashioned idea of "Marrying For Love." Hers is not the only romance blossoming. Although he doesn't realize it, her handsome, Ivy League assistant, Kenneth Gibson (Russell Nype), has fallen for Lichtenburg's Princess Maria (Galina Talva). After watching the natives dance "The Ocarina," he tentatively conveys his feeling by suggesting, since "It's A Lovely Day Today," the princess and he might work together on whatever she has planned. The course of these lovers will not run smoothly if the opposition, led by Sebastian Sebastian (Henry Lascoe), has its way. When the machinations of the other side seem to wreck Cosmo and Sally's ambitions as well as their romance, Sally stalwartly tells Cosmo she wants only what's best for him and she is convinced, "The Best Thing For You Would Be Me." She also has to hold Kenneth's hand, for he is displaying symptoms he doesn't understand, but which she recognizes. "You're Just In Love," she counsels. The opposition succeeds in wangling Sally's recall, but not before everything else has turned out happily for both pairs of lovers. Out-of-town praises were echoed when *Call Me Madam* opened in New York. "You're Just In Love" received four or five encores a night, a thing long-unheard-of in the more reserved atmosphere of the postwar theatre. It was a two-part song patterned after "Simple Melody" from *Watch Your Step* (12-8-14). This old-timer had recently enjoyed a successful revival beyond its original popularity thanks to a recording by Bing Crosby and his son, Gary. Several of Berlin's other songs were almost as much in demand. One number, "They Like Ike," became popular until the networks banned it when Eisenhower became a serious candidate for President. The Republicans played it often during the 1952 campaign, and it became as popular a campaign song as any written in the century. The show ran a year and a half, then toured.

Only one musical appeared in November, but it was a far bigger success than even *Call Me Madam*. It was, in fact, one of the masterworks of the American Musical Theatre. **Guys and Dolls** (11-24-50, 46th St.) was a sassy, irreverent love poem of low-life in New York. Jo Swerling and Abe Burrows' book was based on stories and characters of Damon Runyon, particularly "The Idyll of Miss Sarah Brown."

. . .

Abe Burrows (Abram Borowitz) was born in New York City on December 18, 1910 (six months after the birth of *Guys and Dolls'* composer). Before entering the entertainment field he had studied to be a doctor and an accountant, and had spent several years in selling. Burrows received his apprenticeship as a summer entertainer in the Catskills. He became a successful writer of radio scripts for over a decade and was perhaps even better known as an author and performer of unusual party songs, such as "The Girl With The Three Blue Eyes."

. . .

Frank Loesser created the songs and George S. Kaufman staged the piece. The principals were either unknown when the show opened or at best moderately celebrated: Sam Levene, Robert Alda, Vivian Blaine, and Isabel Bigley. At least for a few seasons thereafter they could all write their own meal-tickets. The show opens with a ballet depicting the hustle and bustle of Manhattan's netherworld: pickpockets, hookers, sandwichmen, and packaged tourists. Three scruffy horseplayers appear and in "A Fugue For Tinhorns" argue their selections. A Salvation Army Mission band appears, lead by Sister Sarah (Miss Bigley), a sinfully beautiful young girl. She exhorts those who would listen (and there are few) to "Follow The Fold," promising, "Put down the bottle and we'll say no more." One of the horseplayers wonders out-loud "why a refined doll like her is mixed up in the Mission dodge," and meets with the response, "Maybe she owns a piece of the Mission." Nathan Detroit (Levene) enters. He runs a crap game, but because of a breaking police scandal (and by convenient coincidence New York was having one of its periodic police scandals when *Guys and Dolls* opened) cops have

been cracking down. Nathan bemoans to his would-be players, "I'm having terrible trouble. Everybody's scared on account of that lousy Brannigan." When he discovers he has made his pronouncement within earshot of the detective he is quick to explain to him, "I hope you didn't think I was talking about you. There are other lousy Brannigans." Nathan tells his friends he is trying to find one thousand dollars to rent the Biltmore Garage. One way or another he will come up with a place for "The Oldest Established"—"the oldest established permanent floating crap game in New York." He is especially anxious to resume when he learns Sky Masterson (Alda) is in town. Young, handsome Sky is the highest player of all. Knowing Sky's betting proclivities, Nathan determines to bet Sky a thousand on a sure thing. But Sky, when he appears, tells Nathan of a warning Sky's father once gave—bet on a sure thing and "You are going to wind up with an earful of cider." They get to talking about girls. Sky scoffs at Nathan for his loyalty to his girl friend, Adelaide (Miss Blaine). To Sky, "all dolls are the same." Nathan wants to know why Sky hasn't a girl of his own, and Sky counters he can pick them up wherever he goes, even in Havana, where he is headed. "Not real high-class dolls," Nathan counters. When Sky boasts he can have any doll he goes after, Nathan gleefully bets him a thousand dollars he's wrong. The bet seems irresistible to Sky. He accepts. Just then the Mission band is heard, and when it appears Nathan demands Sky take Sister Sarah to Havana. All Sky can reply is, "Cider!" In the mission Sky promises to deliver Sarah "one dozen genuine sinners" if she will have dinner with him. She seems ready to accept until he tells her the meal is in Havana. Gamblers, she announces, are not her cup of tea. Sky snarlingly remarks she wants a breakfast-eating Brooks Brothers type. But Sarah is unmoved. She responds that when her love comes along, "I'll Know." When Sky kisses her he is rewarded with a slap. He leaves offering to return "in case you want to take a crack at the other cheek." At the Hot Box night club, Nathan's Adelaide and the Hot Box Farmerettes are entertaining the customers with an appropriate yokelish song, "A Bushel And A Peck." When the show is over, and Nathan and Adelaide are alone, Adelaide reveals she has not been able to admit to her mother that she and Nathan have been engaged fourteen years. During that period she has written her mother that they have been married, and at intervals has announced the birth of five children.

The deception is telling on Adelaide. She has developed a chronic cold, and her doctor has given her a book to explain the illness. She reads from it:

> The average unmarried female, basically insecure
> Due to some frustration, may react
> With psychosomatic symptoms, difficult to endure,
> Affecting the upper respiratory tract.
> In other words, just from waiting around
> For the plain little band of gold,
> A person can develop a cold.

The crap-shooters are concerned not only about their game but about the effects the battle of the sexes, of the "Guys And Dolls," will have on it. Sky learns that General Matilda B. Cartwright is going to close the Mission for lack of attendance. When he repeats his offer of a dozen sinners to the General, she is so enthusiastic Sarah can do nothing but go along. The Mission band marches through, and when Nathan, who has remarked on Sky's absence, notices Sarah is not in the group he collapses on a crapshooter's shoulder.

Masterson and Sarah have indeed gone to Havana, and Sarah has had enough disguised drinks to proclaim she would go "ding, dong," "If I Were A Bell." By four in the morning they are back in Manhattan. Sky confesses this is "My Time Of Day." The two also confess, "I've Never Been In Love Before." Just then the police arrive and the gangsters pour out of the mission. The belief that she's been duped throws cold water on Sarah's new-found feelings. On a lonely street beside an open manhole Sarah stops to rest with an old Mission helper. She would forget Sky, but the old man (Pat Rooney) isn't sure that's really the wisest thing for her. He tells her, "More I Can Not Wish You," than she find her own true love that day. Sky appears to remind her he will keep his part of the bargain. He will have twelve sinners at that evening's meeting. When she rebuffs him, his thoughts turn to the crap game. Nathan has found an outlandish spot for it—down in the manhole! Masterson arrives at the game and, begging "Luck Be A Lady Tonight," rolls the dice. The results become evident when twelve forlorn gamblers are seen slinking toward the Mission. As the gamblers settle down for the service, Brannigan crashes in. He is made to sit and join the others. Nicely-Nicely (Stubby Kaye), one of the gamblers, is asked for his confession. He responds with a rousing revivalist anthem, "Sit Down, You're Rocking The Boat," relating his crapshooting on the way to the Pearly Gates. Brannigan then appeals to Sarah to testify to what she saw the previous night, but Sarah has undergone another change of heart and insists she saw nothing. With Brannigan out of the way, Nathan allows that he, too, has made a bet and lost. As a result he must take a certain young lady on a long-postponed trip. Sarah and Adelaide meet and discover they share the same philosophy, "Marry The Man Today"—and change him later. Sky appears in a Mission uniform, announcing he and Sarah are married. Nathan has a fit of sneezing. Its implications do not go unnoticed by Adelaide.

The most popular song from the show was "A Bushel And A Peck," one of the two night club numbers that had the least pertinence to the plot. "If I Were A Bell" and "I've Never Been In Love Before" both profited from some passing attention. But the score was not the work's principal forte. *Guys and Dolls'* strength was the wit and appropriateness of its lyrics, which fit so neatly into the mirth and movement of the book. This "Fable of Broadway" offered a tonal and structural cohesion rare in the annals of the American Musical Theatre. *Guys And Dolls*—sparked initially by Levene and Miss Blaine's deliciously droll performances—ran just short of three years.

A "musical novelty" was the first of December's three lyric offerings. **Let's Make an Opera** (12-13-50, Golden) had book and lyrics by Eric Crozier and music by Benjamin Britten. It asked its audience to participate as a group of children and their teachers created an opera about a chimneysweep who gets stuck in a chimney and has to be rescued from a wicked master. It was the sort of entertainment that two generations before would have brought in precisely at this holiday season to profit from what was at that time a dependable children's market. The market had long since withered away, so the show was taken from the boards after five performances.

A big, bustling revue, **Bless You All** (12-14-50, Hellinger) offered three fine comedians, Jules Munshin, Mary McCarty, and Pearl Bailey; a graceful dancer, Valerie Bettis; and the handsome leading singer of *Where's Charley?* (10-11-48), Byron Palmer. All it lacked was the material to allow its fine talent to shine. It travestied *Peter Pan* and spoofed the Tennessee Williams–Carson McCullers school of writing in a sketch "Southern Fried Chekhov" and in a song "Don't Wanna

Write About The South." In "Little Things Meant So Much To Me" Miss McCarty explained how her husband's daily insults and jibes had finally driven her to murder. The most interesting bit was the first-act finale, which suggested that someday political campaigns would be conducted largely on television and showed the programing used in the candidacy of Joe Gabriel Blow (Munshin). (Washington and Lincoln give testimonials as if they were advertising soap.) It was not half so funny or horrific as real televised campaigns a few years later.

December's last musical was **Out of This World** (12-21-50, New Century). It reunited Cole Porter with the producers and designers of *Kiss Me, Kate* (12-30-48). Porter composed a lovely score; coproducer Lemuel Ayers designed some of the most spacious and eye-filling settings Broadway had seen, settings that gave Mt. Olympus a star-spangled grandeur the ancient gods might have envied. Porter and his producers arrived at one inspired piece of casting, bringing Charlotte Greenwood out of retirement to play the Goddess, Juno. In most years that might have been enough to make a go of it. But as fine new musicals continued to arrive, *Out of This World*, stranded far uptown, found it was surviving largely on its advance sale. When business dropped at the beginning of spring, it was forced to close; a 20-week failure. Indeed, there were things not right enough about the evening. Dwight Taylor and Reginald Lawrence's book, based on the Jean Giradoux-S. N. Behrman success *Amphitryon 38*, could not recapture the airy grace and sophisticated wit of the original. Nor was all of the casting ideal. The basic story remained. Jupiter (George Jongeyans) falls in love with a newly-wed mortal, Helen (Priscilla Gillette), and sends Mercury (William Redfield) to earth to arrange a tryst. In the musical, unlike the play, the mortals live in modern-day Greece, and when Juno rushes to earth to pursue her husband, she comes into confrontation with a harmlessly snarling gangster, Niki Skolianos (David Burns). In the end, having had a successful fling, Jupiter goes back to Olympus with his spouse, and the earthly Helen is left to resume her more mundane marriage. Porter's score was diverse and melodic but inevitably met with unkind comparisons to his *Kiss Me, Kate* material. Ironically the song that has proven the most popular, "From This Moment On," was cut during the Philadelphia tryout. Admittedly Helen's beguine, "I Am Loved," sounded too much like a revision of *Kate*'s "So In Love," but Porter's gifts and versatility were ingratiatingly displayed. Jupiter's opening number, "I, Jupiter," contained some of Porter's most impish rhymes; such as "sassy air" and "brassiere." In one of Porter's most endearing ballads Mercury begged the audience to "Use Your Imagination." The rest of the score ranged from Juno and Niki's exhilarating "Climb Up The Mountain" to Helen's lilting "Where, Oh Where" and Jupiter's lush, suave "Hark, To The Song Of The Night," which demonstrated Porter's ability to make an obsolete expression such as "Hark" seem at home in a contemporary setting However, for most theatregoers the triumph of the evening was the joyous cavorting of Charlotte Greenwood. Forty years after her first Broadway appearance she still retained her regal bearing, the glow in her eyes, and her incredible loose-jointed, high-kicking eccentric dances. She brought down the house nightly singing and dancing a fetching Porter ditty, "Nobody's Chasing Me."

No new musicals opened in January of 1951, but on the 29th the D'Oyly Carte began a four-week visit presenting the most popular of the Gilbert and Sullivan repertory.

On February 19, the same night the D'Oyly Carte began a one week-run of *Cox and Box* and *The Pirates of Penzance,* a revue called **Razzle Dazzle** opened at the theatre-in-the-round Arena. It was scheduled for an unlimited run but lasted no longer than the final D'Oyly Carte presentation. Besides the novelty of a revue with the audience surrounding the cast, the piece attempted a sketch that continued on and off throughout the evening. It was a travesty on the popular movie "All About Eve" and featured the droll little comedienne, Dorothy Greener. But the diminutive Miss Greener's herculean efforts were insufficient to keep the show alive.

Another outstanding entry, **The King and I** (3-29-51, St. James) was based on Margaret Langdon's novel *Anna and the King of Siam*, which had already been made into a successful movie. Rodgers and Hammerstein had cautiously moved away from the Americana they had made the rage. In their previous offering, *South Pacific* (4-7-49), they had placed their Americans on an exotic island. Now, though they once again rushed back to the 19th century they had ignored in *South Pacific* (4-7-49) and just missed touching in *Allegro* (10-10-47), they set all their action in the colorful, but alien world of Siam, peopling most of their cast of characters with Siamese natives.

Actually, their breakaway wasn't total, for they seized on an incident in the novel to excuse a lengthy ballet based on *Uncle Tom's Cabin*. But essentially the evening represented a distinct change in color and tone. To some extent this change was probably the inspiration of the show's star, Gertrude Lawrence, who brought the story to Rodgers and Hammerstein, and asked them to create a vehicle for her. The show was the only one they ever devised around the talents of a specific performer. Hammerstein faithfully held to the story of Anna Leonowens' arrival at the court of the Siamese king to teach his children and of her making the king her most important pupil. A nervous Anna debarks in Siam in the 1860s, but she openly confesses her fears, acknowledging that to bury them, "I Whistle A Happy Tune." One of the king's concubines, Tuptim (Doretta Morrow), accepts him as "My Lord And Master," although in secret she loves the handsome Lun Tha (Larry Douglas). Anna compassionately greets all the hopeful sweethearts, "Hello, Young Lovers." The king (Yul Brynner), however, is less tolerant and understanding. Anna's ways and Anna's teachings alternately amuse and exasperate him. They are, in fact, "A Puzzlement." But there is no denying Anna's flair with the youngsters of the royal family, and she tells them she enjoys, "Getting To Know You." Sadly, this lightheartedness is denied Tuptim and Lun Tha, who lament, "We Kiss In A Shadow." When the king's unpredictable tantrums disrupt the court and her teachings, the infuriated Anna asks, "Shall I Tell You What I Think Of You?" and before the king can answer does tell him. But his head wife, Lady Thiang (Dorothy Sarnoff), begs Anna's forbearance. The king can be cruel at times, while at other times he will do or say "Something Wonderful." He displays his cruelty when he discovers the furtive affair between Tuptim and Lun Tha. Before they are dragged to their deaths each lover laments "I Have Dreamed" in vain. Even if she cannot bring them back to life, Anna does ultimately prevail on the king to establish a more humane rule. They grow closer together. When Anna asks the king, "Shall We Dance?," he accepts. But the king is fatally stricken. On his deathbed he implores his son to follow the wisdom Anna has attempted to impart.

The long evening, patently sentimental and at times archly humorous, was made even longer by the ballet "The Small House Of Uncle Thomas," an attempt by the Siamese to interpret Harriet Beecher Stowe's novel. But if Hammerstein and choreographer Jerome Robbins sometimes were long-winded, they were still too professional to let the show become insufferable. Moreover, the show was stunningly mounted in glittering golden Oriental sets by Jo Mielziner. Gertrude Lawrence, who contracted first hepatitis, then cancer, during the run and died, was an impeccable Anna, and Yul Brynner was catapulted to stardom for his imperious, physical performance as the king. More than anything else, Rodgers' soaringly beautiful score gave the evening its glow. For his fine singers he was able to write as much arioso music as the market would tolerate, while for Miss Lawrence he wrote gay, simple, appealingly sentimental melodies. Half a dozen songs from the show quickly became standards. (One of these, "Getting To Know You" was originally from *South Pacific*, where "Younger Than Springtime" replaced it.) The show ran 1,246 performances, 46 more than *Guys and Dolls*; just as the romantic *South Pacific* outran the witty *Kiss Me, Kate*. It could be argued that the 46-performance difference was insignificant, but it must also be remember that *The King and I* played in a larger house and had a higher break-even figure to maintain. It would seem to confirm, even if only in a small way, that the American public continued to prefer the sentimentality of the operetta tradition to the best wit of the musical comedy form.

April's two musicals opened one night apart in the middle of the month. **Make a Wish** (4-18-51, Winter Garden) was a musical version of Ferenc Molnar's *The Good Fairy*. It had songs by Hugh Martin and a book by Preston Sturges (whom Abe Burrows assisted without public credit when the show received bad notices in its Philadelphia tryout). The evening depicted the adventures of Janette (Nanette Fabray), a French-orphan on a tour of Paris, who breaks away from her group to visit a Paris not included in guided tours. Courted by a middle-aged millionaire, Marius (Melville Cooper), she ultimately settled for a penniless young artist, Paul (Stephen Douglass). A secondary love interest allowed Helen Gallagher and Harold Lang to bring Gower Champion's challenging choreography to life. Once again an impressive array of fine talent was unable to save weak material, so *Make a Wish* was withdrawn after 103 performances.

An even sadder failure was **A Tree Grows in Brooklyn** (4-19-51, Alvin), for it was a funny, melodic entertainment, marvelously cast, opulently mounted, and greeted with generally favorable notices. It even managed to run 270 performances, but since it was unable to repay its original investment, it ended on the debit side of the ledger. As its title revealed, it was based on Betty Smith's phenomenal best seller. Miss Smith collaborated with George Abbott to produce a libretto that retained the basic story and flavor of her book, while Dorothy Fields and Arthur Schwartz combined to create fitting and beautiful songs. To some extent the show may have suffered because a movie version of the novel had already been released (although the same situation clearly left *The King and I* unaffected) and because the vogue for Americana may have been overplayed. The piece's underlying, inevitable melancholy may also have told against it. Primarily, it suffered because of the tremendous competition it had to buck at a time when the theatre could no longer support so many good attractions. *A Tree Grows in Brooklyn* brought to life again the star-crossed love of Katie (Marcia Van Dyke) for the ne'er-do-well Johnny Nolan (Johnny Johnston). Johnny could swear, "I'm Like A New Broom," and promise, "I'll Buy You A Star," but he was too unstable to keep a job or even his sobriety. This didn't stop Katie from imploring, "Make The Man Love Me," in hopes that her love would somehow reform him. This tragic love story was played out against the background of the equally unsuccessful love-life of the wistfully comic Aunt Cissy (Shirley Booth), who years ago unwittingly entered into a bigamous marriage. She nonetheless longs for her faithless husband until one day he suddenly reappears and she sees him with new eyes. Although the music was probably the most beguiling Schwartz had written since *The Band Wagon*, the score never really became popular. Schwartz' tunes covered a wide variety of styles, from the rollicking polka of Katie's "Look Who's Dancing," to the bittersweet lilt of Cissy's "Love Is The Reason," to the perfect period flavor of the chorus' waltz, "If You Haven't Got A Sweetheart," to a thoroughly contemporary yet in no way inappropriate ballad such as "Make The Man Love Me." Dorothy Fields' lyrics were her best in a long while, too. Words, music, and star met in a perfect match when Shirley Booth stopped the show with reminiscences of her departed spouse, "He Had Refinement." Miss Booth, who had spent most of her career as a wise-cracking comedienne, had shown unsuspected dramatic abilities the preced-

ing season in *Come Back, Little Sheba*. The role of Cissy allowed her to parade both sides of her remarkable talent to great advantage.

An off-beat musical with a libretto by the team that did *Finian's Rainbow* (1-10-47), E.Y. Harburg and Fred Saidy, had been a smash hit in its Philadelphia tryout, but the New York reviewers were as critical as those in Philadelphia had been enthusiastic. Both sets of critics were probably extreme. **Flahooley** (5-14-51, Broadhurst) had an ear-pleasing score and a clever idea for a book. It was delightfully staged with a capital cast that starred Barbara Cook, Jerome Courtland, Ernest Truex, Yma Sumac, and the Baird puppets. The basic idea of the book dealt with the unprecedented sales generated by a laughing doll on a market glutted with dolls that cry. Unfortunately, the book got out of hand. Miss Sumac had a voice with an abnormal range, and her three songs with no lyrics and no real relevance to the story bogged down the action. Moreover a subplot of Arab intrigue had to be created to justify bringing her on stage. A genie not unlike the leprechaun of *Finian's Rainbow* was also involved, and given a pleasant song, "The Springtime Cometh," that reminded too many people of the superior "Something Sort Of Grandish" from the earlier show. At the height of the McCarthy era the librettists added still another turn to the story by having a shrill, reactionary group, the Capsul-anti, attack the unheard-of happiness the new doll is spreading. Big business was also satirized. All through the evening B.G. Bigelow (Truex), head of the vast B.G. Bigelow, Inc., rails against the unethical practices of his competitor, A.E.I.O.U. (and sometimes Y. and W.) Schwartz, only to discover that he owns his competition. Along the way, the charming original conceit got buried. Buried with the show were Sammy Fain's gay, childlike melodies and romantic ballads including the title song, "Here's To Your Illusions," "Who Says There Is No Santa-Claus?," "He's Only Wonderful," and "The World Is Your Balloon"—all of which, except the title song, were sung by Miss Cook and Courtland. The show folded after eight weeks. A revised version called *Pollyanna*, starring Bobby Clark, was later presented on the West Coast. But it, too, missed the requisite innocence and failed.

The season ended on May 29 when *Oklahoma!* cheered Broadway with a return engagement. No major names were featured.

Scene Two
INCREASING PROBLEMS— LOWERING STANDARDS
1951-1964

1951-1952

Had some of the preceding season's shows, such as *Out of This World* and *A Tree Grows in Brooklyn,* waited until the 1951–52 season to make their appearance, they would have met little serious competition. The American Musical Theatre sank to an abysmal state. Only nine new musicals were offered. This was the lowest figure since well back into the 19th century, and this was out of a total of seventy-two plays. Moreover two of these were Yiddish-American revues not usually seen in regular legitimate houses. Furthermore not a single one of the five new book shows realized a return on its investment. Four revivals and one return engagement swelled the lyric total a bit. Yet even here only one of the shows was a success.

The season opened on June 13 with **Courtin' Time** (6-13-51, National), a musical version of Eden Phillpotts' play, *The Farmer's Wife.* The show had encountered star problems on its tryout. Its original star, Lloyd Nolan, was replaced by the show's director, Alfred Drake. Drake chose not to wear two hats, and Joe E. Brown was called in to assume the lead. Brown tempered his usually broad style to play Samuel Rillings, a middle-aged widowed Maine farmer in the late 1890s. The story of Rillings' up-and-down courtship of his housekeeper Araminta (Billie Worth) made a charming rustic idyll. Its songs by Jack Lawrence and Don Walker matched the tenor of its book.

They were simple and unassuming, typified by "Heart In Hand," which a repentant Samuel sang to Araminta as the show's quiet finale. Unfortunately this bit of relatively gentle Americana had more charm than staying power.

Seventeen (6-21-51, Broadhurst) advanced the calendar by a decade to 1907 Indianapolis, where once again Willie Baxter (Kenneth Nelson) suffered all the pangs of his puppy-love romance with Lola Pratt (Ann Crowley), just as he had since Booth Tarkington's novel first appeared. The adaptation was by Sally Benson, famous primarily for her New Yorker tales that became *Junior Miss.* The music was by Walter Kent; the lyrics by Kim Gannon. The show, like *Courtin' Time,* had period charm. *Seventeen* proved more attractive at the box office, playing until November. Its music was a little less rustic, tinged with Broadway sounds. "I Could Get Married Today," a verseless number, was popular in the show but never made its mark outside the theatre, although "Summertime Is Summertime" was heard occasionally.

July's only entry was a lavish summer revue, **Two on the Aisle** (7-19-51, Hellinger), starring Bert Lahr and Dolores Gray. Lahr played a riotous bit as Lefty Hogan, a celebrated but brainless baseball player who can't comprehend that he's being interviewed for a children's program and insists on talking about his booze and his broads. He also plays a hilariously short-sighted Central-Park street sweeper who idiotically fills his trash-bag with $100 bills rather than lose a small award for collecting the most trash. Miss Gray had the best of Jule Styne's songs in "Give A Little, Get A Little Love," and "If You Hadn't, But You Did." The two stars played a pair of vaudevillians who could see hardly any difference between their old act and the nonsense on the stage of the Metropolitan Opera. The show was a far cry from the tasteful, witty, and melodic revues Lahr and his great fellow comedians had done in the thirties. For want of serious competition *Two on the Aisle,* with some forcing, was able to play 281 performances.

The two Jewish revues opened five nights apart in September. **Bagels and Yox** (9-12-51, Holiday) achieved a run of 208 performances, while **Borscht Capades** (9-17-51, Royale) lasted 99 showings. "Yox" was a theatrical term for laughs, and the title was, of course, a play on the familiar Jewish coupling of bagels and lox (smoked salmon).

October's only musical entry was a loving,

opulent revival of Kern and Hammerstein's *Music in the Air* (11-8-32). The show was given a star-filled cast that included Charles Winninger (Dr. Lessing), Dennis King (Bruno), Jane Pickens (Frieda), and Conrad Nagel (Ernst). Because anti-German feelings still ran strong in many quarters, the producers changed the scene to Switzerland. But the thoughtful attention devoted to it failed to elicit a favorable response from playgoers. Lack of business forced its withdrawal after seven weeks.

Phil Silvers and his band of supporting comedians were the principal inducement to see **Top Banana** (11-1-51, Winter Garden). Silver's character of Jerry Biffle was reputedly modeled on Milton Berle, the most successful of early television clowns. The noisy, imperial Biffle is told by his sponsors to establish a love interest on his program. He hires Sally Peters (Judy Lynn) and before long a real love affair develops between her and Cliff Lane (Lindy Doherty). Biffle also falls in love with Sally, but when he realizes where her heart lies he helps her with uncharacteristic selflessness to get her man. Hy Kraft's book and Johnny Mercer's songs were brassy and serviceable. The highlight of the evening remained Silvers and his cohorts running through their old vaudeville and burlesque routines, such as a man carrying a large carton announcing he's taking a case to court, then reappearing with a ladder announcing he's taking the case to a higher court. Alarmingly, the fun was all on stage. The box office told a very unfunny story. *Top Banana* ran almost a year—350 performances—without being able to pay off its initial investment. It was another ominous hint of things to come.

A rollicking, boom-or-bust Gold Rush musical, **Paint Your Wagon** opened at the Shubert on November 12. When gold is found on land owned by Ben Rumson (James Barton), his acreage soon becomes a prosperous mining town. Ben's daughter Jennifer (Olga San Juan) falls in love with one of the miners, Julio Valveras (Tony Bavaar). But Rumson's newly acquired wealth gives him grand ideas for Jennifer, and she is sent to a school back east. In time the gold runs out, and the town becomes deserted. Ben would pick up his stakes and move on, but dies before he can leave. However, Jennifer returns to resume her love affair with Julio, and they plan to turn the town into an irrigated farming community. Alan Jay Lerner's somewhat rambling chronicle told against the forcefulness of the rest of the show, but his lyrics and Frederick Loewe's music were colorful and memorable. Ben was given two soft, pathetic numbers—"I Still See Elisa," in which he recalls his dead wife, and "Wand'rin' Star," which he sings just before he dies. The chorus had the rousing title song and the stirring, "They Call The Wind Maria." But the outstanding song of the evening was given to Julio. It was a beguine-like ballad, "I Talk To The Trees" (with imagery much like "I've Told Every Little Star" from *Music in the Air*). Like *Top Banana, Paint Your Wagon* enjoyed a relatively long run—289 performances. And like *Top Banana*, it lost money.

The once-popular month of December, with its large contingent of holiday theatregoers, saw no new musicals arrive. It was January 3, 1952, just after the holiday crush, when the season's biggest hit opened at the Broadhurst. But the show was not a new one, it was *Pal Joey* (12-25-40). A highly successful revival of its hit song, "Bewitched, Bothered and Bewildered," had recently made it as one of the best-known popular songs of the day. A superb LP recording of the entire score further whetted interest. Postwar attitudes made *Pal Joey*'s cynical, hard-nosed story less unnerving to many. With Vivienne Segal re-creating her original role as Vera and with Harold Lang in the title role, the musical received better reviews and more patronage than the 1940 production, playing 542 performances before embarking on an extended tour. Curiously, a return of *Kiss Me, Kate* (12-30-48) at popular prices found no takers and folded after a single week.

Celtic magic again hoped to weave its spell over Broadway in **Three Wishes for Jamie** (3-21-52, Hellinger). Charles O'Neal and Abe Burrows wrote the book; Ralph Blane, the songs. Just before the turn of the century Jamie McRuin (John Raitt) is granted three wishes by a fairy. He wishes to travel, to marry, and to have a son. The first two wishes are speedily granted. Jamie sails from Ireland to Georgia and there marries Maeve Harrigan (Anne Jeffreys). When Maeve is discovered to be barren, the McRuins must adopt a boy to make the third wish come true. But the boy proves a mute until one day a miracle allows him to speak—in Gaelic. *Jamie*'s whimsy and sentimentality were too treacly for New Yorkers—some, like Brooks Atkinson of the *Times*, condemned it as outdated operetta—and the show survived less than three months.

Two revivals opened in May. Both failed. Ever since its initial production, *Of Thee I Sing* (12-26-

31) had remained popular with amateur and stock groups, particularly as elections approached. George S. Kaufman had tried to convince Morrie Ryskind to work with him on a revival for 1948, but Ryskind, who had swung far to the right politically, refused. For reasons Kaufman was never sure of, Ryskind changed his answer when Kaufman solicited his assistance four years later. With the brash, well-liked Hollywood comedian Jack Carson as Wintergreen and Paul Hartman as Throttlebottom, the revival opened May 5 at the Ziegfeld. There were various schools of thought as to what went wrong. Many felt the stars lacked the panache of William Gaxton and Victor Moore; others resented the changed tempos used for some of the Gershwin score; some contended the new jokes used to update the book (kidding the perennial hopeful, Harold Stassen, and President Truman's flamboyant shirts) were glaringly inferior to the older material, and more than a few critics simply felt the piece had dated itself. There was a certain amount of truth in all these charges, but the show remained viable enough and the production sufficiently professional to deserve more than the 72 hearings it received.

On May 8 at the Broadway, a revival of *Shuffle Along* (5-23-21) fared far worse; it was moot whether it could be considered a revival. All that was left of the original were two songs ("I'm Just Wild About Harry" and "Love Will Find A Way"), a much older Flournoy Miller on stage, and the title. Miller, with Paul Gerard Smith, had written a totally new book detailing the adventures of a troop of Negro soldiers in Italy at the end of World War II and on their return home. Complications arise after WAC Sgt. Lucy Duke (Dolores Martin) is mistakenly informed her former husband, Longitude Lane (Miller), has been killed in action. She begins a second romance with Capt. Harry Gaillard (Napoleon Reed). Longitude suddenly reappears. At a USO performance Longitude decides to remain in the army and sail away. The book was badly written, almost on a par with the claptrap librettos of older black shows. George Jean Nathan, the hellion critic who had so loved the original that he saw it five times, wrote in the *Journal-American*,

Even if some of the original stuff might now seem a bit old-fashioned, it would not seem nearly as old-hat as the substitutions involving a sand-dance, which goes back to 1895, a succession of senescent, gooey music hall ballads

. . . a 1904 vaudeville act in which a comedian on a mountain-top accidentally drops over the edge his sole remaining provisions, and a scene in a dressmaking salon with its parade of models which was already obsolete when Clara Lipman introduced it into a show at the old Herald Square Theatre. . . .

Variety complained more succinctly, "The yarn opens as a musical comedy, presently turns into operetta, and ends as revue." Although Eubie Blake received credit for the whole new score, he later publicly disowned most of the tunes. It was a thoroughly botched affair, mercifully removed after four showings.

The season's final offering was the only new work to have both a long run and realize a profit. **New Faces of 1952** (5-16-52, Royale) was the best in the intermittent series—and would remain so. While none of the young talent ever reached the heights of fame or enjoyed the enduring popularity of Henry Fonda, an alumnus of the 1934 edition, the show started more bright entertainers on the road to success than any earlier version had. Among the fresh faces were Eartha Kitt, Alice Ghostley, Carol Lawrence, Robert Clary, Ronny Graham, and Paul Lynde. The show had diverting sketches and pleasant songs, one of which, "Love Is A Simple Thing" (June Carroll/Arthur Siegel), sung (together with a Charles Addams variation) by virtually all the players enjoyed a certain vogue. Better skits included Paul Lynde's monologue—with Lynde hobbling on crutches describing the trip to Africa won by him and his "late" wife, and Ronny Graham's send-up of Truman Capote. But the revue's highspots were its comic lyrics. "Lizzie Borden" kept insisting, "Oh, you can't chop your poppa up in Massachusetts." Slinky, feline Eartha Kitt made herself comfortable all over a couch as she confessed her irresistible charms had finally made life "Monotonous" (Carroll/Siegel), although traffic will stop for her, stock prices drop for her, and Truman play bop for her. A dowdy, schoolmarmish Alice Ghostley bewailed her frustrating search for romance in "The Boston Beguine" (Sheldon M. Harnick). In her Boston the "Casbah" is an Irish Bar, the underground headquarters of the D.A.R. She and her unnamed lover fall asleep before they can make love. It was good fun from beginning to end, and New Yorkers applauded the revue for 365 showings.

1952-1953

A pattern seemed to be emerging on Broadway of alternate seasons of feast and famine. Although *Variety* listed eleven new musicals, it appeared to have obtained its figure by including a one-woman show and at least one revival. Of conventional new lyric pieces there were once again only nine. To the extent that all, or all but one, were undisguised musical comedies or revues, untouched by the artful pretensions of the still-fashionable "musical play," they happily reverted to a convention that had lately been in no small disrepute. They made no claim to edification or catharsis, although the best, in their insouciant gaiety, were as exhilaratingly cathartic as good musical comedy fun had always been to the tired businessman. Producers were exhilarated, too. Half the new musicals made a profit for their backers.

The season began with one of the most ballyhooed affairs in recent memory. Joshua Logan, Arthur Kober, and Harold Rome had collaborated to create a lyric version of Kober's old hit *Having Wonderful Time*. They used another postcard cliché for their new title, **Wish You Were Here** (6-25-52, Imperial). For their musical picture of life at a Jewish summer camp they went so far as to build a real swimming pool into the theatre's stage. This, coupled with the rest of the production's elaborateness, reflected the American Musical Theatre's feeling it had to compete with the new wide screen and stereophonic sound of the movies and the obvious attractions of home television. All the season's shows but one were mammothly mounted. In the case of *Wish You Were Here*, the extensive stage requirements precluded a customary road tryout and ultimately precluded a workable post-Broadway tour. Previews were substituted for an out-of-town break-in, and devastatingly unfavorable word-of-mouth began to spread as soon as they were inaugurated. The opening was delayed several times, and revisions followed fast and furiously. When the show finally opened, most critics shrugged it off as not worth all the time and effort that had gone into it. Luckily, the delays had given Eddie Fisher's recording of the title song time to become a national best seller, and with the song cleverly repeating the title ten times in its chorus *Wish You Were Here* received inestimable publicity. The song,

plus a huge advance sale, gave the public time to make up its mind. When it decided it liked the show, the musical was able to chalk up a year-and-a-half run, and thumb its nose at its detractors.

As the original had in the 1930s, the story revolved around the romance of Teddy Stern (Patricia Marand) and Chick Miller (Jack Cassidy). Teddy throws over old Herman Fabricant (Harry Clark), whom she has been seeing, when Chick, a young man of her own age, comes into her life. But Camp Karefree's clownish social director, Itchy (Sidney Armus), unwittingly gives Chick to believe that Teddy has spent the night with a garment district lothario named Pinky Harris (Paul Valentine), who specializes in selling "genuine copies of Paris originals." For a moment the romance seems over. However, Teddy is able to clear her name, so everything ends contentedly. The score was Rome's first for a book musical. His lyrics were surprisingly free of the political slant he had heretofore shown; his melodies were memorable and diverse. Itchy had two comedy numbers, "Social Director" and "Don Jose Of Far Rockaway." Even the heavy, Pinky, was allowed to lead a lilting, old-fashioned waltz, "Summer Afternoon." But Chick had the stand-out title ballad and an equally lovely second ballad, "Where Did The Night Go?," that somehow got lost in the attention devoted to the title song.

No musicals arrived between the opening of *Wish You Were Here* and the premiere of **An Evening with Beatrice Lillie** (10-2-52, Booth). Reginald Gardiner and a few minor entertainers assisted Miss Lillie and manned the stage while she changed costumes. Most of the material was from the great revues Miss Lillie had starred in years before. Nobody minded. Broadway was not producing that kind of marvelous revue anymore, so any way to get the hilarious comedienne on stage was acceptable. As she had before, Miss Lillie destroyed a star's opening night and punctured a singer's "Come Into The Garden, Maud." Miss Lillie regaled her fans and any innocents who happened to wander into the theatre until the end of May.

The season's worst musical and one of its biggest failures appeared twelve nights later. Like the preceding season's *Shuffle Along*, **Buttrio Square** (10-14-52, New Century) sought its fun in the confrontation of American soldiers with Italian villagers. Billy Gilbert, sneezing at every turn, starred in the show, for which he shared parital blame for the book. It was gone after seven performances.

S.M. Chartock once again tried to establish an American company devoted to Gilbert and Sullivan. He even succeeded in luring away Martyn Green from his longtime home at the D'Oyly Carte. But Green's performances only served to underscore the lack of style elsewhere in the cast. Time might have smoothed matters, but Chartock's funds were limited, and so, therefore, was his time. He opened with *The Mikado* on October 20, followed with *The Pirates of Penzance* and the double bill of *Trial by Jury* and *H.M.S. Pinafore*. When *Iolanthe* failed to enchant, the engagement was terminated after only four weeks.

Aida was reset in the Confederacy and retitled **My Darlin' Aida** (10-27-52, Winter Garden). The pharaoh became General Farrow, Raadames was rechristened Raymond Demarest, and somehow Amneris wound up as Jessica. "Celeste Aida" evolved into the title song, and "Ritorna Vincitor!" resounded as "March On For Tennessee." Since virtually all of Verdi's difficult score was retained, evenings and matinees featured different principals. The main cast offered Elaine Malbin as Aida, William Olvis as Raymond, Dorothy Sarnoff as Jessica, and Kenneth Schon as Farrow. It was all well intentioned, but a bit ponderous and silly. Nevertheless, it found enough curiosity seekers to survive 11 weeks.

The most notable thing about **Two's Company** (12-15-52, Alvin) was that it marked the return of Bette Davis to Broadway—and in the most unlikely of vehicles, a musical revue. Miss Davis was not a complete stranger to the world of song and dance. She had introduced "They're Either Too Young Or Too Old" in a wartime film. But her métier had been more serious drama. Perhaps she was attracted by the original conception of *Two's Company*, which promised to present a vis-à-vis chronicle of romance and its problems down the ages. However, its authors (Peter De Vries and Charles Sherman on the sketches, Ogden Nash on the lyrics and Vernon Duke on the music) concluded so tight a program was constricting and probably unworkable. By the time the revue premiered, it had dwindled into a conventional mediocrity, with Miss Davis assailing such easy marks as Sadie Thompson. Miss Davis got considerable attention, but Hiram Sherman and David Burns drew most of the applause. Sherman had a droll monologue about an owner of a Frank Lloyd Wright home that blends so completely into the landscape he has never been

able to find it, while Burns played a W.C. Fields-style comedian desperately trying to prevent a child star from stealing a scene. Nash and Duke's songs were especially disappointing. The show depended on its advance sale and theatre parties to run 90 performances.

Three musicals arrived in February. The first was **Hazel Flagg** (2-11-53, Hellinger). It had a clever idea, several talented hands to flesh it out, and a fine cast to give it life. Yet on stage it seemed to have difficulty moving, or even breathing. Hazel is a backwater Vermont girl who is believed to be dying of radium poisoning. A magazine gets hold of her story and brings her to New York where she is the center of attention. She finds time to fall in love with sophisticated Wallace Cook. When it is learned that she is really in the pink of health New York loses interest, but Wallace loves her all the same. Hazel was vigorously sung and danced by Helen Gallagher. Thomas Mitchell, Jack Whiting, Benay Venuta, and John Howard (Wallace) filled the top supporting roles. Ben Hecht provided the book, which he based on the film *Nothing Sacred*, while Bob Hilliard wrote words for Jule Styne's melodies. Styne's score was good. Whiting, as a Jimmy Walker style mayor, had a fine soft shoe number in "Every Street's A Boulevard In Old New York," and another dancer, Sheree North, received her first real Broadway acclaim in a lively bump and grind number that had nothing to do with the plot, but was inserted as a diversion in the mayor's testimonial for Hazel, "Salome." The public seemed to prefer Wallace's slightly overblown ballad, "How Do You Speak To An Angel?" The show had a dream ballet that had become a cliché since *Oklahoma!* (3-31-43). There were enough attractions in the show to keep it on the boards for 190 performances—not long enough to pay back its investors.

A week later a musical version of James Barrie's *What Every Woman Knows* appeared. The story of how Maggie Wylie (Betty Paul) manipulates the fortunes and love life of John Shand (Keith Andes) was faithfully retold, although **Maggie** (2-18-53, National) lacked the charm the play so wisely talked about. Its music was commonplace, and it, too, felt it needed a dream ballet. *Maggie* lasted half a week.

No musical of the season was greeted as effusively as February's final presentation. **Wonderful Town** (2-25-53, Winter Garden) was a musical rendition of Joseph Fields and Jerome Chodorov's *My Sister Eileen*, which in turn was based on Ruth McKenny's semiautobiographical stories for the *New Yorker*. Fields and Chodorov adapted the book themselves. The lyrics were created by Betty Comden and Adolph Green, whose fertile comic talents first delighted theatregoers in *On the Town* (12-26-44). Their collaborator in that hit, the glamorous composer and conductor, Leonard Bernstein, once again did the music. The even more glamorous Rosalind Russell came back to Broadway to play Ruth, a role she had done in the songless movie version of the play.

A tour guide shows gawking out-of-towners the all-too-staged sights of "Christopher Street" in Greenwich Village. When the tour moves on Ruth and her sister, Eileen (Edith Adams), appear, looking for lodging. They have come from Ohio to make good in the big time: Ruth as a writer and Eileen as an actress. A Village urchin grabs Ruth's typewriter but he is stopped by Appopolous (Henry Lascoe), who forces him to relinquish the machine. Ruth can easily identify it. The letter "W" is missing. It fell off after she wrote her thesis on Walt Whitman. Appopolous offers to rent them a basement apartment, and before the girls can refuse he has taken the first month's rent. The room is small, dirty, and dilapidated. Worse, it is shaken periodically by blasts from nearby subway construction. Together the girls wonder "why, oh, why, oh," they left "Ohio." While Eileen quickly finds dates, Ruth forlornly admits that in the mating game she is a born loser. In fact she has come up with "One Hundred Easy Ways To Lose A Man," pointing out that if she shows a man where his grammar errs, a girl can mark her towels with "Hers" and "Hers." Ruth takes her stories to the "Manhattan" magazine, but an editor, Robert Baker (George Gaynes), advises her to go home. After she leaves he thumbs through her manuscripts. They are a mélange of other more famous writers' styles. Several of them come to life before his eyes with Ruth as the principal figure. He decides the stories are awful, but that perhaps Ruth has talent. When he attempts to tell Ruth this later at her flat, she becomes angry and exits in a huff, leaving Baker to muse over his dream of "A Quiet Girl." Life waxes anything but quiet for Ruth when Eileen gets Ruth an assignment to interview some Brazilian sailors at the Brooklyn Navy Yard. She would like to get their opinions on America but all they want to do is dance the "Conga!" In the ensuing melee Eileen manages to slug a policeman and is arrested. The Irish policeman takes a fancy to Eileen, insisting over her protestations she is Irish,

too. The brawl makes the papers and gets the girls dispossessed. To add insult to injury, Baker appears to tell Ruth that his editor liked her stories even less than he did. Yet there are silver linings. Baker had fallen in love with Ruth and promises to get her published. The publicity has also brought an offer of a job in a night club. The evening ends at the Village Vortex, with Ruth and Eileen singing a gloriously cacophonous tribute to life in New York, "The Wrong Note Rag."

The show was clever and knowing. Bernstein's score was a technical tour de force that ran the gamut from straight ballads to parodies of 1930 swing, but it was all facile. Because it worked faultlessly on stage, the show ran over 500 performances, but out of the theatre the public never embraced the songs as they did the material from the next new musical.

Before that show arrived a superb remounting of *Porgy and Bess* (10-10-35), designed to tour internationally, illuminated the Ziegfeld for nine months. One of the singers who alternated in the role of Bess was Leontyne Price, who later went on to become one of grand opera's prima donnas. Cab Calloway sang Sportin' Life. This production had scored a rousing success in Russia before its New York opening.

Can-Can (5-7-53, Shubert) was the first of two May musicals, both of which opened to divided, largely discouraging notices and both of which established themselves as hits. Abe Burrows' libretto for the show was conventional musical comedy frippery. Two stories ran concurrently. In one a handsome young judge, Aristide Forestier (Peter Cookson), is sent to investigate reports of scandalous cancan dancing at a Montmartre café. After he falls in love with both the dance and the café's owner, La Mome Pistache (Lilo), he helps legalize the dance and, of course, marries Pistache. In a comic subplot one of the dancers, Claudine (Gwen Verdon), is pursued by both Boris (Hans Conried), a sculptor, and Hilaire (Erik Rhodes), an art critic. Their rivalry leads the critic to denounce the sculptor's work, and that leads to a hilarious roof-top duel. Lilo, the French star, was given top billing; but Miss Verdon won the lion's share of applause with her exuberant dancing. What made the show the runaway hit of the season—and after an uncertain start it went on to run for 892 times—was Cole Porter's initially unappreciated score. Except for *Anything Goes* and *Kiss Me, Kate*, Porter scores were time and again dismissed as below his previous standard. *Can-Can*'s score was no exception.

It seemed at first as if Aristide's "I Am In Love" was meant to be the hit of the show. But the song was a derivative beguine. One by one Pistache's songs from the musical rose in public esteem: the plaintive "Allez-Vous En," the flowing "C'est Magnifique," the vivacious title song, and, the biggest hit of all, the haunting "I Love Paris" (sung on the same rooftop, now starlit). After the show closed Aristide's "It's All Right With Me" also became nationally known, giving the evening five new Porter standards.

Three weeks after the Porter show raised its curtain, Rodgers and Hammerstein presented what is generally considered their least satisfactory musical, **Me and Juliet** (5-28-53, Majestic). The faults, as usual, were Hammerstein's. His libretto, like his libretto for *Allegro*, was created out of whole cloth and not adapted from a tested work. It had a more self-contained plot than *Allegro*, but the plot was contrived and exaggerated. Exaggeration and contrivance have long been the stock-in-trade of musical comedy, but, given Hammerstein's quest for more purposeful and artful musical theatre, they made his story seem particularly retrogressive and inappropriately inept. The plot purported to be a slice of backstage life, a familiar setting. In his autobiography, Rodgers insisted that he and Hammerstein were determined to depart from expected twists: "One of our aims was to avoid all the clichés usually found in backstage stories. Though the plot focused on various people associated with a stage musical, we established the fact at the beginning that the show within a show was a success. The backer didn't pull out, the star didn't quit and the chorus girl didn't take over. We simply used the production as the framework for a love story, though of course we did take advantage of the theme to reveal some aspects of the world of the theatre."

Like *Can-Can, Me and Juliet* actually told two stories at once. The main tale followed the romance of Jeanie (Isabel Bigley), a chorus girl in a musical named "Me and Juliet," with Larry (Bill Hayes), an assistant stage manager. Larry's jealous rival, an electrician, Bob (Mark Dawson), will not even stop at attempted murder to keep from losing Jeanie. He cuts a spotlight that falls from the flies, but fortunately misses its mark. A comic subplot featured a dancer not unlike *Can-Can*'s Claudine. Betty (Joan McCracken) loves the stage manager Mac (Ray Walston), but Mac has always refused to socialize with the casts of shows he works on. The problem is solved by having Mac change shows. Hammerstein's lyrics were

perhaps more revealing than his book. In the show's opening Jeanie confesses she awakes every day convinced in her heart it will be "a very special day." Not only was the sentiment treacly, but it disclosed his penchant for unpoetic words such as "special." Later in the same song he coupled "munch" with "hunch." His attempts at clever rhymes lacked grace and ease. A song sung by Arthur Maxwell as the lead in the show within the show had the ungainly title, "Marriage Type Love." In "The Big, Black Giant" Hammerstein self-consciously seemed to reach for a phrase that would describe audiences the way "Ol' Man River" had anthropomorphized the Mississippi. Again it was cumbersome and contrived, missing the simple dignity of "Ol' Man River." Jeannie and Larry's ballad "No Other Love" became the hit of the show, although it had already enjoyed a minor vogue as a theme from Rodgers' score for the film, *Victory at Sea*. The faults of the show were minimized by its professionalism. With their names still a potent drawing card, Rodgers and Hammerstein were able to turn a profit on the show's 358-performance run.

1953-1954

The American Musical Theatre continued on its roller coaster of alternating up-and-down seasons. New shows dropped in number and quality during the theatrical year. Only nine new musicals premiered on Broadway, but if three "one-man" shows are excluded, the figure dropped still farther to a mere six (plus two superior off-Broadway mountings).

No shows came in at the very beginning of the season, hoping to span the summer. Of course, two big musicals had arrived in May. The first lyric offering of the season did not appear before the footlights until August 31, and that was a popular-priced revival of *Oklahoma!* (3-31-43) at the City Center. Florence Henderson was its Laurey; Barbara Cook, its Ado Annie.

Anna Russell's Little Show (9-7-53, Vanderbilt) was a little show, indeed. In fact it was simply a one-woman show (with a few other entertainers helping when Miss Russell had to change her costume or catch her breath). Miss Russell's sarcastic attacks hit such prime targets as the old Shubert operettas with "The Prince of Philadelphia," and she went on to analyze "The Decline and Fall of the Popular Song." Her fans supported her loyally at the tiny house for two weeks.

Carnival in Flanders (9-8-53, New Century) was a ponderous affair. Preston Sturges' Hollywood luck had again eluded him. He adapted his book from the 1936 film, *La Kermesse héroïque*. The setting was novel: 17th-century Flanders, but the plot and dialogue were ordinary. When the Spanish Duke d'Olvereas (John Raitt) invades the Flemish village of Flacksenburg, the terrified mayor (Roy Roberts) plays dead. This allows the Duke and the mayor's supposed widow (Dolores Gray) to have a brief romance before the Spaniards move on. A leaden ballet completely bogged down the action at one point. Lyricist James Van Heusen and composer Johnny Burke were co-producers as well. Their idea of a hit tune was the awkwardly titled, "The Very Necessary You," or the modestly popular, "Here's That Rainy Day." *Carnival in Flanders* folded the same week it opened.

At Home with Ethel Waters (9-22-53, 48th St.) welcomed its guests for 23 sessions. Miss Waters and her pianist had the stage to themselves. She sang numbers she had introduced in past hits and a collection of old favorites, but little new material.

The only "one-man" show actually to star a man, **Comedy In Music** (10-2-53, Golden), found Victor Borge accompanying himself on the piano. His verbal and pianistic wit regaled audiences at the bandbox Golden not just through the season but all through the next season and into 1956.

The second conventional musical did not arrive until December. **Kismet** (12-3-53, Ziegfeld) was a resounding hit, and probably would have been so even if there had been competition; but having the field to itself didn't hurt. The show was not especially original. It was a musical version of Edward Knoblock's 1911 romantic hokum of the same name, and used Alexsandr Borodin melodies for its songs. Robert Wright and George Forrest supplied lyrics, as they had for Grieg's music in *Song of Norway* (8-21-44). Both productions had originated on the West Coast with Edwin Lester's fine company. Lester mounted the work with Oriental splendor (bustling Arabian Nights bazaars, moonlit gardens, muezzins crying from minarets) and hired Alfred Drake to re-create Otis Skinner's old role of Hajj. He becomes emir for a day, and marries his daughter Marsinah (Doretta Morrow) to the caliph (Richard Kiley). Drake dominated the evening with his fine singing and bravura acting. But it was to the caliph and to Marsinah that the hit of the evening, "Stranger In Paradise," fell. It was based on Borodin's Polovtsian Dances. Marsinah also sang the lovely "Baubles, Bangles And Beads" from a Borodin string quartet. Drake cavorted in such glittering show pieces as "Rhymes Have I" and "Gesticulate." And he framed the evening with the sentiments of "Sands Of Time" assuring audiences only lovers know all that there is to know. If the lyrics and dialogue had an old-fashioned ring to them, they were nonetheless precisely apposite for such gaudy Edwardian claptrap. *Kismet* led its audiences happily into its world of make-believe for 583 performances.

One week later **John Murray Anderson's Almanac** (12-10-53, Imperial) opened. Anderson had been one of the most innovative figures behind the great extravaganzas of the twenties and shared a large part of the credit for the success of the *Greenwich Village Follies*. He had mounted another *Almanac* in 1929. Skyrocketing costs prevented his making this new edition as lavish as those of bygone days, but it was nonetheless as eye-filling and tasteful an evening as Broadway had seen in many a year. One unique lighting arrangement had slowly revolving lights set in a quilted harlequin pattern. Two rising songwriters, Richard Adler and Jerry Ross, did most of the songs, while the witty Jean Kerr contributed a number of the sketches. For his cast Anderson recruited the popular calypso singer, Harry Belafonte, the droll monologist, Orson Bean, and a personable singer, Polly Bergen. However, two great clowns were the mainstay of the evening: Hermione Gingold in her American debut and Billy De Wolfe. Miss Gingold announced she was particularly impressed on sailing into New York harbor to see the gigantic statue of Judith Anderson; she performed as an old harridan of a cellist grateful for any instrument between her legs and did a number "Which Witch?" (Allan Melville/ Charles Zwar), which left the audience wondering which witch was which. Teamed with De Wolfe in drag, she played a tippling old lady going for a visit to an aunt in Ceylon. The highlight of the evening was "Dinner for One," in which Miss Gingold portrayed a senescent grand dame whose butler—De Wolfe—has set the table to include spaces for four long-dead admirers. The butler then proceeded from chair to chair proposing toasts, getting increasingly drunk as he clattered dishes with each change of course, and when the meal was finished escorted madam to her room.

Anderson revived one of the ballet ballads from the *Greenwich Village Follies*, "The Nightingale and the Rose," mounting it with a shimmering beauty all in white, silver, and pearl gray. Neither the old songs nor the new were particularly distinguished. The best was probably the calypso, "Hold 'Em Joe," composed and sung by Belafonte. The show ran 229 performances, not enough, sadly, to reimburse its backers. Its failure marked the closing chapter in Anderson's illustrious career.

Three years after Sigmund Romberg's death, his last Broadway score was heard in **The Girl in Pink Tights** (3-5-54, Hellinger). Herbert Fields and Jerome Chodorov based their book on the actual events that resulted in the creation of *The Black Crook* (9-12-66), but then peopled their plot with fictitious characters. Lotta Leslie (Brenda Lewis) is concerned that all the attention being paid to a French ballet troupe scheduled to open at the Academy of Music will dampen interest in her production of Clyde Hallam's new play, "Dick, The Renegade." She wonders how she will be able to compete with all the girls in pink tights performing a few block from her Niblo's Garden. But a love affair soon springs up between her playwright (David Atkinson) and the most alluring of the ballerinas, Lisette Gervais (Jeanmaire). Moreover the manager of the French troupe, Maestro Gallo (Charles Goldner), expresses more than a passing interest in Lotta. During a rehearsal the Academy catches fire, and Clyde rushes over to rescue the trapped Lisette. The house and all the costumes and scenery are destroyed. Lotta suggests the ballet be made a part of Hallam's melodrama. An argument over whether Lisette's dances or Hallam's story is more important sunders the lovers. They are reconciled when the new mounting, now called "The Black Crook," proves a wild success. Romberg strove, as he had in *Up in Central Park* (1-27-45), to write in a contemporary style. Unfortunately his native idiom fell somewhere between the styles of 1866 and 1954. The best he could produce was a languid ballad, "Lost In Loveliness." The show's biggest attraction was the dancing of petite Jeanmaire in her legitimate stage debut. But her art and her reputation were insufficient to prolong the run beyond 15 weeks.

On March 10 at the small Theatre de Lys in Greenwich Village the Brecht-Weill masterpiece **The Threepenny Opera** was revived for a limited engagement. The revival was offered in a biting new translation by Marc Blitzstein. Lotte Lenya, Weill's widow, re-created her original role of Jenny. The show had not been successful when it was first done in New York in 1933, and there seemed little chance for more than a modest run. It played until May 30, when it was withdrawn after 96 performances. Persistent calls for its return, especially from the *Times*' Brooks Atkinson, who ended a number of his reviews with a cry to restore the work, encouraged it to reopen at the De Lys on September 20, 1955. An aid to its success was Louis Armstrong's wildly popular recording of "Moritat," in Blitzstein's version called "Mack The Knife." Before it closed, the musical had added an additional 2,611 performances to its record. Although its vogue had no immediate influence on main-stem musicals, a decade or so later *Cabaret* and *Chicago* both proclaimed their debt to its style and form.

The week-old *Girl in Pink Tights* was called to mind the night after *The Threepenny Opera* first returned, when a fresh, imaginative musical began performances not far from the sites of Niblo's Garden and the old Academy. The Phoenix Theatre on Second Avenue and 12th Street invited New Yorkers to partake of **The Golden Apple** beginning March 11. They came in such large numbers after reading the rave reviews that the show was hurriedly transferred uptown on April 20. The musical —almost devoid of dialogue, and propelled by its fetchingly evocative songs and dances—was a retelling of *The Iliad* and *The Odyssey* in a turn-of-the-century America. Angel's Roost is a small town in Washington where, according to the townsfolks, "Nothing ever happens." The biggest events of the year are Ulysses' return from the Spanish-American War and the county fair. Unexpected happenings at the fair do give the citizens something to gossip about. A traveling salesman named Paris (Jonathan Lucas) arrives in a balloon and so beguiles Sheriff Menelaus' wife, Helen (Kaye Ballard), that she runs off with him to Rhododendron. Ulysses (Stephen Douglass) and his neighbors go in pursuit. Hector (Jack Whiting), Rhododendron's mayor, engineers all sorts of delays and temptations for the boys, until Ulysses outclasses Paris in a boxing match. After more delays enroute home, the soldiers return to Angel's Roost, where Ulysses finds Penelope (Priscilla Gillette) waiting faithfully.

John Latouche provided adroit, clever lyrics, while Jerome Moross' music at one and the same time managed to be thoroughly contemporary, yet convey the flavor of an earlier era. Some of their material had little relation to Homer's stories, such as the show's most popular ballad, Helen's languorous "Lazy Afternoon," or the mayor's soft shoe (which gave Whiting a routine not unlike the one he employed so divertingly in *Hazel Flagg*). But the snares in *The Odyssey* offered Latouche and Moross ample opportunity for delicious fun, and they took intelligent advantage of it. Scylla and Charybdis (Dean Michener and Whiting) became unethical stock brokers, singing a parody of Gallagher and Shean's famous number. The sirens, metamorphosed into a burlesque night club act, spoofed ersatz South Sea Island songs in "By Goona-Goona Lagoon," while the intercession of the gods became the meddling of scientists in a lively rag, "Doomed, Doomed, Doomed." Daring and inventiveness were rewarded when the critics bestowed their prize for the best musical of the season on *The Golden Apple*. Yet, although the show cost only $75,000 to mount, the move uptown did not prove popular and when the summer heat hurt business, the musical was taken off the boards at a loss.

The collaborators of *A Tree Grows in Brooklyn* (4-19-51) reunited to try again with **By the Beautiful Sea** (4-8-54, Majestic), a musical set in the same era as their earlier work but with a happier, more showy plot. Their star, Shirley Booth, rejoined them to enliven the festivities. Miss Booth played Lottie Gibson, an old vaudevillian who now runs a theatrical boarding house in Coney Island. She caters to theatrical trade. When Dennis Emery (Wilbur Evans) comes to stay, she promptly falls in love with him. But Emery's ex-wife and his daughter are also among the boarders. Not until she can win the daughter's affection can she win Emery. The plot reminded some of *Panama Hattie* (10-30-40) clothed in popular period costumes. The show also fell back on that curious but apparently comforting ploy of having the title take on an extra significance in the story. In this case "By The Beautiful Sea" is the name Lottie gives her boarding house. Arthur Schwartz' music was inferior to his fine score for *A Tree Grows in Brooklyn*. The show's best moment came when Miss Booth revived "In The Good Old Summertime" as half of a two-part number, with a lively Schwartz countermelody for the chorus to sing. Dorothy Fields invented at least one blunt, startling couplet in Dennis' love song, "Alone Too Long," with Dennis confessing he wants to kiss Lottie but he's scared. Like *A Tree Grows in Brooklyn*, *By the Beautiful Sea* was able to achieve a passable run of 270 showings, thanks largely to Miss Booth's magnetism. But like its predecessor, it was a commercial failure.

May brought revivals of *Show Boat* (12-27-27) and *Fledermaus* into the City Center. *Show Boat*'s cast included Laurel Hurley (Magnolia), Robert Rounseville (Gaylord), Helena Bliss (Julie), Burl Ives (Captain Andy), Marjorie Gateson (Parthy Ann) and Laurence Winters (Joe). Strauss' operetta featured Gloria Lind, Adelaide Bishop, John Tyers, Donald Gramm, and Jack Russell.

Sandwiched between their two openings was the premiere of **The Pajama Game** (5-13-54, St. James). If it was noisy, coarse-grained, and leftish, it was also melodic and comic—an increasingly rare phenomenon among musical comedies. George Abbott and Richard Bissell hammered out the book from Bissell's novel *7½ Cents*. When Hines (Eddie Foy, Jr.), the production manager at the Sleep-Tite Pajama Factory, tries to speed up machines, Babe Williams (Janis Paige), head of the union grievance committee, comes to the factory's superintendent, Sid Sorokin (John Raitt), with a demand for an increase of seven-and-a-half cents. Sid is new on the job and takes an instant liking to Babe, but when he tries to date her she refuses, since they are on opposite sides of the bargaining table. After the workers try a slowdown, Sid threatens to fire all of them. In anger Babe kicks a machine and disrupts the whole plant. She alone is fired. Since Sid is still in love with her, he determines to see if the employees can't get their raise. He invites Gladys (Carol Haney), the bookkeeper, to have drinks with him at an obscure night spot called Hernando's Hideaway, ignoring the fact that Gladys is Hines' girl friend. When she's drunk, Sid wangles the key to the safe. An examination of the ledgers shows him the company already had added the seven-and-a-half cents into their costs. Sid confronts the president and wins the workers their raise. Naturally he also wins his girl.

The book was obviously lopsided and unfair to business, but its attitude could be overlooked thanks to the sunny clowning of a topnotch cast. The choreography established the reputation of both Bob Fosse and his leading dancer, Carol Haney.

. . .

Robert Louis Fosse was born in Chicago on June 23, 1927. His early career was spent dancing in Broadway shows such as *Call Me Mister* and

Make Mine Manhattan (both during their national tours) and *Dance Me a Song*. He also appeared as a dancer in films. More than any other choreographer Fosse became responsible for making the dance director a central figure in many Broadway musicals, so that it would often come to seem the show was conceived to serve as a vehicle for choreographic conceptions. This, however, did not become evident until later.

. . .

In his dance for "Steam Heat," Fosse employed the device that would become his trademark: startling, off-beat, close-knit posturings. He allowed his performers to dance with snapping fingers and clicking tongues as well as with their feet. The best thing in the show, its clever, memorable songs, firmly established the team of Richard Adler and Jerry Ross. Two outstanding numbers emerged: "Hey There," Sid's love ballad whose main theme sounded a little like Mozart in revised tempo, and "Hernando's Hideaway," an irresistible travesty of the sexy Latin tangos that had so long been popular. George Abbott gave the song a memorable staging, beginning it in total darkness, then, following the lyrics' instructions to "light a match," illuminating the stage only with small flickering fires. "Hey There"'s catchy, colloquial lyrics excused any mild plagiarism. Adler and Ross awarded Foy two superior comic numbers, "I'll Never Be Jealous Again" in which his actions belied his oath, and "Think Of The Time I Save," in which he recounted his minute-saving devices. The show ran two-and-a-half years. Happily no one could foresee how tragically foreshortened the careers of both Ross and Miss Haney would be.

1954-1955

The inexplicable swing of good and bad seasons continued. When the pattern held, the new theatrical year proved a banner session. Distressingly, as several of the earlier seasons rich in quality had demonstrated, Broadway could no longer handle many fine musicals. Several musicals failed which in a lesser season or in a former era would have almost certainly made the grade. Not only was the quality unusually high, but the number of musicals took a noticeable jump. There were a dozen new book shows, and twenty or twenty-one lyric works, depending on how *Mrs. Patterson* was listed.

The lone June entry was a return of *Carousel*

(4-19-45) at the customary popular prices of the New York City Center. With no other musical openings all summer long to divert theatregoers attention, the show ran well into August. The revival was strongest in its female leads with Barbara Cook as Carrie, Jo Sullivan as Julie and Bambi Linn back to dance the daughter.

More than a decade before country music became a national craze, a "Hillbilly" revue offered the sound to knowing New Yorkers. Scenery was simple, skits omitted; only the folk music mattered. The line-up of popular figures from the field included stalwarts such as Lester Flatt and Earl Scruggs. But **Hayride** (9-13-54, 48th St.) discovered to its sorrow that knowing New Yorkers were few and far between, so few in fact that the show was withdrawn after three weeks.

September also saw the curtain rise on a "New Musical Comedy of the 1920s." Sandy Wilson's **The Boy Friend** (9-30-54, Royale) was a full-length travesty of the gay, unpretentious confections of the jazz age, carefully and accurately burlesquing the simplistic plot lines, the formula songs (the Charleston number, the dream of a love nest, the exchange of vows, etc.), and the stylized staging of the period. But while it was careful and accurate, it was also affectionate. Those who had sat through the original *No! No! Nanette!* (9-16-25) or *The Girl Friend* (3-17-26) or *Mary* (10-15-20) could now laugh at the excesses and clichés, while still experiencing a warm twinge of nostalgia. The story told how a lordly young English boy and an aristocratic young English lady each pretend to a lowly station to win the other's hand. The situation was precisely the reverse of an earlier American spoof, "The Gladiola Girl" in *Lend An Ear* (12-16-48), in which two poor youngsters pretend to be rich. The aristocratic young lady of the evening was played on Broadway by a young lady with a face of porcelain perfection, a crystal clear voice, and exact diction, Julie Andrews. *The Boy Friend* was an importation from London, where it went on to establish a long-run record. It established no records at all in New York, but it provided delight through the season.

Four nights later Libby Holman brought in her one-woman show, **Blues, Ballads and Sin-Songs** (10-4-54, Bijou). Miss Holman had been absent for some while from Broadway. Time had apparently not been kind to either her artistry or her drawing power, so the show folded after 12 representations.

Nor did most critics feel time had been kind to *On Your Toes* (4-11-36), Rodgers and Hart's memorable hit. It opened in a fine production on October 11 and managed an eight-week run. Bobby Van danced Ray Bolger's part, while Vera Zorina assumed the role Tamara Geva had created. By and large the critics could still praise the "Slaughter on Tenth Avenue" ballet and Rodgers and Hart's songs, but the claptrap of the book seemed to them to belong to a discarded school. With interesting new musicals coming along at a fast clip, the public didn't bother to find out for itself if the critics were right or wrong.

One of the new musicals was **Peter Pan** (10-20-54, Winter Garden), a lyric version of James Barrie's play. It was staged with inventive wit by Jerome Robbins and performed with rare style and panache by Mary Martin as Peter and Cyril Ritchard as Captain Hook. When Peter with the magical word "Indians" gets the Darling children to fly to Neverland, they flew giddily out of their nursery and virtually over the audience. No doubt, too, only this Peter could make the wicked father-figure of Captain Hook to cry "Misericordia." The show originated with Edwin Lester's California organization. When it opened on the West Coast, the music was by Mark (Moose) Charlap and the lyrics by Carolyn Leigh. While they wrote two of Peter's most joyous numbers, "I've Got To Crow" and "I'm Flying," neither song gave promise of being a hit outside the theatre. Jule Styne was invited to write additional music to new Comden and Green lyrics. Most of their material proved more clever than memorable, but they did create one lovely ballad in the "Toyland" tradition, "Neverland." They also wrote "Hook's Waltz" which Ritchard sang with lugubrious hypocrisy, protesting he was merely "Mrs. Hook's little baby boy." The nineteen-week run of the piece was disappointing, and normally would have meant an unprofitable run. But Lester's California subscriptions, plus a lucrative sale of the whole production to television, allowed the production to make a profit. The taping of *Peter Pan*'s second television showing gives future audiences an unusual chance to see an original Broadway cast performing more or less as it did in the theatre.

Although *The Boy Friend, On Your Toes*, and *Peter Pan* all represented some measure of disappointment at the box office, their producers had the consolation that they were mounted with intelligence and taste. It remained for an over-written, over-produced piece to become the first runaway hit of the season. **Fanny** (11-4-54, Majestic) was a musical version of Marcel Pagnol's cinematic trilogy, *Marius, Fanny,* and *César*. The new piece attempted to cover in one evening much the same ground the three films had covered. With equal shortsightedness in the face of the restricting limitations of a Broadway stage, it attempted to show a fully-rigged ship sailing the stage and offer elaborate undersea and circus ballets. Although the distinguished playwright S. N. Behrman collaborated with Joshua Logan on the book, the intimacy and warmth of the original screen masterpieces were lost. Only the story remained. César, the owner of a small waterfront café in Marseilles, hopes his son Marius will wed the young, pretty Fanny, settle down, and take over the business. But Marius prefers the sea. He sails away, leaving Fanny pregnant but unwed. Frightened, Fanny consents to become the wife of a kind, elderly sailmaker, Panisse. Panisse is even prepared to change the name of his small firm to "Panisse And Son," although he knows the child is not his. Years later Marius returns, and both he and Fanny would willingly resume their romance. But César roughly intervenes so that the good-hearted Panisse will not be hurt. Although Panisse hires a whole circus for Césario's twelfth birthday, the boy is more interested in meeting Marius, about whom he has heard so much over the years. He finds him working in a garage in Toulon and tells of his desire to go to sea. Marius discourages him, insisting he must return to his parents. Césario returns to find Panisse dying. Even on his deathbed Panisse can think only of his adopted boy. He begs Fanny to wed Marius so that Césario can grow up in a loving household.

Harold Rome's score pulled out all the sentimental stops. Songs such as "Never Too Late For Love," "Why Be Afraid To Dance?," "Love Is A Very Light Thing," "Other Hands, Other Hearts," and "Be Kind To Your Parents" employed the same unabashed directness of expression and feeling that Oscar Hammerstein regularly offered his public. Rome's most successful number was his title song, sung by Marius. As he had with "Wish You Were Here," he managed to repeat the title so often it acted as a sort of advertisement for the play. With Ezio Pinza as César and Walter Slezak as Panisse in the starring roles and with Florence Henderson and William Tabbert featured, *Fanny* embarked on a run that lasted for over two years. In retrospect, *Fanny* may well be remembered as the debut of the most important producer of the era, David Merrick.

   . . .

David Merrick was born David Margulois in St. Louis on November 27, 1911. He studied to be a lawyer, but found the lure of the theatre irresistible, and, after a brief but thorough apprenticeship, boldly entered producing ranks.

. . .

The critical, if not commercial, success of *The Golden Apple* (3-11-54) prompted the experimental Phoenix Theatre to attempt two more musicals during the season. Both were well received, but learning from the fiasco of the preceding spring, the company rejected thoughts of moving uptown. The first of the two musicals—presented on November 23—was the more off-beat, a "Ballad in Three Acts" called **Sandhog.** Written by Earl Robinson and Waldo Salt and based on Theodore Dreiser's short story "St. Columba and the River," it was a singularly stark, cohesive work which repeated several of its musical passages at intervals throughout the evening in a leitmotif fashion uncommon to Broadway. The story chronicled the career of Johnny O'Sullivan (Jack Cassidy), who gets a job as a sandhog digging tunnels under the river, marries his sweetheart Katie (Betty Oakes), leaves the job after several of his friends are killed in an accident, then returns to the work and is miraculously spared when he is blown to safety in a second mishap. With the prosperity and complacency of the Eisenhower years settling in, the show's slightly thirtyish tone and attitude seemed somewhat out of date, but in no way compromised its integrity.

Mrs. Patterson (12-1-54, National) recounted the conflicting dream lives of a black girl who at times wants to be a sedate, rich, white woman and at other times a dark hellion. She finally accepts reality. Although Eartha Kitt had made her name as a singer and though she sang six of the seven numbers James Shelton wrote for the show, the piece was generally looked on as a straight play. It was in fact one of those borderline affairs more common thirty or forty years before. The music came not from a pit band, but rather was amplified from recordings. In any case it was not a success, although it ran 101 performances.

A musical called **Hit the Trail** opened at the Hellinger the following night, December 2, and closed two nights later. Its plot depicted the plight of a prima donna, Lucy Vernay (Irra Petina), whose troupe is stranded in 19th-century Nevada, and who must choose between a banker (Paul Valentine) and a crook (Robert Wright). The score was Frederico Valerio's sole Broadway effort. Even such fine singers as Miss Petina and Wright couldn't help it. It was unquestionably the one musical of the season that didn't even deserve a production.

The last week in December brought two of the season's most unusual and interesting works. Both failed. On the 27th, Gian-Carlo Menotti offered his latest opera, **The Saint of Bleecker Street,** at the Broadway. Menotti's tale recounted the incestuous passion of Michele for his devout little sister, Annina. When the voluptuous Desideria (Gloria Lane) opens Michele's eyes to the true nature of his feelings, he kills her. Annina takes the veil. David Poleri and Davis Cunningham alternated in the role of Michele, while Virginia Copeland and Gabrielle Ruggiero spelled each other as Annina. Musically, the opera was neither venturesome nor deep, but it was, as all of Menotti's pieces of this period were, unstintingly theatrical. At its own level it had a rare consistency of style and tone. But opera's appeal to regular Broadway playgoers was still limited. Menotti's novelty had worn off, so the best the new work could achieve was 92 performances: a remarkable figure for an opera but a certain indication of indifference and failure in the commercial theatre.

House of Flowers (12-30-54, Alvin), with book and lyrics by Truman Capote, also had an uncommon consistency of style and tone, even if it was worlds away from the drab, urban harshness of Menotti's opera. Some viewers felt the uniformity of tone subtly deteriorated into simple monotony. Whether the show's boosters or detractors were correct, it was amazing that the show had any noteworthy tone at all. It had been plagued during its tryout by some of the most vicious backstage fighting Broadway had heard about in years. One thing that remained gratefully unaffected were the exquisite pastel delicacies of Oliver Messel's poetically imaginative costumes and sets. They depicted life on an unidentified West Indies isle. In this unworldly paradise a very earthy trade war has broken out between two brothels. One is run by Madame Tango (Juanita Hall). The other, "The House of Flowers," is run by the appropriately named Madame Fleur (Pearl Bailey), and filled with young ladies named after blossoms. When a group of sailors introduces an epidemic of mumps in the establishment, Madame Fleur is in desperate straits. She is not above selling one of her girls, Ottilie (professionally known as Violet), to a rich merchant. When Ottilie (Diahann Carroll) protests she intends to marry her own sweetheart, Royal (Rawn Spearman), Madame Fleur arranges to have Royal kidnaped. He escapes in time to prevent Ottilie's marriage. Madame Fleur emerges triumphant when Madame Tango's girls sail on a world cruise. Another part of the show that remained happily above backstage strife was Harold Arlen's luminous score. It was as exquisite and poetic as the settings, able to turn from the sunlit airiness of "Two Ladies In De Shade Of De Banana Tree"—a calypso number sung by Gladiola (Ada Moore) and Pansy (Enid Mosier)—to the subtly modulated languors of Ottilie's "A Sleeping Bee," and the title song, sung by Royal and Ottilie. An intangible gossamer grace rendered the show somehow untheatrical. When an off-Broadway revival attempted to re-create the original conception some years later, it met with no success.

Yet **Plain and Fancy** (1-27-55, Hellinger), which arrived as 1955's first musical show and which also eschewed all the easy theatrical tricks, managed to provide an eminently satisfying evening. Even its setting was novel: the Amish country near Lancaster, Pennsylvania. Two wordly-wise New Yorkers, Ruth Winters (Shirl Conway) and Dan King (Richard Derr), come to the area to sell a farm Dan has inherited. He believes he has a customer in Papa Yoder (Stefan Schnabel). Yoder's daughter, Katie (Gloria Marlowe), has been picked to marry Ezra Reber (Douglas Fletcher Rodgers). Ezra has accepted the arrangement casually. One wife in his eyes is as good or as bad as another, so, "Why Not Katie?" Katie also stoically accepts her father's plans. Just before the wedding her old love, Peter (David Daniels), Ezra's brother, returns and before long both wish they could be "Young And Foolish" again. The Yoders, however, will have none of this. Peter has left the community, a grievous sin among Amish. As Yoder explains to Dan, "Plain We Live." The Amish way of life is simple and clear-cut. Peter has become an outsider to be shunned. When the Yoders' farm burns down, the neighbors all help raise a new one. Peter somehow feels he has brought on the problem and determines to leave. Before he can go, Ezra gets drunk at a carnival, and only Peter's quick action minimizes the disgrace. Papa Yoder reconsiders his opinion of Peter, and Peter reconsiders his plans to leave. About the same time that Peter and Katie announce they will wed, Dan and Ruth come to the same decision. The book was by Joseph Stein and William Glickman; Albert Hague and Arnold B. Horwitt wrote the music and lyrics respectively. The show took a sympathetic look at the stern Amish philosophy and their often hard existence. It made an unexpected applause-getting scene out of an Amish barn-raising. Only in the Carnival Ballet did it employ for any length the accepted and expected Broadway musical devices. *Plain and Fancy*'s willingness to pioneer was re-

warded. "Young And Foolish" became one of the most popular songs of the year and the show had a run of 461 performances.

Silk Stockings (2-24-55, Imperial) arrived a month later. It, too, had the potential for being an off-beat musical. But in an extended tryout, marked by as many battles and revisions as *House of Flowers* had suffered, it was turned into a slick, formula musical. Luckily the old hands working on the show were some of the top professionals in the business, and they made the old formula work well enough to give *Silk Stockings* a run of 478 performances. The piece was a lyric version of a popular 1939 movie, *Ninotchka*. At the musical's world premiere its book was a joint effort of George S. Kaufman and Leueen MacGrath. By the time it arrived in New York, Abe Burrows had contributed a substantial rewriting. Kaufman had also been the original director, and though he insisted that credit be dropped he allowed his name to remain as coauthor of the libretto. The story that Garbo had brought to the screen remained reasonably intact. Steve Canfield (Don Ameche), an American theatrical agent, has made him such attractive offers that Peter Boroff (Philip Sterling), a Russian composer famous for his "Ode to a Tractor," decides to stay in the West. The communists send the unsmiling disciplinarian, Ninotchka (Hildegarde Neff), to retrieve him. Steve makes Paris so attractive for the pretty girl that the Russians must in turn send a whole delegation to bring her back. She returns to Russia, only to have Steve pursue her there. Together they return to the West. A secondary plot that only touched on the principal tale had Janice Dayton (Gretchen Wyler), a Hollywood glamor queen, in Paris to make a movie.

The "Cold War" was going full blast, providing ready-made targets. A leading best seller in the shaky hierarchy of the Kremlin is "Who's Still Who," while a Soviet official when advised Prokofiev is dead, comments, "I didn't even know he was arrested." A superb cast acted and sang surrounded by colorful Jo Mielziner sets. Yet for many the primary appeal of the show was Cole Porter's score. Although its songs never became as standard as his previous *Can-Can* score, they were melodic and varied. The most popular was probably Steve's racy "All Of You." Porter created another solid beguine in Steve's title song and a rippling number in Steve and Ninotchka's "As On Through The Seasons We Sail." Nor did his way with words fail him. "Paris Loves Lovers" at first seemed like a pleasant reworking in reverse of "I Love Paris," but before Porter was through Ninotchka interrupted Steve's picture with fitting communistic replies. The subplot allowed him to have fun at the expense of the wide screens and new sound equipment motion palaces had introduced with a song given to Janice, "Glorious Technicolor, Breath-taking Cinemascope And Stereophonic Sound." Both *Can-Can* (5-7-53) and *Silk Stockings* were set in Paris, as were Porter's first two successes, *Paris* (10-8-28) and *Fifty Million Frenchmen* (11-27-29). Since his new show sadly turned out to be his last, it meant he had come full circle. While Porter was as urbane and civilized as the City of Light he so loved, his most identifiable songs were written in a South American beat derived from the African jungles often with minor key melodies he himself termed "Jewish," and his lyrics were so carefully nuanced and so often knowingly topical they defied translation or even a sea-crossing. Porter's stylish songs were unique products of the proverbial but not always successful American melting pot.

On February 28, Ben Bagley brought the first of his **Shoestring Revues** into the tiny President, an "off-Broadway" house in the heart of the theatrical district. These low-budget productions were among the most consistently witty Broadway ever knew. "In Bed with the Reader's Digest" devastated that magazine's saccharine innocuities. "Medea in Disneyland" reduced Greek tragedy to a puerile animated confection. The shows were filled with deliciously comic songs, such as Sheldon Harnick's "Garbage." Only in their failure to produce durable standards did the *Shoestring Revues* prove disappointing. But the shows nurtured an amazing number of future stars: Dody Goodman, Beatrice Arthur, Chita Rivera, Arte Johnson, and one great comedienne who failed to reach the top, Dorothy Greener.

Another low-budget "diversion in song and dance" called **3 for Tonight** (4-6-55, Plymouth) presented Marge and Gower Champion, Harry Belafonte, and Hiram Sherman in a refreshingly oddball revue that mingled old and new material. None of the new songs made an impression, but the playgoers could leave the theatre whistling such old favorites as "Shine On Harvest Moon" and "When The Saints Go Marching In." Though *3 for Tonight* ran only 85 performances, its miminal initial cost allowed it to make money.

Ankles Aweigh (4-18-55, Hellinger), a raucous, rowdy musical comedy of the old school, sailed in next. By the standards of an earlier era everything was shipshape. The musical had a gag-filled, far-fetched but workable book; an eye-appealing

chorus line; unashamedly old-fashioned tap dancing; coarse, funny comedians, and a hammock-load of songs. That the demand for such diverting claptrap had not yet died was evident from the 22 week stay *Ankles Aweigh* enjoyed. In the days to which it harked back, a similar run almost assuredly would have spelled success, but in 1955 the musical closed without returning its investment. The Guy Bolton-Eddie Davis book described the honeymoon of a Hollywood starlet and a navy flier interrupted in all sorts of exotic Mediterranean settings by the demands of her studio and navy top brass. Jane Kean and Mark Dawson as the lovers were assisted by Jane's sister Betty, Lew Parker, Gabriel Dell, and Thelma Carpenter. Sammy Fain's spunky score ranged from the jaunty "Walk Like A Sailor" to a competent ballad "Nothing At All"—whose Dan Shapiro lyrics reflected the hyperbolic imagery Hammerstein had popularized in *Oklahoma!* (3-31-43).

A more modish evening premiered the following night. **All in One** (4-9-55, Playhouse) was a triple bill that included a staging of Leonard Bernstein's one-act opera, *Trouble in Tahiti*. Although the bill also offered a Tennessee Williams play and a dance program by Paul Draper, the public was unresponsive.

The next night brought a popular price return of *Guys and Dolls* (11-24-50), Walter Matthau was Nathan while Helen Gallagher played Adelaide. *South Pacific* (4-7-49), followed at the house on May 4, while *Finian's Rainbow* (1-10-47) ended the Center's season on May 18 with Will Mahoney as Finian and Miss Gallagher as Sharon.

April's last musical appeared on the 23rd. It was the second of the Phoenix Theatre's two lyric offerings. If it struck a number of critics as a surprisingly conventional piece for the unconventional house to mount, it struck even more critics as a hilarious evening in the theatre. The show was a revue entitled succinctly, **Phoenix '55.** In the teens or the twenties such a title would have hinted at the beginning of a revue series. But everyone knew the success of *Phoenix '55* rested solely on one performer. So it is doubtful that there was any intention of making the show an annual affair. The performer was Nancy Walker, and she was almost singlehandedly responsible for making the material seem hysterically funny. When she was off-stage, particularly when the show's lackluster songs were being sung, the evening sagged. The high spot of the entertainment came when Miss Walker burlesqued the jerky, undisciplined method school of acting, then the rage of the theatre. Miss Walker almost literally chewed the scenery as she reacted to her own emotions—which told her to walk over sofas and actors, and generally create mayhem. Because the show was the Phoenix's final offering of the season, it decided to extend the run after the initial engagement had been played. As a result the show ran until hot weather at the end of July depleted its audience.

Considering the popularity of football in collegiate musicals, and of sports such as golf, prize-fighting, and horse-racing in other musical shows, it is startling to realize that until 1955 no New York musical had ever successfully dealt with the most American of sports, baseball. Most New Yorkers were no doubt unaware Chicago had made a hit of *The Umpire* (12-2-05) at the turn of the century. The oversight was joyously rectified when **Damn Yankees** (5-5-55, 46th St.) hit a metaphoric grand slam. In a couple of ways its timing was perfect. The baseball season had just begun, and the Yankees, who are the inadvertent villains of the piece, were nearing the end of the great epoch that was the starting point for the plot. The story was not new to the more literate baseball fans. George Abbott and Douglass Wallop adapted their libretto from Wallop's best seller, *The Year the Yankees Lost the Pennant,* which had wickedly combined the nation's chagrin at the seeming hopelessness of outclassing the great New York team with the wishful possibilities of the Faust legend. No one is more chagrined than middle-aged Joe Boyd (Robert Shafer) as he sits in his living room watching his beloved Senators take another beating. When he suggests he would sell his soul to see Washington win, a man named Applegate (Ray Walston) appears miraculously at his side and obligingly agrees to accept Joe's soul in exchange for making the Washington Senators world champions. In a flash paunchy Joe Boyd becomes strapping Joe Hardy (Stephen Douglass). Van Buren (Russ Brown), the Senators' manager, is urgently telling his downtrodden team that all they need to turn the tide is "Heart." The players know better. They need something more, something like, "Shoeless Joe From Hannibal, Mo." Joe proves to be just the needed tonic, inaugurating an unprecedented winning streak. Unfortunately, Joe is lonely for his wife (Shannon Bolin). He rents a room in his own home, but his wife, of course, doesn't recognize the handsome, youthful man she sees before her. Applegate, fearing Joe's homing instincts will queer the deal, enlists the support of Lola (Gwen Verdon), a hag who has sold her soul to become a beautiful woman. Lola appears in the locker room and warns the protesting Joe not to resist her charms, for "Whatever Lola Wants," Lola gets. Eventually Joe's longing for his wife grows too strong for him to fight. He reneges on his deal and goes home to watch the Senators start another losing streak.

. . .

Redheaded **Gwyneth Verdon** was born in Culver City, California, on January 13, 1926. Her mother was a dancer. Miss Verdon studied with Jack Cole, and after making her debut in *Bonanza Bound,* which folded on tryout, worked with Cole as assistant choreographer for both *Magdelena* and *Alive and Kicking.* She danced with Cole in the latter. Her dancing in *Can-Can* called her to Broadway's attention. *Damn Yankees* also called attention to her gaminlike, teasing charm.

. . .

Adler and Ross' score was inventive and clever, but in some respects uncomfortably close to their material for *Pajama Game.* "Whatever Lola Wants," like "Hernando's Hideway," was a mock tango; the soft-shoe style of Applegate's "Those Were The Good Old Days" recalled "I'll Never Be Jealous Again"; "Who's Got The Pain," though it used a different rhythm, seemed a first cousin to "Steam Heat." But "Heart," if cornball, was fresh, and some of the minor numbers such as "Near To You" and Joe and Lola's farewell, "Two Lost Souls," displayed promising originality. Unfortunately, which direction Adler and Ross would have taken will never be known. Jerry Ross died shortly after the show opened, and Adler, after some weak solo attempts, disappeared for years from the Broadway scene. *Damn Yankees* played for over a thousand performances and had a road company headed by Bobby Clark in his last important assignment.

The season's last show was a musical version of yet another old film favorite, the Janet Gaynor and Charles Farrell silent-film classic, *Seventh Heaven.* But in some way the magic of the movie's obvious sentimentality was lost in transferring the story from the screen. Although Ricardo Montalban made a suitable Chico and Gloria DeHaven was an attractive Diane, the story of the girl who remains faithful to her street cleaner, even after he is blinded in the war, seemed contrived and maudlin. Stella Unger's lyrics ran to such clichés as "Where Is That Someone For Me?" (almost a spoof of a 1920s title) and to such trite bits as "A Miss You Kiss." Victor Young's score seemed commonplace. Only in Diane and Chico's "Sun At My Window, Love At My Door" did Young come up with a catchy melody and Miss Unger provide reasonably unembarrassing lyrics. They were not enough to buck both the heat and the competition. **Seventh Heaven** (5-26-55, ANTA) survived just over one month.

1955-1956

Did the 1955–56 season continue the pattern of alternate feast and famine? Statistically it would appear so. The number of new lyric pieces fell to a discouraging eight: three revues and five book shows. City Center revivals and a pair of one-man shows fattened the figure slightly, as did a visit by the D'Oyly Carte. Equally discouraging, only two of the commercial ventures made profits. It would be impossible to imagine a more depressing year in the history of the American Musical Theatre, except for one thing: one of the two hits was *My Fair Lady*.

However, *My Fair Lady,* and what little else was interesting, didn't arrive until late in the season. The early months were horrendous. A brightly mounted but vacuous revue, **Almost Crazy** (6-20-55, Longacre), opened the season. Much of its material was by the persistent, if uninspired, James Shelton, while a fine comedienne, Portia Nelson, contributed several numbers that suggested she belonged on stage rather than behind the scenes. The show got the season off to a doubly disheartening beginning by insisting in its curtain raiser, "Everything's Gonna Be Much Worse Next Year." Luckily not too many patrons had a chance to take such Cassandric utterings to heart, for *Almost Crazy* was carted away after two weeks.

A second revue, **Catch a Star!** (9-6-55, Plymouth), fared only a mite better, running three weeks. Its songs were by Sammy Fain, a composer of pleasant melodies that never seemed to make the grade on Broadway, by Phil Charig, a voice out of the past, and by Jerry Bock, a voice soon to be heard more assertively. The evening's sketches were the joint effort of Danny and Neil Simon, the latter, of course, going on to become one of Broadway's top comic playwrights. The Simons parodied a Tennessee Williams play in "Room for Rent," and spoofed *Marty,* a popular film about a homely, ordinary New Yorker, in *Arty.*

On the 27th of the month the D'Oyly Carte began a season of eight Gilbert and Sullivan works that continued until Thanksgiving. The operettas presented were *Iolanthe, The Mikado, The Yeomen of the Guard, The Pirates of Penzance, Princess Ida, Trial by Jury, H.M.S. Pinafore,* and *Ruddigore.*

The night after the Englishmen arrived the popular French boulevardier, Maurice Chevalier, began a six-week stint with his one-man show. He was followed by the season's other solo effort, **Joyce Grenfell Requests the Pleasure** (10-10-55, Bijou). Strictly speaking, Miss Grenfell's was not a solo performance. She had three artists assist her in some of her numbers and entertain while she changed gowns. Nonetheless her fans came to see Miss Grenfell, and she amused them for 65 performances with her droll lyrics set to Richard Addinsell's music.

November brought the season's first two book musicals. Both glittered with promise and both failed. **The Vamp** (11-10-55, Winter Garden) starred Carol Channing, who had had such glorious fun with the roaring twenties and now proposed to have an even more lavish spree in the good, old days ten years or so earlier. Miss Channing played Flora Weems, a hard-working farm girl from the Bronx, who rises to fame as an incongruously gigantic, hilariously wide-eyed siren in the early movie studios of New York and Hollywood. Sadly, the airy wit John Latouche had displayed in *The Golden Apple* deserted him. His lyrics and dialogue (coauthored with Sam Locke) were heavy-handed and obvious, while James Mundy's score contained nothing memorable. Even the sumptuous mounting (especially in sets parodying the Biblical scenery of early movies) seemed to bog down in its own opulence. The show closed while the rest of Broadway was celebrating New Year's Eve.

Opera's Helen Traubel costarred with Bill Johnson in Rodgers and Hammerstein's latest musical, **Pipe Dream** (11-30-55, Shubert), a lyric version of John Steinbeck's *Sweet Thursday.* When a pretty vagrant named Suzy (Judy Tyler) is arrested for stealing food, a good-natured brothel-keeper, Fauna (Miss Traubel), extricates her from the mess and offers her a home. She soon falls in love with an impoverished marine biologist, Doc (Johnson). Doc is so poor he can't even afford the microscope his work requires, so the raffish stumblebums of the neighborhood, men to whom Doc has always been unpatronizingly friendly, stage a rigged lottery. After Doc and Suzy quarrel and Suzy says she will never again see Doc—unless, of course, he needs her—one of the men breaks Doc's arm while Doc is sleeping so that Suzy can tend it. Hammerstein's expected sentimentality oozed forth in songs such as Suzy's "Everybody's Got A Home But Me" and Doc's "The Man I Used To Be," and even Rodgers' attractive melodies were not up to his best. Only one song pleased the public at large, the lovers' "All At Once You Love Her," sung as a first-act finale. Miss Traubel, hefty and regal, seemed uncomfortably cast, and while she had lively "Sweet Thursday" to sing, her most satisfying moment may well have been her lovely second-act reprise of "All At Once You Love Her." Although *Pipe Dream* ran through the season, it failed to repay its investors. The economic outlook in the theatre was growing increasingly grim. One highly praised, six-character, single-set straight comedy, *Fallen Angels,* also ran seven months without being able to recoup reasonable initial costs.

No further musicals appeared until **My Fair Lady** (3-15-56) broke a history of failures that had beset the Mark Hellinger and went on to establish a Broadway long-run record. The musical was based on George Bernard Shaw's *Pygmalion.* Lerner and Loewe's adaptation was uncommonly faithful, and even when it deviated from the original it did so with unerring intelligence, taste, and style. As it did in the Shaw play, the evening opens just after a performance at Covent Garden, where elegantly dressed operagoers mingle with the area's low-life. One of the denizens of the place warns a be-smudged flower-seller, Liza Doolittle (Julie Andrews), that a gentleman is taking notes of everything she says. She begins to bawl and the gentleman tries to comfort her by his assurance he is not a policeman. He also tells her she is from Lisson Grove. She is amazed—and defensive. Liza swears the place wasn't fit to be a pigsty, and that here she earns a bare living legitimately. The gentleman turns out to be Professor Henry Higgins (Rex Harrison), a philologist and phoneticist. His attentions are soon diverted by another gentleman who proves to be Colonel Pickering (Robert Coote), author of "Spoken Sanskrit." To his newfound colleague Higgins complains, "Why can't the English teach their children how to speak?" Higgins offhandedly remarks that he could take an uneducated waif like the flower-seller and make her into a lady by improving her speech. He invites Pickering to move in with him, giving the Colonel his address. After throwing some coins in Liza's basket, they hurry off. Liza would like to be a lady and dreams of its comforts, sighing "Wouldn't It Be Loverly?" Liza's father (Stanley Holloway) is thrown out of a pub for want of money. He decides to ask his daughter to stand him and his friends a round of drinks. Under normal conditions Liza would have prob-ably rebuffed him, but, flush with the coins Higgins has given her and with his hint she might some-day be a lady, she gives her father enough to treat himself and his friends. With a knowing wink the appropriately named Doolittle remarks to his cronies, "With a little bit of luck, someone else'll do the blinkin' work!" At Higgins' house Pickering has settled in when a visitor is announced—none other than Liza come to take Higgins up on his suggestion that he can turn her into a lady. Higgins is appalled, but an amused Pickering presses Higgins to try, so Eliza is carted off by Higgins' house-keeper to be bathed and properly clothed. Higgins is slightly unnerved. He protests "I'm An Ordinary Man" enjoying solitude, and warns:

But let a woman in your life
    And you are up against the wall!
Make a plan and you will find
    She has something else in mind;
And so rather than do either
    You do something else that neither
Likes at all.

After a visit from Doolittle that Higgins sees as a form of blackmail, the professor embarks on a rigorous training program for Eliza, determined to restore her "H's" to their proper place and make her vowel sounds more musical and correct. His persistence drives Eliza into a rage, warning Higgins, "Just You Wait." At the same time Higgins' persistence is rewarded, and, after a seemingly endless struggle, Higgins and Pickering celebrate Eliza's correct pronunciation of "The Rain In Spain" with a giddy fandangoing, tangoing revel. The elated Eliza exults, "I Could Have Danced All Night."

At the Ascot enclosure (beginning the second act) lords and ladies watch the races with a carefully regulated excitement, excitement with as much life in it as a formal gavotte. Higgins and Pickering have determined to risk a public presentation of their pupil. Eliza's diction proves perfect, even when she reveals to their horror, "Gin was mother's milk." Her grammar and startling pronouncements entrance Freddy Eynsford-Hill (John Michael King), who promptly falls in love with her and thereafter spends an inordinate amount of his time "On The Street Where You Live." At an Embassy Ball Higgins brazenly dances Eliza into the arms of a Hungarian named Karpathy, who has publicly professed to spot impostors unfailingly. It becomes obvious from the congratulations Higgins and Pickering exchange when they return home that Karpathy was soundly gulled. Higgins and Pickering each tell the other, "You Did It," ignoring any part Eliza may have played in her own education. This prompts Eliza to leave the house. On the street she meets Freddie, who has continued to mope about and, when Freddie spills out his feelings, she insists, "Show Me." The empty-headed Freddie fails to comprehend or act decisively. She hits him with her suitcase and goes on her way, but she finds she is unrecognized and out of place in her old haunts, until she meets her father. Doolittle is bitter at Higgins. The money Higgins presented him has delivered him "into the hands of middle-class morality." In short, he is about to be married. But before he succumbs he will have one last old-fashioned toot. While urging his cronies to "pull out the stopper" and make his final drink "a whopper," he begs, "Get Me To The Church On Time." Deserted by Eliza, the baffled and hurt Higgins sings a "Hymn To Him," inquiring "why can't a woman be more like a man," then, more specifically, why can't a woman be more like him and Pickering, and finally why a woman can't be just like he himself is. Eliza, meanwhile, visits Henry's mother (Cathleen Nesbitt), seeking advice. But Higgins barges in:

Higgins: Get up and come home and don't be a fool! You've caused me enough trouble for one morning!

Mrs. Higgins: Very nicely put, indeed, Henry. No woman could resist such an invitation.

. . .

Higgins: You mean I'm to put on my Sunday manners for this thing I created out of the squashed cabbage leaves of Covent Garden?

Mrs. Higgins: Yes, dear, that is precisely what I mean.

Higgins: I'll see her damned first.

But Eliza will not be subservient. She informs the startled Higgins that art, music, Keats, and the rain in Spain will all survive "Without You." Higgins storms out. He is furious. Still, he must wistfully acknowledge, "I've Grown Accustomed To Her Face." Alone in his study he replays primitive recordings he made while working on Eliza's speech. Eliza enters quietly. Her return is a tacit admission of her feelings and her situation. Although Higgins is joyous, all he can think to ask is, "Where the devil are my slippers?"

This ending, which Shaw had allowed for a movie version, was the principal deviation from the original play. To Lerner's literate, civilized book and lyrics, Loewe appended a score that, while never inventive, was graceful and melodic. If it

seemed at times derivative, the need to keep period flavor was more to blame than any failing on the composer's part. To many these period costumes and songs echoing an earlier era argued that *My Fair Lady* was a modern day operetta, underscoring how the modern musical play was really a continuation of an older tradition.

The original production added more praiseworthy elements. The nonpareil cast was headed by Rex Harrison, who made a definitive Higgins, and Julie Andrews, who fulfilled the promise of *The Boy Friend* with her superlative performance as Eliza. The rest of the fine cast sparkled under Moss Hart's scintillating direction. Oliver Smith designed magnificent sets (most notably an Ascot conceived in black, gray, and white), and Cecil Beaton came over from England to create ravishing period costumes. Companies of the show established records in major cities and foreign capitals all over the world. The New York company alone entertained patrons for 2,717 performances, or over six years.

One interesting sidelight was CBS-Columbia's sizable investment in the original production in order to secure recording rights. The gamble proved doubly rewarding, for not only did the show turn out to be a gold mine, but the original-cast LP became the biggest selling show album in history until that time.

Despite its period settings and the necessary period flavor of its score, *My Fair Lady* unquestionably represented the glorious fruition of the contemporary school of musical plays with its aim of cohesiveness and tonal integrity. How ironic then that the very next musical to arrive—one week after Lerner and Loewe's masterpiece—was contemporary in setting and contemporary in sound, yet was a clear throwback to the slapdash vehicles of bygone years. The evening was meant to introduce a popular black night club entertainer, Sammy Davis, Jr., to the legitimate stage. **Mr. Wonderful** (3-22-56, Broadway) told an unusually simple, straightforward tale. Charlie Welch is a small-time performer whose fiancée, Ethel (Olga James), and whose white friend, Fred Campbell (Jack Carter), both believe he belongs at the top of his profession. They persuade him to try his act at the Palm Club in Miami Beach. He does, and achieves great success. Most of the second act was merely an on-stage repeat of the act Davis, his father, and his uncle had played to applause as the Will Mastin Trio. Jerry Bock, Larry Holofcener, and George Weiss' score added two new standards to the repertory.

Curiously the hit of the evening was not sung by

Davis, but by Miss James. It was the title song. Davis' big hit was a solid swing number, "Too Close For Comfort." Although Davis and the hit songs kept customers coming to the large Broadway Theatre for nearly a year (383 performances), theatrical economics left the show in the red.

. . .

Jerry Bock was born in New Haven, Connecticut, on November 23, 1928, but moved at the age of two to New York City. His musical education began early and culminated with his majoring in music at the University of Wisconsin. He wrote for college musicals, television, and films before his songs were heard on Broadway for the first time earlier in the season in *Catch a Star.*

. . .

A spring season of revivals at the City Center offered *The King and I* (3-29-51) with Zachary Scott and Jan Clayton on April 18, followed by *Kiss Me, Kate* (12-30-48) with Kitty Carlisle on May 9, and *Carmen Jones* (12-2-43) on May 31.

The season's second commercial success was **The Most Happy Fella** (5-3-56, Imperial). Critics divided sharply on how great an artistic success it was, but even those unhappy with the results unhesitatingly gave it top marks for sincerity. *The Most Happy Fella* was a musical adaptation of Sidney Howard's hit of the 1924–25 season, *They Knew What They Wanted*—and it was the work of one man, Frank Loesser. While there were over forty musical numbers and while the spoken dialogue was kept to a minimum, Loesser refused to brand the work an opera or even a musical play, preferring to consider it an "extended musical comedy." His designation was honest, but it pointed to the great flaw in the work that its detractors harped on. For, although Loesser wrote the piece singlehandedly, he seemed unable or unwilling to imbue it with a consistent style and tone. Some of its passages were floridly arioso; some recalled the inventive, up-to-the-minute idioms he had employed in *Guys and Dolls,* while others were out-and-out musical-comedy turns. The show retained the original drama's division into three acts—rare in modern musicals. As in Howard's play an aging vintner in the Napa Valley, Tony (Robert Weede), is attracted to a young lady he sees working in a San Francisco restaurant. In a letter he asks the girl to send him her photograph. She responds, asking for his photograph in return. But Tony, fearful of her cutting off the correspondence abruptly, sends her a photograph of his young, handsome hired hand, Joe (Art Lund). The girl, Rosabella (Jo Sullivan), arrives at the ranch and greets Joe

warmly. Joe quickly disabuses her. She is ready to make a hasty retreat when word arrives that Tony has been injured in an accident while on his way to meet her. Touched by the sight of the injured man, she agrees to remain, and before much time elapses they are married. But this does not prevent a brief, impassioned love affair between Rosabella and Joe. To make his wife more at home, Tony invites her best friend, Cleo (Susan Johnson), to stay on the farm. Cleo quickly becomes involved with another hired hand, Herman (Shorty Long), and their relationship offers a lighthearted counterpoint to Tony and Rosabella's story. After Rosabella discovers she is pregnant, she decides to leave rather than hurt Tony with an admission of infidelity. When Tony tries to stop her, the truth comes out. At first Tony is livid, threatening to kill Joe. With time to reflect, he realizes that both he and Rosabella will only return to separate lonelinesses. He offers to accept the child as his own, and Rosabella, deeply moved, agrees.

The story was dangerously sentimental, but Loesser adroitly managed to underplay its most maudlin aspects. In singing Tony, Weede became the season's second major opera star to try Broadway. The most operatic of the passages fell to him. Rosabella had more conventional ballads, such as the beautiful, "Somebody, Somewhere." However, an all-but-nameless male quartet was given one of the show's two major hits, "Standing On The Corner," while Cleo, Herman, and the chorus attacked the rousing second hit, a tribute to Dallas called "Big D." Despite its flaws, the evening's sure-fire professionalism and general excellence told. To varying degrees, it pleased and sometimes annoyed theatregoers for a year and a half.

The season's final new offering was another Phoenix Theatre revue on May 22. It was a far cry from the preceding season's *Phoenix '55,* with its broad clowning by Nancy Walker. The new offering was called **The Littlest Revue,** a name that was probably meant to evoke echoes of the suave, intimate *Little Shows* of a quarter of a century before. A galaxy of the theatre's bright names made contributions to one department or another: Ogden Nash, Vernon Duke, John Latouche, Lee Adams, and Charles Strouse, among others. Skits had fun with old-timers who haunted the recently demolished Brevoort Hotel, off-Broadway plays, toilets, diets, and Noel Coward, while songs ran the gamut from love ballads to "Second Avenue And 12th Street Rag" (Nash/Duke), to an untraditional "Summer Is Icumen In" (Latouche/Duke). The material was performed by some equally bright talent that included Joel Grey, Tammy Grimes, and Charlotte Rae—all names on the way up. While the show developed a coterie of staunch admirers, they had little chance to see it in the flesh. The revue opened on May 22 and by June 17 gave its final performance.

No doubt the main reason a group of advocates could develop to sing the real or imagined virtues of so quick a flop was the practice of issuing original cast recordings for almost every musical to reach Broadway. As mentioned earlier this practice began in American only with *Oklahoma!*, though England had been doing it, and benefiting, since the 1900s. Not only did the practice keep alive material that might otherwise have been forgotten— or used to better advantage in a later, more successful show—but on occasion, as with *Pal Joey,* it actually precipitated a major revival. Unfortunately, by the seventies the economics of the record industry put a stop to the issuance of original cast records except for a handful of runaway hits.

1956-1957

The season was intriguing, unorthodox, and ultimately frustrating. Among composers, all the surviving old masters were absent, and only two of the better young songwriters were represented—Jule Styne and Leonard Bernstein. Not unpredictably, they offered the year's best scores. A few dependable names appeared among libretto credits: Lindsay and Crouse, Comden and Green, and George Abbott. One surprising new name was Lillian Hellman, heretofore celebrated for her stark dramas. Yet old hands and newcomers alike failed to find quite the right approach to their stories. Most of the season's musicals relied heavily on the drawing power of their feminine stars. Perhaps the most fascinating aspect of the season's crop was the unlikely source material nearly every show resorted to: Al Capp's comic strip, *Li'l Abner,* Voltaire's *Candide,* Don Marquis' *archy and mehitabel,* and Eugene O'Neill's *Anna Christie.* Most of these works were untheatrical, and those, like the O'Neill drama, which were fine theatre were nonetheless fundamentally unsuited for light musical treatment. They were exciting challenges, irresistible to a musical theatre that craved novelty and a certain degree of artistic daring. But for the time being they proved at once mountable physically and insurmountable esthetically.

The season opened with a seemingly obvious possibility for adaptation, a musical version of James Hilton's novel *Lost Horizon.* Hilton collaborated with Jerome Lawrence and Robert E. Lee, two popular playwrights, on the book, and Harry Warren returned to Broadway after a long, successful sojourn in Hollywood to create the score. An exceptionally strong cast was recruited: Dennis King, Jack Cassidy, Martyn Green, Harold Lang, Carol Lawrence, and Alice Ghostley. Hilton's romantic tale of a group of harried Westerners whose plane crashes in the hidden utopia of **Shangri-La** (6-13-56, Winter Garden) was relived. A few are so taken with the mysterious land they elect never to return home. Somehow a tale and setting that in the mind's eye took on a unique magic seemed cumbersome and contrived in the flesh. A specially built stage of translucent plastic, lit from below, apparently to suggest a landscape covered with glistening snow, managed only to underscore the evening's contrived nature. Warren's music was particularly disappointing. *Shangri-La* survived for just two and a half weeks.

The principal attraction of the latest in the on-again, off-again series, **New Faces of '56** (6-14-56, Barrymore), was the finest female impersonator Broadway had seen since the days of Julian Eltinge and Bert Savoy. So clever was T. C. Jones that many in the audience were unaware the performer was a male until he took off his wig and revealed his bald head during the curtain calls. His best sketch was an easy but riotous spoof of a grand Follies production number. Other skits satirized the popular Japanese films of the time and the successful American motion picture about violence in high schools, *The Blackboard Jungle.* The opening skit, which knocked the United Nations, was by Neil Simon and his brother, Dan. The humor was not always sure-fire, and the songs, in the unfortunate tradition of the series, were largely time-wasters. One attractive young lady, largely unnoticed at the time, went on to distinguish herself on the London stage, Maggie Smith. Although *New Faces of '56* ran over six months, it became one of many longer runs of the era to close in the red.

Nearly five months passed before another musical offering appeared. A lady named Iva Kitchell attempted a one-woman revue entitled **That Girl at the Bijou** (11-9-56, Bijou). Her program progressed alphabetically, running from "Bacchanale (As Seen at the Opera)"—with Saint-Saëns music —to "Ze Ballet" with music by Ponchielli. Most of the material in between had music by her pianist Harvey Brown. But even at the smallest remaining regular Broadway house, Miss Kitchell could only attract enough interest for 11 performances.

When **Li'l Abner** (11-15-56, St. James) bounced in, the denizens of Dogpatch came to life behind the footlights. As she had for so many years on the daily comic page, Daisy Mae (Edith Adams) prepared to catch her beloved Li'l Abner (Peter Palmer) in the annual Sadie Hawkins' Day chase. She is all the more determined this year because Earthquake McGoon (Bern Hoffman) has his eye on her and because Abner will also be pursued by the voluptuous Appassionata Von Climax (Tina Louise). Daisy is abetted, and now and then hindered, by such other notable Dogpatch characters as Mammy and Pappy Yokum, General Bullmoose, Senator Jack S. Phogbound, Mayor Dawgmeat, Marryin' Sam, and Evil Eye Fleagle. Their lives are further complicated after the government, declaring Dogpatch the most useless piece of real estate in the U.S.A., decides to test an atom bomb there. The village is spared when a plaque, in which Abe Lincoln declares Dogpatch a national shrine, is uncovered as the townspeople prepare to remove a statue of Dogpatch's founder. The book could not always sustain the humor of Al Capp's cartoon, but it was serviceable. The evening burst into a foot-stomping exuberance whenever Michael Kidd sent his chorus dancing to Gene de Paul's lively melodies. With Johnny Mercer as his lyricist, de Paul wrote one ballad that enjoyed a modest acclaim, Abner and Daisy Mae's "Namely You." With the help of Marryin' Sam (Stubby Kaye) and the Dogpatch community, they told of the founder of Dogpatch, a latter-day Duke of Plaza-Toro, "Jubilation T. Cornpone."

It had been many years since comic strips had provided material for a Broadway musical. Authors had apparently assumed readers of "the funnies" had left the theatre for cheaper, less intellectual entertainments. *Li'l Abner* shot that theory full of holes, running happily for just short of 700 performances.

An English revue, **Cranks** (11-26-56, Bijou), was the brainchild of John Cranko, who later became the distinguished head of the Stuttgart Ballet. He incorporated no real skits and no songs of any matter. Instead, he offered a highly stylized evening whose "self-conscious posturings, less suggested a revue than the religious rites of the Stanislavsky methodists." It left after 40 showings. With it went one young performer, Anthony Newley, soon to have his brief moment upon the New York musical stage.

November's last show was **Bells Are Ringing** (11-29-56, Shubert), a conventional musical that in many ways was the most satisfying show of the season. Much of its charm derived from its authors' awareness that it was conventional and that nothing would be gained by pretension and over-reaching. The rest of its charm came from Judy Holliday, who costarred with Sydney Chaplin. Betty Comden and Adolph Green—who had started their careers in a nightclub act with Miss Holliday—supplied book and lyrics. Their story was one of only two during the season drawn entirely from its writers' fertile imaginations and not from an older play or novel. Growing demand for telephone-answering services provided the background of the story. Ella Peterson (Miss Holliday) works for "Susanswerphone." She is a pleasant, well-meaning girl, with confused proprieties. Her sense of dignity requires she put on her lipstick before answering the phone, but it in no way prevents her from eavesdropping on conversations or meddling in the lives of her customers. One customer who receives her special attention is Jeff Moss (Chaplin), an aspiring playwright. After Ella overhears a particularly nasty call with a producer she rushes over to Jeff's apartment and coaxes him into rewriting his material. In no time the two are in love. But Ella's life is complicated by another customer, Sandor (Eddie Lawrence), who allows her to take orders for what are ostensibly records. Actually an order for three dozen of Beethoven's Fifth is a bet on the third horse in the fifth race at Belmont. The police enter the picture, and for a while Jeff and Ella's romance seems headed for the rocks, but just when Ella is set to pack and return home, Jeff comes back to her. Jule Styne's score, like Comden and Green's book, was comfortably old hat. The hit of the evening was the lovers' simple ballad that relied on an essentially two-note melody, "Just In Time." Somewhat more expansive was the poignant "The Party's Over," which Ella sings when she believes she has lost Jeff. Comden and Green's clever lyrics abounded in songs such as "Drop That Name" (a dig at social-climbing partygoers) and the expository opening, "It's A Perfect Relationship." Styne's melodies ranged from the contemporary sounds of the same opening to the nostalgic rag at the closing, "I'm Going Back." *Bells Are Ringing* delighted audiences for over two years.

Candide (12-1-56, Martin Beck) was the season's most interesting failure. At least it seemed a failure to everyone at the time, including its librettist, Lillian Hellman, who claims it was the beginning of her disenchantment with the theatre. Since it marked her first efforts for the musical stage, she deferred to suggestions of her collaborators when changes were required in the book, although her instincts insisted her projected alterations were right and theirs wrong. Her instincts indeed may have been correct, for the show that was played at the Martin Beck suffered from a clumsy, uncertain, heavy-handed book. Miss Hellman could not, however, have been accused of tampering with the story line. Young Candide (Robert Rounseville) is again tutored by an ever-optimistic Pangloss (Max Adrian); who assures him everything is for the best in the best of all possible worlds. He even encourages Candide's marriage to Cunegonde (Barbara Cook), for all the problems it will bring. In the middle of the marriage ceremony war between Westphalia and Hesse intervenes, and Cunegonde is carried off. Candide's troubles have begun. He reaches Lisbon in time for the great earthquake. There the Inquisition apparently kills Pangloss. Moving on to Paris, Candide discovers Cunegonde living in kept luxury, determined to "Glitter And Be Gay." Candide, Cunegonde, and an Old Lady (Irra Petina) they have met are carried off on a slave ship to South America. In Buenos Aires the governor proposes to make Cunegonde his mistress, and with the help of the "easily assimilated" Old Lady he convinces Candide to seek his fortune elsewhere. Candide heads for Eldorado, where he does, in fact, find a fortune. Returning to claim Cunegonde, he learns she has fled. The ship in which he sets out after her sinks, so the despairing Candide makes his way to Venice. He discovers the Old Lady working as a shill in a gambling house. She, too, is less confident and tinged with bitterness. Candide discovers Cunegonde reduced to a scrubwoman. He returns with her to Westphalia, where, to his amazement, he encounters the supposedly dead Pangloss. But Candide can no longer subscribe to the philosopher's all-accepting view of life. He and Cunegonde retire to live quietly and to make their garden grow. The show's lyrics were from the pens of three brilliant rhymers—John Latouche (who died, at the age of 38, shortly before the show opened), the Pulitzer prize-winning poet, Richard Wilbur, and Dorothy Parker. At best these lyrics were brittle and witty; at times they labored under the slight burden of the artificiality and formality of the story's period, and now and then they lapsed in Broadway trickery. For them Bernstein created a pyrotechnic, eclectic score that moved from stately 18th-century forms to modern tangos and jazz. The most popular, durable bit of his work turned out to be the overture, whose theme has become familiar to concertgoers. The flaws in the eve-

ning and even its unconventional successes told against the work. It played 73 performances and was put away until a revised production two decades later presented it with such overall flair that the public could no longer resist its charms.

Happy Hunting (12-6-56, Majestic) was the season's second old-fashioned musical comedy, with the season's second original book to come to Broadway. Just as Lindsay and Crouse had used Harry Truman's appointment of Pearl Mesta as the starting point for *Call Me Madam*, they contrived another story for Ethel Merman out of Grace Kelly's marriage to Prince Rainier of Monaco. Miss Merman played a wealthy, pushy Main Line matron, Liz Livingstone, who is so angry at not being invited to the wedding that she determines to marry her daughter, Beth (Virginia Gibson), to someone even more imposing. She sets her sights on the Duke of Granada (Fernando Lamas), a Hapsburg. In her own way she is as naive as Sally Adams was. When she hears Rainier referred to as "His Grace," she inquires, "Is his name Grace, too?" The Duke is captivated by her naiveté; Liz finds that she, and not her daughter, is being wooed. Beth is left with the pleasant young man she wanted in the first place, Sanford Stewart (Gordon Polk). Liz has one last laugh. She learns the Duke's name is Jaime and is amused to contemplate the Main Line's reaction when, given the correct pronunciation, they learn she is Mrs. Jaime Hapsburg. The book was adequate, but Miss Merman was left without any first-class songs to belt out in Matt Dubey and Harold Karr's score. The show's best numbers were two country-style tunes, "Mutual Admiration Society" and "If'n." Both enjoyed momentary replayings, but neither became a Merman standard. Miss Merman, in fact, did not even sing "If'n" in the show. One cleverly staged song was "A New-Fangled Tango," sung by a chorus crammed onto a minuscule dance floor and unable to do little more than move its fingers. Miss Merman kept the show on the boards for a full year, but most of the time to far-from-full houses, and when *Happy Hunting* closed it went down in the books as one of her rare commercial failures.

After November and December's outpouring of new musicals subsided, no more new lyric pieces danced across the boards until March, when a new edition of the **Ziegfeld Follies** (3-1-57, Winter Garden) appeared. It was advertised as a Golden Jubliee edition, fifty years after the unveiling of the initial *Follies*. Most critics felt it was an insult rather than a tribute. Much of its material and physical production had been salvaged from an edition of the *Follies* with Tallulah Bankhead that had folded during its tryout the preceding season. Sets and costumes were skimpy, unimaginative, and shabby. Worse, there were a mere eight girls (on some nights only six) to recall Ziegfeld's breathtaking line of beauties. The show had a fine cast that included Harold Lang and Carol Lawrence (both free after the *Shangri-La* debacle) and wasted the talents of a great clown, Billy De Wolfe. He did the best he could with a take-off of the writhing rock and roll star Elvis Presley and participated in a not very funny spoof of *My Fair Lady*. Only Beatrice Lillie had some passable material. She played a Charles Addams character at a fine restaurant in "Milady Dines Alone," kidded the Japanese craze in "Kabuki Lil," and played an airline stewardess who is forever singing "I've Got A Feeling I'm Falling" in "High and Flighty." She, too, took part in "My Late, Late Lady" singing, "I Had A Bath Last Night." The music was so indifferent no original cast album was released. Miss Lillie's art and Ziegfeld's name kept the show alive into June.

The New York City Center began a somewhat more venturesome than usual series of spring revivals on March 13 with *The Beggar's Opera,* giving New Yorkers a chance to compare the original with the Weill-Brecht *Threepenny Opera* still playing in the Village. Jack Cassidy acted Macheath and Shirley Jones was Polly. *Brigadoon* followed on March 27, with Helen Gallagher and Robert Rounseville among the principals, *The Merry Widow* with Marta Eggerth and Jan Kiepura graced the boards on April 10, and *South Pacific* closed the season on April 24. Robert Wright and Mindy Carson were featured.

Shinbone Alley (4-13-57, Broadway) demonstrated once more that magic created in the mind's eye is easily destroyed by flesh and blood actors on a spotlit stage. In Don Marquis' *archy and mehitabel* stories, archy is a cockroach who writes free verse by throwing himself on the keys of a typewriter. Since he can't hold down two keys at once, all his writing is in lower-case letters. Mehitabel is a friendly neighborhood cat. The producers hired Eartha Kitt, who had often been described as "feline," to portray mehitabel. But the adjective became almost meaningless in the face of human forms and sounds. Eddie Bracken, a fading Hollywood comedian who played archy, bore no known resemblence to any cockroach. What little story there was described archy's persistent, unrequited passion for mehitabel. He remains loyal even when she is lured away and made pregnant by Big Bill

(George S. Irving), a tough tom cat. This almost plotless play was by Joe Darion and Mel Brooks (Brooks later went on to Hollywood acclaim). Darion also provided lyrics to George Kleinsinger's music. Together they devised some cute, if not memorable, songs. But all in all *Shinbone Alley* lacked the stuff of which hits are made, and what pleasures it offered were lost in the vastness of the large Broadway Theatre. It packed its trunks after 49 performances.

The Phoenix Theatre dispensed with the end-of-season revues it had offered the two preceding sessions and instead offered a loosely structured musical based on Mark Twain's Mississippi River stories. All the old favorites were present: Huckleberry Finn, Tom Sawyer, Aunt Polly, Becky Thatcher, and Injun Joe. But they, too, seemed more lovable and somehow more believable on the pages of a book. **Livin' the Life** (4-27-57, Phoenix) sang its unpretentious songs for 25 showings and folded.

The season's final musical was in many ways its most distressing. **New Girl in Town** (5-14-57, 46th St.) was a lyric adaptation of Eugene O'Neill's somber *Anna Christie*. If this drama was ever material for musicalization—and that is questionable —it was probably only workable in the hands of, say, Rodgers and Hammerstein or Frank Loesser or Leonard Bernstein. As it developed, though, it was George Abbott who was responsible for the transition. With the assistance of Bob Merrill, who had written a number of light, "Hit Parade" tunes, he turned it into a noisy, explosive musical comedy. By changing its setting from the days just after World War I to the turn of the century, he also turned it into another of this period's colorful costume pieces. The stark human drama was made to play second fiddle to splashy colors and wild dancing. However, the story line remained largely untouched. Anna, a prostitute recovering from a siege of tuberculosis, seeks a haven with her seafaring father, Chris (Cameron Prud'homme). Chris is ignorant of Anna's recent past. While she is staying with her father, she falls in love with another seaman, Mat (George Wallace). Her idyll is shattered when Mat learns of her old trade and deserts her. But he later returns, convinced Anna is willing to turn over a new leaf. Abbott wrote a workman-like book and Merrill filled the evening with facile, often percussive, melodies. The principal attractions of *New Girl in Town* were its lively Bob Fosse dances, with Gwen Verdon as Anna leading the fancy stepping, and the off-hand comedy of Thelma Ritter in the role of Chris' companion,

Marthy. Miss Ritter had a show-stopping number called "Flings" in which she insisted flings have to be "flung by the young." O'Neill's ghost may have winced, but audiences, beguiled by the stars' performances and unable to find better competition elsewhere, kept the show in business for over a year.

1957-1958

Two of the period's finest musicals were the season's outstanding successes. Although they were strikingly different, both suggested that artistry and integrity were neither lacking nor unwelcome in the commercial theatre. If neither show boasted an abundance of the singable melodies that had enhanced the shows of earlier eras or the better Rodgers' offerings of their own time, both boasted a unique appreciation of style and tone—and good enough songs. The rest of the season's musicals, however, were even less rewarding musically, and none had anything approaching the unity of feeling of the best pieces. Nonetheless almost all the other musicals had something attractive to offer—usually memorable performances—and the public that couldn't buy tickets for *West Side Story* or *The Music Man* was generally able to find some consolation on stages elsewhere.

The black poet, Langston Hughes, was responsible for the book and lyrics of **Simply Heavenly** (8-20-57, Playhouse), a work that moved to the Main Stem after its off-Broadway success. A light-hearted, affectionate look at a small group of Harlem characters, it was a far cry from the stark, poetic material Hughes had contributed to *Street Scene* (1-9-47). Simple (Melvin Stewart) is a likable bungler who has lost his first wife and his job to better men. He is torn between the wholesome Joyce (Marilyn Berry) and the brazenly sensual Zarita (Anna English). For a number of critics the highlight of the evening was the hero's recounting of his dream to be the first Negro to lead white Mississippians into battle. Hughes' material dominated David Martin's weak score, giving the impression the work was a play with music rather than a musical comedy. The public response to black plays was still unpredictable. Despite generally encouraging notices, theatregoers stayed away. *Simply Heavenly* closed October 12.

September's first offering was even less successful, closing the same night as *Simply Heavenly*.

Mask and Gown (9-10-57, Golden) was a revue written around the talents of T. C. Jones. Jones had been the most celebrated discovery in Leonard Sillman's most recent *New Faces,* and Sillman thanked him by mounting the new show. A brief look at theatrical history could have warned the producer he was heading for rocky waters. Even in their heyday, female impersonators such as Julian Eltinge and Bert Savoy never attempted one-artist shows. Eltinge appeared in book musicals that carefully explained how he came to have to dress as a woman. Others in the cast had substantial time to offer respites from what was essentially a single joke. Savoy never attempted to rationalize his transvestite act but performed in large-scale revues that provided a variety of other distractions during the evening. Jones appeared with only four other performers, presenting uneven material by several *New Faces* authors. Jones' lame bits satirized television, Ruby Keeler-style movies, Shakespeare, and T. C. Jones. Had the material been better, there still would have been good reason to question the show's chances of success. The season would show the day of the clown was over on Broadway—at least for the foreseeable future. It was, sadly, for T. C. Jones.

The night after *Mask and Gown* premiered, *Carousel* (4-19-45) was revived briefly at the City Center. Barbara Cook and Howard Keel played the leads, while Victor Moore came out of retirement to portray the star keeper. *Annie Get Your Gun* followed in February, Nancy Walker brought her special comedy to *Wonderful Town* (2-25-52), while *Oklahoma!* (3-31-43) closed the Center's season in March.

West Side Story (9-26-57, Winter Garden), as originally conceived by Jerome Robbins, was to have retold the Romeo and Juliet legend in terms of young Irish and Jewish lovers. However, Robbins and Leonard Bernstein—who was called in to do the music—decided the Irish-Jewish theme had been run dry on Broadway and, in any case, had diminishing contemporary validity. On the other hand the influx of Puerto Ricans onto the New York scene offered a group given to high passion and violence, the very meat of Shakespeare's story. Their gang wars suggested a likely substitute for family feuds. To oppose the Spanish-speaking gang, Arthur Laurents, the librettist, assembled "an anthology of what is called American" and christened the rival group the Jets. The Puerto Ricans became the Sharks. The Jets, boastful and contemptuous of the immigrants, have decided to challenge the Sharks to a street fight, a rumble. They have Riff (Mickey Calin) ask Tony (Larry Kert) to be present. Tony was a founder of the group, but he has become puzzlingly peaceable and drifted away. Riff reminds Tony of his old allegiance and of how menacing the newcomers are. Tony agrees reluctantly, falling in with the peculiar patter of the group:

Tony: What time?
Riff: Ten?
Tony: Ten it is.
Riff: Womb to tomb!
Tony: Sperm to worm! And I'll live to regret this.
Riff: Who knows? Maybe what you're waitin' for'll be twitchin' at the dance!

Suddenly Tony finds himself excited, for "Something's Coming." Meanwhile in a bridal shop, Anita (Chita Rivera), the sweetheart of the Sharks' leader, Bernardo (Ken Le Roy), is converting Maria's communion dress into a gown for the dance. Maria (Carol Lawrence) is Bernardo's sister, and he has brought her from Puerto Rico hoping she will marry his friend, Chino (Jamie Sanchez). At the dance Riff challenges Bernardo and the groups agree to the battle. Tony and Maria spot each other and fall in love instantly. Tony can only apostrophize on his new flame, "Maria." Together Tony and Maria ignore the terror building around them "Tonight." Most of the Puerto Ricans are nervously elated over the coming hassle, but they are confident and determined to embrace the chrome-plated comforts of "America," despite the homesick reminiscences of one of the girls, Rosalia (Marilyn Cooper). A name-calling session is interrupted by a policeman, who orders the Puerto Ricans to disperse:

Clear out, Spics. Sure; it's a free country and I ain't got the right. But its's a country with laws; and I can find the right. I got the badge, you got the skin. It's tough all over. Beat it!

But the fracas is merely delayed. When it does begin and when Tony attempts to halt it, he succeeds only in distracting his own friend Riff long enough to allow Bernardo to fatally stab him. In a fury Tony kills Bernardo with Riff's knife. While all this is going on, Maria is at home singing to herself coquettishly, "I Feel Pretty." Chino appears with the news. Before Maria's feelings have time to take form, Tony arrives, and her love for him overrides her hatred for her brother's killer. He promises to take her away and in a dream ballet ("Somewhere") the battle is re-enacted but this time the lovers are not allowed to meet. The dream turns into a nightmare but Tony and Maria flee, seeking haven in love-making. The gangs, meanwhile, are concerned with their inevitable encounter with the law and, singing "Gee, Officer Krupke," they mockingly imagine how they will handle themselves. Anita savagely taunts Maria for remaining faithful to Tony, but she is prevailed upon to deliver Maria's message for Tony to the Jets. Unfortunately the Jets so cruelly revile her that she is driven to claim Chino has shot and killed Maria. On hearing this Tony goes after Chino, but Chino shoots him just as Tony discovers that Maria is not dead after all. Somewhat ashamed, the Jets and the Sharks jointly remove Tony's body as Maria follows them.

The evening emphasized the jangling noise, the sordidness, and the roughness of tenement life, confining its lyricism to the mere facts of the love story and to the passion of much of Bernstein's score. It also offered a dream ballet as a concession to the still voguish form. And, of course, it let its Juliet live. But none of these deviations or compromises affected the integrity of the work, which remained cohesive and overpowering. At times some theatregoers found the reflections of street language too overpowering. Even though the lyrics were printed as "If the spit hits the fan" and "Every last buggin' gang on the whole buggin' street!" they were conveniently distorted—intentionally or not —by theatrical projection. Of course it could be argued that the use of derogatory epithets such as "wop" and "spic" represented a more socially conscious and artistically responsible employment than their careless usage in the musicals of thirty and forty years before. The old usage implied an indifference or even an acceptance of such demeaning expressions. More explosive language had long been infiltrating the theatre. It had even spread to the once-staid London stage. *Look Back in Anger,* the prime example of the work of that city's new school of "Angry Young Men," opened five nights after *West Side Story.* The musical's lyrics were the first Broadway musical play credits for Stephen Sondheim.

. . .

Stephen Sondheim was born on March 22, 1930, and educated at Williams College. He then studied music in New York with Milton Babbitt. Dropping his musical interests temporarily, Sondheim collaborated on scripts for television's "Topper" series, but returned to the musical field to write background music for the Broadway play, *Girls of Summer.*

. . .

For many the most electrifying parts of the evening were—unfortunately for future generations —Robbins' tense, vibrant dances, particularly the rumble. But everything was in top working order. *West Side Story* ran 981 performances in its hometown (in two slightly separated runs of 732 and 249 performances). It compiled an even greater 1,040 performances in London. Her portrayal of the original Anita launched Chita Rivera on her road to stardom.

. . .

Chita Rivera was born in Washington, D.C., on January 23, 1933, and christened Dolores Conchita del Rivero. After training at the American School of Ballet, she appeared as Conchita del Rivero in *Guys and Dolls,* the road company of *Call Me Madam,* and *Can-Can.* She altered her name when she became a featured dancer in a *Shoestring Revue.*

. . .

The first of October's two musicals brought the hilarious Nancy Walker back to Broadway in **Copper and Brass** (10-17-57, Beck). Miss Walker played the hopelessly jinxed policewoman, Katey O'Shea. When she marches in a police parade all the other policemen somehow march in the opposite direction (shades of Bea Lillie's "March With Me") and when she stoops to pick up a paper she has dropped in the Holland Tunnel (where she has been assigned as punishment), she creates a massive chain crash. Off duty, Katey becomes hopelessly trapped in the depths of a modernistic chair. Miss Walker's antics skillfully concealed the mediocrity of David Craig and David Baker's material. But as T. C. Jones had demonstrated earlier the vogue for broad-styled, visual funmakers had waned. For all her riotous rampaging, she could not attract sufficient patronage. *Copper and Brass* ran just over one month.

On the other hand, the movie's svelte Lena Horne proved a big enough box-office lure to help **Jamaica** (10-31-57, Imperial) to a run of well over a year. *Jamaica* succeeded by presenting in primary colors something *House of Flowers* (12-30-54) had unsuccessfully attempted with pastels. Again the composer was Harold Arlen, but the librettists were the librettists of *Finian's Rainbow* (1-10-47) and *Flahooley* (5-14-51), E. Y. Harburg and Fred Saidy. They found themselves on a tropical, relatively apolitical, paradise called Pigeon's Island, off Jamaica's coast. There a poor, handsome fisherman, Koli (Ricardo Montalban), loves the beautiful Savannah (Miss Horne). But Savannah spends her hours dreaming of living in New York. A hustling dude, Joe Nashua (Joe Adams), has come to the island to exploit pearl-diving possibilities in its

shark-infested water. Savannah sees in him as an all-expenses-paid trip to the big city. However, when Koli saves the life of Savannah's little brother during a hurricane, she comes to face reality and accepts her island suitor. She visits New York only in a dream ballet.

Although Arlen's music was obviously commercial, it was also less inspired and melodic than his *House of Flowers* score. Some numbers such as "Monkey In The Mango Tree" seemed like hand-me-downs. A number of critics preferred the comic songs "Push The Button" (Savannah's song spoofing a life with modern conveniences) and "Napoleon" (in which she sings how the great names of the past are exploited by commercial products). No critic recalled Arlen and Harburg had first used "Napoleon's A Pastry" in *Hooray for What!* (12-1-37). Perhaps the best of Arlen's ballads was Savannah's "Cocoanut Sweet." Since Miss Horne was the attraction and since she was featured in eleven of the twenty-one numbers (including reprises), most customers left satisfied. *Jamaica* was the second hit in David Merrick's burgeoning career.

A carefree lark called **Rumple** (11-6-57, Alvin) had a novel plot. Unless cartoonist Nelson Crandal can recapture some of his original inspiration within forty-eight hours, his comic strip "Rumple" will be discontinued and his beloved little figure consigned to Oblivia, a sort of Valhalla for cartoon figures. At one point Rumple is allowed to visit Oblivia and consort briefly in a comic ballet with The Yellow Kid and other old timers. The whole show had a happy, old-time flavor to it, including Ernest G. Schweikert's soft-shoe numbers, such as "In Times Like These." It also had Eddie Foy, Jr., in the title role and Stephen Douglass as Crandal. But its writers were all inexperienced, and producers Paula Stone and Mike Sloan, who had worked with Foy on their successful revival of *The Red Mill,* couldn't assemble everything with the necessary style. *Rumple* headed for Oblivia after 45 showings.

But another musical with a happy, old-time flavor to it did succeed in putting its components together with a flair. In fact the homey artistry of **The Music Man** (12-19-57, Majestic) made it the biggest hit of the season. It couldn't have been more different from the season's other hit, *West Side Story.* Whereas the Bernstein-Sondheim opus tried to look at the harsh side of contemporary life with something approaching twenty-twenty vision, *The Music Man* gladly donned rose-colored glasses for a glimpse of 1912 America.

A group of traveling salesmen conduct a conversation in time with the rhythm of the train taking them to River City, Iowa. One of them is "con" man Harold Hill, who makes his living selling band instruments and then disappearing with the money before the instruments or his promised lessons can be delivered. His ploy is complicated in River City by Marian Paroo, "Marian, The Librarian," who has a sharp eye for swindlers. When Hill makes the mistake of claiming he was a member of the 1905 class of Gary University, she is prepared to expose him by quoting an article in the Indiana State Educational Journal showing the school had not yet been founded in 1905. Only the touching glee with which her young brother and her fellow townspeople await the Wells Fargo wagon that will deliver the instruments persuades her to rip out and destroy the incriminating page. Harold is forced to stay and teach the children how to play their instruments, although he cannot read a note of music. The interval allows him to fall in love with Marian, whom he had begun to court solely as a strategic maneuver. At last the band is ready for its first public appearance. The results are horrendous, but to the doting parents the ensuing cacophony sounds like angelic harmony.

One reason for the show's pervasive unity of style and tone was that it was the work of one man, Meredith Willson. Willson was born in Iowa and grew up there in the period about which he was now writing. He left to study music in New York, did occasional composing, and for years was a popular orchestra leader on radio.

To a large degree, Willson captured the feeling of the time faithfully, working over his materials with imagination and resourcefulness. The show's big hit was the rousing march "Seventy-six Trombones," in which Hill pictures the rewards in having a school band. Willson used the same melody for Marian's attractive, lullaby-like love-song, "Goodnight, My Someone." He also employed the clever device of using a barbershop quartet to comment on the action, with songs that allowed strong period flavor, such as the lovely "Lida Rose." He gave Harold a modern-day patter song in "Trouble." The only jarring lapse in musical fidelity was the show's most popular love-song, "Till There Was You," sung by the romantic leads, which had a distinctly late thirties or early forties sound. Robert Preston made a persuasive Harold, while Barbara Cook was a comely Marian. Significantly, this show, not *West Side Story*, walked away with all the seasonal awards. The public agreed. They kept the New York company on the boards for 1,375 performances.

A boxing musical, **The Body Beautiful** (1-23-58, Broadway), was knocked out after just 60 showings. It had a book by Joseph Stein and Will Glickman, lyrics by Sheldon Harnick and music by Jerry Bock.

. . .

Sheldon Harnick was born in Chicago on April 30, 1924. Although he was to make a name for himself primarily as a lyricist, he received a thorough musical education. Like his new partner, Bock, he started by writing collegiate musicals, at Northwestern University. His songs were heard in Broadway revues such as *New Faces of 1952* and *Two's Company*.

. . .

Stein and Glickman's story traced the efforts of Dave (Jack Warden), a failing boxer's manager, to make a champion out of a handsome graduate, Bob (Steve Forrest). At first the attempt seems hopeless, but when Bob starts to win he grows so egotistical he virtually wrecks his romance with Ann (Mindy Carson) and leaves everybody wishing a loss would bring him back to earth. It was all noisy and undistinguished. But its creators were intelligent men who would profit from their mistakes and proceed to better things.

Oh, Captain (2-4-58, Alvin), a musicalized stage version of the highly popular Alec Guinness film, *The Captain's Paradise*, kept the saga of Capt. Henry St. James, who has a reserved British wife in one port and a voluptuous foreign mistress in another. But instead of sailing back and forth across the Strait of Gibraltar as he did in the film, St. James cruises the English Channel and his romance unfolds in Paris. In this version Henry finally settles for dutiful monogamy. What *Oh, Captain* lost in transition was the film's light insouciance. The humor suddenly seemed heavy and contrived, and the songs were no help. One trick the show used several times was to repeat the Jay Livingston and Ray Evans songs with varying lyrics. For example, "Life Does A Man A Favor" was sung three times: once by the St. Jameses when they extol life's "simple joys," then by the captain and his crew when life "leads him down to the sea," and finally by St. James when "it puts him in Paree." Although Tony Randall, an intelligent actor, led a fine company that included the ballerina Alexandra Danilova, there was little they could do to save so uninspired an adaptation. It ran 192 showings, folding with a loss.

The worst fiasco of the season, **Portofino** (2-21-58, Adelphi), like *Buttrio Square* (10-14-52), went in search of fun in a confrontation of American tourists and Italian villagers. It didn't seem to find any and left after three performances.

Three musicals, of sorts, came in during April. The first, **Say Darling** (4-3-58, ANTA), was a play based on a book about making a musical out of another book, and had enough new music of its own to allow it to join the musical ranks. Richard Bissell collaborated on the story (from his own novel *Say Darling*), with Abe Burrows and Marian Bissell. Bissell's novel recounted the backstage adventures of turning *7½ cents* into *The Pajama Game*. Names were changed to protect the guilty, but the tough director, the cerebral, gesticulating young producer, and the fading star were all reasonably recognizable. The show had a pleasant Jule Styne score and serviceable Comden and Green lyrics. It also had a remarkably funny performance by Robert Morse. Morse played Ted Snow, the young producer. Some cognoscenti read Hal Prince for Ted Snow.

. . .

Impish **Robert Morse** was born in Boston, Massachusetts, on May 18, 1931. After leaving the navy he took work warming up television-studio audiences. His comic capers landed him in Hollywood, where he was awarded a part in *The Proud and the Profane*. Tyrone Guthrie brought him to New York for a principal role in Thornton Wilder's 1955 hit, *The Matchmaker*.

. . .

While the show was too choppy to be a good straight play and too spiritless to be a good musical, it played for nearly ten months, but it often played to barely profitable houses and was still in the red when it closed.

On April 7 Joyce Grenfell began a three-week run with her one-woman show that included numbers by Richard Addinsell and Donald Swann, with Gershwin medleys while Miss Grenfell was changing costumes.

The season's last lyric entertainment was a "Musical Salmagundi" that included comedian Mort Sahl, a dancer, Anneliese Widman, and a group labeled simply "The Folk Singers." Although the next election year was far off, the evening bore the untimely title **The Next President** (4-9-58, Bijou) and provided each act with a socially significant label. The first act was "The Status Quo," while the second was the more awkward, "A Brand New Attitude with the Same Old Prejudices." One of "The Folk Singers" numbers was "The Chorus of Collective Conscience," but it fell largely to Sahl to deliver the leftish-slanted political satire in adaptations of his night-club free-association mono-logues. This was the era of Eisenhower complacency, and not too many New Yorkers were willing to listen. The show was withdrawn after 13 performances.

1958-1959

The 1958–59 theatrical year marked the seventeenth season of this last great act. The era had run more than two-thirds of its course and gave signs of waning. The new season did bring in one of the towering masterpieces of the period, but except for that one show—*Gypsy*—it was a season of continual disappointment. Only two other regular American musicals proved commercial successes, while a third showed great staying power if no profit. Although not without their attractions, all three owed some of the popularity to lack of solid competition.

Goldilocks (10-11-58, Lunt-Fontanne) inaugurated the season, ending a half-year in which no musicals appeared. The show had a book by Walter and Jean Kerr, who had provided most of the material some years before for *Touch and Go* (10-13-49), and who had both found more congenial niches than the world of musical comedy. The music was by Leroy Anderson, a well-known arranger and composer of light, "semiclassical" instrumental works. The Kerrs went in search of their fun to the same source *The Vamp* (11-10-55) had mined—the silent movie industry—and, although the famous mordant wit of the Kerrs was often evident, they too came back almost empty-handed. They kept their story closer to home, setting it in the 1913 movie colony at Fort Lee, New Jersey. The principal plot concerned the love-hate clashes between Maggie Harris (Elaine Stritch), a sharp-tongued musical comedy actress, and a vain, financially strapped young movie mogul, Max Grady (Don Ameche). They express their feelings early on in "No One'll Ever Love You [like you do]." Max keeps the infuriated Maggie working overtime on extra scenes because he has been warned he will get no further financing after his picture is finished. By the time shooting ends he has enough footage for several flicks. Of course, by the final curtain their associates have witnessed the taming of the two. Maggie has even decided to marry Max instead of socialite George Randolph Brown (Russell Nype), to whom she had been engaged. George finds solace in offering his coat to sweet, simple

Lois (Pat Stanley), a girl who had been pursuing Max. Funny bits of dialogue characterized the Kerr humor. When Max's backer, growling that Max's financial statements are inadequate, spots Lois wandering aimlessly about the sets, he remarks, "I have the feeling I've come face to face with Miscellaneous Expenses." Anderson's score was gay and airily evocative of the epoch, especially such dance numbers as "The Pussy Foot" and "The Town House Maxixe," for which Agnes de Mille provided show-stopping routines. Settings were sumptuous and sunny. Unfortunately, despite flashes of wit, the book was heavy-handed and Anderson's score lacked an outstanding love ballad. *Goldilocks* could find only a limited public, enough to keep it on the boards 20 weeks.

David Merrick, who was quickly becoming the most active, exciting, and responsible producer on Broadway, combined forces with the National Broadcasting Company to bring Menotti's television opera, **Maria Golovin** (11-5-58, Beck), to the stage. Like most Menotti librettos the story was simple. Maria Golovin's husband is a prisoner-of-war. A young, blind boy, Donato (Richard Cross), falls in love with her. When she refuses to desert her husband and marry him, Donato attempts to kill her. Donato's mother (Patricia Neway) tells him where to aim, at the same time motioning Maria (Franca Duval) to flee. Donato is lead to believe Maria is dead and is taken away by his mother. Menotti's appeal had dwindled among rank-and-file theatregoers, and his latest work did not translate effectively from one medium to another. It closed after five performances.

One of the brightest revues Broadway had seen in years arrived on November 11, with Merrick again one of the producers. Its origins were anything but ordinary. **La Plume de Ma Tante** (11-11-58, Royale) began life as a Parisian hit and then moved on to a long London run before crossing the Atlantic. Theatregoers with little or no French had no cause for concern. The show's creator, Robert Dhery, acted as compère and offered laconic, amusing comments on the skits. The skits themselves were virtually silent, relying on a series of impeccably paced sight gags for most of the laughs. The evening's high point was a first-act finale in which four monks enter to a sedate "Frère Jacques" and begin to pull at bell ropes. The music grows faster and more pronouncedly rhythmic. By the curtain the monks are swinging on the ropes and kicking wildly. In its universality *La Plume de Ma Tante* was a latter-day *Chauve Souris* (2-4-22), and, like its predecessor, it had little influence on revues that followed it. But its Frenchmen had a home to return to and, unlike the Russian émigrés' production, when its long run was through it said farewell for once and for all.

Rodgers and Hammerstein had a solid commercial success in **Flower Drum Song** (12-1-58, St. James). It was a musical comedy on the order of their *Me and Juliet* (5-28-53) and *Pipe Dream* (11-30-55), sprinkled with just enough Oriental incense to remind theatregoers of *The King and I* (3-29-51). Oscar Hammerstein and Joseph Fields' libretto was based on C. Y. Lee's novel and set in San Francisco's Chinatown. Its story followed Sammy Fong's uncertain journey to the altar. Sammy (Larry Blyden) loves a nightclub hostess Linda Low (Pat Suzuki), but he is contractually obligated to marry Mei Li (Miyoshi Umeki). By arranging a marriage between Wang Ta (Ed Kenny) and Mei Li, Sammy hopes to break the arrangement and free himself. Since Wang Ta also has eyes only for Linda, Sammy invites the senior Wangs to Linda's nightclub, knowing they will be so appalled by Linda's striptease they will never consent to their son's marrying her. Wang Ta also begins to doubt his feeling for Linda, but Mei Li has seen his jacket at the apartment of her seamstress friend, Helen Chao (Arabella Hong), and has drawn the wrong conclusion. To complicate matters the Three Family Association, which regulates much of Chinatown life, insists Sammy and Mei Li's wedding take place promptly. Seemingly too late, Wang Ta confesses to Mei Li he has fallen in love with her. The wedding begins, but when the bride removes her veil she is discovered to be Linda. Mei Li and Wang Ta are free to pursue their own romance. The show was given a lavish production and Gene Kelly, so long in Hollywood, returned to create the staging, but not the choreography. But a Rodgers and Hammerstein work depended on Rodgers and Hammerstein, and neither disappointed their public. Hammerstein's book and lyrics were filled with the contrived sentimentality and contrived simplicity his admirers adored, and with his almost unfailing professional know how, while Rodgers' music was the best he had done since *The King and I*. It ran the gamut from the soft, flowing poetry of Wang Ta's "You Are Beautiful" to the stronger plaints of Helen's "Love, Look Away" to the joyous exuberance of Linda's "Grant Avenue" and "I Enjoy Being A Girl."

Feuer and Martin broke their string of successes (*Where's Charley?, Guys and Dolls, Can-Can, Silk Stockings*) with a 56-performance dud called

Whoop-Up (12-22-58, Shubert). Although it was set on a modern-day Indian reservation, it was at a loss to capitalize on its rather novel setting. Glenda (Susan Johnson) runs a bar, half of which sits on the reservation. She loves Joe Champlain (Ralph Young), but Joe prefers Billie Mae Littlehorse (Asia). Glenda gets Joe in her debt by accepting parts of his automobile as payment for his drinks. By the end of the evening she not only had Joe's car, she has Joe. Moose Charlap's music was as undistinguished as the book.

The following night **A Party with Betty Comden and Adolph Green** (12-23-58, Golden) was brought to the intimate Golden from off-Broadway. The evening was spent singing songs from all their Broadway shows, Hollywood films, and even the night club act in which they got their start. Enough patrons thought it as pleasant a party as any around to keep it on the boards for 82 showings. With its minimal budget, that was sufficient to let it return a reasonable profit.

1959's first musical, **Redhead** (2-5-59, 46th St.), was a vehicle for Gwen Verdon. Her previous musical, *New Girl in Town*, had resorted to O'Neill's *Anna Christie* for its unlikely source. An equally untoward source offered the starting point for *Redhead*'s plot: the murders of Jack, the Ripper. The book by Herbert and Dorothy Fields, Sidney Sheldon, and David Shaw made no attempt at historical accuracy. Rather, it developed its plot around the search for a killer of actresses at the turn of the century. Essie Whimple (Miss Verdon) works for her aunt in the Simpson Sisters' Waxworks. She meets handsome Tom Baxter (Richard Kiley), who had performed with a lady partner in a strong-man act until his partner was murdered. After Essie helps in a performance, it becomes apparent that she is being stalked by the same killer, and there is evidence to throw suspicion on red-bearded Sir Charles Willingham (Patrick Horgan). The killer turns out to be a fellow entertainer, George Poppett (Leonard Stone), who has been able to disguise himself as Sir Charles. Their common interest and terror throw Essie and Tom together, and by the time Poppett is carted off to jail they have fallen in love. The book was serviceable, as was Albert Hague's score, but nothing more. The evening's strength lay in Miss Verdon's charm and her brilliant dancing to Bob Fosse's imaginative choreography, notably in "Pick-Pocket Tango" and "The Uncle Sam Rag." The show also served to further Kiley's path to stardom.

. . .

Richard Kiley was born in Chicago on March 31, 1922. He studied at Loyola University and Barnum Dramatic School, and did a stint as a navy aerial gunner before calling theatregoers' attention to himself as Stanley Kowalski in a road company of *A Streetcar Named Desire*. Small roles in films followed until Broadway took notice of his singing as the caliph in *Kismet*.

. . .

The show received several awards as the best musical of the season, largely because the season's only truly fine musical, *Gypsy*, opened after the balloting deadlines. Still, as a first-class dance show *Redhead* earned its run of over a year. In retrospect *Redhead* can also be seen as something of a breakaway show, more or less initiating the trend that Fosse would promote to make the choreographer so central a creative figure that his dances could be viewed as the crux of the evening.

The City Center low-priced ticket season began on February 10 with *The Most Happy Fella* (5-3-56), with Art Lund again singing Joe, and proceeded to *Say, Darling* (4-3-58), still with Robert Morse, on the 25th and *Lute Song* (2-6-46) on March 12. Dolly Haas assumed Mary Martin's role.

Just before *Lute Song* was heard, the commercial theatre offered a musical version of Sean O'Casey's *Juno and the Paycock*, with its title abbreviated to **Juno** (3-9-59, Winter Garden). The music and lyrics were by Marc Blitzstein, the adaptation by Joseph Stein. Although Shirley Booth played the title role, she was given little solid comedy, while Melvyn Douglas, her costar, in the role of Jack Boyle, and Jack MacGowran as "Joxer" also found the comic elements in their characters minimized. The new version emphasized O'Casey's melodrama rather than his luminous, redeeming humor. It dealt principally with Juno's heartbreaks: the false hope of an inheritance; the death of her rebel son, Johnny (Tommy Rall); and her abandoning Jack to find a better world elsewhere with her daughter, Mary (Monte Amundsen). To make matters even more difficult for itself, the show was unable fully to integrate its songs, though the opening number, "We're Alive," dramatically punctured its dogged optimism with the shooting of a young rebel. Assailed by a generally unkind reception, *Juno* closed after just two weeks.

Although **First Impressions** (3-19-59, Alvin) was little better, it ran longer. A musical version of Jane Austen's *Pride and Prejudice*, it took its title from Miss Austen's original title for her book. The story of the Bennet family, and particularly of Elizabeth Bennet's romance with Fitzwilliam Darcy, was retold as faithfully as time and physical limitations permitted. Regrettably, in their effort to achieve the leisurely elegance of the book and its era, the authors could do no better than to evoke the woodenness and stiff formality of the time at its worst. The titles of the songs ran to "A Perfect Evening," "The Heart Has Won The Game," "Wasn't It A Simply Lovely Wedding?" and "Love Will Find Out The Way." Only the appeal of Polly Bergen (Elizabeth), Hermione Gingold (Mrs. Bennet), and Farley Granger (Darcy) can account for the twelve-week run of the show.

David Merrick brought in another musical destined for a long run. Yet while **Destry Rides Again** (4-23-59, Imperial), a lyric adaptation of the popular Marlene Dietrich and James Stewart film, ran for more than a year, it was a financial failure. Part of its failure may be attributed to the fact that it lacked tone, wit, and melody. It made do with noise and color and whatever else professional know-how could throw on the stage. Like its movie antecedent, it was set in that persistently beloved piece of Americana, the Wild West, more specifically, in Bottleneck at the turn of the century, where young Destry, the son of an almost legendary lawman, is enlisted to break the murderous, corrupt stranglehold Kent's gang has on the town. The townsfolk are chagrined to discover their new defender is a shy, mild-spoken man, reluctant to employ violence. Kent (Scott Brady) sets his own girl, Frenchy, to seduce Destry, but she fails. Destry is determined to destroy Kent and his killers by lawful means, but when he brings a federal judge to try the murderer of the previous sheriff a gun battle ensues and Destry is forced to shoot it out. At one point Destry's life is saved by Frenchy, who has grown to admire him. With the gang destroyed, Destry is willing to settle down and enjoy the good life with Frenchy. He also persuades the town to set aside its arms and live peacefully. While Harold Rome composed the score, no superior popular hits emerged. The show's strong points were the performances of its stars—Andy Griffith and Dolores Gray—and the superb Michael Kidd choreography. His dance in which three of Kent's gang slash the air with their bullwhips was one of the most stunning in an era of fine dancing.

Once upon a Mattress (5-11-59, Phoenix) offered a more innocent order of merriment. It was essentially the princess and the pea story set to music, telling of the comical fairy tale courtship of Princess Winnifred (Carol Burnett) by Prince Dauntless (Joe Bova). Before Winnifred is allowed to marry Dauntless, Queen Agravain makes her swim a moat, work as a chambermaid, and, of course, sleep on a pile of mattresses under which is hidden a single pea. A more straightforward romance between the dashing Sir Harry (Allen Case) and the comely Lady Larken (Anne Jones) serves as a counterpoint. The book was light and droll. Dauntless loses his heart to Winnifred on hearing her sing "The Swamps Of Home." Asked by the Prince if he can call her "Winnie," she replies her friends call her "Fred." The music was by Richard Rodgers' daughter, Mary. It was skillful and musicianly, but never memorable. For Miss Burnett's scatterbrained comedy the show was a major stop on the road to television celebrity.

The following night a new musical called **The Nervous Set** (5-12-59, Henry Miller's) transported theatregoers back to contemporary New York. Written by a group of unknown, inexperienced hands, and originally mounted in their hometown of St. Louis, it was coolly received and hastily whisked away. The plot described the problem marriage of Brad (Richard Hayes), the staid, nervous publisher of "Nerves" magazine, and his "beatnik" wife, Jan (Tani Seitz). They compromise rather than have two nervous breakdowns.

The season's best musical was its last. **Gypsy** (5-21-59, Broadway) was based on the memoirs of Gypsy Rose Lee. It had a book by Arthur Laurents, lyrics by Stephen Sondheim (who had worked with Laurents on *West Side Story*), and music by Jule Styne. David Merrick and Leland Hayward were coproducers. Although the story told of Miss Lee's start in burlesque, she was not the central figure. The evening was dominated by the presence of her mother, Rose (Ethel Merman), the quintessential pushy stage-mother, who is not above threatening "Uncle Jocko" that she will report his talent contests are rigged if her daughter, Baby June (Jacqueline Mayro), isn't given a satisfactory spot. All her daughter has is a cute little ditty to sing, which begs "Let Me Entertain You." Rose's father isn't smiling. He resents her always being away with the children. But Rose has only contempt for "Some People," stay-at-homes. Rose, June, and June's younger sister, Louise (Karen Moore), leave home to continue their search for fame and fortune. At one tryout Rose meets Herbie (Jack Klugman), who sells candy to vaudeville houses and who tells her that he has noticed her before, waiting outside a manager's office: "You looked like a pioneer woman without a frontier." They take an immediate liking to each other, and Rose is quick to suggest how alike they are. They are both strangers in the same town and doesn't that make it a "Small World." Before long Herbie has agreed to join the act and be its agent. To flickering lights and to the tune of "Let Me Entertain You," June and Louise grow up before the audience's eyes. But "talkies" and the depression have come, and they are hurting both vaudeville and Rose's daughters' chances. Even Herbie wants to leave to try something where he can have an opportunity to make more money. Naturally, Rose won't hear of it, insisting "You'll Never Get Away From Me." She wins, and the tour resumes. As the years wear on, June and Louise (now played by Lane Bradbury and Sandra Church) become disenchanted with living out of a trunk. They wish their mother would marry so they could settle into a house. They themselves are older, and marriage, if they want it, cannot be far off. In fact there is a pleasant young man in the group named Tulsa (Paul Wallace) who has his eye on June. In the guise of describing a soft-shoe act he is developing, Tulsa hints of his affection, "All I Need Is The Girl." Before long June and Tulsa have eloped. At first Rose is livid. It was June for whom she sacrificed everything. When she is calmer she remembers she has another daughter and in a flash her ambitions for Louise grow boundless. Once again "Everything's Coming Up Roses." She tells Louise not to be frightened: "You got Herbie for brains; we got you for talent; and you both got me—to yell at." All three will stick "Together." But vaudeville is dead, and Louise is forced to perform in burlesque. Herbie, concluding he is of no further use, leaves as unobtrusively as anyone can walk out of Rose's life. Initially, Louise has little success. She is too prim. When she realizes that burlesque is the only world in which she can succeed, she discards her inhibitions and performs with style and gusto. After a fellow stripper, Tessie (Maria Karnilova) blares out a trumpet solo to show "You Gotta Have A Gimmick," Louise realizes her own genteelness is her "gimmick." Her success is phenomenal and takes her to the very top, to Minsky's. With nothing further to strive for, Rose becomes introspective. In an extended soliloquy she concludes everything she did was not for her girls but for herself. Awareness, if it cannot bring joy, brings a certain serenity and a small ability to laugh at oneself. As she walks off the empty stage with Louise she confides:

Rose: You know, I had a dream last night. It was a big poster of a mother and daughter—you know, like the cover of that ladies' magazine.
Louise: Yes, Mother?
Rose: Only it was you and me wearing exactly the same gown. It was an ad for Minsky—and the

headline said: MADAM ROSE—AND HER DAUGHTER, GYPSY!

The show offered a plethora of attractions. There was a fine production with Ethel Merman giving the most marvelously bravura performance of her career. Her electric personality made the abrasive, almost unpleasant Rose seem a little lovable. As things developed, it was to be Miss Merman's last major new role. But the show itself was something of a marvel. It was pure musical comedy, filled with all the old musical comedy tricks: burlesque routines, strip-teases, soft-shoe dances, rousing choruses, and love songs. Yet *Gypsy* was clearly something more, something superior. Its book—although it was a chronicle covering a number of years—was taut and relentless, with Robbins' brilliant staging underscoring its cohesiveness and flow. It was packed with laughs, yet few were trite gags. The humor realized the dream of several generations of librettists, stemming naturally, almost inevitably, from situations and characters. And the amazingly brilliant, yet unfailingly colloquial, lyrics propelled the action and deepened the characterizations. They established that Sondheim was, with Lerner, the heir to the earlier masters in the field, all now dead or retired. Most of all, there was Styne's score, the last important, traditional musical comedy (as opposed to musical play) score to be heard on Broadway. It was vibrant and melodic. "Small World," "You'll Never Get Away From Me," "Everything's Coming Up Roses," and "Together" all entered the ranks of standards.

1959-1960

The musical shows offered in the preceding seasons had been distressingly few. With the new theatrical year the American Musical Theatre experienced the beginning of a numerically small, but proportionately not insignificant, rise in new lyric offerings. For the remainder of this history the number of new musicals remained in the "teens" (except for two isolated seasons) and once even reached twenty.

1959–60 introduced a steady parade of highly entertaining musicals. None was as fully achieved as the masterpieces of preceding sessions, but with few exceptions the new shows had much to recommend them. Not all met with success, but most near-misses could console themselves with having offered value for money.

The season began modestly with the **Billy Barnes Revue** (8-4-59, Golden). Barnes wrote the music and lyrics, while Bob Rodgers created the sketches. The small cast featured bright, young unknowns. In its spoof of "The Thirties" it was about ten years ahead of the nostalgic vogue for the period. Everything was pleasant, but nothing was outstanding. The show survived until stronger attractions began to appear.

The popular French entertainer, Yves Montand, brought his one-man show, with his songs and his microphone, in to start the fall season. More than one critic suggested his act would be better if shortened and put in a nightclub.

The season's first book musical was an amateurish dud. **Happy Town** (10-7-59, 54th St.) tried to make an evening out of a single joke—a Texas town without a millionaire. Several big spenders try unsuccessfully to buy the place, named Back-A-Heap. Produced with Texas oil money, it was laughed off the stage after five performances.

England sent Broadway the year's first hit, a delightful two-man show, **At the Drop of a Hat** (10-8-59, Golden). Its authors were its performers. Michael Flanders delivered his material from his wheelchair, while his partner, Donald Swann, sat at a piano and sang his droll, Edward Learish songs. Together they ran out the season.

In 1957 Bob Merrill had provided the score for a musical version of Eugene O'Neill's *Anna Christie*. For this still young season he went to a second O'Neill play, one that was a more likely candidate for musical treatment, *Ah! Wilderness*. With Joseph Stein and Robert Russell working on the libretto, they came up with **Take Me Along** (10-22-59, Shubert), a work that faithfully retained the small-town hominess and comic glow of the original. O'Neill had already set their story in the turn-of-the-century America so cherished by the musicals of this period. The place is Centerville, Connecticut. And the home around which the story revolves is that of Nat Miller (Walter Pidgeon), the town's newspaper editor. Nat's boozy brother-in-law, Sid (Jackie Gleason), is in the throes of a courtship with the Miller's neighbor, Lily (Eileen Herlie). And Nat's adolescent son, Richard (Robert Morse), is having a puppy-love affair with Muriel Macomber (Susan Luckey). The affair is broken off when Muriel's father learns that Richard writes poetry and reads scandalous writers such as Wilde and Ibsen. In his despair Richard imitates his uncle by going on a jag (he also visits a whorehouse). The drinking leads to a dream ballet in which he is pursued by Salome and other characters from his reading. When Richard ascertains that Muriel was forced by her father to break off their friendship, he leaves for college promising he will always love her. Sid also makes a promise: to stay away from the bottle if Lily will marry him. She accepts. Merrill again demonstrated his ability to write songs that were pleasing but rarely strong enough to catch and hold the public's fancy. Nat had a poignant number, "Staying Young," in which he first argues that everyone is growing older except him, and in a second-act reprise wistfully confesses he is growing older too. Sid vividly described the consequences of too much drinking in "Little Green Snake." The show's best number was it title song, with its lilting old-fashioned tune. It was sung by Nat and Sid, then repeated as the finale. Though *Take Me Along* gave Gleason the best role of his career, one that fit him to a tee, and though it ran over a year, it went into the books as another long-run show that never realized a return on its investment.

Some of Broadway's most competent writers joined forces with several of the theatre's greatest clowns to offer a revue called **The Girls against the Boys** (11-2-59, Alvin). Richard Lewine and Albert Hague wrote the music, Arnold B. Horwitt provided the sketches and lyrics. Nancy Walker and Bert Lahr headed the cast. In "Rich Butterfly" Miss Walker played a Japanese war bride, grovelingly subservient until she learns the ways of American wives, at which point she changes her ways with a vengeance. Lahr portrayed an aging stagedoor Johnny seeking an "Old-Fashioned Girl." The chorus girls who leave the theatre are all tough, hard-mouthed, and in slacks. The only bit of femininity Lahr can find is a swishy young chorus boy. The show was uneven. Its musical numbers were particularly weak. With great clowns no longer a sufficient attraction in themselves, the revue was forced to suspend after just 16 showings.

The season's biggest hit arrived two weeks later. **The Sound of Music** (11-16-59, Lunt-Fontanne) was a lyrical stage version of Maria Augusta Trapp's biographical *The Trapp Family Singers*. Howard Lindsay and Russel Crouse collaborated on the book, while Rodgers and Hammerstein provided the songs. The time is 1938; the place, Austria. When Maria (Mary Martin), a postulant, is deemed unprepared for convent life, she is sent to act as governess for the children of a stern, widowed naval officer, Captain Georg von Trapp (Theodore Bikel). Her warm, sympathetic treatment of the children contrasts with their father's inflexible authoritarianism. The Captain leaves for Vienna and reappears with a fiancée. On his return he is surprised and delighted that Maria has been teaching the children how to sing. Maria, fearing she is falling in love with the captain, flees to the refuge of the convent. The abbess, however, sends her back. Georg and his fiancée find their attitudes about the Nazis unreconcilable, and agree to part. For all his authoritarianism Georg is fervently opposed to the new government. When it orders him to report for naval duty, he, his children and Maria all escape to Switzerland. The show's plot was not unlike *The King and I*—a governess sent to work with the children of a strict, imperious father. Furthermore, the show's Austrian setting reminded many of something that *The King and I* had strongly suggested, namely that Rodgers and Hammerstein's shows exemplified the natural, American evolution of operetta, even if its creators strongly rejected the argument. The sentiment, romance, and seeming seriousness of the old form remained. Only ranks and vocal ranges were reduced to comply with the more egalitarian spirit and technical limitations of the day. Not since *The King and I* had Rodgers found a story so inspiring. At least half a dozen of the songs from this score have become Rodgers standards; the opening title song, "My Favorite Things," "Do Re Mi,"—all sung by Maria; "Climb Every Mountain" (used to close both acts); "You Are Sixteen," and "Edelweiss." The show opened to an advance sale of over two million dollars, ran for more than three years, toured extensively, and was well received overseas. Oscar Hammerstein's death, shortly after the show opened, meant *The Sound of Music* marked the end of the most lucrative partnership in the history of the American Musical Theatre. The film version six years later, with Julie Andrews in the lead role, was the leading grossing musical of all time, which showed the great continued appeal of the story.

Far down in Manhattan a new show opened two nights after *The Sound of Music,* professing to spoof the old order of operettas from which the contemporary musical plays were descended. The curtain for **Little Mary Sunshine** (11-18-59, Orpheum) rises on the Colorado Inn, high in the Rocky Mountains. Singing their song, "The Forest Rangers" appear and to her coy embarrassment proclaim their affection for "Little Mary Sunshine," the inn's proprietress. Mary (Eileen Brennan) has missed a mortgage payment on the inn and may be evicted. But she is undaunted, always able to "Look

For A Sky Of Blue." The Rangers' Captain Jim (William Graham) reveals he is searching for a villainous Indian, Yellow Feather (Ray James). When the inn is visited by a great European opera star, Mme. Ernestine (Elizabeth Parrish), who lovingly recalls her own favorite hideaway, "In Izzenschnooken On The Lovely Essenzook Zee," the romantic mood prompts Mary and Jim to admit their love for each other (and their home state) in the "Colorado Love Call." Two youngsters, Corporal Billy (John McMartin) and Nancy Twinkle (Elmarie Wendel), are also attracted to each other and agree they could be loyal, if only "Once In A Blue Moon." A big affair is held, "Such A Merry Party" that no one could possibly be unhappy. But danger, in the person of Yellow Feather, lurks not far away. Nancy dampens Billy's ardor slightly by confessing she is "Naughty, Naughty Nancy." There is momentary confusion when Billy dresses up as Yellow Feather. But the real villain is caught. The good Indians, who own the inn, give the deed to Mary, and Jim ponders joys of marriage in Colorado. The show was absurdly funny, blessed with two adroit performances by Eileen Brennan and John McMartin. But for all the kudos it received and all the success it enjoyed—and it ran nearly three years at its small Second Avenue house—it missed the consistent satire of *The Boy Friend* (9-30-54) or the earlier, shorter "Rose of Arizona" in *Garrick Gaieties* (5-10-26) and "The Gladiola Girl," in *Lend an Ear* (12-16-48). Sandy Wilson's show had kept its sights on one type of twenties musical—the modern, lean, jazzy musical comedy such as *No! No! Nanette!* (9-16-25). Rick Besoyan in *Little Mary Sunshine* drew laughs by attacking all the genres of the era. The show most quickly called to mind the operetta school of *Rose-Marie* (9-2-24), *Naughty Marietta* (11-7-10), and *Rio Rita* (2-2-27), but also harked back to Jerome Kern's commercial hits of the period—"Look For The Silver Lining" from *Sally* (12-21-20)—and Kern's more Continental pieces of a decade later— "In Egern By The Tegern See" from *Music in the Air* (11-8-32). From the early twenties musical comedies it culled numbers such as the party song that sounded joyously like "We'll Have A Wonderful Party" from *Mary* (10-18-20) and "The Best Part Of Every Party" from *Irene* (11-18-19).

A flamboyant, eminently theatrical figure from the very era whose plays Besoyan was burlesquing was the subject of the next musical to appear. And when, later in the season, **Fiorello!** (11-23-59, Broadhurst) was awarded the Pulitzer Prize it brought back to mind another musical of that era, the first to win the award, *Of Thee I Sing* (12-26-31). Comparisons suggested that newer did not mean better, even if George Abbott and Jerome Weidman's book, Jerry Bock's score, and Sheldon Harnick's lyrics were no mean achievement. The deliciously preposterous fictions of the earlier work were absent as was the consistent tone that the fictions allowed and that its authors successfully maintained. To some extent the facts of Fiorello La Guardia's career dictated the broad swings back and forth from nostalgia to muckraking to satire to sentimentality. The show opened with an irresistible bit of nostalgia by showing the famous newsreels of La Guardia's reading comic strips to the children of New York during a newspaper strike. An offhand remark of his about the corrupt politicians who governed the city when he was a young lawyer takes the show back to 1914. His secretary, Marie (Patricia Wilson), who quite obviously loves him, and the rest of his staff are awed to be working for a man so clearly "On The Side Of The Angels." When Marie's friend, Dora (Pat Stanley), tells Fiorello (Tom Bosley) that the leader of their strike, Thea (Ellen Hanley), has been arrested on a trumped-up charge of soliciting, La Guardia personally berates the corrupt policeman, Floyd (Mark Dawson), who made the arrest. But La Guardia is not above associating with Ben Marino (Howard da Silva), the Republican Ward leader who agrees to run him in his district against the Tammany candidate. Ben's enthusiasm is only halfhearted. He and his cronies divide their passion equally between "Politics And Poker." La Guardia takes to the streets in his campaign, impressing on those who will listen, "The Name's La Guardia." His background allows him to repeat the message in Italian and Yiddish as well. It's a message people understand. When the results are in, the boys at Marino's clubhouse are staggered to discover "The Bum Won." Meanwhile Floyd and Dora have become close, and Floyd has begun to climb the Tammany ladder. Dora starts to drift away from Thea, who is being courted by Fiorello. To the caressing melody of "Till Tomorrow," he proposes to her before sailing off to war. Thea dies in the middle of La Guardia's next campaign. At the same time, the excesses of the Walker administration catch up with it during the Seabury investigation—excesses that have given Floyd and Dora a lavish penthouse. Ben and some of his regulars enjoyed the discomfort of their opponents and the unmistakable ridiculousness of their opponents' replies in court, when the Tammany men insist their wealth came from savings in "A Little Tin Box." Seabury has selected La Guardia to run on a Fusion ticket. Fiorello delays accepting only long enough to warn: "And if I should decide to run again, I want all you politicians to know that my chief qualification for Mayor of this great city is my monumental ingratitude." He then fires his long-time secretary, Marie, explaining, "I can't court a girl who's working for me." Together they prepare for the forthcoming campaign.

Saratoga (12-7-59, Winter Garden) opened, filled with promise, and closed, a major disappointment, ten weeks later. In proper hands there was no reason why Edna Ferber's colorful period piece about New Orleans and Saratoga in the 1880s could not have made as rich a musical as had her *Show Boat* (12-27-27). But the fine talents that labored on the new adaptation were distressingly uninspired. Morton Da Costa kept the basic story of Clio Dulaine (Carol Lawrence) and Clint Maroon (Howard Keel), two fortune hunters who join forces to make their way in the world and end up caring about each other. Clio is motivated by society's disdain for her illegitimacy, while Clint is determined to avenge the railroad's stealing of his family's land. He eventually beats the railroad men at their own game. The plot seemingly became entangled in the elaborate moving stage and complicated scenery of the show. Harold Arlen's score, with Johnny Mercer lyrics, was not strong enough to break loose and soar on its own.

Unlike *Saratoga*, **Beg, Borrow or Steal** (2-10-60, Beck) promised little and delivered less. Few were disappointed when it left after five performances. The show starred a number of Hollywood and Broadway names who had seen their best days, and was written for them by creators untried on Broadway. The story dealt with those bohemians the decade referred to as "beatniks." Clara (Betty Garrett) and Pistol (Eddie Bracken) are sister and brother. They live together in The Pad, and run a health-food store. Pistol and his friend, Rafe (Larry Parks), also run a beatnik meeting place, The Pit. They keep alive by the skin of their teeth. Clara must choose romantically between Rafe and a seemingly "square," Junior (Biff McGuire). She chooses Junior, who proves to be Rex All, the beatnik poet laureate. Given the growing association between beatniks and drugs, naming the poet after a drugstore chain was one of the evening's few felicitous touches.

Frank Loesser's **Greenwillow** (3-8-60, Alvin)

was probably the major disappointment of the season, though many serious students feel it deserves a rehearing. An idyll of bygone rural America, based on B. J. Chute's novel, it centered its attention on young Gideon Briggs. Gideon (Anthony Perkins) refuses to court his girl, Dorrie (Ellen McCown), because he fears he has inherited the family wanderlust. Love conquers fear. Loesser's book was so idyllic it ultimately came to seem untheatrical, and Loesser's songs, while often clever, sounded surprisingly thin. There were interesting touches such as the contrapuntal sermons of Reverend Birdsong (Cecil Kellaway) and Reverend Lapp (William Chapman), the one extolling a God of Love, the other warning of a God of Wrath. But the show's principal number, "The Music Of Home," over-reached melodically without any reason and without the necessary backbone to support itself. Thanks largely to an excellent advance sale *Greenwillow* was able to survive three months.

The last major hit of the season, and its most unexpected success, followed five weeks later. **Bye, Bye Birdie** (4-14-60, Beck) was a fresh, unpretentious, funny, and melodic show that kidded the flourishing rock-and-roll rage and its wriggling superstar, Elvis Presley. If the singing sensation Conrad Birdie (Dick Gautier) is drafted, his agent, Albert Peterson (Dick Van Dyke), will lose his commissions and not have enough money to marry Rose Grant (Chita Rivera). This would be a sad state of affairs for everyone except Albert's loving mother (Kay Medford), who practically collapses at even the thought of his marrying and finds herself at death's door when Rose is mentioned specifically. But Rose has a scheme. They will write a song called "One Last Kiss," which Birdie will sing to a carefully selected typical teen-age admirer. If the song clicks, they can live off the royalties until Birdie is discharged. The girl selected is Kim MacAfee (Susan Watson), and the whole entourage heads for Kim's hometown of Sweet Apple. Conrad is given a room in the MacAfee house and before long has come between Kim and her loyal beau, Hugo Peabody (Michael J. Pollard). When Mrs. Peterson's tantrums threaten to come between Albert and Rose, Rose and Hugo go out on a bender, and before long an intoxicated Rose is disrupting a staid, small-town Shriners' meeting. A wild "Shriners' Ballet" ensues. Luckily for Hugo, Kim grows weary of Conrad's egotistical, overbearing ways even before he leaves for the army. She and Hugo, and Albert and Rose are soon hand in hand again. The score with music by Charles Strouse and lyrics

by Lee Adams was as delightful as the book. However, it contained little pure rock and roll. Conrad, Kim, and the teenagers had the hit of the show, "A Lot Of Livin' To Do." Albert had the toe-tapping "Put On A Happy Face" and the love ballad, "Baby, Talk To Me." The town's elders sang a Charleston melody in which they gave vent to their dismay with the younger generation, "Kids," asking why the children can't be like *they* were, "Perfect, in every way!" The show enhanced the growing reputation of Chita Rivera and helped propel Dick Van Dyke, Paul Lynde (as the harrassed Mr. MacAfee), Pollard, and Miss Medford on to bigger things. In rocking, rolling, and wriggling for a joyous year and a half on Broadway it also gave a major leg-up to its librettist, Michael Stewart.

• • •

Michael Stewart Rubin was born in New York City on August 1, 1929. Educated at Yale, he was awarded a Master of Arts there in 1953. He served an apprenticeship writing sketches for such off-Broadway revues as *Razzle Dazzle, The Shoestring Revue,* and *The Littlest Revue,* as well as working on Sid Caesar's television show.

• • •

Hermione Gingold's bad luck pursued her when she arrived in a revue, **From A to Z** (4-20-60, Plymouth). Names soon to be famous in the theatre contributed songs and sketches: Jerry Herman, Woody Allen. But to no avail. The show folded after 20 showings. Its big first-act finale was a travesty on *The Sound of Music*, rechristened, "The Sound of Schmaltz," in which International Nannies, Ltd., send Alice Cadwallader-Smith, a governess given to singing as she swings in a Central Park hammock, to assist in rearing the children of Baron von Klaptrap.

On April 27, when *West Side Story* returned to begin the second engagement already mentioned, the City Center resumed its annual series of revivals, although this year there would be only two. It was a hint that increasing costs were shortly to sound the knell of these low-priced presentations. *Finian's Rainbow*, with Bobby Howes and Jeannie Carson, was first, followed by *The King and I*, with Farley Granger and Barbara Cook, on May 11.

In between the two revivals the season's last original on-Broadway musical appeared. **Christine** (4-28-60, 46th St.) was not unlike *The King and I* (3-29-51) in that it recounted the love story between a Western lady and an Eastern gentleman. In this case the woman is Lady Christine FitzSimons (Maureen O'Hara) of Ireland and the man is her widowed son-in-law, Dr. Rashil Singh (Morley Meredith). The doctor settles for a native beauty, Sita Roy (Janet Pavek), after Christine decides too many disparities separate Rashil's and her worlds. Sammy Fain provided the music. But famed novelist turned librettist Pearl Buck lacked the theatrical know-how of Oscar Hammerstein and Fain's innocuous score was a far cry from the rich beauties Rodgers had offered. Even the lovely and gracious Miss O'Hara could not save the piece.

On May 3, 1960, **The Fantasticks** premiered at the minuscule Sullivan Street Playhouse in the village and at this writing, over seventeen years later, is still playing there. Not many critics were overjoyed and in the early weeks business was so slow that the backers looked certain to lose their meager $16,500 investment. But a small band of devotees plugged it, and it went on to win the Vernon Rice Award for the best off-Broadway show of the season. Attendance picked up, and when "Try To Remember" inched its way into national popularity the success of the show was assured. The Narrator (Jerry Orbach) sings the song, which opens the show, and sets the bittersweet mood. He explains that the parents of The Boy called Matt (Kenneth Nelson) and The Girl called Luisa (Rita Gardner) have built a wall between their homes on the theory that the best way to bring lovers together is to make it seem they are to be kept apart. The parents go so far as to hire a bandit (played by The Narrator) to attempt, and purposely be foiled in, a rape of The Girl. But the Rape Ballet is followed by the youngsters' discovery of their parents' devices. The Boy and The Girl quickly fall out and go their separate ways. Eventually they return, disillusioned with the world, and embrace. The Narrator comments laconically, "Without a hurt the heart is hollow." The show had originally been a one-act musical play suggested by Rostand's *Les Romantiques*. Composer Harvey Schmidt and author Tom Jones expanded it into a full-length work at the request of Lore Noto, who then produced it. None of the rest of Schmidt's score became as popular as "Try To Remember," although The Girl's "Much More" and the youngsters' "Soon It's Gonna Rain" enjoyed brief vogues when Barbra Streisand recorded them. The show did maintain a tone—an odd mixture of poignancy and whimsy. But Schmidt and Jones were never able to re-create it or move on successfully to other achievements either off Broadway or on. In this respect fortune was far less kind to them than it was to their original Narrator, Jerry Orbach.

1960-1961

Just as it was becoming obvious that the latest act was nearing its end, the man most responsible for its shape and tenor passed on. Oscar Hammerstein II died on August 23, 1960, before the season's first new musical appeared. As early as *Rose-Marie* (9-2-24), he had attempted tentative breaks with the traditions of the American Musical Theatre. With the successful *Show Boat* (2-27-27) and the unsuccessful *Rainbow* (11-21-28), both still in the twenties, he had pioneered in the form which, with *Oklahoma!* (3-31-43), established the master mold for more than two decades of lyric-theatre writing. His death, coming in a second season of good but uninspired musicals, underscored the waning of the renaissance he had so strongly influenced.

Not one of the three September offerings was a wholly New York affair, and only one was unequivocally American. The experimental Phoenix Theatre on Second Avenue opened the season with a Stratford, Ontario, production of *H.M.S. Pinafore* by the inventive English director, Tyrone Guthrie. The intention of both Stratford's Shakespearean Festival and Mr. Guthrie was to mount a Gilbert and Sullivan piece without recourse to accepted D'Oyly Carte staging. Critics disagreed as to how genuinely fresh Guthrie's conceptions were. Enough Savoyards flocked to the downtown house to give the work a 55-performance run. But after the production closed most directors assigned to revive *H.M.S. Pinafore* hurried back to traditional prompt books.

September also brought a California revue, **Vintage '60** (9-12-60, Atkinson). A few New York names such as Sheldon Harnick, Fred Ebb, and David Baker added material in hopes of strengthening it for a more demanding Broadway. Since 1960 was an election year, a first-act finale mocked a national political convention, honored by a visit from a man named Richard Nixon. But Broadway continued to prefer foreign and local wines to the western ones, and *Vintage '60* survived only a single week. It was David Merrick's first musical offering of the season.

His second production recompensed him for the failure of his first. He unveiled his importation from France (by way of England), **Irma La Douce** (9-29-60, Plymouth). A saucy, galloping musical about a "poule" and her "mec," it ran well into the next season. Elizabeth Seal and Keith Michell repeated their London successes in the lead roles. Merrick was to have an amazingly busy year, one that established him indisputably as the major producer of the era. The next two shows to arrive on Broadway were his importations of two straight plays, *A Taste of Honey* and *Becket*. They were among the best plays and biggest hits of the season.

Stanley Holloway, who had been kept busy for several years as Doolittle in *My Fair Lady* (3-15-56), returned to appear alone in his one-man show, **Laughs and Other Events** (10-10-60, Barrymore). The other events included selections from Holloway's British music-hall days. Unfortunately they weren't sufficiently appealing to Americans to keep the evening on the boards beyond its initial week.

The first big, new American book musical, **Tenderloin** (10-17-60, 46th St.) had a libretto by Jerome Weidman and George Abbott, lyrics by Sheldon Harnick, and music by Jerry Bock—the team that created the preceding season's winning *Fiorello!* They took as their source a novel by Samuel Hopkins Adams based loosely on the attempts of the Reverend Mr. Parkhurst to clean up the old Tenderloin district near West 23rd Street. But what the librettists ended with was far more fiction than fact. Their Reverend Brock would eradicate his era's corruption with the help of a handsome young scandal-sheet reporter who is also a part-time singer at one of the area's roughest bars. Brock is unaware that Tommy (Ron Husmann), his supposed associate, is in cahoots with a dishonest policeman, Lieutenant Schmidt (Ralph Dunn). The two frame Brock with doctored photographs. But in court Tommy, who has been converted by a choir girl named Laura (Wynne Miller), admits the truth. A cleanup of the area begins. Brock does not remain to witness the change. He moves his crusade on to Detroit. Though *Tenderloin* was able to enlist the noted Shakespearean and Shavian actor, Maurice Evans, for the part of Brock, it had little else in the way of novelty to present. The plot had obvious parallels with *Fiorello*'s, but the age it depicted, "the latter part of the 19th century," was not as flamboyant or as theatrically colorful as La Guardia's times, and the priggish, sometimes comically naïve, minister no match for "The Little Flower." Bock's score was filled with pleasantries that delighted in the theatre but found no lasting popularity on the outside. Most notable were Tommy's sentimental "Artificial Flowers" and Brock's hilariously innocent interpretation of Tenderloin notions about "Good Clean Fun." *Tenderloin* ran over six months, yet closed a commercial failure.

If Bock and his collaborators were drifting away from historical figures, Meredith Willson latched on to a fascinating character who had become a legend in her own lifetime, **The Unsinkable Molly Brown** (11-3-60, Winter Garden). Luckily for Willson her heyday encompassed the most popular period of the era, the turn of the century to 1912. At the beginning Molly is an impoverished but spunky tomboy, determined one day to be rich and grand. But when she moves from Missouri to Colorado she meets an equally impoverished and spunky young miner, Johnny "Leadville" Brown, falls headlong in love and marries him. Her dreams seem to come true when Johnny presents her with $300,000 he receives from selling a claim. Her joy is short-lived, for she hides the money in an oven and forgetfully burns it. The forgiving Johnny soon brings her a second fortune, and they move to Denver. Snubbed by Denver society, they head for Europe, where her wealth and her gaucheries make her the darling of the moment. She returns to Denver to have her revenge, but her gala party is wrecked by the unexpected appearance of the Browns' old mining buddies. Johnny insists on staying in Colorado, but Molly flees to Europe. She is courted by an attractive prince, but, lonely for Johnny, sails to rejoin him. Her ship is the *Titanic*, and when it sinks she proves one of the heroines of the disaster. Her heroism makes her acceptable to society. Willson did only the songs for *The Unsinkable Molly Brown*. The book was by Richard Morris. This may partly explain why the new work lacked something of the stylish consistency and cohesiveness of *The Music Man*. Its bent toward the commercial was undoubtedly furthered by its co-producers, The Theatre Guild. This once-daring organization, in its death throes as a responsible artistic force, had become crassly, even desperately, conscious of the box office. Yet if the show was less artful than Willson's first work, it remained rattling good theatre. Two of Willson's most durable melodies emerged from the evening, Molly's forceful "I Ain't Down Yet" and Johnny's tender love ballad, "I'll Never Say No." The show was lavishly mounted, with scenes, depicting the sinking of the *Titanic* and Molly in her lifeboat, that recalled the elaborate stage effects of prefilm days. Tammy Grimes and the strong-voiced Harve Presnell headed the cast and helped the show to achieve a 532-performance run.

A week after the opening John F. Kennedy defeated Richard M. Nixon for the presidency. Kennedy's inauguration four months later ushered in a brief era during which the arts were embraced and made welcome by the first family.

The season's most eagerly awaited musical, **Camelot** (12-3-60, Majestic), was Lerner and Loewe's first Broadway effort since their triumphant *My Fair Lady* (3-15-56). Based on T. H. White's popular novel, *The Once and Future King,* it continued the team's wanderings through British terrains and centuries by recalling the sunlight and shadow of Arthurian legend that lies on the other side of the Celtic mists, not far from Brigadoon. Just before his marriage to Guenevere, whom he has not met, a nervous, shy Arthur imagines what his people are thinking. He can hear them ask, "I Wonder What The King Is Doing Tonight?" He would like to tell them he is "wishing he were in Scotland fishing tonight." But the appearance of an attractive young maiden sends him scurrying for a hiding spot. She is Guenevere, and she, too, is nervous about the forthcoming marriage. She fears she has missed "The Simple Joys Of Maidenhood" she has read about in romances. "Shall kith not kill their kin for me?" she inquires. Arthur reveals himself, but not his identity. He tells her he has heard some wicked stories about the king, but that Camelot is not a bad place. After the wedding Arthur begins consolidating the Round Table. One of his knights is the dashing Lancelot (Robert Goulet), who falls in love with Guenevere almost at first sight and leaves Camelot rather than stir up trouble. But he cannot remain away and returns to court her furtively. In the show's hit number, "If Ever I Would Leave You," he lists the qualities of the passing seasons to see if any could induce him to leave and concludes none could. When the villainous Mordred (Roddy McDowell) exposes the romance, the lovers are condemned. They escape to France where Arthur pursues them. Arthur meets them before going into a battle with the French that may cost his life. He is forgiving, but only when a youngster begs to be made a member of the Round Table can he catch even a glimmer of hope that Camelot's "one brief shining moment" can be revived.

After President John Kennedy's death, Lerner's lyric about "one brief shining moment" became synonymous with the high noon of his administration.

The comparisons that the critics made to *My Fair Lady* were largely unkind and somewhat unfair. Nonetheless, they were inevitable. Not only

had Lerner and Loewe written the work, but *My Fair Lady*'s costar, Julie Andrews; principal featured player, Robert Coote; and director, Moss Hart, were back as well as its designer (Oliver Smith), choreographer, and conductor. Parenthetically, the show's trouble-plagued tryout is sometimes held responsible for Hart's fatal heart attack a year later. Once again Miss Andrews was costarred with a noted English dramatic actor, this time Richard Burton. Even the hyperbolic sweep of Lancelot's love song reminded many of "On The Street Where You Live." To some extent it could be argued that *Camelot* attempted to impose the biting realistic wit of *My Fair Lady* on the magical fantasy of *Brigadoon*. It became especially disconcerting when Mordred was made into a comic villain. But for all its faults, *Camelot* was a fine evening's entertainment gorgeously set and dressed in medieval splendor. Its advance sale of over three million dollars gave audiences time to spread a generally favorable word-of-mouth after the shock of the initial disappointment. Before it had run its course *Camelot* played over two years in Manhattan, toured and enjoyed international celebrity as well.

Two weeks later audiences were back in 1912. It was not the homey, small-town 1912 of so many recent shows but the rough-and-tumble good old days of the early oil booms. And the **Wildcat** (12-16-60, Alvin) to end all wildcats was television's beloved Lucille Ball. She played Wildcat Jackson, who arrives in Centavo City with her crippled sister Jane (Paula Stewart). Wildcat bluffs the townspeople into believing she has drilling rights and persuades Joe Dynamite (Keith Andes) to be her foreman. Only then does she actually purchase oil leases from a comic recluse, Sookie (Don Tomkins). When Joe becomes discouraged with the prospects on her land and threatens to quit, she has him arrested on trumped-up charges and put in her custody. After further digging proves futile and all her crew seem ready to quit, Wildcat throws a stick of dynamite into a well and comes up with a spectacular gusher. She also wins Joe for a husband. It was not much of a book, although it was written by an accomplished playwright, N. Richard Nash. For most theatregoers the only inducement to see the show was Miss Ball. In June, when she tired of playing it, the show had to fold before it could retrieve its investment. While *Wildcat* was running its show-stopper was a hoe-down routine with Wildcat and Sookie called "What Takes My Fancy," but a second lively number, *Wildcat*'s commanding march, "Hey, Look Me Over," later developed into a standard. The rest of the score, with music by Cy Coleman and lyrics by Carolyn Leigh, ran from the cloyingly cute, "Tippy Tippy Toes" to the mawkish "That's What I Want For Janie" to the pretentious "Tall Hope," a choral number that closed the first act.

The season's only sustained attempt at dealing with the contemporary scene **Do Re Mi** (12-26-60, St. James) closed out 1960. Garson Kanin's libretto was not much better than *Wildcat*'s book. It, too, depended primarily on its clowns for its strength. Fortunately its producer, David Merrick, hired two of the best, Phil Silvers and Nancy Walker. They played a husband and wife, Hubert and Kay Cram, who occasionally are in the money when one of Hubie's pie-in-the-sky schemes momentarily works. When they visit the Casacabana and their table is shoved farther and farther into the rear of the nightclub, the humiliation drives Hubie to attempt to become a big shot in the jukebox business. He kids himself, "It's Legitimate," even though he knows his associates have been racketeers. Before long the big boys muscle in, but Hubie is swimming in money. Kay concludes the old days of middle-class struggle were a more joyous "Adventure." When she complains of Hubie's underworld cronies and he responds that they help pay for the elegant dress she has on, she takes off the dress. After a while, Hubie is over his head and finally forced out. Kay is content, but Hubie is planning his next conquest. A love interest was provided by Tilda Mullen (Nancy Dussault), a waitress Hubie helps make a singing star, and the polished John Henry Wheeler (John Reardon). The show's best production number, "What's New At The Zoo," fell to Tilda. John was given the hit Jule Styne love ballad, "Make Someone Happy": Jule Styne wrote the music, and Gordon and Green the lyrics. Its stars were more loyal to *Do Re Mi* than Miss Ball was to *Wildcat,* and it ran 400 performances. Nevertheless, theatrical economics were responsible for its closing in the loss column.

1961's first musical was billed as a revue, but it was little more than a one-woman show. The one-woman in this case was the towering Carol Channing, given breathers by comedian Jules Munshin and Les Quat' Jeudis. Miss Channing's **Show Girl** (1-12-61, O'Neill) had no connection with Ziegfeld's 1929 production. However, one high spot was a comparison of the musical shows of Ziegfeld's era with the musicals of her own day. With the new era coming to an end and with its clichés falling into perspective, Miss Channing took advantage of a unique opportunity for comic juxtaposition. Culling songs from "The Gladiola Girl" spoof that had rocketed her to fame in *Lend an Ear* (12-16-48), she compared three of them with similarly placed numbers from imaginary contemporary shows. "The Gladiola Girl's" opening "Join Us In A Little Cup Of Tea" was contrasted with "This Is A Darned Fine Funeral," and the 1920's style love song, "In Our Teeny Little Weeny Nest For Two," gave way to "Love Is A Sickness," while the high-kicking Yahoo step was replaced by a balletic "Switchblade Bess." Although the show ran only three months, a low budget and successful road tour helped it show a profit.

Preston Sturges' acclaimed *Hail, the Conquering Hero* was made into a musical by Larry Gelbart, Moose Charlap, and Norman Gimbel. They contracted the title to **The Conquering Hero** (1-16-61, ANTA) but kept the essentials of the movie's story in which a recruit (Tom Poston), discharged after a month's service because of his allergies, is mistaken for a war hero. The picture had been done during World War II and delighted with its zany hilarity. By 1961 both timeliness and zaniness were missing. One week was the length of the new show's welcome.

Only the least bit less unsuccessful was **13 Daughters** (3-2-61, 54th St.), whose main attraction in a year of notable scenery and scenic effects was George Jenkins' colorful Hawaiian settings. Don Ameche found himself playing a turn-of-the-century Chinese pater familias in Hawaii who cannot marry off his twelve younger daughters until he finds a suitable husband for his eldest. In addition, to complicate his life further, a family curse says his daughters mustn't marry at all. Ameche strove with such lines as "A bird in the hand is worth two in the bushel," but he didn't have to struggle for long.

E. Y. Harburg, Fred Saidy, and Henry Myers took Aristophanes' ancient Greek comedy, *Lysistrata*, set it to Offenbach's 19th-century French music, gave the principal, if not the title, role to the best of all British fop portrayers, Cyril Ritchard, and came up with a new Broadway musical, **The Happiest Girl in the World** (4-3-61, Beck). It was charming, but not charming enough to survive long.

The City Center presented four revivals in its annual spring season. For 1961 it began on April 12 with *Show Boat* (12-27-27) with Jo Sullivan, Robert Rounseville, and Joe E. Brown, and continued on April 26 with *South Pacific* (4-7-49), *Porgy And Bess* (10-10-35) on May 17, and *Pal Joey*

(12-25-40) on May 31, with Bob Fosse and Carol Bruce as the principals.

Twice before, with his musical versions of *Anna Christie* and *Ah! Wilderness,* Bob Merrill had demonstrated his willingness to compose scores for challenging adaptations. His derring-do was again displayed when he offered a new work in association with librettist Michael Stewart and producer David Merrick. What was so unusual about **Carnival** (4-13-61, Imperial) was that it was based on a recent and tremendously popular motion picture, *Lili,* whose own score had produced at least one standard. The entire film score was discarded. But the essential story remained. Lili, an orphan, appears at a small European carnival seeking a friend of her dead father, and, she hopes, the offer of a home. She is taken in hand by the carnival folk. At first she becomes enamored of the show's magician, Marco the Magnificent (James Mitchell), but she soon realizes her true future lies with the lame, misanthropic puppeteer Paul Berthalet (Jerry Orbach). She brings out his repressed warmth and goodness, and love ensues. The show lacked the fey enchantments of the film, but had virtues of its own, especially Gower Champion's vital staging. No curtain was used, and the performers often employed aisles for entrances and exits, sometimes even for part of the show. Champion's choreography was as exciting as his staging, culminating in the rousing ensemble dancing for "Grand Imperial Cirque De Paris," with virtually the entire cast swinging arm-in-arm around the stage. Champion found himself in the peculiar position of having to give virtually no dancing to his Lili, even though one of the film's delights had been Leslie Caron's dancing. The star of the show was Anna Maria Alberghetti, a singer, so the burden of providing her with material fell to Merrill. His songs (not only for Lili) kept a seemingly conscious distance in time and place. Their titles often appeared to have come from musicals of fifty years earlier—"Fairyland," "Sword, Rose And Cape," "Tanz Mit Mir," and "Yum Ticky." But he did manage to create a "Theme From 'Carnival' " that became almost as popular as the movie's "Hi Lili, Hi Lo." It was played all through the show and finally sung by Lili and Paul's puppets as the first-act finale. It received national attention under the more workable title of "Love Makes The World Go Round." *Carnival* walked away with most of the season's awards and ran over 700 performances, to the profit of all concerned.

Donnybrook! (5-18-61, 46th St.), the season's final musical, was also based on a film, John Ford's *The Quiet Man.* It was adapted by Robert E. Mc-Enroe, who years before had written one successful play, *The Silver Whistle,* and had songs by Johnny Burke. The story again recounted the trials and tribulations of John Enright (Art Lund), a prizefighter who retires from the ring to Ireland after one of his punches kills an opponent. His hopes to marry Ellen Danaher (Joan Fagan) are dashed when Ellen's brother Will (Philip Bosco) refuses to give her a dowry unless John first fights him. John, fearing he might inadvertently kill Will, demurs. Since Ellen will not marry without her dowry, John has no choice but to fight. *Donnybrook!,* like *The Conquering Hero* and unlike *Carnival,* could not find the secret to moving successfully from one medium to another. Despite some good singing by Lund and some capital clowning by Susan Johnson and Eddie Foy, Jr., it languished for 68 performances before calling it a run.

In one respect the season ended as it began, with the death of a notable figure. Joe Howard had never approached Oscar Hammerstein's importance on Broadway, and indeed he had rarely approached Broadway. He belonged to a time much earlier than Hammerstein's, when Broadway was not the sole production center for the American Musical Theatre. In a day when Chicago was almost as important, Howard was indisputably the best of the Chicago composers. He died at the age of ninety-three, on stage, performing. But his creative days had long since passed, and his very era seemed irretrievably far away.

1961-1962

The new season was the busiest in a dozen years, and like several recent sessions, was packed with good shows whose possibilities were never fully realized. In several ways the season gave further indication of the waning of an era, while at the same time it demonstrated that the period's high artistic principles would not be readily discarded. Almost all the season's musicals were steadfastly set in the present day; none looked back to the America of a half-century or so before. Sentimentality took several severe knockings and even romance was often either relegated to a subservient role or given an unhappy denouement. Although dancing remained generally excellent, there were fewer of the kind of ballets that had become commonplace since *Oklahoma!,* especially "dream ballets." A number of the musicals dealt head-on with growing racial problems, or with life among one important section of theatregoers, the Jews. This, plus their modern settings, gave the season's shows a thirtyish air. Appearances, however, did not bear close scrutiny. The biting social commentary of the more purposeful depression-era musicals was missing, while the cardboard figures and caricatures of that period's lighter pieces gave way to the more lifelike men and women the modern musical play had led audiences to expect.

A lone summer entry was **The Billy Barnes People** (6-13-61, Royale). Barnes and his collaborator, Bob Rodgers, had managed to span the summer two seasons back with the *Billy Barnes Revue*. This time their appeal, or their luck, ran out, and the show survived less than a week, taking with it skits on the order of its *Camelot* travesty, "Damn-Alot."

A Chicago revue, **From the Second City** (9-26-61, Royale), was unusual in that it was a series of clever sketches with almost no music interjected. Most of the material was topical. A new Germany was seen as so eager to reject its recent past that it was determinedly burning Nazi books and seeking a "final solution" to the Nazi problem. A news broadcast, plucked magically from four years in the future, summed up the early achievements of America's latest President. The minimum wage has been reduced to a sensible pittance; social security begins at ninety-five, provided disability can be proved; and the work week has been extended to a productive sixty hours. "So much," the announcer concludes, "for the first hundred days of the Goldwater administration." New Yorkers didn't accept the revue as wholeheartedly as Chicagoans had, but in its eleven-week run it helped further the careers of such bright, young talents as Barbara Harris and Alan Arkin.

Sail Away (10-3-61, Broadhurst) was also unusual, but in a different way. It was the work of England's idolized Noel Coward, but it was presented on Broadway before London was allowed to see it. New Yorkers were not overwhelmed by the courtesy. Less than vintage Coward, this tale of a harassed cruise hostess (Elaine Stritch) on a Cunard Mediterranean voyage left port after 21 weeks. It was the first musical in a busy October.

Given the size of the Jewish segment of Broadway's playgoers and its concern with Israel, it was surprising no musical had used an Israeli setting before. Curiously, although **Milk and Honey** (10-10-61, Beck) ran nearly a year and a half (without showing a profit), only one other major musical later used the same setting. The principal figures in

Milk and Honey were not Israelis, but American Jews in Israel as tourists. Phil is a middle-aged businessman, separated from his wife. His daughter Barbara (Lanna Saunders) and son-in-law David (Tommy Rall) live in a kibbutz. Phil meets an attractive American, Ruth, and they quickly grow fond of each other. When Phil reveals he is still married their idyll seems ended. Watching a joyous Yemenite wedding convinces Ruth that she should at least give the liaison a try, but her qualms persist, and she soon flees to Tel Aviv. Phil pursues her, but when she agrees to return he develops qualms. Ruth decides to go back to America and to wait until Phil gets his divorce. An undercurrent of unhappiness pervades Barbara and David's relationship, too, because Barbara is homesick for the United States and David accepts the probability of having to leave his beloved fatherland to please his wife. The only completely happy romance in the show was that of the central comic figure, a "yenta" named Clara Weiss who comes to Israel specifically to find a husband and succeeds in capturing an appropriately docile "nebbish," Mr. Horowitz. The score was the first by Jerry Herman to be heard on Broadway.

. . .

Jerry Herman was born in New York City on July 10, 1933. He studied music from early childhood and majored in drama at the University of Miami. Three of his musicals—*I Feel Wonderful, Nightcap,* and *Parade*—were done off-Broadway before *Milk and Honey* made the big time. He also trained by writing special material for performers such as Tallulah Bankhead, Jane Froman, and Hermione Gingold. One of his songs was heard in Miss Gingold's revue, *From A to Z*.

. . .

His new score was a superb amalgam of Jewish colorings and rhythms within accepted theatrical forms. The show's hit was Phil and Ruth's warmly inviting "Shalom," which virtually framed the evening. The rest of the songs moved from the irresistible beat of the "Independence Day Hora" to the stirring title song, sung by David and the chorus, to David's poignant cry of "I Will Follow You," to Ruth and Phil's slightly arioso, "There's No Reason In The World," to their lively "That Was Yesterday." Although Herman was destined to have an even greater success, none of his future scores was as melodically inventive or memorable. Two fine singers, formerly of the opera, Mimi Benzell and Robert Weede, played Ruth and Phil, while Second Avenue's popular Molly Picon was Clara.

Television's lackadaisical George Gobel bowed

in a new musical version of *Three Men on a Horse,* now dubbed **Let It Ride!** (10-12-61, O'Neill). An earlier musicalization had appeared twenty years before as *Banjo Eyes* (12-25-41) with Eddie Cantor. Cantor had been able to keep an essentially weak vehicle going singlehandedly. Gobel's version was no worse, but Gobel lacked the theatrical know-how and, surprisingly, the drawing power to keep the show alive. The high moment of the evening was a comic number called "Just An Honest Mistake" which ended, "Mr. Nixon said 'Let's Debate.' " But it was insufficient to overcome duller moments or competition.

Competition became intense two nights later. **How To Succeed in Business without Really Trying** (10-14-61, 46th St.) was based on Shepherd Mead's book of the same name; it was an unromantic, but not unaffectionate, satire, that reunited many of the team responsible for *Guys and Dolls* (11-24-50). Feuer and Martin were once again the producers. Abe Burrows collaborated on the libretto (with Jack Weinstock and Willie Gilbert), and composer Frank Loesser abandoned his more operatic ambitions to return to the world of pure musical comedy. The show even played the same 46th Street Theatre where *Guys and Dolls* had run. The story followed the rise of the disarmingly opportunistic J. Pierrepont Finch (Robert Morse) from window-washer to chairman of the board of World Wide Wickets Company. He does it by coolly following the precepts of Mead's book, which he pulls from his pocket and reads at necessary intervals. Mead extols the virtues of "education and intelligence and ability" but reminds his readers that "thousands have reached the top without any of these qualities." So Finch discards his work clothes and heads for the personnel office of World Wide Wickets. In his rush he literally bumps into the company's president, J. B. Biggley (Rudy Vallee), and in his ignorance is unmoved by Biggley's scolding. His indifference to Biggley catches the eye and heart of one of the company's prettiest secretaries, Rosemary Pilkington (Bonnie Scott). She escorts him to the office of the personnel director, Mr. Bratt (Paul Reed):

Bratt: We're not hiring anyone today.
Finch: Well, I was just speaking to Mr. Biggley . . .
Bratt: J. B. Biggley himself? You were speaking to him?
Finch: Yes, sir. I just bumped into him.
Bratt: Ah, is he a friend of yours?
Finch: Sir, I don't think a man should trade on friendship to get a job.

This timely evasion gets Finch a position in the mail room working alongside Biggley's obnoxious nephew, Bud Frump (Charles Nelson Reilly). Although Finch is unaware of it, it also deepens the affections of Rosemary, who would be "Happy To Keep His Dinner Warm" while he wangles his way up in the world. And while his fellow employees waste time at a "Coffee Break," Finch determines to move above the mail room. He cannot take the executive mail in to Biggley—that's Frump's job. So Finch arranges to pass Biggley's secretary accidentally in the corridor. Pretending he doesn't know who she is, he offers her a flower. When she reveals her position he professes astonishment—and delight—to learn she's not the ogre Frump had described. Twimble (Sammy Smith), head of the mail room, tells Finch he will go far if he only does everything "The Company Way." Finch comprehends quickly. He refuses Twimble's post now that Twimble is to retire, insisting it rightfully belongs to Frump. Finch's knowing diplomacy is rewarded with an even better position and with Frump's jealous enmity. The personnel manager is given a buxom beauty, Hedy La Rue (Virginia Martin), to place in a secretarial slot, and he warns his men, "A Secretary Is Not A Toy." Miss La Rue is Biggley's current mistress. Biggley has another secret. He loves to knit. And Biggley, a graduate of "Grand Old Ivy," is a loyal Groundhog. Finch is able to turn Biggley's pleasures to his advantage. When the not too bright Miss La Rue is assigned to Finch and presents herself as his "assignation," he reads Mead's precept, "The smaller her abilities, the bigger her protector," and correctly surmises who is protecting Hedy. He hastily offers her to the libidinous Mr. Gatch, the director of Plans and Systems, and in no time at all he has replaced the transferred Mr. Gatch. He also leads Biggley to believe he is a Groundhog and is promoted to the head of advertising when he reveals the current head was once a Chipmunk, the Groundhogs' detested rivals. As head of advertising he must come up with a stupendous idea. Frump suggests a television treasure hunt, knowing his uncle has already rejected the plan. Miss La Rue unwittingly saves the day for Finch. Ignoring Biggley's plaint that he cannot live without "Love From A Heart Of Gold," Miss La Rue threatens to leave unless she is given a better job. When Finch suggests the young lady be made the national Treasure Girl, the grateful Biggley revises his feelings about the program. In the men's washroom the confident Finch sings a love song—to himself. Seeing in the mirror "the cool clear eyes of a seeker of wisdom and truth," he assures his reflection, "I Believe In You." Unfortunately Biggley confides to Hedy that the treasure is hidden in World Wide Wickets' offices, and Hedy reveals the hiding place on the television show. The next morning the offices are a wreck. The chairman of the board, Wally Womper (Sammy Smith), appears, out for blood. But when he learns Finch began, like he did, as a window-washer, he is mollified. Womper does not fire Biggley, but he does take Miss La Rue for his wife, and he retires, appointing Finch in his place. Finch, secure at the top, now has time to consider romance. He agrees to take the chairmanship if Rosemary has no objections:

Rosemary: Darling, I don't care if you work in the mail room, or you're chairman of the board, or you're President of the United States, I love you.
Finch: Say that again.
Rosemary: I love you.
Finch: No, before that.

Just before the final curtain Frump is seen washing windows with one hand and reading *How To Succeed* with the other.

The show's superb comedy was made even funnier by impeccable casting. Vallee, a singing idol in the twenties and early thirties, revealed a droll, dead-pan delivery. Morse's gap-toothed smile and deceptively boyish appearance somehow made his double-dealing as lovable as it was hilarious. Reilly's pouting Frump was virtually a caricature of a 19th-century villain. Loesser's score was, for the most part, not hummably melodic. It was strongest when it was satiric. But "I Believe In You," removed from its riotously outlandish situation in the play, gradually received general and long-lasting acceptance. Sadly, it was Loesser's last work. He died at the age of fifty-nine of cancer on July 28, 1969. He lived long enough to see *How To Succeed in Business without Really Trying* become the American Musical Theatre's fourth Pulitzer Prize winner, but not long enough to see it tally a run of 1416 performances.

Kwamina (10-23-61, 54th St.) survived for a mere 32 performances, but it was interesting in several respects. Its songs were by Richard Adler, in his first solo effort after the death of his partner, Jerry Ross. The book was by Robert Alan Arthur, a playwright whose works had met with respect, if not success. Their story recounted the love of a white woman for a black man in a newly freed West African country. The white girl is an attractive lady named Eve (Sally Ann Howes), and her lover is a Western-trained doctor known both as Peter and Kwamina (Terry Carter). The country's in-

ternal struggle between Western enlightenment and African superstition exacerbates an inherently difficult romance. In the end, the pair prudently decide to go their separate ways. The story and the music were a far cry from the boisterous mirth of Adler's previous shows, and neither he nor Arthur could find quite the right treatment for their pioneering, difficult theme. Nor could Agnes de Mille's vibrant African dances—notably a wedding ritual that opened the second act—save the show.

Yves Montand returned the next night with a one-man program of his songs and pleased his followers for 55 performances.

Two elaborate, promising musicals premiered in November, and both failed. **Kean** (11-2-61, Broadway) was given a sumptuous mounting, enlivened by another of Alfred Drake's dependably bravura performances in the title role. The songs were by Robert Wright and George Forrest, who had heretofore contented themselves with setting words to the melodies of classical composers (Grieg's in *Song of Norway*, Borodin's in *Kismet*). The book by the untried Peter Stone was based on a Jean-Paul Sartre play that itself had been inspired by an earlier Alexandre Dumas drama. All three told of Kean's struggle to be accepted as something more than a great actor. But the material was clumsily handled and the music second-rate. It was the only show during the season resorting to the 19th century for its background. But *Kean* went back to the first half of the century, a period generally ignored by librettists. A respectable advance sale and Alfred Drake's name allowed the work to play for three months.

The Gay Life (11-18-61, Shubert) did look back to the turn of the century, but it was a turn-of-the-century Vienna. The evening was based on Arthur Schnitzler's *The Affairs of Anatol*, and the libretto was devised by Fay and Michael Kanin. Both had enjoyed success in Hollywood, while Mrs. Kanin was affectionately remembered on Broadway for her comedy *Goodbye, My Fancy*. To raise expectations even higher Arthur Schwartz and Howard Dietz were reunited for the songs. The plot recounted the relinquishing of determined bachelor and man-about-town Anatol von Huber's (Walter Chiari) tenaciously held independence for the arms of the equally determined Liesl Brandel (Barbara Cook). The evening began drolly when Mac (Jules Munshin), Liesl's brother and Anatol's best friend, awakes the sleeping hero to determine why he is not at his own wedding. The remainder of the history is a flashback. A number of musicologists have hailed Schwartz' score as one of his masterpieces. In his study of American popular song, Alec Wilder gives extensive space to three of the show's numbers, "Why Go Anywhere At All?," sung by a minor character, Liesl's "Something You Never Had Before," and the evening's touching close, Anatol's "For The First Time." But most of the critics and the public, overcome by the current rage, rock and roll, didn't hear its beauties or subtleties—or, if they did, rejected the patently reminiscent melodic lines. Only the simple, slightly stretched melodic line of "Magic Moment" enjoyed any general appeal. Actually neither the book nor the score was very theatrical. Still, Dietz placed most of the blame for the show's failure on its leading man, who, he said, with some understatement, "couldn't act, dance, sing, or speak English, which was a handicap." The show ran only slightly longer than *Kean,* 113 performances.

December's only musical plunked theatregoers back in contemporary New York. Producer David Merrick presented the latest in the Comden-Green-Styne paeans to ordinary, if slightly kooky, Manhattanites. **Subways Are for Sleeping** (12-27-61, St. James) described the rocky course of two love affairs. Tom Bailey (Sydney Chaplin) is a good-looking, polished, professional ne'er-do-well, so out-of-pocket he sleeps in the subway. But he is attractive enough to win the heart of a moderately successful fashion magazine writer, Angie McKay (Carol Lawrence), when she is sent to interview him. Martha Vail (Phyllis Newman) is a beauty contest winner (Miss Watermelon and Miss Southern Comfort) who has lost all her clothing and will lose her apartment if her landlord succeeds in evicting her. She spends most of her day wrapped in a towel and many of her evenings being courted on the phone by Charlie Smith (Orson Bean). Smith is another full-time ne'er-do-well, so poor he attempts to make local calls collect. Not much really happens, although Tom does get temporary employment as a Santa Claus. In the end Tom and Angie agree to write a book, while Charlie and Martha start a coffee-vending service. The show's best numbers followed each other in the second act. In its comic highlight Charlie confesses to Martha, "I Just Can't Wait" ("till I see you with your clothes on"). Angie and Tom settle for a carpe diem philosophy in "Comes Once In A Lifetime." The indifferent notices the show received led to one of the American Musical Theatre's most hilarious and celebrated contretemps. Merrick found seven New Yorkers whose names were identical with those of the seven daily newspaper critics and who were willing to give his show enthusiastic praise.

He then took a large advertisement in the *Herald Tribune* listing the names and quotations. To avoid legal problems he also printed a small photograph alongside each name. There were howls of outrage and laughter. The publicity helped the show run six months, not sufficiently long, however, to put it in the black.

1962's first musical, **A Family Affair** (1-27-62, Rose) had a book by James and William Goldman, both of whom later went on to Hollywood and Broadway success, and music by John Kander. Essentially, it was an extended Jewish joke. Sally Nathan (Rita Gardner) and Gerry Siegel (Larry Kert) would like to marry, and there is really nothing to stand in their way, except Gerry's doting parents (Morris Carnovsky and Eileen Heckart) and Sally's outrageous guardian (Shelley Berman). Once upon a time it might have seemed funny, as a short, furiously paced farce. Songs broke the momentum, and the respite gave audiences time to realize the joke was over before the show was. Fine performances couldn't push the musical beyond eight weeks.

The young performers in **New Faces of 1962** (2-1-62, Alvin) naturally had none of the experience enjoyed by the older performers in *A Family Affair.* Their material was disappointing. Limp skits and weak songs touched on everything from basic education to marital infidelity. A gnawing suspicion whispered these new faces were not quite as bright as some of the neophytes in earlier editions. The show quit after 28 showings.

A second composer whose partner had recently died offered both words and music for his songs on March 15. Unlike Adler, Richard Rodgers was a supreme melodist, and he had written his own lyrics on a few earlier occasions. Like Adler he chose an established playwright for his librettist, although Samuel Taylor had a more successful history than Robert Alan Arthur. Taylor, like Arthur, created an original story, and, coincidently, one that also dealt with an interracial romance. Experience and ability told, and the Rodgers-Taylor offering, **No Strings** (3-15-62, 54th St.), survived both an uneven critical reception and an out-of-the-way theatre to become a long-run hit. David Jordan is an American writer from Maine who has spent the six years since winning a Pulitzer Prize having a good time in Paris. He meets a glamorous black model, Barbara Woodruff, at a photographer's studio. They take an instant liking to one another and are shortly enjoying the attractions of Paris together. Their budding love affair is abruptly terminated when David discovers Barbara has a wealthy, middle-aged admirer. The separation is not long-lasting, and the two are soon together again. They go off to Honfleur, where David hopes to resume his writing career. Inspiration refuses to come. David concludes he must return to Maine if he is to be creative once more. He offers to take Barbara, but she reminds him of the prejudice they would encounter, and of the freedom and income she would leave behind. Although they promise to meet at some future date, they leave each other knowing they will probably never see each other again.

The show was given an imaginative staging with a minimum of movable scenery that suggested a photographer's props, but it was stylishly done, and beautifully costumed. An orchestra played from behind the scenes and sometimes on stage instead of in the pit, and, in keeping with the title, contained no strings. The show was framed in a poignant melody, "The Sweetest Sounds," which Barbara and David sing from opposite sides of the stage before they meet and again as they go their separate ways. Most of the other love ballads in the show had the same flavor, but Rodgers' seemingly limitless melodic gifts kept them enticingly varied: "Nobody Told Me," "Look No Further," and the title song. Early in the show Barbara is given a driving, cynical number which nonetheless managed to also sound romantic, "Loads Of Love." Critics suggested that Rodgers as a lyricist was a happy combination of the best of Hammerstein and Hart. Nevertheless, Rodgers thereafter left the lyric writing chores to others. The show was faultlessly cast with Diahann Carroll as the all-too-worldly, forlorn Barbara and Richard Kiley as the urbane David.

College life and football returned to the Broadway stage with **All American** (3-19-62, Winter Garden) four nights after *No Strings* arrived. It had music by Charles Strouse and lyrics by Lee Adams, whose work was every bit as good as the material they had produced for *Bye Bye Birdie* (4-14-60). And in Ray Bolger they had a beguiling dancer and comedian. But the book by Mel Brooks, who later went on to become one of Hollywood's most creative figures, was inept and ultimately dragged the rest of the evening down with it. An immigrant, Professor Fodorski (Bolger), comes to Southern Baptist Institute of Technology, where he promptly catches the eye of the dean, Elizabeth Hawkes-Bullock (Eileen Herlie). His curious charm even inspires his football team to unaccustomed victory and catapults the professor to national attention. Fame brings headaches. Would-be

exploiters arrive; peace and privacy are destroyed, and the engineering career of SBIT's star fullback, Ed Bricker (Ron Husmann), seems jeopardized by his preoccupation with his Saturday-afternoon success. To restore tranquillity and proportion, Fodorski purposely loses the season's big game by keeping Bricker on the bench. But Fodorski does win the dean and Ed wins pretty Susan Thompson (Anita Gillette). Two numbers in the charming Strouse-Adams score outlived the show: Fodorski's light, tripping soft-shoe, "If I Were You," and the nostalgic, Irish-tinted, "Once Upon A Time," which Fodorski and the dean sing early in the show and which the dean twice reprises. SBIT closed for good about the same time most schools were finishing their semesters.

David Merrick had another musical ready for New York's inspection three nights after *All American* premiered, making for three major openings in just over a week. **I Can Get It for You Wholesale** (3-22-62, Shubert) was adapted by Jerome Weidman from his own novel, with songs by Harold Rome. The musical was set in the thirties, but it made little appeal to the nostalgic. It took a hardboiled look at the cutthroat world of New York's garment district. Even Harold Rome, who rose to prominence with his music for depression revues, eschewed most sounds of the era and most of its propagandizing. As a result, for all its token bows to the thirties, *I Can Get It for You Wholesale* projected itself as a contemporary piece with a dateless story. It seemed to many a sort of *How To Succeed in Business without Really Trying* (10-14-61), stripped of that show's wit and sunny disposition. Harry Bogen (Elliott Gould) is cold, pushy, and determined—determined to rise to the top by whatever means are required. He starts as a small-time strikebreaker, moves into the garment business with a few partners, and then shoves them out of his way. He ignores the pleas of his goodhearted mother (Lillian Roth) and his adoring girl friend and neighbor, Ruthie Rivkin (Marilyn Cooper), to act ethically. He would even ditch Ruthie for a cheap, flamboyant night-club performer, Martha Mills (Sheree North). When, after all his machinations, he ends up a bankrupt, only his mother and Ruthie are there to console him. The ending did not necessarily imply that simplicity and goodness were the best rewards but only that Harry was neither ruthless nor cunning enough to attain his goals.

No standards emerged from Rome's serviceable, unimaginative score, but one number stopped the show nightly. It was the comic lament of a much-put-upon secretary, "Miss Marmelstein." The young lady whose delivery of the song brought down the house was a nineteen-year-old newcomer, Barbra Streisand. Enough cloak-and-suiters used the musical as a busman's holiday to keep it playing for nine months, although it never brought Merrick's backers a profit.

The season took a breather in April, then four shows opened in May to end the season. The first was only the third of the year's new musicals ultimately to show a profit. **A Funny Thing Happened on the Way to the Forum** (5-8-62, Alvin) had a book by Burt Shevelove and Larry Gelbart purportedly based on plays of Plautus. Accordingly, the scenery and costumes were more or less Roman, and so were the names of the characters. But what the musical really represented was a hilarious mixture of burlesque and outrageous comedy, the closest thing the American Musical Theatre could expect to an evening with the Marx Brothers, without the Marx Brothers. The story told of an attempt by the slave, Pseudolus (Zero Mostel), to win his freedom by procuring the beautiful, if vapid, courtesan, Philia (Preshy Marker) for his master, Hero (Brian Davies). His efforts are hindered by dashing Miles Gloriosus (Ronald Holgate), who has purchased Philia from Lycus (John Carradine), a dealer in courtesans and by Hero's father, Senex (David Burns), who has his own plans for the girl. So Pseudolus first spreads the word that Philia is a carrier of plague and then announces that she has died. A mock funeral turns into a mad chase. When Miles learns he is Philia's brother, he gives her to Hero, and Pseudolus is granted his freedom. The show's humor leaned heavily on double entendres and outlandish jokes. When Pseudolus is told a wine is "from the year one" he asks if that was a good year for wine. A eunuch is admonished, "Don't you lower your voice at me!"

The songs not only had lyrics by Stephen Sondheim, they had music by him as well. His tunes—from the opening "Comedy Tonight" to the finale—were light and easy on the ear, with a distinct hint of Rodgers and Hart. One of them, "Lovely," has remained popular. Yet it was Sondheim's masterful way with words that was most telling. The lovesick Hero in "Love, I Hear" wakes "too weak to walk." Pseudolus promises that in his gratitude for being made "Free," "I'll be so conscientious I may vote twice," while Senex suggests "Everybody Ought To Have A Maid." Later Senex and Hero find it outrageously "Impossible" that the other could be in love. Some of Broadway's funniest comedians assisted in the antics with Zero Mostel

leading a contingent that also boasted Jack Gilford as a farcically hysterical Hysterium. The show rocked Broadway with laughter for over two years.

A number of great singers had left opera for Broadway when their careers had begun to flag. But it was almost unheard of for a prominent opera star to assume a Broadway role when still at the height of his powers. Cesare Siepi ventured just that when he appeared in **Bravo Giovanni** (5-19-62, Broadhurst). Handsome, with a fine voice and more than competent acting ability, he might have found a permanent home for himself in the legitimate stage had he chosen a better vehicle to initiate his new career. Regrettably, the new show, which was based on Howard Shaw's novel, *The Crime of Giovanni Venturi,* managed to tell a not uninteresting story uninterestingly. Giovanni Venturi's simple restaurant is hit hard when Signor Bellardi (George S. Irving) opens a branch of his fast-food chain, Uriti, down the street. The new eatery offers cut-price minestrone, tortoni, and chicken chow mein. Its espresso spews forth from a bust of Dante. In desperation Giovanni and his girl friend, Miranda (Michele Lee), decide to dig a tunnel from their kitchen into Uriti's and steal Uriti's food. The digging unearths an Etruscan tomb, and threatens to expose their plan. But in the end the tunnel is so successful Giovanni contemplates opening restaurants next to other Uritis. Even more disappointing than the book was the score. "Ah! Camminare" enjoyed a passing vogue but by and large the score left Siepi without a palpably enchanting number and with little to show off his fine style and range. In two engagements, broken by a summer vacation, the show compiled a total of 76 performances. When it passed into history, Siepi returned to the more steady employment offered by Mozart and Verdi.

The City Center season of revivals began later than usual and lapped over into the following season. The 1962 offerings were *Can-Can* (5-7-53) on May 16, with the French singer, Genevieve, *Brigadoon* (3-13-47) on May 30 with Peter Palmer and Sally Ann Howes and, technically in 1962–63, *Fiorello!* (11-23-59) on June 13.

1962-1963

Statistically at least the American Musical Theatre suffered a dismal year. When importations, revivals, and one-man shows were set aside, only six new offerings remained: five book shows and one revue. Not one of these was a commercial success. Their failure was not a fair reflection of their merit. Two were worthwhile, and a third was a minor, generally unappreciated, gem. Nonetheless English works gave the real excitement and backbone to the season—something London musicals had not done since the beginning of the century.

After the opening of the City Center's *Fiorello!* on June 13, the theatrical calendar showed nothing of interest until October 2 when **Eddie Fisher at the Winter Garden** bowed. It was as much vaudeville as a one-man show, opening with Gordon Jenkins' brief showpiece, "The Broadway Zoo," followed by black comedian Dick Gregory and dancer Juliet Prowse. The star had the second act to himself.

The first of three major English hits premiered the next night. **Stop the World—I Want To Get Off** (10-3-62, Shubert) was the work of Leslie Bricusse and Anthony Newley. Mr. Newley was starred in the role of Littlechap. As the character's name suggests, the piece was an allegory, played out on a single circuslike set. If the allegory was obviously shallow, the evening as a whole was imaginative, lively, colorful, and melodic. The show's finale, "What Kind Of Fool Am I?," became one of the most popular tunes of the year.

In 1950 Howard Lindsay, Russel Crouse, and Irving Berlin had made Broadway a happier, more song-filled part of town with their lighthearted political charade, *Call Me Madam* (10-12-50). It had fun with the world of ambassadorial diplomacy. Now the trio decided to throw their hats in the ring again, and this time set out to reach the very top. They reached it politically, if not artistically. **Mr. President** (10-20-62, St. James) was a solid bit of professional craftsmanship that disappointed largely because something more had been hoped for. A prologue warns the audience not to read any real-life figures into the characters they are about to see. President Stephen Decatur Henderson and his family are all and none of the White House's recent or current occupants. The stage White House is the scene of a lively ball, where sophisticated crowds are all reveling in the dance that was sweeping America in the early sixties, the Twist. When the President and his wife appear, the first lady suggests, "Let's Go Back To The Waltz." The guests comply until the pair leave, then, as one, the whole party goes back to the Twist. In the morning, the President has more serious problems to contend with. An invitation to visit Russia is canceled while he is flying there. He determines to land at Moscow, even though it is a breach of protocol. Only a few workman are present when he arrives. His humiliation costs him the next election. While his wife, Nell, is happy to be back home, Stephen is not. Nonetheless, he turns down a seat in the Senate when compromising conditions are attached. Henderson eventually realizes his love of his country is primary and returns to government at the behest of the new President. The warning of the prologue should have been heeded. Canceling of the Russian tour inevitably recalled Eisenhower's predicament after the U-2 incident, while in their youthful good looks and vigor the Hendersons unmistakably suggested the Kennedys. Furthermore the President's spunkiness and the Hendersons' apparent hominess brought Harry and Bess Truman to mind. As always, Berlin filled his score with pleasing melodies and easy, homey, sentiments. Titles such as the Hendersons' "In Our Hideaway," "Meat And Potatoes," sung by two secret service men, Pat (Jack Haskell) and Charles (Stanley Greger), "Pigtails And Freckles," sung by Miss Henderson (Anita Gillette) and her secret service man, Pat, Mrs. Henderson's "Glad To Be Home," and Henderson's "This Is A Great Country" convey the tone. In the last-named song Berlin struck upon one of his typically felicitous phrases: asking, if patriotic statements are flag waving, "Do you know of a better flag to wave?" For the aging composer *Mr. President* was his last musical in this history. It sounded some eerie echoes of his very first score, *Watch Your Step* (12-8-14), just short of a half-century before. Berlin repeated some uncommon rhymes such as "service" with "nervous," and just as in "What Is Love?" he had managed to introduce some startling ragtime effects into a simple waltz, so in "Let's Go Back To The Waltz" he introduced some unexpected harmonic changes into a bit of forthright nostalgia. The principal difference between the scores was that none of the songs from the new show won wide public acceptance. Nor did the show itself. Glowing performances by Nanette Fabray and Robert Ryan as the First Lady and the President notwithstanding, *Mr. President* ran just eight months.

A trend had been developing toward songless revues. The preceding seasons had witnessed shows such as *A Thurber Carnival* and *From the Second City,* which had the requisite sketches but for all practical purposes no singing and dancing. On October 27 London offered what may have been the most brilliant of these, **Beyond the Fringe** (10-27-62, Golden), a collection of monologues, dialogues, and skits written by its four performers, all recently out of their university. It is hard to gauge to what extent the movement toward integrated songs and the vogue for theatrically effective, but not especially memorable, melodies prompted the revues to drop isolated numbers. The revue would seem to have been the logical refuge for stray, good tunes. But apart from Dudley Moore's brief moments at the piano, *Beyond the Fringe* followed the new vogue by rarely raising its voice in song.

November's first new musical took a ready-made subject, and botched it. Izzy Einstein and Moe Smith were undoubtedly the most flamboyant and theatrical of the twenties' Prohibition agents. Their resourceful disguises and ruses made them popular at a time when there were few less popular people than speakeasy raiders. But their story was told in **Nowhere To Go but Up** (11-10-62, Winter Garden) by two inexperienced writers, James Lipton on the book and lyrics, and Sol Berkowitz for the music. Theirs was not an inept job—the title song was one of the liveliest and catchiest tunes of the year—but the show demanded the sort of zaniness its performers couldn't provide. Tom Bosley impersonated Izzy, while Martin Balsam played Moe. The musical lasted one week.

On November 13 the D'Oyly Carte began a 32-performance run at the City Center, presenting *The Mikado, The Gondoliers, The Pirates of Penzance, Trial by Jury, H.M.S. Pinafore,* and *Iolanthe.*

Hopes were as high for **Little Me** (11-17-62, Lunt-Fontanne) as they had been for *Mr. President.* It was not that the book was by Neil Simon, then thought of only as the author of *Come Blow Your Horn,* nor that the songs were by *Wildcat's* Cy Coleman and Carolyn Leigh. A small flurry of anticipation might have been attributed to the show's source, Patrick Dennis' best seller. What created the lines at the box office before the reviews were out was the presence of Sid Caesar as star. He had not frolicked through a Broadway show since *Make Mine Manhattan* (1-15-48), and in the interval had become one of television's top celebrities. Simon's libretto retained Dennis' account of the rise of Belle Poitrine (née Schlumpfort) from a waif on the wrong side of the tracks in Venezuela, Illinois, to fame and wealth. In her teens she sets her sights on Noble Eggleston, who lives on the right side of the tracks, but whose mother puts an abrupt end to her ambitions. Biding her time, Belle finally succeeds in landing a rich, eighty-year-old skinflint, Mr. Pinchley. When he dies under suspicious circumstances, she is tried for murder and acquitted. The notoriety of the trial brings her a vaudeville offer and a romance with Val du Val, who modestly considers himself the world's greatest entertainer. Further romances follow with myopic Fred Poitrine, Prince Cherney of Rozenzweig, and the imperious film director, Otto Schnitzler. Each romance in some unexpected way advances both Belle's career and fortune. Although it would appear that Belle (Nancy Andrews) was the central figure, Caesar was the star by virtue of his assuming the roles of all the lovers, from the sixteen-year-old Eggleston to the decrepit Pinchley. While the score produced no songs that enjoyed much acclaim outside the theatre at the time, it was bright and more than adequate. Since then, the lively "I've Got Your Number," sung in the show by Belle's old admirer (Swen Swenson), has gained some currency.

The season's biggest hit, a third London importation, opened at the Imperial January 6, 1963, after an extensive national tour. **Oliver** was Lionel Bart's musicalization of Dickens' *Oliver Twist.* It drove critics to expressions such as "jolly bad show," and "popperetta," but the public found it unfailingly appealing. Two standards emerged from the score, the gripping ballad, "As Long As He Needs Me," and the romping "Consider Yourself [At Home]." Excellent performances by Clive Revill and Georgia Brown, plus Sean Kenny's strikingly evocative skeletonized sets and costumes enhanced the performance.

Maurice Chevalier delighted his supporters for a month at the Ziegfeld, where he opened his one-man show on January 28. Two nights after Chevalier appeared, the City Center initiated an uncustomary winter season, presenting *Brigadoon* (3-13-47) on January 30, with Russell Nype, Peter Palmer, and Sally Ann Howes, *Wonderful Town* (2-25-52) on February 13, with Kaye Ballard, and *Oklahoma!,* (3-31-43) on February 27 with Palmer as Curly. The opening of *Oklahoma!* coincided with the arrival of Jack Benny at the Ziegfeld in a vaudeville that also offered singer Jane Morgan and a number of other acts. Unlike Eddie Fisher, earlier in the season, Benny and Miss Morgan performed intermittently all through the evening. April 10 saw Danny Kaye and his vaudeville troupe follow Benny into the Ziegfeld.

Tovarich (3-18-63, Broadway), Jacques Deval and Robert E. Sherwood's 1936-37 hit, came back to the stage as a musical on March 18. Once again Prince Mikail Alexandrovitch Ouratieff (Jean Pierre Aumont) and his wife, the Grand Duchess Tatiana Petrona (Vivien Leigh), have fled Soviet Russia with four billion francs. But they are broke, since the money belongs to the Czar and they intend to hold it for his heirs until the monarchy is restored. They take jobs as a butler and maid with an American family in Paris. But two Soviet agents trail them and ultimately wrest the fortune from them. Since they have grown fond of their American employers, and their employers, who have learned their real identities, remain fond of them, they decide to retain their positions. The adaptation was by untried hands and betrayed their inexperience and lack of inspiration, though some of the music was pleasantly melodic. In a move rare in mid-20th-century book musicals, at least one extraneous number was interpolated to help the proceedings. But what little real help the show received came from its star, Miss Leigh.

Another colorful figure out of the past became the subject of a musical biography in **Sophie** (4-15-63, Winter Garden). Sophie, of course, was Sophie Tucker, the last "Red Hot Mama." William Morris, Marcus Loew, Julian Mitchell, and Nora Bayes were all brought back to life to re-enact their famous contretemps with the volatile coon singer, and Miss Tucker (Libi Staiger) was even given a fling and romance with handsome Frank Westphal (Art Lund). The story tried to cover too much of Miss Tucker's history. It became diffuse and meandering, while the songs by Steve Allen, a well-known television entertainer, were a pale imitation of the lusty originals of Miss Tucker's day. Like the history of Izzy and Moe, which had played the same house, *Sophie* lasted just one week.

Four nights later Judy Holliday came a cropper in a musical about the Peace Corps, **Hot Spot** (4-19-63, Majestic). The story presented a rather startling reversion to the *Sultan of Sulu* (12-29-02) school of scenarios. The eager, incompetent Sally Hopwinder (Miss Holliday) is sent by the Peace Corps to D'Hum. She convinces the Nadir of D'Hum to proclaim a communist threat so that more American money will be forthcoming. In various disguises she helps and hinders her own plan. Sally also has a love affair with the handsome American consul, Gabriel Snapper (Joseph Campanella). The book gave evidence of being all too hastily contrived, while Mary Rodgers' score bore even sadder witness to her lack of her father's great melodic gifts. Miss Holliday braved the odds for a little over a month before calling it quits.

As happened with some frequency in this period, the season's last new American book musical was its best, even if this time its origin and its tone weren't totally American. **She Loves Me** (4-23-63, O'Neill) began life years before as Miklos Laszlo's *Parfumerie* and then became a fondly remembered film, *The Shop around the Corner*. In the skillful, tasteful adaption by Joe Masteroff, who did the book, and by Jerry Bock and Sheldon Harnick, who did the songs, it was turned into the closest thing Broadway had seen to Jerome Kern's Continental confections, *Music in the Air* and *The Cat and the Fiddle*. It was set in the very era of the Kern works, the early thirties, and in the same Mittel-europa ambiance. Maraczek's Parfumerie in Budapest is not thriving and Maraczek is at a loss to know how he will sell a new shipment of music boxes. A young lady, Amalia Balash (Barbara Cook), appears, looking for work. He attempts to turn her away, but when she picks up a music box and sells it to the very first customer to enter the shop, he relents and hires her. Her fellow employees include a dashing philanderer, Steven Kodaly (Jack Cassidy), and a shy, soft-spoken Georg Nowack (Daniel Massey). Georg is nervous because that evening he will meet for the first time a girl with whom he has been corresponding and whom he knows only as "Dear Friend." Amalia is also writing to a "Dear Friend" she has never seen. Of course, they are writing to each other. Their visions of their fellow writers are far more glamorous than the reality, but when Georg arrives at the rendezvous and realizes who his "Dear Friend" is, he keeps the secret from Amalia, claiming his presence is coincidental. Georg's front is doubly brave, for Maraczek, suspecting him of being his wife's lover, has quarreled with him and accepted his resignation. However, a letter informs Maraczek that Kodaly is the lover. Maraczek's attempted suicide is thwarted by an employee. The bullet only wounds him. He makes up with Georg and takes him back. When Amalia reports in sick, Georg arrives at her apartment. Her initial reaction is to accuse him of snooping, to see if she were really ill. But when he presents her with a gift of ice cream and fabricates a tale about a bald-headed man who followed him after their rendezvous to question him on his relation with Amalia, she begins to lose interest in her "Dear Friend" and fall in love with Georg. Georg senses the change and is elated for he has fallen in love with her. At a Christmas party in the shop Amalia drops a package she has meant for a friend. It is a music box. Georg confesses he too likes music boxes, and the conversation takes on a special warmth. Both admit their feelings for each other, and, after Georg quotes excerpts from her letters to "Dear Friend," Amalia realizes she has found a dear friend indeed.

The song, "Dear Friend," one of the loveliest in the work, was used throughout the evening, but never attained any independent popularity. Only the title song enjoyed anything approaching a lasting vogue. But all of the score was attractive and appropriate. The score was so long that it required two LP records. Many of the songs were conversational in tone; all furthered the plot. Set pieces accounted for the changing of the seasons (the action ran from summer to Christmas) or offered charming, incisive character vignettes that cannot readily be excerpted, but that consistently conveyed a uniform tone and style, deftly suggesting the period of the piece while remaining contemporary in their structure and harmony. Neither the dialogue nor the lyrics, taken out of context, were exceptional, but they, too, maintained the integrity of the work. The show was beautifully mounted and excellently cast. Yet for all its virtues *She Loves Me* closed with a loss after a nine-month run.

The City Center's regular spring season began on May 15 with additional performances of *Oklahoma!* (3-31-43), with many principals held over from the preceding year, followed by *Pal Joey* (12-25-40), with Bob Fosse and Viveca Lindfors, on May 29. As it had the preceding year the series ran into the new season.

A revue called **The Beast in Me** (5-16-63, Plymouth) brought the old season to a close. It was based on James Thurber's *Fables for Our Times,* and almost all the characters portrayed in the sketches and songs were animals. James Costigan made the adaptation and Don Elliot composed the music. Some of Broadway's brightest young talent was featured: Allyn Ann McLerie, Kaye Ballard, Richard Hayes, and Bert Convy, as well as Mr. Costigan. But, as it had with *Shinebone Alley* (4-13-57), Broadway found the idea of actors in sheep's clothing too cloyingly cute. The show folded after 4 showings.

1963-1964

The disastrous 1962–63 season should have discouraged producers and writers, but it didn't. Its hit shows, even though they came from England, had reaped tremendous profits. National origins ignored, statistics had disclosed that one out of five musicals returned their investment, compared to one out of twelve straight plays. So the American Musical Theatre bounced back with fervor in the new theatrical year.

After *The King and I* (3-29-51) concluded the City Center openings on June 12, the musical stage took a respite until the last day of September. **The Student Gypsy, or The Prince of Liederkranz** (9-30-63, 54th St.) was, as its titles suggests, a travesty on the old Graustarkian operettas. It told of a not particularly attractive girl, Merry May Glockenspiel (Eileen Brennan), who becomes the belle of a gypsy camp and is courted by Rudolph von Schlump (Don Stewart), a prince in disguise. Their road to the altar is boobytrapped by a villainous gypsy queen, but they surmount every obstacle. The satire was the work of Rick Besoyan and its concentration on one genre served as a tacit admission that his earlier *Little Mary Sunshine,* for all its mirth, had not always been on target. *The Student Gypsy* had another sterling performance by the erstwhile Mary Sunshine, Miss Brennan, and some deliciously melodic spoofs of the Romberg-Friml-Herbert tradition. However, older musicals had long been the butt of burlesque, and *The Boy Friend* (9-30-54) and *Little Mary Sunshine* (11-19-59) had apparently exhausted the market for full-length take-offs. Poor attendance forced it to be withdrawn after a two-week stay.

Meredith Willson's deteriorating flair was disclosed in **Here's Love** (10-3-63, Shubert), his third musical to reach Broadway. As he had with his first effort, *The Music Man*, Willson created the book, lyrics, and music. His task was made somewhat easier for him since he based his new show on the successful 1947 film, *Miracle on 34th Street.* The real Kris Kringle (Laurence Naismith) is hired by Macy's after its regular Santa Claus goes on a binge. Kris' goodness and honesty throw the holiday's shabby commercialism into such turmoil that the United States government hauls him into court. Santa Claus and the true spirit of Christmas prevail. In the process, little Susan Walker (Valerie Lee), who has steadfastly believed in Kris Kringle, finds a new father for herself and a husband for her divorced mother (Janis Paige) in Fred Gailey (Craig Stevens), after Fred defends Santa Claus at his trial. If Willson's artistry had deserted him, his solid professional know-how had not. Everything about the show was appealing, if insistently forgettable. The delightful story lured theatregoers into the Shubert for the rest of the season, and then some.

According to its lyricist, Howard Dietz, **Jennie** (10-17-63, Majestic) had begun life as a musical comedy about a small-town gymnastics instructress. Somewhere along the line Mary Martin, who was to be its star, objected to the slightly off-color humor of the material. Everything was jettisoned, and a new story based on Marguerite Courtney's biography of Laurette Taylor was substituted. Miss Taylor became Jennie Malone; her first husband, Charles Taylor, became James O'Connor. O'Connor (George Wallace), a small-time theatrical promoter, is promiscuous, drunken, distrustful, and cruel. Jennie tolerates him as long as she can, finally leaving him for a more engaging and considerate English playwright, Christopher Lawrence Cromwell (Robin Bailey), who clearly stood for J. Hartley Manners. The book's best moments were spoofs of turn-of-the-century melodramas, which opened and closed the show. Whether the sudden changes or mere exasperation left Arthur Schwartz and Dietz bereft of inspiration will never be known. But their songs fell far below their best work. Miss Martin learned to her dismay that she was not the powerful drawing-card she had believed. Although one early week established a short-lived record gross of $92,000, she and her wholesome show packed their bags after 82 showings.

110 in the Shade (10-24-63, Broadhurst) rather daringly combined the roughhewn talents of playwright N. Richard Nash with the more delicate artistry of *The Fantasticks'* songwriters, lyricist Tom Jones and composer Harvey Schmidt. Nash based the work on his own well-received play, *The Rainmaker*. Lizzie Curry (Inga Swenson) is on the way to becoming a spinster. She is not ugly, but she is plain and shy. To add to her family's woes, the western state is in the middle of a devastating drought. If there seems to be no hope for Lizzie, there is at least a slim chance of rain, for a glib, self-assured young man named Bill Starbuck (Robert Horton) appears at the Curry farm and offers to produce rain for a cash payment of $100. Lizzie warns her father and brother that Starbuck is a fraud, but in their desperation they accept his offer. In the time he claims it will take him to work his miracle he dispels Lizzie's antagonisms, and she finds herself in love. Starbuck confesses that he is a fake, but Lizzie no longer cares. She even discourages another would-be suitor, the sheriff, File (Stephen Douglass), from arresting Starbuck for taking money under false pretenses. To Starbuck's amazement, as much as anyone else's, rain comes just when he said it would. Taking advantage of the lucky break he heads out of town, leaving a more confident and hopeful Lizzie to be courted by the sheriff. The songs Schmidt and Jones wrote for *110 in the Shade* were scarcely replayed outside the theatre, but they were effective in the show.

Lizzie's first number was the poignant, "Love, Don't Turn Away," but she could show a comic side in "Raunchy" when, with patent hypocrisy, she denies her fascination with sex. To some extent they helped put the show's emphasis on her instead of the rainmaker. The show was good theatre and might have run more than the ten months had some stronger competition not come along.

Black poet Langston Hughes continued to be fascinated with the theatre, even if the theatre persistently refused to reciprocate. He presented his adaptation of his own novel, **Tambourines to Glory** (11-2-63, Little), which told of two women who established a gospel-singing church in Harlem. Essie Belle Johnson (Rosetta Le Noire) is genuinely devout; Laura Wright Reed (Hilda Simms) is more opportunistic. After she is involved in a killing, Laura repents and mends her grasping ways. Classic Negro spirituals were used as well as additional material by Jobe Huntley that dovetailed harmoniously with the old favorites. The public, however, showed little interest.

The Golden Age (11-18-63, Lyceum), which advertised itself as "An entertainment in the words and music of the Elizabethan Age," was November's other musical offering. The anthology proved too arcane for Broadway and left after one week.

On November 22 President Kennedy was assassinated in Dallas, sending the nation into shock and mourning. The somber mood did not help the opening of Noel Coward's **The Girl Who Came to Supper** (12-8-63, Broadway), and the show needed all the help it could get. This musical version of Terence Rattigan's play, *The Sleeping Prince,* retold the twenty-four-hour fling of Mary Morgan (Florence Henderson), an American chorus girl in England, and the Grand Duke Charles (Jose Ferrer), Prince Regent of Carpathia, who comes to London for the coronation of George V. Mary is more interested in candlelight suppers and protestations of love than in real love, but it is with genuine regret that the Grand Duke says goodbye. The passing of time at the candlelit dinner was cleverly suggested by trick candles that sank deeper into their holders. The effect was possibly the most memorable bit of the show. Even though Ferrer and Miss Henderson performed valiantly, it was hefty Tessie O'Shea who had the only show-stopper, a gay, music-hall number called "London Is A Little Bit Of All Right." There had been one good, comic song in the show during its tryout, a sardonic commentary on assassinations, "Long Live

The King (If He Can)," but it was hastily pulled after Kennedy's murder.

On December 26, a small Irish revue, **Double Dublin,** followed *Tambourines to Glory* into the intimate Little Theatre, but survived only four showings.

By mid-January of 1964 the country was beginning to recover from its grief and willing to embrace some delightful escapism. With perfect timing David Merrick offered New York what swiftly became the biggest musical hit in years, **Hello, Dolly!** (1-16-64, St. James). The show was in no way innovative and made not the slightest pretense to artistic merit. But it was mounted and staged in rare high style (attractive sliding panels with views of old New York entertained viewers between scenes), faultlessly cast, and in its title song presented the most popular melody to come out of a Broadway musical in many seasons. A lyric version of Thornton Wilder's hit, *The Matchmaker*, it was adapted by Michael Stewart and set to music by Jerry Herman. The scene is New York in the 1890s. Dolly Levi's various business cards list her as available for, among other things, "Financial Consultation, Instruction in the Guitar and Mandolin. . . and Varicose Veins Reduced," but her preoccupation at the moment is "Social Introductions." She states it more succinctly, "I meddle." It is the affairs of Horace Vandergelder (David Burns) in which she is currently meddling. She describes Horace as "half-a-millionaire . . . that means he's got at least sixty thousand cash." She has suggested one of two women for his next wife, Irene Molloy (Eileen Brennan), the owner of a hat shop, or the rich Ernestina Money (Mary Jo Catlett). Both are decoys. Privately, Dolly has decided to capture Horace for herself. At the same time she is conniving to allow Vandergelder's daughter to wed. Dolly is a widow given to communicating aloud with her dead husband, Ephraim. When she asks Ephraim for a sign that he approves of her designs, she is met with a disappointing silence. Dolly persists, leaving Ephraim with the request, "Sometime today!" Vandergelder is about to head from Yonkers to Manhattan to make his choice. He has two shop helpers, Barnaby (Jerry Dodge) and Cornelius (Charles Nelson Reilly), and he elevates the latter from "impertinent fool to chief clerk" in his absence. But Barnaby and Cornelius have their own plans for a day and night in on Broadway, so they explode some cans of tomatoes in order to have an excuse to close the store. In Manhattan they spot Vandergelder coming down the street

and take refuge in the nearest boutique. By coincidence they seek shelter in Irene Molloy's shop, Vandergelder's own destination. Only Dolly's fast-talking saves the day. Dolly had arranged for Mr. Vandergelder to take Ernestine to the Harmonia Gardens Restaurant for dinner. She reserves another table for herself, pleading for some marital bliss and financial security, "Before The Parade Passes By." In still another coincidence Barnaby and Cornelius are wangled into taking Mrs. Molloy and her assistant there. When Dolly, an old favorite at the Harmony Gardens arrives, service halts while the entire staff, trays in hand, sing her their "Hello, Dolly!" Before long she has lured an annoyed Vandergelder away from Miss Money:

Vandergelder: That's the trouble with you, Dolly. Always putting your nose into other people's affairs. Anybody who married you would get as nervous as as cat.

Dolly: What? What's that you're saying?

Vandergelder: I said anybody who married you would . . .

Dolly: Horace Vandergelder, get that idea right out of your head this minute. I'm surprised that you even mentioned such a thing. Understand once and for all that I have no intention of marrying you!

Vandergelder: I didn't mean that!

Dolly: You've been hinting around at such a thing for some time, but from now on put such ideas right out of your head! Horace Vandergelder, you go your way (*She points with her left hand to the left.*) and I'll go mine. (*She points with her right hand also to the left!*)

When the floor show discloses that the young man courting Horace's daughter is a singer and that Horace's own daughter is in the chorus, pandemonium breaks loose, and everyone is hauled into court. Dolly's pleas move the judge to tears, so charges are dismissed. Even Horace recognizes there is no point in resisting Dolly. In admitting defeat, he uses a favorite expression of Dolly's late spouse. Dolly, thanking Ephraim for the sign, consents to marry Horace.

Jerry Herman's score was neither as inventive nor as melodic as his material for *Milk and Honey*, but the title song proved as persistent and as irresistible as Dolly herself and, with a tremendous boost from Louis Armstrong's recording, swept the nation. In the show Dolly and her greeters came down ramps on both sides of the proscenium to sing it within arm's reach of audiences. That the score was not particularly original was borne out when a lawsuit against Herman by Mack David and Paramount-Famous Music Company, claiming the title song was plagiarized from a 1948 tune, "Sunflower," was won by the plaintiffs. One other number, "It Only Takes A Moment," a love ballad, sung somewhat surprisingly by Cornelius in the court scene, also became popular with time. Carol Channing as Dolly had the best role of her career. When she decided to tour with the show, a number of celebrities replaced her on Broadway, including Ginger Rogers, Ethel Merman, and Pearl Bailey (in an all-black cast). Mary Martin originated the part in London. The show ran for 2,844 performances, a new long-run record for a musical, but one it was to hold only briefly.

Paris' darling of the twenties, Josephine Baker, returned briefly on February 4 in what was essentially a one-woman show, although she was assisted by several other artists. Miss Baker sang a large repertory of French songs, as well as "Make Believe," "Hello, Young Lovers," and "April In Paris." The Aviv Dancers, the Larl Becham Trio, and Geoffrey Holder performed the evening's footwork. In two slightly separated engagements she entertained both those who had fond memories of her and a younger set to whom she was a curiosity.

A less acceptable curiosity opened two nights after Miss Baker's return. At various periods French, English, and Viennese musicals have been the rage of the musical stage, but in light lyric entertainments Broadway has never thought twice about Italy. Italian lyric pieces appeared regularly on Broadway stages only in the 18th century, when operas were often mounted in legitimate theatres. The musical, **Rugantino** (2-6-64, Hellinger), had enjoyed an astonishing success in its native land, and Alfred Drake "adapted" it for Broadway. It was brought over with an Italian cast, but, apart from the novelty of the whole affair, Broadway found little of interest in it. The Italians were soon packing for the trip home.

The failure of **Foxy** (2-16-64, Ziegfeld), a musical version of Ben Jonson's *Volpone* reset in the Kondike gold rush, was sad for a number of reasons. First of all, because it was a good show. It had a rousing score by Robert Emmett Dolan that included one ballad, "Talk To Me, Baby," whose popularity survived the production. It was sung in the show by the romantic lead, Ben (John Davidson). Moreover it had an uproarious per-

formance by Bert Lahr in the title role. Lahr's antics included quite literally climbing the theatre's gold proscenium. Sadly, it was Lahr's last appearance before his death.

Budd and Stuart Schulberg adapted the former's novel, **What Makes Sammy Run?** (2-27-64, 54th St.), for the musical stage. With songs by Ervin Drake and with the popular night club singer, Steve Lawrence, as star, it settled down for a run beginning February 27. Although the novel was twenty-three years old and although Hollywood was no longer the unassailable giant it had been, the story was still valid. It was to the motion picture industry what *I Can Get It for You Wholesale* (3-22-62) had been to the garment trade. Sammy Glick rises in the newspaper world by stealing other men's material. A movie script he writes gets him a job in Hollywood, where the famous producer, Sidney Fineman (Arny Freeman), takes him under his wing, and where he earns the affection of a thoughtful, undemanding secretary, Kit Sargent (Sally Ann Howes). But in his greed to reach the top he throws Kit over for Laurette Harrington (Bernice Massi), daughter of the studio's chairman of the board, and pushes Fineman out of his job, after which Fineman commits suicide. He even ignores Laurette's flagrant infidelities once they are married, since his only concern is getting to the top. The score by Drake, who had written such Hollywood successes as "Tico, Tico," gave Lawrence the chance to introduce several hits, especially "My Hometown." Kit sang "A Room Without Windows." But when the public learned that Lawrence, apparently tired of playing Sammy, frequently missed performances, attendance fell and the show closed. Even though it ran 540 performances, it was added to the disheartening list of shows that failed to return their original investment.

The next musical to arrive may have also recalled *I Can Get It for You Wholesale* (3-22-62), for it starred Barbra Streisand, who had called herself to Broadway's attention as Miss Marmelstein. The **Funny Girl** (3-26-64, Winter Garden) of the title was Fanny Brice, and the evening retraced the great comedienne's rise from burlesque to Ziegfeld Follies stardom, her trouble-plagued marriage to the crooked Nicky Arnstein (Sydney Chaplin), and her decision to devote her energies to her career after their marriage broke up. No attempt was made to use songs Miss Brice had made famous, but Jule Styne wrote several in the period idiom, notably "Sadie, Sadie," that were serviceable. His best numbers, however, made no concession to period flavor. "Don't Rain On My Parade," a song strikingly like *Hello, Dolly*'s "Before The Parade Passes By" in both style and sentiment, closed both acts with its fervent plea not to have more obstacles thrown in one's path. The evening's outstanding hit, "People," expressed the recurring loneliness and unhappiness in the life of a performer dedicated to making others laugh. The book by Isobel Lennart was adequate but unexceptional. Even the production could be faulted, especially in scenes purportedly depicting the *Ziegfeld Follies*. Their skimpiness demonstrated the price a modern economy was exacting for the mere suggestion of the opulence of a half-century before. Happily, Miss Streisand overrode any objections or carping. She proved that she alone among performers of her generation could match Fanny Brice's gifts for hilarity and pathos. Typical of her funnier moments was a first-act travesty of a spectacular Ziegfeld number. As a tenor sang "His Love Makes Me Beautiful" the gorgeous chorus girls, decked out in sumptuous bridal gowns, moved regally down a Ziegfeldian staircase. Miss Brice appeared as the final bride. If love had not made her as beautiful as the other girls, it had given her a singular advantage. She was pregnant. The nonplused tenor attempted to proceed with the song as Fanny first coyly tried to hide her embarassment, and then openly advertised her condition. Her comic responses also wreaked havoc with Nick's seduction number, "You Are Woman." Performances of *Funny Girl* without her have shown the work to be sufficiently well crafted to make a pleasant entertainment, but not the electrifying evening into which she transformed it. Next to *Hello, Dolly!*, *Funny Girl* was the biggest hit of the season.

April was a busy month for musicals, at least by modern standards. **Anyone Can Whistle** (4-4-64, Majestic) had an out-of-the-ordinary plot (perhaps, in its fake miracle, a little like *110 in the Shade*). A small town has only one industry, a company that manufactures an item that never wears out. For lack of reorders the plant closes. To create a tourist market the town creates a fake miracle—water pumped to seemingly flow out of rock. The tourists come in droves. But the plan is jeopardized when the local mental institution, The Cookie Jar, brings forty-nine patients to the rock for a cure. The hoax is exposed, but not before Nurse Fay Apple (Lee Remick) and Dr. J. Bowden Hapgood (Harry Guardino) fall in love.

Angela Lansbury also starred. The book by playwright Arthur Laurents seemed diffuse and ineffective. Stephen Sondheim's music and lyrics were fresh and original, but, somehow, they often didn't convey that impression in the theatre. Received with generally unkind notices, the show departed after nine showings.

No musical during the season was more literate or had a more consistent sense of style and tone than **High Spirits** (4-7-64, Alvin), a lyric adaptation of Noel Coward's wartime hit, *Blithe Spirit*. The book and music were not by Coward, but by Hugh Martin and Timothy Gray. As she had twenty years before, the irrepressible and slightly irresponsible spiritualist, Madam Arcati (Beatrice Lillie), disrupts Charles Condomine's happy second marriage by bringing his first wife, Elvira (Tammy Grimes), back from the dead. Elvira is determined to have one last fling, and she does—flying over a posh party on the roof of a London hotel to the consternation of Charles' present wife, Ruth (Louise Troy), and to the not unamused consternation of Charles (Edward Woodward) himself. If the show had a fault, it was the lack of an outstanding tune to make it compellingly attractive to theatregoers at large. Without a "Hello, Dolly!" or a "People," it could not expect to compete for tourist trade after the smaller, solid body of knowledgeable and regular theatregoers had been exhausted. If the show had an overriding virtue—and it had—it was the brilliant clowning of Miss Lillie as the spiritualist. She arrived for her first entrance on a bicycle, removed the clips that kept her skirts in place and turned them into bracelets, glowering at the audience when it had the presumption to laugh. But the supreme moment of the evening was a series of curtain calls she took early in the second act after a song called "Talking To You." Every parting of the curtains revealed her in another of the positions assumed by great stars in answer to applause, an uproarious mockery of curtsies and bravura gestures. Miss Lillie's stylish madness went hand in glove, as it had often before, with Coward's stylish impudence. The show ran nearly a year—375 performances—but suffered the fate of so many long runs of the era, ending its run still a financial failure.

April 8, the night after *High Spirits* breezed in, the City Center unveiled its spring season of revivals. *West Side Story* (9-26-57) was the first, succeeded by *Porgy and Bess* (10-10-35) on May 6 and *My Fair Lady* (3-15-56) on May 20. In this last mounting Russell Nype sang Freddy and Reginald Gardiner was Doolittle.

April's last musical was a quick flop. Even with the popular Sam Levene as its star, **Café Crown** (4-17-64, Martin Beck) could muster only three performances. Levene played Hymie, a busboy in a restaurant. Hymie's theatrical ambition and his backing of a Broadway play were the theme of the show. The action took place in the thirties, a period that seemed ready to replace the turn of the century in librettists' affection.

It was the era chosen for the background of the season's final musical, **Fade Out—Fade In** (5-26-64, Hellinger). In fact, the show's opening number was "The Thirties." And, like *What Makes Sammy Run?*, it was set in Hollywood, in the film capital's heyday. The story was simple, one Hollywood itself employed numerous times during the thirties. An unpromising chorus girl is accidentally given the starring part in a new motion picture. When the mistake is discovered, heads roll and the film is securely stashed away in a vault. But Rudolf (Dick Patterson), the nephew of the studio's top man, takes a liking to the girl, Hope Springfield (Carol Burnett), and arranges for a preview. The movie is a success, Hope is a star, and she and Rudolf go off hand in hand. Unlike *What Makes Sammy Run?*, whose characters were merely Hollywood stereotypes, *Fade Out–Fade In* offered cameo impersonations of great film stars of the thirties, while its delineation of the studio head, Lionel Z. Governor (Lou Jacobi), clearly pointed a wicked finger at Louis B. Mayer. Governor shared Mayer's notorious eye for startlets and his grudging nepotism. The characterization was drolly exaggerated, with Governor requiring a full-time psychiatrist at his side and with his hatred of his fourth nephew so great he can no longer say "four." Jack Cassidy was featured as a suave Hollywood leading man. Like Steve Lawrence in *What Makes Sammy Run,* Miss Burnett became unhappy with the show, and, when no other comedienne could be recruited, the show closed after 271 performances, divided into two runs separated by a three-month hiatus. To some extent Miss Burnett's displeasure was justified, for though Comden and Green did the book, Jule Styne the music (his second score of the season), and George Abbott the staging, it represented far from their best efforts. Even changes made in the book and new songs added during the three-month vacation failed to help. For her fans, Miss Burnett's funniest moment was probably her spoof of Shirley Temple.

1964-1965

This was the last season in the great era of "musical plays." One lone show earned the season its place in the act, for otherwise it was a dismal year. More than twenty years had elapsed since *Oklahoma!* (3-31-43) had set new standards for the American Musical Theatre. *Oklahoma!* had endowed the lyric stage with a new seriousness of purpose, a new sense of cohesiveness and tonal integrity. It had made turn-of-the-century America and its homey sentimentalities stylish. In doing so it had broken long-run and financial records, some of which had remained unassailed for decades. Higher production costs and admission fees, coupled with the shrinking of legitimate theatre offerings and the concentration on major successes of any given season, eventually allowed a few other shows to surpass *Oklahoma!*'s figures. The sole masterwork of the final season, *Fiddler on the Roof,* was alien to its great predecessors in its choices of theme and setting, but in its tenor—its seriousness, its artistry—it was not an unfitting finale. And like *Oklahoma!* it closed holding the long-run record for the American Musical Theatre.

The season began with an unusual importation, the Parisian tourist mecca, the **Folies Bergère** (6-2-64, Broadway). Besides bringing its famous showgirls, it arrived carting fifteen tons of scenery and 1,200 costumes. The day of nudes moving across the stage had not yet come to Broadway, so that one of the main attractions of the Parisian revue had to be somewhat modified. Nonetheless there were still complaints and disputes about the scantiness of some of the costumes. Not a first-rate mounting, the show's renown and its near nudity helped it to run until November 14.

On July 6 the New York State Theatre at the new Lincoln Center welcomed its first legitimate attraction. Plans called for the Music Theatre of Lincoln Center to revive popular Broadway musicals at reduced prices in the pattern of the City Center. The result, although it could not be foreseen at the time, was to kill the City Center series, and thus, when the Music Theater proved economically unfeasible, leave New Yorkers without a program of low-priced revivals. Richard Rodgers was the president and producing director of the new group, and he selected his own *The King and I* (3-29-51), with Risë Stevens and

Darren McGavin, for the premiere presentation. *The Merry Widow* (10-27-07), with Patrice Munsel and Bob Wright, followed on August 17. The operetta, which fifty-seven years before had brought to a close one era and inaugurated another, displayed a curious faculty for reappearing whenever new acts began or ended.

From Czechoslovakia came **Laterna Magika** (8-3-64, Philharmonica Hall), a performance of Offenbach's *Tales of Hoffman* combining live action and motion pictures. Another foreign company, this time from Austria, brought in a revival of **Wiener Blut** (9-11-64, Lunt-Fontanne). The work had been slightly tampered with, including some waltzes Strauss never wrote for it. But it was the first revival of the piece since the turn of the century. Although *The Merry Widow* grossed $98,000 one week, the receptions accorded to the Lehar, Offenbach, and Strauss works suggested that, while an era was coming to an end, it would not be the old operetta that would initiate the new rage.

Fiddler on the Roof (9-22-64, Imperial) was the season's biggest hit and the last of the great masterworks of the era. Based on Sholom Aleichem's stories, it had a book by Joseph Stein, lyrics by Sheldon Harnick, and music by Jerry Bock. Although the adaptation was faithful to the essentials of Aleichem's tales, it eschewed, of necessity, some of their Yiddish parochialism, without denying their Jewishness. By emphasizing ongoing problems of family bonds and religious interaction against a backdrop of disintegrating social order, the authors gave the work a universality that allowed the evening to transcend what might have otherwise been an appeal limited largely to the sizable Jewish segment of playgoers.

The time is 1905. But no carefree, color-strewn turn-of-the-century American small town is revealed as the curtain raises. Instead, audiences see a somber, dilapidated shtetl, a Jewish community, in the Russian village of Anatevka. The scene is the exterior of the house of the community's pious dairyman, Tevye (Zero Mostel). A fiddler is playing on the roof. Tevye addresses the audience:

A fiddler on the roof. Sounds crazy, no? But in our little village of Anatevka, you might say everyone of us is a fiddler of the roof, trying to scratch out a pleasant, simple tune without breaking his neck. It isn't easy. You may ask, why do we stay here if it's so dangerous? We stay because Anatevka is our home. And how

do we keep our balance? That I can tell you in a word—tradition!

The villagers enter and join Tevye in singing of "Tradition," the familial hierarchy that maintains the Jews' strength. Their strength must be maintained in the face of not just local bigotries, but of officially fostered governmental onslaughts as well. When a villager asks the rabbi if there is a proper blessing for the Tsar, the rabbi replies, "Of course. May God bless and keep the Tsar—far away from us!" Tevye has five daughters, three of whom are of marriageable age, so Tevye and his wife, Golde (Maria Karnilova), have employed Yente (Beatrice Arthur), the village matchmaker, to find a mate for their eldest, Tzeitel (Joanna Merlin). The younger girls implore, "Matchmaker, Matchmaker," find mates for them, too. Meanwhile Tevye goes about his business. He comes home exhausted at nights and contemplates a better life, "If I Were A Rich Man." But bad news from elsewhere suggests riches alone would not help. Jews are being evicted from other villages. Closer to home, affairs take a momentarily happier turn. Lazar (Michael Granger), the elderly, relatively well-to-do butcher, has asked for Tzeitel's hand. When Tevye consents, he and Lazar celebrate with a toast "To Life" ("L' Chaim"). But their joy is brief. Two problems arise. A constable warns Tevye to expect trouble in Anatevka. And Tzeitel will not accept Lazar as a husband, preferring the young tailor, Motel (Austin Pendleton). Tevye decides not to go against Tzteitel's wishes. At the wedding Tevye and Golde remember when their children were babies and in "Sunrise, Sunset" remark on how swiftly time has passed. Once more, though, joy is brief. The wedding is disrupted and the community vandalized by the pogrom of which the constable had warned. Tevye's second daughter, Hodel (Julia Miganes), has fallen in love with the community's intellectual and radical, Perchik (Bert Convy). At first Tevye is opposed to this marriage, too, because the youngsters talk of love, and Tevye cannot see what love has to do with arranging a marriage. Reluctantly, he acknowledges old ways are disappearing, conceding, "our old ways were new once." Unfortunately Perchik is arrested and shipped to Siberia for his dangerous antigovernment notions. Hodel elects to follow him, even if she must go, "Far From The Home I Love." Perhaps the hardest blow of all for Tevye comes when he learns his third daughter, Chava (Tanya Everett), wants to marry a Christian.

This time he remains adamant in his opposition, and when Chava and her fiancé, Fydka (Joe Ponazecki), elope, Tevye brokenheartedly declares, "Chava is dead to us!" Chava is hardly gone when the Constable returns bringing news the community has long feared. The Jews must leave Anatevka. Tevye and his family make plans to join their Uncle Abram in America, while the rest of the Jews attempt to plan their own destinies. As they leave, they sing of their beloved "Anatevka" and wonder where else the Sabbath could be so sweet. The fiddler is seen playing on the roof. Tevye beckons to him and, tucking his violin under his arm, he joins the exodus.

The book was unabashedly sentimental, but the insistent cruelties of the story made its sentimentality believable and palpable. Bock's melodic score captured both the vitality and pathos of traditional Jewish song and projected them in undeniably popular molds. Jerome Robbins' direction was at once forceful and compassionate, while Boris Aronson's sets were moodily evocative. Mostel's performance—his dialogues with God, his tragi-comic rendition of "If I Were a Rich Man," his comic business—amounted to a titanic tour de force. Yet Mostel's several replacements as well as Tevye's in the road and international companies proved the work to be so powerful that it did not depend on a star. The show closed on July 2, 1972, after 3,242 performances—the longest run in this history of the American Musical Theatre.

If the age-old problem of anti-Semitism had been poignantly portrayed in *Fiddler on the Roof*, an even more ancient lust for battle was satirized in an English importation, **Oh, What a Lovely War!** (9-30-64, Broadhurst). As generals bungled and horrendous casualty figures soared, a chorus sang the lilting, insouciant tunes of World War I. The show's finale was the soldier's version of Jerome Kern's 1914 hit from *The Girl from Utah*, "They Didn't Believe Me." The wartime lyrics had been composed by a then unknown Cole Porter. Once more it seemed as if subconsciously Broadway wanted to recapitulate the history of the American Musical. Just as *The Merry Widow* harked back to the opening of one era, so "They Didn't Believe Me" sounded the opening notes of the succeeding period. But neither the gay songs nor the antiwar sentiments of *Oh, What a Lovely War!* attracted the public at large. The show closed after a disappointing three-and-a-half-month run.

A second British importation, the revue **Cambridge Circus** (10-6-64, Plymouth), seemed doomed to an even shorter run. However after 23 performances at the Plymouth, it was moved downtown to a tiny off-Broadway house, where in two editions—spoofing everything from Handel to the BBC—it found an audience until spring.

Two big book musicals arrived a week apart in the last half of October. **Golden Boy** (10-20-64, Majestic) was a musical version of Clifford Odets' 1938 hit. Odets himself had begun the adaptation, but when he died in 1963, another playwright, William Gibson, agreed to finish the assignment. Because blacks had generally replaced the white minorities who had comprised the principal fighters of the thirties, the hero was changed to a black man. And because the blacks generally lacked the pervasive cultural heritage and cultural interests of the Italians depicted in the original play, Joe Bonaparte's central dilemma between his love of the violin and his ambitions as a prizefighter was muted. The new black Joe was a young Negro determined to get rich quick. And, of course, his name was no longer Bonaparte. Slyly, Odets or Gibson had rechristened him Joe Wellington. Joe fights his way to the top only to discover his sluttish girl friend, Lorna Moon (Paula Wayne), is having an affair with his manager, Tom Moody (Kenneth Tobey). Upset, he takes off on a wild ride and is killed in a car crash. The show's opening was postponed several times to allow Gibson to give some backbone to the plot, whose heart had been cut out. If he succeeded in making the libretto stronger than the score, it was simply because the Lee Adams–Charles Strouse tunes were so lackluster. The best-received song in the show was a production number, "Don't Forget 127th Street," in which Joe tells his young admirers not to be ashamed of their Harlem home. Donald McKayle's highly praised choreography included a fast-paced boxing match. The show ran 69 performances, thanks primarily to the box-office lure of its star, Sammy Davis, Jr.

The well-liked Robert Preston proved to be a less potent draw, but then his vehicle, **Ben Franklin in Paris** (10-27-64, Lunt Fontanne), was not even as strong as *Golden Boy*. The patriotic old ladies' man gets Louis XVI to recognize America and rekindles the passion of a bygone love with the Countess Diane de Vobrillac (Ulla Sallert). He also abets his grandson's romance with a pretty young revolutionary, Janine Nicolet (Susan Watson). The evening's most spectacular moment occurred when Franklin took off in a large balloon. In spite of a trite book and mediocre score,

Preston kept the show on the boards for six months.

November was busy. A new edition of Victor Borge's one-man show, called **Comedy in Music Opus 2** (11-9-64, Golden), led the parade of November offerings. The next evening witnessed the opening of the short-lived—two weeks—**Something More!** (11-10-64, O'Neill), a musical version of Gerald Green's *Portofino P.T.A.* The book, interspersed with Sammy Fain songs, followed novelist Bill Weems (Arthur Hill) and his family from their unsatisfactory life in suburban Mineola to the vaunted freedom and pleasures of Italy. Included was one scene in which the Italians danced "The Watusi," a briefly voguish American step purportedly suggested by an African tribal celebration. Audiences found such intercontinental diversion an unsatisfactory hodgepodge.

The D'Oyly Carte Opera Company began a five-week stay at the City Center on November 17th, offering *Iolanthe, Trial by Jury* and *H.M.S. Pinafore, The Pirates of Penzance, The Mikado,* and *Ruddigore.* Four nights later, **Zizi**, a "French musical hall dance revue" which starred, appropriately, Zizi Jeanmaire, replaced the *Folies Bergère* at the Broadway Theatre and compiled 49 showings.

In the days of Gilbert and Sullivan and the French music hall, musicals about gypsies had been commonplace. But they were usually operettas, set in the Austro-Hungarian empire. **Bajour** (11-23-64, Shubert) was a gypsy musical with a difference: it was a contemporary musical comedy set in present-day New York. When Johnny Dembo (Herschel Bernardi) and his gypsy family decamp in New York, Lt. MacNiall (Robert Burr) persuades his distant cousin, the anthropologist, Emily Kirsten (Nancy Dussault), to "study" the tribe and report its movements to him. He learns Dembo's main ambition is to marry his son, Steve (Gus Trikonis), to Anyanka (Chita Rivera), daughter of Newark's gypsy king. Anyanka must prove her worth by pulling a successful swindle (a bajour). She succeeds, at the expense of Emily's widowed mother and with Emily's unwitting help. *Bajour* was another of the many musicals of the season that offered no more than a serviceable book and a weak plot, and that, as a result, depended for its strength on its star performer. In the case of *Bajour* that star was Miss Rivera, and her driving performance and fiery dancing as Anyanka gave the evening the muscle it required to run out the season.

December's only new musical, **I Had a Ball** (12-15-64, Martin Beck), dealt with an equally raffish figure, Garside, a Coney Island swami. When, after a concentrated look into his crystal ball, he decides to act as a matchmaker, his couplings turn out to be all wrong. He pairs Brooks (Steven Roland), a loan shark, with Jeannie (Karen Morrow), who runs a Ferris wheel, and attempts to unite Sam the Shpieler (Richard Kiley), a pitchman, with Addie (Luba Lisa), a hustler known as "Miss Under-the-Boardwalk." With time Jeannie and Sam discover they are a suitable couple. Once again a weak book and limp score were propped up by a star's performance. Comedian Buddy Hackett portrayed the swami and, in the greatest of the old clown tradition, Hackett improvised much of his material every night. He, too, kept his show before the footlights for the rest of the season.

The popular-priced revivals at the City Center continued with a mounting of *Brigadoon*, with Peter Palmer, December 23. Another series of popular-priced revivals at the City Center began on April 26 with *Guys and Dolls*. Alan King, Jerry Orbach, Sheila MacRae and Anita Gillette headed the cast. *Kiss Me Kate*, with Patricia Morison and Bob Wright, followed on May 12 and two more offerings arrived at the start of the 1965–66 season.

It was February 6, 1965, before another new musical opened. With **Kelly** (2-6-65, Broadhurst) the season reached its nadir. A leaden, dim-witted affair whose hero, Hop Kelly (Don Francks), was based loosely on Steve Brodie, supposedly the first man to leap from the Brooklyn Bridge, it lasted a single performance. When it folded, *Kelly* took with it $650,000 of its investors' money, a sum beyond Brodie's wildest dreams.

Costs continued to skyrocket, and the season's musicals were forced to price their top ticket at $9.90. As a result, **Baker Street** (2-16-65, Broadway) achieved a record gross of $103,000 for a holiday week in which it played an extra matinee. Incessant increases in costs, admissions, and grosses soon made comparative figures meaningless. *Baker Street* drew a large attendance early in its run because the popular Sherlock Holmes legend was sumptuously and imaginatively mounted, and superbly performed. However, it was the seventh new book musical in a row with a disappointing libretto and, worse, a thin, colorless score. Jerome Coopersmith used three of Conan Doyle's stories—"The Adventure of the Empty House," "A Scandal in Bohemia" and

Act Five: The American Musical as a Conscious Art Form

"The Final Problem"—with a free hand that distressed many Baker Street Irregulars. After Holmes (Fritz Weaver) helps the musical star, Irene Adler (Inga Swenson), retrieve some letters, he discovers she has become infatuated with him. She intrudes into his desperate attempt to prevent Moriarty (Martin Gabel) from stealing Queen Victoria's jewels during the Diamond Jubilee. Goodness and celibacy triumph. The production's most discussed scene was the Diamond Jubilee parade, cleverly depicted by Bill Baird's marionettes. Weaver and Gabel temporarily abandoned their more serious acting careers to give delightfully melodramatic performances.

A tacky re-creation of the stripper shows of the Minsky era was moved uptown after playing several years off-Broadway. At its new home **This Was Burlesque**, with the former burlesque queen, Ann Corio, as headliner, added 114 performances to its record.

The only other musical, aside from *Fiddler On The Roof*, with any real merit that season was **Do I Hear a Waltz?** (3-18-65, 46th St.) It was singularly fitting that what was meritorious in the show derived from the pen of Richard Rodgers, the composer who twenty-two years before had given this era its first durable masterpiece. That the show ultimately was set down in the record books as a failure was attributable to its unpleasant story and an inexplicably slack, draggy production. Arthur Laurents reworked the libretto from his own successful play, *The Time of the Cuckoo*. Its heroine was Leona Samish (Elizabeth Allen), a lonely, naive, but rather grasping and greedy American woman. She is a spinster, convinced that when the right man comes along the air around him will sing a waltz. On vacation in Venice she visits the shop of Renato di Rossi (Sergio Franchi). Leona is captivated by his good looks and glib charm. She accepts his offer of a date, but breaks it when she learns he is married. However, when he presents her with a bejeweled necklace she falls completely under his spell. Of course, Renato is simply a cynical, calculating Casanova. Leona discovers that Renato has not paid for the necklace and that she must pay for it herself. Her disillusion is complete when she learns that Renato has been given a commission on the purchase price. Only the title song, a refreshingly sweeping waltz, sung by Leona, entered the canon of Rodgers' standards. The rest of the music, while not especially memorable, was thoughtful and effective. To Stephen Sondheim's competent lyrics the songs ranged from the introspective "Moon In My Window," in which the principal female characters—Leona, Signora Fioria—examine their ideas of romance, to the humorous "This Week Americans," in which Signora Fioria (Carol Bruce) recounts the cyclical trials of a pensione keeper, to the expected easy musical comedy gaiety of "Perfectly Lovely Couple." With no star of the caliber of Shirley Booth or Katharine Hepburn (who had played the original stage and film Leonas) on which to focus interest and with general disappointment in the offering itself, *Do I Hear a Waltz?* ran only 220 performances, the shortest run accorded a Rodgers work during the era.

On April 1, **Maurice Chevalier at 77** presented the indefatigable star in another one-man show for a 31-performance run. Two weeks later the London musical hit, **Half a Sixpence** (4-25-65, Broadhurst), arrived with the English teen-agers' delight, Tommy Steele, heading the cast. This musical version of H.G. Wells' *Kipps* pleased New York as much as it had the West End, settling in for a long stay.

Two May musicals brought the season and the era to a close. **Flora, the Red Menace** (5-11-65, Alvin), the last American book musical of the act, reverted to the increasingly voguish thirties for its background. This musical version of Lester Atwell's novel, *Love Is Just Around the Corner*, was dramatized by George Abbott and Robert Russell, and set to John Kander's music and Fred Ebb's lyrics. The story told how sweet, accepting Flora, a would-be fashion designer just out of school, is persuaded by her boy friend, Harry Toukarian (Bob Dishy), to join the Communist Party. Harry is a stammerer, determined to cure his impediment by speaking with a mouth filled with pebbles. Flora almost loses him to the voluptuous Comrade Charlotte (Cathryn Damon). All the Communists succeed in doing is to stage a pretentious ballet, "The Tree of Life." Flora and the U.S. survive. The show was another in the depressingly drab chain of new works, and it ran largely on the strength of Liza Minnelli's likable portrayal of the title role. Miss Minnelli was the daughter of Vincente Minnelli, the distinguished stage and screen director, and of Judy Garland, onetime Hollywood musical star. An off-Broadway revival of *Best Foot Forward* had shown that Miss Minnelli had a talent all her own, and *Flora, the Red Menace* confirmed it.

Anthony Newley and Leslie Bricusse created a sequel to *Stop The World!—I Want To Get Off* and entitled it **The Roar of the Greasepaint—The**

Smell of the Crowd (5-16-65, Shubert). Like its predecessor, it was an allegory. In this case a confrontation of the "haves" represented by Sir (Cyril Ritchard) and the "have nots" in the person of "Cocky" (Newley). At times it was hard to distinguish between the two since almost all the costumes were ragged; Cocky and Siro making their first entrance dressed like the leading figures in *Waiting for Godot*. As in the earlier work, a single, skeletonized set served to represent the world. The show had two good tunes, Cocky's "Who Can I Turn To? (When Nobody Needs Me)," a ballad reminiscent of the earlier "What Kind Of Fool Am I?," and Cocky and Sir's sprightly "A Wonderful Day Like Today," which achieved general acceptance only after the show closed. The show struck many as too close a rewrite of the first Bricusse and Newley work. Its run, as a result, was curtailed. The show had been given to New York before London, but after the disappointing New York run no London mounting materialized.

11

EPILOGUE
Exhaustion and the
Search for New Directions
1965-1978

The years covered in this chapter were unhappy ones for both the United States and the American Musical Theatre. A controversial, escalating war in Asia led to domestic turmoil. Rioters burned and looted American cities, and when the very politicians who most loudly decried this breakdown in law and order took over the government they proved as lawless if not as disorderly as the ghetto hordes, and they soon led the nation into its blackest political tragedy. It would have been remarkable had the lyric stage been able to ignore and override these upheavals, but for several seasons the American Musical Theatre had been manifesting unmistakable signs of exhaustion. Beset by the collapse of so much order and decorum, it, too, fell apart.

Merely getting to the theatre became something of an ordeal. New York's aging playhouses were clustered together in an area fast growing sleazy and occasionally dangerous. Honky-tonk bars and shops vending pornography crowded into the Times Square district. Derelicts, female and male prostitutes, and muggers pestered and sometimes molested playgoers. For those still hoping to have a night on the town, the slow, but steady disappearance of night clubs shortened such evenings appreciably. All that was left was dinner and a show.

But dinner and a show were beginning to cost a bundle. Inflation, fueled by the Vietnam War and later by the oil cartel, created havoc on both sides of the footlights. Few theatregoers were old enough to remember that from the Civil War to World War I ticket prices held steady at a top of $1.50, or, at most, $2.00. But many could attest to the relative stability that prevailed from the twenties to the early fifties. Now a $6.00 top gave way to $7.20, which quickly jumped above the $10.00 level and then shot up to $12.00 and $15.00 and $20.00. Of necessity the theatre became increasingly elitist, depending to no small extent on expense-account trade. To compensate for increasing costs producers drastically reduced the ranks of the chorus and cut down on the lavishness of scenery—skeletonized and basic unit sets appeared more frequently.

Largely because of economic pressures the theatre offered less assurance of regular employment. The day when, if she needed it, a Lillian Russell or a Marilyn Miller or an Ethel Merman could be certain of a new show every season was seemingly gone forever. Moreover, except for a very fortunate few, Broadway's financial rewards were meager compared with television or films. As a result a phenomenon that had been a nuisance since sound movies and the depression swelled into a plague. Brilliant young talent would appear, be hailed as a bright hope for tomorrow, and by that tomorrow be in Hollywood never to return. Witness, to name one striking example, Barbra Streisand.

Partly as cause, partly as effect, fewer and fewer genuinely good musicals appeared, while many better offerings seemed wistfully derivative.

Occasional attempts to break out of old molds all somehow led nowhere. Moreover, even these more daring works displayed some unfortunate tendencies. They were lamentably unmelodic, often virtually formless, and given to abrasively scatological language. They seemed at times to be cursing their own inadequacies.

Esthetically three developments forcefully influenced the American Musical Theatre. With the arrival of the British singing group, the Beatles, in 1964, rock music exploded across the land, driving every other musical sound into a panicky retreat. Broadway's older, traditional composers were thrown for a loss. Some, such as Harold Arlen and Harold Rome, have not been heard from in years. Those who remained more or less active found their newer efforts were not awarded the constant replaying on records or radio that their older songs had been given, though here the fault lay partly in an incontestable falling off of memorably melodic invention. As far as memorable melodies went, the American Musical Theatre had suddenly become not very musical. With rare exceptions, audiences rarely left new musicals singing their music.

Instead, in the second important change, Broadway relied more on its librettists, lyricists, and directors. Directors became especially important. Tom O'Horgan, Gower Champion, and, most of all, Bob Fosse gave the period some of its most original and sustained—though, alas, ephemeral—achievements. Directors sometimes assumed dictatorial creative control—originating the very ideas for their musicals and shaping their entire development. Many successful musicals of this epilogue would have been lackluster indeed but for the taut, imaginative artistry of men such as Fosse. Stephen Sondheim, the most notably brilliant of the writers, similarly advocated such "conceptual musicals," bending and subordinating every aspect of the work to an overall vision. As a result, increasingly intellectualized musicals confronted audiences with problems and ideas that a few years before tired businessmen and their wives had gone to musicals to escape. The ordeal that began with getting to the theatre ended by having to sit through the show.

One last major development was the emergence of blacks as both creators and playgoers. If much black writing was either stridently antagonistic or mildly self-pitying, several black shows possessed the exuberance and zest many white musicals lacked. Admittedly exuberance and zest were all that many prejudiced critics of earlier years would give blacks credit for. But given the blacks' gifts for melody, rhythm, and humor it is not inconceivable that they could eventually provide the tonic the ailing American Musical Theatre of this epilogue direly needs. Other minorities—first the Irish, then the Jews—used their talents to lift the lyric stage out of earlier doldrums. Where there is melody, rhythm, and humor, there is always hope.

1965-1966

Statistics for the very first season of this epilogue hint at the malaise that pervaded the period. Although twenty-eight musicals presented themselves for Broadway's approval, twelve of these were revivals mounted by either the New York City Center Light Opera Company or the Music Theatre of Lincoln Center. Of the remaining sixteen lyric works, importations accounted for four, including one revival. A number of the new American books shows, as well as several importations, seemed determined efforts to capitalize on earlier successes.

The City Center had both its productions on the boards before Lincoln Center unveiled its two summer offerings. As was their wont both houses played safe by bringing back recent popular hits. The City Center offered *South Pacific* (4-7-49) with Ray Middleton as de Becque on June 2, 1965 and *The Music Man* (12-19-57) with Bert Parks in the title role on June 16, while the Music Theater followed with *Kismet* (12-3-53) in which Alfred Drake re-created his original role on June 22 and *Carousel* (4-19-45) also featuring its original male lead, John Raitt, on August 10. David Merrick contributed to the flood of revivals by returning *Oliver!* to the New York stage for eight weeks beginning August 2. Before the first new musical of the season appeared the New York City Opera gave theatregoers and opera lovers a chance to re-evaluate Menotti's *The Saint of Bleecker Street* when the company added it to its repertory on September 29. Two more operas originally done as Broadway shows were included in its spring season: *Street Scene* on February 24 and *The Consul* on March 17.

Pickwick (10-4-65, 46th St.) was a West End adaptation of Dickens' material, clearly designed to follow in *Oliver!*'s lucrative footsteps. In London it had met with some modest success; in New

York, where, like *Oliver!*, David Merrick was its sponsor, it was a quick failure.

An even quicker failure, **Drat! The Cat!** (10-10-65, Beck), survived a single week. In spirit the musical was not a little unlike the lyric mock-melodramas the Krimskys had offered at their American Music Hall in the thirties. Its libretto told of the love affair that blossoms between Bob Purefoy (Elliot Gould), a distressingly inept policeman, and Alice Van Guilder (Lesley Ann Warren), a kooky, criminally minded heiress. In one respect Purefoy is a kindred soul to Alice, since both have easy berths in life thanks to their fathers. Purefoy's father was a Chief of Detectives. Unfortunately the drolleries in conception were not quite so amusing in the glare of the spotlights.

One of the most eagerly awaited musicals of the season, **On a Clear Day You Can See Forever** (10-17-65, Hellinger) had at first been announced as *I Picked a Daisy* and promised to offer the fruits of a newly established collaboration of two of the American Musical Theatre's greatest talents, Alan Jay Lerner and Richard Rodgers. But a few months of working together convinced the pair that their habits and theories were too disparate. Lerner retained the rights to the story and joined with composer Burton Lane to create the piece. Lane's score was theatrically effective, and in its title song (sung by the romantic leads) had one superior number that has survived long after the show played its final performance. As always, Lerner created literate dialogue for an imaginative story. But as he so often had before, he failed to tie it all together in a completely viable libretto. To some extent Lerner's problem may have derived from the fact that his was the only libretto of the season not based on an earlier work. In this instance, however, his problem may have been exacerbated by his trying to go too far with his theme of extrasensory perception, allowing his heroine to predict the future as well as to recall a past existence. Although he tied the past and the future together adroitly at the end, he asked his audience in the interim to look both ways at once. Dr. Mark Bruckner (John Cullum), attempting to demonstrate hypnosis to a class at his family's clinic, finds he has unwittingly hypnotized not his intended subject but a highly susceptible young lady, Daisy Gamble (Barbara Harris). When the class leaves, Daisy begs the doctor to cure her addiction to smoking, an addiction which threatens to hinder her prospects for marrying Warren Smith (William Daniels). Bruckner agrees

to work with her, although it is not her addiction that intrigues him. He quickly establishes that she is gifted with extrasensory perception—she knows when a phone is about to ring or where Bruckner has misplaced his keys. She makes plants grow by talking to them. Equally curious is her insistence that she remembers another life as Melinda Wells, a spunky 18th-century wench. Almost against his will Bruckner discovers himself accepting Daisy's stories—and falling in love with her. Although it means missing an interview with Warren's prospective employers, Daisy accompanies Bruckner to the Frick Museum and then on a boat ride, "On The S.S. Bernard Cohn." At subsequent meetings in his office Mark grows increasingly fascinated by Daisy's adventures as Melinda and seems to become even more enamored of the uninhibited Melinda than of Daisy. Melinda marries a painter, and when she learns how unfaithful her husband is, runs away to America on a ship named the Trelawney. But Mark's budding infatuation is jolted when his stolid brother Conrad (Michael Lewis)—who has "been an analyst so long, he invades privacy instinctively"—comes across the tape Mark has made of his sessions with Daisy and warns him he will cause the clinic to become a laughing-stock. When Mark's materials are published, he loses his job. But a rich Greek appears offering Mark almost limitless resources to pursue his study. To Mark's distress Daisy has played one of his tapes, one on which he muses, "Poor sweet nothing little Daisy. It's not your fault you're not Melinda." Hurt, Daisy walks out of his life. Trusting her ESP will hear his pleas, Mark cries "Come Back To Me." She hears and heeds, but only to tell him she has a plane ticket for California. At the airport she has a premonition the plane will meet with an accident. When the announcer advises the name of the plane is the Trelawney, memories of her drowning in a shipwreck flood back. She cannot explain them, but understands she and Mark will work out the riddle together. Faulty as it was, the show ran 280 performances, sparked by Barbara Harris' wide-eyed, captivating Daisy. A later road tour proved disappointing.

November's first two shows also achieved runs that a half-century or so before would probably have assured them a respectable profit, but in the befuddled theatrical economy of their own day placed them on the wrong side of the ledger. **The Zulu and the Zayda** (11-10-65, Cort) had a book by Howard daSilva and Felix Leon, based on a Dan Jacobson story, and music by Harold

Rome. Some critics viewed it as a straight play with songs, but Rome's eleven musical numbers (plus reprises and orchestral passages) suggest it was indeed a musical. The absence of dancing—surprising given the possibilities of its African setting—may have promoted some doubts. But the show's Africa is not the colorful, throbbing jungle of some earlier shows. For the most part the action unfolds in a Jewish suburb of Johannesburg, where the Grossman family hires a towering Zulu called Paulus to be a companion for their grandfather. (Zayda is Yiddish for grandfather.) The principal attraction of the evening was the clowning of the diminutive, sad-eyed Menasha Skulnik, long a favorite downtown in the Yiddish theatres and for a few seasons before *The Zulu and the Zayda* equally popular with Broadway audiences. He kept the show alive until April.

Three nights after Skulnik opened, one of the leading ladies of the American stage, Julie Harris, cast her lot with the musical theatre. It proved an unhappy decision. Her musical, **Skyscraper** (11-13-65, Lunt-Fontanne), was a lyric version of Elmer Rice's 1945 hit, *Dream Girl*. Peter Stone adapted the text, while Sammy Cahn wrote words to James Van Heusen's music. Broadway's once infallible team of Feuer and Martin produced the evening. Looking back in his autobiography, Cahn terms the production "One devastating experience." He is proud of his lyrics for "Everybody Has A Right To Be Wrong" (sung in the show by Peter L. Marshall), and the song did in fact meet with some popularity. The book faithfully retained Rice's basic story of Georgina Allerton, who spends most of her waking hours in Walter Mitty-like dreams of fame, fortune, and romance, but added a contemporary touch by placing her in an old brownstone surrounded by modern high-rise buildings and menaced by developers. Much of Georgina's dreaming centers around her assistant at her antique shop, Roger Somerhill (Charles Nelson Reilly), whom she envisages in such romantic guises as a secret agent and a toreador. Roger proves treacherous, conspiring with the developers who would demolish her house. By the end of the evening she has at least come down to earth enough to agree to marry Timothy Bushman (Marshall), a young architect, and the two arrange to save her home and shop. Two witty Michael Kidd dances had fun at the expense of flirting construction workers and Georgina's ideas of a lady's honor. Robert Randolph's scenery strikingly juxtaposed Georgina's warm rooms against an imposing, impersonal skyline. Miss Harris'

stylish acting, Reilly's hilarious unctuous obnoxiousness, and "two-fers" (cheap tickets, two for the price of one) allowed *Skyscraper* to run out the season.

The season's biggest hit opened on November 22 without much fanfare at a temporary theatre that had been erected on the New York University campus to house the ill-fated repertory company that later played briefly at Lincoln Center. **Man of La Mancha** was a musical version of Cervantes' *Don Quixote* that had tried out at the Goodspeed Opera House in Connecticut. Although it had no advance sale to speak of, generally excellent reviews and favorable word-of-mouth from audiences that no longer demanded the well-mannered niceties of an earlier era soon made it the "hottest" ticket in town. In Dale Wasserman's adaptation, with lyrics by Joe Darion and music by Mitch Leigh, Cervantes' masterpiece became a hard-driving, often rough-talking, frequently compassionate lyric drama. The show made few concession to theatregoers, playing out its entire story in one basic set and without intermission. The dancing, especially one brutal Abduction ballet, was as violent and unyielding as much of the dialogue and lyrics. Wasserman employed a frame device, beginning the evening with the imprisonment of Cervantes and his servant. In reading his tale to his fellow prisoners, the Spaniard is transformed into Don Quixote and his servant becomes Sancho. According to Quixote, "the wild winds of fortune will carry me onward, Oh whithersoever they blow." They blow him, fittingly, to a windmill, although in the Don's eyes the mill is a fearsome ogre. He can bring himself to admit he has tilted at a windmill only by claiming an enchanter had magically reshaped the fiend. Not until a lord of a castle dubs him a knight will he be able to destroy the enchanter. Quixote's addled mind allows a dilapidating roadside inn to become a suitable castle and the innkeeper its lord. Even Aldonza, the inn's sluttish serving girl, is elevated to "Sweet Lady [and] fair virgin." Going still further, the Don rechristens her Dulcinea and apostrophizes, "thy name is like a prayer an angel whispers." He confesses to the baffled girl that his mission in life is, "To dream the impossible dream . . . To reach the unreachable star." No sooner has the obliging innkeeper dubbed Quixote, Knight of the Woeful Countenance, than the new knight's mettle is severely tested. Rough muleteers attack and abduct Aldonza. For a moment, Cervantes becomes himself again as the Inquisition enters to remove one of his fellow prisoners. As the Don, he stumbles into a gypsy encampment, where he recovers the much bedraggled Aldonza, refusing to heed her pleas to accept her for what she is. To a fanfare of trumpets a warrior, the Knight of the Mirrors, appears and jousts with Quixote. In the warrior's mirrors the Don sees his own reflection and is soon brought to realize he is, "A madman dressed for a masquerade!" The warrior reveals himself to be Dr. Carrasco, sent to Cervantes to rid him of his delusions. He succeeds all too well. Even Aldonza, insisting she is Dulcinea and begging the virtually lifeless man to continue his impossible dream, cannot get an encouraging response. The Inquisition arrives to lead Cervantes away, as his fellow prisoners exhort him "To live with your heart striving upward." Leigh's music played as important a part in the show's success as Wasserman's book. The score was in a totally modern idiom. The chromatic progressions of "The Impossible Dream" (called in the program "The Quest") were instantly appealing, and the song became an enormously popular hit. Indeed, it could be considered the last major hit to emerge from Broadway before "rock-and-roll" overwhelmed the nation. Of course, its hymnlike tune played over heavy chords did suggest a certain rock quality. "Dulcinea" and the title song also received significant replaying outside the theatre. The original cast included a number of fine singing actors: Richard Kiley was Cervantes (who sang both hit songs); Joan Diener, Aldonza; Ray Middleton, the Innkeeper; and Robert Rounseville, a priest. In one curious bit of casting Sancho was performed by Irving Jacobson, a refugee from the moribund Yiddish theatre. In its Village auditorium and later at an uptown house *Man of La Mancha* compiled 2,328 performances. Its touring and international companies thrived as well.

Robert Wright and George Forrest, who had embellished their book and lyrics to *Song of Norway* (8-21-44) with Grieg's music and their book and lyrics for *Kismet* (12-3-53) with Borodin's melodies, turned to Rachmaninoff for their tunes in **Anya** (11-29-65, Ziegfeld), their adaptation of Marcelle Maurette and Guy Bolton's popular *Anastasia*. The story once again seemed to support the claim of the young lady who appeared mysteriously in Berlin in 1925 professing to be the sole surviving member of Czar Nicholas' supposedly slaughtered family. In a sizzling encounter in the second act Anya convinces the Dowager Empress she is the real Anastasia. The play had been lush hokum, the musical seemed elaborate ho-hum. A fine cast included Constance Towers and Lillian Gish in the pivotal roles as well as Lawrence Brooks, Irra Petina, and John Michael King in important singing parts. Poor attendance closed the show after two weeks. When it closed, the finest musical theatre New York had known closed with it. Joseph Urban's gorgeous, spacious Ziegfeld was demolished shortly after the departure of its last tenant.

An embarrassingly bad attempt to put Marjorie Kinnan Rawlings' once-popular novel, **The Yearling** (12-10-65, Alvin), on the boards met with almost instant disaster. The stage was simply no place to tell a story in which much of the action revolves around a fawn. Jody Baxter's attachment to his yearling and the understanding of life his yearling's death gives Jody might seem moving, if mawkish, on the printed page or even on the screen, but it proved to be one form of realism the stage could not handle. Three performances was the extent of *The Yearling*'s run.

La Grosse Valise (12-14-65, 54th St.) ran twice as long, compiling a total of seven performances. Its brief stay was obviously disappointing, since this Robert Dhery contrivance (with music by Gerard Calvi) had been touted as a sequel to Dhery's *La Plume de Ma Tante*, and had enjoyed some Paris acclaim. The show was a departure from the earlier work in several ways. It had a thin plot line about an enormous trunk that is opened at customs and out of which pours a parade of songs and sketches. But the trunk was little more than a mute compère, and the show, despite its claim to having a book, was a revue. A more meaningful change was the inclusion of a number of songs that suggested they wanted a separate life outside the theatre. The suggestion was underscored by Harold Rome's creating English lyrics for them. In *La Plume de Ma Tante*, the musical numbers had been an integral, unextractable part of the show.

A revival of *Oklahoma!* (3-31-43) with John Davidson and Susan Watson, began a three-week run at the City Center the night after *La Grosse Valise* opened. The revival was the last lyric offering of the year. The first new musical of 1966 didn't arrive until late January, but in many respects it was worth waiting for. **Sweet Charity** (1-29-66, Palace) was a song-and-dance version of Fellini's film, *Nights of Cabiria*, with a pronounced emphasis on the dancing half. Although the popular playwright Neil Simon transferred the work to the stage and reset the the story in New York and although Dorothy Fields and Cy Cole-

man created lyrics and music that were soon causing coins to be fed into juke boxes, the principal
attractions of the evening were the dancing of
Gwen Verdon and the staging of her choreog-
rapher-husband, Bob Fosse. Fosse's stylized clustered posturings soon became something of a
trademark. In Simon's version Charity is a warm-
hearted, unlucky dance hostess at the honky-tonk
Fan-Dango Ballroom. A lonely walk in Central
Park costs her a purse and a dunking in the lake.
She latches on to a famous Italian movie star
(James Luisi), whose date has left him in a huff,
but, when he takes her to his apartment and she
joyously dances with his top hat and cane, his
contrite date reappears, so Charity is relegated to
a closet while the other two make love. At a
YMHA lecture series she meets an accountant
named Oscar (John McMartin). They are
stranded together in an elevator, where she learns
he is claustrophobic, and later stranded in mid-air
on a Coney Island amusement ride, where he discovers she is acrophobic. She lies about her job,
pretending she works in a bank. But Oscar confesses he had known her real employment all
along. Although he insists her past will not interfere with his kind feelings about her, he finally
admits marriage would be impossible. The show
ends with Charity again alone on a park bench.

Some critics were surprised by the amount of
sentimentality in Simon's book and by the lack of
the consistently sharp comedy his straight plays
presented. Reviewers were often even more critical
of the score, which seemed to them lackluster on
first hearing. The public disagreed and within a
short time both "Big Spender" and "Baby, Dream
Your Dream" were being whistled and sung everywhere. Curiously neither of these songs was performed in the show by Miss Verdon; Helen
Gallagher and Thelma Oliver, playing Charity's
sister hostesses, introduced the pair. *Sweet Charity*
brought with it an additional blessing to Broadway
by capturing the historic Palace Theatre for the
legitimate fold. Once the shrine of vaudeville and
long given over to films, it was completely refurbished and, to a small extent, compensated for the
loss of the Ziegfeld.

A white African revue called **Wait a Minim!**
(3-7-66, Golden) and relying heavily on folk
material and folk instruments not always from
Africa, began a long run, repeating a success it
had enjoyed in its homeland and in London. On
those few occasions when they discarded folk
material, the eight cast members took lighthearted
digs at their homeland's racial policies.

Although Duke Ellington was one of the most
respected and successful of the nation's jazz musicians, good luck had always eluded him when he
attempted something for the Broadway stage.
Nothing changed with **Pousse-Café** (3-18-66, 46th
St.). While the skillful Jerome Weidman adapted
the classic 1930 film *The Blue Angel* for the stage,
and while the equally skillful Lilo and Theodore
Bikel re-created the parts Marlene Dietrich and
Emil Janning had played, the show folded after a
humiliating three performances. Weidman moved
the story of the small-town professor ruined by his
infatuation for a minor nightclub performer to
1920 New Orleans. Neither Ellington nor Weidman seemed to care that only one show set in the
Creole city had ever succeeded and that show—
Louisiana Purchase (5-28-40)—made little attempt
to capitalize on the town's colorful atmosphere.
But the intriguing jinx—if it is a jinx—prevailed.

As it did every so often, Broadway put aside its
pretensions and looked to the comic strips for
musical inspiration. Some critics thought **It's a
Bird   It's a Plane   It's SUPERMAN** (3-29-66,
Alvin) better than average foolery. A small cult
formed; but the public at large did not accept its
judgment, and *SUPERMAN* was dealt a knockout
blow by the summer heat. The story would have
done the strip proud. Underneath his everyday
business clothes a mild-mannered newspaper man
Clark Kent (Bob Holiday) wears the flashy tights,
snug-fitting shirt with the big S on the chest and
cape that reveal he is Superman, child of another
planet sent to earth when that planet was destroyed. Kent generally effects his clothes change
in any convenient telephone booth. He works with
pretty Lois Lane (Patricia Marand), who dreams
of being loved by Superman, never for a moment
suspecting he is typing away at the next desk. For
the moment Superman's nemesis is a mad scientist,
Dr. Sedgwick (Michael O'Sullivan). Sedgwick is
embittered because he has never received a Nobel
Prize. He invites Superman to the dedication of a
physics hall he has obsequiously named for the
hero. When the strongman is helplessly occupied
supporting a speaker's collapsed platform, Sedgwick blows up Metropolis' city hall. Although
Superman is reviled in the papers, Sedgwick wants
more than to humble him. He wants Superman
dead. He lures him into a supposed death trap in
a power station by kidnaping Lois. But in "Bow!
Bam! Zonk!" Superman assails Sedgwick and frees
Lois. Sedgwick inadvertently electrocutes himself.
Lois' love for the hero now knows no bounds, but
it is doomed to remain unrequited. A deadly mis-

sile is heading toward Metropolis, and with his "Up, up and away!" Superman flies off to intercept it. Invisible wiring allowed Superman to fly high above the stage; but no mechanism could make the show soar into the hit column. The failure of the show left its songwriters Lee Adams and Charles Strouse still looking for a successor to their *Bye Bye Birdie* (4-14-60).

On April 20 the New York City Light Opera Co. launched a Frank Loesser festival at the City Center. Three of the four openings fell in the current season: *How to Succeed in Business Without Really Trying* (10-14-64) with Billy DeWolfe as Biggley, *The Most Happy Fella* (5-3-56) with Art Lund again singing Joe, followed on May 11 and *Where's Charley?* (10-11-48) with the small part of Donna Lucia D'Alvadorez played by the former Metropolitan Opera prima donna, Eleanor Steber.

Richard Llewellyn's old novel *How Green Was My Valley* was dusted off and theatricalized as **A Time for Singing** (5-21-66, Broadway). Given its Welsh setting it should have occasioned some fine choral singing—and it did. But the music the singers were given was drab and did little to enhance the grim story of the Morgan family's tribulations during accidents and union agitation in their mining town. The show was another of the season's quick flops, leaving after 11 showings.

Mame (5-24-66, Winter Garden), on the other hand, ran and ran, compiling 1,508 performances in New York. It would have been surprising if it hadn't, for Patrick Dennis' irrepressible auntie had made cash registers jingle happily as a novel, a film, and stage play. Jerome Lawrence and Robert E. Lee, who had made the long-run stage adaptation, fashioned the book, and Jerry Herman, whose *Hello, Dolly!* was still packing them in on 44th Street, composed the score. If the show left critics and audiences generally content, it also left many with a sense of *déjà vu* or perhaps *déjà entendu*. The story and even some of the lines had become familiar, but more to the point Mame Dennis (Angela Lansbury) was a sister under the skin to Dolly Gallagher Levi, and Herman seemed to be consciously trying to rewrite some of his old songs to fit new molds. The title song had much the same lilt as his earlier title song and repeated the heroine's name just as incessantly. Its tone was harder and a little more driving than the sunny, affectionate "Hello, Dolly!" but the difference was one of degree not kind. A number of the other tunes possessed a desperate, martial gaiety that seemed a determined effort to invest the evening

with life. But if there was at once something second-hand and second-rate about the score it nonetheless worked effectively in the theatre, especially in the splashy, professional production.

Miss Lansbury's Mame was interrupted in the middle of a chic cocktail party by the arrival of her orphaned ten-year-old nephew, Patrick Dennis (Frankie Daniels), and his timid, prayerful chaperone, Agnes Gooch (Jane Connell). All Mame can think to do is advise him to "circulate." But when the guests have gone. Mame settles down to plan her young ward's education. Over the protestations of a guardian from the bank she enrolls the boy in a progressive school where children spend part of the day naked. With time the two become close, so close Patrick considers Mame "My Best Girl," although Agnes remains as part of the household. But the year is 1929, and the stock market crash leaves Mame without a cent. A job as manicurist leads to a romance with a rich young Southerner (Charles Braswell). His family is snobbish and conspires to break up the affair, but when she actually catches the fox in a hunt, they have no choice but to salute and welcome "Mame." Years pass. Mame's husband has died, and soon she is again ensconced in a luxurious New York apartment. Patrick (now older and played by Jerry Lanning) is courting a light-headed socialite, Gloria Upson (Diane Walker). Mame decides to put an end to the romance because she rightly concludes Gloria is the wrong girl for Patrick. But she also admits she doesn't really want to lose Patrick, a confession she painfully reveals in, "If He Walked Into My Life." She scares away the Upson clan with her plan to build a home to house unwed mothers next door to their property. Still Patrick is of a marriageable age and disposition, so before long he has wed Pegeen Ryan (Diane Coupe). More time passes, Patrick and Pegeen bring their ten-year-old son Michael to Mame, and Mame offers to take him with her around the world. They agree, provided she brings Michael back for the beginning of school on Labor Day. Mame accepts the condition, privately assuring Michael Labor Day is sometime in November. Mame's most hilarious moment came in a parody of an old-time musical comedy number. Since "The Man In The Moon" is a miss, Mame squirms uncomfortably on a gigantic new moon, finally slipping and wrecking the scene. If Miss Lanbury's performance was pivotal, she was handsomely abetted by the hoarse drolleries of Beatrice Arthur as her fairweather friend, Vera. In a backbiting duet, "Bosom Buddies," they stopped the show, especially when Vera assured Mame that she didn't seem old, merely somewhere between "forty and death."

The season's last offering was a revival on May 31 of *Annie Get Your Gun* (5-16-46) by the Music Theatre of Lincoln Center. Because its original star, Ethel Merman, was playing Annie Oakley again twenty-one years after she created the part, some wags referred to the show as "Granny Get Your Gun," but even in the vastness of the New York State Theater Miss Merman had no problem projecting her songs or her personality. Irving Berlin showed his faith in her by giving her a new song, "Old Fashioned Wedding," a contrapuntal number on the order of "You're Just In Love" and "Simple Melody." The book was also slightly revised to make Miss Merman the absolute cynosure by omitting an unimportant secondary love story. With the love story went the lovers' song "Who Do You Love, I Hope." So successful was the revival, if not the new song, that it was taken on a brief tour when *Show Boat* was due and in the next season brought back to a regular Broadway house.

1966-1967

The season opened with the customary City Center and Lincoln Center revivals. *Guys and Dolls* (11-24-50) arrived on June 8 to complete the Frank Loesser festival the 55th Street house had inaugurated at the end of the preceding session. Vivian Blaine was back to re-create her classic Adelaide, while Hugh O'Brian played Sky. *Show Boat* (12-27-27) sailed into the New York State Theatre on July 19. Kern and Hammerstein's masterpiece was attractively mounted and splendidly cast. David Wayne was Cap'n Andy; Barbara Cook, Magnolia; Stephen Douglass, Ravenal; William Warfield, Joe; and Constance Towers, Julie. *Show Boat* played until September 10 when it was taken on the road, where it had disappointing grosses despite good notices.

September's lone musical entry was **A Hand Is on the Gate** (9-21-66, Longacre), as assemblage of Negro poetry and folk song performed by a small cast that included Josephine Premice, James Earl Jones, and Cicely Tyson. A modest enterprise, it met with a modest reception, surviving two and a half weeks.

The New York City Opera made a bow to Broadway when it again inserted *The Consul* into its repertory on October 6. But the season's first more or less traditional musical did not arrive until October, and in this case it was decidedly less traditional than most. In fact, **The Apple Tree** (10-18-66, Shubert) was three one-act pieces presented together as a complete evening. Mark Twain's *The Diary of Adam and Eve* provided the inspiration for the first act. Only three characters appear: a somewhat nervous, obsessive Adam (Alan Alda), a carefree, tactile Eve (Barbara Harris), and the Snake (Larry Blyden), who destroys the couple's bliss by persuading Eve to eat "the rich ripe round red rosy apples." Life outside Eden transforms Adam into a quietly desperate wage-earner and Eve into a resigned housewife. The second act used Frank R. Stockton's famous short story, *The Lady or the Tiger?*, as its source. Probably only a handful in the audience remembered this same story had provided the frame for De Wolf Hopper's full-length musicalization way back in 1888. In the new retelling King Arik (Marc Jordan) catches his war hero, Captain Sanjar (Alda), kissing Princess Barbara (Miss Harris) and sentences him to open one of two doors. A hungry tiger lurks behind one; a beautiful woman whom he must marry awaits him behind the other. His beloved Barbara signals which door he should open. The curtain falls as Stockton's story concluded, without showing which choice Barbara made. The final playlet, based on Jules Feiffer's *Passionella*, finds a little chimneysweep, Ella (Miss Harris), dreaming she has become the famous and glamorous movie star of the title. Her *Passionella* bears a startling physical resemblance to Hollywood's sex symbol, Marilyn Monroe. (Passionella's career is relived in a giant montage of old footage and stills.) In her dream she marries the black-leather-jacketed, hippie rock sensation, Flip (Alda); she awakes to reality and settles for scruffy little George L. Brown (Alda). Jerry Bock and Sheldon Harnick departed from their practice of only writing songs to create (originally with Jerome Coopersmith) the book (or booklets) for the evening. Their work had an admirably consistent style and tone, but not enough punch to revive the tired businessman; nevertheless the show ran out the season.

Neither of the other two October entries was quite in the Broadway mainstream. A Swedish "marionette" version of **The Threepenny Opera** recorded 13 performances at the Billy Rose. The marionettes were not the expected puppets but actors performing behind cut-out figures. Swedish gave way to French four nights later when a one-man show entitled **Gilbert Becaud on Broadway** raised its curtain. Monsieur Becaud spent 19 performances serenading ticketholders with popular French songs. Still a third alien language was heard on the Broadway stage when **Let's Sing Yiddish** led off the parade of November musicals. Using Yiddish folksongs and folktales, the evening was essentially a revue with its first half set in an old world shtetl and its second act in America. The appeal of Yiddish theatre had long since waned, but enough was left to allow the musical to compile 107 performances.

On November 15 another language foreign to many Americans graced the musical stage: the king's English. The D'Oyly Carte began a limited and not too enriching stay at the City Center, giving *The Pirates of Penzance, The Mikado, Ruddigore, H.M.S. Pinafore,* and *Patience.*

The next evening **The Apparition Theater of Prague** opened. A combination of pantomime, ballet, and drama, it depended for effect largely on black-garbed performers moving against black backdrops and working objects covered with luminous paint. The same night saw yet another foreign musical offering premiere. *Les Ballets Africans* was a collection of native dances from French-influenced areas of Africa. The Czechs entertained New York for 21 showings, the Africans for 85.

Not until late November did a musical at once original and traditional open in New York. For being both comfortably daring and derivative it was rewarded with the longest run of the season. **Cabaret** (11-20-66, Broadhurst) was a lyric version of John Van Druten's hit of fifteen years before, *I Am a Camera,* itself a dramatization of earlier Christopher Isherwood stories. Its book was by Joe Masteroff, its lyrics by Fred Ebb, and its music by John Kander. Because it was set in the heyday of the Weill–Brecht collaboration and because its story had something of the epic-drama undercurrents of that team's pieces, the authors and producer-director more than once mimicked the musical styles, orchestrations, and staging techniques associated with *The Threepenny Opera* or *The Rise and Fall of the City of Mahagonny.* The relationship of *Cabaret* to these earlier works was underscored by the presence in the original cast of Lotte Lenya (Weill's wife and the original Polly) in the important role of the landlady, Frau Schneider. But the Weill-Brecht masterpieces were neither slavishly copied nor parodied. *Cabaret*'s creators were solid contemporary craftsman, attuned to the

requirements of the musical theatre of their day and able to fulfill those requirements handsomely.

The curtain is up as the audience enters. A stylized set suggests a sleazy cabaret, the Kit Kat Klub, against a larger background of jazz-age Berlin. A spotlight reveals a heavily made-up Master of Ceremonies (Joel Grey)—white face, rouged cheeks, heavy lashes, and cupid bow lips —who sings a tinny "Willkommen" to his customers in three languages. On a train heading toward this same Berlin, Cliff Bradshaw (Bert Convy), a fledgling American writer, encounters a pleasant young German, Ernst Ludwig (Edward Winter). Ludwig seems to be engaged in some sort of smuggling, and Cliff, a little amused by the whole thing, helps him through customs. The grateful Ernst promises to become Cliff's friend and help open doors for him. Cliff takes a room at Frau Schneider's. The good lady professes to have once been rich and adored. The fates have not been especially kind to her, but she shrugs them off with "So What?" She lives only for the moment, and at this moment another boarder, a Jew named Herr Schultz (Jack Gilford), seems to be on the verge of proposing marriage to her. Cliff visits the Kit Kat Klub, where he meets an English entertainer, Sally Bowles (Jill Haworth). Sally begins to visit Cliff in his room. He is quickly taken by her forlorn charm, finding her "Perfectly Marvelous." Sally's view of life is wholly carpe diem. She insists, "Why should I wake up? This dream is going so well." But the dream has not long to run. Ernst visits Cliff asking him to aid with further smuggling. By now it is clear that Ernst is a Nazi and that the money he keeps bringing in illegally is to aid the Nazi coffers. Cliff demurs. But Ernst does not leave without warning Frau Schneider not to wed Schultz, "He is not a German." A rock thrown through the rooming-house window convinces the landlady of the sad truth behind the young Nazi's threat. Cliff begs Sally to leave Germany with him. Instead, she returns to the Kit Kat Klub. Cliff follows her, and in an argument there with Ernst he is badly beaten by Ernst's henchmen. Sally continues to sing to the club's patrons, telling them life is "Cabaret" and inviting each and every "old chum" to come to the cabaret. When Cliff learns that Sally has had an abortion, paying for it with her fur coat, he walks out of her life. Alone on the train heading out of Germany, he begins to write his reminiscences. The Master of Ceremonies appears again, and in three languages wishes the audience good-bye.

Although inevitably there was a mixing of

contemporary sounds with sounds of the show's era, *Cabaret* had a generally consistent, evocative sense of time and place. It poignantly portrayed the seediness and forced gaiety of Berlin night life as the Nazi menace grew. Not even intermission was allowed to break the spell. With the curtain remaining up, the Kit Kat Klub's all-girl band played jazzily until the action resumed. Grey had the evening's best notices. His appearances were far more numerous than the brief summary of the show suggests; he appeared in all the scenes at the Kit Kat Klub, singing several numbers with the chorus line. But as so often happens with scenes set in nightclubs, the songs had little relevance to the main action other than to underscore the era's tinselly, unwholesome attempts at escape. In *Cabaret*'s case these nightclub songs were among the weaker numbers in the show, put across largely because of fine staging and Grey's chilly brilliance. Audiences by now had become inured to the realistic librettos of the modern American Musical Theatre. *Cabaret* ran 1,165 performances in New York and toured successfully, although it was one of the rare modern Broadway hits that London failed to take to its heart.

One not insignificant reason for *Cabaret*'s immediate popularity was the relative emptiness of the musicals that followed it. Within a month three more new book musicals appeared. In all three instances the main attraction of the evening was appealing performers. The shows met with varying degrees of success—and failure. The first to arrive was **Walking Happy** (11-26-66, Lunt-Fontanne), a musical version of Harold Brighouse's *Hobson's Choice*. Hobson in this case was not the legendary English liveryman but Maggie Hobson (Louise Troy), daughter of a Lancashire shoemaker. To her father's consternation Maggie falls in love with his meek, bungling apprentice, Will Mossop (Norman Wisdom). In short order she makes Will into a fine shoemaker as well as a husband. The score for the evening was by James Van Heusen with lyrics by Sammy Cahn. The two had provided the songs for the preceding season's *Skyscraper* (11-13-65). Their material for *Walking Happy* represented a decline from even *Skyscraper*'s modest attainments. For most theatregoers the principal inducement to line up at the box office was to watch the antics of the pint-sized English comic Norman Wisdom. Unfortunately, he was not well-known enough to help the show survive more than 20 weeks. The show's closing brought to an unhappy end the once astonishingly successful New York career of it producers, Feuer and Martin.

An even more amazingly successful producing career was slowly winding down when David Merrick escorted in **I Do! I Do!** (12-5-66, 46th St.). The show was a musical version of Jan de Hartog's *The Fourposter,* a two-character comedy that had originally opened on Broadway a few weeks before the premiere of *I Am a Camera, Cabaret*'s source. Once again the bedroom was its sole setting and a husband and wife its only characters. The play begins just before the turn of the century with the wedding of Michael and Agnes, and then follows the couple through the joys and tribulations of fifty years of married life. The joys include the births of their children, celebrated in "My Cup Runneth Over," while tribulations come to a head just before the first-act curtain when Michael reveals he has had an extramarital affair. He staunchly proclaims it is "A Well Known Fact" that midde-aged men are especially attractive to many women. Furious and hurt, Agnes dons an extravagantly feathered hat and announces she will turn herself into a sexually stimulating creature everyone will call "Flaming Agnes." At loggerheads, the two agree "The Honeymoon Is Over." But affection and good sense prevail. The marriage continues on its inexorable road until old age forces Michael and Agnes to give up their large house. Another young couple are taking their place, so just before they depart they leave a bottle of champagne on the bed, covering the bottle with a pillow on which has been inscribed "God is Love."

Inevitably the musicalization of so intimate a play led to additional theatricalization, but Harvey Schmidt and Tom Jones never let their changes vulgarize the material. Unfortunately, their good taste was not matched by any telling inspiration. Nothing from the work achieved the popularity of their material for *The Fantasticks* (5-3-60). *I Do! I Do!*'s run of over a year was attributable to the appeal of its two stars, Mary Martin and Robert Preston, and to Gower Champion's lively staging. Typical of Champion's inventiveness was the dance he gave Preston to accompany "I Love My Wife." Something between a soft-shoe and tap routine, Preston performed it barefoot, in a dressing gown, with top hat and cane.

Ten nights later **A Joyful Noise** (12-15-66, Hellinger) began a brief stay. Based on Borden Deal's novel, *The Insolent Breed*, it recounted the courtship of Jenny Lee (Susan Watson) by the wandering minstrel, Shade Motley (John Raitt). Shade is run out of little Macedonia, Tennessee, by Jenny Lee's father, but he moves on to become a success at Nashville's Grand Ole Opry. The prospect of a rich, settled life in Nashville holds little interest for Shade. His love for Jenny Lee and his wanderlust bring him back to Macedonia. Obviously the show's music relied heavily on the popular country and western folk music styles of the day. But the newly created "folk" songs offered nothing memorable, and the show folded after a mere 12 performances. Raitt must have watched with a certain bittersweet curiosity the revival of *Carousel* (4-19-45), which opened at the City Center the same evening *A Joyful Noise* opened. Raitt, of course, had been *Carousel*'s original Billy Bigelow. The revival outran Raitt's new vehicle by a week.

Donald Swann, playing the piano, and Michael Flanders, reciting from his wheelchair, returned two nights after Christmas with their second two-man show, **At the Drop of Another Hat** (12-27-66, Booth). It suffered the fate of most sequels, falling far short of the vogue of the original. But it was by no means a failure. The Englishmen regaled audiences until early April of 1967.

Oddly it was almost April before another musical arrived. **Sherry!** (3-27-67, Alvin) was a musical version of Kaufman and Hart's 1939 hit, *The Man Who Came to Dinner*. As he had twenty-seven years before, Sheridan Whiteside (Clive Revill) finds himself confined after a fall in the Mesalia, Ohio, home of the confortably bourgeois Stanleys. He proceeds to disrupt the household with his imperious ways until his hosts soon pray for his early departure. Catastrophically, the adaptation was put into relatively inexperienced hands. The show's weaknesse were aggravated by cast problems during the tryout. The show New York finally saw was anything but the riotously festive romp the straight play version had been. *Sherry!* struggled along for nine weeks before throwing in the towel.

April was a remarkably busy month. **Hello, Solly!,** a Yiddish-English vaudeville, began the parade on the 4th. No one seriously confused its title with the musical at the St. James, and David Merrick, *Dolly*'s producer, didn't even attempt to get some free publicity with a prestaged hassle. The new piece ran 68 performances at Henry Miller's lovely theatre (shortly to be converted to a pornographic movie house) and left quietly.

The City Center offered a spring season of three revivals, beginning with *Finian's Rainbow* (1-10-47) with Nancy Dussault as Sharon on April 5. *The Sound of Music* (11-16-59) featuring Bob Wright and Constance Towers followed three weeks later, and *Wonderful Town* (2-25-53), starring Elaine Stritch, brought up the rear on May 14.

Esthetically and commercially, Broadway musicalizations of Hollywood films had rarely proved satisfying, but this disappointing history refused to discourage new attempts. In one respect **Ilya Darling** (4-11-67, Hellinger) seemed to stand a better chance to bridge the forms sucessfully than had most earlier efforts, for the show was a lyric stage version of *Never on Sunday*, with a libretto by the same man, Jules Dassin, who had created the piece for the screen and with its charismatic star, Melina Mercouri, repeating her movie role. Ilya is a prostitute, working the waterfront in modern Piraeus. She is an open-handed and open-hearted girl who plies her trade only from Monday through Saturday, leaving Sunday open to entertain friends and customers lavishly at her own expense. Her carefree life is disrupted by the arrival of an American tourist, a teacher named, curiously, Homer Thrace (Orson Bean). He determines to make a good woman of Ilya. For a while he appears to succeed. He gets her to abandon her old ways and gives her instructions in the liberal arts. Happy with the change he has wrought, he even tries to convert Ilya's fellow prostitutes. He ends by antagonizing them and by making Ilya realize how unnaturally constrained her new existence is. She gratefully reverts to her old ways, and Homer, coming to understand that she was a good woman before he met her, returns home wiser if not happier.

The music for the show was by Manos Hadjidakis, a Greek whose exile had made him a something of a *cause célèbre*. Hadjidakis had written the score for the motion picture, and the popularity of its title song played no small part in the film's success. His new score was often zestful, but never outstandingly memorable. Ilya inevitably suffered from limitations the stage imposed on the free flow of the film script. Although Oliver Smith's scenery moved back and forth between Ilya's apartment, the Acropolis, tavernas, and shipyards in Piraeus, it could not capture the sun-splashed, sea-washed abandon of the film. David Ewen gives a telling example of a scene that could not be transferred to the stage in which Ilya, wearing a revealing bathing suit, goes for a swim in the harbor, prompting scores of sailors and fisherman to jump in after her. The show was most successful in it intimate moments, notably when Ilya teaches an innocent American sailor the facts of life in "Love, Love, Love." Thanks largely to Miss Mercouri's presence, the show was able to run, with some forcing, for 318 performances.

April's last offering was the only new book musical of the season to have a libretto not based on an earlier work. But **Hallelujah, Baby!** (4-26-67, Beck) (exclamation points were the rage of the season) did not resort to a carefully plotted, crescendoing story. Instead it employed the device used some years before in *Love Life*, a chronicle extending over a number of years in which the principals, nonetheless, never age. In this case the principals are Georgina (Leslie Uggams), a twenty-five-year-old black woman; her black boy friend, Clam (Robert Hooks), and her white lover, Harvey (Allen Case). After a brief introduction in which Georgina explains the nature of the evening, the setting hurtles back to the turn of the century. Georgina, made by her mother to clean the floor of their simple home, sings longingly of "My Own Morning." When she discovers Clem has lost their wedding money in a crap game, she leaves for New York to earn her way in show business. She scores a quick success in a 1920 cabaret. When the depression hits, Georgina finds herself in a breadline with only the paltry sums doled out by the Federal Theatre to sustain her hope. World War II brings recovery, and Georgina goes to work in a cheap night club near an army base. By the fifties she is a major night club star. Her success with the white world alienates Clem, who has embraced the civil rights movement. But in the sixties, Georgina contrives a happy ending rousingly assuring everyone "Now's The Time."

The evening had a solidly crafted score by Jule Styne and lyrics by Comden and Green. Though the music was essentially contemporary, Styne was careful to suggest the correct patterns and flavor of each period the show passed through. Curiously, the show was at its best re-creating the black-inspired jazz of the twenties. Georgina sang and the appropriately named Tip and Tap (Winston De Witt Hemsley and Alan Weeks) danced to the infectious beat of "Feet Do Yo' Stuff." Unfortunately, Arthur Laurents' book could not make up its mind whether it wanted to be an entertainment or a politcal tract. His preachings on racism worked against the entertainment of the rest of the show. Happily, Miss Uggams' charm made the show palatable and kept it on stage for nine months.

The season concluded with a third Yiddish musical, **Sing Israel Sing** (5-11-67, Atkinson), built around a joyous kibbutz wedding. The musical's appeal was limited, and it closed after two weeks so that it could be translated into English in hopes of finding a larger audience.

In this season of librettos that were more chronicles than tightly knit plots, the most successful of the off-Broadway shows fell in with the vogue. **You're a Good Man, Charlie Brown** (3-7-67, 80 St. Marks) was populated with youngsters from Charles M. Schulz' adored comic strip *Peanuts*. With becoming and sensible modesty this low-budget show chronicled a very limited time-span—one day in the life of Charlie (Gary Burghoff) and his friends. All the well-known figures were present; Charlie, of course, Lucy (Reva Rose), Linus (Bob Balaban), Schroeder (Skip Hinnant), and even the dog Snoopy (Bill Hinnant). The vignettes depicting them followed no real pattern, seeming almost as haphazard as their childish world. After an opening paean to Charlie ("You could be King. If only you weren't so wishywashy)," Lucy dreams of being a queen and bossing the world ("Queen Lucy"); Linus sings of his need for his security blanket ("My Blanket And Me"); Snoopy plans to capture the Red Baron, while a baseball game (where Charlie's teammates sing a rousing "T.E.A.M.") degenerates into a poll gauging Lucy's popularity. In the end the youngsters and the dog each give his idea of what true happiness is, with Charlie Brown concluding "happiness" is "anyone and anything that's loved by you." Clark Gesner wrote both the libretto and the songs. Although nothing from the evening enjoyed a vogue outside the theatre, the show itself repeated something of the phenomenal success of the comic strip. Road companies were set up to tour regular sized legitimate theaters (one ran a year at the Wilbur in Boston), while the New York contingent tallied 1,597 showings.

1967-1968

The parade of mediocrities continued. One new revue and eleven new book shows presented themselves for New York's evaluation. Almost without exception they received low grades. The single runaway hit of the season, *Hair*, began promisingly downtown, caught on uptown because of sensational publicity accorded a nude scene and ultimately settled down to a long run when its superb score received wide play. Yet for all its deserved success, it was far from flawless. Among the other musical offerings only *George M.* managed a full year's stay. It survived largely on the appeal of its turn-of-the-century Cohan melodies and, to a lesser extent, the performance of Joel Grey in the title role. Star performances were the only explanation for the season's two other relatively long runs. All in all, a sad year for the American Musical Theatre—uptown. But *Hair* was not alone in providing off-Broadway with exciting new ideas for the lyric stage. Throughout the season, small, out-of-the-way houses raised their curtains on innovative, satisfying musicals that put the big time to shame.

The season began with the promised English translation of *Sing Israel Sing*. The new language infused no new life in the show. One additional week was all it could garner.

The Music Theatre of Lincoln Center revived *South Pacific* (4-7-49) with Florence Henderson and the Metropolitan Opera's Giorgio Tozzi on June 12 and ran it until September 9 for a total of 104 performances. Ominously, inflationary costs had prompted the dropping of a two-show season.

When *Sweet Charity* ended its stay at the Palace, the great old flagship of vaudeville spent the summer months, while waiting for its next legitimate offering, hosting a number of contemporary vaudeville bills. The *Best Plays* volume for the year lists them as revues—and indeed they were little different from the one-man shows that recently had played standard auditoriums. But vaudeville at the Palace, if only for sentimental reasons, stands somewhat apart. For the record, headliners included Judy Garland, Eddie Fisher, and Buddy Hackett. Marlene Dietrich competed with them across Times Square at the Lunt-Fontanne.

While Broadway bided its time, off-Broadway came alive. The mushrooming protest against the Vietnam War was the theme of **Now Is the Time for All Good Men** (9-26-67, de Lys), a musical that occupied the same stage so long given over to *The Threepenny Opera*. The new work followed the downfall of a popular young teacher, Mike Butler (David Cryer), after the small, conservative town of Bloomdale, Indiana, discovers he has been imprisoned for refusing to fight. The show was perhaps more preachy than entertaining, but Greenwich Village proved far more sympathetic to its outlook than Bloomdale might have, so the show ran to December 31. In a few weeks *Hair*,

preaching much the same message, would elicit a more enthusiastic response.

Broadway had no interest in preaching, but its very first major musical offering suggested it had little ability to entertain either. Nunnally Johnson, so long successful in Hollywood, adapted his daughter Nora's novel *The World of Henry Orient* first into a film and then into a stage musical, calling the latter **Henry, Sweet Henry** (10-23-67, Palace), with music by Bob Merrill and with Don Ameche as star. The sweet Henry of the title is an unattached man-about-town who finds his footsteps dogged by a lonesome, neglected infatuated teen-ager, Valerie Boyd (Robin Wilson). For the ten weeks the show survived some of the biggest applause was awarded to Alice Playten, who clowned her way through the evening as a second teen-ager, the brattish Kafritz.

Over a month elapsed before another major mounting appeared uptown. But off-Broadway was bursting with energy and song. *Hair* was unveiled for a limited run to October 29 at the New York Shakespeare Festival Public Theater. It received generally favorable notices, and theatregoers responded in sufficient numbers to move it to a second small off-Broadway house until the end of January. By that time demand for seats had reached the point where a run in a larger uptown Broadway house was called for. The show was closed, expanded, and revised. It will be treated more fully under its Broadway opening.

In Circles (11-5-67, Cherry Lane) was an offbeat revue based on Gertrude Stein material and with music by Al Carmines. One critic described it as "A complex arrangement of word, song and dance effects, each one conceived as describing its own circles." Carmines became one of the most praised and sought after of off-Broadway composers, but unlike so many of his associates he never earned the affection of the public at large nor succeeded uptown. He did, however, prosper handsomely with the new show, which ran out the season.

World turmoil and the decline of theatrical creativity sent many benumbed and bored playgoers in search of the joys and certainties of the good old days, even if they were the good old days of the depression. Since Hollywood was not given to burlesquing its old movies, Broadway took it upon itself to do the job. The first of several musical plays kidding screen musicals of the thirties attacked one of the most obvious targets, Shirley Temple. **Curley McDimple** (11-22-67, Wheeler) spent the evening spoofing the inanities of the child star's films so well it compiled a run of 931 performances before New York would let it go. Bayn Johnson was Curley.

When Broadway finally got around to unveiling its second major new musical of the season, it did at least offer something of a rarity—a show based on an "original idea." Regrettably its setting, the world of Wall Street, and its title, **How Now, Dow Jones** (12-7-67, Lunt-Fontanne), seemed suspiciously close to *How To Succeed in Business Without Really Trying* (10-14-61). Even more regrettably, it wasn't a particularly well-written piece. The original idea, however, was the sort that had propped up many a show in a less demanding day. Charley (Anthony Roberts), a young man trying to succeed, has promised to marry his girl Kate (Marilyn Mason), who works on Wall Street, just as soon as the Dow Jones average hits 1000. Kate issues a report showing the figure has been reached, and it takes all of the second act to put things back in order. The show ran out the season, thanks in no small parts to the determination of producer David Merrick.

The City Center gave New Yorkers a pleasant holiday gift with a low-priced revival of *Brigadoon* (3-13-47), with Bill Hayes and Russell Nype, that opened on December 13 and closed New Year's Eve.

From April 25 to May 19 the Center mounted a repertory of Gilbert and Sullivan works that included *The Pirates of Penzance, H.M.S. Pinafore, The Mikado, The Yeomen of the Guard,* and *Patience.* Later the house closed the year by offering a revival of *The King and I* with Constance Towers again Anna. The show had been revived four years earlier at Lincoln Center. Yet, though the City Center was soon to have no competition, it remained steadfastly in the rut of reviving the biggest hits of recent years. This repetition, as much as inflation, was soon to bring its quarter-of-a-century history to an end.

One more play with music appeared before 1967 went on its way. But **How To Be a Jewish Mother** (12-28-67, Hudson) was no more a full-fledged musical than was its first cousin, *The Zulu and the Zayda* (11-10-65). It was a two-character comedy, a series of sketches in which a middle-aged Jewish mother and a slightly baffled Negro interact. Five songs were interspersed. It was also, in any case a quick flop, leaving two fine performers, Molly Picon and Godfrey Cambridge, at liberty again.

The differences and similarities between the first off-Broadway show of 1968 and the first uptown production were revealing. In a sad, curious way the similarities loomed larger in the long run. Both followed the now almost universal practice of deriving their material from an old show. Both relied heavily for effect on the use of filmed projections. And saddest of all, but again typical of the modern American musical, both failed to produce a single song inventive and melodic enough to survive the show. But the off-Broadway show, like *Hair* before it, brought the latest musical sound, rock-and-roll, to the American Musical Theatre, while the big uptown production embraced, however feebly, more traditional idioms. Equally significantly, the little show on the edge of Greenwich Village, using minimal sets and employing unknown performers, depended often on trenchant, relevant wit, while the mammoth mounting just off Times Square required stars to gloss over deficiencies.

The off-Broadway musical, **Your Own Thing** (1-13-68, Orpheum), arrived first. A lyric adaptation of Shakespeare's *Twelfth Night,* it adroitly welded Shakespeare's story and some of his dialogue with the latest in teen-age speech and rock music. In this retelling the action transpires in "Manhattan Island, Illyria" where Orson (Tom Ligon) is a theatrical agent and Olivia (Marcia Rodd) the operator of a discotheque. The confusion between Viola and her brother Sebastian seemed more understandable than it probably had been at anytime since Elizabethan days because of the long hair teen-age boys were wearing during this period. In the show Viola (Leland Palmer) and Sebastian (Rusty Thacker), both rock singers who have been separated and have lost all their music in a shipwreck, coincidentally apply to the same agent when they seek work. Viola, informed that Orson requires a male singer for a rock group, dresses as a boy and calls herself Charlie. When Orson sends Charlie with a love letter to Olivia, the familiar complications ensue. In the end Viola is engaged to Orson and Sebastian to Olivia. Sebastian is not at all disturbed by Olivia's being a good ten years older than he. As he and his rock group, the Apocalypse, enjoin their listeners, "do your own thing —or die." The use of photographs with voiced comments was one of the highlights of the production, brilliantly blending Shakespeare and pertinent contemporary asides. The very first slide showed Everett Dirksen, a Senate leader and flowery orator, while a voice not unlike his read the opening of *Twelfth Night*—"If music be the food of love, play on!"—only to add, "I can't remember if that's Marlowe or Bacon." Queen Elizabeth, Humphrey Bogart, Michelangelo's Sistine God, and John Wayne have a hilarious discourse, with Wayne lamenting he can no longer tell boys from girls because of the long hair. At the very end of the show, the Sistine God calls out to Jesus, and, when Christ responds "Yes father?," God inquires, "When are you going to get your hair cut?" The show ran 933 performances at its small downtown house, but like *You're A Good Man, Charlie Brown,* road companies were sent out to play regular legitimate theatres. The companies established contemporary records on several of their stands.

The uptown show was **The Happy Time** (1-18-68, Broadway), a musical rendering of Samuel Taylor's 1950 hit of the same name, which itself was based on a book by Robert L. Fontaine. It was another David Merrick production which ran as long as it did because of the producer's heavy publicity and timely forcing. Merrick was not aided by his authors, playwright N. Richard Nash and the songwriters of *Cabaret* (11-20-66), composer John Kander and lyricist Fred Ebb. Their work was solid but uninspired. The story recorded the growing up and coming of age of young Bibi Bonnard (Mike Rupert) in the bosom of his loving, eccentric French-Canadian family. Because Robert Goulet and David Wayne were the stars, there was some change of emphasis from the straight play, but there was no change in its warm, affectionate tone. Goulet portrayed a footloose photographer whose recollections shaped the plot, while Wayne was the baffled, but understanding pater familias. In a red top hat, Wayne stopped the show recounting his feats as a ladies' man in "The Life Of The Party." Gower Champion furthered the action with clever filmed sequences. In an urgent quest for novelty to mask a lack of quality, gimmicks such as eschewing an overture appeared. But they neither helped nor hindered the evening.

A small-scale "cabaret revue," with just four performers, devoted entirely to the songs and commentary of one man opened January 22 at the Village Gate. It was not the sort of entertainment one would expect to enjoy a long life, but the Belgian Jacques Brel had gathered about him so loyal, persuasive a cult that by the time **Jacques Brel Is Alive and Well and Living in Paris** closed it had run up an astounding 1,847 performances, making it the third longest engagement in off-Broadway history. The adoration accorded Brel is hinted at in the title. For at the time, when some theologians were asking "Is God dead?" others were replying that God was alive and well in various locations. Mort Shuman helped adapt it and starred, but Ellie Stone was the performer everyone remembered.

On January 27 **Darling of the Day** (1-27-68, Abbott) premiered. Taking as its source a somewhat unlikely prospect for musicalization, Arnold Bennett's *Buried Alive,* it retold in song and dance the courtship by mail of Alice Challice, widow of the valet of the famous artist, Priam Farll, by none other than Farll himself. He stoops to conquer, assuming the identity of a valet. The book was originally credited to Nunnally Johnson, who had perhaps hoped to erase the demerit he received on his return to Broadway earlier in the season for *Henry, Sweet Henry.* But his latest adaptation proved even less stageworthy than his former. By the time *Darling of the Day* reached Broadway, his name had been dropped from the credits and the authorship of the book was left for the audiences to guess at. Composer Jule Styne and lyricist E. Y. Harburg allowed their names to remain on the program, although nothing they offered caught the public's fancy. By common consent the highlight of the evening was the desperate-faced, captivating, clowning of the English comedienne, Patricia Routledge, as Alice. The popular screen actor Vincent Price was her leading man.

In the fourteen years that had passed since the original *House of Flowers* (12-30-54) closed, persistent stories had blamed the show's failure on changes made during its Philadelphia tryout. Saint-Subber, the producer of the ill-fated venture, apparently agreed and retained enough faith in the Harold Arlen–Truman Capote work to chance a revival. Unfortunately, since the new production on January 28 was to be at the tiny off-Broadway Theatre de Lys, the evocative, lavishly praised Oliver Messel sets were not re-created. Five new songs were added. The show was coolly received and quickly closed, leaving unanswered whether the first mounting, before tinkering, had been as good as its boosters believed.

Steve Lawrence and his wife Eydie Gorme were still sufficiently potent drawing cards to let producers ignore Lawrence's unprofessional behavior during the stay of *What Makes Sammy Run?* (2-27-64) and create a new vehicle for the couple, **Golden Rainbow** (2-4-68, Shubert). Arnold Schulman's play of several seasons back, *A Hole in the Head,* was selected for adaptation. Moving the action from Miami to Las Vegas allowed for splashier, noisier production numbers, but the basic story remained. Larry Davis is a widower with two passions in life: his down-at-the-heels hotel and his young son, Ally (Scott Jacoby). But Larry stands to lose both. The hotel may be taken from him if he cannot meet a mortgage payment; his son may be given over to his sister-in-law, who has claimed Ally is not being given a wholesome upbringing. Much of Judy's vehement moralizing masks her love for her brother-in-law. Her real feelings are revealed in the course of the evening and by curtain time she has given Larry the money he needs for the mortgage and accepted his proposal of marriage. Ernest Kinoy's libretto was workmanlike though it sacrificed some depth by concentrating on the stars. At least one of the songs for which Walter Marks wrote both words and music, "I've Got To Be Me," met with popular acclaim. The show ran just short of one year.

Two foreign offerings followed. **The Grand Music Hall of Israel** began a 64-performance stay early in February, while *Les Ballets Africains* returned toward the end of the months to give 55 additional performances.

March's lone entry was a lyric version of John Steinbeck's novel *East of Eden*, retitled confidently **Here's Where I Belong** (3-3-68, Rose). New Yorkers didn't agree, and the piece closed ignominiously after just one showing. The authors were largely untried in the Broadway arena. Although they wisely attempted to cut down to workable size Steinbeck's vast romantic canvas of California farm country during World War I, concentrating on the father and son relationship between Adam Trask (Paul Rogers) and young Caleb (Walter McGinn), the material proved intractable in their inexperienced hands.

A number of other relatively inexperienced hands had only slightly better luck with **The Education of H*Y*M*A*N K*A*P*L*A*N** (4-4-68, Alvin), a musical version of Leo Rosten's collections of short stories. Set in New York on the Lower East Side across the country from *Here's Where I Belong*'s locale, but in almost the same era, the years immediately after World War I, the scenes depicted the eager efforts of a band of Jewish immigrants to make themselves at home in their new world. But again craftsmanship was wanting, and the appeal of Jewish themes was becoming a bit overexploited. Despite Tom Bosley's attractive performance as Hyman, the tailor, the new show lasted a mere three and a half weeks.

But the appeal of George M. Cohan and his songs of a happier Broadway was evident in long lines at the box office even before **George M!** (4-10-68, Palace) opened. A loosely thrown together biography of the great song-and-dance man, with a comparatively small cast that found itself playing a number of roles, it nevertheless was at once reasonably faithful and, when Cohan's songs were being sung, enthralling entertaining. Unlike the film biography of Cohan, *George M!* had no qualms about portraying his first marriage. It moved from his early vaudeville, his initially cool reception, his triumph and his sad disillusionment late in life. Unlike James Cagney, Joel Grey made no attempt to mimic Cohan's mannerisms. Though the *Times'* saluted his performance as "sharp as a whiplash," dissenters missed Cohan's warmth. Cohan might have been better honored by an honest revival of one of his masterpieces, but with little competition around the public asked no questions, so *George M!* ran over a year.

The third and final new musical in April was **I'm Solomon** (4-23-68, Hellinger), another Jewish theme by more inexperienced authors. It ran seven performances. There were a few departures in the show. For one, the setting was biblical, and, two, the authors, apparently aware of their own inadequacies, allowed interpolations—a policy virtually extinct in the American Musical Theatre. One number had lyrics by Erich Segal, a young scholar who went on to write the best-selling novel, *Love Story*. The plot employed a folk motif as old as the musical setting—the look-alike commoner who substitutes for his king. In this case the commoner was Yoni (Dick Shawn), a cobbler in ancient Jerusalem whose resemblance to King Solomon (Shawn) allows the monarch to leave his throne and move among his people. Sadly, the show's failure deprived the theatregoers of a chance to savor Rouben Ter-Arutunian's scenery that poetically mixed Eastern with anachronistic Art Nouveau motifs.

The expanded, revised **Hair** reopened uptown at the Biltmore on April 29. In every respect—commercial, historic, esthetic—it was far and away the most important musical offering of the season, possibly of the era. And yet, inexplicably, it was in some ways a tragic failure. The book uptown first-nighters saw and the book played by the road companies and, in general, by the overseas editions was a decimated version of the already relatively plotless story told earlier downtown. Rambling, almost formless, if it had a central figure at all it was probably Claude (James Rado), a long-haired, sometimes bewildered, rebel against what his hippie culture termed "The Establishment." Brooklyn-bred, he romantically lies that he comes from Manchester, England—perhaps mistaking it as the home of the greatest of all rock groups, The Beatles. He billets himself in the small apartment shared by his friend Berger (Gerome Ragni) and Berger's girl, Sheila (Lynn Kellogg). His own girl,

Jeannie (Sally Eaton), is pregnant with someone else's child. Problems of racial inequality, drugs, homosexuality, poverty, and free love rear their heads, often without motivation or connection with the plot, but long enough to allow strongly worded protests in song. Claude's pivotal dilemma is whether or not to burn his draft card and join the growing draft evasion movement. Puzzlingly, he elects to accept the Establishment's rules, allowing himself to be drafted. He is killed, and his friends gather to mourn his useless, unnecessary death.

At a time when tightly knit librettos were often propping up disappointing, unmelodic, or pretentious scores, the book for *Hair* represented a startling reversion to an older approach to musical theatre. It did follow the pattern of its day by offering some very imaginative, impressive staging. Indeed, staging was coming to outclass even librettos as the mainstay of the modern musical—a phenomenon in itself a reversion to the still earlier musical theatre of *The Black Crook* (9-12-1866) and the Kiralfys. Tom O'Horgan, called in to restage the production for uptown, filled the evening with theatric pyrotechnics. The show's most notorious scene placed a number of nude men and women at the front of the stage during the first-act finale. Flickering, relatively dim lights assured that the scene was more sensational than revealing. At one point cast members dressed as policemen rushed down the aisles from the back of the house scaring more gullible patrons by announcing they were raiding the show. But the telling strength of *Hair* was its score—rich in melody and, more importantly, finally working a thoroughly contemporary musical sound into the Broadway mainstream. *Bye, Bye Birdie* (4-14-60) had employed some rock-and-roll sounds to tell a story in which a rock-and-roll star figured prominently, but its delightful score was, for the most part, doggedly traditional. *Hair* accepted no such compromise. From beginning to end Galt MacDermot's music and Gerome Ragni and James Rado's lyrics—all much expanded for the uptown version—utilized nothing but the chromatics, rhythms, and word patterns of the new form. Somehow, though, MacDermot's strong, memorable melodies imposed themselves over the incessant throbbings of rock orchestration, and even Ragni and Rado's lyrics, while a far cry from the polished rhymes of Broadway's masters, avoided pitfalls presented by the often languid, monotonous, and expository words to most songs in the style. The sweet, soft optimism of "Good Morning Starshine" and the more exulting hopefulness of "Aquarius" quickly attained universal recognition. In the show the irrelevant non sequiturs of "Frank Mills," in which an otherwise unimportant character named Crissy (Shelley Plimpton) stoically accepts the ups and downs of her teen-age passion, were a nightly show-stopper. If the songs' lyrics seemed a bit odd and uncomfortable, it was because in this instance MacDermot had wryly set prose to music. The tremendous popularity of the show's music ultimately outweighed the scandal of the nude scene in accounting for the evening's success. For many staid, older playgoers in the audience *Hair* allowed a brief, vicarious participation in the protest movements of the sixties. *Hair* ran a total of 1,844 performances in its uptown and downtown engagements, three less than *Jacques Brel*. But there was of course no comparison. *Hair* played a large, regular theatre for all but the first three months of its life, and its numerous companies across the country and in foreign theatrical capitals generally played in the best houses. (Still it is noteworthy that the four longest running musicals of the season were off-Broadway creations.)

In a very important sense, though, *Hair* was a failure, for it failed to usher in a new era in the American Musical Theatre. Though rock continued to dominate popular song for years to come, it played little further part on the Broadway musical scene. The contrast in this respect between *Hair* and, say, *Watch Your Step!* (12-8-14)—which also suffered from a weak "book, if any"—or *Lady, Be Good!* (12-1-24), is saddening. The fault cannot be laid at the feet of the new sound, however untheatrical, unmelodic, and uninteresting it often seems. The authors of *Hair* proved this need not be the case. But, as with swing, Broadway had apparently grown too old and decrepit to embrace youthful forms.

Since Leonard Sillman was no longer the producer, but merely the director, some perverse Broadway politicking included his name in the official title of the show, **Leonard Sillman's New Faces of 1968** (5-2-68, Booth). The revue kidded everything from Greek tragedy (in "Hullabaloo at Thebes") to saccharine beauty pageants (in "Missed America"). The evening was not well received and none of the new faces went on to become familiar faces on Broadway as had several performers in earlier editions. This edition has been the last of the series to date, though there are promises every season or two of another.

1968-1969

During the first months of the new season the American Musical Theatre seemed to be sinking deeper into the preceding season's mire. The escalation of the Vietnam War, the shock of President Johnson's decision not to run again, and the ensuing election campaign between Richard Nixon and Hubert Humphrey offered Americans more gripping if less diverting occupation. Not until the middle of November, just after the election, did Broadway come to life. In retrospect some of the excitement and success seems as much a reaction to months of mediocrity as witness to any genuine overriding merit.

The summer months and early fall were rife with revivals. June saw mountings of *My Fair Lady* (3-15-56) with Fritz Weaver and Inga Swenson at the City Center and *West Side Story* (9-26-57) at the New York State. The Lerner and Loewe masterpiece recorded an additional two and a half weeks, while the Laurents-Sondheim-Bernstein opus ran until September. In December the City Center revived *Carnival* (4-13-61), with tiny Pierre Olaf re-creating his poignant role.

Noel Coward's Sweet Potato (9-29-68, Barrymore), a revue anthologizing some of Coward's best material, chalked up 44 showings in two slightly separated engagements.

October was busy although not especially fruitful. In the first week of the month Marlene Dietrich and Gilbert Becaud brought back their one-man programs, the quasi-legendary Miss Dietrich far outrunning M. Becaud.

A Yiddish-English musical, **The Megilla of Itzik Manger,** arrived from Israel and pleased a specialized audience for two months at the small John Golden Theatre. The musical took the biblical story of Esther and transplanted it in a European shtetl.

The season's first original American musical was neither very original nor 100 percent Yankee, being a musical version of George Bernard Shaw's *Ceasar and Cleopatra.* Rechristened **Her First Roman** (10-20-68, Lunt-Fontanne), it had book, lyrics, and music by Ervin Drake, another relatively inexperienced hand. Richard Kiley moved over from playing Don Quixote to portray Caesar, while the young black, Leslie Uggams, impersonated Cleopatra. As in Shaw's comedy, the sometimes naïve, sometimes wily queen has a brief one-sided romance with the great emperor and in the end must accept his promise to send her a handsome young soldier named Marc Antony. If the producers were hoping the great Shaw would provide the basis for another *My Fair Lady* (3-15-56), their hopes were quickly dashed. *Her First Roman* folded after two weeks.

A second new musical by unknowns, **Maggie Flynn** (10-23-68, ANTA), fared only a little better. Its story reflected the same racial ecumenism as its casting and the casting of *Her First Roman.* Set at the time of the Civil War draft riots, when Irish protestors lynched Negroes and destroyed property, it followed its heroine's attempts to save her orphanage and its youthful Negro wards. She not only succeeds, she finds time for romance with a fellow Irishman, Phineas (Jack Cassidy). Thanks largely to the presence of the popular actress Shirley Jones in the title role, *Maggie Flynn* survived for ten weeks despite its mediocrity.

October closed with a financially disappointing visit by the D'Oyly Carte, offering New Yorkers *H.M.S. Pinafore, Patience, The Mikado, The Pirates of Penzance,* and *Iolanthe.*

The first long run of the season began just after campaign politics were set aside. A musical version of Nikos Kazantzakis' magnificently rich, vital novel, *Zorba the Greek*—a novel which had already been translated into a popular motion picture—*Zorba* (11-17-68, Imperial) represented the efforts of librettist Joseph Stein, lyricist Fred Ebb, and composer John Kander. Because they were professionals in a musical theatre increasingly trafficking in tyros, they devised a solidly crafted work that retained much of the original's juices. That their work was not their best was glossed over in a colorful, lively production, mounted and staged by Harold Prince. Boris Aronson's sets often relied heavily on black and white, so that a stylized green tree stood out dramatically. A Greek-like chorus led by Lorraine Serabian performed much the same function that the compère had performed in the team's *Cabaret,* and performed it with almost as much style and success. Added to this was Herschel Bernardi's dynamic performance in the title role. His life-embracing Zorba persuades young Nikos (John Cunningham) to reopen a mine he has inherited, but Zorba recklessly squanders the money Nikos has given him to purchase mine equipment. Nikos' sweetheart is murdered in a family vendetta. Neither failure nor tragedy daunts Zorba. He insists the only way to enjoy life is to accept whatever it offers. Though no song hit emerged, the "production values" were sufficient to allow the show to run nine months.

Promises, Promises (12-1-68, Shubert), an even better and more successful musical, compiled a run of 1,281 showings. This time the source was a popular movie, *The Apartment*. Once again top professionals provided the adaptation. Broadway's most successful playwright, Neil Simon, created the book and Hal David put words to Burt Bacharach's thoroughly contemporary music. Bacharach was the best known of the younger generation of songwriters, although he was a comparative stranger to Broadway. Simon remained faithful to the original Billy Wilder and I. A. L. Diamond story of Chuck Baxter (Jerry Orbach), a young executive who hopes to speed his rise to the top of the corporate ladder by lending the key to his bachelor's apartment to his bosses. When Fran Kubelik (Jill O'Hara), one of the young women brought to his digs, attempts suicide there, Chuck finds he must bring her to her senses in more ways than one. Naturally, romance follows. He succeeds with the help of a wisecracking Jewish doctor who luckily rents the neighboring apartment. *Variety* praised Orbach as "superb" describing his interpretation as "half slickie, half schlemiel, but always endearing—especially in a funny series of audience asides Simon has created for him." Bacharach's score contained at least two songs that enjoyed an immediate popular vogue, the title number, sung by Chuck just before the finale, and Fran and Chuck's "I'll Never Fall In Love Again."

The two big Broadway musicals were followed by the major off-Broadway success of the season, **Dames at Sea** (12-20-68, Bouwerie Lane). A spoof of old Ruby Keeler and Dick Powell movies, it had begun life some years before as a short cabaret sketch, and by the time it reached the Bouwerie Lane had been stretched into a two-hour entertainment with a cast of six and an orchestra of three. To make its twitting obvious it called its heroine, a tap dancer from Utah, Ruby (Bernadette Peters), and its hero, a song-writing sailor, Dick (David Christmas); Ruby gets a part in a Broadway musical with a nautical theme. Its star, Mona (Tamara Long), wangles an opening night on a battleship. Mona also tries to wangle Dick's songs away from him and Dick himself away from Ruby. But when she gets seasick on opening night, Ruby takes over, becomes a star, and captures Dick permanently. The evening was filled with thirtyish touches, umbrellas opening and shutting in musical numbers, tap dances that moved up and down steps, and dialogue such as "your name is gonna go up in lights." Like *Curley McDimple* the preceding season, *Dames at Sea* was the sort of travesty Hollywood might better have done about itself had it been willing. As it was, the musical proved the only major lyric piece of interest in an off-Broadway season that was a marked come-down from the year before. It achieved a run of 575 performances.

1969 began on a dismal note. **The Fig Leaves Are Falling** opened at the Broadhurst on January 2 and closed on January 4. During its half week it recounted the problems in Harry and Lillian Stone's marriage brought about by Harry's flirtation with his secretary, Pookie (Jenny O'Hara). Even the performances of Barry Nelson as Harry and the fine singing comedienne, Dorothy Loudon, as Lillian were to no avail.

The critics, if not the public, found themselves happier with January's second musical, **Celebration** (1-22-69, Ambassador). Written by Tom Jones and Harvey Schmidt, who had created off-Broadway's long-running *The Fantasticks* (5-3-60), it was an allegorical parable. Its narrator-hobo-confidence man, Potemkin (Keith Charles), falls in with Orphan (Michael Glenn-Smith), a young boy who has fled from an institutional home as it was about to be demolished, taking with him a stained glass "Eye of God." Orphan is seeking to re-create the garden he so loved at his orphanage. Together Potemkin and Orphan attend Rich's New Year's Eve party. Rich (Ted Thurston) laments that he was once young, innocent, and happy, but that now he is bitter, impotent, and surrounded by artificiality. Both Rich and Orphan fall in love with Angel (Susan Watson), a girl longing to be somebody, who has been hired to entertain at the party. Somehow Orphan obtains his garden and there seduces Angel before Rich's eyes. Before the vengeful Rich can retaliate, Potemkin initiates a ritual battle between winter and summer in which Rich is destroyed. The sun shines on the young victors as Potemkin sings, "Every day—Make a celebration." The production had only the four principals, a small chorus of masked "revelers," and an even smaller on-stage orchestra of percussion and strings, but it could not draw enough attendance to run beyond 14 weeks.

January's last musical was a show that had been produced successfully in Atlanta. It revolved around Lester Maddox, the Georgia restaurant owner who attained national prominence when he used an ax handle to keep blacks out of his establishment and who later was elected governor of the state. **Red, White and Maddox** (1-26-69, Cort) took Maddox (Jay Garner) on to the presidency of the United States and allowed him virtually to destroy the nation. The satire seemed funnier closer to home. New Yorkers could not foresee that in a number such as "The Impeachment Waltz" the spoof was touching on an issue that would later become a national tragedy. *Red, White and Maddox* survived only 41 performances on Broadway.

Still another disappointment was the London hit, **Canterbury Tales** (2-3-69, O'Neill). Its New York run of 121 showings fell far short of its long West End stay, despite a fine cast led by Martyn Green, Hermione Baddeley, and George Rose. Chaucer's pilgrims became characters in the four bawdy stories retold: "The Miller's Tale," "The Steward's Tale," "The Merchant's Tale," and "The Wife of Bath's Tale." Curiously, another musicalization of Chaucer had opened off-Broadway the preceding week. **Get Thee to Canterbury** (1-25-69, Sheridan Square) fared even more poorly, closing after 20 showings.

A fourth interesting failure was **Dear World** (2-6-69, Hellinger), a lyric version of Giraudoux' *The Madwoman of Chaillot*. Countess Aurelia (Angela Lansbury), the Madwoman of Chaillot and her cronies—the Madwoman of Montmartre (Jane Connell) and the Madwoman of the Flea Market (Carmen Matthews)—confound the saner rich man and help the course of true love. Jerry Herman's title song repeated the title as often and effectively as he had the titles of *Hello, Dolly!* (1-16-64) and *Mame* (5-24-66), although the song failed to catch on. Neither Herman, librettists Jerome Lawrence and Robert E. Lee, nor Miss Lansbury could recapture the peculiar magic of the 1948 production. *Dear World* departed after 132 performances.

1776 (3-16-69, 46th St.) was the season's second major success. Its tremendous success, indeed, its very success, came as a surprise to much of Broadway's smart money. Its librettist, Peter Stone, had been represented on Broadway only by his work on two failures, *Kean* (11-21-61) and *Skyscraper* (11-13-65). Its composer, Sherman Edwards, had never been heard from before. Even more dubious than the work's virtually unknown authors was its subject, the great debate leading to the signing of the Declaration of Independence. What the doubters overlooked was that a great debate is always good theatre. Luckily, Edwards and Stone approached the problem with intelligence and integrity. They eschewed all the standard formulas for easy entertainment. There were no toe-tapping melodies or high-kicking choruses. The one tune that

bordered on being a love song was kept at arm's length by lyrics such as, "Soon, madame, we shall walk in Cupid's grove together." The evening's most poignant moment came when a bedraggled young courier interrupted the convention to describe the ardors of war in, "Momma, Look Sharp." To build dramatic tension there was no intermission. Adams (William Daniels), Franklin (Howard da Silva), Jefferson (Ken Howard), and the other founding father came alive in the give-and-take of its arguments. At the end the delegates stepped up one by one to sign the Declaration, slowly fading behind a projection of the document while the Liberty Bell tolls. For many, Daniels' stiff-necked, but appealing Adams was the evening's hero. The reward for high mindedness was a run of 1,217 performances, just 64 less than that of the more obviously commercial *Promises, Promises*.

The rest of the season ran downhill. Three of the four remaining shows stayed less than a week, the fourth hardly much longer. Two nights after *1776* premiered, Ray Bolger returned to Broadway in a picaresque musical called **Come Summer** (3-18-69, Lunt-Fontanne). Set in the Connecticut River valley in 1840, it followed Phineas Sharp, a peddler, and his young friend, Jude Schribner (David Cryer), on their peregrinations. Though Agnes de Mille choreographed a poetic lovers' idyll and a stirring loggers' dance, and Bolger had a show-stopping routine in "Feather In My Shoe," dancing aside, the evening had little to offer.

The same week saw the one-performance run of a pretentious musical version of Melville's *Billy Budd*, entitled simply, **Billy** (3-22-69, Rose). Like *1776*, it was performed without intermission. But lacking that work's merits, it seemed all the more tedious for the lack of a breather.

A third show to be performed without intermission was **Trumpets of the Lord** (4-29-69, Atkinson). An anthology of sermons and hymns tied together in a supposed black revival meeting, the musical had enjoyed some success off-Broadway in 1963–64. It had clearly exhausted its appeal there, for it could eke out only a single week uptown although it had enjoyed a notable pre-Broadway success at Ford's Theatre in Washington.

The season's last show was a strange hodgepodge of a musical, based on a Spanish zarzuela, *La Verbena de la Paloma*. Although its title was **Fiesta in Madrid** (5-28-69, City Center), it was done in Spanish, leaving anyone not fluent in the language to guess at the details of an apothecary's fling with two young ladies. So peculiar an offering done so late in the year was foredoomed.

1969-1970

A lone, appalling statistic betrays the ghastliness of the 1969–70 season; half of the new musicals—seven out of fourteen—ran a week or less. Three of these each closed after their opening nights. Of the remaining seven none was a runaway success, and two longer runs were attributable to the attractions' stars. Out of all the songs from all the shows, at best a single number—the title song of *Applause*—gives any promise of becoming a standard. Even its chances are moot.

Oklahoma! (3-31-43) was revived by the Music Theater of Lincoln Center on June 23 and ran until September with Bruce Yarnell as Curley and *The Wizard of Oz'* witch, Margaret Hamilton, as Aunt Eller. This marked the sixth major revival of the work since its original production closed. Most of the revivals were produced at City Center or the Music Theatre. With Richard Rodgers and the New York Opera coming to an amicable parting of the ways, *Oklahoma!* marked the end of the Lincoln Center series and, with the City Center having suspended its program, the end of over a quarter of a century of popular-priced revivals. It was gratifyingly appropriate that *Oklahoma!*, which inaugurated the great era whose works filled these revival bills, should consciously or otherwise have been selected to write finis to them.

Nothing further called the critics from the comfort of their firesides until October 2 when **The New Music Hall of Israel**, a revised version of the imported vaudeville that had played the Palace in 1968, returned for a two-month stay.

Three more weeks went by before the first new musical of the season appeared. **Jimmy** (10-23-69, Winter Garden) was a lyric biography of New York's colorful mayor, Jimmy Walker. Its untried authors based their work on Gene Fowler's *Beau James,* although material on Walker was easily accessible. They may have understood a pitfall ignored by a number of hands who, before and after, thought lives of famous figures automatically translate into good theatre. History that is fondly remembered or that comes alive on the printed page does not necessarily answer the requirements of dramatic structure. Oddly enough, Walker's life probably did. His meteoric rise and tragic fall set against a Charlestoning, gaudy jazz age seems almost a natural. However, the authors lacked the ability or know-how to handle the story. They wisely confined their libretto to the seven most vital years in the mayor's life, 1925–31, framing the evening in Walker's embittered departure for Europe. Moreover, they peopled their cast with reincarnations of such celebrities as Eddie Dowling, Texas Guinan, Izzy and Moe, and, of course, Walker's mistress and eventual second wife, Betty Compton. A popular night-club comedian, Frank Gorshin, was enlisted to portray the Mayor. The entertainment fell far short of becoming another *Fiorello!* (11-23-59), surviving a mere 84 showings.

A figure as controversial to his contemporaries as Walker had been to the twenties provided the sole reason for possibly attending **Buck White** (12-2-60, Abbott), Muhammad Ali (né Cassius Clay) was the champion heavyweight prizefighter of the day. He chose to challenge Broadway in a musical version of *Big Time Buck White*, a play which described the turmoil that ensues when its militant Negro titular hero arrives to address the Beautiful Allelujah Days Society. All the action takes place at the society's meeting hall. Ali and the show, another by relatively inexperienced writers, went down for the count of seven performances.

The successful conversion of *Lili*, a film played to a background of a touring French circus, into *Carnival* may have prompted the first of the season's one-performance fiascos. As its name reveals, **La Strada** (12-14-69, Lunt-Fontanne) was a musicalization of Fellini's popular motion picture, retelling the bittersweet romance of Gelsomina (Bernadette Peters) and Mario (Larry Kert) as their troupe wanders across lower Italy. The songs were by Lionel Bart, who, as far as Broadway was concerned, had written nothing but *Oliver!*

Coco (12-18-69, Hellinger) fared much better. What its fate might have been but for the presence of Katharine Hepburn in the title role is unpleasant to contemplate. Like *Jimmy*, this slightly romanticized biography of the great fashion designer, Gabrielle "Coco" Chanel, was framed in a highpoint of Miss Chanel's life, her attempted comeback after World War II. But unlike *Jimmy* the frame was expanded and actually embodied what insubstantial plot there was. Coco's comeback seems thwarted when the French press hands her scathing notices, but Americans from "Ohrbach's, Bloomingdale's, Best and Saks" save the day. A trite subplot injected a love interest between one of Coco's protégés and a young man. Alan Jay Lerner provided the book and lyrics, with his rhymes outshining his libretto as usual. The songs were by André Previn, a well-known young composer and conductor. They were undistinguished. Neither Chanel nor her associates were called upon to create the costumes; Cecil Beaton was enlisted for the chore. His dresses and gowns were as disappointing as the show itself. His gowns seemed far too feminine to suggest Chanel's elegant, slightly masculine lines. The show's obvious prop remained Miss Hepburn, who was on stage virtually from beginning to end, coasting through on her unique glamor. Ewen has perspicaciously compared the show to *Roberta*, another musical whose background is the world of high fashion. His conclusion is that *Coco* had all of *Roberta*'s drawbacks and nothing to equal its enchanting Jerome Kern score. In dollars and cents the musical's record reveals what was happening to Broadway. The show cost close to a million dollars to mount (Paramount Pictures absorbed most of the charges), it could gross $128,000 a week with a break-even mark of $80,000 (Miss Hepburn alone is reputed to have received $15,000 per). Although it ran 332 performances, it failed to recoup its investment.

January, like November, brought no new musicals. The two that arrived in February were among the season's disasters, but before they premiered the popular French singing star, Charles Aznavour, came in with a one-man program of song, offered in English as well as French. Both **Gantry** (2-14-70, Abbott) and **Georgy** (2-26-70, Winter Garden) were by inexperienced hands. *Elmer Gantry,* Sinclair Lewis' tale of a hypocritical opportunistic, hard-drinking revival preacher (Robert Shaw), and his relationship with the evangelistic Sister Sharon (Rita Moreno), provided the source of the former. Lewis' powerful diatribe seemed more watery than boozy on stage; it folded after one performance. *Georgy* lasted half a week. Based on the novel and the well-liked movie, *Georgy Girl,* the evening re-created the love and adventures of an independent-minded young Londoner (Dilys Watling). Her principal heartthrob is a man old enough to be her father, James Leamington (Stephen Elliot).

The abrupt closings of these shows, along with musicals such as *La Strada,* demonstrated the desperation that was masking both a lack of creativity and an absence of any new striking style to pursue. In general the public refused to sit through musicalizations of old novels never meant to be abridged into two-and-a-half-hours' traffic on a stage or of recent movies more at home on the less constricted screen. Yet the failures, as the records show, did little to discourage more of the same.

March was the busiest month of the season, bringing with it five new musicals. The first and the last were the most successful. Ossie Davis, aided by Philip Rose and Peter Udell, turned his 1961 comedy, *Purlie Victorious*, into a libretto for which Gary Geld wrote some appropriately light-hearted music. The flashback–frame device so voguish during the year was again employed to recount the young preacher Purlie's return to his home in southern Georgia bent on improving the lot of his fellow blacks. His plans are opposed by the redneck Ol' Cap'n (John Hefferman), but Cap'n's son, Charlie (C. David Colson) has more liberal views and helps the minister. Purlie also wins the hand of Lutiebelle (Melba Moore). Much of the hilarious humor of **Purlie** (3-15-70, Broadway) came at the expense of bigotry—such as the dismayed Cap'n's complaint that a college education only teaches students to mispronounce "nigger" as if it were spelled "negro." Funny as the show was, it was even better when it was rousing, and it was rousing from its opening revival hymn, "Walk Him Up The Stairs," to the hymn's reprise at the close. Purlie (Cleavon Little) added to the festivities singing "New Fangled Preacher Man," a gospel song set over "a series of rocking rhythmic breaks." The attractive, seemingly-shy Miss Moore lit up the stage singing of her feelings for Purlie in "I Got Love." *Purlie* was such good fun it racked up 686 performances and toured successfully.

Growing outrage at the waste and stupidity of the Vietnam War was given vent in **Blood Red Roses** (3-22-70, Golden), a plotless musical that chose to mask its fury by setting its action during the Crimean War. Queen Victoria, Prince Albert, Florence Nightingale, and Lord Raglan were all recalled from the past. But vitriolic assaults and a lack of inspiration prevented the evening from being in the least entertaining. It was removed from the stage after its initial showing.

Figures from the past were evoked again in **Minnie's Boys** (3-26-70, Imperial), a musical biography of the young Marx Brothers and their famed mother. Once again nostalgia and sentimentality were no substitute for theatrical craftsmanship or inspiration. Although Groucho's son, Arthur, had a hand in the book, the evening was put together by still another contingent of tyros. The antics of the Marx Brothers themselves might have saved it by making it so zany no one would have noticed its flaws. Sadly the great clowns were either dead or too old to play themselves as young men. The young men who did, notably Lewis J. Stadlen as Groucho, avoided re-creating the famous old Marx Brothers routines, settling instead for more impressionistic impersonations. Stadlen had one uproarious scene in which he substituted for Chico while still performing his own bit as Groucho. Shelley Winters played the loving, if pushy, Minnie. The show survived a slightly forced run of ten weeks.

But yet more experienced hands also could come a cropper. Leonard Spigelgass, Jule Styne, and Sammy Cahn learned this as they watched **Look to the Lilies** (3-29-70, Lunt-Fontanne) succumb after 25 showings. Their musical was based on William E. Barrett's novel, *Lilies of the Field,* which had been already used as the source of a popular motion picture. It told a tale of racial ecumenism in which Homer, a vagrant, hostile Negro, is persuaded by some New Mexican nuns to build them a chapel. The chapel built, he moves on. In his autobiography, Cahn places much of the blame for the show's failure on the evening's Homer, Al Freeman, Jr., who Cahn believes couldn't act or sing. Not even Shirley Booth as the Mother Superior could overcome the problems his miscasting produced. Cahn admits his astonishment that he and Styne created "a show without one successful song coming out of it," but suggests "I, Yes, Me! That's Who!" may someday be given a second chance. He adds, "I'm especially proud of that song." The song was the very last number in the show and had to express the love which had developed between the Mother Superior and Homer.

Applause (3-30-70, Palace), the season's biggest hit, was March's last offering. In the manner of so many shows of recent years, it was a lyric redaction of a successful film, the famous Bette Davis vehicle, *All About Eve,* and in the manner of so many of the current season's show it employed a flashback-frame device. At the Tony Awards Margo Channing (Lauren Bacall), the preceding year's winner, presents the trophy to Eve Harrington (Penny Fuller). In the flashback a star-struck, unknown young Eve appears at the stage door of the theatre where Margo is playing, and before Margo realizes what she is doing the actress has all but adopted the youngster. Eve mimics Margo's every action and in no time has insinuated her way into the affection of all the people who are important in Margo's life. The wife of Margo's favorite playwright even arranges to strand the star in the country so that Eve, who

has become Margo's understudy, can go on. The playwright himself, Buzz (Brandon Maggart), decides to write his next work for Eve. By the end of the evening Margo has accepted a proposal of marriage from her director, Bill Sampson (Len Cariou), the only one of her friends who has remained steadfastly loyal, and she has also accepted retirement. The solidly crafted libretto by Comden and Green sizzled with taut, bitchy give-and-takes. When Margo begins to suspect Buzz' affection for Eve, she charges her own performances have covered up his weak playwriting:

Buzz: You empty-headed, conceited bass fiddle! You're just a body and a voice! Don't ever forget—I'm the brain!
Margo: Till the autopsy, there's no proof!

Charles Strouse set Lee Adams' words to music and in the title song (sung by Bonnie Franklin as a bar waitress) came up with the most successful tune to emerge from a Broadway show during the season. Ron Fields, who served both as director and choreographer, kept the action sizzling, especially during a giddy scene in which Margo joins patrons at a gay bar in feeling punchy and bleary, "But Alive." Lauren Bacall's electric cavorting gave the show its biggest boost, propelling it to a run of 896 performances.

Hopes ran high for April's first muscial, a lyric rendering of William Alfred's five-year-old blank verse drama, *Hogan's Goat.* Alfred himself helped with both the libretto and the lyrics, while Mitch Leigh, who composed the score for *Man of La Mancha* (11-22-65), created the songs. The principals included some of Broadway's finest talents: Robert Weede, Helen Gallagher, Tommy Rall, and Joan Diener. Like *Man of La Mancha,* the new musical **Cry for Us All** (4-8-70, Broadhurst) was performed without intermission. It relentlessly followed the destruction of the promising political career of Matt Stanton (Steve Arlen) by Mayor Quinn (Weede). When Quinn reveals that Matt has hidden the facts of his first marriage, the argument that follows leads to the accidental death of his second wife, Kathleen (Miss Diener). The strength of the original play eluded the adapters, and the show closed after nine performances.

A revival of Sandy Wilson's spoof, *The Boy Friend,* began a disappointing run at the Ambassador on April 14. Eight nights later **Park** (4-22-70, Golden), a musical that had first seen the light of day at an experimental theatre in Baltimore, was delivered to New York for inspection. It was intimate, but pretentious, and New York didn't take to it. For five performances a young couple (Don Scardino and Joan Hackett) and an older couple (David Brooks and Julie Wilson) met in a park and talked out their problems.

The only musical of the season other than *Applause* to close with a profit was its last, **Company** (4-26-70, Alvin). It was in some respects an odd-ball piece, as innovative as commercial Broadway was likely to get without tripping over itself. George Furth's book had no plot. It was a chronicle whose action was framed by several birthdays in the life of its protagonist, a New York bachelor named Robert (Dean Jones), Bobby to his friends. His friends are blasé, jaded New Yorkers, one of whom, Joanne (Elaine Stritch), insists, "It's not the gift, it's the cost that counts." Bobby's visits to the supposedly happily married couples prove disenchanting. At Harry and Sarah's, Bobby realizes that Harry (Charles Kimbrough) is an alcoholic and Sarah (Barbara Barrie) has become hostile and sniping. Bobby's married male friends insist marriage pulls one's emotions in two directions at once and that they are forever "Sorry-Grateful." At Peter and Susan's, Bobby discovers the seemingly blissful pair (John Cunningham and Merle Louise) have decided to get a divorce. David (George Coe) and Jenny (Teri Ralston) despair of keeping up with a younger crowd. Bobby escapes into a daydream about his girl friends, only to hear them complain, "You Could Drive A Person Crazy." His men friends reassure him, "Have I Got A Girl For You!," and Bobby himself is certain "Someone Is Waiting." But Bobby's evenings with Marta (Pamela Myers), a kooky left-wing intellectual, and Amy (Beth Howland), an airline stewardess, suggest neither is the someone. At Bobby's next birthday he and his friends celebrate the joys of being "Side By Side By Side" and ask each other, "What Would We Do Without You?" Another year passes, bringing more meetings and more disillusionments, such as a slightly tipsy Joanne's toast to her bored fellow matrons, "The Ladies Who Lunch." When Bobby's next birthday rolls around, his friends arrange a surprise party—but Bobby never appears. A little reluctantly Bobby has decided to go his way alone. A single skeletonized set served on its various levels to house whatever byplay was transpiring. Stephen Sondheim created the songs. His melodies were intelligent and musicianly, but in the unfortunate pattern of the day, not demandingly memorable. His lyrics, however, were the high point of the evening, again confirming that he alone—possibly with Lerner at his best—was keeping alive the lit-

erate, brittle tradition of the old masters. One of his songs, "The Ladies Who Lunch," with which Miss Stritch won rounds of applause, remains for many playgoers their fondest memory of the show. Michael Bennett's novel choreography for "Side By Side By Side" took old-fashioned straw hats and canes and made "the hats slash the air and the canes slap the floor to stress the harshness of what is being stomped out."

The off-Broadway season produced nothing that promised to be any more memorable or enduring than the shows which raised their curtains in the big houses near Times Square. But in one respect there was a distinct, noteworthy difference. The majority of off-Broadway musicals gave forth with an unmistakably contemporary sound: rock. Despite the success of *Hair,* Broadway, with rare exceptions, was determinedly avoiding the idiom. But in the smaller houses *The Last Sweet Days of Isaac, The Me Nobody Knows* (to be discussed when it reaches Broadway in the next season), *Salvation, Mod Donna,* and others sang to the melodies and rhythms of the sound. In *The Best Plays of 1969–1970* Otis L. Guernsey devoted an entire chapter to excerpts from the lyrics of these shows insisting, "The Rock Lyric is a literary form developed in this decade; as different from the June-moon cadences of our rose-colored memory as the Beatles from the Lombardo brothers." Of course he is correct about the difference, however unfair his adjective "rose-colored" and his recalling the Lombardos may be. Regrettably, he makes no attempt to define the new style. Rock lyrics tend to be prosey, quietly preachy, and given to folklorish repetitiveness. For those accustomed to the brillance and precision of Cole Porter, Lorenz Hart, and Ira Gershwin they take some getting used to. One example Guernsey quotes from **Salvation** (9-24-69, Jan Hus), a song called "In Between," runs;

You, I wanted you, in the mornin' and over again
You, I wanted you, in the evenin' and over again
And in between, and in between and in between
I wanted all of your friends!

A few regular off-Broadway composers, especially Al Carmines, stuck more closely to older traditions.

Off-Broadway shows tended to be more loosely constructed, with plots, when they had them, that defiantly rejected a boy-meets-girl formula. For example, **Sambo** (12-12-69, Public), "a black opera with white spots," was essentially an accounting of black alienation from white society seen through the eyes of characters perverted from children's fairy tales, such as Untogether Cinderella and Jack

Horney. **Mod Donna** (4-24-70, Public) was a four-character piece in which a bored couple agree to exchange partners (while a chorus comments on the women's liberation movement and sexual exploitation). The treatment was a far remove from the lighthearted or elegant handling similar stories had received in, say, *So Long, Letty* (10-23-16) or *Apple Blossoms* (10-7-19). *Salvation* was a revue principally satirizing the religious and moral extremes of the day. **The Last Sweet Days of Isaac** (1-26-70, East Side) imprisoned a young boy and girl first in a stalled elevator, then in a jail. Even Carmines' **Promenade** (6-4-69, Promenade), with a book by Maria Irene Fornes, spent the night mischievously seeing the world through the eyes of two prisoners, 105 and 106. The most successful off-Broadway musical was a revue called **Oh, Calcutta!**, its title a fanciful Anglicization of some French scatology. Devised by the English drama critic, Kenneth Tynan, its contributors, besides Tynan himself, included Samuel Beckett, Jules Feiffer, and John Lennon (of the Beatles). Their material was at best lackluster. But from June 17 on the show packed the Eden Theatre (not long since the Phoenix) because so much of the show was performed completely in the nude. What must have been the reaction of the ghosts of chorus girls in *The Black Crook* (9-12-1866), who had played just a few blocks away?

1970-1971

One discouraging season followed another. Statistically, the count of new musicals dropped still further. Eliminating revivals, moves uptown from off-Broadway, and Yiddish tune shows that arrived in the fall, only nine new lyric pieces were unveiled. (By stretching definitions *Variety* was able to list a total of seventeen.) A number of shows, *Paul Sills' Story Theater,* for one, were straight plays interlarded with songs.

The potent Jewish influence on Broadway which stemmed from extensive, loyal patronage manifested itself conspicuously at the beginning of the season. The first new musical arrived nearly six months after the last musical premiere and celebrated the rise of the most important Jewish family of the modern era, **The Rothschilds** (10-19-70, Lunt-Fontanne). Based on Frederic Morton's popular account of the clan, Sherman Yellen's book followed the fortunes of the family from their hum-ble German beginnings to their powerful influence at the Congress of Vienna. Son Nathan (Paul Hecht) was sent to London and given the requisite love interest in the second act. *The Rothschilds'* songs were by Jerry Bock and Sheldon Harnick, who together had been responsible for the songs in *Fiddler on the Roof* (9-22-64), still running at the time their new show premiered. The new melodies lacked the fiber and melodic inspiration of their earlier material; not a single hit emerged. For many the high spot of the evening was the performance of Keene Curtis, impersonating several of the historic figures who crossed the Rothschilds' paths, from Prince William at the beginning of the show to Metternich at the end. But Hal Linden as Meyer Rothschild was equally fine, walking away at the end of the season with a Tony Award. Advance interest and lack of stiff competition enabled the musical to run out the season.

Light, Lively and Yiddish, a Yiddish musical with an English-speaking compère, and **The President's Daughter,** which mixed English and Yiddish dialogue, followed in late October and early November. Both found limited markets.

Probably the most eagerly awaited musical of the season was **Two by Two** (11-10-70, Imperial). As it had in *The Rothschilds,* Jewish lore provided its story. But in this instance the material was of somewhat more universal appeal, since the evening was a recounting of the Old Testament's legend of Noah. Peter Stone's book leaned heavily on Clifford Odets' *The Flowering Peach,* which Menasha Skulnik had starred in during the 1954–55 season. Expectations ran high for two reasons. First, the new show's score was by Richard Rodgers. Second, the musical was to bring Danny Kaye back to Broadway after several decades' absence. Stone, who had written the solidly competent book for *1776* (3-16-69), wrote a reasonably serviceable libretto for the new piece. It discovered the pious Noah obeying God's commandments in a world increasingly remote from God. Noah cannot even impart his piety to his sons and their wives. Their father's pleas to build an ark to ride out the coming flood are met with derision. Noah finally succeeds in building the boat and gets his family and the world's animals on board before the rain begins. Noah's rescue deepens his religious convictions. That his God would stop to create and save so small a living thing as a tiny bird fills the old man with wonder. Regrettably, Rodgers' score, like the book, was no more than serviceable. Martin Charnin wrote the lyrics for the songs, the best of which was supposed to be "I Do Not Know A Day I Did

Not Love You." It remained for Kaye to sustain the evening, and he did, in a way that infuriated Rodgers. Shortly after the opening Kaye tore a ligament in his leg. Once out of the hospital he returned to perform in a wheelchair or on crutches. Disregarding the text and staging, he turned *Two by Two* into what Rodgers disgustedly termed "one-by-one vaudeville." His antics probably saved the show, which he kept going for just short of a year and which closed with a small profit.

In the preceding May an unusual musical had opened off-Broadway. **The Me Nobody Knows** (12-18-70, Hayes) took its lyrics and dialogue from the writing of underprivileged school children in the greater New York City area. Though the adapters necessarily revised substantial portions of the material, they left four poems untouched, "Fugue For Four Girls," "Rejoice," "The Horse," and "War Babies." Essentially a revue singing a song of sociological significance, it possessed a fetching blend of worldliness and naïveté that aided its young performers in compiling a record of 586 performances.

1953's long-run hit, *The Teahouse of the August Moon,* was the source of **Lovely Ladies, Kind Gentlemen** (12-28-70, Majestic), which appeared after an extended transcontinental tour. The evening again recounted the stratagems employed by the wily Sakini (Kenneth Nelson) to build a teahouse for his fellow Okinawans during the American occupation. Sakini had the sometimes helpless sympathy of young Captain Fisby (Ron Husmann) as both took on the doltish, befuddled old army man, Colonel Purdy (David Burns). At one point the almost completed teahouse has to be taken down. But by the end of the night it sits serenely in its Japanese garden. If Sakini was a latter-day Sultan of Sulu, his show was not. Musicalized, as were so many of the shows of the period, by generally untried or uninspired hands, it sat lumberingly on the stage. After two weeks the teahouse was dismantled for good.

On January 12, 1971, the Ritz Theatre, for years given over to radio and television, returned to the legitimate fold with "a rock opera," **Soon.** Its story followed an ambitious rock group in its climb to the top. Early success and drive bring them quickly to New York, but club dates and recording sessions show them some ugly aspects of the professional musical world, and they soon take to the road again. The show itself never took to the road. It folded after three showings, leaving the small, old Ritz seeking a new tenant.

Broadway's huge Jewish market was tapped again when **Ari** (1-15-71, Hellinger), a musical version of Leon Uris' Zionist novel, *Exodus,* premiered. Uris himself adapted the book and wrote the lyrics. Walt Smith composed the melodies. Both men were novices on the Broadway musical scene, and their labors were inept. David Cryer played Ari Ben Canaan, whose attempt to lead a band of Jewish refugees out of Cyprus and into Palestine was withdrawn after 19 representations.

A revival of *No! No! Nanette!* (9-16-25) proved the biggest hit of the year, even before it opened at the 46th Street on January 19. When the show went into rehearsals, songs not in the original were added and a substantially revised book was in hand. By some curious theatrical chemistry the interpolated songs disappeared during the tryouts, and the score first-nighters heard was with a few discreet omissions, the same that had delighted first-nighters of forty-six years before. Though much of the dialogue was rewritten and some of the steeliest barbs inexplicably removed, the story hewed close to the original. Its carefree spirit, if not its cynical letter, was faithfully retained. Ruby Keeler, Patsy Kelly, and choreographer Busby Berkeley made much heralded returns to the stage. Miss Keeler, Jack Gilford, Helen Gallagher, Bobby Van, and a large, frenetically tapping chorus made this revival a dancing show such as Broadway hadn't thrilled to in years. Night after night the beloved old songs stopped the proceedings and elicited repeated encores. In this version "I Want To Be Happy" was sung by Jimmy (Gilford) and Nanette (Susan Watson), then rousingly danced by Mrs. Smith (Miss Keeler) and the chorus. Tom (Roger Rathburn) and Nanette once more embraced in "Tea For Two." Nostalgia par excellence, the New York company rolled up 861 performances, far outrunning the original New York stay. Road companies thrived, although by and large their runs fell far short of runs the original's touring troupes enjoyed in the same cities. If nostalgia and trivia go hand in hand, scholars may choose to ponder why, in an era given to titles with exclamation points, the three exclamation points featured in the original title were dropped for the revival.

A week after this glorious bit of past nonsense regaled Broadway, the rage of off-Broadway, *Oh, Calcutta!,* moved uptown to the Belasco to continue its stay—nudes, exclamation point, and all.

Neither February nor March brought any musicals, but a comparatively busy April began with the season's most interesting new musical, **Follies** (4-4-71, Winter Garden). In one sense *Follies,* by hinting at the lavishness and tunefulness of the great old annuals, catered to the same craving for nostalgia that *No! No! Nanette!* attempted to appease. But its very lack of prodigal opulence and endearingly memorable songs suggested how irretrievably far away that bygone theatre now was. *Follies'* loose, essentially plotless, structure, its intelligent, if necessarily superficial introspection suggested the inadequacy of contemporary alternatives. Although the show was highly praised and had a reasonably long, if slightly forced, run, it wound up in the red, and a projected road tour collapsed after several weeks. The show's initial $800,000 cost precluded a return on investment (none of Ziegfeld's far more opulent *Follies* ever cost even $300,000). The demolition of the Ziegfeld possibly suggested the story, which takes place in a partially torn-down theatre. A reunion of old-timers who had starred or played in the old "Weismann Follies" is in progress. Weismann, unlike Ziegfeld, was portrayed as still alive, and his shows were not said to go back as far as the real *Follies,* but the analogy was unmistakable. Most of the glittering figures have not aged well, nor have their late years been especially successful. The principal couples are Sally and Buddy Plummer (Dorothy Collins and Gene Nelson) and Phyllis and Ben Stone (Alexis Smith and John McMartin). Sally had loved Ben in their younger days. The reunion revives the old passions, but Ben had run away from Sally before and runs away again. The show was presented without intermission. Throughout the story "memory-figures" appeared in the background. (At least one real Ziegfeld favorite—Ethel Shutta—played a brief scene.) Often these "memory figures" were merely gorgeously costumed chorus girls parading out of the past. Just as often they were youthful versions of the old-timers. Sally and Ben's memory-figures (Marti Rolph and Kurt Peterson), for example, reappear to relive their old heartbreaks as the older Sally and Ben attempt to handle rekindled ardors. Playwright James Goldman created the literate book that looked on unblinkingly as illusions were destroyed, and Stephen Sondheim the songs. Sondheim's tunes were frequently gentle parodies of melodies that had graced long-gone shows, but his lyrics had the expected Sondheim brilliance, a brilliance lyrics from the old annuals rarely approached. One girl, describing the years that followed her Follies glamor rhymed "Abie's Irish Rose" with "Dionne-babies, Major Bowes."

In a season turning desperately to the joys of another era, a revival of Paul Green and Kurt Weill's bleak musical tract, *Johnny Johnson* (11-

19-36), was singularly ill-timed. Its first performance on April 11 was its last.

Sadly, a gay, harmless romp whose title recalled the advertisements for shows of Nanette's and Ziegfeld's days, **70, Girls 70** (4-15-71, Broadhurst), didn't survive much longer, less than five weeks. The show had been beset with problems on the road; its leading male comic, David Burns, died during the tryout. But its innocent tale of denizens from an old folks' home who set out to rob the rich and feed the poor was brought to life by a fine cast that included Mildred Natwick, Lillian Roth, Hans Conried, and Joey Faye.

A musical version of *Frank Merriwell's School Days* entitled **Frank Merriwell, or Honor Challenged** (4-24-71, Longacre) fared less well, running no longer than *Johnny Johnson.* The scenes were treated as chapters and given chapter headings such as "The Blow of a Coward," "Terror at the Junction" and "Death by Dynamite." It was a cute idea, but as close as its neophyte authors came to attractive innovation.

Earl of Ruston (5-7-71, Rose) was the season's final musical. Only the third major show to employ rock, it met with the fate attending most rock shows uptown—complete failure. Again much of the problem stemmed from its authors' lack of experience. The librettists and lyricists, C. C. Courtney and Regan Courtney, claimed the story was a threnody for their cousin, Earl Woods, who spent most of his life in mental institutions. Both Courtneys played Earl during the voguishly intermission-less evening.

After Broadway closed up shop for the season, off-Broadway offered what proved to be its major achievement for the year. **Godspell** was a musical based on the Gospel according to St. Matthew, with a book by John-Michael Tebelak and songs by Stephen Schwartz. Originally performed at Café La Mama, the celebrated off-off-Broadway house, it moved to the Cherry Lane on May 17 and then uptown. It ran into 1977. A small cast costumed in raggedy-Ann style reinterpreted the Bible story in consciously naïve, simplistic terms, singing and dancing to the strains of a minuscule orchestra. Schwartz' contemporary revival songs were typified by "Day by Day," introduced by Robin Lamont and company.

. . .

Stephen Schwartz was born in New York City on March 6, 1948. He began to study piano at the age of seven, and later majored in drama at Carnegie Tech. His first work on Broadway was a theme song for the 1969 play, *Butterflies Are Free.*

Young Schwartz also collaborated with Leonard Bernstein on the lyrics for Bernstein's "Mass."

1971-1972

In one sense this was the most interesting, promising season since the end of the last great act. Three of its biggest hits sang out loudly and uncompromisingly in rock terms, suggesting that Broadway would finally manipulate the latest musical rage to its own advantage. Of the three long runs with rock scores only *Jesus Christ Superstar*'s music had any strong appeal outside the theatre, while both *Jesus Christ Superstar* and *Grease* betrayed the formless librettos endemic among rock musicals. *Grease* also demonstrated that Broadway was embracing the "latest musical rage" when the rage was about to wane, for *Grease*'s songs reflected the rock-and-roll sounds of twenty years earlier at the time the idiom was first taking hold across the country. To this extent *Grease* fell in curiously with the "nostalgia craze" making one of its periodic reappearances. The preceding season's revival of *No! No! Nanette!* had fueled the craze. *Grease* allowed a younger generation to recapture the sounds and joys of its youth. The season also saw a number of revivals that might have seemed part of this same need to recall the past. Significantly, at least one of the old shows brought back to life had never elicited affection in the first place. Its revival suggested rather that Broadway could on occasions exercise a surprising sense of responsibility.

A revival of a show too new to elicit twinges of nostalgia opened the season. *You're a Good Man, Charlie Brown* (3-7-67) arrived at the tiny Golden Theatre on June 1 and ran out the month. No further lyric pieces appeared until **Jesus Christ Superstar** (10-12-71, Hellinger) exploded in a circus of gaudy color and amplified sound. Originally a wildly successful rock LP album, written and recorded in England, it recounted the last seven days of Jesus in contemporary terms. Tom O'Horgan, the pyrotechnical young director made famous by *Hair*, was responsible for bringing it very much alive on stage. Alone of the season's shows its music attained national popularity, though actually the music was well known long before the piece went into rehearsal. The uncanny blending of rock sound with revivalist fervor made Andrew Lloyd Webber's melody for the chorus' title song a momentary anthem, while Tim Rice's thoughtful lyrics, coupled with a second memorable Webber tune, help spread the appeal of "I Don't Know How To Love Him," sung in the show by Mary Magdalene (Yvonne Elliman). *Jesus Christ Superstar* ran out the season, although complaints of irreverence and anti-Semitism were leveled at the show.

A second show to run out the year and into the next arrived eight nights later. Like *Jesus Christ Superstar,* **Ain't Supposed To Die a Natural Death** (10-20-63, Barrymore) had been a recording before it became a show and, like *Superstar,* it was more chronicle than plot. Indeed it lacked even the thread of biblical narrative that tied Webber and Rice's work together. Its author, Melvin Van Peebles, was, like Webber and Rice, new to Broadway. A black bursting with things to say and the need to say them, he was to be heard from again later in the season. Although Peebles subtitled these vignettes of lower-class black life, "Tunes from Blackness," he gave more emphasis to his words than to his melodies, insisting the lyrics be spoken rather than sung, so that their meaning would project more clearly. The show's nineteen numbers mirrored all sides of black life: yowling, griping, and defiance on the one hand, optimism and warmth on the other. Unfortunately, hostility prevailed. The show was framed in hatred. Its opening number, "Just Don't Make No Sense" (sung by Arthur French) complained, "Everybody be getting in the race to keep me in my place"; its last number found a harridan (Minnie Gentry) hoping to "Put A Curse On You." In its all-black cast, a policeman wore a white mask.

Having appealed to Christians and blacks in its first two fall offerings, Broadway almost inevitably turned to its large Jewish constituency, providing an Israeli revue, **To Live Another Summer, To Pass Another Winter.** Its small cast entertained at the Helen Hayes (normally given over to straight plays) until March. A second Israeli show, **Only Fools Are Sad,** was a November entry, running like its compatriot until March.

October's final offering was a lavish revival of Comden-Green-Bernstein's World War II hit, *On the Town* (12-28-44). If the show had lost something of its timeliness, it lost nothing of its style and wit. Regrettably, its producers—although they were more intelligent and responsible than most of the breed merchandising revivals for Broadway—could not come up with performers to equal the originals—Nancy Walker, Sono Osato, or Comden and Green themselves. A second-rate cast deprived the show of the necessary élan and the ability to click. *On the Town* closed after 73 showings, a major disappointment.

November's only new American musical was **The Grass Harp** (11-2-71, Beck), a lyric version of Truman Capote's novel. Capote's own dramatization had failed in 1952, and this musical version by two inexperienced hands was an even quicker failure twenty years later, running a mere week. As she had in the book and in the play, Dolly Talbo (Barbara Cook) takes to life in a treehouse to escape from the world and especially from what she believes are attempts of her sister to commercialize a dropsy cure. The show was yet one more musical falling in with the practice of omitting intermissions.

The play critics later proclaimed the best musical of the season, **Two Gentlemen of Verona** (12-1-71, St. James) had originally been performed in the summer at Joseph Papp's outdoor New York Shakespeare Festival in Central Park. It was played now in a regular theatre on a brightly colored multi-level skeleton set with the theatre's rear wall painted "a luminous Mediterranean blue, a Botticelli blue, stolen from the sky behind Venus being born." In this modern-day lyrical rendering, Milan and Verona came to have a distinctly Puerto Rican tinge, not unlike *Romeo and Juliet* turned into *West Side Story* (9-26-57). In this tale of a fickle gentleman who turns on both his friend and sweetheart, Raul Julia played the undependable Proteus. Galt MacDermot's music was good, although nowhere near as melodic nor as popular as his masterful *Hair* score. John Guare and Mel Shapiro did the book and Guare alone composed the lyrics. His lyrics were often simplistic, one line merely repeating the word "love" nine times. Disgracefully, the repetitious, innocuous "love" gave way to unabashedly scatological lines. The show, for all its offensive passages, finally caught on, after meeting initial resistance from patrons, who resented a $15 top for much the same show that had been given free months earlier. During its run, however, *Two Gentlemen of Verona* exposed the lamentable state of musical production and talent on Broadway when a performance had to be canceled as a result of a breakdown of its amplification system. Singing in "live" Broadway shows was rarely fully "live" anymore.

More newcomers tried their hand at a Broadway musical and failed with **Wild and Wonderful** (12-7-71, Lyceum). Though the show had an up-to-the-minute theme, telling of the CIA's attempt to infiltrate the youth movement, its ineptness was even more telling. Its first performance was its last.

Tom O'Horgan was director for the second time in the season when **Inner City** (12-14-71, Barrymore) raised its curtain. The evening was based on Eve Merriam's book, *The Inner City Mother Goose*, and fell in with the social protest so rampant on the musical stage. To music by Helen Miller, the cast sang Miss Merriam's muckraking parodies of beloved old nursery rhymes. "Three Blind Mice," for example, became "You'll Find Mice." Subtitled "A Street Cantata," the show, essentially a revue, ran three months.

1971's last musical originated in Canada and enjoyed a modest London run before tackling Broadway. **Anne of Green Gables** was a musicalization of L. M. Montgomery's novel. Brought to the City Center on December 21 for a two-week run, New Yorkers rejected its old-fashioned sentimentality, and no one pleaded for an extended engagement.

Grease (2-14-72, Eden) opened off-Broadway. Public response was so immediate and so enthusiastic that by the summer the musical was playing at the Broadhurst, a regular Times Square house. Like so many of the season's lyric works, *Grease* sang in rock-and-roll, but its sounds harked back to early days of the idiom as a group of youngsters gather for a high-school reunion and relive the joys and pains of adolescence in the fifties. In those seemingly halcyon days, Danny Deitch (Barry Bostwick), a member of the "Burger Palace Boys," a greaser (slicked hair) gang at Rydall High, loves Sandy Dumbrowski (Carole Demas), an innocent who has transferred from Immaculata. When Danny refuses to conform to her prim idea of behavior, she dons tight jeans, a bouffant hair-do and stoops to conquer. As she does, she also gives a would-be rival, Betty Rizzo (Adrienne Barbeau), her comeuppance. In the first act Betty Rizzo had taunted her with, "Look At Me, I'm Sandra Dee." Sandy's swinging second-act reprise puts Betty in her place. The fads of the fifties were all made fun of: pajama parties, singers such as Elvis Presley and Fabian, and a wriggling dance called the Hully Gully. For the most part, *Grease* was another loosely constructed chronicle. Affectionate and funny, if not memorably melodic, it has retained the public's fancy. At this writing, five years after its opening, it remains one of Broadway's attractions, while road companies and foreign productions have spread its cheer in lengthy runs elsewhere.

March brought in two shows: a new musical and a revival of a not too old hit. Both failed. The new work was based on journalist Joe McGinness' successful study of commercialization in national elections, **The Selling of the President** (3-22-72, Shubert). Although the title was retained, the history of President Nixon's bid for a second term was fictionalized. The scandal-beset incumbent was replaced by an imaginary Senator George W. Mason (Pat Hingle), and his campaign controlled not by issues but by public relations men and television executives. It seemed a bitter, almost true-to-life expansion of a spoof Jules Munshin had done years before in *Bless You All* (12-14-50). As had become so commonplace in a distressed Broadway, the writing was in the hands of optimistic, but untested, tyros. The job, if it could have been done successfully at all, was botched; *The Selling of the President* closed after five showings.

But a revival of *A Funny Thing Happened on the Way to the Forum* (5-8-62) seemed to have everything going for it. Its original colibrettist and director, Burt Shevelove, was back in his old stand, and Stephen Sondheim added new numbers to freshen his still fresh score. Fine clowns such as Phil Silvers, Lew Parker, and Larry Blyden were on hand to dish out the merriment. But despite good notices, the public refused to line up at the box office and the show folded with the summer.

Another array of fine talent had better luck with inferior material in **Sugar** (4-9-72, Majestic). David Merrick, no longer as active as he once was, produced this stage version of the popular film *Some Like It Hot*. The book was adapted by Peter Stone—of *1776* (3-16-69)—while Jule Styne put melodies to Bob Merrill's lyrics. Stone's libretto adhered closely enough to the original story of two musicians of the prohibition era who witness a gang slaying and are forced to disguise themselves as members of an all-girl orchestra to avoid being silenced. One of the men's disguises is so successful he must spend the evening warding off the advances of an old lecher. The freedom of movement afforded by films was lacking and, as had happened with earlier translations of film farces to the musical stage, much of the wild zaniness was lost. Still Cyril Ritchard and Robert Morse were such capital comedians they often made audiences forget the show's inadequacies. Elaine Joyce played Sugar Kane, a candied variant of Marilyn Monroe's role in the original film. Sparked by Ritchard and Morse's performances as the old man and the "girl" of his dreams, they kept the show on the boards all through the season and well into the next.

That's Entertainment (4-14-72, Edison) proved far less entertaining. An anthology of song hits by Howard Dietz and Arthur Schwartz performed by a small cast, it was withdrawn after 4 performances.

April's next offering was a revival of Maxwell Anderson and Kurt Weill's *Lost in the Stars* (10-30-49). Since the original production had been at best a *succès d'estime,* its resurrection could not seriously be considered part of the nostalgia craze. The new production, mounted initially for the Kennedy Center in Washington, confirmed the judgments of nearly a quarter of a century earlier. With Brock Peters singing the minister, *Lost in the Stars* remained a melodic, richly textured but fatally static piece. Years before, Broadway's theatrical columnist, Walter Winchell, had said something to the effect that it is difficult to revive an old hit, impossible to revive an old flop. The musical's 39 performances recalled and underscored his sentiment.

Lost in the Stars had a racially mixed cast, performing the work of two white men. A sort of revue by a black and sung entirely by blacks arrived the next night. Micki Grant's **Don't Bother Me, I Can't Cope** (4-19-72, Playhouse) often put new lyrics to familiar old melodies to sing its songs of black men's attitudes to a world they don't own. Less strident and more infectiously rhythmic than some other black musicals of the season, it proved popular both in New York and on the road.

Four musicals arrived in May, a surprising figure considering the lateness of the season and the number of musicals that had already found audiences. All four failed. **Different Times** (5-1-72, ANTA) was another loosely structured chronicle spread over sixty-five years from 1905 to 1970, depicting the problems engendered by changing mores and the influx of foreign blood into American families. Entirely written and directed by Michael Brown, it found few takers and left after three weeks.

The religious bent evidenced in musicals during this time reappeared when **Hard Job Being God** (5-15-72, Edison) attempted to follow in the footsteps of *Godspell* and *Jesus Christ Superstar*. Although it used the same rock sound as its predecessors, it concentrated its attention on the Old Testament (and the Apocrypha) rather than the New Testament. Its small cast, with the exception of the actor who portrayed God (Tom Martel), assumed several roles in a history that ranged from Sarah and Abraham through Moses and David to Susanna. The musical lacked the professional know-how of the earlier hits, and folded after six showings.

The night after *Hard Job Being God* opened,

Melvin Van Peebles had his second musical of the season ready. Peebles, in fact, produced and directed **Don't Play Us Cheap!** (5-16-72, Barrymore) as well as putting it all on paper. His simple plot had two bungling demons—Trinity (Joe Keyes, Jr.) and David (Avon Long)—attempt to throw monkey wrenches into an uninhibited Harlem party. They get their comeuppance. The show was less hostile than Peebles' *Ain't Supposed To Die a Natural Death*, but the market for musicals in general and black musicals in particular was momentarily satiated. *Don't Play Us Cheap* struggled into the hot weather before surrendering.

Heathen (5-21-72, Rose), the season's last musical, chalked up a single performance. Not quite a chronicle, it juxtaposed the world of 1819 with that of 1972. A young 19th-century missionary, the Reverend Jonathan Beacon (Russ Thacker), sets out from Boston to convert heathen Hawaiians. A latter-day Jonathan seems more secular but finds religion in his own way.

1972-1973

Broadway groped aimlessly and flailed helplessly all season long. There seemed to be little the musical theater would not resort to in an attempt to revitalize itself, to find a new style and, perhaps, to begin a new era. At one time or another during the theatrical year the lyric stage housed *commedia dell'arte*, rock, a faithless revival of a half-century old musical comedy filled with juicy old songs, a tasteful attempt to write a modern operetta disappointing only for its juiceless new melodies, formless librettos ineptly derived from original ideas, well-plotted librettos ineptly adapted from other works. Often, directors showed more daring and imagination than writers. Three shows earned themselves long runs, though only one—*A Little Night Music*—earned it solely on its own merits.

The season began with two revivals. *Man of La Mancha* opened at the Vivian Beaumont Theatre in Lincoln Center on June 22 with Richard Kiley again in the title part and remained until the Center's repertory company was ready to resume its operations at the end of October. Nothing else appeared until September 15, when *Jacques Brel Is Alive and Well and Living in Paris* was brought in for a limited engagement.

Two importations were among the early October offerings. Each played a week at the Palace. The first was an Israeli army revue, **From Israel with Love,** the second, a Maori revue that had enjoyed a successful run in its native New Zealand, **Pacific Paradise.** Sandwiched between these two foreign offerings was the first new musical of the season, **Dude** (10-9-72, Broadway), subtitled, *The Highway Life. Dude* was created by two of the young writers of *Hair*, Gerome Ragni and Galt MacDermot. Ragni's libretto was even more incohesive, some said incoherent, than his material for *Hair*. It took Dude, first as a boy (Ralph Carter), later as man (Nat Morris), into all parts of the cosmos, as well as into all parts of the specially reconstructed Broadway Theatre, in his search for religious and secular truths. Ragni peopled his cast with such odd-ball characters as #33, Mother Earth, Bread, Esso, Texaco, Noname, World War Too, and the Theater Wings. The show made it sorely obvious that Ragni was not going to sit down and learn the art of theatrical construction. Unfortunately for him, MacDermot's rock score, lacking the melody and appeal of his earlier music for *Hair*, could do nothing to save the evening. Nor could its stager, Tom O'Horgan, for all his free employment of the whole auditorium, devise anything as notorious as his former nude scene to win the musical some sensational publicity. The show closed after 16 performances. The shock of *Dude*'s failure—after such high hopes—no doubt dampened Broadway's infatuation with rock and youth culture.

Three nights after *Dude* opened, another musical with a similar theme appeared. **Hurry, Harry** (10-12-72, Ritz) kept its hero, Harrison Fairchild IV (Samuel D. Ratcliffe), earthbound and confined within the proscenium arch, but sent him, between frequent visits to his psychiatrist, as far afield as Greece and Africa, in search of many of the same truths Dude was seeking. Written by unknowns and denied the ballyhoo that preceded *Dude*'s premiere, *Hurry, Harry* survived a mere 2 performances. The alliterative lilt of the show's title, so reminiscent of titles of a long-gone day, underlined how far librettos had strayed from the era when they hoped only to entertain.

Revues followed the trend as well. **Mother Earth** (10-19-72, Belasco) spent an entire evening pleading in songs and sketches for an understanding of ecological necessities and for an end to our exploitation of our resources. Not many people wanted to be preached to so the revue closed after 12 showings.

Pippin (10-23-72, Imperial), with a libretto by Roger O. Hirson and songs by *Godspell*'s Stephen

Schwartz, was the biggest hit of the season and October's last new musical. Oddly enough it employed much the same story both *Dude* and *Hurry, Harry* had used. Quests for "identity" were, as a popular expression of the day went, "In." The show also employed the increasingly popular device of playing without an intermission. But *Pippin* departed from the contemporary settings the other musicals had, turning instead to the times of Charlemagne. Charlemagne's son Pepin, respelled Pippin (John Rubinstein), looks for meaning in a succession of scenes, whose titles reveal the direction in which the boy has turned: War, The Flesh, Revolution. Nothing satisfied, and Pippin settles for a life of indolent ease. If there was a connection between weak plots and more or less unhappy endings no one stopped to consider it. Even the merely competent writing was glossed over by the clever, stylized staging choreographed by Bob Fosse. His cast was transformed into a collection of *commedia dell'arte* clowns cavorting in whatever manner the mood of the moment demanded. Performing honors went to Ben Vereen as a compère capable of playing both God and the Devil. Assisted by what has become acknowledged as one of the most astute television advertising campaigns, *Pippin*, despite its essential emptiness, ran and ran.

A young composer, Peter Link, heard his music played for first-nighters at two shows which opened one evening apart in November. This apparent streak of good fortune soured a bit when the first show, the New York Shakespeare Festival's *Much Ado About Nothing*, for which he wrote only incidental numbers, proved one of the hits of the season, while **Lysistrata** (11-13-72, Atkinson), for which he created a more traditional Broadway score, folded after a single week. Not even the presence of Melina Mercouri in the title role helped. Three more flops followed in fast succession.

Oscar Wilde's self-destructive life was musicalized as **Dear Oscar** (11-16-72, Playhouse). Unhesitatingly depicting even his homosexual leanings, it found no ready audience and left after five showings. On the very night it closed, **Ambassador** (11-19-72, Lunt-Fontanne), a lyric adaptation of Henry James' *The Ambassadors,* offered itself for inspection. Its American authors, unable to get a hearing, had produced the musical first in London where it had a short run. Its New York run was even shorter, 19 performances. The show was lavishly mounted, with Howard Keel portraying Lambert Strether, a proper New England lawyer sent to Paris on business, where he falls in love with Marie de Vionnet. The popular French actress Danielle Darrieux played Marie.

The spanking new Uris Theatre was opened with a musical that boasted the second Galt MacDermot score of the season, **Via Galactica.** Set a thousand years in the future—2972—in a world destructive of individuality, it narrated the adventurous expedition of Gabriel Finn (Raul Julia), and his girl, Omaha (Virginia Vestoff), to set up a "New Jerusalem" in another solar system. As he had in *The Rothschilds* (10-19-70), Keene Curtis almost stole the show, this time as the intellectual, disembodied head of Dr. Isaacs, wheeling around in a heart-lung machine. Like O'Horgan with *Dude,* Peter Hall ignored the boundaries imposed by the proscenium, flying space ships out over the audience. A trampoline-covered stage allowed performers to bounce up and down to simulate weightlessness. Yet the show's possibilities were never successfully realized, the show folded after one week, and the new Uris embarked on what for several years seemed to be a luckless career.

The procession of failures continued into January. **Tricks** (1-8-73, Alvin), a musical version of Molière's *Les Fourberies de Scapin,* bedecked itself in *commedia dell'arte* finery and presented René Auberjonois in the leading role. The show had met with acclaim and some success in the Actors Theater in Louisville and the Arena Stage in Washington, but New York would have none of it. It was gone after one week.

February's first musical also closed on the wrong side of the ledger. Nonetheless, **Shelter** (2-6-73, Golden) had the small consolation of running a full month (at least double the run of any other flop that had opened during the season) and of garnering favorable or respectful reviews from a number of leading critics. The show had book and lyrics by Gretchen Cryer and music by Nancy Ford, two artists who had earned good reputations for themselves off-Broadway. Its story dared to suggest that boy-girl relationships were still of interest, even though it framed its hero's love-life in a decidedly off-beat narrative and setting. Michael (Terry Kiser) is a young man who writes television commercials and lives in a television studio with a talking computer named Arthur ("talked" by an unseen Tony Wells). Arthur follows his roommate's amours with interest, helping or hindering as he sees fit, especially when a young lady named Maud (Marcia Rodd) comes along. A second young lady who entered the picture had the unlikely name of Wednesday November (Susan Browning). Much the best part of the evening may have been Tony Walton's stunningly conceived single set, a television studio whose ambiance was constantly changed by various pictures projected against its walls.

Just when the season was beginning to look hopeless, **A Little Night Music** raised its curtain. This musical version of Ingmar Bergman's film, *Smiles of a Summer Night,* opened February 25 at the Shubert to general critical cheering. Its old-world elegance led several of the cheering critics to label it an operetta, and Stephen Sondheim's waltz-filled score seemed to confirm the judgment. Yet Bergman's tale, as retold by Hugh Wheeler, interwove a series of love stories that were the essence of worldly cynicism, bathing them in warm, deceptively sentimental glows. True operetta had always been doggedly sentimental, however cynical its veneer. Set in the eerie, romantic light of a turn-of-the-century Swedish summer, *A Little Night Music* concerned itself primarily with the attempt of middle-aged Fredrik Egerman (Len Cariou), to free himself from an unwise, unconsummated second marriage to a girl his son's age. Frederik finds he is falling in love with his former mistress, Desirée (Glynis Johns), the beautiful actress daughter of old Mme. Armfeldt (Hermione Gingold), who herself had enjoyed memorable "Liaisons" in her younger days. Desirée's present lover, Count Carl-Magnus (Laurence Guittard), suspecting Frederik's intentions, sends his wife to indiscreetly make the young Mme. Egerman (Victoria Mallory) aware of them. A candle-lit dinner party at Mme. Armfeldt's brings matters to a head. Fredrik's son, Henrik (Mark Lambert), elopes with his stepmother, the count returns to his wife, and Fredrik has Desirée all to himself. Having rearranged the latest liaisons, Mme. Armfeldt dies unobserved in her chair. As in all of Sondheim's works, his lyrics outshone his music. However, for the first time since *A Funny Thing Happend on the Way to the Forum* (5-8-62), Sondheim did create one melody that enjoyed wide and instant popular appeal. After a not entirely satisfactory meeting with Fredrik in her room, Desirée covers her real emotions by suggesting they "Send In The Clowns." Gorgeously mounted in the subtly tinted, free-flowing sets of Boris Aronson, the show ran 600 performances. Its touring companies and international companies prospered as well. The production was another feather in the cap of Harold Prince who, with *Fiddler on the Roof* (9-22-64), *Cabaret* (10-20-66), and all the recent Sondheim shows, had replaced David Merrick as the major producer in the American Musical Theatre. Prince went one step further than most of his predecessors, staging his own productions.

Hugh Wheeler, in collaboration with Joseph Stein, had a second book ready for the first of March's two musicals on the 13th. The show was, ostensibly, a revival of *Irene* (11-18-19), but it was a revival that demonstrated little faith in the value of the original. Not only was a new book created for the evening, but most of the original numbers were discarded and replaced by either other old songs or by entirely new tunes. The new libretto managed to salvage the names of the original principals and thoughtfully retained the basic Cinderella motif—a motif the original *Irene* had helped make the dominant theme of the early twenties musicals. Once again Irene O'Dare, now a poor little Irish piano-tuner, is called to the home of the rich Marshalls, falls in love with handsome Donald Marshall (Monte Markham), and, aided by a male dress designer who trades under the name of Madame Lucy (George S. Irving), wins Donald over the objections of both families. The old songs added to the show included "They Go Wild, Simply Wild, Over Me" (with lyrics by *Irene*'s original lyricist, Joseph McCarthy and music by Fred Fisher) and "You Made Me Love You" (McCarthy/James Monaco). Audiences out for pure entertainment and unbothered by historical accuracy applauded them as much as they did "Alice Blue Gown." Ignoring the suggestions of intimacy in the original, the show was gaudily mounted and vigorously staged by Gower Champion. Its latter-day Irene, Debbie Reynolds, crooned her songs into a microphone, projecting a flavor far different from the soaring soprano of Edith Day and her followers. To justify her costarring billing, Patsy Kelly clowned broadly in the expanded role of Mrs. O'Dare. The show surpassed the run of the original, dancing merrily on at the new Minskoff for two years. But it left Broadway under a cloud when its accounting practices prevented it from showing a profit after so lengthy a stay.

The best of the season's more traditional, non-innovative lyric works was **Seesaw** (3-18-73, Uris), March's other musical. The show was adapted by Michael Bennett from William Gibson's two-character comedy, *Two for the Seesaw,* which Henry Fonda and Anne Bancroft had played so memorably in 1958. The demands of musical comedy necessitated some expansion in the cast of characters, but Bennett wisely kept them peripheral and, as a result, managed to convey much of the original's intimacy. Of the sixteen numbers in the show, the two principals fail to appear only in three and had nine of thirteen remaining songs to themselves. Oddly, although all of Cy Coleman's music was easy on the ears and Dorothy Fields' lyrics were skillful, if a bit tougher than was her wont, the writers gave the evening's single show-stopper, "It's Not Where You Start," to a minor character and the dancers. Tommy Tune sang this most patently old-fashioned of the evening's melodies while dancing with an avalanche of multicolored balloons. Ken Howard played Jerry Ryan, the young but mature, Midwest attorney whose brief romance with the volatile, gesticulating Manhattanite, Gittel Mosca (Michele Lee), occupied the evening. In the end of the two go their separate ways. *Seesaw,* with numerous cast changes, ran out the season and into the next. But its run was slightly forced, and it never returned its initial investment.

Three musicals, opening six days apart in the middle of May, brought the season to a close. None succeeded. The best of the lot was indubitably **Cyrano** (5-13-73, Palace), which the popular English novelist, Anthony Burgess, adapted from the Rostand play and for which he provided lyrics. Much of the strength of the evening came a bravura performance by the Canadian actor, Christopher Plummer. But the score was weak and, as Victor Herbert and his associates had learned, three-quarters of a century before, *Cyrano de Bergerac* seemingly defies musicalization.

A revue called **Nash at Nine** (5-17-73, Hayes) was devoted, appropriately, to the verse of Ogden Nash. Set to music by Milton Rosenstock, one of Broadway's leading conductors, and performed without intermission by a small cast that included the distinguished actor, E. G. Marshall, it learned to its dismay that although Nash's admirers were legion few of them would pay to sit through an evening of nothing but his rhymes.

The season ended as it began, with a young man searching for his "identity." Walter Smith (Don Murray) is not a little unlike Walter Mitty. He works as dutifully as he can for Mr. Baggett (Mort Marshall) of Baggett Nitrates, but he is given to uncontrollable dreaming. The big dream of the evening finds him as the star of an imaginary musical comedy singing his heart out to a young lady called The Dancing Melody (Bonnie Walter). A clever idea, **Smith** (5-19-73, Eden) was executed with some charm, but not enough. The dream was shattered for good after two weeks.

Off-Broadway had a generally dull season. But the successful **Oh, Coward!** (10-4-72, New) and the not quite so successful **Berlin to Broadway with Kurt Weill** (10-1-72, de Lys) presented homages to leading composers in a form of musical montage Broadway would quickly emulate.

1973-1974

The American Musical Theatre had become barren. To fill the empty playhouses, producers rushed in one-man and one-woman shows, montages and revivals. In desperation a great film was translated, songs and all, onto the stage. Almost nothing worked. For the first time in years, no musical was awarded a place in the *Best Play* series.

No shows appeared throughout the height of the summer. The season opened on September 5, at the Uris, ominously, with a low-budget revival of *The Desert Song* (11-30-26). Some of the minor numbers, especially the comic numbers, were given new lyrics and the setting was advanced inexplicably into the voguish thirties. The reception was anything but cordial, although, significantly, the skimpy production itself was attacked as much or more than was the idea of reviving an old-style operetta. The Red Shadow (David Cryer) and his Riffs rode off after two weeks.

A month and a half elapsed before another musical appeared. When the first new lyric work of the season finally did appear it was warmly welcomed and quickly settled down to become one of the two major hits of the theatrical year. **Raisin** (10-18-73, 46th St.) was a musical version of Lorraine Hansberry's 1959 success, *A Raisin in the Sun,* depicting the efforts of the Younger clan to leave their ghetto existence behind them. Widowed Lena Younger (Virginia Capers) is the matriarch of the group. She hopes to put her daughter, Beneatha (Deborah Allen), through medical school; to help her married son Walter (Joe Morton) buy a liquor store; and to move her family to a better home. Walter's would-be partner absconds with all their savings, but Lena at least contrives to buy a home in a better neighborhood. Like most of the period's musicals, *Raisin* was created by names that were meaningless to most Broadway theatregoers, but librettists Charlotte Zaltzberg and Robert Nemiroff (Nemiroff was also the show's producer), lyricist Robert Brittan and composer Judd Woldin provided material that came to life effectively in the theatre—especially in Donald McKayle's sizzling African dance number—even if it was not particularly memorable after the final curtain.

Molly (11-1-73, Alvin) was based on the once

popular radio series, "The Goldbergs," a series that had long since been made into a moderately successful play, *Me and Molly,* for the show's original star, Gertrude Berg. Miss Berg was dead, and Kaye Ballard assumed the principal role. Set in the voguish thirties, *Molly* watched its heroine help her family and friends through the rigors of the depression. Although Miss Ballard was a skilled comedienne, there was something ersatz about her Yiddish warmth. Indeed there was more of 1973 Broadway than of the 1933 Bronx about the whole evening. The show closed after 68 performances, probably allowing the Goldberg family to rest peacefully hereafter in radio history.

Perhaps no show of this period demonstrated the dire plight of the American Musical Theatre as cruelly as **Gigi** (11-13-73, Uris). For *Gigi* was simply Lerner and Loewe's enchanting film musical lifted off the screen and set down a little uncomfortably on a legitimate stage. The show originated in California with Edwin Lester's Los Angeles and San Francisco Light Opera Company. In years past the group had been responsible for some unusual made-to-order presentations such as *Song of Norway* (8-21-44) and *Gypsy Lady* (9-17-46). But even though all these works used older material, material often not initially conceived for the stage, they were assembled with a discernible iota of creativity. The translation of *Gigi* from film script to play script was mere hack work. Lester was careful to give his show a sumptuous mounting, and he was thoughtful in his casting. Alfred Drake, Daniel Massey, Agnes Moorehead, and a newcomer, Karin Wolfe, played the pivotal roles. For want of competition the show was able to run three months.

Good Evening (11-14-73, Plymouth), a two-man revue by and with half of the team responsible for *Beyond the Fringe,* was imported on November 14. Peter Cook and Dudley Moore's civilized nonsense, called *Beyond the Frinde* in London, ran out the season.

The growing awareness of a large potential black audience, so profitably revealed by *Raisin,* was manifest by the unusual casting of Cab Calloway in the revival of *The Pajama Game* (5-13-54). Calloway was assigned the comic lead of Hines, created by Eddie Foy Jr. Casting of the rest of the primarily white players was not as noteworthy. A number of the more faddish critics, reviewing the December 9 opening at the Lunt-Fontanne, also rued the show's having reached an age which could allow it to be considered "dated."

New Year's Eve brought **An Evening with Jose-**phine **Baker** into the Palace for a one-week stay. Although she was surrounded by an array of competent musical-hall talent, Miss Baker was indeed the whole evening, even if to some her glamor and material (much of which she had offered in her 1964 appearance) were more than a bit frayed.

Up the street at the Winter Garden a much younger lady raised the curtain on her one-woman show six nights later, January 6, 1974. **Liza,** of course, was Liza Minnelli. Assisted by four youthful dancers and by some new material Fred Ebb and John Kander designed around her talents, she delighted her fans for 23 showings.

Lorelei (1-27-74, Palace) was almost a one-woman show. Without Carol Channing it would have been nothing. The musical illustrated almost as poignantly as *Gigi* the exhausted state of the musical theatre. The show's subtitle, *Gentlemen Still Prefer Blondes,* betrayed its genesis, for the show was a collection of the best scenes and songs from the 1949 musical, framed by a prologue and epilogue in which an aging, widowed but wealthy Lorelei Lee Esmond elaborated on her past. For the show Jule Styne wrote several new songs to lyrics by Comden and Green. None approached the popularity of the original's best numbers. Like *Gigi, Lorelei* had no stiff competition. As a result, she ran out the season.

Only one musical arrived in February, called **Rainbow Jones** (2-13-74, Music Box); it survived for a single performance. The young lady of the title (played by Ruby Pearson) spent most of her day in Central Park cavorting with fantasy animals such as Leona (Peggy Hagen Lamprey) and C. A. Fox (G. I. Robbins).

March was busier and happier, although it got off to an unpromising start with a six-character musical, entitled fittingly, **Sextet** (3-3-74, Bijou). Following the growing trend, the show was performed without intermission. Played entirely on a single apartment setting, it dissected the heterosexual and homosexual longings of four boys and two girls. All its "trendiness" wasn't enough. The musical was withdrawn after 9 showings.

A gaudy, stomping evocation of the era of boogie-woogie and jitter-bugging, **Over Here** (3-6-74, Shubert), trucked in next, bringing with it as stars the two surviving of the original Three Andrews Sisters. Played out on a single basic set that simulated the late art-déco stage frames often employed by the big bands, it told a simple story of two singers, Pauline and Paulette de Paul (Maxene and Patty Andrews), embarking on a trip to entertain soldiers during World War I and searching for a third voice to fill out their act. They also find themselves searching for a German spy in their midst. The spy turns out to be the very girl they have hired to make a threesome, Mitzi (Janie Sell). She is unmasked by her all too thorough German indoctrination. Asked to sing the second chorus of "The Star Spangled Banner," she knows all the words—something no true-blooded American can claim. The show's music and orchestrations unerringly captured the sounds and textures of the swing era, but the songs were therefore too consciously out of date to receive any play away from the theatre. The show ran a year on Broadway, closing when the Andrews Sisters and the producers could not come to terms on a contract for a tour.

The most surprising and the biggest hit of the year first saw the light of day in Brooklyn as part of that borough's Chelsea Theater Center program. It moved to Manhattan on March 8. A number of well-known Broadway hands assisted in turning the revival of Bernstein's *Candide* (12-1-56) into a success that must have gone far to heal the hurts the earlier production's failure had inflicted. Hugh Wheeler's new book at once tightened and liberated the tale (for example, Pangloss was minimized). Lewis J. Stadlen, who played Pangloss, also undertook several other roles; Mark Baker was Candide and Maureen Brennan, Cunegonde. If their singing fell below the original's standards, their lively acting compensated. Bernstein's orchestrations were also cut down. Ignited by Harold Prince's electrifying staging, *Candide* exploded all over the house. In this respect, the producers were fortunate that the old barn of a theatre, the Broadway, had been done over the preceding year to meet the same expansive requirements of *Dude* (10-9-72). Some spectators could even sit in specially constructed "bleachers." Stephen Sondheim contributed new lyrics, and some previously unused ones by the late John Latouche were employed. All in all, they combined to make *Candide* a rousing triumph and find for it a place in the permanent repertory.

The rest of the season was downhill. April brought in two montages and a one-man show. The montages arrived first, five nights apart. Alan Jay Lerner's "cavalcade of American music" from 1895 to the present, called without much imagination, **Music! Music!** (4-11-74, City Center), was unveiled at the City Center. It covered a range of styles and composers from ragtime to rock. No doubt some confusion was created when Sammy Cahn opened his revue and called it **Words and Music** (4-16-74, Golden). The words were all by

Cahn and the music by various songsmiths he had worked with for the past forty years. Since Hollywood had been kinder to him than Broadway, much of the material he and three young assistants performed came out of films. The evening proved the popular adage "less is more," and Cahn's limited selection played into the summer, while Lerner's extensive potpourri was gone after 37 representations.

Sammy, a one-man show for Sammy Davis Jr. (actually assisted by a handful of other artists), played the troubled Uris for two weeks beginning April 23.

An unusual setting and subject—11th-century Japan and its Samurai warriors—were not sufficient novelty to save **Ride the Winds** (5-16-74, Bijou), a musical written entirely by John Driver. It lasted a mere three showings.

Just before the calendar brought the season to a halt, an off-beat, appealing little musical show appeared at the Cort. **The Magic Show** (5-28-74, Cort) had a book by Bob Randall and songs by Stephen Schwartz. Schwartz, with the scores for *Godspell* (5-17-71) and *Pippin* (10-23-72) already to his credit, demonstrated a propensity for choosing such odd-ball works. As always, his music was pleasant, lively and forgettable. The book, which told how a fading New Jersey night club, The Passaic Top Hat, saves itself from insolvency by hiring a magic act, was merely an excuse on which to hang the spectacular illusions. Its small cast, small orchestra, and single set kept its running costs low so that in 1978 this intermissionless entertainment, eminently suitable for children, was still thriving.

1974-1975

Two smash hits were the sole commercial bright spots of the new season, yet both succeeded despite often unenthusiastic notices. Their popularity had to be attributed to something other than genuine artistic merit. Except for the profits enjoyed by these two shows—*The Wiz* and *Shenandoah*—and for one revival brought back for a limited stay, the season was a washout.

The fine revival came first, on September 23 at the Winter Garden. Seeing *Gypsy* (5-21-59) fifteen years after the original opening night led most critics to rejoice that the musical remained

"Still Mysteriously Perfect Theatre." Wisely, the revival remained absolutely faithful to the text, while not attempting to mimic slavishly the original mounting. Both the production and the performances tended to be warmer than the first, yet, in sum, equally valid. Angela Lansbury, who had played Ethel Merman's role in London, re-created her more humane interpretation of Rose. If she seemed at first glance too young and beautiful to be believable, her thoughtful acting and stylish, energetic rendering of the songs quickly won over skeptics. *Gypsy* delighted again for 120 performances.

Whenever Broadway has sought to have fun at the expense of silent movies, it has fallen flat on its face. **Mack and Mabel** (10-6-74, Majestic) proved no exception. Old-timers probably guessed even before the curtain rose that Mack (Robert Preston) was Mack Sennett and Mabel (Bernadette Peters) Mabel Normand. In Michael Stewart's book Mabel is swooped from her job in a delicatessen and made a star by the great director. But Mabel wants more than stardom; she wants Mack's love. When Mack remains too preoccupied with his films to notice, Mabel takes to drugs and hits the skids. While Preston's forthright Mack and Miss Peters wide-eyed, waif-like Mabel were both appealing, Gower Champion's imaginative staging frequently stole the show. Champion resorted to films, as he had in *The Happy Time* (1-18-68), for *Mack and Mabel,* offering a montage of silent film comedy that to many was the high point of the evening. He had bathing beauties slide down a giant, multicolored corkscrew, and, in keeping with the popular pretense that prosceniums had disappeared, swung Mack out over the audience on a camera dolly. Jerry Herman's music was lively, but not memorable. For all its happier moments, the show could not sustain its festive gaiety, folding after eight weeks.

Some years back in *Show Girl* (1-12-61), Carol Channing had mocked the lugubrious propensities of modern musicals, singing songs such as "This Is A Darned Fine Funeral" and "Love Is A Sickness." A "play with music" that was a one-performance flop suggested there were no lengths the new musical would not go to in its search for suffering. **Mourning Pictures** (11-10-74, Lyceum) spent the evening with a young poet (Kathryn Walker) as she watched her mother (Leora Dana) die of cancer.

A stager as imaginative as Gower Champion, Tom O'Horgan was responsible for what life **Sgt.**

Pepper's Lonely Hearts Club Band on the Road (11-17-74, Beacon) displayed. His heroine (Kay Cole) made her first appearance singing from the audience; his other performers threw multi-colored Frisbees at patrons. Horgan and Robin Wagner derived their entertainment from a popular Beatles album, adding seventeen additional McCartney and Lennon songs to fill out the evening. A thread of plot watched Billy Shears (Ted Neeley) sell his soul to become a rock star. Only at the end, when Sgt. Pepper (David Patrick Kelly) appears as a sort of deus ex machina and destroys a pair of silver eyeglasses Billy has been wearing, does Billy give promise of reaching his goal. The show was offered at a large, converted film house far uptown from the theatre heartland. It ran just one performance more than *Mack and Mabel*.

Two revivals followed. On December 20, at the new Circle In The Square, Ted Mann brought back *Where's Charley?* (10-11-48). Its new Charley, Raul Julia, was far closer to college age than Bolger had been, even if he was not as lithe and supple as the great dancer. Faithfully resuscitated, and with a redeeming sense of style, the musical played out a limited engagement of 76 performances.

No such sense of style, or anything else redeeming, graced a tasteless revival of *Good News* (9-6-27) on December 23 at the St. James. This wonderful, melodic glimpse of 1927 collegiate shenanigans was not even allowed to retain its roaring twenties setting, but instead, was moved up to the fadingly voguish thirties. Two relatively minor roles were expanded for its stars, two long-unheard-from movie favorites, Alice Faye and John Payne. De-Sylva, Brown, and Henderson songs from other shows, or from their Hollywood and Tin Pan Alley output, were inserted to enhance a score that needed no enhancing. The producers played safe by touring the show for months around the country and by giving weeks of previews in New York before allowing the critics in. During the previews Payne withdrew and was replaced by Gene Nelson. Once the critics reported their findings, the revival was doomed. It closed 16 performances later.

The season's two smash hits arrived two nights apart at the beginning of January 1975. **The Wiz** (1-5-75, Majestic) was an all-black re-creation of *The Wizard of Oz,* far more faithful to the original (and to the story millions knew from the film version) than was Fred Stone and Dave Montgomery's 1903 vehicle. Once again a tornado blew little Dorothy (Stephanie Mills) from her home to the wonderful land of Oz. Only after she helps a

Scarecrow (Hinton Battle), the Tinman (Tiger Haynes), and a cowardly Lion (Ted Ross) achieve their ambitions does she return to earth. The new book and score were adequate, even if some critics complained the latter was "vastly overamplified." At least one song from Charlie Smalls' "soul"-tinged score, "Ease On Down The Road," enjoyed some popularity. The show's clever production was its strong point. Costumes and sets both were eye-catching and witty. The witches' flowing, brightly painted dresses and weird headpieces suggested extravagant Ziegfeld costumes gone amok. The wizard's balloon had a gondola made of old iron stoves and musical instruments, while one of its three balloons looked like a monstrous electric light bulb. In a ballet, the tornado was personified by a dancer (Evelyn Thomas) in long, slender clouds of dark drapes.

Production was anything but the strong point of **Shenandoah** (1-7-75, Alvin). Its scenery was dismissed as "drab and unimaginative," while its staging was condemned as "undistinguished." Indeed, its book, based on a James Stewart movie of the same name, and its music were little better. The story recounted the attempts of the Anderson family to stay clear of the Civil War's bloody turmoil. Only when the family's youngest son (Joseph Shapiro) is kidnapped by Union soldiers, do Charlie Anderson (John Cullum) and his older boys get fighting mad. *Shenandoah* had been preceded by some glowing reports. Critical reception in New York was anything but ecstatic, though Cullum's solemn, strong-voiced performance received general praise, and the show got off to a slow start. Word soon spread that for all its faults the show was wholesome and sentimental. Aided by cut-rate tickets, the show kept its head above water. In time momentum told. Although it rarely played to capacity, it rarely had a losing week. It was even able to send out a road company.

A leader in the "pop art" field, Andy Warhol, produced January's last musical, **Man on the Moon** (1-29-75, Little), a work with book, music, and lyrics by John Phillips a former member of a popular singing group. His story told how Dr. Bomb (Harlan S. Foss) sends his brother and sister-in-law to establish a hotel on Canis Major. Later he launches a bomb that will hurl the moon at the hotel. Somehow in all this nonsense an astronaut (Eric Lang) finds time to fall in love with Bomb's niece (Genevieve Waite). Curiously, Warhol did not design the show's sets, which were dreary. In his bitingly witty review for the *Times*, Clive Barnes insisted

the best part of the evening was watching the "beautiful people" walk in late. Although the musical played the smallest theatre remaining on Broadway, Barnes snidely noted that Lang "sings with a strong microphone." The critic cried longingly, "Bring back 'Via Galactica!' " Warhol quickly withdrew his mistake.

A revue written by and starring a popular singer of country rock, Harry Chapin, was February's only entrant. The songs, mostly with a radical bent, belonged to what one critic described as the "somebody done somebody wrong" school. There were no skits. A revolving geodesic bandstand and the use of closed circuit television brought some novelty to the staging, but the songs' restricted appeal confined the run of **The Night That Made America Famous** (2-26-75, Barrymore) to just over one month.

Goodtime Charley (3-3-75, Palace) propelled audiences back to the 15th century, and retold the effects of Joan of Arc (Ann Reinking) on the young Dauphin (Joel Grey). The show and the production were a collection of contradictions that ultimately proved self-defeating, taking the evening off the boards after three months. The book could not make up its mind whether it wanted to be flippant or serious. Despite its title and its star, Grey, Charley was not its pivotal figure; Joan was. Even its assets worked against the show in some way. For example, Rouben Ter-Arutunian designed an attractive basic set, a semicircle of steps backed with Romanesque pillars and arches. Unfortunately, the set took up so much space it cramped the action and, especially, the dances.

Having already witnessed musicals about a woman dying of cancer and a saint burned at the stake, Broadway was probably not too surprised when a musical appeared treating the "My Lai Incident," in which American soldiers had massacred innocent Vietnamese. The trial of the officer in charge, Lt. William L. Calley, had made headlines for weeks. In a rock opera, devoid of spoken dialogue and laced with relentless dancing, the **Lieutenant** (3-9-75, Lyceum) was not named Calley, but the identification was unmistakable. The show proffered the argument that American militarism, not the officer (Eddie Mekka), must shoulder the real blame. The Prosecutor (Burt Rodriquez) summed up the author's sentiments in "The Conscience Of A Nation." Wartime massacres proved no more palatable to theatregoers than cancer or martyrdom, so *Lieutenant* folded after nine showings.

The next night the musical stage progressed from massacres to monsters. **The Rocky Horror Show** (3-10-75, Belasco) originally opened unheralded in London at a dilapidated cinema house that reinforced the very atmosphere for which the evening strove. The show was a travesty of old horror movies, centering on a character named Frank N. Furter (Tim Curry), a creature with a baritone voice and black lips, dressed as a transvestite in fish net tights. The work's author, Richard O'Brien, took part in the performance under the name Ritz O'Brien, impersonating a hunchbacked butler, Riff-Raff. The entertainment was presented in cabaret style, without intermission. In order to create the proper ambiance, the Belasco was drastically remodeled, even to having boxes removed. In doing so the theatre-owners apparently destroyed some Everett Shinn murals and permanently defaced one of America's unique auditoriums. They probably never retrieved the costs of their remodeling, for *The Rocky Horror Show* couldn't survive a full month.

For years Buster Davis had been a prominent conductor and orchestrator for Broadway musicals. When he at last attempted to write an entire evening on his own, he came a cropper with a five-performance flop called **Doctor Jazz** (3-19-75, Winter Garden). Davis' book followed the rise of a young man (Bobby Van) from his days of a hustler for New Orleans prostitutes to his realization of his dream to be a jazz trumpeter. Although Davis supplemented his own score with songs by Eubie Blake, King Oliver, and Harry Von Tilzer, the evening failed to catch fire or evoke a proper sense of period. Even Raoul Pène du Bois' art-déco scenery was out of place in a story purporting to unfold between 1917 and 1925. While Van did some fine tap dancing that included an interesting slide-walking step, his talents were never fully utilized.

A kooky revue, centering upon the talents of Bette Midler, **Clams on the Half Shell** (4-17-75, Minskoff), depended largely on her popularity to see it through its 88 performances. It was largely a concert, presented in the guise of a cabaret and heavily amplified. Lionel Hampton assisted.

A second song revue came in a month later. **Rodgers and Hart** (5-13-75, Hayes) employed twelve young performers to sing ninety-eight of the team's songs in whole or in part. Romantic numbers monopolized the first half; satiric, the second. The pastiche found enough of an audience to run until mid-August.

1975-1976

In reviewing the original cast recordings for the season's first two shows—the season's two biggest hits—the *Times* headed its notice, "Musicals To Be Seen, Not Heard." As the season progressed, this sad truism had to be applied to every new lyric work that premiered. Theatregoers could on occasion walk out whistling memorable melodies, but only if they had been attending one of the season's revivals or pastiches—or, just possibly, if they had sat through a fascinating work Broadway was enjoying for the first time but that had been written nearly seventy years before. Good mounting, clever staging, and superb dancing accounted for much of the season's excitement.

Chicago (6-3-75, 46th St.), a musicalization of Maurine Dallas Watkins' 1926 hit of the same name, began the season on a up-beat note. The adaptation by Bob Fosse and Fred Ebb, with music by John Kander and lyrics by Ebb, remained faithful to the original tale of Roxy Hart (Gwen Verdon), who kills her lover, enjoys the notoriety, but is relieved to be acquitted thanks to the hanky-panky of her shyster lawyer (Jerry Orbach). In her freedom she forms a nightclub act with another released murderess (Chita Rivera). The *Times* was right in insisting the show was easier on the eye than on the ear. The songs were commonplace, the music and singing annoyingly amplified, the lyrics and dialogue often more than impolite. On the other hand, Fosse's staging was taut; his cakewalks, Charlestons (the show retained its 1926 setting), and soft-shoes vivacious and identifiably angular. Tony Walton employed a basic art-déco unit set, flanked by translucent columns depicting vaudeville and other long-gone greats; and with an onstage band performing from a platform in the rear. Suggestions of vaudeville were furthered by songs that recalled two-a-day favorites. For example, Roxy's trusting husband (Barney Martin) complained he is as transparent as "Cellophane" in a song clearly patterned after Bert Williams' "Nobody." Julian Eltinge and Bert Savoy were evoked when a lady newspaperwoman called Mary Sunshine (M. O'Haughey), a lady with a soaring soprano voice, was revealed to be a man. One especially impressive feat was Fosse's ingenious use of a very small chorus, made to seem larger than it was. Choruses were getting smaller each year.

The next show to open used no chorus at all,

since all the principals were young hopefuls auditioning for **A Chorus Line** (7-25-75, Shubert). Originally mounted the preceding April 15 at Joseph Papp's New York Shakespeare Festival, the musical was conceived by its director and choreographer, Michael Bennett. Its book was by James Kirkwood and Nicholas Dante; its songs had music by Marvin Hamlisch and lyrics by Edward Kleban. The work, performed without intermission, without any real scenery (except a mirrored rear wall) and with the entire cast in work clothes, described how a choreographer, Zach (Robert LuPone), selects his chorus of eight from seventeen applicants not merely by watching the youngsters dance but by having each recite his or her history. Sagas of neurosis, frustration, homosexuality, and hope follow. The most painful for Zach is the plea of his former mistress, Cassie (Donna McKechnie), who had held more important parts, only to lose ground when she couldn't act. She is determined to dance, even if she has to be just another chorus girl. After Zach makes his choices, the entire cast in satiny top hats and dress clothes—the only major costume change of the evening—strut in a high-kicking finale, "One." No one could question the integrity of *A Chorus Line,* which proceeded to grab almost every major award within reach. Possibly it will prove a beacon, pointing the way toward a new type of tightly-knit chamber musical. But the show seemed to many theatregoers taxing in its demand to listen to other people's problems and disappointing in its lack of memorable music. Still, its relatively low initial cost and running costs will keep it on the boards for a long time and possibly prompt less honest and thoughtful imitations.

John Houseman's touring troupe, the Acting Company, opened its repertory season on October 7 with a new musical, *The Robber Bridegroom.* While it stayed only two weeks, its reception was so encouraging, it returned in the next season for an unlimited run (and will be taken up in detail at that time).

In 1953 Menasha Skulnik had left the fading Yiddish theatre and delighted Broadway with his lovable antics in a comedy about the clothing industry, *The Fifth Season.* He played a harassed partner whose associate prefers watchings beautiful models to watching the business. On October 12 the Eden, an off-Broadway house in the heart of Times Square, raised its curtain on a musicalized version, partly in English, partly in Yiddish, produced by Jewish Nostalgic Production, Inc. The original title was retained. Joseph Buloff assumed Skulnik's old role, but he was given only one song

to sing. Even so, the offering proved attractive enough to run until the end of January at the small house.

The next musical was something of a curiosity, and something of a marvel. Scott Joplin had written his ragtime opera, **Treemonisha** (10-21-75, Palace), in 1907 but was never able to see it beyond a run-through. In the intervening years, his orchestrations were lost. The mid-seventies revival of ragtime and especially of Joplin's rag "The Entertainer" prompted Gunther Schuller to study old ragtime orchestrations in the Red Back Book and re-create an approximation of Joplin's intentions. It began as a production of the Houston Grand Opera, conducted by Schuller, and later toured briefly before reaching Broadway. Designer Franco Colavecchia mixed African voodoo and Southern rural motifs with warm, vibrant colors, and choreographer Louis Johnson moved from joyous swinging and jumping dances in "Goin' Around" and "Aunt Dinah Has Blowed De Horn" to fantastically conceived animals cavorting in a ballet, "The Frolic Of The Bears," to a stately, classic rag at the end in "A Real Slow Drag." A fine cast of black singing actors brought Joplin's simple story irresistibly to life. A childless couple, Ned (Willard White) and Monisha (Betty Allen and Lorna Myers, alternating), find a baby under a tree, and so name it Treemonisha (Carmen Balthrop or Kathleen Battle). They persuade white people to educate her. The opera begins when Treemonisha is eighteen. A voodoo conjurer, Zodzetrick (Ben Harney), abducts her to stop her from enlightening her neighbors. A friend, Remus (Curtis Rayam), disguised as a scarecrow, leads her rescuers. Once free, she forgives the kidnaper, and her neighbors elect her to lead them. Excellent as the production and performance were, Joplin's superb melodic gifts outshone them. Moving from the touching pathos of Monisha's "I Want To See My Child," to a quartet of cotton-pickers "We Will Rest Awhile" to the exuberant dance numbers, they gave Broadway its most rewarding score of the season. The show, brought in for a limited engagement, played eight weeks, but no further tour followed, ostensibly because the physical production was too cumbersome for most road theatres to handle.

Another long-gone black entertainer figured prominently in the next musical to open on Broadway. The accurately titled piece was essentially a two-woman show, and one of those women was dead. **Me and Bessie** (10-22-75, Ambassador) offered Linda Hopkins narrating the tragic history of Bessie Smith and singing the songs Miss Smith made famous. When the Ambassador Theatre proved much too large for so intimate an evening, *Me and Bessie* was moved to the smaller Edison, another off-Broadway house in the Times Square area. There it settled in comfortably for a long run.

A third black company arrived at the Minskoff on November 6, with a revival of *Hello, Dolly!* (1-16-64) starring Pearl Bailey. Supported by Billy Daniels as Horace, Miss Bailey and her troupe added another 51 performances to the show's Broadway record.

One week later an all-star cast (Lillian Gish, Tammy Grimes, Larry Kert, John Raitt, Cyril Ritchard, Patrice Munsel, and Dick Shawn) presented a potpourri claiming to demonstrate the development of the American musical. Whether tunes such as "Sweet Betsy From Pike," "Skip To My Lou" or "Mademoiselle From Armentiers" were ever sung in legitimate musicals was moot, while assigning songs from operettas of the 1920s and 1930s to "Early Broadway" suggested either an ignorance or disdain of the American Musical Theatre. Apparently theatregoers weren't interested in so careless a hodgepodge, so **A Musical Jubilee** (11-13-75, St. James) was withdrawn after 92 showings.

Boccaccio (11-24-75, Edison), an inept attempt to translate the more bawdy moments of *The Decameron* to the musical stage, folded after a single week.

One of the joys of an earlier Broadway, *Very Good Eddie* (12-23-15) was revived at the Booth on December 21. The production had originated at the Goodspeed Opera House in East Haddam, Connecticut. Although the revival was tasteless and insensitive, so good was the original and so barren was the competition that the show ran out the season. Much of Jerome Kern's original score was discarded. In its stead songs from other Kern shows were added, including, "Hot Dog," from as late as 1922. Worse, the material was not even played straight, but rather was mocked in a style fashionably known as "camp."

Home Sweet Homer (1-4-76, Palace) came in after a ten-month tour that relied on the lure of Yul Brynner to overcome scathing notices. When Broadway's critics proved just as damning, the show's first New York performance was also its last. Acted out on a single dark-hued set, the work was an intermissionless and interminable retelling of the *Odyssey* with Brynner as Odysseus, Joan Diener as Penelope, and Russ Thacker as Telemachus.

Several of the musical theatre's giants promised new works during the season. Stephen Sondheim's appeared first. **Pacific Overtures** (1-11-76, Winter Garden) was daring and innovative—too daring, innovative, and untheatrical for many. Sondheim and his librettist, John Weidman, attempted to portray Commodore Perry's opening of Japan from a Japanese viewpoint. The entire cast was Asian—even the Americans were played by Asians. (All the players took several roles.) At first the Japanese are frightened and reluctant, but at the very end the scene switches to 20th-century Japan, and the American intrusion is seen as justification for Japan's expansionist policies. Sondheim used not only Oriental instruments to convey his moods, but poetry highly suggestive of Japanese haiku. The mounting drew strongly on the Japanese Kabuki Theatre. Boris Aronson's poetic sets had a distinctly Oriental tinge. He designed Perry's ship to resemble a dragon as much as a vessel. Accordingly, the "Americans" used makeup that suggested they were not only foreign, but possibly fearful monsters. The show made no concession to the tired businessman, so its run was modest and its profits nil.

A free rock adaptation of *Hamlet*—**Rockabye Hamlet** (2-17-76, Minskoff)—sometimes went to Shakespeare for its dialogue and occasional lyrics in songs such as "That It Should Come To This" and "Tis Pity, Tis True," but more often was content to employ contemporary jargon in its speech and in songs on the order of "He Got It In The Ear," "Have I Got A Girl For You," and "The Rosencrantz And Guildenstern Boogie." Even so resourceful a director as Gower Champion couldn't find a way to make the mixture palatable. The show folded after a single week.

An all-black revue attempted much the same retrospective of a bygone Harlem that *A Musical Jubilee* had tried for our lyric stage. Some of the songs in **Bubbling Brown Sugar** (3-2-76, ANTA) were new, but the evening's best moments came when it sang its older songs and did its older dances, notably when Vernon Washington recalled Bill Robinson's brand of tapping and when Avon Long sang Bert Williams' "Nobody." The great Harlem night spots, the Savoy Theatre, and Lenox Avenue all provided backgrounds for fondly remembered melodies by "Fats" Waller, Duke Ellington, Shelton Brooks, Maceo Pinkard, and Eubie Blake. The show ran out the season and through the next.

A twentieth anniversary remounting of *My Fair Lady* (3-15-56) faithfully re-created not only Oliver Smith's sumptuous settings and Cecil Beaton's beautiful gowns, but also Moss Hart's staging and Hanya Holm's choreography. With Ian Richardson as Higgins and Christine Andreas as Eliza the work played on for nearly a year.

Shirley MacLaine, assisted by a chorus of three men and two girls, brought in her one-woman show for two weeks. Between bits of dancing and monologues written for her by Fred Ebb, Miss MacLaine sang songs from as far back as *Madame Sherry*'s "Every Little Movement" to *Sweet Charity*'s "Big Spender."

Richard Rodgers suffered one of his most embarrassing failures when his **Rex** (4-25-76, Lunt-Fontanne) closed after just 41 performances. Rodgers himself was not at fault. His score was attractive, and the show's demise probably deprived "No Song More Pleasing" of a place in his canon. Sheldon Harnick's lyrics were also pleasant. Unfortunately, Sherman Yellen's book was unwieldy, dealing with Henry VIII and his wives in the first act, and in the second with Henry's love-hate relationship to his daughter Elizabeth (played by Penny Fuller, who also played a wife in the first act). The mercurial English actor Nicol Williamson portrayed Henry.

An at times delightful bit of fluff, **So Long, 174th Street** (4-27-76, Harkness) was probably booked far too uptown at the out-of-the-way Harkness to have a chance to find an audience. The show itself was second-rate, but its flaws were frequently glossed over by the clowning of Robert Morse and George S. Irving. Morse brought his perennial boyish charm to the role of a young man in the depression whose parents want him to be a pharmacist but who dreams of being a great star. The show was cleverly framed, beginning as he is interviewed in a dressing room just before he is to receive an honor and ending as he walks up the podium to deliver his thanks for being elected pharmacist of the year. In between, his dreams allow him to dance with a hat and cane in a big production number of the title song and allow his butler (Irving) a hilarious, if smutty, song suggesting the young star is busy making love to every glamor girl in Hollywood.

If Sondheim and Rodgers met with bad luck during the season, their lot was fortunate compared to Leonard Bernstein and Alan Jay Lerner's. Their **1600 Pennsylvania Avenue** (5-4-76, Hellinger) was a one-week fiasco. It took a servant's eye-view of the White House from Washington to Teddy Roosevelt. Handsome Ken Howard played all the Presidents, the fine English comedienne with the desperate smile, Patricia Routledge, played all the First Ladies, and Gilbert Price played an apparently eternal butler. The show turned "The Star Spangled Banner" into a minuet and the post-Civil War boom into "The Robber Baron Minstrel Parade." But Lerner's continuing inability to write well-constructed librettos from original ideas undermined the entertainment.

Joseph Papp's venturesome New York Shakespeare Festival brought back Bertolt Brecht and Kurt Weill's *Threepenny Opera,* decked out in late Victorian costumes and settings, and using a new, scatological translation by Ralph Manheim and John Willett that purported to be closer to Brecht's original than Blitzstein's fine reworking. With Raul Julia as Mack the Knife, the revival, which opened at the Vivian Beaumont on May 1, quickly found a receptive audience and ran for months.

England's D'Oyly Carte had found its visits increasingly short and less profitable. When it returned the night after *1600 Pennsylvania Avenue*'s premiere, it confined its visit to less than three weeks and performed only the most popular, sure-fire works: *The Mikado, The Pirates of Penzance,* and *H.M.S. Pinafore.* The response was not overwhelming.

A small, charming, unpretentious musical ended the season. A group of novices used a story much like Agatha Christie's *Ten Little Indians* to create a comical musical mystery about ten people marooned on an island estate, Rancour's Retreat, and murdered one by one. One of the characters was the appropriately named Miss Tweed, a combination of Miss Christie and her Miss Marple. Played by the hefty English music hall favorite, Tessie O'Shea, she helped underscore the show's debt in "I Owe It All (To Agatha Christie)." Even the somber, cumbersome Victorian furniture was as witty as it was murderous. Sadly, audiences couldn't be corraled, so **Something's Afoot** (5-27-76, Lyceum) departed when summer came.

1976-1977

This was a season of revivals rather than revival. Broadway had seen over half the musicals offered to it before, while one "new" show had actually premiered in Berlin nearly fifty years earlier. By coincidence Salvation Army dolls and their shady guys framed the season.

Guys and Dolls (11-24-50), with an all-black cast, braved the hot weather to open on July 22 at the Broadway. If this version smacked more of Harlem than of Brooklyn, Queens, or the seedier sections of white Manhattan, it nonetheless had style, gusto, and a gratifying faithfulness to the original. Adelaide (Norma Donaldson), Nathan (Robert Guillaume), Sarah (Ernestine Jackson), and Sky (James Randolph) replayed their adventures well into the season. The revival prompted Clive Barnes of the *Times* to note that the great songs of the old shows were "the element that keeps [them] alive." All through the year only the old shows really sent audiences away singing.

Going Up (12-25-17) was another oldie—a virtually forgotten one—filled with buoyant, hummable melodies. The revival originated at the Goodspeed Opera House in East Haddam, Connecticut, and came to the Golden on September 19. If Goodspeed had a tradition of bravely resuscitating obscure past hits, it also had a tradition of presenting them faithlessly and tastelessly. *Going Up* was no exception. The book was altered, songs written for other shows interpolated, and the whole mounting, even what were meant to be its tender moments, played for laughs. For all its faults, the second-string critic the *Times* sent to review the show could still quite rightly find it full of charm. But the revival had more charm than staying power.

Debbie Reynolds brought a vaudeville into the Minskoff briefly, while the nudist revue, *Oh, Calcutta!* was revived at the Edison.

Porgy and Bess (10-10-35) was actually more than a revival. The version unveiled at the Uris on September 25 was Broadway's first chance to hear virtually the complete score Gershwin wrote, including such generally omitted passages as the extended opening and "The Buzzard Song" in its proper place. The production had originated with the Houston Grand Opera Company as its contribution to the nation's bicentennial celebration. As they often had in earlier revivals, several singers alternated in each of the principal roles. For opening night Porgy was sung by Donnie Ray Albert and Bess by Clamma Dale.

A handful of New Yorkers had seen **The Robber Bridegroom** (10-9-76, Biltmore) when it had visited Broadway a year earlier as part of the repertory of John Houseman's band, the Acting Company. Based on a novella by Eudora Welty, the musical had book and lyrics by Alfred Uhry and music by Robert Waldman. Its story followed the picaresque adventures of Jamie Lockhart (Barry Bostwick) after he is separated from his be-

loved through the machinations of her wicked stepmother. Folksy and light, if not insistently memorable, the show played through most of the season.

On the other hand, a show from which much had been expected closed immediately after it opened. With Richard Adler and Will Holt writing the songs, George Abbott attempted to turn Shakespeare's *Twelfth Night* into much the same sort of romp he had created out of *A Comedy of Errors*, *The Boys from Syracuse* (11-23-38). That a number of relatively unknown hands had done the job superbly eight years before in *Your Own Thing* (1-13-68) failed to daunt the eighty-nine-year-old Abbott. Unlike *The Boys from Syracuse*, which employed only a single line from Shakespeare, **Music Is** (12-20-76, St. James) leaned frequently on the original text, much more than had *Your Own Thing*. But *Your Own Thing* had brought to its adaptation a point of view, a deliciously irreverent two-faced stance that allowed it to josh the very story it was following. Somehow *Music Is* lost itself shunting between two worlds. Its high moments came fitfully. Sebastian (Joel Higgins) and Olivia (Sherry Mathis) had one pleasant song, "Please Be Human," while Malvolio (Christopher Hewitt) had his day with "I Am It." Choreographer Patricia Birch offered a splended *galop* for her Offenbachian first-act finale.

An adaptation of the Gospel according to St. Matthew, presented with black revival meeting fervor, **Your Arm's Too Short To Box with God** (12-22-76, Lyceum) set feet stomping and hands clapping. Amusingly, this show, which had been created for the Spoleto Festival, sent enthusiastic critics back to the very words they had used to salute the happy black musicals of half a century before: "the best singing and dancing on Broadway," "rollicks with contagious high spirits." Vinnette Carroll, Micki Grant, and Alex Bradford—all associates in *Don't Bother Me, I Can't Cope* (4-19-72)—shaped the evening, which included William Hardy, Jr., a remarkable baritone capable of soaring above "the highest register ordinarily associated with the most adventurous male voice."

Fiddler on the Roof (9-22-64) returned on December 28 with Zero Mostel once again its Tevye. The stay at the Winter Garden was announced as limited, though the limits were set not by attendance but by Mostel's willingness to remain with the show. His willingness lasted through the spring.

In an odd, sad way, the black shows of the twenties were again recalled by **Ipi-Tombi** (1-11-77, Harkness). Though the show had been a major hit in London, this collection of South African native dances was coolly received by New York critics and hounded by left-wing pickets. It struggled on for a brief time before calling it quits. Shortly after it closed the Harkness was sold for demolition or conversion. In recent years the out-of-the-way house had served unsuccessfully as a dance auditorium and legitimate theatre. Before that it had been a television studio and a grind movie house. But in the twenties, as the Colonial Theatre, it had been used for lesser vaudeville and legitimate attractions, including black shows held unworthy of Times Square.

Eighteen years had passed since New Yorkers were first invited to *A Party with Betty Comden and Adolph Green* (12-23-58). The two were "at home" again, accompanied only by a pianist, on February 10 at the Morosco. Singing lyrics they set to Jule Styne's or Leonard Bernstein's or Cy Coleman's music, they delighted their loyal admirers. That these admirers were fewer in number than they had a right to hope was revealed when they moved their entertainment to the smaller Little Theatre and shortly thereafter sent the last of their guests home.

Three hits arrived over a six-night span in mid-April. **Side by Side by Sondheim** (4-15-77, Music Box) was a low-budget (cast of four) anthology of Stephen Sondheim's songs. Curiously, the show had originated in London. As a slightly premature retrospective, it confirmed Sondheim's brilliance as a lyricist—Clive Barnes in the *Times* went further, asserting the show proved he was "the master lyricist of American popular music." But even Barnes had to make excuses for Sondheim's failings as a melodist. Still, Sondheim's word wizardry was intriguing enough to make the evening worthwhile.

Barnes began his review for **I Love My Wife** (4-17-77, Barrymore) noting that Broadway was bound to get around to wife-swapping, since Hollywood had done it years ago. Barnes was clearly too young to remember Broadway got there first, with *So Long, Letty* (10-23-16). The small cast was abetted by a small on-stage orchestra. The musicians—dressed as devils, or in pajamas—acted as a sort of modern-day Greek chorus might, commenting flippantly on the liaisons which, by the by, never got very far. Barnes and most other critics singled out lanky Lenny Baker as the best of the straying spouses. Baker's Alvin employs every conceivable delaying tactic—needing ages to undress, painstakingly folding every garment, then insisting on finishing off a banana cream pie. Michael Stewart wrote the book and lyrics to Cy Coleman's music, the best of which was probably the lively "Hey There, Good Times" and the title song.

The season's biggest hit was the last of April's trio, **Annie** (4-21-77, Alvin). Based on the once-famous comic strip, *Little Orphan Annie*, the musical sent its waif (Andrea McArdle) from an orphanage run by the comically villainous Miss Hannigan (Dorothy Loudon) into the arms of fabulously rich, totally bald Daddy Warbucks (Reid Shelton). Under his aegis Annie gets to meet Franklin D. Roosevelt and even has J. Edgar Hoover enlisted to help find her real parents. Annie and Warbucks share all their adventures with her loyal dog, Sandy. Thomas Meehan's book, Martin Charnin's lyrics, and Charles Strouse's music were serviceable. Peter Gennaro had fun allowing a small band of ragged waifs to strut and kick as if they were the long line of Radio City Music Hall Rockettes that Gennaro still supervised.

A sumptuous revival of Rodgers and Hammerstein's *The King and I* (3-29-51) on May 2 at the Uris brought Yul Brynner back to re-create the role of the king. Constance Towers played his Anna. At a time when musicals were generally unmelodic, often formless, and frequently preachy or scatological, the revival was poignantly hailed as a "Reminder of [a] Golden Age." The public responded in such numbers that, even in the record-breaking heat of July, *The King and I* played to 98 percent capacity.

From an even earlier, perhaps more golden age, came a musical New York had never really seen before, Kurt Weill and Bertolt Brecht's **Happy End** (5-7-77, Beck). With its tale of underworld guys and Salvation Army dolls, it was originally written for Berlin in 1929, at almost a halfway point between the time New York first saw *The Belle of New York* (9-28-97) and the Broadway premiere of *Guys and Dolls* (11-24-50). Brecht's Salvation Army lass is Hallelujah Lil (Meryl Streep). When she capitulates to the charms of the murderous Bill Cracker (Bob Gunton), she is stripped of her uniform. She reforms Cracker and his gang in time to put her uniform back on before the final curtain. The show, in Michael Feingold's translation, had originated at the Chelsea in Brooklyn. Despite critical kudos and superior Weill melodies such as "Surabaya Johnny" and "The Bilbao Song," theatregoers stayed away, so *Happy End* ended its run unhappily with the coming of warm weather.

Two oddities deserve passing mention. An ice show played the Palace briefly in the spring, while at the Winter Garden something called **Beatle-mania** played weeks and weeks of previews without, apparently, ever opening officially. The entertainment surrounded four young men impersonating the rock stars with "slides, film, and video projections, read-outs from a giant ticker tape and a great many lights." In a sense *Beatlemania* helps tie together this epilogue—at least as far as it has gone—since the Beatles' arrival here in 1964 set the rock movement in full gear and played no small part in throwing the American Musical Theatre off balance.

1977-1978

Like the preceding season, 1977–78 was one of revivals rather than revival. Certainly the early months offered little more than a parade of old faces. On August 4, *Hair* (4-29-68) returned to the Biltmore and added another 108 performances to its record. *Man of La Mancha* (11-22-65) came into the Palace on September 15 for a limited stay as part of a national tour. It chalked up 124 performances. October's revival was Victor Borge in his popular one-man show, *Comedy in Music*. Borge added much fresh material to his evening, but *Hair* and *Man of La Mancha* were presented with a large degree of fidelity to their originals (with Kiley again in his starring role). Here and there, critics suggested these book shows had lost something of their old lustre—a criticism also voiced when *Jesus Christ Superstar* (10-12-71) appeared at the Longacre on November 23. But carping critics were in the minority. Still, *Superstar* failed to find the hoped-for audience and was withdrawn after 96 showings.

But another "superstar" had arrived in October with the first original musical of the season. **The Act** (10-29-77, Majestic) was created solely as a vehicle for Liza Minnelli. John Kander and Fred Ebb, who had written material for her earlier, did the songs, while George Furth developed the thinnest of books. Miss Minnelli played Michelle Craig, a once-important film star whose career collapses after she loses her husband. She determines to make a comeback with a nightclub act for Las Vegas. Little enthusiasm was shown for the book or lyrics, but there was general rejoicing over Miss Minnelli's skills as an entertainer. However, the rejoicing was soon soured when it was learned Miss Minnelli had prerecorded some of her songs and was merely mouthing them on stage. Walter Kerr led the protests with an article in the *Times* headed, "A Theater Critic Gets That 'Synching' Feeling." The disclosures brought out in the open a growing displeasure with the abuse—indeed, with the very use—of amplification in what was supposedly "live" theatre. Proponents insisted that today's audiences, lulled by films and television, no longer had an ear for naturally voiced singing and dialogue. Still, for the first time in years, in review after review of musicals that followed, complaints were expressed about the unnatural sounds emanating from loudspeakers on the proscenium. Most theatregoers would probably be surprised to learn that the battle had first been joined thirty-seven years before when Richard Watts, Jr., and Brooks Atkinson had bewailed Earl Carroll's use of microphones in his last *Vanities* (1-13-40). Miss Minnelli aggravated matters later in the run when she insisted even mouthing songs was too arduous for the customary eight performances a week. Tantrums, fainting spells, and dramatic exits were the stock-in-trade of early prima donnas such as Lillian Russell or Della Fox, but these ladies had at least performed in a theatre that required muscle and vocal chords.

The next musical to arrive, **On the Twentieth Century** (2-19-78, St. James), tried to be a good, old-fashioned musical comedy. It was lavishly mounted, star-studded, blessed with a solid, funny story, and offered songs that, for this day and age, could be considered slightly arioso. Based on *Twentieth Century*, an old play by Ben Hecht and Charles MacArthur, and remembered by most theatregoers for the film version with John Barrymore and Carole Lombard, it told another tale of a theatrical has-been desperately seeking a comeback. In this case the has-been is the flamboyant producer Oscar Jaffe (John Cullum), and key to his resurrection is his former star and mistress, Lily Garland (Madeline Kahn). His attempts to woo her back while they travel by train cross-country are sometimes interrupted by a zany religious fanatic (Imogene Coca). Betty Comden and Adolph Green devised the book and lyrics, and Cy Coleman the music. But for many the star of the evening was Robin Wagner's "brilliantly effective" re-creation of the famous old train. *Variety* began its notice, "It's ominous when an audience leaves a musical whistling the scenery." Still, for all its faults, the evening was rattling good fun. If the audiences that left whistling the scenery were not always capacity they were close to it for a long while.

By the standards of the time, March was busy. Four musicals appeared: three new and one old. Actually the first of the "new" musicals was an old friend in disguise: **Timbuktu** (3-1-78, Hellinger) was merely *Kismet* (12-3-53) revised to meet the requirements of its all black cast. New songs, often based on African folk music rather than on Borodin, were added to give some tonal verisimilitude to the change of venue from Baghdad to the half-legendary African watering spot. Geoffrey Holder's costumes and Tony Straiges' sets had a Ziegfeldian opulence. Eartha Kitt, Melba Moore, and Gilbert Price were starred. Though all three were capital performers, none had Alfred Drake's commanding theatrical presence. One result was that some critics felt the show lacked a certain backbone. As with *On the Twentieth Century,* however, the show's attractions helped minimize its shortcomings, and *Timbuktu* did good, though not sellout, business.

Four nights later New Yorkers once again had a chance to say *Hello, Dolly!* (1-16-64). With Carol Channing returned to head the fun at the Lunt-Fontanne, the show, which had enjoyed a profitable pre-Broadway tour, settled in for a run.

March's next entry underscored the importance of choreographers to contemporary Broadway. The musical was the brain child of Bob Fosse and was devoted entirely to **Dancin'** (3-27-78, Broadhurst). There was no story, nor any dialogue or new songs as Broadway normally understood them. Instead, sixteen talented hoofers danced in a variety of styles to music "from Bach through John Philip Sousa and George M. Cohan to Johnny Mercer and Cat Stevens." Without a story or lavish sets to hang the dances on, some critics felt the dances failed to provide a totally satisfactory evening. Other critics were ecstatic. At least in its early weeks the show seemed to attract hordes of playgoers willing to decide for themselves.

If complaints about amplification were growing, Broadway's reception of the next musical stood to revive an even older complaint, namely that Broadway critics often killed shows the road loved. **A History of the American Film** had been mounted at several important regional theatres, generally to resounding acclaim. The evening was a series of vignettes spoofing famous films and film stars from the silent era to the present. Christopher Durang wrote the book and lyrics to Mel Marvin's score. What many American cities had viewed as stylish drollery, New York rejected as a crass, humorless hodgepodge. It was just this sort of reaction that has inspired Richard Adler to attempt to found a hospitable base for new musicals in North Carolina. Adler has not had a New York success since *Damn Yankees* (5-5-55), although a number of distinguished critics, led by Richard Coe of the *Washington Post,* have praised his later works, especially *Music Is* (12-20-76).

Like *A Chorus Line* (7-25-75), **Runaways** (5-6-78, Plymouth) began life in one of Joseph Papp's off-Broadway auditoriums. And like *A Chorus Line* it was essentially a chamber musical allowing a collection of people to come forward with their histories and personal problems. Conceived and written by Elizabeth Swados, the evening recounts the often humorous, often harrowing experiences of children who have run away from home. Daringly, Swados employed several real runaways in her cast. As a result, the *Times* found one of the pleasures of the production "its rough edges and its freshness" and also hailed "a lowdown travesty of punk rock" called "Where Are Those People Who Did 'Hair'?" *Variety* also singled out the song. The trade paper may have also given this sort of show an official label when it tagged it a "musical collage."

A collection of songs by "Fats" Waller provided the meat for an entire evening named after his most famous song, **Ain't Misbehavin'** (5-9-78, Longacre). A small cast presented at least two songs which have long been credited to Jimmy McHugh, but which the producers have announced Waller actually wrote and sold the rights to: "I Can't Give You Anything But Love" and "Sunny Side Of The Street."

The next night brought the premiere of **Angel** (5-10-78, Minskoff). To music by Gary Geld, Peter Udell and Ketti Frings provided a libretto adapted from Frings' prize-winning stage version of Thomas Wolfe's *Look Homeward, Angel.* The bittersweet saga of Eugene Gant's adolescence in North Carolina, of his soured-on-life father and his dreamy mother, was re-created in homey, sentimental terms. Since so many of the people behind the scenes had been responsible for *Shenandoah* (1-7-75), Broadway had some advance inkling of the musical's tenor. The initial pre-opening advertisement confirmed this, reprinting Kevin Kelly's notice, from the Boston *Sunday Globe,* that underscored *Angel's* kinship to the earlier show.

May's fourth musical was **Working** (5-14-78), a lyric version of Studs Terkel's slices of lower-class life. A group effort to an even greater extent than many musicals, its advertisements listed songs by six writers, including Micki Grant, Mary Rodgers, and Stephen Schwartz.

Two oddball musicals were also seen during the

season. A Spanish importation called **Estrada** played a brief stand at the Majestic in September, while a glorified rock concert, not unlike the preceding season's *Beatlemania*, ran for a few weeks at the Palace. Just as the earlier show had concentrated on the music of the group its title celebrated, the new piece honored a famous rock figure, insisting in its title, **Elvis the Legend Lives.**

APPENDIX

This appendix is provided as an adjunct to the index and is not to be regarded as an all-inclusive listing of the works of the major figures cited.

ABBOTT, GEORGE: Barefoot Boy with Cheek ('47); Beat the Band ('42); Best Foot Forward ('41); Boys from Syracuse, The ('38); Damn Yankees ('55); Fade Out-Fade In ('64); Fiorello! ('59); Flora, the Red Menace ('65); Look Ma, I'm Dancin' ('48); Music Is ('76); New Girl in Town ('57); On the Town ('44); On Your Toes ('36); Pajama Game, The ('54); Tenderloin ('60); Tree Grows in Brooklyn, A ('51); Where's Charley? ('48)

ASTAIRE, FRED and/or ADELE: Apple Blossoms ('19); Band Wagon, The ('31); Bunch and Judy, The ('22); For Goodness Sake ('22); Funny Face ('27); Gay Divorce ('32); Lady, Be Good! ('24); Love Letter, The ('21); Over the Top ('17); Passing Show of 1918, The; Smiles ('30)

BLOSSOM, HENRY: All for the Ladies ('12); Candy Shop, The ('09); Follow the Girl ('18); Man from Cook's, The ('12); Mlle. Modiste ('05); Only Girl, The ('14); Prima Donna ('08); Princess Pat, The ('15); Red Mill, The ('06); Trip to Washington, A ('13); Velvet Lady, The ('19); Yankee Consul, The ('04)

BOCK, JERRY: Apple Tree, The ('66); Catch a Star ('55); Fiddler on the Roof ('64); Fiorello! ('59); Mr. Wonderful ('56); Rothschilds, The ('70); She Loves Me ('63); Tenderloin ('60)

BOLTON, GUY: Ankles Aweigh ('55); Daffy Dill ('22); Five O'Clock Girl ('27); Follow the Girls ('44); Girl Behind the Gun, The ('18); Girl Crazy ('30); Have A Heart ('17); Hold on to Your Hats ('40); Hotel Mouse, The ('22); Jackpot ('44); Lady, Be Good! ('24); Leave It to Jane ('17); Nightingale, The ('27); Ninety in the Shade ('15); Nobody Home ('15); Oh, Boy! ('17); Oh, Kay! ('26); Oh, Lady! Lady!! ('18); Oh, My Dear! ('18); Polly ('29); Ramblers, The ('26); Rio Rita ('27); Riviera Girl, The ('17); Rosalie ('28); Rose of China, The ('19); Sally ('20); Simple Simon ('30); Sitting Pretty ('24); Tangerine ('21); Tip Toes ('25); Top Speed ('29); Very Good Eddie ('15); Walk with Music ('40)

CARYLL, IVAN: Canary, The ('18); Chin-Chin ('14); Circus Girl, The ('97); Duchess of Dantzic ('05); Earl and the Girl, The ('05); Girl Behind the Gun, The ('18); Girl from Kay's, The ('03); Girl from Paris, The ('96); Girls of Gottenberg, The ('08); Hotel Mouse, The ('22); Jack o' Lantern ('17); Kissing Time ('20); Ladies' Paradise, The ('01); Little Cafe, The ('13); Little Cherub, The ('06); Little Christopher Columbus ('94); Marriage à la Carte ('11); Oh! Oh! Delphine ('12); Orchid, The ('19); Our Miss Gibbs ('07); Pink Lady, The ('11); Runaway Girl, A ('98); Shop Girl, The ('95); Spring Chicken, The ('06); Toreador, The ('02)

COHAN, GEORGE M.: American Idea, The ('08); Billie ('28); Cohan Revue, The ('16 and '18); Fifty Miles from Boston ('08); Forty-five Minutes from Broadway ('06); George Washington, Jr. ('06); Hello, Broadway! ('14); Honeymooners, The ('07); I'd Rather Be Right ('37); Little Johnny Jones ('04); Little Millionaire, The ('11); Little Nellie Kelly ('22); Man Who Owns Broadway, The

689

('09); Mary ('20); Merry Malones ('27); O'Brien Girl, The ('21); Rise of Rosie O'Reilly, The ('23); Royal Vagabond, The ('19); Running for Office ('03); Talk of New York, The ('07); Yankee Prince, The ('08)

COMDEN, BETTY and GREEN, ADOLPH: Applause ('70); Bells Are Ringing ('56); Billion Dollar Baby ('45); Do Re Mi ('60); Fade Out —Fade In ('64); Hallelujah, Baby! ('67); Lorelei ('74); On the Town ('44); Party with Comden and Green, A ('58); Peter Pan ('54); Say, Darling ('58); Subways Are for Sleeping ('61); Wonderful Town ('53)

DEKOVEN, REGINALD: Algerian, The ('93); Beauty Spot, The ('09); Begum, The ('87); Don Quixote ('89); Fencing Master, The ('93); Foxy Quiller ('00); Girls of Holland, The ('07); Golden Butterfly, The ('08); Happyland ('05); Her Little Highness ('13); Highwayman, The ('97); Jersey Lily, The ('03); Knickerbockers, The ('92); Little Duchess, The ('01); Maid Marian ('02); Mandarin, The ('96); Papa's Wife ('99); Red Feather, The ('03); Robin Hood ('90); Rob Roy ('94); Student King ('06); Three Dragoons, The ('99); Tzigane, The ('95); Wedding Trip, The ('11)

DE SYLVA, B. G. (BUDDY), BROWN, LEW and/or HENDERSON, RAY: Calling All Stars ('34); Captain Jinx ('25); Du Barry Was a Lady ('39); Flying High ('30); Follow Thru ('29); George White's Scandals ('25, '26, '28, '31, '35); Good News ('27); Hold Everything! ('28); Hot-Cha! ('32); La La Lucille ('19); Louisiana Purchase ('40); Manhattan Mary ('27); Panama Hattie ('40); Piggy ('27); Say When ('34); Strike Me Pink ('33); Take a Chance ('32); Yokel Boy ('39); Ziegfeld Follies ('43)

DIETZ, HOWARD: At Home Abroad ('35); Band Wagon, The ('31); Between the Devil ('37); Dear Sir ('24); Flying Colors ('32); Gay Life, The ('61); Inside U.S.A. ('48); Jackpot ('44); Jennie ('63); Little Show, The ('29); Merry-Go-Round ('27); Sadie Thompson ('44); Second Little Show, The ('30); Three's A Crowd ('30)

DILLINGHAM, CHARLES: Babette ('03); Better Times ('22); Big Show, The ('16); Canary, The ('18); Century Girl, The ('16); Cheer Up ('17); China Rose ('25); City Chap, The ('25); Girl from Home, The ('20); Hip-Hip Hooray ('15); Everything ('18); Jack o' Lantern ('17); Lady of the Slipper, The ('12); Love Letter, The ('21); Miss 1917; Mlle. Modiste ('05); New Faces ('34); Night Boat, The ('20); Old Town, The ('10); One Kiss ('23); Over the River ('12); Sidewalks of New York ('27); Sunny ('25); Red Mill, The ('06); Watch Your Step ('14)

ENGLANDER, LUDWIG: Caliph, The ('96); Daughter of the Revolution, A ('95); Half a King ('97); In Gayest Manhattan ('97); In Gay Paree ('99); Jewel of Asia, The ('03); Little Corporal, The ('98); Madame Moselle ('14); Madcap Princess, A ('04); Miss Innocence ('08); Monks of Malabar, The ('00); New Yorkers, The ('01); Office Boy, The ('03); Passing Show, The ('94); Prince Consort, The ('93); Rich Mr. Hoggenheimer, The ('06); Sally in Our Alley ('02); Strollers, The ('01); Twentieth Century Girl, The ('95); Two Roses, The ('04); Wild Rose, The ('02)

FIELDS, DOROTHY: Annie Get Your Gun ('46); Arms and the Girl ('50); Blackbirds of 1928; By the Beautiful Sea ('54); Hello, Daddy ('28); International Revue ('30); Let's Face It! ('41); Mexican Hayride ('44); Seesaw ('73); Something for the Boys ('43); Stars in Your Eyes ('39); Sweet Charity ('66); Tree Grows in Brooklyn, A ('51); Up in Central Park ('45)

FIELDS, HERBERT: America's Sweetheart ('31); Annie Get Your Gun ('46); Arms and the Girl ('50); By the Beautiful Sea ('54); Chee-Chee ('28); Connecticut Yankee, A ('27); Dearest Enemy ('25); Du Barry Was a Lady ('39); Fifty Million Frenchmen ('29); Girl Friend, The ('26); Hello, Daddy ('28); Hit the Deck ('27); Let's Face It ('41); Mexican Hayride ('44); New Yorkers, The ('30); Panama Hattie ('40); Pardon My English ('33); Peggy-Ann ('26); Present Arms ('28); Something for the Boys ('43); Up in Central Park ('45)

FRIML, RUDOLF: Blue Kitten, The ('22); Cinders ('23); Firefly, The ('12); Glorianna ('18); High Jinks ('13); June Love ('21); Katinka ('15); Kitty Darlin' ('17); Little Whopper, The ('19); Luana ('30); Music Hath Charms ('34); Peasant Girl, The ('15); Rose-Marie ('24); Sometime ('18); Three Musketeers, The ('28); Tumble In ('19); Vagabond King, The ('25); White Eagle, The ('27); Wild Rose, The ('26); You're In Love ('17)

GERSHWIN, GEORGE: Funny Face ('27); George White's Scandals ('20 to '24); Girl Crazy ('30); Lady, Be Good! ('24); La La Lucille ('19); Let 'Em Eat Cake ('33); Of Thee I Sing ('31); Oh, Kay! ('26); Our Nell ('22); Pardon My English ('33); Porgy and Bess ('35); Rosalie ('28); Show Girl ('29); Song of the Flame ('25); Strike Up the Band ('30); Sweet Little Devil ('24); Tell Me More! ('25); Tip-Toes ('25); Treasure Girl ('28)

GERSHWIN, IRA (shows without George): Firebrand of Florence, The ('45); Lady in the Dark ('41); Life Begins at 8:40 ('34); Park Avenue ('46); Two Little Girls in Blue ('21); Ziegfeld Follies ('34)

HAMMERSTEIN, OSCAR, II: Allegro ('47); Always You ('20); Ballyhoo ('30); Carmen Jones ('43); Carousel ('45); Daffy Dill ('22); Desert Song, The ('26); East Wind

('31); Flower Drum Song ('58); Free for All ('31); Gang's All Here, The ('31); Golden Dawn ('27); Good Boy ('28); Jimmie ('20); King and I, The ('51); Mary Jane McKane ('23); May Wine ('35); Me and Juliet ('53); Music in the Air ('32); New Moon, The ('28); Oklahoma! ('43); Pipe Dream ('55); Queen o' Hearts ('22); Rainbow ('28); Rose-Marie ('24); Show Boat ('46); Song of the Flame ('25); Sound of Music ('59); South Pacific ('49); Sunny ('25); Sunny River ('41); Sweet Adeline ('29); Tickle Me ('20); Wildflower ('23); Wild Rose, The ('26)

HARBACH, OTTO: Blue Kitten, The ('22); Bright Eyes ('10); Cat and the Fiddle, The ('31); Criss Cross ('26); Desert Song, The ('26); Dr. Deluxe ('11); Firefly, The ('12); Forbidden Melody ('36); Girl of My Dreams, The ('11); Going Up ('17); Golden Dawn ('27); Good Boy ('28); High Jinks ('13); Jimmie ('20); Kid Boots ('23); Kitty Darlin' ('17); Kitty's Kisses ('26); Lucky ('27); Madame Sherry ('10); Mary ('20); No! No! Nanette! ('25); O'Brien Girl, The ('21); Oh, Please ('26); Roberta ('32); Rose-Marie ('24); Song of the Flame ('25); Sunny ('25); Three Twins ('08); Tickle Me ('20); Tumble In ('19); Wildflower ('23); Wild Rose, The ('26)

HARRIGAN, EDWARD and/or HART, TONY: Are You Insured? ('85); Cordelia's Aspirations ('83); Dan's Tribulations ('84); Donovans, The ('75); Grip, The ('85); Investigation ('84); Last of the Hogans, The ('91); Leather Patch, The ('86); Lorgaire, The ('89); Maid and the Moonshiner, The ('86); Major, The ('81); McAllister's Legacy ('85); McNooney's Visit ('87); McSorley's Inflation ('82); Mordecai Lyons ('82); Muddy Day, The ('83); Mulligan Guards' Ball, The ('79); Mulligan Guards' Chowder, The ('79); Mulligan Guards' Christmas, The ('79); Mulligan Guards' Nominee, The

('80); Mulligan Guards' Picnic, The ('78); Mulligan Guards' Surprise, The ('80); Mulligans' Silver Wedding, The ('80); Old Lavender ('77); O'Regan's, The ('86); Pete ('87); Reilly and the Four Hundred ('90); Squatter Sovereignty ('82); Toy Pistol, A ('86); Waddy Googan ('88); Woolen Stocking, The ('93)

HART, LORENZ: America's Sweetheart ('31); Babes in Arms ('37); Betsy ('26); Boys from Syracuse, The ('38); By Jupiter ('41); Chee-Chee ('28); Connecticut Yankee, A ('27); Dearest Enemy ('25); Garrick Gaieties, The ('25 and '26); Girl Friend, The ('26); Heads Up! ('26); Higher and Higher ('40); I'd Rather Be Right ('37); I Married an Angel ('38); Jumbo ('35); On Your Toes ('36); Pal Joey ('40); Peggy-Ann ('26); Poor Little Ritz Girl ('20); Present Arms ('28); She's My Baby ('28); Simple Simon ('30); Spring Is Here ('29); Too Many Girls ('39)

HERBERT, VICTOR: Algeria ('80); Ameer, The ('99); Angel Face ('19); Babes in Toyland ('03); Babette ('03); Century Girl, The ('16); Cyrano de Bergerac ('99); Debutante, The ('14); Dream City ('06); Dream Girl, The ('24); Duchess, The ('11); Eileen ('17); Enchantress, The ('11); Fortune Teller, The ('98); Girl in the Spotlight, The ('20); Gold Bug, The ('96); Her Regiment ('17); Idol's Eye, The ('97); It Happened in Nordland ('04); Lady of the Slipper, The ('12); Little Nemo ('08); Madcap Duchess, The ('13); Magic Knight ('06); Miss Dolly Dollars ('05); Miss 1917; Mlle. Modiste ('05); My Golden Girl ('20); Naughty Marietta ('10); Old Dutch ('09); Only Girl, The ('14); Orange Blossoms ('22); Prima Donna, The ('08); Prince Ananias ('94); Princess Pat, The ('15); Red Mill, The ('06); Rose of Algeria, The ('09); Serenade, The ('97); Singing Girl, The ('99); Sweethearts ('13); Tattooed Man, The ('07); Velvet Lady, The

('19); Viceroy, The ('00); When Sweet Sixteen ('11); Wizard of the Nile, The ('95); Wonderland ('05)

HOPPER, DE WOLF (plays in which starred): Castles in the Air ('90); Charlatan, The ('98); Dr. Syntax ('94); El Capitan ('96); Erminie ('21); Everything ('18); Fiddle-Dee-Dee ('00); Happyland ('05); Hoity Toity ('01); Hop o' My Thumb ('13); Lieber Augustin ('13); Matinee Idol, A ('10); Mr. Pickwick ('03); Panjandrum ('93); Passing Show, The ('17); Pied Piper, The ('08); Snapshots ('21); Some Party ('22); Wang ('91)

HOWARD, WILLIE and/or EUGENE: Ballyhoo of 1932; Crazy with the Heat ('41); George White's Music Hall Varieties ('32); George White's Scandals ('26, '27, '28, '36, '39); Girl Crazy ('30); Passing Show, The ('12, '15); My Dear Public ('43); Priorities of '42; Sally ('48); Show of Wonders, The ('16); Sky High ('25); Whirl of the World, The ('14); Ziegfeld Follies ('34)

HUBBELL, RAYMOND: Air King, The ('09); Big Show, The ('16); Cheer Up ('17); Fad and Fancies ('15); Fantana ('05); Girl at the Helm, The ('08); Good Times ('20); Happy Days ('19); Hip-Hip Hooray ('15); Jolly Bachelors, The ('10); Kiss Burglar, The ('18); Knight for a Day ('07); Mam'selle Sallie ('06); Man from Cook's, The ('12); Mexicana ('06); Midnight Sons, The ('09); Miss Millions ('19); Never Homes, The ('11); Runaways, The ('03); Three Cheers ('28); Three Romeos, The ('11); Winsome Widow, A ('12); Yours Truly ('27); Ziegfeld Follies ('11 to '14, '17)

JOLSON, AL: Big Boy ('25); Bombo ('21); Dancing Around ('14); Hold on to Your Hats ('40); Honeymoon Express, The ('13); La Belle Paree ('11); Robinson Crusoe, Jr. ('16); Sinbad ('18); Vera Violetta ('11); Whirl of Society, The ('12); Wonder Bar, The ('31)

KAUFMAN, GEORGE S.: Animal Crackers ('28); Band Wagon, The ('31); Be Yourself ('24); Cocoanuts, The ('25); Face the Music ('32); 49ers, The ('22); Guys and Dolls ('50); Helen of Troy, New York ('23); Hollywood Pinafore ('45); I'd Rather Be Right ('37); Let 'Em Eat Cake ('33); Music Box Revue, 1923–24; Of Thee I Sing ('31); Park Avenue ('46); Silk Stockings ('55); Sing Out the News ('38); Strike Up the Band ('30)

KERKER, GUSTAVE: American Beauty, An ('96); Belle of New York, The ('98); Billionaire, The ('02); Blonde in Black, The ('03); Castles in the Air ('90); Fascinating Flora ('07); Girl from Up There, The ('01); In Gay New York ('96); Kismet ('95); Lady from Lane's, The ('07); Lady Slavey, The ('96); Little Christopher Columbus ('94); Man in the Moon, The ('99); Pearl of Pekin, The ('88); Prince Kam ('94); Social Whirl, The ('06); Telephone Girl, The ('98); Tourists, The ('06); Two Little Brides ('12); Two Roses, The ('04); Whirl of the Town, The ('97); White Hen, The ('07); Winsome Winnie ('03); Yankee Doodle Dandy ('98)

KERN, JEROME: Bunch and Judy, The ('22); Cat and the Fiddle, The ('31); City Chap, The ('25); Criss Cross ('26); Dear Sir ('24); Good Morning, Dearie ('21); Have a Heart ('17); Head Over Heels ('18); Hitchy Koo ('20); Leave It to Jane ('17); Love o' Mike ('17); Lucky ('27); Miss Information ('15); Miss 1917; Mr. Wix of Wickham ('04); Music in the Air ('32); Night Boat, The ('20); Ninety in the Shade ('15); Nobody Home ('15); Oh, Boy! ('17); Oh, I Say! ('13); Oh, Lady! Lady!! ('18); Red Petticoat, The ('12); Roberta ('33); Rock-a-bye Baby ('18); Sally ('20); She's a Good Fellow ('19); Show Boat ('27); Sitting Pretty ('24); Stepping Stones ('23); Sunny ('25); Sweet Adeline ('29); Toot-Toot! ('18);

Very Good Eddie ('15); Very Warm for May ('39)

LERNER, ALAN JAY: Brigadoon ('47); Camelot ('60); Coco ('69); Day Before Spring, The ('45); Gigi ('73); Love Life ('48); Music! Music! ('74); My Fair Lady ('56); On a Clear Day You Can See Forever ('65); Paint Your Wagon ('51); 1600 Pennsylvania Avenue ('76); What's Up ('43)

LILLIE, BEATRICE: At Home Abroad ('35); Charlot's Revue ('24); Charlot's Revue of 1926; Evening with Beatrice Lillie, An ('52); High Spirits ('64); Inside USA ('48); Oh, Please! ('26); Set to Music ('39); Seven Lively Arts ('44); She's My Baby ('28); Show Is On, The ('36); Third Little Show, The ('31); This Year of Grace ('28); Ziegfeld Follies ('57)

MARTIN, MARY: I Do! I Do! ('66); Jennie ('63); Leave It to Me ('38); Lute Song ('46); One Touch of Venus ('43); Peter Pan ('54); Sound of Music, The ('59); South Pacific ('49)

MERMAN, ETHEL: Annie Get Your Gun ('46); Anything Goes ('34); Call Me Madam ('50); Du Barry Was a Lady ('39); George White's Scandals ('31); Girl Crazy ('30); Gypsy ('59); Happy Hunting ('56); Panama Hattie ('40); Red, Hot and Blue ('36); Something for the Boys ('43); Stars in Your Eyes ('39); Take a Chance ('32)

MERRICK, DAVID: Carnival ('61); Destry Rides Again ('59); Do Re Mi ('60); Fanny ('54); Gypsy ('59); Happy Time, The ('68); Hello, Dolly! ('64); How Now Dow Jones ('67); I Do! I Do! ('66); Irma la Douce ('60); Jamaica ('57); La Plume de Ma Tante ('58); Maria Golovin ('58); Pickwick ('65); Subways Are for Sleeping ('61); Sugar ('72); Take Me Along ('59); Vintage '60

MOORE, VICTOR: Allez-Oop! ('27);

Anything Goes ('34); Carousel ('57); Forty-five Minutes from Broadway ('06); Funny Face ('27); Happiest Night of His Life, The ('11); Heads Up! ('29); Hold Everything ('28); Hollywood Pinafore ('45); Leave It to Me! ('38); Let 'Em Eat Cake ('33); Louisiana Purchase ('40); Of Thee I Sing ('31); Oh, Kay! ('26); Princess Charming ('30); Talk of New York, The ('07)

PORTER, COLE: Anything Goes ('34); Around the World in 80 Days ('46); Can-Can ('53); Du Barry Was a Lady ('39); Fifty Million Frenchmen ('29); Gay Divorce ('32); Hitchy-Koo ('19); Jubilee ('35); Kiss Me, Kate ('48); Leave It to Me! ('38); Let's Face It! ('41); Mexican Hayride ('44); New Yorkers, The ('30); Out of This World ('50); Panama Hattie ('40); Paris ('28); Red, Hot and Blue ('36); See America First ('16); Seven Lively Arts ('20); Silk Stockings ('55); Something for the Boys ('43); You Never Know ('38)

RICE, EDWARD E.: Adonis ('84); Ballet Girl, The ('98); Billie Taylor ('81); Bottle of Ink, A ('85); Corsair, The ('87); Evangeline ('74); Excelsior, Jr. ('95); 1492 ('93); French Maid, The ('97); Girl from Paris, The ('96); Hiawatha ('80); H.M.S. Pinafore ('79); Iolanthe ('82); Monte Carlo ('98); Mr. Wix of Wickham ('04); Origin of the Cake Walk; or, Clorindy ('98); Patience ('81); Pearl of Pekin, The ('88); Polly ('85); Pop ('83); Revels ('80); Rice's Summer Nights ('98); Show Girl, The ('02)

RODGERS, RICHARD: Allegro ('47); America's Sweetheart ('31); Babes in Arms ('37); Betsy ('26); Boys from Syracuse, The ('38); By Jupiter ('41); Carousel ('45); Chee-Chee ('28); Connecticut Yankee, A ('27); Dearest Enemy ('25); Do I Hear a Waltz? ('65); Flower Drum Song ('58); Garrick Gaieties, The ('25 and '26); Girl Friend, The ('26); Heads Up!

('26); Higher and Higher ('40); I'd Rather Be Right ('37); I Married an Angel ('38); Jumbo ('35); King and I, The ('51); Me and Juliet ('53); No Strings ('62); Oklahoma! ('43); On Your Toes ('36); Pal Joey ('40); Peggy-Ann ('26); Pipe Dream ('55); Poor Little Ritz Girl ('20); Present Arms ('28); Rex ('76); She's My Baby ('28); Simple Simon ('30); Sound of Music, The ('59); South Pacific ('49); Spring Is Here ('29); Too Many Girls ('39); Two by Two ('70)

ROMBERG, SIGMUND: Artists and Models ('24); Blossom Time ('21); Blue Paradise, The ('15); Blushing Bride, The ('22); Bombo ('21); Cherry Blossoms ('27); Dancing Around ('14); Dancing Girl, The ('23); Desert Song, The ('26); Doing Our Bit ('17); East Wind ('31); Follow Me ('16); Forbidden Melody ('36); Girl from Brazil, The ('16); Girl in Pink Tights, The ('54); Hands Up ('15); Her Soldier Boy ('16); Louie the 14th ('25); Love Birds ('21); Love Call, The ('27); Magic Melody, The ('19); Maid in America ('15); Maytime ('18); May Wine ('35); Melody ('33); Melting of Molly, The ('18); Monte Cristo, Jr. ('19); My Lady's Glove ('17); My Maryland ('27); My Princess ('27); My Romance ('48); New Moon, The ('28); Nina Rosa ('30); Passing Show, The ('14, '16, '17, '18, '19, '23, '24); Poor Little Ritz Girl ('20); Princess Flavia ('25); Robinson Crusoe, Jr. ('16); Rosalie ('28); Show of Wonders, The ('16); Sinbad ('18); Springtime of Youth ('22); Student Prince, The ('24); Sunny River ('41); Up in Central Park ('45); Whirl of the World, The ('14); World of Pleasure, A, ('15)

RUSSELL, LILLIAN: American Beauty, An ('96); Apollo ('91); Belle Hélène, La ('99); Billy Taylor ('83); Brigands, The ('89); Cigale, La ('91); Dorothy ('87); Erminie ('99); Fiddle-Dee-Dee ('00); Giroflé-Girofla ('91); Goddess of

Truth, The ('96); Grand Duchess, The ('89); Grand Mogul, The ('81); Hoity Toity ('01); Hokey Pokey ('12); Iolanthe ('82); Lady Teazle ('04); Little Duke, The ('95); Maid and the Moonshiner, The ('86); Mountebanks, The ('91); Patience ('81); Pepita ('86); Périchole, La ('95); Polly ('84); Poor Jonathan ('90); Prince Methusalem ('83); Princess Nicotine ('93); Princess of Trebizonde ('83); Queen of Brilliants, The ('94); Queen's Mate, The ('88); Twirly Whirly ('02); Tzigane, The ('95); Wedding Day, The ('97); Whirl-i-Gig ('99)

SCHWARTZ, ARTHUR: At Home Abroad ('35); Band Wagon, The ('31); Between the Devil ('37); By the Beautiful Sea ('54); Flying Colors ('32); Gay Life, The ('61); Grand Street Follies, The ('29); Inside U.S.A. ('48); Jennie ('63); Little Show, The ('29); Park Avenue ('46); Revenge with Music ('34); Second Little Show, The ('30); Stars in Your Eyes ('39); Three's a Crowd ('30); Tree Grows in Brooklyn, A ('51)

SHUBERT BROTHERS (Over 200 musicals produced. These are selected highlights): At Home Abroad ('35); Blossom Time ('21); Blue Paradise, The ('15); Bombo ('21); Chinese Honeymoon, A ('02); Dream Girl, The ('24); Fantana ('05); Girl Behind the Counter, The ('07); Hellzapoppin ('38); La Belle Paree ('11); Lady Teazle ('04); Love o' Mike ('17); Maytime ('17); My Maryland ('27); My Romance ('48); Oh, I Say ('13); Passing Show, The ('12 onward); Pioneer Days ('06); Red Petticoat, The ('12); Sally, Irene and Mary ('22); Show Is On, The ('36); Student Prince, The ('24)

SLOANE, A. BALDWIN: Aunt Hannah ('00); Belle of Broadway, The ('02); Broadway to Tokio ('00); China Rose ('25); Comin' Through the Rye ('06); Giddy Throng, The ('00); Gingerbread Man, The ('05); Greenwich Village Follies ('19, '20); Hall of

Fame, The ('02); Hanky Panky ('12); Hen Pecks, The ('11); Hokey Pokey ('12); Jack and the Beanstalk ('96); King's Carnival, The ('01); Ladies First ('18); Lady Teazle ('04); Million Dollars, A ('00); Mimic and the Maid, The ('07); Mocking Bird, The ('02); Nell Go In ('00); Never Homes, The ('11); Prince of Bohemia, The ('10); Seeing New York ('06); Sergeant Kitty ('04); Summer Widowers, The ('10); Tillie's Nightmare ('10); Wizard of Oz, The ('03)

SMITH, HARRY B. (With lyrics or librettos for nearly 150 shows to his credit, this is merely a selection of highlights): Angel Face ('19); Babette ('03); Begum, The ('87); Casino Girl, The ('00); Countess Maritza ('26); Fortune Teller, The ('98); Free Lance, The ('06); Girl from Utah, The ('14); Hurly Burly ('98); Little Duchess, The ('01); Marching By ('32); Office Boy, The ('03); Rich Mr. Hoggenheimer, The ('06); Robin Hood ('91); Serenade, The ('97); Singing Girl, The ('99); Stop! Look! Listen! ('15); Watch Your Step ('14); Ziegfeld Follies ('07 to '10, '12)

SONDHEIM, STEPHEN: Anyone Can Whistle ('64); Company ('70); Do I Hear a Waltz? ('65); Follies ('71); Funny Thing Happened on the Way to the Forum, A ('62); Gypsy ('59); Little Night Music, A ('73); Pacific Overtures ('76); West Side Story ('57)

STYNE, JULE: Bells Are Ringing ('56); Darling of the Day ('68); Do Re Mi ('60); Fade Out—Fade In ('64); Funny Girl ('64); Gentlemen Prefer Blondes ('49); Gypsy ('59); Hallelujah, Baby! ('67); Hazel Flagg ('53); High Button Shoes ('47); Look to the Lilies ('70); Lorelei ('74); Say, Darling ('58); Subways Are for Sleeping ('61); Sugar ('72); Two on the Aisle ('51)

TEMPLETON, FAY: Broadway to Tokio ('00); Catherine ('99);

Evangeline ('85); Excelsior, Jr. ('95); Fiddle-Dee-Dee ('00); Forty-five Minutes from Broadway ('06); Helter-Skelter ('99); Hendrik Hudson ('90); H.M.S. Pinafore ('14, '26, '31); Hoity Toity ('01); Hokey Pokey ('12); Hurly Burly ('98); In Newport ('04); Little Bit of Everything, A ('04); Mascot, The ('81); Roberta ('33)

WEBER, JOE and/or FIELDS, LEW: About Town ('06); All Aboard ('13); Art of Maryland, The ('96); Blue Eyes ('21); Catherine ('99); Chee-Chee ('28); Concurers, The ('98); Connecticut Yankee, A ('27); Cyranose de Bricabrac ('98); Dream City ('06); Fiddle-Dee-Dee ('00); Geezer, The ('96); Girl Behind the Counter, The ('07); Girl Friend, The ('26); Glad Hand, The ('97); Glimpse of the Great White Way, A ('13); Hanky-Panky ('12); Hello, Daddy ('28); Helter-Skelter ('99); Hen Pecks, The ('11); Higgledy-Piggledy ('04); Hip! Hip! Hooray! ('07); Hoity Toity ('01); Hokey-Pokey ('12); Hurly-Burly ('98); It Happened in Nordland ('04); Jolly Bachelors, The ('10); Lonely Romeo, A ('19); Magic Knight, The ('06); Merry Widow Burlesque, The ('08); Midnight Sons, The ('09); Miss 1917; Never Homes, The ('11); Old Dutch ('09); Poor Little Ritz Girl ('20); Pousse Café ('97); Roly Poly ('12); Rose of Algeria, The ('09); Step This Way ('16); Summer Widowers, The ('10); Sun Dodgers, The ('12); Tillie's Nightmare ('10); Twiddle Twaddle ('06); Twirly Whirly ('02); Under the Red Globe ('97); Vanderbilt Revue ('30); Whirl-i-gig ('99); Whoop-Dee-Doo ('03); Wife Haters, The ('11)

ZIEGFELD, FLORENZ, JR.: Annie Dear ('24); Betsy ('26); Bitter Sweet ('29); Century Girl, The ('16); Higgledy Piggeldy ('04); Hot Cha! ('32); Kid Boots ('23); Little Duchess, The ('01); Louie the 14th ('25); Mam'selle Napoleon ('03); Miss Innocence ('08); Miss 1917; No Foolin' ('26); Over the River ('12); Papa's Wife ('99); Parisian Model, A ('06); Parlor Match ('96); Red Feather, The ('03); Rio Rita ('27); Rosalie ('28); Sally ('20); Show Boat ('27); Show Girl ('29); Simple Simon ('30); Smiles ('30); Three Musketeers, The ('28); Whoopee ('28); Winsome Widow, A ('12); Ziegfeld Follies ('07–'27, '31)

INDEX

This index is divided into three parts. The first lists all the musicals mentioned in this book, except certain operas performed in repertory with lighter pieces. At the end of this section is a supplementary index listing sources (plays, books, etc.) on which these musicals are based, unless the name of the musical and its source are the same. The second section lists songs from these musicals, if they are mentioned in the text. The third section covers everything else, but is primarily a listing of major people associated with the musicals. We have attempted to list all authors mentioned in the book, but actors, choreographers, set designers, etc., have generally been listed only if they appear at least three times in the text. There are a few exceptions, especially if the figure was celebrated in other fields or is a distinguished foreigner. A complete list of credits will be available when Oxford publishes the second volume mentioned in the preface.

SHOWS AND SOURCES

Index: Shows and Sources

SONGS

Index: Songs

Index: Songs

Index: Songs

Index: Songs

Index: Songs

Index: Songs

Index: Songs

Index: Songs

Index: Songs

PEOPLE

(Page citations for biographical material are in boldface type. In this part of the Index the following theatres are included: Casino, Gaiety, Hippodrome, La Salle, New Amsterdam, Niblo's, Princess, Winter Garden, Ziegfeld.)

Index: People

Index: People

Index: People

Index: People

Index: People

Index: People